Learning Microsoft® Office 2010: Deluxe Edition

Lisa Bucki

Chris Katsaropoulos

Christy Parrish

Suzanne Weixel

Faithe Wempen

PEARSON

Prentice Hall

Boston • Columbus • Indianapolis • New York • San Francisco • Upper Saddle River
Amsterdam • Cape Town • Dubai • London • Madrid • Milan • Munich • Paris • Montreal • Toronto
Delhi • Mexico City • Sao Paulo • Sydney • Hong Kong • Seoul • Singapore • Taipei • Tokyo

Editor in Chief: Michael Payne
Product Development Manager: Eileen Bien Calabro
Editorial Assistant: Nicole Sam
Director of Marketing: Kate Valentine
Marketing Manager: Tori Olson Alves
Marketing Coordinator: Susan Osterlitz
Marketing Assistant: Darshika Vyas
Senior Managing Editor: Cynthia Zonneveld
Associate Managing Editor: Camille Trentacoste
Production Project Manager: Mike Lackey
Operations Director: Alexis Heydt
Senior Operations Specialist: Diane Peirano
Text and Cover Designer: Vanessa Moore
AVP/Director of Online Programs, Media: Richard Keaveny
AVP/Director of Product Development, Media: Lisa Strite
Media Project Manager, Editorial: Alana Coles
Media Project Manager, Production: John Cassar
Editorial and Product Development: Emergent Learning, LLC
Composition: Vanessa Moore
Printer/Binder: R.R. Donnelly Menasha
Cover Printer: Lehigh-Pheonix Color
Text: 10/12 Helvetica

Credits and acknowledgements borrowed from other sources and reproduced, with permission, in this textbook are as follows: All photos courtesy of Shutterstock.com.

Softcover ISBN 10: 0-13-510838-1
Softcover ISBN 13: 978-0-13-510838-3

Hardcover ISBN 10: 0-13-510840-3
Hardcover ISBN 13: 978-0-13-510840-6

PEARSON

2 3 4 5 6 7 8 9 10 12 11

Table of Contents

Microsoft Excel 2010

Microsoft Access 2010

Chapter 1 Getting Started with Microsoft Access 2010. 572

Chapter 2 Working with Queries. 640

Chapter 3 Working with Queries. 710

Microsoft PowerPoint 2010

Chapter 1 Getting Started with Microsoft PowerPoint 2010 784

Chapter 2 Working with Lists and Graphics 840

Chapter 3 Enhancing a Presentation . . 896

The following Bonus Chapters are provided in pdf format on the CD that comes with the book. The data files for these Chapters can also be found on the CD.

Word Chapter 4 Learning More about Merge, and Exploring the World Wide Web

Excel Chapter 5 Advanced Printing, Formatting, and Editing

PowerPoint Chapter 4 Finalizing a Presentation

Introduction

Microsoft Office 2010 is Microsoft's suite of application software. The Standard version includes Word, Excel, Outlook, and PowerPoint. Other editions may also include Access, Publisher, OneNote, and InfoPath. This book covers Word (the word processing tool), Excel (the spreadsheet tool), PowerPoint (the presentation tool), and Access (the database tool). Because Microsoft Office is an integrated suite, the components can all be used separately or together to create professional-looking documents and to manage data.

HOW THE BOOK IS ORGANIZED

Learning Microsoft Office 2010 Deluxe Edition is made up of five sections:

- **Basics.** This chapter introduces essential Microsoft Office 2010 skills—including starting Microsoft Office, using the mouse and keyboard, screen elements, and an overview of the applications. If you are completely new to the Office suite, you should start with this chapter.
- **Word 2010.** With Word you can create letters, memos, Web pages, newsletters, and more.
- **Excel 2010.** Excel, Microsoft's spreadsheet component, is used to organize and calculate data, track financial data, and create charts and graphs.
- **Access 2010.** Access is Microsoft's powerful database tool. Using Access you will learn to store, retrieve, and report on information.
- **PowerPoint 2010.** Create dynamic onscreen presentations with PowerPoint, the presentation graphics tool.

Lessons are comprised of short exercises designed for using Microsoft Office 2010 in real-life business settings. Each lesson is made up of seven key elements:

- **What You Will Learn.** Each lesson starts with an overview of the learning objectives covered in the lesson.
- **Software Skills.** Next, a brief overview of the Microsoft Office tools that you'll be working with in the lesson is provided.
- **Application Skills.** The objectives are then put into context by setting a scenario.
- **Words to Know.** Key terms are included and defined at the start of each lesson, so you can quickly refer back to them. The terms are then highlighted in the text.
- **What You Can Do.** Concise notes for learning the computer concepts.
- **Try It.** Hands-on practice activities provide brief procedures to teach all necessary skills.
- **Create It.** These projects give students a chance to create documents, spreadsheets, database objects, and presentations by entering information. Steps provide all the how-to information needed to complete a project.
- **Apply It.** Each lesson concludes with a project that challenges students to apply what they have learned through steps that tell them what to do, without all the how-to information. In the Apply It projects, students must show they have mastered each skill set.
- Each chapter ends with two assessment projects: **Make It Your Own** and **Master It**, which incorporate all the skills covered throughout the chapter.

WORKING WITH DATA AND SOLUTION FILES

As you work through the projects in this book, you'll be creating, opening, and saving files. You should keep the following instructions in mind:

- For many of the projects you can use the data files provided on the CD-ROM that comes with this book. Other projects will ask you to create new documents and files, and then enter text and data into them, so you can master creating documents from scratch.
- The data files are used so that you can focus on the skills being introduced—not on keyboarding lengthy documents. The files are organized by application in the folders on the CD-ROM.
- When the project steps tell you to open a file name, you can open the data file provided on CD.
- All the projects instruct you to save the files created or to save the project files under a new name that includes your first and last name as part of the file name. This is to make the project file your own, and to avoid overwriting the data file in the storage location.
- Follow your instructor's directions for where to access and save the data files on a network, local computer hard drive, or portable storage device such as a USB drive.
- Many of the projects also provide instructions for including your name in a header or footer. Again, this is to identify the project work as your own for grading and assessment purposes.
- Unless the book instructs otherwise, use the default settings for text size, margin size, and so on when creating a file. If someone has changed the default software settings for the computer you're using, your exercise files may not look the same as those shown in this book. In addition, the appearance of your files may look different if the system is set to a screen resolution other than 1024 x 768.

WHAT'S ON THE CD

The CD contains the following:

- Data Files for many of the projects.
- Glossary of all the key terms from the book.
- Bonus Chapters, including:
  - Word Chapter 4 – Learning More about Merge, and Exploring the World Wide Web
  - Excel Chapter 5 – Advanced Printing, Formatting, and Editing
  - PowerPoint Chapter 4 – Finalizing a Presentation
  - Microsoft Office 2010, Windows 7, and Internet Explorer Procedure Reference provided in PDF format contains all of the step-by-step procedures needed to complete the activities in the book.

TO ACCESS THE FILES INCLUDED ON CD

1. Insert the Learning Microsoft Office 2010 Deluxe CD in the CD-ROM drive.
2. Navigate to your CD-ROM drive; right-click and choose Explore from the shortcut menu.
3. Right-click the folder that you wish to copy.
4. Navigate to the location where you wish to place the folder.
5. Right-click and choose Paste from the Shortcut menu.

COMPANION WEB SITE

Visit the Learning Microsoft Office 2010 Web site at www.pearsonhighered.com/learningseries for crossword puzzles, word searches, quizzes, challenge projects, videos, and additional bonus content.

Learning Microsoft® Office 2010: Deluxe Edition

Chapter 1

Using the Common Features of Microsoft Office 2010

Lesson 1
Microsoft Office 2010 Basics
Projects 1-2

- Analyzing Information Technology
- Analyzing Microsoft Office 2010
- Using the Mouse
- Using the Keyboard
- Analyzing Data Storage
- Navigating with Windows Explorer
- Creating and Deleting a Folder
- Starting and Exiting Microsoft Office Programs

Lesson 2
Saving, Printing, and Closing Microsoft Office Files
Projects 3-4

- Identifying Common Microsoft Office Screen Elements
- Entering and Editing Text
- Correcting Errors
- Saving a File
- Printing a File
- Closing a File

Lesson 3
Working with Existing Files
Projects 5-6

- Opening an Existing File
- Saving a File with a New Name
- Viewing File Properties
- Using the Ribbon
- Using Access Keys
- Selecting Text
- Formatting Text

Lesson 4
Using Command Options
Projects 7-8

- Using the Quick Access Toolbar
- Using the Mini Toolbar
- Using Shortcut Menus
- Using Dialog Box Options
- Using Task Panes
- Formatting Pages

Lesson 5
Managing Program Windows
Projects 9-10

- Changing the View
- Using Window Controls
- Zooming
- Scrolling
- Using Multiple Windows
- Using the Microsoft Office Clipboard

Lesson 6
Using Microsoft Office Help
Projects 11-12

- Using Microsoft Office Help
- Searching for Help
- Using the Help Table of Contents
- Viewing Application Options
- Using AutoRecover and Autosave

Lesson 7
Managing Information Technology
Projects 13-14

- Copying Files and Folders
- Moving Files and Folders
- Compressing Files
- Recognizing Types of Business Documents
- Determining the Risks and Rewards of Developing an IT Strategy
- Identifying Needed Equipment and Supplies
- Establishing, Scheduling, and Following Maintenance Procedures

End of Chapter Assessments
Projects 15-16

WORDS TO KNOW

Byte
A unit used to measure storage capacity. One byte equals about one character.

Communications technology
Technology that makes communication easier and more efficient.

Current file
The file currently open and active. Actions and commands affect the current file.

Folder
A location on disk where you can store files.

Hardware
Computers, printers, and other devices.

Hyperlink
Text or graphics that are linked to another location. When you click a hyperlink, the destination is displayed. Often referred to simply as "link."

Icon
A picture used to identify an element onscreen, such as a toolbar button.

Information technology (IT)
The use of computers to collect, store, and distribute information. Also the various technologies used in processing, storing, and communicating business and personal information.

Lesson 1

Microsoft Office 2010 Basics

➤ What You Will Learn

Analyzing Information Technology
Analyzing Microsoft Office 2010
Using the Mouse
Using the Keyboard
Navigating with Windows Explorer
Creating and Deleting a Folder
Starting and Exiting Microsoft Office Programs

Software Skills Anyone trying to succeed in today's competitive business world benefits from an understanding of information technology. A good place to start is by learning how to use Microsoft® Office 2010, a suite of programs that may be used independently or together to create simple documents, such as letters and memos, as well as complex reports, data tables, and budget spreadsheets.

Application Skills You have just been hired as the office manager at Restoration Architecture, a growing firm that specializes in remodeling, redesign, and restoration of existing properties. One of your responsibilities is to analyze how information technology can help the company succeed and grow. You must also practice using your computer storage system and familiarizing yourself with the Microsoft Office 2010 programs.

What You Can Do

Analyzing Information Technology

- **Information technology**, or IT, refers to the use of computers to collect, store, and distribute information.
- **Communications technology** is part of information technology. It refers to the use of technology to make communication easier and more efficient.
- Businesses rely on technology of many types to make sure employees have the tools they need to complete assignments, tasks, and other responsibilities.
- Technology purchases include **hardware** and **software**.
- At the very least, almost all businesses require a computer, a printer, a connection to the Internet, and software such as Microsoft Office for basic business applications, such as word processing, data management, and spreadsheet functions.
- Other IT needs depend on the type and size of business. Some common IT equipment includes **scanners** to convert printed material to digital format. Some businesses may use other input devices such as voice recognition software, digital cameras, touch screen monitors or tablet PCs, and microphones.
- Other technology a company might need includes projectors, bar code readers, cash registers, and video conferencing systems.
- Departments must evaluate the needs of each employee, research the available technologies and then purchase and install the appropriate systems. They must also be sure employees know how to use the new systems.
- Requirements vary from department to department and from company to company. For example, a large financial services company will have different technology needs than a small travel agency.
- When evaluating technology, consider the following:
  - Tasks you need to accomplish
  - Cost
  - Ease-of-use
  - Compatibility with existing systems
- You can learn more about hardware and software technology using the Internet, consulting a magazine or buyer's guide, or by visiting a retailer in your area to talk to a salesperson.

Analyzing Microsoft Office 2010

- Microsoft Office 2010 is a newest version of the popular Microsoft Office **software suite**.
- You use the Microsoft Office programs for many business tasks, including to create various types of documents, to communicate with co-workers and customers, and to store and manage information.
- The Microsoft Office 2010 software suite is available in different editions.

WORDS TO KNOW

Insertion point
The flashing vertical line that indicates where typed text will display.

Library
In Microsoft Windows 7, a location where you can view files and folders that are actually stored in other locations on your computer system.

Menu
A list of commands or choices.

Mouse
A device that allows you to select items onscreen by pointing at them with the mouse pointer.

Mouse pad
A smooth, cushioned surface on which you slide a mouse.

Mouse pointer
A marker on your computer screen that shows you where the next mouse action will occur.

Object
Icon, menu, or other item that is part of an onscreen interface.

Random access memory (RAM)
Temporary memory a computer uses to store information while it is processing.

WORDS TO KNOW

Read-only memory (ROM)
Fixed memory stored on a chip in a computer that provides startup and other system instructions.

Scanner
A device that converts printed documents into digital file formats.

Scroll
To page through a document in order to view contents that is not currently displayed.

Scroll wheel
A wheel on some mouse devices used to navigate through a document onscreen.

Software
Programs that provide the instructions for a computer or other hardware device.

Software suite
A group of software programs sold as a single unit. Usually the programs have common features that make it easy to integrate and share data.

Storage
A computer device or component used to store data such as programs and files.

Subfolder
A folder stored within another folder.

Window
The area onscreen where a program or document is displayed.

- Most editions include the following core Microsoft Office programs:
  - Microsoft® Word, a word processing program.
  - Microsoft® Excel®, a spreadsheet program.
  - Microsoft® PowerPoint®, a presentation graphics program.
  - Microsoft® Outlook®, a personal information manager and communications program.
- Some editions may include the following additional programs:
  - Microsoft® Access®, a database application.
  - Microsoft® Publisher, a desktop publishing program.
  - Microsoft® OneNote®, a note-taking and management program.
  - Microsoft® InfoPath™, an information gathering and management program.
- This book covers the most commonly used programs in the Microsoft Office 2010 suite: Word, Excel, Access, and PowerPoint.
- Microsoft Office 2010 can run with different versions of the Microsoft® Windows® operating system, including Microsoft® Windows® 7, Microsoft® Vista®, and Microsoft® Windows® XP®.
- There may be slight differences in the programs depending on the operating system you are using.
- For example, features that involve browsing for storage locations are different depending on the operating system. This includes opening and saving a file, and selecting a file to insert.
- In addition, there may be some minor visual differences in the way the programs look onscreen.
- The procedures in this book assume you are using Microsoft Windows 7. Ask your teacher for information on procedures that may be different on systems using Vista or Windows XP.

Using the Mouse

- Use your **mouse** to point to and select commands and features of Microsoft Office 2010 programs.
- Most mouse devices work using light. Others may use a wireless connection. Some older models work by sliding a tracking ball on your desk.
- Notebook computers may have a touchpad or trackball to move the pointer on the screen in place of a mouse.
- When you move the mouse on your desk, the **mouse pointer** moves onscreen. For example, when you move the mouse to the left, the mouse pointer moves to the left.
- Hovering the pointer over an **object** such as an **icon** or menu name usually displays a ScreenTip that identifies the object.
- When you click a mouse button, the program executes a command. For example, when you move the mouse pointer to the Save button and then click, the program saves the current document or file.
- Clicking a mouse button can also be used to move the **insertion point** to a new location.
- A mouse may have one, two, or three buttons. Unless otherwise noted, references in this book are to the use of the left mouse button.

- Your mouse might have a **scroll wheel**. Spin the scroll wheel to **scroll**—move—through the file open on your screen.
- The mouse pointer changes shape depending on the program in use, the object being pointed to, and the action being performed. Common mouse pointer shapes include an arrow for selecting, an I-beam, and a hand with a pointing finger to indicate a **hyperlink**.
- You should use a mouse on a **mouse pad** that is designed specifically to make it easy to slide the mouse.
- You can move the mouse without moving the mouse pointer by picking it up. This is useful if you move the mouse too close to the edge of the mouse pad or desk.

Table 1-1 Mouse Actions

Action	Description
Point to	Move mouse pointer to touch specified element.
Click	Point to element then press and release left mouse button.
Right-click	Point to element then press and release right mouse button.
Double-click	Point to element then press and release left mouse button twice in rapid succession.
Drag	Point to element, hold down left mouse button, then move mouse pointer to new location.
Drop	Release the mouse button after dragging.
Scroll	Rotate center wheel backward to scroll down, or forward to scroll up.
Pan	Press center wheel and drag up or down.
Auto-Scroll	Click center wheel to scroll down; move pointer up to scroll up.
Zoom	Hold down Ctrl and rotate center wheel.

Try It! Using the Mouse

1. Start your computer if it is not already on. Log in to your user account, if necessary.

   ✓ *Ask your teacher how to log in to your user account.*

2. Move the mouse pointer to point at the Recycle Bin icon (see picture at right).
3. Right-click the Recycle Bin icon. A shortcut menu displays.
4. On the shortcut menu, click Open. The Recycle Bin window opens and displays files and folders that have been deleted.
5. Click the Close button in the upper-right corner of the Recycle Bin window.
6. Double-click the Recycle Bin icon. This is another method of opening an object.

   ✓ *Some systems are set to open objects with a single click.*

7. Click the Close button in the upper-right corner of the Recycle Bin window.

Right-click to display a shortcut menu

Using the Keyboard

- Use your keyboard to type characters, including letters, numbers, and symbols. The keyboard can also be used to access program commands and features.
- Function keys (F1–F12) often appear in a row above the numbers at the top of the keyboard. They can be used as shortcut keys to perform certain tasks.
- Modifier keys such as Shift [SHIFT], Alt [ALT], and Ctrl [CTRL] are used in combination with other keys or mouse actions to select certain commands or perform actions. In this book, key combinations are shown as: the modifier key followed by a plus sign followed by the other key or mouse action. For example, [CTRL] + [S] is the key combination for saving the **current file**.
- The 17-key keypad to the right of the main group of keyboard keys on an enhanced keyboard includes the numeric keys.
- Most notebook computers and portable devices integrate the numeric keys into the regular keyboard.
- When the Num Lock [NUM LOCK] feature is on, the keypad can be used to enter numbers. When the feature is off, the keys can be used as directional keys to move the insertion point in the current file.
- The Escape key [ESC] is used to cancel a command.
- Use the Enter key [ENTER] to execute a command or to start a new paragraph when typing text.
- Directional keys are used to move the insertion point.
- Editing keys such as Insert [INS], Delete [DEL], and Backspace [BACKSPACE] are used to insert or delete text.
- The Windows key (sometimes called the Winkey or the Windows Logo key) is used alone to open the Windows Start **menu**, or in combination with other keys to execute certain Windows commands.
- The Application key is used alone to open a shortcut menu, or in combination with other keys to execute certain application commands.
- Some keyboards also have keys for opening shortcut menus, launching a Web browser, or opening an e-mail program.

Try It! Using the Keyboard

1. Press on your keyboard to open the Start menu.
2. Press [ESC] to cancel the action, which closes the menu.
3. Press [TAB] to select the object to the right of the Start button on your Windows Taskbar.
4. Press [TAB] repeatedly until the Recycle Bin icon is selected.
5. Press [ENTER] to open the Recycle Bin window.
6. Press [ALT] + [F4] to close the window. [ALT] + [F4] is the key combination for closing the current window.

Analyzing Data Storage

- Data **storage** is any device or component which can record and retain data, or information.
- Without storage, you would not be able to save files or access computer programs.
- Storage capacity is measured in bytes. One **byte** is equal to about one character.
- A typical hard disk drive today may have a capacity of 800 gigabytes (GB) or more!
- The type of storage you have available depends on your computer system.
- Some common storage devices include the following:
  - Internal hard disk drive, which is a device mounted inside a computer, and used to store programs and data files.
  - External hard disk drive, which is similar to an internal hard disk drive except that it connects to the outside of the computer via a cable and a port, such as a Universal Serial Bus (USB).
  - Network drive, which is a hard disk drive attached to a network, Computers attached to the same network can access the information on the drive.

- Flash drive, which is a small, portable device that can be attached to a USB port on the outside of a computer. A flash drive is convenient for transporting files from one computer to another.
- Memory card, which is a small card that is usually inserted into a slot in a computer or other device, such as a digital camera or printer.
- DVD, which is a disk that you insert into a DVD drive to record or read data. DVDs are often used for storing video, music, and pictures.
- CD, which is an older form of storage disk.
- Virtual drive, which is an area on a storage device that is identified as a separate drive.
- Online storage, which allows you to save, access, and share data using storage space on the Internet. The data is protected from unauthorized access using a password. For example, SkyDrive, offered by Microsoft Corp., allows free access to up to 25 GB of online storage for saving and sharing files.

■ Memory is also a type of storage. There are two types of computer memory:
- **Read-only memory** (ROM) which is stored on a chip inside the computer. It provides the instructions your computer needs to start and begin operation, and it cannot be changed under normal circumstances,
- **Random access memory** (RAM) is the temporary memory your computer uses to store information it is currently processing. Information stored in RAM is lost when then computer shuts down; you must save it on a storage device if you want to use it in the future.

Navigating with Windows Explorer

■ You use Windows Explorer, a feature of your Windows operating system, to navigate among your system components to find and use the information you need.

■ For example, you navigate to a storage device such as a disk drive to locate and open a file or program. You navigate to an output device such as a printer to perform maintenance, adjust settings, or use the device.

■ Windows comes with built-in **folders** that organize your computer components to make it easier to find the object you need. When you open a folder in Windows Explorer, its contents display in a **window** on your monitor.

■ For example, open the Computer folder window in Windows Explorer to display devices such as hard disk drives. Open the Libraries folder window to display **libraries** organized on your system. Open the Network window to display the devices connected to the same network as your system.

✓ *Libraries are only available in Windows 7.*

■ Most windows can be opened using links on the Start menu.

■ To select an item displayed in a window, click it. To open an item, double-click it.

✓ *This book assumes your system is set to open an object using a double click. If your system is set to open an object on a single click, you will use that method instead.*

■ Every computer system has different components. For example, one system might have a DVD drive, and another system might not. One might connect to a networked printer, while another has a printer directly connected to a USB port. No matter what the system components might be, the methods for navigating are the same:
- Use the Back and Forward buttons to move through windows you have opened recently.
- Use the Recent Pages menu to go directly to a window you have opened recently.
- Click a location in the Address bar to open it.
- Click an arrow between locations in the Address bar to display a menu, then click a location on the menu to open it.
- Each window displays a navigation pane which provides links to common locations. Click a location in the Navigation pane to display its contents in the window.

Try It! Navigating with Windows Explorer

1. If you have a removable storage device to use for storing your work in this class, connect it to your computer. For example, insert a removable disk in a drive, or connect a flash drive to a USB port.

   ✓ *If an AutoPlay dialog box displays, close it without taking any action.*

2. Click Start.

3. Click Computer in the right pane of the Start menu to open the computer window to view the storage devices that are part of your computer system.

4. In the Content pane of the Computer window, double-click the location where you are storing your work for this class. For example, double-click the icon for the removable device you connected in step 1.

   OR

   If you are storing your work for this class on a network location, click Network in the Navigation pane of the Computer window to open the Network window to view the components that are part of your computer network.

   ✓ *The Computer and Network components are specific to your system and may be different from those shown in the illustration.*

5. Click the Back button in the upper-left corner of the window to display the previous storage location.

6. Click the Forward button to move forward to the last window you had opened.

7. Click the Close button to close the window. If other windows are open, close them as well.

Navigate with Windows Explorer

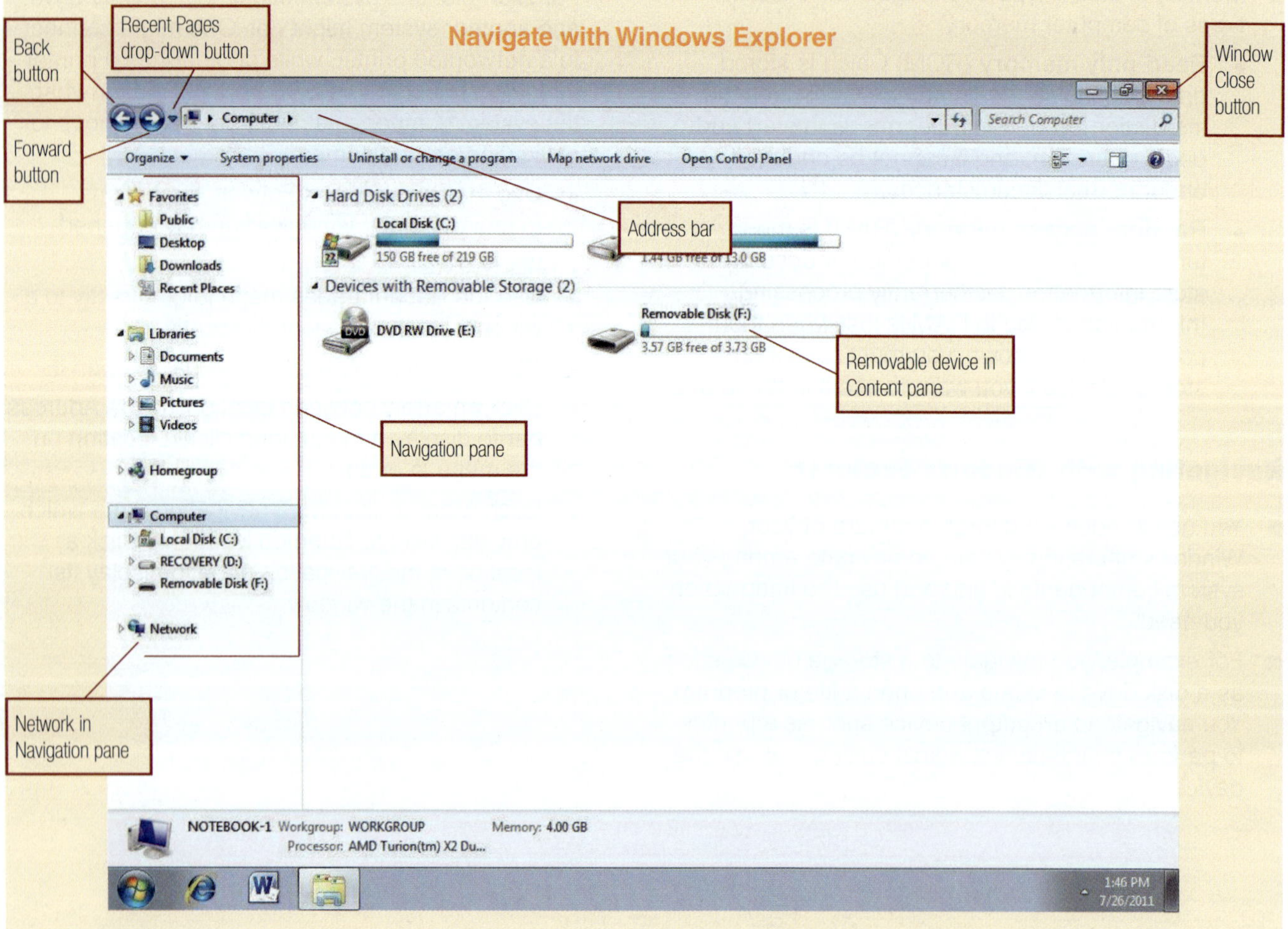

Creating and Deleting a Folder

- A folder is a named location on a storage device that you create using the Windows operating system.
- To create a folder, you specify where you want it on your computer system, and then give it a name.
- Folders help you keep your data organized, and make it easier to find the files you need when you need them.
- For example, you might store all the documents you use for planning a budget in a folder named Budget. You might store all the documents you use for a marketing project in a folder named Marketing Project.
- You can create a folder within an existing folder to set up layers of organization. A folder within another folder may be called a **subfolder**.
- You can delete a folder you no longer need. Deleting removes the folder from its current location and stores it in the Recycle Bin.

Try It! Creating a Folder

1. Click Start > Computer.

   ✓ *In this book, the symbol > is used to indicate a series of steps. In this case, click the Start button and then click Computer on the Start menu.*

2. In the Content pane of the Computer window, double-click the location where you are storing your work for this class.
3. Click New folder on the menu bar.

   OR

   a. Right-click a blank area of the window.

   b. Click New.

   c. Click Folder.

4. Type **BTry01**.
5. Press ENTER .

Create a Folder

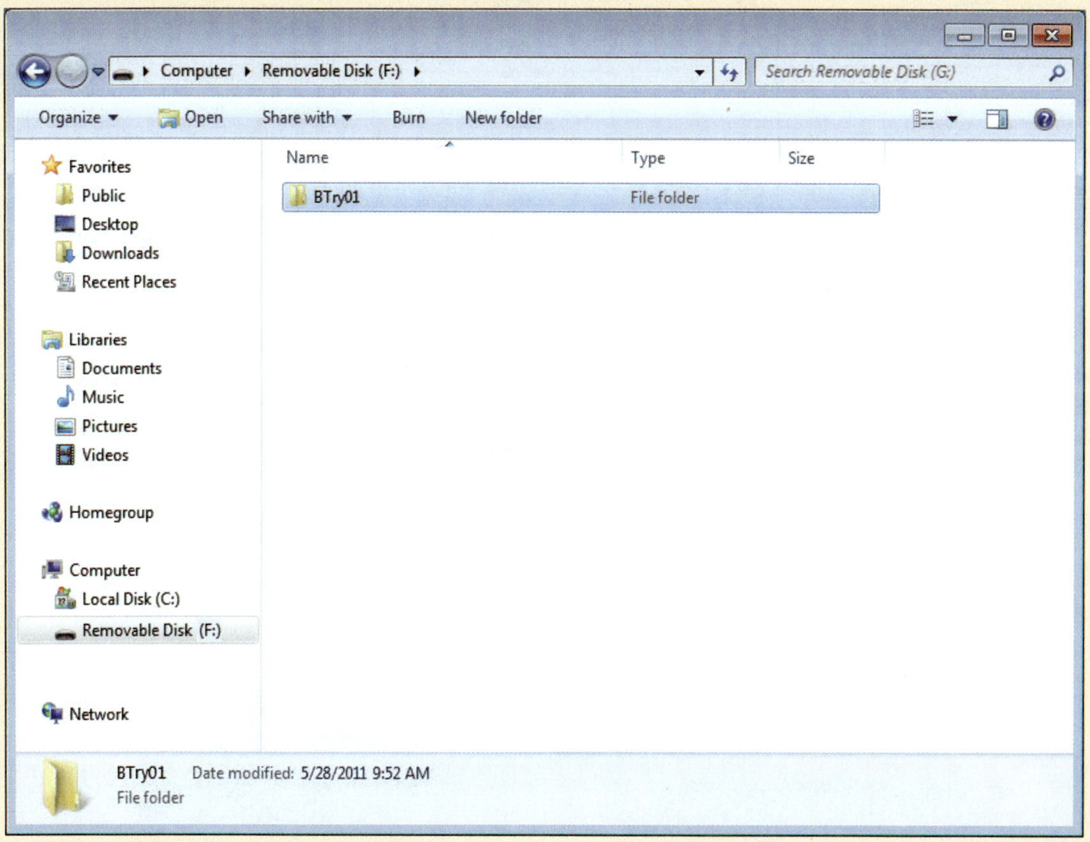

Try It! Deleting a Folder

1. Right-click the **BTry01** folder.
2. Click Delete.
3. Click Yes to move the folder to the Recycle Bin.
4. Click the Close button in the storage location window to close Windows Explorer.

Starting and Exiting Microsoft Office Programs

- To use a Microsoft Office 2010 program you must first start it so it is running on your computer.
- Use Windows to start a Microsoft Office program.
- You can select the program you want to start from the Microsoft Office folder accessed from the Windows All Programs menu.
- Depending on your system configuration, you may be able to use one of these alternative methods:
  - If the program has been used recently, or pinned to the Windows Start menu, you can select it directly from the Windows Start menu.
  - If the program shortcut icon displays on your Windows desktop, you can double-click it:
  - If the program icon has been added to the Taskbar, you can click it.
- When you are done using a Microsoft Office program, close it to exit. If you have a file open, the program prompts you to save, or to exit without saving.

✓ *You learn about saving files in Basics, Lesson 2.*

Try It! Starting a Microsoft Office Program

1. Click Start > All Programs. If necessary, scroll until you see the Microsoft Office folder icon.
2. Click the Microsoft Office folder icon.
3. Click Microsoft Word 2010.
4. Leave the file open for the next Try It.

Options for Starting a Microsoft Office Program

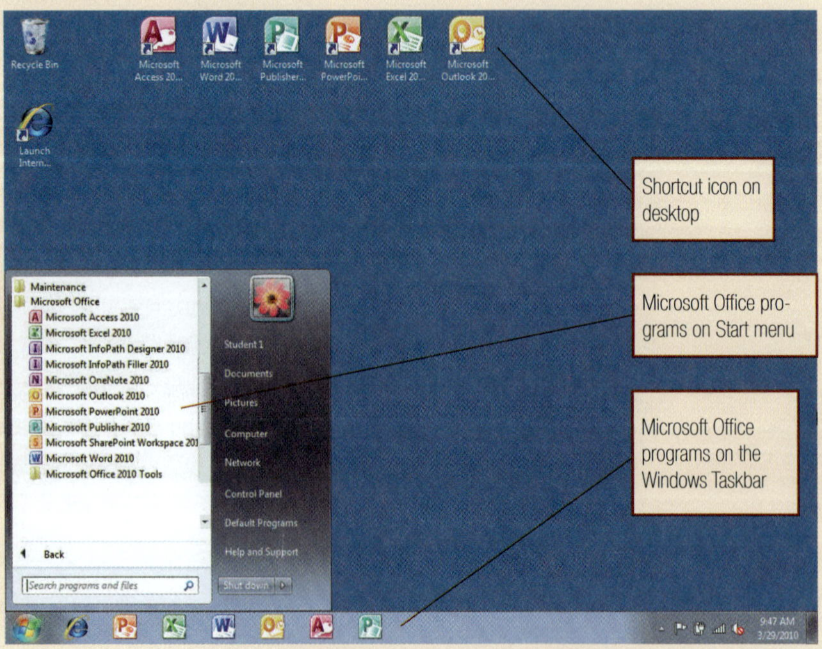

Try It! **Exiting a Microsoft Office Program**

1. In the Microsoft Word program window, click the Close button × at the right end of the program's title bar.

OR

1. Click the File tab.
2. Click Exit.
3. If you have a file open, a dialog box displays. Click Save to save changes to the file and exit, or click Don't Save to exit without saving.

Project 1—Create It

Create a Folder

DIRECTIONS

1. If you have a removable storage device to use for storing your work in this class, connect it to your computer. For example, insert a removable disk in a drive, or connect a flash drive to a USB port. (Close the AutoPlay dialog box without taking any action, if necessary.)
2. Click the **Start** button on the Windows Taskbar.
3. Click **Computer** in the right pane of the Start menu. The computer window opens. It displays the storage devices that are part of your computer system.
4. Follow your teacher's directions to navigate to and open the specific location where you will store the files and folders for this book.
5. Rest the mouse pointer on the Show/Hide **Preview pane** button in the upper right of the window. If the ScreenTip says Hide the preview pane, click the button to hide the pane. If it says Show the preview pane, go to step 6.
6. Click the **View** button drop-down arrow to display a menu of view options.
7. Click **Medium Icons** on the View drop-down menu to change the way the items in the window display.
8. Click **New Folder** on the window menu bar to create a new folder.
9. Type **BProj01_studentfirstname_ studentlastname**.

   ✓ *Throughout this book, replace the text studentfirstname with your own first name and studentlastname with your own last name when naming files and folders.*
10. Press ENTER to name the new folder. The window should look similar to Figure 1-1 on the next page.
11. Double-click the new folder to open it.
12. Click the **Back** button in the upper-left corner of the window to display the previous storage location.
13. Click the **Forward** button to move forward to the **BProj01** folder window.
14. Click the **Close** button to close the window.
15. Click the **Start** button on the Windows Taskbar.
16. Click **All Programs**.
17. Click the **Microsoft Office** folder.
18. Click **Microsoft Excel 2010**.
19. Click the **File** tab.
20. Click **Exit**. Click **Don't Save** if prompted, to exit without saving the file.

Figure 1-1

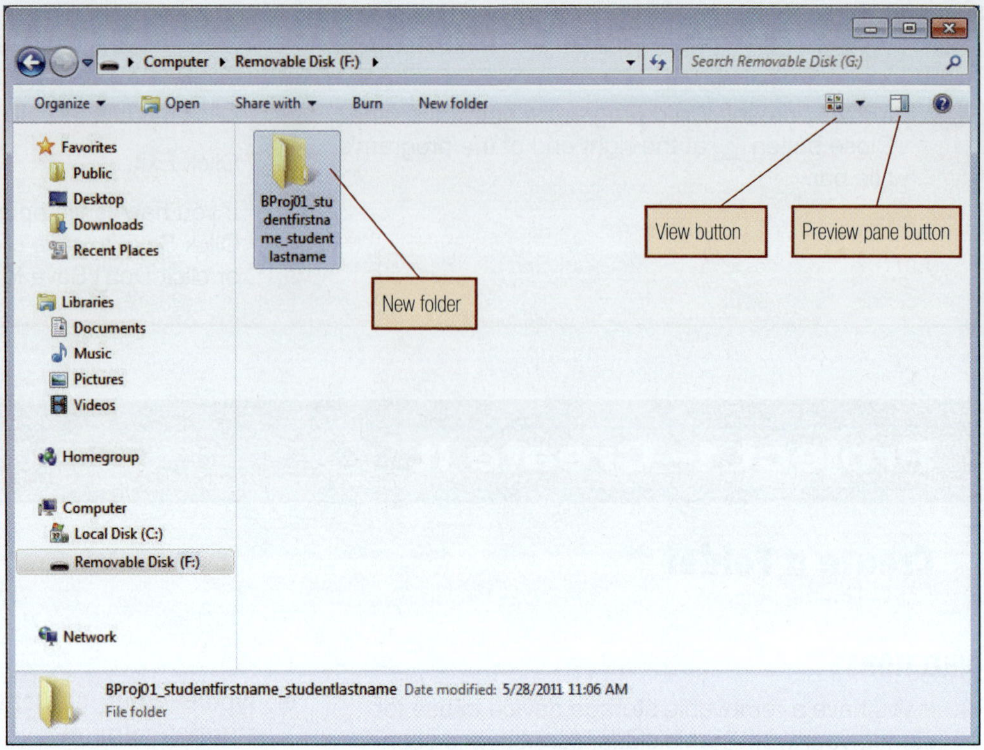

Project 2—Apply It

Create and Delete a Subfolder

DIRECTIONS

1. Click **Start** > **Computer**.
2. Navigate to and open the **BProj01_studentfirstname_studentlastname** folder you created in Project 1.
3. Create a new folder named **BProj02__studentfirstname_studentlastname**.
4. Open the **BProj02 _studentfirstname_studentlastname** folder, then navigate back to the **BProj01_studentfirstname_studentlastname** folder.
5. Navigate forward to the **BProj02_studentfirstname_studentlastname** folder.
6. Navigate back to the **BProj01_studentfirstname_studentlastname** folder.
7. Delete the **BProj02_studentfirstname_studentlastname** folder.
8. Close the **BProj01_studentfirstname_studentlastname** folder window, and then delete it.
9. Click **Start** > **All Programs** > **Microsoft Office**.
10. Click **Microsoft Word 2010**.
11. Exit Word.
12. Click **Start** > **All Programs** > **Microsoft Office**.
13. Click **Microsoft PowerPoint 2010**.
14. Exit PowerPoint.

Lesson 2

Saving, Printing, and Closing Microsoft Office Files

➤ What You Will Learn

- Identifying Common Microsoft Office Screen Elements
- Entering and Editing Text
- Correcting Errors
- Saving a File
- Printing a File
- Closing a File

WORDS TO KNOW

Backstage view
A feature of Microsoft Office 2010 from which you access file and program management commands.

Software Skills The programs in the Microsoft Office 2010 suite share common elements. That means that once you learn to accomplish a task in one program, you can easily transfer that skill to a different program. For example, the steps for saving a file are the same, no matter which program you are using.

Application Skills As the new office manager at Restoration Architecture, you have been asked to analyze how the company might use Microsoft Office to achieve its business goals. To do so, you will explore and compare the different programs, and practice creating, saving, and printing files.

What You Can Do

Identifying Common Microsoft Office Screen Elements

- When a program is running, it is displayed in a window on your screen.
- The program windows for each of the Microsoft Office applications contain many common elements.
- You will find more information about the individual program windows in the other sections of this book.
- Refer to Figure 2-1 to locate and identify these common window elements:
  - Ribbon. Displays buttons for accessing features and commands.

    ✓ *Note that the way items display on the Ribbon may depend on the width of the program window. If your program window is wider than the one used in the figures, more or larger buttons may display. If your program window is narrower, fewer or smaller buttons may display. Refer to Lesson 3 for more information on using the Ribbon.*

  - Ribbon tabs. Used to change the commands displayed on the Ribbon.
  - Quick Access Toolbar. A toolbar that displays buttons for commonly used commands. You can customize the Quick Access Toolbar to display buttons you use frequently.
  - Close button. Used to close the program window. It is one of three buttons used to control the size and position of the program window.
  - Mouse pointer. Marks the location of the mouse on the screen.
  - Scroll bar. Used with a mouse to shift the onscreen display up and down or left and right.
  - Status bar. Displays information about the current document.
  - Document area. The workspace where you enter text, graphics, and other data.

    ✓ *The appearance of the document area is different in each program.*

Figure 2-1

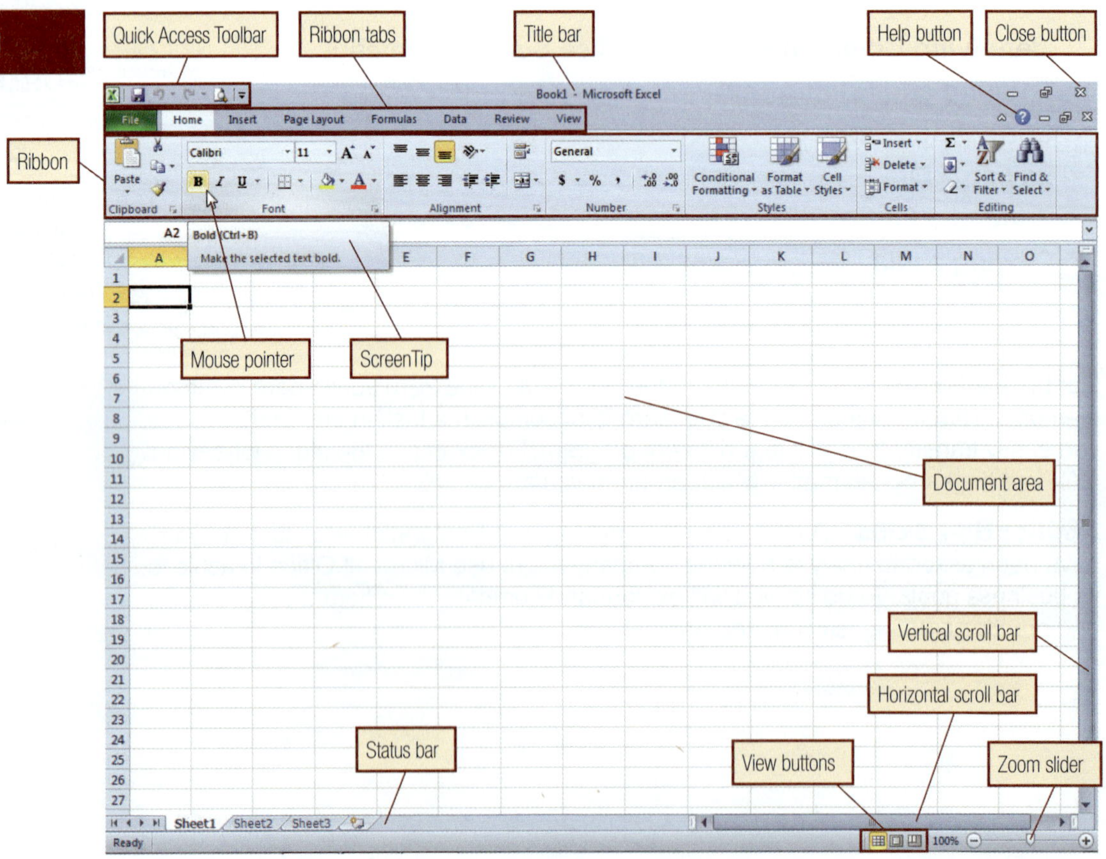

- ScreenTip. Displays information about the element on which the mouse pointer is resting.
- Title bar. Displays the program and file names.
- Zoom slider. Used to increase or decrease the size of the document onscreen.
- Help button. Used to start the program's Help system.
- View buttons. Used to change the document view.

Entering and Editing Text

- Use your keyboard to enter or edit text in a file.
- Characters you type are inserted to the left of the insertion point.
- You position the insertion point using your mouse or the directional keys on your keyboard.
- Press BACKSPACE to delete the character to the left of the insertion point.
- Press DEL to delete the character to the right of the insertion point.

✓ *When you are working in a program such as Access or Excel, text is entered into the selected cell. You learn about entering information in specific programs in each section of this book.*

Table 2-1 Positioning the Insertion Point with the Keyboard

Action	Keys	Action	Keys
One character left	←	Up one paragraph	CTRL + ↑
One character right	→	Down one paragraph	CTRL + ↓
One line up	↑	Beginning of document	CTRL + HOME
One line down	↓	End of document	CTRL + END
Previous word	CTRL + ←	Beginning of line	HOME
Next word	CTRL + →	End of line	END

Try It! Entering and Editing Text

1. Start Microsoft Word.
2. Use the keyboard to type your first name, press SPACEBAR and then type your last name.
3. Press ENTER twice to start two new paragraphs.
4. Move the mouse so the pointer I-beam is positioned to the left of the first letter in your last name.
5. Click to position the insertion point.
6. Type your middle initial followed by a period and a space.
7. Press CTRL + END to position the insertion point at the end of the document.
8. Press BACKSPACE twice.
9. Position the insertion point to the left of your middle initial.
10. Press DEL three times to delete your initial, the period, and the space.
11. Exit Word without saving any changes.

Correcting Errors

- Press ESC to cancel a command or close a menu or dialog box before the command affects the current file.
- Use the Undo button on the Quick Access Toolbar to reverse a single action made in error, such as deleting the wrong word.
- Use the Undo drop-down list to reverse a series of actions. The most recent action is listed at the top of the list; click an action to undo it and all actions above it.
- Use the Redo button on the Quick Access Toolbar to reinstate any actions that you reversed with Undo.
- If the Undo button is dimmed, there are no actions that can be undone.
- If the Redo button is dimmed, there are no actions that can be redone.
- Sometimes when there are no actions to redo, the Repeat button is available in place of Redo. Use Repeat to repeat the most recent action.

Try It! Correcting Errors

1. Start Microsoft Excel.
2. Use the keyboard to type your first name in the first cell (the rectangular area in the upper-left corner) and then press ENTER.
3. Click the **Undo** button on the Quick Access Toolbar. The previous action—typing your first name—is undone.
4. Click the Redo button on the Quick Access Toolbar. The undone action is redone.
5. Press the down arrow key three times to select the cell in the fourth row of column A.
6. Type today's date and press ENTER.
7. Click the Undo drop-down arrow to display the Undo menu.
8. Press ESC. The menu closes without any action taking place.
9. Click the Close button and then click Don't Save to exit Excel without saving any changes.

Saving a File

- When you start Word, Excel, or PowerPoint a new file displays.

  ✓ *Creating a database file with Access is different. You learn how in the Access section of this book.*

- If you want to have a file available for future use, you must save it on a storage device.
- The first time you save a new file you must give it a name and select the location where you want to store it.
- Each Microsoft Office program is set to save files in a default storage location.
- You can select a different storage location in the Save As dialog box.
- After you save a file for the first time, you save changes to the file in order to make sure that you do not lose your work.
- Saving changes updates the previously saved version of the file with the most recent changes.

Try It! Saving a File

1. Start Word.
2. Click Save on the Quick Access Toolbar.

   OR

   a. Click the File tab.

   b. Click Save.
3. Select the contents in the File name text box if it is not selected already.

   ✓ *To select the contents, drag across it with your mouse.*
4. Type **BTry02_studentfirstname_studentlastname**.

   ✓ *Replace the text studentfirstname with your own first name, and studentlastname with your own last name. For example, if your name is Mary Jones, type BTry02_Mary_Jones. This will be the standard format for naming files throughout this book.*
5. Use the Navigation pane to navigate to the location where your teacher instructs you to store the files for this lesson. If necessary, create and name a new folder.

   ✓ *If the Navigation pane is not displayed, click Browse Folders.*
6. Click Save or press ENTER.
7. If a confirmation dialog box displays, click OK.
8. Leave the **BTry02_studentfirstname_studentlastname** file open to use in the next Try It.

Save As dialog box

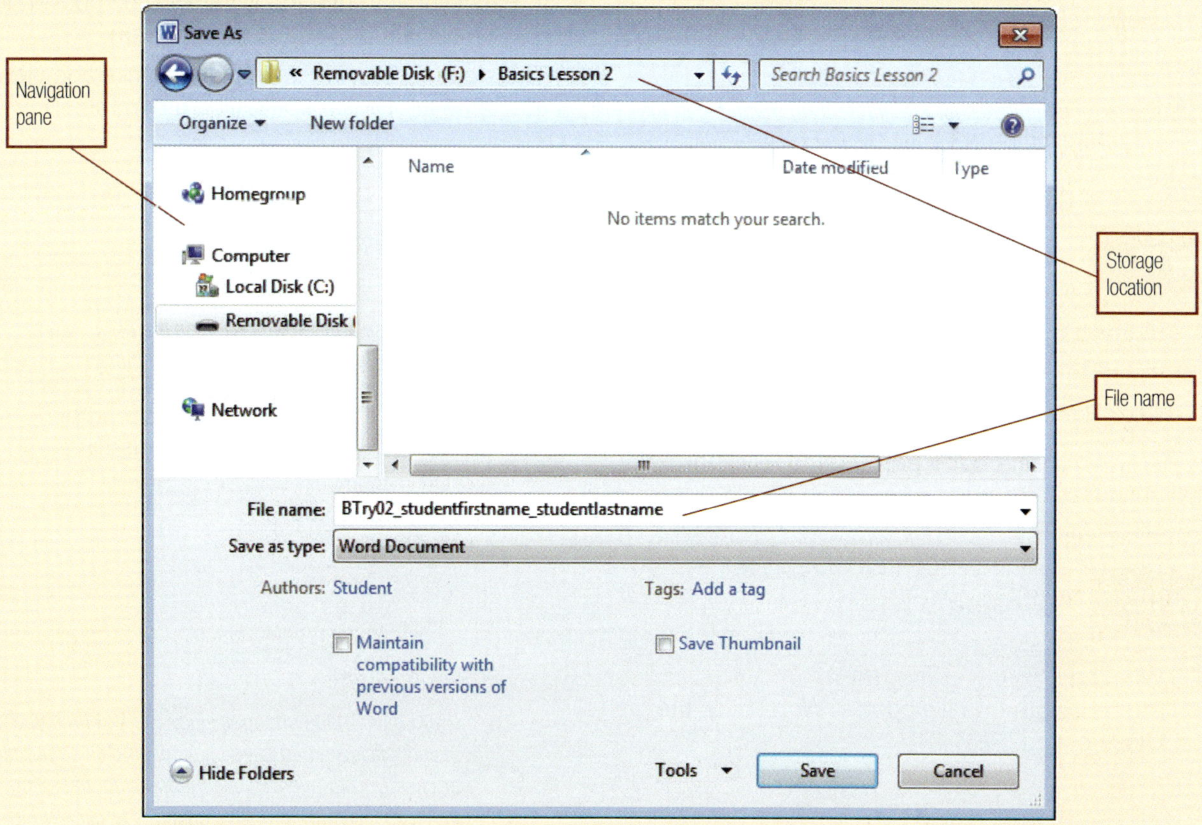

Try It! Saving Changes to a File

1. In the BTry02_studentfirstname_studentlastname file, type your first name, press SPACEBAR, type your last name, and then press ENTER.
2. Type today's date.
3. Click Save on the Quick Access Toolbar.

   OR

   a. Click File.

   b. Click Save.

   ✓ *You can also press CTRL + S to save changes.*
4. Leave the BTry02_studentfirstname_studentlastname file open to use in the next Try It.

Printing a File

- Printing creates a hard copy version of a file on paper.
- In Microsoft Office 2010 programs you use the Print tab in **Backstage view** to preview and print a file.
- You can also select printer settings such as the number of copies to print and which printer to use.

  ✓ *Printer setting options vary depending on the system configuration.*
- Your computer must be connected to a printer loaded with paper and ink in order to print.
- Ask your teacher for permission before printing any file.

  ✓ *Steps for printing in Access are different from printing in the other Microsoft Office programs. You learn how to print in Access in the Access section of this book.*

Closing a File

- A file remains open onscreen until you close it.
- If you try to close a file without saving, the program prompts you to save.
- You can close a file without saving it if you do not want to keep it for future use.
- In Word, PowerPoint, and Access you can use the Close button to close the file and exit the program; if there are multiple files open, the program remains running.
- In Excel you can use the Window Close button to close a file without exiting the program.
- The steps for closing a file using Backstage view are the same in all Microsoft Office programs.

Try It! Printing the Current File

1. In the BTry02_studentfirstname_studentlastname file, click File.
2. Click Print.
3. **With your teacher's permission,** click the Print button.

   ✓ *You can select settings such as the printer and number of copies to print before printing.*
4. Leave the BTry02_studentfirstname_studentlastname file open to use in the next Try It.

Try It! Closing a File

1. With the BTry02_studentfirstname_studentlastname file open in Word, click the Close button.

   OR

   a. Click File.

   b. Click Close.

   ✓ *If you have made changes since the last time you saved, click Save to save changes and close the file, or click Don't Save to close the file without saving. In Access, click Yes to save changes or click No to close without saving.*

Project 3—Create It

Create, Save, and Print a File in Word

DIRECTIONS

1. If you have a removable storage device to use for storing your work in this class, connect it to your computer. For example, insert a removable disk in a drive, or connect a flash drive to a USB port.
2. Click **Start** > **All Programs** > **Microsoft Word 2010** to start the Word program.
3. Move the mouse pointer so it is resting on the **Save** button on the Quick Access Toolbar. The ScreenTip displays Save (CTRL + S).
4. Point to the Zoom slider on the right end of the status bar.
5. Click the **Insert** tab on the Ribbon.
6. Click the **File** tab.
7. Click **Save** to display the Save As dialog box.
8. Type **BProj03_studentfirstname_studentlastname**.
9. Navigate to the location where your teacher instructs you to store the files for this lesson.

   ✓ *If necessary, create a new folder for storing the files.*
10. Click **Save** in the Save As dialog box to save the file, and click **OK** in the confirmation dialog box
11. In the new file, type your first name and your last name and press ENTER to start a new line.
12. Type today's date and press ENTER .
13. Type **Notes on using Microsoft Office 2010**.
14. Click the **Undo** button on the Quick Access Toolbar to undo the typing.
15. Click the **Redo** button to redo the action.
16. Click the **Save** button on the Quick Access Toolbar to save the changes to the file.
17. Click the **File** tab to display Backstage view.
18. Click **Print**. Backstage view should look similar to Figure 2-2.
19. **With your teacher's permission,** click the **Print** button to print the file.

    ✓ *If necessary, click the Printer drop-down arrow and select the printer your teacher wants you to use.*
20. Click the **File** tab, then click **Close** to close the file.
21. Exit Word.

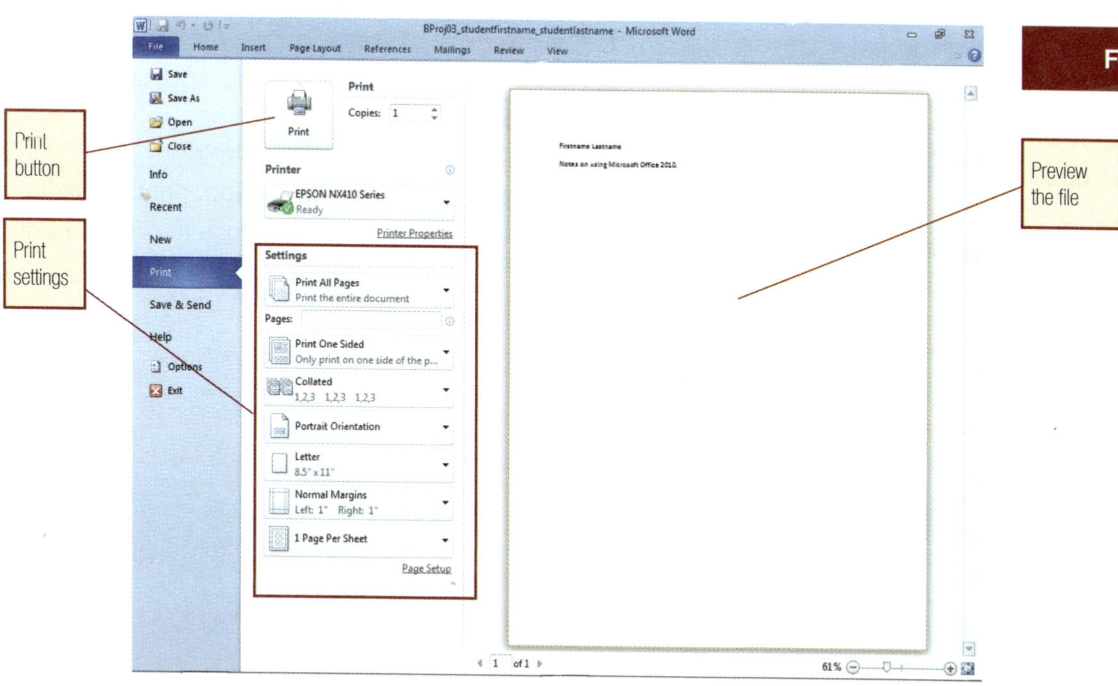

Figure 2-2

Project 4—Apply It

Compare Microsoft Office Programs

DIRECTIONS

1. Start Microsoft Excel.
2. Point to the following common elements in the Excel window: Zoom slider, Save button on the Quick Access Toolbar, View buttons, and the vertical scroll bar.
3. Click the **Insert** tab on the Ribbon.
4. Click the **File** tab to display Backstage view and then click **Save**.
5. Type **BProj04a_studentfirstname_studentlastname**.
6. Navigate to the location where your teacher instructs you to store the files for this lesson, and then click **Save** to save the file.
7. In the new file, type your first name and your last name and press ENTER.

   ✓ *In Excel, typing displays in the current, or selected, cell, and pressing ENTER moves to the next cell down.*

8. Type today's date and press ENTER.

   ✓ *Excel might apply date formatting to the entry. You learn more about formatting in a worksheet in the Excel section of this book.*

9. Click **Undo**.
10. Click **Undo** again.
11. Click **Redo** twice.
12. Click the **Save** button on the Quick Access Toolbar to save the changes to the file.
13. Click the **File** tab and then click **Print**.
14. **With your teacher's permission,** print the file.
15. Click the **Close** button to close the file and exit Excel.
16. Start Microsoft PowerPoint.
17. Point to the following common elements in the PowerPoint window: Zoom slider, Save button on the Quick Access Toolbar, View buttons, and the Close button.
18. Click the **Insert** tab on the Ribbon.
19. Click the **File** tab to display Backstage view and then click **Save**.
20. Type **BProj04b_studentfirstname_studentlastname**.
21. Navigate to the location where your teacher instructs you to store the files for this lesson, and then click **Save** to save the file.
22. In the new file, type your first name and your last name and press ENTER. Type today's date.

    ✓ *In PowerPoint, typing displays in the current, or selected, placeholder. Pressing ENTER starts a new line.*

23. Click **Undo**.
24. Click **Redo**.
25. Click the **Save** button on the Quick Access Toolbar to save the changes to the file.
26. Click the **File** tab and then click **Print**.
27. **With your teacher's permission,** print the file.
28. Click the **Close** button to close the file and exit PowerPoint.

Lesson 3

Working with Existing Files

➤ What You Will Learn

- Opening an Existing File
- Saving a File with New Name
- Viewing File Properties
- Using the Ribbon
- Using Access Keys
- Selecting Text
- Formatting Text

Software Skills You can open an existing file in the program used to create it. You can then use Microsoft Office program commands to save it with a new name so you can edit or format it, leaving the original file unchanged. Formatting improves the appearance and readability of text.

Application Skills As a public relations assistant at the Michigan Avenue Athletic Club you are responsible for preparing press releases. In this lesson, you will open an existing press release file in Word and save it with a new name. You will then enter, edit, and format the text to prepare it for distribution.

WORDS TO KNOW

Access keys
Keys you can use to select or execute a command.

Command
Input that tells the computer which task to execute.

Contextual tab
A Ribbon tab that is only available in a certain context or situation.

Contiguous
Adjacent or in a row.

Dialog box launcher
A button you click to open a dialog box.

File properties
Information about a file.

Font
A complete set of characters in a specific face, style, and size.

Font color
The color of characters in a font set.

Font size
The height of an uppercase letter in a font set.

Font style
The slant and weight of characters in a font set.

Format
To change the appearance of text or other elements.

Gallery
A menu that displays pictures instead of plain text options.

WORDS TO KNOW

Highlighted
Marked with color to stand out from the surrounding text.

KeyTip
A pop-up letter that identifies the access key(s) for a command.

Live Preview
A feature of Microsoft Office that shows you how a command will affect the selection before you actually select the command.

Noncontiguous
Not adjacent.

Select
Mark text as the focus of the next action.

Selection bar
A narrow strip along the left margin of a page that automates selection of text. When the mouse pointer is in the selection area, the pointer changes to an arrow pointing up and to the right.

Toggle
A type of command that can be switched off or on.

What You Can Do

Opening an Existing File

- To view or edit a file that has been saved and closed, open it again.
- You can open a recently used file on the Recent tab in Backstage view by clicking it.
- You can use the Open dialog box to locate and open any file.

Try It! Opening an Existing File

1. Start Microsoft Excel.
2. Click File.
3. Click Open.
4. Navigate to the location where the data files for this lesson are stored.
5. Double-click **BTry03a** to open it.

   OR

   a. Click **BTry03a**.

   b. Click Open.
6. Close the file, but leave Excel open to use in the next Try It.

Open dialog box

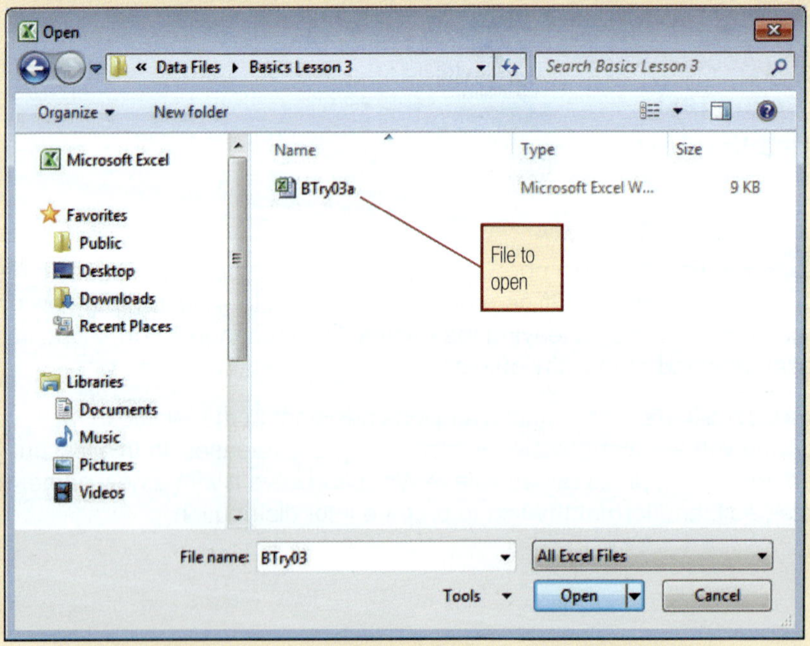

Try It! Opening a Recently Opened Document

1. In Excel, click File.
2. Click Recent.
3. Click BTry03a in the list on the right side of the screen.
4. Leave the file open in Excel to use in the next Try It.

Recent tab in Backstage view

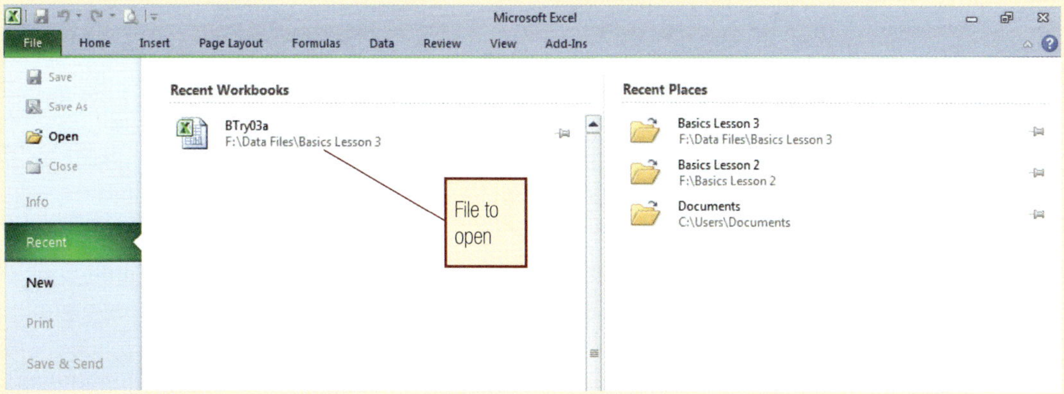

Saving a File with a New Name

- Use the Save As command to save a copy of a file in a different location or with a different file name.
- The original file remains unchanged.

Viewing File Properties

- You can view **file properties** on the Info tab in Backstage view.
- File properties include information about the file, such as how big it is and when it was created or modified.

Try It! Saving a File with a New Name

1. In Excel, with the BTry03a file open, click File.
2. Click Save As.
3. Type BTry03a_studentfirstname_ studentlastname, using your own first and last name.
4. Navigate to the location where your teacher instructs you to store the files for this lesson.
5. Click Save.
6. Close the file and exit Excel.

Try It! Viewing File Properties

1. Start PowerPoint.
2. Click File > Open.
3. Navigate to the location where the data files for this lesson are stored.
4. Double-click **BTry03b** to open it.
5. Click File.
6. Click Info. View the file properties on the right side of the Info tab.
7. Close the file and exit PowerPoint.

File properties on the Info tab in Backstage view

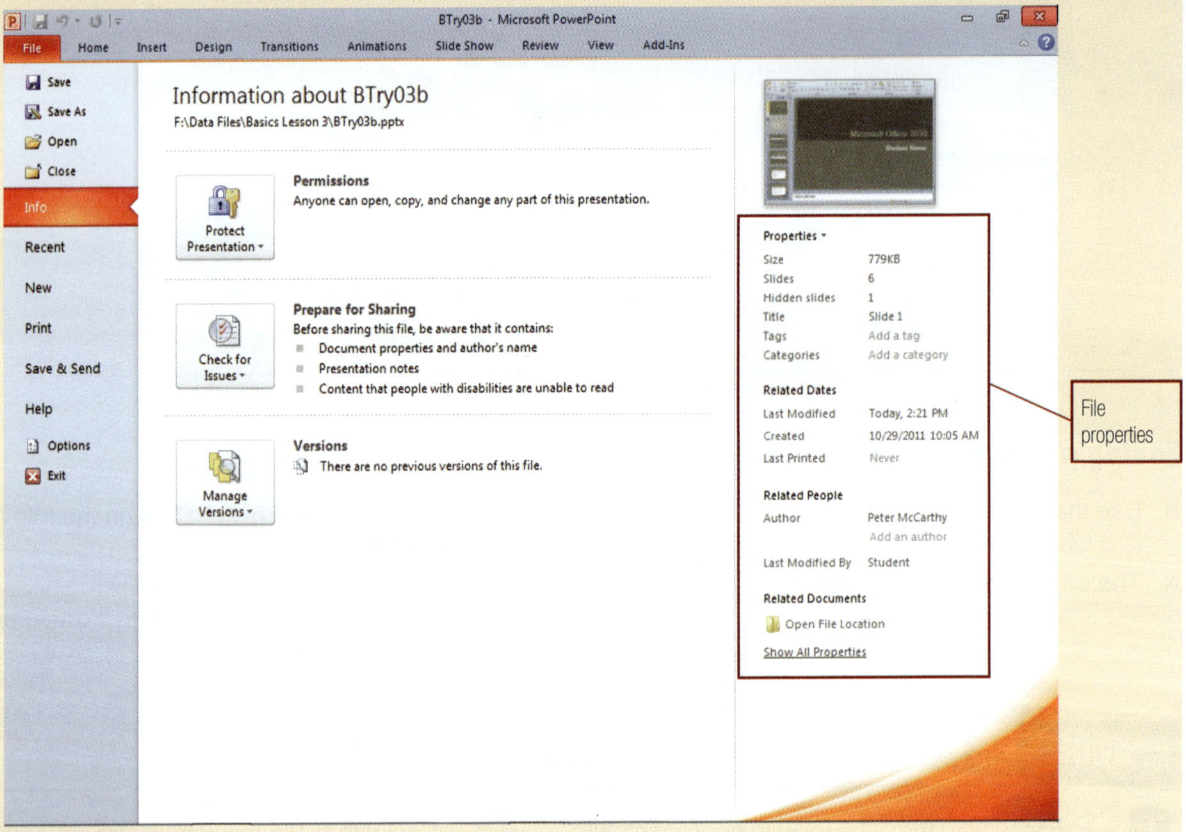

Using the Ribbon

- To accomplish a task in a Microsoft Office 2010 program, you execute **commands**. For example, Save is the command for saving a file.
- Most commands are available as buttons on the Ribbon. Refer to Figure 3-1 to identify parts of the Home tab of the Ribbon.
- The Ribbon is organized into tabs based on activities, such as reviewing a file or inserting content. On each tab, commands are organized into groups.
- **Contextual tabs** are only available in certain situations. For example, if you select a picture, the Picture Tools tab becomes available. If you deselect the picture, the Picture Tools tab disappears.
- You can minimize the Ribbon to display only the tabs if you want to see more of a file, and expand it when you need to use the commands.
- When you point to a button on the Ribbon with the mouse, the button is highlighted and a ScreenTip displays information about the command.
- Buttons representing commands that are not currently available are dimmed.
- Some buttons are **toggles**; they appear highlighted when active, or "on."
- If there is a drop-down arrow on a button, it means that when you click the arrow, a menu or **gallery** displays so you can make a specific selection.

  ✓ *In this book, when it says "click the button" you should click the button; when it says "click the drop-down arrow" you should click the arrow on the button.*

- Sometimes, the entire first row of a gallery displays on the Ribbon.
- You can rest the mouse pointer on a gallery item to see a **Live Preview** of the way your document will look if you select that item.
- You can scroll a gallery on the Ribbon, or click the More button to view the entire gallery.
- Some Ribbon groups have a **dialog box launcher** button. Click the dialog box launcher to display a dialog box, task pane, or window where you can select additional options, or multiple options at the same time.
- Note that the way items display on the Ribbon may depend on the width of the program window.
  - If the window is wide enough, groups expand to display all items.
  - If the window is not wide enough, groups collapse to a single group button. Click the button to display a menu of commands in the group.
  - The size of icons in a group may vary depending on the width of the window.
- If your program window is narrower or wider than the one used in this book, the Ribbon on your screen may look different from the one in the figures.
- In addition, the steps you must take to complete a procedure may vary slightly.
  - If your screen is narrower than the one in this book, you may have to click a group button to display the commands in that group before you can complete the steps in the procedure.
  - If your screen is wider, you may be able to skip a step for selecting a group button and go directly to the step for selecting a specific command.

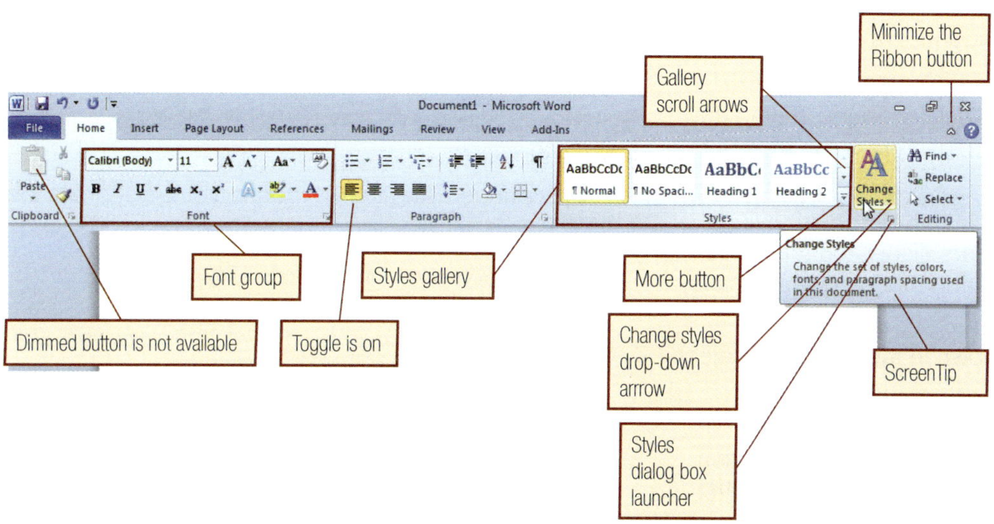

Figure 3-1

Try It! Using the Ribbon

1. Start Microsoft Word.
2. Save the open file as **BTry03c_studentfirstname_studentlastname** in the location where your teacher instructs you to store files for this lesson.
3. Point to the Center button on the Ribbon. The ScreenTip displays the button name, shortcut keys, and a description.
4. Click the Center button. The insertion point moves to the center of the current line.
5. Type your first name, press ENTER, and then type your last name.
6. Press CTRL + ENTER, the shortcut key combination for starting a new page, and type today's date.
7. Click the View tab on the Ribbon to make it active.
8. Click the Two Pages button Two Pages. This command changes the view to display two pages at the same time.
9. Click the One Page button One Page. This command changes the view to display one page at a time.
10. Save the changes to **BTry03c_studentfirstname_studentlastname**, and keep it open to use in the next Try It.

Try It! Minimizing/Expanding the Ribbon

1. In **BTry03c_studentfirstname_studentlastname**, click the Minimize the Ribbon button. The Ribbon is hidden, and the Minimize the Ribbon button is replaced by the Expand the Ribbon button.

   ✓ *CTRL + F1 is the shortcut key combination for minimizing the Ribbon.*

2. Click the Expand the Ribbon button to restore the Ribbon.
3. Double-click the View tab. Double-clicking any tab is an alternative way to minimize the Ribbon.
4. Double-click the Insert tab. Double-clicking any tab when the Ribbon is minimized is an alternative way to expand the Ribbon.
5. Save the changes to **BTry03c_studentfirstname_studentlastname**, and keep it open to use in the next Try It.

Using Access Keys

- Microsoft Office 2010 programs are designed primarily for use with a mouse.
- Some people prefer to select commands using the keyboard. In that case, you can press the Alt key to activate **access keys**.
- When access keys are active, **KeyTips** showing one or more keyboard letters display on the screen over any feature or command that can be selected using the keyboard.
- You press the letter(s) shown in the KeyTip to select the command or feature.
- If there is more than one access key for a command, you may press the keys in combination (at the same time) or consecutively (press the first key and then immediately press the next key).
- If a KeyTip is dimmed, the command is not available.
- The KeyTips remain active if you must press additional keys to complete a command.
- Once a command is executed, the KeyTips disappear.
- To continue using the keyboard, you must press the Alt key to activate the access keys again.

  ✓ *People accustomed to the shortcut key combinations in previous versions of Microsoft Office will be happy to know that they function in Microsoft Office 2010 programs as well. For example, you can still press CTRL + SHIFT + F to open the Font dialog box.*

Try It! Using Access Keys

1. With the **BTry03c_studentfirstname_ studentlastname** file still displayed, press ALT . The KeyTips for the Ribbon tabs display.
2. Press W to make the View tab active. The KeyTips for the View tab display.
3. Press 2 to change to Two Page view.
4. Press ALT , W , 1 to change to One Page view.
5. Press ALT , W , J to change the view to show the file at 100% magnification.
6. Press ALT , H to make the Home tab of the Ribbon active.
7. Press ESC twice to cancel the KeyTips.
8. Save the changes to **BTry03c_ studentfirstname_studentlastname**, and keep it open to use in the next Try It.

KeyTips on the View tab

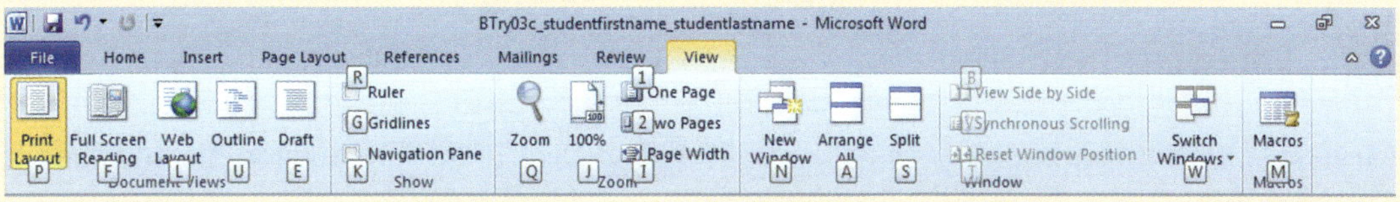

Selecting Text

- **Select** text in order to edit it or format it.
- You can select any amount of **contiguous** or **noncontiguous** text.
- You can also select non-text characters, such as symbols; nonprinting characters, such as paragraph marks; and graphics, such as pictures.
- By default, selected text appears **highlighted** onscreen as black characters on a blue background.
- When you first select text, the transparent Mini toolbar may display. The toolbar will fade away completely if you do not use it.
- When text is selected, any command or action affects the selection. For example, if text is selected and you press DEL , the selection is deleted.
- Refer to Table 3-1 for keyboard selection commands. Refer to Table 3-2 on the next page for mouse selection commands.

Table 3-1 Keyboard Selection Commands

To Select	Press
One character right	SHIFT + →
One character left	SHIFT + ←
One line up	SHIFT + ↑
One line down	SHIFT + ↓
To end of line	SHIFT + END
To beginning of line	SHIFT + HOME
To end of document	SHIFT + CTRL + END
To beginning of document	SHIFT + CTRL + HOME
Entire document	CTRL + A

Table 3-2 Mouse Selection Commands

To Select	Do This
One word	Double-click word.
One sentence	CTRL + click in sentence.
One line	Click in **selection bar** to the left of the line.
One paragraph	Double-click in selection bar to the left of the paragraph.
Document	Triple-click in selection bar.
Noncontiguous text	Select first block, Press and hold CTRL, select additional block(s).

Try It! Selecting Text

1. In **BTry03c_studentfirstname_studentlastname**, press CTRL + HOME, the shortcut key combination to move the insertion point to the beginning of a Word document.
2. Position the mouse pointer to the left of the first character in your first name.
3. Hold down the left mouse button.
4. Drag the mouse across your first name to select it.
5. Click anywhere outside the selection to cancel it.
6. Double-click your last name to select it.
7. Press DEL. The selected text is deleted.
8. Save the changes to **BTry03c_studentfirstname_studentlastname**, and keep it open to use in the next Try It.

Formatting Text

- You can **format** text to change its appearance.
- Formatting can enhance and emphasize text, and set a tone or mood for a file.
- Microsoft Office 2010 programs offer many options for formatting text; you will learn more in the other sections of this book.
- Some common formatting options include:
  - **Font**
  - **Font size**
  - **Font style**
  - **Font color**
- You can change the formatting of selected text, or you can select formatting before you type new text.
- You can preview the way selected text will look with formatting by resting the mouse pointer on the formatting command on the Ribbon.

Try It! Formatting Selected Text

1. In **BTry03c_studentfirstname_studentlastname**, double-click your first name to select it.
2. On the Home tab, in the Font group, click the Bold button .
3. On the Home tab, in the Font group, click the Font Size drop-down arrow to display a list of font sizes, and rest the mouse pointer on the number 28 to preview the text with the formatting.
4. Click 16 on the Font size drop-down list to change the font size to 16 points.
5. On the Home tab, in the Font group, click the Underline button .
6. On the Home tab, in the Font group click the Italic button .
7. Click anywhere outside the selection in the document to deselect the text.
8. Save the changes to **BTry03c_studentfirstname_studentlastname**, and keep it open to use in the next Try It.

Try It! Formatting New Text

1. In **BTry03c_studentfirstname_studentlastname**, move the insertion point to the end of your first name and press ENTER to start a new line.
2. Type your middle name (If you do not have a middle name, type any name.) Notice that the current formatting carries forward to the new line.
3. Press ENTER to start a new line. Click the Bold , Italic , and Underline buttons to toggle those commands off.
4. Click the Font drop-down arrow and click Cambria on the list of available fonts.
5. Click the Font Color drop-down arrow and click Purple.
6. Type your last name. The text displays in purple 16-point Cambria, without bold, italic, or underline formatting.
7. Close **BTry03c_studentfirstname_studentlastname**, saving the changes, and exit Word.

Select a font color

Project 5—Create It

Press Release

DIRECTIONS

1. If you have a removable storage device to use for storing your work in this class, connect it to your computer. For example, insert a removable disk in a drive, or connect a flash drive to a USB port.
2. Start Microsoft Word.
3. Click the **File** tab on the Ribbon and then click **Open**.
4. Navigate to the location where the data files for this lesson are stored.
5. Double-click the file **BProj05** to open it.
6. Click the **File** tab and then click **Save As** to open the Save As dialog box.
7. Type **BProj05_studentfirstname_studentlastname** in the File name box.
8. Navigate to the folder where your teacher instructs you to store the files for this lesson.
9. Save the file.
10. Select the headline: *Voyager Travel Adventures Announces Exciting Summer Tours*.
11. Click the **Bold** button [B].
12. Click the **Font Size** drop-down arrow [11] and click **14**.
13. Select the text *Denver, Colorado – Today's Date –* and then click the **Italic** button [I].
14. Select the text *Today's Date*, press [DEL] to delete it, and then type the actual date.
15. Press [CTRL] + [END] to move the insertion point to the end of the document, and press [ENTER] to start a new line.
16. Click the **Font** drop-down arrow [Calibri (Body)] and click Cambria.
17. Click the **Font Size** drop-down arrow [11] and click **12**.
18. Type **For more information contact:** and press [ENTER].
19. Click the **Bold** button [B].
20. Click the **Font Color** drop-down arrow [A] and click **Red**.
21. Type your full name. The file should look similar to Figure 3-2.
22. Save the changes to file.
23. Click the **File** tab. Click **Info**, if necessary, to view the file properties. Note the date and time the file was created and modified.
24. **With your teacher's permission**, print the file.
25. Close the file.

Figure 3-2

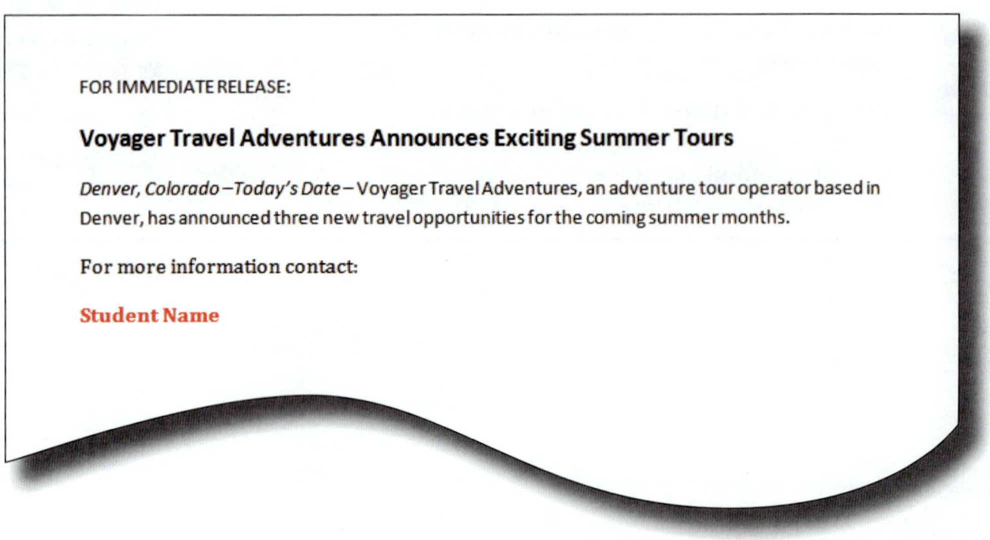

FOR IMMEDIATE RELEASE:

Voyager Travel Adventures Announces Exciting Summer Tours

Denver, Colorado – Today's Date – Voyager Travel Adventures, an adventure tour operator based in Denver, has announced three new travel opportunities for the coming summer months.

For more information contact:

Student Name

Project 6—Apply It

Press Release

DIRECTIONS

1. Start Microsoft Word, if necessary.
2. Open the file **BProj06** from the location where the data files for this lesson are stored.
3. Save the file as **BProj06_studentfirstname_studentlastname** in the location where your teacher instructs you to store the files for this lesson.
4. Change the font of the headline to Cambria and the font size to 16.
5. Replace the text *Today's Date* with the current date.
6. Position the insertion point at the end of the main paragraph and insert the paragraph shown in Figure 3-3, applying formatting as marked.
7. Move the insertion point to the end of the document, press ENTER, and type your full name in 12-point Cambria, bold, as shown in Figure 3-3.
8. Change the color of the first line of text to Light Blue and increase the font size to 12.

   ✓ *Use ScreenTips to identify the correct color.*
9. Save the changes.
10. **With your teacher's permission**, print the file.
11. Close the file, saving changes, and exit Word.

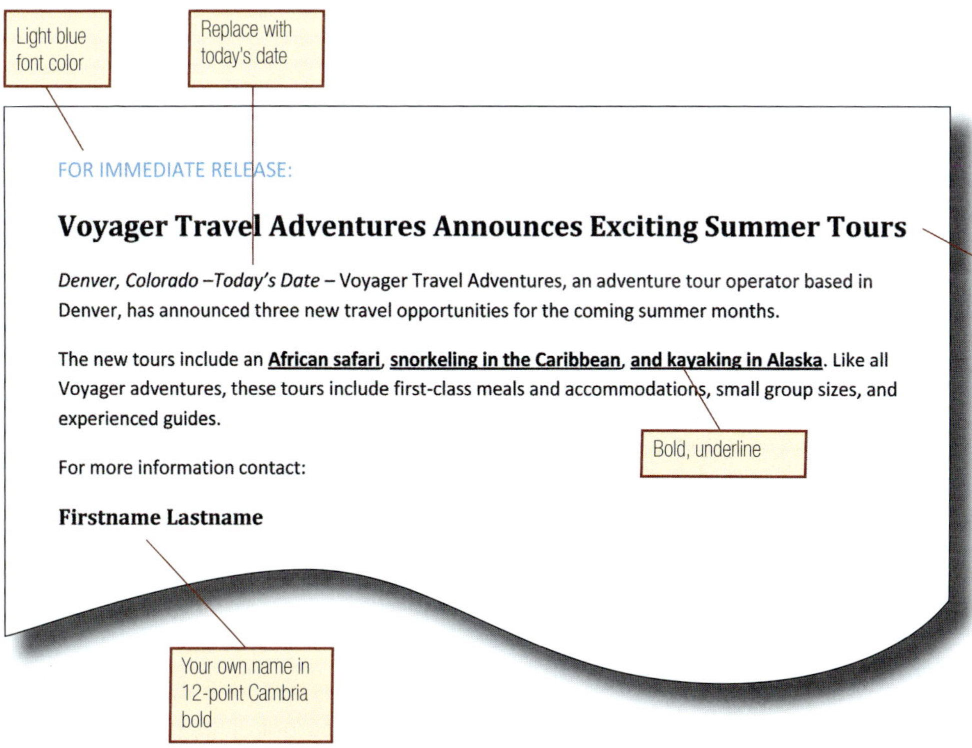

FOR IMMEDIATE RELEASE:

Voyager Travel Adventures Announces Exciting Summer Tours

Denver, Colorado –Today's Date – Voyager Travel Adventures, an adventure tour operator based in Denver, has announced three new travel opportunities for the coming summer months.

The new tours include an **African safari**, **snorkeling in the Caribbean**, **and kayaking in Alaska**. Like all Voyager adventures, these tours include first-class meals and accommodations, small group sizes, and experienced guides.

For more information contact:

Firstname Lastname

Figure 3-3

WORDS TO KNOW

Dialog box
A window in which you select options that affect the way the program executes a command.

Landscape orientation
Rotating document text so it displays and prints horizontally across the longer side of a page.

Margins
The amount of white space between the text and the edge of the page on each side.

Portrait orientation
The default position for displaying and printing text horizontally across the shorter side of a page.

Shortcut menu
A menu of relevant commands that displays when you right-click an item. Also called a context menu.

Task pane
A small window that displays additional options and commands for certain features in a Microsoft Office 2010 program.

Toolbar
A row of command buttons.

Lesson 4

Using Command Options

➤ What You Will Learn

- Using the Quick Access Toolbar
- Using the Mini Toolbar
- Using Shortcut Menus
- Using Dialog Box Options
- Using Task Panes
- Formatting Pages

Software Skills As you have learned, to accomplish a task in a Microsoft Office 2010 program, you must execute a command. Most commands are available on the Ribbon, but you may also use toolbars, menus, dialog boxes, or task panes. Page formatting includes settings such as margins and page size. To prepare a file for printing or other types of distribution you may have to change the page formatting, such as adjusting the margin width, or selecting a page size.

Application Skills As the store manager for Whole Grains Bread, a bakery, you must prepare a contact list of your employees for the franchise owner. In this lesson, you will use Excel to complete and format the contact list. You will also prepare the same information in a Word document, in case the owner is not able to work with Excel.

What You Can Do

Using the Quick Access Toolbar

- The Quick Access Toolbar displays in the upper left corner of the program window.
- To select a command from the Quick Access Toolbar, click its button.

- By default, there are three buttons on the Quick Access Toolbar: Save, Undo, and Repeat. The Repeat button changes to Redo once you use the Undo command.
- Use the Customize Quick Access Toolbar button to add or remove buttons from the **toolbar**.
- The buttons on the Quick Access Toolbar are not available in Backstage view.

Try It! Adding and Removing Quick Access Toolbar Buttons

1. Start Microsoft Word and save the default blank document as **BTry04a_studentfirstname_studentlastname** in the location where your teacher instructs you to store the files for this lesson.
2. Click the Customize Quick Access Toolbar button to display a menu of common commands.

   ✓ *A check mark next to a command indicates it is already on the Quick Access Toolbar.*
3. Click Print Preview and Print on the menu. The button for Print Preview and Print is added to the Quick Access Toolbar.
4. Right-click the Paste button on the Home tab of the Ribbon.
5. Click Add to Quick Access Toolbar.
6. Click the Customize Quick Access Toolbar button to display a menu of common commands.
7. Click Print Preview and Print. The button is removed from the Quick Access Toolbar.
8. Right-click the Paste button on the Quick Access Toolbar.
9. Click Remove from Quick Access Toolbar.
10. Save the changes to **BTry04a_studentfirstname_studentlastname**, and keep it open to use in the next Try It.

Using the Mini Toolbar

- The Mini toolbar displays when the mouse pointer rests on selected text or data that can be formatted.
- At first, the Mini toolbar is semi-transparent, so you can easily ignore it if you don't need it.
- When you move the mouse pointer over the Mini toolbar, the Mini toolbar becomes opaque.
- Select a command from the Mini toolbar the same way you select a command from the Ribbon.

Try It! Using the Mini Toolbar

1. In the **BTry04a_studentfirstname_studentlastname** document, type your first name, and then select it. The Mini toolbar displays semi-transparent, so you can barely see it.
2. Move the mouse pointer over the Mini toolbar.
3. Click the Bold button **B** on the Mini toolbar.
4. Save the changes to **BTry04a_studentfirstname_studentlastname**, and leave it open to use in the next Try It.

Formatting with the Mini toolbar

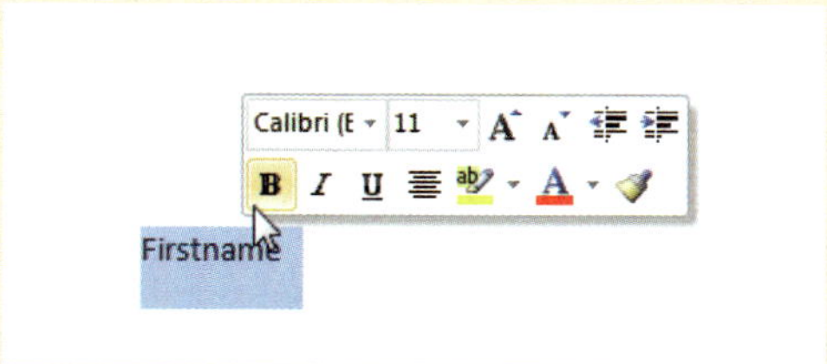

Using Shortcut Menus

- When you right-click almost any element on the screen in any Microsoft Office 2010 program, a **shortcut menu** displays.
- Shortcut menus include options relevant to the current item.

✓ *Shortcut menus are sometimes called context menus.*

- Click an option on the shortcut menu to select it.
- Alternatively, press the access key—the key that is underlined in the command name.

✓ *Sometimes, selecting an option on a shortcut menu opens a submenu, which is simply one menu that opens off another menu.*

- If you right-click selected data, the Mini toolbar may display in addition to the shortcut menu. The Mini toolbar disappears when you select an option on the menu.

Try It! Using a Shortcut Menu

1. In **BTry04a_studentfirstname_studentlastname**, click anywhere outside the selected text to deselect it.
2. Right-click the Home tab of the Ribbon to display a shortcut menu.
3. Click Show Quick Access Toolbar Below the Ribbon on the shortcut menu. The Quick Access Toolbar moves below the Ribbon.
4. Right-click the status bar at the bottom of the Word window.

Use a shortcut menu to toggle screen elements off and on in Word

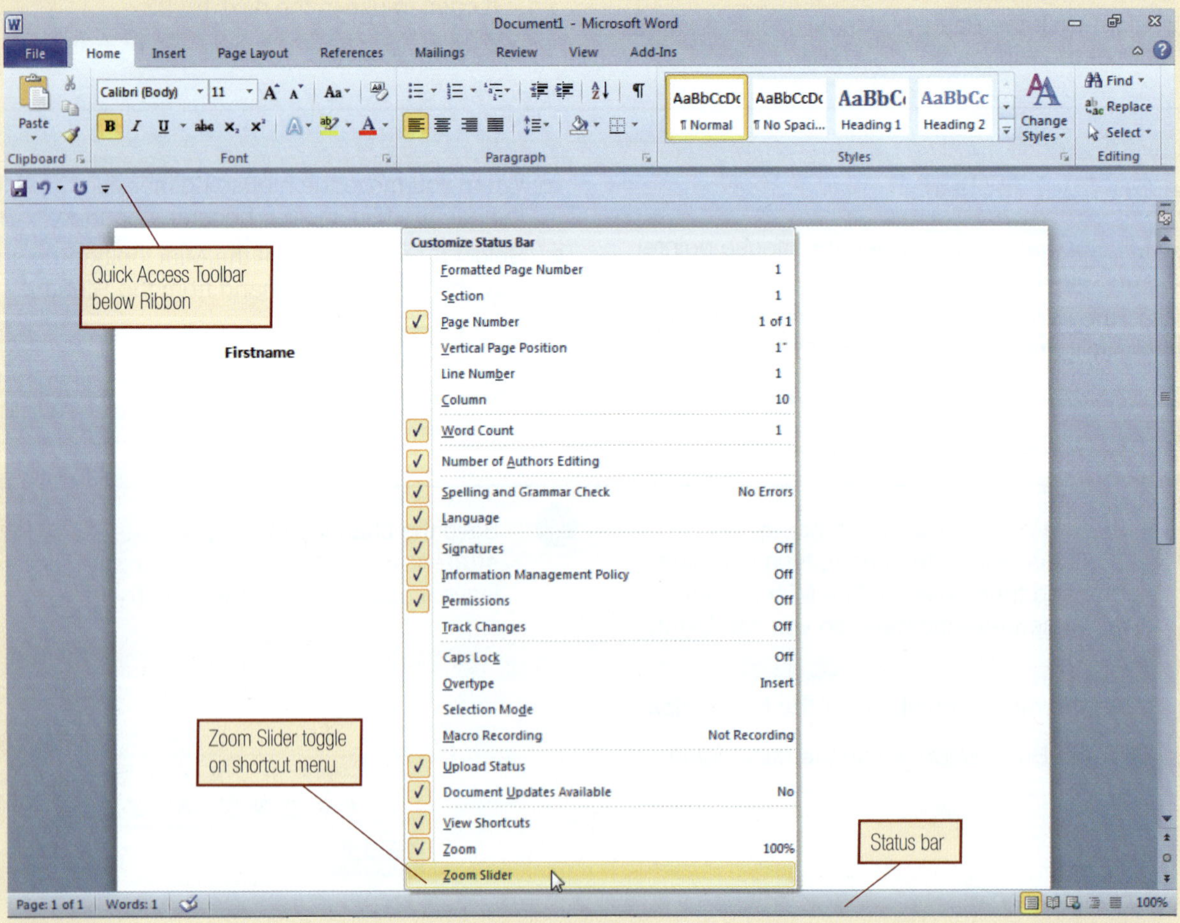

(continued)

Try It! **Using a Shortcut Menu** *(continued)*

5. Click Zoom Slider on the shortcut menu to toggle the Zoom slider display off.
6. Click Zoom Slider on the shortcut menu again, to toggle the Zoom Slider display on.
7. Right-click the View tab of the Ribbon to display a shortcut menu.
8. Click Show Quick Access Toolbar Above the Ribbon on the shortcut menu to move the toolbar back to its default position.
9. Leave the **BTry04a_studentfirstname_studentlastname** file open to use in the next Try It.

Using Dialog Box Options

- When you must provide additional information before executing a command, a **dialog box** displays.
- You enter information in a dialog box using a variety of controls (refer to Figures 4-1 and 4-2):
  - **List box**—A list of items from which selections can be made. If more items are available than can fit in the space, a scrollbar is displayed.
  - **Palette**—A display, such as colors or shapes, from which you can select an option.
  - **Drop-down list box**—A combination of text box and list box; type your selection in the box or click the drop-down arrow to display the list.
  - **Check box**—A square that you click to select or clear an option. A check mark in the box indicates that the option is selected.
  - **Command button**—A button used to execute a command. An ellipsis on a command button means that clicking the button opens another dialog box.

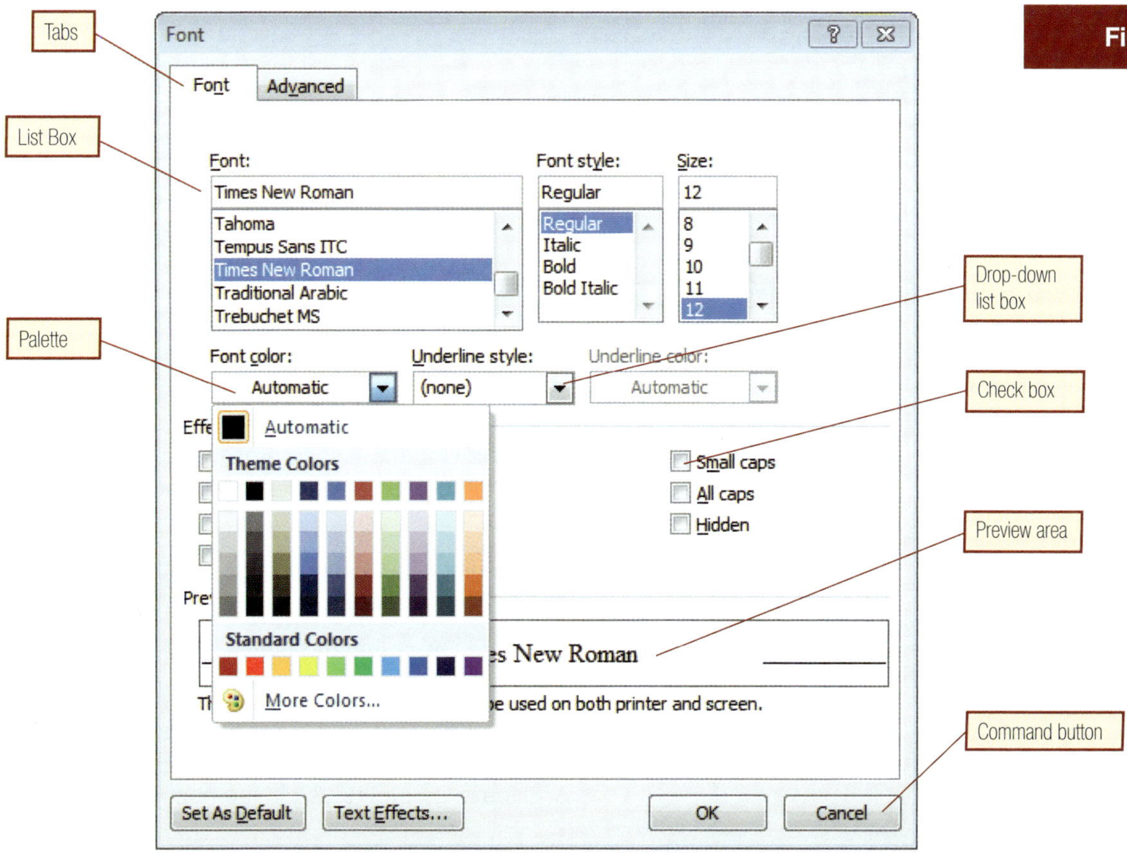

Figure 4-1

- **Tabs**—Markers across the top of the dialog box that, when clicked, display additional pages of options within the dialog box.
- **Preview area**—An area where you can preview the results of your selections before executing the commands.
- **Increment box**—A space where you type a value, such as inches or numbers, or use increment arrows beside the box to increase or decrease the value with a mouse. Sometimes called a spin box.
- **Text box**—A space where you type variable information, such as a file name.
- **Option buttons**—A series of circles, only one of which can be selected at a time. Click the circle you want to select it.

■ To move from one control to another in a dialog box you can click the control with the mouse, or press TAB.

■ Some dialog box controls have access keys which are underlined in the control name. Press ALT and the access key to select the control.

Figure 4-2

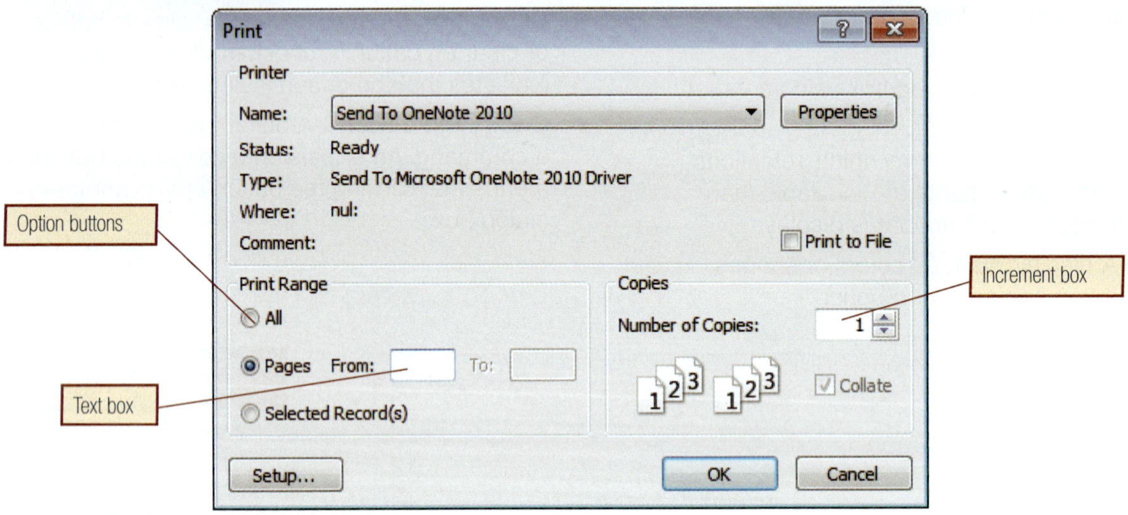

Try It! Using Dialog Box Options

1. In **BTry04a_studentfirstname_studentlastname**, select your first name.
2. On the Home tab, click the Font group dialog box launcher to open the Font dialog box.

Font group on the Home tab

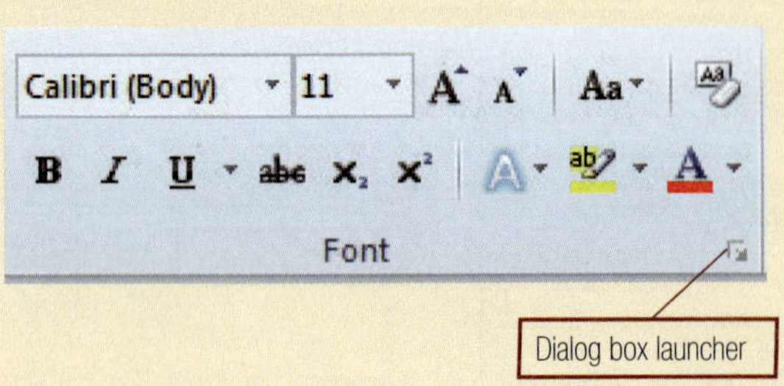

3. In the Font style list box, click Italic.
4. In the Size box, click 8.
5. Click the Underline style drop-down arrow, and click the double underline that is second from the top.
6. In the Effects section, click the Small caps check box to select it.
7. Click the OK command button to apply the formatting to the selected text.
8. Deselect the text, then save the changes to **BTry04a_studentfirstname_studentlastname**, and leave it open to use in the next Try It.

Displaying Task Panes

- Some commands open a **task pane** instead of a dialog box. For example, if you select to insert a clip art picture, the Clip Art task pane displays.
- Task panes have some features in common with dialog boxes. For example, some have text boxes in which you type text as well as drop-down list boxes, check boxes, and options buttons.
- Unlike a dialog box, you can leave a task pane open while you work, move it, or close it to get it out of the way. You can also have more than one task pane open at the same time.

✓ *You learn how to accomplish tasks using task panes in the lesson in which that feature is covered. For example, in Basics Lesson 5 you learn how to use the Windows Clipboard task pane to copy or move a selection.*

Try It! Displaying Task Panes

1. In the **BTry04a_studentfirstname_studentlastname** document, on the Home tab, click the Styles group dialog box launcher [launcher icon] to open the Styles task pane.
2. In the document window, click to position the insertion point at the end of your name.
3. In the Styles task pane, click Clear All. This clears the formatting from the text.
4. Press ENTER to start a new line, and then type your last name.

   ✓ *If the task pane moves you can point at its title bar and drag it to its original position.*

5. On the Home tab, click the Clipboard group dialog box launcher [launcher icon] to open the Clipboard task pane. Now, both the Styles task pane and the Clipboard task pane are open.
6. Click the Close button [×] in the upper-right corner of the Styles task pane to close it.
7. Click the Close button [×] in the upper-right corner of the Clipboard task pane to close it.
8. Close **BTry04a_studentfirstname_studentlastname** saving all changes, and exit Word.

Open multiple task panes

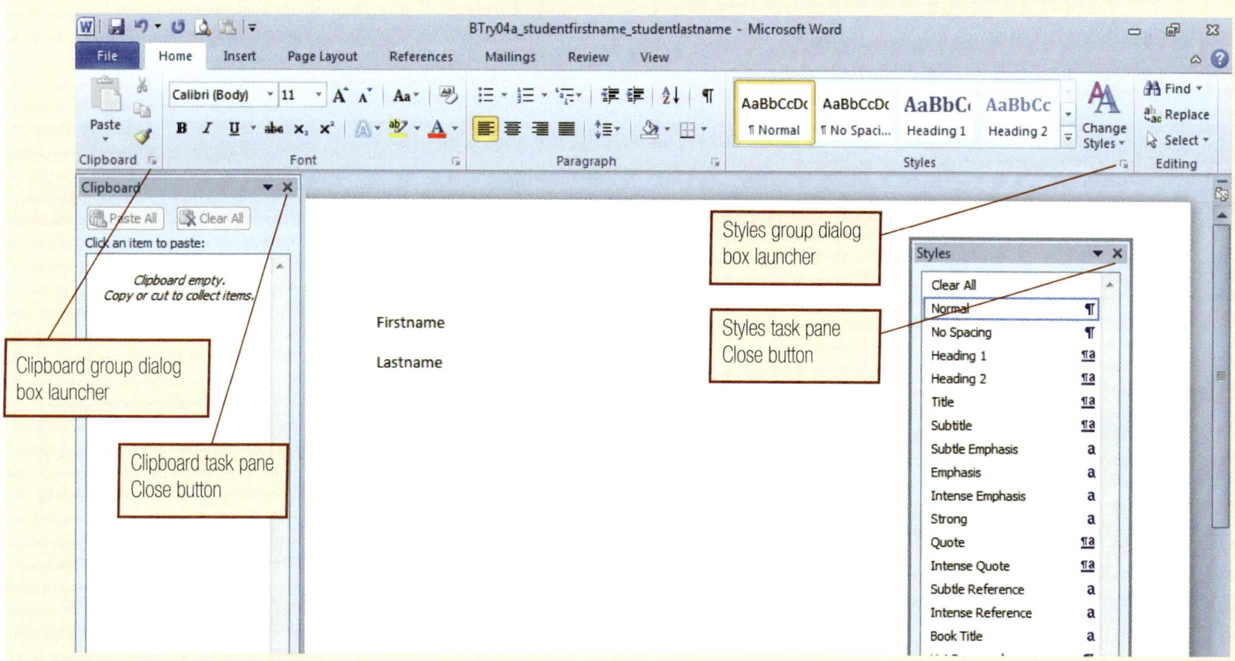

Formatting Pages

- Before you print or otherwise distribute a file, you may need to adjust the page formatting.
- Use the Print tab in Backstage View to select basic page formatting settings.
- In Access, use the options on the Print Preview tab.
- You can select an orientation, a paper size, and **margin** widths.
- Orientation is either portrait or landscape.
  - Select **Portrait orientation**—the default—when you want data displayed across the shorter length of a page.
  - Select **Landscape orientation** when you want data displayed across the wider length of a page.

✓ *You will learn about more advanced page formatting settings, such as setting custom margins and adjusting the alignment, in the program sections of this book.*

- You can select from a list of preset margins, including Normal, Wide, and Narrow. Margins are measured in inches.

Try It! Formatting Pages

1. Start Excel and open **BTry04b** from the data files for this lesson. Save the file as **BTry04b_studentfirstname_studentlastname** in the location where your teacher instructs you to store the files for this lesson.
2. Click the File tab and then click Print to display the Print tab in Backstage view. In the preview, you see that not all columns fit on the first page.
3. Click the Margins down arrow and click Narrow on the menu. This changes the width of the margins from 1" on all sides to 0.75" on the top and bottom and 0.25" on the left and right. Now, only the Total column is still on page 2.
4. Click the Orientation down arrow and click Landscape Orientation. Now, all columns fit, with room to spare.
5. Click the Margins down arrow and click Wide to increase the width of the margins.
6. Click the File tab to close Backstage view.
7. Close **BTry04b_studentfirstname_studentlastname**, saving all changes, and exit Excel.

Project 7—Create It

Contact List in Excel

DIRECTIONS

1. Click **Start** > **All Programs** > **Microsoft Excel** to start the Excel program.
2. Open the file **BProj07** from the data files for this lesson, and save it as **BProj07_studentfirstname_studentlastname** in the location where your teacher instructs you to store the files for this lesson.
3. Double-click on the word *Position* (in cell A2). This positions the insertion point in the cell.
4. Select the word *Position*. The semi-transparent Mini toolbar displays.
5. Move the pointer over the Mini toolbar to make it opaque as shown in Figure 4-3 on the next page, and then click the **Bold** button on it.
6. Click the next cell down the column, containing the text **Clerk**, and drag down to the cell in row 12, containing the text **Manager**. This selects the cells.
7. On the Home tab, click the **Font group** dialog box launcher to open the Font dialog box.

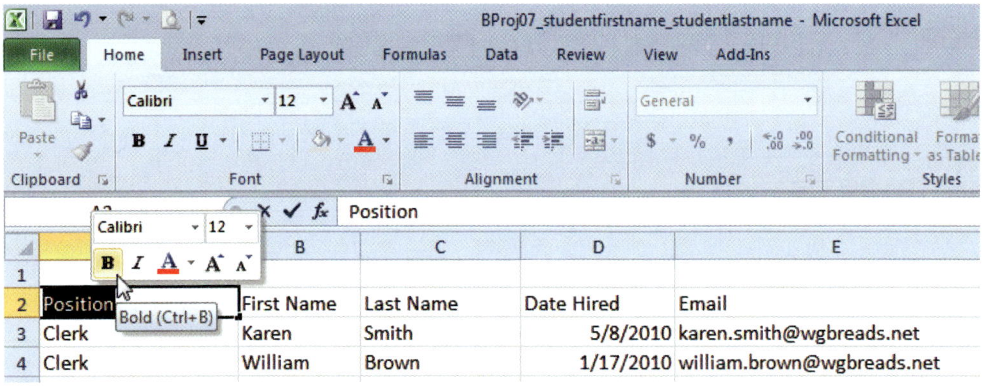

Figure 4-3

8. In the Font style list box, click **Italic**.
9. Click the **Underline** drop-down arrow and click **Double**.
10. Click **OK** to close the dialog box and apply the formatting.
11. Click cell **B12**—the blank cell to the right of the text *Manager* and below the text *Kevin*.
12. Type your own first name, and then press TAB.
13. Type your last name, and then press TAB.
14. Type today's date, and then press TAB.
15. Type your e-mail address, and then press TAB.
16. Right-click your e-mail address to display a shortcut menu
17. On the shortcut menu, click **Remove Hyperlink**. This removes the hyperlink formatting from your e-mail address.
18. Click the **Customize Quick Access Toolbar** button and click **Print Preview and Print** to add the Print Preview and Print button to the Quick Access Toolbar.
19. Click the **Print Preview and Print** button on the Quick Access Toolbar to display the Print tab in Backstage view.
20. Click the **Orientation** down arrow and click **Landscape Orientation** to change the page formatting to Landscape orientation.
21. Click the **Margins** down arrow and click **Normal** to change the page formatting to the default Normal margin widths. The screen should look similar to Figure 4-4.
22. **With your teacher's permission**, print the file.
23. Click the **File** tab to close Backstage view, click the **Customize Quick Access Toolbar** button, and click **Print Preview and Print** to remove the Print Preview and Print button from the Quick Access Toolbar
24. Close the file, saving all changes, and exit Excel.

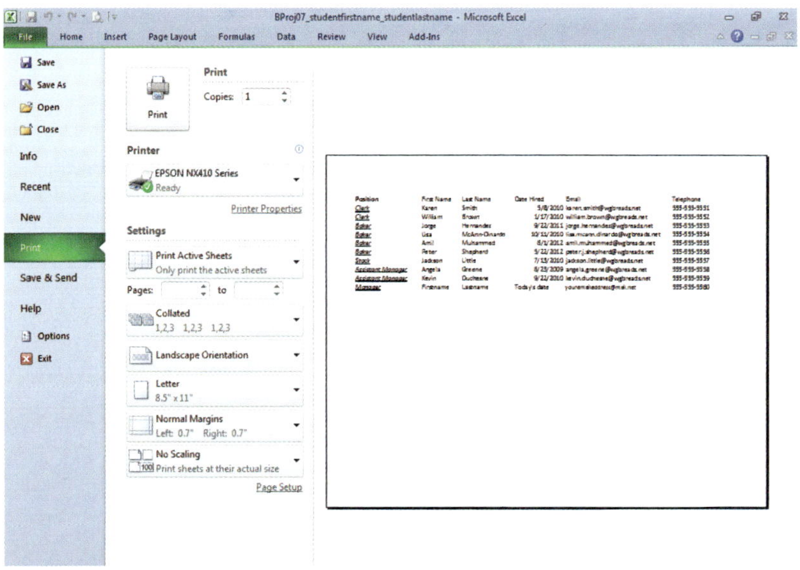

Figure 4-4

Project 8—Apply It

Contact List in Word

DIRECTIONS

1. Start **Microsoft Word**.
2. Open the file **BProj08** from the data files for this lesson, and save it as **BProj08_studentfirstname_studentlastname** in the location where your teacher instructs you to store the files for this lesson.
3. Display the Print tab in Backstage view and change to Landscape Orientation.
4. Set the margins to Normal.
5. Close Backstage view.
6. Select all data in the document, and use the Mini toolbar to increase the font size to **12** points.
7. Display the Quick Access Toolbar below the Ribbon.
8. Type your name, today's date, and your e-mail address into the appropriate cells in the document.
9. Use a shortcut menu to remove the hyperlink formatting from your e-mail address.
10. Select the first line of text only, and use the Styles task pane to clear all formatting, then close the Styles task pane.
11. With the first line of text still selected, open the Font dialog box, and apply **Bold, Green, 14-point** formatting. Your screen should look similar to Figure 4-5.
12. **With your teacher's permission**, print the file.
13. Return the Quick Access Toolbar to its position above the Ribbon.
14. Close the file, saving all changes, and exit Word.

Figure 4-5

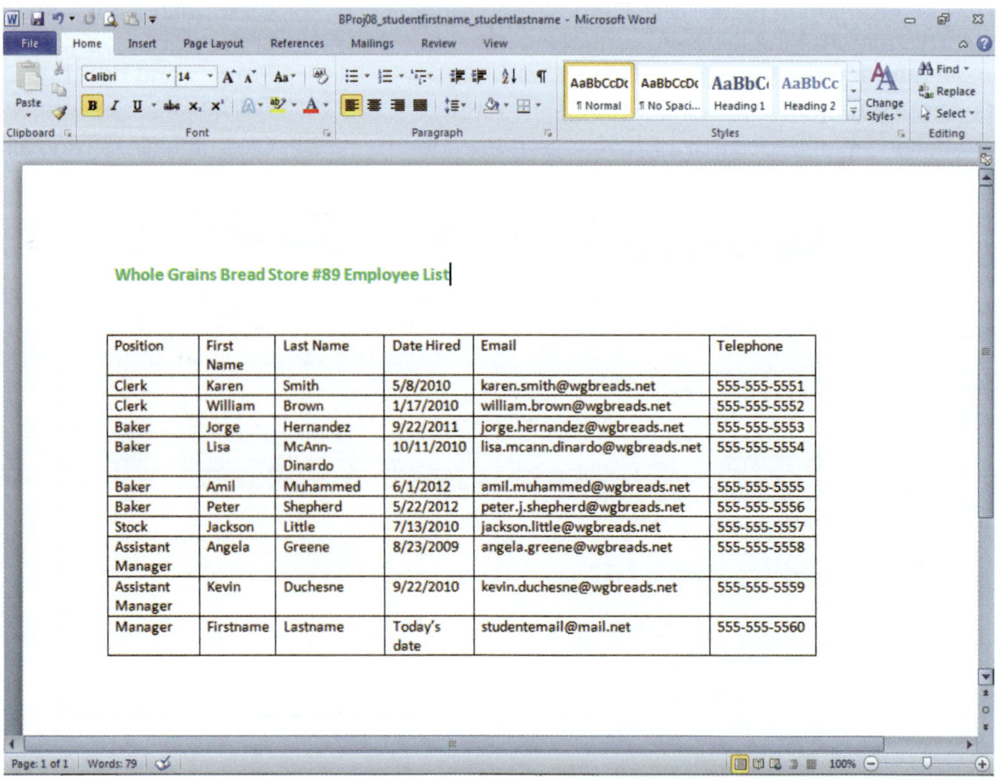

Whole Grains Bread Store #89 Employee List

Position	First Name	Last Name	Date Hired	Email	Telephone
Clerk	Karen	Smith	5/8/2010	karen.smith@wgbreads.net	555-555-5551
Clerk	William	Brown	1/17/2010	william.brown@wgbreads.net	555-555-5552
Baker	Jorge	Hernandez	9/22/2011	jorge.hernandez@wgbreads.net	555-555-5553
Baker	Lisa	McAnn-Dinardo	10/11/2010	lisa.mcann.dinardo@wgbreads.net	555-555-5554
Baker	Amil	Muhammed	6/1/2012	amil.muhammed@wgbreads.net	555-555-5555
Baker	Peter	Shepherd	5/22/2012	peter.j.shepherd@wgbreads.net	555-555-5556
Stock	Jackson	Little	7/13/2010	jackson.little@wgbreads.net	555-555-5557
Assistant Manager	Angela	Greene	8/23/2009	angela.greene@wgbreads.net	555-555-5558
Assistant Manager	Kevin	Duchesne	9/22/2010	kevin.duchesne@wgbreads.net	555-555-5559
Manager	Firstname	Lastname	Today's date	studentemail@mail.net	555-555-5560

Lesson 5

Managing Program Windows

➤ What You Will Learn

- Changing the View
- Using Window Controls
- Zooming
- Scrolling
- Using Multiple Windows
- Using the Microsoft Office Clipboard

Software Skills Controlling the way Microsoft Office 2010 programs and documents are displayed on your computer monitor is a vital part of using the programs successfully. For example, you can control the size and position of the program window onscreen, and you can control the size a document is displayed. In addition, you can open more than one window onscreen at the same time, so that you can work with multiple documents and even multiple programs at once. Use the Office Clipboard to copy or move a selection from one location in a file to another, and even to a location in a different file.

Application Skills You are a marketing assistant at Voyager Travel Adventures, a tour group operator. You have pictures in a PowerPoint presentation that you want to use to illustrate tour descriptions in Word. In this lesson, you will manage program windows and use the Office Clipboard to copy and move pictures from one file to another.

WORDS TO KNOW

Active window
The window in which you are currently working.

Cascade
Arrange windows so they overlap, with the active window in front. Only the title bars of the nonactive windows are visible.

Copy
To duplicate a selection. The original remains unchanged.

Cut
To delete a selection from its original location and move it to the Clipboard.

Default
A standard setting or mode of operation.

Group button
A Taskbar button that represents all open windows for one application.

Maximize
Enlarge a window so it fills the entire screen.

Minimize
Hide a window so it appears only as a button on the Windows Taskbar.

Office Clipboard
A temporary storage area that can hold up to 24 selections at a time.

Paste
To insert a selection from the Clipboard into a document.

Restore
Return a minimized window to its previous size and position on the screen.

WORDS TO KNOW

Restore down
Return a maximized window to its previous size and position on the screen.

Scroll
Shift the displayed area of the document up, down, left, or right.

Tile
Arrange windows so they do not overlap.

Zoom
Adjust the magnification of the content displayed on the screen. This does not affect the actual size of the printed document.

Zoom in
Increase the size of the document as it is displayed onscreen.

Zoom out
Decrease the size of the document as it is displayed onscreen.

What You Can Do

Changing the View

- The Microsoft Office 2010 programs provide different ways to view your data in the program window.
- Although the view options vary depending on the program, most offer at least two different views.
- In Word, Excel, and PowerPoint, you can change views using the View shortcut buttons on the status bar or the commands on the View tab of the Ribbon.
- In Access, you usually use the Views button.
- You learn more about changing the view in the program sections of this book.

Try It! Changing the View

1. Start Excel.
2. Click the View tab.
3. In the Workbook Views group, on the View tab of the Ribbon, click the Page Layout button to change from Normal view to Page Layout view. In Excel, Page Layout view displays the header and footer areas and rulers.
4. On the status bar, click the Normal view button.

Page Layout view in Excel

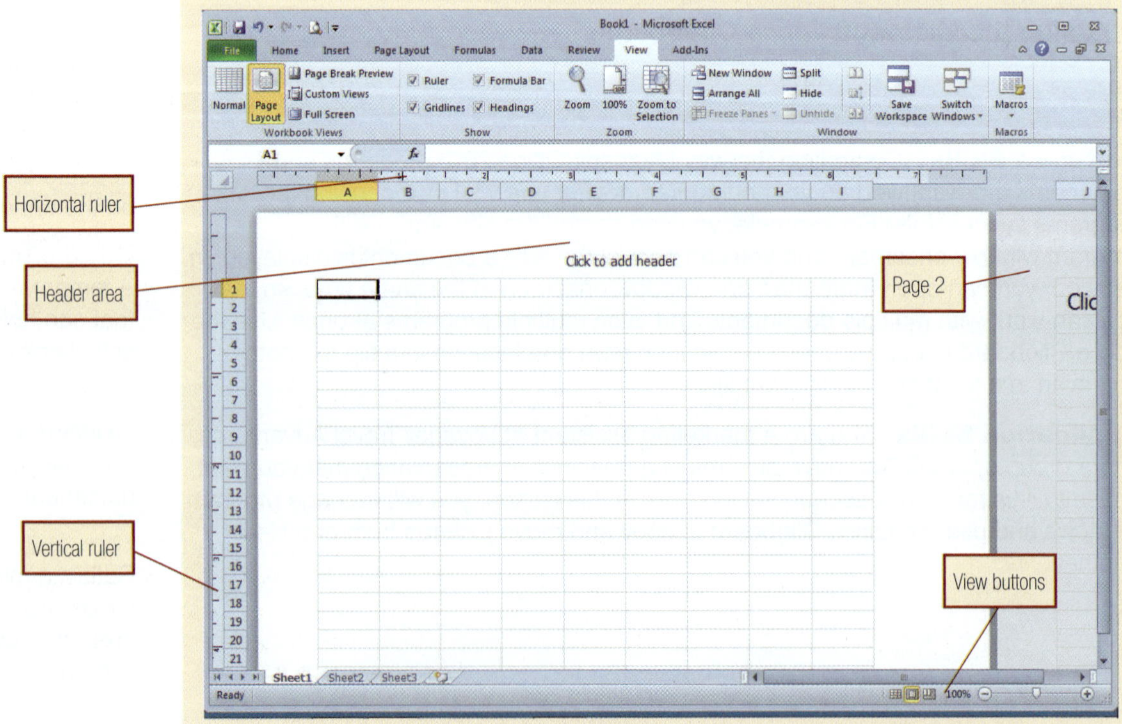

Using Window Controls

- When you start a Microsoft Office 2010 program, it opens in a program window using **default** settings.
- You can control the size and position of the program window.
  - You can **maximize** the window to fill the screen.
  - You can **minimize** the window to a Taskbar button.
  - You can **restore** a minimized window to its previous size and position.
  - You can **restore down** a maximized window to its previous size and position.
- There are three ways to control a program window:
  - Use the Control buttons located on the right end of the title bar.

    Minimize

    Maximize

    Restore Down

    ✓ *Restore Down is only available in a maximized window.*
  - Use the Windows' Taskbar button shortcut menu.
  - Use the program's control menu.

Try It! Using Window Controls

1. In the Excel window, click the Minimize button. When the program window is minimized, it displays as a button on the Windows Taskbar.
2. Click the Excel program icon on the Windows Taskbar to restore the window to its previous size and position.
3. In the Excel window, click the Maximize button.

   ✓ *If the Maximize button is not displayed, the window is already maximized. Continue with step 4.*
4. Click the Restore Down button to restore the window to its previous size and position.
5. Exit Excel without saving any changes.

Zooming

- In Word, Excel, and PowerPoint, you can adjust the **zoom** magnification setting to increase or decrease the size a program uses to display a file onscreen.

  ✓ *The Zoom options may be different depending on the program you are using.*
- There are three ways to set the zoom:
  - The Zoom slider on the right end of the program's status bar
  - The commands in the Zoom group of the View tab on the Ribbon
  - The Zoom dialog box
- **Zoom in** to make the data appear larger onscreen. This is useful for getting a close look at graphics, text, or data.

  ✓ *When you zoom in, only a small portion of the file will be visible onscreen at a time.*
- **Zoom out** to make the data appear smaller onscreen. This is useful for getting an overall look at a document, slide, or worksheet.
- You can set the zoom magnification as a percentage of a document's actual size. For example, if you set the zoom to 50%, the program displays the document half as large as the actual, printed document would appear. If you set the zoom to 200%, the program displays the document twice as large as the actual printed file would appear.
- Other options may be available depending on your program.
  - In Word, you can select from the following preset sizes:
    - Page width. Word automatically sizes the document so that the width of the page matches the width of the screen. You see the left and right margins of the page.

- Text width. Word automatically sizes the document so that the width of the text on the page matches the width of the screen. The left and right margins may be hidden.
- One page (or Whole page). Word automatically sizes the document so that one page is visible on the screen.
- Two pages. Word automatically sizes the document so that two pages are visible on the screen.
- Many pages. Word automatically sizes the document so that the number of pages you select can all be seen onscreen.

✓ *Some options may not be available, depending on the current view. Options that are not available will appear dimmed.*

- In Excel you can Zoom to Selection, which adjusts the size of selected cells to fill the entire window.
- In PowerPoint you can Fit to Window, which adjusts the size of the current slide to fill the entire window.

Try It! Zooming Using the Slider

1. Start Microsoft Word, and open **BTry05a** from the data files for this lesson. Save the file as **BTry05a_studentfirstname_studentlastname** in the location where your teacher instructs you to store the files for this lesson.
2. Drag the Zoom slider to the left to zoom out, or decrease the magnification. At 10% magnification, the document page is so small you cannot view the content.
3. Drag the Zoom slider to the right to zoom in, or increase the magnification. At 500% magnification, the document page is so large you can only view a small portion of the content.
4. Click the Zoom Out button at the left end of the Zoom slider. Each time you click, the magnification zooms out by 10%.
5. Click the Zoom In button at the right end of the Zoom slider. Each time you click, the magnification zooms in by 10%.
6. Leave the **BTry05a_studentfirstname_studentlastname** file open to use in the next Try It.

Zoom out to 10%

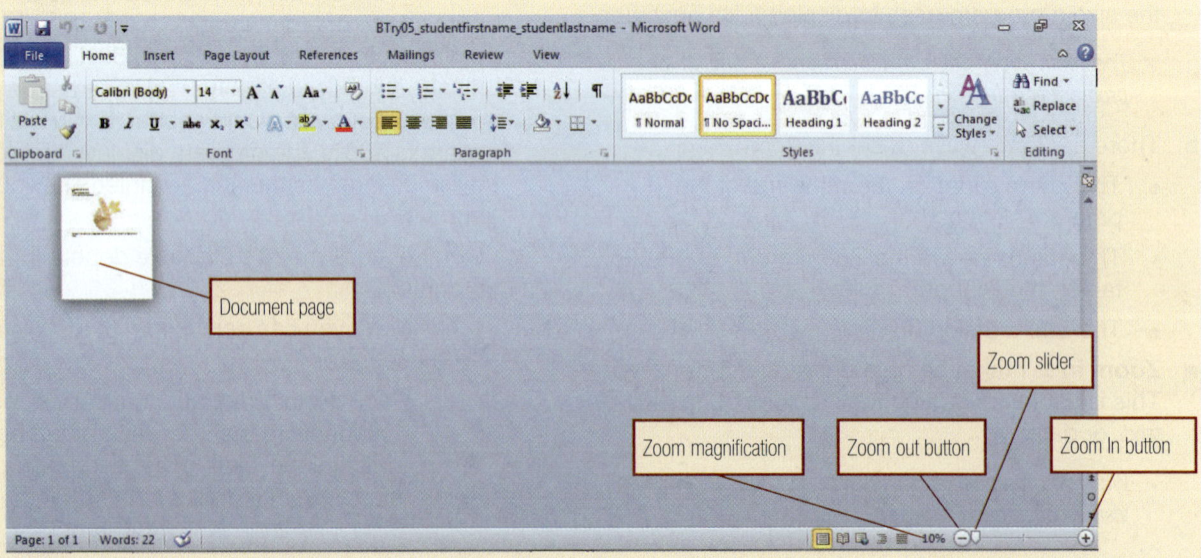

Try It! Zooming Using the View Tab

1. With the **BTry05a_studentfirstname_studentlastname** file open, click the View tab on the Ribbon and locate the Zoom group of commands.
2. Click the 100% button in the Zoom group. The magnification adjusts to display the document at its actual size.
3. Click the Zoom button in the Zoom group to open the Zoom dialog box.
4. Click the 75% option button and then click OK to apply the change and close the dialog box.
5. Click the Zoom button in the Zoom group again, and use the Percent increment arrows to set the zoom magnification to 150%.

   ✓ *In Excel, set the percentage in the Custom box.*
6. Click OK.
7. Save the changes to **BTry05a_studentfirstname_studentlastname**, and leave it open to use in the next Try It.

Zoom using the Zoom group on the View tab

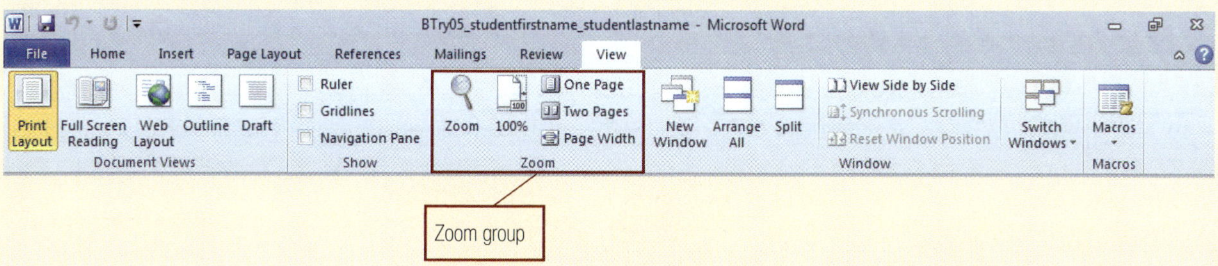

Scrolling

- When there is more data in a window or dialog box than can be displayed onscreen at one time, or when the zoom magnification is set high, you must **scroll** to see the hidden parts.
- You can scroll up, down, left, or right.
- You can scroll using the directional keys on the keyboard, or using the arrows and boxes on the scroll bars.

  ✓ *Some mouse devices have scroll wheels that are used for scrolling.*
- The size of the scroll boxes change to represent the percentage of the file visible on the screen.
- For example, in a very long document, the scroll boxes will be small, indicating that a small percentage of the document is visible. In a short document, the scroll boxes will be large, indicating that a large percentage of the document is visible.
- Scrolling does not move the insertion point.

Try It! Scrolling

1. In the **BTry05a_studentfirstname_studentlastname** file, click the down scroll arrow at the bottom of the vertical scroll bar on the right side of the window. The content in the window scrolls down.

   ✓ *If you have a wide screen, you may have to increase the zoom for the vertical scroll bar to display.*

2. Drag the vertical scroll box about halfway to the bottom of the scroll bar to scroll down in the file until you can see the line of text below the picture.

3. Click the right scroll arrow at the right end of the horizontal scroll bar above the status bar at the bottom of the window to scroll to the right so you can see the entire line of text.

4. Drag the vertical scroll box all the way to the top of the scroll bar to scroll to the top of the document page.

5. Save the changes to **BTry05a_studentfirstname_studentlastname**, and leave it open to use in the next Try It.

Tools for scrolling in a document

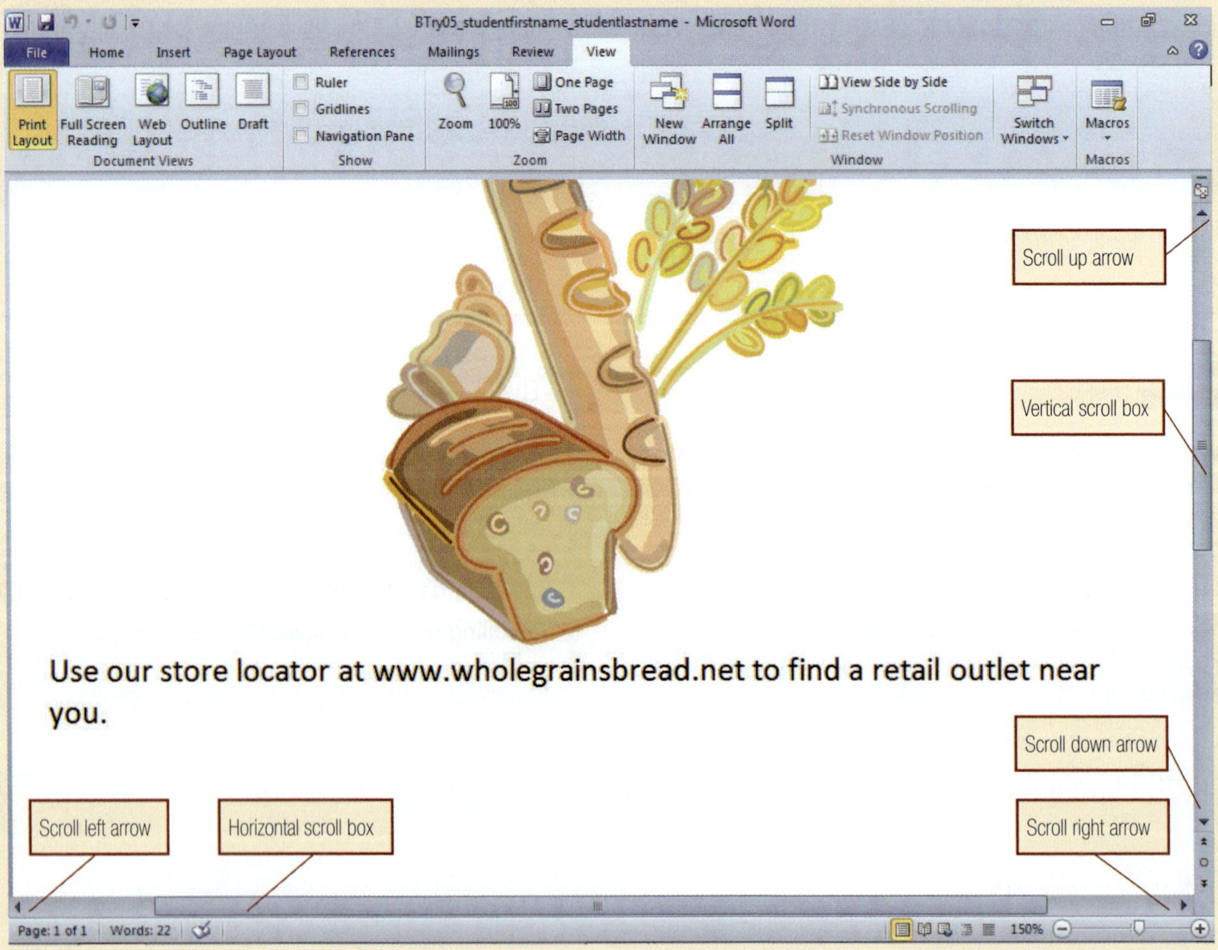

Using Multiple Windows

- You can open multiple program windows at the same time.
- You can also open multiple document windows in Word, PowerPoint, and Excel.
- Each open window is represented by a button on the Windows Taskbar.
- If there is not room on the Taskbar to display buttons for each open window, Windows displays a **group button**.

  ✓ *The Taskbar may not be visible onscreen if Windows is set to hide the Taskbar, or to display windows on top of the Taskbar. To see the Taskbar, move the mouse pointer to the edge of the screen where it usually displays.*

- Only one window can be active—or current—at a time.
- The **active window** is displayed on top of other open windows. Its title bar is darker than the title bars of other open windows, and its Taskbar button appears pressed in.
- You can switch among open windows to make a different window active.
- You can **tile** windows if you want to see all of them at the same time. Tiled windows do not overlap; they are arranged side by side or stacked so you see the full width of each window across the screen.
- The more windows you have open, the smaller they display when tiled.
  - If necessary in smaller windows, the program may hide or condense common screen elements such as the Quick Access Toolbar and Ribbon and display only a program icon on the left end of the title bar.
  - You can click the program icon to display a shortcut menu of commands including Maximize, Minimize, and Close.
- You can **cascade** windows if you want to see the active window in its entirety, with the title bars of all open windows displayed behind it.
- You can also open and arrange multiple files in Word, PowerPoint, and Excel.

Try It! Using Multiple Program Windows

1. With the **BTry05a_studentfirstname_studentlastname** file still open in Word, start Excel.
2. Start PowerPoint.
3. Right-click on a blank area of the Windows Taskbar to display a shortcut menu.
4. Click Cascade windows to overlap the three program windows; the active window displays on top.
5. Right-click on a blank area of the Windows Taskbar.
6. Click Show windows stacked to tile the three windows so you see the full width of each window; the window height is reduced.
7. Right-click on a blank area of the Windows Taskbar.
8. Click Show windows side by side to tile the three windows so you see the full height of each window; the window width is reduced.
9. Click at the beginning of the text in the **BTry05a_studentfirstname_studentlastname** document window. Now, the **BTry05a_studentfirstname_studentlastname** window is active. Notice the insertion point in the window, and that the title bar displays darker.
10. Press and hold ALT and press TAB. A bar of icons representing open windows displays. Press TAB to move through the icons until the one you want is selected, then release ALT.
11. Close the PowerPoint program window, without saving changes.
12. Close the Excel program window, without saving changes.
13. Maximize the Word program window.
14. Save the changes to **BTry05a_studentfirstname_studentlastname**, and leave it open to use in the next Try It.

Try It! Arranging Multiple Files in Word

1. With the **BTry05a_studentfirstname_studentlastname** window open, click File > Open.
2. Open **BTry05b** from the data files for this lesson. Now, both files are open in Word at the same time.
3. Rest the mouse pointer on the Word icon on the Taskbar to view a list of all open Word files.
4. Click **BTry05a_studentfirstname_studentlastname** on the list to make that window active.
5. Click the View tab on the Ribbon.
6. In the Window group, click the Arrange All button. The two open files are tiled in the program window.

   ✓ *If nothing happens when you click Arrange All, you may have to Restore down the BTry05a_studentfirstname_studentlastname window.*

7. Close both files, without saving any changes, and exit Word.

Use the Taskbar button to change the active window

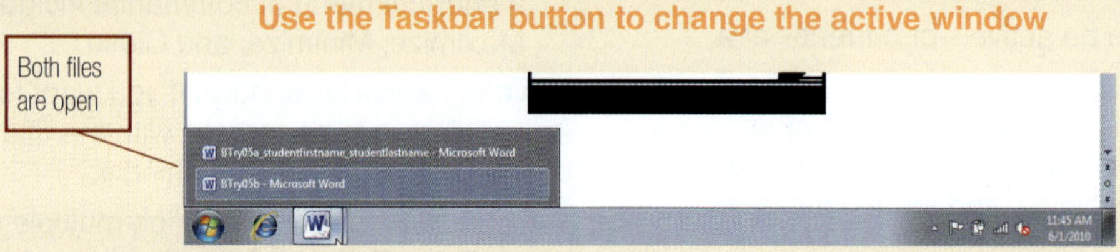

Try It! Arranging Multiple Files in Excel

1. Start Excel and maximize the window, if necessary. Open **BTry05c** from the data files for this lesson.
2. Click File > Open, and then open **BTry05d** from the data files for this lesson. Both files are now open in Excel.
3. Click the View tab on the Ribbon.
4. In the Window group, click the Arrange All button. The Arrange Windows dialog box opens.
5. Click the Horizontal option button and then click OK to tile the open files one above the other (stacked).
6. Click in the **BTry05c** window to make it active.
7. Click the Arrange All button again to open the dialog box, click the Vertical option button, and then click OK. The files are tiles side by side.
8. Close both files, without saving any changes, and exit Excel.

Try It! Arranging Multiple Files in PowerPoint

1. Start PowerPoint and Maximize the window, if necessary. Open **BTry05e** from data files for this lesson.
2. Click File > Open, and then open **BTry105f** from the data files for this lesson. Both files are now open in PowerPoint.
3. Click the View tab on the Ribbon.
4. In the Window group, click the Cascade button to overlap the windows with the active window on top.
5. In the Window group, click the Switch Windows down arrow to display a list of open windows. A check mark displays beside the active window.
6. Click **BTry05e** on the Switch Windows drop-down list to make it active.
7. Click the View tab, then, in the Window group, click the Arrange All button to tile the windows side by side.
8. Close both files, without saving any changes, and exit PowerPoint.

Using the Microsoft Office Clipboard

- Use the Microsoft **Office Clipboard** with the Cut, Copy, and Paste commands to copy or move a selection from one location to another.
- The **Copy** command stores a duplicate of the selection on the Office Clipboard, leaving the original selection unchanged.
- The **Cut** command deletes the selection from its original location, and stores it on the Office Clipboard.
- You can then use the **Paste** command to paste the selection from the Office Clipboard to the insertion point location in the same file or a different file.
- By default, the last 24 items cut or copied display in the Office Clipboard task pane.
- You can paste or delete one or all of the items.
- You can turn the following Office Clipboard options off or on (a check mark indicates the option is on):
  - Show Office Clipboard Automatically. Sets the Clipboard task pane to open automatically when you cut or copy a selection.
  - Show Office Clipboard When Ctrl+C Pressed Twice. Sets Word to display the Clipboard task pane when you press and hold CTRL and then press C on the keyboard twice.
  - Collect Without Showing Office Clipboard. Sets the Clipboard task pane so it does not open automatically when you cut or copy data.
  - Show Office Clipboard Icon on Taskbar. Adds a Clipboard icon to the Show Hidden Icons group on the taskbar.
  - Show Status Near Taskbar When Copying. Displays a ScreenTip with the number of items on the Clipboard when you cut or copy a selection.

Try It! Using the Microsoft Office Clipboard

1. Start Word and maximize the window, if necessary. Open **BTry05g** from the location where the data files for this lesson are stored, and save it as **BTry05g_studentfirstname_studentlastname** in the location where your teacher instructs you to store the files for this lesson.
2. On the Home tab click the Clipboard group dialog box launcher to display the Clipboard task pane.
3. Select the text **Whole Grains Bread**.

(continued)

Try It! Using the Office Clipboard *(continued)*

4. Right-click the selection and click Copy. The selected text is copied to the Office Clipboard. Notice that it remains in its original location in the document, as well.
5. In the document window, click on the picture to select it. (A selection box displays around a selected picture.)
6. Right-click the selection and click Cut. The selection is deleted from the document, and displays in the Clipboard task pane.
7. In Word, open **BTry05h** from the location where the data files for this lesson are stored. The Clipboard task pane is still displayed.
8. Save the file as **BTry05h_studentfirstname_studentlastname** in the location where your teacher instructs you to store the files for this lesson. Make sure the insertion point is at the beginning of the document, and then press ENTER to insert a blank line. Press the up arrow key ↑ to move the insertion point to the blank line.
9. In the Clipboard task pane, click the picture of the bread. It is pasted into the document at the insertion point location. It also remains on the Clipboard so you can paste it again, if you want.
10. Right-click the picture of the runner in the document and click Copy to copy it to the Clipboard. Now, there are three selections stored on the Clipboard.
11. Save the changes to **BTry05h_studentfirstname_studentlastname**, and close it. **BTry05g_studentfirstname_studentlastname** is still open.
12. Position the insertion point at the end of the document and press ENTER to insert a new line.
13. Click the picture of the runner in the Clipboard task pane. It is pasted into the document. Even though the original file is closed, you can still paste a selection that is stored on the Clipboard. Save the changes to the file and leave it open to use in the next Try It.

Try It! Deleting Selections from the Office Clipboard

1. With **BTry05g_studentfirstname_studentlastname** still open, click the Options button at the bottom of the Clipboard task pane. A menu of settings that affect the Clipboard displays. A check mark indicates that an option is selected.
2. In the Clipboard task pane, rest the mouse pointer on the picture of the runner, and click the down arrow that displays.
3. Click Delete on the drop-down menu. The selection is removed from the Clipboard, but it remains in place in the document.
4. Rest the mouse pointer on the picture of the bread in the Clipboard task pane, click the down arrow that displays, and click Delete.
5. Rest the mouse pointer on the text *Whole Grains Bread*, click the down arrow, and click Delete. Now, the Office Clipboard is empty.

   ✓ *Click the Clear All button at the top of the Clipboard task pane to quickly delete all selections.*
6. Close the Clipboard task pane.
7. Close **BTry05g_studentfirstname_studentlastname**, saving all changes, and exit Word.

Project 9—Create It

Kayaking Tour Description

DIRECTIONS

1. Click **Start** > **All Programs** > **Microsoft Word** to start the Word program.
2. Save the default, blank Document1 file as **BProj09a_studentfirstname_studentlastname** in the location where your instructor tells you to store the files for this lesson.
3. Click the **View** tab.
4. In the Zoom group, click the **100%** button to set the zoom to 100% magnification.
5. On the first line of the document, type the text **Kayak in the Land of the Midnight Sun** and then press ENTER .
6. Click the **Home** tab.
7. Select the text, and then change the font to Cambria and the font size to 28 points.
8. Move the insertion point to the end of the document, set the font size to 12 points, and type: **Join Voyager Travel Adventures on a 10-day sea kayaking trip in one of the most beautiful and exciting places on earth! Experience the thrill of seeing whales, bears, and other wildlife up close, while enjoying a comfortable base camp and first-class dining.**
9. Press ENTER and then save the changes.
10. Click the **Draft** view button on the status bar to change to draft view.
11. Click the **View** tab on the Ribbon, and then, in the Document Views group, click the **Print Layout** button to change to Print Layout view.
12. Click the **Zoom In** button on the Zoom slider as many times as necessary to increase the zoom magnification to 150%.
13. Save the changes to the file, and then click the **Minimize** button to minimize the Word program window.
14. Start PowerPoint and maximize the window if necessary. Open the file **BProj09b** from the location where the data files for this lesson are stored.
15. Click the **Word** button on the Windows Taskbar to restore the Word program window.
16. Right-click a blank area of the Windows Taskbar and click **Show windows Side by Side** to view both the Word and PowerPoint windows.

    ✓ *If you have other windows open, they will be arranged as well. Minimize them, and then repeat step 16.*
17. Click the **Maximize** button in the PowerPoint window.
18. Click the **Home** tab, if necessary, and then click the **Clipboard group dialog box launcher** .
19. In the list of slides on the left side of the PowerPoint window, right-click **slide 2**—Kayaking in Alaska.
20. Click **Copy** on the shortcut menu to copy the selection to the Clipboard.
21. Close the PowerPoint window without saving any changes.
22. Click the **Maximize** button in the Word window.
23. Click the **Home** tab and then click the **Clipboard group dialog box launcher** to open the Clipboard task pane. The picture copied from the presentation in step 20 should display.
24. Make sure the insertion point is at the end of the **BProj09a_studentfirstname_studentlastname** document, and then click **Kayaking in Alaska** in the Clipboard task pane to paste the selection into the Word document.
25. Click the **Zoom Out** button on the Zoom slider until the magnification is set to 80%.
26. Rest the mouse pointer on the picture in the Clipboard task pane, click the **down arrow** that displays, and click **Delete**.
27. Click the **Close** button in the Clipboard task pane.
28. **With your teacher's permission**, print the file.
29. Close the file, saving all changes, and exit Word.

Project 10—Apply It

Safari Tour Description

DIRECTIONS

1. Start Word and open **BProj10a** from the data files for this lesson.
2. Save the file as **BProj10a_studentfirstname_studentlastname** in the location where your teacher instructs you to store the files for this lesson.
3. Zoom out to 80% so you can see all content in the document.
4. Display the Clipboard task pane.
5. Cut the picture from the document to the Clipboard.
6. Start PowerPoint and maximize the window, if necessary.
7. Open **BProj10b** from the location where the data files for this lesson are stored. Save it as **BProj10b_studentfirstname_studentlastname** in the location where your teacher instructs you to store the files for this lesson.
8. Display the Clipboard task pane, if necessary.
9. Click slide 3 in the list of slides to make that slide active. On the slide in the main area of the window, right-click the picture and click **Cut**.
10. Click the dotted line bordering the placeholder for content on the slide to select it, as shown in Figure 5-1 on the next page.
11. In the Clipboard task pane, click the picture you cut from the Word document to paste it on to the slide.
12. Close the Clipboard task pane and save the changes to the PowerPoint presentation.
13. Arrange the PowerPoint presentation and the Word document side by side.
14. Arrange them stacked.
15. Minimize the PowerPoint presentation window.
16. Maximize the Word window.
17. Paste the picture you copied from the PowerPoint presentation on to the last line of the Word document.
18. Close the Clipboard task pane and zoom out so you can see the entire document.
19. **With your teacher's permission**, print the file.
20. Close the file, saving all changes, and exit Word.
21. Maximize the PowerPoint window.
22. Close the file, saving all changes, and exit PowerPoint.

Figure 5-1

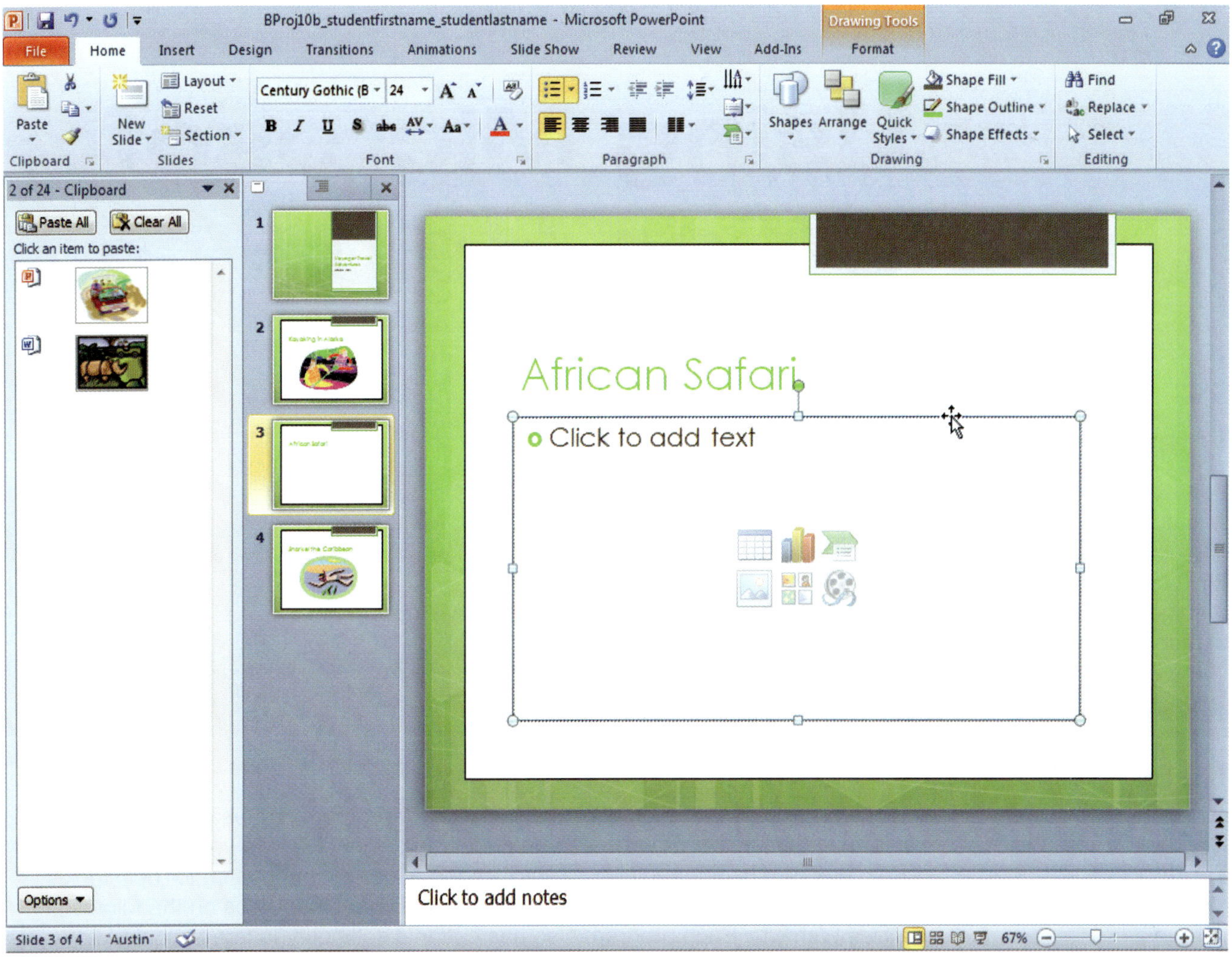
BProj10b_studentfirstname_studentlastname - Microsoft PowerPoint
Drawing Tools
File
Home
Insert
Design
Transitions
Animations
Slide Show
Review
View
Add-Ins
Format
Paste
Layout
Reset
New Slide
Section
Clipboard
Slides
Century Gothic (B
24
Font
Paragraph
Shapes
Arrange
Quick Styles
Shape Fill
Shape Outline
Shape Effects
Drawing
Find
Replace
Select
Editing
2 of 24 - Clipboard
Paste All
Clear All
Click an item to paste:
Options
African Safari
Click to add text
Click to add notes
Slide 3 of 4
"Austin"
67%

Lesson 6

Using Microsoft Office Help

WORDS TO KNOW

AutoRecover
A feature in some Microsoft Office 2010 programs that automatically saves files at a set interval so that in the event of a system failure the files may be recovered.

Read-only mode
A mode in which the open file can be viewed but not edited.

➤ What You Will Learn

Using a Help Program
Searching for Help
Using the Help Table of Contents
Viewing Application Options
Using AutoRecover and AutoSave

Software Skills Each Microsoft Office 2010 program comes with Help information that you can access and display in a window while you work. Use the Help program to get help about using a specific command, search for help topics, access the Help table of contents, or link to additional resources on the Microsoft Office Web site. Each program also has optional settings you use to control how the program operates. For example, you can specify how often the program should automatically save an open file.

Application Skills As a new employee at Restoration Architecture, it's important to learn how to solve problems on your own. In this lesson, you will practice using the Help system to locate information about printing and formatting files. You will also investigate program options, and learn about options for recovering damaged or unsaved files.

What You Can Do

Using Microsoft Office Help

- Each Microsoft Office program has its own Help program.
- You can start Help using four methods:
  - Click the Help button which displays in the upper right corner of the program window.

- Press F1.
- Click a Help button in a dialog box.
- Use the Help tab in Backstage view.

■ Help opens in a window that you can keep open while you work.

■ By default, the Help Home page displays, listing links to Help categories.

■ When the mouse pointer touches a link, it changes to a hand with a pointing finger.

■ Click a link to display subcategories or topics in a category, and then click a topic to display the specific Help information.

■ Other links might go to related content on different pages.

■ The links are formatted in blue so they stand out from the surrounding text.

■ Some words or phrases link to definitions or explanations. These links are formatted in dark red.

■ If the link Show All displays on a Help page, click it to display all definitions and explanations on that page.

■ Use the buttons on the Help window toolbar to control the Help display.

- **Back**
  Displays the previously viewed page.
- **Forward**
  Returns to a viewed page.
- **Stop**
  Cancels a search.
- **Refresh**
  Updates the current page.
- **Home**
  Displays the Help Home page.
- **Print**
  Prints the current page.
- **Change Font Size**
  Displays an option to change the size of the characters in the Help window.
- **Show Table of Contents**
  Displays the Help table of contents page.
- **Keep on Top**
  Sets the Help window to always display on top of other windows.

✓ *At the bottom of most Help pages there is a question asking if you found the information helpful. If you are connected to the Internet, click Yes, No, or I don't know to display a text box where you can type information that you want to submit to Microsoft.*

Try It! Using Office Help

1. Start Microsoft Access.
2. Click the File tab and then click Help to display the Help tab in Backstage view.
3. Click the Help button in the upper-right corner of the window

   OR

   Click the Help button under the heading Support.
4. Click Access basics to display a list of topics related to Access basics.
5. Click Database basics to display an article about database basics.
6. Maximize the window.
7. Click the Back button on the toolbar to display the previously viewed page—the list of Access basics topics.
8. Click the Home button on the toolbar to display the Help Home page.
9. Click see all to display a list of all Access Help and How-to topics.
10. Click Saving and printing to display a list of topics on that subject.
11. Click Save As to display an article about using the Save As command. Notice that this article provides information about using the command in all Microsoft Office programs.
12. Click the Home button to return to the Home page.
13. Close the Help program window, and exit Access.

Searching for Help

- You can search for a Help topic from any Help page.
- Simply type the term or phrase for which you want to search in the Search box, and then click the Search button .
- A list of topics that contain the term or phrase displays in the Help window.
- Click a topic to display the Help information.

✓ *If your computer is connected to the Internet, you can use the Bing search box to search the Internet.*

Try It! Searching for Help

1. Start Microsoft PowerPoint.
2. Press F1 to start the Help program.
3. Click in the Search box, and type **Print**.
4. Click the Search button . A list of topics related to the term *Print* displays.
5. Click the topic Preview and print a file to display that article.
6. Close the Help window, and exit PowerPoint.

Using the Help Table of Contents

- The Table of Contents is a list of all categories for which Help is available.
- When you open the Table of Contents, the list displays in a task pane on the left side of the Help window.
- Each category in the Table of Contents has a book icon next to it.
- Click a category to display a list of related topics and subcategories; then click a topic to display the article in the Help window.

Try It! Using the Help Table of Contents

1. Start Microsoft Excel.
2. On the Home tab of the Ribbon, click the Font group dialog box launcher to open the Format Cells dialog box, and then click the Help button to start the Help program.
3. On the Help toolbar, click the Show Table of Contents button . The Table of Contents task pane displays.

   ✓ *If the Table of Contents task pane is already displayed, clicking the button closes it. Click it again to open it.*
4. In the Table of Contents, click Printing. The category expands to display a list of related topics.
5. Click Printing, again. The category collapses to hide the related topics.
6. Click Customizing to view the related topics.
7. Click Customize the Quick Access Toolbar to display the article in the Help window.
8. Click Customizing in the Table of Contents to collapse the topic, then click the Hide Table of Contents button on the Help toolbar.
9. Close the Help window, and cancel the Format Cells dialog box. Leave Excel open to use in the next Try It.

Viewing Application Options

- Each of the Microsoft Office programs has options for controlling program settings.
- The settings depend on the program, although some are the same for all of Microsoft Office. For example, you can enter a user name, and set a default storage location for files.
- You view and set program options in the program's Options dialog box, which is accessed from Backstage view.

Try It! Viewing Application Options

1. In Excel, click the File tab to display Backstage view, and then click Options to open the Excel Options dialog box. The General options display.
2. Click Save in the list on the left side of the dialog box to display the Save options.
3. Click Proofing to display the Proofing options.
4. Click Cancel to close the dialog box without making any changes, and then exit Excel.

Using AutoRecover and AutoSave

- By default the **AutoRecover** feature in Word, Excel, and PowerPoint is set to automatically save open files every ten minutes.
- The files are listed under Versions on the Info tab in Backstage view; click one to open it.
- The AutoSave feature automatically saves a version of a file if you close it without saving.
  - If you were working in a new, unsaved file, you can recover a version from the UnsavedFiles folder, which you can open from the Recent tab in Backstage view.
  - If you were working in a file that had been saved, but not since your most recent changes, you can recover a version from the Info tab in Backstage view.
- An autosaved file opens in **read-only mode**, which means you must save it with a new name, or replace the existing file with the same name if you want to edit it. AutoRecovered files are stored for up to four days or until you edit the file, and then deleted.
- If a program closes unexpectedly due to a system failure or power outage, the Document Recovery task pane may display the next time you start the program.
- Up to three autosaved versions of the file(s) you were working on before the program closed are listed in the task pane. You may select the version you want to save, and delete the others.

Try It! Setting AutoRecover and AutoSave Options

1. Start Excel and open **BTry06** from the location where the data files for this lesson are stored, and save it as **BTry06_studentfirstname_studentlastname** in the location where your teacher instructs you to store the files.
2. Click the File tab to display Backstage view.
3. Click Options > Save to display the Save options in the Excel Options dialog box.
4. Use the Save AutoRecover information every increment arrows to set the time to 1 minute.
5. Verify that there is a check mark in the Keep the last autosaved version if I close without saving check box.

   ✓ *A check mark indicates the option is selected. If it is not, click the check box to select it.*
6. Verify that there is no check mark in the Disable AutoRecover for this workbook only check box.
7. Click OK to apply the changes and close the dialog box. Leave **BTry06_studentfirstname_studentlastname** open in Excel to use in the next Try It.

Try It! Opening an Autosaved File

1. In the **BTry06_studentfirstname_studentlastname** file, click on cell B6, where the total sales figure displays, if it is not already selected.
2. Press DEL to delete the information.
3. Wait at least one minute without saving the file.
4. Click File > Close > Don't Save.

   ✓ *Notice the text in the file delete confirmation dialog box indicating that a recent copy of the file will be temporarily available.*

5. Open the **BTry06_studentfirstname_studentlastname** file in Excel. The Info tab should display in Backstage view. A list of autosaved versions of the file displays under Versions. It includes files closed without saving and files automatically saved by the AutoRecover feature, if there are any.

   ✓ *If the Info tab does not display, click it.*

6. Click the autosaved file to open it in read-only mode. Notice the information bar that indicates that it is a recovered file that is temporarily stored on your computer. Notice also that the content of cell B6 has been deleted.
7. Close both versions of the file without saving any changes. Leave Excel open to use in the next Try It.

Open an autosaved file

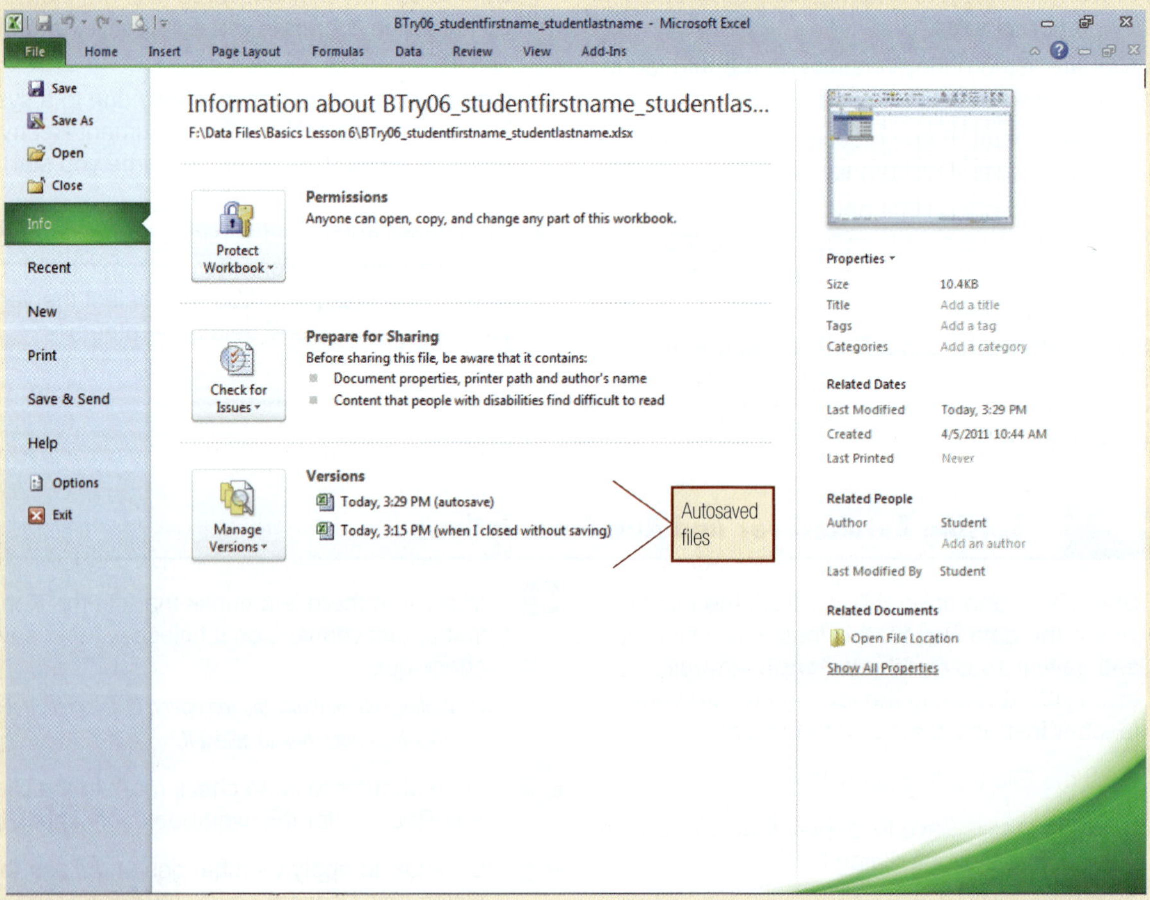

Try It! Opening a Draft Version of an Unsaved File

1. In Excel, click File > New > Create to create a new blank workbook.
2. Type your first name, press ENTER, type your last name, and press ENTER.
3. Wait at least a minute without saving the file.
4. Close the file without saving.
5. Click File. The Recent tab should display in Backstage view.
6. Below the Recent Places pane on the right side of the window, click Recover Unsaved Workbooks to display the contents of the UnsavedFiles folder in the Open dialog box.
7. Click the unsaved file at the top of the list, and then click Open to open it in Excel.
8. Close the file without saving the changes.
9. Click File > Options > Save to display the Save tab of the Excel Options dialog box.
10. Change the Save AutoRecover information setting back to 10 minutes.
11. Click OK to apply the changes and close the dialog box. Exit Excel.

Project 11—Create It

Use Help to Investigate Document Recovery

DIRECTIONS

1. Click **Start** > **All Programs** > **Microsoft Word** to start the Word program.
2. Click the **Help** button in the upper-right corner of the program window to start the Help program.
3. If the Table of Contents is displayed, click the Hide Table of Contents button. Type **recover** in the Search text box, and then click the **Search** button to display a list of articles about recovering files.
4. Click **Use the Document Recovery task pane to recover your files** to display that article.
5. Maximize the **Help** window to make it easier to read the content.
6. Click the link to **My Office program did not open a recovered file** to display that article.
7. **With your teacher's permission**, click the **Print** button and print the article.
8. Click the **Back** button to display the previous page.
9. Click the **Home** button to display the Home page.
10. Close the Help program window.
11. Exit Word.

Project 12—Apply It

Locate Information About Formatting Text

DIRECTIONS

1. Start Microsoft Word and open the file **BProj12** from the data files for this lesson.
2. Save the file as **BProj12_studentfirstname_studentlastname** in the location where your teacher instructs you to store the files for this lesson.
3. On the first line of the file, type your first name and last name. Press ENTER and type today's date, and then press ENTER to insert a blank line.
4. Start the Help program.
5. Search for information about how to format text with superscript and subscript.
6. Use the information in the Help article to apply superscript to the *nd* and *rd* in the sentence.
7. Use the information in the Help article to apply subscript to the *2* in H_2O.
8. Close the Help program window. The **BProj12_studentfirstname_studentlastname** document should look similar to Figure 6-1.
9. Save the changes to the document.
10. **With your teacher's permission**, print the file.
11. Close the file, saving all changes, and exit Word.

Figure 6-1

Firstname Lastname

Today's date

Superscript is a character that displays slightly above other characters on the line. For example, a footnote number is formatted as superscript, as are trademark symbols, and ordinals.

Take the 2nd left and then the 3rd right.

Subscript is a character that displays slightly below other characters on the line. For example, chemical formulas use subscript numbers.

H_2O is the chemical formula for water.

Lesson 7

Managing Information Technology

➤ What You Will Learn

- Copying Files and Folders
- Moving Files and Folders
- Compressing Files
- Recognizing Types of Business Documents
- Determining the Risks and Rewards of Developing an IT Strategy
- Identifying Needed Equipment and Supplies
- Establishing, Scheduling, and Following Maintenance Procedures

Software Skills Every employee benefits from knowing how to identify the equipment and supplies he or she needs to accomplish tasks, and how to manage information technology resources to achieve goals. A basic place to start is by learning how to recognize types of business documents and the programs you need to create, view, and edit them. You can also save money and time by understanding the importance of maintaining IT equipment so that it performs efficiently.

Application Skills You have been hired by the Michigan Avenue Athletic Club to set up policies for purchasing and maintaining information technology equipment and supplies. In this lesson, you use Word to create a memo to the office manager asking him to conduct an inventory of hardware currently owned by the club, the software programs currently in use, and the current maintenance schedules. You also ask him to provide you with a list of needed equipment and supplies. You will create a folder where you can store the files he submits, and you will organize the files so you can use the information to develop an IT purchasing and maintenance plan.

WORDS TO KNOW

Business document
A professional document used to communicate information within a company, or between one company and another.

Compress
Minimize the size of something.

Destination location
The location where a folder or file is stored after it is moved.

Extract
Remove, or separate from.

IT strategy
A plan that identifies how information technology will be put in place over time to help an organization achieve its overall business goals.

Source location
The original location where a folder or file is stored.

Technology infrastructure
The computer systems, networking devices, software, and other technologies used to collect, store, and distribute information.

What You Can Do

Copying Files and Folders

- You can copy a file or folder from one storage location to another.
- When you copy a file or folder, the original remains stored in it its **source location** and the copy is stored in the **destination location**.
- Both the original and the copy have the same name; you can tell them apart because they are stored in different locations.
- You copy a file or folder using the Copy and Paste commands, or by dragging the item from its source to its destination while holding down CTRL.
- When you copy a folder, all the items stored in the folder are copied as well.
- If you try to copy a folder or file to a location that already contains a folder or file with the same name, Windows offers three options:
  - Copy and Replace. Select this option to replace the existing file with the copy.
  - Don't copy. Select this option to cancel the command.
  - Copy, but keep both files. Select this option to continue with the copy command. Windows leaves the existing file unchanged and adds (2) to the copied file's name.

Try It! Copying Files and Folders

1. Click Start > Computer to open Windows Explorer and navigate to the location where your teacher instructs you to store the files for this lesson.
2. Create a new folder named **BTry07_Copy_studentfirstname_studentlastname**. Leave the window open.
3. Click Start > Computer to open Windows Explorer in another window. Using Windows Explorer, navigate to the location where the data files for this lesson are stored.
4. Click a blank area of the Windows Taskbar and click Show Side by Side to arrange the two windows so you can see the contents of both.
5. In the location where the data files are stored, right-click the file named **BTry07a** and click Copy on the shortcut menu.
6. Right-click a blank area in the **BTry07_Copy_studentfirstname_studentlastname** folder and click Paste on the shortcut menu.
7. Press and hold CTRL and drag the **BTry07b** file from the data files storage location to the **BTry07_Copy_studentfirstname_studentlastname** folder.
8. Drop the file and release CTRL when the ScreenTip displays *Copy to BTry07_Copy_studentfirstname_studentlastname*.
9. Close the window where the data files for this lesson are stored. Double-click the **BTry07_Copy_studentfirstname_studentlastname** folder to open it. The two copied files are in the folder. The originals are still in the original location.
10. Click the Back button to return to the location where the files for this lesson are stored.
11. Right-click the **BTry07_Copy_studentfirstname_studentlastname** folder and click Copy.
12. Navigate to the desktop, right-click a blank area, and click Paste. The folder is copied to the desktop.
13. Open the **BTry07_Copy_studentfirstname_studentlastname** folder on the desktop. Note that the two files were copied as well.
14. Close the **BTry07_Copy_studentfirstname_studentlastname** folder, and delete it from the desktop.
15. In Windows Explorer, navigate to the location where the files for this lesson are stored, and delete the **BTry07_Copy_studentfirstname_studentlastname** folder. Leave the Windows Explorer window open to use in the next Try It.

(continued)

Try It! **Copying Files and Folders** *(continued)*

Copy by dragging

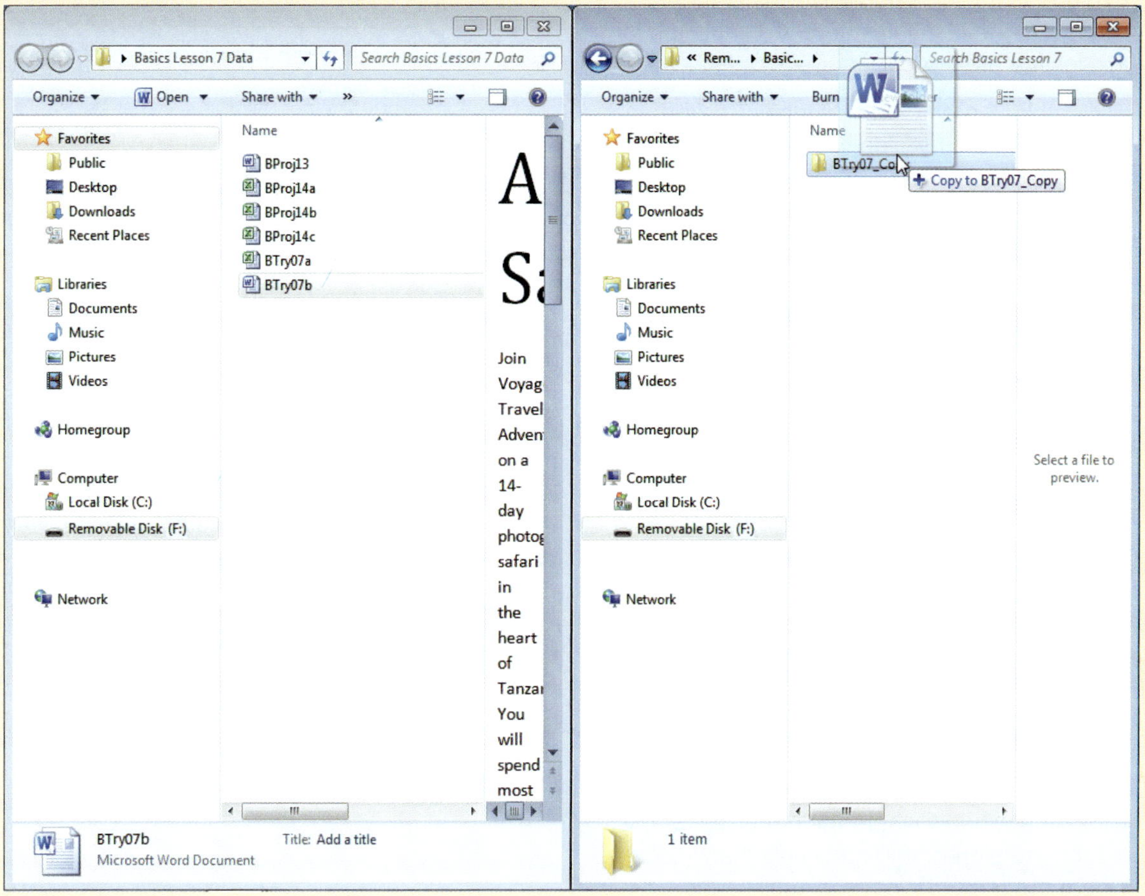

Moving Files and Folders

- You can move a file or folder from one storage location to another.
- When you move a file or folder, it is deleted from its source location and is stored in the destination location.
- You move a file or folder using the Cut and Paste commands, or by dragging it to the destination.
- When you move a folder, all the items stored in the folder are moved as well.
- If you try to move a folder or file to a location that already contains a folder or file with the same name, Windows offers three options:
  - Move and Replace. Select this option to replace the existing file with the one you are moving.
  - Don't move. Select this option to cancel the command.
  - Move, but keep both files. Select this option to continue with the move command. Windows leaves the existing file unchanged and adds (2) to the copied file's name.

Try It! Moving Files and Folders

1. Click Start > Computer to open Windows Explorer in a new window. Navigate in that window to the location where the data files for this lesson are stored.
2. Click a blank area of the Windows Taskbar, and click Show Side by Side to arrange the two windows so you can see the contents of both.
3. Right-click the **BTry07a** file, and click Cut on the shortcut menu.
4. In the window displaying the location where you are storing the files for this lesson, right-click a blank area and click Paste on the shortcut menu. The file is deleted from its original location and pasted into the new location.
5. In the location where the files for this lesson are stored create a new folder named **BTry07_Move**.
6. Right-click the **BTry07b** file, and click Cut on the shortcut menu.
7. Right-click the **BTry07_Move** folder, and click Paste on the shortcut menu. The file is deleted from its original location, and pasted into the **BTry07_Move** folder.
8. Close the window where the data files for this lesson are stored, and maximize the window where the **BTry07_Move** folder and the **BTry07a** file are stored.
9. Drag the **BTry07a** file to the **BTry07_Move** folder.
10. Drop the file when the ScreenTip displays *Move to BTry07_Move*.
11. Double-click the **BTry07_Move** folder to open it. The two files are now stored only in this folder.
12. Click the Back button to return to the location where the files for this lesson are stored.
13. Right-click the **BTry07_Move** folder, and click Cut.
14. Navigate to the desktop, right-click a blank area, and click Paste. The folder is moved to the desktop.
15. Open the **BTry07_Move** folder on the desktop. Note that the two files were moved as well.
16. Select both files, right-click the selection, and click Cut.
17. Navigate to the location where the files for this lesson are stored, right-click a blank area of the window, and click Paste.
18. Delete the **BTry07_Move** folder from the desktop.

Compressing Files

- **Compress**, or zip, a file to minimize its size, making it easier to store or transmit.
- You use Windows to compress files.
- When you compress a file, you create a compressed, or zipped, folder in which the file is stored.
- By default, the compressed folder has the same name as the compressed file, but you can rename it, if you want.
- You can compress multiple files together into one folder.
- You can even compress entire folders.
- To use the compressed files, you must extract them from the folder.
- When you **extract** the files, you copy them from the compressed folder to a destination location. By default, the location is a new folder with the same name as the compressed folder, but you can select a different location.

Try It! Compressing Files

1. Open Windows Explorer and navigate to the location where the data files for this lesson are stored.
2. Right-click the **BTry07c** file to display a shortcut menu.

Use Windows to compress a file

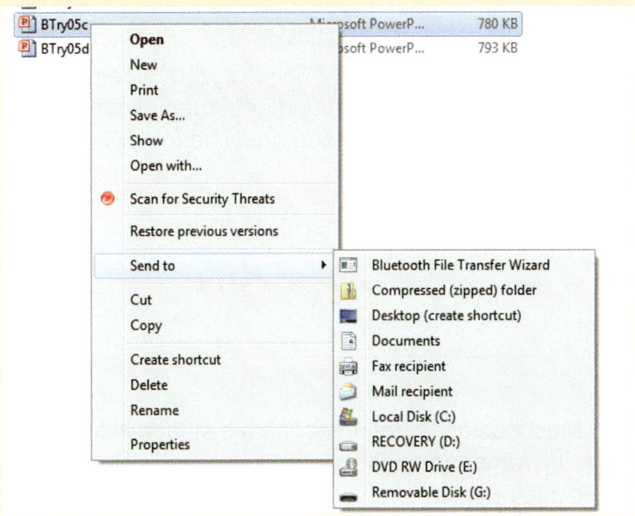

3. Click Send to on the shortcut menu, and then click Compressed (zipped) folder. Windows compresses the file into a compressed folder. The new folder name is selected so you can type a new name.
4. Type **BTry07_compressed**, and press ENTER. Notice that the compressed folder has fewer kilobytes (KB) than the original file. Kilobytes are a measurement of size.
5. Right-click the **BTry07d** file and click Copy on the shortcut menu.
6. Right-click the **BTry07_compressed** folder and click Paste on the shortcut menu. This copies the **BTry07d** file into the compressed folder.
7. Double-click the **BTry07_compressed** folder to open it and view its contents. It contains both the **BTry07c** and **BTry07d** files. Close Windows Explorer.

A compressed file is smaller than the original

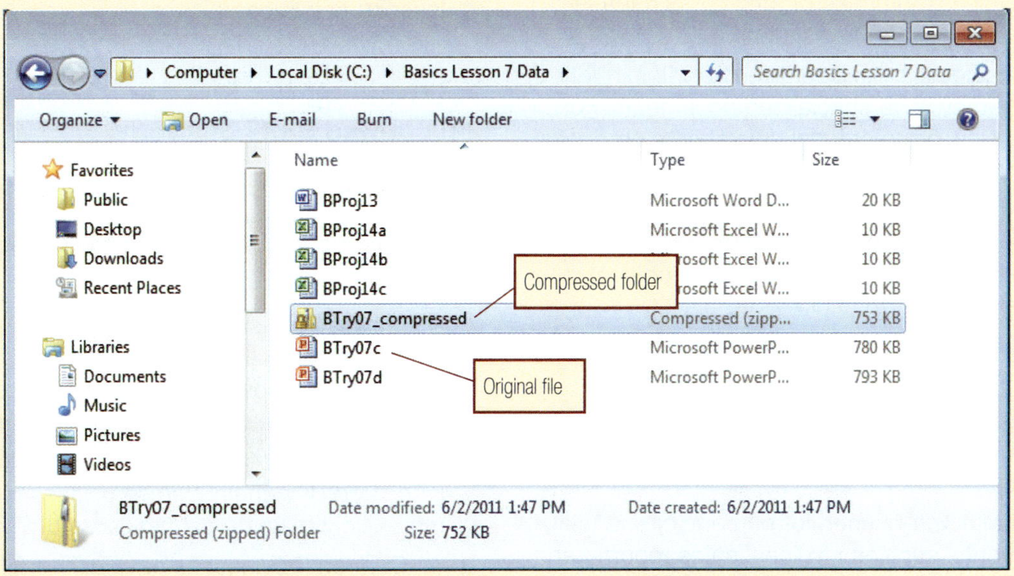

Try It!

Extracting Compressed Files

1. Click Start > Computer and then, in Windows Explorer, navigate to the location where the data files for this lesson are stored.
2. Right-click the **BTry07_compressed** folder and click Extract All. Windows displays the name of the default folder where it will store the extracted files.
3. Select the text *compressed* at the end of the folder name and then type **extracted** to change the name.
4. Click Extract. Windows creates a new folder in the current location and copies the files to it. By default, it opens the new folder in a separate window. You can see the extracted files.

   ✓ *If the window does not open by default, double-click the BTry07_extracted folder to open it.*
5. Close the **BTry07_extracted** folder window. The window for the location where the data files for this lesson are stored should still be open.
6. Right-click the **BTry07_compressed** folder (with the zipped folder icon), click Delete on the shortcut menu, then click Yes in the confirmation dialog box. The compressed folder is sent to the Recycle Bin. The regular folder containing the extracted files remains.
7. Right-click the **BTry07_extracted** folder, click Delete on the shortcut menu, then click Yes in the confirmation dialog box. The folder is sent to the Recycle Bin.

Recognizing Types of Business Documents

- Some common **business documents** used by most companies include letters, memos, fax covers, marketing presentations, training slide shows, invoices, purchase orders, press releases, agendas, reports, and newsletters.
- Certain businesses—or departments within a larger company—may have specialized documents. For example, a law office or legal department produces legal documents such as wills, contracts, and bills of sale.
- In additional, individuals create personal business documents such as letters, research papers, and resumes.
- Each Microsoft Office program is designed for creating specific types of business documents.
  - Microsoft Word is used for text-based documents, such as letters, memos, and reports.
  - Microsoft Excel is used for numeric or financial documents, such as invoices, sales reports, and graphic analysis.
  - Microsoft PowerPoint is used for slide shows and presentation graphics.
  - Microsoft Access is used to store data and create forms, tables, and reports based on that data.
- Most business documents have standard formats, which means each type of document includes similar parts.
- You will learn about the standard formats for different types of documents throughout the lessons in this book.

Determining the Risks and Rewards of Developing an IT Strategy

- An **IT strategy** is a road map or plan that identifies how information technology will be put in place over time to help an organization achieve its overall business goals.
- A successful IT strategy prepares a business for future growth and puts the technology in place that a company needs to make the best use of available resources, solve problems, and compete.
- Companies that take the time and make the effort to include IT in their overall business plans are more likely to implement successful IT strategies.
  - Different businesses have different IT needs.
  - A small business might require only a desktop computer, an all-in-one printer/scanner device, and an Internet connection.

- A large business might require hundreds of desktop PCs, notebook and tablet computers, one or more internal networks, corporate servers, a telephone system, printers, scanners, and copier machines, projection systems, and more.

- Some businesses might require specialized IT tools.
  - A construction company might require rugged portable devices that can withstand extreme weather or rough conditions.
  - A design firm might require high-end computer-aided design software, while an investment firm requires high-end financial applications.
- A successful IT strategy takes into consideration factors such as the current needs of the company, how to best use systems currently in place, and how to implement new technologies that support the business.
- It also takes into consideration the cost of new equipment, maintenance, and training, as well as the physical environment in which IT will be installed. For example, a small business must consider if there is space to install new computer systems. A large company might need to install a climate control system for a new data center.
- There are two primary risks of locking in to a particular IT strategy: a plan that is too advanced, and a plan that is not advanced enough.
  - If a company puts a plan in place that is more advanced than it can support, it wastes money on unnecessary technology that employees do not know how to use.
  - If a company puts a plan in place that is not advanced enough, the company may lose ground to its competition or find that it has to spend money to upgrade systems sooner than expected.
- When an IT strategy balances the needs, costs, and corporate goals, the risks are minimized and the rewards are achievable.

Identifying Needed Equipment and Supplies

- Almost every business has a **technology infrastructure**, which is the computer systems, networking devices, software, and other technologies used to collect, store, and distribute information.
- No matter how large or small a business may be, it is vital that someone monitor, manage, and maintain the technology infrastructure in order to keep the business running.
  - In a small organization, each employee might be responsible for his or her own technology. That might mean changing the ink in a desktop printer.
  - In larger organizations, the employees in the IT department are responsible for the IT systems.
- Performing an inventory of the current IT situation is a good first step in developing an IT strategy. Knowing what is already in place and how well it meets current needs helps define future needs.
- Researching and budgeting for an IT project is much like planning any project. You can check pricing online, get bids from various consultants and vendors, or use a combination of those techniques.
- When budgeting for IT systems, it is important to factor in the costs of ongoing support, maintenance, and training.

Establishing, Scheduling, and Following Maintenance Procedures

- Technology systems require maintenance to operate properly. In a large company, maintenance is a constant need. A dedicated staff of technicians responds to employee requests, services hardware, and upgrades software, or outside technicians are hired to provide service.
- In a small company, maintenance might be as basic as keeping a computer keyboard clean, installing a virus protection program, and changing the ink in the printer, when necessary.
- All systems will be more reliable and effective if maintenance is performed on a regular basis.
- Establishing maintenance schedules enables you to plan and perform maintenance appropriately, provide notice to users when maintenance is due, and budget for ongoing maintenance costs.
- Many maintenance tasks can be automated, including data backup, virus scans, and program updates.

- Manufacturers provide maintenance procedures for all equipment and programs. If the user does not follow the manufacturer's recommended maintenance procedures, warranties and service contracts become void, and the company becomes responsible for costs associated with damage and repair.
- In addition, qualified IT professionals are able to diagnose and solve problems individually and as a team to keep the systems running efficiently.

Project 13—Create It

Copy, Move, and Compress Files and Folders

DIRECTIONS

1. Click **Start** > **All Programs** > **Microsoft Word** to start the Word program.
2. Open the file **BProj13** from the data files for this lesson, and save it as **BProj13_studentfirstname_studentlastname** in the location where your teacher instructs you to store the files for this lesson.
3. Replace the text *Student's Name* with your own first and last name.
4. Replace the text *Today's Date* with the current date.
5. Press CTRL + END to move the insertion point to the last line of the document and type the following paragraph:

   Tom, as a first step in developing policies for purchasing and maintaining the club's IT equipment and supplies, I need to know what we have and what we need. Please take an inventory of the hardware we currently own, the software we currently use, and the maintenance schedule currently in place. I would also like a list of any equipment and supplies we need.
6. Press ENTER twice and type the following paragraph:

   I would like to receive this information by the end of the week. Thanks so much for your assistance. Let me know if you have any questions.
7. Save the document. It should look similar to Figure 7-1 on the next page.
8. **With your teacher's permission**, print the file.
9. Close the file and exit Word.
10. In Windows, navigate to the desktop.
11. Create a folder named **BProj13_studentfirstname_studentlastname** on the desktop.
12. Right-click the **BProj13_studentfirstname_studentlastname** folder and click **Cut** on the shortcut menu. This cuts the folder from the desktop and stores it on the Clipboard.
13. Navigate to the location where your teacher instructs you to store the files for this lesson.
14. Right-click a blank area of the window, and click **Paste** on the shortcut menu to paste the folder from the Clipboard into the selected storage location.
15. Right-click the **BProj13_studentfirstname_studentlastname** Word file, and click **Copy** on the shortcut menu.
16. Right-click the **BProj13_studentfirstname_studentlastname** folder, and click **Paste** on the shortcut menu. This copies the file into the folder. The original file remains stored in its current location.
17. Right-click the original **BProj13_studentfirstname_studentlastname** Word file, click Send to, and then click Compressed (zipped) folder. The file is sent to a compressed folder with the default name **BProj13_studentfirstname_studentlastname**.
18. Type **BProj13_studentfirstname_studentlastname_compressed**, and press ENTER to rename the compressed folder.

19. Right-click the original **BProj13_studentfirstname_studentlastname** Word file, and click **Delete** on the shortcut menu.

20. Click **Yes** to delete the file. Now, you have a regular folder named **BProj13_studentfirstname_studentlastname**, which contains the Word memo file, and a compressed folder named **BProj13_studentfirstname_studentlastname_compressed**, which contains a compressed version of the Word memo file.

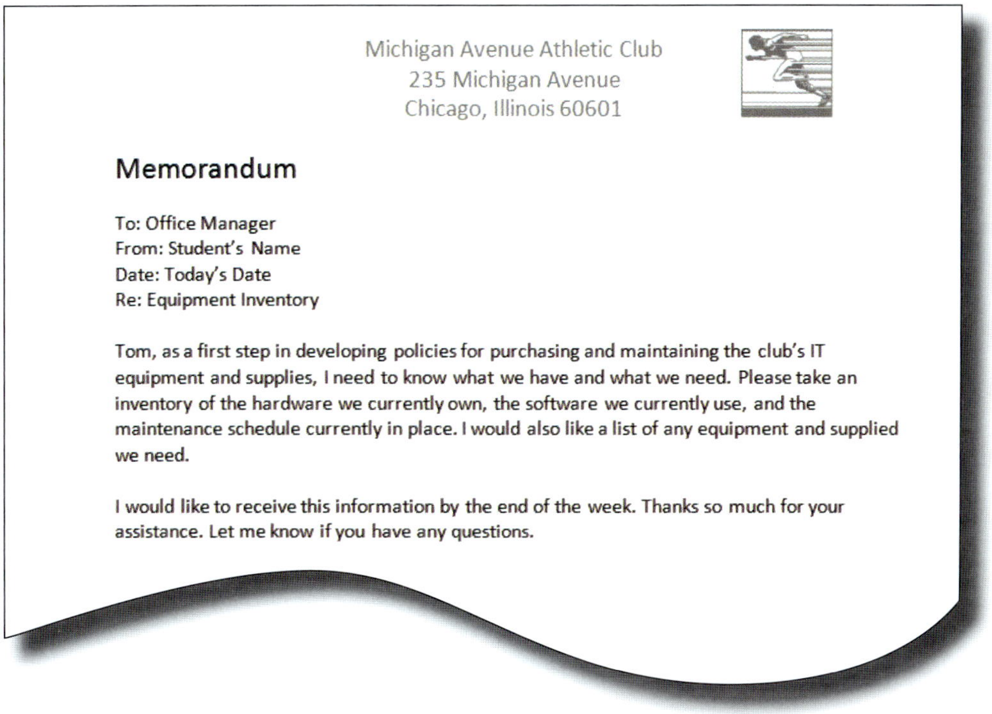

Michigan Avenue Athletic Club
235 Michigan Avenue
Chicago, Illinois 60601

Memorandum

To: Office Manager
From: Student's Name
Date: Today's Date
Re: Equipment Inventory

Tom, as a first step in developing policies for purchasing and maintaining the club's IT equipment and supplies, I need to know what we have and what we need. Please take an inventory of the hardware we currently own, the software we currently use, and the maintenance schedule currently in place. I would also like a list of any equipment and supplied we need.

I would like to receive this information by the end of the week. Thanks so much for your assistance. Let me know if you have any questions.

Figure 7-1

Project 14—Apply It

Copy, Move, and Compress Files

DIRECTIONS

1. Navigate to the location where your teacher instructs you to store the files for this lesson.
2. Create a new folder named **BProj14_studentfirstname_studentlastname**.
3. Copy **BProj14a** from the location where the data files for this lesson are stored to the **BProj14_studentfirstname_studentlastname** folder.
4. Copy **BProj14b** from the location where the data files for this lesson are stored to the **BProj14_studentfirstname_studentlastname** folder.
5. Copy **BProj14c** from the location where the data files for this lesson are stored to the **BProj14_studentfirstname_studentlastname** folder.
6. Compress the **BProj14_studentfirstname_studentlastname** folder and its contents into a compressed folder named **BProj14_studentfirstname_studentlastname_compressed**.
7. Move the **BProj13_studentfirstname_studentlastname** regular folder into the **BProj14_studentfirstname_studentlastname_compressed** compressed folder.
8. Open the **BProj14_studentfirstname_studentlastname_compressed** compressed folder.
9. Extract all files from **BProj14_studentfirstname_studentlastname_compressed** into a regular folder named **BProj14_studentfirstname_studentlastname_extracted**.

Chapter Assessment and Application

Project 15—Make It Your Own

Create an IT Strategy

You are responsible for developing a list of ways a group, organization, or business might use Microsoft Office 2010 as part of an IT strategy. Start by selecting the group. It might be a club, team, or organization to which you belong, the place where you work, or any business of your choice. Research its goals, current IT infrastructure, and requirements. Then, use Microsoft Office 2010 and the skills you have learned in this chapter to develop your list.

DIRECTIONS

1. Create a folder named **BProj15_studentfirstname_studentlastname** in the location where your teacher instructs you to store the files for this chapter.
2. Start the Microsoft Office 2010 program you want to use to create the list. For example, you might use Word or Excel.
3. Save the file as **BProj15a_studentfirstname_studentlastname** in the **BProj15_studentfirstname_studentlastname** folder.
4. Type your name in the file.
5. Type the date in the file.
6. Type a title for your list and format the title using fonts, font styles, and font color.
7. Type the list of ways the group, organization, or business might use Microsoft Office 2010 as part of an IT strategy.
8. Save the changes to the file.
9. Start Word, if necessary, and open **BProj15b**. Save it as **Proj15b_studentfirstname_studentlastname** in the **Proj15_studentfirstname_studentlastname** folder.
10. Type your name on the first line of the file and the date on the second line. Then, move the insertion point to the blank line above the picture, and type a paragraph explaining the list you typed in step 7.
11. Save the changes to the file.
12. **With your teacher's permission**, print the file. If necessary, adjust page formatting such as orientation and margins so its fits on a single page. It should look similar to Illustration A on the next page.
13. Copy the picture in the file to the Clipboard, and then close the file, saving all changes.
14. Make the **BProj15a_studentfirstname_studentlastname** file active, and paste the picture at either the beginning or end of the file.
15. Save the changes, and, **with your teacher's permission**, print the file. If necessary, adjust page formatting such as orientation and margins so it fits on a single page. It should look similar to Illustration B on the next page.
16. Close the file, saving all changes, and exit all programs.
17. Compress the **BProj15_studentfirstname_studentlastname** folder into a compressed folder named **BProj15_studentfirstname_studentlastname_compressed**.

Illustration A

Firstname Lastname
Today's Date

Ways the Marching Band Might Use Microsoft Office 2010

Use Microsoft Word to create memos to band members, letters to parents, and fundraising letters to send to neighborhood businesses.
Use Microsoft Excel to create worksheets tracking income and expenses, to create a budget, and to create graphs illustrating the data.
Use Microsoft Access to set up and maintain a database of members, parents, volunteers, and community supporters.
Use Microsoft Publisher to create postcard mailings, flyers, and even brochures.
Use Microsoft Outlook for communication.

Illustration B

Firstname Lastname

Today's Date

Explanation of My List

I think the marching band could benefit from using all of the Microsoft Office 2010 programs. It will be faster to use Microsoft Word to create all text-based documents such as letters and memos. Old files can be reused and updated, and it is easier to make corrections. It also looks professional. Microsoft Excel automates calculations so it is easier to keep track of income and expenses and to identify ways to save and spend. It makes it easy to create charts that illustrate the data which might help the band convince the school committee to increase funding. By creating databases in Microsoft Access the band can easily keep track of the people and equipment it has. The databases can be used to generate mass mailings and reports. With Microsoft Publisher, the band can create professional quality publications. Microsoft Office makes it easy to create and store email messages, to schedule appointments and meetings, and to keep track of tasks that must be accomplished.

Project 16—Master It

Create a Memo

Voyager Travel Adventures is opening a new office. You have been asked to make a list of IT equipment and supplies needed to get the office up and running. In this project, you will create a folder for storing your work. You will start Microsoft Office 2010 programs and create, save, and print files. You will also open and save existing files, use the Office Clipboard to copy a selection from one file to another, and prepare a file for distribution. Finally, you will compress the files.

DIRECTIONS

1. On the Windows desktop, create a new folder named **BProj16_studentfirstname_ studentlastname**.
2. Move the folder to the location where your teacher instructs you to store the files for this chapter.
3. Start Microsoft Word, and create a new file. Save the file in the **BProj16_studentfirstname_ studentlastname** folder with the name **BProj16a_ studentfirstname_studentlastname**.
4. On the first line of the document, type today's date. Press ENTER and type your full name. Press ENTER and type the following:

   I recommend the following IT equipment to get the new Voyager Travel Adventures office up and running:
5. Press ENTER and type the following list, pressing ENTER at the end of each line to start a new line.

   4 personal computers running Microsoft Windows 7, with Microsoft Office 2010

   2 notebook computers to be shared as necessary, also running Microsoft Windows 7, with Microsoft Office 2010

   Wireless network devices

   1 printer

   1 printer/fax/copier all-in-one

   1 external hard drive for backing up data

   Internet telephone system
6. Save the changes to the document.
7. Format the date in bold and increase the font size to 14, then format your name in bold italic, and increase the font size to 12.
8. Start the Help program and locate information about how to format a bulleted list.
9. Use the Help information to apply bullet list formatting to the list of equipment.

   If you cannot find information about bullet list formatting, select the items in the list, and then click the Bullets button in the Paragraph group on the Home tab of the Ribbon.
10. Save the changes to the file.
11. Start Microsoft Excel and open the file **BProj16b** from the data files for this chapter. Save the file in the **BProj16_studentfirstname_studentlastname** folder as **BProj16b_studentifrstname_ studentlastname**.
12. Copy the picture in the Excel file to the Clipboard.
13. Arrange the Excel and Word windows side by side.
14. Make the Word window active and display the Clipboard task pane.
15. Exit Excel without saving any changes, and maximize the Word window.
16. Paste the picture on to the last line of the document, and then delete it from the Clipboard.
17. Close the Clipboard task pane.
18. Save the changes to the Word document.
19. Change the margins for the document to Wide.
20. **With your teacher's permission**, print the document. It should look similar to Illustration A on the next page.
21. Close the file, saving all changes, and exit Word.
22. Navigate to the location where you are saving the files for this lesson.
23. Compress the entire **BProj16_studentfirstname_ studentlastname** folder into a compressed folder named **BProj16_studentfirstname_ studentlastname_compressed**.
24. If you have completed your session, log off your computer account.

Illustration A

Today's Date

Firstname Lastname

I recommend the following IT equipment to get the new Voyager Travel Adventures office up and running:

- 4 personal computers running Microsoft Windows 7, with Microsoft Office 2010
- 2 notebook computers to be shared as necessary, also running Microsoft Windows 7, with Microsoft Office 2010
- Wireless network devices
- 1 printer
- 1 printer/fax/copier all-in-one
- 1 external hard drive for backing up data
- Internet telephone system

Chapter 1

Getting Started with Microsoft Word 2010

Lesson 1
Creating Word Documents with Headers and Footers
Projects 1-2

- Starting and Exiting Microsoft Word 2010
- Exploring the Microsoft Word 2010 Window
- Changing the Microsoft Word 2010 Window
- Showing or Hiding Nonprinting Characters
- Typing in a Document
- Typing in the Header or Footer
- Splitting a Word Window
- Saving a Document

Lesson 2
Formatting Documents with Themes and Styles
Projects 3-4

- Creating a New, Blank Document
- Closing a Document
- Using Click and Type
- Opening a Saved Document
- Saving a Document with a New Name
- Applying a Built-In Style
- Changing the Style Set
- Applying a Theme
- Analyzing a Press Release

Lesson 3
Editing and Correcting Documents
Projects 5-6

- Inserting Text
- Using Overtype Mode
- Selecting and Replacing Text
- Canceling a Command
- Using Undo, Redo, and Repeat

Lesson 4
Adjusting Alignment and Spacing
Projects 7-8

- Aligning Text Horizontally
- Aligning a Document Vertically
- Setting Line Spacing
- Setting Paragraph Spacing
- Analyzing Memos

Lesson 5
Creating Letters and Envelopes
Projects 9-10

- Indenting Text
- Setting and Modifying Tabs
- Inserting the Date and Time
- Writing a Business Letter
- Creating an Envelope

Lesson 6
Formatting Text with Fonts and Effects
Projects 11-12

- Changing the Font
- Changing the Font Size
- Changing the Font Color
- Applying Font Styles and Effects
- Applying Underlines
- Clearing Formatting
- Writing a Personal Business Letter

Lesson 7
Formatting and Sorting Lists
Projects 13-14

- Creating a Bulleted List
- Creating a Numbered List
- Changing the Bullet or Number Formatting
- Sorting Paragraphs

Lesson 8
Inserting Pictures, Text Boxes, and Shapes
Projects 15-16

- Analyzing Objects
- Inserting Pictures
- Inserting a Text Box
- Inserting Shapes
- Resizing and Deleting Objects
- Scanning Content into Microsoft Clip Organizer

Lesson 9
Formatting Graphics Objects
Projects 17-18

- Wrapping Text Around an Object
- Moving and Positioning an Object
- Formatting Objects
- Modifying Pictures
- Modifying a Text Box
- Adding Text to a Shape
- Changing a Shape

Lesson 10
Working with SmartArt Graphics, Text Effects, and Page Borders
Projects 19-20

- Inserting a SmartArt Graphic
- Entering Text in a SmartArt Graphic
- Modifying the Design of a SmartArt Graphic
- Applying Text Effects
- Applying a Page Border

End of Chapter Assessments
Projects 21-22

Lesson 1

Creating Word Documents with Headers and Footers

➤ What You Will Learn

Starting and Exiting Microsoft Word 2010
Exploring the Microsoft Word 2010 Window
Changing the Microsoft Word Window
Showing or Hiding Nonprinting Characters
Typing in a Document
Typing in the Header or Footer
Splitting a Word Window
Saving a Document

Software Skills Microsoft Word 2010 is the word processing application included in the Microsoft Office 2010 suite. You use Word to create text-based documents such as letters, memos, reports, flyers, and newsletters. The first step in mastering Word is learning how to start the program and create a document.

Application Skills You are the office manager at the Michigan Avenue Athletic Club in Chicago, Illinois. Two new employees have recently joined the staff, and you must type up brief biographies that will be made available at the club and sent to members. In this lesson, you will start Word, create and save documents, and exit Word.

WORDS TO KNOW

Active pane
The pane in which the insertion point is currently located. Commands and actions occur in the active pane.

Default
Standard.

Footer
Text or graphics printed at the bottom of all pages in a document.

Header
Text or graphics printed at the top of all pages in a document.

Insertion point
The flashing vertical line that indicates where the next action will occur in a document onscreen.

Nonprinting characters
Characters such as paragraph marks and tab symbols that are not printed in a document but that can be displayed on the screen.

Paragraph mark
A nonprinting character inserted in a document to indicate where a paragraph ends.

Word wrap
A feature that causes text to move automatically from the end of one line to the beginning of the next line.

What You Can Do

Starting and Exiting Microsoft Word 2010

- To use Microsoft Word 2010 you must first start it so it is running on your computer.
- Use the Microsoft Windows Start menu to start Word.
- Depending on the way your system is set up, you may also be able to use the Word icons on the Windows desktop or the Windows Taskbar. When you are done using a Microsoft Office program, close it to exit.

Try It! Starting and Exiting Microsoft Word 2010

1. Click Start > All Programs. If necessary, scroll until you see the Microsoft Office folder icon.

   ✓ *In this book, the symbol > is used to indicate a series of steps. In this case, click Start and then click All Programs.*

2. Click the Microsoft Office folder icon.
3. Click Microsoft Word 2010.

OR

1. Click Start.
2. Click Microsoft Word 2010 in the list of recently used programs.

OR

1. Double-click the Microsoft Word 2010 shortcut icon on the desktop.

OR

1. Click the Word icon on the Taskbar.

To exit Microsoft Word:

4. Click the Close button at the right end of the Word title bar.

OR

4. Click the File tab.
5. Click Exit.

   ✓ *If you have made changes to the open document, Word displays a dialog box. Click Save to save the changes and then exit, or click Don't Save to exit without saving. Refer to Basics Lesson 6 for information on recovering files you accidentally close without saving.*

Options for Starting Microsoft Word 2010

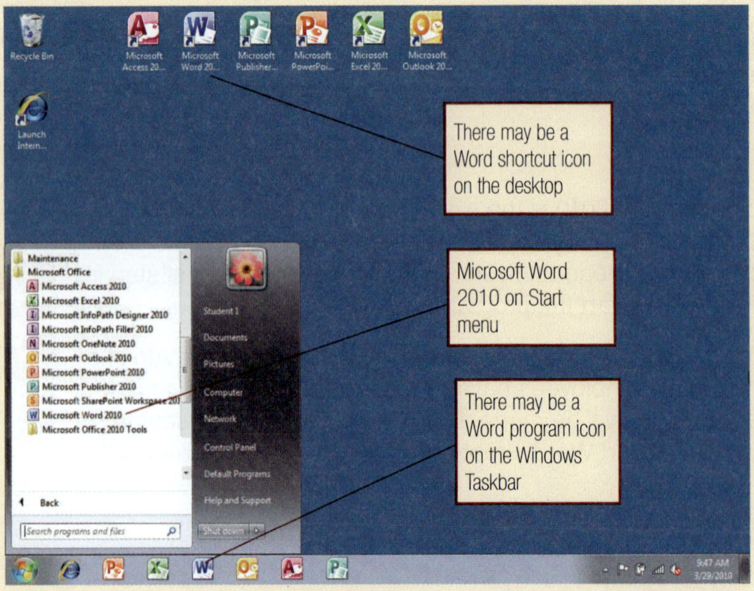

Exploring the Microsoft Word 2010 Window

- When Word starts, it opens a new, blank document using standard, or **default**, settings. Default settings control features such as the margins, the line spacing, the character font, and the font size.

  ✓ *If the text [Compatibility Mode] displays on the Word title bar, it indicates that your software is set to open in a mode that is compatible with older versions of the program.*

- By default, the new document displays in Print Layout view, showing the most common tools you need to create, edit, format, and distribute a document.
- Many of the elements in the Word window are the same as those in other Microsoft Office 2010 programs, such as the Ribbon and the Quick Access Toolbar. Other elements are unique to Word, such as the Rulers.
- Following are some of the typical elements you will see in the Word window:
  - Quick Access Toolbar. A toolbar that displays buttons for commonly used commands. You can customize the Quick Access Toolbar to display buttons you use frequently.
  - Ribbon. Displays buttons for accessing features and commands.

    ✓ *Note that the way items display on the Ribbon may depend on the width of the program window. If your program window is wider than the one used in the figures, more or larger buttons may display. If your program window is narrower, fewer or smaller buttons may display.*

  - Close button. Used to close the program window. It is one of three buttons used to control the size and position of the program window.
  - Title bar. Displays the program and document name.
  - Ribbon tabs. Used to change the commands displayed on the Ribbon.
  - Document area. The workspace where you enter text, graphics, and other data.
  - Rulers. The horizontal ruler measures the width of the document page; it displays information such as margins, tab stops, and indents. The vertical ruler measures the height of the document page.

    ✓ *The rulers may not display by default. You can click the View Ruler button above the vertical scroll bar or click the Ruler check box in the Show/Hide group on the View tab of the Ribbon to toggle them on or off.*

  - Insertion point. A blinking vertical line that displays to the right of the space where characters are inserted in a document.
  - Scroll bars. Used with a mouse to shift the onscreen display up and down or left and right.
  - Status bar. Displays information about the current document.
  - Zoom slider. Used to increase or decrease the size of the document onscreen.
  - Help button. Used to start the program's Help system.
  - View buttons. Used to change the document view.

Try It! Exploring the Microsoft Word 2010 Window

1. Start Microsoft Word 2010.
2. Rest your mouse pointer on a window element to display a descriptive ScreenTip.

The Word Window

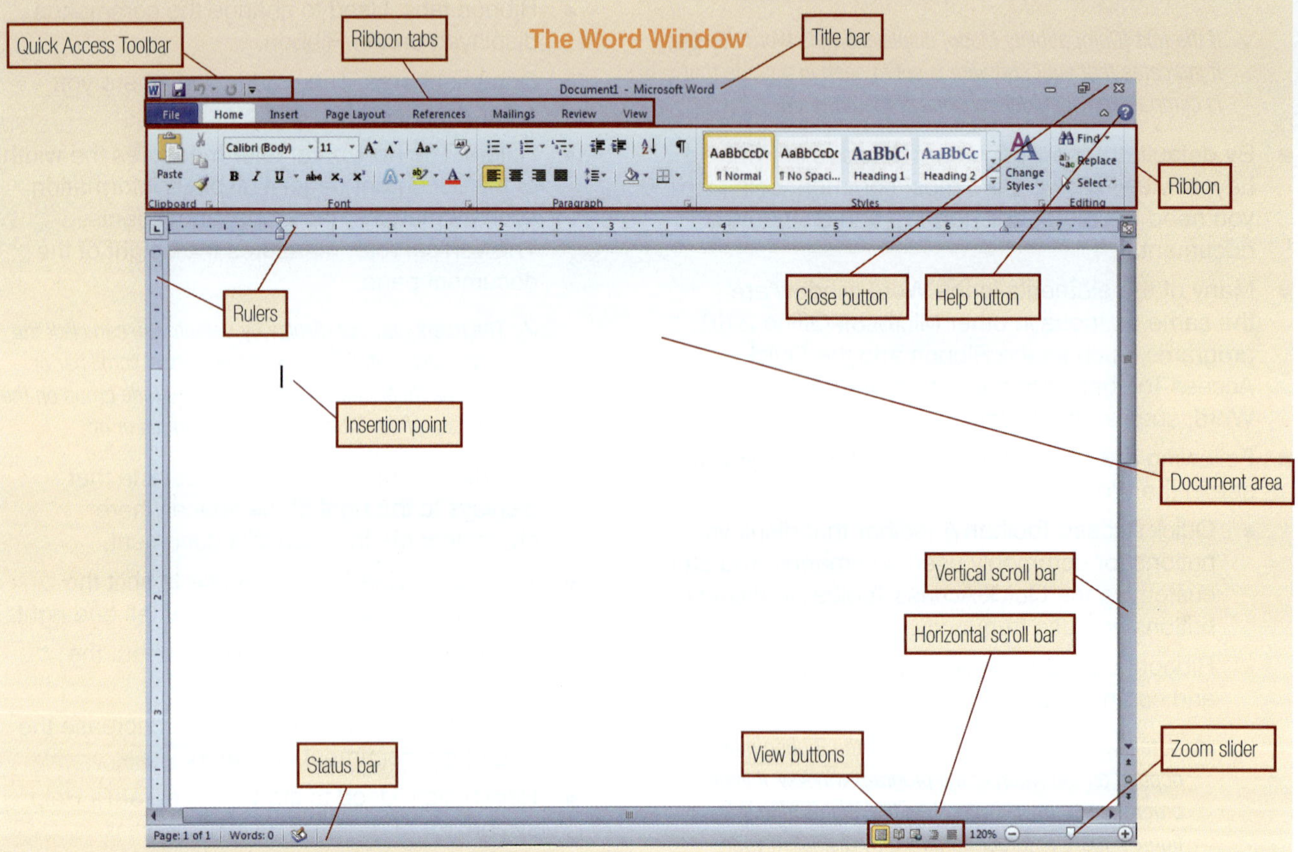

Changing the Microsoft Word Window

- You can control whether certain Word elements display while you work.
- You can show or hide rulers.
- You can minimize the Ribbon.
- You can change views using the View shortcut buttons on the status bar or the commands in the Document Views group on the View tab of the Ribbon. Each view displays the tools you need to work in that view.
  - Print Layout view displays a document onscreen the way it will look when it is printed. It is the default view.
  - Web Layout view wraps text to fit the window, the way it would on a Web page document.
  - Outline view is used to create and edit outlines.
  - Full Screen Reading view adjusts the display of text to make it easier to read documents onscreen.
  - Draft view can be used for most typing, editing, and formatting, but some formatting does not show onscreen.

Try It! Changing the Word Window

1. Start Word, if necessary, or continue working in the open document.
2. Click the View Ruler button above the vertical scroll bar.

OR

1. Click the View tab.
2. In the Show group, click to select the Ruler check box.

✓ *A check in the check box indicates the ruler is displayed.*

3. Click the Minimize the Ribbon button . The Ribbon is hidden, and the minimize button is replaced by the Expand the Ribbon button.
4. Click the Expand the Ribbon button to restore the Ribbon.
5. Double-click any tab on the Ribbon. This is an alternative way to minimize the Ribbon.
6. Double-click any tab on the Ribbon. This is an alternative way to expand the minimized Ribbon.
7. Click the View tab.
8. In the Document Views group, click the Draft button to change from Print Layout view to Draft view.
9. On the status bar, click the Full Screen Reading button .
10. Click the Web Layout button .
11. Click the Outline button .
12. Click the Print Layout button .

Options for displaying the rulers

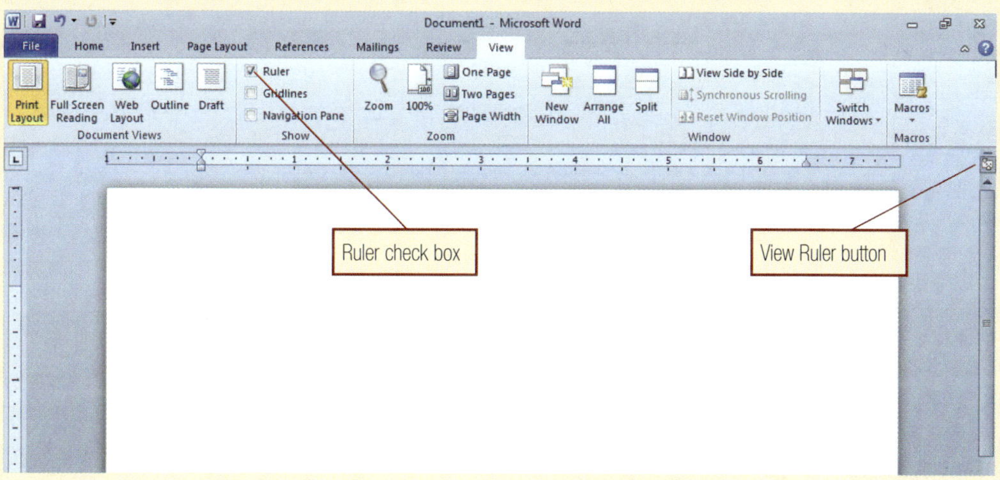

Showing or Hiding Nonprinting Characters

- When you type in Word you insert **nonprinting characters** such as spaces, tabs, and paragraph marks along with printing characters such as letters and numbers.
- Displaying nonprinting characters onscreen is helpful because you see where each paragraph ends and if there are extra spaces or unwanted tab characters.
- The command for showing and hiding nonprinting characters is a toggle; use it to turn the feature off and on.
- Onscreen, the most common nonprinting characters display as follows:

  Space: dot (·)

  Paragraph: paragraph symbol (¶)

  Tab: right arrow (→)

✓ *Other nonprinting characters include optional hyphens, page breaks, and line breaks.*

Try It! Showing or Hiding Nonprinting Characters

1. Start Word, if necessary, or continue working in the open document.
2. Click the Home tab. In the Paragraph group, click Show/Hide ¶ [¶].

   OR

   Press [CTRL] + [*].

   ✓ *If the feature was already on, it is now toggled off. Repeat the steps to turn it back on.*
3. Press [ENTER]. Word starts a new paragraph. You can see the paragraph mark at the end of the previous line.
4. Press [SPACE] five times. You can see the space characters to the left of the insertion point.
5. Press [TAB]. You can see the tab character to the left of the insertion point.
6. Click Show/Hide ¶ [¶] to toggle off nonprinting characters. Leave the document open in Word to use in the next Try It.

Display nonprinting marks in a document

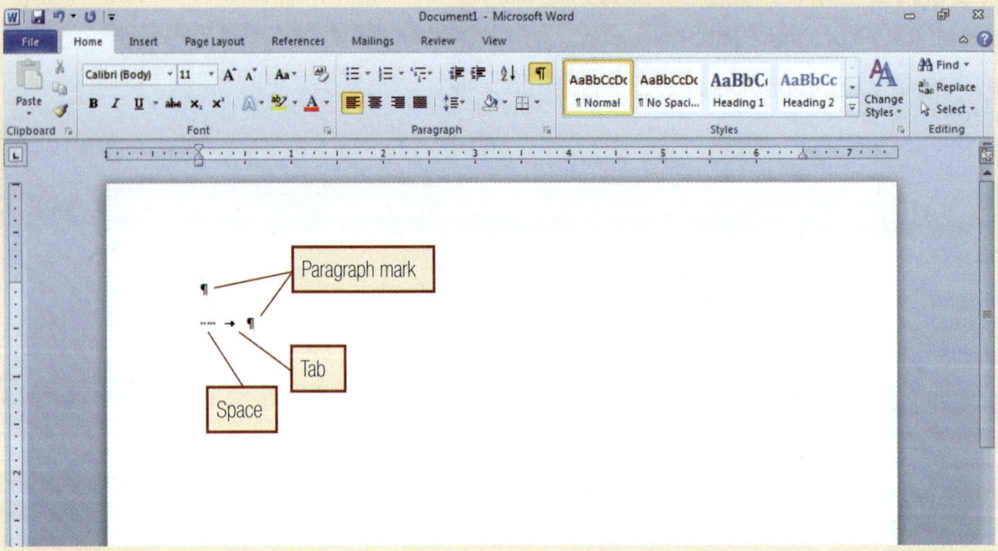

Typing in a Document

- The **insertion point** indicates where text will be inserted or deleted.
- By default, the insertion point is positioned at the beginning (left end) of the first line of a new document.
- You simply begin typing to insert new text.
- Characters you type are inserted to the left of the insertion point.
- Press [BACKSPACE] to delete the character to the left of the insertion point; press [DEL] to delete the character to the right of the insertion point.
- You can move the insertion point anywhere in the existing text with keystrokes or mouse clicks.
- Scrolling to shift the document view does not move the insertion point.
- **Word wrap** automatically wraps the text at the end of a line to the beginning of the next line.
- When you press [ENTER], Word inserts a **paragraph mark** and starts a new paragraph.
- After you type enough text to fill a page, Word automatically starts a new page.

  ✓ *Note that Word includes many features designed to make your work easier, such as a spelling checker. These features are often displayed automatically onscreen as colored underlines or buttons. Simply ignore these features for now; you learn to use them later in this book.*

Table 1-1 Keystrokes for Moving the Insertion Point

Movement	Keystroke	Movement	Keystroke
One character left	←	Up one paragraph	CTRL + ↑
One character right	→	Down one paragraph	CTRL + ↓
One line up	↑	Beginning of document	CTRL + HOME
One line down	↓	End of document	CTRL + END
Previous word	CTRL + ←	Beginning of line	HOME
Next word	CTRL + →	End of line	END

Try It! Typing in a Document

1. With the default Document1 file open in Word, click Show/Hide ¶ [¶] to toggle on nonprinting characters.
2. Press ENTER and then use the keyboard to type the following paragraph:

   Microsoft Word 2010 is the word processing program that comes with the Microsoft Office 2010 suite of programs. I can use it to create, edit, and format text-based documents such as letters, memos, and reports.
3. Press ENTER at the end of the paragraph. Move the mouse so the pointer I-beam is positioned to the left of the first paragraph mark on the first line of the document.
4. Click to position the insertion point.
5. Type your first name, a space, and then your last name.
6. Press ENTER to start a new paragraph.
7. Press CTRL + HOME to position the insertion point at the beginning of the document.
8. Press DEL enough times to delete all the characters in your name. Leave the document open to use in the next Try It.

Typing in the Header or Footer

- Type in a **header** when you want text to display at the top of every page of a document.
- Type in a **footer** when you want text to display at the bottom of every page of a document.
- For example, type your name in the header so it displays at the top of every page; insert page numbers in the footer so they display at the bottom of every page.
- The header area consists of the top 1 inch of the page. The footer area is the bottom 1 inch.
- To type in a header or footer, you first double-click in the area to make it active.
- When the header or footer is active, the main document area is not active, and the Header & Footer Tools tab displays on the Ribbon.
- When you are finished working in the header or footer, the main document area is made active again.
- Headers and footers do not display in Draft view; use Print Layout view to see them on the screen.

Try It! Type in the Header or Footer

1. With the default Document1 file open in Word, double-click in the header area—the white space between the first paragraph mark and the top of the page—to make the header active. Word moves the insertion point into the header.
2. Type your full name.
3. Double-click in the main document area to make it active. You can see the text in the header, but it is not active.

   OR

   On the Header & Footer Tools tab of the Ribbon, in the Close group, click the Close Header and Footer button.
4. Scroll down to the bottom of the page and double-click in the footer area—just above the bottom of the page—to make it active.

   ✓ *For information on scrolling, refer to Basics, Lesson 5. If you have trouble making the footer area active, click the Insert tab, then, in the Header & Footer group, click Footer, and then click Edit Footer.*
5. Type today's date.
6. On the Header & Footer Tools Design tab, in the Navigation group, click the Go to Header button. The insertion point moves up to the header area.
7. Click the Go to Footer button. The insertion point moves to the footer.
8. Double-click in the main document area.

   OR

   On the Header & Footer Tools tab of the Ribbon, in the Close group, click the Close Header and Footer button on the Ribbon.
9. Leave the file open in Word to use in the next Try It.

Typing in the header

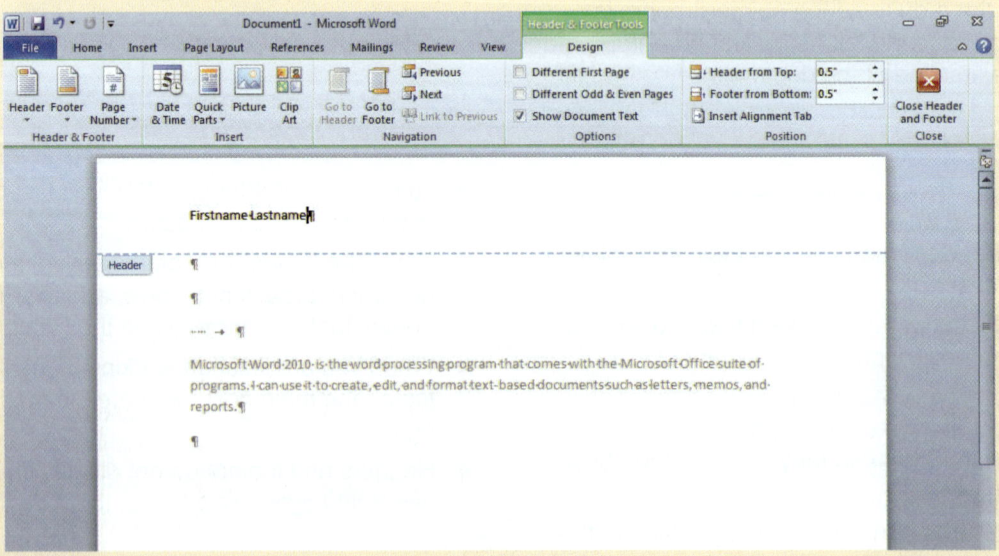

Splitting a Word Window

- Split the Word window into two panes so you can see and work in different sections of a single document.
- Word tiles the panes one above the other within the program window, separated by a split bar.
- Each pane has its own scroll bars so you can scroll each section independently from the other.
- Each pane also has its own rulers.
- There is only one menu bar, one title bar, and one Ribbon.
- Commands affect the **active pane**. For example, you can change the zoom in the top pane if it is active without affecting the inactive bottom pane.
- To switch from one pane to the other to make edits and formatting changes, simply click in the pane you want to make active.

Try It! Splitting a Word Window

1. In the default document, click the View tab.
2. In the Window group, click the Split button. The mouse pointer changes to the resize pointer, and a dark gray bar extends horizontally across the screen.
3. Click halfway down the document. The window splits at the location where you click.

   ✓ *You can also double-click the Split box at the top of the vertical scroll bar to split the window into two equally sized panes.*

4. In the default document, click the View tab.
5. In the Window group, click the Remove Split button.

   ✓ *You can also double-click the Split bar that divides the panes.*

Saving a Document

- If you want to have a Word file available for future use, you must save it on a storage device.
- The first time you save a new file you use the Save As dialog box to give it a name and select the location where you want to store it.
- If Microsoft Word 2010 is running in compatibility mode, it prompts you to confirm you want to save in the most current Word document format.
- After you save a file for the first time, you save changes to the file in order to make sure that you do not lose your work.
- Saving frequently ensures that no work will be lost if there is a power outage or you experience computer problems.

  ✓ *The AutoRecover feature also helps ensure that you won't lose your work. Refer to Basics Lesson 6 for more information on AutoRecover.*

- Saving changes updates the previously saved version of the file with the most recent changes.

Try It! Saving a File

1. In the default document, click Save on the Quick Access Toolbar.

   OR

   a. Click File.

   b. Click Save.

2. Select the File name text box if it is not selected already.
3. Type **WTry01_studentfirstname_studentlastname**.

   ✓ *Replace the text studentfirstname with your own first name, and studentlastname with your own last name. For example, if your name is Mary Jones, type WTry01_Mary_Jones.*

(continued)

Try It! Saving a File *(continued)*

4. Use the Navigation pane to navigate to the location where your teacher instructs you to store the files for this lesson. Create a new folder, if necessary.

   ✓ *Refer to Lesson 1 of the Basics section of this book for information on navigating in Windows Explorer.*

5. Click Save or press ENTER.
6. If a confirmation dialog box displays, click OK.
7. On the first line of the **WTry01_studentfirstname_studentlastname** file, type your teacher's name and then press ENTER.
8. Type the period or class time.
9. Click Save on the Quick Access Toolbar.

   OR

   a. Click File.

   b. Click Save.

   ✓ *You can also press CTRL + S to save changes.*

10. Click File > Exit to close the document and exit Word.

Save As dialog box

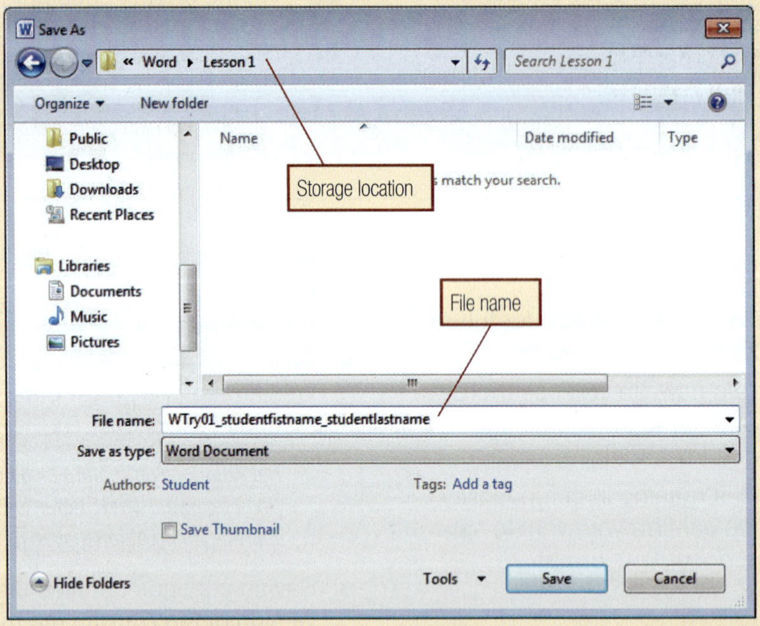

Project 1—Create It

Personal Trainer Biography

DIRECTIONS

1. Click **Start** > **All Programs** > **Microsoft Office** > **Microsoft Word 2010** to start the Word program.
2. Save the file as **WProj01_studentfirstname_studentlastname** in the location where your teacher instructs you to store the files for this lesson.

   ✓ *Remember to replace the sample text studentfirstname with your own first name and studentlastname with your own last name.*

3. Click the **View Ruler** button at the top of the vertical scroll bar to display the rulers, if necessary.
4. On the **Home** tab, in the **Paragraph** group, click the **Show/Hide ¶** button ¶ to display nonprinting characters. If nonprinting characters are already displayed, skip this step.
5. Type the following paragraph. Do not press ENTER at the end of each line. Word wrap automatically moves the text to the next line as necessary.

   Michigan Avenue Athletic Club is pleased to announce that David Fairmont has joined our staff. David is a licensed personal trainer with extensive experience in cardiovascular health. He holds a master's degree in health management from the University of Vermont in Burlington, Vermont. After graduation, he remained at UVM as an instructor. He recently moved to the Chicago area with his family.

   ✓ *If you make a typing error, press BACKSPACE to delete it, and then type the correct text.*

6. At the end of the paragraph, press ENTER to start a new paragraph.
7. Type the following paragraph:

   We are certain that David will be a valuable addition to our staff. His skills and experience make him highly qualified and his attitude and personality make him a lot of fun to have around. David is available for private, semi-private, and group sessions. Please contact the club office for more information or to schedule an appointment.

8. Proofread the document for errors, and correct any that you find.

   ✓ *Word marks spelling errors with a red wavy underline, and grammatical errors with a green wavy underline. If you see these lines in the document, proofread for errors.*

9. Click the **Save** button on the Quick Access Toolbar to save the changes to the document.
10. Click the **Web Layout** shortcut button on the status bar to change to Web Layout view.
11. Click the **Draft** shortcut button on the status bar to change to Draft view.
12. On the **View** tab, in the **Document Views** group, click the **Full Screen Reading** button to change to Full Screen Reading view.
13. In the **Document Views** group, click the **Print Layout** button to change to Print Layout view.
14. Click the **Minimize the Ribbon** button in the upper-right corner of the window.
15. Double-click in the header area and type your full name. The document should look similar to Figure 1-1 on the next page.
16. Click the **Expand the Ribbon** button in the upper-right corner of the window to expand the Ribbon.
17. On the **Header & Footer Tools Design** tab, in the **Navigation** group, click the **Go to Footer** button to move the insertion point to the footer area.
18. Type today's date.
19. Double-click in the document area to make it active.
20. On the **View** tab, in the Show group, click to deselect the **Ruler** check box. This hides the rulers.
21. On the **Home** tab, in the **Paragraph** group, click the **Show/Hide ¶** button ¶ to turn off the display of nonprinting characters.
22. **With your teacher's permission**, print the document.

    ✓ *Refer to Lesson 2 of the Basics section of this book for information on printing a file.*

23. Close the document, saving all changes, and exit Word.

Figure 1-1

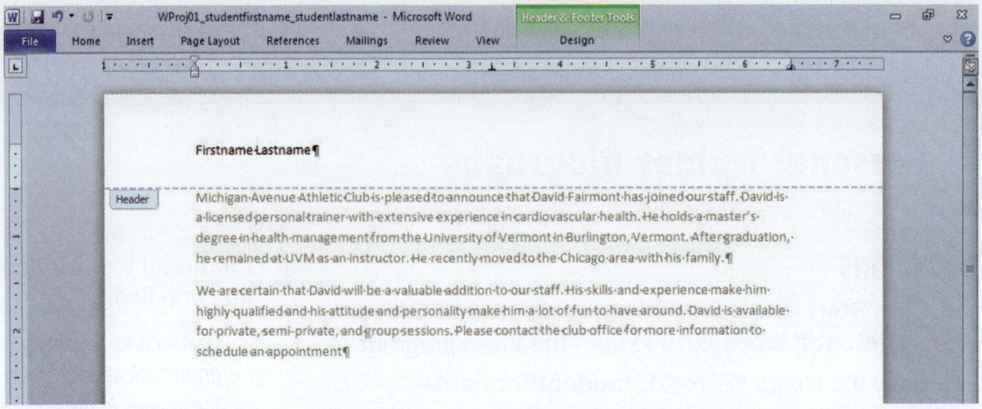

Project 2—Apply It

Nutritionist Biography

DIRECTIONS

1. Start Word.
2. Save the default Document1 file as **WProj02_studentfirstname_studentlastname** in the location where your teacher instructs you to store the files for this lesson.
3. Display the rulers.
4. Display nonprinting characters.
5. Type the two paragraphs shown in Figure 1-2.
6. Type your name in the header area.
7. Type today's date in the footer area.
8. Save the changes to the document.
9. See how the document looks in Full Screen Reading view.
10. See how the document looks in Draft view.
11. Change back to Print Layout view.
12. Hide the rulers.
13. Hide nonprinting characters.
14. **With your teacher's permission**, print the document.
15. Close the document, saving all changes, and exit Word.

Figure 1-2

Firstname Lastname

Michigan Avenue Athletic Club is pleased to announce that Sandra Tsai has joined our staff as Chief Nutritionist. Sandra received both her Bachelor of Science degree in Nutrition Science and her master's degree in Food Science and Human Nutrition at the University of Illinois. She previously worked as a dietitian at the Shady Grove senior center, and as a sports nutrition consultant at the Manor Academy school.

Sandra plans to work closely with the staff at the club's coffee shop to improve the nutritional quality of the food and snacks. She will also offer classes in diet and nutrition, and will work one-on-one with interested club members. Please contact the club office for more information or to schedule an appointment.

Closing a Document

- A file remains open onscreen until you close it.
- If you try to close a document without saving, the program prompts you to save.
- You can close a document without saving it if you do not want to keep it for future use.
- In Word you can use the Close button to close the document if there are multiple documents open.
- If there is one document open, use the Close button to close it and exit Word, or use the Close command in Backstage view to close the document and leave Word running.

Try It! Closing a Document

1. With the Document2 file open in Word, click the Close button.

   ✓ *If you have made any changes to the file, Word asks if you want to save it before closing. Click Save to save the changes or Don't Save to close it without saving.*

2. Word remains running, and the Document1 file remains open.
3. Click File to display Backstage view.
4. Click Close. Word remains running, but there are no open documents.

   ✓ *Again, if you have made any changes to the file, Word asks if you want to save it before closing. Click Save to save the changes or Don't Save to close it without saving.*

Using Click and Type

- Use the click and type feature in Print Layout view to position the insertion point to begin typing.
- When click and type is active, the mouse pointer changes to indicate the **horizontal alignment** of the new text, as follows:

  Text will be flush—even with—with the left margin.

  Text will be centered.

  Text will be flush with the right margin.

  The first line of text will be indented 0.5".

✓ *Click and type is usually active by default. If it is not active on your system, you can turn it on by clicking File > Options. In the Word Options dialog box, click Advanced. Click to select the Enable click and type check box, and then click OK.*

Try It! Using Click and Type

1. Start Word.
2. Display nonprinting characters.
3. Position the mouse pointer in the center of the document area so it changes to look like this.
4. Double-click to position the insertion point, and type **Centered**.
5. Position the mouse pointer at the right side of the document area along the same line so it changes to look like this.
6. Double-click to position the insertion point, and type **Right**.
7. Position the mouse pointer down one or two lines along the left side of the document area along the same line so it changes to look like this.
8. Double-click to position the insertion point, and type **Left**.
9. Position the mouse pointer down one or two lines and about 0.5" in from the left margin, so it changes to look like this.
10. Double-click to position the insertion point, and type **Use click and type to indent the first line of text in a paragraph by one-half inch. The other lines remain flush left.**
11. Click the Close button, and then click Don't Save to close the file and exit Word without saving any changes.

Opening a Saved Document

- To view or edit a document that has been saved and closed, open it again.
- You can open a recently used document on the Recent tab in Backstage view by clicking it.
- You can use the Open dialog box to locate and open any document.

✓ *You can also use Windows to open a saved document. Use Windows Explorer to navigate to the location where the document is stored and then double-click the file name.*

Try It! Opening a Saved Document

1. Start Microsoft Word 2010.
2. Click File > Open.
3. Navigate to the location where the data files for this lesson are stored.
4. Double-click WTry02a to open it.

   OR

   a. Click WTry02a.

   b. Click Open.
5. Click File > Close to close the document without saving any changes, but leave Word open to use in the next Try It.

Try It! Opening a Recently Used Document

1. In Word, click File > Recent.
2. Click WTry02a under Recent Documents on the left side of the screen.
3. Leave the WTry02a document open in Word to use in the next Try It.

Saving a Document with a New Name

- Use the Save As command to save a copy of a file in a different location or with a different file name.
- The original file remains unchanged.

Try It! Saving a Document with a New Name

1. In Word, with the WTry02a file open, click File > Save As.
2. Type WTry02a_studentfirstname_studentlastname.
3. Navigate to the location where your teacher instructs you to store the files for this lesson.
4. Click Save.
5. Close the document and exit Word.

Applying a Built-In Style

- **Styles** make it easy to apply a collection of formatting settings to characters or paragraphs all at once.
- Word 2010 comes with built-in Quick Styles for formatting common document parts, such as titles, headings, and subheadings.

  ✓ *There are also Quick Styles for formatting other elements, such as pictures and tables. You learn how to use them later in this book.*

- The Quick Styles display in the Styles gallery in the Styles group on the Home tab of the Ribbon, and in the Styles task pane.
- To apply a style to a paragraph, click anywhere within the paragraph, and then click the style name in the Styles gallery or task pane.
- To apply a style to text, select the text and then click the style name.
- You can also select a style before you type new text.
- The default style for new text is called Normal.
- Only one row of styles displays in the Styles gallery at a time, but you can scroll the gallery, or click the More button to display the entire gallery.
- You can preview how a style will affect text by resting the mouse pointer on the style in the Styles gallery.

Try It! Applying a Built-In Style

1. Start Word and open the file **WTry02b** from the data files for this lesson.
2. Save the file as **WTry02b_studentfirstname_studentlastname** in the location where your teacher instructs you to store the files for this lesson.
3. Click anywhere within the first line of text.
4. On the Home tab, in the Styles group, click the Heading 1 style in the Styles gallery. The Style is applied to the current paragraph—in this case, the first line.

   ✓ *Any amount of text followed by a paragraph mark is a paragraph in Word—even a single character.*

5. Click the More button on the Styles gallery to display additional styles.
6. Click the Title style to apply it to the current paragraph.
7. Click the Home tab and then click the Styles gallery dialog box launcher to display the Styles task pane.
8. Click anywhere within the second line of text.
9. Click the Subtitle style in the Styles task pane to apply it to the paragraph.
10. Select the text *Denver, Colorado*, and then click the Emphasis style in the Styles task pane to apply it to the selection.

    ✓ *For more on selecting, refer to Lesson 3 of the Basics section of this book.*

11. Close the Styles task pane.
12. Save the changes to the document and keep it open to use in the next Try It.

Changing the Style Set

- The fonts used for Quick Styles depend on the current theme; formatting depends on the current **style set**.
- For example, in the Modern style set, the Heading 1 style uses 10 point, bold, all caps, with a shaded background, while in the Simple style set, the Heading 1 style uses 11 point, small caps.
- You can change the style set.

Try It! Changing the Style Set

1. With the **WTry02b_studentfirstname_studentlastname** file open, click the Home tab, then, in the Styles group, click the Change Styles button. A menu displays.
2. Click Style Set on the menu to display a list of available style sets.
3. Rest the mouse pointer on Elegant to see how the change affects the document.
4. Rest the mouse pointer on Modern.
5. Click Formal to change to the Formal style set.
6. Click the Change Styles button again.
7. Click Style Set on the menu, and then click Word 2010 to change back to the default style set.
8. Save the changes to the document and keep it open to use in the next Try It.

Applying a Theme

- Office 2010 comes with built-in **themes** that you can apply to documents.
- Each theme includes a set of coordinated colors, fonts, styles, and effects.
- The default theme is Office.
- Click the Themes button on the Page Layout tab of the Ribbon to display the Themes gallery.
- To preview how a theme will affect the current document, rest your mouse pointer on it in the gallery.
- The same themes are available in other Microsoft Office 2010 programs.
- By using a theme, you can easily create different types of documents that have a consistent and professional appearance.

Try It! Apply a Theme

1. In the **WTry02b_studentfirstname_studentlastname** file, click the Page Layout tab.
2. In the Themes group, click the Themes button to display the Themes gallery.
3. Rest the mouse pointer on the Apex theme in the gallery. Notice that the appearance of the text in the current document changes to show how it would look formatted with the Apex theme.
4. Rest the mouse pointer on the Equity theme in the gallery to see how the text changes.
5. Scroll down in the gallery and click the Newsprint theme to apply it to the document.
6. Click the Themes button again and click the Office theme to change back to the default theme.
7. Close the **WTry02b_studentfirstname_studentlastname** file, saving all changes, and exit Word.

Analyzing a Press Release

- Use a press release to announce information about your company to media outlets, such as Web sites, newspapers, and magazines.
- For example, you can issue a press release about new products, trends, developments, and even to provide tips or hints.
- The media outlet may provide you with publicity by reporting the information.
- A press release should be no more than one page in length. It should provide the basic facts, details that define why the content is newsworthy, and who to contact for more information.

- The basic parts of a press release include the following:
  - Contact information
  - Headline
  - Location
  - Lead paragraph
  - Additional information and details

Project 3—Create It

Press Release

DIRECTIONS

1. Start Word.
2. Click **File** > **Close** to close the default Document1.
3. Click **File** > **New** to display the New tab in Backstage view.
4. Click the **Blank document** icon and then click the **Create** button to create a new blank document.
5. Save the document as **WProj03a_studentfirstname_studentlastname** in the location where your teacher instructs you to store the files for this lesson.
6. Display nonprinting characters and the rulers.
7. On the first line of the document, type **For Immediate Release**.
8. Position the mouse pointer at the middle of the next line, and when the Center pointer icon displays, double-click to position the insertion point.
9. Type **Voyager Travel Adventures Announces New Winter Tours**.
10. Position the mouse pointer flush left on the next line and double-click to position the insertion point.
11. Type **Denver, Colorado**, and press ENTER twice.
12. Type today's date, press ENTER twice, and type **Voyager Travel Adventures, an adventure tour operator based in Denver, has announced its winter tour schedule, which includes exciting new offerings.**

    ✓ *Word's AutoCorrect feature replaces the double hyphens with an em dash character. You learn about AutoCorrect in Word, Lesson 18.*

13. Press ENTER to start a new paragraph and type **This winter, you have the option of joining Voyager Travel Adventures for cross-country ski touring in either Yellowstone National Park in Wyoming or the White Mountain National Forest in New Hampshire. For travelers who prefer warmer adventures, the company is also adding a tour of Central America. Highlights include a visit to the Costa Rican rain forest and a trip through the Panama Canal.**
14. Press ENTER and type **For more information contact:**.
15. Press ENTER and type your full name.
16. Save the changes to the document. It should look similar to Figure 2-1 on the next page.
17. Click **File** > **Close** to close the document.
18. Click **File** > **Open** to display the Open dialog box.
19. Navigate to the **WProj03a_studentfirstname_studentlastname** file and double-click to open it.
20. Click **File** > **Save As** to open the Save As dialog box.
21. Save the file with the name **WProj03b_studentfirstname_studentlastname**.
22. Click the Page Layout tab, then, in the Themes group, click the Themes button to display the Themes gallery.
23. Click **Executive** in the Themes gallery to apply the theme to the document.
24. Click anywhere in the first line of text, click the Home tab, click the **More** button in the Styles gallery, and click the **Title** Quick Style to apply it to the paragraph.

Figure 2-1

For Immediate Release

Voyager Travel Adventures Announces New Winter Tours

Denver, Colorado—Today's date—Voyager Travel Adventures, an adventure tour operator based in Denver, has announced its winter tour schedule, which includes exciting new offerings.

This winter, you have the option of joining Voyager Travel Adventures for cross-country ski touring in either Yellowstone National Park in Wyoming or the White Mountain National Forest in New Hampshire. For travelers who prefer warmer adventures, the company is also adding a tour of Central America. Highlights include a visit to the Costa Rican rain forest and a trip through the Panama Canal.

For more information contact:

Firstname Lastname

25. Click anywhere in the second line of text and click the **Subtitle** Quick Style in the Styles gallery.
26. Select the text *Denver, Colorado*, and then click the **Emphasis** Quick Style in the Styles gallery.
27. Select today's date, and then click the **Emphasis** Quick Style in the Styles gallery.
28. On the Home tab, in the Styles group, click the Change Styles button.
29. On the Change Styles menu, click **Style Set**, and then click **Distinctive**.
30. Save the changes to the document.
31. **With your teacher's permission**, print the document. It should look similar to Figure 2-2.
32. Close the document, saving all changes, and exit Word.

Figure 2-2

FOR IMMEDIATE RELEASE

Voyager Travel Adventures Announces New Winter Tours

Denver, Colorado*—*Today's date—Voyager Travel Adventures, an adventure tour operator based in Denver, has announced its winter tour schedule, which includes exciting new offerings.

This winter, you have the option of joining Voyager Travel Adventures for cross-country ski touring in either Yellowstone National Park in Wyoming or the White Mountain National Forest in New Hampshire. For travelers who prefer warmer adventures, the company is also adding a tour of Central America. Highlights include a visit to the Costa Rican rain forest and a trip through the Panama Canal.

For more information contact:

Firstname Lastname

Project 4—Apply It

Press Release

DIRECTIONS

1. Start Word.
2. Open the file **WProj04** from the data files for this lesson.
3. Save the file as **WProj04_studentfirstname_studentlastname** in the location where your teacher instructs you to store the files for this lesson.
4. Display the rulers and nonprinting characters if they are not already displayed.
5. Replace the sample text *Today's date* with the actual date, and *Firstname Lastname* with your own first and last names.
6. Position the mouse pointer on the right side of the header area so the Right pointer displays, and then double-click to position the insertion point flush right in the header.
7. Type **Page 1 of 1**.
8. Close Header and Footer view to make the main document active.
9. Apply the **Heading 1** Quick Style to the first line of text.
10. Apply the **Subtitle** Quick Style to the second line of text.
11. Apply the **Intense Emphasis** Quick Style to the text *Denver, Colorado* and to today's date.
12. Apply the **Essential** theme to the document.
13. Change the style set to **Modern**.
14. Save the changes to the document.
15. **With your teacher's permission**, print the document. It should look similar to Figure 2-3.
16. Close the document, saving all changes, and exit Word.

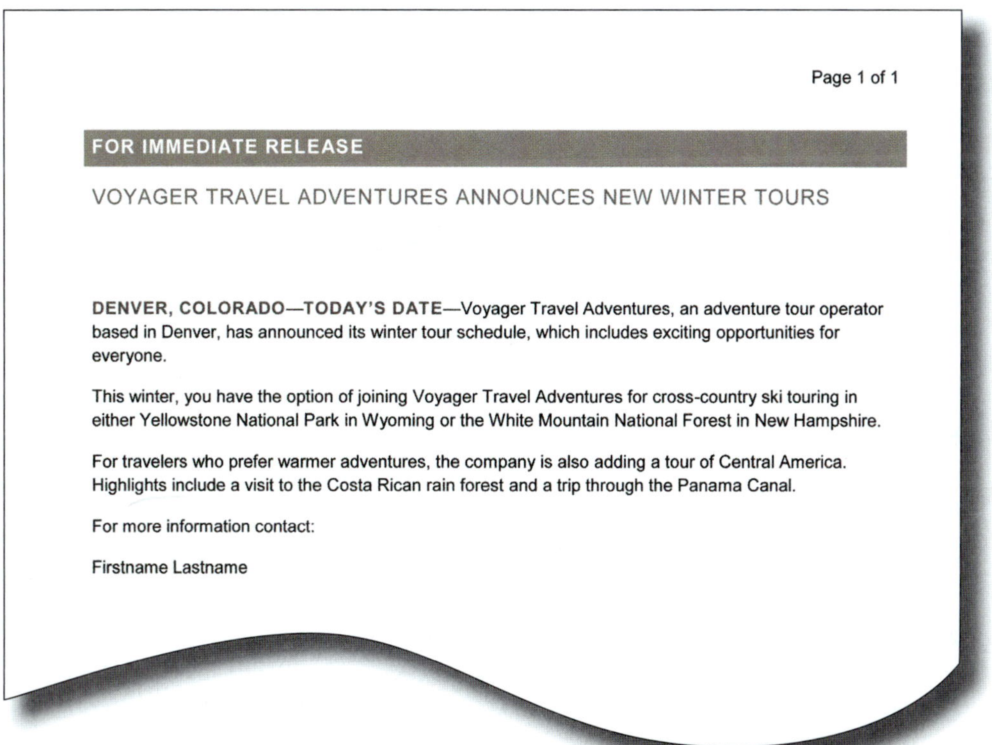

Page 1 of 1

FOR IMMEDIATE RELEASE

VOYAGER TRAVEL ADVENTURES ANNOUNCES NEW WINTER TOURS

DENVER, COLORADO—TODAY'S DATE—Voyager Travel Adventures, an adventure tour operator based in Denver, has announced its winter tour schedule, which includes exciting opportunities for everyone.

This winter, you have the option of joining Voyager Travel Adventures for cross-country ski touring in either Yellowstone National Park in Wyoming or the White Mountain National Forest in New Hampshire.

For travelers who prefer warmer adventures, the company is also adding a tour of Central America. Highlights include a visit to the Costa Rican rain forest and a trip through the Panama Canal.

For more information contact:

Firstname Lastname

Figure 2-3

Lesson 3

Editing and Correcting Documents

WORDS TO KNOW

Insert mode
The method of operation used for inserting new text within existing text in a document. Insert mode is the default.

Overtype mode
The method of operation used to replace existing text in a document with new text.

➤ What You Will Learn

Inserting Text
Using Overtype Mode
Selecting and Replacing Text
Canceling a Command
Using Undo, Redo, and Repeat

Software Skills Microsoft Word 2010 includes many tools for editing and correcting documents. You can easily insert and replace existing text. You can also undo actions and then redo them, if necessary. In some cases, you can use the Repeat command to repeat an action, which might save you time and keystrokes.

Application Skills Voyager Travel Adventures wants you to make changes to two press release documents. In this lesson, you will open existing press release documents so you can make edits and corrections.

What You Can Do

Inserting Text

- By default, you insert new text in a document in **insert mode**. Existing text moves to the right as you type to make room for new text.
- You can insert text anywhere in a document.
- You can also insert nonprinting characters as you type, including paragraph marks to start a new paragraph (press ENTER), tabs (press TAB), and spaces (press SPACE).

Try It! Inserting Text

1. Open **WTry03** from the data files for this lesson and save it as **WTry03_studentfirstname_studentlastname** in the location where your teacher instructs you to store the files for this lesson.
2. Position the insertion point to the right of the *R* in the word *FOR* on the first line.
3. Press SPACE, type **IMMEDIATE** and then press SPACE. The text is inserted between the words *FOR* and *RELEASE*.
4. Save the changes to the document and keep it open to use in the next Try It.

Using Overtype Mode

- To replace text as you type, use **overtype mode**.
- In overtype mode, existing characters do not shift right to make room for new characters. Instead, new characters delete existing characters as you type.
- Overtype mode is off by default. You can change Word options to make overtype mode active all the time, or to set the Insert key to toggle overtype mode off and on.
- Most editing should be done in insert mode, so you do not accidentally type over text that you need.
- You can customize the status bar with a typing mode indicator that displays Insert when you are working in insert mode or Overtype when you are working in overtype mode.

Try It! Using Overtype Mode

1. With the **WTry03_studentfirstname_studentlastname** document open, right-click the status bar to display a shortcut menu.
2. Click Overtype on the menu. The typing mode indicator displays near the left end of the status bar.

   ✓ *A check mark next to the command on the shortcut menu indicates that it is selected.*
3. Click Overtype on the menu again to hide the indicator.
4. Press ESC to close the menu.
5. Click File > Options to open the Word Options dialog box.
6. Click Advanced to display the advanced options.
7. Click to select the Use the Insert key to control overtype mode check box. A check mark indicates that the option is selected.
8. Click to select the Use overtype mode check box.
9. Click OK.
10. Position the insertion point to the left of the *I* in the word *Illinois*.

    ✓ *You can increase the zoom magnification to make it easier to position the insertion point, if you want.*
11. Press INS. This toggles on overtype mode.
12. Type **Colorado**. Each character that you type replaces an existing character in the document.
13. Press INS. This toggles off overtype mode.
14. Click File > Options.
15. Click Advanced to display the advanced options.
16. Click to clear the check mark from the Use the Insert key to control overtype mode check box.
17. Click OK.
18. Save the changes to the document and leave it open to use in the next Try It.

Selecting and Replacing Text

- You select text in order to edit it or format it.

  ✓ *Refer to Lesson 3 of the Basics section of this book for more information on selecting and formatting text.*

- You can also select non-text characters, such as symbols; nonprinting characters, such as paragraph marks; and graphics, such as pictures.
- When text is selected, any command or action affects the selection.
- Press DEL to delete the selection.
- Type new text to replace the selection.
- Refer to Table 3-1 for keyboard selection commands. Refer to Table 3-2 for mouse selection commands.

Table 3-1 Keyboard Selection Commands

To Select	Press
One character right	SHIFT + →
One character left	SHIFT + ←
One line up	SHIFT + ↑
One line down	SHIFT + ↓
To end of line	SHIFT + END
To beginning of line	SHIFT + HOME
To end of document	SHIFT + CTRL + END
To beginning of document	SHIFT + CTRL + HOME
Entire document	CTRL + A

Table 3-2 Mouse Selection Commands

To Select	Do This
One word	Double-click word.
One sentence	CTRL + click in sentence.
One line	Click in selection bar to the left of the line.
One paragraph	Double-click in selection bar to the left of the paragraph.
Document	Triple-click in selection bar.
Noncontiguous text	Select first block, Press and hold CTRL, select additional block(s).

Try It! Selecting and Replacing Text

1. In the **WTry03_studentfirstname_studentlastname** document, hold down the left mouse button.
2. Drag the mouse pointer across the date to select it.
3. Type today's date. The selected text is deleted and replaced with the text you type.
4. Double-click on the word *guides* at the end of the document to select it. Notice that the period is not selected.
5. Type the word **leaders** but do not type a period. The text you type replaces the selected text.
6. Save the changes to the document and leave it open to use in the next Try It.

Canceling a Command

- Press ESC to cancel a command or close a menu or dialog box before the command affects the current file.
- You can also click anywhere outside a menu to close it without selecting a command.

Try It! Canceling a Command

1. In the **WTry03_studentfirstname_studentlastname** document, press CTRL + A, the shortcut key combination for selecting all text in a document.
2. Click anywhere in the document to cancel the selection.
3. Right-click the status bar to display the shortcut menu.
4. Press ESC to close the menu without making a selection.
5. On the Home tab, click the Font group dialog box launcher to open the Font dialog box.
6. Press ESC to close the dialog box without changing any options.
7. On the Home tab, in the Styles group, click the Change Styles button to display the Change Styles menu.
8. Click anywhere in the document outside the menu to close it without making a selection.
9. Leave the document open to use in the next Try It.

Using Undo, Redo, and Repeat

- Use the Undo button on the Quick Access Toolbar to reverse a single action made in error, such as deleting the wrong word.
- Use the Undo drop-down list to reverse a series of actions.

✓ *The most recent action is listed at the top of the list; click an action to undo it and all actions above it.*

- Use the Redo button on the Quick Access Toolbar to reinstate any actions that you reversed with Undo.
- If the Undo button is dimmed, there are no actions that can be undone.
- If the Redo button is dimmed, there are no actions that can be redone.
- Sometimes when there are no actions to redo, the Repeat button is available in place of Redo. Use Repeat to repeat the most recent action.

Try It! Using Undo, Redo, and Repeat

1. In the **WTry03_studentfirstname_ studentlastname** document, press CTRL + A to select all text in the document.
2. Press DEL. The entire selection is deleted.
3. Click the Undo button on the Quick Access Toolbar. The previous action—deleting the selection—is undone.
4. Click the Redo button on the Quick Access Toolbar. The undone action is redone—the selection is deleted again.
5. Click the Undo button again to undo the deletion.

   ✓ *CTRL + Z is the shortcut key combination for undoing an action. CTRL + Y is the shortcut key combination for redoing an action.*

6. Select the second line of text and press DEL. The line is deleted from the document.
7. Position the insertion point in the first line of text and then click Heading 1 in the Styles gallery to apply the Quick Style.
8. Click the Undo down arrow on the Quick Access Toolbar. Both actions display on the Undo menu; the most recent action is at the top.
9. Click Clear on the Undo menu. All actions between the action you click and the top of the menu are undone.

Use the Undo menu to undo a series of actions

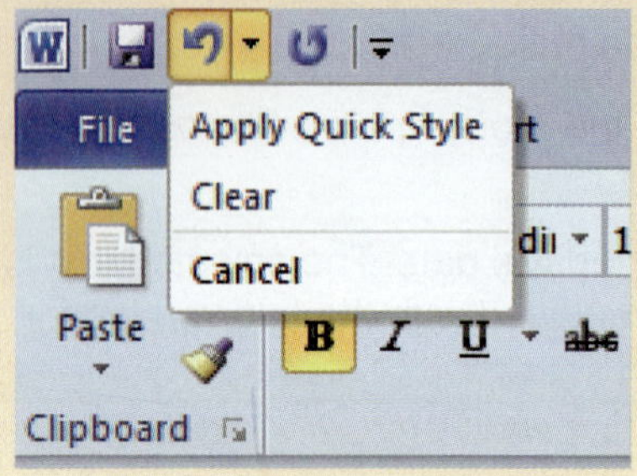

10. Position the insertion point in the first line of text.
11. On the Home tab, in the Styles group, click Heading 1 in the Styles gallery to apply the Quick Style.
12. Position the insertion point anywhere in the second line of text and then click the Repeat button on the Quick Access Toolbar. Word repeats the most recent action—applying the Heading 1 Quick Style.

    ✓ *CTRL + Y is the shortcut key combination for repeating an action.*

13. Close the **WTry03_studentfirstname_ studentlastname** document, saving all changes, and exit Word.

Project 5—Create It

Press Release

DIRECTIONS

1. Start Word, if necessary, and open **WProj05** from the data files for this lesson.
2. Save it as **WProj05_studentfirstname_ studentlastname** in the location where your teacher instructs you to store files for this lesson.
3. Click **File** > **Options** to open the Word Options dialog box.
4. Click the **Advanced** tab to display the advanced options, and then click to select the **Use the Insert key to control overtype mode** check box.
5. Click **OK** to apply the setting and close the dialog box.

6. Right-click the status bar and click to select **Overtype** on the shortcut menu to display the indicator on the status bar.
7. Press ESC to close the shortcut menu.
8. Delete the first line of text, and then click the **Undo** button to reverse the delete action.
9. Click the **Redo** button to redo the action and delete the line.
10. Select *New Winter Tours* in the second line of text and type **Two Cross-Country Ski Adventures** to replace the selection.
11. Select the text *CO* and type **Colorado**, followed by two hyphens and today's date.
12. Press INS to make overtype mode active.
13. Position the insertion point to the left of the *e* in the word *exciting*, and type: **two amazing cross-country ski adventures.**
14. Press INS to make insert mode active.
15. Apply the **Title** style to the first line of the press release.
16. Position the insertion point in the second line of the press release and click the **Repeat** button on the Quick Access Toolbar to apply the Title style to the paragraph.
17. Click the **Undo** button on the Quick Access Toolbar to undo the action and remove the Title style.
18. Apply the Subtitle style to the second line.
19. Select the text *Denver, Colorado* and apply the **Intense Emphasis** style.
20. Select today's date and click the **Repeat** button on the Quick Access Toolbar to apply the **Intense Emphasis** style to the selection.
21. Click the **arrow** on the **Undo** button to display the Undo menu, and click the second action in the list—**Style**. The last two actions are undone.
22. Select the text *Denver, Colorado* and apply the **Emphasis** style.
23. Select today's date and click the **Repeat** button on the Quick Access Toolbar to apply the **Emphasis** style to the selection.
24. Move the insertion point to the end of the document, press ENTER to start a new paragraph and type your full name.
25. **With your teacher's permission,** print the document. It should look similar to Figure 3-1.
26. Click **File** > **Options** to open the Word Options dialog box.
27. Click the **Advanced** tab to display the Advanced options, and then click to clear the check mark from the **Use the Insert key to control overtype mode** check box.
28. Click **OK** to apply the setting and close the dialog box.
29. Right-click the status bar and click to deselect **Overtype** on the shortcut menu to hide the indicator on the status bar.
30. Click anywhere in the document area outside the shortcut menu to close it.
31. Close the document, saving changes, and exit Word.

For Immediate Release

Voyager Travel Adventures Announces Two Cross-Country Ski Adventures

Denver, Colorado—Today's date—Voyager Travel Adventures, an adventure tour operator based in Denver, has announced its winter tour schedule, which includes two amazing cross-country ski adventures.

This winter, you have the option of joining Voyager Travel Adventures for cross-country ski touring in either Yellowstone National Park in Wyoming or the White Mountain National Forest in New Hampshire.

For travelers who prefer warmer adventures, the company is also adding a tour of Central America. Highlights include a visit to the Costa Rican rain forest and a trip through the Panama Canal.

For more information contact:

Firstname Lastname

Figure 3-1

Project 6—Apply It

Press Release

DIRECTIONS

1. Start Word and open the file **WProj06** from the data files for this lesson.
2. Save the file as **WProj06_studentfirstname_studentlastname** in the location where your teacher instructs you to store the files for this lesson.
3. Open the Word Options dialog box and display the Advanced options.
4. Select the option to **Use the Insert key to control overtype mode** check box.
5. Click **OK** to apply the setting and close the dialog box.
6. Right-click the status bar and click to select **Overtype** on the shortcut menu; then close the shortcut menu.
7. Press INS to turn on overtype mode.
8. Position the insertion point to the left of *Announces Two Cross-Country Ski Adventures* in the second line of text and type **Adds a Central American Getaway to its Winter Schedule**.
9. Undo the action, and then redo it.
10. Press INS to turn on insert mode.
11. Select the text *Costa Rica* and type **Denver, Colorado**, followed by two hyphens and today's date.
12. Select the text *This winter, you have the option of joining*, and type **For those who prefer colder weather,**.
13. Select the word *for* between *Adventures* and *cross-country* and type **is offering**.
14. Apply the **Subtitle** style to the first line of the press release, then undo the action and apply the **Title** style.
15. Apply the **Heading 3** style to the second line, and then repeat the action to apply it to the last line.
16. Move the insertion point to the end of the document, press ENTER to start a new paragraph and type your full name.
17. **With your teacher's permission**, print the document. It should look similar to Figure 3-2.
18. Open the Word Options dialog box, display the Advanced options, and clear the **Use the Insert key to control overtype mode** check box.
19. Click **OK** to apply the setting and close the dialog box.
20. Remove the overtype indicator from the status bar.
21. Close the document, saving all changes, and exit Word.

Figure 3-2

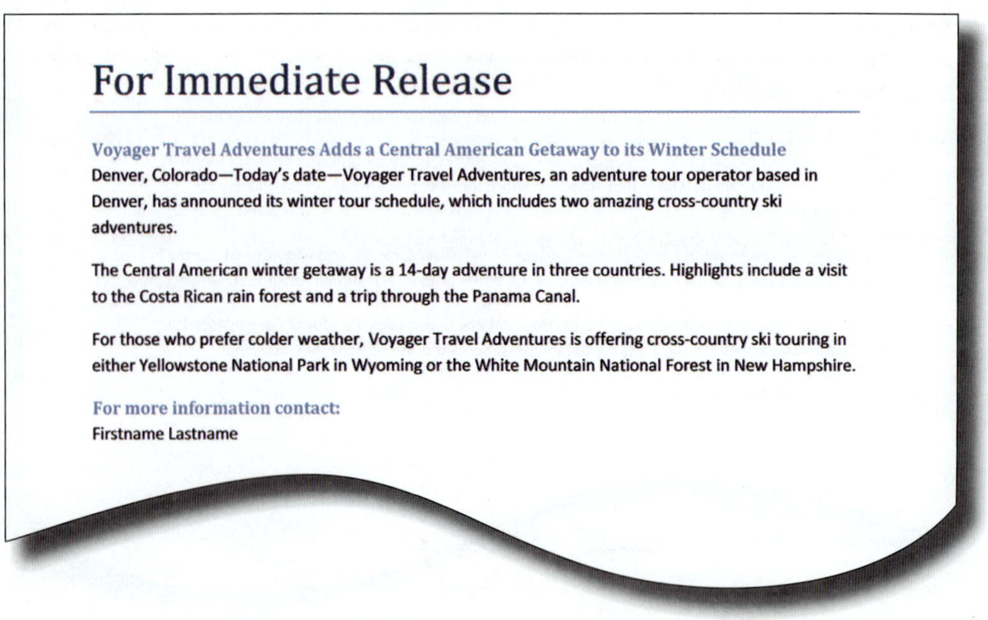

For Immediate Release

Voyager Travel Adventures Adds a Central American Getaway to its Winter Schedule

Denver, Colorado—Today's date—Voyager Travel Adventures, an adventure tour operator based in Denver, has announced its winter tour schedule, which includes two amazing cross-country ski adventures.

The Central American winter getaway is a 14-day adventure in three countries. Highlights include a visit to the Costa Rican rain forest and a trip through the Panama Canal.

For those who prefer colder weather, Voyager Travel Adventures is offering cross-country ski touring in either Yellowstone National Park in Wyoming or the White Mountain National Forest in New Hampshire.

For more information contact:

Firstname Lastname

Lesson 4

Adjusting Alignment and Spacing

➤ What You Will Learn

- Aligning Text Horizontally
- Aligning a Document Vertically
- Setting Line Spacing
- Setting Paragraph Spacing
- Analyzing Memos

Software Skills Changing the horizontal and vertical alignment can improve the appearance of a document and make it easier to read. Format documents using the right amount of space between lines and paragraphs to make the pages look better and the text easier to read, and to achieve the standard page setup for documents such as memos and letters.

Application Skills You are an assistant in the personnel department at Whole Grains Bread, a manufacturer of specialty breads and pastries based in Larkspur, California. In this lesson, your supervisor has asked you to type a memo to employees about a new automatic payroll deposit option.

WORDS TO KNOW

Horizontal alignment
The position of text across a line in relation to the left and right margins.

Leading
Line spacing measured in points.

Line spacing
The amount of white space between lines of text in a paragraph.

Paragraph spacing
The amount of white space between paragraphs.

Point
A unit of measurement used in desktop publishing and graphic design.

Vertical alignment
The position of text in relation to the top and bottom page margins.

What You Can Do

Aligning Text Horizontally

- **Horizontal alignment** is used to adjust the position of paragraphs in relation to the left and right margins of a page.

  ✓ *You have already used click and type to align text horizontally in a document.*

- There are four horizontal alignments:
  - Left
    Text is flush with left margin. The text along the right side of the page is uneven (or ragged). Left is the default horizontal alignment.
  - Right
    Text is flush with right margin. The text along the left side of the page is uneven (or ragged).
  - Center
    Text is centered between margins.
  - Justify
    Text is spaced so it runs evenly along both the left and right margins.
- You can use different alignments in a document.
- Buttons for changing the alignment are available in the Font group on the Home tab of the Ribbon.
- The Center align button is available on the Mini toolbar that displays when you select text.
- You can also use shortcut key combinations:
  - Align Text Left.............. CTRL + L
  - Center.......................... CTRL + E
  - Align Text Right .... CTRL + R
  - Justify .... CTRL + J

Try It! Aligning Text Horizontally

1. Open **WTry04a** and save it as **WTry04a_studentfirstname_studentlastname** in the location where your teacher instructs you to store the files for this lesson.
2. Click anywhere in the first paragraph.
3. On the Home tab, in the Paragraph group, click the Align Text Left button. The text, which was aligned right, is now aligned left.
4. Select the second and third paragraphs.
5. In the Paragraph group, click the Center button. Both paragraphs are centered.
6. Click in the fourth paragraph.
7. In the Paragraph group, click the Align Text Right button. The three lines in the paragraph are aligned flush with the right margin.
8. Click in the last paragraph.
9. In the Paragraph group, click the Justify button. Word adjusts the spacing between words so that both margins are even.
10. Save the changes to **WTry04a_studentfirstname_studentlastname**, and close it. Leave Word open to use in the next Try It.

(continued)

Try It! Aligning Text Horizontally *(continued)*

Horizontal alignments

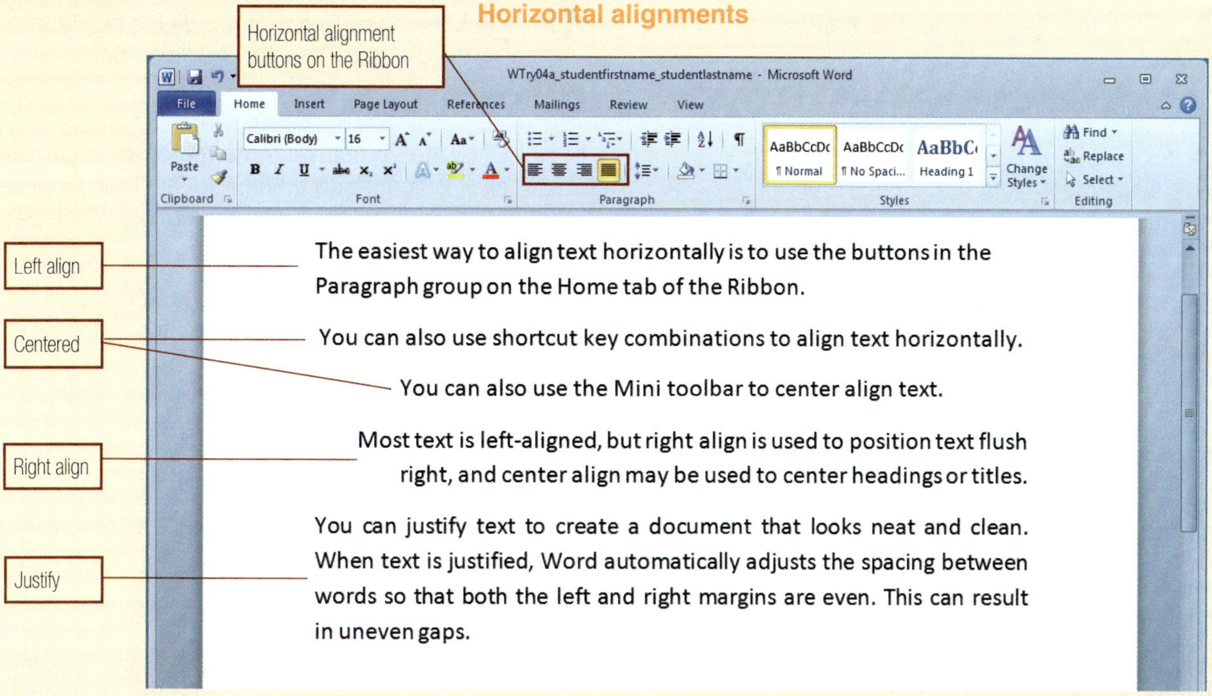

Aligning a Document Vertically

- **Vertical alignment** is used to adjust the position of all text on a page in relation to the top and bottom margins.
- There are four vertical alignments:
  - Top: Text begins below the top margin. Top is the default vertical alignment.
  - Center: Text is centered between the top and bottom margins. Centering can improve the appearance of some one-page documents, such as flyers or invitations.
  - Justified: Paragraphs are spaced to fill the page between the top and bottom margins. Vertical justification improves the appearance of documents that contain nearly full pages of text.
  - Bottom: The last line of text begins just above the bottom margin.

Try It! Aligning a Document Vertically

1. Start Word and open **WTry04b**. Save it as **WTry04b_studentfirstname_studentlastname** in the location where your teacher instructs you to store the files for this lesson. Notice that by default, the vertical alignment is set to Top.
2. On the View tab, in the Zoom group, click the One Page button. This enables you to see the entire page on your screen.

   ✓ *For more on adjusting the zoom, refer to Lesson 5 in the Basics section of this book.*
3. On the Page Layout tab, click the Page Setup group dialog box launcher to open the Page Setup dialog box.
4. Click the Layout tab.
5. Click the Vertical alignment drop-down arrow to display a menu of alignment options.
6. Click Center, and then click OK. The document is centered vertically.

(continued)

Try It! Aligning a Document Vertically *(continued)*

7 Click the Page Layout tab, if necessary.

8 Click the Page Setup group dialog box launcher button ⧉ to open the Page Setup dialog box.

9 Click the Layout tab, if necessary.

10 Click the Vertical alignment drop-down arrow, click Justified, and then click OK. The document is justified vertically.

11 Click the Page Layout tab, if necessary.

12 Click the Page Setup group dialog box launcher ⧉ to open the Page Setup dialog box.

13 Click the Layout tab, if necessary.

14 Click the Vertical alignment drop-down arrow, click Bottom, and then click OK. The document is vertically aligned with the bottom of the page.

14 Save the changes to **WTry04b_studentfirstname_studentlastname** and close it. Leave Word open to use in the next Try It.

Setting Line Spacing

- **Line spacing** sets the amount of vertical space between lines in a paragraph. In the Normal style, which is the default, line spacing in Word is set to 1.5 lines.
- Line spacing can be measured in either lines (single, double, etc.) or in **points**.
- When line spacing is measured in points, it is called **leading** (pronounced *ledding*).
  - Increase leading to make text easier to read.
  - Decrease leading to fit more lines on a page.

  ✓ *Decreasing leading too much can make text difficult to read.*
- You can set line spacing using the Line spacing button in the Paragraph group on the Home tab of the Ribbon, or in the Paragraph dialog box.

Try It! Setting Line Spacing

1 Start Word and open **WTry04c** from the data files for this lesson. Save it as **WTry04c_studentfirstname_studentlastname** in the location where your teacher instructs you to store the files for this lesson.

2 Increase the zoom to 100%.

3 Position the insertion point in the first paragraph.

4 Click the Home tab, then, in the Paragraph group, click the Line and Paragraph Spacing button ⧉.

5 Click 2.0 on the menu to change the line spacing to 2.0 lines. Notice that the line spacing in the other paragraphs is not affected.

✓ *The shortcut key combination to set line spacing to 2.0 lines is* CTRL + 2*. Use* CTRL + 1 *for single line spacing, or* CTRL + 5 *for 1.5 line spacing.*

6 Select the first and second paragraphs.

7 On the Home tab, click the Paragraph group dialog box launcher ⧉ to open the Paragraph dialog box.

✓ *You can also click the Line Spacing Options item on the Line and Paragraph Spacing menu to open the dialog box.*

8 If necessary, click the Indents and Spacing tab.

9 Click the Line spacing drop-down arrow to display a menu of line spacing options.

10 Click Single. This would set the line spacing to 1 line.

11 Click the Line spacing drop-down arrow again, and click Exactly.

✓ *Exactly is one of three leading options you can use if you want to set line spacing in points. The other leading options are At least, which you can use to set a minimum leading, and Multiple, which you can use to specify a percentage by which to increase leading.*

12 Use the At box increment arrows to set the leading to 15 pts.

13 Click OK to apply the change to the selection.

14 Save the changes to the document and leave it open in Word to use in the next Try It.

Setting Paragraph Spacing

- **Paragraph spacing** affects space before and after paragraphs.
- The amount of space is usually specified in points. In the Normal style, paragraph spacing in Word is set to 10 points after each paragraph.
- You can set paragraph spacing in the Paragraph group on the Page Layout tab of the Ribbon, or in the Paragraph dialog box.
- Use the Paragraph dialog box when you want to set multiple paragraph formatting options at the same time, such as line spacing and paragraph spacing.
- Use increased paragraph spacing in place of extra returns or blank lines.

✓ *To quickly remove all paragraph and line spacing, apply the No Spacing style.*

Try It! Setting Paragraph Spacing

1. In the **WTry04c_studentfirstname_studentlastname** document, click anywhere in the second paragraph.
2. Click the Page Layout tab.
3. In the Paragraph group, use the Spacing Before box increment arrows to set the spacing before the paragraph to 24 points.
4. Use the Spacing After box increment arrows to set the spacing after the paragraph to 36 points.
5. On the Page Layout tab, click the Paragraph group dialog box launcher to open the Paragraph dialog box.

   ✓ *You can also open the Paragraph dialog box by clicking the Paragraph dialog box launcher in the Paragraph group on the Home tab.*

6. Under Spacing, click in the Before box and replace the 24 with 14.
7. Click in the After box and replace 36 with 16.
8. Click OK to apply the changes.
9. Make sure the insertion point is within the second paragraph.
10. Click the Home tab, and then, in the Paragraph group, click the the Line and Paragraph Spacing button.
11. Click Remove Space After Paragraph. All space after the paragraph is removed.

Set paragraph spacing on the Page Layout tab

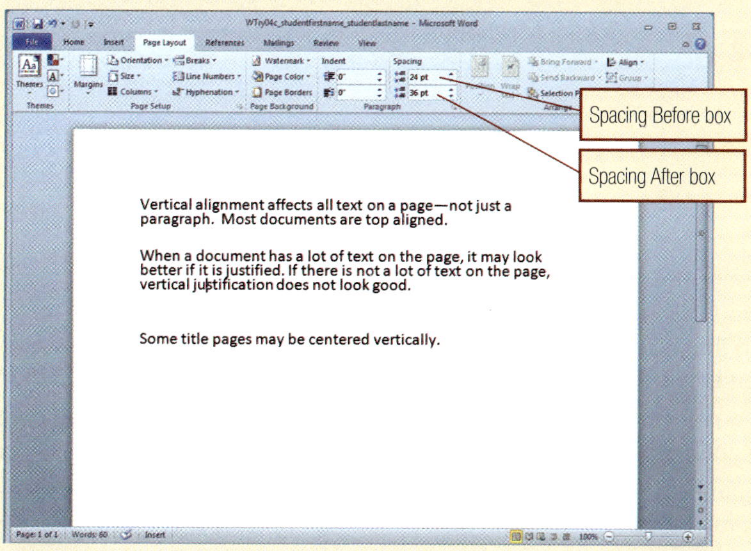

(continued)

Try It! Setting Paragraph Spacing *(continued)*

12. Click the Line and Paragraph Spacing button again.

    ✓ *Notice that now the Add Space After Paragraph command is available in place of Remove Space After Paragraph.*

13. Click Remove Space Before Paragraph to remove the space before the paragraph.

    ✓ *There is still space between the first and second paragraphs because there is space after the first paragraph.*

14. Close **WTry04c_studentfirstname_studentlastname**, saving all changes, and exit Word.

Analyzing Memos

- A memo, or memoranda, is a business document commonly used for communication within a company.
- Unlike a letter, a memo may or may not be addressed to a particular individual and does not include a formal closing.

  ✓ *Word, Lesson 5 explains letter formatting.*
- Usually, a memo includes the company name, the word memo, the headings To:, From:, Date:, and Subject:, and the memo text.
- Line spacing in a memo is usually set to Single, so that no extra space is left between lines.
- One blank line, or spacing equal to one line, may be used to separate parts of a memo.
- The writer may include his or her name, title, and/or signature at the end of the memo text or it may be in the From line at the beginning of the memo.
- If someone other than the writer types the memo, that person's initials should be entered below the memo text. In addition, if there is an attachment or an enclosure, the word *Attachment* or *Enclosure* should be entered after the text (or the typist's initials).
- Some variations on this memo format include typing headings in all uppercase letters, typing the subject text in all uppercase letters, and leaving additional spacing between memo parts. Also, the word *memo* may be omitted.

Project 7—Create It

Memo

DIRECTIONS

1. Start Word, if necessary, and save the default Document1 as **WProj07_studentfirstname_studentlastname** in the location where your teacher instructs you to store the files for this lesson.
2. Display nonprinting characters, if necessary.
3. Before you begin typing, on the Home tab, click the Paragraph group dialog box launcher to open the Paragraph dialog box.
4. Click the **Indents and Spacing** tab, if necessary.
5. Click the **Line spacing** drop-down arrow and click **Single**.
6. Use the **After increment arrows** to set the spacing after paragraphs to **0**.
7. Click **OK** to apply the settings.
8. On the Home tab, in the Paragraph group, click the **Center** button. Type **MEMO**, and press ENTER.
9. On the Home tab, in the Paragraph group, click the **Align Text Left** button. Type **To: All Employees** and press ENTER.

10. Type **From: Human Resources**, and press ENTER.
11. Type **Date:**, press SPACE, type today's date, and then press ENTER.
12. Type **Subject: New Option**, and then press ENTER.
13. Save the changes.
14. Type the following paragraph: **We are pleased to offer a new automatic deposit option for all payroll checks. This new option provides security as well as convenience, because you do not run the risk of misplacing your paycheck.**
15. Press ENTER and type the following paragraph: **Additional information and enrollment forms will be available starting Monday at 9:00 a.m. in the human resources department.**
16. Press ENTER. On the Home tab, in the Paragraph group, click the **Align Text Right** button and type your full name.
17. Press ENTER and type **Human Resources Assistant**.
18. Click the Page Layout tab, and then click the **Page Setup** group dialog box launcher to open the Page Setup dialog box.
19. Click the **Layout** tab, if necessary.
20. Click the **Vertical alignment** drop-down arrow and click **Center**. Click OK to vertically center the document on the page.
21. **With your teacher's permission**, print the document. It should look similar to Figure 4-1.
22. Close the document, saving all changes, and exit Word.

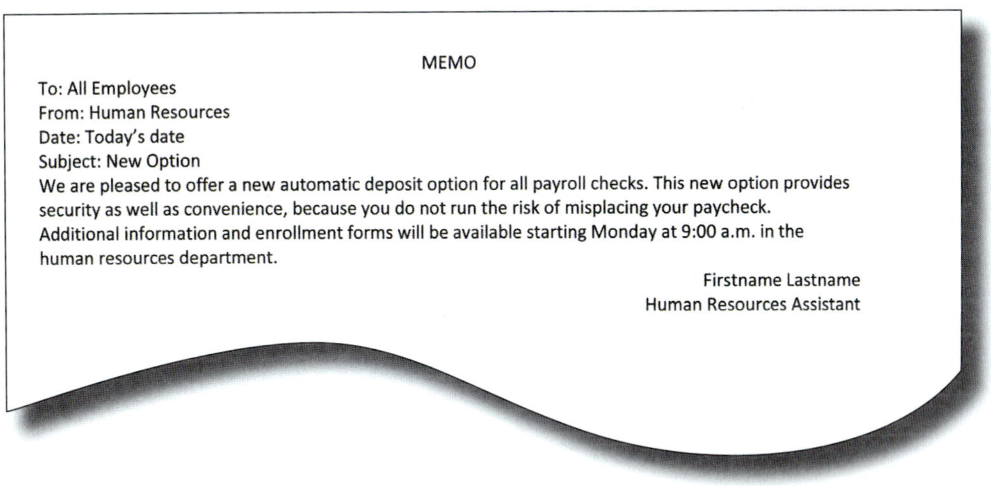

MEMO

To: All Employees
From: Human Resources
Date: Today's date
Subject: New Option
We are pleased to offer a new automatic deposit option for all payroll checks. This new option provides security as well as convenience, because you do not run the risk of misplacing your paycheck.
Additional information and enrollment forms will be available starting Monday at 9:00 a.m. in the human resources department.

Firstname Lastname
Human Resources Assistant

Figure 4-1

Project 8—Apply It

Memo

DIRECTIONS

1. Start Word and open **WProj08** from the data files for this lesson.
2. Save it as **WProj08_studentfirstname_studentlastname** in the location where your teacher instructs you to store the files for this lesson.
3. Replace the sample text *Today's date* with the actual date, then double-click in the header area to make it active.
4. Type **Whole Grains Bread** and center the text.
5. Press ENTER and type **320 Magnolia Avenue, Larkspur, California**.
6. Make the main document active, and click the **Page Layout** tab.
7. Click in the word **MEMO**, and set paragraph spacing **Before** to **24** points and paragraph spacing **After** to **36** points.
8. Click in the word **Subject** and set paragraph spacing **After** to **18** points.

9. Select the two paragraphs of text in the main body of the memo.
10. Open the Paragraph dialog box and set line spacing to **Exactly 18** points.
11. Set paragraph spacing **After** to **16** points.
12. Justify the selected paragraphs horizontally.
13. Move the insertion point to the end of the document and press ENTER to start a new line.
14. Set the horizontal alignment to **Right**, and then type your full name.
15. Remove the spacing after the paragraph.
16. Press ENTER and type **Human Resources Assistant**.
17. Open the Page Layout dialog box and set the vertical alignment to **Top**.
18. Save the changes to the document.
19. **With your teacher's permission**, print the document. It should look similar to Figure 4-2.
20. Close the document, saving all changes, and exit Word.

Figure 4-2

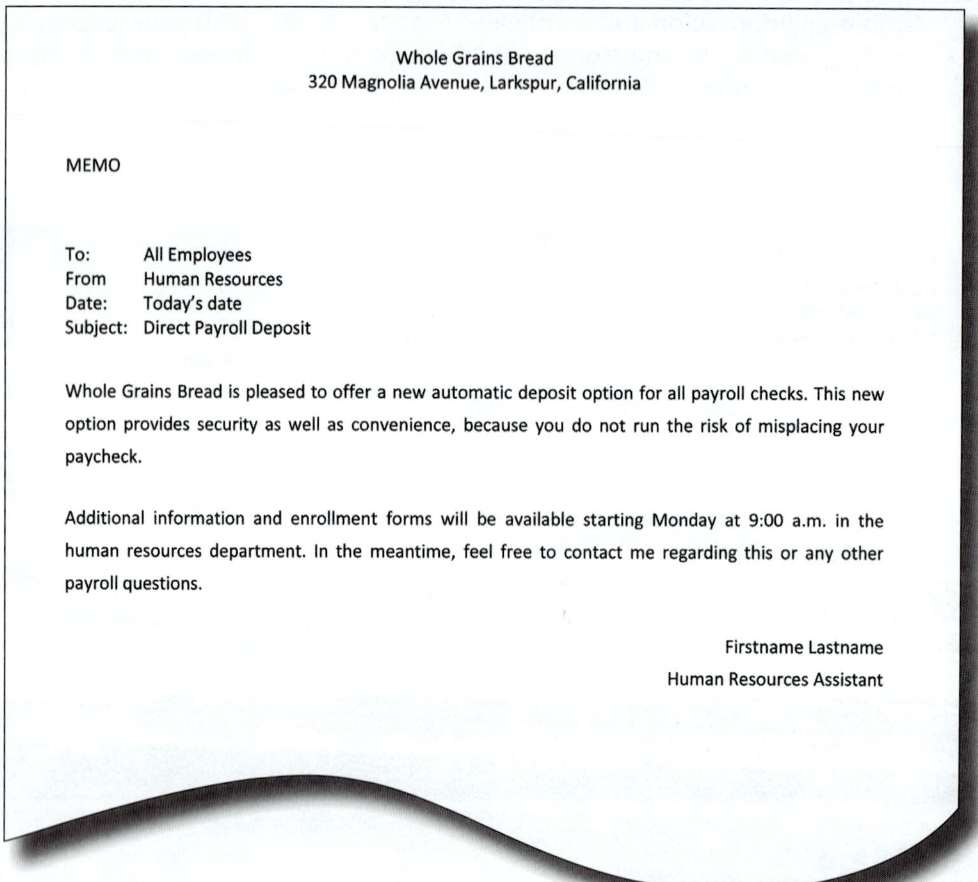

Whole Grains Bread
320 Magnolia Avenue, Larkspur, California

MEMO

To: All Employees
From Human Resources
Date: Today's date
Subject: Direct Payroll Deposit

Whole Grains Bread is pleased to offer a new automatic deposit option for all payroll checks. This new option provides security as well as convenience, because you do not run the risk of misplacing your paycheck.

Additional information and enrollment forms will be available starting Monday at 9:00 a.m. in the human resources department. In the meantime, feel free to contact me regarding this or any other payroll questions.

Firstname Lastname
Human Resources Assistant

Lesson 5

Creating Letters and Envelopes

➤ What You Will Learn

- Indenting Text
- Setting and Modifying Tabs
- Inserting the Date and Time
- Writing a Business Letter
- Creating an Envelope

Software Skills Write business letters as a representative of your employer to communicate with other businesses, such as clients or suppliers, or to communicate with individuals, such as prospective employees. You use tabs to position text along a line in a document and indents to call attention to a paragraph, to achieve a particular visual effect, or to leave white space along the margins for notes or illustrations.

Application Skills You are the assistant to Mr. Frank Kaplan, the Franchise Manager for Whole Grains Bread. He has asked you to type letters to people interested in opening store franchises outside of California. The first letter will be in full-block format; the second will be modified block. You will create envelopes for both.

WORDS TO KNOW

Computer's clock
The clock/calendar built into your computer's main processor to keep track of the current date and time.

Delivery address
A recipient's address printed on the outside of an envelope.

Field
A placeholder for data that might change.

Full block
A style of letter in which all lines start flush with the left margin—that is, without indents.

Indent
A temporary left and/or right margin for lines or paragraph.

Inside address
The recipient's address typed in the letter above the salutation.

Modified block
A style of letter in which some lines start at the center of the page.

Return address
The writer's address, typically appearing at the very top of the letter as well as in the upper-left corner of an envelope.

Salutation
The line at the start of a letter including the greeting and the recipient's name, such as Dear Mr. Doe.

WORDS TO KNOW

Tab
The measurement of the space the insertion point advances when you press the Tab key.

Tab leader
A series of characters inserted along the line between the location of the insertion point when you press the Tab key and the tab stop.

Tab stop
The location on a horizontal line to which the insertion point advances when you press the Tab key.

What You Can Do

Indenting Text

- There are four types of **indents**:
  - *Left* indents text from the left margin.
  - *Right* indents text from the right margin.
  - *First line* indents just the first line of a paragraph from the left margin.
  - *Hanging* indents all lines but the first line from the left margin.

  ✓ *You can also use the mirror indents option to set inside and outside indents for bound pages. Inside indents from the margin along the binding; outside indents from the margin opposite the binding.*
- To set any type of indent, use the Paragraph dialog box.
- You can also drag the indent markers on the horizontal ruler.
- Use the Increase Indent button in the Paragraph group on the Home tab of the Ribbon or on the Mini toolbar to move the current left indent 0.5" to the right.
- Use the Decrease Indent button to move the current left indent 0.5" to the left.
- You can set precise left and/or right indents in the Paragraph group on the Page Layout tab of the Ribbon.
- You can apply indents before you type new text, for the current existing paragraph, or for selected multiple paragraphs.
- Once you set indents, the formatting is carried forward each time you start a new paragraph.

Try It! Adjusting the Left Indent by 0.5"

1. Start Word and open **WTry05a** from the data files for this lesson. Save the document as **WTry05a_studentfirstname_studentlastname** in the location where your teacher instructs you to store the files for this lesson.
2. Display the rulers, and then click anywhere in the second paragraph.
3. Click the Home tab, if necessary, and then, in the Paragraph group, click the Increase Indent button to increase the left indent by 0.5".
4. Click the Increase Indent button again. Now, the left indent is set at 1.0" on the horizontal ruler.
5. In the Paragraph group, click the Decrease Indent button to decrease the left indent by 0.5". It is now set at 0.5" on the horizontal ruler.
6. Save the changes to the document and leave it open in Word to use in the next Try It.

(continued)

Try It! Adjusting the Left Indent by 0.5" *(continued)*

Adjust the left indent

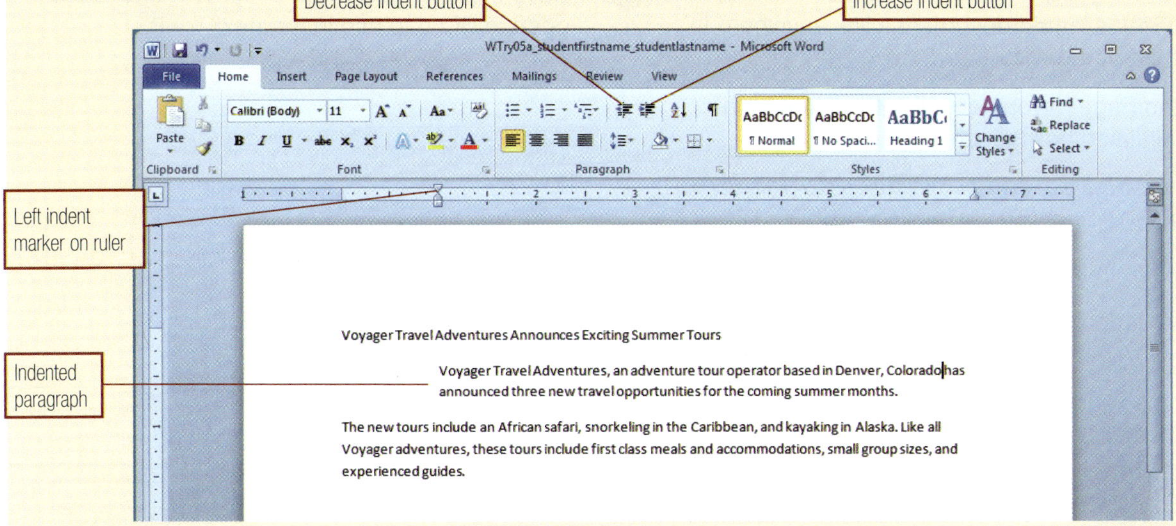

Try It! Setting a Left or Right Indent Precisely

1. In the **WTry05a_studentfirstname_studentlastname** document, select the first two paragraphs.
2. Click the Page Layout tab.
3. In the Paragraph group, use the Indent Left increment arrows to set the left indent to 1.2".
4. Use the Indent Right increment arrows to set the right indent to 0.8".

   ✓ *When you indent a paragraph from both the left and right margins it is called a double indent.*
5. Save the changes to the document and leave it open in Word to use in the next Try It.

Set precise left and right indents

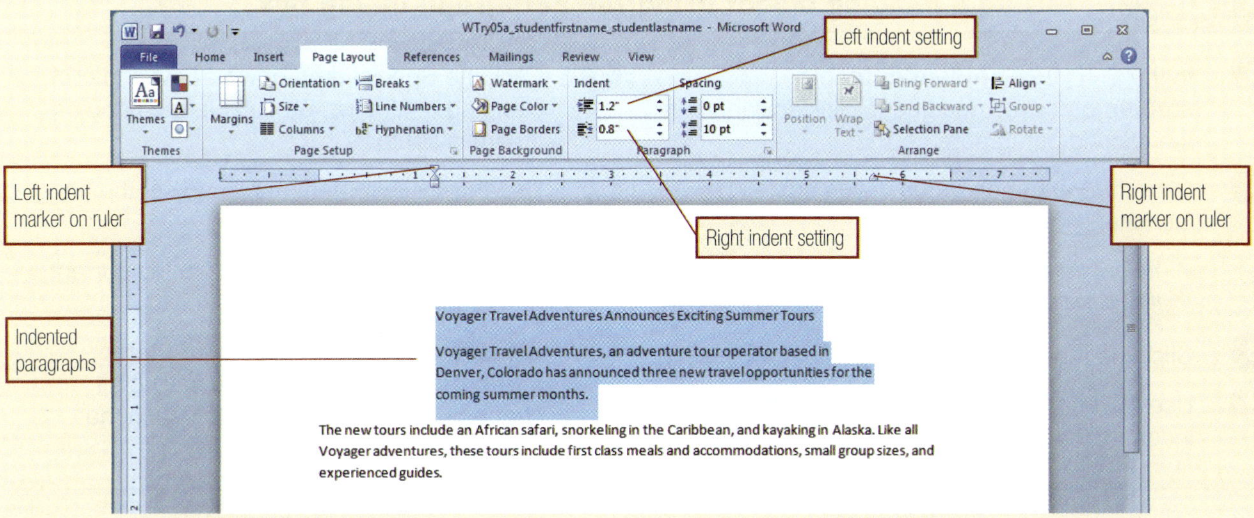

Try It! Setting Indents Using the Paragraph Dialog Box

1. In the **WTry05a_studentfirstname_studentlastname** document, click anywhere in the third paragraph.
2. On the Page Layout tab, click the Paragraph group dialog box launcher .

   ✓ *You can use the Paragraph group dialog box launcher on the Home tab or the Page Layout tab.*

3. Click the Indents and Spacing tab, if necessary.
4. Under Indentation, use the Left increment arrows to set the left indent to 0.4".
5. Use the Right increment arrows to set the right indent to 0.6".

   ✓ *If you were setting indents for a bound publication, you could select the Mirror indents check box and set inside and outside indents instead of left and right indents.*

6. Click the Special drop-down arrow and click First line on the list. By default, the first line indent is set to 0.5".
7. Use the By increment arrows to set the first line indent to 0.8".
8. Click OK to apply the settings to the current paragraph.

   ✓ *To quickly apply a first line indent, press TAB at the beginning of a paragraph.*

9. Save the changes to the document and leave it open in Word to use in the next Try It.

Paragraph dialog box

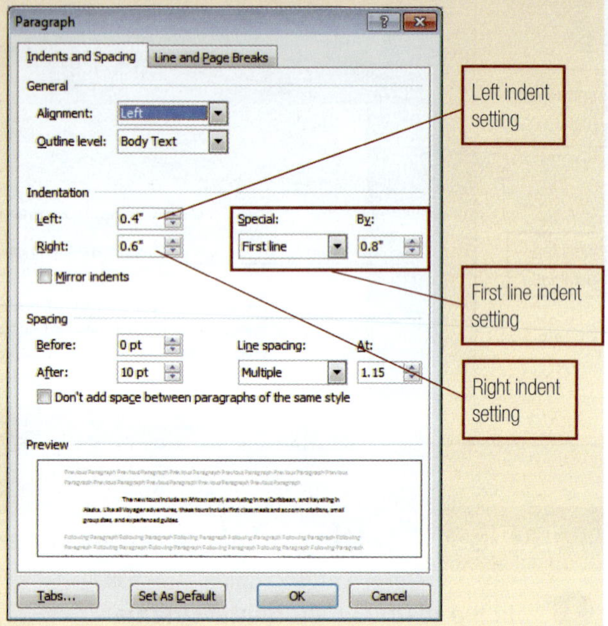

Try It! Setting a Hanging Indent Using the Paragraph Dialog Box

1. In the **WTry05a_studentfirstname_studentlastname** document, click anywhere in the second paragraph.
2. Click the Paragraph group dialog box launcher .

   ✓ *You can use the Paragraph group dialog box launcher on the Home tab or the Page Layout tab.*

3. Click the Indents and Spacing tab, if necessary.
4. Use the Left increment arrows to set the left indent to 0.4".
5. Click the Special drop-down arrow and click Hanging on the list. By default, the hanging indent is set to 0.5".
6. Use the By increment arrows to set the hanging indent to 0.8".
7. Click OK to apply the settings to the current paragraph.
8. Close the **WTry05a_studentfirstname_studentlastname** document, saving all changes. Leave Word open to use in the next Try It.

Setting and Modifying Tabs

- **Tabs** are used to indent a single line of text.
- Each time you press the Tab key, the insertion point advances to the next set **tab stop**.
- There are five types of tab stops:
  - *Left*: Text starts flush left with the tab stop.
  - *Right*: Text ends flush right with the tab stop.
  - *Center*: Text is centered on the tab stop.
  - *Decimal*: Decimal points are aligned with the tab stop.
  - *Bar*: A vertical bar is displayed at the tab stop position.
- By default, left tab stops are set every ½" on the horizontal ruler.
- You can set any type of tab stop at any point along the ruler.
- To select a tab type, click the Tab selector box at the left end of the ruler until the tab you want to use displays.

  ✓ *Note that after the five tab types display on the Tab selector, the first line indent and hanging indent markers display.*

- You can use the Tabs dialog box to set precise tab stops.
- You can also select a **tab leader** in the Tabs dialog box.
- You can set tabs before you type new text, for the current paragraph, or for selected multiple paragraphs.
- Once you set tabs, the formatting is carried forward each time you press ENTER to start a new paragraph.

Try It! Setting Left and Center Tabs Using the Horizontal Ruler

1. Create a new document in Word. Save the document as **WTry05b_studentfirstname_studentlastname** in the location where your teacher instructs you to store the files for this lesson. Notice that by default, the Left Tab type displays in the Tab selector box.
2. Display nonprinting characters.
3. Click at the 1.0" mark on the horizontal ruler. This sets a left tab stop at that point.
4. Press TAB. The insertion point advances to the tab stop.
5. Type your first name.
6. Click the Tab selector box once to change the tab type to Center Tab.
7. Click at the 4.0" mark on the horizontal ruler.
8. Press TAB to advance the insertion point to the Center tab stop, and then type **Microsoft Word 2010**. The text is centered on the tab stop.
9. Press ENTER to start a new line. Notice that the tab settings carry forward to the new line.
10. Save the changes to the document and leave it open in Word to use in the next Try It.

Try It! Setting Right, Decimal, and Bar Tabs Using the Horizontal Ruler

1. In the Word document **WTry05b_studentfirstname_studentlastname**, click the Tab selector box once to change the tab type to Right Tab.
2. Click at the 3.0" mark on the horizontal ruler to set a right tab stop.
3. Press TAB. The insertion point advances to the left tab stop.
4. Press TAB again. The insertion point advances to the right tab stop. Type your last name.
5. Click the Tab selector box once to change the tab type to Decimal Tab.
6. Click at the 5.0" mark on the horizontal ruler to set a decimal tab stop.
7. Press TAB. The insertion point advances to the center tab stop.
8. Press TAB again. The insertion point advances to the decimal tab stop. Type **$123.75**. The decimal point in the dollar value aligns with the decimal tab stop.
9. Click the Tab selector box once to change the tab type to Bar Tab, then click at the 6.0" mark on the horizontal ruler to set a bar tab stop. A vertical bar displays at the tab stop location.
10. Save the changes to the document and leave it open in Word to use in the next Try It.

Set tabs on the horizontal ruler

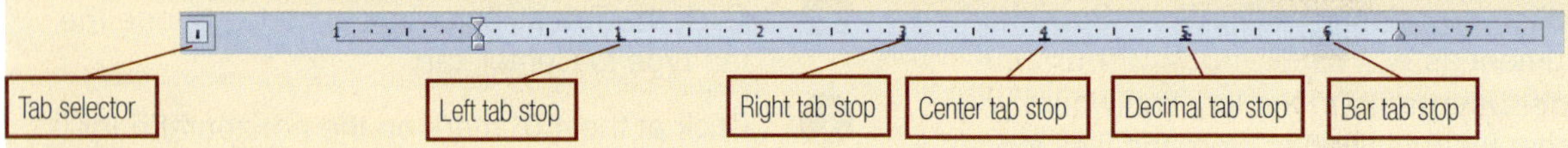

Try It! Setting Tabs in the Tab Dialog Box

1. In the **WTry05b_studentfirstname_studentlastname** document, select the first line of text.
2. Click the Home tab, if necessary, and then click the Paragraph group dialog box launcher.
3. Click the Tabs button in the lower left of the Paragraph dialog box to open the Tabs dialog box. Notice that the two tabs that are currently set in the selected text are listed under the Tab stop position box, and that the Left tab type is selected by default.
4. Click the Clear All button to remove all tabs from the selection.

   ✓ *To remove only one tab, select it in the Tab stop position list, and then click the Clear button.*

(continued)

Try It! Setting Tabs in the Tab Dialog Box *(continued)*

5. Type **.75** in the Tab stop position box, and then click the Set button. This sets a left tab stop at 0.75" on the horizontal ruler.

   ✓ *If you only want to set one tab stop, you can click OK instead of Set.*

6. Click the Center option button to change the tab type to Center tab, and then select the value in the Tab stop position box.
7. Type **3.0** and then click the Set button. This sets a Center tab stop at 3.0" on the horizontal ruler.
8. Click OK to apply the settings. In the document, the text adjusts to the new tab stop settings.
9. Save the changes to the document and leave it open in Word to use in the next Try It.

Set tabs in the Tabs dialog box

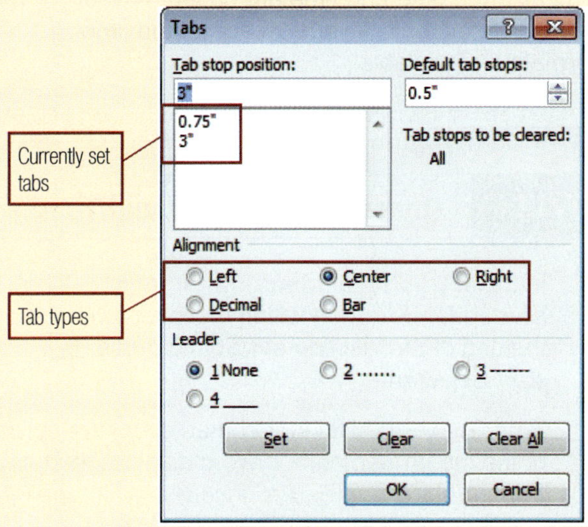

Try It! Using the Horizontal Ruler to Adjust and Clear Tab Stops

1. In the **WTry05b_studentfirstname_studentlastname** document, position the insertion point anywhere along the second line of text.
2. Drag the Bar Tab stop off the horizontal ruler. This is a quick method of removing a tab stop.
3. Drag the Right Tab stop from the 3.0" mark on the ruler, to the 2.5" mark on the ruler. The text adjusts to the new tab stop position.
4. Save the changes to the document and leave it open in Word to use in the next Try It.

Try It! Selecting a Tab Leader

1. Move the insertion point to the end of the **WTry05b_studentfirstname_studentlastname** document and press ENTER to start a new line.
2. Click the Home tab, if necessary, and then click the Paragraph group dialog box launcher.
3. Click the Tabs button in the lower left of the Paragraph dialog box to open the Tabs dialog box.
4. In the Leader area, click option 2 to select a dotted line tab leader, and then click OK to apply the change.
5. In the document, press TAB to advance the insertion point to the first set tab stop. Word inserts the dotted tab leader.
6. Type your first name. The text begins after the tab leader.
7. Save the changes to **WTry05b_studentfirstname_studentlastname** and leave it open to use in the next Try It.

Inserting the Date and Time

- Use the Insert Date & Time feature to automatically enter today's date and/or time into a document.
- The inserted date and time are based on your **computer's clock**. A variety of date and time formats are available.
- If you want, you can insert the date and/or time as a **field**, so that they update automatically whenever you save or print the document.
- To quickly insert the current date, type the first four letters of the name of the current month. When Word displays the date in a ScreenTip press ENTER. If the month has fewer than four characters, you do not have to press ENTER.

Try It! Inserting the Date and Time

1. In the **WTry05b_studentfirstname_studentlastname**, position the insertion point at the end of the last line of text and press ENTER to start a new line.
2. Type **Sept** – the first four characters of the name of the month September. Word displays the text *September (Press ENTER to Insert)* in a ScreenTip.
3. Press ENTER.
4. Press ENTER to start a new line.
5. Click the Insert tab, then, in the Text group, click the Date &Time button to open the Date and Time dialog box. The default format is mm/dd/yyyy.
6. Click the second format in the list of Available formats, and then click OK. Word inserts the date in the selected format.

   ✓ *Select the Update automatically check box if you want the date to update automatically every time you save or print the document.*
7. Press ENTER, then click the Date & Time button again.
8. Click the last format in the list of available formats, and then click OK to insert the time into the document.
9. Close **WTry05b_studentfirstname_studentlastname**, saving all changes. Leave Word open to use in the next Try It.

Writing a Business Letter

- A business letter is written to communicate with other businesses, such as clients or suppliers, or to communicate with individuals, such as prospective employees. For example, a bank manager might write a business letter to a customer to explain changes in an account, or a marketing representative might write a business letter to an advertising agency requesting rates.
- Traditionally, business letters are printed and mailed, but in some circumstances they may be sent via e-mail.
- Refer to Figure 5-1 on the next page to identify the parts of a business letter.
  - **Return address (**may be omitted if the letter is printed on letterhead stationery)
  - Date
  - **Inside address**
  - **Salutation**
  - Body
  - Signature line
  - Job title line (the job title of the letter writer)
  - Reference initials (the initials of the person who wrote the letter, followed by a slash, followed by the initials of the person who typed the letter).

Figure 5-1

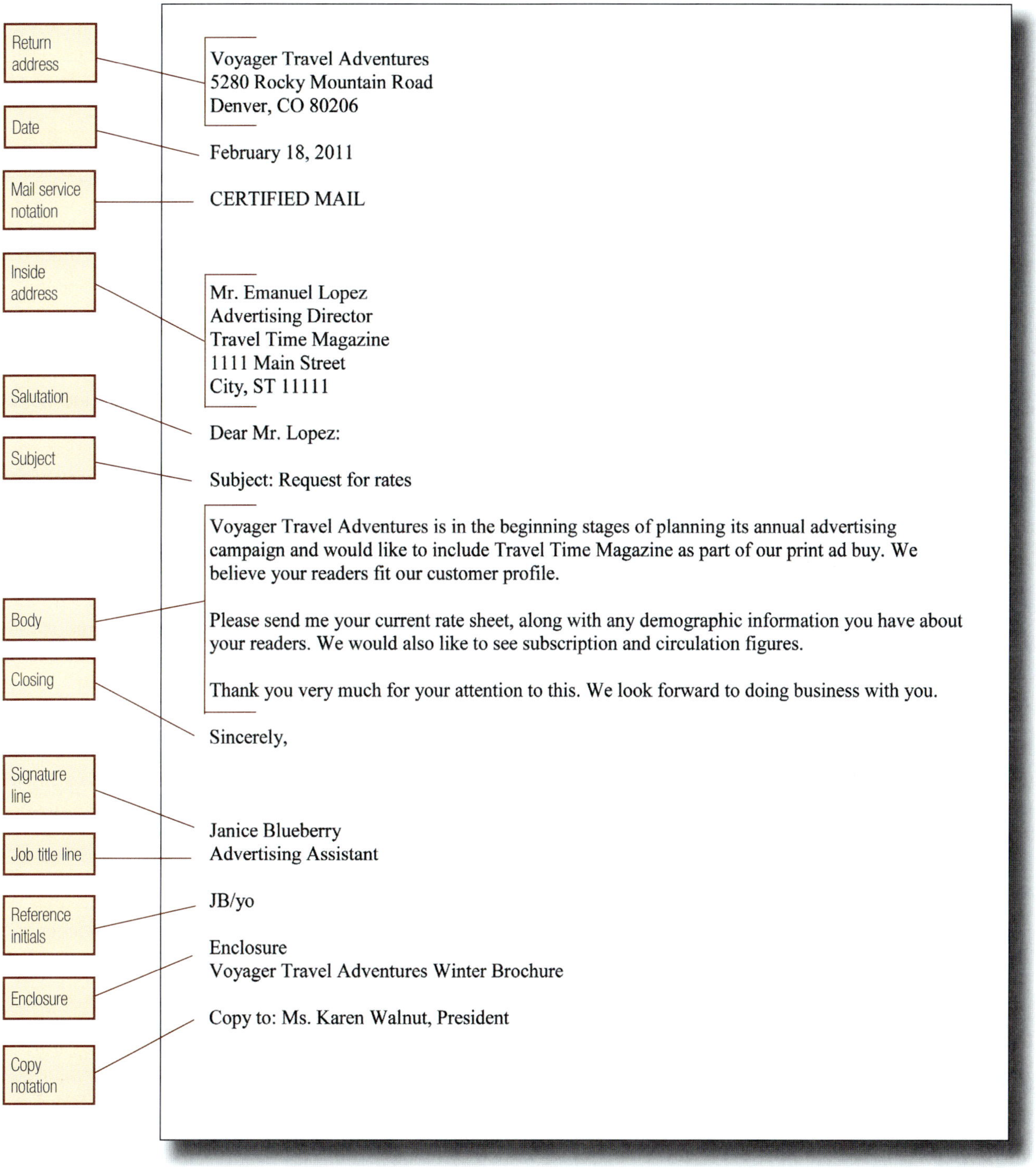
Voyager Travel Adventures
5280 Rocky Mountain Road
Denver, CO 80206

February 18, 2011

CERTIFIED MAIL

Mr. Emanuel Lopez
Advertising Director
Travel Time Magazine
1111 Main Street
City, ST 11111

Dear Mr. Lopez:

Subject: Request for rates

Voyager Travel Adventures is in the beginning stages of planning its annual advertising campaign and would like to include Travel Time Magazine as part of our print ad buy. We believe your readers fit our customer profile.

Please send me your current rate sheet, along with any demographic information you have about your readers. We would also like to see subscription and circulation figures.

Thank you very much for your attention to this. We look forward to doing business with you.

Sincerely,

Janice Blueberry
Advertising Assistant

JB/yo

Enclosure
Voyager Travel Adventures Winter Brochure

Copy to: Ms. Karen Walnut, President

- Special notations (included only when appropriate):
  - Mail service notation indicates a special delivery method. It is typed in all capital letters, two lines below the date. Typical mail service notations include CERTIFIED MAIL, REGISTERED MAIL, or BY HAND.
  - Subject notation identifies or summarizes the letter topic. The word Subject may be typed in all capital letters or with just an initial capital. It is placed two lines below the salutation.

  ✓ *The text Re (meaning with regard to) is sometimes used in place of the word Subject.*

- Enclosure or Attachment notation indicates whether there are other items in the envelope. It is typed two lines below the reference initials in any of the following styles: ENC., Enc., Encl., Enclosure, Attachment. The name of the item(s) may be listed under the notation.

  ✓ *If there are multiple items, the number may be typed in parentheses following the notation.*

- Copy notation indicates if any other people are receiving copies of the letter. It is typed two lines below either the enclosure notation, or reference initials, whichever is last. It may be typed as Copy to:, cc:, or pc: (photocopy) with the name(s) of the recipient(s) listed after the colon.

■ There are different styles of business letters. The most common are full-block and modified block.
- In a **full block** business letter all lines start flush with the left margin.
- In a **modified block** business letter the return address, date, closing, signature, and job title lines begin at the center of the page at a left tab stop.

■ The parts of a business letter are the same regardless of the style.

Creating an Envelope

■ Use Word's Envelopes and Labels dialog box to set up an envelope for printing.

■ If a letter document is open onscreen, you can select the inside address to identify it as the **delivery address**.

■ Alternatively, you can type any delivery address you want.

■ You can type a return address or select to omit the return address if you are printing on an envelope that has the return address pre-printed, or if you plan to use return address labels.

■ If you type a return address, Word asks if you want to make it the default return address.

■ Before printing an envelope, you should be certain the envelope is correctly inserted in your printer, and that the printer is set to print an envelope.

■ Consult your printer's manual or ask your teacher for information on using the available printer to print envelopes.

✓ *For this lesson, your teacher may instruct you to print the envelope on standard paper.*

■ You can print the envelope immediately or add it to the beginning of the open document and save it to print later.

Try It! Creating an Envelope

1. In Word, open **WTry05c** from the data files for this lesson. Save it as **WTry05c_studentfirstname_studentlastname** in the location where your teacher instructs you to store the files for this lesson.
2. On the Mailings tab, in the Create group, click the Envelopes button to open the Envelopes and Labels dialog box.
3. In the Delivery address box, type your name and address, using proper address formatting.

   ✓ *Refer to the following figure to see proper address formatting.*

4. Click to clear the Omit check box, if necessary, then click in the Return address box and type your school's address.

   ✓ *Click the Omit check box if there is a return address printed on your envelopes already, or if you plan to use return address labels.*

5. Follow your teacher's instructions to properly insert envelopes or paper into the printer.

(continued)

Try It! Creating an Envelope *(continued)*

6. **With your teacher's permission**, click the Print button to print the envelope.
7. Click No to continue without making the return address the default.
8. In the document, select the five lines of the inside address, beginning with *Mr. Emanuel Lopez*.
9. Click the Mailings tab on the Ribbon, then, in the Create group, click the Envelopes button to open the Envelopes and Labels dialog box.
10. Click in the Return address box and type your own address.
11. Click Add to Document.
12. Click No to continue without making the return address the default. Word inserts the envelope as the first page in the current document. Once you save the document, you can print the envelope by printing just the first page.
13. Close the document, saving all changes, and exit Word.

Envelopes tab of the Envelopes and Labels dialog box

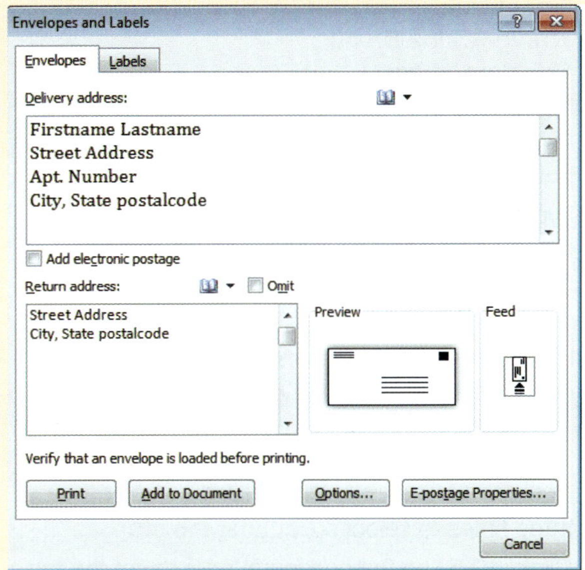

Project 9—Create It

Full Block Business Letter

DIRECTIONS

1. Start Word, if necessary, and save the default document as **WProj09_studentfirstname_studentlastname** in the location where your teacher instructs you to store the files for this lesson.
2. Display the rulers and nonprinting characters, if necessary.
3. Apply the **No Spacing** style to set the line spacing to single and the paragraph spacing to **0 points** before and after.
4. Type the following return address, pressing ENTER after each line:

   Whole Grains Bread
   320 Magnolia Avenue
   Larkspur, CA 94939
5. Press ENTER to leave a blank line.
6. Click the **Insert tab**, and then, in the Text group, click the **Date &Time** button to open the Date and Time dialog box.
7. Click the **third format** in the list and then click **OK** to insert the date.

8. Press ENTER twice, type **CERTIFIED MAIL**, and then press ENTER four times.
9. Type the following inside address, pressing ENTER after each line:

   Ms. Lindsey Parks
   Franchisee
   Whole Grains Bread
   456 Main Street
   Brentwood, CA 94513
10. Press ENTER to leave a blank line, then type **Dear Ms. Parks:** and press ENTER twice.
11. Type **Subject: New franchise opportunity** and press ENTER twice.
12. Type the following paragraph:

    Thanks for your interest in opening an additional franchise outside of California. In response to your question, I have enclosed a financing brochure. In general, we believe you will need the following funds:
13. Press ENTER twice, and then click the **Tab selector** three times to select a **Decimal tab stop**.
14. Click at **1.5"** on the horizontal ruler to set the tab stop, then press TAB to advance the insertion point.
15. Type **$125,500.00**, press ENTER, press TAB, and type **$21,250.00**. Press ENTER, press TAB, type **$5,400.00**, and press ENTER twice.
16. Drag the **Decimal Tab stop** off the horizontal ruler, and then type: **The challenges and rewards of starting a new Whole Grains Bread franchise can be summed up by the following quote from our founder:** and press ENTER twice.
17. Click the **Page Layout** tab, then use the **Left increment arrows** to set the left indent to **1.5"** and the **Right increment arrows** to set the right indent to **1.5"**.
18. Type the following: **"Starting a new Whole Grains franchise is both expensive and difficult. However, when done properly, it brings financial rewards and a strong sense of personal satisfaction."**
19. Press ENTER, and use the **Left increment arrows** to set the left indent to **0"** and the **Right increment arrows** to set the right indent to **0"**.
20. Press ENTER, type **Sincerely,** and press ENTER four times.
21. Type your name, press ENTER, and type **Manager**.
22. Press ENTER twice, type **Enclosure**, press ENTER, and type **Financing brochure**.
23. Press ENTER twice and type **Copy to: Mr. Anthony Splendora, CEO**.
24. Save the changes to the document.
25. Select the **inside address**, and then click the **Mailings** tab on the Ribbon.
26. Click the **Envelopes** button in the Create group to open the Envelopes and Labels dialog box.
27. Click in the **Return address** box and type

    320 Magnolia Avenue
    Larkspur, CA 94939
28. Click **Add to Document** to add the envelope to the document.
29. Click **No** to continue without making the return address the default. Word inserts the envelope as the first page in the current document. The document should look similar to Figure 5-2 on the next page.
30. **With your teacher's permission**, print both the letter and the envelope.
31. Close the document, saving all changes, and exit Word.

Figure 5-2

320 Magnolia Avenue
Larkspur, CA 94939

Ms. Lindsey Parks
Franchisee
Whole Grains Bread
456 Main Street
Brentwood, CA 94513

Voyager Travel Adventures
5280 Rocky Mountain Road
Denver, CO 80206

February 18, 2011

CERTIFIED MAIL

Mr. Emanuel Lopez
Advertising Director
Travel Time Magazine
1111 Main Street
City, ST 11111

Dear Mr. Lopez:

Subject: Request for rates

Voyager Travel Adventures is in the beginning stages of planning its annual advertising campaign and would like to include Travel Time Magazine as part of our print ad buy. We believe your readers fit our customer profile.

Please send me your current rate sheet, along with any demographic information you have about your readers. We would also like to see subscription and circulation figures.

Thank you very much for your attention to this. We look forward to doing business with you.

Sincerely,

Janice Blueberry
Advertising Assistant

JB/yo

Enclosure
Voyager Travel Adventures Winter Brochure

Copy to: Ms. Karen Walnut, President

Project 10—Apply It

Modified Block Business Letter

DIRECTIONS

1. Start Word, if necessary, and open **WProj10** from the data files for this lesson.
2. Save the file as **WProj10_studentfirstname_studentlastname** in the location where your teacher instructs you to store the files for this lesson.
3. Display the rulers and nonprinting characters, if necessary.
4. Press CTRL + A to select all text in the document.
5. Open the Paragraph dialog box, and click the **Tabs** button to open the Tabs dialog box.
6. Verify that **Left** is the selected alignment, type **3.25** in the **Tab stop position box**, and then click **OK**. This sets a left tab stop in the center of the document page.
7. Position the insertion point at the beginning of the first line of the return address, and press TAB. The text on the line advances to the tab stop.
8. Tab the remaining two lines in the return address to the tab stop.
9. Delete the sample text **Today's date**, and press TAB to advance the insertion point to the tab stop.
10. Insert the 8th format in the Available formats list in the Date and Time dialog box.
11. Select the inside address and replace it with the following:

    Mr. Cameron McGill
    Franchisee
    Whole Grains Bread
    222 Oak Hill Avenue
    Omaha, NE 68180
12. Edit the salutation line to **Dear Mr. McGill:**
13. Position the insertion point at the beginning of the Closing line (*Sincerely,*) and press TAB to advance the text.
14. Delete the sample text **Student's Name**, press TAB to advance the insertion point to the tab stop, and type your name.
15. Tab the Job Title line in to the tab stop.
16. Save the changes to the document.
17. Create an envelope for the letter, using the inside address as the delivery address and **320 Magnolia Avenue, Larkspur, CA 94939** as the return address.
18. Add the envelope to the document without changing the default return address. The document should look similar to Figure 5-3 on the next page.
19. **With your teacher's permission**, print both the letter and the envelope.
20. Close the document, saving all changes, and exit Word.

Figure 5-3

320 Magnolia Avenue
Larkspur, CA 94939

Mr. Cameron McGill
Franchisee
Whole Grains Bread
222 Oak Hill Avenue
Omaha, NE 68180

Whole Grains Bread
320 Magnolia Avenue
Larkspur, CA 94939

Apr. 19, 10

CERTIFIED MAIL

Mr. Cameron McGill
Franchisee
Whole Grains Bread
222 Oak Hill Avenue
Omaha, NE 68180

Dear Mr. McGill:

Subject: New franchise opportunity

Thanks for your interest in opening an additional franchise outside of California. In response to your question, I have enclosed a financing brochure. In general, we believe you will need the following funds:

$125,500.00
$21,250.00
$5,400.00

The challenges and rewards of starting a new Whole Grains Bread franchise can be summed up by the following quote from our founder:

> "Starting a new Whole Grains franchise is both expensive and difficult. However, when done properly, it brings financial rewards and a strong sense of personal satisfaction."

Sincerely,

Firstname Lastname
Manager

Enclosure
Financing brochure

Copy to: Mr. Anthony Splendora, CEO

WORDS TO KNOW

Cover letter
A personal business letter that you send with your resume when you apply for a job.

Font
A complete set of characters in a specific design, style, and size.

Font color
The color of characters in a font set.

Font effects
Enhancements applied to font characters.

Font size
The height of an uppercase letter in a font set.

Font style
The slant and weight of characters in a font set.

Sans serif
A font that has straight edges.

Script
A font that looks like handwriting.

Serif
A font that has curved or extended edges.

Theme fonts
The default font sets applied with a theme.

Lesson 6

Formatting Text with Fonts and Effects

➤ What You Will Learn

- Changing the Font
- Changing the Font Size
- Changing the Font Color
- Applying Font Styles and Effects
- Applying Underlines
- Clearing Formatting
- Writing a Personal Business Letter

Software Skills Write personal business letters to communicate with businesses such as your bank or your insurance company, or to apply for a job. Fonts are a basic means of applying formatting to text and characters. They can set a mood, command attention, and convey a message.

Application Skills You are looking for a summer job in recreation management. In this lesson, you will write personal business letters to Voyager Travel Adventures and Michigan Avenue Athletic Club asking about job opportunities. You will try out different font and text formatting options to see how they affect the document.

What You Can Do

Changing the Font

- Microsoft Office 2010 comes with built-in **fonts**; you can install additional fonts.
- Each font set includes upper- and lowercase letters, numbers, and punctuation marks.
- There are three basic categories of fonts:
  - **Serif** fonts are easy to read and are often used for document text.
  - **Sans serif** fonts are often used for headings.
  - **Script** fonts are often used to simulate handwriting on invitations or announcements.
- A fourth font category includes decorative fonts which may have embellishments such as curlicues or double lines designed to dress up or enhance the characters.
- The current font name displays in the Font box on the Home tab of the Ribbon.
- The default font for the Office theme Normal style is Calibri.
- Click the Font box drop-down arrow in the Font group or on the Mini toolbar to display a gallery of available fonts. The fonts display in alphabetical order, but **theme fonts** and recently used fonts are listed at the top.

  ✓ *Refer to Word, Lesson 2 for information about themes.*
- You can also type the name of the font you want to use directly into the Font box or select a font in the Font dialog box.
- You can set the tone of a document by putting thought into the fonts you select.
- More than two or three fonts in one document look disjointed and unprofessional.
- You can change the font of existing text, or you can select a font before you type new text.
- To preview how selected text will look in a particular font, rest the mouse pointer on the font name in the Font list.

Try It! Changing the Font

1. Start Word and open **WTry06** from the data files for this lesson. Save it as **WTry06_studentfirstname_studentlastname** in the location where your teacher instructs you to store the files for this lesson.
2. Select the text *African Safari*.
3. On the Home tab, in the Font group, click the Font drop-down arrow Calibri (Body) to display a list of available fonts.
4. Scroll down the list and click Broadway to change the font of the selected text.

   ✓ *You can quickly scroll the list by typing the first character or two of a font name. For example, type* B R *to scroll to fonts beginning with the letters BR.*
5. Select the two full paragraphs of text.
6. In the Font group, click the Font drop-down arrow Calibri (Body), scroll down the list, and click Times New Roman.

   ✓ *The fonts installed on your system may not be the same as those shown in the figure.*
7. Save the changes to the document and leave it open in Word to use in the next Try It.

Change the font

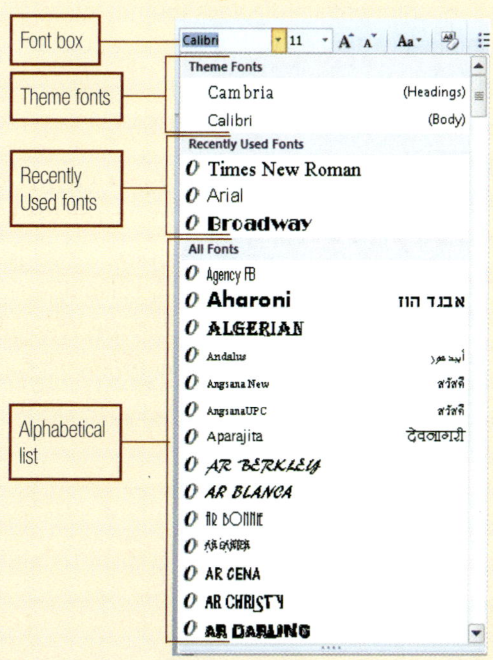

Changing the Font Size

- **Font size** is measured in points. There are 72 points in an inch.
- The default font size for the Office theme Normal style is 11 points.
- The current font size displays in the Font Size box on the Home tab of the Ribbon.
- Click the Font Size drop-down arrow [11 ▾] in the Font group or on the Mini toolbar to display a gallery of font sizes.
- Alternatively, you can select a font size in the Font dialog box, or type a specific font size in the Font Size box.
- You can also use the Grow Font [A˄] and Shrink Font [A˅] buttons to adjust the font size by one point.

Try It! Changing the Font Size

1. In the **WTry06_studentfirstname_studentlastname** document, select the text *African Safari*.
2. On the Home tab, in the Font group, click the Font Size drop-down arrow [11 ▾] to display a list of font sizes.
3. Click 28 to change the font size of the selected text.
4. Select the two full paragraphs of text.
5. In the Font group, click the Shrink Font button [A˅] to reduce the font size by 1 point to 10 points.
6. In the Font group, click Grow Font [A˄] button twice to increase the font size by 2 points to 12 points.
7. Save the changes to the document and leave it open in Word to use in the next Try It.

Changing the Font Color

- Use the Font Color palette in the Font group on the Home tab of the Ribbon, on the mini toolbar, or in the Font dialog box to change the **font color**.
- The font color palette displays theme colors, which are the colors applied with a theme, and standard colors.
- When you select a font color, consider how people will be viewing the document. For example, will it be printed or displayed on a monitor?
- Also consider who will be viewing the document. For example, a business letter to a bank should not include pastel colors such as light blue or pink, or bold colors such as bright orange or yellow.

Try It! Changing the Font Color

1. In the **WTry06_studentfirstname_studentlastname** document, select the text *African Safari*.
2. On the Home tab, in the Font group, click the Font Color drop-down arrow [A ▾] to open the color palette.
3. Under Standard Colors, click Blue (third from right) to change the color of the selected text.
4. Save the changes to the document and leave it open in Word to use in the next Try It.

Applying Font Styles and Effects

- The most common **font styles** are bold [B] and italic [I].
- When no style is applied to a font, it is called regular.
- Font styles can be combined, such as bold italic.
- Font styles are available in the Font group on the Home tab of the Ribbon, on the Mini toolbar, or in the Font dialog box.
- You can also use shortcut key combinations to apply font styles.
  - Bold [B] .... CTRL + B
  - Italic [I] .... CTRL + I
- **Font effects** include formatting options applied to regular font characters. Common font effects include strikethrough, superscript, and subscript.
- Some font effects are available in the Font group on the Home tab of the Ribbon; they are all available in the Font dialog box.
- Font styles and effects are toggles; click the button once to apply the formatting, and then click it again to remove the formatting.

✓ *Font effects are not the same as text effects. Text effects are covered in Word, Lesson 10.*

Try It! Applying Font Styles and Effects

1. In the WTry06_studentfirstname_studentlastname document, select the text *Voyager Travel Adventures* in the first sentence.
2. On the Home tab, in the Font group, click the Bold [B] button to apply the bold style to the selected text.
3. Click the Font group dialog box launcher to open the Font dialog box.
4. In the Effects area, click to select the Small caps check box.
5. Click OK to close the dialog box and apply the effect.
6. Save the changes to the document and leave it open to use in the next Try It.

Font dialog box

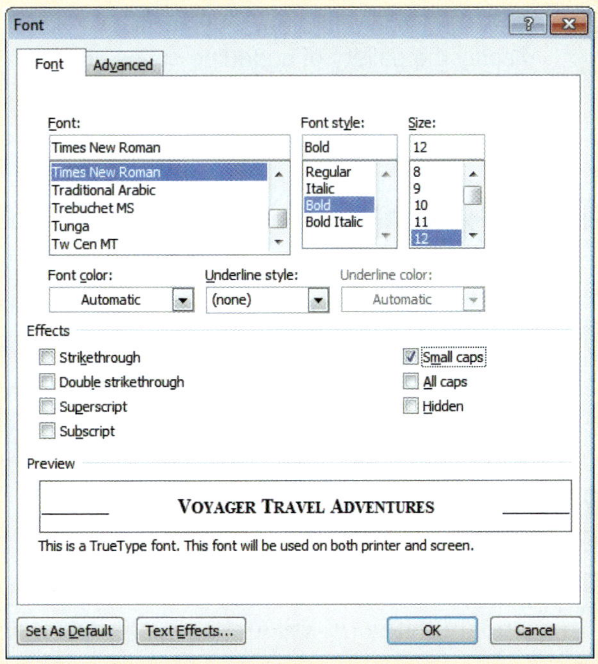

Applying Underlines

- There are 17 types of underline styles available in Word, which include:
  - Single (underlines all characters, including nonprinting characters such as spaces and tabs)
  - Words only
  - Double
  - Dotted
- Some underlines are available from the Underline gallery in the Font group on the Home tab of the Ribbon, or you can select from the complete list in the Font dialog box.
- Press CTRL + U to apply the default single underline.
- By default, the underline color matches the current font color. You can select a different color from the Underline color palette off the Underline gallery or in the Font dialog box.

Try It! Applying Underlines

1. In the **WTry06_studentfirstname_studentlastname** document, select the text *African Safari*.
2. On the Home tab, in the Font group, click the Underline U button to apply a single underline.
3. Click the Underline drop-down arrow U to display the gallery of underline styles and then click Wave underline to apply it to the text.
4. Click the Underline drop-down arrow U again and click Underline Color to display the underline color palette.
5. Under Standard Colors, click Dark Red (the first color on the left) to change the color of the underline.
6. Save the changes to the document and leave it open to use in the next Try It.

Clearing Formatting

- Use the Clear Formatting button in the Font group on the Home tab of the Ribbon to remove all formatting from a selection.
- You can also use the shortcut key combination CTRL + SPACE.

Try It! Clearing Formatting

1. Select all text in the **WTry06_studentfirstname_studentlastname** document.
2. On the Home tab, in the Font group, click the Clear Formatting button to remove all formatting from the selection.
3. Close **WTry06_studentfirstname_studentlastname** saving all changes, and exit Word.

Writing a Personal Business Letter

- A personal business letter is written on behalf of an individual instead of on behalf of another business.
- A personal business letter may be full-block or modified block. It usually includes a return address and contact information such as telephone number or e-mail address—unless it is printed on paper that has a letterhead. It does not usually include a title line or reference initials.
- A **cover letter** is a personal business letter that you send with your resume when you apply for a job. You use a cover letter to introduce yourself and to highlight the qualities that make you suitable for the position.
- A cover letter should be short and to the point. You address it to the person who is responsible for hiring. If you do not know the person's name, title, and address, you should call the company and ask.
- Include the following in any cover letter:
  - The job title for the position you want.
  - Where you learned about the position.
  - The skills that qualify you for the position.
  - Your contact information.
- Be sure to thank the reader for his or her time and consideration, and to correct all spelling and grammatical errors.
- A well-written and well-organized cover letter helps you make a positive impression. It shows that you have taken the time to match your qualifications with a specific job.

✓ *For information on writing other types of business letters, refer to Word, Lesson 5.*

Project 11—Create It

Cover Letter 1

DIRECTIONS

1. Start Word, if necessary and save the default document as **WProj11_studentfirstname_studentlastname** in the location where your teacher instructs you to store the files for this lesson.
2. Display the rulers and nonprinting characters, if necessary.
3. Apply the **No Spacing** style to set the line spacing to single and the paragraph spacing to 0 points before and after.
4. On the Home tab, in the Font group, click the **Font** drop-down arrow [Calibri (Body)] and click **Times New Roman** to change the font.
5. Click the **Font Size** drop-down arrow [11] and click **12** to change the font size.
6. Type your own return address, pressing [ENTER] after each line.
7. Press [ENTER] to leave a blank line. Click the **Insert** tab, then, in the Text group, cick the **Date & Time** button to open the Date and Time dialog box.
8. Click today's date in the month day, year format (third from the top) and then click **OK** to insert the date.
9. Press [ENTER] four times to leave blank space, then type the following inside address, pressing [ENTER] after each line:

   Ms. Maria Sanchez
   Human Resources Manager
   Voyager Travel Adventures
   1635 Logan Street
   Denver, CO 80205
10. Press [ENTER] to leave a blank line, then type **Dear Ms. Sanchez:** and press [ENTER] twice.

11. Type the following paragraphs, pressing ENTER twice to leave space between them, as shown in Figure 6-1:

    I am writing to inquire about summer job opportunities or internships as a tour leader at Voyager Travel Adventures. My uncle, who traveled with your company to Costa Rica last year, suggested that I contact you.

    I am currently pursuing a degree in recreation management and I think a position at Voyager Travel Adventures would fit my interests and abilities. Last summer, I worked as a camp counselor. My responsibilities included leading groups of campers on backpacking and kayaking trips. I am also a certified lifeguard. I believe that my experience, education, and knowledge of nature and first aid make me uniquely qualified to work for you.

    I would appreciate the opportunity to meet with you to discuss possible employment options. I look forward to hearing from you.

12. Press ENTER twice, type **Sincerely,** and press ENTER four times.
13. Type your name, press ENTER, and type your phone number.
14. Press ENTER and type your e-mail address.
15. Select the text **Human Resources Manager** in the inside address.
16. Click the **Home** tab, then, in the Font group, click the **Italic** button I to apply italic to the selection.
17. Click the **Italic** button I again to remove the style.
18. Select the text *Voyager Travel Adventures* in the inside address.

Figure 6-1

Student Street Address
City, State postal code

Today's Date

Ms. Maria Sanchez
Human Resources Manager
VOYAGER TRAVEL ADVENTURES
1635 Logan Street
Denver, CO 80205

Dear Ms. Sanchez:

I am writing to inquire about summer job opportunities or internships as a tour leader at Voyager Travel Adventures. My uncle, who traveled with your company to Costa Rica last year, suggested that I contact you.

I am currently pursuing a degree in recreation management and I think a position at Voyager Travel Adventures would fit my interests and abilities. Last summer I worked as a camp counselor. My responsibilities included leading groups of campers on backpacking and kayaking trips. I am also a certified lifeguard. I believe that my experience, education, and knowledge of nature and first aid make me uniquely qualified to work for you.

I would appreciate the opportunity to meet with you to discuss possible employment options. I look forward to hearing from you.

Sincerely,

Firstname Lastname
Phone number
Email address

19. Click the **Font group dialog box launcher** [icon] to open the Font dialog box.
20. Click to select the **Small caps** check box, and then click **OK** to apply the effect.
21. With the text still selected, click the **Bold** button [B] to apply bold to the selection.
22. With the text still selected, click the **Font Color** drop-down arrow [A] to display the Font Color palette.
23. Under Standard Colors, click **Purple** (last color on the right) to apply it to the selection.
24. With the text still selected, click the **Underline** button arrow [U] to display the gallery of underline styles.
25. Click the **Thick underline** style (third in the list) to apply it to the selection.
26. **With your teacher's permission**, print the letter. It should look similar to Figure 6-1 on the previous page.
27. Close the document, saving all changes, and exit Word.

Project 12—Apply It

Personal Business Letter

DIRECTIONS

1. Start Word, if necessary, and open **WProj12** from the data files for this lesson.
2. Save the file as **WProj12_studentfirstname_studentlastname** in the location where your teacher instructs you to store the files for this lesson.
3. Display the rulers and nonprinting characters, if necessary.
4. Press CTRL + A to select all text in the document.
5. Click the **Clear Formatting** button to remove all formatting in the document, and then apply the **No Spacing** style.
6. Click the **Font group dialog box launcher** [icon] to open the Font dialog box.
7. Type **Arial** in the **Font** box, type **13** in the Size box, and then click **OK** to change the font to 13 point Arial.
8. Replace the sample return address with your own address.
9. Replace the sample date with the current date.
10. Replace the inside address with the following:

    Mr. Daniel Costello
    Personnel Director
    Michigan Avenue Athletic Club
    235 Michigan Avenue
    Chicago, IL 60601

11. Change the font of the company name to **Cambria** and increase the font size to **14** points.
12. Edit the salutation line to **Dear Mr. Costello:**
13. Edit the first paragraph of the letter body to the following:

    I am writing to inquire about summer job opportunities or internships as a recreation assistant at Michigan Avenue Athletic Club. My cousin, who is a member, suggested that I contact you.

14. Edit the second paragraph of the letter body to the following:

    I am currently pursuing a degree in recreation management and I think a position at Michigan Avenue Athletic Club would fit my interests and abilities. Last summer, I worked as a camp counselor at Pine Acres Day Camp. My responsibilities included teaching swimming classes, organizing H2O Fun Day, and leading fitness sessions for campers and counselors of all ages. I am a certified lifeguard. I believe that my experience and education make me uniquely qualified to work for you.

15. Select the text *Pine Acres Day Camp* and apply italic with a double underline.
16. Select the character *2* in H_2O and apply the subscript font effect.

17. Replace the sample text *Student's Name* with your own name.

18. Replace the sample text *Telephone number* with your own number.

19. Replace the sample text *Email address* with your own e-mail address.

20. **With your teacher's permission**, print the letter. It should look similar to Figure 6-2.

21. Close the document, saving all changes, and exit Word.

Figure 6-2

Street Address
City, State postal code

Today's Date

Mr. Daniel Costello
Personnel Director
Michigan Avenue Athletic Club
235 Michigan Avenue
Chicago, IL 60601

Dear Mr. Costello:

I am writing to inquire about summer job opportunities or internships as a recreation assistant at Michigan Avenue Athletic Club. My cousin, who is a member, suggested that I contact you.

I am currently pursuing a degree in recreation management and I think a position at Michigan Avenue Athletic Club would fit my interests and abilities. Last summer, I worked as a camp counselor at ***Pine Acres Day Camp***. My responsibilities included teaching swimming classes, organizing H_2O Fun Day, and leading fitness sessions for campers and counselors of all ages. I am a certified lifeguard. I believe that my experience and education make me uniquely qualified to work for you.

I would appreciate the opportunity to meet with you to discuss possible employment options. I look forward to hearing from you.

Sincerely,

Firstname Lastname
Telephone number
Email address

Lesson 7

Formatting and Sorting Lists

➤ What You Will Learn

- Creating a Bulleted List
- Creating a Numbered List
- Changing the Bullet or Number Formatting
- Sorting Paragraphs

Software Skills Lists are an effective way to present items of information. Use a bulleted list when the items do not have to be in any particular order, like a grocery list or a list of objectives. Use a numbered list when the order of the items is important, such as directions or instructions. Use Sort to organize a list into alphabetical or numerical order.

Application Skills As the customer service manager at the Michigan Avenue Athletic Club, you have recently received a number of complaints about the club's check-in policy for members who forget their ID badges. In this lesson, you will create a memo to employees about the proper check-in procedure. You will use a bulleted list and a numbered list, and you will sort the bulleted list into alphabetical order. You will revise the memo to send to members.

WORDS TO KNOW

Bullet
A dot or symbol that marks an important line of information or designates items in a list.

Picture
A graphics image stored in a graphics file format.

Sort
To organize items into a specified order.

Symbol
A visual element such as a shape or mathematical or scientific notation that you can insert as a character into a document.

What You Can Do

Creating a Bulleted List

- Use **bullets** to mark items in a list when the order does not matter.
- To apply the current bullet formatting, click the Bullets button in the Paragraph group on the Home tab of the Ribbon or on the Mini toolbar.
- By default, the bullet symbol for the Office theme is a simple black dot, indented 0.25" from the left margin. The symbol is followed by a 0.25" left tab, and the text on subsequent lines is indented to 0.25".
- You can select a different bullet from the Bullet Library.
- You can also define a new bullet using a **symbol** or a **picture**.
- Once you select a different bullet, it becomes the current bullet. It is also added to the Recently Used Bullets area in the Bullet Library.
- You can select bullet formatting before you start a list, or you can apply it to existing paragraphs.
- Word automatically carries bullet formatting forward to new paragraphs in a list.
- To end a bulleted list, press ENTER twice or click the Bullets button.
- To remove bullet formatting, select the bulleted paragraph(s) and select None in the Bullet Library.

Try It! Creating a Bulleted List

1. Start Word. Save the default blank document as **WTry07a_studentfirstname_studentlastname**.
2. On the Home tab, in the Paragraph group, click the Bullets button.
3. Type **Milk**, and then press ENTER.
4. Type **Orange juice**, and then press ENTER twice to turn off bullet formatting.
5. Select the two items in the bulleted list.
6. Click the Bullets drop-down arrow to open the Bullet Library.
7. Click the check mark bullet symbol.
8. Select the two items in the bulleted list.
9. Click the Bullets drop-down arrow to open the Bullet Library.
10. Click Define New Bullet to open the Define New Bullet dialog box.
11. Click Symbol to open the Symbol dialog box. The characters that are part of the Symbol font set display.

    ✓ *You can select a different font set from the Font drop-down list.*

Bullet Library

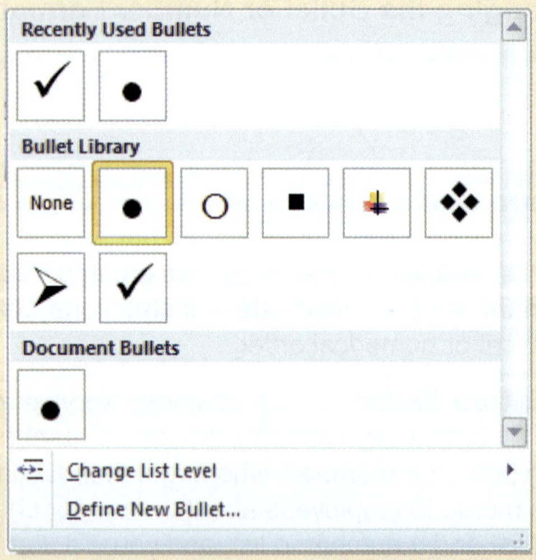

12. Scroll up a line or two and click the heart-shaped symbol, then click OK.
13. Click OK in the Define New Bullet dialog box to apply the symbol as the bullet.
14. Select the two items in the bulleted list.
15. Click the Bullets drop-down arrow to open the Bullet Library.

(continued)

Try It! Creating a Bulleted List *(continued)*

16. Click Define New Bullet to open the Define New Bullet dialog box.
17. Click Picture to open the Picture Bullet dialog box. A collection of picture bullets that come with Microsoft Office 2010 displays.

    ✓ *You can include picture bullets from Office.com by selecting the Include content from Office.com check box, and you can import any picture by clicking the Import button. You learn more about working with pictures in Word, Lesson 8.*
18. Scroll down and click the round, greenish bullet (ScreenTip says bullets, icons, network blitz...), then click OK.
19. Click OK in the Define New Bullet dialog box to apply the picture as the bullet.
20. Save the changes to the document and leave it open to use in the next Try It.

Creating a Numbered List

- Use numbers to mark items in a list when the order matters, such as for directions or how-to steps.
- Word automatically renumbers a list when you add or delete items.
- By default, Word continues list numbering sequentially. You can select to restart numbering in the middle of a list, and you can set the numbering value if you want to start at a number other than 1.
- To apply the current number formatting, click the Numbering button in the Paragraph group on the Home tab of the Ribbon.
- The default numbering style for the Office theme is an Arabic numeral followed by a period.
- You can select a different number format from the Numbering Library.
- You can also change the list level by increasing or decreasing the indent of the paragraph. For example, you can demote a numbered item from a main level 1) to a sublevel a. Or, you can promote a numbered item from a sublevel a) to a main level 1).
- Once you select a different number format, it becomes the current format. It is also added to the Recently Used Number Formats area in the Numbering Library.
- You can select number formatting before you start a list, or you can apply it to existing paragraphs.
- Word automatically carries numbering forward to new paragraphs in a list.
- To end a numbered list, press ENTER twice, or click the Numbering button.

Try It! Creating a Numbered List

1. In **WTry07a_studentfistname_studentlastname**, move the insertion point to the end of the document and press ENTER.
2. On the Home tab, in the Paragraph group click the Numbering button.
3. Type **Turn left on Main Street.** Press ENTER.
4. Type **Bear right at the fork.** Press ENTER.
5. Type **Go straight for 3 miles to destination.** Press ENTER.
6. Right-click the list number 4 to display a shortcut menu.
7. Click Restart at 1. Word changes the 4 to a 1.
8. Right-click the number 1 marking the fourth item in the list.
9. On the shortcut menu, click Continue Numbering. Word changes the 1 back to a 4.
10. Type **Park behind the building.** Press ENTER.
11. With the insertion point positioned on line five in the numbered list, click the Increase Indent button. The item is demoted one level.

(continued)

Try It! Creating a Numbered List *(continued)*

12. Type **You will need quarters for the meter.** Press ENTER .
13. In the Paragraph group, click the Decrease Indent button. The current line is promoted one level.
14. Right-click the number 1 marking the first item in the numbered list.
15. On the shortcut menu, click Set Numbering Value.
16. Use the Set value to increment arrows to enter 5 in the box, and then click OK. Word changes the first number to a 5, and renumbers the other items in the list accordingly.
17. Select all the lines in the numbered list.
18. In the Paragraph group, click the Numbering drop-down arrow to open the Numbering Library.
19. Click the list that uses lowercase letters followed by parentheses.
20. Save the changes to the document and leave it open in Word to use in the next Try It.

Changing the Bullet or Number Formatting

- You can create a customized bullet or number by changing the font and/or paragraph formatting.
- The commands for changing the font and paragraph formatting are the same as for changing the formatting of regular text.

Try It! Changing the Bullet or Number Formatting

1. In the **WTry07a_studentfistname_ studentlastname** document, right-click the first picture bullet and click Font on the shortcut menu to open the Font dialog box.
2. Type **16** in the Size box (or click 16 on the Size list).
3. Click OK to apply the formatting.
4. Right-click the first picture bullet and click Paragraph on the shortcut menu to open the Paragraph dialog box.
5. Select the value in the By text box and type **.75** to increase the Hanging indent setting to 0.75".
6. Click OK to apply the formatting. Notice that is applied to the current line only.
7. Right-click any of the numbers (the letters followed by parentheses) and click Font on the shortcut menu to open the Font dialog box.
8. Click Bold Italic in the Font style list.
9. Click 18 on the Size list.
10. Click the Font color drop-down arrow and click Red under Standard Colors.
11. Click OK to apply the formatting.
12. Select all the lines in the numbered list.
13. Right-click the selection and click Paragraph on the shortcut menu to open the Paragraph dialog box.
14. Use the Left increment arrows to increase the left indent setting to 1.0".
15. Click OK to apply the formatting.
16. Save the changes to the document and close it. Leave Word open to use in the next Try It.

Sorting Paragraphs

- Use the Sort feature to **sort** paragraphs into alphabetical, numerical, or chronological order. Word identifies the type of sort automatically.
- A sort can be ascending (A to Z or 0 to 9) or descending (Z to A or 9 to 0).
- The default sort order is alphabetical ascending.

Try It! Sorting Paragraphs

1. Open WTry07b from the data files for this lesson. Save the file as WTry07b_studentfirstname_studentlastname in the location where your teacher instructs you to store the files for this lesson.
2. Select the items in the bulleted list.
3. On the Home tab, in the Paragraph group, click the Sort button [A↓Z] to open the Sort Text dialog box.
4. Click OK to sort the list in ascending alphabetical order.
5. Click the Sort button [A↓Z] again to open the Sort Text dialog box.
6. Click the Descending option, then click OK to reverse the sort into descending alphabetical order.
7. Select the four numbers.
8. In the Paragraph group, click the Sort button [A↓Z] to open the Sort Text dialog box. Notice that Word selects Number as the sort type. The sort order is still set to Descending, because that was the last option you used.
9. Click OK to sort the list into descending numerical order.
10. Click the Sort button [A↓Z] again, click the Ascending option, and then click OK to reverse the sort into ascending numerical order.
11. Close the document, saving all changes, and exit Word.

Project 13—Create It

Memo with Lists

DIRECTIONS

1. Start Word, if necessary.
2. Create a new blank document and save it as **WProj13_studentfirstname_studentlastname** in the location where your teacher instructs you to store the files for this lesson.
3. Display the rulers and nonprinting characters, if necessary.
4. Set paragraph spacing **Before** to **24** points and paragraph spacing **After** to **36** points.
5. Type **MEMO**, and press ENTER.
6. Apply the **No Spacing** style, type **To:**, press TAB, and type **Desk Management Associates**. Press ENTER.
7. Set a left tab stop at 0.75" on the horizontal ruler.
8. Type **From:**, press TAB, and type your own name. Press ENTER.
9. Type **Date:**, press TAB, and type or insert today's date. Press ENTER.
10. Type **Subject:**, press TAB, and type **Check-in Procedures**. Press ENTER twice.
11. Apply the Normal style and type the following paragraph: **In an effort to reduce the wait at the reception desk for members who forget to bring their ID badges, we are implementing new procedures. Please review the following, and post this memo where you can refer to it as necessary.**

12. Press ENTER, then type **Check-in Procedure** and press ENTER.
13. On the Home tab, in the Paragraph group, click the **Numbering** button to apply the default numbered list format—an Arabic numeral followed by a period—and then type the following four list items, pressing ENTER between each item:

    Greet member politely.

    Ask to see picture identification, such as a driver's license or school ID card.

    Enter the member's name and the type of ID in the Forgotten Badge Log book.

    Press buzzer to allow member to enter.
14. Press ENTER twice to turn off numbering.
15. Type **Check-in Guidelines** and press ENTER.
16. On the Home tab, in the Paragraph group, click the **Bullets** drop-down arrow to display the Bullets Library.
17. Click the diamond pattern bullet (refer to Figure 7-1 on the next page).
18. Type the following list items, pressing ENTER between each item:

    Never let a member wait more than two minutes.

    Call a manager if there is a problem.

    Always be polite and patient.

    Remember that members take priority over telephone calls and co-workers.
19. Press ENTER twice and type **Thank you for your cooperation.**
20. Select the items in the bulleted list. On the Home tab, in the Paragraph group, click the **Sort** button to open the Sort Text dialog box.
21. Verify that the **Ascending** option is selected, and then click **OK** to sort the list into ascending alphabetical order.
22. **With your teacher's permission**, print the memo. It should look similar to Figure 7-1.
23. Close the document, saving all changes, and exit Word.

Figure 7-1

MEMO

To: Desk Management Associates
From: Firstname Lastname
Date: Today's Date
Subject: Check-in Procedures

In an effort to reduce the wait at the reception desk for members who forget to bring their ID badges, we are implementing new procedures. Please review the following and post this memo where you can refer to it as necessary.

Check-in Procedure

1. Greet member politely.
2. Ask to see picture identification, such as a driver's license or school ID card.
3. Enter the member's name and the type of ID in the Forgotten Badge Log book.
4. Press buzzer to allow member to enter.

Check-in Guidelines

- ❖ Always be polite and patient.
- ❖ Call a manager if there is a problem.
- ❖ Never let a member wait more than two minutes.
- ❖ Remember that members take priority over telephone calls and co-workers.

Thank you for your cooperation.

Project 14—Apply It

Revised Memo with Lists

DIRECTIONS

1. Start Word, if necessary, and open **WProj14** from the data files for this lesson.
2. Save it as **WProj14_studentfirstname_studentlastname** in the location where your teacher instructs you to store the files for this lesson.
3. Display the rulers and nonprinting characters, if necessary.
4. Select the text **MEMO** and change the font to **Cambria** and the font size to **18 points**.
5. Replace the sample text *Student's Name* with your own name.
6. Replace the sample text *Today's Date* with the current date.
7. Select the text *If you forget your badge:* and apply the **Bold** font style and a **single underline**.
8. Select the next four lines and apply the numbering format that uses Arabic numbers followed by a parenthesis.
9. Select the four lines beginning with the word *Attend*.
10. Apply bullet list formatting using the check mark bullet symbol.
11. Sort the bulleted list into descending alphabetical order.
12. **With your teacher's permission**, print the memo. It should look similar to Figure 7-2.
13. Close the document, saving all changes, and exit Word.

Figure 7-2

Michigan Avenue Athletic Club
235 Michigan Avenue. Chicago, Illinois 60601

MEMO

To: Club Members
From: Firstname Lastname
Date: Today's Date
Subject: Forgotten badge procedures

Many of you have pointed out that the procedures used to check in members who forget their ID badges are slow and frustrating. As a result, we have implemented new procedures which should make it easier and faster to gain access to the club facilities without scanning your badge.

<u>If you forget your badge:</u>

1) Proceed directly to the reception desk.
2) Tell the desk management associate on duty your name and that you forgot your badge.
3) Show the associate a photo ID, such as a driver's license or school ID card.
4) Enter the facility when the associate presses the entrance buzzer.

Keep in mind that this procedure is for your safety and the security of all club members. Use the following guidelines if you have a problem or complaint with this or any other club policy:

- ✓ Write a letter to the club manager explaining the problem or complaint.
- ✓ Submit a suggestion in the Suggestion Box in the lobby or on the club's Web site.
- ✓ Politely discuss the policy with a club employee.
- ✓ Attend a members' forum to publicly discuss your problem or complaint.

Thank you for your cooperation.

WORDS TO KNOW

AutoShapes
Pre-drawn shapes that come with Word 2010.

Bounding box
A border that displays around the edges of a selected object.

Clip art
Files such as pictures, sounds, and videos that you can insert in an Office document.

Clip collection
A folder used to store clip files in the Microsoft Clip Organizer.

Device driver
A software program that provides the instructions your computer needs to communicate with a device, such as a scanner.

Floating object
An object that is positioned independently from the document text.

Microsoft Clip Organizer
A folder that comes with Office. It contains drawings, photographs, sounds, videos, and other media files that you can insert and use in Office documents.

Object
A graphic, picture, chart, shape, text box, or other element that can be inserted in a document.

Scanner
A device that converts printed documents into digital file formats.

Lesson 8

Inserting Pictures, Text Boxes, and Shapes

➤ What You Will Learn

- Analyzing Objects
- Inserting Pictures
- Inserting a Text Box
- Inserting Shapes
- Resizing and Deleting Objects
- Scanning Content into Microsoft Clip Organizer

Software Skills Use graphics objects, such as pictures, shapes, and text boxes, to illustrate and add visual interest to a document. You can insert picture files from any storage location connected to your computer, including the Microsoft Clip Organizer. You can also use a scanner to convert a printed picture to a file. Once you insert an object, you can resize it to fit properly on the page.

Application Skills The Michigan Avenue Athletic Club has asked you to create flyers announcing classes with the new trainers. In this lesson, you create the flyers using pictures, shapes, and text boxes.

What You Can Do

Analyzing Objects

- **Objects** are elements that can be selected, edited, resized, positioned, and formatted independently from the surrounding text.
- Common objects include pictures, shapes, text boxes, diagrams, charts, and tables.
- When you select an object in a Word document, a **bounding box** and **sizing handles** display around its borders (see Figure 8-1).
- In addition, tabs specifically for use in editing and formatting the object become available on the Ribbon.
- For example, when you select a picture, the Picture Tools Format tab becomes available (see Figure 8-1); when you select a shape, the Drawing Tools Format tab becomes available.
- Many of the commands you use to edit or format one type of object are the same as or similar to those you use to edit or format other types of objects.

Figure 8-1

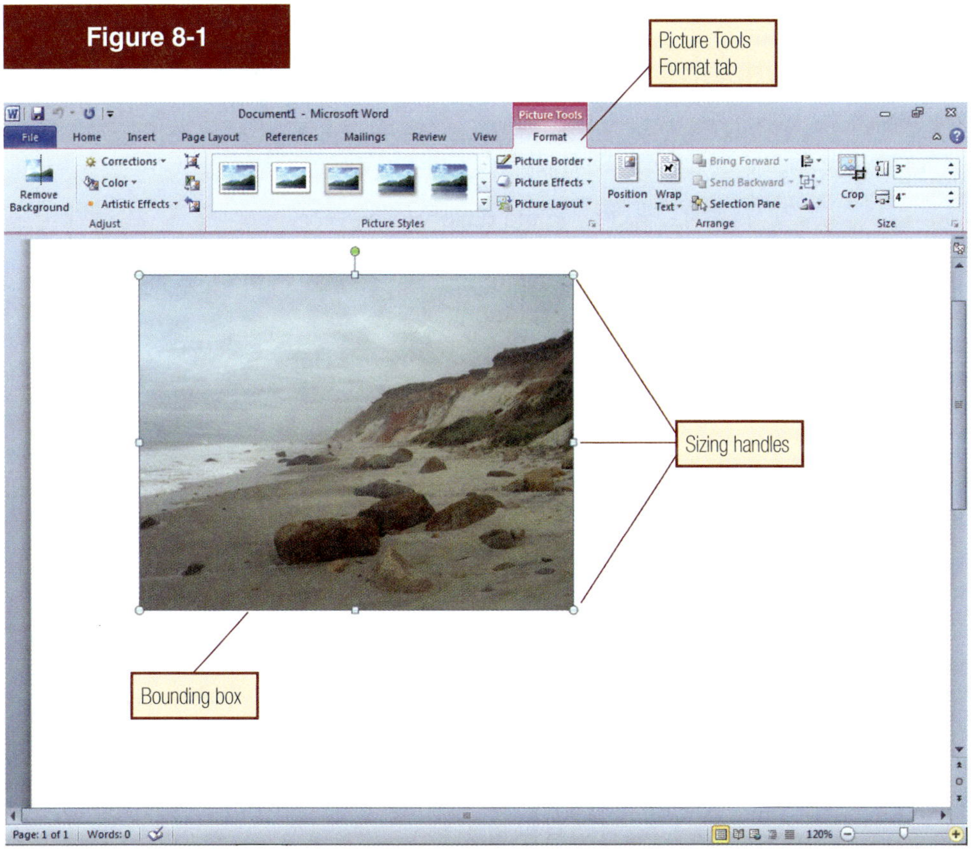

WORDS TO KNOW

Screenshot
A picture of the content currently displayed in a window open on your computer desktop.

Screen clipping
A picture of selected content currently displayed in a window open on your computer desktop.

Sizing handles
Small symbols around the edges of a selected object that you use to resize the object. Corner handles are round, and side handles are square.

Text box
A rectangular drawing object in which text or graphics images can be inserted and positioned anywhere on a page.

USB
Universal Serial Bus. A type of connection used to attach devices such as flash drives, scanners, cameras, and printers to a computer.

Inserting Pictures

- Pictures are graphics files that are inserted as objects in your Microsoft Office documents.
- Some pictures are **clip art**, some are photographs, and some are drawings.

  ✓ *Clip art files also include sound, videos, and animations.*

- You use the Insert Picture command to insert a picture file stored in a location that can be accessed from your computer.
- You use the Insert Clip Art command and the Clip Art task pane to locate and insert clip art files that are stored in the Microsoft Clip Organizer or on the Internet at Office.com.
- You can also insert a **screenshot** or **screen clipping** of any window currently open on your computer desktop.

Try It! Inserting Pictures

1. Start Word and save the default blank document as **WTry08a_studentfirstname_studentlastname** in the location where your teacher instructs you to store the files for this lesson.
2. Click the Insert tab then, in the Illustrations group, click the Picture button.

   ✓ *The Insert Picture dialog box displays*

3. Navigate to the location where the data files for this lesson are stored.
4. Click **WTry08a_picture**.
5. Click Insert.
6. Click anywhere outside the picture to deselect it.
7. Press ENTER twice to move the insertion point down two lines.
8. Click the Insert tab, then, in the Illustrations group, click the Clip Art button.
9. Click in the Search for text box and delete any existing text.
10. Type **computer** and click Go.

    ✓ *The pictures that display in the Clip Art task pane will vary, depending on the Clip Art you have installed on your system.*

11. Click a picture to insert it in the document.
12. Click the Clip Art task pane Close button ×.
13. Scroll up so you can see the top of the document on your screen.
14. Click Start > Microsoft Office Word 2010 to open another Word window, with a blank document displayed. Save the document as **WTry08b_studentfirstname_studentlastname** in the location where your teacher instructs you to store the files for this lesson.
15. Click the Insert tab, then, in the Illustrations group, click the Screenshot button. A gallery of all windows currently open on your desktop displays.
16. In the gallery, click **WTry08a_studentfirstname_studentlastname** to insert a picture of that entire window into the current document.
17. In **WTry08b_studentfirstname_studentlastname**, move the insertion point to the end of the document and press ENTER twice.
18. Click the Insert tab, then, in the Illustrations group, click the Screenshot button.
19. Click Screen Clipping. Word makes the **WTry08a_studentfirstname_studentlastname** document active in clipping mode. It appears dim, and the mouse pointer resembles a cross hair +.
20. Position the mouse pointer in the upper-left corner of the Font group on the Ribbon, then click and drag to the lower-right corner of the Font group.
21. Release the mouse button. Word inserts just the area you selected—the Font group—into the **WTry08b_studentfirstname_studentlastname** document.
22. Close both documents, saving all changes. Leave Word open to use in the next Try It.

Inserting a Text Box

- Insert a **text box** to position several blocks of text on a page or to change the direction of the text.
- You can create a text box by selecting a text box style from the Text Box gallery and then typing text in the text box.
- The text box gallery includes styles for setting up quotes and sidebars, as well as for a simple text box.
- Alternatively, you can draw your own blank text box, or draw a text box around existing text.

Try It! Inserting a Text Box

1. Start Word, if necessary, and open **WTry08c**. Save the file as **WTry08c_studentfirstname_studentlastname** in the location where your teacher instructs you to store the files for this lesson.
2. Move the insertion point to the end of the document.
3. Click the Insert tab, then, in the Text group, click the Text Box button.
4. Click the Austere Quote text box style.
5. Type **"Martha's Vineyard is beautiful even when the ocean is raging and the clouds block the sun."**
6. Click outside the text box to deselect it.

Text Box gallery

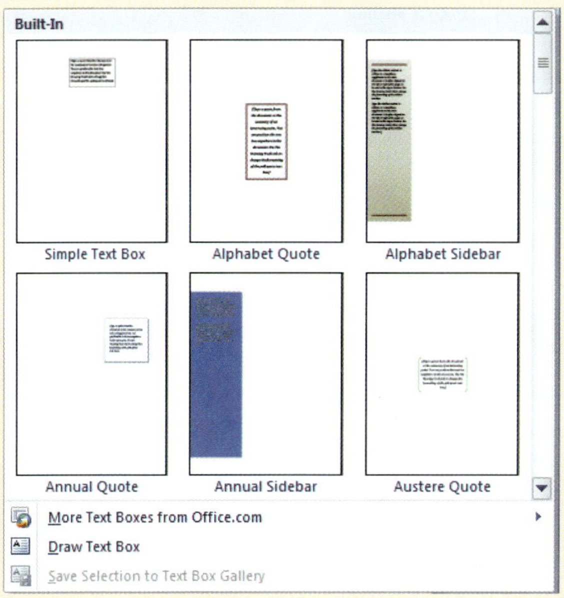

7. Click the boundary, or edge, of the text box to select it.
8. Press DEL.

   ✓ *If the text box remains, you may have positioned the insertion point in the text box instead of selecting the text box. Click the boundary again and make certain the text box is selected before you press* DEL.
9. On the Insert tab, in the Text group, click the Text Box button.
10. Click Draw Text Box. The mouse pointer changes to a crosshair +.
11. Click below the second paragraph of text, where you want to position a corner of the text box, then drag diagonally to draw the box.
12. Release the mouse button when the box is the size you want. The insertion point is inside the box.
13. Type **"Martha's Vineyard is beautiful even when the ocean is raging and the clouds block the sun."**
14. Select the text *Martha's Vineyard Beach Scene*.
15. Click the Insert tab, then, in the Text group, click the Text Box button.
16. Click Draw Text Box.
17. Save the changes to the document and close it. Leave Word open to use in the next Try It.

Inserting Shapes

- Shapes, like pictures and text boxes, are objects you insert into documents.
- You can insert closed shapes, such as ovals and rectangles; lines, such as curves and arrows; or **AutoShapes**, such as hearts, stars, and lightning bolts.
- When you click the Shapes button in the Illustrations group on the Insert tab of the Ribbon, Word displays a gallery of shapes organized into palettes.

  ✓ *Rest the mouse pointer on a shape in the gallery to display a ScreenTip describing the shape.*

- Click a shape in the gallery to select it, and then click and drag in the document to insert the shape in the desired size.
- To insert a shape in the default size, select it and then click in the document.
- When you select an inserted shape, the Insert Shapes gallery becomes available on the Drawing Tools Format tab, so you can easily insert additional shapes.
- By default, Word inserts shapes as **floating objects** so they can be positioned anywhere on a page.
- You can insert a single shape, or combine multiple shapes to create a larger drawing.
- If you use multiple shapes, you can group them together so you can edit and format them as one.
- Use Print Layout view to insert and edit drawing objects.

Try It! Inserting Shapes

1. Create a new blank document in Word, and save it as **WTry08d_studentfirstname_studentlastname** in the location where your teacher instructs you to store the files for this lesson.
2. Click the Insert tab, then, in the Illustrations group, click the Shapes button to display the Shapes gallery.
3. Under Basic Shapes, click the Oval—second from the left in the first row. The mouse pointer changes to a crosshair +.
4. Click and drag diagonally to draw the oval.

   ✓ *Press and hold SHIFT while you drag with the Oval tool to draw a circle. Use the same technique with the rectangle tool to draw a square.*

5. On the Drawing Tools Format tab, in the Insert Shapes group, click the 5-Point Star.
6. Click a blank area on the page. Word inserts the shape in the default size.
7. Click the Insert tab, then, in the Illustrations group, click the Shapes button to display the Shapes gallery.

   ✓ *If a shape is selected in the document, you can click the Line tool on the Drawing Tools Format tab in the Insert Shapes gallery.*

Shapes gallery

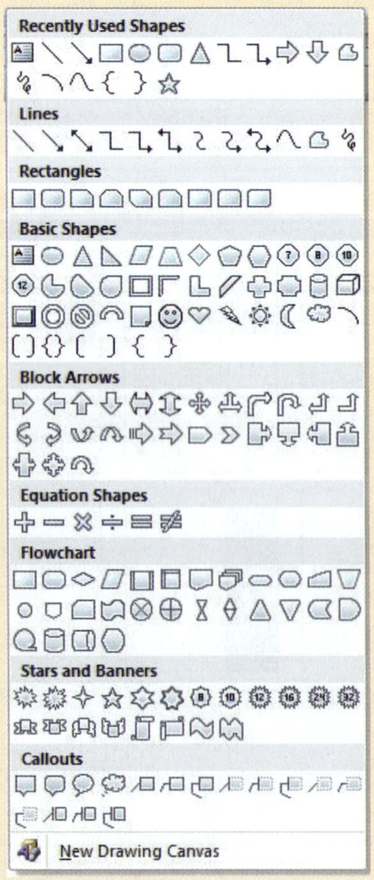

(continued)

Try It! Inserting Shapes *(continued)*

8. Under Lines, click the Line tool—first on the left. The mouse pointer changes to a crosshair.
9. Click and drag in the document below the other two shapes to draw the line.
10. Click Insert > Shapes.
11. Under Lines, click the Curve tool—third from the right. The mouse pointer changes to a crosshair.
12. Click a blank area of the document where you want the line to begin.
13. Click at the first point where you want the line to curve.
14. Click at the next point where you want the line to curve.
15. When you have created all the curves, double-click to end the line.
16. Click Insert > Shapes.
17. Under Lines, click the Freeform tool—second from the right. The mouse pointer changes to a crosshair.
18. Click and hold the mouse button in a blank area of the document where you want the line to begin, then drag to draw freehand as if you are using a pencil, or release the mouse button and click to draw straight lines.
19. When you are finished drawing, double-click to end the line.
20. Click Insert > Shapes.
21. Under Lines, click the Scribble tool—last one on the right. The mouse pointer changes to a crosshair.
22. Click and hold the mouse button in the area of the document where you want the line to begin. The mouse pointer changes to a pencil icon.
23. Drag to draw freehand as if you are using a pencil. For example, sign your name.
24. When you are finished drawing, release the mouse button to end the line.
25. Save the changes to the document and leave it open in Word to use in the next Try It.

Resizing and Deleting Objects

- You can resize an object to make it larger or smaller.
- You can resize it evenly so the height and width remain proportional, or you can resize it unevenly, distorting the image.
- Drag the sizing handles to resize a picture using the mouse.
- Enter a precise size using the Shape Height and Shape Width boxes in the Size group on the Format tab of the Ribbon.

Try It! Resizing and Deleting Objects

1. In the **WTry08d_studentfirstname_studentlastname** document, click the oval shape to select it.
2. Rest the mouse pointer over the sizing handle in the upper-right corner until the pointer resembles a diagonal double-headed arrow.
3. Drag the handle down and to the left to decrease the height and width of the shape at the same time. (When you press the left mouse button, the pointer changes to a crosshair.)
4. Drag the sizing handle in the middle of the right side to the right to increase the width of the object. The height does not change.

(continued)

Try It! Resizing and Deleting Objects *(continued)*

5 Click the Drawing Tools Format tab. In the Size group, use the Shape Height increment arrows [1.5"] to set the height to 3.0".

✓ *If the Height and Width tools are not visible, click the Size button.*

6 Use the Shape Width increment arrows [1.37"] to set the width of the shape to 2.5".

✓ *When you resize some objects, such as photographs, Word may automatically adjust the dimensions to keep the object in proportion.*

7 Position the mouse pointer over the scribble shape.

8 When the Select pointer displays, click to select the shape.

9 Press DEL.

10 Save the changes to the document and leave it open in Word.

Scanning Content into Microsoft Clip Organizer

- Use a **scanner** to convert printed documents into digital files.
- You can scan an image for use in a Microsoft Office program by using the **Microsoft Clip Organizer**, or you can use the software that comes with the scanner.
- You can insert the scanned image into an Office file, such as a Word document.
- You may also copy the image from the Clip Organizer to store it in a different location

  ✓ *For information on copying files, refer to Basics Lesson 7.*

- Other technologies are available for importing content into digital format, including digital cameras, digital video cameras, tablet PCs, and voice recognition devices.
- Before use, a scanner must be connected to the computer system. Most scanners connect via a **USB** cable.
- The first time the device is connected, Windows automatically installs the necessary **device driver** software. If Windows cannot find the correct driver, you may download the driver from the hardware manufacturer's Web site, or insert a driver installation CD that comes with the hardware.
- Images scanned into the Clip Organizer are saved in .jpg format with a default file name, and are stored in a **clip collection** under the scanner identification, which is usually the make and model number.
- The Clip Organizer also includes the following clip collections:
  - My Collections—includes clips that you have stored on your system and sorted into folders such as Favorites. It may also include a Windows folder containing clips that come with Windows, other Windows programs, or clips that you had before you installed Microsoft Office 2010.
  - Office Collections—includes the clips that come with Office and sorted into folders such as People, Animals, Emotions, and Food.
  - Web Collections, which automatically use an open Internet link to access clips stored on Microsoft Office Clip Art and Media online Web site.

Try It! Scanning Content into Microsoft Clip Organizer

1. Follow the manufacturer's instructions to install the scanner for use with your computer, if necessary.
2. Connect the scanner to your computer and turn it on.
3. Place the printed content face down on the scanner surface.
4. Click Start > All Programs > Microsoft Office > Microsoft Office 2010 Tools > Microsoft Clip Organizer.
5. Click File > Add Clips to Organizer > From Scanner or Camera.

   ✓ *Follow the prompts for your scanner to select resolution and other options.*
6. Click Insert.

   ✓ *The scanned image is saved in the Clip Organizer in .jpg format.*

Try It! Inserting a Picture from the Clip Organizer

1. Click Start > All Programs > Microsoft Office > Microsoft Office 2010 Tools > Microsoft Clip Organizer.
2. In the Collection list, click the clip collection named for your scanner make and model. If you did not scan a picture, click the Expand button next to Office Collections and then click Animals.
3. Click the image to insert. When a clip is selected, a drop-down arrow becomes available.
4. Click the clip's drop-down arrow and click Copy on the shortcut menu.
5. Make **WTry08d_studentfirstname_studentlastname** active, and position the insertion point on the first line of the document.
6. On the Home tab, in the Clipboard group, click the Paste button.
7. Close the document saving all changes. Close the Clip Organizer, and exit Word.

   ✓ *If a dialog box displays asking you if you want the clip to be available after the Clip Organizer is closed, click No.*

Project 15—Create It

Fairmont Flyer

DIRECTIONS

1. Start Word, if necessary and save the default document as **WProj15_studentfirstname_studentlastname** in the location where your teacher instructs you to store the files for this lesson.
2. Display the rulers and nonprinting characters, if necessary.
3. Press ENTER five times and type **Spin with David!**
4. Press ENTER to start a new line.
5. On the Home tab, in the Font group, click the **Font Size** drop-down arrow and click **14** to increase the font size to 14 points.

6. Type the following paragraph: **David Fairmont, licensed personal trainer, is starting an early morning spinning class designed specifically to improve cardiovascular health. The 45-minute class will be held Monday through Friday beginning at 5:30 a.m.**
7. Press ENTER four times, click the **Font Size** drop-down arrow and click **18** to increase the font size to 18 points.
8. Type the following paragraph: **David Fairmont is one of the club's new trainers. He holds a master's degree in health management from the University of Vermont in Burlington, Vermont, and specializes in fitness and cardiovascular health.**
9. Click the **Insert** tab and then, in the Illustrations group, click the **Shapes** button to display the Shapes gallery.
10. Under Stars and Banners, click the **Explosion 1** AutoShape (the first shape on the left).
11. Position the mouse pointer over the first paragraph mark at the beginning of the document, then click and drag diagonally down and to the right to draw a shape about 1.0" high by 1.0" wide.
12. On the Drawing Tools Format tab, in the Size group, use the **Shape Height** increment arrows to set the height to **2.0"** and the **Shape Width** increment arrows to set the width to **2.0"**.
15. Select the text **Spin with David!** Click the **Home** tab and click **Heading 1** style in the Styles gallery to apply the style.
16. In the Paragraph group, click the **Center** button to center the text.
17. Click the **Font Size** drop-down arrow and click **48** to increase the font size to 48 points.
18. Click the **Paragraph** group dialog box launcher to open the Paragraph dialog box.
19. Use the **Before** increment arrows to set the Before spacing to **36 pts**, and then click **OK**.
20. Click the **Insert** tab, then, in the Text group, click the **Text Box** button, and click **Draw Text Box**.
21. Position the insertion point about 3.5" down from the top margin and about 1.0" in from the left margin.
22. Click and drag diagonally down and to the right to draw a text box approximately 0.75" high by 5.0" inches wide.
23. Click the **Home** tab, then, in the Font group, click the **Font Size** drop-down arrow and click **24**.
24. Type **Class size is limited so sign up now!**
25. Position the insertion point at the beginning of the last paragraph of text in the document.
26. Click the **Insert** tab and then in the Illustrations group, click the **Picture** button to display the Insert Picture dialog box.
27. Navigate to the location where the data files for this lesson are stored.
28. Click **WProj15_picture** and then click **Insert**.

   ✓ *You may use a scanned picture instead.*

29. On the **Picture Tools Format** tab, in the Size group, use the **Shape Height** increment arrows to set the picture height to **2.0"**. The width should increase automatically to keep the picture in proportion.
30. Double-click in the header area and type your first and last name. Press TAB twice to move to the right tab stop and type or insert today's date.
31. Close the header.
32. Save the changes to the document.
33. **With your teacher's permission**, print the document. It should look similar to Figure 8-2 on the next page.
34. Close the document, saving all changes, and exit Word.

Figure 8-2

Firstname Lastname Today's Date

Spin with David!

David Fairmont, licensed personal trainer, is starting an early morning spinning class designed specifically to improve cardiovascular health. The 45-minute class will be held Monday through Friday beginning at 5:30 a.m.

Class size is limited so sign up now!

David Fairmont is one of the club's new trainers. He holds a master's degree in health management from the University of Vermont in Burlington, Vermont, and specializes in fitness and cardiovascular health.

Project 16—Apply It

Tsai Flyer

DIRECTIONS

1. Start Word, if necessary, and open **WProj16** from the data files for this lesson.
2. Save the file as **WProj16_studentfirstname_studentlastname** in the location where your teacher instructs you to store the files for this lesson.
3. Display the rulers and nonprinting characters, if necessary.
4. Type your full name and today's date in the header.
5. Position the insertion point on the first line of the document and display the Clip Art task pane.
6. Search for pictures using the search text **heart**, and insert an appropriate picture, such as the one shown in Figure 8-3 on the next page. Resize the picture to 1.5" high by 2.18" wide. Close the Clip Art task pane.

7. Insert a Heart AutoShape in the upper-right corner of the page. Resize the shape to 2.0" × 2.0".
8. Apply the **Title** style to the text *Eat Heart Healthy with Sandra!*
9. Increase the font size of the first paragraph to 14 pts.
10. Increase the font size of the text *Class size is limited. Register now so you won't be left out!* to 24 points, and center the text horizontally.
11. Draw a text box around the text.

    ✓ *If one line of text displays below the text box make sure the text box is selected, then press ↓ to nudge the text box down in the document so it displays below the paragraph.*
12. Increase the font size of the last paragraph to 14 pts.
13. Position the insertion point on the blank line between the text box and the last paragraph and insert the data file **WProj16_picture**.

    ✓ *You may use a scanned picture instead.*
14. Resize the picture height to 2.5". The width should adjust automatically to keep the picture in proportion.
15. Save the changes to the document.
16. **With your teacher's permission**, print the document. It should look similar to Figure 8-3.
17. Close the document, saving all changes, and exit Word.

Figure 8-3

Firstname Lastname
Today's Date

Eat Heart Healthy with Sandra!

Are all sugars bad? Do carbs really boost my endurance? Do I need extra protein to maintain lean muscle? Should I be taking supplements? These are some of the questions Sandra Tsai, licensed dietitian, will answer in her new class, Nutrition Facts and Fiction. The class will be held Monday evenings at 7:00 p.m. for four weeks, beginning October 11.

Class size is limited. Register now so you won't be left out!

Sandra Tsai is one of the club's new trainers. She holds a master's degree in Food Science and Human Nutrition from the University of Illinois. She specializes in sports diet and nutrition.

Lesson 9

Formatting Graphics Objects

➤ What You Will Learn

- Wrapping Text Around an Object
- Moving and Positioning an Object
- Formatting Objects
- Modifying Pictures
- Modifying a Text Box
- Adding Text to a Shape
- Changing a Shape

Software Skills You can position and format objects to integrate them into a Word document, making the document easier to read and more interesting for the reader. For example, you can apply styles, or add effects such as shadows or borders.

Application Skills Voyager Travel Adventures is preparing a booklet describing some of the wildlife travelers might encounter while on an African Safari. In this lesson, you will prepare a page describing lions and zebras, formatting pictures, shapes, and text boxes to illustrate the document.

WORDS TO KNOW

3D
A perspective added to a border to give the appearance of three dimensions.

Brightness
The amount of white or black added to a color; sometimes called tint.

Contrast
The difference between color values in different parts of the same image.

Fill
The inside area of a shape or other object.

Outline
The border that defines the outer boundary of a shape or other object.

Saturation
The intensity or depth of a color.

Shadow
An effect designed to give the appearance of a shadow behind a border.

Tone
The amount of gray added to a color.

What You Can Do

Wrapping Text Around an Object

- You can change the wrapping style to affect the way a picture is integrated into the document text. Select from seven wrapping options:
  - In Line with Text: Picture is positioned on a line with text characters.
  - Square: Text is wrapped on the sides of the picture.
  - Tight: Text is wrapped to the contours of the image.
  - Behind Text: Picture is layered behind the text.
  - In Front of Text: Picture is layered on top of the text.
  - Top and Bottom: Text is displayed above and below picture but not on the left or right sides.
  - Through: Text runs through the picture.
- By default, pictures are in line with text.

Try It! Wrapping Text Around an Object

1. Start Word if necessary and open **WTry09**. Save the document as **WTry09_studentfirstname_studentlastname** in the location where your teacher instructs you to store the files for this lesson.
2. Display nonprinting characters and rulers.
3. Click the picture to select it.
4. On the Picture Tools Format tab, in the Arrange group, click the Wrap Text button.
5. Click Square. The text wraps on the right and bottom of the picture.
6. Click the Wrap Text button and click Behind Text.
7. Click the Wrap Text button and click In Line with Text.
8. Save the changes to the document and leave it open to use in the next Try It.

Square text wrapping

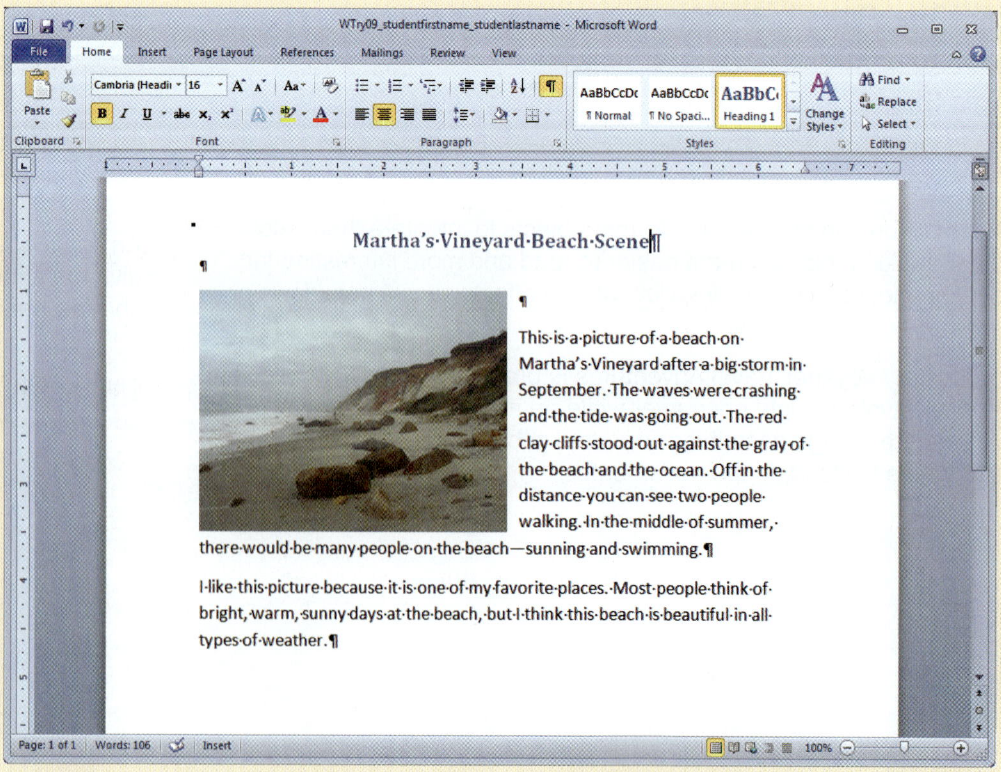

Moving and Positioning an Object

- You can drag an object to a new location.
- You can nudge an object that is not in line with text using the directional arrow keys on your keyboard.
- You can use the Cut and Paste commands to move an inline object the way you would move any character.
- You can position an object relative to the top, bottom, left, right, and middle of a page.
- You can align an object vertically with the top, bottom, or middle or horizontally with the left, right, or middle of the margin or the page.
- You can rotate an object around its center axis or flip it horizontally or vertically.
- Layer objects that overlap to designate which will be in front and which will be in back.
- Group multiple objects together so you can edit or format them as one.

Try It! Moving and Positioning an Object

1. In the **WTry09_studentfirstname_studentlastname** document, click the picture to select it, if necessary
2. Position the mouse pointer over the selected picture until the mouse pointer changes to a four-headed arrow.
3. Drag the picture to the end of the first paragraph of text. As you drag the Move pointer displays.
4. When the vertical bar in the move pointer displays between the period at the end of the paragraph and the paragraph mark, release the mouse button to move the picture.
5. Click the picture to select it, if necessary
6. Click the Picture Tools Format tab, then, in the Arrange group, click the Position button.
7. Under With Text Wrapping, click the style on the right end of the top row—Position in Top Right with Square Text Wrapping.
8. Click the Position button again and click the middle option under With Text Wrapping—Position in Middle Center with Square Text Wrapping.
9. Click the picture to select it, if necessary
10. Click the Picture Tools Format tab, then, in the Arrange group, click the Align button.
11. Verify that the Align to Margin option is selected, and then click Align Left.

    ✓ *A check mark next to the option indicates it is selected. If Align to Page is selected, click Align to Margin, and then repeat steps 10 and 11.*
12. Click the Align button again and click Align Top.
13. Scroll down and click the sun AutoShape to select it.
14. Press → to nudge the shape to the right.
15. Press ↑ five times.
16. Position the mouse pointer over the shape's green rotation handle so it resembles a circular arrow.
17. Drag the handle about one inch to the right to rotate the object clockwise (to the right).
18. Drag the rotation handle about 0.5 inches to the left to rotate the picture counterclockwise (to the left).
19. Scroll up and click the picture to select it.
20. Click the Picture Tools Format tab, then, in the Arrange group, click the Rotate button.
21. Click Flip Vertical.

(continued)

Try It! Moving and Positioning an Object *(continued)*

22. Click the Rotate button and click Flip Horizontal.

23. Click the Rotate button and click Flip Vertical.

24. Save the changes to the document and leave it open to use in the next Try It.

Flip an object

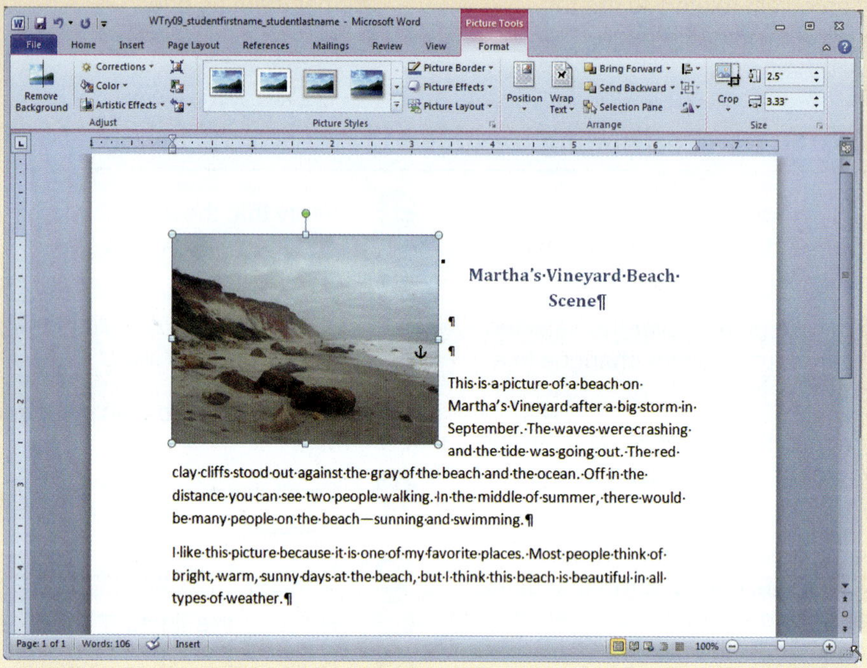

Try It! Layering and Grouping Objects

1. In the **WTry09_studentfirstname_studentlastname** document click the picture to select it, if necessary.

2. Click the Picture Tools Format tab, then, in the Arrange group, click the Position button.

3. Click the style on the left end of the bottom row—Position in Bottom Left with Square Text Wrapping. Scroll down so you can see the objects at the bottom of the page.

4. With the picture still selected, in the Arrange group, click the Send Backward button to move the picture back behind the shape.

5. Click the Bring Forward button to move the picture forward in front of the shape.

6. Click the picture to select it, if necessary.

7. Press and hold SHIFT.

8. Click the shape to select it, and then release SHIFT.

9. On the Picture Tools Format tab, in the Arrange group, click the Group button.

   ✓ *You can select any available Format tab.*

10. Click Group.

11. In the Arrange group, click the Position button and click the style in the middle of the top row—Position in Top Center with Square Text Wrapping. Scroll up to the top of the document to see the grouped objects.

(continued)

Try It! Layering and Grouping Objects *(continued)*

Grouped and layered objects

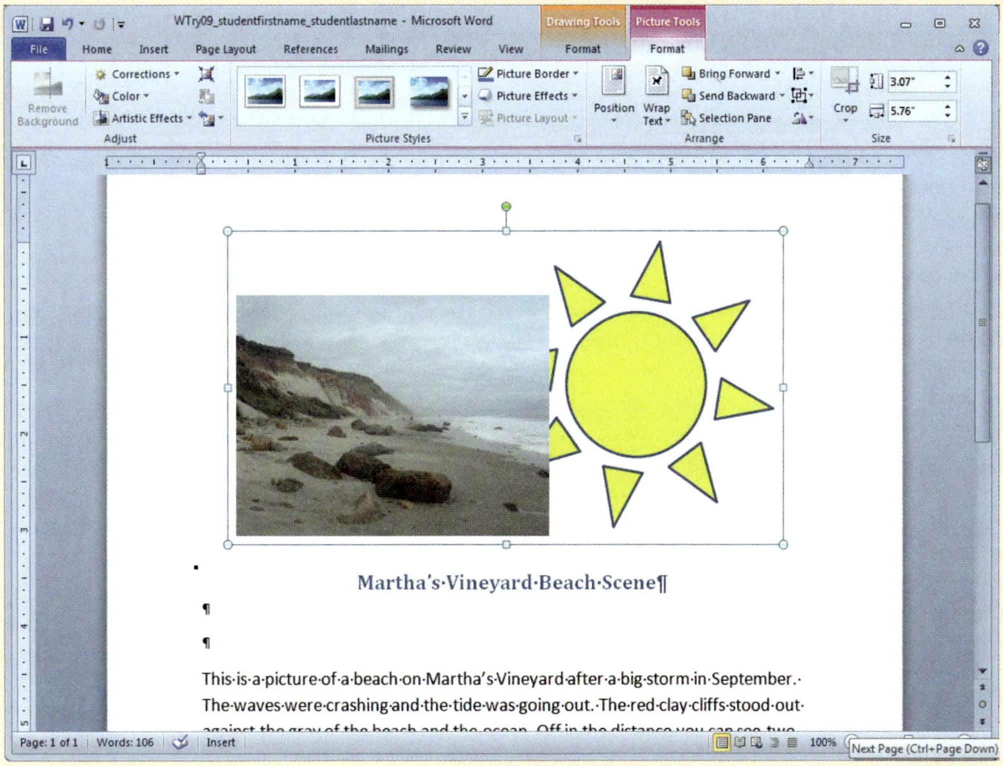

12. Click the group to select it, if necessary.
13. On the Picture Tools Format tab in the Arrange group, click the Group button.

    ✓ *You can select any available Format tab.*

14. Click Ungroup, then click anywhere outside the selected objects to deselect them.
15. Save the changes to the document and leave it open to use in the next Try It.

Formatting Objects

- When you select a graphics object, commands for editing and formatting become available on a Format tab of the Ribbon.
- Each type of object has a gallery of styles you can use to apply a collection of formatting settings, such as **outlines** and **fills**.
- You can also apply outlines and fill settings independently.
- You can use effects such as **3-D** and **shadows** to format objects, as well.

Try It! Formatting Objects

1. In the **WTry09_studentfirstname_studentlastname** document, click the sun AutoShape and drag it to the blank area near the bottom of the page.

   ✓ *You might find it easier to drag the object if you decrease the zoom so you can see the entire page in the document window. Once you move the object, increase the zoom again.*

2. Click the Drawing Tools Format tab, then, in the Shape Styles group, click the More button, ▾ and then click the last style in the gallery—Intense Effect—Orange, Accent 6.
3. Click the picture to select it.
4. Click the Picture Tools Format tab, then, in the Picture Styles group, click the More button, ▾ and then click the last style in the gallery—Metal Oval.
5. Click the picture to select it, if necessary.
6. On the Picture Tools Format tab, in the Picture Styles group, click the Picture Effects button.
7. Click Shadow to display a gallery of shadow styles.
8. Under Perspective, click the first style on the left—Perspective Diagonal Upper Left.
9. Click the AutoShape to select it.
10. On the Drawing Tools Format tab, in the Shape Styles group, click the Shape Fill drop-down arrow.

    ✓ *To quickly apply the color displayed on the button, click the button instead of the drop-down arrow.*

11. Under Theme Colors, click Red, Accent 2.
12. Click the AutoShape to select it, if necessary.
13. On the Drawing Tools Format tab, in the Shape Styles group, click the Shape Outline drop-down arrow.

    ✓ *On the Picture Tools Format tab, it is called the Picture Border button.*

14. Under Theme Colors, click Purple, Accent 4.
15. Click the Shape Outline drop-down arrow again, and click Weight to display a gallery of line weights.
16. Click 6 pt.
17. Save the changes to the document and leave it open to use in the next Try It.

Modifying Pictures

- Use the buttons in the Adjust group on the Picture Tools Format tab to modify the appearance of a picture.
  - Use the Corrections gallery to sharpen or soften a picture, or adjust the **brightness** and **contrast**.
  - Use the Color gallery to change the color palette, **saturation**, or **tone** of the picture.
  - Use the Artistic Effects gallery to apply an effect to make a picture look more like a sketch, drawing, or painting.

Try It! Modifying Pictures

1. In the **WTry09_studentfirstname_studentlastname** document, click the picture to select it.
2. On the Picture Tools Format tab, in the Adjust group, click the Corrections button.
3. Under Brightness and Contrast, click the second style from the left in the bottom row—Brightness: –20%Contrast: +40%.

(continued)

Try It! Modifying Pictures *(continued)*

Corrections gallery

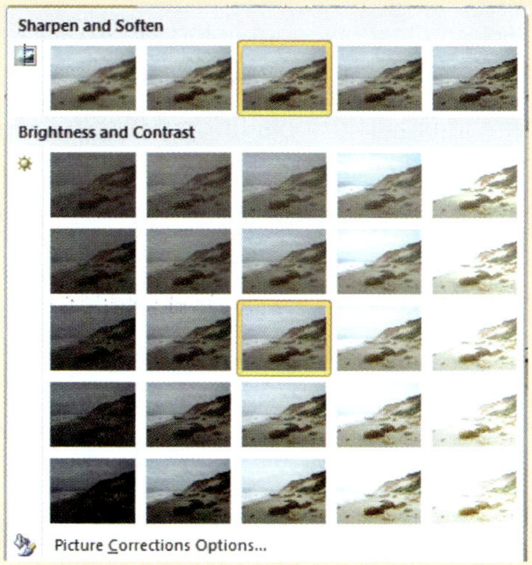

4 On the Picture Tools Format tab, in the Adjust group, click the Color button.

5 Under Recolor, click the style at the right end of the bottom row—Orange, Accent color 6 Light.

6 On the Picture Tools Format tab, in the Adjust group, click the Reset Picture button.

✓ *To reset the picture formatting and size, click the Reset Picture drop-down arrow and click Reset Picture & Size.*

7 On the Picture Tools Format tab, in the Adjust group, click the Artistic Effects button.

8 Rest the mouse pointer on any effect to preview what it does to the picture.

9 Click the style in the middle of the third row—Film Grain.

✓ *Zoom in to get a good look at the effects.*

Color gallery

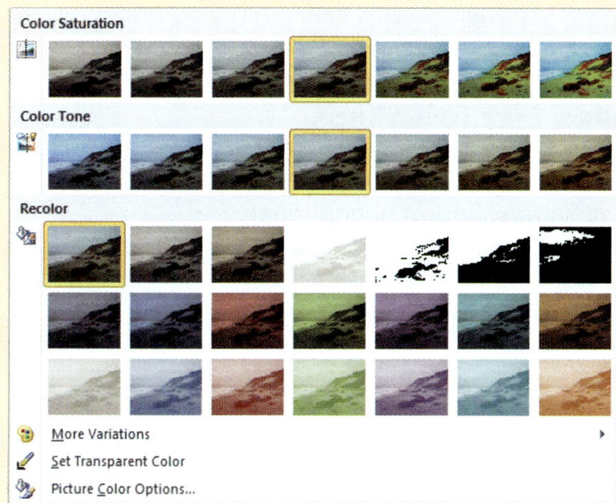

10 Move the picture down about 1.0" and align it with the left margin.

11 Save the changes to the document and leave it open to use in the next Try It.

Modifying a Text Box

- You can format text within a text box using the same commands as you would to format regular text. For example, you can apply fonts and font styles, or change the font size.
  - Select the text box to apply formatting to all text within the box.
  - Select specific text to apply formatting to the selection.
- You can change the direction of text within a text box so it runs horizontally up or down.
  - Rotate the text 90° if you want it to run from the top of the box to the bottom.
  - Rotate the text 270° if you want it to run from the bottom of the box to the top.

Try It! Modifying a Text Box

1. In **WTry09_studentfirstname_studentlastname**, select the title, *Martha's Vineyard Beach Scene*.
2. Click the Insert tab, then, in the Text group, click the Text Box button and click Draw Text Box.
3. With the text box selected, click the Home tab, then, in the Font group, click the Font Size drop-down arrow and click 18.
4. Select the text *Martha's Vineyard* within the text box.
5. Click the Italic button.
6. Click the text box containing the text *Martha's Vineyard Beach Scene* to select it.
7. On the Drawing Tools Format tab, in the Text group, click the Text Direction button.
8. Click Rotate all text 270°.
9. Save the changes to the document and leave it open to use in the next Try It.

Adding Text to a Shape

- You can add text to a shape by inserting a text box within the shape's boundaries.
- By default, the text box does not display borders, so it looks as if the text is inserted in the shape itself.

Changing a Shape

- You can change the shape of an object without affecting the style or formatting.
- For example, you can change a rectangular text box into an oval, or change a star shape into a moon.

Try It! Adding Text to a Shape

1. In the **WTry09_studentfirstname_studentlastname** document, right-click the sun AutoShape.
2. Click Add Text on the shortcut menu.

   ✓ *If there is already text in the shape, the command is Edit Text.*
3. Type **Wow!**.
4. Select the text *Wow!* and increase the font size to 22 points.
5. Save the changes to the document and leave it open to use in the next Try It.

Try It! Changing a Shape

1. In the **WTry09_studentfirstname_studentlastname** document, click the sun AutoShape to select, if necessary.
2. On the Drawing Tools Format tab, in the Insert Shapes group, click the Edit Shape button, then click Change Shape to display the Shapes Gallery.
3. Under Basic Shapes, click the Heart.
4. Close **WTry09_studentfirstname_studentlastname**, saving all changes, and exit Word.

Project 17—Create It

Booklet Page: Lion

DIRECTIONS

1. Start Word, if necessary and save the default document as **WProj17_studentfirstname_studentlastname** in the location where your teacher instructs you to store the files for this lesson.
2. Display the rulers and nonprinting characters, if necessary.
3. Double-click in the header area and type your full name and today's date.
4. Move the insertion point to the first line of the document, type **Lion** and press ENTER.
5. Select the text *Lion* and click **Title** in the Styles gallery to format the text.
6. On the Home tab, in the Paragraph group, click the **Center** button to center the selected text.
7. Move the insertion point to the blank line below the title. Click the **Font Size** drop-down arrow and click **18** to increase the font size, and then type the following two paragraphs:

   One of the most thrilling moments of a Voyager Travel Adventures African Safari is when you encounter a pride of lions. Lions are called the King of Beasts for a reason. They are majestic, huge, and dangerous. They are found in savannas, grasslands, dense bush, and woodlands.

   Lions generally sleep during the day and hunt at night. We often find them lounging on rock formations enjoying the sun. They live in groups called prides, so when we come across one lion there are likely to be others nearby. Usually, there is one male with multiple females. Viewing a pride with cubs is a particularly exciting event.
8. Click the **Insert** tab and, in the Illustrations group, click the **Picture** button to open the Insert Picture dialog box.
9. Navigate to the data files for this lesson and select **WProj17_picture**.
10. Click **Insert** to insert the picture in the document.
11. On the **Picture Tools Format** tab, in the Size group, use the **Height** increment arrows to set the picture height to 2.5". The width should adjust automatically.
12. In the Arrange group, click the **Wrap Text** button, and then click **Square** to apply the Square text wrapping style to the picture.
13. In the Arrange group, click the **Align** button and click **Align Right** to align the picture with the right margin, then click anywhere outside the picture to deselect it.
14. Click the **Insert** tab and, in the Text group, click the **Text Box** button.
15. In the Text Box gallery, scroll down and click the **Stacks Quote** style to insert it into the document.
16. Type **"Seeing a pride of lions was the highlight of my African Safari."**
17. On the Drawing Tools Format tab, in the Arrange group, click the **Wrap Text** button and then click **In Line with Text**. The text box should move up to the beginning of the first paragraph (refer to Figure 9-1 on the next page).
18. On the Drawing Tools Format tab, click the **Shape Styles More** button and click the style in the middle of the fourth row—**Subtle Effect, Olive Green – Accent 3**.
19. Click the **Insert** tab and then, in the Illustrations group, click the **Shapes** button to display the Shapes gallery.
20. Under Stars and Banners, click the **Explosion 1 AutoShape**.

    ✓ *The shape may also be available under Recently Used Shapes.*
21. Click to the right of the title text, *Lion*, and drag to draw a shape 2.0" high by 2.0" wide.

    ✓ *Use the Height and Width increment boxes in the Size group on the Drawing Tools Format tab to adjust the size, if necessary.*

Figure 9-1

Firstname Lastname
Today's Date

Lion

One of the most thrilling moments of a Voyager Travel Adventures African Safari is when you encounter a pride of lions. Lions are called the King of Beasts for a reason. They are majestic, huge, and dangerous. They are found in savannas, grasslands, dense bush, and woodlands.

> *"Seeing a pride of lions was the highlight of my African Safari."*

Lions generally sleep during the day and hunt at night. We often find them lounging on rock formations enjoying the sun. They live in groups called prides, so when we come across one lion there are likely to be others nearby. Usually, there is one male with multiple females. Viewing a pride with cubs is a particularly exciting event.

22. On the **Drawing Tools Format tab,** click the **Shape Styles More** button and click the style in the middle of the second row—**Colored Fill – Olive Green, Accent 3**.
23. Right-click the shape and click **Add Text**.
24. Type **King of the Beasts!**
25. Select the text you just typed. Then, click the **Home** tab. In the Font group, click the **Font Size** drop-down arrow and click **14** to increase the font size.
26. Click the **Drawing Tools Format** tab, click the **Shape Effects** button . Click **Preset**, and click the **Preset 5** style.
27. Click the **Drawing Tools Format** tab. In the Arrange group, click the **Position** button , and then click the style on the right end of the middle row under With Text Wrapping – **Position in Middle Right with Square Text Wrapping**. This positions the shape overlapping the lion picture (refer back to Figure 9-1).
28. With the shape selected, press and hold SHIFT and click the picture to select it, too.
29. Click the **Drawing Tools Format** tab, then, in the Arrange group, click the **Group** button . Click **Group** to group the two objects.
30. Click the **Drawing Tools Format** tab, then, in the Arrange group, click the **Position** button , and then click the style on the right end of the top row under With Text Wrapping – **Position in Top Right with Square Text Wrapping**. This moves the group to the top right.
31. Save the changes to the document.
32. **With your teacher's permission**, print the document. It should look similar to Figure 9-1 on the previous page
33. Close the document, saving all changes, and exit Word.

Project 18—Apply It

Booklet Page: Zebra

DIRECTIONS

1. Start Word, if necessary, and open **WProj18** from the data files for this lesson.
2. Save the file as **WProj18_studentfirstname_studentlastname** in the location where your teacher instructs you to store the files for this lesson.
3. Display the rulers and nonprinting characters, if necessary.
4. Type your full name and today's date in the header.
5. Resize the **Explosion 2** shape in the upper-left corner of the page to 2.0" high by 2.5" wide, and format it with the **Subtle Effect – Red, Accent 2** shape style. Modify the shape outline to increase the outline weight to 3 pts.
6. Add the text **How many zebra can you see?** to the shape, setting the font size to 12 pts.
7. Position the shape in the bottom right of the page with square text wrapping.
8. Resize the **Explosion 1** shape in the upper-right corner of the page to 2.5" high by 2.0" wide.
9. Format it with the **Colored Fill – Red, Accent 2** shape style. Modify the shape outline to increase the outline weight to 3 pts.
10. Position the shape in the bottom right of the page with square text wrapping, so it layers behind the Explosion 2 shape.
11. Group the two shapes.
12. Select the second sentence in the document and draw a text box around it. Rotate the text direction 270° and resize the height of the text box to 4.5".
13. Apply the **Light 1 Outline, Colored Fill – Black, Dark 1** shape style to the text box.

14. Set the text wrapping for the picture to **Square**, increase its height to **2.5"** and align it in the middle right of the document.
15. Drag the grouped shapes up to overlap the lower right of the picture. Bring the group forward to layer it on top of the picture.
16. Save the changes to the document.
17. **With your teacher's permission**, print the document. It should look similar to Figure 9-2.
18. Close the document, saving all changes, and exit Word.

Figure 9-2

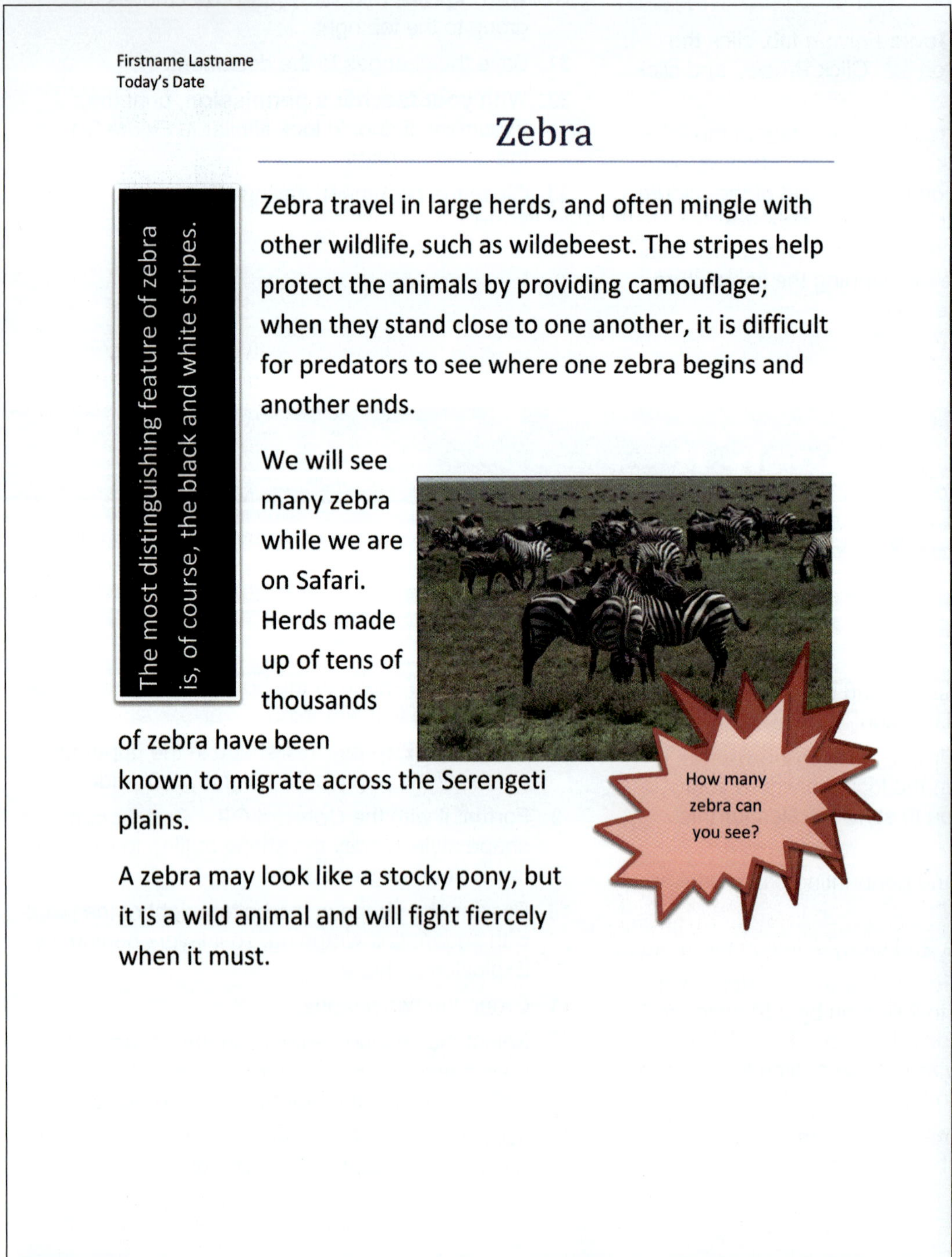

Firstname Lastname
Today's Date

Zebra

The most distinguishing feature of zebra is, of course, the black and white stripes.

Zebra travel in large herds, and often mingle with other wildlife, such as wildebeest. The stripes help protect the animals by providing camouflage; when they stand close to one another, it is difficult for predators to see where one zebra begins and another ends.

We will see many zebra while we are on Safari. Herds made up of tens of thousands of zebra have been known to migrate across the Serengeti plains.

How many zebra can you see?

A zebra may look like a stocky pony, but it is a wild animal and will fight fiercely when it must.

Lesson 10

Working with SmartArt Graphics, Text Effects, and Page Borders

➤ What You Will Learn

- Inserting a SmartArt Graphic
- Entering Text in a SmartArt Graphic
- Modifying the Design of a SmartArt Graphic
- Applying Text Effects
- Applying a Page Border

Software Skills Use Word 2010's SmartArt feature to create diagrams and charts to illustrate data in reports and other documents. You can also apply effects such as shadows or borders to text characters to make the text stand out.

Application Skills Restoration Architecture has recently reorganized its management structure. In this lesson, you use SmartArt graphics to draw a company organization chart in a document. You then use SmartArt graphics to draw a diagram illustrating the new procedures for requesting vacation time off. You apply text effects and page borders to enhance the appearance of the documents.

WORDS TO KNOW

Border
A line placed on one or more sides of a paragraph(s), page, or text box.

Diagram
A chart or graph usually used to illustrate a concept or describe the relationship of parts to a whole.

What You Can Do

Inserting a SmartArt Graphic

- Word comes with a set of SmartArt graphics objects that you can insert to create **diagrams**, such as organization charts or Venn diagrams, in a document.
- Use SmartArt graphics to illustrate information, concepts, and ideas such as the relationship between employees in an organization, or the steps in a procedure.
- To insert SmartArt, click the SmartArt button in the Illustrations group on the Insert tab of the Ribbon to display the Choose a SmartArt Graphic dialog box.
- From that dialog box, you can select a category of diagrams, and then a specific object to insert.
- When you select an object, a description of it and how to use it also displays in the dialog box.

Try It! Inserting a SmartArt Graphic

1. Start Word and open **WTry10**. Save the document as **WTry10_studentfirstname_studentlastname** in the location where your teacher instructs you to store the files for this lesson.
2. Position the insertion point on the last line of the document.
3. Click the Insert tab, then, in the Illustrations group, click the SmartArt button.

   ✓ *The Choose a SmartArt Graphic dialog box displays.*
4. Click Hierarchy in the left pane.
5. Click Organization Chart in the center pane.
6. Click OK.
7. Save the changes to the document and leave it open in Word to use in the next Try It.

Choose a SmartArt Graphic dialog box

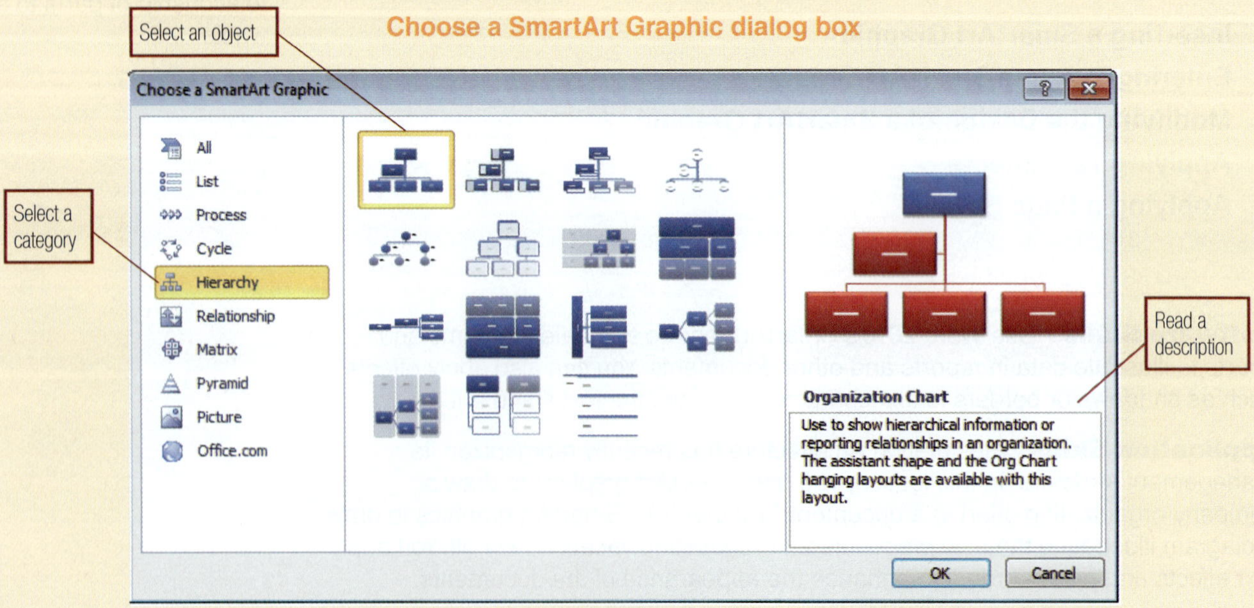

Entering Text in a SmartArt Graphic

- SmartArt objects are comprised of shapes, to which you can add text labels.
- New SmartArt graphics have placeholders in text boxes grouped with the shapes. Select the placeholder to type the text.
- You can edit and format the text using the same commands used to edit and format text in a text box.
- Most SmartArt graphics also have a Text pane as an alternative location for typing text. Select the placeholder in the Text pane and type the text.
- The Text pane is similar to a task pane; you can drag it to move it around the desktop, open it when you need it, and close it when you don't.

Try It! Entering Text in a SmartArt Graphic

1. In the **WTry10_studentfirstname_studentlastname** document with the SmartArt object selected, click the SmartArt Tools Design tab.
2. In the Create Graphic group, click the Text Pane button Text Pane. The button is a toggle; if the Text pane was displayed, clicking the button hides it. If the Text pane was hidden, clicking the button shows it.

   ✓ *You can also click the arrows on the control on the left side of the SmartArt object to display the Text pane.*

3. Click to select the shape at the top of the chart, and then type **President**.
4. Click to select the shape in the middle row and type **Executive Assistant.**
5. In the Text pane, click to select the next placeholder and type **V.P. Sales**.
6. In the Text pane, click to select the next placeholder and type **V.P. Operations**.
7. In the Text pane, click to select the next placeholder and type **V.P. Finance**.
8. Click the Text pane Close button ☒.
9. Save the changes to the document and leave it open in Word to use in the next Try It.

Add text to SmartArt objects

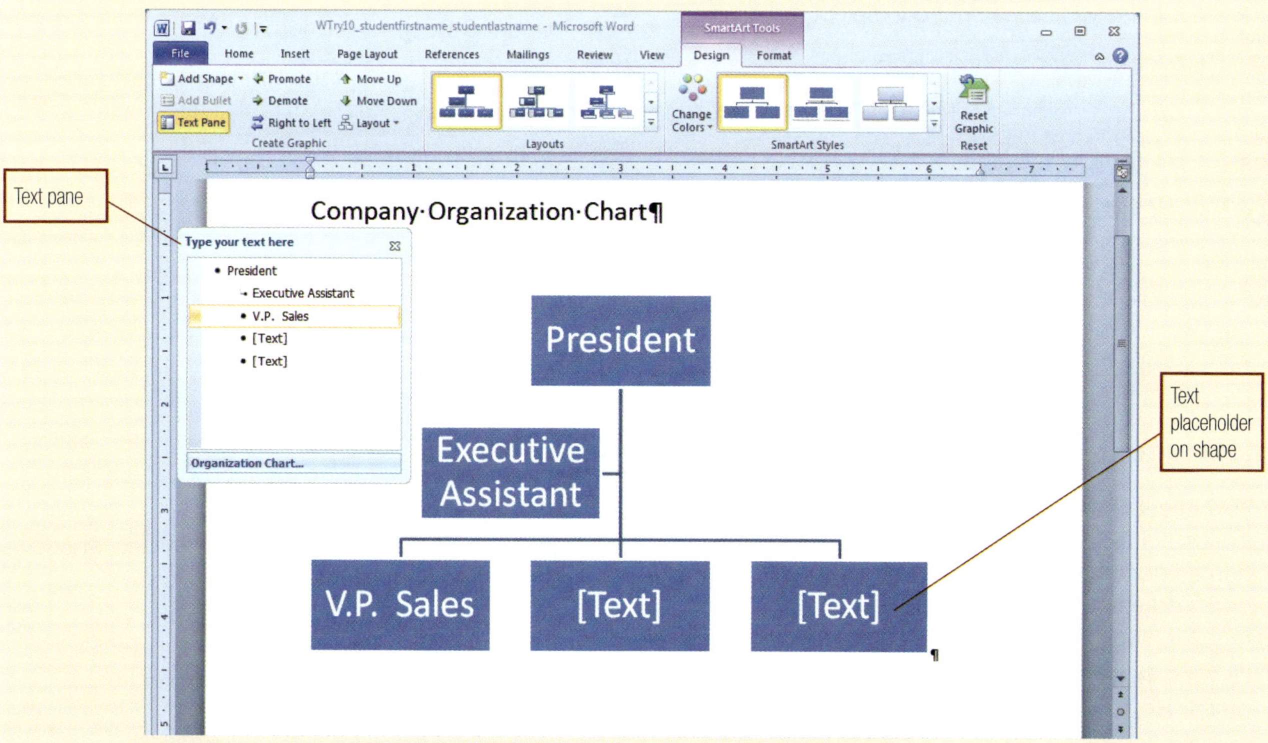

Modifying the Design of a SmartArt Graphic

- SmartArt graphics are inserted using the default design for the selected graphic type.
- You can modify the design of most SmartArt graphics, although the changes depend on the type of graphic you insert. For example, in an organization chart you can promote or demote a shape.
- Use the options on the SmartArt Tools Design tab of the Ribbon to modify the design.
- For most SmartArt graphics, you can add shapes, change the order or position of shapes in the graphic, or change the layout.
- You can usually change colors and styles, as well.
- To apply formatting to a SmartArt graphic or the shapes in a SmartArt graphic, use the commands on the SmartArt Tools Format tab on the Ribbon.

✓ *For more on formatting objects, refer to Word, Lesson 9.*

Try It! Modifying the Design of a SmartArt Graphic

1. In the **WTry10_studentfirstname_studentlastname** document, click the V.P. Sales shape to select it.
2. Click the SmartArt Tools Design tab, then, in the Create Graphic group, click the Add Shape button [Add Shape].
3. Type **Regional Manager**, and then click the President shape.
4. Click the Add Shape drop-down arrow [Add Shape] and click Add Shape Above.
5. Type **CEO**.
6. Click the V.P. Sales shape to select it.
7. Click the Demote button [Demote].
8. Click the Regional Manager shape to select it.
9. Click the Move Up button [Move Up].
10. Click the border around the object to select the entire object.
11. On the SmartArt Tools Design tab, in the Layouts group, click the More button.
12. Click the Hierarchy layout (use ScreenTips to identify the layout).
13. If necessary, select the SmartArt object and then click the SmartArt Tools Design tab.
14. In the SmartArt Styles group, click the Change Colors button.
15. Under Colorful, click Colorful – Accent Colors.
16. Select the SmartArt object and then click the SmartArt Tools Design tab.
17. In the SmartArt Styles group, click the More button.
18. Under 3-D, click Cartoon.
19. If necessary, select the SmartArt object and then click the SmartArt Tools Design tab.
20. In the Reset group, click the Reset Graphic button.
21. Save the changes to the document and leave it open in Word to use in the next Try It.

Applying Text Effects

- Text effects such as shadows, fills, and outlines are useful for adding visual interest to text in printed documents, including flyers, brochures, or advertisements, or in documents viewed on a monitor, such as Web pages or presentations.
- Use the Text Effects button in the Font group on the Home tab of the Ribbon to apply text effects.
- When you click the button, a gallery of text effects displays, or you can use the individual effects options to create your own style.
- Individual effects options include outlines, shadows, reflections, and glows.
- Text effects are not appropriate for use in a business letter or other serious professional document, such as a resume or report.

Try It! Applying Text Effects

1. In the **WTry10_studentfirstname_studentlastname** document, select the text *Company Organization Chart*.
2. Click the Home tab, and then, in the Font group, click the Text Effects button.
3. Click the style at the right end of the bottom row—Gradient Fill – Purple, Accent 4, Reflection.
4. Save the changes to the document and leave it open in Word to use in the next Try It.

Applying a Page Border

- You can apply a **border** to pages in a document.
- Basic border and shading options include line style, line width (weight), and line color.
- Additional border options include 3-D or Shadow effects.
- Word also has a built-in list of artwork designed for page borders. Art borders are useful for stationery, invitations, and other informal, decorative documents.
- You apply page borders using the options in the Borders and Shading dialog box which you access from the Page Background group on the Page Layout tab of the Ribbon.

Try It! Applying a Page Border

1. In the **WTry10_studentfirstname_studentlastname** document, adjust the zoom so you can see the entire page on your monitor.
2. On the Page Layout tab, in the Page Background group, click the Page Borders button.
3. Click the Page Border tab, if necessary.
4. Click the Color drop-down arrow and under Standard Colors, click Purple.
5. Click the Width drop-down arrow and click 1 pt.
6. In the Setting list, click Box.
7. Click OK.
8. Click the Page Layout tab and then click the Page Borders button.
9. Click the Page Border tab, if necessary.
10. Click the Art drop-down arrow to display a gallery of art borders.
11. Scroll down the gallery and click a border of globes.
12. Click OK.
13. Close **WTry10_studentfirstname_studentlastname** saving all changes, and exit Word.

Project 19—Create It

Organization Chart

DIRECTIONS

1. Start Word, if necessary and save the default document as **WProj19_studentfirstname_studentlastname** in the location where your teacher instructs you to store the files for this lesson.
2. Display the rulers and nonprinting characters, if necessary.
3. Double-click in the header area and type your full name. Press ENTER and type today's date.
4. Double-click in the main document area to position the insertion point at the beginning of the document. Type **Restoration Architecture,** press ENTER, and type **Upper Management Organization Chart**.
5. Press ENTER to start a new line.
6. Select the two lines of text. On the Home tab, in the Font group, click the **Font** drop-down arrow and click **Arial** in the list of available fonts.
7. On the Home tab in the Font group, click the **Font Size** drop-down arrow 11 and click **26** to increase the font size.
8. On the Home tab in the Paragraph group, click the **Center** button to center the text.
9. Move the insertion point to the blank line and click the **Insert** tab on the Ribbon.
10. Click the **SmartArt** button to display the Choose a SmartArt Graphic dialog box.
11. In the left pane of the dialog box, click **Hierarchy**.
12. In the center pane of the dialog box, click the **Half Circle Organization Chart**, and then click **OK** to insert the graphic.
13. Verify that the shape at the top of the chart is selected, and type **President/CEO**.
14. Click the **SmartArt Tools Design** tab, then, in the Create Graphic group, click the **Text Pane** button Text Pane to display the Text pane.

    ✓ *If the Text pane is already displayed, skip this step.*
15. In the Text pane, click the second text placeholder and type **Vice President of Operations**.
16. Click the third text placeholder and type **Director of Marketing**.
17. Click the fourth text placeholder and type **Director of Architectural Design**.
18. Click the fifth text placeholder and type **Director of Construction Management**.
19. Click the **Text Pane** button Text Pane to hide the Text pane.
20. On the **SmartArt Tools Design** tab, in the **SmartArt Styles** group, click the **Change Colors** button. Under Accent 2, click the **Colored Outline – Accent 2** style.
21. Click the **SmartArt Styles More** button and, under Best Match for Document, click the **Intense Effect** style.
22. Click the **SmartArt Tools Format** tab and click the **Size** button.
23. Use the Shape Height increment arrows 1.5" to set the **Shape Height** to **5.0"** and the Shape Width increment arrows 1.37" to set the **Shape Width** to **6.5"**.
24. On the SmartArt Tools Format tab, in the Shape Styles group, click the **Shape Outline** drop-down arrow and under Theme Colors, click **Red, Accent 2**.
25. Click the **Director of Marketing** shape to select it, then click the **SmartArt Tools Design** tab.
26. In the Create Graphics group, click the **Add Shape** drop-down arrow Add Shape, click Add Shape Below, and then type **Communications Manager**.
27. Save the changes to the document.
28. Select the text *Upper Management Organization Chart*.
29. Click the **Home** tab on the Ribbon and, in the Font group, click the **Text Effects** button.
30. Click the style on the right end of the third row—**Fill – Red, Accent 2, Double Outline – Accent 2**.
31. Click the **Page Layout** tab and, in the Page background group, click the **Page Borders** button. Click the **Page Borders** tab if necessary.
32. Click the **Color** drop-down arrow and under Theme Colors, click **Red, Accent 2, Lighter 40%.**

33. Click the **Width** drop-down arrow and click **3 pt**.
34. In the **Setting** area, click **Box**, and then click **OK**.
35. Save the changes to the document.
36. **With your teacher's permission**, print the document. It should look similar to Figure 10-1.
37. Close the document, saving all changes, and exit Word.

Figure 10-1

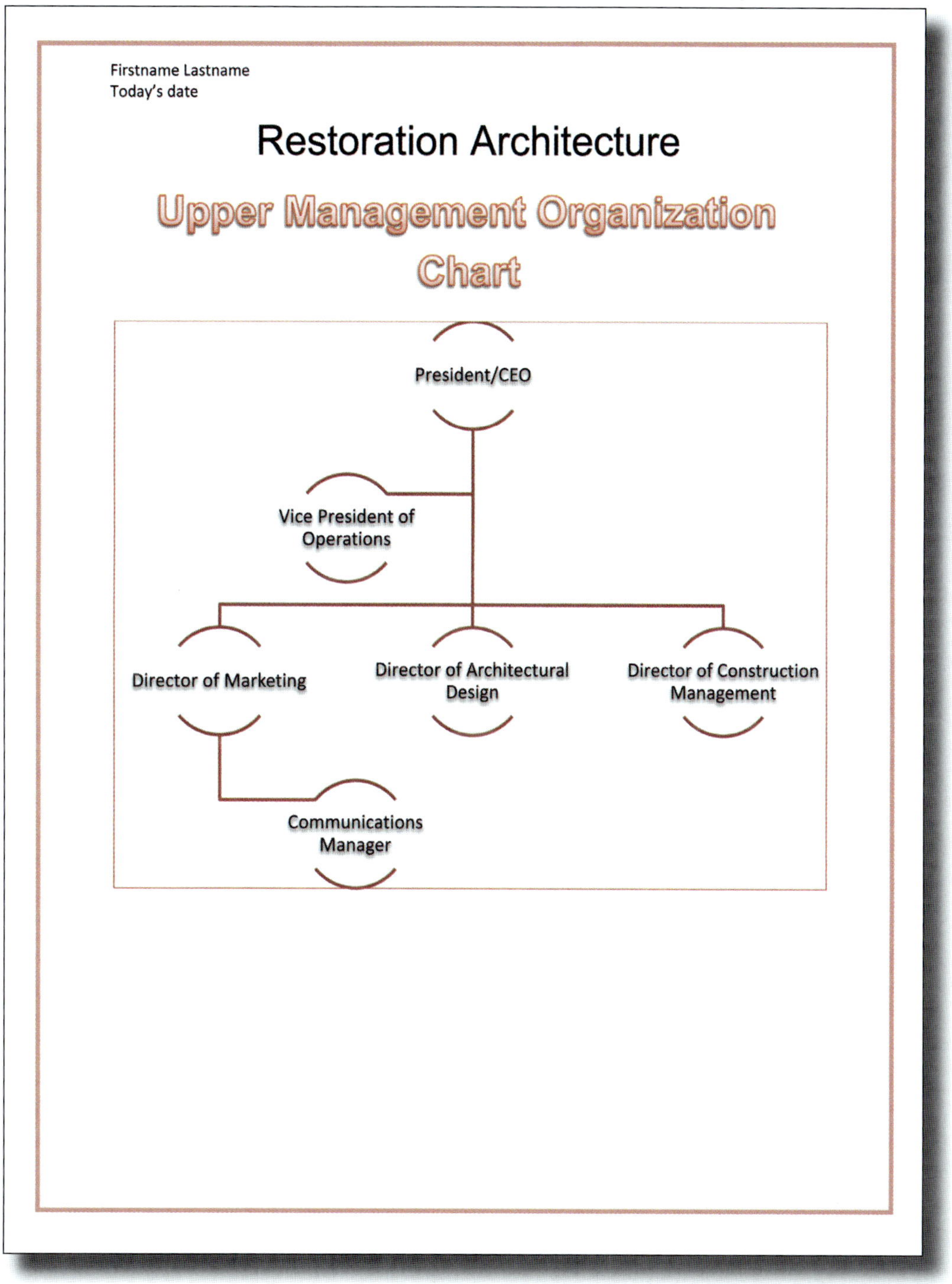

Project 20—Apply It

Process Diagram

DIRECTIONS

1. Start Word, if necessary, and open **WProj20** from the data files for this lesson.
2. Save the file as **WProj20_studentfirstname_studentlastname** in the location where your teacher instructs you to store the files for this lesson.
3. Display the rulers and nonprinting characters, if necessary.
4. Type your full name and today's date in the header.
5. Position the insertion point on the last line of the document.
6. Click the **Insert** tab, and click the **SmartArt** button.
7. Select the **Process** category and then select the **Basic Process** diagram. Click **OK** to insert the diagram in the document.
8. In the first shape on the left, type the text label **1. Discuss schedule with supervisor.**
9. In the middle shape, type the text label **2. Obtain vacation request form from Human Resources dept.**
10. In the shape on the right, type the text label **3. Complete form and submit to supervisor for signature.**
11. With the third shape selected, select to add a shape after.
12. In the new shape, type the text label **4. Submit signed form to Human Resources dept. for approval.**
13. Change the diagram layout to **Step Down Process**.
14. Change the colors to **Dark 1 Outline**.
15. Apply the **Polished 3-D** SmartArt style.
16. Click the border around the object to select it, then resize the height of the object to 4.5" inches. Leave the width at 6.0".
17. Position the object in the **Middle Center with Square Text Wrapping**.
18. Left align the object horizontally on the page.
19. Save the changes to the document.
20. Select the text *Restoration Architecture*.
21. Apply the **Gradient Fill – Blue, Accent 1, Outline – White, Glow – Accent 2** text effects style.
22. Select the text *Vacation Request Procedure* and apply the **Gradient Fill – Blue, Accent 1** text effects style.
23. Apply a **Dark Blue, Text 2, 1½ pt. box** border to the page.
24. **With your teacher's permission**, print the document. It should look similar to Figure 10-2 on the next page.
25. Close the document, saving all changes, and exit Word.

Figure 10-2

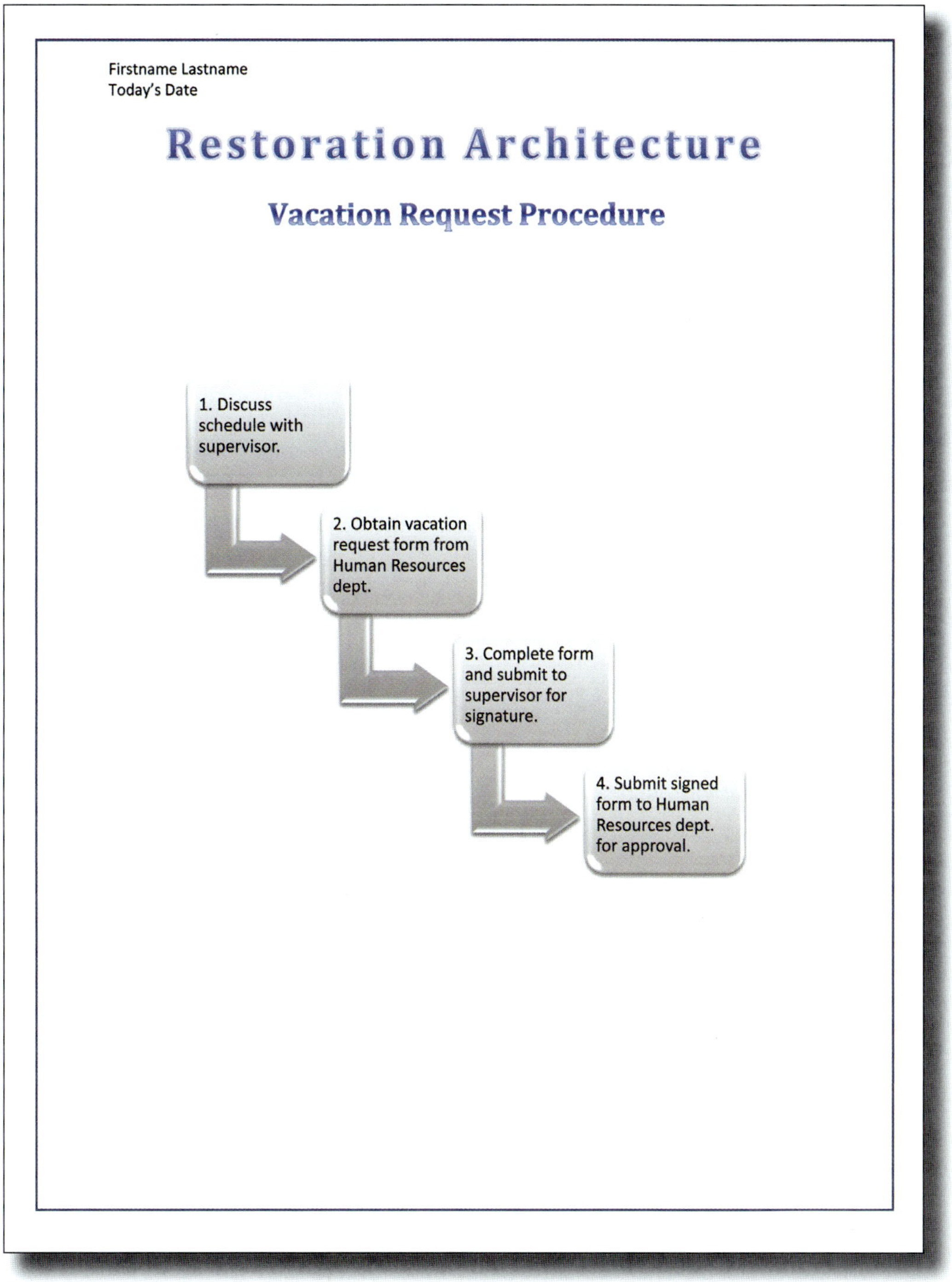
Firstname Lastname
Today's Date

Restoration Architecture

Vacation Request Procedure

1. Discuss schedule with supervisor.

2. Obtain vacation request form from Human Resources dept.

3. Complete form and submit to supervisor for signature.

4. Submit signed form to Human Resources dept. for approval.

Chapter Assessment and Application

Project 21—Make It Your Own

Write a Letter and Create a Flyer

Becoming involved in a student organization such as Future Business Leaders of America-Phi Beta Lambda, Business Professionals of America, or Family, Career and Community Leaders of America, can lead to many opportunities. They sponsor conferences and competitions, encourage leadership, and often offer scholarships for summer programs and college.

In this project, plan an event to publicize student organizations at your school. For example, you might plan a fair at which all organizations have booths or tables where they hand out information, or it might be an assembly at which representatives of the organizations give presentations.

Write a personal business letter to the school principal explaining the event, and asking for permission to hold it. Then design a flyer publicizing the event.

DIRECTIONS

Write the Letter and Create an Envelope

1. Start Word, if necessary. Save a new blank file as **WProj21a_studentfirstname_studentlastname** in the location where your teacher instructs you to store the files for this project.
2. Select a theme and a style set and type a letter to the school principal using full-block or modified block business letter formatting. Be sure to set up the letter correctly, including all the necessary parts, such as a return address, date, and inside address.
3. In the letter, explain your project and why it is important. Politely ask for permission to continue planning the event, and to hold the event, if possible. Be specific about the date and time, and where the event would take place.
4. Proofread the letter to find any spelling or grammatical errors, and correct them.
5. Create an envelope for the letter, using the inside address as the delivery address and your own address as the return address.
6. Add the envelope to the document without changing the default return address.
7. **With your teacher's permission**, print both the letter and the envelope.
8. Close the document, saving all changes.

Create the Flyer

1. Create a new blank document and save it as **WProj21b_studentfirstname_studentlastname** in the location where your teacher instructs you to store the files for this lesson.
2. Select a theme and a style set.
3. Enter and format text and graphics to create a flyer publicizing your event.
4. Use text boxes to make it easier to integrate the text with graphics. Use at least two types of graphics—pictures, clip art, scanned images, shapes, text boxes, or SmartArt.
5. Use font formatting and text effects to enhance the appearance of the document.
6. Use styles and effects to format the graphics objects.
7. Size and position the objects and text to make the document attractive, fun, and easy to read.
8. Use line and paragraph spacing to make the text easy to read, and use list formatting where appropriate.
9. As you work, consider the overall organization and appearance of the document. Use colors that work together, and do not overload the page with too much text or formatting.

10. Include your name and the current date somewhere in the header or footer of the document.
11. When you are satisfied with the document, ask a classmate to review it and make comments or suggestions that will help you improve it.
12. Make changes and corrections, as necessary.
13. **With your teacher's permission**, print the document.
14. Close the document, saving all changes, and exit Word.

Project 22—Master It

Write a Letter and Create an Invitation

Michigan Avenue Athletic Club recently renovated its lobby and locker room. Restoration Architecture was responsible for the design and construction. The club manager has asked you to write a letter to the project manager thanking him for his support during the process and inviting him to the grand reopening celebration.

In this project, you will create and type the letter and an accompanying envelope using modified-block business letter formatting. You will also create an invitation to include with the letter, using graphics, styles, and effects.

DIRECTIONS

Write the Letter and Create an Envelope

1. Start Word, if necessary. Save a new blank file as **WProj22a_studentfirstname_studentlastname** in the location where your teacher instructs you to store the files for this project.
2. Apply the **No Spacing** style, change the font to **12 point Times New Roman**, and type the letter shown in Illustration A on the next page.
   - Type the business name and address in the header.
   - Set a left tab at 3.25" and use it to position the date, closing, signature, and job title lines.
   - Replace the sample text **Today's Date** with the actual date and **Student Name** with your own full name.
   - Apply the Title style to both lines in the header, and then center them horizontally.
3. Proofread the letter to find any spelling or grammatical errors, and correct them.
4. Create an envelope for the letter, using the inside address as the delivery address and **235 Michigan Avenue, Chicago, IL 60601** as the return address.
5. Add the envelope to the document without changing the default return address.
6. **With your teacher's permission**, print both the letter and the envelope.
7. Close the document, saving all changes.

Create the Invitation

1. Open **WProj22b** from the data files for this lesson. Save it as **WProj22b_studentfirstname_studentlastname** in the location where your teacher instructs you to store the files for this lesson.
2. Apply the **Verve** theme and the **Traditional** style set to the document.
3. Select the first line of text, center it horizontally and increase the font size to 36 points. Apply the **Gradient Fill – Dark Purple, Accent 4, Reflection** text effect.
4. Select the second paragraph and apply the **Title** style, then justify the text.

Illustration A

Michigan Avenue Athletic Club
235 Michigan Avenue, Chicago, IL 60601

Today's Date

Mr. George Hernandez
Project Manager
Restoration Architecture
5566 Elm Street, Suite 25B
Chicago, IL 60601

Dear Mr. Hernandez:

I am writing on behalf of the members and employees of Michigan Avenue Athletic Club to thank you for the excellent job designing and renovating the club's lobby and locker rooms. Everyone is very pleased with the completed results.

All the representatives of Restoration Architecture and all the construction workers were courteous and professional. The work was completed with a minimum of disruption. Best of all, it was done on time and within budget.

We are holding our grand reopening on Sunday, April 14 from 2:00 p.m. to 6:00 p.m. (see the enclosed invitation). There will be refreshments, tours, and complimentary access to the club's facilities, including the pool, racquetball courts, and fitness rooms. We hope you will be able to join us so we can express our gratitude in person.

Again, thank you very much for an excellent job, well done.

Sincerely,

Student's Name
Assistant Manager

Enclosure
Invitation

5. Draw a text box around the selection, and resize the box to 3.0" high by 5.5" wide. Format the text box to have no outline, and align it in the center middle of the page.
6. Select the date and time, increase the font size to 20 points and draw a text box around the selection. If necessary, increase the size of the text box so all the text displays.
7. Apply the **Light 1 Outline, Colored Fill – Pink, Accent 1** shape style to the text box, and then apply the **Dark Purple, 18 pt. glow, Accent color 4** Glow shape effect.
8. Position the text box in the **Top Right with Square Text Wrapping**, then change the text wrapping to **Top and Bottom**.
9. Select the five items at the end of the document and increase the font size to 16 points.
10. Format the items as a bulleted list, using the bullet symbol shown in Illustration B on the next page.
11. Change the font color to **Plum, Accent 3, Darker 25%.** Change the hanging indent setting to 0.5".
12. Draw a text box around the list. Resize the box to 1.8" high by 4.0" wide, and apply the **Colored Outline – Pink, Accent 2** shape style. Position the text box in the **Bottom Center with Square Text Wrapping**.
13. Insert an **Explosion 1** shape sized to 1.5" high by 1.7" wide. Add the text **Food!** to the shape, and format the text as **12 pt. Bold**. Apply the **Subtle Effect – Plum, Accent 3** shape style and then rotate the shape about 0.5" to the left.
14. Insert an **Explosion 2** shape sized to 1.5" high by 2.0" wide. Add the text **Fun!** to the shape, and format the text as **12 pt. Bold**. Apply the **Subtle Effect – Dark Blue, Accent 6** shape style and then rotate the shape about 0.5" to the right.
15. Move the **Explosion 2** shape so it overlaps the **Explosion 1** shape, and layer it behind the Explosion 1 shape (refer to illustration B on the next page).
16. Group the two shapes together, and align them above the list text box, centered horizontally on the page. They may overlap the top of the text box.
17. Use the Clip Art task pane to search for a picture of balloons to insert in the document, or insert the picture file **WProj22b_picture**.
18. Recolor the picture to **Pink, Accent color 1 Light**.
19. Resize the picture to 4.5" high by 4.5" wide, and set the text wrapping to **Behind Text**.
20. Align the picture in the top left of the page.
21. Complete the invitation by adding an art page border of balloons.
22. Save the changes to the document. It should look similar to Illustration B on the next page.
23. Type your name and today's date in the footer of the document. (If the text is hidden by the border, Click the Header & Footer Tools Design tab, and change the Footer from Bottom setting to 0.6".)
24. **With your teacher's permission**, print the document.
25. Close the document, saving all changes, and exit Word.

Illustration B

Chapter 2

Editing Documents and Working with Tables

Lesson 11
Checking Spelling and Grammar
Projects 23-24

- Correcting Spelling and Grammar as You Type
- Checking Spelling and Grammar
- Using the Thesaurus
- Controlling Hyphenation
- Analyzing the Use of Hyphens
- Inserting a Non-Breaking Space

Lesson 12
Moving a Selection
Projects 25-26

- Moving Text
- Using Drag-and-Drop and Cut and Paste
- Using Paste Options
- Using Paste Special

Lesson 13
Copying a Selection
Projects 27-28

- Using Copy and Paste
- Using Drag-and-Drop Editing to Copy

Lesson 14
Inserting a Table
Projects 29-30

- Analyzing Tables
- Inserting and Deleting a Table
- Entering Text in a Table
- Selecting in a Table
- Selecting Multiple Components in a Table
- Changing Table Structure
- Formatting a Table
- Viewing Gridlines

Lesson 15
Aligning Tables
Projects 31-32

- Converting Text to a Table
- Inserting Existing Text into a Table Cell
- Setting Column Width and Row Height
- Setting Alignment in a Table Cell
- Setting Tabs in a Table Cell
- Setting Cell Margins
- Aligning a Table Horizontally on the Page

Lesson 16
Drawing a Table
Projects 33-34

- Drawing a Table
- Merging and Splitting Cells
- Changing Text Direction in a Table Cell
- Moving and Resizing Tables
- Setting Text Wrapping Around a Table

Lesson 17
Performing Calculations in a Table
Projects 35-36

- Performing Addition in a Table
- Applying a Number Format
- Sorting Rows in a Table
- Applying Cell Borders and Shading

Lesson 18
Improving a Document with Find and Replace and AutoCorrect
Projects 37-38

- Using Find
- Using Advanced Find
- Using Find and Replace
- Using Go To
- Using the Navigation Pane
- Browsing by Object
- Using AutoCorrect
- Editing the AutoCorrect List

Lesson 19
Working with Templates and Web Pages
Projects 39-40

- Recognizing File Types
- Opening and Saving Compatible Files
- Analyzing Web Page Files
- Saving a Word Document as a Web Page
- Using Web Layout View
- Saving a Word Document as PDF
- Analyzing a Resume
- Creating a Document Based on a Template
- Using Content Controls
- Saving a Word Document as a Template
- Exploring Templates on Office.com

End-of-Chapter Assessments
Projects 41-42

Lesson 11

Checking Spelling and Grammar

➤ What You Will Learn

- Correcting Spelling and Grammar as You Type
- Checking Spelling and Grammar
- Using the Thesaurus
- Controlling Hyphenation
- Analyzing the Use of Hyphens
- Inserting a Non-Breaking Space

Software Skills A professional document should be free of spelling and grammatical errors. While it is important to always proofread your work for errors, Word can check the spelling and grammar in a document and recommend corrections. You can also use Word to control hyphenation, and to recommend alternative words to improve your writing.

Application Skills The Marketing Director at Michigan Avenue Athletic Club has asked you to create a mission statement for the club. A mission statement is used to define the purpose and goals of a business or organization. In this lesson, you will create two versions of the statement. You will check and correct spelling and grammar, and use the thesaurus to select synonyms. You will also use automatic and manual hyphenation in the documents.

WORDS TO KNOW

Antonyms
Words with opposite meanings.

Compound modifier
Two words combined to act as an adjective.

Compound word
Two or more words combined to create a new or more specific word.

Hyphen
A horizontal bar character used to indicate a split or incomplete word.

Hyphenation zone
The maximum space Word allows between a word and the right margin without inserting a hyphen.

Synonyms
Words with the same meaning.

Thesaurus
A listing of words with synonyms and antonyms.

What You Can Do

Correcting Spelling and Grammar as You Type

- Word checks spelling and grammar as you type and marks suspected errors with a wavy underline. The color of the underline indicates the type of error:
  - Red wavy underlines are spelling errors.
  - Green wavy underlines are grammatical errors such as incorrect punctuation, mismatched case or tense, sentence fragments, and run-on sentences.
  - Blue wavy underlines are possible word choice errors, which are words that are spelled correctly but may be used in the wrong context. For example, if you type *I red the book*, Word applies a blue wavy underline to the word *red*.
- You can ignore the wavy lines and keep typing, or use a shortcut menu to select a correction. Note that these wavy lines do not appear in the document when printed.
- You can also choose to ignore the error, which removes the underline.
- Any word not in the Word dictionary is marked as misspelled, including proper names, words with unique spellings, and many technical terms. You can add words to the Word dictionary so that Word does not mark them as misspelled in the future.
- By default, Word checks for grammar only. You can select to check for grammar and style, and you can even select specific grammar and style rules to check.
- If the wavy underlines distract you from your work, you can turn off the feature.

Try It! Selecting Spelling and Grammar Options

1. Start Word and open **WTry11a** from the data files for this lesson. Save the file as **WTry11a_studentfirstname_studentlastname** in the location where your teacher instructs you to store the files for this lesson.
2. Click File > Options.
3. Click Proofing.
4. Verify that the Check spelling as you type check box is selected.
5. Verify that the Use contextual spelling check box is selected.
6. Verify that the Mark grammar errors as you type check box is selected.
7. Verify that the Check grammar with spelling check box is selected.

   ✓ *A check mark in a box means the option is already selected. If there is no check mark, click the box to select it.*

8. Click OK.
9. Save **WTry11a_studentfirstname_studentlastname**, and leave it open to use in the next Try It.

Word's spelling and grammar options

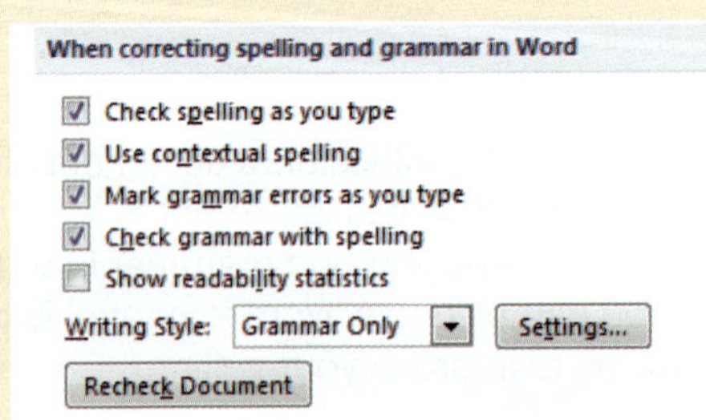

Try It! Correcting Spelling as You Type

1 In the **WTry11a_studentfirstname_studentlastname** file, right-click the first word that has a red, wavy underline: *Advetners*.

2 On the shortcut menu, click Adventures—the correct spelling.

3 Right-click the word *Deshawn*, which also has a red, wavy underline.

4 Click Add to Dictionary.

✓ *When you add a word to the dictionary, it is no longer marked as misspelled.*

5 Right-click the word *Weitzel*.

6 Click Ignore.

✓ *When you ignore an error, the underline is removed from that occurrence only. When you Ignore All, it is removed from all occurrences in the document.*

7 Right-click the word that has a blue wavy underline: *companies*.

8 Click company's on the shortcut menu.

9 Save the changes to the **WTry11a_studentfirstname_studentlastname** file, and leave it open to use in the next Try It.

Use a shortcut menu to correct errors as you type

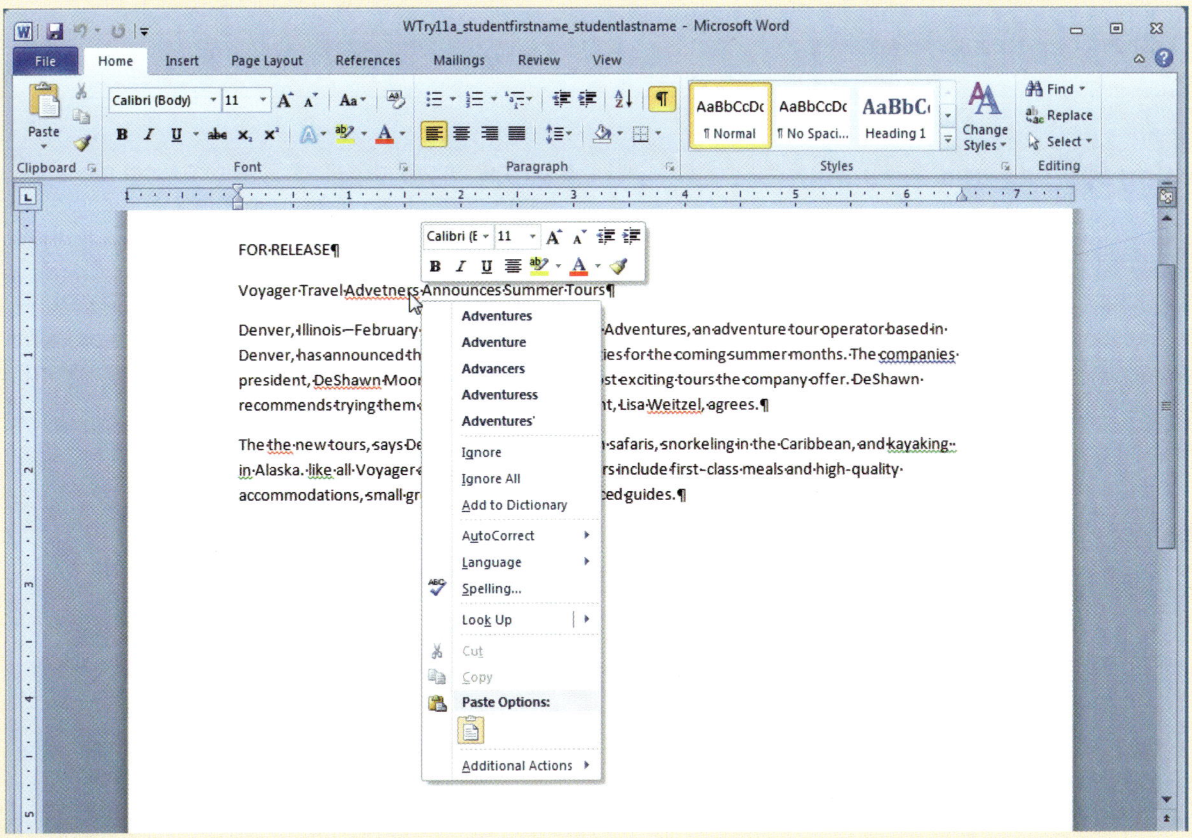

Try It! Correcting Grammar as You Type

1. In the **WTry11a_studentfirstname_studentlastname** file, right -click the first text marked with a green, wavy underline: *company offer.*
2. On the shortcut menu, click company offers.
3. Right-click the third text marked with a green, wavy underline: *like.*
4. On the shortcut menu, click Like.
5. Save the **WTry11a_studentfirstname_studentlastname** file and close it.
6. In Word open **WTry11b** from the data files for this lesson, and save it as **WTry11b-studentfirstname_studentlastname** in the location where your teacher instructs you to store the files for this lesson.
7. Click File > Options > Proofing.
8. Next to Writing Style, click the Settings button.
9. Scroll through the list to see which options are selected.
10. Click the Writing Style drop-down arrow and click Grammar & Style.
11. Scroll through the list to see which options are selected.
12. Click the Writing Style drop-down arrow and click Grammar Only.
13. Click OK.
14. Click OK.
15. Save the changes to the **WTry11b_studentfirstname_studentlastname** file, and leave it open to use in the next Try It.

Checking Spelling and Grammar

- You can check the spelling and grammar in an entire document or in part of a document.
- To check part of a document, you must first select the section you want to check.
- When Word identifies a word that may be misspelled, you can correct the error, ignore it, or add the word to the dictionary.
- When Word identifies a grammatical mistake, you can correct the error or ignore it. You can also click the Explain button to display information about the error.
- To check only the spelling, you can clear the Check grammar check box in the Spelling and Grammar dialog box or on the Proofing tab of the Word Options dialog box.

Try It! Checking Spelling and Grammar

1. In the **WTry11b_studentfirstname_studentlastname** file, click the Review tab. In the Proofing group, click the Spelling & Grammar button.

   ✓ *F7 is the shortcut key to start the spelling and grammar check.*
2. For the first misspelled word, *Advetners*, click the correct spelling, Adventures, in the Suggestions list, and then click Change.
3. For the possible word choice error, click the correct word in the Suggestions list and click Change.
4. For the Subject-Verb Agreement, click company offers and then click Change.
5. For the proper name *Weitzel*, click Ignore Once.
6. For the Repeated Word error, click Delete.

(continued)

Try It! Checking Spelling and Grammar *(continued)*

7 For the error with extra space between words, click *kayaking* in the Suggestions list, and then click Change.

8 For the Number Agreement, click on *African safari* in the Suggestions list, and then click Change.

9 For the Capitalization error, click *Like*, and then click Change.

10 For the last error, press BACKSPACE twice to delete the word a in the error box, and then click Change.

11 Click OK.

12 Save the changes to the file, and leave it open to use in the next Try It.

Use the Spelling and Grammar checker

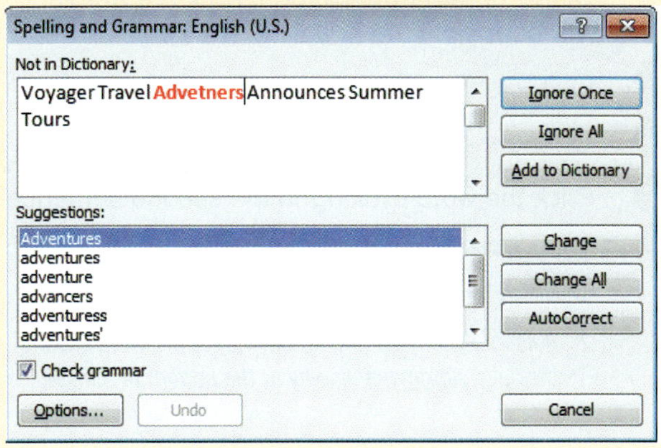

Try It! Editing the Custom Dictionary

1 Click File > Options.

2 Click Proofing.

3 Click Custom Dictionaries.

4 Click Edit Word List.

5 Click DeShawn.

6 Click Delete.

7 Click OK.

8 Click OK.

9 Click OK.

10 Leave the file open to use in the next Try It.

Using the Thesaurus

- A **thesaurus** can improve your writing by helping you eliminate repetitive use of common words and to choose more descriptive words.
- You can use a shortcut menu to quickly find a **synonym** for any word in a document.
- Use Word's thesaurus to look up synonyms, definitions, and **antonyms** for any word. Word displays a list of results in the Research task pane.
  - Click a plus sign to expand the list to show additional words.
  - Click a minus sign to collapse the list to hide some words.
- Use the available drop-down list to insert a word from the results list at the current insertion point location, copy it at a different location, or look it up in the thesaurus.
- Use the Back [Back button] and Forward [Forward button] buttons in the Research task pane to browse through the content you previously viewed in the Research pane.
- By default, Word searches an English thesaurus, but you can select to search different reference sources, including all available reference books, a thesaurus in a different language, or a Web site such as the Microsoft Encarta Dictionary.

Try It! Using the Thesaurus

1. In the WTry11b_studentfirstname_studentlastname file, right-click the word *Announces* in the headline.
2. On the shortcut menu, click Synonyms.
3. On the submenu, click Reveals.
4. Click the word *exciting* in the second sentence.
5. On the Review tab, click the Thesaurus button Thesaurus.

   ✓ *A list of synonyms and antonyms for the word* exciting *displays. Antonyms display at the bottom of the list.*
6. In the Research task pane, click *thrilling*.

   ✓ *A list of synonyms and antonyms for the word* thrilling *displays.*
7. Click the Back button to display the synonyms for exciting again.
8. Rest the mouse pointer on the word *breathtaking*, click the down arrow that displays, and click Insert.
9. Close the Research task pane.
10. Save the changes to WTry11b_studentfirstname_studentlastname, and leave it open to use in the next Try It.

Controlling Hyphenation

- You can set Word to use **hyphens** to break long words at the end of a line instead of wrapping them to the next line.
- Use automatic hyphenation to automatically insert hyphens to break long words at the end of lines in a document or selection. When you edit the document, Word adjusts, or re-hyphenates, the words, as necessary.
- Use optional hyphens to indicate where you want to insert a hyphen if a word falls at the end of a line. Word only uses the optional hyphen if necessary, but you can see it by displaying nonprinting characters.
- Use non-breaking hyphens to prevent a word from breaking at the end of a line. Non-breaking hyphens are useful for hyphenated text that you want to keep together on the same line, such as phone numbers.
- Word uses the **hyphenation zone** to determine whether to automatically hyphenate a word.
  - Make the hyphenation zone wider to reduce the number of automatic hyphens in a document, which usually make the right margin look ragged.
  - Make the hyphenation zone narrower to increase the number of hyphens, which usually makes the right margin neater.

Try It! Controlling Hyphenation

1. In the WTry11b_studentfirstname_studentlastname file, display nonprinting characters, if they are not already displayed.
2. On the Page Layout tab, click the Hyphenation button.
3. Click Automatic.
4. On the Page Layout, click Hyphenation > None.
5. On the Page Layout tab, click Hyphenation > Manual.

   ✓ *Word looks for long words that may require hyphenation, and displays the Manual Hyphenation dialog box. It suggests logical positions for hyphens. The cursor flashes on the selected location.*
6. Click Yes.
7. Click OK.
8. Click to position the insertion point to the right of the letter *h* in the word *breathtaking*.
9. Press CTRL + -.

(continued)

Try It! Controlling Hyphenation *(continued)*

Optional hyphens display as nonprinting characters

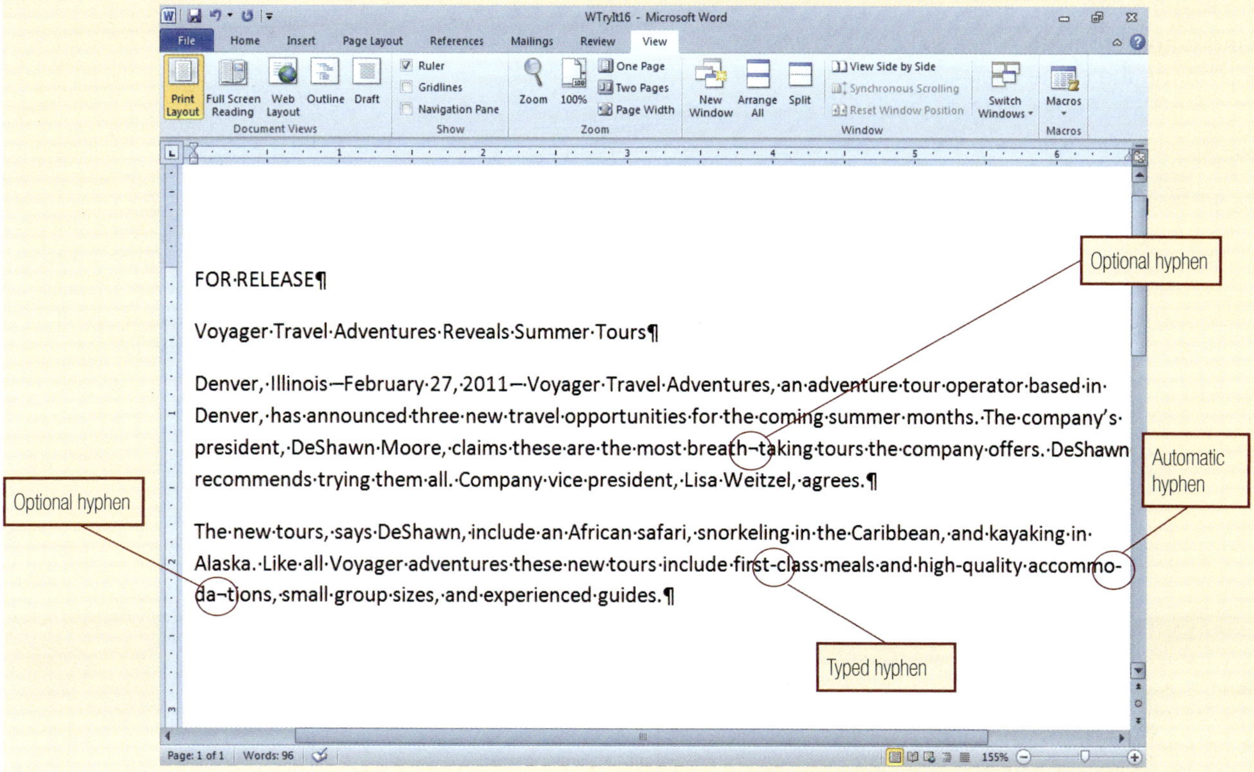

10. Position the insertion point to the right of the hyphen in the word *high-quality*.
11. Press BACKSPACE to delete the hyphen.
12. Press CTRL + SHIFT + -.
13. Click Page Layout > Hyphenation > Hyphenation Options.
14. Use the increment arrows to change the Hyphenation zone setting to 1.0".
15. Click OK.
16. Save the changes to **WTry11b_studentfirstname_studentlastname**, and leave it open to use in the next Try It.

Analyzing the Use of Hyphens

- Most of the time, it is best not to hyphenate; it makes text harder to read.
- When you do hyphenate, insert the hyphen between syllables at a logical point for pausing. Visually, it looks best if the word is split evenly.
- Hyphens may be used in some **compound words** to make them easier to read. For example, mother-in-law is usually hyphenated.
- Hyphens are usually used in **compound modifiers** that come before the noun they describe. For example, She has a ten-year-old brother includes hyphens; Her brother is ten years old, does not.
- They should also be used if the compound modifier can be misinterpreted. Consider the different meanings of the following two sentences:
  - My first-class teacher assigns a lot of homework.
  - My first class teacher assigns a lot of homework.

Inserting a Non-Breaking Space

- When Word wraps text from one line to the next, it breaks the line at a space or—if hyphenation is on—at a hyphen.
- Insert a non-breaking space to keep two words together on the same line.

Try It! **Inserting a Non-Breaking Space**

1. In the **WTry11b_studentfirstname_studentlastname** file, delete the space between the words *in* and *Alaska* in the first sentence of the second paragraph.
2. Position the insertion point between the n and the A, and press CTRL + SHIFT + SPACE. Word insert the non-breaking space—it looks like a small superscript circle, and keeps the two words together on the same line.
3. Close **WTry11b_studentfirstname_studentlastname**, saving all changes, and exit Word.

Project 23—Create It

Mission Statement

DIRECTIONS

1. Start Word, if necessary, and save the default document as **WProj23_studentfirstname_studentlastname** in the location where your teacher instructs you to store the files for this lesson.
2. Display the rulers and nonprinting characters, if necessary.
3. Double-click in the header area and type your full name and today's date.
4. Starting on the first line of the document, type the following:

   The Michigan Avenue Athletic Club is cometted to
5. Right-click the misspelled word **cometted**, and select the correct spelling **committed**.
6. Reposition the insertion point and continue typing:

   excellence. We encourages our employees and our members to strive for the highest goals, meet all challenges with spirit and enthusiasm, and work diligently to achieve personel and professionel harmony.
7. Press ENTER.
8. Right-click the **green wavy underline** in the second sentence and select the correct word, **encourage**. Do not correct the remaining errors.
9. Reposition the insertion point and type the following second paragraph:

   At MAAC, we respects individuality and value diversity. Under the first-rate guidance of General Manager Raimond Petersun and Exercise Director Chardutta Saroj we hope to provide an enviromnent where people feel comfortable, safe,, and free to pursue there physical fitness goals.

10. Save the changes to the document.
11. Move the insertion point to the beginning of the document.
12. Click the **Review** tab and click the **Spelling & Grammar** button to start the spelling checker.
13. When Word stops on the misspelled word **personel**, click the correct spelling, **personal**, in the Suggestions list and then click **Change**.
14. When it stops on **professionel**, click **professional** in the Suggestions list and then click **Change**.
15. When Word stops on the Subject-Verb Agreement for **respects**, click the correct word, **respect**, in the Suggestions list, and then click **Change**.
16. Click **Ignore Once** to skip over the proper name **Raimond**.
17. Click **Add to Dictionary** to add the proper name **Petersun** to the dictionary.
18. Click **Ignore Once** to skip over the proper names **Chardutta** and **Saroj**.
19. For the Possible Word Choice Error, click **their** in the Suggestions list and then click **Change**.
20. For the incorrect punctuation, click **Change** to replace the two commas with one.
21. Correct any other errors that Word identifies, and then click **OK** when the spelling and grammar check is complete.
22. Save the changes to the document.
23. Right-click the word **encourage** in the second sentence, click **Synonyms** on the shortcut menu, and click **embolden** in the list of synonyms.
24. Click on the word **guidance** in the second sentence of the second paragraph.
25. Click **Review** > **Thesaurus**.
26. In the Research task pane, rest the mouse pointer on the word **leadership**, then click the down arrow and click **Insert**.
27. Close the Research task pane.
28. Click **Page Layout** > **Hyphenation** > **Automatic** to automatically hyphenate long words at the end of lines.
29. Click the **Hyphenation** button again, and then click **Manual**.
30. In the first **Manual Hyphenation** dialog box, click **Yes** to accept the hyphen location in the word Manager.
31. Click on the hyphen between the t and the l in the word diligently in the Hyphenate at box to move the hyphen location, and then click **Yes**, and then click **OK**.
32. **With your teacher's permission**, print the document. It should look similar to Figure 11-1.
33. Close the document, saving all changes, and exit Word.

Figure 11-1

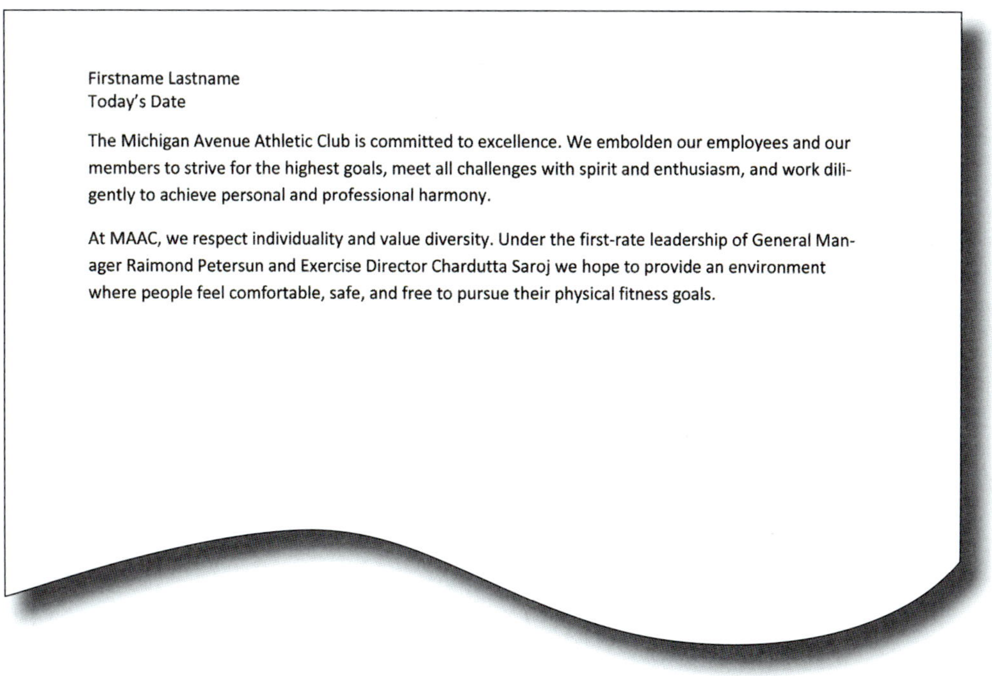

Firstname Lastname
Today's Date

The Michigan Avenue Athletic Club is committed to excellence. We embolden our employees and our members to strive for the highest goals, meet all challenges with spirit and enthusiasm, and work dili-gently to achieve personal and professional harmony.

At MAAC, we respect individuality and value diversity. Under the first-rate leadership of General Man-ager Raimond Petersun and Exercise Director Chardutta Saroj we hope to provide an environment where people feel comfortable, safe, and free to pursue their physical fitness goals.

Project 24—Apply It

Mission Statement

DIRECTIONS

1. Start Word, if necessary, and open **WProj24** from the data files for this lesson.
2. Save the file as **WProj24_studentfirstname_studentlastname** in the location where your teacher instructs you to store the files for this lesson.
3. Display the rulers and nonprinting characters, if necessary.
4. Type your full name and today's date in the header.
5. Right-click the misspelled word *dilligently* in the first paragraph and use the shortcut menu to select the correct spelling.
6. Right-click the grammatical error in the second paragraph. The suggested correction of a single semicolon is incorrect.
7. Press ESC to cancel the shortcut menu and correct the error by selecting the two semicolons and typing a comma.
8. Move the insertion point to the beginning of the document and start the spelling and grammar checker.
9. Click goals in the Suggestions box and then click **Change All** to correct the misspelling of the word *goles* throughout the document.
10. For the number agreement error, select the correct option, **a positive attitude**, and click **Change**.
11. Ignore all proper names that Word marks as not in the dictionary.
12. Click different in the Suggestions box and then click **Change All** to correct the misspelling of the word *diferent* throughout the document.
13. Correct the subject-verb agreement in the first sentence of the third paragraph, and correct both word choice errors in the second sentence of the third paragraph. Select **their** in the Suggestions list to replace the word *there*.
14. Click **OK** when the spelling and grammar check is complete, and save the changes to the document.
15. Use a shortcut menu to replace the word *excellent* in the second sentence of the first paragraph with its synonym *outstanding*.
16. Click the word **things** in the first sentence of the third paragraph and use the thesaurus to display a list of synonyms in the Research task pane.
17. Scroll down the list, and click the word **points** to display its synonyms, then scroll down and click the word **aims** to display its synonyms.
18. Under *goals*, rest the mouse pointer on the word **objectives** and click **Insert**, then close the Research task pane.
19. Start manual hyphenation.
20. Select to insert an optional hyphen between the second and third syllables in the words *responsibility*, *employees*, and *leadership*. Close the dialog box.
21. Display the Hyphenation dialog box and change the **Hyphenation zone** setting to **1.0"**. Click OK.
22. Change the hyphenation setting back to **Automatic**.
23. Change the **Hyphenation zone setting** to **0.1"**.
24. Apply the **Title style** to the text *Michigan Avenue Athletic Club*, and the **Heading 1 style** to the text *Mission Statement*, and then save the changes to the document.
25. **With your teacher's permission**, print the document. It should look similar to Figure 11-2 on the next page.
26. Close the document, saving all changes, and exit Word.

Figure 11-2

Firstname Lastname
Today's Date

Michigan Avenue Ahthletic Club

Mission Statement

The Michigan Avenue Athletic Club is committed to excllence. We encourage our outstanding employees and our loyal members to strive for the highest goals, meet all challenges with spirit, and a positive attitude, and to work diligently to achieve personal and professional harmony.

At Michigan Avenue Athletic Club, we respect individuality and value diversity. Under the first-rate leadership of General Manager Raimond Petersun and Exercise Director Chardutta Saroj we hope to provide an environment where people feel comfortable, safe, and free to pursue their physical fitness goals.

At MAAC, we recognize that different people are motivated by different objectives. We take our responsibility for making sure every individual can achieve their goals very seriously. Our mission, in a nutshell, is to make the highest quality resources available and to provide a safe and nurturing environment.

Lesson 12

Moving a Selection

WORDS TO KNOW

Cut
To delete a selection from its original location and move it to the Clipboard.

Drag-and-drop editing
The action of using a mouse to drag a selection from its original location and drop it in a new location.

Embed
To insert an object created with one program into a file created with a different program.

Link
To create a connection between two files, or the connection itself.

Office Clipboard
A temporary storage area where a selection may be held until it is pasted into a new location.

Paste
To insert a selection from the Clipboard into a document.

➤ What You Will Learn

- Moving Text
- Using Drag-and-Drop and Cut and Paste
- Using Paste Options
- Using Paste Special

Software Skills Move text to rearrange a document quickly without retyping existing information. You can move any amount of text, from a single character to an entire page. You can also move selected graphics and other objects.

Application Skills A summer intern at Voyager Travel Adventures tried to combine multiple documents to create pages for a travel brochure, but was not successful. All of the information you need is in the pages, but it is in the wrong order. In this lesson, you will use different methods to rearrange the contents of two documents into the proper order.

What You Can Do

Moving Text

- Word has many features that make it easy to move text from one location to another.
- One of the simplest methods for moving selected text is to use the F2 key on your keyboard.
- You can use the up arrow key in combination with ALT and SHIFT to move a paragraph up into place before the previous paragraph.
- You can use the down arrow key in combination with ALT and SHIFT to move a paragraph down into place after the next paragraph.
- Be sure to consider nonprinting characters when you select text to move:
  - Select the space following a word or sentence to move along with text.
  - Select the paragraph mark following a paragraph or line to move paragraph formatting and blank lines with text.
- Use Undo to reverse a move that you make unintentionally.

Try It! Moving Text

1. Start Word and open **WTry12** from the data files for this lesson. Save the file as **WTry12_studentfirstname_studentlastname** in the location where your teacher instructs you to store the files for this lesson.
2. Display nonprinting characters.
3. Select the line with the title *Spin with David!* Select the entire line, including the paragraph mark.
4. Press F2.
5. Position the insertion point to the left of the word *David* in the last paragraph.
6. Press ENTER.
7. Click anywhere in the title *Eat Heart Healthy with Sandra!*

   ✓ *Recall that any amount of text that ends with a paragraph mark is a paragraph.*
8. Press ALT + SHIFT + ↑.
9. Press ALT + SHIFT + ↓.
10. Save the changes to **WTry12_studentfirstname_studentlastname**, and leave it open to use in the next Try It.

Using Drag-and-Drop and Cut and Paste

- Use **drag-and-drop editing** to move a selection by dragging it with the mouse.
- Drag-and-drop editing is convenient when you can see the selection to move and the new location on the screen at the same time.
- Use the Cut and Paste commands to move a selection in a document.

  ✓ *For more information on using Cut and Paste and the Office Clipboard, refer to Lesson 5 of the Basics section of this book.*
- The **Cut** command deletes selected text from its original location and moves it to the **Office Clipboard**.
- The **Paste** command copies the selection from the Clipboard to the insertion point location.
- The Cut and Paste commands are in the Clipboard group on the Home tab of the Ribbon or on the shortcut menu when you right-click a selection.
- The shortcut key combination for cutting a selection is CTRL + X.
- The shortcut key combination for pasting a selection is CTRL + V.

Try It! Using Drag-and-Drop and Cut and Paste

1. In the **WTry12_studentfirstname_studentlastname** file, adjust the zoom to 90% so you can see all text in the document.
2. Select the line with the title *Eat Heart Healthy with Sandra!* Include the paragraph mark. (It may still be selected from the previous Try It.)
3. Move the mouse pointer anywhere over the selection.
4. Press and hold the left mouse button.
5. Drag the mouse to position the insertion point at the beginning of the first line of text—*Are all sugars bad?*

   ✓ *As you drag, the mouse pointer changes to the move pointer, which is a box with a dotted shadow attached to an arrow* .
6. Release the mouse button.
7. Select the text *Do carbs really boost my endurance?*
8. On the Home tab, in the Clipboard group, click the Cut button .
9. Position the insertion point at the beginning of the paragraph, to the left of the word *Are*.
10. On the Home tab, click the Paste button . (If necessary, type a space.)
11. Save the changes to **WTry12_studentfirstname_studentlastname**, and leave it open to use in the next Try It.

Using Paste Options

- Use paste options to select formatting for a pasted selection.
- Paste options vary depending on the selection. For text, they usually include the following:
  - *Keep Source Formatting* to maintain formatting from original location
  - *Merge Formatting* to apply formatting used in the destination location to the pasted selection
  - *Keep Text Only* to remove formatting
- For graphics and other objects, paste options may also include:
  - *Use Destination Styles* to apply formatting used in the destination location to the pasted object.
  - *Link & Keep Source Formatting* to **link** the object to the source file and maintain the source formatting.
  - *Link and Use Destination Styles* to link the object to the source file, but apply formatting used in the destination location.
  - *Picture* to insert the object as a picture.
- The available paste options display when you click the drop-down arrow on the Paste button in the Clipboard group on the Home tab.
- Rest the mouse pointer over a paste option before selecting it to preview how completing the paste will affect the document.
- When you paste a selection in a document, Word displays the Paste Options button . Click the button to access a menu of available paste options.

✓ *If the Paste Options button does not display, click File > Options > Advanced, and select the Show Paste Options button when content is pasted check box.*

Try It! Using Paste Options

1. In the **WTry12_studentfirstname_studentlastname** file, select the line *Eat Heart Healthy With Sandra!* including the paragraph mark.
2. On the Home tab, click the Cut button.
3. Position the insertion point at the end of the fourth sentence in the paragraph, to the right of the question mark.
4. On the Home tab, click the Paste drop-down arrow.
5. Under Paste Options, rest the mouse pointer over the Keep Source Formatting button.
6. Look at the document to preview how the text will look if you keep the source formatting.
7. Under Paste Options, click the Merge Formatting button.
8. In the document, click the Paste Options button.
9. Click the Keep Text Only button.
10. Save the changes to **WTry12_studentfirstname_studentlastname**, and leave it open to use in the next Try It.

Using Paste Special

- As an alternative to paste options, you can use the Paste Special dialog box to choose the formatting you want to apply to a pasted selection.
- Paste Special provides additional options, and lets you select specific formatting, such as pasting the selection as a .jpg picture or a .gif picture.
- You also use Paste Special to **link** or **embed** an object created in a different program into a Word document. You will learn about linking and embedding Excel objects in Word documents in Lesson 28 of the Excel section of this book.

Try It! Using Paste Special

1. In the **WTry12_studentfirstname_studentlastname** file, select the line *Spin with David!* including the paragraph mark.
2. On the Home tab, click the Cut button.
3. Position the insertion point at the end of the paragraph, to the left of the paragraph mark.
4. Click the Paste drop-down arrow.

   ✓ *Notice that there are three paste options available.*
5. Click Paste Special to display the Paste Special dialog box.

   ✓ *Notice there are more than three paste options available in the As list in the Paste Special dialog box. The options in the box vary depending on the type of content on the Clipboard.*

(continued)

Try It! **Using Paste Special** *(continued)*

6. In the As list, click Picture, and then click OK.
7. In the document, click on the pasted selection. Note that it is now a picture object: a bounding box and sizing handles display, and the Picture Tools Format tab becomes available on the Ribbon.
8. Close **WTry12_studentfirstname_studentlastname** saving all changes, and exit Word.

Paste Special dialog box

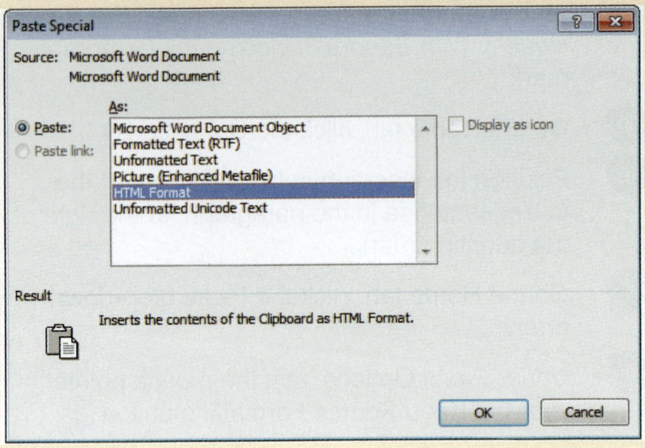

Project 25—Apply It

Safari Brochure Page

DIRECTIONS

1. Start Word, if necessary, and open **WProj25** from the data files for this lesson. Save the file as **WProj25_studentfirstname_studentlastname** in the location where your teacher instructs you to store the files for this lesson.
2. Display the rulers and nonprinting characters, if necessary.
3. Double-click in the header area and type your full name and today's date.
4. Take a moment to look over the document and note how the paragraphs are in the wrong order.
5. Select the first paragraph under the title *Wildebeest!*.
6. Press F2.
7. Scroll down and position the insertion point at the beginning of the second paragraph under the title *Lion!*.
8. Press ENTER.
9. Select the first sentence under the title *Lion!*.
10. Adjust the zoom so you can see the selection and the top of the document on your screen at the same time.
11. Position the mouse pointer over the selection.
12. Press and hold the left mouse button and drag the selection to position the insertion point between the first and second sentences under the title *Wildebeest*.
13. Release the mouse button to drop the selection.
14. Select the text *Zebra!* at the beginning of the last paragraph in the document.
15. Click the **Home** tab, and then click the **Cut** button.
16. Position the insertion point at the beginning of the document to the left of the title **Wildebeest!**.
17. Click the **Paste** drop-down arrow.
18. Under **Paste Options**, rest the mouse pointer on the **Keep Source Formatting** button.
19. Click the **Merge Formatting** button.

20. Delete the text *Wildebeest!*.
21. Click anywhere in the last sentence in the document.
22. Press ALT + SHIFT + ↑ four times to move the paragraph up into position as the middle paragraph in the description of zebra.
23. Save the changes to the document.
24. **With your teacher's permission**, print the document. It should look similar to Figure 12-1.
25. Close the document, saving all changes, and exit Word.

Figure 12-1

Firstname Lastname
Today's Date

Zebra!

Zebra travel in large herds, and often mingle with other wildlife, such as wildebeest. The most distinguishing feature of zebra is, of course, the black and white stripes. The stripes help protect the animals by providing camouflage; when they stand close to one another, it is difficult for predators to see where one zebra begins and another ends.

A zebra may look like a stocky pony, but it is a wild animal and will fight fiercely when it must.

We will see many zebra while we are on Safari. Herds made up of tens of thousands of zebra have been known to migrate across the Serengeti plains.

Lion!

One of the most thrilling moments of a Voyager Travel Adventures African Safari is when you encounter a pride of lions. Lions are called the King of Beasts for a reason. They are majestic, huge, and dangerous. They are found in savannas, grasslands, dense bush, and woodlands.

Lions generally sleep during the day and hunt at night. We often find them lounging on rock formations enjoying the sun. They live in groups called prides, so when we come across one lion there are likely to be others nearby. Usually, there is one male with multiple females. Viewing a pride with cubs is a particularly exciting event.

Project 26—Apply It

Safari Animal Descriptions

DIRECTIONS

1. Start Word, if necessary, and open **WProj26** from, the data files for this lesson.
2. Save the file as **WProj26_studentfirstname_studentlastname** in the location where your teacher instructs you to store the files for this lesson.
3. Display the rulers and nonprinting characters.
4. Type your full name and today's date in the header.
5. Select the paragraph under the title *Lion* and press F2.
6. Position the insertion point under the title *Hyena* and press ENTER.
7. Click anywhere within the paragraph that describes zebra and press SHIFT + ALT + ↑ as many times as necessary to position it under the title *Zebra*.
8. Select the paragraph that describes elephants and use drag-and-drop editing to move it under the title *Elephant*.
9. Select the paragraph that describes cheetahs and use drag-and-drop editing to move it under the title *Cheetah*.
10. Cut the paragraph that describes giraffes.
11. Position the insertion point under the title *Giraffe*, and preview the available paste options. Paste the selection, keeping the source formatting.
12. Cut the paragraph describing lions and paste it under the title *Lion*.
13. Using any or all of the methods for moving text, arrange the titles and their descriptive paragraphs into alphabetical order.
14. Save the changes to the document.
15. **With your teacher's permission**, print the document.
16. Close the document, saving all changes, and exit Word.

Lesson 13

Copying a Selection

➤ What You Will Learn

Using Copy and Paste
Using Drag-and-Drop Editing to Copy

WORDS TO KNOW

Copy
To create a duplicate of a selection.

Software Skills Copy a selection from one location to another when you need to reuse content already entered into a document. You can leave the copied selection intact, or edit it. You can copy or move any amount of text, from a single character to an entire document, and you can copy graphics and objects such as pictures, as well.

Application Skills Whole Grains Bread has asked you to type up a page listing three new franchise locations. The information about each location is similar. Once you type one, you can copy it to use for the other two. To accompany the list, you will use copying techniques to complete a press release announcing new developments at the company.

What You Can Do

Using Copy and Paste

- Use the Copy and Paste commands to copy a selection from one location and paste it to another location.

  ✓ *For more information on using Copy and Paste and the Office Clipboard, refer to Lesson 5 of the Basics section of this book.*

- The **Copy** command stores a duplicate of the selection on the Clipboard, leaving the original selection unchanged.
- You can then use the Paste command to paste the selection from the Clipboard to the insertion point location.

- The Copy and Paste commands are in the Clipboard group on the Home tab of the Ribbon or on the shortcut menu when you right-click a selection.
- The shortcut key combination for copying a selection is CTRL + C.
- The shortcut key combination for pasting a selection is CTRL + V.
- Use Paste Options and Paste Special to control formatting when copying a selection just as you use it when moving text.

✓ *For more information about Paste Options and Paste Special, refer to Lesson 12.*

Using Drag-and-Drop Editing to Copy

- Use drag-and-drop editing to copy a selection by dragging it with the mouse.
- Drag-and-drop is convenient when you can see the content to copy and the new location on the screen at the same time.

Try It! Using Copy and Paste

1. Start Word and open **WTry13** from the data files for this lesson. Save the file as **WTry13_studentfirstname_studentlastname** in the location where your teacher instructs you to store the files for this lesson.
2. Select the text *Eat Heart Healthy with Sandra!,* including the paragraph mark.
3. On the Home tab, in the Clipboard group, click the Copy button.
4. Press CTRL + END to move the insertion point to the end of the document.
5. On the Home tab, in the Clipboard group, click the Paste button.
6. In the document, click the Paste Options button, and click the Merge Formatting button.
7. Save **WTry13_studentfirstname_studentlastname**, and leave it open to use in the next Try It.

Try It! Using Drag-and-Drop Editing to Copy Text

1. In the **WTry13_studentfirstname_studentlastname** file, select the text *Spin with David! without the paragraph mark.*
2. Move the mouse pointer anywhere over the selection.
3. Press and hold CTRL.
4. Press and hold the left mouse button and drag the mouse to the end of the document.

   ✓ *As you drag, the mouse pointer changes to the copy pointer, which is a box with a dotted shadow attached to an arrow.*
5. Release the mouse button.
6. In the document, click the Paste Options button, and click the Merge Formatting button.
7. Close **WTry13_studentfirstname_studentlastname,** saving all changes, and exit Word.

Project 27—Create It

Franchise List

DIRECTIONS

1. Start Word and save the new blank document as **WProj27_studentfirstname_studentlastname** in the location where your teacher instructs you to store the files for this lesson.
2. Display the rulers and nonprinting characters.
3. Double-click in the header area and type your full name and today's date.
4. On the first line of the document, type **New Franchise Information**, and format it using the **Title** style.
5. Press ENTER at the end of the line to start a new paragraph, and type **Park City, Utah**. Format the text using the **Heading 1** style.
6. Press ENTER at the end of the line to start a new paragraph, increase the font size to 12 points, and type **The Park City store is scheduled to open on April 1. It includes a bakery and a cafe that serves sandwiches, pastries, and other light meals. It uses the standard Whole Grains Bread interior design and color scheme, but the exterior has been customized to complement the unique character of the neighborhood.**
7. Press ENTER to start a new line.
8. Type **Seattle, Washington**. Format the text using the **Heading 1** style, and then press ENTER to start a new line.
9. Select the paragraph of text under the heading *Park City, Utah*.
10. On the **Home** tab, in the Clipboard group, click the **Copy** button.
11. Position the insertion point on the blank line under the heading *Seattle, Washington*.
12. On the Home tab, in the Clipboard group, click the **Paste** button.
13. Edit the text in the pasted paragraph to replace the text *Park City* with the text **Seattle**, and the date *April 1* with the date **April 15**.
14. Move the insertion point to the blank line at the end of the document and type **Taos, New Mexico**.
15. Format the text using the **Heading 1** style, and then press ENTER to start a new line.
16. Select the paragraph of text under the heading *Seattle, Washington*.
17. Press and hold CTRL, press and hold the left mouse button, and drag the selection to the blank line under the heading *Taos, New Mexico*.
18. Release the mouse button when the insertion point is in the correct location.
19. Edit the text in the copied paragraph to replace the text *Seattle* with the text **Taos**, and the date *April 15* with the date **May 1**.
20. Save the changes to the document.
21. **With your teacher's permission**, print the document. It should look similar to Figure 13-1 on the next page
22. Close the document, saving all changes, and exit Word.

Figure 13-1

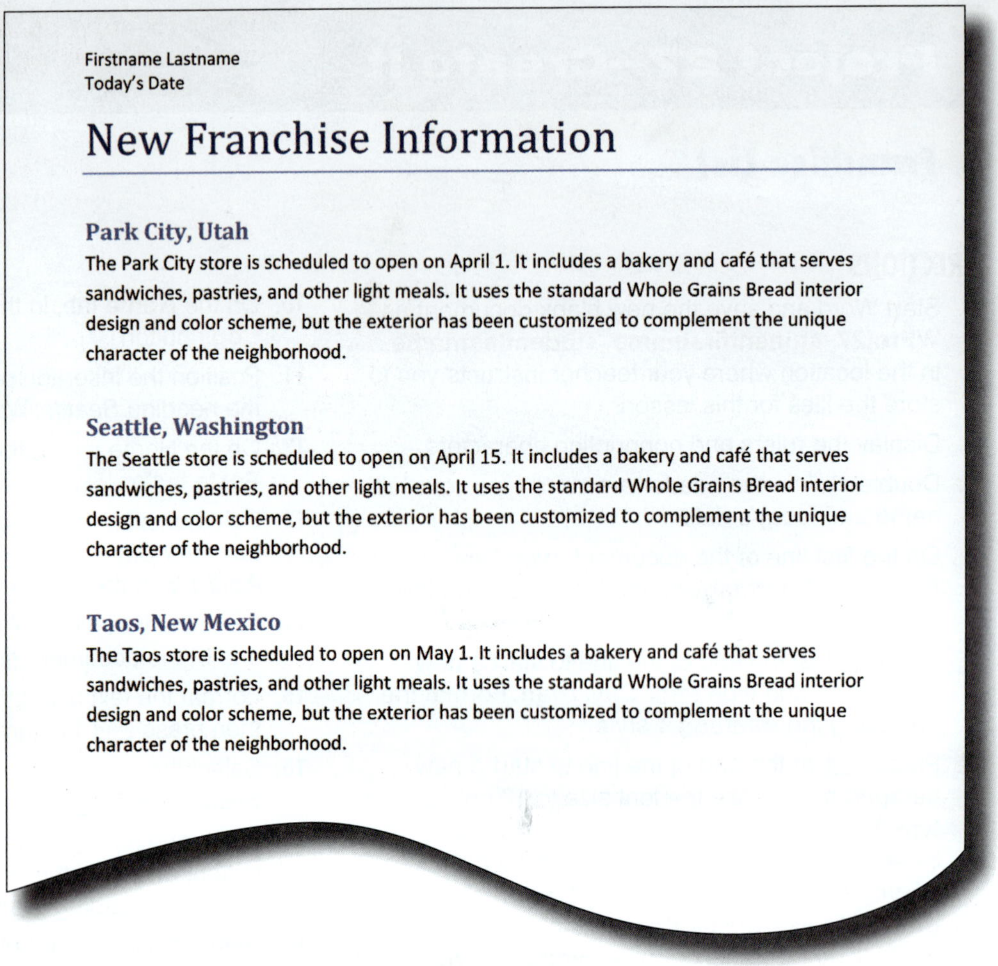
Firstname Lastname
Today's Date

New Franchise Information

Park City, Utah

The Park City store is scheduled to open on April 1. It includes a bakery and café that serves sandwiches, pastries, and other light meals. It uses the standard Whole Grains Bread interior design and color scheme, but the exterior has been customized to complement the unique character of the neighborhood.

Seattle, Washington

The Seattle store is scheduled to open on April 15. It includes a bakery and café that serves sandwiches, pastries, and other light meals. It uses the standard Whole Grains Bread interior design and color scheme, but the exterior has been customized to complement the unique character of the neighborhood.

Taos, New Mexico

The Taos store is scheduled to open on May 1. It includes a bakery and café that serves sandwiches, pastries, and other light meals. It uses the standard Whole Grains Bread interior design and color scheme, but the exterior has been customized to complement the unique character of the neighborhood.

Project 28—Apply It

Press Release

DIRECTIONS

1. Start Word, if necessary, and open **WProj28** from the data files for this lesson.
2. Save the file as **WProj28_studentfirstname_studentlastname** in the location where your teacher instructs you to store the files for this lesson.
3. Display the rulers and nonprinting characters.
4. Replace the sample text *Today's Date* with the actual date, and *Student's Name* with your own name.
5. Move the insertion point to the end of the last paragraph, above the text *For more information contact*.
6. Press ENTER to start a new line and type **New franchise opening dates:**.
7. Press ENTER to start a new line. Change the style to **No Spacing**.
8. Set a left indent at **0.5"**, and a left tab stop at **2.5"**.
9. Select the text *Park City, Utah* in the first paragraph, and copy it to the new blank line you inserted in step 7.

10. Press TAB.
11. Select the text *April 1* in the second paragraph, and copy it to the right of the tab stop. Press ENTER to start a new line.
12. Copy the text *Seattle, Washington* and the date *April 15* to the new blank line.
13. Press ENTER to start a new blank line, and copy the text *Taos, New Mexico* and the date *May 1* to the new blank line.
14. Save the changes to the document.
15. **With your teacher's permission**, print the document. It should look similar to Figure 13-2.
16. Close the document, saving all changes, and exit Word.

For Immediate Release

Whole Grains Bread Announces Exciting New Developments

Larkspur, California—Today's Date—Whole Grains Bread is pleased to welcome three new franchise stores to the family. These three, based in Park City, Utah, Seattle, Washington, and Taos, New Mexico, represent the first wave of an expansion into areas outside of California.

According the company president, Frank Kaplan, the stores are scheduled to open on April 1, April 15, and May 1. The staggered dates provide the company with time to supervise and assist each store with the critical start.

"We have been looking for the right locations, the right franchisees, and the right time to expand for quite a while, now. We look forward to continued success and future growth," said Kaplan.

Whole Grains Bread is a franchise company that operates all natural and organic bakeries and cafes throughout California.

New franchise opening dates:

Park City, Utah	April 1
Seattle, Washington	April 15
Taos, New Mexico	May 1

For more information contact:

Firstname Lastname

Figure 13-2

Lesson 14

Inserting a Table

➤ What You Will Learn

Analyzing Tables
Inserting and Deleting a Table
Entering Text in a Table
Selecting in a Table
Selecting Multiple Components in a Table
Changing Table Structure
Formatting a Table
Viewing Gridlines

Software Skills Create tables to organize data into columns and rows. Any information that needs to be presented in side-by-side columns can be set up in a table. For example, a price list, an invoice, and a resume are all types of documents for which you could use a table. The table format lets you align information side by side and across the page so the information is easy to read.

Application Skills Restoration Architecture is offering in-house computer training courses. In this lesson, you will create a memo that uses a table to list the names of instructors teaching the courses. You will edit the memo to add a course schedule.

What You Can Do

Analyzing Tables

- A **table** is an object that you insert in a Word document.
- Tables are easier to use than tabbed columns when setting up and organizing data in **columns** and **rows**.

WORDS TO KNOW

Border
A line drawn around the edges of an element, such as a table or a table cell. Borders can also be drawn around graphics, paragraphs, and pages.

Cell
The rectangular area at the intersection of a column and a row in a table, into which you enter data or graphics.

Column
A vertical series of cells in a table.

Column markers
Markers on the horizontal ruler that indicate column dividers.

Column width
The width of a column in a table, measured in inches.

Contiguous
Adjacent, or next to, each other.

Dividers
The lines that indicate the edges of cells in a table. Dividers do not print, although they are indicated onscreen by either gridlines or borders.

End of row/cell markers
Nonprinting characters used to mark the end of a cell or a row in a table.

Gridlines
Nonprinting lines that can be displayed around cells in a table.

- You can format an entire document using a table, or integrate a table with text and other objects on a page.
    - You might use a table to format a Web page, because it makes it easy to arrange different elements such as graphics, buttons, and text.
    - You might insert a table in a report so you can include statistical data.
- When you select a table, the Table Tools Design and Table Tools Layout tabs become available on the Ribbon. You use the commands on these tabs to edit, design, and format the table.

Inserting and Deleting a Table

- Use the Table drop-down menu in the Table group on the Insert tab to select commands for inserting a table.
    - You can use the Table grid to select the number of columns and rows you want in the table.
    - You can open the Insert Table dialog box to specify the number of columns and rows.
- Word inserts the table at the insertion point location.
- **Column markers** on the horizontal ruler show the location of the right **divider** of each column.
- By default, Word places a ½-pt. **border** around all **cells** in a table.
- Tables also have three nonprinting elements:
    - **End of cell markers**, which display at the end of all content entered in a cell.
    - **End of row markers**, which display at the end of each row.
    - **Gridlines**, which you can choose to display along the row and column dividers if there are no printing table borders applied to the table.
- When you delete a table, you delete all the data in the table as well.

WORDS TO KNOW

Noncontiguous
Not adjacent, or not next to, each other.

Row
A horizontal series of cells in a table.

Row height
The height of a row in a table, measured in inches.

Table
A grid comprised of horizontal rows and vertical columns into which you can enter data.

Try It! Inserting and Deleting a Table

1. Start Word and open **WTry14** from the data files for this lesson. Save the file as **WTry14_studentfirstname_studentlastname** in the location where your teacher instructs you to store the files for this lesson.
2. Display the rulers and nonprinting characters.
3. Position the insertion point on the blank line between the two lines of text.
4. Click Insert > Table.
5. On the grid, position the mouse pointer over the third cell from the left in the third row, so a grid of three rows and three columns is highlighted. The label at the top of the grid displays *3x3 Table*.
6. Click to insert a table with 3 columns and three rows.
7. Move the insertion point to the end of the document.
8. On the Insert tab, click the Table button.
9. Click Insert Table.
10. Use the Number of columns increment arrows to set the value to 4.

(continued)

Try It! Inserting and Deleting a Table *(continued)*

Inserting a table with 3 columns and 3 rows

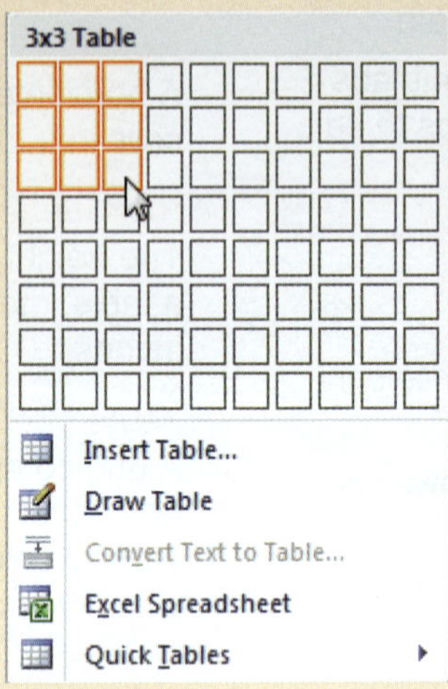

11. Use the Number of rows increment arrows to set the value to 3.
12. Click OK.
13. Click in any cell in the second table.
14. On the Table Tools Layout tab, click the Delete button , and then click Delete Table.
15. Save the changes to **WTry14_studentfirstname_studentlastname** and leave it open to use in the next Try It.

Entering Text in a Table

- You enter text in the cells of a table.
- **Row height** increases automatically to accommodate the text.
- **Column width** does not change automatically when you type. Text wraps at the right margin of a cell the same way it wraps at the right margin of a page.
- To move to the next cell you press TAB, →, or click the cell with the mouse.
- When you press ENTER in a cell, Word starts a new paragraph within the cell.
- The keyboard shortcuts for moving the insertion point within a table are listed in Table 14-1 on the next page.

Try It! Entering Text in a Table

1. In the **WTry14_studentfirstname_studentlastname** file, click in the top left cell in the table.
2. Type **Group A**.
3. Press TAB.
4. Type **Group B**.
5. Press TAB.
6. Type **Group C**.
7. Press TAB.
8. Type **Manufacturing**.
9. Press TAB.
10. Type **Marketing**.
11. Press TAB
12. Type **Accounting**.
13. Save the changes to **WTry14_studentfirstname_studentlastname** and leave it open to use in the next Try It.

Table 14-1 Keyboard Shortcuts for Moving the Insertion Point in a Table

To Select	Press
One cell left	SHIFT + TAB
One cell right	TAB
One cell up	↑
One cell down	↓
First cell in column	ALT + PG UP
Last cell in column	ALT + PG DN
First cell in row	ALT + HOME
Last cell in row	ALT + END

Selecting in a Table

- As with other Word features, you must select table components before you can affect them with commands.
- You select text within a cell using the standard selection commands. For example, double-click a word to select it, or drag across the text to select.
- You can select one or more columns, one or more rows, one or more cells, or the entire table.
- The commands for selecting table components are in the Table group on the Table Tools Layout tab of the Ribbon.
- You can also use your mouse to select components in a table.
- Selected table components are highlighted.

Try It! Selecting in a Table

1. In the **WTry14_studentfirstname_studentlastname** file, click in the middle cell of the top row.
2. On the Table Tools Layout tab, click the Select button.
3. Click Select Cell.
4. Click in the middle cell of the top row.
5. On the Table Tools Layout tab, click Select > Select Column.
6. Click in the middle cell of the top row.
7. On the Table Tools Layout tab, click Select > Select Row.
8. Click in the middle cell of the top row.
9. On the Table Tools Layout tab, click Select > Select Table.
10. In the cell on the right end of the second row, position the insertion point over the area to the left of the text and the right of the column divider. When the pointer changes to a small black arrow pointing diagonally up and right, click.
11. Position the mouse pointer above the cell on the right end of the first row—outside the table border. When the pointer changes to a small black arrow pointing down, click.
12. Position the mouse pointer to the left of the first cell in the first row—outside the table border. When the pointer changes to a typical selection pointer, click.
13. In the upper-left corner of the table, click on the Table Selector button.
14. Save **WTry14_studentfirstname_studentlastname** and leave it open to use in the next Try It.

Selecting Multiple Components in a Table

- Sometimes you may want commands to affect more than one component at a time.
- For example, you may want to apply the bold font style to all text in the top row, or increase the font size of numbers in multiple cells.
- Press and hold SHIFT to select **contiguous** components.
- Press and hold CTRL to select **noncontiguous** components.
- You can also drag across contiguous components to select them.

Try It! Selecting Multiple Components in a Table

1. In the **WTry14_studentfirstname_studentlastname** file, in the cell on the left end of the first row, position the insertion point to the left of the text and the right of the column divider, and click.

   ✓ *This selects the first cell.*

2. Press and hold SHIFT.
3. In the cell on the left end of the second row, position the insertion point to the left of the text and the right of the column divider, and click.

   ✓ *This selects the second, contiguous, cell.*

4. Press and hold CTRL.
5. In the cell on the right end of the first row, position the insertion point to the left of the text and the right of the column divider, and click.
6. Save **WTry14_studentfirstname_studentlastname** and leave it open to use in the next Try It.

Changing Table Structure

- Change a table's structure by inserting and deleting columns, rows, or cells.
- To quickly add a row to the bottom of a table, position the insertion point in the last cell and press TAB.
- The commands for inserting and deleting columns and rows are on the Table Tools Layout tab in the Rows & Columns group.
  - You can insert rows above or below the current row.
  - You can insert columns to the left or right of the current column.
- Use the Insert Cells or Delete Cells dialog box to insert or delete individual cells.
  - When you insert a cell, you choose whether to shift existing cells to the right or down to make room for the new cell.
  - When you delete a cell, you choose whether to shift existing cells left or up to fill in the space left by the deleted cell.
- To insert multiple components select that number before selecting the insert command. For example, to insert three rows, select three rows.

Try It! Changing Table Structure

1. In the **WTry14_studentfirstname_studentlastname** file, click in the middle cell of the top row.
2. On the Table Tools Layout tab, click the Insert Below button.
3. Click in the right cell of the top row.
4. On the Table Tools Layout tab, click the Insert Right button.
5. Click in the right cell of the bottom row.
6. On the Table Tools Layout tab, click the Rows & Columns dialog box launcher.

(continued)

Try It! Changing Table Structure *(continued)*

Insert columns, rows, and cells to change table structure

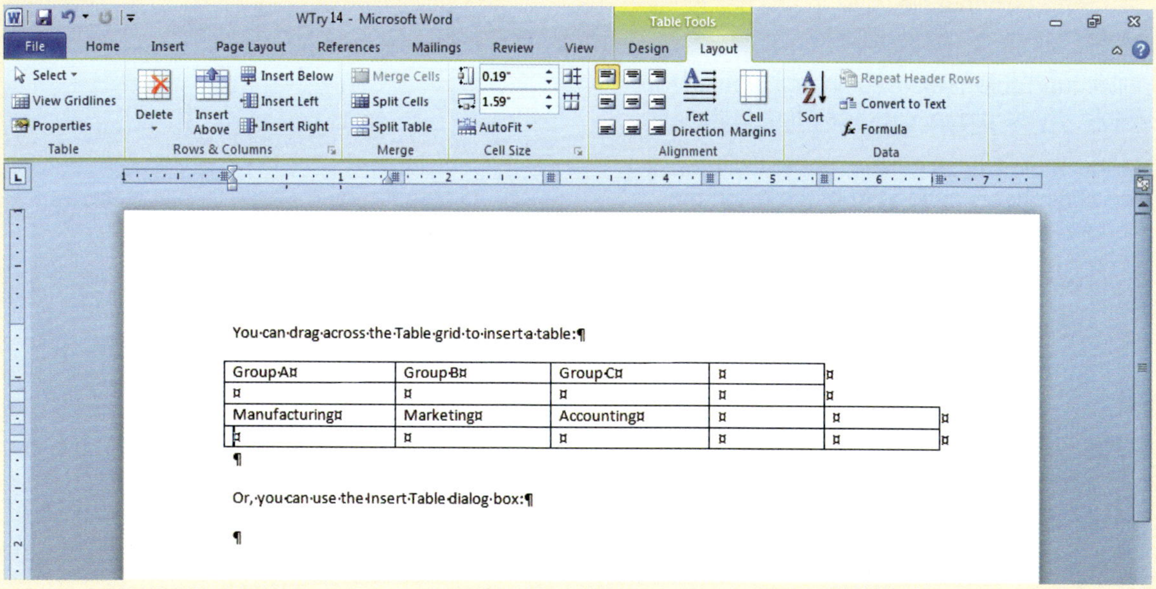

7. In the Insert Cells dialog box, click Shift cells right, and then click OK.
8. Click in the right cell of the bottom row—the one you inserted in step 7.
9. Press TAB.
10. Click in any cell in the bottom row.
11. On the Table Tools Layout tab, click Delete > Delete Rows.
12. Click in the cell on the right end of the top row.
13. On the Table Tools Layout tab, click Delete > Delete Columns.
14. Click in the cell on the right end of the bottom row.
15. On the Table Tools Layout tab, click Delete > Delete Cells.
16. In the Delete Cells dialog box, click Shift cells left, and then click OK.
17. Save the changes to **WTry14_studentfirstname_studentlastname** and leave it open to use in the next Try It.

Formatting a Table

- You can format text within a table using standard Word formatting techniques. For example, use font formatting and alignments to enhance text in a table.
- You can apply formatting to selected text, or to selected cells, columns, or rows.
- To quickly apply a set of formatting effects to an entire table, you can select a Table Style from the gallery of styles in the Table Styles group on the Table Tools Design tab of the Ribbon.
- Rest the mouse pointer on a Table style in the gallery to preview how it will affect the current table, and to see the style name in a ScreenTip.
- When you select a table style, it overrides existing formatting. Therefore, you should apply a style first, and then modify the formatting as needed.

Try It! Formatting a Table

1. In the **WTry14_studentfirstname_studentlastname** file, click in any cell in the table.
2. Click the Table Tools Design tab, then, in the Table Styles group, click the More button.
3. In the Table Styles gallery, under Built-In, click the style that is second from the left in the second row—Light list – Accent 1.
4. Double-click the text **Manufacturing** in the left cell of the bottom row.
5. Click Home > Bold **B** to toggle the Bold style off.
6. Select the top row in the table.
7. On the Home tab, click the Font Size drop-down arrow and click 14.
8. With the first row still selected, on the Home tab, click the Center button.
9. Save the changes to **WTry14_studentfirstname_studentlastname** and leave it open to use in the next Try It.

Table Styles gallery

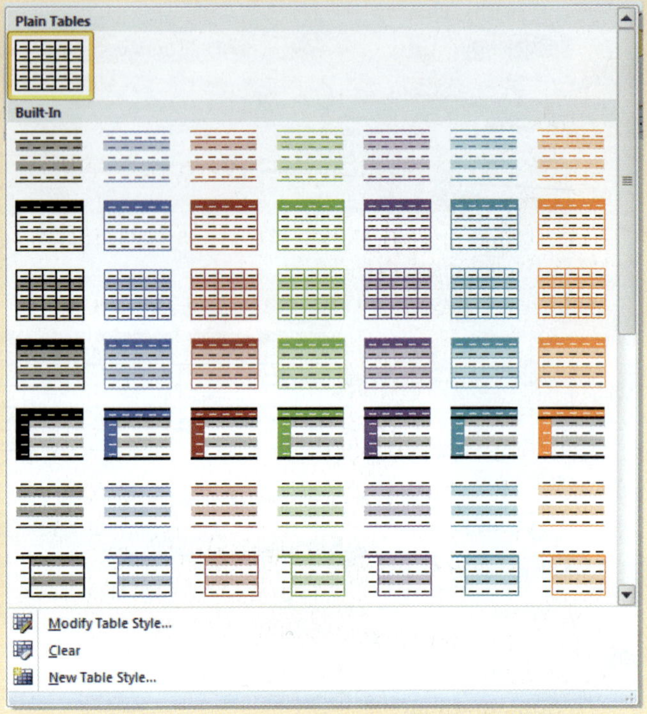

Viewing Gridlines

- When a table is not formatted with printing gridlines, you cannot see the cell dividers onscreen.
- Toggle nonprinting gridlines on so you can identify where one cell ends and the next begins.
- Gridlines display as dotted lines.

Try It! Viewing Gridlines

1. In the **WTry14_studentfirstname_studentlastname** file, click in any cell in the table.
2. Click the Table Tools Layout tab, then click the View Gridlines button.

   ✓ *Click the button again to toggle gridlines off.*
3. Close **WTry14_studentfirstname_studentlastname**, saving all changes, and exit Word.

Project 29—Create It

Table List

DIRECTIONS

1. Start Word and save the new blank document as **WProj29_studentfirstname_studentlastname** in the location where your teacher instructs you to store the files for this lesson.
2. Display the rulers and nonprinting characters.
3. On the **Page Layout** tab set paragraph spacing **Before** to **24** points and paragraph spacing **After** to **36** points.
4. Type **MEMO**, and press ENTER.
5. Click **Home**, then apply the **No Spacing** style.
6. On the horizontal ruler, set a left tab stop at 0.75".
7. Type **To:**, press TAB, and type **All Employees**. Press ENTER.
8. Type **From:**, press TAB, and type your own name. Press ENTER.
9. Type **Date:**, press TAB, and type or insert today's date. Press ENTER.
10. Type **Subject:**, press TAB, and type **Training Courses**. Press ENTER twice.
11. Apply the **Normal** style and type the following: **In response to many requests, here are the names of the instructors who will be teaching the courses next week.**
12. Press ENTER.
13. Click **Insert** > **Table**.
14. Move the mouse pointer across the table grid to select two columns and two rows, and then click in the lower right selected cell to insert the table.
15. Click in the cell in the top left, and type **Course Name**. Press TAB and type **Instructor Name**.
16. Press TAB and type **Word for Beginners**. Press TAB and type **Marilyn Pak**.
17. Press TAB and type **Advanced Excel**. Press TAB and type **Ben Thompson**.
18. Click **Table Tools Layout** > **Insert Above**.
19. In the new row, click in the cell on the left and type **Introduction to the Internet**. Press TAB and type **Suni Patel**.
20. On the **Table Tools Design** tab, in the Table Styles group, click the **More** button.
21. In the Table Styles gallery, click the style on the left end of the second to last row—**Colorful List**.
21. Click the **Table Selection** button to select the entire table.
22. Click **Home** > **Font Size** drop-down arrow > **12** to increase the font size.
23. Check and correct the spelling and grammar in the document, and then save the changes.
24. **With your teacher's permission**, print the document. It should look similar to Figure 14-1 on the next page.
25. Close the document, saving all changes, and exit Word.

Figure 14-1

MEMO

To: All Employees
From: Firstname Lastname
Date: Today's Date
Subject: Training Courses

In response to many requests, here are the names of the instructors who will be teaching the courses next week.

Course Name	Instructor Name
Word for Beginners	Marilyn Pak
Introduction to the Internet	Suni Patel
Advanced Excel	Ben Thompson

Project 30—Apply It

Table Schedule

DIRECTIONS

1. Start Word, if necessary, and open **WProj30** from the data files for this lesson.
2. Save the file as **WProj30_studentfirstname_studentlastname** in the location where your teacher instructs you to store the files for this lesson.
3. Display the rulers and nonprinting characters.
4. Replace the sample text *Student's Name* with your own name, and *Today's Date* with the actual date.
5. Press CTRL + END to move the insertion point to the end of the document.
6. Press ENTER and type: **Following is the schedule and location of courses:** and press ENTER.
7. Insert a table with three columns and four rows.
8. Enter the following data in the table:

Course Name	Location	Time
Word for Beginners	Conference Room A	8:30 – 11:45
Advanced Excel	Conference Room B	8:30 – 11:45
Introduction to the Internet	Media Lab	1:30 – 3:30

   To enter an en dash between the times, simply type a space, a hyphen, and a space. By default, AutoFormat automatically replaces the hyphen and spaces with an en dash after the second number is typed.

9. Select the last two rows in the table and insert two rows above them.

10. Enter the following data in the new rows:

Advanced Word	Conference Room A	8:30 – 11:45
Excel for Beginners	Conference Room B	1:30 – 3:30

11. Insert a column to the right of the Time column.
12. Starting in the top cell, enter the following data in the new column:

    Days
    Tuesday, Thursday
    Monday, Wednesday
    Tuesday, Wednesday
    Monday, Thursday
    Friday

13. Delete the row for the Word for Beginners course.
14. Apply the **Colorful Grid - Accent 2** table style to the table.
15. Increase the font size of all text in the table to 12 points.
16. Check and correct the spelling and grammar in the document, and then save the changes.
17. **With your teacher's permission**, print the document. It should look similar to Figure 14-2.
18. Close the document, saving all changes, and exit Word.

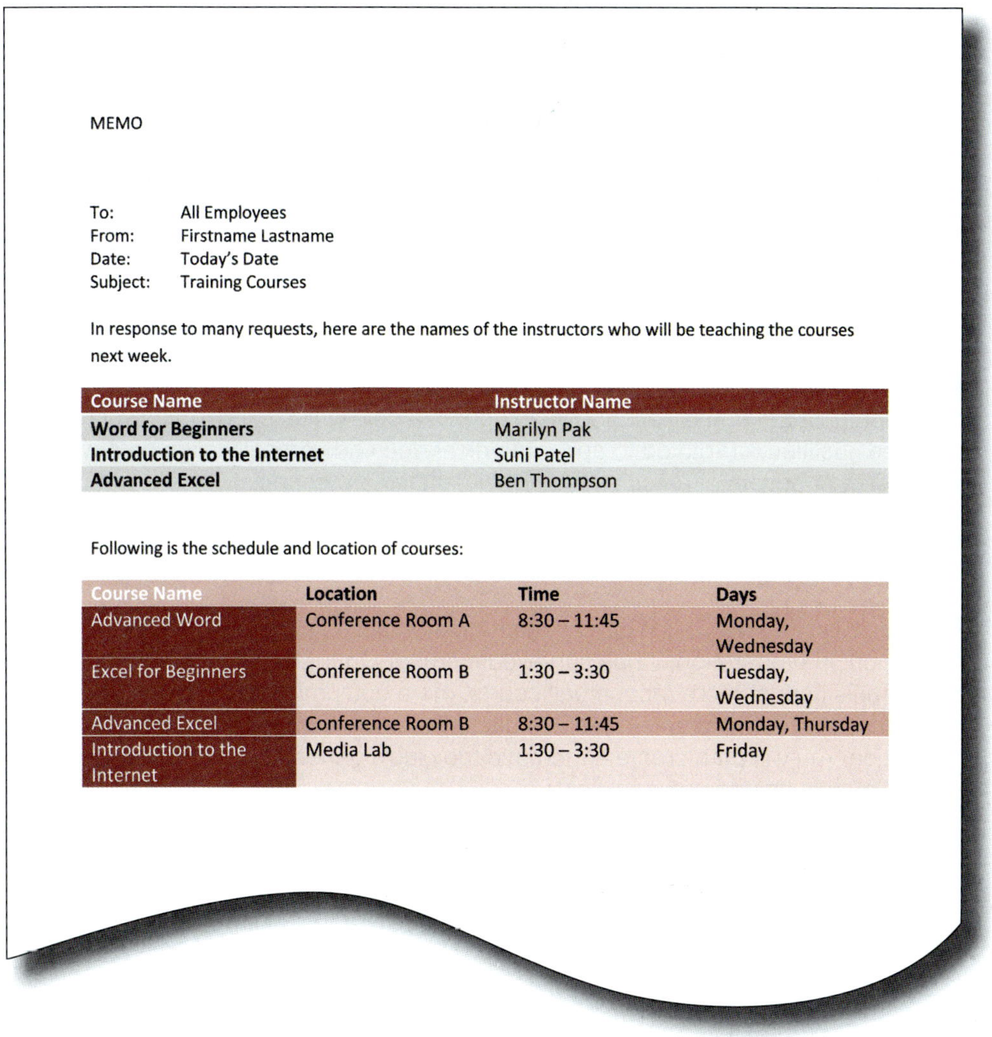

MEMO

To: All Employees
From: Firstname Lastname
Date: Today's Date
Subject: Training Courses

In response to many requests, here are the names of the instructors who will be teaching the courses next week.

Course Name	Instructor Name
Word for Beginners	Marilyn Pak
Introduction to the Internet	Suni Patel
Advanced Excel	Ben Thompson

Following is the schedule and location of courses:

Course Name	Location	Time	Days
Advanced Word	Conference Room A	8:30 – 11:45	Monday, Wednesday
Excel for Beginners	Conference Room B	1:30 – 3:30	Tuesday, Wednesday
Advanced Excel	Conference Room B	8:30 – 11:45	Monday, Thursday
Introduction to the Internet	Media Lab	1:30 – 3:30	Friday

Figure 14-2

Lesson 15

Aligning Tables

➤ What You Will Learn

Converting Text to a Table
Inserting Existing Text into a Table Cell
Setting Column Width and Row Height
Setting Alignment in a Table Cell
Setting Tabs in a Table Cell
Setting Cell Margins
Aligning a Table Horizontally on the Page

Software Skills Use alignment options and tabs to make tables easy to read. Numbers are usually aligned flush right in a cell, while text can be flush left, centered, justified, or rotated to appear vertical. You can vertically align data with the top, center, or bottom of a cell as well. Decimal tabs are especially useful in tables for aligning dollar values. Other ways to improve the appearance of a table include aligning the table horizontally on the page and adjusting column width and row height.

Application Skills Michigan Avenue Athletic Club is planning a major renovation. In preparation, it has surveyed members to find whether they want more tennis courts, more racquetball courts, more equipment rooms, or a lap pool. In this lesson, you will create a table to display the potential cost of each area or renovation. You will then create a memo to the club's general manager that includes the survey results and potential costs.

What You Can Do

Converting Text to a Table

- You can convert existing text to a table using commands in the tables group on the Insert tab of the Ribbon.
- If the existing text includes paragraph marks, Word will start a new row at every paragraph mark.
- If the existing text includes tabs, Word will start a new column at every tab.
- You can choose to separate text at a different character in the Convert Text to Table dialog box.

Try It! Converting Text to a Table

1. Start Word and open **WTry15** from the data files for this lesson. Save the file as **WTry15_studentfirstname_studentlastname** in the location where your teacher instructs you to store files for this lesson.
2. Select the line beginning with *Paper goods* and the three lines below it.
3. Click the Insert tab, then click the Table button.
4. Click Convert Text to Table to open the Convert Text to Table dialog box.
5. Click OK.
6. Save **WTry15_studentfirstname_studentlastname**, and leave it open to use in the next Try It.

Inserting Existing Text into a Table Cell

- You can copy or move existing text into a table cell.
- Inserting existing text into a table cell saves you the time and effort of retyping information.
- You can change the formatting of text you insert in a cell, using standard text formatting commands. For example, you can apply font formatting, and even bullet or numbered list formats.

Try It! Inserting Existing Text into a Table Cell

1. In the **WTry15_studentfirstname_studentlastname** file, position the insertion point in any cell in the top row.
2. Click Table Tools Layout > Insert Above.
3. Select the text *Party Budget*. (Do not select the paragraph mark
4. Right-click the selection and click Cut on the shortcut menu.
5. Click in the blank cell on the left of the new row.
6. Click Home > Paste.
7. Select the left column.
8. On the Home tab, click the Bullets button.
9. Click in the top left cell of the column, and click the Bullets button again to remove the formatting from the text in that cell.
10. Save the changes to **WTry15_studentfirstname_studentlastname** and leave it open to use in the next Try It.

Setting Column Width and Row Height

- By default, Word creates table columns of equal column width, sized so the table extends from the left margin to the right margin.
- Rows are sized according to the line spacing on the line where the table is inserted. Row height automatically increases to accommodate lines of text typed in a cell.
- You can automatically adjust the column width and row height to fit the contents of each cell, or to fit the width of the current window.
- You can drag with your mouse to change column width or row height:
  - You can drag column dividers to increase or decrease column width.
  - In Print Layout view, you can drag row dividers to increase or decrease row height.

  ✓ *Press and hold* ALT *as you drag the divider to see measurements displayed on the ruler.*
- You can set precise measurements for column width and row height using the options in the Cell Size group on the Table Tools Layout tab of the Ribbon.
- Alternatively, you can select to automatically distribute the height of the rows equally among the total height of selected rows.
- You can also automatically distribute the width of the columns equally across the total width of selected columns.

Try It! Setting Column Width and Row Height

1. In the **WTry15_studentfirstname_studentlastname** file, click in the cell at top left.
2. Click Table Tools Layout > AutoFit > AutoFit Contents.

   ✓ *To quickly resize a column to automatically fit the contents, double-click the column divider. To resize a row automatically to fit the contents, double-click the row divider.*
3. Click the AutoFit button again, and then click AutoFit Window.
4. Rest the mouse pointer on the column divider between the left and right columns.

   ✓ *The pointer changes to a double vertical line with arrows pointing left and right.*
5. Click and drag the divider about 0.5" to the left.

Drag to resize a column

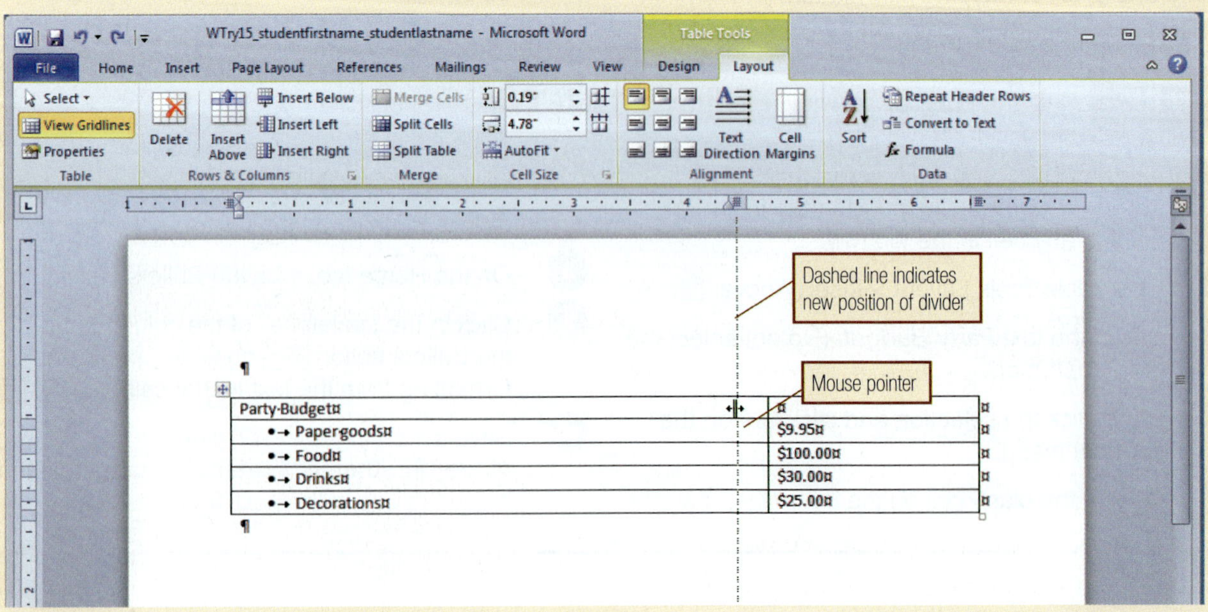

(continued)

Try It! Setting Column Width and Row Height *(continued)*

6. Release the mouse button to resize the columns.
7. Rest the mouse pointer on the divider between the first and second rows.

   ✓ *The pointer changes to a double horizontal line with arrows pointing up and down.*

8. Click and drag down about 0.5".
9. Release the mouse button to resize the row.
10. Click in any cell in the right column.
11. On the Table Tools Layout tab, use the Table Column Width increment arrows to set the column width to 1.5".
12. Select rows two through five.
13. On the Table Tools Layout tab, use the Table Row Height increment arrows to set the row height to 0.5".
14. Click the Table Selector button to select the entire table.
15. On the Table Tools Layout tab, click the Distribute Rows button.
16. Click the Distribute Columns button.
17. Save the changes to **WTry15_studentfirstname_studentlastname** and leave it open to use in the next Try It.

Setting Alignment in a Table Cell

- You can set horizontal and vertical alignment within a cell.
- Set alignment for the cell in which the insertion point is currently located, or for all cells in a selection.
- There are nine possible alignments available on the Table Tools Layout tab in the Alignment group:
  - Align Top Left
  - Align Top Center
  - Align Top Right
  - Align Center Left
  - Align Center
  - Align Center Right
  - Align Bottom Left
  - Align Bottom Center
  - Align Bottom Right
- You can also use the horizontal alignment buttons in the Font group on the Home tab to align text horizontally in a cell.

  ✓ *If you justify text in a cell, be sure you have at least three lines of text.*

Try It! Setting Alignment in a Table Cell

1. In the **WTry15_studentfirstname_studentlastname** file, click in the cell where the text **Party Budget** displays.
2. On the Table Tools Layout tab, click the Align Center button to center the text horizontally and vertically in the cell.
3. Select the four cells containing the bulleted items.
4. Click the Align Bottom Right button.
5. Select the four cells containing the dollar values, and then click the Align Bottom Left button.
6. Save the changes to **WTry15_studentfirstname_studentlastname** and leave it open to use in the next Try It.

Setting Tabs in a Table Cell

- All tab stops can be used within a table cell.
- Decimal tab stops are often used in a table to automatically align numbers such as dollar values within a cell or a column.
- To advance to a tab stop within a table cell you must press CTRL + TAB.

  ✓ *For more information on tabs, refer to Lesson 5.*

Try It! Setting Tabs in a Table Cell

1. In the **WTry15_studentfirstname_studentlastname** file, select the four cells containing dollar values.
2. Verify that the left tab indicator displays in the tab selector box. If not, click the Tab selector box until the left tab indicator displays.
3. Click at 4.0" on the horizontal ruler to set a left tab.
4. Click the Tab selector box until the decimal tab indicator displays.
5. Click at 5.0" on the horizontal ruler to set a decimal tab.
6. Position the insertion point to the left of the dollar value in the second row and press CTRL + TAB to advance the data to the left tab stop.
7. Press CTRL + TAB again to advance the data to the decimal tab stop.
8. Repeat steps 6 and 7 to advance the dollar values in rows 3, 4, and 5 so they align on the decimal tab.
9. Save the changes to **WTry15_studentfirstname_studentlastname** and leave it open to use in the next Try It.

Setting Cell Margins

- By default, top and bottom margins in a cell are set to 0" and left and right margins are set to 0.08".
- You can use the Table Options dialog box to set margins within a cell.
- The margins affect all cells in the table.
- By default, Word resizes the cells so the content fits.

Try It! Setting Cell Margins

1. In the **WTry15_studentfirstname_studentlastname** file, click in any cell.
2. On the Table Tools Layout tab, click the Cell Margins button.
3. In the Table Options dialog box, use the Top increment arrows to set the top margin to 0.1".
4. Use the Left increment arrows to set the left margin to 0.1".
5. Use the Bottom increment arrows to set the bottom margin to 0.1".
6. Use the Right increment arrows to set the right margin to 0.1".
7. Click OK.
8. Save the changes to **WTry15_studentfirstname_studentlastname** and leave it open to use in the next Try It.

Aligning a Table Horizontally on the Page

- You can left-align, right-align, or center a table on the page.
- The options for aligning a table on the page are found in the Table Properties dialog box, which you can open from the Table group on the Table Tools Layout tab of the Ribbon.

Try It! Aligning a Table Horizontally on the Page

1. In the **WTry15_studentfirstname_studentlastname** file, position the insertion point anywhere in the table.
2. On the Table Tools Layout tab, click the Properties button.
3. Click the Table tab if it is not already active.
4. Under Alignment, click the Center button.
5. Click OK.
6. Click the Properties button again.
7. Under Alignment, click the Right button.
8. Click OK.
9. Close **WTry15_studentfirstname_studentlastname** saving all changes, and exit Word.

Table Properties dialog box

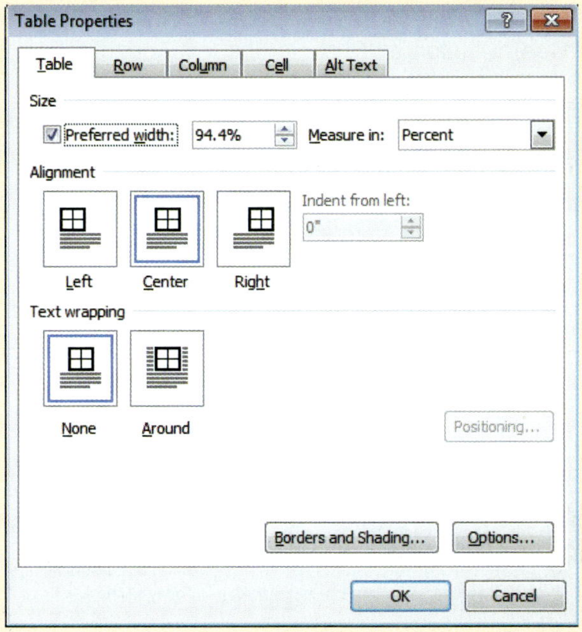

Project 31—Create It

Potential Cost Table

DIRECTIONS

1. Start Word and save the new, blank document as **WProj31_studentfirstname_studentlastname** in the location where your teacher instructs you to store the files for this lesson.
2. Display the rulers and nonprinting characters.
3. Double-click in the header area and type your full name and today's date.
4. In the main document area, type the following list, separating the area names from the potential cost values using a left tab stop:

Area	Potential Cost
Reception	$8,500.00
Tennis court	$50,000.00
Racquetball court	$50,000.00
Equipment room	$75,000.00
Lap pool	$115,000.00

5. Select the six lines you typed in step 4.
6. Click **Insert** > **Table** > **Convert Text to Table** to display the Convert Text to Table dialog box.
7. Click **OK** to create the table.
8. Select the cells in rows 2 through 6 in the left column (the area names).
9. Click **Home** > **Bullets**.
10. Click the **Table Selector** button to select the entire table.
11. Click **Table Tools Layout** > **AutoFit** > **AutoFit Contents**.
12. With the entire table still selected, use the Table Row Height increment arrows to set the row height to 0.4".

13. Click in any cell in the right column, and use the Table Column Width increment arrows to set the right column width to 1.5".
14. Select the top row.
15. On the **Table Tools Layout** tab, click the **Align Center** button to center the text horizontally and vertically in the cell.
16. Select rows 2 through 6.
17. On the **Table Tools Layout** tab, click the **Align Center Left** button.
18. Select the cells in rows 2 through 6 in the right column (the dollar values).
19. Click the **Tab selector** box until the decimal tab indicator displays.
20. Click at **3.0"** on the horizontal ruler to set a decimal tab. Word automatically aligns the selected data with the tab stop.
21. Click in the left cell in the top row.
22. On the **Table Tools Layout** tab, click the **Cell Margins** button to display the Table Options dialog box.
23. Use the **Top** increment arrows to set the top cell margin to 0.05" and the **Bottom** increment arrows to set the bottom cell margin to 0.05".
24. Click **OK**.
25. On the **Table Tools Layout** tab, click the **Properties** button to display the Table Properties dialog box.
26. On the **Table** tab, under Alignment, click **Center**, and then click **OK**.
27. **With your teacher's permission**, print the document. It should look similar to Figure 15-1.
28. Close the document, saving all changes, and exit Word.

Figure 15-1

Firstname Lastname
Today's Date

Area	Potential Cost
• Reception	$8,500.00
• Tennis court	$50,000.00
• Racquetball court	$50,000.00
• Equipment room	$75,000.00
• Lap pool	$115,000.00

Project 32—Apply It

Survey Results Memo

DIRECTIONS

1. Start Word, if necessary, and open **WProj32** from the data files for this lesson.
2. Save, and save the file as **WProj32_studentfirstname_studentlastname** in the location where your teacher instructs you to store the files for this lesson.

3. Display the rulers and nonprinting characters.
4. Replace the sample text *Student's Name* with your own name, and *Today's Date* with the actual date.
5. Use the following steps to create the document shown in Figure 15-2.
6. Select the six lines where the tabbed survey results are listed.
7. Convert the selection into a table with 5 columns and 6 rows, separating the text at the tabs.
8. In column 1, apply the **Align Bottom Center** alignment.
9. In columns 2, 3, and 4, apply the **Align Bottom Right** alignment.
10. In column 5, apply the **Align Bottom Left** alignment.
11. In row 1, apply the **Align Center** alignment.
12. In the cells that contain dollar values, insert a decimal tab at **6.25"** on the horizontal ruler to align the costs.
13. Change the font formatting of the text in the first column and the first row to 12 point Arial, bold.
14. Set the widths of column 1 and 5 to **1.5"**.
15. Set the width of columns 2, 3, and 4 to **0.8"**.
16. Set the height of all rows to **0.5"**.
17. Center the entire table horizontally on the page.
18. Apply the **Title** style to the text **Memo**.
19. **With your teacher's permission**, print the document. It should look similar to Figure 15-2.
20. Close the document, saving all changes, and exit Word.

Figure 15-2

MEMO

To: General Manager
From: Firstname Lastname
Date: Today's Date
Subject: Renovation Survey Results

Here are the results of the member survey. I have also included information about the potential costs associated with each item. We can use this data to help us decide where we want to focus our resources during the renovation.

Area	Want	Do not Care	Do not Want	Potential Cost
Reception	15	18	2	$8,500.00
Tennis court	19	10	5	$50,000.00
Racquetball court	25	15	7	$50,000.00
Equipment room	45	22	2	$75,000.00
Lap pool	8	5	12	$115,000.00

Lesson 16

Drawing a Table

WORDS TO KNOW

Header row
A row across the top of a table in which heading information is entered.

Merge
Combine multiple adjacent cells together to create one large cell.

Sizing handle
A nonprinting icon that displays outside the lower right corner of a table that you use to resize the table.

Split
Divide one cell into multiple cells, either vertically to create columns or horizontally to create rows.

➤ What You Will Learn

Drawing a Table
Merging and Splitting Cells
Changing Text Direction in a Table Cell
Moving and Resizing Tables
Setting Text Wrapping Around a Table

Software Skills Word's Draw Table tool gives you great flexibility to organize tables. You can lay out the table cells exactly as you want them; not necessarily in rigid columns and rows. You can then move and resize the table, if necessary, merge and split cells, and rotate the text to achieve the exact effect you need.

Application Skills The exercise director at Michigan Avenue Athletic Club has asked you to design a flyer announcing a series of new classes. In this lesson, you will create a draft of the table you will use in the flyer. You will then create the flyer that includes the table and other information.

What You Can Do

Drawing a Table

- Word's Draw Table feature lets you create tables with uneven or irregular columns and rows by dragging the mouse.
- Access Draw Table from the Tables group on the Insert tab of the Ribbon, or in the Draw Borders group on the Table Tools Design tab.
- You can draw a new table, or add columns, rows, or cells to an existing table.
- When you draw a table, the mouse pointer looks and functions like a pencil.
- You drag the pointer to draw one cell, then drag to draw lines vertically or horizontally to create cell dividers.

- Word creates straight lines at 90 degree angles to existing cell dividers, even if you do not drag in a straight line.
- You can draw a diagonal line across a cell as a visual element or border, not to split the cell diagonally.
- New cells can be drawn anywhere. Rows and columns do not have to extend across the entire table.
- The Draw Table tool remains active until you turn it off.
- You must use Print Layout view to draw a table.

Try It! Drawing a Table

1. Start Word and open **WTry16** from the data files for this lesson, and save it as **WTry16_studentfirstname_studentlastname** in the location where your teacher instructs you to store the files for this lesson. Display nonprinting characters and the rulers.
2. Click the Insert tab, then click the Table button.
3. Click Draw Table on the Insert Table drop-down menu.

   ✓ *The mouse pointer change to resemble a pencil.*
4. Position the mouse pointer just below the paragraph mark at the end of the document, press and hold the left mouse button, and drag diagonally down and to the right.

   ✓ *Notice that lines on the rulers indicate the current position of the mouse.*
5. When the cell is approximately 2" high by 5" wide, release the mouse button.
6. Position the mouse pointer at the mid-point along the top border of the cell.
7. Click and drag straight down. When the dotted divider line reaches the bottom border, release the mouse button.
8. Position the mouse pointer at the mid-point along the cell divider you drew in step 7, and then click and drag to the right. When the divider line reaches the right border, release the mouse button.
9. Press ESC to turn off Draw Table
10. Click Table Tools Design > Draw Table.

    ✓ *The mouse pointer change to resemble a pencil.*
11. Position the mouse pointer on the lower left corner of the table.
12. Click and drag down about .5" and to the right until the new cell is the same width as the current table.
13. Release the mouse button.
14. Click and drag to draw eight vertical cell dividers across the new cell you drew in step 4.
15. Click the Draw Table button again to turn the feature off.
16. Save the changes to **WTry16_studentfirstname_studentlastname** and leave it open to use in the next Try It.

Merging and Splitting Cells

- You can **merge** horizontally or vertically adjacent cells using commands in the Merge group on the Table Tools Layout tab of the Ribbon.
- You can use the Eraser tool in the Draw Borders group on the Table Tools Design tab to erase dividers between cells, thus merging the cells.
- If you erase a divider on the outer edge of the table, you simply erase the border line, not the divider.
- Merging is useful for creating a **header row** across a table.
- **Split** a cell to insert dividers to create additional columns or rows in an existing table.
- You can split a cell using the Split Cells dialog box to select the number of columns or rows you want to create.

  ✓ *Alternatively, use the Draw Table tool to draw divider lines, as you learned in the previous Try It.*

Try It! Merging and Splitting Cells

1. In the **WTry16_studentfirstname_studentlastname** file, select the two cells on the left end of the bottom row.
2. Click Table Tools Layout > Merge Cells.
3. Click anywhere in the table.
4. Click Table Tools Design > Eraser.

   ✓ *The mouse pointer changes to resemble an eraser.*
5. Click on a vertical divider line in the bottom row.
6. Click another vertical divider line in the bottom row.
7. Press ESC to turn off the feature.
8. Click in the cell in the top right corner of the table.
9. Click Table Tools Layout > Split Cells to open the Split Cells dialog box.
10. Use the Number of columns increment arrows to set the number of columns to 3.
11. Use the Number of rows increment arrows to set the number of rows to 2.
12. Click OK.
13. Save the changes to **WTry16_studentfirstname_studentlastname** and leave it open to use in the next Try It.

Changing Text Direction in a Table Cell

- By default, when you type text in a table cell it runs from left to right, like text in a document.
- You can change the text direction so it runs from top to bottom or from bottom to top.

Try It! Changing Text Direction in a Table Cell

1. In the **WTry16_studentfirstname_studentlastname** file, click in the top left cell in the table and type **Voyager Travel Adventures**.
2. On the Table Tools Layout tab, click the Text Direction button to rotate the text so it runs top to bottom.

   ✓ *Notice that the Text Direction button changes to show the direction of the text in the current cell.*
3. Click the Text Direction button again to rotate the text so it runs bottom to top.

   ✓ *The Text Direction button changes again.*
4. Click the Text Direction button again to rotate the text so it runs left to right.
5. Save the changes to **WTry16_studentfirstname_studentlastname** and leave it open to use in the next Try It.

Moving and Resizing Tables

- Drag the table selector button to move a table anywhere on the page.
- Existing text will wrap around the table in its new position.
- Drag the table's **sizing handle** to change the table size.
- The table selector button and sizing handle only display when the mouse pointer is resting on the table or if the table is selected.

Try It! Moving and Resizing Tables

1. In the **WTry16_studentfirstname_studentlastname** file, rest the mouse pointer over the table so the table selector button displays.
2. Click and drag the table selector button straight up.

   ✓ *As you drag, the mouse pointer changes to a four-headed arrow, and a dotted line moves with the pointer to indicate the new location.*

3. Release the mouse button when the pointer is positioned on the blank line between the two paragraphs to drop the table in the new location.

   ✓ *Notice that the text now wraps around the table.*

4. Rest the mouse pointer over the table so the sizing handle displays.
5. Click and drag the sizing handle diagonally up and to the left.

   ✓ *As you drag, the mouse pointer changes to resemble a cross-hair, and a dotted outline moves with the pointer to show the new size.*

6. Release the mouse button when the table is about 2" high by 4" wide.
7. Save the changes to **WTry16_studentfirstname_studentlastname** and leave it open to use in the next Try It.

Drag the table sizing handle to resize a table

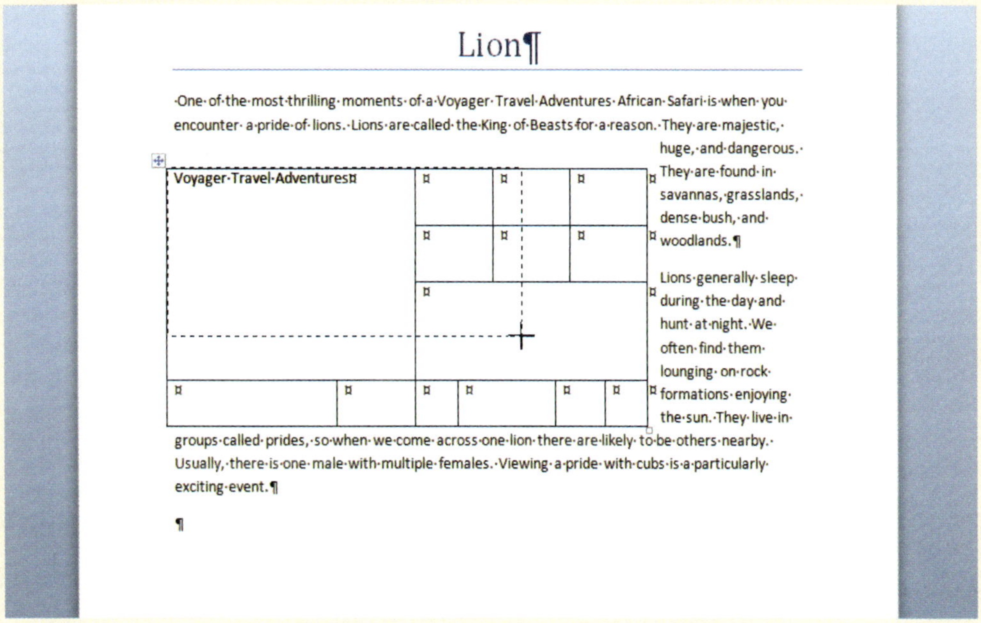

Setting Text Wrapping Around a Table

- There are two text-wrapping options in the Table Properties dialog box for integrating a table with text on a page.
  - Choose None to display text above and below the table.
  - Choose Around to wrap text around the sides of the table.
- By default, tables are inserted on a blank line above or below existing text.
- When you drag a table to a new location, text automatically wraps around the table.
- Wrapping text around a table integrates the table object into the text so text appears above, below, and on either side of the table.

Try It! Setting Text Wrapping Around a Table

1. In the **WTry16_studentfirstname_studentlastname** file, click in any cell in the table.
2. Click Table Tools Layout > Properties to open the Table Properties dialog box.
3. Under Text Wrapping, click None.
4. Click OK. Word removes text wrapping so text flows above and below the table.

   ✓ *The position of the table in relation to the text depends on the size of your table. It may not look exactly like the figures.*
5. On the Table Tools Layout, click the Properties buttons again.
6. Under Text Wrapping, click Around, and then click OK. Word wraps the text around the table.

   ✓ *The position of the table in relation to the text depends on the size of your table. It may not look exactly like the figures.*
7. Close **WTry16_studentfirstname_studentlastname** saving all changes and exit Word.

Text wrapping is set to None (left) and Around (right)

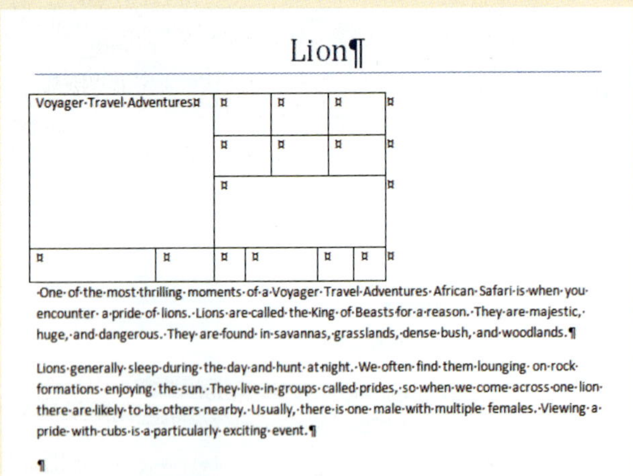

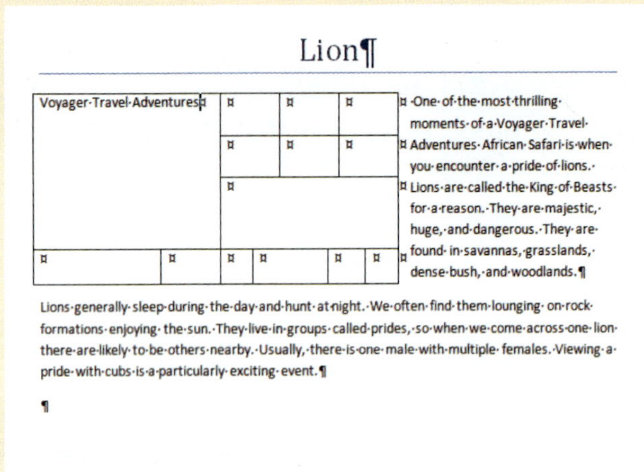

Project 33—Create It

Draw a Table

DIRECTIONS

1. Start Word and save the new, blank document as **WProj33_studentfirstname_studentlastname** in the location where your teacher instructs you to store the files for this lesson.
2. Display the rulers and nonprinting characters.
3. Double-click in the header area and type your full name and today's date.
4. On the first line of the document, increase the font size to 12 points and then type the following paragraph:

   Work Out with David is a series of three classes designed to introduce members to some of the exercise opportunities here at Michigan Avenue Athletic Club. Each hour-long session focuses on two complementary types of exercises.

5. Press ENTER to start a new line.
6. Click **Insert** > **Table** > **Draw Table**.
7. Starting at the current insertion point location, click and drag down and to the right with the mouse pointer to draw a cell approximately 3" wide by 3" high.
8. Click and drag to draw a vertical line dividing the cell into two columns so that the left column is 1" wide and the right column is 2" wide.
9. Click and drag to draw two horizontal lines dividing the table into three 1" high rows.
10. On the Table Tools Design tab, click the **Draw Table** button to turn the feature off.
11. Select the left column of the table.
12. Click **Table Tools Layout** > **Merge Cells**.
13. Change the font size to 22 points and then type **Work Out with David**.
14. Click **Table Tools Layout** > **Text Direction** twice to rotate the text so it runs bottom to top.
15. Click in the top cell in the right column.
16. Click the **Split Cells** button to open the Split Cells dialog box.
17. Use the **Number of columns** increment arrows to set the value to **1**.
18. Use the **Number of rows** increment arrows to set the value to **2**.
19. Click **OK**.
20. Click in what is now the third row in the right column, and then click the **Repeat** button on the Quick Access Toolbar.
21. Click in what is the fifth row in the right column, and then click the **Repeat** button on the Quick Access Toolbar again.
22. Rest the mouse pointer anywhere over the table so the sizing handle displays.
23. Click and drag the **sizing handle** to the right to increase the width of the table to **4"**.
24. Rest the mouse pointer anywhere over the table so the table selector button displays.
25. Click and drag the **table selector** button up and release the mouse button when the mouse pointer is even with the beginning of the first line of text.
26. Check and correct the spelling and grammar in the document, and then save the changes.
27. **With your teacher's permission**, print the document. It should look similar to Figure 16-1.
28. Close the document, saving all changes, and exit Word.

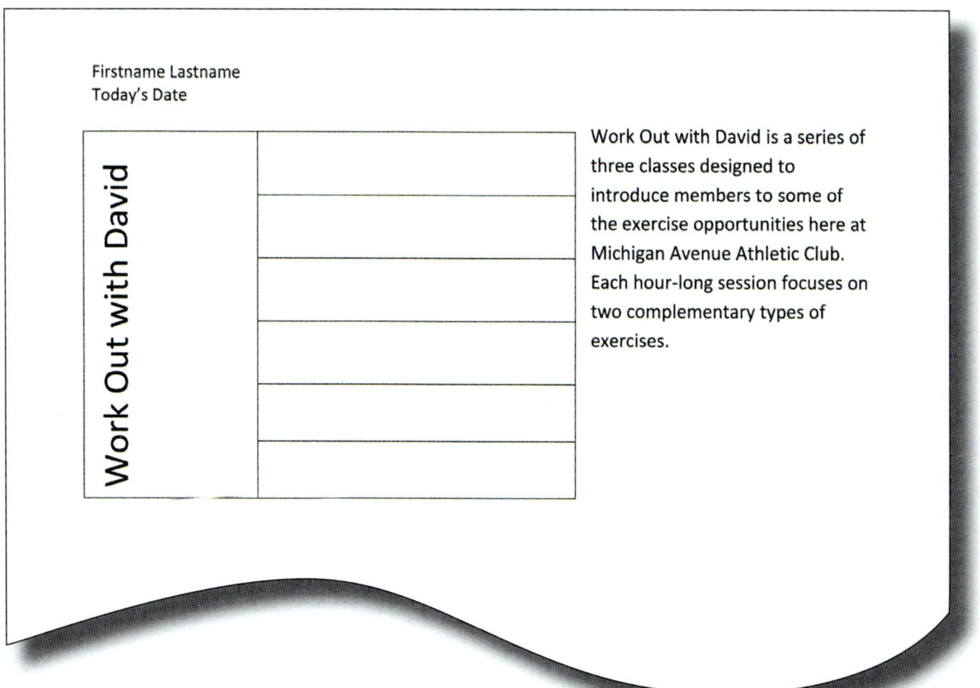

Figure 16-1

Project 34—Apply It

Flyer with Table

DIRECTIONS

1. Start Word, if necessary, and open **WProj34** from the data files for this lesson.
2. Save, and save the file as **WProj34_studentfirstname_studentlastname** in the location where your teacher instructs you to store the files for this lesson.
3. Display the rulers and nonprinting characters.
4. Type your full name and today's date in the header area.
5. Use the following steps to complete the table and format the document as shown in Figure 16-2 on the next page.
6. Click anywhere in the table and then use the **Draw Table** tool to draw a vertical line to split the current column into two columns of equal width.
7. Use the **Draw Table** tool to merge the top two cells in the left column into one cell.
8. Select what are now the second and third cells in the left column and merge them.
9. Select what are now the bottom two cells in the left column and merge them.
10. Draw a new row across the bottom of the table, sized 0.5" high.
11. Draw a new column along the left side of the table, sized about 0.5" wide.
12. Drag the **table selector** button [⊞] to move the entire table on the page so its top aligns with the top of the second paragraph, and its left edge aligns with the left margin.
13. Draw a new row across the top of the table, sized 0.5" high.
14. Drag the **table sizing handle** to resize the table so it is about 4" wide by 4" high.
15. Enter the text as shown in Figure 16-2 on the next page.
    a. Set the font size of the header row and the dates to 20 points, and center align the text horizontally and vertically.
    b. Set the font size of the class names to 18 points and align them with the bottom left of the cells.
    c. Set the font size in the bottom row to 14 points and center align the text horizontally and vertically.
    d. Set the text direction for the left column to run from bottom to top, set the font size to 28 points, and center align the text horizontally and vertically.
16. Change the font of the first three lines of text in the document to 16 point Cambria, and center them horizontally.
17. Add 18 points of space after the third line.
18. Check and correct the spelling and grammar in the document, and then save the changes.
19. **With your teacher's permission**, print the document. It should look similar to Figure 16-2 on the next page.
20. Close the document, saving all changes, and exit Word.

Figure 16-2

Firstname Lastname
Today's Date

Work Out with David
A series of introductory exercise classes with
Personal Trainer David Fairmont

Work Out with David is a series of three classes designed to introduce members to some of the exercise opportunities here at Michigan Avenue Athletic Club. Each hour-long session focuses on two complementary types of exercises.

Schedule		
Work Out with David	January 8	Step Aerobics
		Pilates
	January 15	Spinning
		Yoga
	January 22	Kickboxing
		Free Weights
	Space is limited. Please sign up as soon as possible!	

The first 15 minutes of each class will be spent learning about the exercises, including the equipment that may be involved. The rest of each class includes a warm up, active participation, followed by cool down exercises and stretching.

David Fairmont is out newest personal trainer. He holds a master's degree in health management from the University of Vermont in Burlington, VT, and he is certified in cardiovascular exercise and strength training.

Work Out with David is geared toward those who are new to our exercise class offerings, but all members are welcome to join. There is no fee for participation but class size is limited. Please see Katie at the front desk to enroll.

Lesson 17

Performing Calculations in a Table

WORDS TO KNOW

Formula
A mathematical equation.

Function
A built-in formula for performing calculations, such as addition, in a table.

Line style
The appearance of a line.

Line weight
The thickness of a line.

Shading
A color or pattern used to fill the background of a cell.

Spreadsheet
A document created with an application, such as Microsoft Office Excel 2010, used for setting up mathematical calculations.

➤ What You Will Learn

- Performing Addition in a Table
- Applying a Number Format
- Sorting Rows in a Table
- Applying Cell Borders and Shading

Software Skills Perform basic calculations in a table to total values in a column or row. If the values change, you can update the result without redoing the math. At the same time, you can format the calculation results with one of Word's built-in number formats. Sorting rows helps you keep your tables in order, while cell borders and shading let you dress up your tables to make them look good as well as to highlight important information.

Application Skills A Whole Grains Bread franchise is offering a special gift basket for Earth Day. In this lesson, you will create a document to advertise the gift basket. You will use a table to organize the information and to calculate costs. You will format the table using cell borders and shading.

What You Can Do

Performing Addition in a Table

- Use Word's **Formula** command to access basic **spreadsheet** functions so you can perform calculations on data entered in a table.
- The Formula command is in the Data group on the Table Tools Layout tab.
- Word enters the result in a field, so it can be updated if the values in the table change.
- You must update the total each time one of the values used in the formula is changed. The total does not update automatically.
- By default, Word assumes you want to use the SUM **function** to add the values entered in the column above the current cell or in the row beside the current cell.
- You can enter a different formula by typing it into the Formula text box in the Formula dialog box.
- You can also select a function from the Paste function drop-down list in the Formula dialog box.
- For anything other than basic calculations, use an Excel worksheet, not a Word table.

✓ *For information on using Excel functions, and formulas, refer to the Excel section in this book.*

Try It! Performing Addition in a Table

1. Start Word and open **WTry17** from the data files for this lesson. Save the file as **WTry17_studentfirstname_studentlastname** in the location where your teacher instructs you to store the files for this lesson.
2. In the first table, click in the bottom cell in the right column.
3. Click Table Tools Layout > Formula.
4. Verify that the Formula box displays the formula for adding the values in the cells above the current cell: =SUM(ABOVE).
5. Click OK.
6. Click in the bottom cell of the left column in the first table (Total).
7. On the Table Tools Layout tab, click the Insert Above button.
8. Click in the left column of the new row and type **Taxi**.
9. Press TAB and type **$53.65**.
10. Right-click on the value in the bottom cell of the right column.
11. On the shortcut menu, click Update Field.

    ✓ *The shortcut key for updating a total is* F9.
12. Save the changes to **WTry17_studentfirstname_studentlastname** and leave it open to use in the next Try It.

Applying a Number Format

- When you set up a calculation in a table, you can select a number format in the Formula dialog box to apply to the calculation result.
- Number formats include dollar signs, commas, percent signs, and decimal points.

Try It! Applying a Number Format

1. In the **WTry17_studentfirstname_studentlastname** file, click in the last cell in the right column of the second table.
2. On the Table Tools Layout tab, click the Formula button *fx*.
3. Verify that the Formula box displays the formula for adding the values in the cells to the left of the current cell: =SUM(LEFT).
4. Click the Number format drop-down arrow.
5. Click the third format from the top of the list: $#,##0.00;($#,##0.00).
6. Click OK. Word inserts the result of the formula and applies the selected format.
7. Save the changes to **WTry17_studentfirstname_studentlastname** and leave it open to use in the next Try It.

Select a Number format in the Formula dialog box

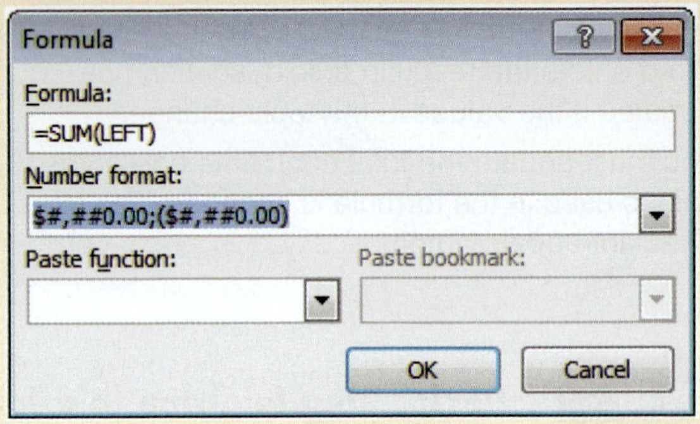

Sorting Rows in a Table

- Sort rows in a table using the Sort dialog box, the same way you sort lists or paragraphs.

  ✓ *See Word, Lesson 7.*

- For tables, the Sort command is available in the Data group on the Table Tools Layout tab of the Ribbon.
- Rows can be sorted according to the data in any column.
- Word rearranges the rows in the table but does not rearrange the columns.
- For example, in a table of names and addresses, rows can be sorted alphabetically by name or by city, or numerically by postal code.
- By default, Word identifies the type of data in the selected column as Text, Number, or Date.
- The default sort order is ascending, but you can select descending if you want.
- You can specify whether or not the table includes a header row that you do not want to include in the sort.
- Word identifies the columns by the label in the header row, if there is one. If not, it numbers the columns consecutively from left to right. For example, in a three-column table, Column 1 is on the left, Column 2 is in the middle, and Column 3 is on the right.
- You can even sort by up to three columns. For example, you can sort a single table alphabetically by name and then numerically by postal code.
- You cannot sort rows containing merged cells.

Try It! Sorting Rows in a Table

1. In the **WTry17_studentfirstname_studentlastname** file, select the right column in the first table.
2. On the Table Tools Layout Tab, click the Sort button.
3. In the Sort dialog box, verify that Column 2 is entered in the Sort by text box, that the data type is Number, that the Sort order is Ascending, and that the No header row option button is selected.
4. Click OK to sort the rows in ascending order based on the dollar values in the right column.

(continued)

Try It! Sorting Rows in a Table *(continued)*

Sort dialog box

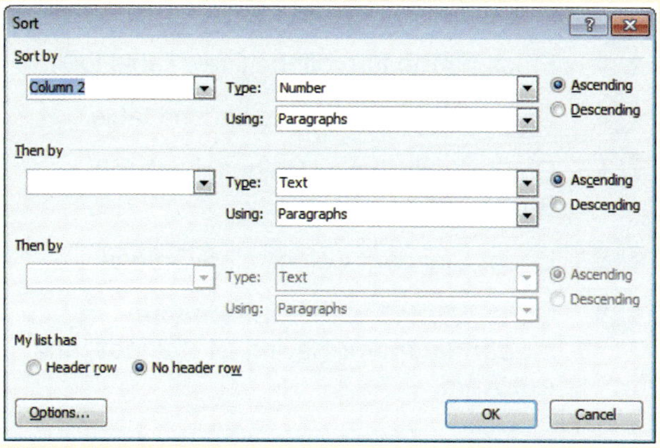

6. Insert a row above the current row so you can set up a header row.
7. In the left column, type **Expense**.
8. In the right column, type **Amount**.
9. On the Table Tools Layout tab, click the Sort button.
10. In the Sort dialog box, verify that Expense is entered in the Sort by text box, that the data type is Text, and that the sort order is Ascending.
11. Click the first Then by drop-down arrow and click Amount. Verify that the data type is Number, the sort order is Ascending, and that the Header row option button is selected.
12. Click OK.
13. Save the changes to **WTry17_ studentfirstname_studentlastname** and leave it open to use in the next Try It.

Applying Cell Borders and Shading

- By default, Word applies a ½-pt. black solid line border around all table cells.
- You can select to display or hide border lines along one or more sides of a cell.
- To change the appearance of the borders, you select a **line style**, **line weight**, and pen color, and then select the border style you want to apply.
- For example, you might apply a green, dashed border around the outside of selected cells, or a purple triple-line border across the bottom of the selected cells.
- When you select border formatting, the Draw Table tool becomes active so you can use it to draw a new table or cells using the selected formatting.
- You can apply background color or **shading** to a cell.
- Selected border and shading formatting remain in effect until new formatting is selected.
- Table style formatting takes precedence over direct border and shading formatting. Apply Table styles first, then modify the styles if necessary using the direct formatting.

✓ *When table borders are removed, you can see table cells onscreen by displaying gridlines. Refer to Word, Lesson 14 for information on showing and hiding gridlines.*

Try It! Applying Cell Borders and Shading

1. In the **WTry17_studentfirstname_ studentlastname** file, select the first table.
2. Click Table Tools Design > Line Style.
3. From the Line Style gallery, click the double-line line style.

   ✓ *Notice that the Draw Table tool becomes active.*

(continued)

Try It! Applying Cell Borders and Shading *(continued)*

4. Click Table Tools Design > Line Weight [½ pt].
5. From the Line Weight gallery, click 1½ pt.
6. Click the Pen Color drop-down arrow.
7. Under Standard Colors, click Red.
8. Click the Borders drop-down arrow.
9. From the Borders gallery, click Outside Borders. Word applies an outside border around the selected cells, using the selected border formatting.

✓ *Border styles are toggles—click on to display border; click off to hide border.*

10. Press ESC to turn off the Draw Table tool.
11. Select the top row in the second table.
12. On the Table Tools Design tab, click the Shading drop-down arrow.
13. Under Standard Colors, click Orange.
14. Close **WTry17_studentfirstname_studentlastname** saving all changes, and exit Word.

Project 35—Create It

Gift Basket Flyer

DIRECTIONS

1. Start Word and save the new, blank document as **WProj35_studentfirstname_studentlastname** in the location where your teacher instructs you to store the files for this lesson.
2. Display the rulers and nonprinting characters.
3. Double-click in the header area and type your full name and today's date. Close the Header area.
4. Set the font to 14-point Calibri and type:
   Celebrate Earth Day by sending someone you love a beautiful gift basket filled with organic treats. The basket includes all of the items listed below, as well as an Earth Day surprise. The basket is beautifully arranged and wrapped using recycled materials. Local delivery is included in the special price.
5. Press ENTER.
6. Click **Insert** > **Table**. Drag across the Insert Table grid to insert a table with two columns and three rows.
7. Enter the following data in the table cells:

Muffins	15.99
Fruit Preserves	12.99
Granola	10.99

8. Select the left column.
9. Click **Table Tools Layout** > **Sort**.
10. Verify that Column 1 is entered in the Sort by text box, that the data type is Text, that the sort order is Ascending, and that the No header row option is selected.
11. Click **OK**.
12. Insert a new row at the bottom of the table.
13. In the left column of the new row, type **Total**.
14. Click in the right column of the new row, then, click **Table Tools Layout** > **Formula** *fx*.
15. Verify that the formula is =SUM(ABOVE).
16. Click the **Number format** drop-down arrow and click the third format from the top of the list: $#,##0.00;($#,##0.00).
17. Click **OK**.
18. Select the bottom row.
19. Click **Table Tools Design** > **Line Style** and click the solid line style.
21. Click the **Line Weight** button [½ pt] and click **3 pt**.

22. Click the **Pen Color** drop-down arrow and, under Theme Colors, click **Dark Blue, Text 2**.
23. Click the **Borders** drop-down arrow and click **Top Border**.
24. Select the right column of the table and set a decimal tab stop at 4.0" on the ruler.
25. Check and correct the spelling and grammar in the document, and then save the changes.
26. **With your teacher's permission**, print the document. It should look similar to Figure 17-1.
27. Close the document, saving all changes, and exit Word.

Figure 17-1

Firstname Lastname
Today's Date

Celebrate Earth Day by sending someone you love a beautiful gift basket filled with organic treats. The basket includes all of the items listed below, as well as an Earth Day surprise. The basket is beautifully arranged and wrapped using recycled materials. Local delivery is included in the special price.

Fruit Preserves	12.99
Granola	10.99
Muffins	15.99
Total	$ 39.97

Project 36—Apply It

Gift Basket Flyer

DIRECTIONS

1. Start Word, if necessary, and open **WProj36** from the data files for this lesson.
2. Save the file as **WProj36_studentfirstname_studentlastname** in the location where your teacher instructs you to store the files for this lesson.
3. Display the rulers and nonprinting characters.
4. In the header, type your full name and today's date. Use the following steps to complete and format the table, as shown in Figure 17-2 on the next page.
5. Click in the bottom right cell in the table and insert a formula to add the values in the cells above. Format the result as dollars.
6. Insert a row at the top of the table. In the left cell of the new row, type **Organic Whole Grain Banana Bread**. In the right cell of the new row, type **16.35**.
7. Update the result of the formula in the bottom left cell to include the new value.
8. Sort the table rows into ascending order based first on the data in column 1 and then by the data in column 2.
9. Insert another new row at the top of the table.

10. In the left cell of the new row, type **Basket Includes:**.
11. In the right cell of the new row, type **Regular Price:**.
12. Select the top row of the table and apply the **Red, Accent 2** shading.
13. With the top row still selected, remove all borders from the top row.
14. Select the bottom row of the table and apply a **solid-line, 2¼ pt. Red, Accent 2** outside border.
15. With the bottom row still selected, apply **Red, Accent 2, Lighter 80%** shading.
16. Check and correct the spelling and grammar in the document, and then save the changes.
17. **With your teacher's permission**, print the document. It should look similar to Figure 17-2.
18. Close the document, saving all changes, and exit Word.

Figure 17-2

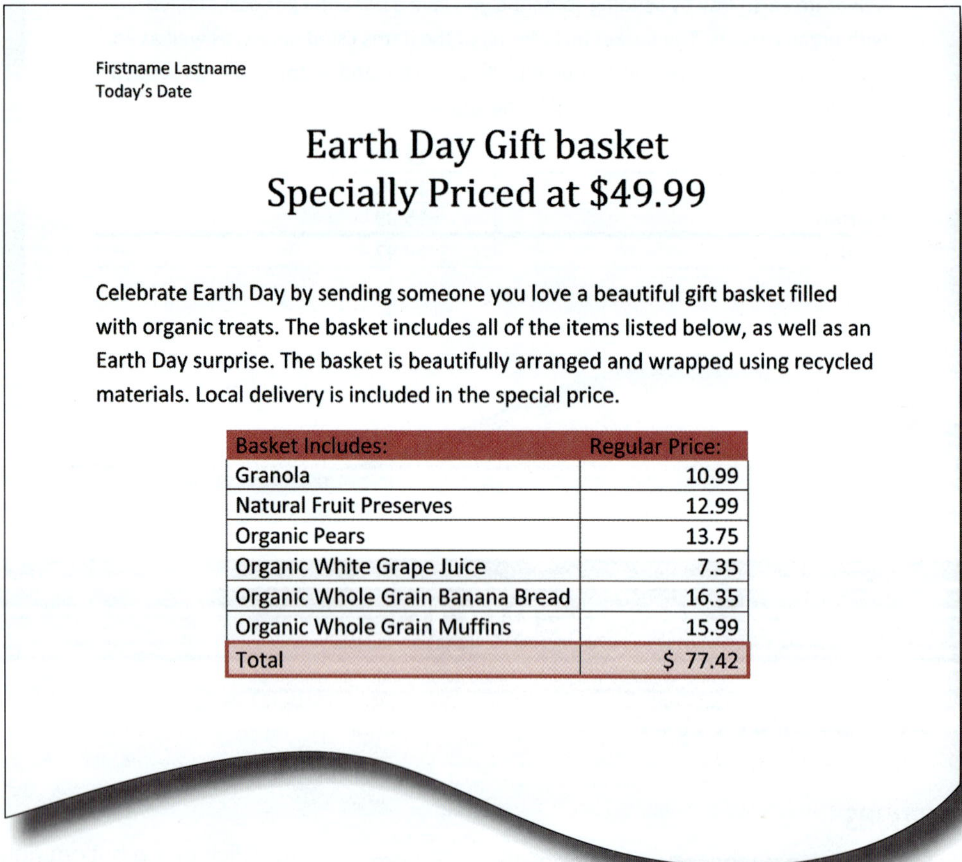

Firstname Lastname
Today's Date

Earth Day Gift basket
Specially Priced at $49.99

Celebrate Earth Day by sending someone you love a beautiful gift basket filled with organic treats. The basket includes all of the items listed below, as well as an Earth Day surprise. The basket is beautifully arranged and wrapped using recycled materials. Local delivery is included in the special price.

Basket Includes:	Regular Price:
Granola	10.99
Natural Fruit Preserves	12.99
Organic Pears	13.75
Organic White Grape Juice	7.35
Organic Whole Grain Banana Bread	16.35
Organic Whole Grain Muffins	15.99
Total	$ 77.42

Lesson 18

Improving a Document with Find and Replace and AutoCorrect

➤ What You Will Learn

- Using Find
- Using Advanced Find
- Using Find and Replace
- Using Go To
- Using the Navigation Pane
- Browsing by Object
- Using AutoCorrect
- Editing the AutoCorrect List

WORDS TO KNOW

AutoCorrect
A feature available in most Microsoft Office 2010 programs that automatically corrects common spelling errors as you type.

Navigation pane
A task pane that opens on the left side of the document window. Features in the Navigation pane help you quickly locate and go to a specific location in a document.

Thumbnails
Small pictures.

Software Skills Word's Navigation pane provides access to tools such as Find, Browse Headings, and Browse Pages that help you quickly move to a specific location in a document. Word's AutoCorrect feature automatically replaces typed characters with something else. You can use it to correct common spelling errors—such as to replace *teh* with *the*—or to insert formatted text and graphics by simply typing two or three characters.

Application Skills You have been working to complete a report on exercise for Michigan Avenue Athletic Club. In this lesson, you will edit a version of the document using Find and Replace. You will use the Navigation pane to navigate through the document to find headings and paragraphs, and AutoCorrect to correct typing errors and to insert a header.

What You Can Do

Using Find

- Use Word's Find feature to locate and highlight all occurrences of a word or phrase within a document
- You type the text to find in the **Navigation pane**; Word displays a list of occurrences in the Navigation pane and highlights the text in the document. Click an item in the list to move the insertion point to it.

Try It! Using Find

1. Start Word and open **WTry18a** from the data files for this lesson. Save the file as **WTry18a_studentfirstname_studentlastname** in the location where your teacher instructs you to store the files for this lesson.
2. On the Home tab, click the Find button to display the Navigation pane.

   ✓ *By default, the most recently searched for text displays in the Navigation pane text box.*
3. In the text box at the top of the Navigation pane, delete any text that displays and type **business**. Word displays a list of occurrences in the Navigation pane, and highlights the text throughout the document.
4. Delete the text *business* in the Navigation pane text box and type **entre**. Word finds and highlights the text throughout the document.
5. Click the third occurrence of the text in the list in the Navigation pane. Word moves the insertion point to that occurrence.
6. Click the Navigation pane Close button.
7. Save the changes to **WTry18a_studentfirstname_studentlastname**, and leave it open to use in the next Try It.

Use Find in the Navigation pane

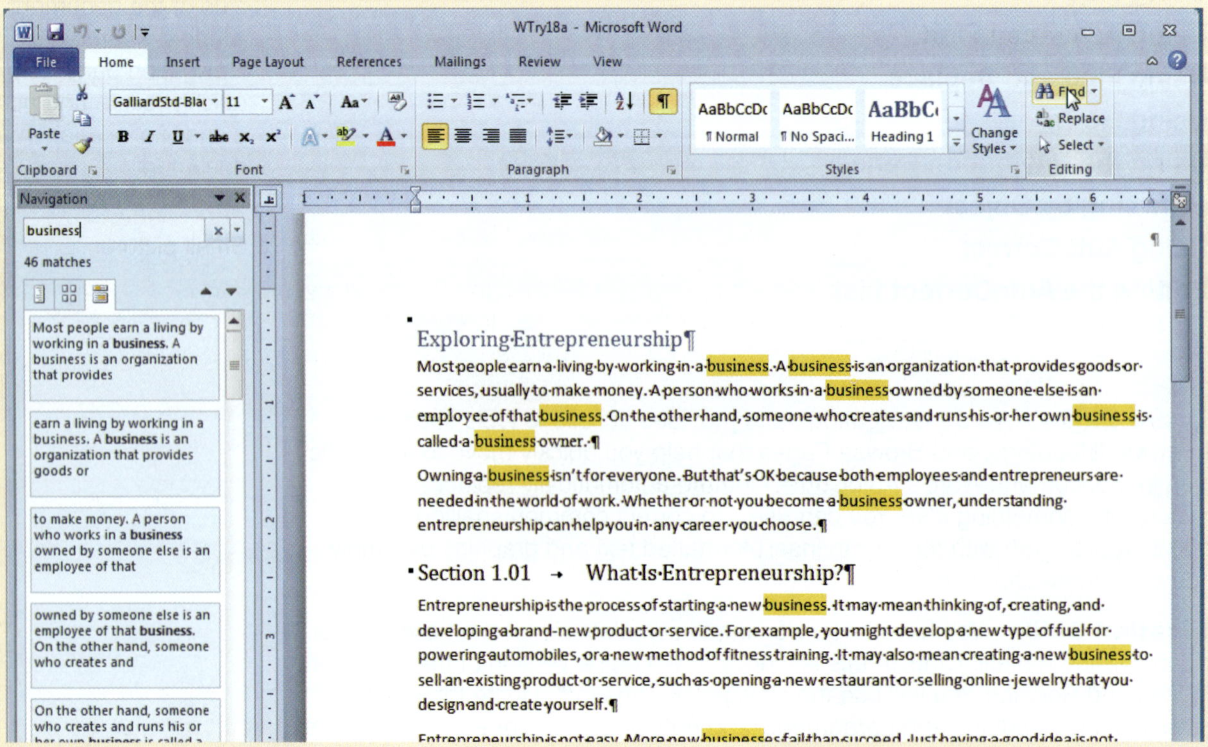

Using Advanced Find

- Use Advanced Find in the Find and Replace dialog box when you want to find and/or replace text or other content, such as formatting, nonprinting characters such as spaces or paragraph marks, symbols, graphics, objects, or other items.
- You can also use Advanced Find to expand the search options to look through headers and footers as well as the main document, to move one by one through each occurrence of the Find text, and to specify criteria, such as matching upper- or lowercase or finding whole word matches only.

Try It! Using Advanced Find

1. In the **WTry18a_studentfirstname_studentlastname** file, press CTRL + HOME to move the insertion point to the beginning of the document.
2. On the Home tab, click the Find drop-down arrow and then click Advanced Find to open the Find and Replace dialog box.

   ✓ *You can also open the Find and Replace dialog box from the Navigation pane. Click the drop-down arrow in the text box at the top of the pane, and click Advanced Find.*
3. In the Find what text box, replace the existing text by typing **Business Owner**.
4. Click Find Next. Word finds and highlights the first occurrence of the text. Notice that even though you typed *Business Owner* with initial capitalization, Word highlights the text *business owner*. By default, case does not matter.

   ✓ *You can drag the dialog box out of the way, if necessary.*
5. Click the More button to expand the dialog box to show all of the search options.
6. Click to select the Match case check box.

   ✓ *A check mark indicates the option is selected.*
7. Click Find Next. Word highlights the text *Business Owner*, matching the case you typed.
8. In the Find and Replace dialog box, click Cancel.
9. Save **WTry18a_studentfirstname_studentlastname** and leave it open to use in the next Try It.

Using Find and Replace

- Use options on the Replace tab of the Find and Replace dialog box when you want to replace occurrences of a word or phrase with something else.
- Replace is useful for correcting errors that occur several times in a document, such as a misspelled name.
- You can use the expanded search options to refine the procedure just as with Advanced Find.

Using Go To

- Use the Go To tab in the Find and Replace dialog box to move the insertion point to a particular part of the document, such as a page, heading, table, or graphic.

Try It! Using Find and Replace

1. In the **WTry18a_studentfirstname_studentlastname** file, press CTRL + HOME to move the insertion point to the beginning of the document.
2. On the Home tab, click the Replace button to open the Find and Replace dialog box. The Replace tab should be active, with the criteria for the previous search still entered.
3. In the Find what text box, replace any existing text by typing **a business owner**.
4. Click in the Replace with text box and type **an entrepreneur**.
5. Verify that the Match case check box is still selected, and then click Find Next. Word finds and highlights the first occurrence of the text *a business owner*.
6. Click Replace. Word replaces the text *a business owner* with the text *an entrepreneur*, and highlights the next occurrence.
7. Click Replace All. Word replaces all occurrences, and displays a dialog box telling you how many replacements it made.
8. Click OK. In the Find and Replace dialog box, click Close.
9. Save the changes to **WTry18a_studentfirstname_studentlastname** and leave it open to use in the next Try It.

Use Find and Replace

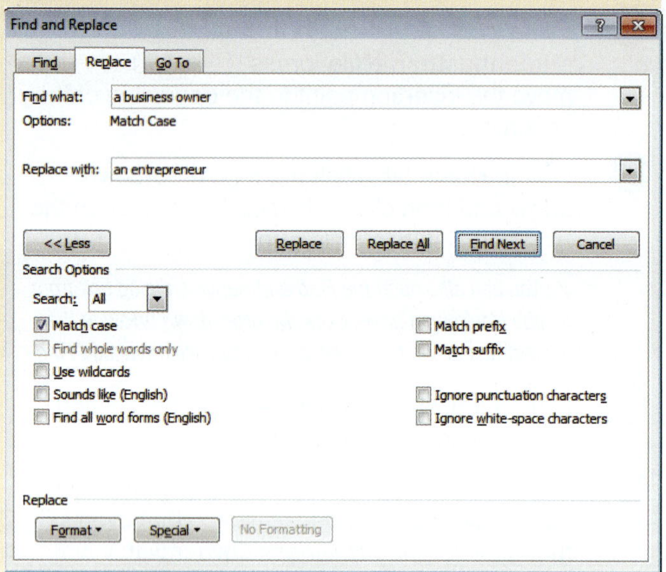

Try It! Using Go To

1. In the **WTry18a_studentfirstname_studentlastname** file, on the Home tab, click the Find drop-down arrow and then click Go To to open the Find and Replace dialog box with the Go To tab active.
2. In the Enter page number text box, type **2**, and then click Go To. Word moves the insertion point to the top of page 2.
3. In the Go to what list box, scroll down and click Heading, and then click the Next button. Word moves the insertion point to the next heading.
4. Click in the Enter heading number text box and type **-2**.
5. Click Go To. Word moves the insertion point back two headings.
6. In the Find and Replace dialog box, click Close.
7. Save the changes to **WTry18a_studentfirstname_studentlastname** and leave it open to use in the next Try It.

(continued)

Try It! Using Go To *(continued)*

Use Go To

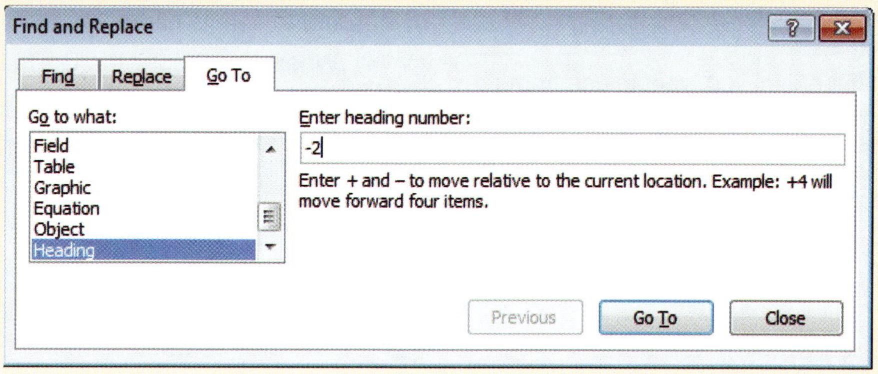

Using the Navigation Pane

- The Navigation pane provides access to two tools that are useful for navigating through long documents: Browse Headings and Browse Pages.
- On the Browse Headings tab, paragraphs formatted as headings display in an outline format.
- Click a heading to move the insertion point to that location in the document.
- If there are no headings, the tab is empty.
- On the Browse Pages tab Word displays **thumbnails** representing each page in the document.
- Click a thumbnail to go to that page.

Try It! Using the Navigation Pane

1. In **WTry18a_studentfirstname_studentlastname**, click the View tab, and then click the Navigation Pane check box to select it.

3. Click the Navigation Pane check box again to clear the check mark and close the pane.

4. Display the Navigation pane.

5. In the Navigation pane, under the Search Document text box, click the Browse Headings tab.

   ✓ *The Browse Headings tab is the left of the three tabs. The ScreenTip displays Browse the headings in your document.*

6. In the Navigation pane, click the heading Section 1.04. Word moves the insertion point to that heading.

7. In the Navigation pane, click the heading Section 1.01. Word moves the insertion point to that heading.

8. In the Navigation pane under the Search Document text box, click the Browse Pages tab.

   ✓ *The Browse Pages tab is the middle of the three tabs. The ScreenTip displays Browse the pages in your document.*

9. Click the page 1 thumbnail. Word moves the insertion point to the beginning of page 1.

10. Click the page 2 thumbnail. Word moves the insertion point to the beginning of page 2.

11. Click the Navigation pane Close button.

12. Save the **WTry18a_studentfirstname_studentlastname** and leave it open to use in the next Try It.

Browsing by Object

- Use Words Browse by feature to scroll to a specific object or feature in a document.
- The feature is accessed using buttons below the vertical scroll bar.
- First, you select the object you want to use from the Browse Object gallery, then you use the Previous and Next buttons to move to that object.

✓ *The ScreenTips for the Previous and Next buttons change depending on the selected browse object.*

- There are twelve browse objects from which to choose; rest the mouse pointer on an object in the gallery to see its name.
  - When you choose the Go To browse object, you must specify the object to go to.
  - When you choose the Find browse object, you must enter text to Find and/or Replace.

Try It! Browsing by Object

1. In the **WTry18a_studentfirstname_studentlastname** file, click the Select Browse Object button to display the gallery of browse objects.

Gallery of browse objects

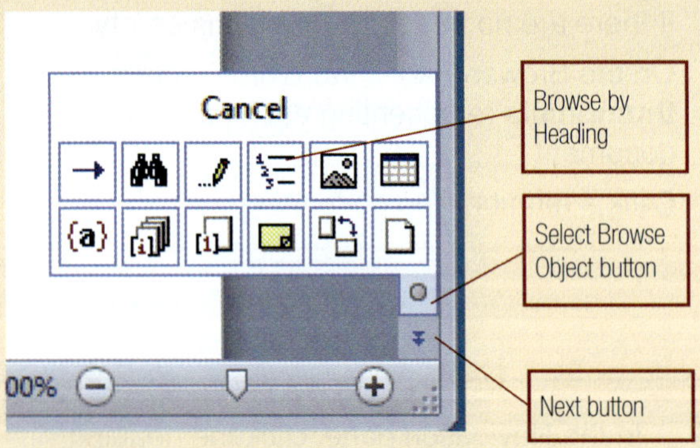

2. Click Browse by Heading.
3. Click the Previous Heading button to move the insertion point to the previous heading.

   ✓ *The shortcut key combination for browsing to the previous object is* CTRL + PG UP.

4. Click the Next Heading button to move the insertion point to the next heading.

   ✓ *The shortcut key combination for browsing to the next object is* CTRL + PG DN.

5. Close the **WTry18a_studentfirstname_studentlastname** file, saving all changes, and leave Word open to use in the next Try It.

Using AutoCorrect

- **AutoCorrect** automatically replaces typed characters with something else as soon as you press the spacebar after typing.
- It is particularly useful for correcting common spelling errors.
- Word comes with a built-in list of AutoCorrect entries including common typos like *adn* for *and* and *teh* for *the*.
- There are also AutoCorrect entries for replacing regular characters with symbols, such as the letters T and M enclosed in parentheses (TM) with the trademark symbol, ™, and for inserting accent marks in words such as café, cliché, crème, and déjà vu.
- By default, AutoCorrect corrects capitalization errors as follows:
  - TWo INitial CApital letters are replaced with one initial capital letter.
  - The first word in a sentence is automatically capitalized.
  - The days of the week are automatically capitalized.
  - Accidental use of the cAPS LOCK feature is corrected if the Caps Lock key is set to ON.
- If AutoCorrect changes text that was not incorrect, you can use Undo or the AutoCorrect Options button to reverse the change.
- If you find AutoCorrect distracting, you can disable it.
- The AutoCorrect list is shared among the Microsoft Office programs.

Try It! Using AutoCorrect

1. In Word, create a new blank file and save it as **WTry18b_studentfirstname_studentlastname** in the location where your teacher instructs you to store the files for this lesson.
2. Type **Mike adn Jane**. Notice that as soon as you press the spacebar after the misspelled word *adn*, Word corrects the spelling.
3. Type **recieved a package**. Again, as soon as you press the spacebar after the misspelled word *recieved*, Word corrects the spelling.
4. Move the mouse pointer over the corrected word *received*. A small blue rectangle displays below the word.
5. Rest the mouse pointer on the rectangle to display the AutoCorrect Options button.
6. Click the AutoCorrect Options button to display available options.
7. Click anywhere in the document outside the AutoCorrect Options menu.
8. Save the **WTry18b_studentfirstname_studentlastname** and leave it open to use in the next Try It.

Editing the AutoCorrect List

- You can add words to the AutoCorrect list in the AutoCorrect dialog box. For example, if you commonly misspell someone's name, you can add it to the list.
- You can even use AutoCorrect to replace a code with a phrase, paragraph, and even objects, such as pictures. For example, you can set AutoCorrect to replace the text *MyAddress* with your actual address, or the word *letterhead* with a company letterhead.
- You can delete AutoCorrect entries.
- If you want to permanently stop AutoCorrect from replacing certain words, you can add them to the Exceptions list. Access the Exceptions list by clicking the Exceptions button in the AutoCorrect dialog box.

Try It! Editing the AutoCorrect List

1. In Word, click File > Options to open the Word Options dialog box.
2. Click Proofing.
3. Click AutoCorrect Options to open the AutoCorrect dialog box.
4. Click in the Replace text box and type **Suzie**.
5. Click in the With text box and type **Suzy**.
6. Click Add.
7. Click OK.
8. Click OK to close the Word Options dialog box.
9. In the **WTry18b_studentfirstname_studentlastname** file, press ENTER to start a new line, type **Suzie**, and press SPACE. As soon as you press the spacebar, Word replaces *Suzie* with *Suzy*.

(continued)

Try It! Editing the AutoCorrect List *(continued)*

AutoCorrect dialog box

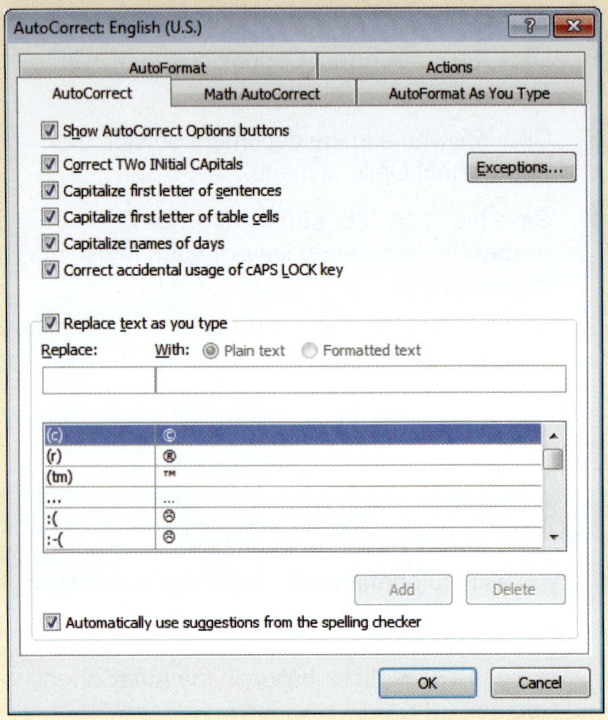

10. Press ENTER, type your full name and address as you would if you were addressing an envelope.
11. Apply the No Spacing style to the address, increase the font size to 14 points, and apply the Bold font style.
12. Select all lines in the address.
13. Click File > Options > Proofing.
14. Click AutoCorrect Options. Notice that the selected text displays in the With text box.
15. Click in the Replace text box and type **MyAddress**.
16. Click Add.
17. Click OK.
18. Click OK to close the Word Options dialog box.
19. In the **WTry18b_studentfirstname_ studentlastname** file, double-click in the header area.
20. Type **MyAddress** and press SPACE. As soon as you press the spacebar Word replaces the text with your formatted address.
21. In Word, click File > Options > Proofing > AutoCorrect Options.
22. Click in the Replace text box and type **Suzie**.
23. In the list of AutoCorrect entries, click Suzie|Suzy.
24. Click Delete.
25. Click in the Replace text box and replace the text *Suzie* by typing **MyAddress**.
26. In the list of AutoCorrect entries, click MyAddress.
27. Click Delete.
28. Click OK.
29. Click OK to close the Word Options dialog box.
30. Save the **WTry18b_studentfirstname_ studentlastname** file, close it, and exit Word.

Project 37—Create It

Athletic Club Report

DIRECTIONS

1. Start Word and open **WProj37a** from the data files for this lesson.
2. Select the line of text in the document.
3. Click **File** > **Options** > **Proofing**.
4. Click **AutoCorrect Options**. Notice that the selected text displays in the With text box.
5. Click in the **Replace** text box and type **letterhead**.
6. Click **Add**.
7. Click **OK**.
8. Click **OK** to close the Word Options dialog box.
9. Close **WProj37a** without saving any changes.
10. Open **WProj37b** from the data files for this lesson. Save it and save as **WProj37b_studentfirstname_studentlastname** in the location where your teacher instructs you to store the files for this lesson.
11. Format the first line of the document with the **Title** style.
12. Replace the sample text *Student's Name* with your own name, and replace the sample text *Today's Date* with the actual date.
13. On the Home tab, click the **Find** button to display the Navigation task pane.
14. In the text box at the top of the Navigation pane, delete any text that displays and type **<H1>**.
15. In the document, click in the text *Introduction* next to the highlighted *<H1>*, and apply the **Heading 1** style.
16. Click in the text box at the top of the Navigation pane and press ENTER to repeat the search.
17. Repeat steps 15 and 16 to format the text next to each occurrence of *<H1>* in the Heading 1 style.
18. Select the text *<H1>* in the Navigation pane text box and replace it with the text **<H2>**.
19. In the document, click in the text *Disease Control* next to the first highlighted *<H2>*, and apply **Heading 2** style.
20. Click in the text box at the top of the Navigation pane and press ENTER to repeat the search.
21. Repeat steps 19 and 20 to format the text next to each occurrence of *<H2>* in the Heading 2 style.
22. In the Navigation pane, click the **Browse Pages** tab (the middle of the three tabs below the text box).
23. Click the page 1 thumbnail to move the insertion point to the beginning of the document.
24. Double-click in the header area and type **letterhead**, then press SPACE to insert the letterhead AutoCorrect entry.
25. Double-click in the document area to close the header and make the document active.
26. Click the Navigation pane **Close** button to close the pane.
27. On the Home tab, click the **Replace** button to open the Find and Replace dialog box.
28. Delete the text in the Find what box and type **<H1>**. Delete all text from the Replace with text box. Clear the Match case check box, if necessary.
29. Click **Replace All**. Word replaces all occurrences of <H1> with nothing.
30. Click **OK**.
31. Edit the text in the Find what text box to **<H2>**, and click **Replace All**. Word replaces all occurrences of <H2> with nothing.
32. Click **OK**, and then click **Close** in the Find and Replace dialog box.
33. Check and correct the spelling and grammar in the document, and then save the changes.
34. **With your teacher's permission**, print the document. Page 1 should look similar to Figure 18-1 on the next page.
35. Close the document, saving all changes, and exit Word.

Figure 18-1

Michigan Avenue Athletic Club

Exercise for Life

Prepared by
Firstname Lastname
Today's Date

Introduction

The benefits of regular exercise cannot be overstated. Studies have shown that people who exercise regularly live longer, are healthier, and enjoy a better quality of life than those who do not exercise. It is now generally accepted knowledge that even moderate physical activity performed regularly improves the health and well-being of all individuals.

Despite this knowledge, studies show that more than 60% of American adults are not regularly active and that an astonishing 25% of adults are not active at all. Therefore, the government recommends that schools and communities provide education to promote exercise to people of all ages.

This report has been prepared for Michigan Avenue Athletic Club in order to help spread the word on the importance of physical activity for the health of our members. It is meant as an introduction only. For more information about the health benefits of exercise, or about a particular type of exercise program, please contact any member of our staff. He or she will be happy to help you find the information you need.

The Impact on Your Health

It is believed that lack of physical activity and poor diet taken together are the second largest underlying cause of death in the United States. Studies show that even the most inactive people can gain significant health benefits if they accumulate 30 minutes or more of physical activity per day. Some of the known benefits of exercise include disease prevention and control, weight control, and improved mental health.

Exercise can also have an impact on your lifestyle as well. Exercising may improve your social life by giving you an opportunity to meet new people. It may open up opportunities for your career as well. For example, it is commonly believed that a lot of business is conducted on the golf course or tennis court!

Disease Control

Daily physical activity can help prevent heart disease and stroke by strengthening the heart muscle, lowering blood pressure, raising the levels of good cholesterol and lowering bad cholesterol, improving blood flow, and increasing the heart's working capacity.

By reducing body fat, physical activity helps prevent obesity and may help to prevent and control noninsulin-dependent diabetes.

By increasing muscle strength and endurance and improving flexibility and posture, regular exercise helps to prevent back pain. Regular weight-bearing exercise promotes bone formation and may prevent many forms of bone loss associated with aging.

Project 38—Apply It

Athletic Club Report

DIRECTIONS

1. Start Word, if necessary, and open **WProj38** from the data files for this lesson.
2. Save the file as **WProj38_studentfirstname_studentlastname** in the location where your teacher instructs you to store the files for this lesson.
3. Replace the sample text *Student's Name* with your own name, and *Today's Date* with the actual date.
4. Make the header active and type **letterhead**. Press SPACE to insert the letterhead AutoCorrect entry.

   ✓ *If the letterhead AutoCorrect entry is not available on your system, follow steps 1 through 10 of Project 37 to create it.*
5. Close the header area.
6. Open the Find and Replace dialog box.
7. Find all occurrences of the text *Obese people*, and replace it with **Those who are overweight**. Be sure to match the case.
8. Replace all occurrences of the text *obese people*, with **those who are overweight**.
9. When the procedure is complete, close the Find and Replace dialog box.
10. Display the **Navigation Pane**.
11. In the Navigation pane, display the **Browse Headings** tab.
12. Go to the heading, *Doctor Supervision*. Close the Navigation pane.
13. Click at the end of the paragraph under the heading and type **The doctor will check for signs that your body might not be able to withstand physical activity. If there is a problem, he or she might place limitations on the type of activity you can do.**
14. Click **File** > **Options** > **Proofing** > **AutoCorrect Options**.
15. Click in the **Replace** text box and type **letterhead**.
16. In the list of AutoCorrect entries, click **letterhead**.
17. Click **Delete**.
18. Click **OK**.
19. Close the Word Options dialog box.
20. Check and correct the spelling and grammar in the document, and then save the changes.
21. **With your teacher's permission**, print the document.
22. Close the document, saving all changes, and exit Word.

Lesson 19

Working with Templates and Different File Types

WORDS TO KNOW

Content controls
Automated features such as a pop-up calendar or drop-down list that make it easier to enter or format information.

Domain name
The name that identifies a Web site.

File extension
A dot followed by three or four characters at the end of a file name, used to indicate the file type.

File icon
The icon used to represent a file in a file list.

File type
The format in which a file is stored. Usually, the file type corresponds to the program used to create the file.

HTML
Hypertext Markup Language. A file format used for storing Web pages.

Path
The route through storage folders and devices to the location where a file is stored.

Placeholder
Sample text or graphics that marks a location in a document where content should be placed.

➤ What You Will Learn

- Recognizing File Types
- Opening and Saving Compatible Files
- Analyzing Web Page Files
- Saving a Word Document as a Web Page
- Using Web Layout View
- Saving a Word Document as PDF
- Analyzing a Resume
- Creating a Document Based on a Template
- Using Content Controls
- Saving a Word Document as a Template
- Exploring Templates on Office.com

Software Skills Templates help you create consistent documents efficiently—and time after time. Templates include page setup and formatting settings to ensure that new documents will be uniform. In many cases they include standard text and graphics as well. You can use Word to open files created with different word processing programs, and to save Word documents in different formats. For example, you can save a Word document as a Web page so that you can display it on the World Wide Web or on a company intranet.

Application Skills Vocation Opportunities, Inc., a career counseling company, offers a service helping clients develop effective job search materials. In this lesson, you will use a Word template to create a resume for a client. You will save the resume in different file formats so it can be viewed using different programs or in different situations, including as a Web page.

What You Can Do

Recognizing File Types

- Files are saved in different **file types**, depending on the application used to create, save, and open the file.
- File types are sometimes referred to as file formats.
- All files have a **file extension** that indicates the file type. For example, a Word 2010 file has a .docx file extension.
- By default, file extensions do not display in Windows. Instead, the name of the program and the **file icon** indicate the file type.
- Table 19-1 lists some common file types and their extensions.

Table 19-1 Common File Types

File Type	File Extension
Word 2010 and 2007 documents	.docx
Word 2010 and 2007 templates	.dotx
Word 97-2003 documents	.doc
Word 97-2003 templates	.dot
Text files	.txt
Web pages	.htm
Excel 2010 and 2007 workbooks	.xlsx
Excel 97-2003 workbooks	.xls
PowerPoint 2010 and 2007 files	.pptx
PowerPoint 97-2003 files	.ppt
Portable document format	.pdf
Graphics Interchange files	.gif
Joint Photography Experts Group	.jpg
Windows media audio file	.wma
Windows media video file	.wmv
MPEG audio	.mp3

WORDS TO KNOW

Protocol
A set of rules that computers use to communicate with each other across a network.

Resume
A document summarizing an individual's employment experience, education, and other information a potential employer needs to know.

Uniform resource locator (URL)
The address that identifies the storage location of a file or page on the Internet.

Web browser
Software designed for locating and viewing information stored on the Internet.

Web page
A document stored on the World Wide Web.

Web page title
A descriptive name or title that displays in the title bar when the page is open in a Web browser.

Web server
A computer connected to the Internet used to store Web page documents.

Web site
A set of linked Web pages relating to the same topic.

World Wide Web
A system for finding information on the Internet through the use of linked documents.

Figure 19-1

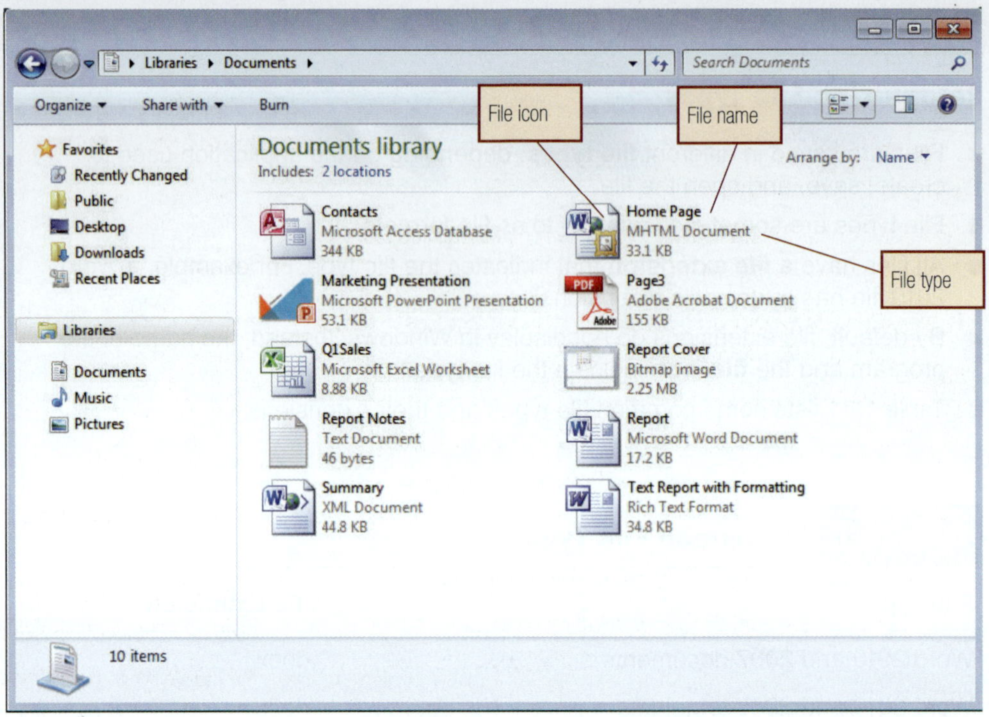

Opening and Saving Compatible Files

- You can save a Word document in a variety of file types, including .pdf, .htm, .txt, and .rtf.
- Use the Save As dialog box to save a Word file in a compatible file type, or to save a compatible file in its original file type or as a Word document.
- Word 2010 can open documents saved in compatible file types. For example, Word can open text files, Web page files, XML files, and files created with other versions of Word.
- Use the Open dialog box to open any file type that is compatible with Word 2010.
- By default, only Word documents display in the Open dialog box, but you can select to display a specific file type, or all files.
- Compatible files open in Compatibility Mode in Word; the text [Compatibility Mode] displays in the title bar.
- If some Word 2010 features are not supported by the selected file type when you save or open the file, Word displays a File Conversion or Compatibility Checker dialog box that shows you how the new format will affect the document contents.
- For example, a plain text file cannot display graphics or style formatting.

Try It! Opening and Saving Compatible Files

1. Start Word and open **WTry19a** from the data files for this lesson.
2. Click File > Save As.
3. Type **WTry19a_studentfirstname_studentlastname**.
4. Click the Save as type button to display a list of compatible file types.
5. Click Plain Text.
6. Navigate to the location where your teacher instructs you to store the files for this lesson.
7. Click Save.
8. Click OK in the File Conversion dialog box.
9. Close **WTry19a_studentfirstname_studentlastname**. Leave Word open.
10. Click File > Open.
11. Click the File Type button to display a list of available file types.

    ✓ *The text on the File Type button changes depending on your most recent selection. If you have never changed the file type, it will display All Word Documents.*
12. Click All Files to display all files in the current storage location.
13. Click the text document **WTry19a_studentfirstname_studentlastname**.
14. Click Open.
15. If Word displays a File Conversion dialog box, click OK.
16. Double-click the word *Zebra* to select it, and then on the Home tab, in the Font group, click the Bold button [B].
17. Click the Save button on the Quick Access Toolbar.
18. In the warning dialog box, click Yes to save the file in the current format—plain text.

    ✓ *Click No to open the Save As dialog box so you can save the file in Word document format. You can select any file format in the Save As dialog box, change the storage location, and enter a new file name, if you want.*
19. Close the **WTry19a_studentfirstname_studentlastname** file, but leave Word open to use in the next Try It.

Analyzing Web Page Files

- **Web pages** are documents that are stored on a **Web server** so they can be accessed on the **World Wide Web** by anyone with a computer, an Internet connection, and Web **browser** software.
- Web page files must be in a file format that is compatible with the World Wide Web and browser software. Most files on the Web are in some form of **HTML**, which stands for Hypertext Markup Language. Some are in PDF format. Other file formats may also be used.
- Web pages are usually linked into **Web sites** which have a common topic. For example, www.whitehouse.gov is a Web site about the White House.

  ✓ *You learn about linking Web pages in Word, Lesson 33.*
- To access a Web page, you use your browser to go to a **uniform resource locator (URL),** which is the address of the file stored online.
- Microsoft Office 2010 comes with the Internet Explorer Web browser, although your computer may be set up to use a different browser.
- The main parts of a URL are:
  - The **protocol**, which tells the browser software the type of server where the page is stored. Web page servers use the http: protocol.
  - The **domain name** (sometimes called a host name), which identifies the company or organization to whom the Web site is registered. microsoft.com, whitehouse.gov, and harvard.edu are all domain names.
  - The **path**, which identifies the specific Web page or document to open.

- The end of the domain name—the last dot followed by two to four letters—is called the *top level domain*. It helps identify the type or location of the company or organization. You can use the top level domain to help you determine if a Web site is a good and accurate source for information.
- For example .gov indicates a government Web site and .edu indicates an educational institution. Both are generally reliable sources.
- The .com domain indicates a commercial business, so you might assume the information on the site is intended to support or promote the business in order to make money.
- The .org domain indicates a nonprofit business, so you might assume the information on the site is intended to promote a point of view or to encourage fundraising.
- Table 19-2 lists some common top level domains.

Table 19-2 Common Top Level Domains

Top Level Domain	Type or Location
.com	commercial business
.edu	educational organization
.gov	government agency
.org	nonprofit organization
.net	network-related business
.us	Websites in the United States
.ca	Web sites in Canada
.mx	Web sites in Mexico
.uk	Web sites in Great Britain
.cn	Web sites in China

Saving a Word Document as a Web Page

- You can save a Word document as a Web page so it can be stored on a Web server and viewed online.
- When you save a document as a Web page you can choose from three Web page formats:
  - Single File Web Page. Saves a Web page and all associated text and graphics in a single file in MHTML format. This is the default option.
  - Web Page. Saves the document in HTML format. Associated graphics files such as bullets, lines, and pictures are stored in a separate folder that is linked to the HTML file. The folder has the same name as the HTML file, followed by an underscore and the word files, like this: Filename_files.

    ✓ *Use caution when moving or renaming the graphics files or the folder they are stored in. If Word cannot identify the files, the page will display without graphics elements.*
  - Web Page, Filtered. Saves a file in HTML format without Microsoft Office tags. This reduces the file size, but limits some functionality for editing the file.

    ✓ *This option is recommended for advanced users only.*
- No matter which Web page format you choose, you can change the **Web page title** to something descriptive that will help the viewer know what the page displays.
- You can save a Web page in any storage location; in order to be available to viewers on the Web, it must be uploaded and stored on a Web server.
- When you save the file as a Web page, Word displays a list of features that are not compatible with the selected Web page format in the Compatibility Checker dialog box.

Try It! Saving a Word Document as a Web Page

1. In Word, open **WTry19b** from the data files for this lesson.
2. Click File > Save As.
3. Type **WTry19b_studentfirstname_studentlastname**.
4. Click the Save as type button to display a list of compatible file types.
5. Click Single File Web Page.
6. Click Change Title.
7. In the Page title text box, type **The Zebra**, and then click OK.
8. In the Save As dialog box, navigate to the location where your teacher instructs you to store the files for this lesson.
9. Click Save. Leave the **WTry19b_studentfirstname_studentlastname** file open to use in the next Try It.

Using Web Layout View

- Web Layout view displays documents in Word as they will look on the Web.
- Word automatically switches to Web Layout view when you display a Web page document.
- You can also switch to Web Layout view by clicking the Web Layout button in the Document Views group on the View tab of the Ribbon or from the View buttons on the status bar.
- Web Layout view lets you edit a document for viewing onscreen, instead of for printing on a page.
- Features of Web Layout view include:
  - Word wrapping to fit the window, not a page.
  - Graphics positioned as they would be in a Web browser.
  - Backgrounds (if there are any) displayed as they would be in a browser.
- You may have to adjust design features that look good in a Word document so that they look good on a Web page. For example, you may have to adjust the width of tables or the position of graphics.

Try It! Using Web Layout View

1. With the **WTry19b_studentfirstname_studentlastname** single file Web page document open in Word, click the Print Layout button on the status bar.

   ✓ *The document displays in Print Layout view.*
2. Click the Web Layout button on the status bar.

   ✓ *The document displays as it would look in a Web browser.*
3. Close the **WTry19b_studentfirstname_studentlastname** file, and leave Word open to use in the next Try It.

Saving a Word Document as PDF

- Portable Document Format is a file type that can be opened in many different programs.
- You can use the Save As dialog box to save a Word document in .pdf format.

Try It! Saving a Word Document as PDF

1. In Word, open **WTry19c** from the data files for this lesson.
2. Click File > Save As.
3. Type **WTry19c_studentfirstname_studentlastname**.
4. Click the Save as type button to display a list of compatible file types.
5. Click PDF.
6. In the Save As dialog box, navigate to the location where your teacher instructs you to store the files for this lesson.
7. Click Save.

   ✓ *The pdf file may display in Adobe Reader. Click the Close button to exit the program.*

8. Close **WTry19c** without saving any changes, and leave Word open to use in the next Try It.

Analyzing a Resume

- When you apply for a job you submit a **resume** which summarizes your qualifications, education, and experience. A resume is sometimes called a CV, which stands for Curriculum Vitae, which is Latin for "course of life."

  ✓ *You usually send a cover letter along with your resume. Refer to Word, Lesson 6 for information on writing a cover letter.*

- A resume is usually the first way a potential employer learns about you, so it is important to make it easy to read and informative.
- To make a positive impression, a resume should be neatly printed on white paper, truthful, and free of any typographical, grammatical, or spelling errors.
- An employer may spend less than a minute looking at your resume; the way it is formatted can help make important information stand out. For example, you should not crowd too much on the page, or use a font that is difficult to read. Using bullets can help the reader identify key points quickly.
- An effective resume has four main parts:
  - Your contact information, including name, address, phone, and e-mail.
  - An objective that describes your career goals.
  - A list of your educational experience, including the names of all schools where you earned a degree, with the most recent school at the top. You can also include special courses or certificates you have earned.
  - A list of your work experience, including all full-time and part-time jobs, internships, and volunteer experience, with the most recent at the top. Include the dates of employment, the job title, company name, and company location. You should briefly list your responsibilities and accomplishments.
- You may also include a section for listing skills, such as an ability to speak multiple languages or to use computer programs, and interests, such as co-curricular activities, awards, honors, and club or organization memberships.

Creating a Document Based on a Template

- All new Word documents are based on a template, which is a file that includes settings for page and text formatting.
- Blank documents are based on the Normal template, which includes settings for creating typical business documents. For example, the Normal template page size is 8.5 inches by 11 inches.

- All new documents based on the same template will have the same default formatting settings and will display the same placeholder text and graphics.
- Word comes with sample templates for creating common documents, such as memos, letters, Web pages, and resumes. Many additional templates are available online at Office.com.

✓ *You can also use templates you create yourself, or use an existing Word document as a template for a new document.*

- You select and preview templates in Backstage view.
- Templates usually come in a variety of themes. Each theme includes different formatting, so you can select a theme that best suits your purpose.
- For a professional, consistent look, you can coordinate your documents by theme. For example, you can select a letter template and a resume template in the same theme.

Try It! Creating a Document Based on a Template

1. In Word, click File > New. Available templates display in Backstage view.
2. Click Sample templates.
3. Scroll down the available templates and click Executive Report. Word displays a preview of the selected template.
4. Click Executive Resume.
5. Click the Create button.
6. Save the file as **WTry19d_studentfirstname_studentlastname** in the location where your teacher instructs you to store the files for this lesson, and leave it open to use in the next Try It.

Using Content Controls

- Most templates include sample text, formatting, graphics, and **content controls** that prompt you to enter information to complete the document.
- You replace the sample text, change the formatting, or replace or delete the graphics using standard editing and formatting commands. For example, you can select and replace text by typing.
- Content controls display with brackets around them, like this: [Type your address]; sample, or **placeholder**, text does not have brackets.
- To enter text in a content control, click it, and type the text.
- When you click a content control, a handle displays. Some content control handles have a drop-down arrow. Click the arrow to display a list of options you can use to automatically insert information into the document.
- You can remove content controls you do not need.

Try It! Using Content Controls

1. In the **WTry19d_studentfirstname_studentlastname** file, click the name on the first line. The content control for the name is called Author. It is part of a larger content control called Resume Name.

   ✓ *Word picked up the name from the user information you use to log in to the system.*

2. If necessary, edit the name to display your full first name and last name.
3. Click the Resume Name content control handle to select the entire content control.
4. Click the drop-down arrow on the Resume Name content control handle to display a gallery of options.

(continued)

Try It! Using Content Controls *(continued)*

5. Click the Name with Picture option.
6. Click the drop-down arrow on the Resume Name content control handle again, and click the Name option.
7. Click the Type your e-mail content control and type your e-mail address.
8. Click the Type your address content control and type your school address.
9. Click the Type your phone number control and type your school phone number.
10. Right-click the Type your website content control.
11. On the shortcut menu, click Remove Content Control.
12. Save the **WTry19d_studentfirstname_studentlastname** file and close it. Leave Word open to use in the next Try It.

Use Content Controls to enter and edit information

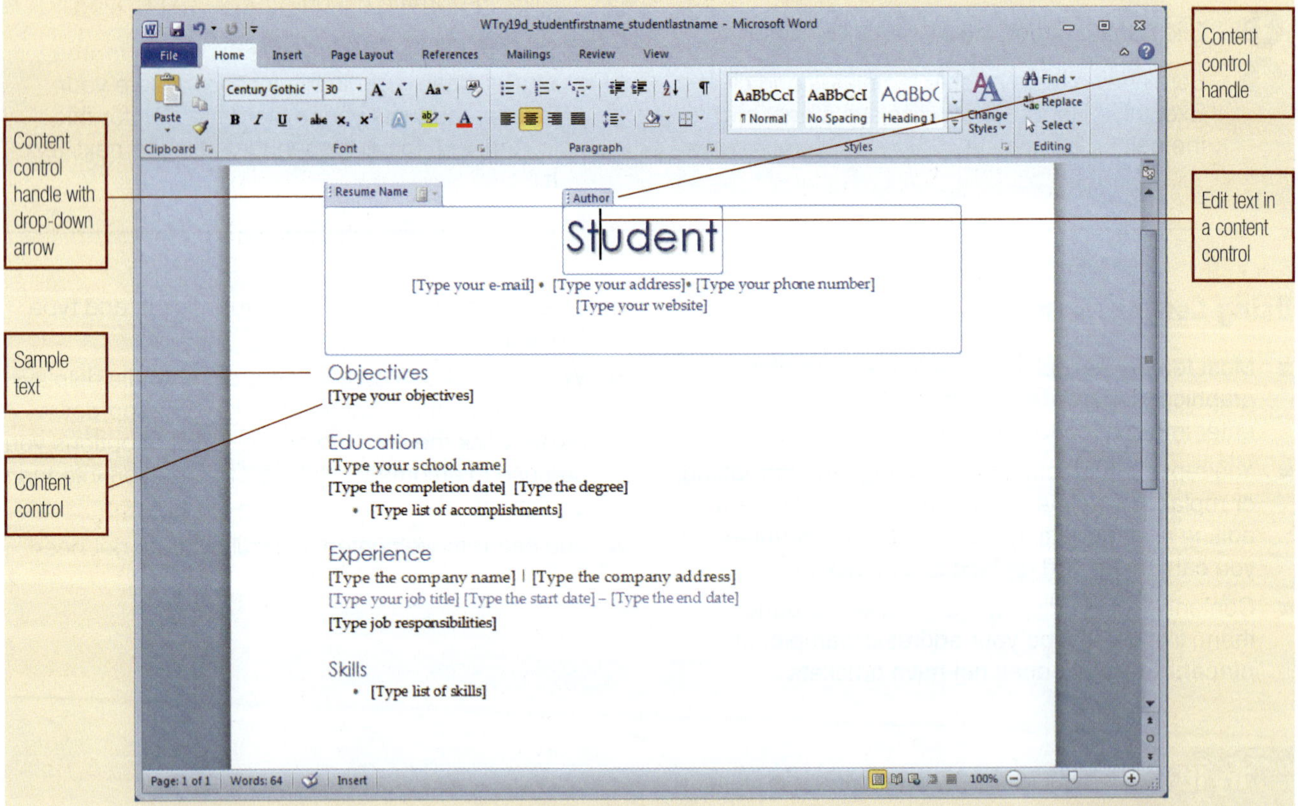

Saving a Word Document as a Template

- You can create your own template by saving a Word document as a template file.
- Template files in the most recent version of Word have a .dotx file extension.
- Template files from Word versions prior to 2010 have a .dot file extension.
- Template file icons look similar to Word file icons, with a yellow bar across the top.
- You can include formatting, themes, style sets, and sample text in your template.

  ✓ *You can also insert content controls to help others create documents based on the template.*

- New documents you create based on the template will include the elements you save with the template file.

Try It! Saving a Word Document as a Template

1. In Word, create a new, blank document.
2. Click Page Layout > Themes > Essential.
3. Click Home > Change Styles > Style Set > Perspective.
4. On the first line of the document, type your full name, and format it with the Title style.
5. Click File > Save As.
6. Type **WTry19e_studentfirstname_studentlastname**.
7. Click the Save as type button and click Word Template in the list of file types.
8. Navigate to the location where your teacher instructs you to store the files for this lesson.

   ✓ *To make a template available in the My templates folder, make the Templates folder under Microsoft Word in the Navigation bar the storage location.*

9. Click Save.

   ✓ *Click OK if Word displays a warning about new file formats.*

10. Close the **WTry19e_studentfirstname_studentlastname** file, but leave Word open.
11. Click File > New.
12. Click New from existing.

    ✓ *If you saved the template file in the Templates folder, click My templates, and skip step 13.*

13. Navigate to the location where you save the files for this lesson.
14. Click the **WTry19e_studentfirstname_studentlastname** file.
15. Click Create New. Word creates a new document that has the same formatting and sample text as the template file.
16. Close the new document without saving changes. Leave Word open to use in the next Try It.

Exploring Templates on Office.com

- If you have a connection to the Internet, you can explore the lengthy list of templates that are available on Office.com.
- The templates are organized by category. For example, you can browse templates for creating reports, or templates for creating calendars.
- Some of the templates are provided by Microsoft, but many are created by users, like you. The name of the person who created the template is listed above the preview in Backstage view, along with a rating.
- You can explore and preview the available templates without actually downloading one; before you download any file, you must have permission from your teacher.

Try It! **Exploring Templates on Office.com**

1. In Word, click File > New.
2. Under Office.com Templates, click Award certificates.
3. Click the folder labeled Business.
4. Click Employee of the Month to preview it.
5. Under Available Templates, click Home to return to Backstage view.
6. Under Office.com Templates, click Flyers.
7. Click Marketing.
8. Click Event flyer.
9. Exit Word.

Project 39—Create It

Resume

DIRECTIONS

1. Start Word.
2. Click **File** > **New** > **Sample templates**.
3. Scroll down the list of templates and click **Origin Resume**.
4. Click **Create** to create a document based on the Origin Resume template.
5. Save the document as **WProj39a_studentfirstname_studentlastname** in the location where your teacher instructs you to store the files for this lesson. Type your name and today's date in the footer of the document.
6. Click the **Author** content control, select the text, and type **Sandra Tsai**.
7. Click the **Resume Name** content control handle drop-down arrow and click **Name with Photo**.
8. Click the **Type your address** content control and type **2555 North Clark, Chicago, IL 60614**.
9. Click the **Type your phone number** content control and type **555-555-5555**.
10. Click the **Type your e-mail address** content control and type **sandrat@emailservice.net**.
11. Right-click the **Type your website** content control and click **Remove Content Control** on the shortcut menu.
12. Select the text **Website:** and press DEL.
13. Replace the remaining content control and sample text using the information shown in Figure 19-2 on the next page.
14. Check and correct the spelling and grammar in the document, and then save the changes.
15. **With your teacher's permission**, print the document. It should look similar to Figure 19-2 on the next page.
16. Click **File** > **Save As**.
17. Type **WProj39b_studentfirstname_studentlastname**.
18. Click the **Save as type** button to display a list of compatible file types.
19. Click **Rich Text Format**.
20. Navigate to the location where your teacher instructs you to save the files for this lesson.
21. Click **Save**. If necessary, click **Continue** in the Microsoft Word Compatibility Checker.
22. Close the document, and exit Word.

Figure 19-2

Sandra Tsai

2555 North Clark, Chicago, IL 60614
Phone: 555-555-5555
E-mail: sandrat@emailservice.net

Objectives

To work as a dietitian in a university environment where I can combine my knowledge of food and nutrition with my experience as an educator.

Education

Masters of Food Science and Nutrition (2011)

- GPA: 3.8
- Wrote thesis on the effects of protein on the development of lean muscle

Experience

Chief Nutritionist (April 1, 2012 -present)
Michigan Avenue Athletic Club (235 Michigan Ave., Chicago, IL 60601)
Taught classes in diet and nutrition
Advised club café on methods for improving nutritional quality
Worked one-on-one with individual club members to develop healthy eating habits

Skills

- Certified dietitian
- Accomplished cook
- Completed Chicago Marathon in under 3 hours

Firstname Lastname

Today's Date

Project 40—Apply It

Resume Web Page

DIRECTIONS

1. Start Word, if necessary, and open **WProj40** from the data files for this lesson.
2. Save the file as a Word document with the name **WProj40a_studentfirstname_studentlastname** in the location where your teacher instructs you to store the files for this lesson. Type your name and today's date in the footer of the file, and save the changes.
3. Save the file again as a **Single File Web Page** in the location where your teacher instructs you to store the files for this lesson with the name **WProj40b_studentfirstname_studentlastname** and the page title **Sandra Tsai Resume**.
4. Click **Continue** in the Microsoft Word Compatibility Checker dialog box. The document in Web Layout view should look similar to Figure 19-3.
5. Type your name and today's date at the bottom of the document.
6. **With your teacher's permission**, print the document.
7. Close the document, saving all changes, and exit Word.

Figure 19-3

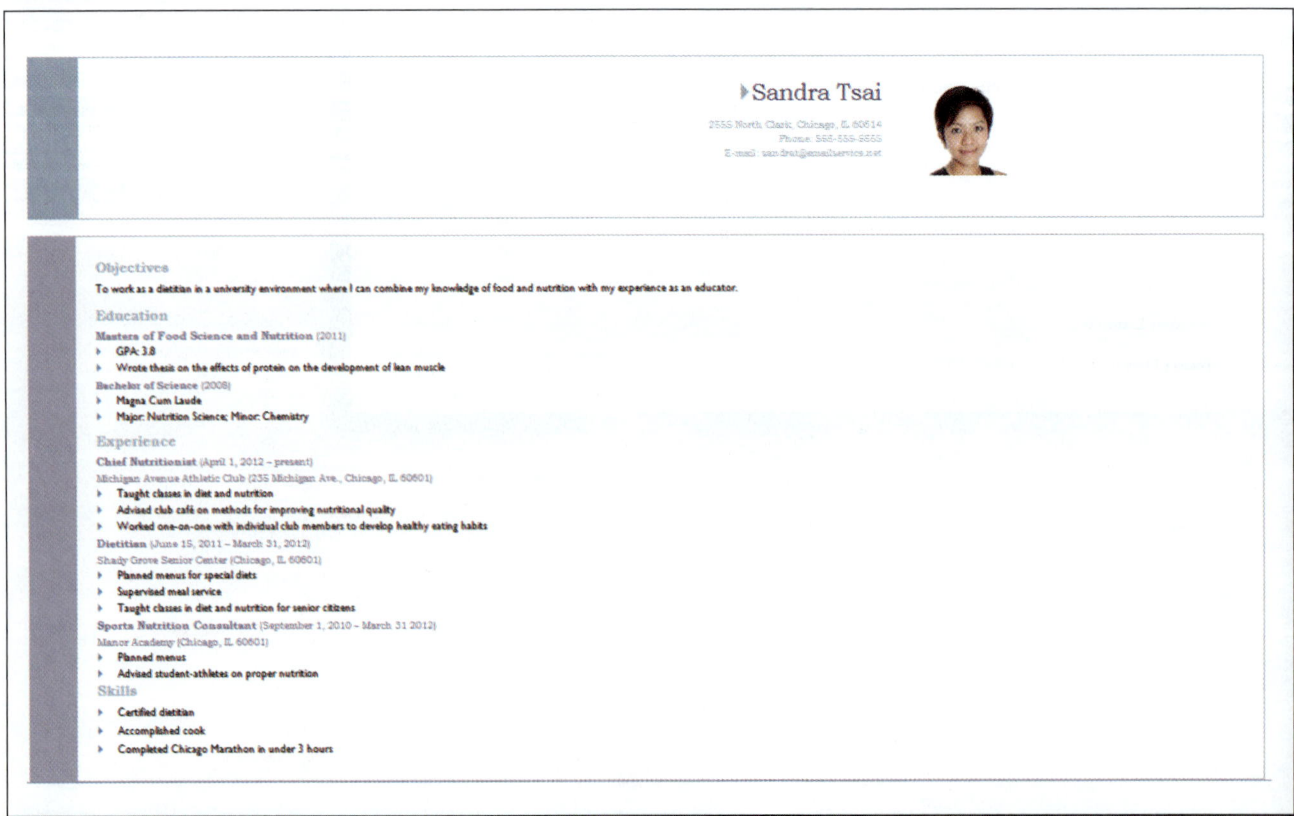

Chapter Assessment and Application

Project 41—Make It Your Own

Create a Resume

Your resume may be the most important job search document you ever create. As such, it is important to take the time to get it right. Once you have a resume that you feel accurately describes you and your goals, you can keep it up-to-date and ready to send any time you want to apply for a job.

In this project, explore the available resume templates and choose one that best highlights your education, work and volunteer experience, and skills so they stand out to someone who might just glance at it quickly. If you do not like any of the resume templates, create your own using table and document formatting skills you have learned in the first two chapters in this section of the book.

Use the template to create your own resume. Before you begin, you may want to research resume writing tips online or in your school's library or career center.

DIRECTIONS

1. Start Word. Explore the available sample resume templates.
2. **With your teacher's permission**, explore the resume templates on Office.com.
3. Select a resume template. If you are not satisfied with any of the templates, create a resume template of your own, using a theme, style set, and tables to align content professionally on the page.
4. Create a new document based on the selected template, and save the document as **WProj41a_studentfirstname_studentlastname** in the location where your teacher instructs you to store the files for this project.
5. Enter your own information into the document.
6. Include your contact information, education and work experience, and your interests and skills.
7. Include contact information for your employers or teachers, as necessary, and specific dates.
8. Be truthful and accurate.
9. Check the spelling and grammar in the document and correct any errors. If you make the same spelling errors frequently, add them to the AutoCorrect list.
10. Ask a classmate to review your resume and offer suggestions on how you might improve the information and the design. For example, it is good to use interesting action words to describe your experience. If you have worked at a sandwich shop, instead of writing *I made sandwiches*, you might write *Prepared sandwiches in a busy shop*. You can use the thesaurus to help you make interesting and accurate word choices.
11. Make the improvements to the resume, and check the spelling and grammar again.
12. **With your teacher's permission**, print the resume.
13. Save it as a single file Web page as **WProj42b_studentfirstname_studentlastname** so you can post it online, if the opportunity presents itself.
14. Close the document, saving all changes, and exit Word.

Project 42—Master It

Customer Demographics Fax

Voyager Travel Adventures has been collecting demographic information about clients who participate in adventure travel vacations. The information is available in a text document. In this project, you will open the text document and save it in Word document format.

You will create tables, apply formatting, and use features such as cut and paste, find and replace, and AutoCorrect to complete the document. You will save the document as a Web page so it can be viewed online. You will then use a sample template to create a fax cover sheet so you can fax the document to the vice president of marketing, who is at an offsite meeting.

DIRECTIONS

Open a Plain Text File and Save it as a Word Document

1. Start Word, if necessary.
2. Open the plain text file **WProj42**. Move the insertion point to the end of the file, insert a blank line and then type your full name and today's date.
3. Save the file in plain text format as **WProj42a_studentfirstname_studentlastname** in the location where your teacher instructs you to store the files for this project.
4. Apply the **Title** style to the first two lines of text, and center both lines horizontally, apply the **Heading 1** style to the third line—*Respondant Survey Results*—and apply the **Normal** style to the rest of the text in the document.
5. Use the Thesaurus to look up synonyms for the word *Favored*. Insert **Preferred** in its place.
6. Save the document in Word document format as **WProj42b_studentfirstname_studentlastname** in the location where your teacher instructs you to store the files for this lesson.
7. Move your name and today's date into the footer of the document.
8. Add an entry to the AutoCorrect list to replace the word **Motto** with the first two lines of the document formatted in the **Title** style.
9. Add an entry to the AutoCorrect list to replace the word **respondant** with the correctly spelled word **respondent**.
10. Check the spelling and grammar in the document and make all necessary corrections.
11. Find and replace all occurrences of the word **Respondent** with the word **Customer**.
12. Save the changes to the document.

Create and Format Tables

1. Select the six lines of text under the heading *Customer Survey Results* and convert them into a table with 3 columns, separated at tabs.
2. Insert a new row at the top of the table.
3. Merge the three cells in the new row.
4. In the new row, type the text **CUSTOMER DEMOGRAPHICS** in all uppercase letters.
5. Apply the **Light Grid** table style to the table.
6. Increase the font size of all text in the table to **12 points**, and then adjust the column width to automatically fit the contents.
7. Change the alignment of the cells displaying percentages to **Align Top Right**.
8. On the second blank line below the table, insert a new table with 3 columns and 3 rows.
9. Change the font size to **12 points**, and then enter the following text to complete the table:

Gender	
Male	**54%**
Female	**46%**

10. Apply the **Medium List 1** table style to the table, and adjust the column width to automatically fit the contents.
11. Apply a **1½ point solid line Blue, Accent** border around the outside of the table, and center the table horizontally on the page.

12. Select the last six lines of text in the document and move them above the *Customer Demographics* table.
13. Convert the six lines of text to a table with 2 columns and 6 rows, separated at the tabs.
14. Delete the top row.
15. Sort the remaining five rows into alphabetical order based on the content in column 1.
16. Insert a new row across the bottom of the table. In the left column type **Total**. In the right column, insert a formula to add the values in the cells above.
17. Right-align the text **Total** and increase the font size for all the text in the table to 12 points.
18. Adjust the column width to automatically fit the contents of the table, and center the table horizontally on the page.
19. Use the Draw Table tool to draw a cell on the left side of the table. Size it to the same height as the current table, and 0.75" wide.
20. In the new cell, change the text direction to **Bottom to Top**. Set the font to **12-point Arial** and type **Preferred Activity (Per Respondant)**. Note that AutoCorrect should correct the misspelled word respondent.
21. Apply **Blue, Accent 1, Lighter 60%** shading to the cell, and a **1½ point solid line Blue, Accent** border around the outside of the entire table.
22. Add 24 points of space after the *Customer Survey Results* heading.
23. Check the spelling and grammar in the document and correct any errors. Save the document.
24. **With your instructor's permission**, print the document. It should look similar to Illustration A on the next page.
25. Save the document as a single file Web page with the file name **WProj42c_studentfirstname_studentlastname** and the Web page title **Voyager Travel Adventures**.
26. On the last line of the document, type your name and today's date.
27. In Web Layout view, it should look similar to Illustration B on page 271.
28. Close the Web page file, saving all changes.

Create Fax Cover Sheet Based on a Template

1. In Word, create a new document based on the **Urban Fax** sample template.
2. Save the file as **WProj42d_studentfirstname_studentlastname** in the location where your teacher instructs you to store the files for this project.
3. In the header, type **Motto** and press SPACE to insert the AutoCorrect entry.
4. Replace the content controls in the template using the following information:

   Company name: **Voyager Travel Adventures**

   Company address: **1635 Logan Street, Denver, CO 80205**

   Phone number: **555-555-5550**

   Remove the Web address content control.

   Date: **Today's date**

   To: **Dan Euell, V.P. Marketing**

   Recipient company name: **Voyager Travel Adventures**

   Fax: **555-555-5552**

   Phone: **555-555-0005**

   From: Your Name

   Pages: **2, including cover**

   Fax: **555-555-5551**

   Phone: **555-555-5550**

   Remove the CC: content control and delete the sample text.

   RE: **Survey results**

   Comments: **Dan – I thought you might want a preview of these survey results. Based on the responses, we should consider targeting families with teenagers, and focusing on trips that involve water!**
5. Check the spelling and grammar in the document and correct any errors.
6. **With your instructor's permission**, print the document. It should look similar to Illustration C on page 272.
7. Delete the **Motto** AutoCorrect entry.
8. Delete the **Respondant/Respondent** AutoCorrect entry.
9. Close the document, saving all changes, and exit Word.

Illustration A

Voyager Travel Adventures
"Active Vacations for All Ages"

Customer Survey Results

Preferred Activity (Per Respondent)		
	Backpacking	25
	Biking	43
	Kayaking	95
	River Rafting	77
	Sightseeing	10
	Total	250

CUSTOMER DEMOGRAPHICS		
Age	0 – 18	3%
	19 – 25	17%
	26 – 35	20%
	36 – 45	30%
	46 – 55	20%
	55 +	10%

Gender	
Male	54%
Female	46%

Firstname Lastname

Today's Date

Illustration B

Voyager Travel Adventures
"Active Vacations for All Ages"

Customer Survey Results

Preferred Activity (Per Respondent)		
	Backpacking	25
	Biking	43
	Kayaking	95
	River Rafting	77
	Sightseeing	10
	Total	250

CUSTOMER DEMOGRAPHICS		
Age	0 – 18	3%
	19 – 25	17%
	26 – 35	20%
	36 – 45	30%
	46 – 55	20%
	55 +	10%

Gender		
	Male	54%
	Female	46%

Firstname Lastname Today's date

Illustration C

Voyager Travel Adventures
"Active Vacations for All Ages"

VOYAGER TRAVEL ADVENTURES
1635 Logan Street, Denver, CO 80205
555-555-5550

Today's Date

Fax

TO: Dan Euell, V.P. Marketing	**FROM: Firstname Lastname**
VOYAGER TRAVEL ADVENTURES	PAGES: 2, including cover
FAX: 555-555-5552	FAX: 555-555-5551
PHONE: 555-555-0005	PHONE: 555-555-5550

RE: Survey results

COMMENTS:
Dan – I thought might want a preview of these survey results. Based on the responses we should consider targeting families with teenagers, and focusing on trips that involve water!

☐ Urgent

☐ Please review

☐ Please comment

☐ For your records

Chapter 3

Creating Reports and Newsletters

Lesson 20
Changing Case and Managing Document Properties
Projects 43-44

- Using Uppercase Mode
- Changing Case
- Managing Document Properties

Lesson 21
Formatting a One-Page Report
Projects 45-46

- Analyzing Document Production
- Setting Margins
- Inserting a Section Break
- Setting Page Orientation
- Inserting Page Numbers
- Checking the Word Count
- Formatting a One-Page Report

Lesson 22
Managing Sources and Controlling Text Flow
Projects 47-48

- Inserting a Hard Page Break
- Controlling Pagination
- Inserting Footnotes and Endnotes
- Inserting Citations
- Analyzing Citations
- Creating a Reference Page

Lesson 23
Working with Newsletter Columns
Projects 49-50

- Understanding Desktop Publishing
- Creating Newsletter Columns
- Setting Column Width
- Inserting a Column Break
- Balancing Columns
- Analyzing Page Layout and Design

Lesson 24
Enhancing Paragraphs with Dropped Capitals, Borders, and Shading
Projects 51-52

- Inserting Dropped Capitals
- Enhancing a Paragraph with Borders and Shading
- Analyzing Time Management

Lesson 25
Copying Formatting
Projects 53-54

- Copying Formatting
- Highlighting Text
- Analyzing Teamwork

Lesson 26
Inserting Symbols
Projects 55-56

- Inserting Symbols

Lesson 27
Merging Mailing Labels
Projects 57-58

- Creating Mailing Labels Using the Mail Merge Wizard

End of Chapter Assessments
Projects 59-60

Lesson 20

Changing Case and Managing Document Properties

WORDS TO KNOW

Case
The specific use of upper- or lowercase letters.

Document properties
Categories of information about a document.

Keywords
Important words found in a document. Keywords can be used to classify a document.

Metadata
Data about data, such as the size of a file. Another term for document properties.

➤ What You Will Learn

Using Uppercase Mode
Changing Case
Managing Document Properties

Software Skills Document properties are details that help you to identify a file, such as the name of the author and the main topic. The properties remain attached to the file so you can use them for recordkeeping and data management.

Application Skills You work in the personnel department at Voyager Travel Adventures. In this lesson you will write two job offer letters to prospective employees. The first is to offer the position of communications director to Jeremy LeBlanc. The second is to offer the position of tour leader to Annabel Martin. In this lesson, you will prepare the letters using Word's features for controlling case and managing document properties.

What You Can Do

Using Uppercase Mode

- Use uppercase mode to type all capital letters without pressing the Shift key.
- When uppercase mode is on, press SHIFT to insert a lowercase letter.
- The Caps Lock key on your keyboard is a toggle that turns uppercase mode off and on.
- When uppercase mode is on, the Caps Lock indicator on your keyboard is lit.
- You can add the Caps Lock indicator to the status bar to display whether uppercase mode is off or on.
- Uppercase mode affects only letter characters.

Try It! Using Uppercase Mode

1. Start Word and save the default blank document as **WTry20_studentfirstname_studentlastname** in the location where your teacher instructs you to store the files for this lesson.
2. Right-click the status bar, click to select Caps Lock on the shortcut menu, and then press ESC.
3. On your keyboard, press CAPS LOCK.
4. Type today's date and press ENTER. Press and hold SHIFT and type the first character of your first name. Release SHIFT and type the rest of your first name.
5. Press CAPS LOCK again to turn uppercase mode off.
6. Type your last name.
7. Right-click the status bar, click to clear the check mark from the Caps Lock option, and then press ESC.
8. Save the changes to **WTry20_studentfirstname_studentlastname** and leave it open to use in the next Try It.

Changing Case

- You can easily change the **case** of selected text in a document using the Change Case button in the Font group on the Home tab of the Ribbon.
- There are five case options:
  - Sentence case: First character in a sentence is uppercase.
  - lowercase: All characters are lowercase.
  - UPPERCASE: All characters are uppercase.
  - Capitalize Each Word: First character in each word is uppercase.
  - tOGGLE cASE: Case is reversed for all selected text.

Try It! Changing Case

1. In the **WTry20_studentfirstname_studentlastname** file, press ENTER to start a new line and type: **Microsoft Word 2010 provides many features that make it easier to create professional documents.**
2. Select the sentence you typed in step 1.
3. On the Home tab, click the Change Case button Aa.
4. Click lowercase.
5. Click the Change Case button Aa and click Capitalize Each Word.
6. Click the Change Case button Aa and click tOGGLE cASE.
7. Save the changes to **WTry20_studentfirstname_studentlastname** and leave it open to use in the next Try It.

Managing Document Properties

- **Document properties**, or **metadata**, are bits of unique information that you save as part of a document.
- Document properties display on the Info tab in Backstage view.
- Some properties are updated automatically when you create or modify a document, such as the file name and type, the author, and the file size.
- You can enter more specific properties to help differentiate the file from other similar documents.
- You can also use the Document Panel to view, enter, and edit summary properties, such as Author, Title, Subject, and **Keywords**, or you can use the Properties dialog box to manage advanced document properties.
- You can print a table listing the document properties.

Try It! Managing Document Properties

1. In the **WTry20_studentfirstname_studentlastname** file, click File to display the Info tab in Backstage view.
2. In the Preview pane, under Properties, click the content control Add a title, and then type **Changing Case**.
3. Click the content control Add a tag and type **uppercase, properties**.
4. Click Add comments and type **Practice document for lesson 20**.
5. Click Show All Properties to expand the list to display all properties.
6. Click Show Fewer Properties to collapse the list.
7. Save the changes to **WTry20_studentfirstname_studentlastname** and leave it open to use in the next Try It.

Try It! Using the Document Information Panel

1. In the **WTry20_studentfirstname_studentlastname** file, click File to display the Info tab in Backstage view.
2. In the Preview pane, click Properties, and then click Show Document Panel to display the panel below the Ribbon.
3. Click in the Subject box in the Document Information Panel and type **Learning Word 2010**.
4. Click the Close the Document Information Panel button ☒.
5. Save the changes to **WTry20_studentfirstname_studentlastname** and leave it open to use in the next Try It.

Try It! Viewing a Properties Dialog Box

1. In the **WTry20_studentfirstname_studentlastname** file, click File to display the Info tab in Backstage view.
2. In the Preview pane, click Properties, and then click Advanced Properties to display the document's Properties dialog box.
3. Click the Summary tab.
4. Click the Statistics tab.
5. Click OK to close the dialog box.

   ✓ *Alternatively, right-click a document name in Windows Explorer or an Office dialog box and click Properties to open the Properties dialog box.*
6. Save the changes to **WTry20_studentfirstname_studentlastname**, and leave it open to use in the next Try It.

Try It! Printing Document Properties

1. In the **WTry20_studentfirstname_studentlastname** file, click File > Print.
2. Under Settings, click the top button—it may display Print All Pages—to display a list of items you can choose to print.
3. Click Document Properties.

   ✓ *Select other print settings and options as necessary.*
4. Click the Print button.
5. Save the changes to **WTry20_studentfirstname_studentlastname**, close it, and exit Word.

Project 43—Create It

Communications Director Offer Letter

DIRECTIONS

1. Start Word, if necessary, and save the default blank document as **WProj43_studentfirstname_studentlastname** in the location where your teacher instructs you to store the files for this lesson.
2. Type the full-block business letter shown in Figure 20-1 on the next page.
   a. Use uppercase mode as necessary to type all text that displays in all uppercase letters.
   b. Replace the sample text *Today's Date* with the actual date.
   c. Replace the sample text *Student's Name* with your own name.
3. Select the *company name* in the return address.
4. On the **Home** tab, click the **Change Case** button [Aa▾] and click **Capitalize Each Word**.
5. Select the *company name* in the first sentence of the letter, click the **Change Case** button [Aa▾] and click **Capitalize Each Word**.
6. Select the text *ACCEPT THIS OFFER OF THE POSITION OF* above the first signature line near the end of the document.
7. Click **Home** > **Change Case** [Aa▾], and click **lowercase**.
8. Select the text *COMMUNICATIONS DIRECTOR* at the end of the sentence above the first signature line.

Figure 20-1

VOYAGER TRAVEL ADVENTURES
1635 Logan Street
Denver, CO 80205

Today's Date

Mr. Jeremy LeBlanc
555 Main Street
Boulder, CO 80309

Dear Mr. LeBlanc:

JOB OFFER

Voyager travel adventures is pleased to offer you a position as Communications Director. We believe that your experience, skills, and abilities will make you a valuable member of our team.

The position comes with the following compensation:

- Salary: annual gross salary of $67,500 paid in monthly installments.
- Performance bonus: up to three percent of your annual gross salary, paid quarterly.
- Benefits: standard benefits for salaried, exempt employees, including the following:
    - 401(k) retirement account
    - Health, dental, life, and disability insurance
    - Educational assistance
    - Personal days for vacation, illness, and family care based on length of employment
    - One voyager travel adventures trip per calendar year

To accept or decline this offer, please sign and date this letter where indicated below and return it to my attention at the address listed above by May 1, 2011.

We hope that you will accept this offer, and we look forward to working with you. Please contact me if you have any questions or concerns.

Sincerely,

Student's Name
Personnel Director

I, Jeremy LeBlanc, ACCEPT THIS OFFER OF THE POSITION OF COMMUNICATIONS DIRECTOR.
Signature:______________________________ Date:________________

I, Jeremy LeBlanc, DECLINE THIS OFFER OF THE POSITION OF COMMUNICATIONS DIRECTOR.
Signature:______________________________ Date:________________

9. Click **Home** > **Change Case** Aa, and click **Capitalize Each Word**.
10. Select the text *DECLINE THIS OFFER OF THE POSITION OF* above the second signature line at the end of the document.
11. Click **Home** > **Change Case** Aa, and click **lowercase**.
12. Select the text *COMMUNICATIONS DIRECTOR* at the end of the sentence above the second signature line.
13. Click **Home** > **Change Case** Aa, and click **Capitalize Each Word**.
14. Check and correct the spelling and grammar in the document, and then save the changes.
15. **With your teacher's permission,** print the document.
16. Click **File** to display the Info tab in Backstage view.
17. In the Preview pane under Properties, click **Add a title** and type **Job Offer Letter**.

18. Click **Add a tag** and type **letter, job offer, Jeremy LeBlanc**.
19. Click **Properties** and then click **Show Document Panel**.
20. In the Subject box, type **Communications Director Position**.
21. In the Category box, type **Personnel Department**.
22. In the Status box, type **Open**.
23. Click the **Close the Document Information Panel** button ☒.
24. Save the changes to the file.
25. Click **File** > **Print**.
26. Under Settings, click the top button to display a list of items you can choose to print, and click **Document Properties**.
27. **With your teacher's permission,** click the **Print** button to print the document properties.
28. Close the document, saving all changes, and exit Word.

Project 44—Apply It

Tour Guide Offer Letter

DIRECTIONS

1. Start Word, if necessary, and open **WProj44** from the data files for this lesson.
2. Save the file as **WProj44_studentfirstname_studentlastname** in the location where your teacher instructs you to store the files for this lesson.
3. Edit the document to create the letter shown in Figure 20-2 on the next page.
   a. Replace the sample text *Student's Name* with your own name, and *Today's Date* with the actual date.
   b. Turn on uppercase mode and type the subject **JOB OFFER**, between the salutation and the first sentence of the letter.
   c. Use the Change Case feature to change all text in tOGGLE cASE to Capitalize Each Word.
   d. Edit the recipient's name from *Jeremy LeBlanc* to **Annabel Martin** in all three places it displays, and *Mr. LeBlanc* to **Ms. Martin** where it displays.
   e. Edit the inside address as shown.
   f. Edit the job title from *Communications Director* to **Tour Guide** in all three places it displays.
   g. Edit the salary from *$67,500* to **$28,000**.
4. Check and correct the spelling and grammar in the document, and then save the changes.
5. **With your teacher's permission,** print the document.
6. Display the Info tab in Backstage view.
7. In the Subject box, change *Communications Director Position* to **Tour Guide Position**.
8. In the Keywords box, change *Jeremy LeBlanc* to **Annabel Martin**.
9. In the Comments box, type **Excellent travel experience; certified teacher**.
10. Close the Document Information Panel.
11. Save the changes to the file.
12. **With your teacher's permission,** print the document properties.
13. Close the document, saving all changes, and exit Word.

Figure 20-2

Voyager Travel Adventures
1635 Logan Street
Denver, CO 80205

Today's Date

Ms. Annabel Martin
1001 South Street
Taos, NM 87571

Dear Ms. Martin:

JOB OFFER

Voyager Travel Adventures is pleased to offer you a position as Tour Guide. We believe that your experience, skills, and abilities will make you a valuable member of our team.

The position comes with the following compensation:

- Salary: annual gross salary of $28,000 paid in monthly installments.
- Performance bonus: up to three percent of your annual gross salary, paid quarterly.
- Benefits: standard benefits for salaried, exempt employees, including the following:
    - 401(k) retirement account
    - Health, dental, life, and disability insurance
    - Educational assistance
    - Personal days for vacation, illness, and family care based on length of employment
    - One voyager travel adventures trip per calendar year

To accept or decline this offer, please sign and date this letter where indicated below and return it to my attention at the address listed above by May 1, 2011.

We hope that you will accept this offer, and we look forward to working with you. Please contact me if you have any questions or concerns.

Sincerely,

Firstname Lastname
Personnel Director

I, Annabel Martin, accept this offer of the position of Tour Guide.
Signature:______________________________________ Date:_____________________

I, Annabel Martin, decline this offer of the position of Tour Guide.
Signature:______________________________________ Date:_____________________

Lesson 21

Formatting a One-Page Report

➤ What You Will Learn

- Analyzing Document Production
- Setting Margins
- Inserting a Section Break
- Setting Page Orientation
- Inserting Page Numbers
- Checking the Word Count
- Formatting a One-Page Report

Software Skills Format a one-page report so that it is attractive and professional. Set margins to meet expected requirements and to improve the document's appearance and readability. For example, leave a wider margin in a report if you expect a reader to make notes or comments; leave a narrower margin to fit more text on a page.

Application Skills Member Services at Michigan Avenue Athletic Club has decided to publish a series of information sheets on various topics. The goal is to keep each report to fewer than 250 words so they fit on one page, and to make them available to members in print and online. In this lesson, you will create and format two of the sheets. The first explains what a personal trainer is and how to select one. The second explores the relationship between diet and exercise.

WORDS TO KNOW

Gutter
Space added to the margin to leave room for binding.

Landscape orientation
Positioning document text so it displays and prints horizontally across the longer side of a page.

Margins
The amount of white space between the text and the edge of the page on each side.

Portrait orientation
The default position for displaying and printing text horizontally across the shorter side of a page.

Section
In Word, a segment of a document defined by a section break. A section may have different page formatting from the rest of the document.

Word count
The number of words in a document or selection.

What You Can Do

Analyzing Document Production

- There are three basic steps to producing any business document: planning, creating, and publishing.
- The planning stage requires you to think about such questions as the type of document you want to create, who will receive the document, and whether there are any special publishing requirements.
- For example, you might consider what paper to print on, if color ink should be used, how many copies to print, or whether you will need to print on both sides of a page.
- If the project seems too complex, you may decide to use a desktop publishing package, such as Microsoft Publisher, instead of using a word processing package, such as Microsoft Word.
- During the planning stage you should create a schedule that includes milestones, such as how long it will take to gather the information you need, when the first draft will be complete, how long it will take for a review process, and when the final document will be complete.
- The creation stage involves selecting page and document settings, such as margins and page size, and entering and formatting the text and graphics.
- The publishing stage involves outputting the document using either your desktop printer or a commercial printer. In some cases, the document may be published electronically on a Web site.

Setting Margins

- **Margins** are measured in inches.
- The normal default margins in Word 2010 are 1" on the left, right, top, and bottom.

✓ *In versions of Word prior to 2007, the default margins are 1.25" on the left and right and 1" on the top and bottom.*

- You can select from a list of preset margins by clicking the Margins button in the Page Setup group on the Page Layout tab or in Backstage view.

✓ *For information on setting margins in Backstage view, refer to Basics Lesson 4.*

- Alternatively you can set custom margins.
- If you set custom margins, you can also specify a **gutter** width to leave room for binding multiple pages.
- Margin settings can affect an entire document, or the current section.

✓ *To set margins for a single paragraph, use indents.*

- On the rulers, areas outside the margins are shaded gray, while areas inside the margins are white.
- Light gray bars mark the margins on the rulers.
- You can set Word to display margins on the page as nonprinting lines called text boundaries.

Try It! Selecting a Preset Margin

1. Start Word and open **WTry21a** from the data files for this lesson.
2. Save the file as **WTry21a_studentfirstname_studentlastname** in the location where your teacher instructs you to store the files for this lesson.
3. Display non-printing characters.
4. On the Page Layout tab, in the Page Setup group, click the Margins button.
5. Click Narrow.
6. In the Page Setup group click the Margins button again, and click Wide.
7. Save the changes to **WTry21a_studentfirstname_studentlastname** and leave it open to use in the next Try It.

Try It! Setting Custom Margins

1. In the **WTry21a_studentfirstname_studentlastname** file, click Page Layout > Margins .
2. Click Custom Margins to open the Page Setup dialog box.
3. Under Margins, use the increment arrows to set the Top, Bottom, Left, and Right margins to 1.3".
4. Click OK.
5. Save the changes to **WTry21a_studentfirstname_studentlastname** and leave it open to use in the next Try It.

✓ *To quickly set a margin, drag a margin marker on the ruler. Press and hold ALT while you drag to see the margin width.*

Try It! Showing or Hiding Text Boundaries

1. In the **WTry21a_studentfirstname_studentlastname** file, click File > Options > Advanced.
2. Under Show document content, click to select the Show text boundaries check box.
3. Click OK.
4. Repeat the steps to clear the check box to hide the boundaries.
5. Save the changes to **WTry21a_studentfirstname_studentlastname** and leave it open to use in the next Try It.

Inserting a Section Break

- A default Word document contains one **section**.
- Using commands in the Page Setup group on the Page Layout tab, you can divide a document into multiple sections to apply different formatting to each section. For example, you can set different margins, headers, or footers for each section.
- There are four types of section breaks:
  - Next page: Inserts a section break and a page break so that the new section will start on the next page.
  - Continuous: Inserts a section break so that the new section will start at the insertion point.
  - Even page: Inserts a section break and page breaks so the new section will start on the next even-numbered page.
  - Odd page: Inserts a section break and page breaks so the new section will start on the next odd-numbered page.
- In Print Layout view, section breaks display only if nonprinting characters display.
- In Draft view, section breaks display as solid double lines across the width of the page with the words Section Break in the middle, followed by the type of break in parentheses.

Try It! Inserting a Section Break

1. In the **WTry21a_studentfirstname_studentlastname** file, position the insertion point at the beginning of the heading *Zebra*.
2. On the Page Layout tab, in the Page Setup group, click the Breaks button.
3. From the Breaks gallery, under Section Breaks, click Continuous.
4. Click on the section break in the document and press DEL to remove it.
5. Click the Breaks button again.
6. From the Breaks gallery, under Section Breaks, click Next Page.
7. Save the changes to **WTry21a_studentfirstname_studentlastname** and leave it open to use in the next Try It.

A continuous section break

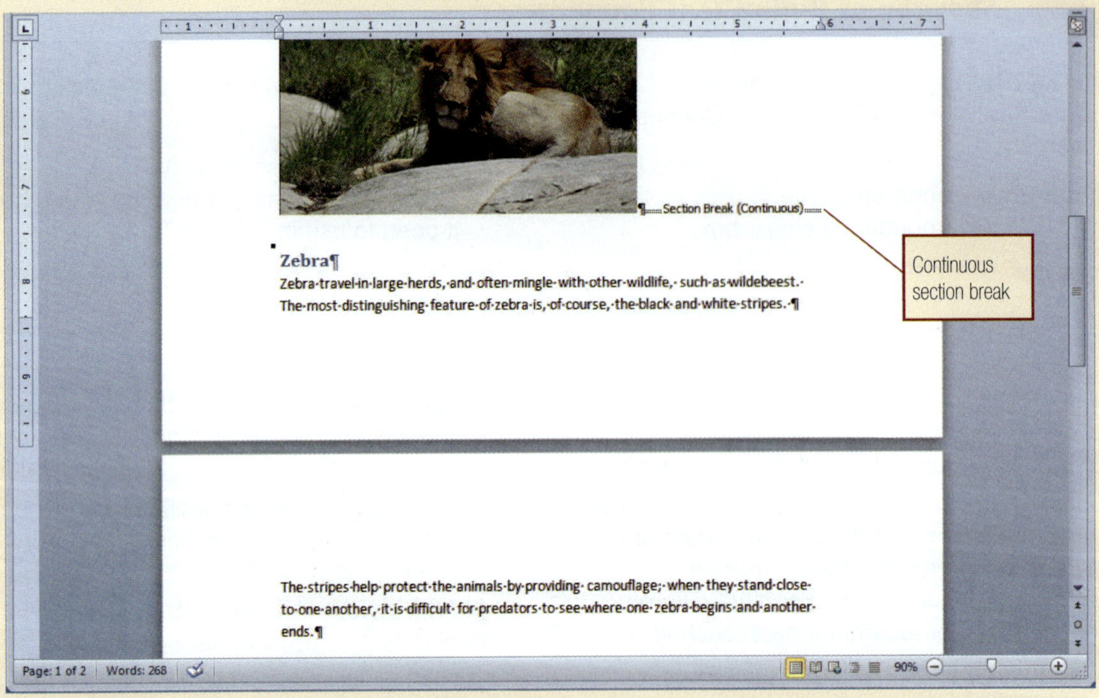

Setting Page Orientation

- Orientation is either **portrait** or **landscape**.
  - Select Portrait orientation—the default—when you want data displayed across the shorter length of a page.
  - Select Landscape orientation when you want data displayed across the wider length of a page.
- Portrait orientation is used for most documents, including letters, memos, and reports.
- Use landscape orientation to display a document across the wider length of the page. For example, if a document contains a table that is wider than the standard 8.5" page, Word will split it across two pages. When you change to landscape orientation, the table may fit on the 11" page.
- You can set the orientation for the entire document, or for a section.
- The Page Orientation options are in the Page Setup group on the Page Layout tab or the Print tab in Backstage view.

✓ *For information on setting page orientation in Backstage view, refer to Basics Lesson 4.*

Try It! Setting Page Orientation

1. In the **WTry21a_studentfirstname_studentlastname** file, make sure the insertion point is still on the same line as the heading *Zebra*.

   ✓ *The heading should be at the top of page 2, at the beginning of the second section.*

2. On the Page Layout tab, click the Orientation button.

3. Click Landscape. The orientation for the second section of the document changes to Landscape; the first section remains in Portrait.

4. Save the changes to **WTry21a_studentfirstname_studentlastname** and leave it open to use in the next Try It.

Change the orientation

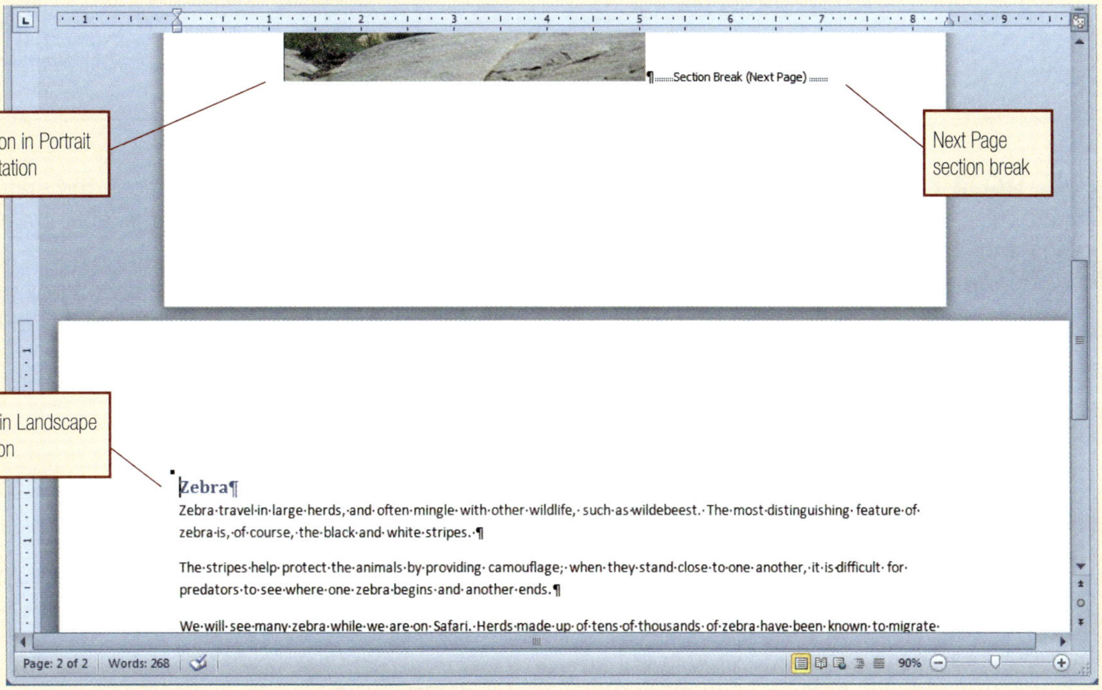

Inserting Page Numbers

- You can insert a page number into the header or footer of a document. Numbers automatically display on each page, numbered consecutively.
- You can select from a collection of built-in page number styles, or you can apply your own formatting.
- Once you insert a page number, you can select options such as to restart numbering for a new section, or to include a chapter number.
- Restarting page numbering is useful when your document has a title page that you do not want numbered.

Try It! Inserting Page Numbers

1. In the **WTry21a_studentfirstname_studentlastname** file, press SHIFT + HOME to move the insertion point to the beginning of the document.
2. Click Insert > Page Number.
3. Click Top of Page to display a gallery of page number formats to display in the header, and then click Plain Number 3.
4. On the Header & Footer Tools Design tab, click the Show Next button to move the insertion point to the page number in the header on page 2.
5. Click the Page Number button on the Ribbon and click Format Page Numbers to open the Page Number Format dialog box.
6. Under Page numbering, click the Start at option button. Leave the page number set to 1, and click OK.
7. Click the Close Header & Footer button, then save the changes to **WTry21a_studentfirstname_studentlastname** and leave it open to use in the next Try It.

✓ *To remove all page numbers, on either the Insert tab or the Header & Footer Tools Design tab, click the Page Number button and click Remove Page Numbers.*

Viewing the Word Count

- Word keeps track of the **word count** as part of the statistics properties for each document.

  ✓ *For more about document properties refer to Word, Lesson 20.*

- By default the word count displays on the status bar.
- If you select part of the document, the status bar displays the word count of the selection and the total word count.
- You can open the Word Count dialog box to view additional statistics such as the number of lines, paragraphs, and characters.

Try It! Viewing the Word Count

1. In the **WTry21a_studentfirstname_studentlastname** file, locate the word count on the status bar and take note of the number of words in the document.

   ✓ *If the word count does not display, right-click the status bar, click to select Word Count, and then close the shortcut menu.*

2. Move the insertion point to the end of the title *Safari with Voyager*, press the spacebar, and type **Travel Adventures**.
3. Locate the word count on the status bar again. The value should have increased by 2 to 270.
4. Select the title. Now, the word count on the status bar displays 5/270, indicating that 5 of the total 270 words are selected.
5. Cancel the selection, and then click the Review tab.
6. In the Proofing group, click the Word Count button to open the Word Count dialog box where you can view the number of words, pages, characters with or without spaces, paragraphs, and lines.
7. Click Close.
8. Save the changes to **WTry21a_studentfirstname_studentlastname** and close it. Leave Word open to use in the next Try It.

Formatting a One-Page Report

- Traditionally, a one-page report is set up as follows:
  - Left and right margins are 1".
  - Orientation is Portrait.
  - The title is positioned 1" to 2" from the top of the page.

    ✓ *The position of the title depends on the amount of text on the page.*
  - The report title is centered and in either all uppercase or title case.
  - Spacing after the title is 54 points (1").
  - Body text is in a 12-point serif font, such as Times New Roman.
  - Text is justified.
  - Lines are double-spaced.
  - First-line indents are between 0.5" and 1".
  - Spacing before and after paragraphs is 0.
  - Author's name and the date are right-aligned in the header.
- There are many variations of one-page report formatting that are acceptable, and your teacher may request that you use alternative formatting. For example, some teachers request a wider margin so there is room for writing comments, and want the teacher's name and class information left-aligned above the title, or in the header.

Try It! Formatting a One-Page Report

1. In Word, open **WTry21b** from the data files for this lesson.
2. Save the file as **WTry21b_studentfirstname_studentlastname** in the location where your teacher instructs you to store the files for this lesson.
3. Select the four paragraphs of body text and change the font to 12 pt. Times New Roman. Justify the paragraph alignment.
4. Change the line spacing to Double and the spacing before and after paragraphs to 0.

   ✓ *Refer to Word, Lesson 4 for a refresher on changing spacing.*
5. Apply a first-line indent of 0.5".
6. Click Page Layout > Margins > Normal.
7. Center the title and apply 54 pts. of space before and after.
8. Double-click in the header, type your name, press ENTER, and type today's date.
9. Right-align your name and the date in the header.
10. Save the changes to **WTry21b_studentfirstname_studentlastname**, close it, and exit Word.

Project 45—Create It

Personal Trainer Information Worksheet

DIRECTIONS

1. Start Word, if necessary, and save the blank default document as **WProj45_studentfirstname_studentlastname** in the location where your teacher tells you to store the files for this lesson.
3. Double-click in the header, type your name, press ENTER, and type today's date.
4. Right-align your name and the date in the header.
5. On the first line of the document, type the title **Is Personal Training Right for You?**
6. Apply the **Title** style to the text, and center it horizontally. Set the spacing before and after the title to 54 pt. and press ENTER to start a new line.
7. Change the font and font size to 12-point Times New Roman.
8. Set the line spacing to **Double**. Set the alignment to **Justified**. Set the first line indent to **0.5"**. Set the spacing before and after paragraphs to **0**.
9. Type the following paragraphs of text:

   Almost everyone could benefit from the services of a personal trainer. In addition to designing a personalized workout program, a good trainer provides motivation and encouragement. He or she helps you understand how to fit exercise into your life and teaches you how to make the most out of your exercise time. The lessons you learn from a trainer help ensure a safe, effective workout, even when you are exercising on your own.

   Working with a trainer should be a satisfying and rewarding experience. There are many different reasons for hiring a personal trainer. Some people want the motivation of a workout partner, others require specialized services for rehabilitation, and still others are interested in achieving weight loss goals. Before hiring a trainer, make sure he or she has experience helping people with goals similar to your own. Ask for references and then contact at least three of them. You should also interview the trainer to find out if you are compatible. You should feel comfortable talking and working together, and you should trust the trainer to respect your time and efforts.

   Verify that the trainer is certified by a nationally recognized organization such as the American Council on Exercise, the American College of Sports Medicine, or the National Strength and Conditioning Association. Many trainers have degrees in subjects such as sports medicine, physical education, exercise physiology, or anatomy and physiology.

   For more information about personal training at Michigan Avenue Athletic Club, contact Candace at extension 765.

10. Click **Review** > **Word Count**. Check the word count in the document. It should be 255. Note how many words you must delete to meet the 250 word limit.
11. Close the Word Count dialog box.
12. In the last sentence of the document, delete the eight words: *about personal training at Michigan Avenue Athletic Club*. Check the word count again to verify that it is now less than 250.
13. Click **Insert** > **Page Number**.
14. Click **Bottom of Page** and then click **Plain Number 2**.
15. Click **Page Layout** > **Orientation** > **Landscape**. Adjust the zoom so you can see the entire document on your screen.
16. Click **Page Layout** > **Orientation** > **Portrait**. Increase the zoom to at least 100%.
17. Check the spelling and grammar in the document and correct errors as necessary.
18. **With your teacher's permission,** print the document. It should look similar to Figure 21-1 on the next page.
19. Close the document, saving all changes, and exit Word.

Figure 21-1

Firstname Lastname
Today's Date

Is Personal Training Right For You?

Almost everyone could benefit from the services of a personal trainer. In addition to designing a personalized workout program, a good trainer provides motivation and encouragement. He or she helps you understand how to fit exercise into your life and teaches you how to make the most out of your exercise time. The lessons you learn from a trainer help ensure a safe, effective workout, even when you are exercising on your own.

Working with a trainer should be a satisfying and rewarding experience. There are many different reasons for hiring a personal trainer. Some people want the motivation of a work out partner, others require specialized services for rehabilitation, and still others are interested in achieving weight loss goals. Before hiring a trainer, make sure he or she has experience helping people with goals similar to your own. Ask for references and then contact at least three of them. You should also interview the trainer to find out if you are compatible. You should feel comfortable talking and working together, and you should trust the trainer to respect your time and efforts.

Verify that the trainer is certified by a nationally recognized organization such as the American Council on Exercise, the American College of Sports Medicine, or the National Strength and Conditioning Association. Many trainers have degrees in subjects such as sports medicine, physical education, exercise physiology, or anatomy and physiology.

For more information, contact Candace at extension 765.

1

Project 46—Apply It

Diet and Exercise Information Sheet

DIRECTIONS

1. Start Word, if necessary, and open **WProj46** from the data files for this lesson.
2. Save the file as **WProj46_studentfirstname_studentlastname** in the location where your teacher instructs you to store the files for this lesson.
3. Display the text boundaries, and then set the margins to **Normal—1"** on each side.
4. Apply the **Title** style to the first line of the document, and center it horizontally. Set the spacing before and after the title to **54 pt**.
5. Capitalize every word in the title except *As*.
6. Select the rest of the text in the document and apply formatting as follows:
   a. Change the font and font size to 12-point Times New Roman.
   b. Set the line spacing to **Double**.
   c. Set the alignment to **Justified**.
   d. Set the first line indent to **0.5"**.
   e. Set the spacing before and after paragraphs to **0**.
7. Check the word count. Note how many words you must delete to be under the 250 word limit.
8. In the second paragraph of body text, delete the sentence *But that's exactly what it is: the fuel your body needs to operate.*
9. Check the word count again. In the last sentence of the fifth paragraph, delete the text *Although there is no magic diet that will dramatically increase athletic ability or endurance,* and change the *B* in the word *by* to uppercase.
10. Check the word count again.
11. Insert a page number flush left in the footer.
12. Hide the text boundaries.
13. Check the spelling and grammar in the document and correct errors as necessary.
14. **With your teacher's permission,** print the document. It should look similar to Figure 21-2 on the next page.
15. Close the document, saving all changes, and exit Word.

Figure 21-2

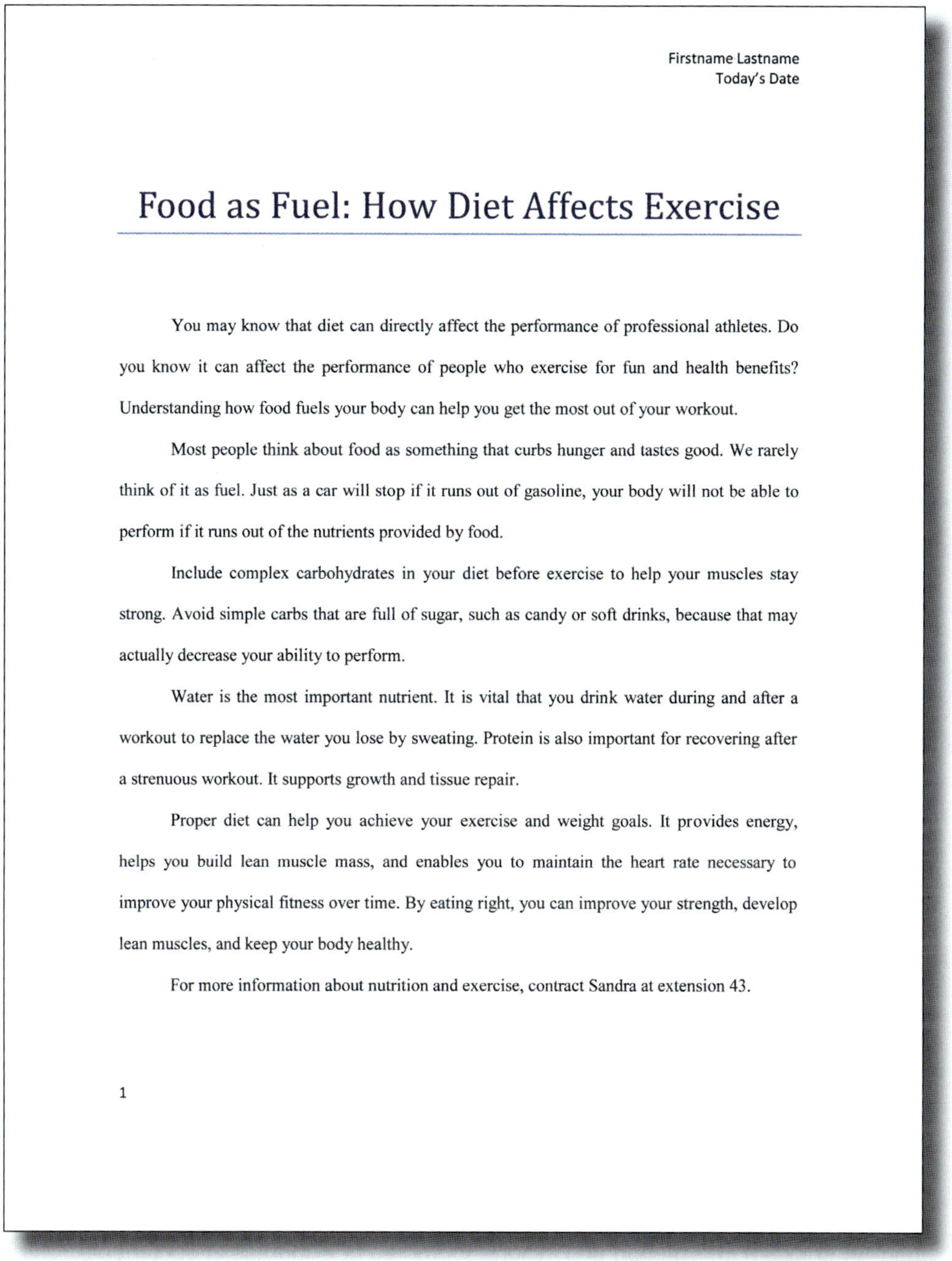

Firstname Lastname
Today's Date

Food as Fuel: How Diet Affects Exercise

You may know that diet can directly affect the performance of professional athletes. Do you know it can affect the performance of people who exercise for fun and health benefits? Understanding how food fuels your body can help you get the most out of your workout.

Most people think about food as something that curbs hunger and tastes good. We rarely think of it as fuel. Just as a car will stop if it runs out of gasoline, your body will not be able to perform if it runs out of the nutrients provided by food.

Include complex carbohydrates in your diet before exercise to help your muscles stay strong. Avoid simple carbs that are full of sugar, such as candy or soft drinks, because that may actually decrease your ability to perform.

Water is the most important nutrient. It is vital that you drink water during and after a workout to replace the water you lose by sweating. Protein is also important for recovering after a strenuous workout. It supports growth and tissue repair.

Proper diet can help you achieve your exercise and weight goals. It provides energy, helps you build lean muscle mass, and enables you to maintain the heart rate necessary to improve your physical fitness over time. By eating right, you can improve your strength, develop lean muscles, and keep your body healthy.

For more information about nutrition and exercise, contract Sandra at extension 43.

1

Lesson 22

Managing Sources and Controlling Text Flow

WORDS TO KNOW

Bibliography
A list of sources.

Citation
A reference to a source of information. In legal documents, it is a reference to previous court decisions or authoritative writings.

Common knowledge
Facts that can be found in many—at least three—independent sources and are known by a lot of people.

Copyright
The exclusive right to perform, display, copy, or distribute an artistic work or form of expression, such as words, music, images, or objects.

Endnote
An explanation or reference to additional material that prints at the end of a document.

Fair Use doctrine
Part of copyright law that provides for the limited use of copyrighted work without permission.

Footnote
An explanation or reference to additional material that prints at the bottom of a page.

Hard page break
A nonprinting character inserted to force the start of a new page.

Note reference mark
A number or character inserted in the document to refer to footnote or endnote text.

➤ What You Will Learn

- Inserting a Hard Page Break
- Controlling Pagination
- Inserting Footnotes and Endnotes
- Inserting Citations
- Analyzing Citations
- Creating a Reference Page

Software Skills Make a long document easier to read and work in by using page breaks and pagination to control where a new page should start. Use the Internet to locate information and include footnotes or endnotes in documents to provide information about the source of quoted material, or to supplement the main text. Insert citations to mark references and to create a reference page or bibliography for your report.

Application Skills In this lesson, you will work to develop a report on exercise for the Michigan Avenue Athletic Club. You will use page breaks and pagination features to control the position of text at the top and bottom of pages. You will also insert footnotes and endnotes, and add citations. Finally, you will create a reference page.

What You Can Do

Inserting a Hard Page Break

- A default Word document page is the size of a standard 8.5" by 11" sheet of paper.
- With 1" top and bottom margins, a page has 9" of vertical space for entering text.

✓ *The number of lines depends on the font size and spacing settings.*

- Word inserts a **soft page break** to start a new page when the current page is full.
- Soft page breaks adjust automatically if text is inserted or deleted, so a break always occurs when the current page is full.
- Insert a **hard page break** to start a new page before the current page is full. For example, insert a hard page break before a heading that falls at the bottom of a page; the break forces the heading to the top of the next page.
- You can insert a hard page break using the Breaks button in the Page Setup group on the Page Layout tab or the Page Break button in the Pages group on the Insert tab.

✓ *Press The shortcut key combination for inserting a hard page break is* CTRL + ENTER.

- Breaks move like characters when you insert and delete text. Therefore, you should insert hard page breaks after all editing is complete to avoid having a break occur at an awkward position on the page.
- In Draft view, a soft page break is marked by a dotted line across the page.
- By default, in Print Layout view page breaks are indicated by a space between the bottom of one page and the top of the next page; if you have nonprinting characters displayed, the space where you insert a hard page break is marked by a dotted line with the words *Page Break* centered in it.
- You can double-click the space between pages to hide it in Print Layout view. If you do, page breaks are marked by a solid black line. Double-click the black line to show the space.
- In Draft view, a hard page break is marked by a dotted line with the words *Page Break* centered in it.

WORDS TO KNOW

Note text
The text of the footnote or endnote citation.

Orphan
The first line of a paragraph printed alone at the bottom of a page.

Pagination
The system used for numbering pages in a document. In Word, it also means using features to control the way paragraphs and lines break at the top and bottom of a page.

Plagiarism
The unauthorized use of another person's ideas or creative work without giving credit to that person.

Soft page break
The location where Word automatically starts a new page because the current page is full.

Widow
The last line of a paragraph printed alone at the top of a page.

Try It! Inserting a Hard Page Break

1. Start Word and open **WTry22a** from the data files for this lesson.
2. Save the file as **WTry22a_studentfirstname_studentlastname** in the location where your teacher instructs you to store the files for this lesson.
3. Display nonprinting characters.
4. Position the insertion point at the beginning of the heading *Zebra*.
5. On the Insert tab, in the Pages group, click the Page Break button.
6. Click Undo on the Quick Access Toolbar.
7. On the Page Layout tab, in the Page Setup group, click the Breaks button and click Page.
8. Double-click the space between pages, then double-click the black line to reveal the space again.
9. Select the line on which the nonprinting page break displays and press DEL.
10. Save the changes to **WTry22a_studentfirstname_studentlastname** and leave it open in Word to use in the next Try It.

Controlling Pagination

- Use **pagination** options to control the way Word breaks paragraphs and lines at the top and bottom of a page. For example, you can control whether or not a heading stays on the same page as the paragraph that follows it.
- The following pagination options are available on the Line and Page Breaks tab of the Paragraph dialog box:
  - **Widow/Orphan** control. Select this option to prevent either the first or last line of a paragraph from printing on a different page from the rest of the paragraph.
  - Keep with next. Select this option to prevent a page break between the current paragraph and the following paragraph.
  - Keep lines together. Select this option to prevent a page break within a paragraph.
  - Page break before. Select this option to force a page break before the current paragraph.
- You can also press SHIFT + ENTER to manually insert a hard line break. A hard line break forces Word to wrap text before reaching the right margin.

✓ *To see hard line breaks onscreen, display nonprinting characters.*

Try It! Controlling Pagination

1. In the **WTry22a_studentfirstname_studentlastname** file, position the insertion point in the heading *Photography Tips*.
2. On the Page Layout tab, click the Paragraph group dialog box launcher to display the Paragraph dialog box.

   ✓ *You can also click the Paragraph group dialog box launcher on the Home tab.*
3. Click the Line and Page Breaks tab.
4. Under Pagination, click to select the Keep with next check box, and then click OK. The heading is now kept with the next paragraph.
5. Save the changes to **WTry22a_studentfirstname_studentlastname** and leave it open in Word to use in the next Try It.

Inserting Footnotes and Endnotes

- **Footnotes** or **endnotes** are required in documents that include quoted material, such as research papers.
- Standard footnotes and endnotes include the following information:
  - The author of the quoted material (first name first) followed by a comma.

    ✓ *This information may not always be available.*
  - The title of the book (in italics) followed by the city of publication followed by a colon, the publisher followed by a comma, and the date.
  - If the source is not a book, the title of the article (in quotation marks), or Web page (in quotation marks) followed by a comma, the name of the publication if it is a magazine or journal (in italics), the publication volume, number, and/or date (date in parentheses) followed by a colon.
  - The page number(s) where the material is located, followed by a period.
  - If the source is a Web page, the citation should also include the URL address, enclosed in angle brackets <> and the date you accessed the information, followed by a period.

✓ *There are other styles used for footnotes and endnotes. If you are unsure which style to use, ask your teacher for more information.*

- Footnotes or endnotes can also provide explanations or supplemental text. For example, an asterisk footnote might provide information about where to purchase a product mentioned in the text.
- The commands for inserting footnotes and endnotes are in the Footnotes group on the References tab of the Ribbon.

- When you insert a footnote, Word first inserts a **note reference mark** in the text, then a separator line following the last line of text on the page, and finally the note number corresponding to the note mark below the separator line. You then type and format the **note text** in the note area below the separator line.
- Endnotes include the same parts as footnotes but are printed on the last page of a document.
- Word uses Arabic numerals for footnote marks; if endnotes are used in the same document, the endnote marks are roman numerals.
- You can select a different number format or a symbol for the note mark.
- By default, numbering is consecutive from the beginning of the document. You can set Word to restart numbering on each page or each section. You can also change the starting number if you want.
- Word automatically updates numbering if you add or delete footnotes or endnotes, or rearrange the document text.
- To delete a footnote or endnote, position the insertion point to the right of the note mark in the text and press BACKSPACE twice.

Try It! Inserting Footnotes

1. In the **WTry22a_studentfirstname_studentlastname** file, position the insertion point at the end of the last sentence in the first paragraph under the heading *Lions*. The point should be between the period and the paragraph mark.

   ✓ *Insert footnotes after punctuation marks.*

2. Click References > Insert Footnote AB¹.

3. Type **"African Wildlife Foundation: Wildlife: Lion," <http://www.awf.org/content/wildlife/detail/lion>, Today's date.**

   ✓ *If Word automatically removes the brackets and/or formats the URL as a hyperlink, you can right-click the text, click Remove Hyperlink,, and then retype the brackets, if necessary.*

4. Save the changes to **WTry22a_studentfirstname_studentlastname** and leave it open in Word to use in the next Try It.

Insert a footnote

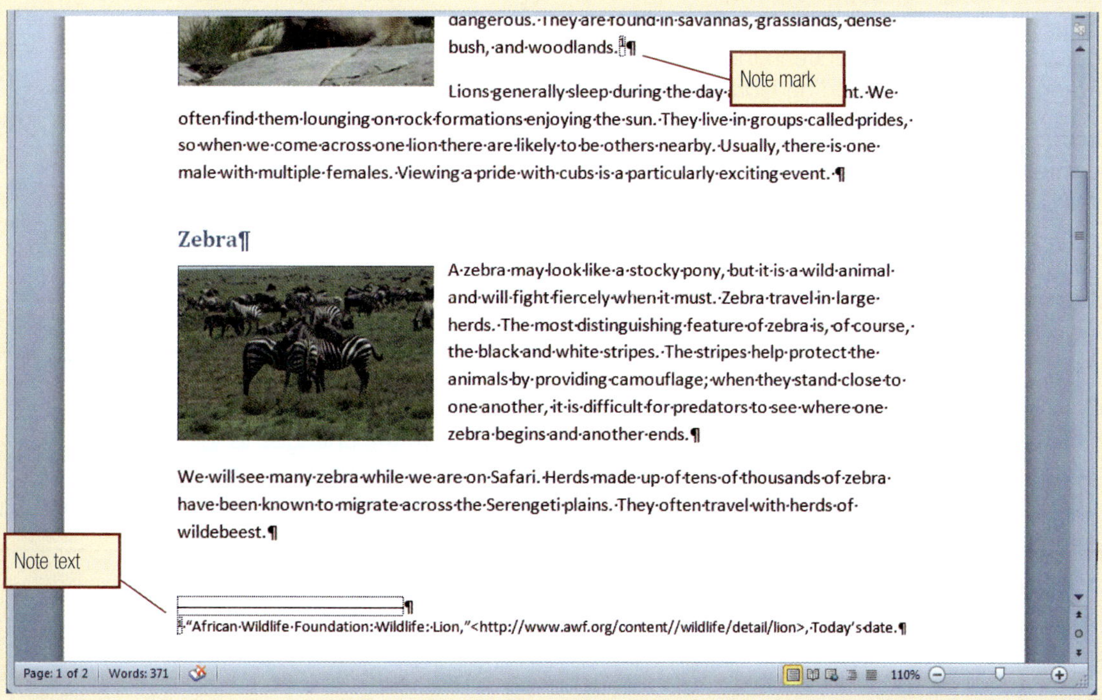

Try It! Inserting Endnotes

1. In the **WTry22a_studentfirstname_studentlastname** file, position the insertion point at the end of the last sentence in the second paragraph under the heading *Zebra*.
2. Click References > Insert Endnote.
3. Type **The movement of wildebeest, zebra, and other grazing animals across the plains is known as the Great Migration.**
4. Save the changes to **WTry22a_studentfirstname_studentlastname** and leave it open in Word to use in the next Try It.

Inserting Citations

- When you use words, pictures, video, sounds, or ideas that come from someone else in a paper or report, you must insert a **citation** to identify the source.
- A proper citation gives credit to the source, and provides the tools a reader needs to locate the source on his or her own.
- To create a citation you select the citation style, then enter source information such as the type of source, the author, the publisher, and the publication date into a Create Source dialog box.
- The citation displays inline at the insertion point location; the format depends on the selected citation style.
- For example, in MLA (Modern Language Association) style, the author's last name displays in parentheses.
- The citations are stored with the document. They are also added to a master list of sources which is available for use with any Word document you create or edit.
- The commands for entering a citation are on the References tab in the Citations & Bibliography group.

Try It! Inserting Citations

1. In the **WTry22a_studentfirstname_studentlastname** file, position the insertion point after the third sentence in the second paragraph under the heading *Lions*.
2. On the References tab, click the Style drop-down arrow Style: APA Fiftl to display a list of available citation styles.
3. Click MLA Sixth Edition.
4. Click the Insert Citation button and click Add New Source to display the Create Source dialog box.
5. Verify that the Type of Source is Book.

   ✓ *If necessary, click the Type of Source down arrow and click Book.*
6. Fill in the information as follows:
   - Author: **George B. Schaller**
   - Title: **The Serengeti Lion: A Study of Predator-Prey Relations**
   - Year: **2009**
   - City: **Chicago**
   - Publisher: **The University of Chicago Press**
7. Click OK.

   ✓ *To insert a citation using the same information you have already inserted in the same document, click the Insert Citation button and click the source to insert.*
8. Save the changes to **WTry22a_studentfirstname_studentlastname** and close it. Leave Word open to use in the next Try It.

Analyzing Citations

- Citations can help you ensure that the material you are using comes from an accurate and reliable source.
- If you do not cite your sources, you are guilty of **plagiarism**.
- You should insert a citation when you quote someone else, summarize or paraphrase another's work, use an idea that has been expressed by someone else, and when you make reference to someone else's work.
- When you reference information that is considered **common knowledge**, you do not have to include a citation; however, the definition of common knowledge varies. It is better to be safe and cite the source.
- Sometimes, a citation is not enough to ensure that you are in compliance with the law. Artistic creations such as music, text, and artwork—both printed and electronic—are protected by **copyright**.
- You must have permission from the copyright holder in order to use the work.
- Part of copyright law referred to as the **fair use doctrine** allows you to use a limited amount of copyrighted material without permission, as long as the purpose is not to make money from the material. For example, you can quote a few lines of a song or a passage from a book.

Creating a Reference Page

- Use Word's Bibliography feature to automatically create a reference page or **bibliography** by compiling a list of all citations in the document.
- Commands for creating a reference page are on the References tab in the Citations & Bibliography group.
- A reference page may also be called a Works Cited page.
- The page is inserted as a content control and formatted in the selected citation style.
- Word comes with built-in designs for one bibliography and one works cited page, or you can simply insert the bibliography as a list.
- If you add or edit sources, you can update the reference page.

Try It! Creating a Reference Page

1. In Word, open **WTry22b** from the data files for this lesson.
2. Save the file as **WTry22b_studentfirstname_studentlastname** in the location where your teacher instructs you to store the files for this lesson.
3. Press CTRL + END to move the insertion point to the end of the document.
4. Press CTRL + ENTER to insert a hard page break.
5. On the References tab, click the Bibliography button to display a gallery of available designs.
6. Click the Works Cited design. Word inserts the bibliography at the insertion point location.

   ✓ *To update a bibliography if you add or edit citations, click in the list to select the content control, and then click Update Citations and Bibliography on the Content Control handle.*
7. Save the changes to **WTry22b_studentfirstname_studentlastname**, close it, and exit Word.

Project 47—Create It

Exercise Report

DIRECTIONS

1. Start Word, if necessary, and open **WProj47** from the data files for this lesson.
2. Save the file as **WProj47_studentfirstname_studentlastname** in the location where your teacher instructs you to store the files for this lesson.
3. Double-click in the header and type your full name, press ENTER, and type today's date. Align the text flush right.
4. Position the insertion point at the beginning of the heading *The Impact on Your Health*.
5. Click **Page Layout** > **Breaks** > **Page**.
6. Select the heading *Mental Health* and the paragraph after it.
7. On the **Page Layout** tab, click the **Paragraph** group dialog box launcher to open the Paragraph dialog box.
8. Click the **Line and Page Breaks** tab.
9. Under Pagination, click to select the **Keep with next** check box and then **Keep lines together** check box, and then click **OK**.
10. Position the insertion point at the beginning of the heading *Safety*.
11. Click **Page Layout** > **Breaks** > **Page**.
12. Position the insertion point at the end of first paragraph of the introduction—to the right of the final punctuation.
13. Click **References** > **Insert Footnote** AB[1].
14. Type **National Center for Chronic Disease Prevention and Health Promotion, "Physical Activity and Health: A Report of the Surgeon General," Executive Summary (11/17/99): page 12.**
15. Position the insertion point at the end of the second paragraph under the heading *The Impact on Your Health*.
16. Click **References** > **Insert Endnote**.
17. Type **For more information, write to the President's Council on Physical Fitness and Sports, Room 738-H Humphrey Building, 200 Independence Avenue, SW, Washington, DC 20201-0004.**
18. Position the insertion point at the end of the first sentence under the heading *The Impact on Your Health*.
19. Click **References** > **Style** drop-down arrow Style: APA Fifth > **Chicago Fifteenth Edition**.
20. Click the **Insert Citation** button and click **Add New Source**.
21. Click the **Type of Source** down arrow and click **Document From Web site**.
22. Click to select the **Corporate Author** check box and then fill in the source information as follows:
    - Corporate Author: **National Institute on Aging**
    - Name of Web Page: **Exercise and Physical Activity: Getting Fit For Life**
    - Name of Web Site: **U.S. National Institutes of Health**
    - Year: **2010**
    - Month: **May**
    - Day: **28**
    - Year Accessed: **2011**
    - Month Accessed: **October**
    - Day Accessed: **11**
    - URL: **http://www.nia.nih.gov/HealthInformation/Publications/exercise.htm**
23. Click OK.
24. Position the insertion point at the end of the paragraph under the heading *Mental Health*.
25. Click **References** > **Insert Citation** > **Add New Source**.
26. Click the **Type of Source** down arrow and click **Book**.

27. Fill in the source information as follows:
    - Author: **G. Faulkner**
    - Title: **Exercise, Health and Mental Health: Emerging Relationships**
    - Year: **2006**
    - City: **Oxford**
    - Publisher: **Routledge**
28. Click **OK**.
29. Press CTRL + END to move the insertion point to the end of the document and then press CTRL + ENTER to insert a hard page break.
30. Click **References** > **Bibliography**.
31. Click the **Works Cited** design to insert the bibliography.
32. Check and correct the spelling and grammar in the document, and then save the changes.
33. **With your teacher's permission,** print the document. The last page should look similar to Figure 22-1.
34. Close the document, saving all changes, and exit Word.

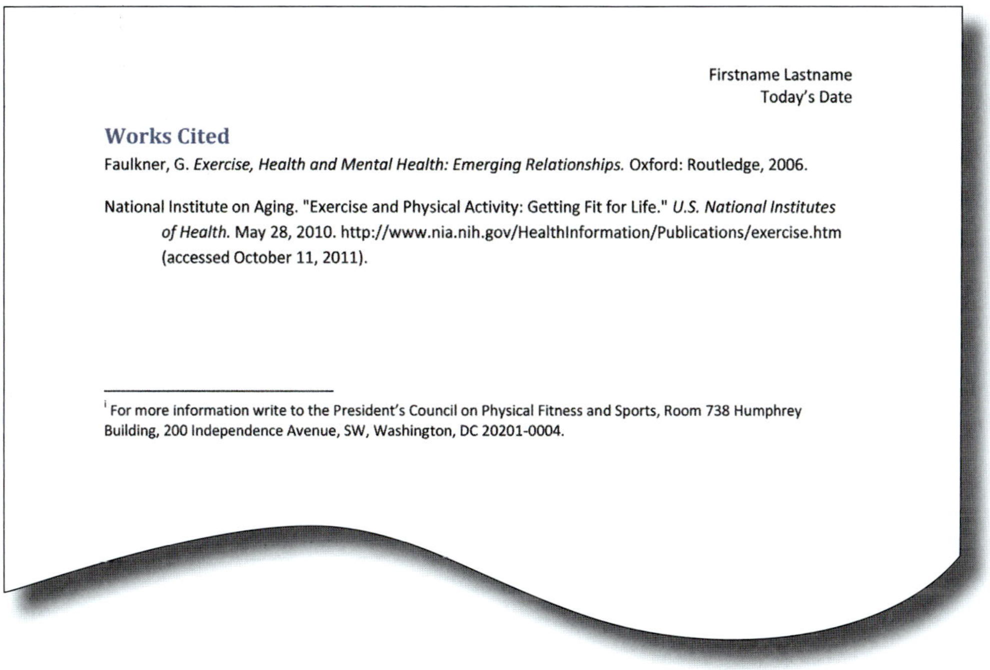

Firstname Lastname
Today's Date

Works Cited

Faulkner, G. *Exercise, Health and Mental Health: Emerging Relationships.* Oxford: Routledge, 2006.

National Institute on Aging. "Exercise and Physical Activity: Getting Fit for Life." *U.S. National Institutes of Health.* May 28, 2010. http://www.nia.nih.gov/HealthInformation/Publications/exercise.htm (accessed October 11, 2011).

[i] For more information write to the President's Council on Physical Fitness and Sports, Room 738 Humphrey Building, 200 Independence Avenue, SW, Washington, DC 20201-0004.

Figure 22-1

Project 48—Apply It

Exercise Report

DIRECTIONS

1. Start Word, if necessary, and open **WProj48** from the data files for this lesson.
2. Save the file as **WProj48_studentfirstname_studentlastname** in the location where your teacher instructs you to store the files for this lesson.
3. Double-click in the header and type your full name, press ENTER, and type today's date. Align the text flush right.
4. Insert a page break before the heading *The Impact on Your Health*.

5. Use the Keep with next and Keep lines together pagination options to keep the heading *Weight Control* and the next paragraph together on the same page and to keep the bulleted list items and the preceding line together on the same page.
6. Position the insertion point after the paragraph under the heading *Weight Control* and insert the following footnote: **Faithe Wempen, *Food & Nutrition for You* (Upper Saddle River: Pearson Education, Inc., 2010): 94.**
7. Position the insertion point after the second paragraph under the heading *Disease Control*. Select the citation style **MLA Sixth Edition** and insert a citation using the following information:
   - Type of Source: **Book**
   - Author: **Faithe Wempen**
   - Title: **Food & Nutrition for You**
   - Year: **2010**
   - City: **Upper Saddle River**
   - Publisher: **Pearson Education, Inc.**
8. Position the insertion point at the end of the second paragraph under the heading *Introduction*, click the **Insert Citation** button, and click the **National Institute on Aging** source to insert it in the document.
9. Start a new page at the end of the document and create a Works Cited page.
10. Check and correct the spelling and grammar in the document, and then save the changes.
11. **With your teacher's permission,** print the document. The first page should look similar to Figure 22-2.
12. Close the document, saving all changes, and exit Word.

Figure 22-2

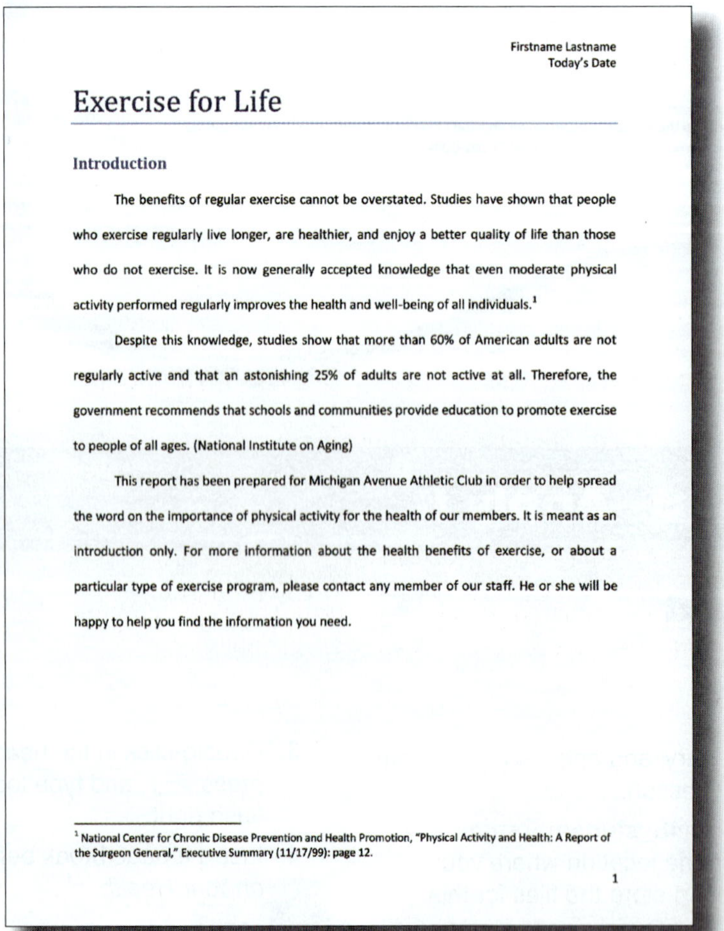

Firstname Lastname
Today's Date

Exercise for Life

Introduction

The benefits of regular exercise cannot be overstated. Studies have shown that people who exercise regularly live longer, are healthier, and enjoy a better quality of life than those who do not exercise. It is now generally accepted knowledge that even moderate physical activity performed regularly improves the health and well-being of all individuals.[1]

Despite this knowledge, studies show that more than 60% of American adults are not regularly active and that an astonishing 25% of adults are not active at all. Therefore, the government recommends that schools and communities provide education to promote exercise to people of all ages. (National Institute on Aging)

This report has been prepared for Michigan Avenue Athletic Club in order to help spread the word on the importance of physical activity for the health of our members. It is meant as an introduction only. For more information about the health benefits of exercise, or about a particular type of exercise program, please contact any member of our staff. He or she will be happy to help you find the information you need.

[1] National Center for Chronic Disease Prevention and Health Promotion, "Physical Activity and Health: A Report of the Surgeon General," Executive Summary (11/17/99): page 12.

1

Lesson 23

Working with Newsletter Columns

➤ What You Will Learn

- Understanding Desktop Publishing
- Creating Newsletter Columns
- Setting Column Width
- Inserting a Column Break
- Balancing Columns
- Analyzing Page Layout and Design

Software Skills Word's desktop publishing features let you design and publish eye-catching documents such as newsletters using your computer and printer. Designing a document with columns lets you present more information on a page, as well as create a visually interesting page. Newsletter-style columns are useful for creating documents such as newsletters, pamphlets, articles, or brochures.

Application Skills As a communications assistant at Vocation Opportunities, Inc., a career counseling company, you are responsible for producing publications such as newsletters, articles, and brochures. In this lesson, you will create and format two articles for clients. The first is about proper business attire and the second is about how to interview for a job.

WORDS TO KNOW

Balance
A basic principle of design that describes the visual weight of objects on a page, and the way the objects are arranged in relation to each other.

Column gutter
The space between column margins.

Commercial printer
A business that provides printing, copying, and publishing services.

Consistency
The use of repetition to create a uniform and predictable design or layout.

Contrast
A basic design principle in which elements with opposite or complementary features are positioned to create visual interest. Also, the degree of separation of color values within a picture.

Desktop publishing
The process of designing and printing a document using a computer and printer.

Newsletter-style columns
Columns in which text flows from the bottom of one column to the top of the next column.

Page layout
The way text, graphics, and space are organized on a document page.

Publish
Output a document so it can be distributed to readers.

What You Can Do

Understanding Desktop Publishing

- **Desktop publishing** refers to designing and producing printed documents using a desktop computer.
- Some common documents you can create with desktop publishing include reports, newsletters, brochures, booklets, manuals, and business cards.
- Most word-processing programs, such as Microsoft Word 2010, include desktop publishing features that are sufficient for producing many types of published documents.
- Some programs, such as Microsoft Publisher 2010, are designed exclusively for desktop publishing applications. These programs offer more sophisticated features for designing documents for publication.
- Many documents can be **published** using the computer, printer, and software that you already have at home, work, or school.
- If you have complex publishing requirements such as color matching or binding, you may be able to design the document on your own equipment, but you may need to use a **commercial printer** to produce the final product.
- A third alternative for publishing a document is to create a file, then deliver it or e-mail it to a copy shop for reproduction.

Creating Newsletter Columns

- Use Word's Columns feature to divide a document into more than one **newsletter-style column**.
- There are five preset column styles available on the Page Layout tab, in the Page Setup group, which you can apply to the entire document or the current section:
  - One is the default format. It has one column the width of the page from the left margin to the right margin.
  - Two creates two columns of equal width.
  - Three creates three columns of equal width.
  - Left creates a narrow column on the left and a wider column on the right.
  - Right creates a narrow column on the right and a wider column on the left.
- By dividing a document into sections using section breaks, you can combine different numbers of columns within a single document. For example, you can have a title or headline across the width of the page, and then divide the body text into multiple columns.

Try It! Creating Newsletter Columns

1. Start Word and open WTry23 from the data files for this lesson.
2. Save the file as WTry23_studentfirstname_studentlastname in the location where your teacher instructs you to store the files for this lesson.
3. Adjust the zoom so you can see the entire page on screen at once, and display nonprinting characters and the ruler.

   ✓ *Notice that there is a continuous section break between the title and the first heading.*
4. Move the insertion point anywhere in the second section of the document.
5. On the Page Layout tab, click the Columns button.
6. Click Three.
7. Save the changes to WTry23_studentfirstname_studentlastname and leave it open in Word to use in the next Try It.

(continued)

Try It! Creating Newsletter Columns *(continued)*

Newsletter-style columns

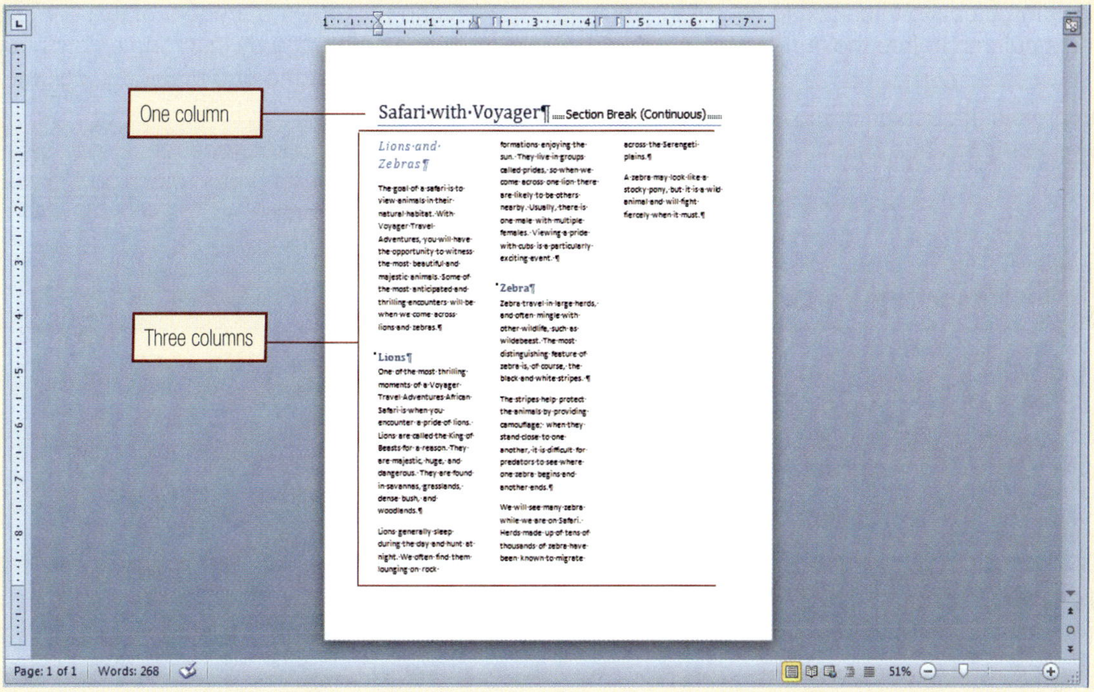

Setting Column Width

- Use the Columns dialog box to customize column formatting.
- You can create more than three columns, set a specific column width, and adjust the **column gutter** spacing.
- You can also select to display a line between columns.
- You can also drag the column margins on the ruler to adjust column widths and gutter spacing. Press and hold ALT as you drag to see the width and/or spacing measurement.

Try It! Setting Column Width

1. In the WTry23_studentfirstname_studentlastname file, verify that the insertion point is anywhere within the second section.
2. Click Page Layout > Columns > More Columns to open the Columns dialog box.
3. Under Presets, click Left.
4. Under Width and spacing, use the increment arrows to change the width of column 1 to 2".
5. Use the increment arrows to change the Spacing between the columns to 1".
6. Click to select the Line between check box.
7. Click OK.
8. Save the changes to WTry23_studentfirstname_studentlastname and leave it open in Word to use in the next Try It.

Inserting a Column Break

- By default, text flows to the top of the next column when the current column is filled.
- Use a column break to force text to flow to the top of the next column before the current column is filled.
- Column breaks are useful for moving headings or headlines to the top of a column.

Balancing Columns

- If there is not enough text to fill the last column in a document, the columns will appear uneven.
- You can balance the amount of text in multiple columns on a page by inserting a continuous section break at the end of the last column on the page.
- Column breaks take precedence over balancing; if there is a column break, the columns will not balance as expected.

Try It! Inserting a Column Break

1. In the **WTry23_studentfirstname_ studentlastname** file, click Page Layout > Columns > Two to divide section 2 of the document into two columns of equal width.
2. Position the insertion point at the beginning of the heading *Zebra*.
3. Click Page Layout > Breaks > Column to insert a column break.
4. Save the changes to **WTry23_ studentfirstname_studentlastname** and leave it open in Word to use in the next Try It.

Insert a column break

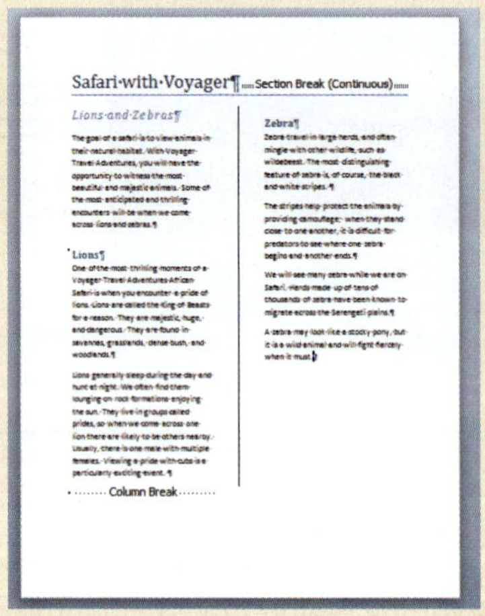

Try It! Balancing Columns

1. In the **WTry23_studentfirstname_ studentlastname** file, position the insertion point on the column break at the bottom of the left column and press DEL to delete it.
2. Position the insertion point at the end of text in the right column.
3. Click Page Layout > Breaks > Continuous.
4. Save the changes to **WTry23_ studentfirstname_studentlastname**, close it, and exit Word.

Balanced columns

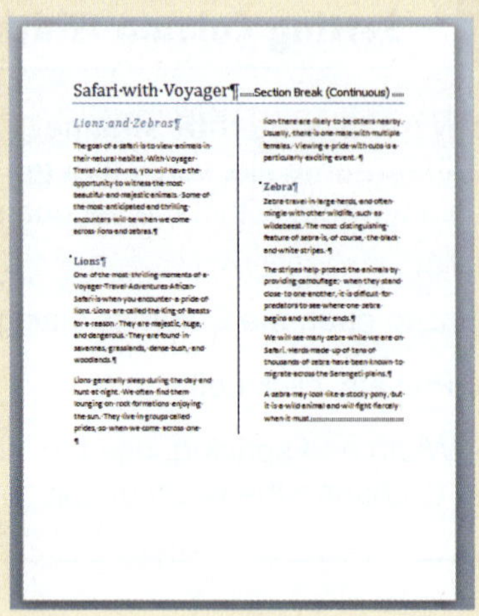

Analyzing Page Layout and Design

- The way you set up a page affects the way the reader sees and interprets the textual information.
- Effective **page layout** uses the basic principles of design, including **contrast**, **balance**, and **consistency** to highlight the text and capture the reader's attention.
- In addition to newsletter columns, you can use features such as themes, style sets, tables, borders, font formatting, lists, alignment, pictures, and spacing to create interesting and informative documents.

Project 49—Create It

Business Attire Article

DIRECTIONS

1. Start Word, if necessary, and open **WProj49** from the data files for this lesson.
2. Save the file as **WProj49_studentfirstname_studentlastname** in the location where your teacher instructs you to store the files for this lesson.
3. Click **Page Layout** > **Themes** > **Elemental**.
4. Click **Home** > **Change Styles** > **Style Set** > **Perspective**.
5. Position the insertion point at the beginning of the first line of text, type **Dress for Success** and press ENTER.
6. Type the following paragraph:

   "What should I wear?" Whether you are heading out to a job interview, your first day at a new job, or your company has started a "casual Friday" policy, it is important to understand the type of clothing that you should wear. In this article we will discuss the three levels of business attire: traditional, general, and business casual. Selecting appropriate attire shows your supervisor and your co-workers that you are professional, responsible, and worthy of respect.
7. Press ENTER.
8. Apply the **Title** style to the title, *Dress for Success*.
9. Apply the **Strong** style to the headings *Traditional Business Attire*, *General Business Attire*, *Business Casual Attire*, *Specific Circumstances*, and *The Bottom Line*.
10. Position the insertion point at the beginning of the heading *Traditional Business Attire*.
11. Click **Page Layout** > **Breaks** > **Continuous**.
12. Click **Page Layout** > **Columns** > **Two**.
13. Position the insertion point at the beginning of the heading *Business Casual Attire*.
14. Click **Page Layout** > **Breaks** > **Column**.
15. Click **Page Layout** > **Columns** > **More Columns** to open the Columns dialog box.
16. Click to select the **Line between check box**, and then click **OK**.
17. Type your full name and today's date in the header.
18. Check and correct the spelling and grammar in the document, and then save the changes.
19. **With your teacher's permission,** print the document. It should look similar to Figure 23-1 on the next page.
20. Close the document, saving all changes, and exit Word.

Figure 23-1

Firstname Lastname
Today's Date

Dress for Success

"What should I wear?" Whether you are heading out to a job interview, your first day at a new job, or your company has started a "casual Friday" policy, it is important to understand the type of clothing that you should wear. In this article we will discuss the three levels of business attire: traditional, general, and business casual. Selecting appropriate attire shows your supervisor and your co-workers that you are professional, responsible, and worthy of respect.

Traditional Business Attire

Traditional—or formal—business attire means a suit and dress shirt for both men and women. Suits should be conservative in color—black or blue is most appropriate.

Men should wear a properly tied necktie and dress shoes. Women should wear hosiery—stockings or pantyhose and closed-toe, closed-heeled shoes.

It is important to note the difference between "formal" business attire and formalwear. Formalwear refers to evening dress for a black-tie party, such as a gown for women and a tuxedo for men. No one expects you to wear a tuxedo to the office.

General Business Attire

General business attire is similar to traditional attire, but is not strictly limited to suits. A sport coat or a jacket may be worn with tailored slacks, but a tie is still called for. Women may wear a dress, or a skirt or slacks coordinated with an appropriate top.

Business Casual Attire

In some businesses, casual attire is appropriate, and even encouraged. Of course, business casual does not mean shorts and flip-flops. Rather, it means chinos and khakis, a collared shirt such as a polo, and sweaters. Men may leave off the tie, and casual shoes are appropriate.

Specific Circumstances

Some modern or contemporary offices develop their own dress code. When the environment is more relaxed, so are the expectations for what to wear. Clean jeans with no holes and fresh sneakers may be acceptable. If you wear a uniform be sure it fits properly, and that you keep it clean and neat. Use safety equipment when necessary.

The Bottom Line

You will be judged by your appearance. Keep yourself clean and well-groomed. Never show too much skin. Make sure your clothing fits properly. Tone down hair color, makeup, and piercings. When you are unsure, ask a co-worker or someone in the personnel department what is appropriate.

Project 50—Apply It

Interviewing Article

DIRECTIONS

1. Start Word, if necessary, and open **WProj50** from the data files for this lesson.
2. Save the files as **WProj50_studentfirstname_studentlastname** in the location where your teacher instructs you to store the files for this lesson.
3. Apply the **Concourse** theme.
4. Apply the **Formal** style set.
5. Apply the **Title** style to the title, *Interviewing Skills for the Job-Seeker*.
6. Apply the **Strong** style to the headings *The Interview Process* and *Making the Most of a Job Interview*.
7. Insert a continuous section break between the introductory paragraph and the heading *The Interview Process*.
8. Format the second section with the **Left** column preset.
9. Apply numbered list formatting to the five lines under the heading *The Interview Process* in the narrow, left column.
10. Apply bulleted list formatting to the 11 items following the full paragraph under the heading *Making the Most of a Job Interview*.
11. Insert a column break to force the heading *Making the Most of a Job Interview* to the top of the right column.
12. Increase the column gutter spacing to **0.6"**.
13. Type your full name and today's date in the footer.
14. Check and correct the spelling and grammar in the document, and then save the changes.
15. **With your teacher's permission,** print the document.
16. Close the document, saving all changes, and exit Word.

Lesson 24

Enhancing Paragraphs with Dropped Capitals, Borders, and Shading

WORDS TO KNOW

Dropped capital
An enlarged capital letter that drops below the first line of body text in the paragraph.

Goal-setting
A plan to obtain or achieve something.

Opacity
A measurement of the transparency of a color.

Prioritize
Rank in order of importance.

Responsibilities
Things people expect you to do or that you must accomplish.

Time management
Controlling and organizing a schedule so you can accomplish tasks and meet responsibilities.

➤ What You Will Learn

Inserting Dropped Capitals
Enhancing a Paragraph with Borders and Shading

Software Skills Dropped capital letters, borders, and shading can call attention to a single word, a line, a paragraph, or an entire page. They make a document visually appealing and interesting to the reader, so the reader will be more likely to take the time to read and remember the text.

Application Skills The articles for Vocation Opportunities have been very well received. Your supervisor would like you to combine them to create a two-page newsletter. She is leaving for an off-site meeting in the morning and would like to bring a draft of the newsletter with her to show off. In this lesson, you will use time management techniques to make sure you complete your assigned tasks on time. You will set up the newsletter and then format the articles using dropped capitals, borders, and shading.

What You Can Do

Inserting Dropped Capitals

- A **dropped capital** letter, called *drop cap*, is used to call attention to an opening paragraph.
- Word 2010 comes with two preset drop cap styles that drop the character three lines.
  - The Dropped style places the drop cap within the paragraph text.
  - The In margin style places the drop cap in the margin to the left of the paragraph.
- You can select options in the Drop Cap dialog box to change the font of the drop cap, the number of lines that the character drops, and the distance the drop character is placed from the paragraph text.
- Selecting a font that is different and more decorative than the paragraph font can enhance the drop cap effect.
- Options for applying and formatting drop caps are in the Text group on the Insert tab of the Ribbon.

Try It! Inserting Dropped Capitals

1. Start Word and open **WTry24** from the data files for this lesson.
2. Save the file as **WTry24_studentfirstname_studentlastname** in the location where your teacher instructs you to store the files for this lesson.
3. Click in the first paragraph under the heading *Lions*.
4. Click Insert > Drop Cap.
5. Click In margin.
6. Click in the first paragraph under the heading *Zebra*.
7. Click Insert > Drop Cap > Dropped.

   ✓ *Click None in the Drop Cap gallery to remove a drop cap style from selected text.*
8. Save the changes to **WTry24_studentfirstname_studentlastname** and leave it open in Word to use in the next Try It.

Try It! Customizing a Dropped Capital

1. In the **WTry24_studentfirstname_studentlastname** file, make sure the insertion point is in the first paragraph under the heading *Zebra*.
2. Click Insert > Drop Cap > Drop Cap Options to open the Drop Cap dialog box.
3. Click the Font down arrow and click Algerian.
4. Use the increment arrows to set the Lines to drop to 5.
5. Click OK.
6. Save the changes **WTry24_studentfirstname_studentlastname** and leave it open in Word to use in the next Try It.

(continued)

Try It! **Customizing a Dropped Capital** *(continued)*

Two styles of drop cap

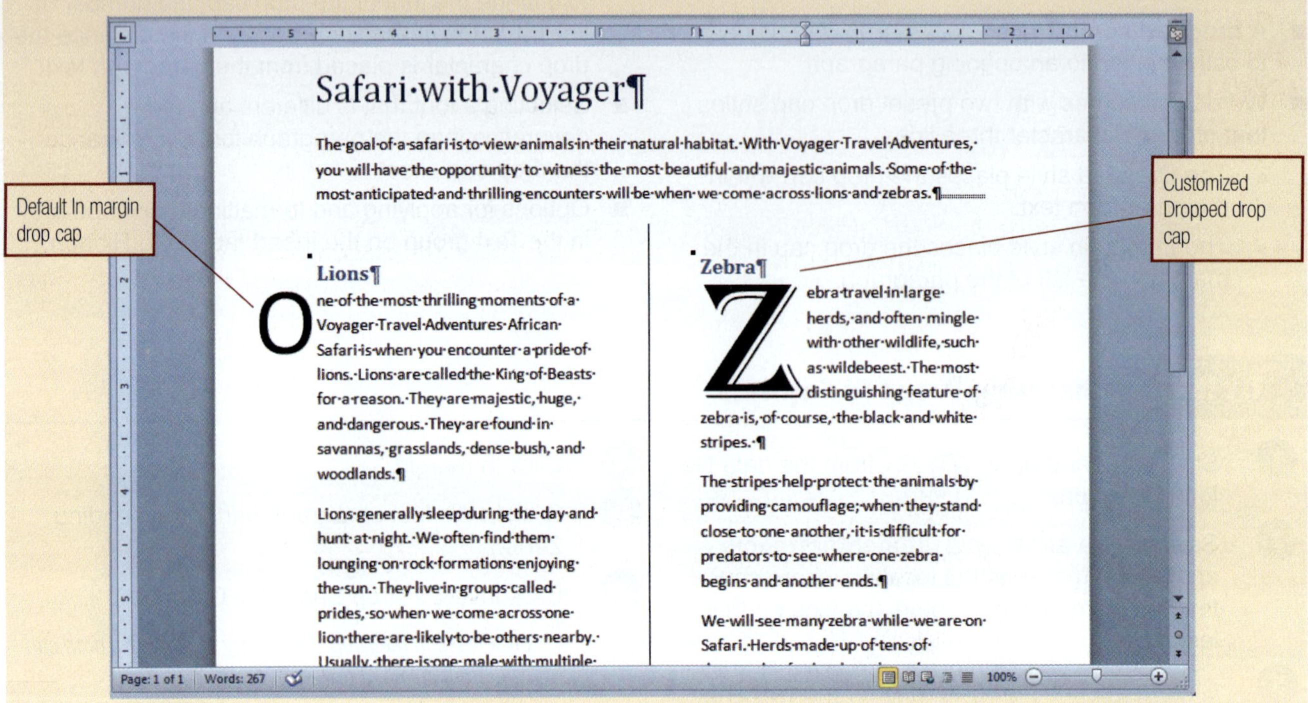

Enhancing a Paragraph with Borders and Shading

- You can apply borders and/or shading to paragraphs.
- Paragraph borders and shading can be applied to a single paragraph or selected paragraphs.
- Paragraph border and shading options are similar to those for tables and pages.

✓ *Refer to Word, Lesson 10 for information on applying page borders; refer to Word, Lesson 17 for information on table borders and shading.*

- Border options include line style, line width (weight), and line color. You can also apply 3D or shadow effects.
- Shading options include solid color fills or you can select a pattern style and color.
- The pattern styles include built-in geometric patterns as well as percentages of **opacity**.
  - The higher the percentage, the more opaque the color, with 100% being solid.
  - The lower the percentage, the more transparent the color, with 0% being no color.

Try It! Enhancing a Paragraph with Borders

1. In the **WTry24_studentfirstname_studentlastname** file, position the insertion point in the title *Safari with Voyager*.
2. Click Page Layout > Page Borders to open the Borders and Shading dialog box.
3. Click the Borders tab.
4. In the Style list box, scroll down and click the border that has a thin line above and below a thick middle line.
5. Click the Color drop-down arrow and under Theme Colors, click Red, Accent 2.
6. Click the Width drop-down arrow and click 3 pt.
7. In the Setting list, click None, and then in the Preview area, click the bottom border button.

   ✓ *The border buttons in the Preview area and in the Setting list are toggles; click once to select and again to clear.*
8. Click OK.
9. Save the changes **WTry24_studentfirstname_studentlastname** and leave it open in Word to use in the next Try It.

Try It! Enhancing a Paragraph with Shading

1. In the **WTry24_studentfirstname_studentlastname** file, position the insertion point in the title *Safari with Voyager*.
2. Click Page Layout > Page Borders to open the Borders and Shading dialog box.
3. Click the Shading tab.
4. Click the Fill drop-down arrow and under Theme Colors, click Tan, Background 2.
5. Click OK.
6. Click the Page Borders button again, and click the Shading tab.
7. Under Patterns, click the Style drop-down arrow and click 10%.
8. Click the Color drop-down arrow and under Theme Colors, click Red, Accent 2.
9. Click OK.
10. Save the changes to **WTry24_studentfirstname_studentlastname**, close it, and exit Word.

Analyzing Time Management

- **Time management** is a critical skill for succeeding at school and at work.
- Use time management techniques to organize and **prioritize** the tasks you must accomplish, and to make sure you meet your **responsibilities**.
- Time management techniques include analyzing exactly how you currently spend your time, making a list of tasks you must accomplish, ranking the tasks in order of importance, and creating a realistic schedule to complete each task.
- Combining **goal-setting** with time management is an effective way to make sure you get things done.
- You can practice time management in class and at home to ensure that you complete your work on time.

Project 51—Create It

Newsletter 1

DIRECTIONS

Time Management

1. Before beginning this project, make a time journal listing how you spend your time every day. The journal will help you analyze your current use of time.
2. Make a to-do list of tasks you must accomplish today. Include the projects for this lesson on your list.
3. Prioritize the tasks, putting this project at the top.
4. Create a schedule that clearly shows how you will spend the time you have available to complete the tasks on your to-do list.

Create the Newsletter

1. Start Word, if necessary, and save the default blank document as **WProj51_studentfirstname_studentlastname** in the location where your teacher instructs you to store the files for this lesson.
2. Apply the **Newsprint** theme and the **Newsprint** style set.
3. Double-click in the header and type your full name and today's date.
4. On the first line of the document, type **Opportunity Knocks**. Format it with the **Title** style.
5. Press ENTER and type **A Publication of Vocation Opportunities, Inc.** Format it with the **Heading 2** style and center it horizontally on the line.
6. Press ENTER. Change the font size to 12 points, set the paragraph spacing before to 12 points, and type the following paragraph: **Welcome to the first edition of Opportunity Knocks, a monthly newsletter published by Vocation Opportunities, Inc. Our goal with this newsletter is to provide information that will help you achieve your career goals. Content will include articles, tips, and interviews with industry insiders. We hope you find it useful and entertaining!**
7. Press ENTER.
8. Click in the paragraph you typed in step 6.
9. Click **Insert** > **Drop Cap** > **Dropped**. Justify the paragraph text.
10. Select the second line in the document—*A Publication of Vocation Opportunities, Inc*.
11. Click **Page Layout** > **Page Borders**.
12. Click the **Borders** tab.
13. In the Style list, click the single solid line border.
14. Click the **Color** drop-down arrow and, under Theme Colors, click **Dark Red, Accent 1**.
15. Click the **Width** drop-down arrow and click **2¼ pt**.
16. In the preview area, click to toggle on the **Top Border** button and the **Bottom border** button, and to toggle off the **Left Border** button and the **Right Border** button.
17. Click the **Shading** tab in the Borders and Shading dialog box.
18. Click the **Fill** drop-down arrow and under Theme Colors, click **Gray-25%, Background 2**.
19. Click **OK**.
20. Check and correct the spelling and grammar in the document, and then save the changes.
21. **With your teacher's permission,** print the document. It should look similar to Figure 24-1 on the next page.
22. Close the document, saving all changes, and exit Word.

Firstname Lastname
Today's date

Opportunity Knocks

A Publication of Vocation Opportunities, Inc.

Welcome to the first edition of Opportunity Knocks, a monthly newsletter published by Vocation Opportunities, Inc. Our goal with this newsletter is to provide information that will help you achieve your career goals. The newsletter content will include articles, tips, and interviews with industry insiders. We hope you find it useful and entertaining!

Figure 24-1

Project 52—Apply It

Newsletter 2

DIRECTIONS

1. Start Word, if necessary, and open **WProj52** from the data files for this lesson.
2. Save the file as **WProj52_studentfirstname_studentlastname** in the location where your teacher instructs you to store the files for this lesson.
3. Type your full name and today's date in the header.
4. Insert page numbers flush right in the footer.
5. Insert continuous section breaks before the headings *Dress for Success*, *Interviewing Skills for the Job-Seeker*, *The Interview Process*, and *Time Management Tips*.
6. Apply two-column formatting to section 2 (*Dress for Success*) and apply Left column formatting to section 4 (*The Interview Process*).
7. Insert a column break in section 4 before the heading *Making the Most of a Job Interview*.
8. In the first paragraph under the heading *Dress for Success*, insert a drop cap using the Dropped style customized to drop 5 lines.
9. In the first paragraph under the heading *Interviewing Skills for the Job Seeker*, insert a drop cap using the default Dropped style.
10. Select the heading *The Bottom Line* and the paragraph following it and apply a single line, **4½ pt., Dark Red, Accent 1 Shadow** border and a **Gray-25%, Background 2** fill.
11. Select the heading *Time Management Tips*, the paragraph, and the four numbered items following it and apply a single line, **Gray-80% Text 2, 2¼ pt. Box** border on all sides, and a **20% Blue-Gray, Accent 4** color pattern.
12. Check and correct the spelling and grammar in the document, and then save the changes.

13. **With your teacher's permission,** print the document. (Use two-sided printed if available.) It should look similar to Figure 24-2.

14. Close the document, saving all changes, and exit Word.

Figure 24-2

Firstname Lastname
Today's date

Opportunity Knocks

A Publication of Vocation Opportunities, Inc.

Welcome to the first edition of Opportunity Knocks, a monthly newsletter published by Vocation Opportunities, Inc. Our goal with this newsletter is to provide information that will help you achieve your career goals. The newsletter content will include articles, tips, and interviews with industry insiders. We hope you find it useful and entertaining!

Dress for Success

Whether you are heading out to a job interview, your first day at a new job or your company has started a "casual Friday" policy, it is important to understand the type of clothing that you should wear. In this article we will discuss the three levels of business attire: traditional, general, and business casual. Selecting appropriate attire shows your supervisor and your co-workers that you are professional, responsible, and worthy of respect.

Traditional Business Attire

Traditional—or formal—business attire means a suit and dress shirt for both men and women. Suits should be conservative in color—black or blue is most appropriate.

Men should wear a properly tied necktie and dress shoes. Women should wear hosiery—stockings or pantyhose and closed-toe, closed-heeled shoes.

It is important to note the difference between "formal" business attire and formalwear. Formalwear refers to evening dress for a black-tie party, such as a gown for women and a tuxedo for men. No one expects you to wear a tuxedo to the office.

General Business Attire

General business attire is similar to traditional attire, but is not strictly limited to suits. A sport coat or a jacket may be worn with tailored slacks, but a tie is still called for. Women may wear a dress, or a skirt or slacks coordinated with an appropriate top.

Business Casual Attire

In some businesses, casual attire is appropriate, and even encouraged. Business casual usually means chinos and khakis, a collared shirt, and sweaters. Men may leave off the tie, and casual shoes are appropriate.

Specific Circumstances

Some offices have a more relaxed environment. Clean jeans with no holes and fresh sneakers may be acceptable. If you wear a uniform be sure it fits properly, and that you keep it clean and neat. Use safety equipment when necessary.

The Bottom Line

You will be judged by your appearance. Keep yourself clean and well-groomed. Never show too much skin. Make sure your clothing fits properly. Tone down hair color, makeup, and piercings. When you are unsure, ask a co-worker or someone in the personnel department what is appropriate.

1

Firstname Lastname
Today's date

Interviewing Skills for the Job-Seeker

You only get one chance to make a first impression. Based on your resume and cover letter, and possibly a phone conversation, the employer has decided you are a qualified candidate. The interview is your opportunity to seal the deal.

The Interview Process

1. Schedule the interview for a time when you are available.
2. Prepare by researching the company and thinking of questions to ask.
3. Practice by rehearsing with a partner or in front of a mirror.
4. After the interview write a thank-you note.
5. Follow-up by phone or e-mail to learn if you got the job.

Making the Most of a Job Interview

A job interview is like a test—if you pass, you will receive a job offer. Use these tips to get that offer!

- Wear clean, neat clothes that fit. Tone down makeup, hair styles, and piercings.
- Make sure your hands, teeth, and fingernails are clean.
- Arrive ten minutes early.
- Introduce yourself to the receptionist, and explain who you are there to meet.
- Be polite and respectful to everyone you meet.
- Shake hands with your interviewer when you arrive and before you leave.
- Listen carefully, using positive body language.
- Use proper English when you speak; no slang.
- Avoid chewing gum, fidgeting, or other behavior that indicates you are bored or uninterested.
- Turn off your cell phone. If you forget and it rings, apologize and ignore it or turn it off without checking to see who called.
- Ask the interviewer for his or her business card before you leave so you know how to make contact to say thank-you or to follow-up.

Time Management Tips

Searching for a job is full-time work. It is important to stay focused and organized and to manage your time effectively. Use these time management tips to help stay on track:

1. Create a daily schedule including a to-do list with specific job search tasks to accomplish. For example, write down the people you need to contact, the letters you need to send out, and the resources you need to check for leads.
2. Create a weekly schedule for tasks such as researching companies, informational interviews, and other networking opportunities.
3. Keep job search materials organized so you do not waste time looking for them or repeating tasks you have already completed.
4. Let a vocational counselor help you plan and organize your job search.

2

Lesson 25

Copying Formatting

➤ What You Will Learn

Copying Formatting
Highlighting Text

Software Skills Use the Format Painter to quickly copy formatting from one location to another. The Format Painter saves you time and makes it easy to duplicate formatting throughout a document. You can highlight text to change the color around the text without changing the font color. Highlighting is useful for calling attention to text and for making text stand out on the page.

Application Skills You have been working as part of a team planning new winter tours at Voyager Travel Adventures. The team member responsible for writing press releases about the tours is having trouble completing his assignments, and the other team members are chipping in to help. In this lesson, you will use the format painter to copy formatting to complete the documents. You will highlight text you think might be incorrect so another team member can check the facts.

WORDS TO KNOW

Conflict
A disagreement between two or more people who have different ideas.

Leader
Someone who unites people to work toward common goals.

Team
A group of two or more people who work together to achieve a common goal.

What You Can Do

Copying Formatting

- Use the Format Painter to copy formatting from existing formatted text to another part of the document.
- You can copy formatting one time, or leave the Format Painter active so you can copy the same formatting to multiple locations.
- The Format Painter button is in the Clipboard group on the Home tab of the Ribbon.

Try It! Copying Formatting

1. Start Word and open **WTry25** from the data files for this lesson.
2. Save the file as **WTry25_studentfirstname_studentlastname** in the location where your teacher instructs you to store the files for this lesson.
3. Click in the heading *Lions*.
4. Click Home > Format Painter.

   ✓ *The mouse pointer changes to the Painter pointer.*
5. Click the heading *Zebra* at the top of the right column.
6. Click in the paragraph under the heading *Lions*, then double-click the Format Painter button.
7. Select the first paragraph under the heading *Zebra*.
8. Select the remaining paragraphs under the heading *Zebra*.
9. Click the Format Painter button to turn the feature off.
10. Save the changes to **WTry25_studentfirstname_studentlastname** and leave it open to use in the next Try It.

Highlighting Text

- Highlighting calls attention to text by applying a color background.
- You can highlight text as a decorative or visual effect, but Word's Highlighter feature is commonly used like a highlighter pen on paper to mark text that requires attention.
- The Text Highlight Color button is in the Font group on the Home tab of the Ribbon.
- Click the button to apply the current color displayed on the button, or click the drop-down arrow to select a different color from the Text Highlight Color palette.

Try It! Highlighting Text

1. In the **WTry25_studentfirstname_studentlastname** file, select the text *sleep at night and hunt during the day* in the first sentence of the second paragraph under the heading *Lions*.
2. Click Home > Text Highlight Color.
3. In the last sentence of the first paragraph under the heading *Zebra*, select the text *the red and white stripes*.
4. Click Home > Text Highlight Color drop-down arrow and click Pink on the color palette.
5. Select the text *and white stripes* again.
6. Click the Text Highlight Color drop-down arrow again and click No Color.
7. Click the Text Highlight Color drop-down arrow and click Bright Green on the color palette.

   ✓ *The mouse pointer changes to the Highlight Text pointer.*
8. Drag across the last sentence in the second paragraph under the heading *Lions*: *Viewing a pride with cubs is a particularly exciting event.*
9. Click the Text Highlight Color button to turn the feature off.
10. Save the changes to **WTry25_studentfirstname_studentlastname**, close it, and exit Word.

Analyzing Teamwork

- Being able to work as part of a **team** is an important skill for succeeding at school and at work.
- A successful team is made up of people who trust and respect one another. They work together to make decisions, solve problems, and achieve common goals.
- **Conflict** can interfere with the team's ability to achieve its goals. Effective communication is an important way to avoid or resolve conflict.
- Team members must be committed to the group's success, and willing to work hard to meet their responsibilities.
- Teams are more likely to succeed when the members are open-minded, cooperative, trustworthy, and friendly, and when they feel comfortable speaking out, listening, and compromising when necessary.
- Often, a team **leader** keeps the team on track and focused on achieving its goals. He or she organizes the team's activities, encourages communication, and motivates team members.

Project 53—Create It

Sailing Tour Description

DIRECTIONS

1. Start Word, if necessary, and open **WProj53** from the data files for this lesson.
2. Save the file as **WProj53_studentfirstname_studentlastname** in the location where your teacher instructs you to store the files for this lesson.
3. Replace the sample text *Student's Name* with your own name, and *Today's Date* with today's date.
4. Click in the blue, bold text *Voyager Travel Adventures* in the first paragraph.
5. Click **Home** > **Format Painter** .
6. Drag across the text *Voyager Travel Adventures* at the beginning of the last paragraph to copy the blue, bold formatting.
7. Click in the paragraph that begins with the text *While on board*.
8. Click **Home** > **Format Painter** .
9. Drag across the first indented paragraph.
10. Drag across the last two lines of the document.
11. Select the text *8-day/7-night*.
12. Click **Home** > **Text Highlight Color** button to apply the default yellow highlight to the selection.

    ✓ *If yellow is not the color displayed on the button, click the drop-down arrow and click Yellow on the Text Highlight Color palette.*

13. Click the **Text Highlight Color** drop-down arrow and click **Bright Green** on the color palette.
14. Drag across the text *48-foot, fully-equipped catamaran*.
15. Drag across the word *spelunking*.
16. Drag across the year *1998*.
17. Click the **Text Highlight Color** button to turn the feature off.
18. Check and correct the spelling and grammar in the document, and then save the changes.
19. **With your teacher's permission,** print the document.
20. Close the document, saving all changes, and exit Word.

Project 54—Apply It

Winter in Yellowstone Tour Description

DIRECTIONS

1. Start Word, if necessary, and open **WProj54** from the data files for this lesson.
2. Save the file as **WProj54_studentfirstname_studentlastname** in the location where your teacher instructs you to store the files for this lesson.
3. Replace the sample text *Student's Name* with your own name, and *Today's Date* with today's date.
4. Copy the blue, bold formatting from the text *Voyager Travel Adventures* in the first paragraph to the text *Voyager Travel Adventures* in the last paragraph.
5. Copy the paragraph formatting from the first paragraph to the second, third, fourth, and fifth paragraphs.
6. Highlight the word *wasteland* in turquoise.
7. Highlight the text *5-day/6-night* and the year *1998* in pink.
8. Highlight in yellow the sentence, *This rugged adventure is for experienced winter campers only*.
9. Check and correct the spelling and grammar in the document, and then save the changes.
10. **With your teacher's permission,** print the document. It should look similar to Figure 25-1.
11. Close the document, saving all changes, and exit Word.

Figure 25-1

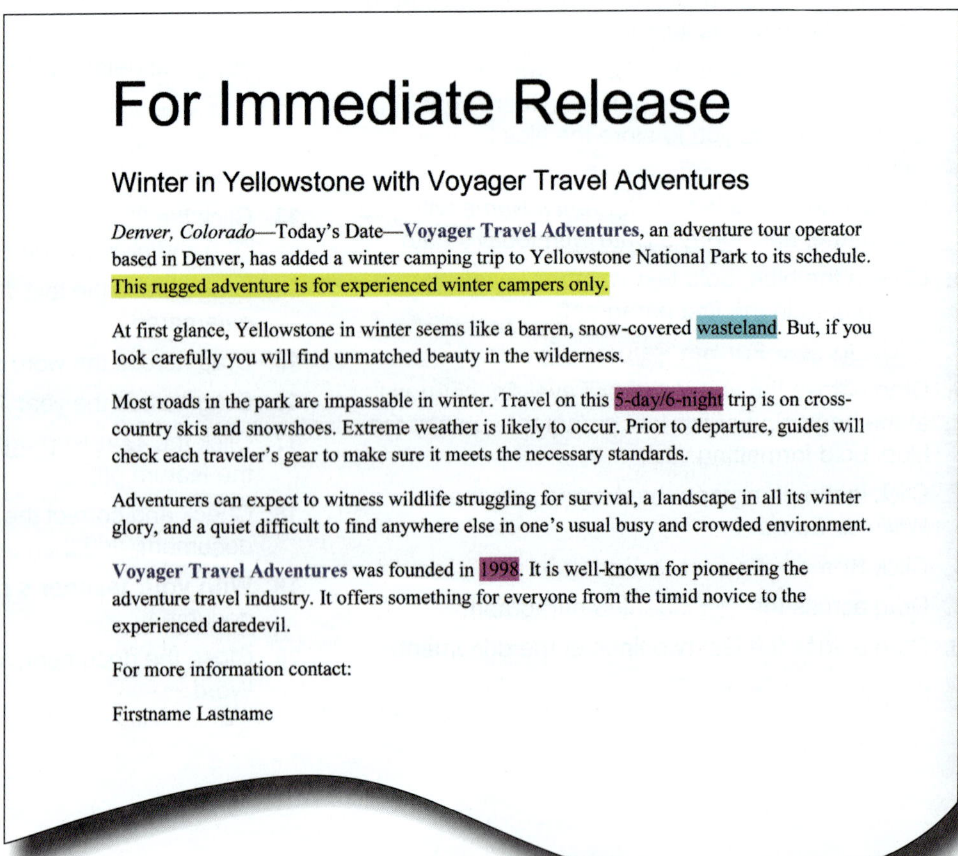

For Immediate Release

Winter in Yellowstone with Voyager Travel Adventures

Denver, Colorado—Today's Date—**Voyager Travel Adventures**, an adventure tour operator based in Denver, has added a winter camping trip to Yellowstone National Park to its schedule. This rugged adventure is for experienced winter campers only.

At first glance, Yellowstone in winter seems like a barren, snow-covered wasteland. But, if you look carefully you will find unmatched beauty in the wilderness.

Most roads in the park are impassable in winter. Travel on this 5-day/6-night trip is on cross-country skis and snowshoes. Extreme weather is likely to occur. Prior to departure, guides will check each traveler's gear to make sure it meets the necessary standards.

Adventurers can expect to witness wildlife struggling for survival, a landscape in all its winter glory, and a quiet difficult to find anywhere else in one's usual busy and crowded environment.

Voyager Travel Adventures was founded in 1998. It is well-known for pioneering the adventure travel industry. It offers something for everyone from the timid novice to the experienced daredevil.

For more information contact:

Firstname Lastname

Lesson 26

Inserting Symbols

➤ What You Will Learn

Inserting Symbols

Software Skills Use symbols to supplement the standard characters available on the keyboard and to add visual interest to documents. For example, you can insert symbols such as hearts and stars into documents as borders or separators.

Application Skills In this lesson, you will use symbols to create and complete a flyer for Whole Grains Bread.

WORDS TO KNOW

Symbol
Shapes, mathematical and scientific notations, currency signs, and other visual elements you can insert in documents by using the Symbol dialog box.

What You Can Do

Inserting Symbols

- **Symbols** are characters that cannot be typed from the keyboard, such as hearts, stars, and other shapes, as well as foreign alphabet characters.
- Symbols can be selected, edited, and formatted in a document just like regular text characters.
- Several symbol fonts come with Microsoft Office 2010 and others are available online for download.
- Many regular fonts also include some symbol characters.
- You can also insert special characters such as paragraph marks and ellipses.
- You can select from a gallery of common and recently used symbols by clicking the Symbol button on the Insert tab, or you can select from all available symbols in the Symbol dialog box.

- Some symbols have number codes you can use for identification, and some have shortcut keys you can use to insert the symbol into a document.
- When you insert symbols, the default font formatting is applied to the character. You can change the font size, style, and effects just as you can for regular text characters.

Try It! Inserting Symbols

1. Start Word and open **WTry26** from the data files for this lesson.
2. Save the file as **WTry26_studentfirstname_studentlastname** in the location where your teacher instructs you to store the files for this lesson.
3. Position the insertion point on the blank line between the first paragraph and the section break.
4. Click Insert > Symbol > More Symbols to open the Symbol dialog box.

   ✓ *If the symbol you want displays in the Symbols gallery, click it to insert it in the document.*
5. Click the Font drop-down arrow and click Wingdings.
6. Click the flower symbol in the sixth row—Wingdings 123—and then click Insert. The dialog box stays open.
7. Click the flower symbol to the right—Wingdings 124—and click Insert.
8. Click Close to close the dialog box.
9. Save the changes to **WTry26_studentfirstname_studentlastname** and leave it open to use in the next Try It.

Try It! Inserting a Special Character

1. In the **WTry26_studentfirstname_studentlastname** file, position the insertion point after the word *Safari* in the first sentence of the first paragraph under the heading *Lions*.
2. Click Insert > Symbol > More Symbols to open the Symbol dialog box.
3. Click the Special Characters tab.
4. Click the Registered symbol and then click Insert.
5. Click Close to close the dialog box.
6. Save the changes to **WTry26_studentfirstname_studentlastname**, close it, and exit Word.

Special Characters tab in the Symbol dialog box

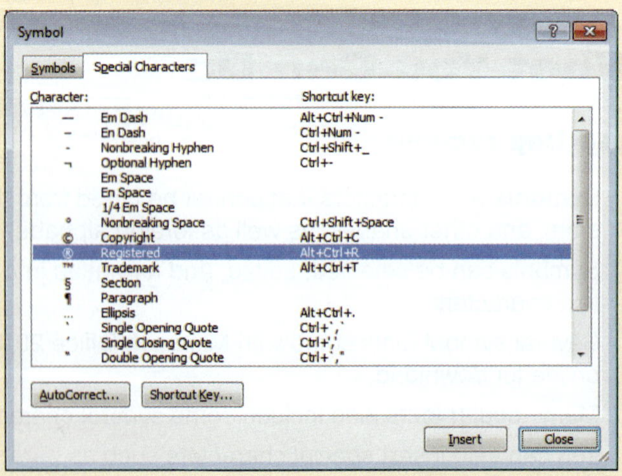

Project 55—Create It

Grand Opening Flyer

DIRECTIONS

1. Start Word, if necessary, and save the default blank document as **WProj55_studentfirstname_studentlastname** in the location where your teacher instructs you to store the files for this lesson.
2. Apply the **Solstice** theme.
3. Double-click in the header and type your full name and today's date.
4. On the first line of the document, type **GRAND OPENING**. Increase the font size to **20** points and center it horizontally on the line.
5. Press ENTER twice and type **Whole Grains Bread**. Format it in the **Heading 1** style. Increase the font size to **36** points, apply the **Small Caps** font effect, and center the text horizontally on the line.
6. Press ENTER twice and type **Announces**. Copy the formatting from the first line in the document to this line.
7. Move the insertion point up to the blank line between the first two lines of text.
8. Click **Insert** > **Symbol** Ω > **More Symbols** to open the Symbol dialog box.
9. If necessary, click the **Font** drop-down arrow and click **Wingdings** to change to the Wingdings font set.
10. Click the five-pointed star on line 10 (**Wingdings 182☆**), and click **Insert**. Click **Insert** nine more times to insert a total of 10 stars.
11. Click **Close** to close the dialog box.
12. Select the line of star symbols and increase the font size to **26** points.
13. Click **Home** > **Text Effects** A and click the effect on the right end of the top row—**Fill – Red, Accent 3, Outline – Text 2**. .
14. Move the insertion point to the blank line between the second and third lines of text.
15. Click **Insert** > **Symbol** Ω > **More Symbols** to open the Symbol dialog box.
16. Click the five-pointed star in a black circle on line 10 (Wingdings 181✪), and click **Insert** ten times. Click **Close** to close the dialog box.
17. Select the line of star symbols and increase the font size to **26** points.
18. Click **Home** > **Text Effects** A and click the effect on the right end of the top row—**Fill – Red, Accent 3, Outline – Text 2**. Center the line horizontally.
19. Check and correct the spelling and grammar in the document, and then save the changes.
20. **With your teacher's permission,** print the document. It should look similar to Figure 26-1 on the next page.
21. Close the document, saving all changes, and exit Word.

Figure 26-1

Project 56—Apply It

Grand Opening Flyer

DIRECTIONS

1. Start Word, if necessary, and open **WProj56** from the data files for this lesson.
2. Save the file as **WProj56_studentfirstname_studentlastname** in the location where your teacher instructs you to store the files for this lesson.
3. Type your full name and today's date in the header.
4. Use the Format Painter to copy the formatting from the first line of five-pointed star symbols to the text *The Grand Opening of its Newest Shop*.
5. Select the next three lines, center them horizontally, and increase the font size to **20** points. Apply the **Gradient Fill – Aqua, Accent 1** text effects to the selection.
6. Click at the beginning of the line *Tasty Treats* and insert the **Wingdings symbol 70**—a hand with a finger pointing to the right.
7. Insert the same symbol at the beginning of the lines *Contests* and *And more...*
8. Use the Format Painter to copy the formatting from the line *Tasty Treats* to the date and the two address lines.
9. On the next blank line, insert 10 five-pointed star symbols (**Wingdings 182**). Center the stars and format them with **Fill – Red, Accent 3, Outline – Text 2** text effects. Increase the font size to 26 points.

10. On the blank line below the address, insert 10 five-pointed star in a black circle symbols (**Wingdings 181✪**). Center the stars and format them with **Fill – Red, Accent 3, Outline – Text 2** text effects. Increase the font size to 26 points. (Alternatively, you can copy the formatting from the symbols inserted in step 9.)
11. Increase the font size in the last paragraph to 20 points and justify the alignment.
12. Insert a trademark symbol (™) after the text *Whole Grains Bread* all three times it displays in the document.
13. Check and correct the spelling and grammar in the document, and then save the changes.
14. **With your teacher's permission,** print the document. It should look similar to Figure 26-2.
15. Close the document, saving all changes, and exit Word.

Figure 26-2

Firstname Lastname
Today's Date

GRAND OPENING

☆☆☆☆☆☆☆☆☆☆

WHOLE GRAINS BREAD™

✪✪✪✪✪✪✪✪✪✪

Announces

The Grand Opening of its Newest Shop

☞Tasty Treats
☞Contests
☞And more...

☆☆☆☆☆☆☆☆☆☆

Thursday, December 12
2020 Main Street
Park City, Utah 84060

✪✪✪✪✪✪✪✪✪✪

Whole Grains Bread™ features freshly baked breads and pastries as well as soups, salads, and sandwiches. Park City is the first Whole Grains Bread™ location in Utah.

Lesson 27

Merging Mailing Labels

WORDS TO KNOW

Address list
A simple data source file which includes the information needed for an address list, such as first name, last name, street, city, state, and so on.

Data source
A file containing the variable data that will be inserted during the merge.

Mail Merge
A process that inserts variable information into a standardized document to produce a personalized or customized document.

Main document
The document containing the standardized text that will be printed on all documents.

Merge block
A set of merge fields stored as one unit. For example, the Address block contains all the name and address information.

Merge field
A placeholder in the main document that marks where an item of variable data such as a first name, a last name, or a ZIP Code will be inserted from the data source document.

Recipient
The entity—a person or organization—who receives a mailing. The recipient's contact information is stored in the data source.

➤ What You Will Learn

Creating Mailing Labels Using the Mail Merge Wizard

Software Skills Use Mail Merge to create mailing labels for a mass mailing. You can select from a long list of standard mailing labels so you can be certain the labels will print correctly.

Application Skills Vocation Opportunities, Inc. needs mailing labels to send out copies of its newsletter. In this lesson, you will use Mail Merge to create labels to send the newsletter to clients and to employers.

What You Can Do

Creating Mailing Labels Using the Mail Merge Wizard

- Word's **Mail Merge** Wizard prompts you through the steps for creating customized mailing labels.

  ✓ *You learn how to use Mail Merge to create form letters, envelopes, e-mail messages, and directories in Word, Chapter 4.*

- There are six steps involved in creating the labels:
  1. Select labels as the **main document**. The label main document is set up using a table, so the Table Tools Ribbon tabs become available.
  2. Select the label type and size so that the label layout onscreen is the same as the actual labels on which you will print.
  3. Select or create the **data source** where the **recipient** addresses are stored. If you have a data source in a compatible file format—such as Excel, Access, or Microsoft Office **Address List**—you may select it as an existing data source. The columns must match the Word merge fields. Alternatively, you can create a new data source by typing the recipient information into columns in the New Address List dialog box. Typing in the New Address List dialog box is similar to typing in a table.
  4. Insert the **merge block** or **merge fields** on the first label. Word automatically inserts the <<Next Record>> field on the other labels, telling Word to duplicate the layout of the first label. Once the first label is complete, you update the remaining labels to match. For labels, it is easiest to use the Address merge block, which includes all fields for a standard mailing address. If you insert individual fields, such as First Name, Last Name, and ZIP Code, you must type the required punctuation, such as the comma between the city and state.
  5. Preview the labels. Onscreen, field names are enclosed in merge field characters (<< >>). The field may be shaded, depending on your system's field code option settings.

     ✓ *Field code option settings are under Show document content on the Advanced tab of the Options dialog box.*
  6. Print the labels. Alternatively, you can save the file to print at a later time.

Try It! Starting the Mail Merge Wizard

1. Start Word and save the default blank document as **WTry27a_studentfirstname_studentlastname** in the location where your teacher instructs you to store the files for this lesson.
2. Click the Mailings tab.
3. In the Start Mail Merge group, click the Start Mail Merge button and click Step by Step Mail Merge Wizard. The Mail Merge task pane displays.
4. In the Mail Merge task pane, click the Labels option button and then click Next: Starting document.
5. Under Change document layout, click Label options.
6. Click the Label vendors drop-down arrow and click Avery US Letter.

   ✓ *Avery is a company that sells mailing labels; you would select the type of label you have on which to print.*
7. In the Product number list, click 5660 Easy Peel Address Labels, and then click OK. Word creates a table that has cells the same size and in the same layout as the labels you selected.

   ✓ *If you cannot see the cells in the document, click the Table Tools Layout tab and, in the Table group, click the View Gridlines button* View Gridlines.
8. Save the changes to **WTry27a_studentfirstname_studentlastname** and leave it open to use in the next Try It.

Label Options dialog box

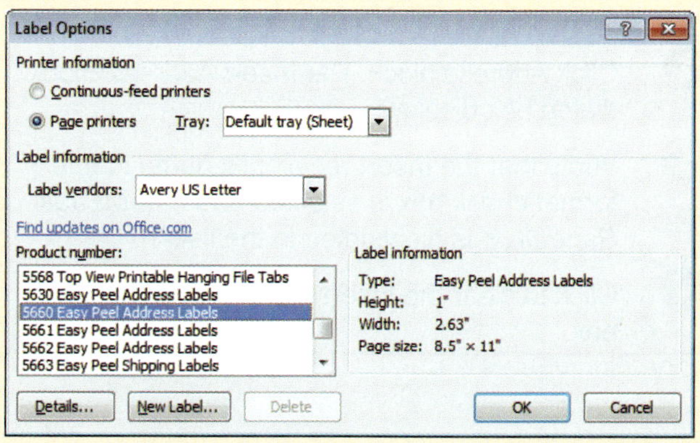

Try It! Creating an Address List and Selecting Recipients

1. In the **WTry27a_studentfirstname_studentlastname** file, in the Mail Merge task pane, click Next: Select recipients.
2. Under Select recipients, click the Type a new list option button, and then click Create. The New Address List dialog box displays.
3. Type **Mr.**, press TAB, type **John**, press TAB, and type **Smith**.
4. Press TAB twice, type **111 Main Street**, and press TAB twice.
5. Type **New York**, press TAB, type **NY**, press TAB, and type **11783**.
6. Click the New Entry button. Word completes the first entry and moves to a new row so you can type the information for another entry.
7. Repeat steps 3 through 6 to enter the following information for two more recipients:
8. Click OK. The Save Address List dialog box displays.
9. Save the address list as **WTry27b_studentfirstname_studentlastname** in the location where your teacher instructs you to store the files for this lesson. It is saved in Microsoft Office Address List format, which is compatible with Microsoft Access. The Mail Merge Recipients dialog box displays, with all entries selected.

   ✓ *Once you create and save an address list data source file, you can use it again for other merges.*
10. Click OK. Word positions the insertion point in the first cell of the label document, and inserts the <<Next Record>> field in the other cells.
11. Save the changes to **WTry27a_studentfirstname_studentlastname** and leave it open to use in the next Try It.

Title	First Name	Last Name	Address Line 1	Address Line 2	City	State	ZIP Code
Ms.	**Kendra**	**Johnson**	**902 Chestnut Street**	**Apt. 5**	**Newtown**	**CT**	**02211**
Mr.	**Oliver**	**White**	**61 Frederick Street**		**Omaha**	**NE**	**68101**

Try It! Arranging the Labels

1. In the **WTry27a_studentfirstname_studentlastname** file, in the Mail Merge task pane, click Next: Arrange your labels.
2. Click Address block. The Insert Address Block dialog box displays.
3. Verify that the Insert recipient's name in this format check box is selected and that *Mr. Joshua Randall Jr.* is highlighted in the list.
4. Click to clear the Insert company name check box.
5. Verify that the Insert postal address check box is selected and that the Only include the country/region if different than option button is selected.
6. Verify that the Format address according to the destination country/region check box is selected.
7. Click OK. Word inserts the <<AddressBlock>> merge block in the first cell.

(continued)

Try It! Arranging the Labels *(continued)*

8. In the Mail Merge task pane, click Update all labels to copy the layout from the first cell to the remaining cells.

9. Save the changes to **WTry27a_studentfirstname_studentlastname** and leave it open to use in the next Try It.

Insert Address Block dialog box

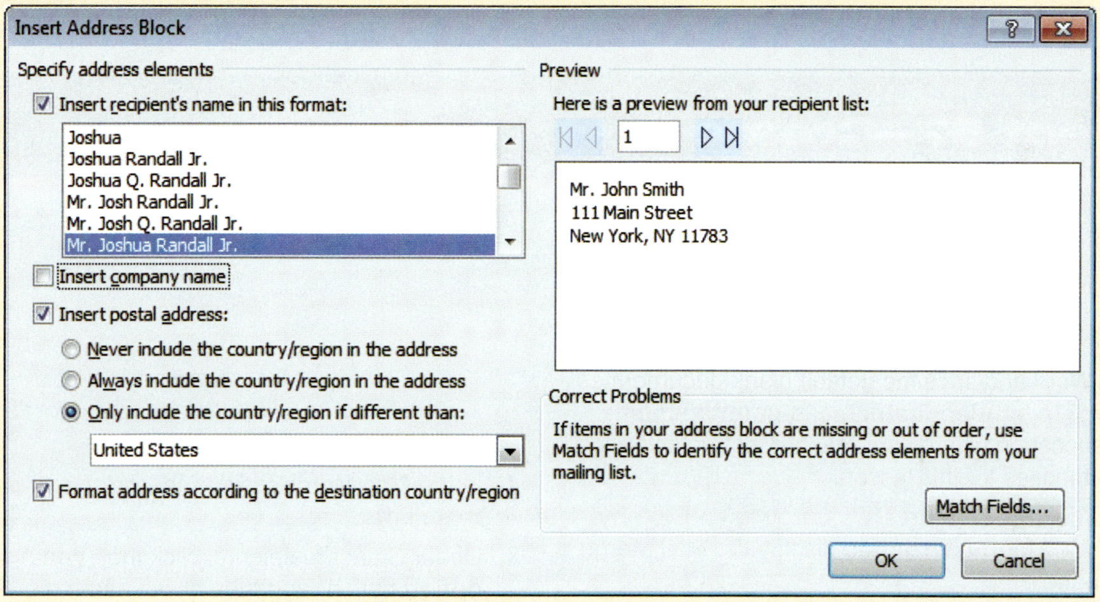

Try It! Previewing the Labels

1. In the **WTry27a_studentfirstname_studentlastname** file, in the Mail Merge task pane, click Next: Preview your labels.

2. Word displays the label document with the actual addresses in place of the merge block fields. Note that the text in the label with four lines does not fit within the cell.

3. In the Mail Merge task pane, click Previous: Arrange your labels.

4. Select the first cell, click the Page Layout tab, and use the Spacing Before increment arrows to set the spacing to 0.

5. In the Mail Merge task pane, click Update all labels.

6. In the Mail Merge task pane, click Next: Preview your labels.

7. Save the changes to **WTry27a_studentfirstname_studentlastname** and leave it open to use in the next Try It.

Try It! **Printing the Labels**

1. In the **WTry27a_studentfirstname_studentlastname** file, in the Mail Merge task pane, click Next: Complete the merge.
2. **With your teacher's permission,** click Print. The Merge to Printer dialog box displays.
3. Click OK to print the labels.

   ✓ *You can print the labels on plain paper.*
4. Save the changes to **WTry27a_studentfirstname_studentlastname**, close it, and exit Word.

Project 57—Create It

Client Mailing Labels

DIRECTIONS

1. Start Word and save the default blank document as **WProj57a_studentfirstname_studentlastname** in the location where your teacher instructs you to store the files for this lesson.
2. Click **Mailings** > **Start Mail Merge** > **Step by Step Mail Merge Wizard** to display the Mail Merge task pane.
3. In the Mail Merge task pane, click the **Labels** option button and then click **Next: Starting document**.
4. Under Change document layout, click **Label options** to open the Label Options dialog box.
5. Click the **Label vendors** drop-down arrow and click **Avery US Letter**.
6. In the Product number list, click **8563 Shipping Labels**. Click OK.

   ✓ *If you cannot see the cells in the document, click the Table Tools Layout tab and, in the Table group, click the View Gridlines button* View Gridlines.
7. In the Mail Merge task pane, click **Next: Select recipients**.
8. Under Select recipients, click the **Type a new list option** button, and then click **Create**.
9. In the New Address List dialog box, type **Ms.**, press TAB, type **Elizabeth**, press TAB, and type **Brown**. Press TAB twice, type **64A State Road**, and press TAB twice. Type **Tampa**, press TAB, type **FL**, press TAB, and type **33601**.
10. Click the **New Entry** button.
11. Enter the following information at the bottom of the page for four more recipients:

Title	First Name	Last Name	Address Line 1	Address Line 2	City	State	ZIP Code
Ms.	**Maria**	**Valero**	**8990 Ocean Way**	**Apt. 2B**	**Tampa**	**FL**	**33601**
Mr.	**Seth**	**McGraw**	**433 Manatee Avenue**		**Citrus Park**	**FL**	**33624**
Mr.	**John**	**Arbedian**	**1123 East Sunset Highway**		**Tampa**	**FL**	**33601**
Mr.	**Patrick**	**Costello**	**9 Plantation Boulevard**		**Tampa**	**FL**	**33601**

12. Click **OK**. The Save Address List dialog box displays.
13. Save the address list as **WProj57b_studentfirstname_studentlastname** in the location where your teacher instructs you to store the files for this lesson.
14. Click **OK**. Word positions the insertion point in the first cell of the label document, and inserts the <<Next Record>> field in the other cells.
15. In the Mail Merge task pane, click **Next: Arrange your labels**.
16. Click **Address Block**. The Insert Address Block dialog box displays. Verify that the Insert recipient's name in this format check box is selected and that *Mr. Joshua Randall Jr.* is highlighted in the list.
17. Click to clear the **Insert company name** check box.
18. Verify that the **Insert postal address** check box is selected, that the **Only include the country/region if different than** option button is selected, and that the **Format address according to the destination country/region** check box is selected.
19. Click **OK**. Word inserts the <<AddressBlock>> merge block in the first cell.
20. In the Mail Merge task pane, click **Update all labels** to copy the layout from the first cell to the remaining cells.
21. In the Mail Merge task pane, click **Next: Preview your labels**.
22. In the Mail Merge task pane, click **Next: Complete the merge**.
23. **With your teacher's permission,** click the **Print** button. The Merge to Printer dialog box displays.
24. Click **OK** to print the labels. The page should look similar to Figure 27-1.

    ✓ *You can print the labels on plain paper.*
25. Close the document, saving all changes, and exit Word.

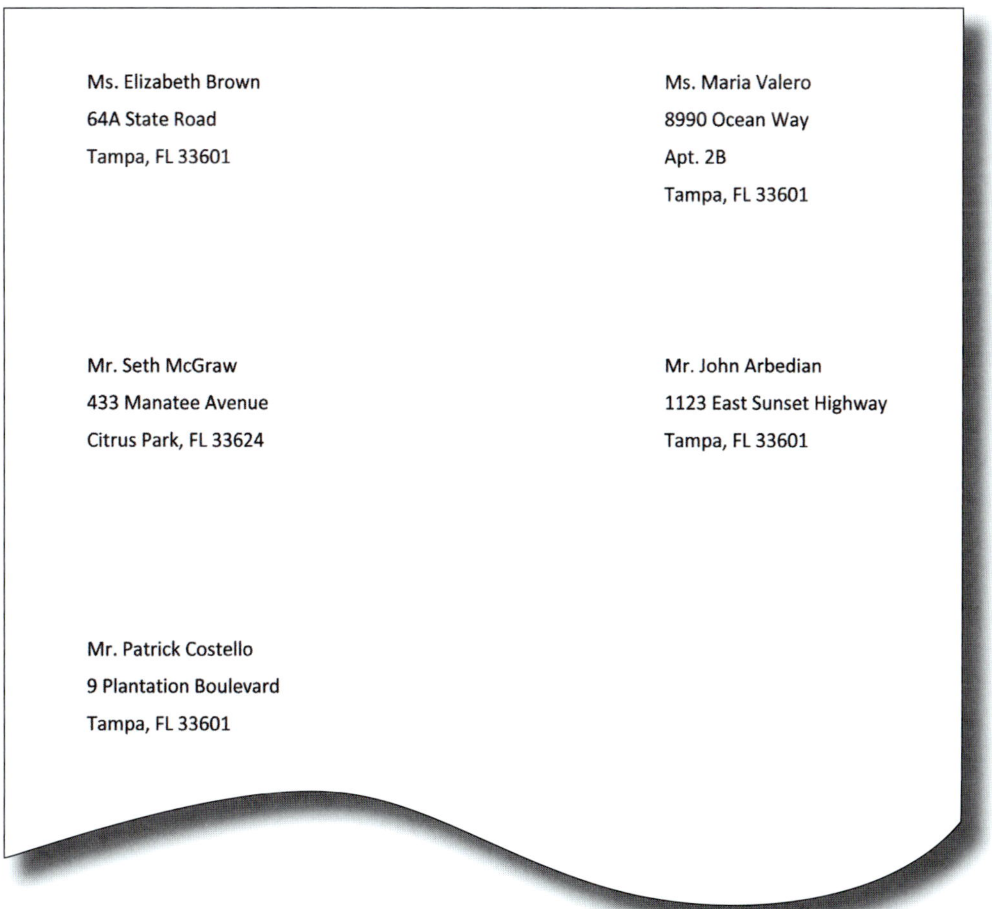

Ms. Elizabeth Brown
64A State Road
Tampa, FL 33601

Ms. Maria Valero
8990 Ocean Way
Apt. 2B
Tampa, FL 33601

Mr. Seth McGraw
433 Manatee Avenue
Citrus Park, FL 33624

Mr. John Arbedian
1123 East Sunset Highway
Tampa, FL 33601

Mr. Patrick Costello
9 Plantation Boulevard
Tampa, FL 33601

Figure 27-1

Project 58—Apply It

Employer Mailing Labels

DIRECTIONS

1. Start Word and save the default blank document as **WProj58a_studentfirstname_studentlastname** in the location where your teacher instructs you to store the files for this lesson.
2. Start the Mail Merge Wizard.
3. Select to create a **Labels** main document using **Avery US Letter 5263 Shipping Labels**.
4. Select to use an existing list. Click the **Browse** button and navigate to the location where the data files for this lesson are stored. Select **WProj58b** and click **Open**. Click **OK** to use all of the recipients in the Mail Merge Recipients dialog box.
5. Insert an Address Block on the first label, including the company name.
6. Update the labels.
7. Preview the labels.
8. Complete the merge.
9. **With your teacher's permission,** print the labels.

   ✓ *You can print the labels on plain paper.*
10. Close the document, saving all changes, and exit Word.

Chapter Assessment and Application

Project 59—Make It Your Own

Technology Trends Newsletter

Trends in technology impact the way we work. For example, thanks to collaborative technologies such as cloud computing and videoconferencing, teams can work together even when they are located hundreds of miles apart. They also impact career opportunities by making some old careers obsolete and making new careers possible. For example, the Internet allows retailers to market world-wide, but robots have replaced many manufacturing jobs.

In this project, work with a team to create a multipage newsletter about emerging trends in computer technology and how they affect employment opportunities. To complete the project, use the skills you have learned in this chapter, set goals, prioritize tasks, and develop a realistic schedule that you will be able to achieve.

DIRECTIONS

1. As a team, work together to plan the project. Develop a schedule, allocate assignments, and set goals. Assign each team member the responsibility of writing at least one article for the newsletter.
2. Use the Internet, magazines, and books to research current trends in technology to gather the information you will need to write your articles. Be sure to use reliable sources. Take notes and record source information so you can enter citations as necessary.
3. Work cooperatively to develop and edit the articles. Meet as a team to read and discuss each other's work, offering and accepting constructive criticism.
4. When the articles are complete, start Word and create a new document.
5. Save the document as **WProj59_studentfirstname_studentlastname** in the location where your teacher instructs you to store the files for this chapter.

   ✓ *Pick one member of the team and use that student's name in the document file name.*
6. Select a theme and style set for the document. Set the margins and page orientation, and insert page numbers.
7. Type in the article text, or copy and paste the text from each team member's original document.
8. Design the newsletter using section breaks and newsletter-style columns. For example, you probably want the newsletter title in one column, but the articles in two or three columns.
9. Adjust spacing and select options to control pagination and make the text easier to read.
10. Enhance the document using drop caps, borders, and shading. Insert symbols as accents or illustrations.
11. At the end of the document insert a page break and create a Works Cited page to accompany the newsletter.
12. Enter document properties to help identify the document. Put the names of all team members in the footer.
13. Check the spelling and grammar in the document and correct errors as necessary.
14. Ask a classmate who is not part of your team to review the newsletter and make suggestions for how you might improve it. Incorporate your classmate's suggestions into the document.
15. **With your teacher's permission,** print the newsletter and share it with your class.
16. Close the document, saving all changes, and exit Word.

Project 60—Master It

Job Search Strategies Report

Vocation Opportunities, Inc. wants to create a report of no more than 350 words about strategies for getting a job search started. In this project, you will create the one-page report. You will include endnotes and enhance the document with borders, shading, and drop caps. When the document is complete, you will create labels using an existing address list so you can mail the report to clients.

DIRECTIONS

Create a One-Page Report

1. Start Word and open **WProj60a** from the data files for this chapter.
2. Save the file as **WProj60a_studentfirstname_studentlastname** in the location where your teacher instructs you to store the files for this chapter.
3. Type your full name and today's date in the header, flush right.
4. Apply the **Perspective** style set and the **Horizon** theme.
5. Apply the **Title** style to the first line of text. Center it, and change the paragraph spacing to **30** points before and after.
6. Format the first paragraph in 12 pt. Times New Roman, justified. Set the line spacing to double. Apply a first line indent of **0.5"** and set paragraph spacing before and after to **0**.
7. Copy the formatting from the first paragraph to the rest of the paragraphs in the document.
8. Insert an endnote after the first sentence as follows: **Bill Vick, How Long Will it Take Me to Find a Job?, <http://employmentdigest.net/2009/08/how-long-will-it-take-me-to-find-a-job/> (August 2009).**
9. Insert an endnote after the second paragraph as follows: **Why Learn About Me?, <http://www.careeronestop.org/ExploreCareers/Self-Assessments/WhylearnAboutMe.aspx> (2010).**
10. Insert an endnote after the comma in the last sentence of the third paragraph as follows: **Bureau of Labor Statistics, Job Search Methods, <http://www.bls.gov/oco/oco20042.thm> (December 2009).**
11. Insert page numbers in the center of the footer.
12. Change the page margins to **Moderate**.
13. Apply an In margin drop cap to the first paragraph, customized to drop two lines.
14. Apply a solid line, 2¼ pt. border to the top and bottom of the report title. Apply a Teal, Accent 5, Lighter 60% shading to the title as well.
15. Enter the following document properties:
    - Title: **Getting a Job Search Started**
    - Subject: **Job search strategies**
    - Keywords: **job search, careers, tips, strategies, networking, online resources**
    - Category: **job search**
    - Status: **mailed**
16. Check the page count to see if it is under 350 words.
17. Check the spelling and grammar in the document and correct errors as necessary.
18. **With your teacher's permission,** print the document. It should look similar to Illustration A shown on the next page.
19. Close the document, saving all changes. Leave Word open to use in the next part of this project.

Illustration A

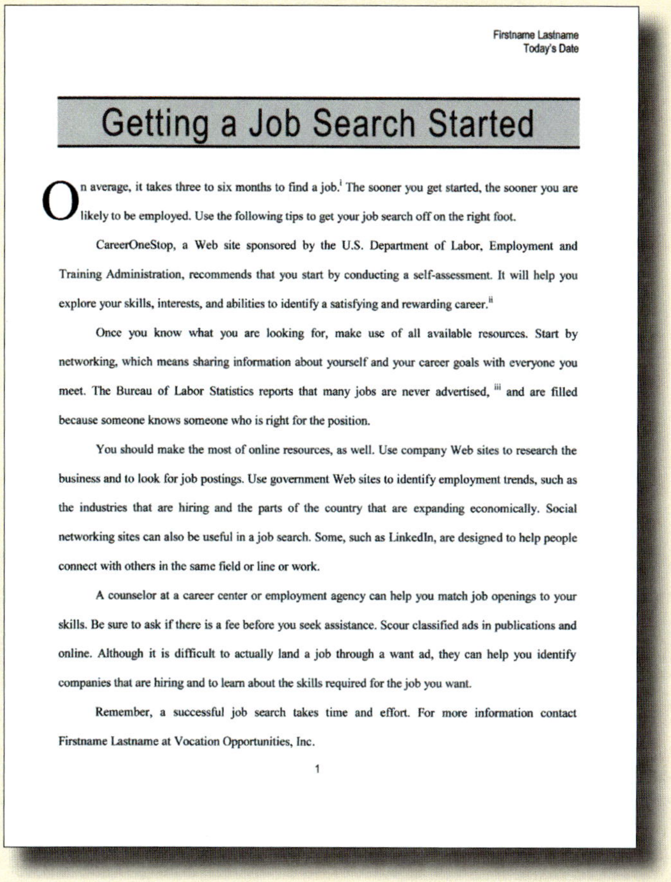

Firstname Lastname
Today's Date

Getting a Job Search Started

On average, it takes three to six months to find a job.[i] The sooner you get started, the sooner you are likely to be employed. Use the following tips to get your job search off on the right foot.

CareerOneStop, a Web site sponsored by the U.S. Department of Labor, Employment and Training Administration, recommends that you start by conducting a self-assessment. It will help you explore your skills, interests, and abilities to identify a satisfying and rewarding career.[ii]

Once you know what you are looking for, make use of all available resources. Start by networking, which means sharing information about yourself and your career goals with everyone you meet. The Bureau of Labor Statistics reports that many jobs are never advertised, [iii] and are filled because someone knows someone who is right for the position.

You should make the most of online resources, as well. Use company Web sites to research the business and to look for job postings. Use government Web sites to identify employment trends, such as the industries that are hiring and the parts of the country that are expanding economically. Social networking sites can also be useful in a job search. Some, such as LinkedIn, are designed to help people connect with others in the same field or line or work.

A counselor at a career center or employment agency can help you match job openings to your skills. Be sure to ask if there is a fee before you seek assistance. Scour classified ads in publications and online. Although it is difficult to actually land a job through a want ad, they can help you identify companies that are hiring and to learn about the skills required for the job you want.

Remember, a successful job search takes time and effort. For more information contact Firstname Lastname at Vocation Opportunities, Inc.

1

Firstname Lastname
Today's Date

[i] Bill Vick, *How Long Will it Take Me to Find a Job?*, <http://employmentdigest.net/2009/08/how-long-will-it-take-me-to-find-a-job/> (August 2009).
[ii] *Why Learn About Me?*, <http://www.careeronestop.org/ExploreCareers/Self-Assessments/WhyLearnAboutMe.aspx> (2010).
[iii] Bureau of Labor Statistics, *Job Search Methods*, <http://www.bls.gov/oco/oco20042.htm> (December 2009).

2

Create Mailing Labels

1. In Word, create a new, blank document and save it as **WProj60b_studentfirstname_studentlastname** in the location where your teacher instructs you to store the files for this lesson.
2. Use the Mail Merge Wizard to create mailing labels to print on Microsoft 30 Per Page Address Labels that are 1" high and 2.63" wide.
3. Use all the names in the **WProj60c** data file as the data source.
4. Adjust formatting as necessary so the addresses fit on the labels
5. **With your teacher's permission**, print the labels.

   ✓ *You can print the labels on plain paper.*

6. Close the document, saving all changes, and exit Word.

Chapter 1

Getting Started with Microsoft Excel 2010

Lesson 1
Touring Excel
Projects 1-2

- Starting Excel
- Naming and Saving a Workbook
- Exploring the Excel Window
- Exploring the Excel Interface
- Navigating the Worksheet
- Changing Between Worksheets
- Changing Worksheet Views
- Exiting Excel

Lesson 2
Worksheet and Workbook Basics
Projects 3-4

- Creating a New (Blank) Workbook
- Entering Text and Labels
- Editing Text
- Using Undo and Redo
- Clearing Cell Contents
- Inserting a Built-In Header or Footer
- Previewing and Printing a Worksheet
- Closing a Workbook

Lesson 3
Adding Worksheet Contents
Projects 5-6

- Opening an Existing Workbook and Saving it with a New Name
- Entering and Editing Numeric Labels and Values
- Using AutoComplete
- Using Pick From List
- Using AutoCorrect
- Checking the Spelling in a Worksheet

Lesson 4
Worksheet Formatting
Projects 7-8

- Choosing a Theme
- Applying Cell Styles
- Applying Font Formats
- Merging and Centering Across Cells
- Applying Number Formats

Lesson 5
More on Cell Entries and Formatting
Projects 9-10

- Entering Dates
- Filling a Series
- Aligning Data in a Cell
- Wrapping Text in Cells
- Changing Column Width and Row Height
- Using Keyboard Shortcuts

Lesson 6
Working with Ranges
Projects 11-12

- Selecting Ranges
- Entering Data by Range
- Making a Range Entry Using a Collapse Button

Lesson 7
Creating Formulas
Projects 13-14

- Entering a Formula
- Using Arithmetic Operators
- Editing a Formula
- Copying a Formula Using the Fill Handle
- Using the SUM Function

Lesson 8
Copying and Pasting
Projects 15-16

- Copying and Pasting Data
- Copying Formats
- Copying Formulas Containing a Relative Reference
- Copying Formulas Containing an Absolute Reference

Lesson 9
Techniques for Moving Data
Projects 17-18

- Inserting and Deleting Columns and Rows
- Cutting and Pasting Data
- Using Drag-and-Drop Editing

Lesson 10
Chart, Sheet, Display, and Print Operations
Projects 19-20

- Creating a Column Chart
- Deleting Unused Sheets in a Workbook
- Displaying, Printing, and Hiding Formulas
- Previewing and Printing a Worksheet

End of Chapter Assessments
Projects 21-22

Lesson 1

Touring Excel

➤ What You Will Learn

- Starting Excel
- Naming and Saving a Workbook
- Exploring the Excel Window
- Exploring the Excel Interface
- Navigating the Worksheet
- Changing Between Worksheets
- Changing Worksheet Views
- Exiting Excel

Software Skills When you want to analyze business, personal, or financial data and create reports in a table format consisting of rows and columns, use the Microsoft Excel 2010 spreadsheet application in the Microsoft Office 2010 suite.

Application Skills You've recently been hired as a marketing specialist for Bike Tours and Adventures, and you've enrolled yourself in a class to learn to use Excel. In this exercise, you will start Excel, familiarize yourself with the Excel window, change your view of the worksheet, and practice moving around the worksheet using the mouse and the keyboard.

WORDS TO KNOW

Active cell
The active cell contains the cell pointer. There is a dark outline around the active cell.

Cell
A cell is the intersection of a column and a row on a worksheet. You enter data into cells to create a worksheet.

Cell address or cell reference
The location of a cell in a worksheet as identified by its column letter and row number. Also known as the cell's address.

Formula bar
As you enter data in a cell, it simultaneously appears in the formula bar, which is located above the worksheet.

Scroll
A way to view locations on the worksheet without changing the active cell.

Sheet tabs
Tabs that appear at the bottom of the workbook window, which display the name of each worksheet.

Tab scrolling buttons
Buttons that appear just to the left of the sheet tabs, which allow you to scroll hidden tabs into view.

WORDS TO KNOW

Workbook
An Excel file with one or more worksheets.

Worksheet
The work area for entering and calculating data made up of columns and rows separated by gridlines (light gray lines). Also called a spreadsheet.

What You Can Do

Starting Excel

- Start Excel using the Windows Start menu.
- When Excel starts, it displays an empty **workbook** with three **worksheets.**
- A worksheet contains rows and columns that intersect to form **cells.**
- Gridlines mark the boundaries of each cell.

Try It! Starting Excel

1. Click the Start button.

   ✔ *If your keyboard has a Windows key (a key with the Windows logo on it), you can press that key at any time to display the Start menu.*
2. Click All Programs.
3. Scroll down, if needed, and click Microsoft Office.
4. Click Microsoft Excel 2010.
5. Explore the features of the Excel program window.
6. Leave the file open to use in the next Try It.

The Excel window

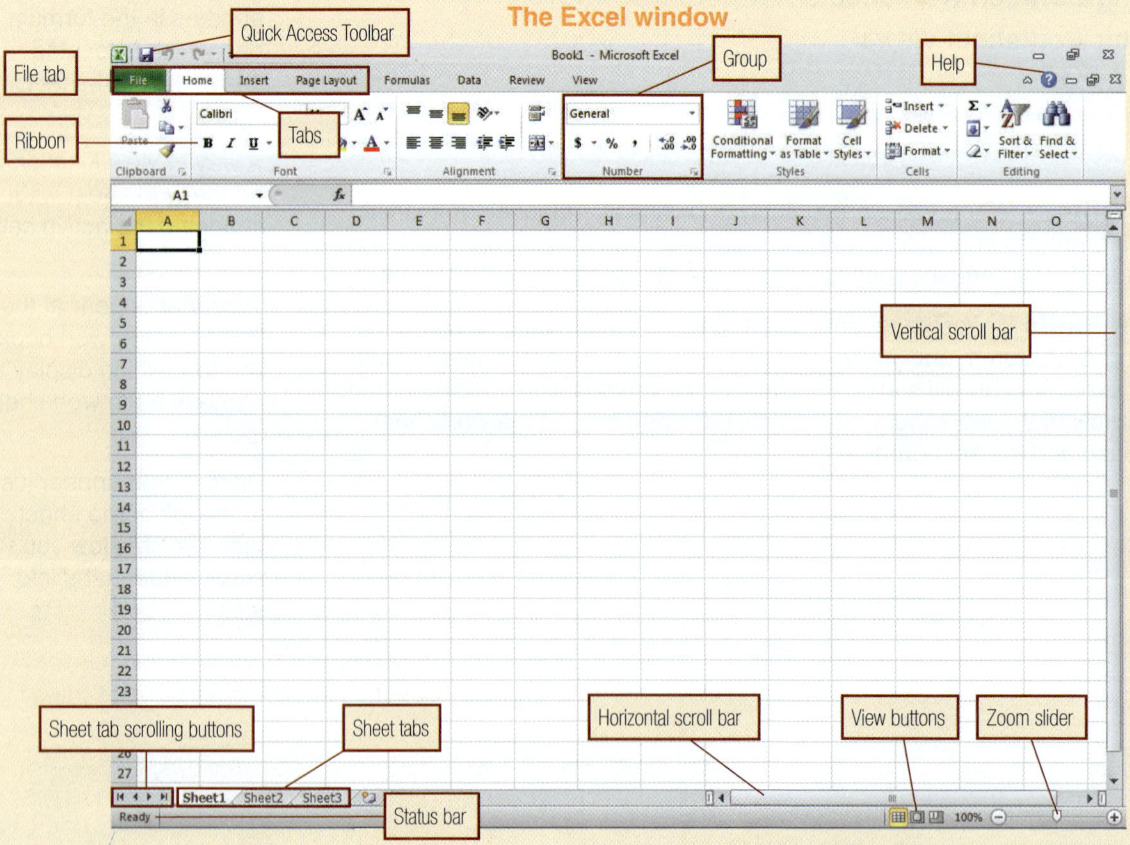

Naming and Saving a Workbook

- After entering data in a workbook, you must save it, or that data will be lost when you exit Excel.
- A workbook may be saved on a hard disk or a removable disk for future use. A saved workbook is referred to as a file.
- You must provide a name for the file when you save it. File names should be descriptive, with a limit of 255 characters for the name, disk drive, and path.
- A file name may contain letters, numbers, and spaces, but not \ / : * ? " < > or | .
- Excel automatically adds a period and a file type extension (usually .xlsx) to the end of a file name when you save it.
- Workbooks are saved in the Documents library in Windows 7 by default, although you may select another location if you like. You can also create new folders in which to store your workbooks.
- The default Excel file format is .xlsx, which is XML based. This new file format allows your workbooks to integrate more easily with outside data sources and results in smaller workbook file sizes than in earlier versions of Excel.

  ✔ *You can install updates to older versions of Excel so they can read the new .xlsx format.*

- Data can also be saved in other formats, such as HTML, Excel Binary (a new file format for very large workbooks), or older versions of Excel (.xls).

  ✔ *You might want to save data in a different format in order to share that data with someone who uses a different version of Excel, or a Web browser to view your data.*

- Once you've saved a workbook, you need only click the Save button as you work to resave any changes made since the last save action. You will not need to reenter the file name.

Try It! Naming and Saving a Workbook

1. Click the File tab.
2. Click Save.

   OR

   Click the Save button on the Quick Access Toolbar.
3. Click in the File name text box, and type **ETry01_studentfirstname_studentlastname**.

   ✓ *Replace the text studentfirstname with your own first name, and studentlastname with your own last name. For example, if your name is Mary Jones, type* **ETry01_Mary_Jones**.
4. Use the Navigation pane to navigate to the location where your teacher instructs you to store the files for this lesson.

   ✓ *Use the drop-down lists at the top of the Save As dialog box or the locations in the Navigation pane at the left to select the folder to save to. Clicking the triangle beside any disk or folder in the Navigation pane displays or hides that location's contents. If saving to a USB drive, make sure it is inserted. Scroll down the Navigation pane at left, and click the USB drive under Computer. Refer to Lesson 1 of the Basics section of this book for more information on navigating.*
5. Click the Save button.
6. Leave the file open to use in the next Try It.

Exploring the Excel Window

- In the worksheet, a black border appears around the **active cell.**
- You can change the active cell using the mouse or the keyboard.
- Data is entered into the active cell.
- The Name box, located on the left side of the **formula bar,** displays the **cell reference** or **cell address** of the active cell (its column letter and row number). For example, A1 is the cell in the first row of the first column. B5 is the address for the cell in the fifth row of the second column.
- To help you identify the cell reference for the active cell, Excel surrounds the cell with a dark border and highlights its column letter (at the top of the worksheet) and row number (to the left of the worksheet). The column letters and row numbers are also known as the column and row headings.
- You can use the arrow keys ↑ ↓ ← → (alone or in combination with other keys), special key combinations, the mouse, or Go To F5 to select a cell on the current worksheet.

Try It! Exploring the Excel Window

1. In the ETry01_studentfirstname_studentlastname file, press [Tab] twice.
2. Press [↓] four times.
3. Click in the Name box, type b3, and press [ENTER].
4. Press [↓].
5. Click cell F13.
6. Press [F5], type z155 in the Reference text box of the Go To dialog box, and click OK.

✓ *You also can open the Go To dialog box by clicking the Find & Select button in the Editing group on the Home tab of the Ribbon, and then clicking Go To. You will learn about the Ribbon next.*

7. Press [CTRL] + [HOME].
8. Save the ETry01_studentfirstname_studentlastname file, and leave it open to use in the next Try It.

Key worksheet features

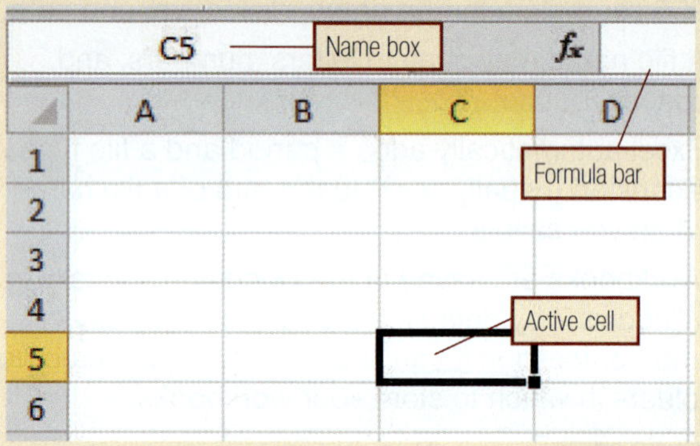

Exploring the Excel Interface

- In the Microsoft Office Basics section, you learned that you can access common program commands such as Save and Undo through the buttons on the Quick Access Toolbar.
- Through the File tab, you can access commands for managing files such as New, Open, Save, and Print. Clicking the File tab displays Backstage view.
- The Ribbon, located at the top of the Excel window, offers buttons for the most common Excel commands.
- The Ribbon offers several tabs, and on each tab, related command buttons are arranged in groups. Click a tab to display its contents, and then click a button to choose a command or display further choices.
- Some tabs, called contextual tabs, appear only when you've selected an item to which the tab's commands apply.
- To access Help, click the Help button.

Try It! Exploring the Excel Interface

1. In the ETry01_studentfirstname_studentlastname file, click the File tab.
2. In the list at the left of Backstage view, click Print.
3. Click the Home tab.
4. Click the Formulas tab.
5. On the Formulas tab, in the Function Library group, click the Date & Time button.
6. Press [ESC].
7. Click the Home tab.
8. Save the ETry01_studentfirstname_studentlastname file, and leave it open to use in the next Try It.

Navigating the Worksheet

- There are 16,384 columns and 1,048,576 rows available in a worksheet, but you don't need to fill the entire worksheet in order to use it—just type data in the cells you need.
- Since the workbook window displays only a part of a worksheet, you scroll through the worksheet to view another location.
- With the mouse, you can scroll using the horizontal or vertical scroll bars.

✔ *Using the mouse to scroll does not change the active cell.*

- With the keyboard, you can scroll by pressing specific keys or key combinations.

✔ *Scrolling with the keyboard does change the active cell.*

- You can move to a specific cell that's not on screen using Go To or the Name box, as you've just learned.

✔ *You can also use the Name box to go directly to a named cell or range. This is discussed in Lesson 13.*

Try It! Navigating the Worksheet

1. In the **ETry01_studentfirstname_studentlastname** file, click the down scroll arrow on the vertical scroll bar to scroll one row down.
2. Click the right scroll arrow on the horizontal scroll bar to scroll one column right.
3. Move the mouse pointer over the vertical scroll bar, and roll the mouse wheel down. (Do not press the wheel, just lightly roll it with your fingertip.) Repeat until row 52 comes into view.
4. Move the mouse pointer from the vertical scroll bar to the center of the worksheet. Press and hold the mouse wheel down while dragging right to pan to the right until column Z comes into view.
5. Click above the scroll box on the vertical scroll bar once or twice to redisplay row 1.
6. Drag the scroll box on the horizontal scroll bar all the way to the left to redisplay column A.
7. Save the **ETry01_studentfirstname_studentlastname** file, and leave it open to use in the next Try It.

Changing Between Worksheets

- By default, each workbook has three worksheets. You can add or delete worksheets as needed, as explained in Lessons 10 and 19.
- You can enter related data on different worksheets within the same workbook.

✔ *For example, you can enter January, February, and March sales data on different worksheets within the same workbook.*

- You can change between worksheets using the **sheet tabs** located at the bottom of the Excel window.
- If a particular worksheet tab is not visible, use the **tab scrolling buttons** to display it. The middle two buttons display the previous and next sheet tabs, and the left and right buttons display the first and last sheet tabs.

Try It! Changing Between Worksheets

1. In the **ETry01_studentfirstname_studentlastname** file, click the Sheet2 tab.
2. Click the Sheet3 tab.
3. Click the Sheet1 tab.
4. Save the **ETry01_studentfirstname_studentlastname** file, and leave it open to use in the next Try It.

Changing Worksheet Views

- To view or hide the formula bar, ruler, column and row headings, or gridlines, select or deselect them by checking or clearing the applicable check box in the Show group on the View tab.

  ✔ *Hiding screen elements shows more rows onscreen.*

- To hide and redisplay the Ribbon, double-click the active tab.
- Normal view is the default working view.
- Page Layout view is used to view data as it will look when printed, and make adjustments.
- Page Break Preview is used before printing, to adjust where pages break.
- Full Screen view hides the title bar and Ribbon. Press Esc to leave this view.

  ✔ *You'll learn more about Page Layout view and Page Break Preview in later lessons.*

- You can use the view buttons on the Status bar to change to the most common views.
- You also can use the buttons in the Workbook Views group on the View tab to change views.
- Use Zoom to magnify cells in a worksheet by any amount.
- Change the zoom using the Zoom slider on the status bar.
- You can also change the zoom using the mouse, or the buttons in the Zoom group on the View tab.

Try It! Changing Worksheet Views

1. In the **ETry01_studentfirstname_studentlastname** file, click the View tab on the Ribbon.
2. In the Show group, click one of the following:
   - Ruler
   - Gridlines
   - Formula Bar
   - Headings
3. Click the item you clicked in step 2 again to redisplay it.
4. Double-click the View tab.
5. Double-click the View tab again to redisplay the Ribbon.
6. Click the Page Layout button in either the Workbook Views group or near the zoom slider to change to Page Layout view.
7. On the View tab, in the Workbook Views group, click the Full Screen button.
8. Press ESC to return to Page Layout view.
9. In the Zoom group, click the Zoom button. The Zoom dialog box offers the following magnifications:
   - 200%
   - 100%
   - 75%
   - 50%
   - 25%
   - Fit Selection
   - Custom
10. Click 50%, and then click OK.
11. On the status bar, click Zoom In once.
12. On the status bar, use the Zoom slider to change the view to more than 100%.
13. On the View tab, in the Zoom group, click the 100% button.
14. In the Workbook Views group, click the Normal button.
15. Save the **ETry01_studentfirstname_studentlastname** file, and leave it open to use in the next Try It.

Key worksheet features

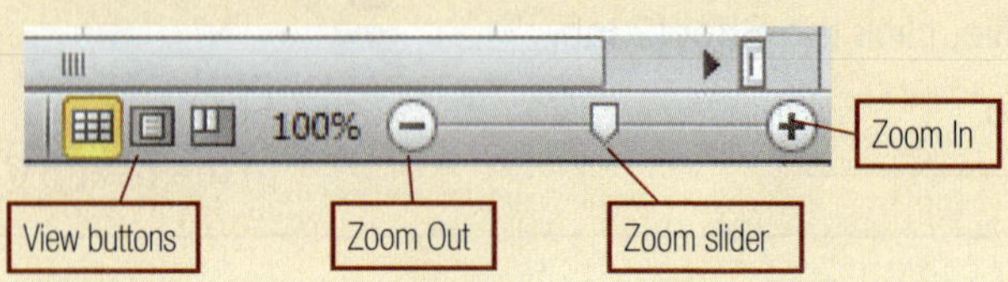

Exiting Excel

- When your worksheet is complete and you want to close the Excel application, use the Exit command after clicking on the File tab.
- Excel prompts you to save any unsaved changes when you exit.

Try It! Exiting Excel

1. In the **ETry01_studentfirstname_studentlastname** file, click the File tab on the Ribbon.
2. Click Exit.
3. Click the Save button to save your changes to the file.
4. Close the file, and exit Excel.

Project 1—Create It

Navigate

DIRECTIONS

1. Click **Start** > **All Programs** > **Microsoft Office** > **Microsoft Excel 2010**.
2. Press → four times to select cell E1.
3. Press ↓ four times to select cell E5.
4. Click cell **H9** to make it the active cell, and then view its cell address in the Name box.
5. Press F5 to open the Go To dialog box.
6. In the Reference text box, type **T98**.
7. Click **OK**. The active cell changes to T98.
8. Click in the Name box to change the active cell to the following, pressing ENTER after typing each new cell address:
   a. **B1492** (row 1492, column B)
   b. **XFD1048576** (bottom right of worksheet)
9. Press CTRL + HOME to move to cell A1.
10. Click the **Sheet2** tab.
11. Click cell **D4**.
12. Point to the horizontal scroll bar and click the right scroll arrow. The worksheet moves right by one column but the active cell does not change.
13. Point to the horizontal scroll bar and click to the left of the scroll box. The worksheet moves back left but the active cell does not change.
14. Point to the horizontal scroll bar, and then drag the scroll box all the way to the right. The view of the worksheet has changed again but the active cell does not change.
15. Click the down scroll arrow on the vertical scroll bar three times. The worksheet moves down three rows but the active cell does not change.
16. Click the **Sheet1** tab. The active cell for Sheet1 remains the same (A1). It did not change even as you changed the active cell on Sheet2.
17. On the **View** tab, in the Show group, deselect the **Formula Bar** check box to hide the formula bar.
18. Change to the **Page Layout** view by clicking its button on the status bar. Notice that the rulers have appeared just above the column headings and to the left of the row numbers.
19. On the **View** tab, in the Workbook Views group, click the **Full Screen** button to change to Full Screen view. The rulers are still there because you changed to Full Screen view from Page Layout view where they are normally shown. Other screen elements are removed, however.
20. Return to Page Layout view by pressing ESC.
21. On the **View** tab, change to Normal view by clicking the **Normal** button.
22. In the Show group, select the **Formula Bar** check box to redisplay the formula bar.
23. In the Zoom group, click the **Zoom** button to display the Zoom dialog box.

24. Click in the Custom box, type **150**, and then click **OK**. The Zoom changes to 150%, so cells appear much larger.
25. Click the **Zoom Out** button on the Status bar twice. The Zoom changes to 130%.
26. Drag the **Zoom slider** to the left until the zoom is set to **90%**. The current zoom percentage shows on the Zoom button as you drag. You may have trouble setting the zoom to an exact percentage using the slider. If so, drag the slider to roughly 90%, then click the Zoom Out or Zoom In button as needed to jump to exactly 90%.
27. Click the **File** tab and then click **Exit** to exit Excel. If asked to save the workbook, click **Don't Save**.

Project 2—Apply It

Tour Data

DIRECTIONS

1. Start Excel, if necessary, and open **EProj02** from the data files for this lesson.
2. Save the file as **EProj02_studentfirstname_studentlastname** in the location where your teacher instructs you to store the files for this lesson.

   ✔ *Replace the text studentfirstname with your own first name, and studentlastname with your own last name.*
3. Click cell **B1**, type your name, and press ENTER.
4. Increase the zoom to **150%**. Your document should appear as shown in Figure 1-1.
5. Hide and redisplay these screen elements:
   - **a.** Ribbon.
   - **b.** Formula bar.
   - **c.** Gridlines.
6. Change to **Page Layout** view, and then back to **Normal** view.
7. Go to **Sheet3**, change its zoom to **150%**, and press CTRL + END.
8. Select cell **B26**, and copy the cell's contents.
9. Return to **Sheet1**, and paste the cell's contents to cell **F5**.
10. Go to **Sheet2**, select cell **B11**, and copy the cell's contents.
11. Return to **Sheet1** and paste the cell's contents to cell **G8**.
12. **With your teacher's permission**, print Sheet1.
13. Close the workbook, saving all changes, and exit Excel.

Figure 1-1

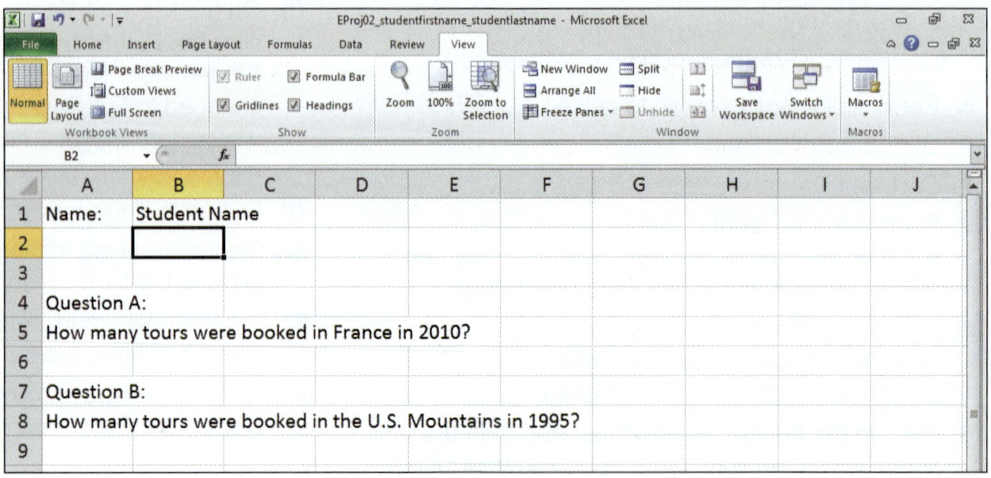

Lesson 2

Worksheet and Workbook Basics

➤ What You Will Learn

- Creating a New (Blank) Workbook
- Entering Text and Labels
- Editing Text
- Using Undo and Redo
- Clearing Cell Contents
- Inserting a Built-in Header or Footer
- Previewing and Printing a Worksheet
- Closing a Workbook

Software Skills Building a workbook involves creating a new file, entering text to identify the data that will be calculated, making changes, and adding an identifying header and footer, among other information. You also can save and print a workbook before closing it. You'll learn these skills in this lesson.

Application Skills You are the Accounts Receivable Supervisor at the Serenity Health Club. A member has charged several services but has not yet paid for them. You need to create an invoice detailing the charges.

WORDS TO KNOW

Blank workbook
A new, empty workbook contains three worksheets (sheets).

Clear
To remove a cell's contents or formatting.

Default
The standard settings Excel uses in its software, such as column width or number of worksheets in a workbook.

Footer
Descriptive text, such as page numbers, that appears at the bottom of every page of a printout.

Header
Descriptive text, such as page numbers, that appears at the top of every page of a printout.

Label
Text entered to identify the type of data contained in a row or column.

Preview
To see how a worksheet will look when printed.

Redo
The command used to redo an action you have undone.

Text
An alphanumeric entry in a worksheet that is not a cell or range address.

Undo
The command used to reverse one or a series of editing actions.

What You Can Do

Creating a New (Blank) Workbook

- You can create a new workbook file any time after you begin working in Excel.
- A **blank workbook** file that you create has three worksheets by default, just like the blank workbook that appears when you start Excel.

- Use the Blank workbook choice on the New tab in Backstage view to create a blank file.

  ✔ *You also can press* CTRL + N *at any time to create a blank file without displaying Backstage view.*

- You can create a workbook using a template in the Backstage view. You can choose from sample templates installed with Excel, or templates in a variety of categories on Office.com.

- During the current work session, Excel applies a temporary name to any new workbook you create. The first blank workbook that appears is named Book1 until you save it with a new name. Subsequent blank files you create are named Book2, Book3, and so on.

Try It! Creating a New Workbook in Excel

1. Click Start > All Programs > Microsoft Office > Microsoft Excel 2010. Excel starts and opens a blank workbook file.

   ✔ *If your keyboard has a Windows key (a key with the Windows logo on it), you can press that key at any time to display the Start menu.*

2. Click File > New.

   ✔ *Throughout this book, you will see instruction provided in a sequence format; for example, "Click File > New" means to click the File tab and then click New.*

3. Make sure that Blank workbook is selected, and click the Create button. The new, blank workbook appears, with its sequentially numbered temporary name, *Book2*.

4. Save the file as **ETry02_studentfirstname _studentlastname** in the location where your teacher instructs you to store the files for this lesson.

5. Leave the file open for the next Try It.

The new file shown in title bar

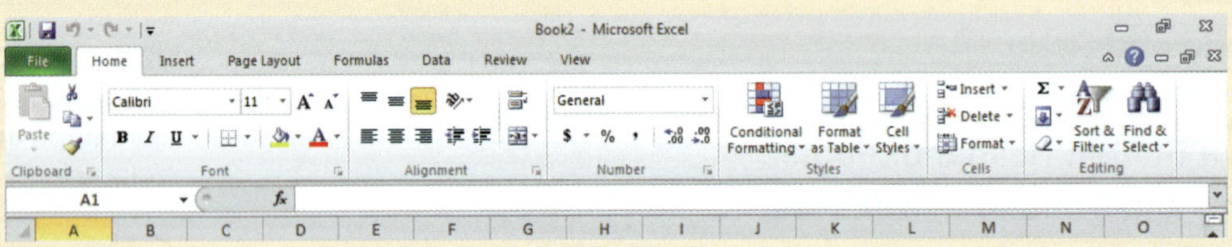

Entering Text and Labels

- The first character entered in a cell determines what type of cell entry it is—a label or text, number, or formula.
- If you enter an alphabetical character or a symbol (` ~ ! # % ^ & * ( ) _ \ I { } ; : ' " < > , ?) as the first character in a cell, you are entering a label.
- A label may be text data, such as the labels: Blue, Sally Smith, Ohio, or Above Average.
- Or, a label may be used to identify data in the row beside it or the column below it, such as the labels: Sales, Qtr 1, or January.
- As you type a label in a cell, it appears in the cell and in the formula bar.
- To enter the label in the cell, type the text and then do any of the following to finalize the entry: press the ENTER key, an arrow key, the TAB key, click another cell, or click the Enter button ✔ on the formula bar.

  ✔ *To enter multiple lines in a cell such as* Overtime above *and* Hours below, *type* Overtime, *press* ALT + ENTER. *Type* Hours *on the second line in the cell and press* ENTER *to finalize the entry.*

- You also can press CTRL + ENTER to finish a cell entry and leave the current cell selected. This is a good technique to use if you later need to copy the cell's contents.
- The default width of each cell is 8.43 characters in the standard font (Calibri, 11 point).

- A label longer than the cell width displays fully only if the cell to the right is blank, or if you make the column wider to fit the long entry.
- If you enter a lot of text in a cell, that text may not fully display in the formula bar. You can expand the formula bar (make it taller) by clicking the Expand Formula Bar button at the right end of the formula bar.
- A label automatically aligns to the left of the cell, making it a left-justified entry.

Try It! Entering Labels (Text)

1. In the **ETry02_studentfirstname_studentlastname** file, click cell A1, type **Client Survey**, and press ENTER twice.
2. Type **Client ID**, and press ENTER twice.
3. Type the following entries, pressing ENTER after each one:

Was the room temperature appropriate?
Were the staff members cordial?
Was your appointment administered on time?
Were your treatments explained in advance?
Were your treatments explained in advance?
Were you offered a beverage?

4. Click cell E4. Type **A Rating**, and press TAB.
5. Type **B Rating** and **C Rating** in the next two cells to the right, pressing TAB to complete each entry.
6. Click the Save button on the Quick Access Toolbar to save the file, and leave it open for the next Try It.

The file with label entries

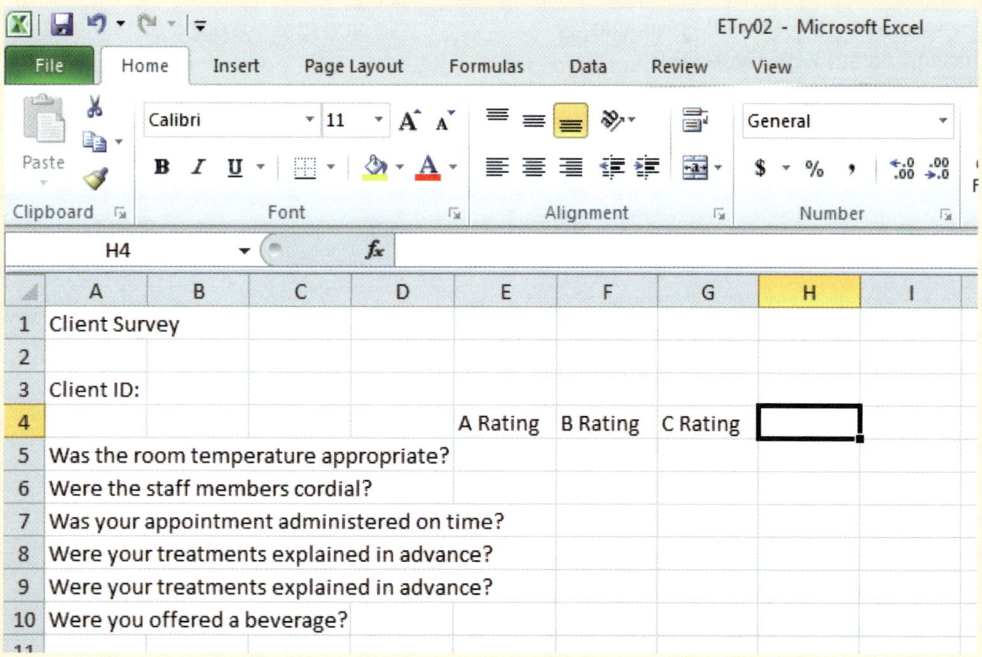

Editing Text

- As you type data in a cell, if you notice a mistake before you press ENTER (or any of the other keys that finalize an entry), you can press the BACKSPACE key to erase characters to the left of the insertion point.
- Before you finalize an entry, you can press the ESC key or click the Cancel button ✕ on the formula bar to cancel it.
- After you enter data, you can make the cell active again (by clicking it, pressing an arrow key, etc.) and then type a new entry to replace the old one.
- You also can double-click a cell in which the entry has been finalized to enable in-cell editing (also called Edit mode) and then make changes to only part of the entry.

✔ *Pressing* F2 *also enables in-cell editing.*

- When in Edit mode, the word *Edit* displays at the left end of the status bar.
- Use the BACKSPACE, DEL, and other keys and selection techniques (as in Word) as needed to select and replace data.

Try It! Editing Text

1. In the **ETry02_studentfirstname_studentlastname** file, click cell A9. This cell has a repeated entry that you want to replace.
2. Type **Were you relaxed during the process?**, and press CTRL + ENTER to finish the entry.
3. Click cell A5 and press F2. Drag over *temperature appropriate* to select those words, type **comfortable**, and press ENTER.
4. Double-click cell A7, and press HOME to make sure the insertion point is at the beginning of the cell entry. Press and hold SHIFT while pressing → three times to select *Was*. Type **Did**.
5. With the cell still in Edit mode, double-click *administered* to select it.
6. Type **start**, and press ENTER.
7. With cell A8 selected, click in the formula bar to the right of the word *explained*, press SHIFT and click to the right of the word *advance*, press DEL, and then press ENTER. This finishes the current edits.
8. Press CTRL + S to save your changes to the **ETry02_studentfirstname_studentlastname** file and leave it open to use in the next Try It.

Editing a text entry

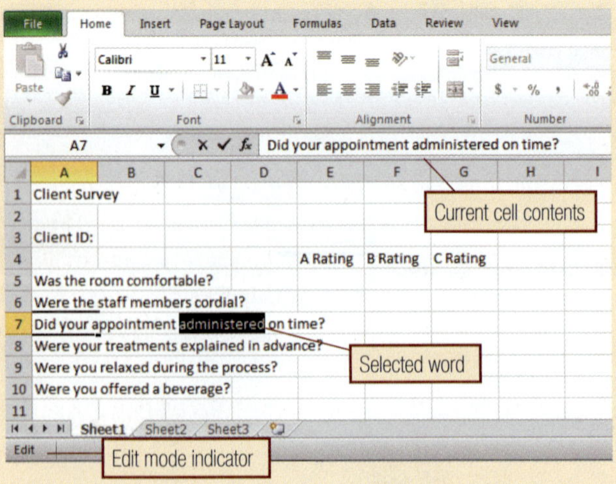

The edited text

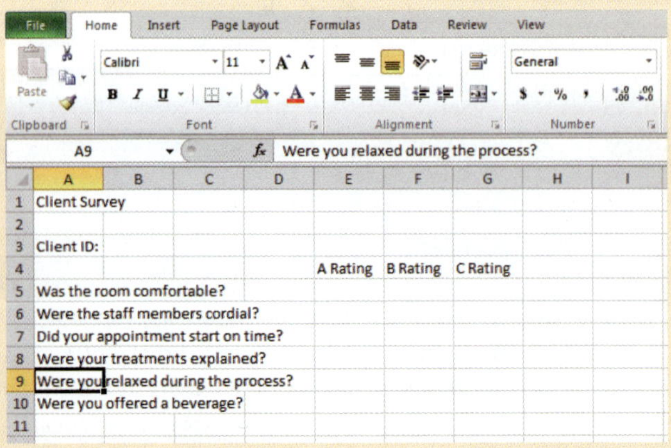

Using Undo and Redo

- Use the **Undo** button on the Quick Access Toolbar to reverse any editing action.
- Some actions can't be undone (such as saving a workbook); in such cases, the Undo button will not be available and will be grayed out.
- You can reverse up to 100 previous editing actions with Undo.
- The Undo button's name changes to reflect the most recent editing action.
- You can also redo (reinstate any action you've undone in error) up to 100 reversed actions using the **Redo** button .
- Both the Undo and Redo buttons include a drop-down list that enables you to undo or redo multiple edits at once.

Try It! Using Undo and Redo

1. In the **ETry02_studentfirstname _studentlastname** file, click cell E4.
2. Type **Yes**, and press TAB.
3. In cell F4, type **No** and press CTRL + ENTER to finish the entry.
4. On the Home tab, in the Font group, click the Bold button **B**.
5. Click the Undo button on the Quick Access Toolbar.
6. Click the Redo button on the Quick Access Toolbar.
7. Click the Undo drop-down arrow on the Quick Access Toolbar, and click the third choice in the menu, which should be **Typing 'Yes' in E4**.
8. Click the **Redo** button on the Quick Access Toolbar twice.
9. Save the **ETry02_studentfirstname _studentlastname** file, and leave it open to use in the next Try It.

Clearing Cell Contents

- Press ESC or click the Cancel button ✕ on the formula bar to clear a cell's contents before finalizing any cell entry.
- To erase a finished cell entry, select the cell and then press DEL.
- You also can use the **Clear** button in the Editing group of the Home tab to delete the cell's contents or to selectively delete its formatting or contents only.
- Right-click a selected cell or range and click Clear Contents on the shortcut menu to remove contents only.

Try It! Clearing Cell Contents

1. In the **ETry02_studentfirstname _studentlastname** file, drag over the range E4:G4 to select it.

   ✔ *The above instruction means to drag the mouse from cell E4 across to cell G4. The shorthand E4:G4 is the address for the range of cells. Lesson 6 provides more detail about selecting and working with ranges.*
2. In the Font group of the Home tab, click the **Bold** button **B**.
3. Click cell G4, and press DEL.
4. Click the Undo button on the Quick Access Toolbar.
5. With cell G4 still selected, click Home > Clear , and then click Clear All.
6. Drag over the range E4:F4 to select it.
7. Click Home > Clear , and then click Clear Formats.
8. Save the **ETry02_studentfirstname _studentlastname** file, and leave it open to use in the next Try It.

Inserting a Built-In Header or Footer

- When you want to repeat the same information at the top of each printed page, create a **header**.
- When you want to repeat the same information at the bottom of each printed page, create a **footer.**
- Header and footer information only appears in the Page Layout view or the printed worksheet.
- You can select a pre-designed header or footer or create customized ones.
- To create a pre-designed header or footer, first click the Header & Footer button in the Text group on the Insert tab of the Ribbon to display the Header & Footer Tools Design tab. Then click either the Header or Footer buttons, and choose one of the predefined headers or footers.
- To customize the header/footer from there, type text in the appropriate section of the header or footer area: left, center, or right.

✔ *From here on, you will need to add a header with your name, the current date, and a page number print code to all the project workbooks.*

- You can also click buttons in the Header & Footer Elements group to insert print codes for the page number, total pages, current date, current time, file path, file name, or sheet name.
- You can also insert a graphic (such as a company logo) in a header or footer.
- You can change the font, font style, and font size of the header or footer using the tools on the Home tab.
- Press ESC to finish editing a custom header or footer and close the Header & Footer Tools Design tab.

Try It! Inserting a Built-in Header or Footer

1. In the **ETry02_studentfirstname _studentlastname** file, click cell A1.
2. On the Insert tab, in the Text group, click the Header & Footer button .
3. On the Header & Footer Tools Design tab, in the Header & Footer group, click the Header button , and then click **ETry02_studentfirstname_ studentlastname**, Page 1 on the menu. The header appears in Page Layout view.

   ✔ *If you've entered your name as the user name in Excel's options, you can choose a predefined header or footer that includes your name.*

4. Click Insert > Header & Footer .
5. On the Header & Footer Tools Design tab, click the Go to Footer button .
6. With the insertion point in the center box of the footer, type your name, and then press TAB to move the insertion point to the right box.
7. On the Header & Footer Tools Design tab, click the Current Date button to insert a code that will display and print the current date.
8. Press TAB to finish the entry in the right box.
9. Press ESC to finish working with the header and footer.
10. Review the footer you created, then scroll up and view the header.
11. Click View > Normal to return to Normal view.
12. Save the **ETry02_studentfirstname _studentlastname** file, and leave it open to use in the next Try It.

Previewing and Printing a Worksheet

- You may print the selected worksheet(s), an entire workbook, or a selected data range.
- You can **preview** a worksheet before you print it. Previewing enables you to see a more accurate representation of how the worksheet will look when printed, so you don't waste paper printing a sheet with the wrong settings.

✔ *In Lesson 20, you learn how to print an entire workbook and a selected range.*

- Before you print a worksheet, you have the opportunity to review its appearance in Backstage view.
- You also can specify print options in Backstage view.
- If you decide not to print, click the Home tab to leave Backstage view.

Try It! Previewing and Printing a Worksheet

1. In the **ETry02_studentfirstname_studentlastname** file, click File > Print.
2. Review the document preview at the right side of Backstage view. The preview shows the placement of headers and footers and all entries on the page. If the worksheet you were printing consisted of multiple pages, you could use the buttons at the lower left to move between them.
3. The various print settings appear in the middle area of Backstage view.
4. Make sure that Print Active Sheets is selected under Settings.
5. **With your teacher's permission**, click the Print button. Otherwise, click the Home tab.
6. Save the **ETry02_studentfirstname_studentlastname** file, and leave it open to use in the next Try It .

The print preview

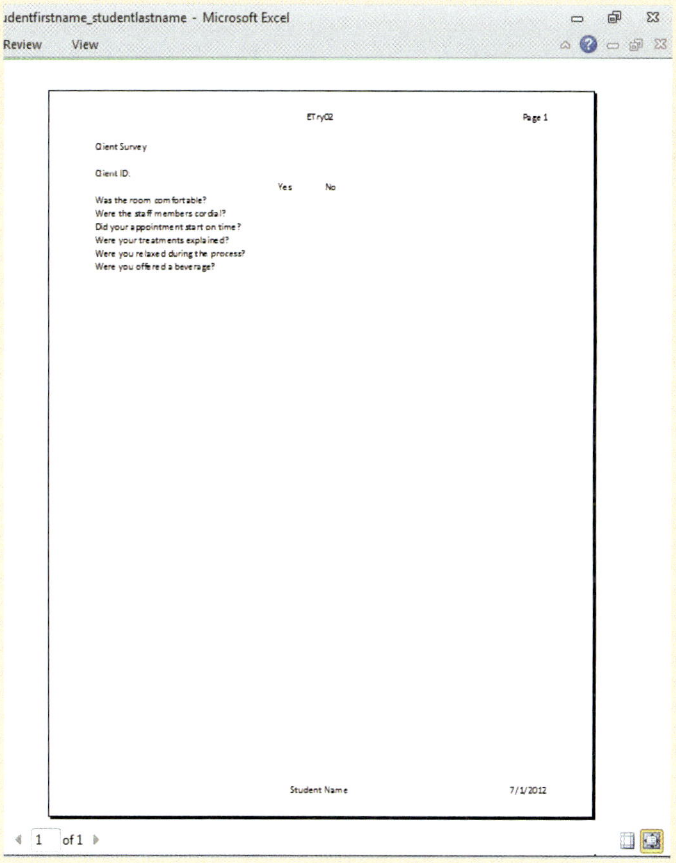

Print settings

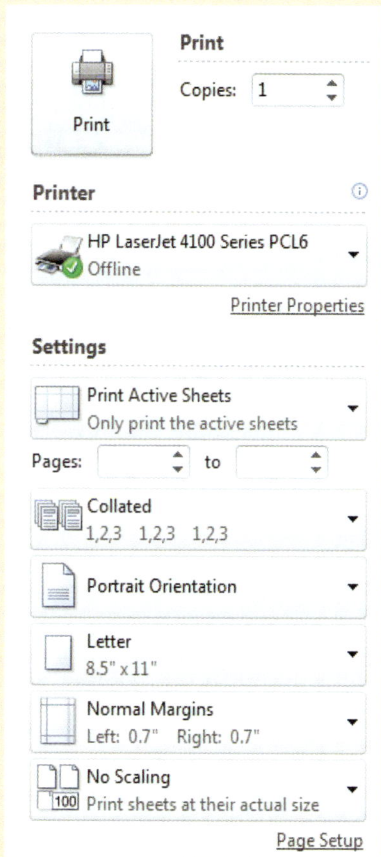

Closing a Workbook

- Closing a workbook file removes it from the screen without exiting Excel.
- Save a workbook before you close it or you will lose the current data or updated entries that you made.
- If you attempt to close a workbook or close Excel before saving, you will be prompted to save the changes.
- If you have more than one file open, Excel allows you to close and save all of the files before you exit the program.

Try It! Closing a Workbook

1. In the **ETry02_studentfirstname_studentlastname** file, click the File tab on the Ribbon.
2. Click Close.
3. Exit Excel.

Project 3—Create It

Basic Invoice

DIRECTIONS

1. Start Excel, if necessary.
2. Click **File** > **New**, make sure **Blank workbook** is selected, and click the **Create** button.
3. Save the blank file that appears as **EProj03_studentfirstname_studentlastname** in the location where your teacher instructs you to store the files for this lesson.
4. Click **Insert > Header & Footer**.
5. Click **Header & Footer Tools Design > Header**, and click the **Page 1** choice.
6. Click **Insert > Header & Footer**.
7. Type **your name** in the left header box, and press TAB twice to move to the right header box.
8. Click **Header & Footer Tools Design > Current Date** to insert a date printing code.
9. Press TAB and then ESC to finish creating the header.
10. Click **View > Normal** to return to Normal view.
11. Type **Invoice** in cell **A1**, and press ENTER twice.
12. Type **Remit To:** and press TAB.
13. Type **Serenity Health Club**, press ENTER, and press ← if needed to select cell B4.
14. Type **200 W. Michigan Ave.** and press ENTER.
15. In cell **B5**, type **Chicago, IL 60614**, and press ENTER.
16. In cell **B6**, type **606-555-1200**, and press ENTER.
17. Click cell **A8,** and type the following three entries, pressing ENTER after each:
    a. **Time:**
    b. **Number:**
    c. **Due Date:**
18. Press ENTER again to select cell **A12**, and make the following two entries, pressing ENTER after each:
    a. **Client ID:**
    b. **Client:**
19. Click the **Undo** button on the Quick Access Toolbar twice to undo the previous two entries.
20. Click the **Redo** button on the Quick Access Toolbar twice to redo your entries.
21. Drag over the range **B3:B6** to select it.
22. Click **Home > Clear**, and then click **Clear Contents**.
23. Click the **Undo** button on the Quick Access Toolbar.
24. Click cell **A8**, type **Date:**, and press ENTER to replace that cell's entry.

25. With cell **A9** selected, press F2, press CTRL + ← to move the insertion point to the beginning of the cell, type **Invoice**, press SPACE , and press ENTER .

26. Drag over cell **A10's** entry in the formula bar, type **Terms:**, and click the **Enter** button ✔ on the formula bar to replace the entry. The finished worksheet appears as shown in Figure 2-1.

27. Click **File** > **Print**.

28. **With your teacher's permission**, click the **Print** button. Otherwise, click the **Home** tab.

29. Click the **Save** button on the Quick Access Toolbar, and then click **File** > **Exit** to close the file and exit Excel.

Figure 2-1

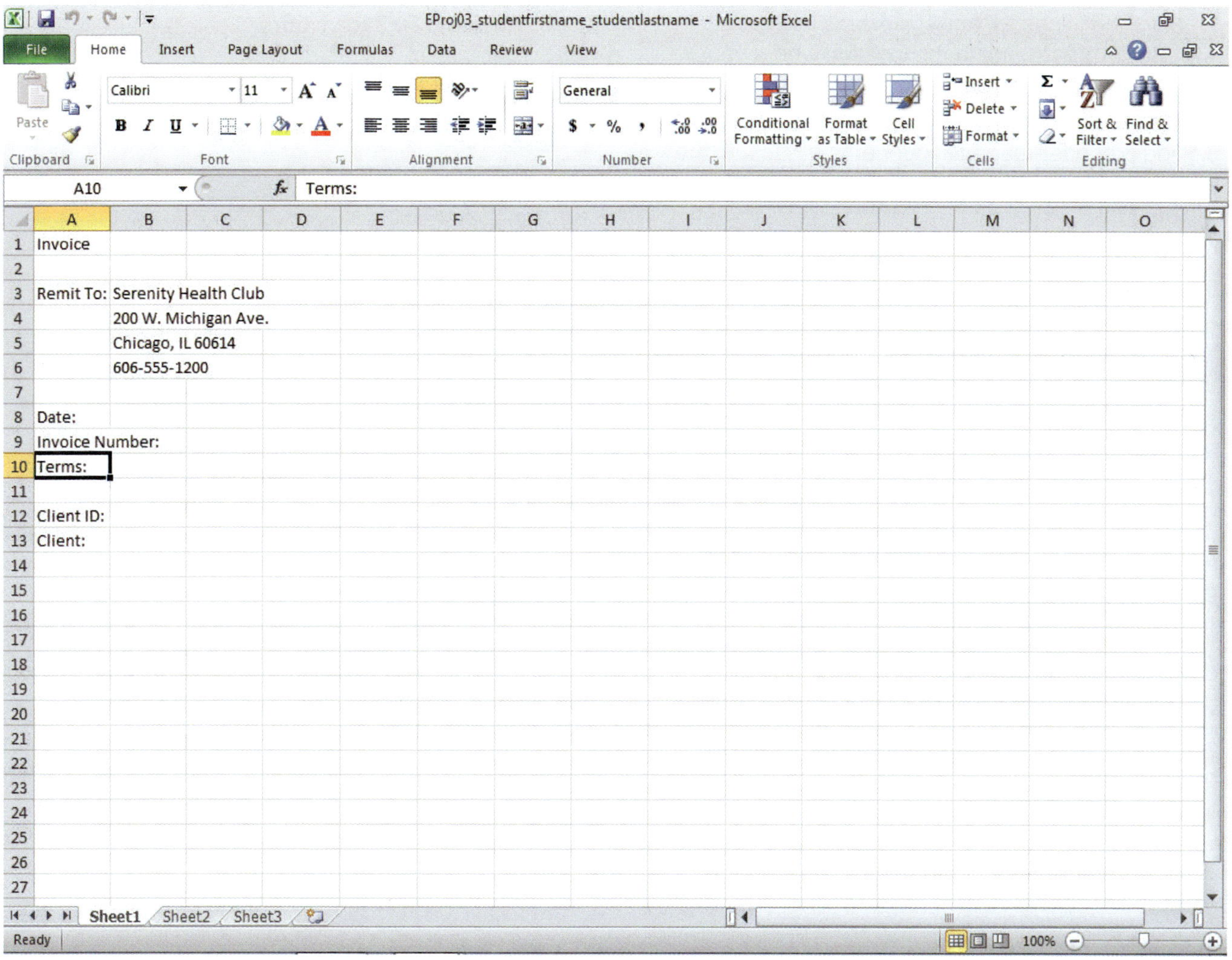

Project 4—Apply It

Member Invoice

DIRECTIONS

1. Start Excel, if necessary, and open **EProj04** from the data files for this lesson.
2. Save the file as **EProj04_studentfirstname_studentlastname** in the location where your teacher instructs you to store the files for this lesson.
3. Add a header that has your name at the left, the date code in the center, and the page number at the right.
4. Change back to **Normal** view.
5. Enter the following data in cells **B8:B10:**
   a. **1/3/13**
   b. **546**
   c. **Due on receipt**
6. Click cell **A9** and replace **Number** with **No**.
7. Click cell **B10**, and then click **Home > Align Text Right**.
8. Clear the formatting you just applied in cell B10.
9. Click the **Undo** button on the Quick Access Toolbar to undo the formatting change.
10. Change the entries in cells **A12:A13** to the following:
    a. **Member ID:**
    b. **Member:**
11. Click cell **B12**, and enter **A1054**.
12. Enter the following data in cells **B13:B15**:
    a. **Joy Wen**
    b. **12 W. 21st St.**
    c. **Chicago, IL 60602**
13. Make entries in the portion of the invoice that calculates the invoice charges, as follows:
    a. cell **A18: 2**
    b. cell **B18: Massage Hours**
    c. cell **C18: 45**
    d. cell **A19: 1**
    e. cell **B19: Facial**
    f. cell **C19: 75**
    g. cell **A20: 3**
    h. cell **B20: Personal Trainer Hours**
    i. cell **C20: 50**
14. Scroll down. Notice that the worksheet already has calculations built in, so it calculates values in the Amount column and Total cell for you.
15. You have been informed that the rate for personal training has changed. Click the **Undo** button on the Quick Access Toolbar, and then enter a rate of **55** in cell C20.
16. Click **File** > **Print** to preview the file in Backstage view.
17. **With your teacher's permission**, click the **Print** button. Otherwise, click the **Home** tab. Submit the printout or the file for grading as required.
18. Close the workbook, saving all changes, and exit Excel.

Lesson 3

Adding Worksheet Contents

➤ What You Will Learn

Opening an Existing Workbook and Saving it with a New Name
Entering and Editing Numeric Labels and Values
Using AutoComplete
Using Pick From List
Using AutoCorrect
Checking the Spelling in a Worksheet

Software Skills Save a workbook with a new name to use it as the basis for another workbook. You also need to know how to enter numeric values, which are the basis for calculations. When entering data, take advantage of the many time-saving features Excel offers: Excel's AutoComplete feature, for example, automatically completes certain entries based on previous entries that you've made. AutoCorrect automatically corrects common spelling errors as you type, while the spelling checker checks your worksheet for any additional errors.

Application Skills You're the team leader at Whole Grains Bread, and you need to complete the baking schedule for today so the other chefs will know what all needs to be done for delivery tomorrow. You want to compare today's schedule with yesterday's, in order to compile a list of any items that were not completed on time. Those items will be given the highest priority.

WORDS TO KNOW

AutoComplete
A feature used to complete an entry based on previous entries made in the column containing the active cell.

AutoCorrect
A feature used to automate the correction of common typing errors.

Numeric label
A number entered in the worksheet as a label, not as a value—such as the year 2012 used as a column label.

Pick From List
A shortcut used to insert repeated information.

Spelling checker
A tool used to assist you in finding and correcting typographical or spelling errors.

Value
A cell entry that consists of a number and numeric formatting only.

What You Can Do

Opening an Existing Workbook and Saving It with a New Name

- When you have saved and closed a workbook file, you can open it from the same disk drive, folder, and file name you used during the save process.

- In the Open dialog box, use the arrows in the text box at the top to navigate the disks, libraries, and folders on your computer.
- You also can use the Navigation pane at the left to go to the location of the workbook. Clicking the triangle beside any location there displays the location's contents, and clicking again hides its contents.
- The default file location, the Documents library in Windows 7, appears in the Navigation pane by default. You can navigate to other libraries, favorite locations (under Favorites), locations on your computer, and locations on the network. You also can navigate to Homegroup (local network) locations if that feature is enabled.
- Click the Change your view button in the Open dialog box to preview a file, change the list to display file details, or display the properties of a file.
- You can access a recently used file without opening the Open dialog box. When you click the File tab, click the Recent tab in Backstage view to show recently opened workbooks and locations. Click a workbook or location to open it.
- You can pin a recently used workbook or location to the Recent lists so it is always easily accessible.
- A newly opened workbook becomes the active workbook and hides any other open workbook.

Try It! Opening an Existing Workbook and Saving It with a New Name

1. Start Excel.
2. Click File > Recent. The middle area of the Backstage view lists files you've opened recently. You could click a file there to open it, or click a folder in the Recent Places list to open it.
3. Click Open.
4. Use the drop-down lists at the top of the Open dialog box or the Navigation pane to select the folder containing the data files for this lesson.
5. Click the **ETry03** file.
6. Click the Open button. The file appears onscreen.
7. Add a header that has your name at the left, the date code in the center, and the page number code at the right, and change back to Normal view.
8. Click File > Save As.

Click a recent file to open it

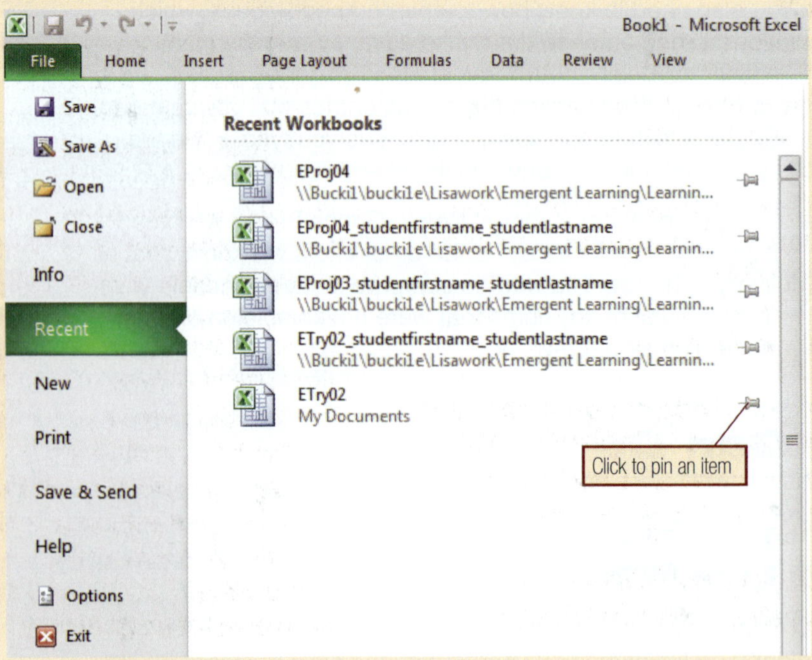

(continued)

Try It! Opening an Existing Workbook and Saving It with a New Name *(continued)*

9 Use the drop-down lists at the top or the Navigation pane to navigate to the folder where your teacher instructs you to store the files for this lesson.

10 Click in the File name text box, and edit the file name to read **ETry03_studentfirstname _studentlastname**.

11 Click the Save button to finish saving the file, and leave it open to use in the next Try It.

Renaming the File

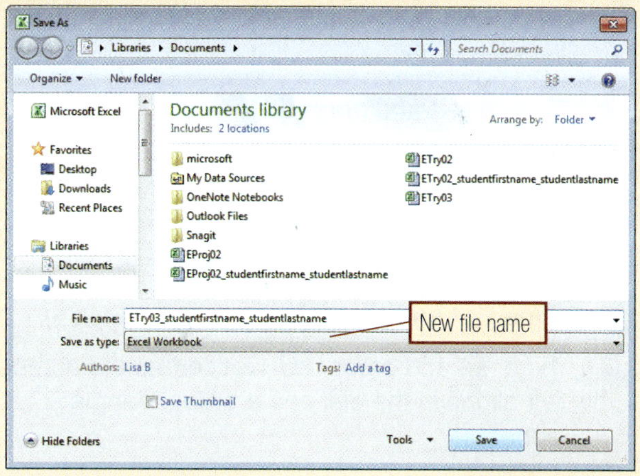

Entering and Editing Numeric Labels and Values

- A cell contains a **value** when its first character begins with either a number or one of the following symbols (+, – , =, $).
- Type the value, and then do one of the following to enter it in the cell:
  - Press ENTER.
  - Press an arrow key.
  - Click the Enter button ✓ on the formula bar.
  - Click another cell.
- If you enter a value that contains 12 or more digits in a cell that uses the default format, Excel will display the number in scientific notation. For example, the entry 123,456,789,012 appears as 1.23457E+11.
- If a number is displayed in scientific notation, widen the column and apply a different format to the cell. This is explained in Lesson 4.
- To display any number in a different format, apply the number format you want to use, as explained in Lesson 4.
- If you see pound signs displayed in a cell instead of a number, widen the column to display the value.
- You can enter some numbers with their formatting and Excel will recognize them as numbers, including:
  - Thousands: You can enter numbers with thousands separators, as in 1,543,009.24
  - Currency values: You can enter values with currency formatting, as in $1,299.60.
  - Percentages: You can enter a percent symbol to specify a percentage, as in 54%.
- When you enter numbers that contain hyphen formatting—such as Social Security numbers, phone numbers, and Zip codes—Excel treats the entries as text, and they cannot be used in calculations.
- A **numeric label**, such as a year number above a column of data that identifies the data's timing, is a number that typically will not be used in calculations.
- Begin the entry of a numeric label with an apostrophe (') as a label prefix to indicate that the number should be treated as a label (text) and not as a value. The entry will align at the left of the cell, unlike other value entries, which align right.
- Although the label prefix (') is shown on the formula bar, it is not displayed on the worksheet or printed.
- When you enter a value with an apostrophe, Excel displays a green triangle in the upper left-hand corner of the cell. Select the cell again, and an error button appears. You can:
  - Click the button and click Ignore Error to confirm that the number is really a label.
  - Click the button and click Convert to Number if the apostrophe was entered in error and the entry should be treated as a number.
- Edit a cell with a value or numeric label using the same techniques as editing a cell with a text entry.

Try It! Entering and Editing Numeric Labels and Values

1. In the **ETry03_studentfirstname_studentlastname** file, click cell A12, type **Roll**, and press TAB.
2. Type **Spelt** and press TAB.
3. Type **8** and press TAB.
4. Type **$.35** and press ENTER.
5. In cell A13 type **Mini Roll**, and press TAB.
6. Type **Oat** and press TAB.
7. Type **'24** and press TAB. Notice that the number left aligns in the cell and a green triangle appears.
8. Click cell C13, click the Error button, and click Convert to Number. The entry right aligns in the cell.
9. Press TAB, type **$.20**, and press CTRL + ENTER.
10. Click cell D8, type **$1.15**, and press ENTER to replace the current entry.
11. Click cell C10, press F2, press BACKSPACE, type **8**, and press ENTER.
12. Save the **ETry03_studentfirstname_studentlastname** file, and leave it open to use in the next Try It.

Converting a numeric label to text

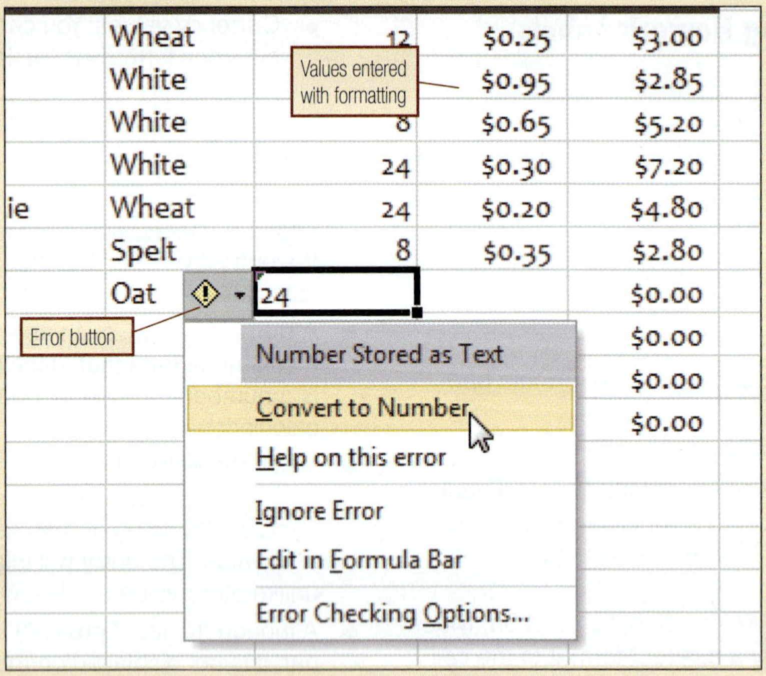

Using AutoComplete

- When you need to repeat a label that has already been typed in the same column, the **AutoComplete** feature allows you to enter the label automatically.
- Type part of the label. If an entry with the same characters has already been entered in the column above, a suggestion for completing the entry appears in black.
- To accept the AutoComplete suggestion, press TAB or ENTER. Otherwise, continue typing the rest of the entry.

Try It! Using AutoComplete

1. In the **ETry03_studentfirstname_ studentlastname** file, click cell A14.
2. Type **Pan**. An AutoComplete suggestion appears in the cell.
3. Press TAB to accept the AutoComplete entry and move to cell B14.
4. Type **Whe**, and press TAB to accept the AutoComplete entry and move to cell C14.
5. Type **8**, and press TAB.
6. Type **$.70**, and press ENTER .
7. Save the **ETry03_studentfirstname_ studentlastname** file, and leave it open to use in the next Try It.

An AutoComplete suggestion

Using Pick From List

- If several labels are entered in a list and the next items to be typed are repeated information, you also can use the **Pick From List** feature to make entries. Right-click a cell and then click the Pick From Drop-down List command on the shortcut menu.

✔ *The cells in the list and the cell to be typed must be contiguous and in the same column. Use the Undo button on the Quick Access Toolbar to reverse any editing action.*

- Click the desired choice in the list of entries that appears to enter it in the cell, and then press TAB or ENTER to move to the next cell, if needed.

Try It! Using Pick From List

1. In the **ETry03_studentfirstname_ studentlastname** file, right-click cell A15, and click Pick From Drop-down List.
2. In the list that appears, click Roll.
3. Right-click cell B15, and click Pick From Drop-down List.
4. In the list that appears, click White, and then press TAB.
5. Type **36**, and then press TAB.
6. Type **$.23**, and then press TAB.
7. Save the **ETry03_studentfirstname_ studentlastname** file, and leave it open to use in the next Try It.

Using AutoCorrect

- If you type a word incorrectly and it is in the AutoCorrect list, Excel automatically changes the word as you type.
- AutoCorrect automatically capitalizes the names of days of the week; corrects incorrectly capitalized letters in the first two positions in a word; and undoes accidental use of the Caps Lock key.
- When certain changes are made with AutoCorrect, you're given an option to remove the corrections by clicking the arrow on the AutoCorrect Options button that appears, and selecting the action you want.
- You can add words to the AutoCorrect list that you often type incorrectly. Click File > Options. In the Excel Options dialog box, click Proofing in the list at the left. Click the AutoCorrect Options button. Type entries in the Replace and With text boxes, and then click the Add button. Repeat as needed, and then click OK to close both dialog boxes.

Try It! Using AutoCorrect

1. In the **ETry03_studentfirstname_ studentlastname** file, click cell A16.
2. Type **Cafe Biscotti**, and press TAB. Notice that when you press SPACE to finish the first word, Excel adds the accent to correct its spelling.
3. Type **O**, and then press TAB. AutoComplete fills in the word *Oat* for you.
4. Type **92**, and then press TAB.
5. Type **$.28**, and then press TAB.
6. Click File > Options.
7. In the Excel Options dialog box, click Proofing in the list at the left.
8. Click the AutoCorrect Options button.
9. Type **quantty** in the Replace text box, and **quantity** in the With text box.
10. Click the Add button.
11. Click the OK button twice.

    ✔ *If your teacher asks you to do so later, reopen the AutoCorrect Options dialog box, select the quantty correction, and click Delete to delete it.*
12. Save the **ETry03_studentfirstname_ studentlastname** file, and leave it open to use in the next Try It.

Checking the Spelling in a Worksheet

- To check the spelling of text in a worksheet and obtain replacement word suggestions, use the **spelling checker** feature.
- Start the spelling check from cell A1 to ensure it checks all sheet contents.

  ✔ *If you don't start the spell check from the beginning of the worksheet, Excel completes the spell check and then displays "Do you want to continue checking at the beginning of the sheet?"*
- To start the spelling checker, click the Review tab and in the Proofing group, click the Spelling button.

  ✔ *Pressing F7 also starts a spelling check.*

  ✔ *Checking spelling in Excel works much as it does in Word. See Lesson 11 in Word Chapter 2 to learn more about the various options for handling misspellings in the Spelling dialog box.*

Try It! Checking the Spelling in a Worksheet

1. In the **ETry03_studentfirstname_ studentlastname** file, click cell A1.
2. Click Review > Spelling.
3. At the first misspelling, *Quantty*, make sure the proper spelling is selected in the Suggestions list, and click the Change button.
4. At the next misspelling, *Pannini*, make sure the proper spelling is selected in the Suggestions list, and click the Change All button.
5. Close **ETry03_studentfirstname_student lastname**, saving all changes, and exit Excel.

Project 5—Create It

Bakery Schedule Entries

DIRECTIONS

1. Start Excel, if necessary.
2. Click **File > New**, make sure **Blank workbook** is selected, and click the **Create** button to open a new file.
3. Save the file as **EProj05_studentfirstname_studentlastname** in the location where your teacher instructs you to store the files for this lesson.
4. Add a header that has your name at the left, the date code in the center, and the page number code at the right, and change back to **Normal** view.
5. Type **Whole Garins Bread (r)** in cell A1, and press SPACE. (Type the entry exactly as shown, as errors will be corrected later.) Notice that the AutoCorrect feature changes the (r) entry to a register mark: ®
6. Press ENTER three times.
7. Type **Bakery Schedule**, and press ENTER.
8. Type **10/10/12**, and press ENTER twice.
9. Type the following cell entries, pressing TAB after each:
   a. **Customer**
   b. **Item**
   c. **Qty Needed**
   d. **Qty Shipped**
   e. **Qty to Bake**
10. Click cell **A8**, type the following cell entries exactly as shown, pressing ENTER after each (note Auto-Correct in action again):
    a. **Cafe Latte**
    b. **Java Cafe**
    c. **Villige Green**
11. Click cell **B8**, type the following cell entries exactly as shown, pressing ENTER after each:
    a. **Bagel Assortment**
    b. **Croissants**
    c. **Wheat Bread**
12. Click cell **C8**, type the following cell entries exactly as shown, pressing ENTER after each:
    a. **325**
    b. **100**
    c. **25**
13. Click cell **D8**, type the following cell entries exactly as shown, pressing ENTER after each:
    a. **300**
    b. **100**
    c. **25**
14. Click cell **A11**, type **J**, and press TAB to complete the cell entry using AutoComplete.
15. Type the following cell entries, pressing TAB after each:
    a. **Pastry Assortment**
    b. **150**
    c. **125**
16. Click cell **A1**.
17. Click **Review > Spelling**.
18. At the first misspelling, *Garins*, make sure that **Grains** is selected in the Suggestions list, and then click the **Change** button.
19. At the next misspelling, *Qty*, click the **Ignore All** button.
20. At the next misspelling, *Villige*, make sure that **Village** is selected in the Suggestions list, and then click the **Change** button.
22. In the message box that informs you that the spelling check is complete, click the **OK** button. The finished spreadsheet appears as shown in Figure 3-1.
23. **With your teacher's permission**, print the worksheet. Submit the printout or the file for grading as required.
24. Close the workbook, saving all changes, and exit Excel.

Figure 3-1

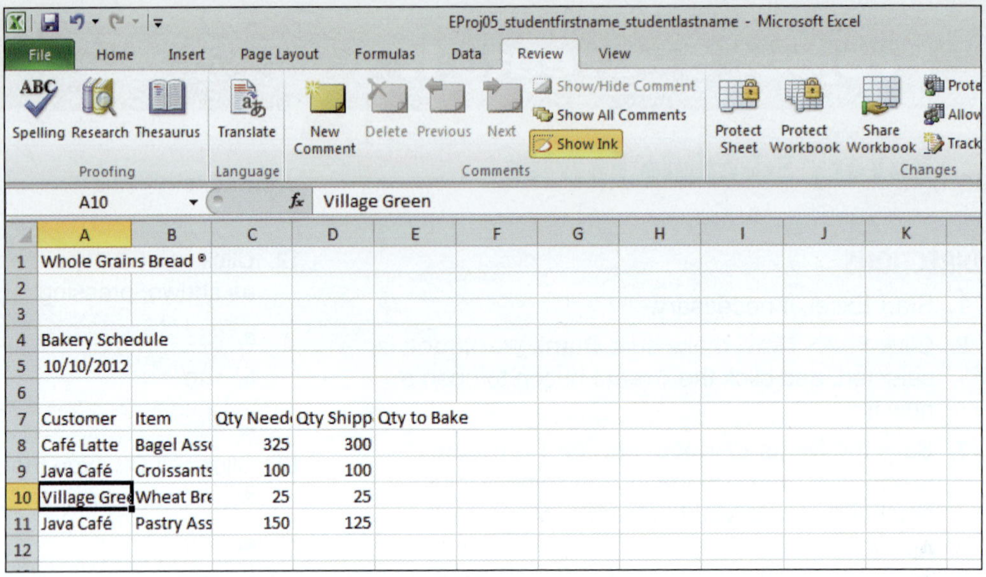

Project 6—Apply It

Finishing the Bakery Schedule

DIRECTIONS

1. Start Excel, if necessary, and open the **EProj06** file from the data files for this lesson.
2. Save the file as **EProj06_studentfirstname_studentlastname** in the location where your teacher instructs you to store the files for this lesson.
3. Add a header that has your name at the left, the date code in the center, and the page number code at the right, and change back to **Normal** view.
4. In cell **A12**, use **Pick From Drop-down List** to enter **Village Green**.
5. Click cell **A13**, and make the following entries, using AutoComplete where applicable and pressing ENTER after each:
   a. **Mikes Steak House**
   b. **Gribaldi's Risorante**
   c. **Java Café**
   d. **Café Latte**
   e. **Village Green**
6. Click cell **B12**, and make the following entries exactly as shown, using AutoComplete where applicable and pressing ENTER after each:
   a. **White Bread**
   b. **Pastry Assortment**
   c. **Garlic Bread**
   d. **Muffin Assortment**
   e. **Muffin Assortment**
   f. **Wheat Rolls**
7. Click cell **C12**, and make the following entries, pressing ENTER after each:
   a. **9**
   b. **200**
   c. **125**
   d. **100**
   e. **225**
   f. **700**

8. Click cell **D12**, and make the following entries, pressing [ENTER] after each:
   a. **9**
   b. **200**
   c. **125**
   d. **100**
   e. **175**
   f. **650**
9. Click cell **D10**, and change the entry to **0**.
10. Click cell **D13**, and change the entry to **160**.
11. Click cell **D15**, and change the entry to **48**.
12. Click cell **A1**.
13. Check the spelling in the worksheet.
14. At the first misspelling, *Qty*, click the **Ignore All** button.
15. At the next misspelling, *Gribaldi's*, click the **Ignore Once** button.
16. At the next misspelling, *Risorante*, edit the entry to read **Ristorante**, and then click the **Change** button. Click **Yes** to change the word even though it's not in the dictionary.
17. At the next misspelling, *Assotment*, make sure the right correction is selected in the Suggestions list, and click the **Change** button.
18. In the message box that informs you that the spelling check is complete, click **OK**.
19. **With your teacher's permission**, print the worksheet. Submit the printout or the file for grading as required.
20. Close the workbook, saving all changes, and exit Excel.

Figure 3-2

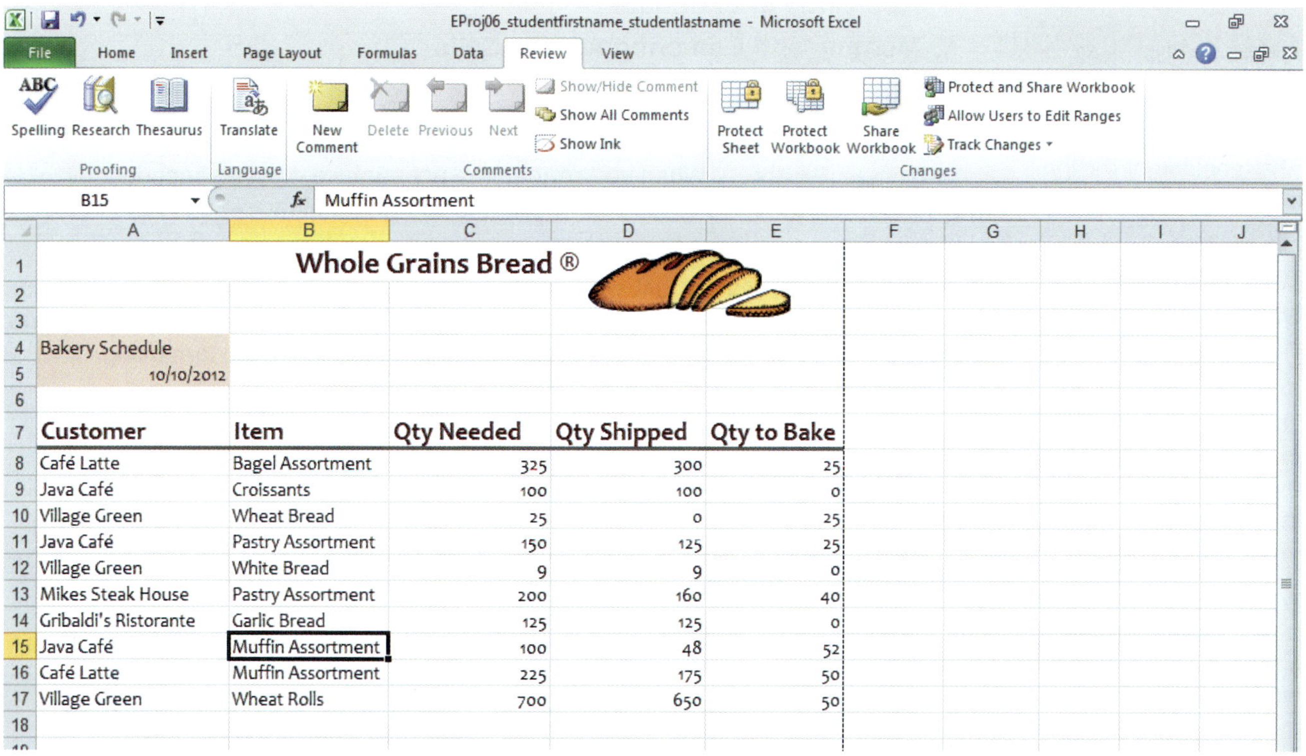

Lesson 4

Worksheet Formatting

WORDS TO KNOW

Accounting format
A style that vertically aligns with dollar signs ($), thousands separators (,), and decimal points.

Cell style
A combination of a font, text color, cell color, and other font attributes applied to a single cell.

Comma format
A style that displays numbers with a thousands separator (,).

Currency format
A style that displays dollar signs ($) immediately preceding the number and includes a thousands separator (,).

Fill
A color that fills a cell, appearing behind the data.

Font
The typeface or design of the text.

Font size
The measurement of the typeface in points (1 point = 1/72 of an inch).

Format
To apply attributes to cell data to change the appearance of the worksheet.

Live Preview
A feature that shows you how a gallery formatting choice will appear in the worksheet when you move the mouse pointer over that choice.

➤ What You Will Learn

Choosing a Theme
Applying Cell Styles
Applying Font Formats
Merging and Centering Across Cells
Applying Number Formats

Software Skills When you change the appearance of worksheet data by applying various formats, you also make that data more attractive and readable.

Application Skills As the Inventory Manager of the Voyager Travel Adventures retail store, you want to enhance the appearance of an inventory worksheet you have created. You have already compiled the inventory data, and you want to spruce up the worksheet prior to printing by adding some formatting.

What You Can Do

Choosing a Theme

- To make your worksheet readable and interesting, you can manually apply a set of formats.
- You manually format data by selecting cells and then clicking options on the Home tab, such as the Font Calibri and Font Color A buttons.
- Using too many manual formats can make the worksheet seem disjointed and chaotic.
- To make your worksheet more professional looking, use a theme to apply a coordinated set of formats.

- By default, the Office theme is applied to all new workbooks; if you select a different theme, the fonts and colors in your workbook will automatically change.
- If you don't want to change the fonts in your worksheet, you can apply just the theme colors from a theme.
- Likewise, you can change theme fonts and the theme effects applied to graphics without affecting the colors already in your worksheet.
- You select a theme from the Themes gallery in the Themes group on the Page Layout tab.
- As you move the mouse over the themes shown in the gallery, the worksheet automatically shows a Live Preview of the data.
- When you type data in a cell, it's automatically formatted using the font in the current theme.
- You can apply a cell color (called a fill) or a text color. Click the down arrow on the Fill Color or Font Color buttons in the Font group of the Home tab, and then click one of the choices under Theme Colors.
- If you apply a theme color to text or as a fill and later switch themes, Excel updates the color according to the new theme.
- If you choose one of the standard colors or use the More Colors option, the selected color will not change if you later change the theme.

WORDS TO KNOW

Merge and Center
A feature that enables you to automatically combine cells and center the contents of the original far left cell in the new cell.

Number format
A format that controls how numerical data is displayed, including the use of commas, dollar signs (or other symbols), and the number of decimal places.

Percent format
A style that displays decimal numbers as a percentage.

Theme
A collection of coordinated fonts, colors, and effects for graphic elements, such as charts and images, that can be quickly applied to all sheets in a workbook.

Try It! Choosing a Theme

1. Start Excel.
2. Open the **ETry04** file from the data files for this lesson.
3. Save the file as **ETry04_studentfirstname_studentlastname** in the location where your teacher instructs you to store the files for this lesson.
4. Add a header that has your name at the left, the date code in the center, and the page number code at the right, and change back to Normal view.
5. On the Page Layout tab, click the Themes button.

Previewing a theme

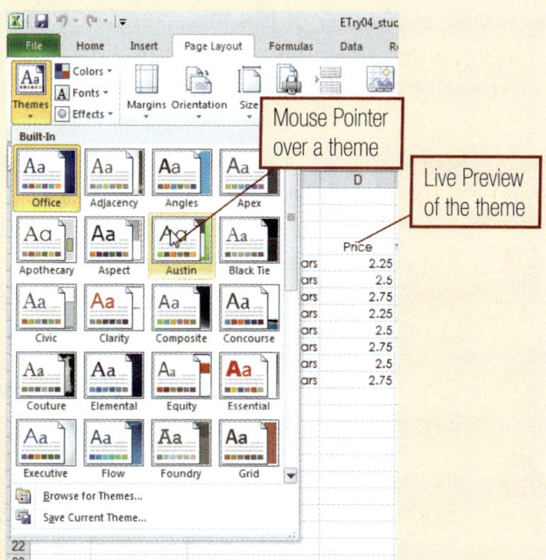

(continued)

Try It! Choosing a Theme *(continued)*

6 Move the mouse pointer over the Austin choice in the Themes gallery. Notice how the fonts applied on the worksheet change.

7 Click the Concourse theme.

8 Double-click the right column header border for columns C and E to make them wider to accommodate the text due to the theme font change. (Lesson 5 covers this technique in more detail.)

9 Drag over the range B2:F2 to select it.

10 On the Home tab, click the Fill Color drop-down arrow. Under Theme Colors, click the Red, Accent 2, Lighter 40% fill color in the sixth column. The selected range shows a Live Preview of the color. Click the color to apply it.

11 Click cell F13.

12 Click Home > Font, and then click the Fill Color drop-down arrow. Under Standard Colors, click the Green color.

13 Save the **ETry04_studentfirstname_studentlastname** file and leave it open to use in the next Try It.

Applying a theme color

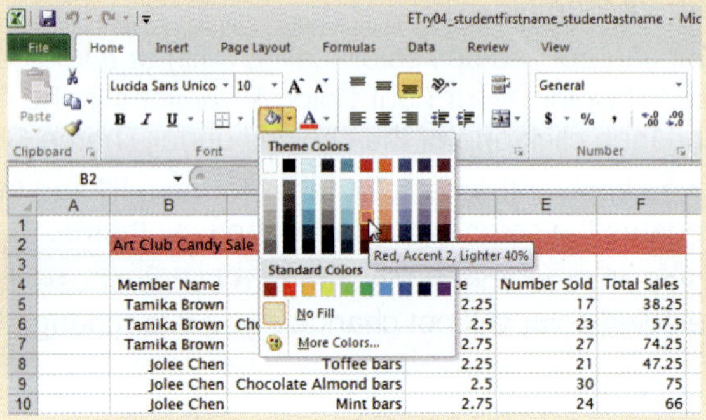

Applying Cell Styles

- Themes contain a coordinated set of colors, fonts, and other elements, such as **cell styles**.
- Cell styles in a theme include various styles you can apply to column headings or totals and title and heading styles.
- If you apply any of the title, headings, or themed cell styles, the cells using that style will update automatically if you change themes.
- You also can apply cell styles that aren't changed if you change themes, such as formats you might use to highlight good or bad values, a warning, or a note.
- There are also some number format cell styles available that won't change if you change themes.

✓ *Sometimes applying a cell style to a cell holding a label causes the label to be cut off rather than spilling over into the cell to the right as you might expect. If this happens and you don't want to change the column width, also apply the style to the next cell to the right.*

Try It! Applying Cell Styles

1 In the **ETry04_studentfirstname_studentlastname** file, drag over the range B4:F4 to select it.

2 On the Home tab, click the Cell Styles button. The gallery of cell styles appears.

3 In the second column under Themed Cell Styles, move your mouse pointer over the 60% Accent2 choice. The selected range shows a Live Preview of the cell style. Click the cell style to apply it.

4 Drag over the range E13:F13 to select it.

5 Click Home > Cell Styles.

6 Under Titles and Headings, click the Total choice in the far right column.

✓ *Notice that the standard color you applied to cell F13 doesn't change when you apply the cell style.*

7 Double-click the right column header border for columns B, E, and F to adjust the column widths due to the new styles.

8 Save the **ETry04_studentfirstname_studentlastname** file, and leave it open to use in the next Try It.

Applying Font Formats

- The Font group on the Home tab of the Ribbon offers choices for formatting text, including font size, color, and attributes such as bold and italics.

  ✔ *This type of formatting is sometimes called direct formatting.*

- The Font group settings you apply override the formatting applied by the current theme.
- If a cell has formatting you applied directly using the Font group tools, such as bold or underlining, that formatting will NOT change if you change themes.
- Theme fonts, font colors, and cell colors appear at the top of the selection list when you click the appropriate button. For example, if you click the Font drop-down arrow, the theme fonts appear at the top of the list.
- Standard fill or text colors will not change if you select a different theme.
- The way in which your data appears after making font and font size changes is dependent on your monitor and printer.
- The available fonts depend on those installed in Windows.
- When you change **font size**, Excel automatically adjusts the row height but does not adjust the column width.

Try It! Applying Font Formats

1. In the **ETry04_studentfirstname_studentlastname** file, click cell B2.
2. Click Home, and then click the Font drop-down arrow.
3. Scroll down the list, and click Arial Black.
4. Click Home, and then click the Font Size drop-down arrow.
5. Move the mouse pointer over the 24 size, view the Live Preview, and then click 24.

   ✔ *When you increase the font size, the row height increases automatically.*

6. Save the **ETry04_studentfirstname_studentlastname** file, and leave it open to use in the next Try It.

Applying a new font size

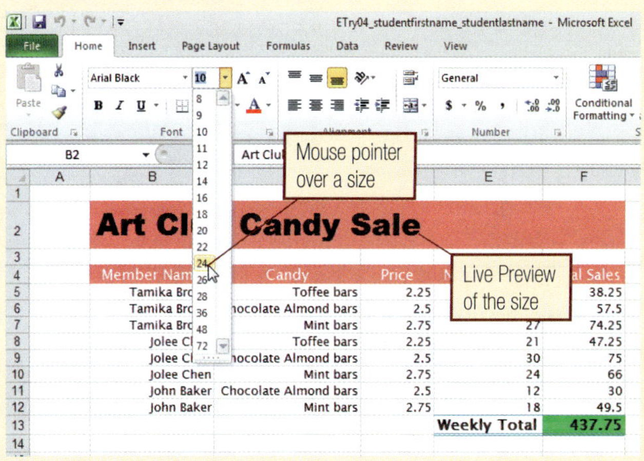

Merging and Centering Across Cells

- You can center a worksheet's title across the columns that contain the worksheet data.
- To center a label across several columns, use the **Merge & Center** button in the Alignment group of the Home tab.

  ✔ *The Merge & Center command actually merges the selected cells into one large cell and then centers the data in the newly merged cell.*

  ✔ *You can align merge cells left or right instead of centering the data. Click the Merge & Center drop-down arrow and click Merge Across to merge the cells with the current alignment (left or right).*

- For Merge & Center to work properly, enter the data in the first cell in a range, and then select adjacent cells to the right.
- Merged cells act as a single cell. Applying formatting to a merged cell formats the entire merged area.
- You can unmerge, or separate, merged cells by selecting the cell and clicking the Merge & Center button again.

Try It! Merging and Centering Across Cells

1. In the **ETry04_studentfirstname_ studentlastname** file, drag over the range B2:F2 to select it.
2. On the Home tab, in the Alignment group, click the Merge & Center button.
3. Drag over the range B13:E13 to select it.
4. On the Home tab, in the Alignment group, click the Merge & Center button.
5. Leave the merged cell selected. Click Home > Cell Styles, and then click Total in the gallery of styles.
6. Save the **ETry04_studentfirstname_ studentlastname** file, and leave it open to use in the next Try It.

Merge & Center aligns headings over all the data

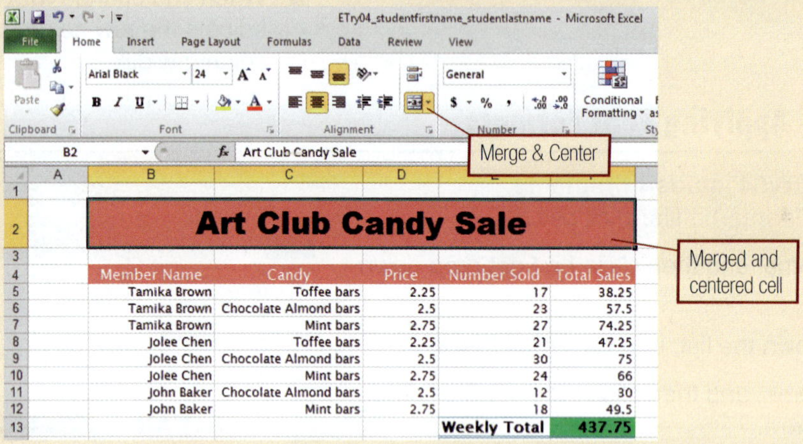

Applying Number Formats

- When formatting numerical data, you may want to change more than just the font and font size—you may want to also apply a **number format.**
- Number formats are grouped together in the Number group on the Home tab.
- The number format determines the number of decimal places and the display of zeros (if any) before/after the decimal point.
- Number formats also include various symbols such as dollar signs, percentage signs, or negative signs.
- Changing the format of a cell does not affect the actual value stored there or used in calculations—it affects only the way in which that value is displayed.
- There are buttons for quickly applying three commonly used number formats:
  - **Accounting format** $ 21,008.00, which includes a decimal point with two decimal places, the thousands separator (comma), and a dollar sign aligned to the far left of the cell.
  - **Percent format** 32%, which includes a percent sign and no decimal points.

    ✔ *32% is entered as* ***.32*** *in the cell. If you type 32 and apply the Percent format, you'll see 3200%.*

  - **Comma format** 178,495.00, which includes two decimal places and the thousands separator (comma).
- Using the Number Format list, you can also apply a variety of other number formats such as Currency, Long Date, and Fraction.
- The **Currency format** is similar to Accounting format, except that the dollar sign is placed just to the left of the data, rather than left-aligned in the cell.
- If you don't see a number format you like, you can create your own by applying a format that's close. For example, you might apply the Accounting format and then change the number of decimal places using the Increase Decimal or Decrease Decimal buttons.
- You can also make selections in the Format Cells dialog box to design a custom number format. Click the Number group dialog box launcher to open the dialog box.

Try It! Applying Number Formats

1. In the ETry04_studentfirstname_studentlastname file, click cell F5.
2. On the Home tab, in the Number group, click the Accounting Number Format button. Excel formats the cell with the Accounting format.
3. Click cell D5.
4. On the Home tab, and then click the Number Format drop-down arrow. Click Currency. Excel formats the cell with the Currency format. Notice the difference between it and the Accounting format in cell F5.
5. Drag over the range D6:D12 to select it.
6. Click Home > Number Format arrow > Currency.
7. Drag over the range F6:F13 to select it.
8. Click Home > Accounting Number Format.
9. Drag over the range E5:E12 to select it.
10. In the Number group, click the Increase Decimal button twice.
11. In the Number group, click the Decrease Decimal button twice.
12. Close the ETry04_studentfirstname_studentlastname file, saving all changes, and exit Excel.

Applying Currency format

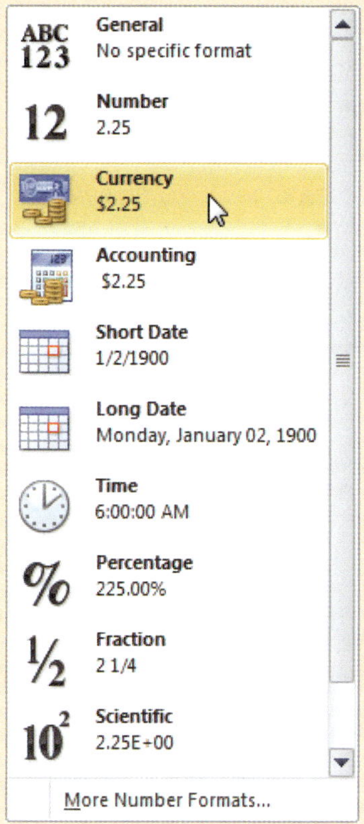

Project 7—Create It

Inventory Sheet Entries and Formatting

DIRECTIONS

1. Start Excel, if necessary, and open the EProj07 file from the data files for this lesson.
2. Save the file as EProj07_studentfirstname_studentlastname in the location where your teacher instructs you to store the files for this lesson.
3. Add a header that has your name at the left, the date code in the center, and the page number code at the right, and change back to Normal view.
4. Drag over the row headers for rows 1 through 4 to select them.
5. Click Home > Clear > Clear Formats.
6. Click cell A4, type 11/30/12, and press CTRL + ENTER.
7. On the Home tab, in the Number group, click the dialog box launcher to open the Format Cells dialog box. Date should already be selected in the Category list.
8. Click 14-Mar in the Type list, and then click OK.
9. Click Page Layout > Themes button.
10. Move the mouse pointer over the Executive theme to view a Live Preview of its appearance.
11. Click the Elemental theme to apply it.
12. Drag over the range A1:I1 to select it.
13. Click Home > Merge & Center.

14. Click **Home > Cell Styles > Title**.
15. Drag over the range **A3:I3** to select it.
16. Click **Home > Merge & Center**.
17. Click **Home > Cell Styles > Heading 2**.
18. Drag over the range **A4:I4** to select it.
19. Click **Home > Merge & Center**.
20. Click **Home > Bold** **B**.
21. Drag over the range **D5:G5** to select it.
22. Click **Home > Merge & Center**.
23. Click **Home > Cell Styles > 20% -Accent4**.
24. Click cell **D7**, and type the following cell entries, pressing ENTER after each:
    - **a.** 1
    - **b.** 3
    - **c.** 2
    - **d.** 2
25. Click cell **E7**, and type the following cell entries, pressing ENTER after each:
    - **a.** 2
    - **b.** 4
    - **c.** 2
    - **d.** 1
26. Drag over the range **C7:C29** to select it.
27. Click **Home > Accounting Number Format** $.
28. Press CTRL + HOME. Your worksheet should look like the one shown in Figure 4-1.
29. **With your teacher's permission**, print the worksheet. Submit the printout or the file for grading as required.
30. Close the workbook, saving all changes, and exit Excel.

Figure 4-1

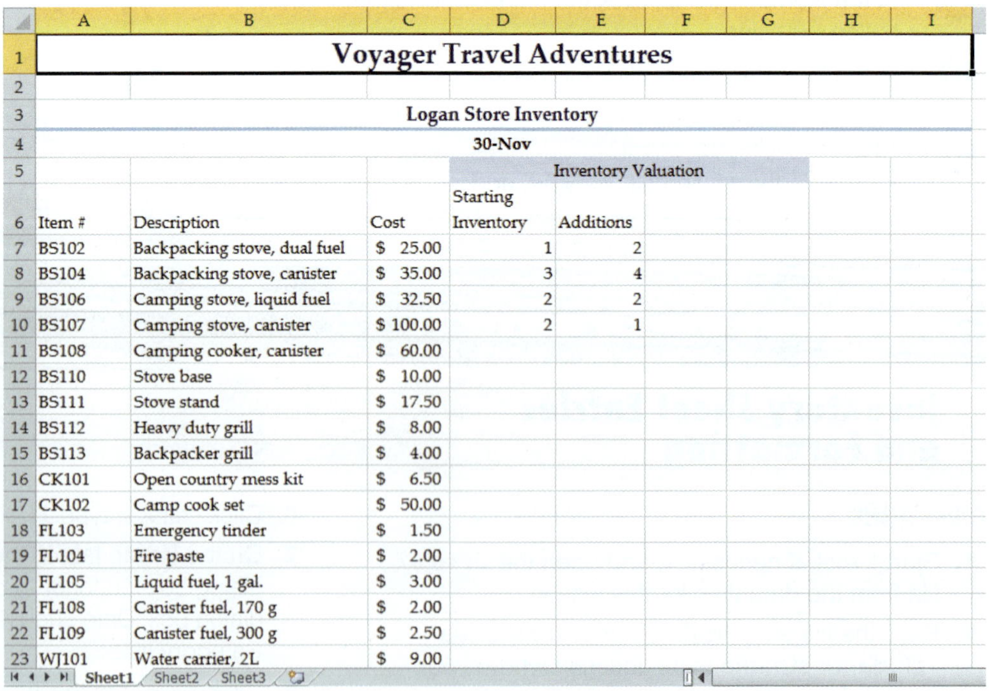

	A	B	C	D	E	F	G	H	I
1	Voyager Travel Adventures								
2									
3	Logan Store Inventory								
4	30-Nov								
5				Inventory Valuation					
6	Item #	Description	Cost	Starting Inventory	Additions				
7	BS102	Backpacking stove, dual fuel	$ 25.00	1	2				
8	BS104	Backpacking stove, canister	$ 35.00	3	4				
9	BS106	Camping stove, liquid fuel	$ 32.50	2	2				
10	BS107	Camping stove, canister	$ 100.00	2	1				
11	BS108	Camping cooker, canister	$ 60.00						
12	BS110	Stove base	$ 10.00						
13	BS111	Stove stand	$ 17.50						
14	BS112	Heavy duty grill	$ 8.00						
15	BS113	Backpacker grill	$ 4.00						
16	CK101	Open country mess kit	$ 6.50						
17	CK102	Camp cook set	$ 50.00						
18	FL103	Emergency tinder	$ 1.50						
19	FL104	Fire paste	$ 2.00						
20	FL105	Liquid fuel, 1 gal.	$ 3.00						
21	FL108	Canister fuel, 170 g	$ 2.00						
22	FL109	Canister fuel, 300 g	$ 2.50						
23	WJ101	Water carrier, 2L	$ 9.00						

Sheet1 Sheet2 Sheet3

Project 8—Apply It

Finishing the Inventory Worksheet

DIRECTIONS

1. Start Excel, if necessary, and open the **EProj08** file from the data files for this lesson.
2. Save the file as **EProj08_studentfirstname_studentlastname** in the location where your teacher instructs you to store the files for this lesson.
3. Add a header that has your name at the left, the date code in the center, and the page number code at the right, and change back to **Normal** view.
4. Apply the **Clarity** theme to the file. Notice how the fonts and colors in the worksheet change.
5. Select the range **I7:I29** and apply the **Percent** style. Then, format the data for two decimal places.
6. Select the range **G7:G29** and apply the **Accounting** number format.
7. Select the range **A6:I6** and apply the **Accent3** cell style and **Center** alignment.
8. Select the range **A7:A29** and apply the **60%-Accent3** cell style.
9. Click cell **A4** and apply the ***Wednesday, March 14, 2001** date format.
10. Go to cell **A1**. Your worksheet should look like the one shown in Figure 4-2.
11. **With your teacher's permission**, print the worksheet. Submit the printout or the file for grading as required.
12. Close the workbook, saving all changes, and exit Excel.

	A	B	C	D	E	F	G	H	I
1	Voyager Travel Adventures								
2									
3	Logan Store Inventory								
4	Friday, November 30, 2012								
5				Inventory Valuation					
6	Item #	Description	Cost	Starting Inventory	Additions	Ending Inventory	Value	Full Stock Level	Current Stock Percentage
7	BS102	Backpacking stove, dual fuel	$ 25.00	1	2	3	$ 75.00	4	75.00%
8	BS104	Backpacking stove, canister	$ 35.00	3	4	7	$ 245.00	8	87.50%
9	BS106	Camping stove, liquid fuel	$ 32.50	2	2	4	$ 130.00	5	80.00%
10	BS107	Camping stove, canister	$ 100.00	2	1	3	$ 300.00	5	60.00%
11	BS108	Camping cooker, canister	$ 60.00	2	0	2	$ 120.00	2	100.00%
12	BS110	Stove base	$ 10.00	1	1	2	$ 20.00	3	66.67%
13	BS111	Stove stand	$ 17.50	2	1	3	$ 52.50	3	100.00%
14	BS112	Heavy duty grill	$ 8.00	2	0	2	$ 16.00	3	66.67%
15	BS113	Backpacker grill	$ 4.00	5	4	9	$ 36.00	10	90.00%
16	CK101	Open country mess kit	$ 6.50	4	3	7	$ 45.50	10	70.00%
17	CK102	Camp cook set	$ 50.00	2	1	3	$ 150.00	4	75.00%
18	FL103	Emergency tinder	$ 1.50	9	7	16	$ 24.00	15	106.67%
19	FL104	Fire paste	$ 2.00	12	6	18	$ 36.00	24	75.00%
20	FL105	Liquid fuel, 1 gal.	$ 3.00	18	15	33	$ 99.00	36	91.67%
21	FL108	Canister fuel, 170 g	$ 2.00	20	5	25	$ 50.00	36	69.44%
22	FL109	Canister fuel, 300 g	$ 2.50	21	13	34	$ 85.00	36	94.44%
23	WJ101	Water carrier, 2L	$ 9.00	10	2	12	$ 108.00	15	80.00%
24	WJ102	Water carrier, 32 oz	$ 4.50	12	6	18	$ 81.00	24	75.00%
25	WJ103	Water carrier, 48 oz.	$ 5.00	3	15	18	$ 90.00	24	75.00%
26	WJ104	Dromedary, 6L	$ 15.00	6	6	12	$ 180.00	15	80.00%
27	WJ105	Water bag, 4L	$ 10.00	10	2	12	$ 120.00	15	80.00%

Sheet1 Sheet2 Sheet3

Figure 4-2

WORDS TO KNOW

Auto Fill
The feature that enables Excel to create a series automatically.

Date
A cell entry that indicates a date or time and is stored as a date code in Excel.

Wrap text
A feature that causes long cell entries to appear on multiple lines within a cell.

Default column width
The default number of characters that display in a column based on the default font.

Fill handle
A black box on the lower-right corner of the selected cell or range that you can use to fill (copy) a series or formula.

Key Tips
Keyboard shortcuts for choosing Ribbon commands that you display by pressing Alt.

Keyboard shortcuts
Specific keyboard keys that you press together or in sequence to execute commands or apply settings.

Series
A list of sequential numbers, dates, times, or text.

Wrap text
A feature that causes long cell entries to appear on multiple lines.

Lesson 5

More on Cell Entries and Formatting

➤ What You Will Learn

- Entering Dates
- Filling a Series
- Aligning Data in a Cell
- Wrapping Text in Cells
- Changing Column Width and Row Height
- Using Keyboard Shortcuts

Software Skills Use dates to identify when you created a worksheet or to label a column or row of data by time period. After typing dates, labels, and numbers in a worksheet, you can improve its appearance by changing the alignment of data and the widths of columns. If you need to enter a series of labels (such as Monday, Tuesday, Wednesday) or values (such as 1, 2, 3), using Excel's Auto Fill feature saves data entry time and reduces errors.

Application Skills You are the Accounts Receivable Supervisor at the Serenity Health Club. You need to compile data on client payments and extra services sold in a worksheet and improve its formatting.

What You Can Do

Entering Dates

- Enter a **date** when you need to indicate the timing for data. Excel stores dates as special date codes, but automatically applies a Date number format depending on how you type in the date.

- You can enter a date using one of these date formats:
  - **mm/dd/yy**, as in 1/14/12 or 01/14/12
  - **mm/dd**, as in 1/14
  - **dd-mmm-yy**, as in 14-Jan-12
  - **dd-mmm**, as in 14-Jan

  ✔ *The current year is assumed for any date entry that doesn't include a year.*

- To enter today's date quickly, press CTRL + ; and then press ENTER.
- To enter the current time, press CTRL + SHIFT + ; and then press ENTER.
- After entering a date, you can change its number format as needed. For example, you can change the date 1/14/12 to display as January 14, 2012.
- To enter a time, follow a number with a or p to indicate AM or PM, like this: 10:43 p.
- You can enter a date and time in the same cell, like this: 10/16/12 2:31 p.

Try It! Entering Dates

1. Start Excel.
2. Open the **ETry05** file from the data files for this lesson.
3. Save the file as **ETry05_studentfirstname_studentlastname** in the location where your teacher instructs you to store the files for this lesson.
4. Add a header that has your name at the left, the date code in the center, and the page number code at the right, and change back to Normal view.
5. Click cell C3 to select it.
6. Press CTRL + ;, and then press ENTER to insert the current date. It appears in the mm/dd/yyyy format.

A date code

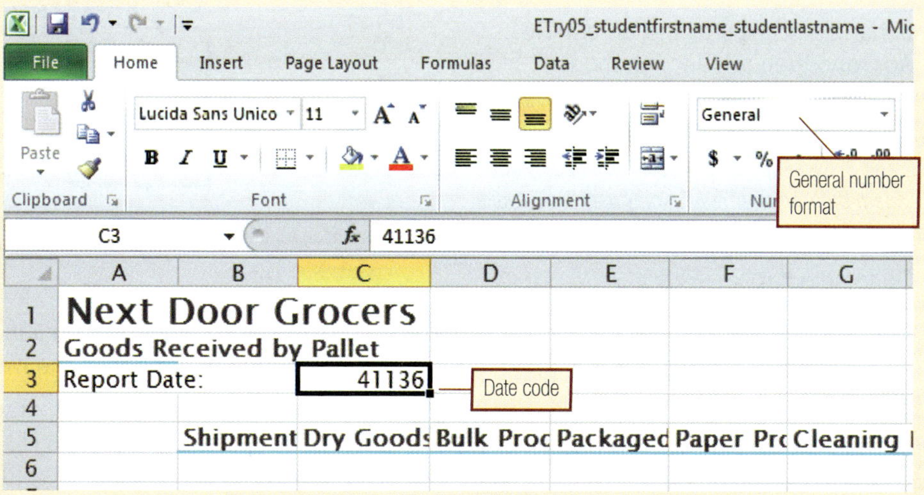

7. Click cell C3 to select it again.
8. Click Home > Number Format drop-down arrow, and then click General. The date code for the date appears in the cell. The date code that you see will vary depending on the date you entered.
9. Click Home > Number Format drop-down arrow, and then click Short Date.
10. Save the **ETry05_studentfirstname_studentlastname** file, and leave it open to use in the next Try It.

Filling a Series

- A **series** is a sequence of numbers (such as 1, 2, 3), dates (such as 10/21/12, 10/22/12, 10/23/12), times (such as 2:30, 2:45, 3:00), or text (such as January, February, March). The feature or process for creating a series in Excel is called **Auto Fill.**
- To enter a series based on the active cell, drag the **fill handle**, a small square in the lower-right corner of the active cell that turns into a plus sign (+), over the range of cells you want to fill with the series.
- Excel can create some series automatically. For example, type January in a cell, and then drag the fill handle down or to the right to create the series January, February, March, and so on.
- A yellow ScreenTip appears under the mouse pointer, displaying the cell values of the series as you drag. The series values appear in the cells after you release the mouse button.
- To create an incremental series (i.e., 1, 3, 5, 7), enter the data for the first and second cells of a series, select the two cells, and then drag the fill handle over the range of cells to fill.
- You can also use the fill handle to copy formatting only (such as bold, italics, and so on) from one cell to adjacent cells, and not its value, or the value only without formatting. To do so, click the Auto Fill Options button that appears when you perform the fill, and then click Fill Formatting Only or Fill Without Formatting.

Try It! Filling in a Series

1. In the **ETry05_studentfirstname_studentlastname** file, click cell B6 to select it.
2. Type **4/2** and press ENTER. This enters the date with the format 2-Apr.
3. Type **4/9** and press ENTER. This is the second date in the sequence that you're entering.
4. Drag over the range B6:B7 to select it.
5. Drag the fill handle down until the ScreenTip reads *30-Apr*, and then release the mouse button.

   ✔ *When you enter dates with the abbreviated format used in steps 2 and 3, Excel applies the year specified by your current system date, so your results may vary from those shown in this chapter.*
6. Click cell C6 to select it.
7. Type **1** and press CTRL + ENTER.
8. Drag the fill handle right through cell G1, and then release the mouse button.

   ✔ *Notice that a single number just repeats and doesn't automatically increment.*
9. Click cell C7 to select it.
10. Type **2** and press ENTER.
11. Drag over the range C6:C7 to select it.

Filling a series

12. Drag the fill handle down until the ScreenTip reads *5*, and then release the mouse button.
13. With the range still selected, drag the fill handle right through column G. This fills the values across the columns, replacing the 1s already in row 6.
14. Save the **ETry05_studentfirstname_studentlastname** file, and leave it open to use in the next Try It.

Aligning Data in a Cell

- When you type a label, Excel automatically aligns it to the left of the cell. Excel aligns values and dates to the right by default.
- In addition, cell entries are aligned along the bottom edge of the cell.
- To improve the appearance of a worksheet, you can change the alignment (both vertically and horizontally) of column labels, row labels, and other data.
- To align data, select the cells to format and use the buttons in the Alignment group on the Home tab.
- Align data between the top and bottom sides of a cell using the Top Align, Middle Align, or Bottom Align buttons.
- Align data between the left and right sides of a cell using the Align Text Left, Center, or Align Text Right buttons.

✔ *Use the Decrease Indent and Increase Indent buttons to add or remove space at the left end of the cell for left-aligned entries.*

Try It! Aligning Data in a Cell

1. In the **ETry05_studentfirstname_studentlastname** file, drag over the range B6:B10 to select it.
2. On the Home tab, click the Align Text Left button.
3. Drag over the range C6:G10 to select it.
4. On the Home tab, click the Center button.
5. Drag over the range A1:H1 to select it.
6. Click Home > Merge & Center.
7. Click Home > Cell Styles, and then click Accent5.
8. Click Home > Increase Font Size five times.
9. Click Home > Middle Align.

   ✔ *You will only see a subtle vertical alignment change in cell A1 at this point.*

10. Save the **ETry05_studentfirstname_studentlastname** file, and leave it open to use in the next Try It.

Center aligned cells

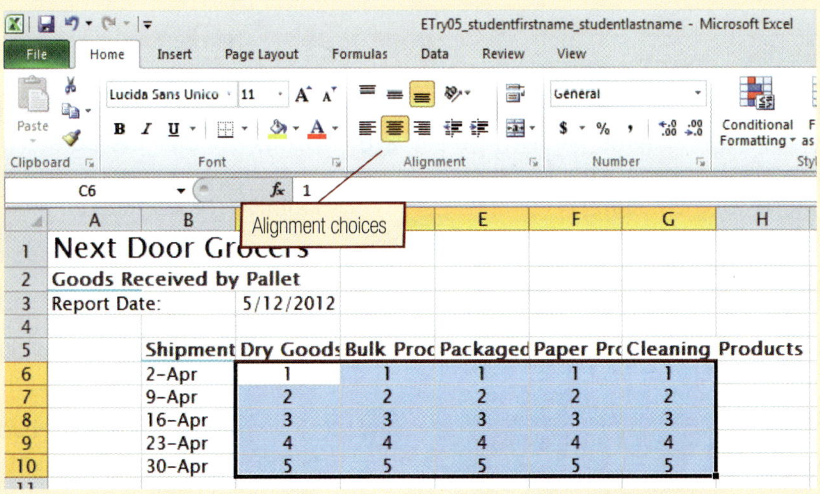

Wrapping Text in Cells

- When a cell with a long label entry is too wide to display, you can use the **wrap text** feature to wrap the text to multiple lines.
- The Wrap Text button is in the Alignment group on the Home tab of the Ribbon. Click it to apply and remove wrapping in the selected cell or range.
- Wrapping sometimes causes a line of text to break within a word, so you may need to adjust the column width for some columns after applying the wrapping.

Try It! Wrapping Text in Cells

1. In the **ETry05_studentfirstname _studentlastname** file, click cell A2 to select it.
2. On the Home tab, click the Wrap Text button.
   ✔ *You will correct the column widths soon.*
3. Drag over the range B5:G5 to select it.
4. Click Home > Wrap Text.
5. Save the **ETry05_studentfirstname _studentlastname** file, and leave it open to use in the next Try It.

Changing Column Width and Row Height

- In a workbook file using the default Office theme, the default column width is 8.43 characters in the Calibri, 11 point font. The **default column width** varies in characters depending on the theme applied.
- You can quickly adjust a column to fit the longest entry in that column by double-clicking the right border of the column header, as you've seen in earlier lessons. Drag the right border to resize the width manually.
- The default row height in a workbook using the Office theme is 15 points.
- In some cases, such as when you apply a new number format, the column width increases automatically.
- In some cases, such as when you increase the font size of text or wrap text in a cell, the row height increases automatically.
- Double-click the bottom border of the row header to fit the row size automatically. Drag the border to resize it manually.
- Drag over multiple column or row headers or over cells in multiple columns or rows to resize all the selected rows or columns at once.
- Clicking the Format button in the Cells group on the Home tab opens a menu with commands for automatically sizing (AutoFit Row Height and AutoFit Column Width) or manually sizing (Row Height and Column Width) rows and columns.

Try It! Changing Column Width and Row Height

1. In the **ETry05_studentfirstname_ studentlastname** file, move the mouse pointer over the right border of the column A column header until you see the resizing pointer, which is a vertical bar with left and right arrows.

Changing column width by dragging

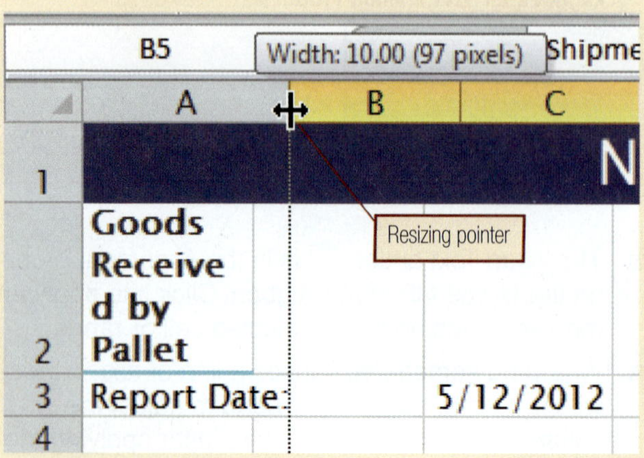

2. Drag right until the ScreenTip shows a width of 10.00, and then release the mouse button to finish resizing the column.
3. Drag over the range B5:G5 to select it.
4. Click Home > Format > Column Width.
5. Type **9.5** in the Column width text box of the Column Width dialog box, and then click OK.
6. Move the mouse pointer over the bottom border of the row 1 row header until you see the resizing pointer.
7. Drag down until the ScreenTip shows a height of 42.00, and then release the mouse button to finish resizing the row.
8. Save the **ETry05_studentfirstname_ studentlastname** file, and leave it open to use in the next Try It.

Using Keyboard Shortcuts

- You can use **keyboard shortcuts**—combinations of two or more keys pressed together or in sequence—to perform many commands in Excel.

✔ *Many keyboard shortcuts are the same as they've been in previous versions of Excel, such as* CTRL + O *to display the Open dialog box.*

- Several of the formatting choices have keyboard shortcuts, such as CTRL + B for applying bold. Move the mouse pointer over a Ribbon button, and the ScreenTip lists a keyboard shortcut if one exists.
- Pressing the ALT key displays **Key Tips**, which are keys you can press to select commands on the Ribbon.
- After pressing ALT, press the Key Tip for the desired Ribbon tab, and then the Key Tip for the command.

✔ *The Help topic "Keyboard shortcuts in Excel 2010" explains Key Tips in detail and lists all the available keyboard shortcuts.*

- You learned earlier about keyboard techniques for navigating and making selections, such as using the arrow keys to move from cell to cell.

Try It! Using Keyboard Shortcuts

1. In the **ETry05_studentfirstname_studentlastname** file, click cell C3 to select it.
2. Press ALT. The tab Key Tips appear onscreen.
3. Press P. The Page Layout tab appears.
4. Press ALT twice to redisplay the tab Key Tips.
5. Press H. The Home tab appears.
6. Press J. The Cell Styles gallery opens.
7. Press ↓ four times to select the 20%-Accent1 style, and then press ENTER.
8. Press ↓ three times and ← once to select cell B6.
9. Press and hold SHIFT and press ↓ four times to select the range B6:B10.
10. Press CTRL + B to apply bold to the selection.
11. Press CTRL + I to apply italics to the selection.
12. Press CTRL + S to save the file.
13. Press ALT + F to display the Backstage view.
14. Press X to exit Excel.

Project 9—Create It

Client Account Tracking Worksheet

DIRECTIONS

1. Start Excel, if necessary, and open the **EProj09** file from the data files for this lesson.
2. Save the file as **EProj09_studentfirstname_studentlastname** in the location where your teacher instructs you to store the files for this lesson.
3. Add a header that has your name at the left, the date code in the center, and the page number code at the right, and change back to **Normal** view.
4. Click cell **H3**, type **7/6/12**, and press ENTER.
5. Click cell **A7** to select it.
6. Double-click the **fill handle**. This automatically fills the range A7:A14 with a series of incrementing entries.
7. Click cell **B6**, type **Jan**, and press CTRL + ENTER.
8. Drag the **fill handle** right through cell **G6** to automatically fill with the series of month labels.
9. Drag over the range **B7:G7** to select it.
10. Drag the **fill handle** down through cell **G13**. This fills all the selected cells with the values from the selection.

11. Click cell **B14**, type **25**, and press TAB.
12. Type **50**, and press TAB.
13. Drag over the range **B14:C14** to select it.
14. Drag the **fill handle** right through cell **G14**. Excel fills the cells with a series that increments based on the first two entries.
15. Drag over the range **A6:H6** to select it.
16. Press ALT + H to select the Home tab and display its Key Tips.
17. Press A + R to align the labels to the right.
18. Click cell **A3** to select it.
19. Click **Home > Wrap Text**.
20. Click cell **B5** to select it.
21. Click **Home > Wrap Text**.
22. Drag over the column headers for columns A through H to select them.
23. Double-click the **column H** column header right border. This automatically AutoFits the selected columns, but notice that column B is too wide due to the entry in cell B5.
24. Press CTRL + Z to undo the column resizing.
25. Drag over the column headers for columns A through H to select them, if necessary.
26. Move the mouse over the **column H** column header right border until you see the resizing pointer, and drag left until the ScreenTip displays a width of **7.70**. The columns resize when you release the mouse button.
27. Click cell **A1** to select it.
28. Click **Home > Format > Row Height**.
29. Type **52** in the Row height text box in the Row Height dialog box, and then click **OK**.
30. Click **Home > Middle Align**. Press CTRL + S to save the file. Your worksheet should look like the one shown in Figure 5-1.
31. **With your teacher's permission**, print the worksheet. Submit the printout or the file for grading as required.
32. Press ALT + F and then C to close the file.

Figure 5-1

	A	B	C	D	E	F	G	H
1	Serenity Health Club							
2								
3	Client Account Tracking							7/6/2012
4								
5		Payments by Month						
6	Client ID	Jan	Feb	Mar	Apr	May	Jun	Total
7	A1001	$150	$150	$150	$150	$150	$150	$900
8	A1002	$150	$150	$150	$150	$150	$150	$900
9	A1003	$150	$150	$150	$150	$150	$150	$900
10	A1004	$150	$150	$150	$150	$150	$150	$900
11	A1005	$150	$150	$150	$150	$150	$150	$900
12	A1006	$150	$150	$150	$150	$150	$150	$900
13	A1007	$150	$150	$150	$150	$150	$150	$900
14	A1008	$25	$50	$75	$100	$125	$150	$525
15	Totals	$1,075	$1,100	$1,125	$1,150	$1,175	$1,200	$6,825
16								

Project 10—Apply It

Extra Services Tracking Worksheet

DIRECTIONS

1. Start Excel, if necessary, and open the **EProj10** file from the data files for this lesson.
2. Save the file as **EProj10_studentfirstname_studentlastname** in the location where your teacher instructs you to store the files for this lesson.
3. Click the **Extra Services** worksheet tab.
4. Add a header that has your name at the left, the date code in the center, and the page number code at the right, and change back to **Normal** view.
5. Click cell **A3**, type **07-06-12**, and press ENTER.
6. Click cell **F3** to select it.
7. Wrap the text and align the text right.
8. Click cell **A1** and top align the data.
9. Adjust the height of row 1 using AutoFit.
10. Click cell **B6** and fill to cell **F6** to fill with a series of label entries.
11. Click cell **A8**. Double-click the **fill handle** to fill four week labels.
12. Select the range **B8:B9.**
13. Drag the **fill handle** down to cell **B11** to fill with a series of increasing values.
14. Select the range **C8:C9**.
15. Drag the **fill handle** down to cell **C11** to fill a series of decreasing values.
16. Select the range **A5:F6.**
17. Wrap the text in the selection.
18. With the range still selected, apply bold to the entries.
19. With the range still selected, change the column width to **12**.
20. With the range still selected, apply Center alignment.
21. Resize row 7 to a height of **6.00**. A thin filled row or column like this is another method for creating a border.
22. Select the range **B11:F11** and apply the Underline style.
23. Go to cell **A1**. Your worksheet should look like the one in Figure 5-2.
24. **With your teacher's permission**, print the worksheet. Submit the printout or the file for grading as required.
25. Close the workbook, saving all changes, and exit Excel.

Figure 5-2

	A	B	C	D	E	F
1	Serenity Health Club					
2						
3	7/6/2012					Extra Services Sold
4						
5	Service Name	Swedish Massage	Aromatherapy Massage	Hot Stone Massage	Exfoliating Salt Scrub	Aromatherapy Facial
6	Service Code	Serv001	Serv002	Serv003	Serv004	Serv005
7						
8	Week 1	$525	$600	$445	$75	$150
9	Week 2	$550	$575	$550	$225	$300
10	Week 3	$575	$550	$575	$300	$450
11	Week 4	$600	$525	$425	$225	$300
12		$2,250	$2,250	$1,995	$825	$1,200

WORDS TO KNOW

Contiguous range
A block of adjacent cells in a worksheet.

Noncontiguous range
Cells in a worksheet that act as a block, but are not necessarily adjacent to each other.

Collapse Dialog box button
A button in a dialog box that you click to downsize a dialog box to make a selection on the sheet, and then click again to restore the dialog box to its regular size.

Range
A block of cells in an Excel worksheet.

Lesson 6

Working with Ranges

➤ What You Will Learn

Selecting Ranges
Entering Data by Range
Making a Range Entry Using a Collapse Dialog Box Button

Software Skills Select a group of cells (a range) to copy, move, or erase the data in them in one step, or to quickly apply the same formatting throughout the range. You also can fill a range of cells with an entry, or perform calculations on cell ranges—creating sums and averages, for example. Some dialog boxes include a Collapse Dialog box button that enables you to specify a range entry in a text box.

Application Skills You are the Principal of Overview Academy, a small private school. You want to create a worksheet to track instructor performance ratings from two prior years. You need to finish entering some of the worksheet data, including the ratings, apply some formatting, and specify the range to print.

What You Can Do

Selecting Ranges

- A **range** is an area made up of two or more cells.
- When you select cells A1, A2, and A3, for example, the range is indicated as A1:A3.
- The range A1:C5 is defined as a block of cells that includes all the cells in columns A through C in rows 1 through 5.
- A range of cells can be **contiguous** (all cells are adjacent to each other or in a solid block) or **noncontiguous** (not all cells are adjacent to each other).

- To select a contiguous range, drag over it. You also can click the first cell, press and hold SHIFT, and use the arrow keys to extend the selection or click the cell that's at the lower-right corner of the range to select.
- To select a noncontiguous range, select the first portion of the range. Then press and hold the CTRL key while dragging over additional areas or clicking additional cells. Release the CTRL key when finished selecting all the noncontiguous areas.
- When a range is selected, the active cell is displayed normally (with a white background), but the rest of the cells appear highlighted.

✔ *You also can assign a name to a range and use it to select or refer to the range. See "Using Named Ranges" in Lesson 13.*

- Clicking the column or row header selects the entire row or column. You also can press CTRL + SPACE to select the column holding the active cell or SHIFT + SPACE to select the row holding the active cell.

Try It! Selecting Ranges

1. Start Excel.
2. Open the **ETry06** file from the data files for this lesson.
3. Save the file as **ETry06_studentfirstname_studentlastname** in the location where your teacher instructs you to store the files for this lesson.
4. Add a header that has your name at the left, the date code in the center, and the page number code at the right, and change back to Normal view.
5. With cell A1 selected, press and hold the SHIFT key while pressing ↓ four times.
6. Click Home > Merge & Center.
7. Drag over the range A5:A10 to select it.

A noncontiguous range selection

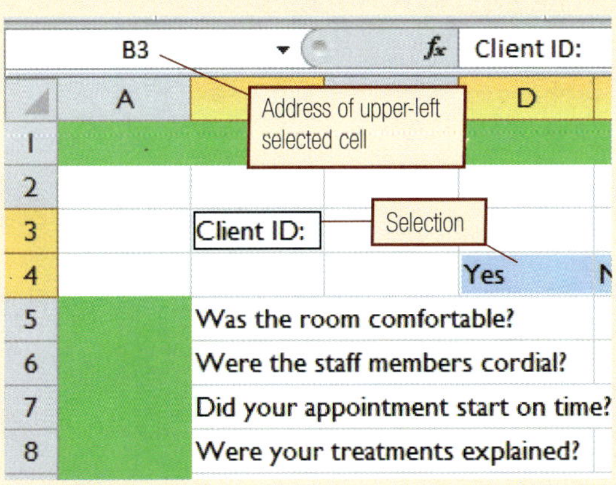

8. Click Home > Cell Styles, and then click Accent1.
9. Drag over the range D4:E4 to select it. Press and hold the CTRL key, and click cell B3.
10. Click Home > Cell Styles, and then click Accent1.
11. Click the column C column header to select the column.
12. Click Home > Cell Styles, and then click Accent1.
13. Drag over the range B5:B10 to select it.
14. Click Home > Wrap Text.
15. Move the mouse pointer over the right border of the column B column header and drag right until the ScreenTip shows a width of 20.00.
16. Click Home > Format > AutoFit Row Height.
17. Move the mouse pointer over the right border of the column C column header and drag left until the ScreenTip shows a width of 1.00.
18. Save the **ETry06_studentfirstname_studentlastname** file, and leave it open to use in the next Try It.

Entering Data by Range

- In the last lesson, you learned how to enter data by using the fill handle. There are a couple of other methods you can use to fill a range.
- To fill all the cells in a selected range with the same entry, first select the range. Then type the desired entry, and press CTRL + ENTER.
- The Fill button in the Editing group on the Home tab offers choices that enable you to fill cells in the desired direction in a selected range and to create custom series. For example, you can click Down to fill down the column, or Right to fill across the row. Click Series to create a series to fill.

Try It! Entering Data by Range

1. In the ETry06_studentfirstname_studentlastname file, drag over the range A5:A10 to select it.
2. Type 1 and press ENTER.
3. Click Home > Fill > Series.
4. In the Series dialog box, make sure the Columns and Linear options are selected and that 1 appears in the Step value text box, and then click OK.
5. Drag over the range D5:D6 to select it.
6. Press and hold CTRL, and click cells E7, D8, D9, and E10.

   ✔ *Be sure to release the CTRL key when you finish.*
7. Type X, and press CTRL + ENTER. Excel fills all the selected cells with the entry.
8. Close ETry06_studentfirstname_studentlastname, saving all changes and exit Excel.

Filling a range

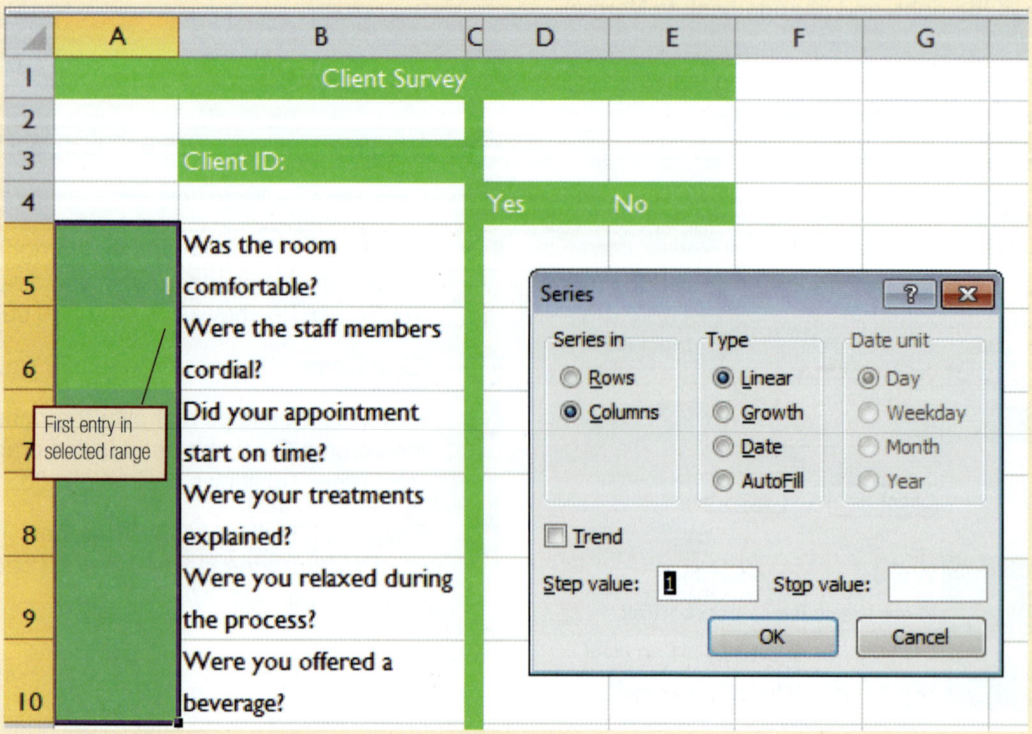

Making a Range Entry Using a Collapse Dialog Box Button

- You will most likely set options in Excel using the buttons on the Ribbon, however, occasionally, you may use a dialog box.
- Dialog boxes appear when you click the dialog box launcher within a particular group on the Ribbon.
- To enter cell addresses or ranges in a dialog box, you can click the **Collapse Dialog box button** on the right end of the text box to shrink the dialog box so you can see the worksheet and select the range, rather than type it.
- After selecting the range, click the Collapse Dialog button to restore the dialog box to its normal size, and then finalize your selections.

Try It! Making a Range Entry Using a Collapse Dialog Box Button

1. In the ETry06_studentfirstname_studentlastname file, on the Page Layout tab, in the Page Setup group, click the dialog box launcher.
2. Click the Sheet tab.
3. Click the Collapse button at the right end of the Print area text box.
4. Drag over the range A1:E10 to select it and enter it in the text box.
5. Click the Collapse button again.
6. Click OK.
7. Save the ETry06_studentfirstname_studentlastname file, and close it.

Using the Collapse button

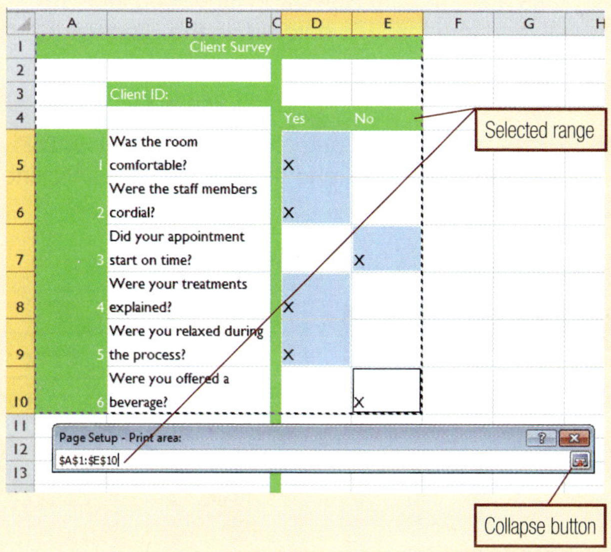

Project 11—Create It

Starting the Instructor Performance Ratings Worksheet

DIRECTIONS

1. Start Excel, if necessary, and open the **EProj11** file from the data files for this lesson.
2. Save the file as **EProj11_studentfirstname_studentlastname** in the location where your teacher instructs you to store the files for this lesson.
3. Add a header that has your name at the left, the date code in the center, and the page number code at the right, and change back to **Normal** view.
4. Click cell **B25**, type **Freida**, and press TAB.
5. Type **Randall**, and press ENTER. Cell B26 should be the active cell. If not, click cell **B26**.
6. Type **John**, and press TAB.
7. Type **Henson**, and press ENTER.
8. Drag over the range **A1:E1** to select it, and click **Home > Merge & Center**.
9. Drag over the range **A2:E2** to select it, and click **Home > Merge & Center**.

10. Drag over the range **A4:E5** to select it, and click **Home** > **Cell Styles** > **Accent2**.
11. Drag over the range **A9:E9** to select it, and click **Home** > **Cell Styles** > **Accent2**.
12. Drag over the range **A5:E5** to select it, and click **Home** > **Wrap Text** and then **Home** > **Center**.
13. Click cell **A6** to select it.
14. Type **1**, and press [ENTER].
15. Drag over the range **A6:E6** to select it.
16. Click **Home > Fill > Series**.
17. Make sure that the Rows and Linear options are selected and that **1** is entered as the Step value, and click **OK**.
18. Drag over the range **D11:D12** to select it.
19. Press and hold [CTRL], and click cells **D15**, **D18**, **D21**, **D22**, and **D26**. Be sure to release [CTRL] after clicking the last cell.
20. Type **3**, and press [CTRL] + [ENTER].
21. Click cell **D19** to select it.
22. Type **4**, and press [CTRL] + [ENTER].
23. Select the range **D19:D20** to select it.
24. Click **Home** > **Fill** > **Down**.
25. Drag over the column headings for columns **A** through **E**.
26. Right-click the selected column headings, and click **Column Width**.
27. Type **11** in the Column width text box, and click OK.
28. Press [CTRL] + [HOME]. Your worksheet should look like the one in Figure 6-1.
29. **With your teacher's permission**, print the worksheet. Submit the printout or the file for grading as required.
30. Close the workbook, saving all changes, and exit Excel.

Figure 6-1

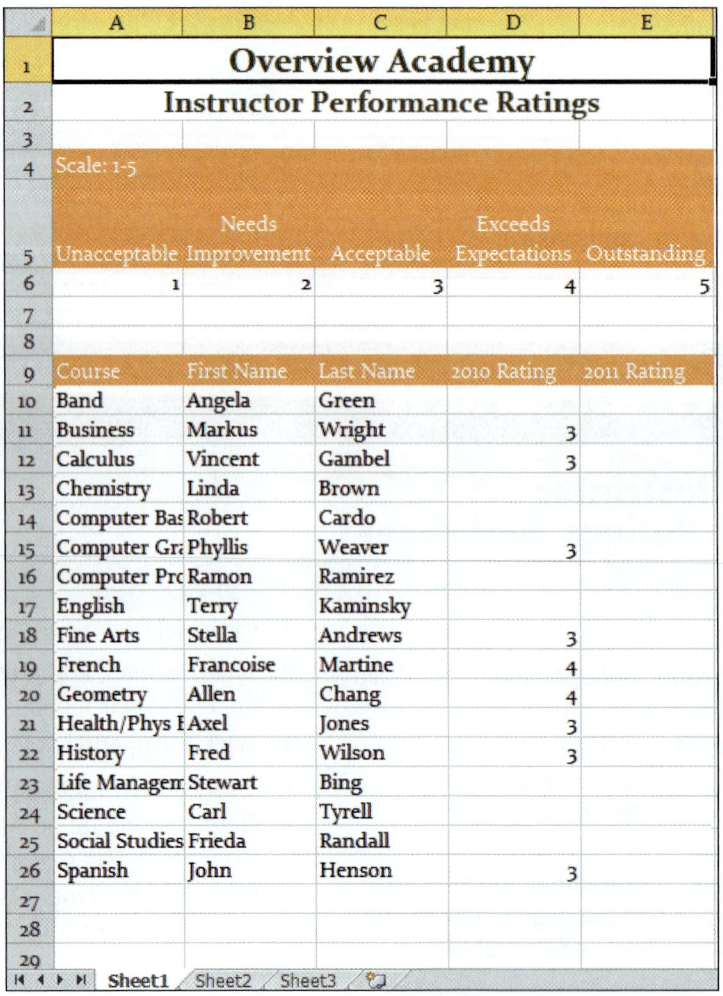

	A	B	C	D	E
1	Overview Academy				
2	Instructor Performance Ratings				
3					
4	Scale: 1-5				
5	Unacceptable	Needs Improvement	Acceptable	Exceeds Expectations	Outstanding
6	1	2	3	4	5
7					
8					
9	Course	First Name	Last Name	2010 Rating	2011 Rating
10	Band	Angela	Green		
11	Business	Markus	Wright	3	
12	Calculus	Vincent	Gambel	3	
13	Chemistry	Linda	Brown		
14	Computer Bas	Robert	Cardo		
15	Computer Gra	Phyllis	Weaver	3	
16	Computer Pro	Ramon	Ramirez		
17	English	Terry	Kaminsky		
18	Fine Arts	Stella	Andrews	3	
19	French	Francoise	Martine	4	
20	Geometry	Allen	Chang	4	
21	Health/Phys E	Axel	Jones	3	
22	History	Fred	Wilson	3	
23	Life Managem	Stewart	Bing		
24	Science	Carl	Tyrell		
25	Social Studies	Frieda	Randall		
26	Spanish	John	Henson	3	
27					
28					
29					

Project 12—Apply It

Completing the Instructor Performance Ratings Worksheet

DIRECTIONS

1. Start Excel, if necessary, and open the **EProj12** file from the data files for this lesson.
2. Save the file as **EProj12_studentfirstname_studentlastname** in the location where your teacher instructs you to store the files for this lesson.
3. Add a header that has your name at the left, the date code in the center, and the page number code at the right, and change back to **Normal** view.
4. Adjust the width of **column A** using AutoFit.
5. Drag over the range **A8:E8** to select it.
6. Open the **Alignment** dialog box, and click the **Alignment** tab, if necessary.
7. Open the **Horizontal** drop-down list and click **Fill**. Then click **OK**. This fills the selected range with the symbol character in cell A8, another way of creating a border.
8. Select the following non-contiguous cells: **D10**, **E10**, **E17**, **E18**, **E22**, **E23**, and **E25**.
9. Type **4**, and press CTRL + ENTER.
10. Click cell **E11** to select it.
11. Type **5**, and press CTRL + ENTER.
12. Fill the range **E12:E14** with the same value.
13. Enter the following data in the blank cells in column D:
    a. 5
    b. 5
    c. 2
    d. 2
    e. 5
    f. 5
    g. 2
14. Enter the following data in the blank cells in column E:
    a. 3
    b. 3
    c. 5
    d. 5
    e. 4
    f. 3
    g. 2
15. Open the **Page Setup** dialog box, and on the **Sheet** tab, set the Print area to **A1:E26**.
16. **With your teacher's permission**, print the worksheet. Submit the printout or the file for grading as required.
17. Close the workbook, saving all changes, and exit Excel.

Lesson 7

Creating Formulas

WORDS TO KNOW

Arithmetic (mathematical) operators
Symbols used in mathematical operations: + for addition, - for subtraction, * for multiplication, / for division, and ^ for exponentiation.

Formula
An instruction Excel uses to calculate a result.

Order of precedence
The order in which Excel performs the mathematical operations specified in a formula, based on the types of mathematical operators used.

SUM function
A built-in calculation used to add a range of values together.

➤ What You Will Learn

Entering a Formula
Using Arithmetic Operators
Editing a Formula
Copying a Formula Using the Fill Handle
Using the SUM Function

Software Skills Creating formulas to perform calculations in Excel provides one if its powerful benefits: automatic recalculation. When you make a change to a cell that is referenced in a formula, Excel automatically recalculates the formula to reflect the change and displays the new formula result.

Application Skills You are the Accounts Receivable Supervisor at the Serenity Health Club. You have some new data in a spreadsheet, and need to add basic formulas to calculate the data.

What You Can Do

Entering a Formula

- A **formula** is a worksheet instruction that performs a calculation.
- Enter a formula in the cell where the result should display.
- As you type a formula, it displays in the cell and in the formula bar.
- If you enter a long formula in a cell, that text may not fully display in the formula bar. You can expand the formula bar (make it taller) by clicking the Expand Formula Bar button at the right end of the formula bar.
- After you enter a formula in the cell, the answer displays in the cell while the formula appears in the formula bar when the cell is selected.
- Use cell or range references, values, and mathematical operators in formulas.

✔ *A formula can also contain Excel's predefined functions, which are covered in Lesson 11, or use named ranges, which are covered in Lesson 13.*

- You must start each formula by typing the equal sign (=). For example, the formula =B2+B4+B6 adds the values in those three cell locations together.
- When you change the value in a cell that is referenced in a formula, the answer in the formula cell automatically changes.
- When typing a percentage as a value in a formula, you can enter it with the percent symbol or as a decimal.
- You can click a cell or drag a range to enter its address in the formula. This method can be more accurate than typing in cell or range addresses.

Try It! Entering a Formula

1. Start Excel.
2. Open the **ETry07** file from the data files for this lesson.
3. Save the file as **ETry07_studentfirstname_studentlastname** in the location where your teacher instructs you to store the files for this lesson.
4. Add a header that has your name at the left, the date code in the center, and the page number code at the right, and change back to Normal view.
5. Click cell F4 to select it.
6. Type **=D4+E4**, and press ENTER.
7. Click cell D5 to select it.
8. Type **=**, click cell B5, type *****, and click cell C5.

Entering a formula

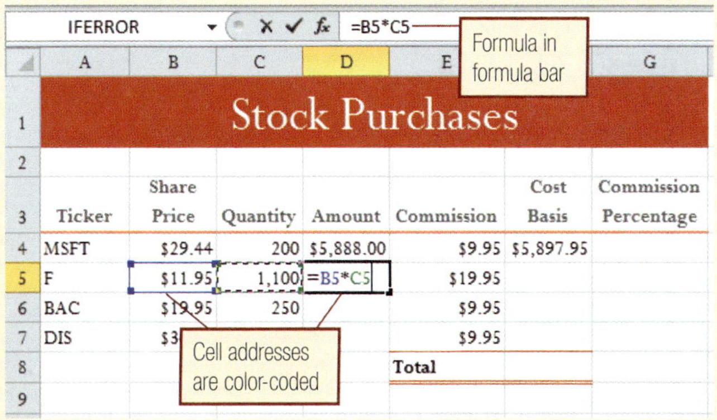

9. Press ENTER to finish the formula.
10. Save the **ETry07_studentfirstname_studentlastname** file, and leave it open to use in the next Try It.

Using Arithmetic Operators

- Use the following standard **arithmetic (mathematical) operators** in formulas:
  - \+ Addition
  - \- Subtraction
  - * Multiplication
  - / Division
  - ^ Exponentiation
- Excel performs mathematical operations in a particular order, called **order of precedence**. This is the order in which Excel calculates:
  1. Operations enclosed in parentheses.
  2. Exponentiation.
  3. Multiplication and division.
  4. Addition and subtraction.
- When a formula has multiple operators of the same precedence level, such as multiple multiplication operations, Excel performs the calculations from left to right.
- Keeping the order of mathematical operations in mind, the easiest way to control which part of a complex formula is calculated first is to simply use parentheses. Here are two examples:

  =8+3*5 result: 23
  Excel multiplies first, then adds

  =(8+3)*5 result: 55
  Excel adds the values in parentheses, then multiplies

Try It! Using Arithmetic Operators

1. In the **ETry07_studentfirstname_studentlastname** file, click cell G4 to select it.
2. Type **=E4/F4** and press ENTER.
3. Press ← to select cell F5.
4. Type **=B5*C5+E5** and press TAB.
5. Type **=E5/(B5*C5+E5)** and press ENTER.

   ✔ *The two formulas you just entered are alternate ways of performing calculations you created earlier. You could also enter these formulas as* ***=D5+E5*** *and* ***=E5/F5****, and they would also calculate the correct results.*
6. Save the **ETry07_studentfirstname_studentlastname** file, and leave it open to use in the next Try It.

Editing a Formula

- Excel automatically provides assistance in correcting common mistakes in a formula (for example, omitting a closing parenthesis).
- You can edit a formula as needed to update its calculation or if you see an error message such as #NUM! or #REF! in the cell.
- Editing a formula works just like editing any other data in a cell. Click the cell, and then press F2 or double-click the cell to enter edit mode. Work in the cell or the formula bar to make the changes, and then press ENTER or click the Enter button ✓ on the formula bar to finish the entry.

Try It! Editing a Formula

1. In the **ETry07_studentfirstname_studentlastname** file, click cell F5 to select it, and press F2 to enter edit mode.
2. Drag over B5*C5 in the cell, click cell D5 to replace the selection, and press TAB to finish the change.
3. With cell G5 selected, drag over (B5*C5+E5) in the formula bar to select it.
4. Type **F5** to replace the selected part of the formula, and press ENTER.
5. Save the **ETry07_studentfirstname_studentlastname** file, and leave it open to use in the next Try It.

Editing in the formula bar

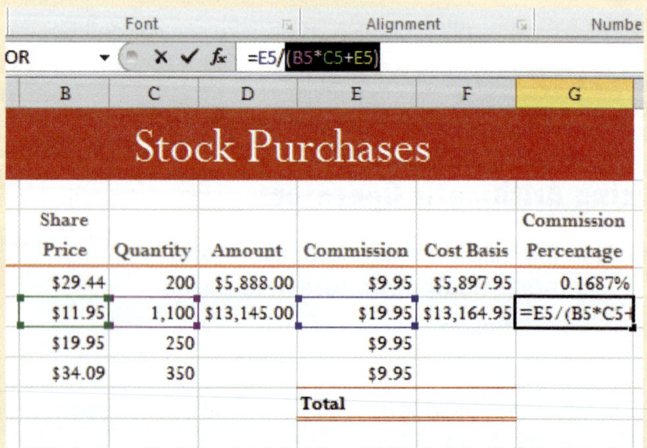

Copying a Formula Using the Fill Handle

- You can use the fill feature to copy a formula that you've created to the cells below or to the right of it.
- Excel automatically adjusts cell addresses so the filled formulas apply to the correct data.

  ✔ *Lesson 8 explains more about how and why Excel adjusts cell and range addresses.*
- Drag the fill handle over the range of cells to fill with the formula.
- Also use the Fill button in the Editing group on the Home tab to fill formulas.

Try It! Copying a Formula Using the Fill Handle

1. In the **ETry07_studentfirstname_ studentlastname** file, click cell D5 to select it.
2. Drag the fill handle down through cell D7 to fill the formula.
3. Click cell F5 to select it.
4. Drag the fill handle down through cell F7 to fill the formula.
5. Click cell G5 to select it.
6. Drag the fill handle down through cell G7 to fill the formula.
7. Save the **ETry07_studentfirstname_ studentlastname** file, and leave it open to use in the next Try It.

Using the SUM Function

- The most basic and perhaps most often used function is the **SUM function**, which adds the values in the specified cells or range together.
- You can enter the SUM function by typing it into the cell just like any other cell entry. For example, you could enter =SUM(A6,A9,B12) or =SUM(A6:B9).

  ✔ *Formulas and functions are not case sensitive, so an entry like =sum(a6:b9) would calculate correctly. This book shows cell addresses, formulas, and functions in uppercase to make them easier to read in the text.*

- Enclose the cell addresses or range to sum in parentheses, and use commas to separate individual cell references.
- Enter the SUM function more quickly using one of the following three methods:
  - Press ALT + =.
  - Click the Sum button Σ ▾ in the Editing group on the Home tab. Note that this button is also called the AutoSum button, because it looks identical to the AutoSum button found in earlier versions of Excel.
  - Click the AutoSum button Σ AutoSum ▾ in the Function Library group on the Formulas tab.

Try It! Using the Sum Function

1. In the **ETry07_studentfirstname_ studentlastname** file, click cell F8 to select it.
2. Click Home > Sum Σ ▾. Excel automatically starts the formula and selects the range above it.

   ✔ *If the selected range is incorrect, you can drag to change it.*

3. Press ENTER to finish the SUM formula.
4. Close **ETry07_studentfirstname_student lastname**, saving all changes, and exit Excel.

Summing a column of data

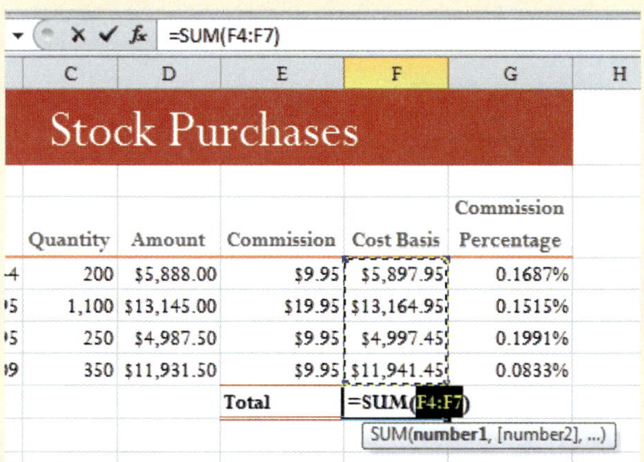

Project 13—Create It

Entering First Formulas in the Extra Services Worksheet

DIRECTIONS

1. Start Excel, if necessary, and open the **EProj13** file from the data files for this lesson.
2. Save the file as **EProj13_studentfirstname_studentlastname** in the location where your teacher instructs you to store the files for this lesson.
3. Add a header that has your name at the left, the date code in the center, and the page number code at the right, and change back to **Normal** view.
4. Click cell **B12**, type **=B8+B9+B10+B11**, and press ENTER twice.
5. Type **=B12/G12**, and press ENTER. Excel should display a #DIV/0! error message, as cell G12 is currently empty.
6. Click cell **C12** to select it.
7. Type **=sum(C8:C11)**, and press ENTER.
8. Click cell **G8** to select it.
9. Type **=B8+C8+D8+E8+F8**, and press ENTER. Your worksheet should look like the one shown in Figure 7-1.
10. **With your teacher's permission**, print the worksheet. Submit the printout or the file for grading as required.
11. Close the workbook, saving all changes, and exit Excel

Figure 7-1

	A	B	C	D	E	F	G
1	Serenity Health Club						
2							
3	9/4/2012						Extra Services Sold
4							
5	Service Name	Swedish Massage	Aromatherapy Massage	Hot Stone Massage	Exfoliating Salt Scrub	Aromatherapy Facial	Weekly Total
6	Service Code	Serv001	Serv002	Serv003	Serv004	Serv005	
7							
8	Week 1	$665	$600	$445	$400	$150	$2,260
9	Week 2	$550	$600	$550	$225	$300	
10	Week 3	$575	$550	$575	$300	$450	
11	Week 4	$600	$550	$625	$225	$300	
12	Total	$2,390	$2,300				
13							
14	Percentage	#DIV/0!					

Project 14—Apply It

Completing the Formulas in the Extra Services Worksheet

DIRECTIONS

1. Start Excel, if necessary, and open the **EProj14** file from the data files for this lesson.
2. Save the file as **EProj14_studentfirstname_studentlastname** in the location where your teacher instructs you to store the files for this lesson.
3. Add a header that has your name at the left, the date code in the center, and the page number code at the right, and change back to **Normal** view.
4. Click cell **D12** to select it and sum the values in the cells above.
5. Drag the fill handle right through cell **G12** to fill the formula.
6. Click cell **G8** and double-click the fill handle to fill the entry down the column.
7. Click cell **B14** and drag the fill handle right through cell **F14**. When you release the mouse button, you should see the error message #DIV/0! in each of the filled cells. This is because Excel changed the reference to cell G12, which holds the overall total, and you don't want it to do that.
8. Edit each of the formulas in the range **C14:F14** to change the divisor (the right cell address) to **G12**.
9. Select the range **B14:F14**. Look in the status bar next to the view buttons. The sum displayed there should be 100.00%, meaning that the corrected formulas each accurately calculate the percentage of the total. Your worksheet should look like the one shown in Figure 7-2.

   ✔ *When you want to see a quick sum of cells without building a formula, drag over the cells and check the status bar.*

10. **With your teacher's permission**, print the worksheet. Submit the printout or the file for grading as required.
11. Close the workbook, saving all changes, and exit Excel.

Figure 7-2

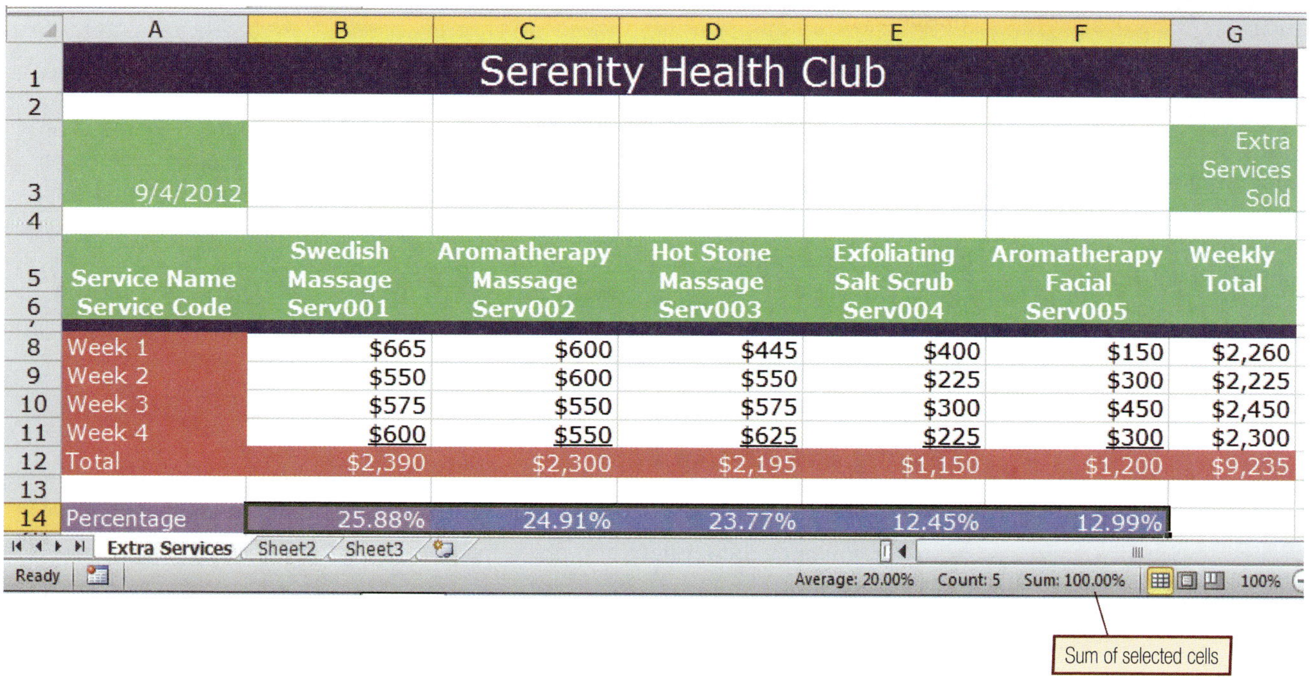

	A	B	C	D	E	F	G
1	Serenity Health Club						
2							
3	9/4/2012						Extra Services Sold
4							
5	Service Name	Swedish Massage	Aromatherapy Massage	Hot Stone Massage	Exfoliating Salt Scrub	Aromatherapy Facial	Weekly Total
6	Service Code	Serv001	Serv002	Serv003	Serv004	Serv005	
8	Week 1	$665	$600	$445	$400	$150	$2,260
9	Week 2	$550	$600	$550	$225	$300	$2,225
10	Week 3	$575	$550	$575	$300	$450	$2,450
11	Week 4	$600	$550	$625	$225	$300	$2,300
12	Total	$2,390	$2,300	$2,195	$1,150	$1,200	$9,235
13							
14	Percentage	25.88%	24.91%	23.77%	12.45%	12.99%	

Lesson 8

Copying and Pasting

WORDS TO KNOW

Absolute reference
A cell address in a formula that will not change when you copy the formula to another location. Dollar signs in the cell reference indicate when it's absolute.

Clipboard
A Windows feature that holds data or graphics that you cut or copy prior to pasting into another location.

Copy
The command used to place a copy of data from the selected cell or range on the Clipboard.

Format Painter
A tool that enables you to copy formatting from a cell and apply it to another cell or range.

Paste
The command used to place data from the Clipboard to a location on the worksheet.

Relative reference
A cell address that can change in a copied formula, so the new address is expressed in relation to the cell containing the copied formula. If you copy a formula to a cell one row down, the row numbers in all relative references increase by one, for example A5 becomes A6.

➤ What You Will Learn

Copying and Pasting Data
Copying Formats
Copying Formulas Containing a Relative Reference
Copying Formulas Containing an Absolute Reference

Software Skills Excel provides many time-saving shortcuts to help you enter data and build formulas in your worksheets. For example, you can use the copy and paste features to reuse data and formulas in the same worksheet, in another worksheet, or in another workbook. You also can copy formats. When copying formulas, you need to understand how to keep a cell reference from changing when needed.

Application Skills As an Adventure Coordinator for Voyager Travel Adventures, you make all the arrangements necessary to create a unique and thrilling adventure vacation for your clients. Today, the Tell City Thrill Seekers Club has asked for an estimate of expenses per person for a special trip that combines white water rafting, back country hiking, and rock climbing. You have started both a trip budget for the club and a profit worksheet. To complete the two worksheets, you need to copy formulas, data, and formatting.

What You Can Do

Copying and Pasting Data

- When you **copy** data, the copy is placed on the **Clipboard.**
- After you copy data, **paste** it to place the copy from the Clipboard to the new location.

- You can copy labels, values, and formulas to another cell, a range of cells, another worksheet, or another workbook. You also can copy Excel data to documents created in other programs, such as Word.
- To copy a selected cell or range of data to a new location, use the Copy and Paste buttons in the Clipboard group on the Home tab of the Ribbon.

  ✔ *CTRL + C and CTRL + V are the shortcuts for copying and pasting.*
- If the cells to which you want to copy data are adjacent to the original cell, you can use the fill handle to copy the data.
- Excel automatically copies the formats applied to data, which overrides any formatting in the destination cell.
- You can copy just the data and formulas without copying formatting.
- Pasting overwrites data in the destination cell or range.
- You can link data as you paste it so the data changes automatically whenever the original data changes. Lesson 36 explains how to link data.

Try It! Copying and Pasting Data

1. Start Excel.
2. Open the **ETry08** file from the data files for this lesson.
3. Save the file as **ETry08_studentfirstname_studentlastname** in the location where your teacher instructs you to store the files for this lesson.
4. Add a header that has your name at the left, the date code in the center, and the page number code at the right, and change back to Normal view.
5. Drag over the range A3:E4 to select it.

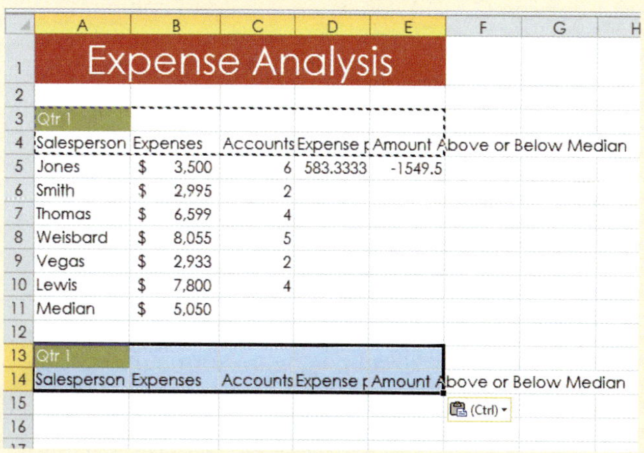

6. Click Home > Copy.
7. Click cell A13 to select it.
8. Click Home > Paste.
9. Drag over the range A5:C11 to select it.
10. Click Home > Copy.
11. Click cell A15 to select it.
12. Click Home > Paste drop-down arrow > Values. Excel pastes the range without pasting the formatting applied in the original range.

    ✔ *Clicking the bottom half of the Paste button, with the arrow on it, displays a menu with additional paste options. For example, you can paste formulas, formulas with number formatting, keep the column widths, and so on.*
13. Press ESC to remove the selection marquee from the copied range.
14. Click cell B21 to select it. You still need a formula in this cell, so you need to update it.
15. Type **=MEDIAN(B15:B20** and press ENTER. Excel automatically fills in the closing parenthesis for you.
16. Save the **ETry08_studentfirstname_studentlastname** file, and leave it open to use in the next Try It.

Copying Formats

- You can copy formatting from one cell to another, without copying the original cell's value.
- The Format Painter button in the Clipboard group on the Home tab enables you to copy formatting from one cell to another.
- **Format Painter** copies a cell's font, font size, font color, border, fill color, number formats, column widths (in some cases), cell alignment, and conditional formatting (formatting that depends on the current value in a cell).
- Select the cell with the formatting to copy, and then on the Home tab, in the Clipboard group, click Format Painter . Click a destination cell or drag over a destination range to apply formatting in that location.
- To paste the formatting to multiple areas, double-click the Format Painter button . It will remain on until you click it again or press ESC to turn it off.

Try It! Copying Formats

1. In the **ETry08_studentfirstname_studentlastname** file, click cell E4 to select it.
2. Click Home > Wrap Text .
3. Click Home > Format Painter .
4. Drag over cells A4:D4 to copy the wrapping to them.
5. Click the column header for column C, and drag its right border to the right to resize the column to a width of 9.00.
6. Click cell E4 to select it.
7. Click Home > Format Painter .
8. Drag over cells D14:E14 to copy the wrapping to them.
9. Click cell B5 to select it.
10. Double-click the Format Painter button .
11. Drag over cells D5:E11 to copy the number formatting.
12. Scroll down and drag over cells B15:B21 to copy the number formatting.
13. Press ESC .
14. Save the **ETry08_studentfirstname_studentlastname** file, and leave it open to use in the next Try It.

Copying Formulas Containing a Relative Reference

- Formulas often have **relative references** to cells. This means that if you copy the formula to another location, the cell reference changes to reflect the position of its copied location relative to the original location.
- For example, the formula =B4+B5 entered in column B becomes =C4+C5 when copied to column C, =D4+D5 when copied to column D, and so on.
- Relative references make it easy to copy formulas across a row to total values above, for example.
- Relative references also work best when you want to fill formulas across a row or down a column.

Try It! Copying Formulas Containing a Relative Reference

1. In the **ETry08_studentfirstname_studentlastname** file, scroll down so row 4 is the first row visible.
2. Click cell D5 to select it.
3. Click Home > Copy .
4. Drag over the range D6:D10 to select it.
5. Press ENTER . Excel pastes the formula to fill the destination range.

   ✔ *In some cases, you can select a range or click in the upper-left cell of a range and press ENTER to complete a paste rather than using the Paste button.*
6. Drag over the range D5:D10 to select it.

(continued)

Try It! Copying Formulas Containing a Relative Reference *(continued)*

A pasted formula with relative references

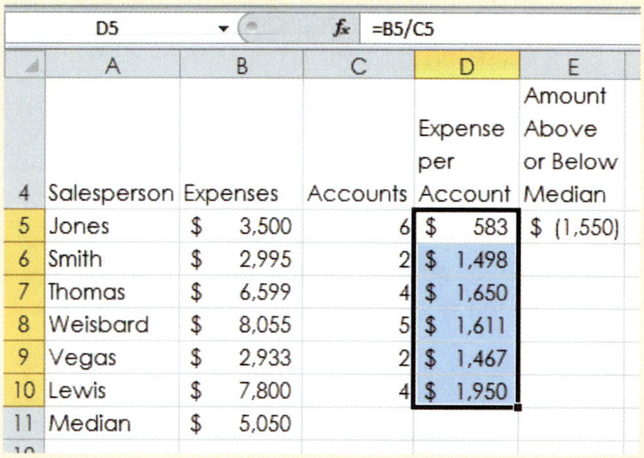
D5 =B5/C5

	A	B	C	D	E
4	Salesperson	Expenses	Accounts	Expense per Account	Amount Above or Below Median
5	Jones	$ 3,500	6	$ 583	$ (1,550)
6	Smith	$ 2,995	2	$ 1,498	
7	Thomas	$ 6,599	4	$ 1,650	
8	Weisbard	$ 8,055	5	$ 1,611	
9	Vegas	$ 2,933	2	$ 1,467	
10	Lewis	$ 7,800	4	$ 1,950	
11	Median	$ 5,050			

7. Press [CTRL]+[C].
8. Click cell D15 to select it.
9. Press [CTRL]+[V].
10. Click cell B15 to select it.
11. Type **4240** and press [ENTER]. The value in cell D15 recalculates as you'd expect.
12. Click cell D15 to select it. The cell references in the formula have been updated to refer correctly to other cells on row 15.
13. Save the **ETry08_studentfirstname_studentlastname** file, and leave it open to use in the next Try It.

Copying Formulas Containing an Absolute Reference

- Sometimes, you do not want a cell reference to change when you copy the formula, so you need to create an **absolute reference**.
- To make a cell reference absolute, enter a dollar sign ($) before both the column letter and row number of that cell in the formula.
- For example, the formula =$B$4+$B$5 contained in a cell in column B remains =$B$4+$B$5 when copied to column C. The cell addresses do not adjust based on the new formula location.
- You can also create mixed cell references, where the column letter part of a cell address is absolute, and the row number is relative, or vice-versa.
- For example, the formula =B$4+B$5 contained in a cell in column B changes to =C$4+C$5 when copied to any cell in column C. The cell addresses partially adjust based on the new formula location.
- Press the [F4] key as you type a cell reference in a formula to change to an absolute reference. Pressing [F4] additional times cycles through the mixed references and then returns to a relative reference.

Try It! Copying a Formula Using an Absolute Reference

1. In the **ETry08_studentfirstname_studentlastname** file, click cell E5 to select it.
2. Drag the fill handle down through cell E10 to fill the formula. Cell E8 displays an error message, so you know there must be a problem with the copied formula.
3. Click cell E5 to select it again. Notice that it subtracts the median value calculated in cell B11 from Jones' expenses. You need for each of the formulas in the column to subtract the value in B11 rather than changing, so you need to change to an absolute reference for cell B11.

Copying a formula with an absolute reference

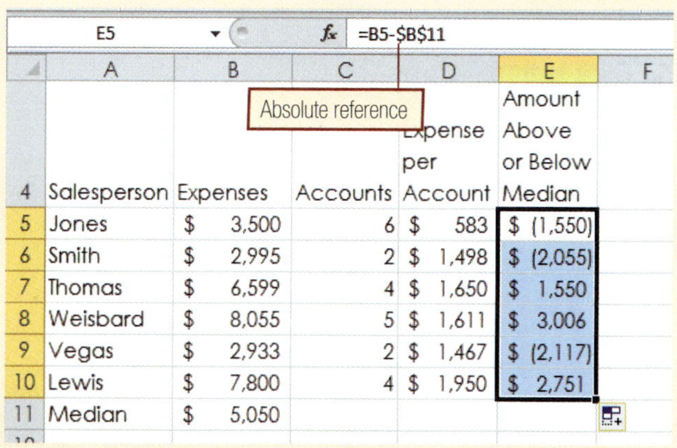

E5 =B5-$B$11

	A	B	C	D	E	F
4	Salesperson	Expenses	Accounts	Expense per Account	Amount Above or Below Median	
5	Jones	$ 3,500	6	$ 583	$ (1,550)	
6	Smith	$ 2,995	2	$ 1,498	$ (2,055)	
7	Thomas	$ 6,599	4	$ 1,650	$ 1,550	
8	Weisbard	$ 8,055	5	$ 1,611	$ 3,006	
9	Vegas	$ 2,933	2	$ 1,467	$ (2,117)	
10	Lewis	$ 7,800	4	$ 1,950	$ 2,751	
11	Median	$ 5,050				

(continued)

Try It! Copying a Formula Using an Absolute Reference *(continued)*

4. Press F2 to enter edit mode.
5. Press F4 to add dollar signs for the row letter and column number for cell B11 in the formula, and then press ENTER to finish the change.
6. Click cell E5 to select it.
7. Drag the fill handle down through cell E10 to fill the formula. Now it fills correctly.
8. With the range E5:E10 still selected, click Home > Copy.
9. Click cell E15 to select it.
10. Click Home > Paste. Look at the formula bar. The absolute reference in the formula still refers to cell B11, but for this set of data, you need for it to refer to cell B21.
11. Click cell E15 to select it.
12. Use the method of your choice to change the absolute reference in the formula from $B$11 to **$B$21**.
13. With cell E15 selected, drag the fill handle down through cell E20 to fill the formula.
14. Close the **ETry08_studentfirstname_studentlastname** file, saving all changes, and exit Excel.

Project 15—Create It

Copying Between the Trip Budget and Profit Worksheets

DIRECTIONS

1. Start Excel, if necessary, and open the **EProj15** file from the data files for this lesson.
2. Save the file as **EProj15_studentfirstname_studentlastname** in the location where your teacher instructs you to store the files for this lesson.
3. Add a header that has your name at the left, the date code in the center, and the page number code at the right for each sheet, and change back to **Normal** view.
4. Click cell **D9** to select it.
5. Click **Home > Copy**.
6. Drag over the range **D10:D19** to select it.
7. Click **Home > Paste**.
8. Drag over the range **A9:D19** to select it.
9. Click **Home > Copy**.
10. Click the **Profit** worksheet tab.
11. Click cell **A9** to select it.
12. Click **Home > Paste**. Your worksheet should look like the one shown in Figure 8-1.
13. **With your teacher's permission,** print both worksheets. Submit the printouts or the file for grading as required.
14. Close the workbook, saving all changes, and exit Excel

	A	B	C	D	E	F	G
1	Voyager Travel Adventures						
2							
3	Eco Wilderness Adventure						
4	Tell City Thrill Seekers Club			Discount amount			35%
5	10/6/12-10/12/12			Commission			0
6							
7							
8	Item	Their Cost per Unit	Units	Their Total Cost	Our Cost per Unit	Our Total Cost	Our Profit
9	Bus to white water launch point (30 adventurers, max)	$1,125	1	$1,125	731.25		
10	White water raft, first day (4 adventurers max)	$450	3	$1,350			
11	White water raft, second day (4 adventurers max)	$450	3	$1,350			
12	River gear rental	$110	12	$1,320			
13	Transportation of gear to hike point	$1,500	1	$1,500			
14	Camping gear rental per person	$25	12	$300			
15	Hiking guides (1 per 4 adventurers), three days	$150	9	$1,350			
16	Rock climbing gear rental per person	$125	12	$1,500			
17	Food and water, per person	$275	12	$3,300			
18	Bus return trip (30 adventurers, max)	$1,675	1	$1,675			
19	Adventurer's insurance	$315	12	$3,780			
20				$18,550		0	0
21							

Figure 8-1

Project 16—Apply It

Finishing the Trip Profit Worksheet

DIRECTIONS

1. Start Excel, if necessary, and open the **EProj16** file from the data files for this lesson.
2. Save the file as **EProj16_studentfirstname_studentlastname** in the location where your teacher instructs you to store the files for this lesson.
3. Add a header that has your name at the left, the date code in the center, and the page number code at the right for each sheet, and change back to **Normal** view.
4. Go to the **Profit** sheet.
5. Select cell **E9,** copy the formula, and paste the formula to the range **E10:E19**. There is an error message in cell E13, so you know there's a problem with the formula.
6. Undo the paste.
7. Click cell **E9**. Notice that to calculate the discounted price, the formula has to use the discount percentage in cell G4. That cell reference needs to be changed to an absolute reference for the formula to copy correctly.
8. In Edit mode, change the **G4** cell reference, to an absolute reference.
9. Copy cell **E9** again and paste it to the range **E10:E19**.
10. Enter the formula **=C9*E9** in cell **F9**. Copy or fill the formula down through cell **F19**.
11. Enter the formula **=D9-F9** in cell **G9**. Copy or fill the formula down through cell **G19**.
12. Format cell **E9** with the **Currency** number format with two decimal places, if it doesn't already appear with that format.
13. Copy the format in cell **E9** to the ranges **E10:E19** and **F9:G20**.
14. Select cells **F20:G20**, and apply the **Total** cell style to them.
15. Click cell **G5** and apply the **Currency** number format to it. Your worksheet should look like the one shown in Figure 8-2.
16. **With your teacher's permission**, print the **Profit** worksheet. Submit the printout or the file for grading as required.
17. Close the workbook, saving all changes, and exit Excel.

Figure 8-2

	A	B	C	D	E	F	G
2							
3	Eco Wilderness Adventure						
4	Tell City Thrill Seekers Club			Discount amount			35%
5	10/6/12-10/12/12			Commission			$649.25
6							
7							
8	**Item**	**Their Cost per Unit**	**Units**	**Their Total Cost**	**Our Cost per Unit**	**Our Total Cost**	**Our Profit**
9	Bus to white water launch point (30 adventurers, max)	$1,125	1	$1,125	$731.25	$731.25	$393.75
10	White water raft, first day (4 adventurers max)	$450	3	$1,350	$292.50	$877.50	$472.50
11	White water raft, second day (4 adventurers max)	$450	3	$1,350	$292.50	$877.50	$472.50
12	River gear rental	$110	12	$1,320	$71.50	$858.00	$462.00
13	Transportation of gear to hike point	$1,500	1	$1,500	$975.00	$975.00	$525.00
14	Camping gear rental per person	$25	12	$300	$16.25	$195.00	$105.00
15	Hiking guides (1 per 4 adventurers), three days	$150	9	$1,350	$97.50	$877.50	$472.50
16	Rock climbing gear rental per person	$125	12	$1,500	$81.25	$975.00	$525.00
17	Food and water, per person	$275	12	$3,300	$178.75	$2,145.00	$1,155.00
18	Bus return trip (30 adventurers, max)	$1,675	1	$1,675	$1,088.75	$1,088.75	$586.25
19	Adventurer's insurance	$315	12	$3,780	$204.75	$2,457.00	$1,323.00
20				**$18,550**		**$12,057.50**	**$6,492.50**
21							
22							

Lesson 9

Techniques for Moving Data

WORDS TO KNOW

Cut
The command used to remove data from a cell or range of cells and place it on the Clipboard.

Drag-and-drop
A method used to move or copy the contents of a range of cells by dragging the border of a selection from one location in a worksheet and dropping it in another location.

➤ What You Will Learn

Inserting and Deleting Columns and Rows
Cutting and Pasting Data
Using Drag-and-Drop Editing

Software Skills After you create a worksheet, you may want to rearrange data or add more information. For example, you may need to insert additional rows to a section of your worksheet because new employees have joined a department or been promoted. With Excel's editing features, you can easily add, delete, and rearrange entire rows and columns. You can also move or drag and drop sections of the worksheet with ease.

Application Skills You are the Payroll Manager at Whole Grains Bread. The conversion to an in-house payroll system is next week, and you want to test out a payroll worksheet the staff will use to collect and enter payroll data in the computer system. You need to finish entering data and formulas in the worksheet. This will require adding and deleting rows and columns, moving data by cutting and pasting, and drag-and-drop techniques.

What You Can Do

Inserting and Deleting Columns and Rows

- You can insert or delete columns or rows when necessary to change the arrangement of the data on the worksheet.
- Use the Insert and Delete buttons in the Cells group on the Home tab to insert and delete columns and rows. You also can click the drop-down arrows for these buttons for more commands, or right-click a selected column or row's heading and use the Insert and Delete commands on the shortcut menu.

✔ *Drag over multiple row or column headings to select multiple rows or columns. Then, using the shortcut menu to insert or delete will add or remove the number of rows or columns specified by your selection.*

- When you insert column(s) in a worksheet, existing columns shift their position to the right. For example, if you select column C and then insert two columns, the data that was in column C is shifted to the right, and becomes column E.
- If you insert row(s) in a worksheet, existing rows are shifted down to accommodate the newly inserted row(s). For example, if you select row 8 and insert two rows, the data that was in row 8 is shifted down to row 10.
- After inserting a column or row, you can use the Insert Options button to choose whether or not formatting from a nearby row or column should be applied to the new rows or columns.
- When you delete a column or row, existing columns and rows shift left or up to close the gap. Any data in the rows or columns you select for deletion is erased.

✔ *Instead of deleting columns or rows, you can hide them temporarily and then redisplay them as needed. Right-click the column/row heading and click Hide. Drag over headings surrounding the hidden row/column, right-click, and click Unhide.*

Try It! Inserting and Deleting Columns and Rows

1. Start Excel.
2. Open the **ETry09** file from the data files for this lesson.
3. Save the file as **ETry09_studentfirstname_studentlastname** in the location where your teacher instructs you to store the files for this lesson.
4. Add a header that has your name at the left, the date code in the center, and the page number code at the right, and change back to Normal view.
5. Click the column B column heading to select the column.
6. Click Home > Delete. Excel removes the column.

   ✔ *Be sure to click the top part of the Delete button, not the drop-down arrow on the bottom part.*

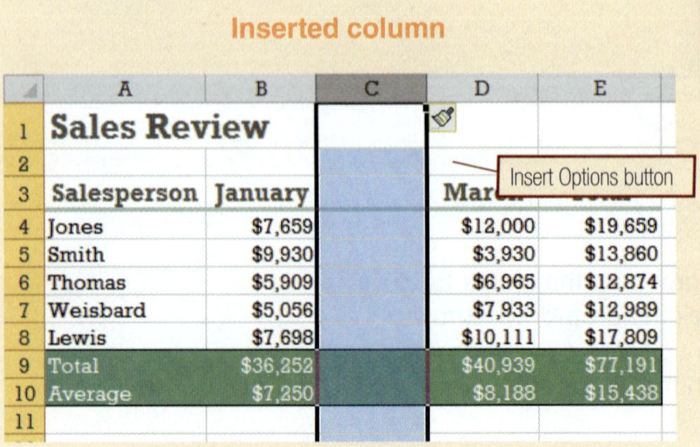

7. Click the column C column heading to select it.
8. Click Home > Insert.

   ✔ *Be sure to click the top part of the Insert button, not the drop-down arrow on the bottom part.*

9. Make the following entries in the new column, starting in cell C3:

   February
   8282
   9087
   10443
   9731
   8367

10. Fill the formulas from cells B9 and B10 to the right to cells C9 and C10.
11. Click the row 8 row heading to select it.
12. Click Home > Insert.
13. Make the following entries in the new row, starting in cell A8:

    Vegas
    8042
    6639
    8088

14. Save the **ETry09_studentfirstname_studentlastname** file, and leave it open to use in the next Try It.

Cutting and Pasting Data

- To move data from one place in the worksheet to another, use the Cut and Paste options in the Clipboard group on the Home tab. This removes the data from its original location.
- When you **cut** data from a location, it is temporarily stored on the Clipboard. That data is then copied from the Clipboard to the new location when you paste.
- If data already exists in the location you wish to paste to, Excel overwrites it.
- Instead of overwriting data with the Paste command, you can insert the cut cells and have Excel shift cells with existing data down or to the right.
- When you move data, its formatting moves with it.
- You can override this and move just the data using choices on the Paste button's drop-down list.

Try It! Cutting and Pasting Data

1. In the **ETry09_studentfirstname_studentlastname** file, drag over the range **A8:E9** to select it.
2. Click Home > Clipboard > Cut.
3. Click cell G4 to select it.
4. Click Home > Clipboard > Paste.

   Be sure to click the top part of the Paste button, not the drop-down arrow on the bottom part.
5. Close **ETry09_studentfirstname_studentlastname** file, saving all changes and exit Excel.

Using Drag-and-Drop Editing

- The **drag-and-drop** feature enables you to use the mouse to copy or move a range of cells simply by dragging them.
- To use drag-and-drop, select a range to copy or move, and then you use the border surrounding the range to drag the data to a different location. When you release the mouse button, the data is "dropped" in that location.
- An outline of the selection appears as you drag it to its new location on the worksheet.
- You can use drag-and-drop to move data and to copy it. To copy data using drag-and-drop, simply hold down the CTRL key as you drag.
- Insert, delete, move, and copy operations may affect formulas, so you should check the formulas after you have used drag-and-drop to be sure that they are correct.
- When a drag-and-drop action does not move data correctly, use the Undo feature to undo it.

Try It! Using Drag-and-Drop Editing

1. In the **ETry09_studentfirstname_studentlastname** file, drag over the range A7:E7 to select it.
2. Point to the border of the selection. When the mouse pointer changes to a four-headed arrow, drag down one row. When the ScreenTip reads *A8:E8*, release the mouse button.
3. Drag over the range G4:K4 to select it.
4. Use drag-and-drop to move the selection to row 7 of the sales data.

Moving a range with drag-and-drop

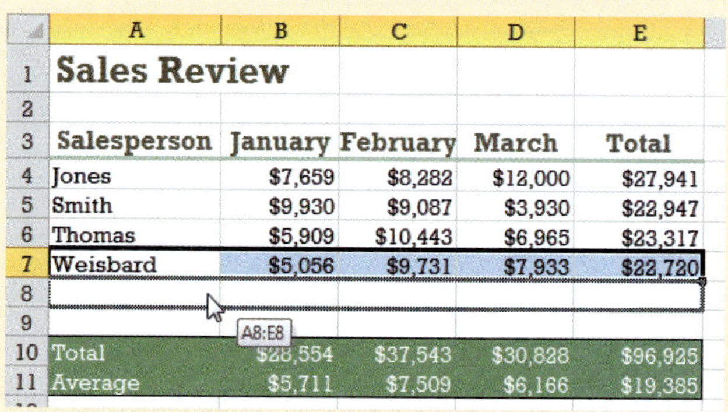

(continued)

Try It! **Using Drag-and-Drop Editing** *(continued)*

5. Click the row 9 row heading to select it.
6. Click Home > Delete.
7. Drag over the range G5:K5 to select it.
8. Click Home > Clear Contents.
9. Close **ETry09_studentfirstname_studentlastname** file, saving all changes, and exit Excel.

Project 17—Create It

Working with Columns and Rows in the Payroll Worksheet

DIRECTIONS

1. Start Excel, if necessary, and open the **EProj17** file from the data files for this lesson.
2. Save the file as **EProj17_studentfirstname_studentlastname** in the location where your teacher instructs you to store the files for this lesson.
3. Add a header that has your name at the left, the date code in the center, and the page number code at the right, and change back to **Normal** view.
4. Click the **row 14** row heading to select it.
5. Click **Home** > **Insert**.
6. Click the **row 4** row heading to select it.
7. Move the mouse pointer over the border of the selection, press and hold CTRL, and drag the selection down to **row 15**. When you release the mouse button, Excel copies the selection.
8. Click cell **A15** to select it, type **Hourly Employees**, and press ENTER.
9. Click the **column D** column heading to select it.
10. Click **Home** > **Delete**.
11. **With your teacher's permission**, print the worksheet. Submit the printout or the file for grading as required.
12. Close the workbook, saving all changes, and exit Excel

Project 18—Apply It

Moving and Copying Data in the Payroll Worksheet

DIRECTIONS

1. Start Excel, if necessary, and open the **EProj18** file from the data files for this lesson.
2. Save the file as **EProj18_studentfirstname_studentlastname** in the location where your teacher instructs you to store the files for this lesson.
3. Add a header that has your name at the left, the date code in the center, and the page number code at the right, and change back to **Normal** view.
4. Select the range **B5:J13** and move it left one column.
5. Select the range **B16:H24** and move it left one column.
6. Adjust column widths as needed.
7. Select the range **G5:I13** and use drag-and-drop to copy the data to the range **H16:J24**.
8. Select **row 12**, and insert a new row.
9. Cut the range **A22:D22**, and paste it in the new **row 12**.

10. In row 12, change the Rate to **765**. For the rest of the columns, fill the formulas down from the row above to row 12.
11. Delete **row 22**. Your worksheet should look like the one shown in Figure 9-1.
12. **With your teacher's permission**, print the worksheet. Submit the printout or the file for grading as required.
13. Close the workbook, saving all changes, and exit Excel.

Figure 9-1

	A	B	C	D	E	F	G	H	I	J	K
5	Employee Name	Employee ID	Rate	Regular Hours	Gross Pay	Fed Tax	SS Tax	State Tax	Net Pay		
6	Anthony Splendoria	38748	$ 2,175.00	40.00	$ 2,175.00	$ 543.75	$ 169.65	$ 65.25	$ 1,396.35		
7	Eileen Costello	21544	$ 1,895.00	40.00	$ 1,895.00	$ 473.75	$ 147.81	$ 56.85	$ 1,216.59		
8	Carol Chen	38448	$ 895.00	40.00	$ 895.00	$ 223.75	$ 69.81	$ 26.85	$ 574.59		
9	Marty Gonzales	61522	$ 684.00	40.00	$ 684.00	$ 171.00	$ 53.35	$ 20.52	$ 439.13		
10	Maria Nachez	34789	$ 1,665.00	40.00	$ 1,665.00	$ 416.25	$ 129.87	$ 49.95	$ 1,068.93		
11	Mika Gritada	22785	$ 1,023.00	40.00	$ 1,023.00	$ 255.75	$ 79.79	$ 30.69	$ 656.77		
12	Vickie Helms	31851	$ 765.00	40.00	$ 765.00	$ 191.25	$ 59.67	$ 22.95	$ 491.13		
13	Randall Lohr	38514	$ 1,545.00	40.00	$ 1,545.00	$ 386.25	$ 120.51	$ 46.35	$ 991.89		
14	Abe Rittenhouse	22854	$ 1,231.00	40.00	$ 1,231.00	$ 307.75	$ 96.02	$ 36.93	$ 790.30		
15											
16	Hourly Employees										
17	Employee Name	Employee ID	Rate	Regular Hours	Overtime Hours	Gross Pay	Fed Tax	SS Tax	State Tax	Net Pay	
18	Thomas Cortese	21875	$ 8.25	40.00	2.00	$ 354.75	$ 53.21	$ 27.67	$ 10.64	$ 263.22	
19	Javier Cortez	21154	$ 7.75	40.00	3.00	$ 344.88	$ 51.73	$ 26.90	$ 10.35	$ 255.90	
20	Allen Gaines	23455	$ 7.25	40.00	6.00	$ 355.25	$ 53.29	$ 27.71	$ 10.66	$ 263.60	
21	Freda Gage	27855	$ 8.00	40.00	3.00	$ 356.00	$ 53.40	$ 27.77	$ 10.68	$ 264.15	
22	Isiah Herron	33252	$ 10.95	40.00	5.50	$ 528.34	$ 79.25	$ 41.21	$ 15.85	$ 392.03	
23	Thomas Kaminski	37881	$ 9.75	40.00	4.00	$ 448.50	$ 67.28	$ 34.98	$ 13.46	$ 332.79	
24	Chris Nakao	29958	$ 11.25	40.00	3.00	$ 500.63	$ 75.09	$ 39.05	$ 15.02	$ 371.46	
25											
26											
27											
28											
29											

Payroll

WORDS TO KNOW

Chart
A graphical representation of data that enables you to identify comparisons and trends.

Chart sheet
A sheet that contains a chart only.

Column chart
The default chart type that displays each data point as a vertical column.

Show Formulas
A command that enables you to display the formulas in a worksheet so that you can check them.

Lesson 10

Chart, Sheet, Display, and Print Operations

➤ What You Will Learn

Creating a Column Chart
Deleting Unused Sheets in a Workbook
Displaying, Printing, and Hiding Formulas
Previewing and Printing a Worksheet

Software Skills Before you finalize a workbook, you may want to chart some of the data and delete unused worksheets. You might also want to display and print formulas to review them, and preview the worksheet so you can see how it will look when printed.

Application Skills You are the Chief Financial Officer for Hyland Manufacturing. You are finalizing the company's balance sheet for fiscal year 2012. You want to chart the basic data, remove blank sheets, review and print the formulas, and preview and print the finished worksheet and charts.

What You Can Do

Creating a Column Chart

- Create a **chart** of data in a worksheet to depict the data graphically.
- A chart can help you identify trends, analyze problems, and track progress, among other benefits.
- Excel offers numerous chart types and subtypes. The **column chart** is the default chart type.
- Select the data to chart—including labels for the data—and then press the F11 key to create a column chart.

- This method places the chart on its own sheet called a **chart sheet.**

✔ *Pressing* ALT + F1 *inserts the chart on the current sheet, instead.*

✔ *Chapter 3, "Charting Data," provides more detail about creating and formatting charts.*

- The theme applied to the workbook file determines the chart's color scheme.

Try It! Creating a Column Chart

1. Start Excel.
2. Open the **ETry10** file from the data files for this lesson.
3. Save the file as **ETry10_studentfirstname_studentlastname** in the location where your teacher instructs you to store the files for this lesson.
4. Add a header that has your name at the left, the date code in the center, and the page number code at the right, and change back to Normal view.
5. Drag over the range A3:D8 to select it. This range holds the labels for the data and the data itself.
6. Press F11. The chart immediately appears on a new chart sheet named Chart1. Contextual tabs for working with the chart also appear.
7. Click Chart Tools > Layout > Chart Title > Above Chart.

✔ *Throughout this book, you will see instruction provided in a sequence format; for example,* "Click Chart Tools Layout > Chart Title > Above Chart" *means to click the Chart Tools tab and the Layout sub-tab, click the Chart Title button, and then click the Above Chart option.*

8. Type **Sales**, and press ENTER .
9. Save the **ETry10_studentfirstname_studentlastname** file, and leave it open to use in the next Try It.

Deleting Unused Sheets in a Workbook

- You do not need to delete unused sheets from a workbook because they do not add greatly to the file size.
- However, if you plan on sharing the file, you may want to remove unused sheets to create a more professional look.
- Right-click a sheet tab and click Delete to remove it from the workbook.
- You also can click the drop-down arrow for the Delete button in the Cells group on the Home tab, and click Delete Sheet to remove the sheet.
- If the sheet contains data, a message asks you to confirm the deletion. Click Delete to do so.

Try It! Deleting Unused Sheets in a Workbook

1. In the **ETry10_studentfirstname_studentlastname** file, click the Sheet2 sheet tab.
2. Click Home > Delete drop-down arrow > Delete Sheet.
3. Right-click the Sheet3 sheet tab and click Delete.
4. Select the Sheet1 sheet if necessary, and go to cell A1.
5. Save the **ETry10_studentfirstname_studentlastname** file, and leave it open to use in the next Try It.

Displaying, Printing, and Hiding Formulas

- The **Show Formulas** command displays formulas in cells in which they are entered rather than formula results.
- Showing formulas enables you to review the worksheet to ensure that the formulas refer to the correct cells and ranges and accurately perform the desired calculations.
- Print the worksheet with the formulas displayed to create a printout of the formulas for later reference.
- Use the Show Formulas button in the Formula Auditing group on the Formulas tab to turn formula display on and off. You also can press CTRL + `.

✔ *The accent grave character (`) is on the same key as the tilde, typically found to the left of the 1 on the row of numbers at the top of the keyboard or beside the Spacebar in rarer cases.*

Try It! Displaying, Printing, and Hiding Formulas

1. In the **ETry10_studentfirstname_studentlastname** file, click Formulas > Show Formulas.
2. Click File > Print.
3. Under Settings, click No Scaling, and then click Fit Sheet on One Page.

   ✔ *It's often necessary to scale the sheet when formulas are displayed because the formula display makes the columns wider.*

4. **With your teacher's permission,** print the worksheet by clicking the Print button. Otherwise, click Home.
5. Press CTRL + ` to toggle off the formula display.
6. Save the **ETry10_studentfirstname_studentlastname** file, and leave it open to use in the next Try It.

Formulas displayed in worksheet

	A	B	C	D	E
1	Sales Review				
2					
3	Salesperson	January	February	March	Total
4	Jones	7659	8282	12000	=SUM(B4:D4)
5	Smith	9930	9087	3930	=SUM(B5:D5)
6	Thomas	5909	10443	6965	=SUM(B6:D6)
7	Vegas	8042	6639	8088	=SUM(B7:D7)
8	Weisbard	5056	9731	7933	=SUM(B8:D8)
9	Total	=SUM(B4:B8)	=SUM(C4:C8)	=SUM(D4:D8)	=SUM(E4:E8)
10	Average	=SUM(B4:B8)/5	=SUM(C4:C8)/5	=SUM(D4:D8)/5	=SUM(E4:E8)/5
11					

Previewing and Printing a Worksheet

- You may print the selected worksheet(s), an entire workbook, or a selected data range.

  ✔ *You learn how to print an entire workbook and a selected range in Lesson 20.*

- When you choose File>Print, the Backstage view automatically shows you a preview of the printout. Review it carefully and adjust print settings there before printing.
- Settings you can change appear in the middle column of Backstage view. These include specifying how many copies to print, what printer to use, page orientation, page size, margins, and scaling.

Try It! Previewing and Printing a Worksheet

1. In the **ETry10_studentfirstname_studentlastname** file with Sheet1 selected, click File > Print.
2. Click the Orientation option and click Landscape Orientation in the menu that appears.
3. Under Settings, click the Page Setup link.
4. In the Page Setup dialog box, click the Margins tab.
5. Click the Horizontally and Vertically check boxes under Center on page to select them, and then click OK.
6. Review the changes in the preview.
7. **With your teacher's permission,** print the worksheet by clicking the Print button. Otherwise, click Home.
8. Close the **ETry10_studentfirstname_studentlastname** file, saving all changes and exit Excel.

Preparing and previewing before printing

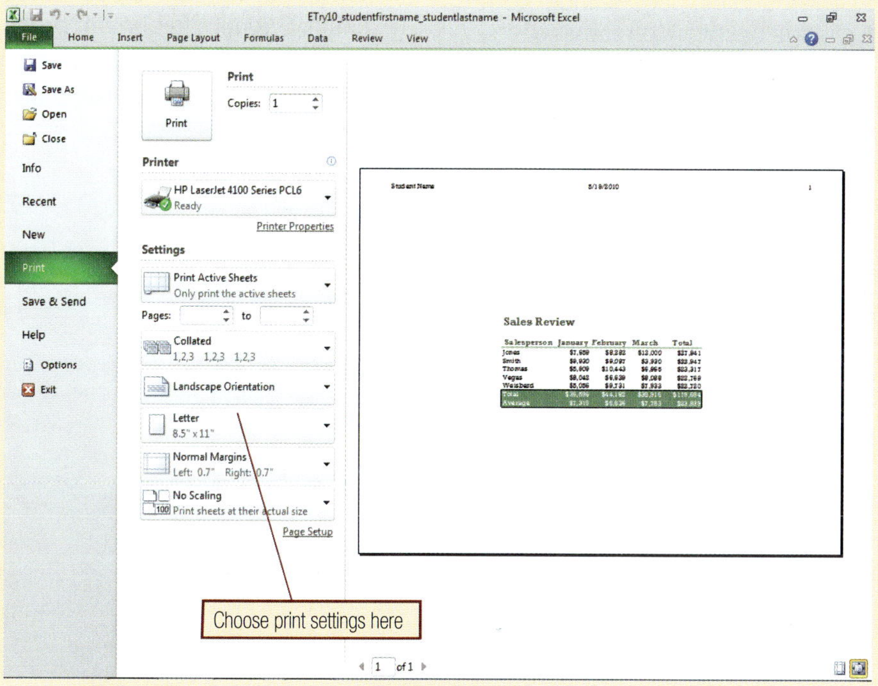

Project 19—Create It

Adding a Chart in the Balance Sheet Worksheet

DIRECTIONS

1. Start Excel, if necessary, and open the **EProj19** file from the data files for this lesson.
2. Save the file as **EProj19_studentfirstname_studentlastname** in the location where your teacher instructs you to store the files for this lesson.
3. Add a header that has your name at the left, the date code in the center, and the page number code at the right, and change back to **Normal** view.
4. Select the range **A12:B12**, press and hold CTRL, and then select **A21:B22**. Release the CTRL key when finished.
5. Press F11. A column chart immediately appears on its own sheet. (See Figure 10-1.)
6. Click **Chart Tools > Layout > Legend > None** to remove the legend at the right.
7. Click **Chart Tools > Layout > Chart Title > Above Chart**.
8. Type **Student Name Assets** (using your name in place of Student Name), and press ENTER. Your chart should look like the one in Figure 10-1.
9. **With your teacher's permission**, print the chart sheet. Submit the printout or the file for grading as required.
10. Close the workbook, saving all changes, and exit Excel

Figure 10-1

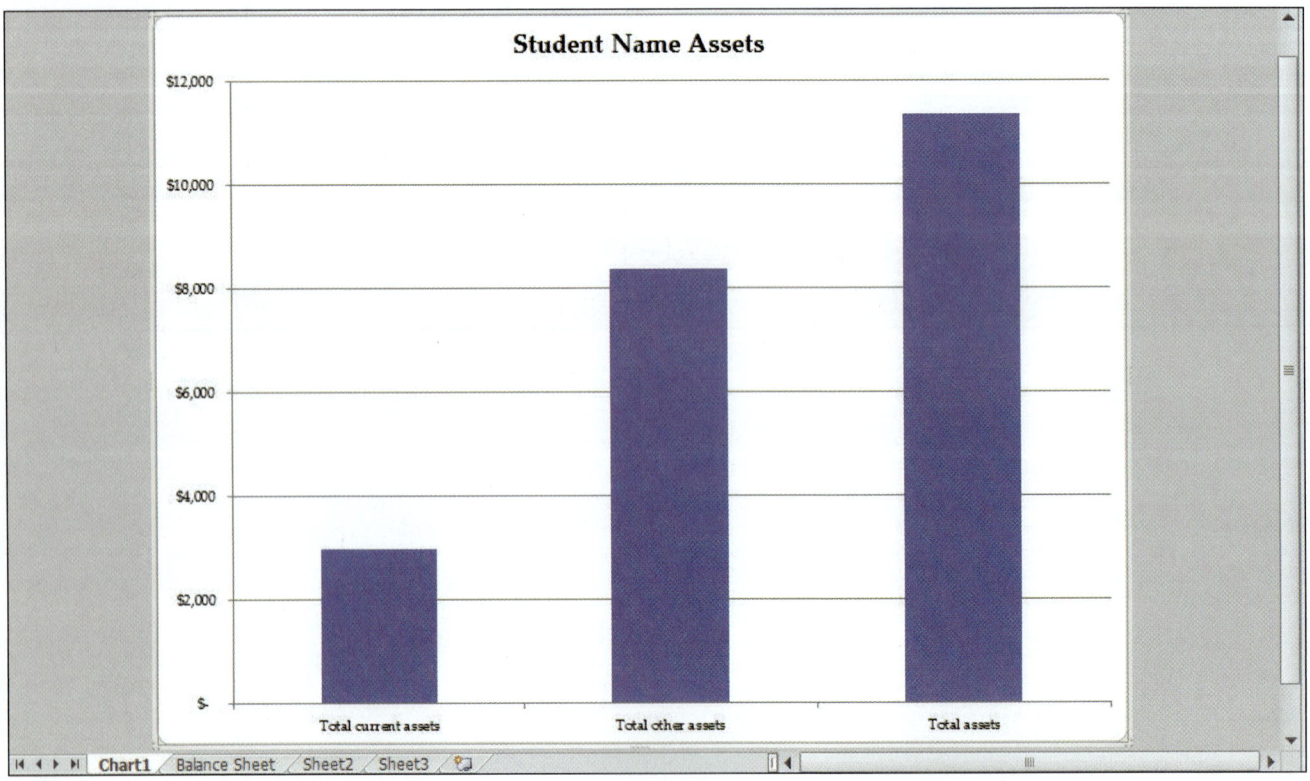

Project 20—Apply It

Reviewing and Printing the Balance Sheet Worksheet

DIRECTIONS

1. Start Excel, if necessary, and open the **EProj20** file from the data files for this lesson.
2. Save the file as **EProj20_studentfirstname_studentlastname** in the location where your teacher instructs you to store the files for this lesson.
3. Add a header that has your name at the left, the date code in the center, and the page number code at the right, and change back to **Normal** view.
4. Delete **Sheet2** and **Sheet3**.
5. Display formulas instead of formula results on the worksheet.
6. Change the print settings so that the sheet fits on one page.
7. **With your teacher's permission**, print the worksheet. Submit the printout or the file for grading as required.
8. Close the workbook, saving all changes, and exit Excel.

Chapter Assessment and Application

Project 21—Make It Your Own

Safety Consulting Services

You have recently started your own business providing safety consulting services to large businesses. You need to create a worksheet to help you track, report, and bill work for each client at two billing rates. You will create and format the sheet, and then enter example data to test how it works.

DIRECTIONS

1. Start Excel, if necessary, and create a new, blank file if necessary.
2. Save the file as **EProj21_studentfirstname_studentlastname** in the location where your teacher instructs you to store the files for this chapter.
3. Add a header that has your name at the left, the date code in the center, and the page number code at the right, and change back to **Normal** view.
4. Enter the following data:

A1	**Timesheet**
A3	**Client Name**
A5	**Rate A**
A6	**Rate B**
B5	**50**
B6	**75**
D5	**Weekly Retainer**
F5	**1750**
A8	**Day**
B8	**Date**
C8	**Hours Rate A**
D8	**Hours Rate B**
E8	**Amount Rate A**
F8	**Amount Rate B**
G8	**Total**
D17	**Total**
E18	**Percent of Retainer**

5. Enter **Monday** in cell **A9**. Fill the days Monday through Sunday down through cell A15.
6. Enter **4/2/12** in cell **B9**. Fill the date entry down the column through 4/8/2012 in cell B15.
7. Enter the formula **=C9*$B$5** in cell **E9**. Fill the formula down through cell E15.
8. Enter the formula **=D9*$B$6** in cell **F9**. Fill the formula down through cell F15.
9. In cell **G9**, enter a formula that adds the values in cells **E9** and **F9**. Fill the formula down through cell G15.
10. In cell **E17**, enter a formula with the SUM function that totals the values above. Fill the formula right through cell **G17**.
11. In cell **G18**, enter a formula that divides the overall total in cell **G17** by the weekly retainer amount in cell **F5**.
12. Apply the **Solstice** theme to the file.
13. Apply the **Title** cell style to cell A1, and merge and center cells **A1:G1**.
14. Apply the **60% - Accent1** style to the label in cell **A3**, then copy the formatting to the other labels in the document (except for the dates).
15. Wrap and center align the range **A8:G8**.
16. Apply the **Currency** format with zero decimal places to the entries in cells **B5**, **B6**, and **F5**.
17. Apply the **Currency** format with two decimal places to all the other cells calculating dollar values.
18. Format cell **G18** as a **Percentage** with one decimal place.
19. Enter the following sample data to test the sheet:

C9	**2.25**
D9	**4.5**
C10	**2**
D10	**1.25**

20. **With your teacher's permission**, print the worksheet. Submit the printout or the file for grading as required. Your worksheet should look like the one in Illustration A.

21. Close the workbook, saving all changes, and exit Excel.

Illustration A

	A	B	C	D	E	F	G
1				Timesheet			
2							
3	Client Name						
4							
5	Rate A	$50		Weekly Retainer		$1,750	
6	Rate B	$75					
7							
8	Day	Date	Hours Rate A	Hours Rate B	Amount Rate A	Amount Rate B	Total
9	Monday	4/2/2012	2.25	4.5	$112.50	$337.50	$450.00
10	Tuesday	4/3/2012	2	1.25	$100.00	$93.75	$193.75
11	Wednesday	4/4/2012			$0.00	$0.00	$0.00
12	Thursday	4/5/2012			$0.00	$0.00	$0.00
13	Friday	4/6/2012			$0.00	$0.00	$0.00
14	Saturday	4/7/2012			$0.00	$0.00	$0.00
15	Sunday	4/8/2012			$0.00	$0.00	$0.00
16							
17				Total	$212.50	$431.25	$643.75
18					Percent of Retainer		36.8%
19							
20							
21							
22							

Sheet1 Sheet2 Sheet3

Project 22—Master It

Personal Budget

You want to save for a car, and need to get a better handle on your income and expenses in order to do so. In this project, you finish a basic budget worksheet by adding formulas and by making sure items are arranged properly. You'll apply attractive formatting and chart your savings progress.

DIRECTIONS

1. Start Excel, if necessary, and open the **EProj22** file from the data files for this chapter.
2. Save the file as **EProj22_studentfirstname_studentlastname** in the location where your teacher instructs you to store the files for this chapter.
3. Add a header that has your name at the left, the date code in the center, and the page number code at the right, and change back to **Normal** view.
4. Enter the formula **=B5+B6** in cell **B7**. Fill the formula across through cell G7.
5. In cell **B13**, enter a formula that sums **B9:B12**. Fill the formula across through cell G13.
6. Insert a blank row between the *Income* and *Expenses* sections.
7. Review the items in the *Expenses* section. You realize that the Gifts row really belongs up on the *Income* area.
8. Insert a new row 6, drag-and-drop row 13 to row 6, and then delete the blank row 13.
9. Click cell **B8** and review its formula in comparison with the original formula you created in step 4. Because it totals specific cells, it does not include the Gifts data that you have moved to the *Income* section. Edit the formula to correct the calculation, and then copy or fill it across the row.
10. In cell **B15**, enter a formula that subtracts the expense subtotal from the income subtotal. Fill the formula across through cell G15.
11. Add a blank row above the *Surplus* row.
12. Apply a different theme to the workbook.
13. Format the labels as desired and apply the **Accounting** format with zero decimal places to the numeric data.
14. Select the ranges **B3:G3** and **B16:G17** and create a column chart based on the data.
15. Hide the legend and add **Student Name Budget Surplus** as a title above the chart.
16. Delete the blank worksheets in the file.
17. On Sheet1, display formulas.
18. Preview the sheet, scaling to fit the sheet on one page with the formulas displayed.
19. **With your teacher's permission**, print the worksheet. Submit the printouts or the file for grading as required.
20. Close the workbook, saving all changes, and exit Excel.

Chapter 2

Working with Formulas, Functions, and Charts

Lesson 11
Getting Started with Functions
Projects 23-24

- Using Functions (SUM, AVERAGE, MEDIAN, MIN, and MAX)
- Inserting a Function
- Using AutoCalculate

Lesson 12
Using Excel Tables
Projects 25-26

- Creating an Excel Table
- Sorting and Filtering an Excel Table
- Converting a Table to a Range

Lesson 13
The NOW Function and Named Ranges
Projects 27-28

- Using the NOW Function to Display a System Date
- Using Named Ranges

Lesson 14
Working with IF Functions
Projects 29-30

- Understanding IF Functions
- Nesting Functions
- Using SUMIF() and SUMIFS() Functions
- Using COUNTIF() and COUNTIFS() Functions

Lesson 15
Using Frozen Labels and Panes
Projects 31-32

- Freezing Labels While Scrolling
- Splitting a Worksheet into Panes

Lesson 16
Using Conditional Formatting and Find and Replace
Projects 33-34

- Applying Conditional Formatting
- Using Find and Replace

Lesson 17
Rotating Entries and Resolving #### Errors
Projects 35-36

- Rotating Cell Entries
- Resolving a #### Error Message

Lesson 18
Adding Print Titles and Scaling a Printout
Projects 37-38

- Printing Titles
- Changing Orientation
- Scaling to Fit

Lesson 19
Managing Worksheets and Performing Multi-worksheet Operations
Projects 39-40

- Inserting, Deleting, Copying, Moving, and Renaming Worksheets
- Changing the Color of a Worksheet Tab
- Hiding Sheets
- Grouping Worksheets for Editing

Lesson 20
Summary Worksheets and Advanced Printing
Projects 41-42

- Constructing Formulas that Summarize Data from Other Sheets
- Changing Values in a Detail Worksheet to Update a Summary Worksheet
- Printing a Selection
- Printing All the Worksheets in a Workbook

End of Chapter Assessments
Projects 43-44

Lesson 11

Getting Started with Functions

WORDS TO KNOW

Argument
The values and other inputs that a function uses to calculate the result. You specify the cell or range that holds the value(s) for each argument or input a particular value.

AutoCalculate
A feature that temporarily performs the following calculations on a range of cells without the user having to enter a formula: AVERAGE, COUNT, MIN, MAX, or SUM.

Formula AutoComplete
A feature that speeds up the manual entry of functions.

Function
A predefined formula that performs a specific calculation using the inputs you specify.

Function name
The name given to one of Excel's predefined formulas.

Nest
To use a function as an argument within another function.

➤ What You Will Learn

Using Functions (SUM, AVERAGE, MEDIAN, MIN, and MAX)
Inserting a Function
Using AutoCalculate

Software Skills Use an Excel function to help you write a formula to perform more advanced calculations in your worksheets. Excel's Insert Function feature provides a list of available functions and "fill-in-the-blanks" assistance to complete a formula. The Function Library group also enables you to select functions by category.

Application Skills You're the owner of Restoration Architecture, a large design and construction firm specializing in the remodeling, redesign, and restoration of existing properties. You submitted a bid to restore several homes purchased by a neighborhood revitalization organization. The group solicited bids from a number of firms. You want to analyze the bidding results to evaluate how competitive your bid was.

What You Can Do

Using Functions (SUM, AVERAGE, MEDIAN, MIN, and MAX)

- Excel provides built-in formulas called **functions** to perform special calculations.
- To create a formula with a function, enter these elements in the following order:
  - The equal sign (=).
  - The **function name**, in upper- or lowercase letters.
  - An open parenthesis to separate the arguments from the function name.

- The **argument(s)** identifying the data required to perform the function.
- A close parenthesis ends the argument.

- For example, =SUM(A1:A40) adds the values in the cells specified by the argument, which in this case is a single range of cells A1 through A40.
- Most functions allow multiple arguments, separated by commas. For example, =SUM(A1:A40,C1:C40) adds the values in the ranges A1:A40 and C1:C40.
- A function may be inserted into a formula. For example, =B2/SUM(C3:C5) takes the value in cell B2 and divides it by the sum of the values in the range C3:C5.
- When a function is used as an argument for other functions, it is **nested** within those functions.
- For example, =ROUND(SUM(B12:B23),2)) totals the values in the range, B12:B23, and then rounds that total to two decimal places.
- Following are commonly used functions:
  - =SUM( ) adds the values in a range of cells.
  - =AVERAGE( ) returns the arithmetic mean of the values in a range of cells.
  - =COUNT( ) counts the cells containing numbers in a range of cells (blank cells or text entries are ignored).
  - =COUNTA( ) counts the number of non-blank cells.
  - =MAX( ) finds the highest value in a range of cells.
  - =MIN( ) finds the lowest value in a range of cells.
  - =ROUND( ) adjusts a value to a specific number of digits.

✓ *When a cell is formatted to a specified number of decimal places, only the display of that value is affected. The actual value in the cell is still used in all calculations. For example, if a cell contains the value 13.45687, and you decide to display only the last two decimal places, then the value 13.46 will display in the cell, but the value, 13.45687, will be used in all calculations.*

- If you are familiar with a formula and its required arguments, you can type it into the cell where you want the result to display. The formula name must be typed correctly.
- After you type =, the function name, and the opening parenthesis, a ScreenTip shows you what argument(s) to enter for the function.
- When you type = and then type the beginning of a function name, the **Formula AutoComplete** feature displays a list of possible matching function names. Use the ↓ key to select the desired function, and then press TAB to enter it in the formula.

✓ *You also can use Formula AutoComplete to enter other listed items such as a range name.*

- Use the drop-down arrow on the Sum button Σ ▾ in the Editing Group on the Home tab to quickly insert a SUM, AVERAGE, COUNT, MAX, or MIN function. The AutoSum button Σ in the Function Library group of the Formulas tab can also be used to insert those functions.

Try It! Using Functions (SUM, AVERAGE, MEDIAN, MIN, and MAX)

1. Start Excel.
2. Open the **ETry11** file from the data files for this lesson.
3. Add a header that has your name at the left, the date code in the center, and the page number code at the right, and change back to Normal view.

(continued)

Try It! Using Functions (SUM, AVERAGE, MEDIAN, MIN, and MAX) *(continued)*

4. Click cell B10 to select it.
5. Type **=sum(**, and then drag over the range B5:B9 to select it.
6. Press [ENTER]. Excel adds the closing parenthesis for you and displays the formula result in the cell.
7. Press [↓] to select cell B12.
8. Type **=av**. Press [↓] once to select AVERAGE.
9. Press [tab], type **B5:B9** to specify that range as the argument, and press [ENTER] to finish the formula and select cell B13.
10. On the Home tab, in the Editing group, click the AutoSum drop-down arrow Σ ▾, and then click Max. Type or select the range **B5:B9**, and press [ENTER] to complete the formula and select cell B14.
11. On the Formulas tab, in the Function Library group, click the AutoSum drop-down arrow Σ, and then click Min. Type or select the range **B5:B9**, and press [ENTER] to complete the formula and select cell B15.
12. Save the **ETry11_studentfirstname_studentlastname** file, and leave it open to use in the next Try It.

Typing a Function

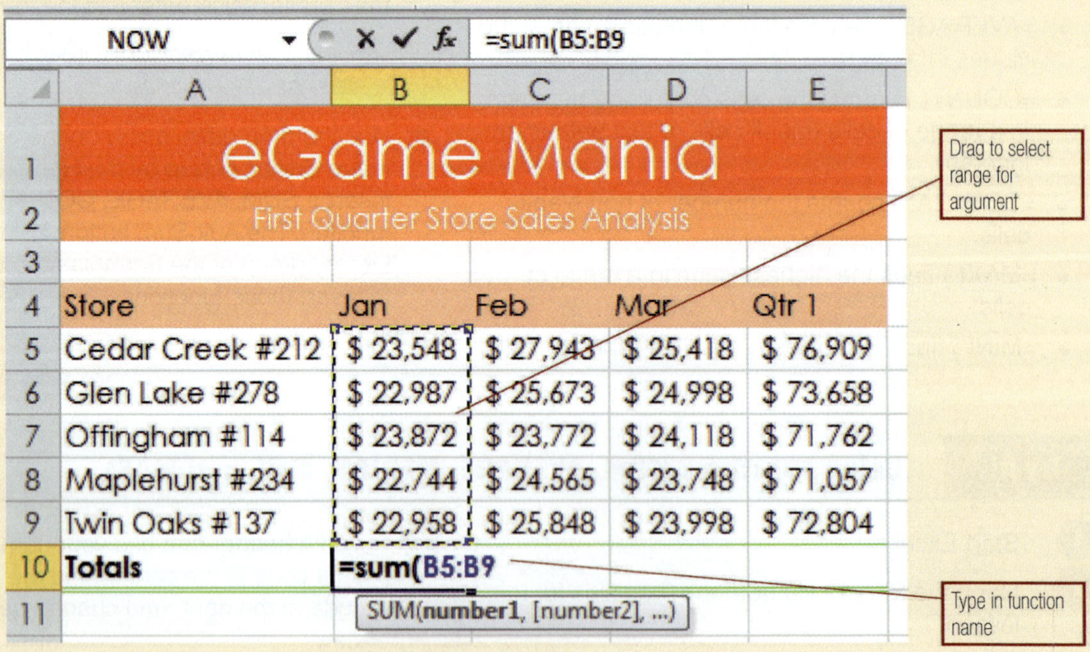

Selecting a function with Formula AutoComplete

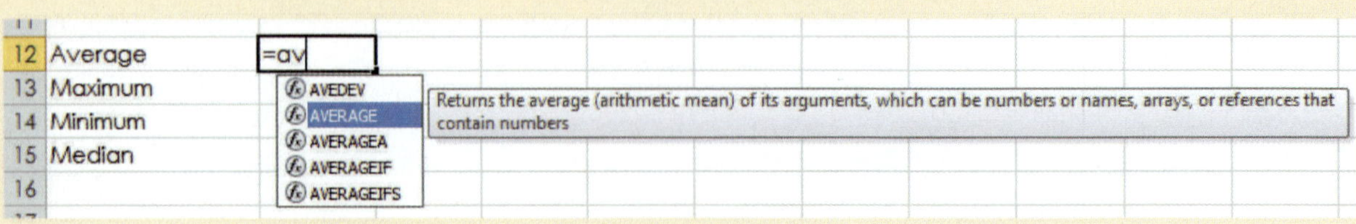

Inserting a Function

- If you know what category a function falls in, you can insert it by clicking the Formulas tab, clicking the category name in the Function Library group, and then clicking the function.
- Clicking More Functions displays a menu with additional categories. Click the desired category, and then the desired function.
- If you need to search for a function, click the Insert Function button on the formula bar. You also can click the Insert Function button *fx* in the Function Library group of the Formulas tab. Either method opens the Insert Function dialog box.
- In the Insert Function dialog box, you can type a brief description of the function you want to use to display a list of corresponding functions.
- For example, you could type the description "add numbers" to find a function you could use to add a column of numbers.
- You can also display functions by typing the name of the function (if you know it), or by choosing a category from the Or select a category list.
- When you enter a formula using Insert Function, Excel automatically enters the equal sign (=) in the formula.
- After you select a function and click OK in the Insert Function dialog box, the Function Arguments dialog box appears to prompt you to enter the arguments needed for the function.
- In the Function Arguments dialog box, you can select cells instead of typing them by using the Collapse Dialog button located at the right of each text box.

✓ *You also can type another function as an argument for the current function.*

- Required argument names appear in bold.
- As you enter the arguments, the value of that argument is displayed to the right of the text box.
- Excel calculates the current result and displays it at the bottom of the dialog box.

✓ *If you need help understanding a particular function's arguments, click the Help on this function link, located in the lower left-hand corner of the dialog box.*

Try It! Inserting a Function

1. With cell B15 still selected in the **ETry11_studentfirstname_studentlastname** file, click Formulas > More Functions > Statistical, and then scroll down and click MEDIAN.
2. In the Number1 text box of the Function Arguments dialog box, type **B5:B9** to replace the suggested entry, and click OK.
3. Click cell C10 to select it.
4. Click the Insert Function button on the formula bar.
5. Click the Or select a category list down arrow, and click Math & Trig if it does not appear.
6. Scroll down the Select a function list, click SUM, and then click OK.
7. In the Function Arguments dialog box, make sure that C5:C9 appears in the Number1 text box, and then click OK.
8. Use the fill handle to copy the formula from cell C10 to D10:E10.

The Insert Function dialog box

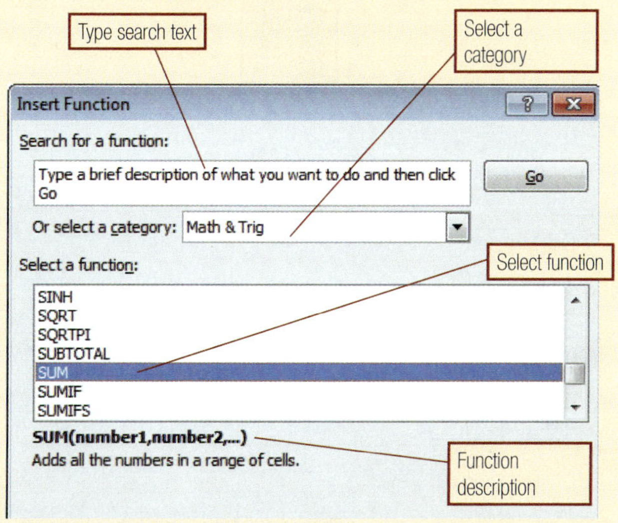

(continued)

Try It! Inserting a Function *(continued)*

9. Select the range B12:B15, and use the fill handle to copy the formulas from those cells to C12:E15 to the right.
10. Adjust column widths if needed.
11. Save the **ETry11_studentfirstname_studentlastname** file, and leave it open to use in the next Try It.

Using AutoCalculate

- To quickly calculate the AVERAGE, COUNT, COUNTA, MAX, MIN, or SUM for a cell range without entering a formula, use **AutoCalculate**.
- Select the range, and the Average, Count (COUNTA), and Sum results appear on the Status bar.
- To control which function results appear on the Status bar, right-click the Status bar and click one of the six functions that appear.

Try It! Using AutoCalculate

1. In the **ETry11_studentfirstname_studentlastname** file, drag over the range E5:E9 to select it.
2. Observe the Status bar. The Average calculated by AutoComplete should match the result in cell E12. The Sum calculated by AutoComplete should match the result in cell E10.
3. With the range E:5:E9 still selected, right-click the Status bar, click Maximum, and press ESC.
4. Observe the Status bar. It now includes a Max value that should match the result shown in cell E13.

Working with AutoCalculate

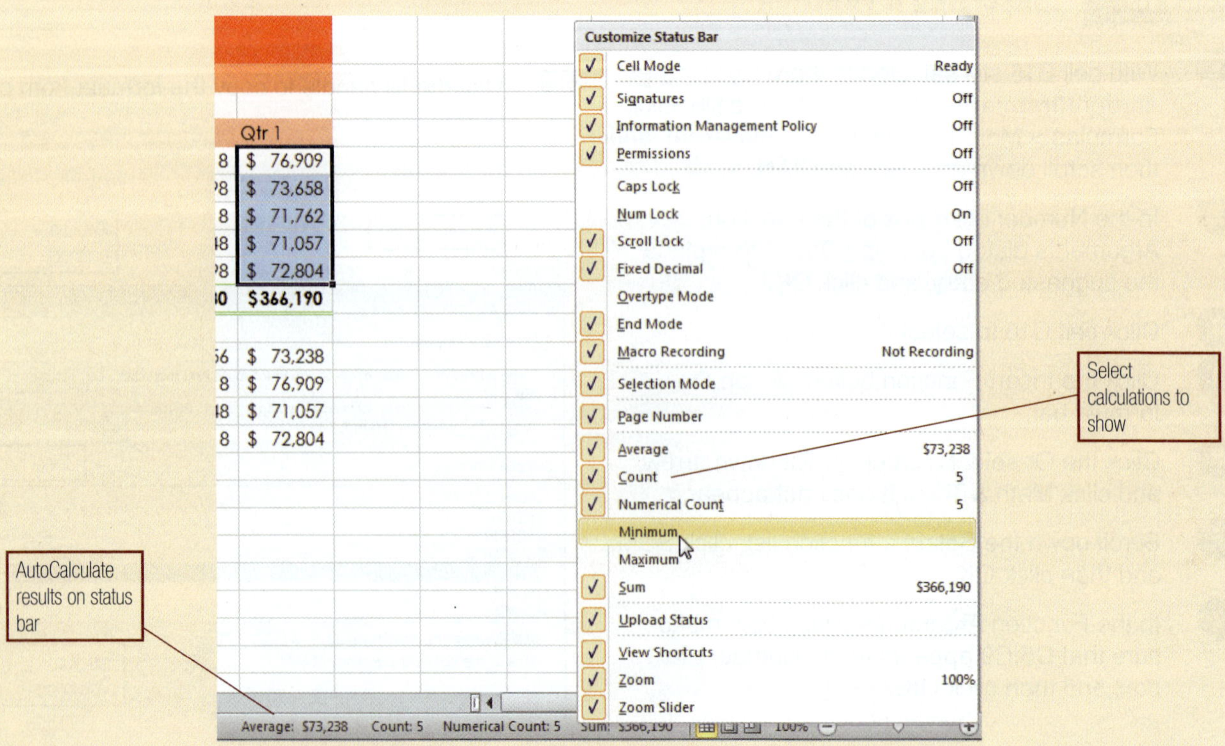

(continued)

Try It! **Using AutoCalculate** *(continued)*

5. Right-click the Status bar, click Maximum, and press ESC.
6. Click cell A1 to select it.
7. Save the **ETry11_studentfirstname_studentlastname** file, and close it.

Project 23—Create It

Type Functions in Formulas

DIRECTIONS

1. Start Excel, if necessary, and open the **EProj23** file from the data files for this lesson.
2. Save the workbook as **EProj23_studentfirstname_studentlastname** in the location where your teacher instructs you to store the files for this lesson.
3. Add a header that has your name at the left, the date code in the center, and the page number code at the right, and change back to **Normal** view.
4. In cell **E6**, enter the formula **=sum(B6,C6)**, and press TAB.
5. In cell **E7**, enter the formula **=sum(B6,D6)**, and press CTRL + ENTER.
6. Drag over the range **E6:F6** to select it, and then double-click the fill handle to copy the formulas down through row 16.
7. Click cell **B19** to select it.
8. Type **=B13**, and press CTRL + ENTER.
9. Drag the fill handle right through cell **F19** to fill the formula across.
10. Press CTRL + HOME. Your worksheet should look like the one shown in Figure 11-1.
11. **With your teacher's permission**, print the worksheet. Submit the printout or the file for grading as required.
12. Save and close the file.

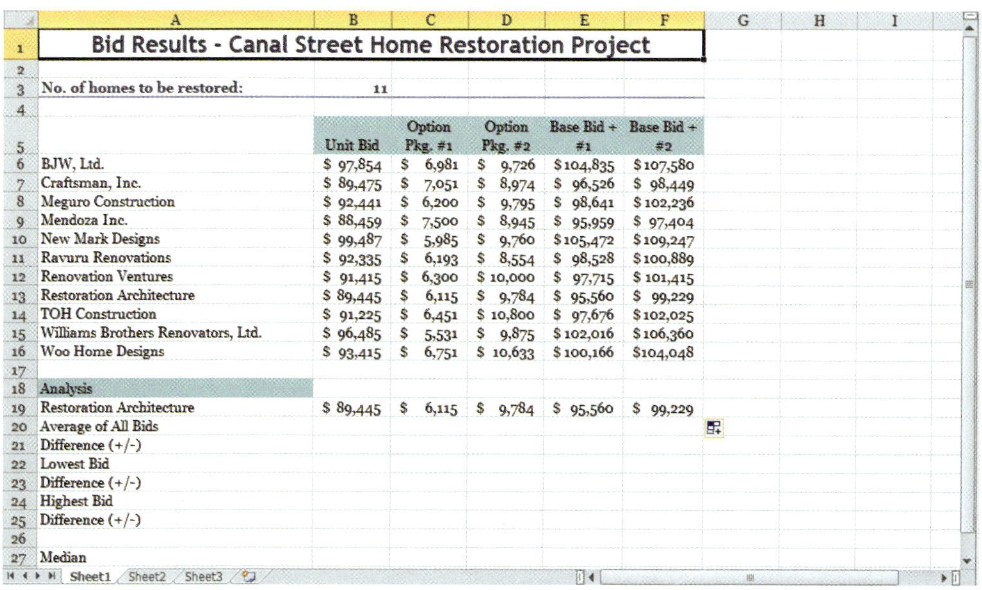

	A	B	C	D	E	F
1	Bid Results - Canal Street Home Restoration Project					
2						
3	No. of homes to be restored:	11				
4						
5		Unit Bid	Option Pkg. #1	Option Pkg. #2	Base Bid + #1	Base Bid + #2
6	BJW, Ltd.	$ 97,854	$ 6,981	$ 9,726	$104,835	$107,580
7	Craftsman, Inc.	$ 89,475	$ 7,051	$ 8,974	$ 96,526	$ 98,449
8	Meguro Construction	$ 92,441	$ 6,200	$ 9,795	$ 98,641	$102,236
9	Mendoza Inc.	$ 88,459	$ 7,500	$ 8,945	$ 95,959	$ 97,404
10	New Mark Designs	$ 99,487	$ 5,985	$ 9,760	$105,472	$109,247
11	Ravuru Renovations	$ 92,335	$ 6,193	$ 8,554	$ 98,528	$100,889
12	Renovation Ventures	$ 91,415	$ 6,300	$ 10,000	$ 97,715	$101,415
13	Restoration Architecture	$ 89,445	$ 6,115	$ 9,784	$ 95,560	$ 99,229
14	TOH Construction	$ 91,225	$ 6,451	$ 10,800	$ 97,676	$102,025
15	Williams Brothers Renovators, Ltd.	$ 96,485	$ 5,531	$ 9,875	$102,016	$106,360
16	Woo Home Designs	$ 93,415	$ 6,751	$ 10,633	$100,166	$104,048
17						
18	Analysis					
19	Restoration Architecture	$ 89,445	$ 6,115	$ 9,784	$ 95,560	$ 99,229
20	Average of All Bids					
21	Difference (+/-)					
22	Lowest Bid					
23	Difference (+/-)					
24	Highest Bid					
25	Difference (+/-)					
26						
27	Median					

Figure 11-1

Project 24—Apply It

Insert Functions in Formulas

DIRECTIONS

1. Start Excel, if necessary, and open the **EProj24** file from the data files for this lesson.
2. Save the workbook as **EProj24_studentfirstname_studentlastname** in the location where your teacher instructs you to store the files for this lesson.
3. Add a header that has your name at the left, the date code in the center, and the page number code at the right, and change back to **Normal** view.
4. Set up AutoCalculate to display all six functions in the status bar if it isn't set up that way already.
5. Click cell **B20**, type **=av**, click **AVERAGE** in the Formula AutoComplete list, and press TAB. Drag over the range **B6:B16** to enter it in the formula, and finish the formula.
6. Use the fill handle to fill the formula across the row.
7. In cell **B21**, enter a formula that subtracts the value in cell **B20** from the value in cell **B19**. Fill the formula across the row.
8. Use the **Sum** button Σ ▾ to enter a formula in cell **B22** that finds the lowest (MIN) value in the range **B6:B16**. Fill the formula across the row.
9. In cell **B23**, enter a formula that subtracts the value in cell **B22** from the value in cell **B19**. Fill the formula across the row.
10. Use the **More Functions** button **Statistical** submenu to enter a formula in cell **B24** that finds the highest (MAX) value in the range **B6:B16**. Fill the formula across the row.
11. In cell **B25**, enter a formula that subtracts the value in cell **B24** from the value in cell **B19**. Fill the formula across the row.
12. Use the **Insert Function** button *fx* on the formula bar to enter a formula in cell **B27** that finds the median value in the range **B6:B16**. Fill the formula across the row.
13. Select the range **F6:F16**. Observe the AutoCalculate results in the Status bar.
14. Change the status bar settings so that AutoCalculate only shows the Average, Count, and Sum results. Your worksheet should look like the one shown in Figure 11-2.
15. **With your teacher's permission**, print the worksheet. Submit the printout or the file for grading as required.
16. Save and close the file, and exit Excel.

Figure 11-2

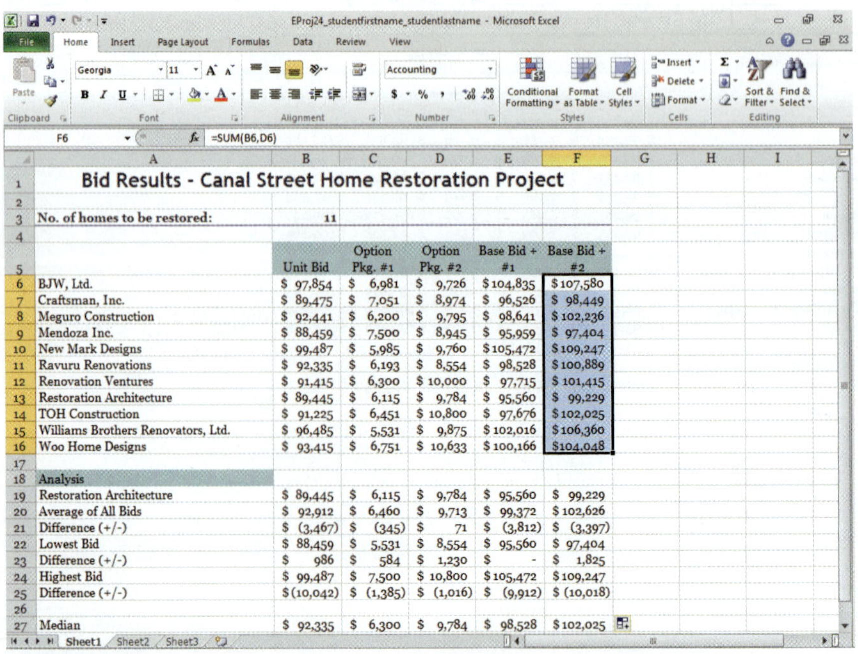

Bid Results - Canal Street Home Restoration Project

No. of homes to be restored: 11

	Unit Bid	Option Pkg. #1	Option Pkg. #2	Base Bid + #1	Base Bid + #2
BJW, Ltd.	$ 97,854	$ 6,981	$ 9,726	$104,835	$107,580
Craftsman, Inc.	$ 89,475	$ 7,051	$ 8,974	$ 96,526	$ 98,449
Meguro Construction	$ 92,441	$ 6,200	$ 9,795	$ 98,641	$102,236
Mendoza Inc.	$ 88,459	$ 7,500	$ 8,945	$ 95,959	$ 97,404
New Mark Designs	$ 99,487	$ 5,985	$ 9,760	$105,472	$109,247
Ravuru Renovations	$ 92,335	$ 6,193	$ 8,554	$ 98,528	$100,889
Renovation Ventures	$ 91,415	$ 6,300	$ 10,000	$ 97,715	$101,415
Restoration Architecture	$ 89,445	$ 6,115	$ 9,784	$ 95,560	$ 99,229
TOH Construction	$ 91,225	$ 6,451	$ 10,800	$ 97,676	$102,025
Williams Brothers Renovators, Ltd.	$ 96,485	$ 5,531	$ 9,875	$102,016	$106,360
Woo Home Designs	$ 93,415	$ 6,751	$ 10,633	$100,166	$104,048
Analysis					
Restoration Architecture	$ 89,445	$ 6,115	$ 9,784	$ 95,560	$ 99,229
Average of All Bids	$ 92,912	$ 6,460	$ 9,713	$ 99,372	$102,626
Difference (+/-)	$ (3,467)	$ (345)	$ 71	$ (3,812)	$ (3,397)
Lowest Bid	$ 88,459	$ 5,531	$ 8,554	$ 95,560	$ 97,404
Difference (+/-)	$ 986	$ 584	$ 1,230	$ -	$ 1,825
Highest Bid	$ 99,487	$ 7,500	$ 10,800	$105,472	$109,247
Difference (+/-)	$(10,042)	$ (1,385)	$ (1,016)	$ (9,912)	$ (10,018)
Median	$ 92,335	$ 6,300	$ 9,784	$ 98,528	$102,025

Lesson 12

Using Excel Tables

➤ What You Will Learn

Creating an Excel Table
Sorting and Filtering an Excel Table
Converting a Table to a Range

Software Skills Formatting a range as an Excel table enables you to apply formatting and create calculations with more ease. You also can sort and filter the data in the table to organize it for analysis. You'll learn how to create a table, perform calculations, and sort and filter in this lesson, as well as how to convert a table back to a regular range of cells.

Application Skills You are the Chief Financial Officer (CFO) of Restoration Architecture, and it's time for the quarterly revenue recap. You want to organize the information in a table so that you can add formulas and sort and filter to make the information easier to follow.

What You Can Do

Creating an Excel Table

- An **Excel table** is a range of data with special features that enable you to reference a column of data in a formula more naturally and build formulas more easily.
- You can perform other functions with the special column headers in an Excel table such as sorting and filtering data.
- Excel tables are best for data that's organized primarily by columns, because automatic totals and other functions can be inserted per column, but not by row.

WORDS TO KNOW

Column specifier
The structured reference to a table column, which consists of the table column header name in square brackets.

Criterion
A value, some text, or an expression that defines the type of content you want to see.

Excel table
Data arranged in columns and specially formatted with column headers that contain commands that allow you to sort, filter, and perform other functions on the table.

Filter
Hide nonmatching rows in a table or list of data according to the criterion or criteria you specify.

Sort
Arrange the rows in a table or list of data in a new order according to the entries in one or more columns.

Structured references
Using the table name or a table column header in a formula to refer to data in the entire table or specified column.

Total row
A row you can display below a table to calculate data in the columns above using a function you choose.

- You create a table by clicking in a range of data that includes headings for every column, and then using the Table button in the Tables group of the Insert tab.
- You select an overall table format and other formatting settings on the Table Tools Design tab.
- Excel automatically names the table, although you can change the table name.
- You can reference the table name and table column headers in formulas. References to the table and columns are called **structured references**.
- Adding a formula in a cell in the column to the right of the table automatically creates a calculated column that becomes part of the table.
- Structured references make the formulas easy to understand and also adjust automatically when you add data to the table.
- For example, =SUM(SalesDept[Jan]) totals the range of cells in the Jan column in the SalesDept table.
- The structured reference to a table column header is called a **column specifier.**
- To enter formulas that reference table data, use Formula AutoComplete so it can supply you with valid table names, column specifiers, and other structured references.
- In a formula, you enclose column specifiers and structured references in square brackets, and precede them with the table name, as in =AVERAGE(Sales[June])
- Excel provides several structured references you can use to refer to specific areas in a table.
  - [#ALL]—refers to the entire table range, including column headers, table data, and the totals row (if any).
  - [#DATA]—refers to the table data range.
  - [#HEADERS]—refers to the cells in the header row.
  - [#TOTALS]—refers to the cells in the total row.
  - [#THISROW]—refers to table cells located in the same row as the formula. This might include non-data cells.
- For example, =SUM(SalesDept[[#TOTALS], [April]:[June]]) totals the values in the Totals cells in columns April through June.
- You can display the **total row** below the table data range and set it up to perform calculations using the functions you specify.

Try It! Creating an Excel Table

1. Start Excel.
2. Open the **ETry12** file from the data files for this lesson.
3. Save the workbook as **ETry12_studentfirstname_studentlastname** in the location where your teacher instructs you to store the files for this lesson.

Creating an Excel table

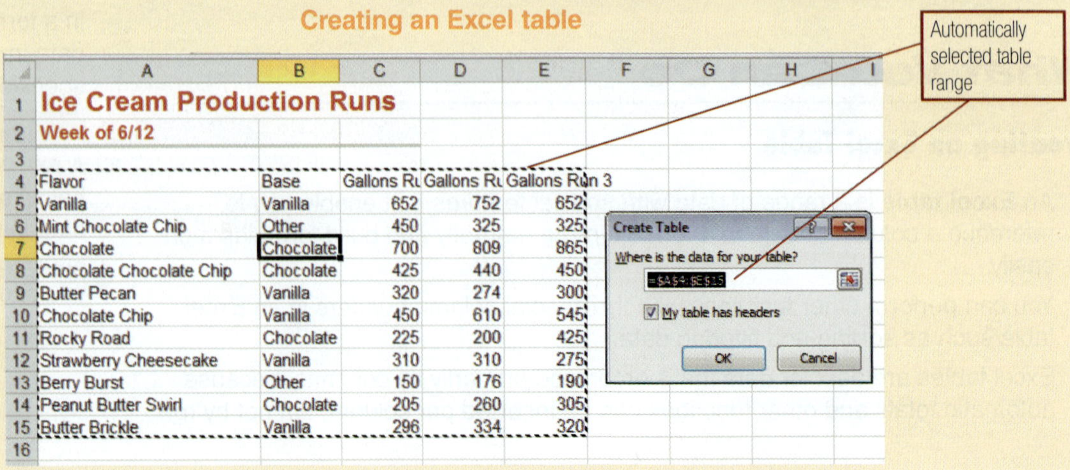

(continued)

Try It! Creating an Excel Table *(continued)*

4 Add a header that has your name at the left, the date code in the center, and the page number code at the right, and change back to Normal view.

5 Click cell B7 to select it.

6 Click Insert > Table. The Create Table dialog box appears, suggesting the correct range as the data range for the table.

✓ *Because the selected cell is in a range of data that has column header labels, Excel can identify the proper range for the table. Otherwise, you can drag to select the desired range.*

7 Click OK. Excel automatically creates the table, applies a table style, and displays the Table Tools Design tab.

8 On the Table Tools Design tab, in the Table Styles group, click the More button and then click Table Style Medium 7 under Medium in the gallery.

9 Click cell F5 to select it.

10 Type **= [Gallons Run 1]+[Gallons Run 2] +[Gallons Run 3]** and press ENTER. Excel automatically adds a new column to the table and copies the formula with structured references in the whole column.

✓ *This formula's structured references are the column headers, or column labels for the table. Notice that you didn't need to type in the table name in this instance.*

11 Press CTRL + Z three times to undo the new column.

12 With cell F5 still selected, click Home >Sum Σ, and press ENTER. This method also creates a formula with structured references and adds a new column to the table.

13 Change the entry in cell F4 to Gallons Total.

14 Click Table Tools Design > Total Row. The total row appears below the table data. Note that by default, Total is entered in cell A16, and a sum formula in cell F16.

✓ *Note that the function used to create the sum is actually a SUBTOTAL function.*

15 Change the entry in cell A16 to **Averages**.

Calculating with structured references

Structured references in range reference

F5 =SUM(Table1[@[Gallons Run 1]:[Gallons Run 3]])

	A	B	C	D	E	F
1	Ice Cream Production Runs					
2	Week of 6/12					
3						
4	Flavor	Base	Gallons Run 1	Gallons Run 2	Gallons Run 3	Gallons
5	Vanilla	Vanilla	652	752	652	2056
6	Mint Chocolate Chip	Other	450	325	325	1100
7	Chocolate	Chocolate	700	809	865	2374
8	Chocolate Chocolate Chip	Chocolate	425	440	450	1315
9	Butter Pecan	Vanilla	320	274	300	894
10	Chocolate Chip	Vanilla	450	610	545	1605
11	Rocky Road	Chocolate	225	200	425	850
12	Strawberry Cheesecake	Vanilla	310	310	275	895
13	Berry Burst	Other	150	176	190	516
14	Peanut Butter Swirl	Chocolate	205	260	305	770
15	Butter Brickle	Vanilla	296	334	320	950
16						

(continued)

Try It! Creating an Excel Table *(continued)*

16. Click cell F16, click the down arrow button, and then click None to remove the sum.
17. Click cell C16, click the down arrow button, and click Average.
18. Add Average calculations for cells D16 and E16.
19. Drag over the range C16:E16 to select it.
20. On the Home tab, click the dialog box launcher for the Number group.
21. In the Format Cells dialog box, click the Number tab, if necessary. In the Category list, click Number. Reduce the Decimal places entry to 0, and then click OK.
22. Save the **ETry12_studentfirstname_studentlastname** file, and leave it open to use in the next Try It.

Sorting and Filtering an Excel Table

- Each column header in an Excel table has a down arrow button. Clicking the button displays a menu with choices for changing the display of the table rows.
- Using a column header menu, you can **sort** the table, or change the order of the rows according to the entries in the column header by which you're sorting.
- You can sort in ascending order: A to Z, lowest to highest, or least recent to most recent.
- You also can sort in descending order: Z to A, highest to lowest, or most recent to least recent.
- Clearing a sort does not undo the sort. So, either use Undo to remove a sort immediately or add a column that numbers the rows so that you can return the rows to their original order.
- To sort by multiple columns, use the Sort button in the Sort & Filter group on the Data tab. In the Sort dialog box, specify the top level sort in the first Sort by row, then to sort within those results, use the Add Level button to sort by another field within those results.
- To limit the list to display only rows that have a particular entry (**criterion**) in one of the columns, **filter** the list.
- For example, you can filter a list of sales transactions to show transactions for only one client or salesperson.

  ✓ *You also can use a text filter to filter by a phrase or filter by color if you've applied conditional formatting.*
- Choose (Select All) or Clear Filter from *"Column"* in the column header menu to remove the filter.

Try It! Sorting and Filtering an Excel Table

1. In the **ETry12_studentfirstname_studentlastname** file, click the down arrow button for the Base column header.
2. In the menu, click Sort A to Z. Notice that the rows change order and are listed according to the entry in the Base column.

   ✓ *Look at the entries in the Flavor column. They are not sorted. For example, the rows with the Vanilla base appear in this order according to Flavor: Vanilla, Butter Pecan, Chocolate Chip, Strawberry Cheesecake, and Butter Brickle.*
3. Click Data > Sort.
4. In the Sort dialog box, click the Add Level button. In the Then by drop-down list that appears, choose Flavor. Open the Order drop-down list for that row, and click Z to A.
5. Click OK.

   ✓ *The rows reorder so that the Flavor column entries now appear in descending order within each Base grouping. The rows with the Vanilla base now appear in this order according to Flavor: Vanilla, Strawberry Cheesecake, Chocolate Chip, Butter Pecan, and Butter Brickle.*
6. Click the down arrow button for the Base column header.

(continued)

Try It! Sorting and Filtering an Excel Table *(continued)*

7. In the menu, click the check box beside (Select All) to uncheck it. Then, click the check box beside Chocolate to check it and click OK.

   ✓ *The total row recalculates to show results based on the filtered data only.*

8. Click the down arrow button for the Base column header.

9. In the menu, click Clear Filter from "Base".

10. Click Data > Sort .

11. Click the Delete Level button twice, and then click OK.

12. Save the **ETry12_studentfirstname_studentlastname** file, and leave it open to use in the next Try It.

Use a column header menu to sort or filter the table

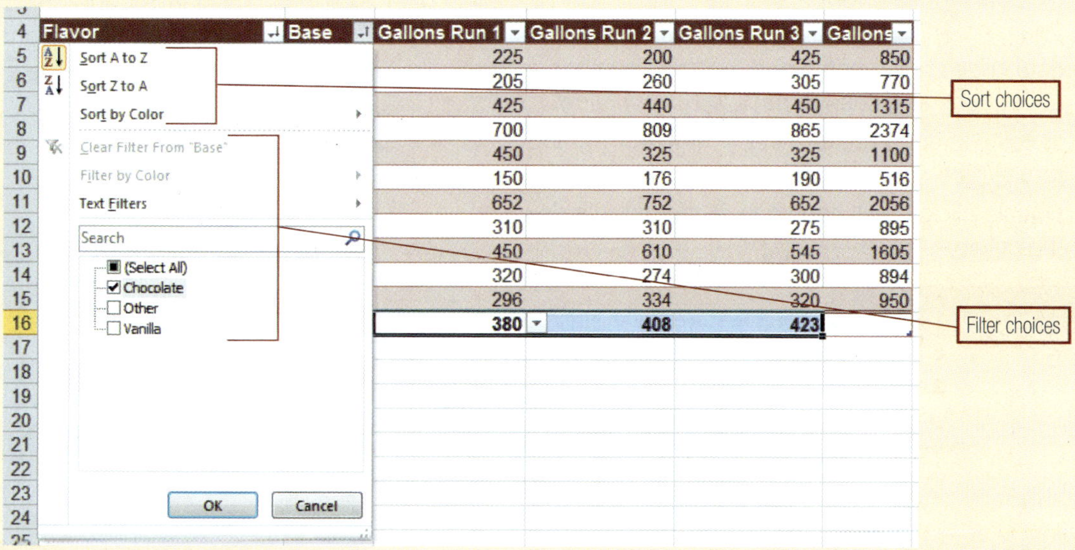

Converting a Table to a Range

- Converting a table to a range removes the special table functionality.
- The converted range retains any formatting you applied.
- Use the Convert to Range button in the Tools group of the Table Tools Design tab to convert the table, or right-click the table, point to Table, and click Convert to Range in the submenu.

Try It! Converting a Table to a Range

1. In the **ETry12_studentfirstname_studentlastname** file, click any cell in the table.

2. Click Table Tools Design > Convert to Range .

3. In the dialog box that appears to ask you to confirm the conversion, click Yes.

4. Click cell F6 to select it. Notice that the structured references have been converted to regular references.

5. Click cell C16 to select it. Notice that the formula is a subtotal formula.

6. Save the **ETry12_studentfirstname_studentlastname** file, and close it.

Project 25—Create It

Revenue Table

DIRECTIONS

1. Start Excel, if necessary, and open the **EProj25** file from the data files for this lesson.
2. Save the workbook as **EProj25_studentfirstname_studentlastname** in the location where your teacher instructs you to store the files for this lesson.
3. Add a header that has your name at the left, the date code in the center, and the page number code at the right, and change back to **Normal** view.
4. In cell **G5**, enter the formula **=sum(D5:F5)**, and press CTRL + ENTER.
5. Double-click the fill handle to fill the formula down the column.
6. Click cell **C8** to select it.
7. Click **Insert** > **Table**.
8. In the Create Table dialog box, click **OK**.
9. On the **Table Tools Design** tab, in the **Table Styles** group, click the **More** button, and click **Table Style Medium 23** under Medium.
10. Change the label in cell **A4** to **Project**. Your worksheet should look like the one in Figure 12-1.
11. **With your teacher's permission,** print the worksheet. Submit the printout or the file for grading as required.
12. Save and close the file.

Figure 12-1

Restoration Architecture

3rd Qtr Revenues by Project

Project	Type	Project Manager	July	August	September	Qtr 3 Totals
Rossen House	Residential	Jansen	$ 328,118	$ 456,221	$ 298,485	$ 1,082,824
Faster Library	Public	Nolo	$ 41,325	$ 78,945	$ 85,664	$ 205,934
512 N. Oak Street	Residential	Nolo	$ 32,995	$ 28,445	$ 18,445	$ 79,885
18 South Pendleton Ave.	Commercial	Jansen	$ 7,855	$ 27,958	$ 31,225	$ 67,038
Old Barn Quilts	Commercial	Nolo	$ 4,522	$ 12,889	$ 18,645	$ 36,056
Cramer Theater	Public	Timson	$125,995	$285,941	$ 275,884	$ 687,820
Freemont Park Amphitheater	Public	Jansen	$ 72,145	$ 63,145	$ 21,778	$ 157,068

Project 26—Apply It

Enhance the Revenue Table

DIRECTIONS

1. Start Excel, if necessary, and open the **EProj26** file from the data files for this lesson.
2. Save the workbook as **EProj26_studentfirstname_studentlastname** in the location where your teacher instructs you to store the files for this lesson.
3. Add a header that has your name at the left, the date code in the center, and the page number code at the right, and change back to **Normal** view.
4. In cell **H5**, enter a function to calculate the average revenues for July, August, and September. Copy the formula for the rest of the projects.

5. Change the column header for the new calculated column to **Qtr 3 Averages** and adjust the column
6. Add a total row to the table using the Table Tools Design tab.
7. Change the entry in cell **A12** to **Averages**.
8. Remove the calculation from cell **H12**, and add average calculations to cells **D12:G12**.
9. Sort the table in ascending order by **Type**.
10. Filter the table to show only projects by **Jansen**.
11. Adjust column widths if needed. Your worksheet should look like the one in Figure 12-2.
12. **With your teacher's permission,** print the worksheet. Submit the printout or the file for grading as required.
13. Save and close the file, and exit Excel.

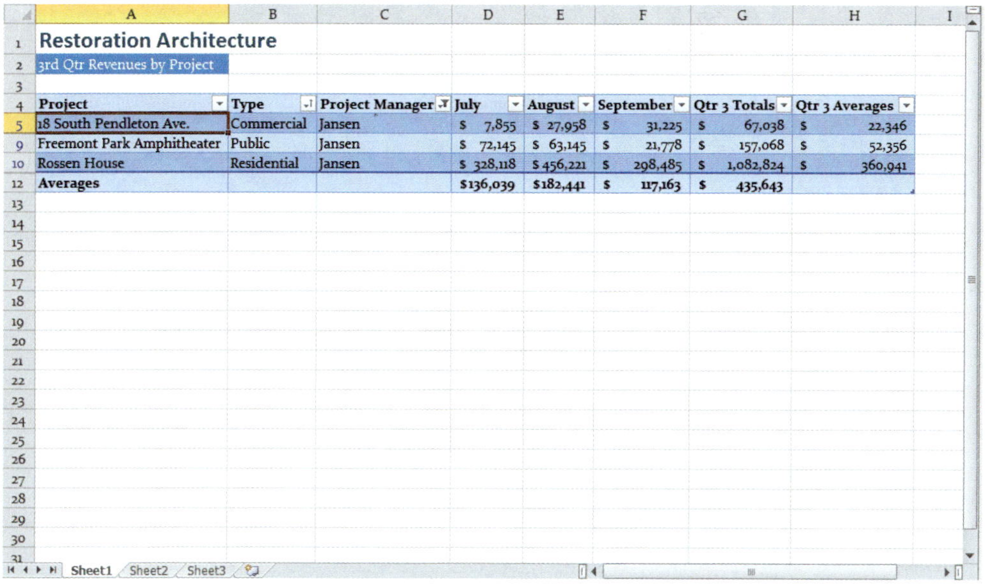

	A	B	C	D	E	F	G	H
1	Restoration Architecture							
2	3rd Qtr Revenues by Project							
3								
4	Project	Type	Project Manager	July	August	September	Qtr 3 Totals	Qtr 3 Averages
5	18 South Pendleton Ave.	Commercial	Jansen	$ 7,855	$ 27,958	$ 31,225	$ 67,038	$ 22,346
9	Freemont Park Amphitheater	Public	Jansen	$ 72,145	$ 63,145	$ 21,778	$ 157,068	$ 52,356
10	Rossen House	Residential	Jansen	$ 328,118	$ 456,221	$ 298,485	$ 1,082,824	$ 360,941
12	Averages			$136,039	$182,441	$ 117,163	$ 435,643	

Figure 12-2

Lesson 13

The NOW Function and Named Ranges

WORDS TO KNOW

Name Box
The box at the far-left end of the formula bar that you can use to create and navigate to named ranges.

Range name
An identifying label assigned to a group of cells. Also known as defined name.

Volatile
A function that updates and displays a new result each time you open the workbook.

➤ What You Will Learn

Using the NOW Function to Display a System Date
Using Named Ranges

Software Skills If you don't add a header or footer including the date print code to a worksheet, you can instead insert the NOW function to add the system date and time to any cell on the sheet. Many users find it easier to reference a cell or range of cells using a descriptive name rather than cell addresses. Using range names makes worksheet formulas easier to understand, as well as helping with other operations such as formatting and printing.

Application Skills As the CFO of Restoration Architecture, you review a great deal of financial and other data. So you want to add features that make your worksheets faster to use, such as a date that updates automatically and named ranges to make it easier to build and review formulas. In this exercise, you'll modify a recent revenue analysis worksheet so it updates with the current date and time and includes range names for use in calculations.

What You Can Do

Using the NOW Function to Display a System Date

- When you need to include a date and time that automatically updates on the worksheet, insert the NOW function. Rather than performing a calculation, this function displays the current system date and time.

- The NOW function doesn't require any arguments, so you enter it as =NOW().
- The results of the now function are **volatile**, meaning that they change based on the current system date and time when you open the workbook file rather than reflecting values on a worksheet.
- When you enter the NOW function in a cell, Excel automatically applies a date format that includes the time to the cell. You can change to another format if desired.
- You can enter the NOW function by typing it in, using Formula AutoComplete, or inserting it as you've learned earlier in the chapter.

Try It! Using the NOW Function to Display a System Date

1. Start Excel.
2. Open the **ETry13** file from the data files for this lesson.
3. Save the file as **ETry13_studentfirstname_studentlastname** in the location where your teacher instructs you to store the files for this lesson.
4. Add a header that has your name at the left, the date code in the center, and the page number code at the right, and change back to Normal view.
5. Click cell A2 to select it.
6. Type **=NOW()** and press CTRL + ENTER. The date and time appear in the cell.

The result of the NOW function

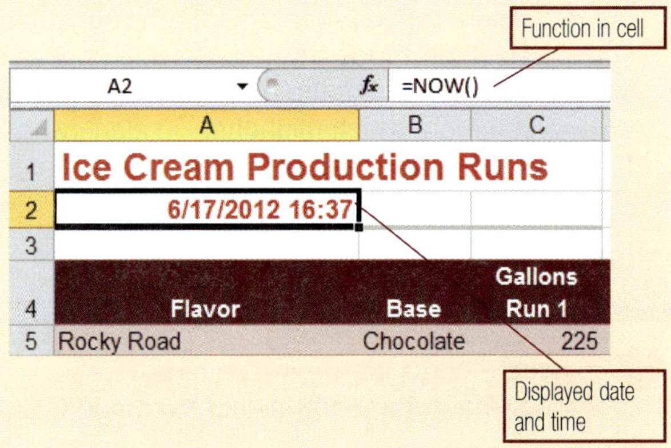

7. Save the **ETry13_studentfirstname_studentlastname** file, and leave it open to use in the next Try It.

Using Named Ranges

- Create a descriptive **range name** for a range of cells (or a single cell) in order to reference it by name rather than by cell addresses.
- After naming a range, you can use the range name any place the range address might otherwise be entered—within a formula, defining the print range, selecting a range to format, and so on.
- As you learned in Lesson 13, you don't have to name ranges to use column labels in formulas. Instead, you can format your data as an Excel table.
- If you use the range name in a formula, you can use Formula AutoComplete to enter it quickly.
- You can also insert range names in a formula using the Use in Formula button list in the Defined Names group of the Formulas tab.
- If a range name is defined within a worksheet, it can only be used within that sheet, unless you precede it with the sheet name and an exclamation point, as in *Sheet1!RangeName*.
- If defined within a workbook, the range name can be used on any sheet in that workbook.
- A range name may use up to 255 characters, although short descriptive names are easier to read and remember.
- Range naming rules include:
  - No spaces allowed. Use the underscore character in place of a space.
  - Do not use range names that could be interpreted as a cell address or a number, such as Q2 or Y2012.
  - A range name may include letters, numbers, underscores (_), backslashes (\), periods (.), and question marks (?).
  - Do not begin a range name with a number.

- Range names are not case sensitive, so you can use uppercase or lowercase letters.
- Avoid using your column labels as range names, because they could create errors if you should format the range as a table and attempt to use range names as table names or vice-versa.

- You can define a range name using the **Name Box** at the left end of the formula bar. Type a name and press ENTER.
- You also can use the Define Name button button in the Defined Names group of the Formulas tab to define a range name. This method enables you to select the scope where the name applies (a particular worksheet or the entire workbook), and to enter a comment which might help in identifying the purpose of the range name.
- Right-click a selected range, and click Define Range to begin the naming process.
- If you have a lot of named ranges in a workbook, you can insert a list of named ranges with their corresponding cell references in the worksheet.
- If you are working with a list or table of data, you may need to sort the data prior to assigning range names.
- Use the Name Manager dialog box, opened from the Defined Names group on the Formulas tab, to edit or delete named ranges.

Try It! Using Named Ranges

1. In the **ETry13_studentfirstname_studentlastname** file, select the range C5:C8.
2. Click in the Name Box, type **ChocRun1**, and press ENTER.
3. Use the technique in step 2 to assign the following names to the specified ranges:
   D5:D8................**ChocRun2**
   E5:E8................**ChocRun3**
   F5:F8................**ChocTotal**
4. Select the range C9:C10, right-click it, and click Define Name. Type **OthRun1** in the Name text box of the New Name dialog box, and then click OK.
5. Use the technique in step 4 to assign the following names to the specified ranges:
   D9:D10................**OthRun2**
   E9:E10................**OthRun3**
   F9:F10................**OthTotal**
6. Select the range C11:C15. Click Formulas > Define Name. Type **VanRun1** in the Name text box of the New Name dialog box, and then click OK.
7. Use the technique in Step 6 to assign the following names to the specified ranges:
   D11:D15.............**VanRun2**
   E11:E15.............**VanRun3**
   F11:F15.............**VanTotal**
8. Click in the Name Box, type **ChocRun1**, and press ENTER. Excel selects the range that you named ChocRun1 earlier.
9. Click cell C16. Type **=sum(ChocRun1,OthRun1,VanRun1)**, and press TAB.
10. Type **=sum(cho**, press ↓ to select ChocRun2, and press TAB. Type **,OthRun2,VanRun2** and press TAB.

✓ *Step 10 is an example of using Formula AutoComplete to enter a range name.*

(continued)

Try It! Using Named Ranges *(continued)*

11 Use the techniques of your choice to enter formulas that total the Gallons Run 3 and Gallons Total columns.

✓ *Named ranges are absolute references, so you can't fill them.*

12 Select cell C18, and enter the formula **=sum(ChocRun1)**. Continue by entering the following formulas:

C19 .... **=sum(OthRun1)**
C20 .... **=sum(VanRun1)**
D18 .... **=sum(ChocRun2)**
D19 .... **=sum(OthRun2)**
D20 .... **=sum(VanRun2)**
E18 .... **=sum(ChocRun3)**
E19 .... **=sum(OthRun3)**
E20 .... **=sum(VanRun3)**
F18 .... **=sum(ChocTotal)**
F19 .... **=sum(OthTotal)**
F20 .... **=sum(VanTotal)**

13 Save the **ETry13_studentfirstname_studentlastname** file, and close it.

Using range names in formulas

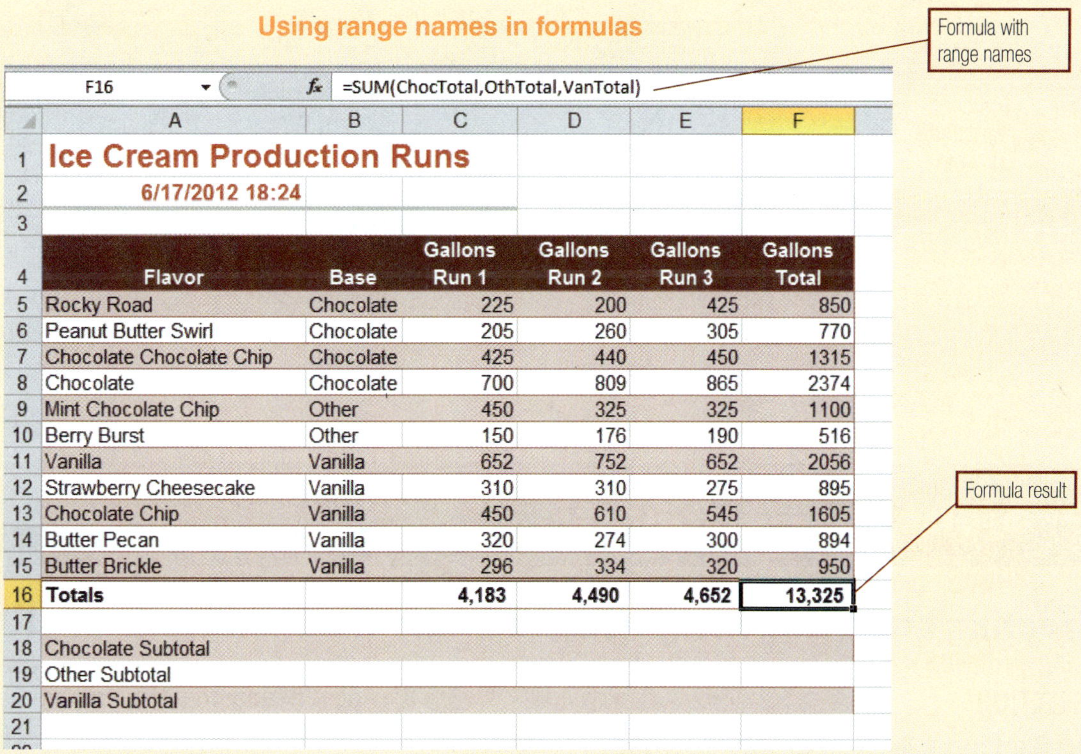

	A	B	C	D	E	F
1	Ice Cream Production Runs					
2	6/17/2012 18:24					
3						
4	Flavor	Base	Gallons Run 1	Gallons Run 2	Gallons Run 3	Gallons Total
5	Rocky Road	Chocolate	225	200	425	850
6	Peanut Butter Swirl	Chocolate	205	260	305	770
7	Chocolate Chocolate Chip	Chocolate	425	440	450	1315
8	Chocolate	Chocolate	700	809	865	2374
9	Mint Chocolate Chip	Other	450	325	325	1100
10	Berry Burst	Other	150	176	190	516
11	Vanilla	Vanilla	652	752	652	2056
12	Strawberry Cheesecake	Vanilla	310	310	275	895
13	Chocolate Chip	Vanilla	450	610	545	1605
14	Butter Pecan	Vanilla	320	274	300	894
15	Butter Brickle	Vanilla	296	334	320	950
16	Totals		4,183	4,490	4,652	13,325
17						
18	Chocolate Subtotal					
19	Other Subtotal					
20	Vanilla Subtotal					
21						

Project 27—Create It

Revenue Worksheet Preparation

DIRECTIONS

1. Start Excel, if necessary, and open the **EProj27** file from the data files for this lesson.
2. Save the workbook as **EProj27_studentfirstname_studentlastname** in the location where your teacher instructs you to store the files for this lesson.
3. Add a header that has your name at the left, the date code in the center, and the page number code at the right, and change back to **Normal** view.
4. In cell **C2**, enter the formula **=NOW()**, and press CTRL + ENTER.
5. Drag over the range **A4:H11** to select it.
6. Click **Data > Sort**.
7. In the Sort dialog box, click the **Sort by** down arrow, and click **Project Manager**.
8. Click **OK**.
9. Drag over the range **A5:H11** to select it.
10. Click **Home > Cell Styles > 40% Accent1**. Your worksheet should look like the one shown in Figure 13-1.
11. **With your teacher's permission,** print the worksheet. Submit the printout or the file for grading as required.
12. Save and close the file.

Figure 13-1

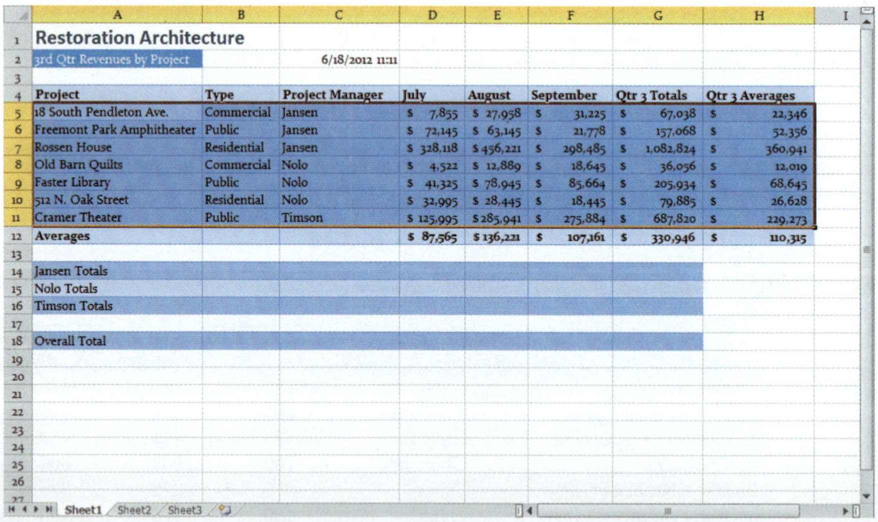

	A	B	C	D	E	F	G	H
1	Restoration Architecture							
2	3rd Qtr Revenues by Project		6/18/2012 11:11					
3								
4	Project	Type	Project Manager	July	August	September	Qtr 3 Totals	Qtr 3 Averages
5	18 South Pendleton Ave.	Commercial	Jansen	$ 7,855	$ 27,958	$ 31,225	$ 67,038	$ 22,346
6	Freemont Park Amphitheater	Public	Jansen	$ 72,145	$ 63,145	$ 21,778	$ 157,068	$ 52,356
7	Rossen House	Residential	Jansen	$ 328,118	$ 456,221	$ 298,485	$ 1,082,824	$ 360,941
8	Old Barn Quilts	Commercial	Nolo	$ 4,522	$ 12,889	$ 18,645	$ 36,056	$ 12,019
9	Faster Library	Public	Nolo	$ 41,325	$ 78,945	$ 85,664	$ 205,934	$ 68,645
10	512 N. Oak Street	Residential	Nolo	$ 32,995	$ 28,445	$ 18,445	$ 79,885	$ 26,628
11	Cramer Theater	Public	Timson	$ 125,995	$ 285,941	$ 275,884	$ 687,820	$ 229,273
12	Averages			$ 87,565	$ 136,221	$ 107,161	$ 330,946	$ 110,315
13								
14	Jansen Totals							
15	Nolo Totals							
16	Timson Totals							
17								
18	Overall Total							

Project 28—Apply It

Creating and Using Range Names in the Revenue Worksheet

DIRECTIONS

1. Start Excel, if necessary, and open the **EProj28** file from the data files for this lesson.
2. Save the workbook as **EProj28_studentfirstname_studentlastname** in the location where your teacher instructs you to store the files for this lesson.
3. Add a header that has your name at the left, the date code in the center, and the page number code at the right, and change back to **Normal** view.

4. Select the range **D5:D7**. Use the Name Box to assign the name **JansenJuly** to the range.
5. Also use the Name Box to assign the following range names:
   a. **E5:E7** **JansenAugust**
   b. **F5:F7** **JansenSeptember**
   c. **G5:G7** **JansenTotal**
6. Select the range **D8:D10**. Right-click the range and click **Define Name**. Type **NoloJuly** in the **Name** text box of the New Name dialog box, change the **Scope** to **Sheet1**, and click **OK**.
7. Use the same technique used in step 6 to assign the following range names and limit their scope to Sheet1:
   a. **E8:E10** **NoloAugust**
   b. **F8:F10** **NoloSeptember**
   c. **G8:G10** **NoloTotal**
8. Use the method of your choice to assign the following range names:
   a. **D11** **TimsonJuly**
   b. **E11** **TimsonAugust**
   c. **F11** **TimsonSeptember**
   d. **G11** **TimsonTotal**
9. Click **D14**, and enter a formula that sums the **JansenJuly** range.
10. Enter formulas that total the other three Jansen ranges in cells **E14:G14**.
11. Enter formulas that sum the ranges for the other two project managers in the applicable cells in the range **D15:G16**.
12. Click cell **D18** and enter a formula that sums the July ranges for all three project managers. (Hint: The first formula is =SUM(JansenJuly,NoloJuly,TimsonJuly).)
13. Enter formulas that sum the August, September, and Total data for the three project managers in cells **E18:G18**. Your worksheet should look like the one shown in Figure 13-2.
14. **With your teacher's permission,** print the worksheet. Submit the printout or the file for grading as required.
15. Save and close the file, and exit Excel.

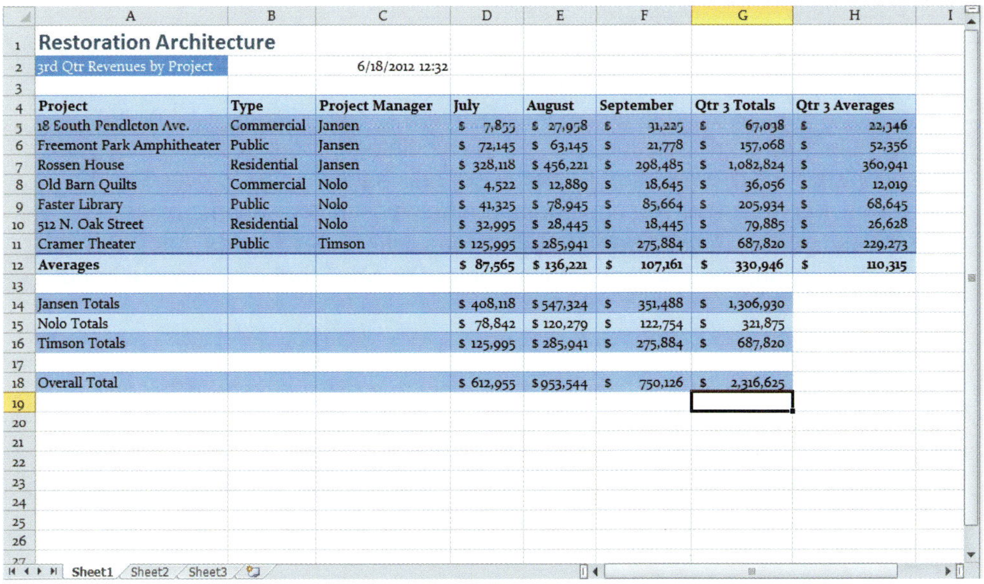

	A	B	C	D	E	F	G	H
1	Restoration Architecture							
2	3rd Qtr Revenues by Project		6/18/2012 12:32					
3								
4	Project	Type	Project Manager	July	August	September	Qtr 3 Totals	Qtr 3 Averages
5	18 South Pendleton Ave.	Commercial	Jansen	$ 7,855	$ 27,958	$ 31,225	$ 67,038	$ 22,346
6	Freemont Park Amphitheater	Public	Jansen	$ 72,145	$ 63,145	$ 21,778	$ 157,068	$ 52,356
7	Rossen House	Residential	Jansen	$ 328,118	$ 456,221	$ 298,485	$ 1,082,824	$ 360,941
8	Old Barn Quilts	Commercial	Nolo	$ 4,522	$ 12,889	$ 18,645	$ 36,056	$ 12,019
9	Faster Library	Public	Nolo	$ 41,325	$ 78,945	$ 85,664	$ 205,934	$ 68,645
10	512 N. Oak Street	Residential	Nolo	$ 32,995	$ 28,445	$ 18,445	$ 79,885	$ 26,628
11	Cramer Theater	Public	Timson	$ 125,995	$ 285,941	$ 275,884	$ 687,820	$ 229,273
12	Averages			$ 87,565	$ 136,221	$ 107,161	$ 330,946	$ 110,315
13								
14	Jansen Totals			$ 408,118	$ 547,324	$ 351,488	$ 1,306,930	
15	Nolo Totals			$ 78,842	$ 120,279	$ 122,754	$ 321,875	
16	Timson Totals			$ 125,995	$ 285,941	$ 275,884	$ 687,820	
17								
18	Overall Total			$ 612,955	$ 953,544	$ 750,126	$ 2,316,625	

Figure 13-2

Lesson 14

Working with IF Functions

WORDS TO KNOW

Expression
A sort of equation (such as B6>25) that returns a value, such as TRUE or FALSE. Excel uses expressions to identify cells to include in certain formulas such as IF and SUMIF.

Nesting
Using a function as an argument within another function.

➤ What You Will Learn

Understanding IF Functions
Nesting Functions
Using =SUMIF() and SUMIFS() Functions
Using =COUNTIF() and COUNTIFS() Functions

Software Skills IF functions enable you to test for particular conditions and then perform specific actions based on whether those conditions exist or not. For example, with an IF function, you could calculate the bonuses for a group of salespeople on the premise that bonuses are only paid if a sale is over $1,000. With the SUMIF function, you could total up the sales in your Atlanta office, even if those sales figures are scattered through a long list of sales figures. And, with the COUNTIF function, you could count the number of sales that resulted in a bonus being paid.

Application Skills You're the Manager of a Whole Grains Bread store in Olympia, Washington, and you've been developing a new worksheet for tracking retail bread sales. You've just learned about various IF functions, and, along with some other new functions you've discovered, you know you can refine the worksheet so that it's simple for your employees to use. With the sales analysis the worksheet will provide, you can refine the retail end of your business to maximize your profits.

What You Can Do

Understanding IF Functions

- IF() is a Logical function.
- With an IF function, you can tell Excel to perform one of two different calculations based on whether your data matches a logical test.

- For example, you can use an IF function to have Excel calculate a 10% bonus if total sales are over $500,000 and just a 3% bonus if they are not.
- The format for an IF function is:

  =IF(logical_test,value_if_true,value_if_false)
  - The *logical test* is a condition or **expression** whose result is either true or false.
  - If the condition is true, the formula displays the *value_if_true* argument in the cell.
  - If the condition is false, the formula displays the *value_if_false* argument in the cell.
- For example, to calculate the bonus described above, you would type **=IF(B2>500000,B2*.10,B2*.03)**
- The above function says, "If total sales (cell B2) are greater than $500,000, then take total sales times 10% to calculate the bonus. Otherwise, take total sales times 3%."
- Notice that in the IF function, the value, $500,000, is entered without the dollar sign or the comma.
- You can have text appear in a cell instead of a calculated value. For example, you might type **=IF(B2>500000,"We made it!","Good try.")** to display the words *We made it!* if total sales are over $500,000, or the words *Good try.* if they are not.
- Surround the text you want to appear with quotation marks (" ") in the formula.
- IF functions may use the comparison operators below to state the condition:

  = Equals

  <> Not equal to

  > Greater than

  >= Greater than or equal to

  < Less than

  <= Less than or equal to

  & Used for joining text
- Like any other function, you can enter an IF function manually, use Formula AutoComplete, or use the Insert Function dialog box or Function Library group drop-down lists to help.

Try It! Understanding IF Functions

1. Start Excel.
2. Open the **ETry14** file from the data files for this lesson.
3. Save the workbook as **ETry14_studentfirstname_studentlastname** in the location where your teacher instructs you to store the files for this lesson.
4. Add a header that has your name at the left, the date code in the center, and the page number code at the right, and change back to Normal view.
5. Click cell F4 to select it.
6. Click Formulas > Logical > IF. The Function Arguments dialog box appears.
7. Type **d4>=20** in the Logical_test text box, and press TAB.
8. Type **Yes** in the Value_if_true text box, and press TAB.

   ✓ *The Function Arguments dialog box adds the quotation marks around text entries for you.*

(continued)

Try It! Understanding IF Functions *(continued)*

9. Type **No** in the Value_if_false text box, and press TAB.
10. Click OK. Because the entry in cell D4 is 17 (less than 20), a result of No displays in cell F4.
11. Drag the fill handle down to fill the formula through cell F21.
12. Save the **ETry14_studentfirstname_studentlastname** file, and leave it open to use in the next Try It.

Building an IF function

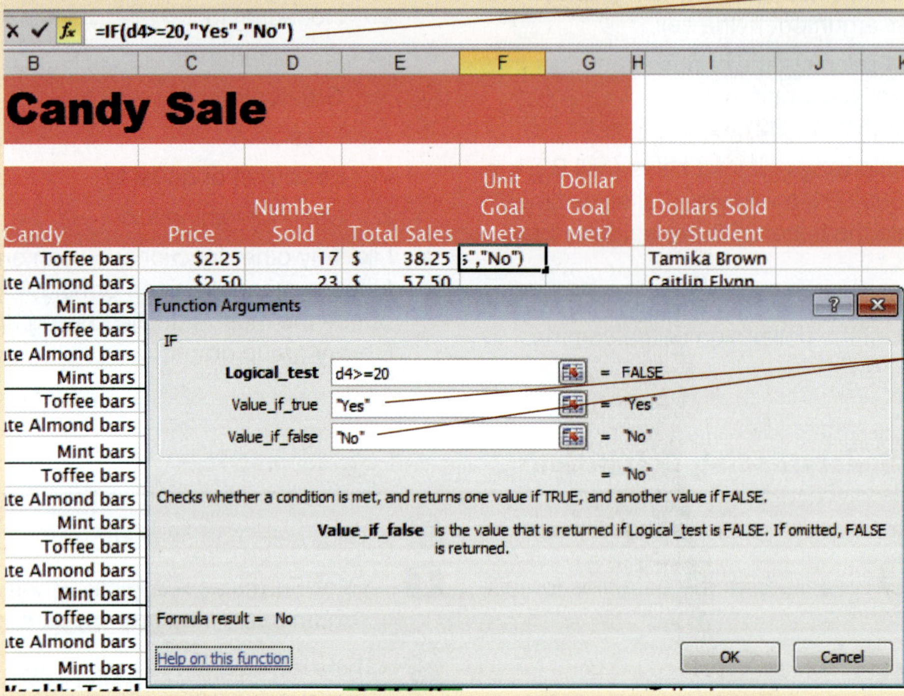

Nesting Functions

- You can **nest** any function as one of the arguments for another function in a formula.
- The arguments in IF functions often use nested functions, either in the logical test or of the possible outcome values, or both.
- For example, consider the formula:
  =IF(C3>92,"A",IF(C3>83,"B",IF(C3>73,"C",IF(C3>65,"D","F"))))
- The above formula says that if the average score in cell C3 is greater than 92, then the student gets an A; if the score is less than or equal to 92 but greater than 83, the student gets a B; if the score is less than or equal to 83 but greater than 73, the student gets a C; and so on.

Try It! **Nesting Functions**

1. In the **ETry14_studenfirstname_ studentlastname** file, click cell G4 to select it.
2. Click the Insert Function button *fx* on the formula bar.
3. Open the Or select a category list, and click Logical. In the Select a function list, click IF. Click OK. The Function Arguments dialog box appears.
4. Type **E4>=60** in the Logical_test text box, and press TAB.
5. Type **Yes** in the Value_if_true text box, and press TAB.
6. Type **No** in the Value_if_false text box, and press TAB.
7. Click OK. Because the entry in cell E4 is $38.25 (less than 50), a result of No displays in cell G4.
8. Drag the fill handle down to fill the formula through cell G21.
9. Click Home > Border to reapply bottom border formatting to cells in rows 6, 9, 12, 15, 18, and 21 of columns F and G.
10. Save the **ETry14_studentfirstname_ studentlastname** file, and leave it open to use in the next Try It.

Using SUMIF() and SUMIFS() Functions

- SUMIF() is a Math & Trig function that uses a condition to add certain data.
- If the condition is true, then data in a corresponding cell is added to the total; if it is false, then the corresponding data is skipped.
- Here is how you enter a SUMIF function: =SUMIF(range,criteria,sum_range)
  - The *range* is the range of cells you want to review.
  - The *criteria* is an expression that is either true or false, and defines which cells should be added to the total.
  - If you specify an optional *sum_range*, values from the sum_range on the rows where the range data results in a true result for the *criteria* are added to the total.
  - If you do not specify a sum_range, the formula adds the values from the *range* rows that evaluate as true.
- Use the same comparison operators (such as >,<>, etc.) as for an IF function in the criteria. However, here, you must enclose the condition in quotation marks (" ") if it is not a cell reference.
- For example, if you had a worksheet listing sales for several different products, you could total only sales for widgets by using this formula: =SUMIF(D2:D55,"Widget",G2:G55)
- Assume in the previous formula example that column D contains the name of the product being sold and column G contains the total amount for that sale. If column D contains the word "Widget," then the amount for that sale (located in column G) is added to the running total.
- You can leave the last argument off if you want to sum the same range that you're testing; for example: =SUMIF(G2:G10,"<=500"). This formula calculates the total of all values in the range G2 to G10 that are less than or equal to 500.
- SUMIFS() is a function similar to SUMIF() except that it allows you to enter multiple qualifying conditions.
- The format for a SUMIFS statement is: =SUMIFS(sum_range,criteria_ range1,criteria1,criteria_range2,criteria2,etc.).
  - The *criteria_range1* is the first range of cells you want to test.
  - The *criteria1* is an expression that is either true or false, and defines which cells should be added to the total.
  - If the criteria1 result is true, the corresponding cell in sum_range is added to the total.
  - If the criteria1 result is false, the corresponding cell in sum_range is not added to the total.
  - You can add conditions and additional ranges to test as needed. You can specify the same range to test or use a different one.
  - All ranges, the sum_range and the criteria ranges, must be the same size and shape.

- Using the earlier example, if you wanted to total all the sales of Widgets and Whatsits, you could use a formula such as: =SUMIFS(G2:G55, D2:D55," Widget",D2:D55,"Whatsits").
- Again, column D contains the name of the product being sold, and column G contains the total amount for that sale.

Try It! Using SUMIF() and SUMIFS() Functions

1. In the **ETry14_studentfirstname_ studentlastname** file, click cell K4 to select it.
2. Click the Insert Function button *fx* on the formula bar.
3. Open the Or select a category list, and click Math & Trig. In the Select a function list, click SUMIF. Click OK. The Function Arguments dialog box appears.
4. Drag over the range A4:A21 to specify it in the Range text box, press [F4] to make the range address absolute, and press [TAB].

   ✓ *Because you will be copying the formula, you need to make the range references absolute.*
5. Click cell I4 to specify it in the Criteria text box, and press [TAB].

   ✓ *Using a cell reference rather than typing in the student name in this case will enable you to fill the formula down and get an accurate result for each student.*
6. Drag over the range E4:E21 to specify it in the Sum_range text box, press [F4] to make the range address absolute, and press [TAB].
7. Click OK. Excel calculates a total of $170.00 in sales for the specified student.
8. Drag the fill handle down to fill the formula through cell K9.

   ✓ *To verify the total calculated for any student, use the AutoCalculate feature. Drag over the sales values for the student in column E, and compare the Sum that appears in the Status bar with the value calculated by the SUMIF function in column K.*
9. Click cell K12 to select it.
10. Click the Insert Function button *fx* on the formula bar.
11. Open the Or select a category list, and click Math & Trig. In the Select a function list, click SUMIFS. Click OK. The Function Arguments dialog box appears.
12. Drag over the range E4:E21 to specify it in the Sum_range text box, press [F4] to make the range address absolute, and press [TAB].

Using the SUMIF function

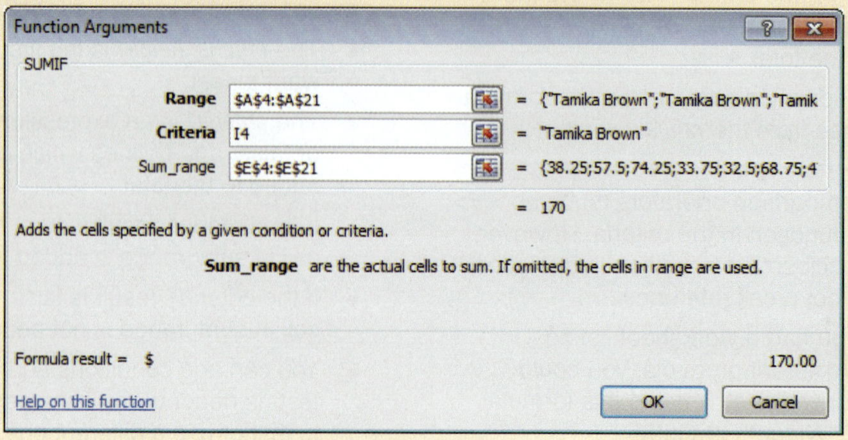

(continued)

Try It! Using SUMIF() and SUMIFS() Functions *(continued)*

13 Drag over the range A4:A21 to specify it in the Criteria_range1 text box, press F4 to make the range address absolute, and press TAB.

14 Click cell I12 to specify it in the Criteria1 text box, and press TAB.

15 Drag over the range D4:D21 to specify it in the Criteria_range2 text box, press F4 to make the range address absolute, and press TAB.

16 Type >20 in the Criteria2 text box.

17 Click OK. Excel calculates a total of $131.75 for sales where the specified student sold more than 20 units of a product.

18 Drag the fill handle down to fill the formula through cell K17.

19 Save the **ETry14_studentfirstname_studentlastname** file, and leave it open to use in the next Try It.

Specify as many criteria as needed with the SUMIFS function

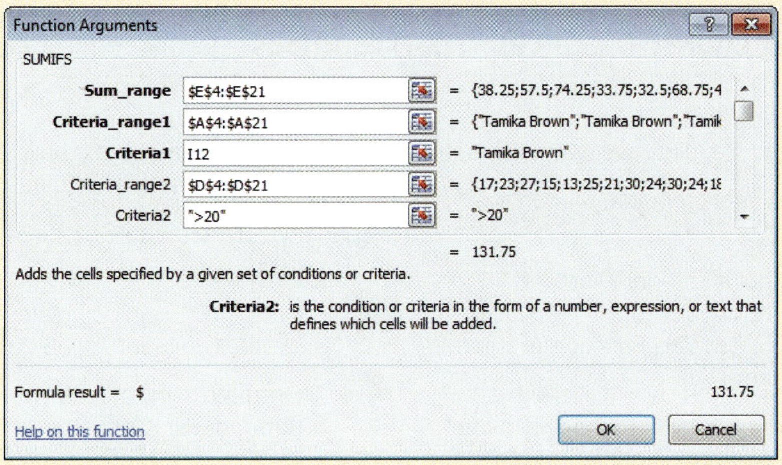

Using COUNTIF() and COUNTIFS() Functions

- COUNTIF is a Statistical function that uses a criteria to count the number of items in a range.
  - ✓ *You learned about two similar functions, COUNT and COUNTA, in Lesson 11.*
- If the result of the criteria is true, then the item is added to a running count; if it is false, then the item is skipped.
- The format for a COUNTIF function is: =COUNTIF(range, criteria).
  - ✓ *The* range *is the range of cells holding the values to test (and count).*
  - ✓ *The* criteria *is an expression that is either true or false, defining which cells should be counted.*
- Use the same comparison operators as for the IF function when writing the criteria. As for SUMIF, you must enclose the condition in quotation marks (" ") if it is not a cell reference.
- For example, if you want to count the number of individual Widget sales in the earlier example, you could use this formula: =COUNTIF(D2:D55,"Widget"). Assume here that column D contains the name of the product being sold; for each cell in column D that contains the word "Widget," 1 is added to the running total of the number of widget sales.
- Because Widget is a text label, you must enclose it in quotation marks (" ").
- To compute the number of widgets sold or the value of those sales, use SUMIF.
- You can combine functions to create complex calculations: =SUMIF(D3:D13,"PASS",C3:C13)/COUNTIF(D3:D13,"PASS").
- The above formula computes the average score of all the students who passed the course. Assume that column D contains the words "Pass" or "Fail" based on the student's final score. The final score is located in column C. The formula sums the scores of all the students who passed and divides that by the number

of students who passed, calculating an average score for passing students.

- COUNTIFS() is a function similar to COUNTIF() except that it allows you to enter multiple qualifying conditions.
- The format for a COUNTIFS statement is: =COUNTIFS(criteria_range1,criteria1,criteria_range2,criteria2,etc.).
  - The *criteria_range1* is the range of cells you want to test.
  - The *criteria1* is an expression that is either true or false, and defines which cells should be counted.
  - You can add additional conditions and ranges to test as needed. You can specify the same range to test or use a different one.
  - All ranges must be the same shape and size.
- Using the earlier example, if you wanted to count all Widget sales with a value over $100, you could use a formula such as: =COUNTIFS(D2:D55,"Widget",G2:G55,">100").
- Again, column D contains the name of the product being sold, and column G contains the total amount for that sale.
- Since there are 54 rows in the two ranges, the highest answer you might get is 54. A row is counted only if it contains both the word Widget in column D, and a value greater than 100 in column G.

Try It! Using COUNTIF() and COUNTIFS() Functions

1. In the **ETry14_studentfirstname_studentlastname** file, click cell K20 to select it.
2. Click the Insert Function button fx on the formula bar.
3. Open the Or select a category list, and click Statistical. In the Select a function list, click COUNTIFS. Click OK. The Function Arguments dialog box appears.
4. Drag over the range B4:B21 to specify it in the Criteria_range1 text box, press F4 to make the range address absolute, and press TAB.
5. Click cell I20 to specify it in the Criteria1 text box, and press TAB.
6. Drag over the range D4:D21 to specify it in the Criteria_range2 text box, press F4 to make the range address absolute, and press TAB.
7. Type **>20** in the Criteria2 text box, and press TAB.
8. Click OK. Excel calculates a total of 3 sales of over 20 units for Toffee bars.
9. Drag the fill handle down to fill the formula through cell K22.
10. Save the **ETry14_studentfirstname_studentlastname** file, and close it.

Using multiple criteria to count with the COUNTIFS function

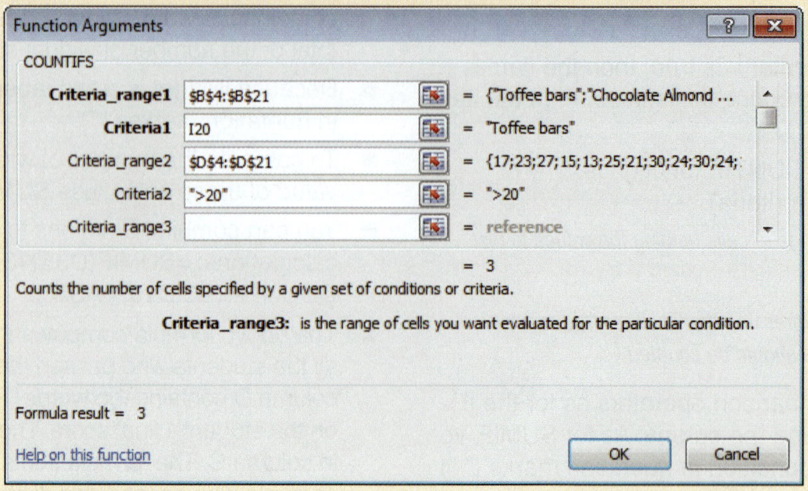

Project 29—Create It

Setting Up Monday Discounts in the Bread Sales Workbook

DIRECTIONS

1. Start Excel, if necessary, and open the **EProj29** file from the data files for this lesson.
2. Save the workbook as **EProj29_studentfirstname_studentlastname** in the location where your teacher instructs you to store the files for this lesson.
3. For each sheet, add a header that has your name at the left, the date code in the center, and the page number code at the right, and change back to **Normal** view.
4. Enter the date **12/3/12** in cell **B4**, and increase the column width as needed to display the date.
5. Display the **Price List** sheet, and click cell **B3**. Notice that the Name Box displays the name already assigned to this cell. All the cells holding prices have names assigned.
6. Because your company gives a discount for white bread on Mondays, you need to enter a formula in cell B3 to calculate the discounted amount for that day of the week. Use the **IF** function with a nested **WEEKDAY** function in the formula. The formula should return a value of $2.00 if the date in cell B4 on the Daily Sales sheet is a Monday, and $2.55 if it is not.

   ✓ *Hint: Use =IF(WEEKDAY(argument)=something,then do this, else do this).*

   The WEEKDAY function requires one argument, in parentheses. The required argument is the address of the cell that contains the date to look at, which in this case is cell B4 on the Daily Sales sheet. WEEKDAY returns a value from 1 to 7, telling you what day of the week the date you provide as the first argument is. By default, Sunday is counted as day 1, so if the date in cell 'Daily Sales'!B4 is a Monday, WEEKDAY() will return a value of 2.
7. Enter a similar formula in cell **B4** of the Price List sheet, charging $2.00 for wheat bread if it's Monday and $2.60 if it's not.
8. Return to the **Daily Sales** sheet, and observe the values calculated in the Order Total column.
9. Change the date in cell **B4** to **12/4/12**. Notice how the Order Total values recalculate to reflect that the date is now a Tuesday.
10. Undo the change to return the date in cell B4 to 12/3/12.
11. Redisplay the **Price List** sheet, and show formulas, increasing the width of column B so that the two new formulas display completely. Your worksheet should look like the one in Figure 14-1.
12. **With your teacher's permission,** print the Price List worksheet. Submit the printout or the file for grading as required.
13. Save and close the file.

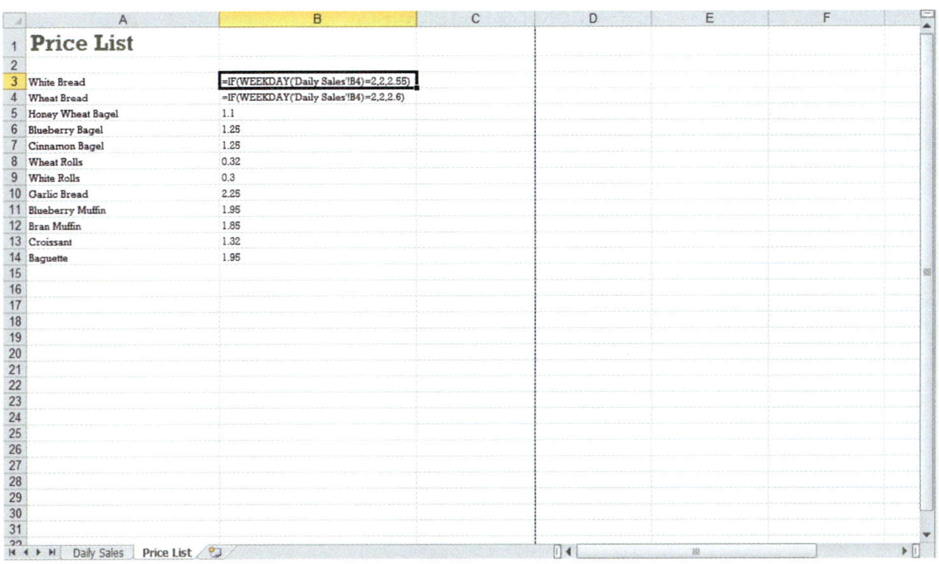

Figure 14-1

Project 30—Apply It

Counting in the Bread Sales Workbook

DIRECTIONS

1. Start Excel, if necessary, and open the **EProj30** file from the data files for this lesson.
2. Save the workbook as **EProj30_studentfirstname_studentlastname** in the location where your teacher instructs you to store the files for this lesson.
3. On the **Daily Sales** sheet add a header that has your name at the left the date code in the center, and the page number code at the right, and change back to **Normal** view.
5. In cell **C36**, use the **COUNT** function to create a formula that counts the number of coupon sales. (Refer to Figure 14-2 throughout this exercise to double-check that you are getting the correct results.) Remember that the COUNT function counts how many cells in the range contain numbers (values or formula results).
6. In cell **C37**, use the **COUNTBLANK** function to create a formula that counts the number of non-coupon sales.
7. In cell **C38**, use the **COUNTIF** function to create a formula that counts the number of credit card sales, using x as the criteria.
8. In cell **C39**, use the **COUNTIF** function to create a formula that counts the number of cash sales, using x as the criteria.
9. In cell **C40**, use the **COUNT** function to count the number of sales for the day, based on the Total Sale column.
10. In cell **C41**, use the **COUNTIFS** function to create a formula that counts the number of credit card sales for less than $10.

✓ *Calculations like this could help you determine whether your business should continue to accept credit card payments for small purchases.*

11. In cell **D36**, use the **SUMIF** function to create a formula that calculates the revenue from coupon sales.
12. In cell **D37**, use the **SUMIF** function to create a formula that calculates the revenue from non-coupon sales.

✓ *Hint: You want to find blank values ("") in the Coupon column and add the values from the corresponding rows in the Total Sale column.*

13. In cell **D38**, use the **SUMIF** function to create a formula that calculates the revenue from credit card sales.
14. In cell **D39**, use the **SUMIF** function to create a formula that calculates the revenue from cash sales.
15. In cell **D40**, use the method of your choice to enter the sum of Total Sales.
16. In cell **D41**, use the **SUMIFS** function to total the value of credit card sales less than $10.
17. Apply the **Currency** cell style to **D36:D41**, and adjust column widths as needed. Your worksheet should look like Figure 14-2.
18. **With your teacher's permission,** print the worksheet. Submit the printout or the file for grading as required.
19. Save and close the file, and exit Excel.

Figure 14-2

35	Daily Summary		
36	Coupon Sales	11	$ 146.46
37	Sales w/o Coupon	13	$ 289.84
38	Credit Sales	14	$ 271.98
39	Cash Sales	10	$ 164.32
40	Total Sales	24	$ 436.30
41	Credit Sales < $10	2	$ 15.48

Lesson 15

Using Frozen Labels and Panes

➤ What You Will Learn

Freezing Labels While Scrolling
Splitting a Worksheet into Panes

Software Skills When working with a large worksheet, you can freeze row and/or column labels to keep them in view, so that you can always identify your data no matter how far you've scrolled. You also can split the worksheet window into two or four panes, enabling you to view multiple parts of a worksheet at the same time—in order to compare or copy data, for example.

Application Skills You manage the Logan retail store for Voyager Travel Adventures. You've made some updates to your inventory worksheet, and need to use the features that enable you to freeze labels and divide the worksheet into panes so that you can complete your evaluation of current inventory levels for summer outdoor gear.

WORDS TO KNOW

Freeze
A method to keep specified rows and columns—usually ones containing labels for data—in view when scrolling through a worksheet.

Panes
Sections or areas in a window that enable you to see different parts of the worksheet at the same time.

What You Can Do

Freezing Labels While Scrolling

- When you need to keep labels or titles in view at the top or left edge of the worksheet as you scroll through it, you can **freeze** them in place.

  ✓ *Note that freezing rows and columns onscreen does not freeze them in a printout. Lesson 18 explains how to freeze labels for a printout.*

- Position the insertion point in the column to the right or the row below the data to be frozen, and then use the Freeze Panes button in the Window group on the View tab of the Ribbon.
- You can freeze just the column labels, the row labels, or both.
- Click a cell to specify which rows and columns to freeze. Rows above and columns to the left of the selected cell will be frozen. To freeze only rows, make sure you click a cell in column A. To freeze only columns, click a cell in row 1.
- You also can instantly freeze either the top row or the first column of the worksheet.
- Thin lines indicate the borders of the frozen area. You can scroll the area outside of these borders, and the frozen row/column labels will remain in view.
- To remove the freeze, use the Unfreeze Panes command found on the Freeze Panes drop-down list.

Try It! Freezing Labels While Scrolling

1. Start Excel.
2. Open the **ETry15** file from the data files for this lesson.
3. Save the workbook as **ETry15_studentfirstname_studentlastname** in the location where your teacher instructs you to store the files for this lesson.
4. Add a header that has your name at the left, the date code in the center, and the page number code at the right, and change back to Normal view.
5. Click cell C4 to select it.
6. Click View > Freeze Panes > Freeze Panes.

   ✓ *Use the Freeze Top Row or Freeze First Column choices to freeze row 1 or column A.*
7. Scroll down and to the right until cell I70 is visible. Notice how rows 1 through 3 and columns A and B remain visible onscreen.
8. Click View > Freeze Panes > Unfreeze Panes. The scrolling panes are removed and the worksheet scrolls back up.
9. Save the **ETry15_studentfirstname_studentlastname** file, and leave it open to use in the next Try It.

Frozen panes

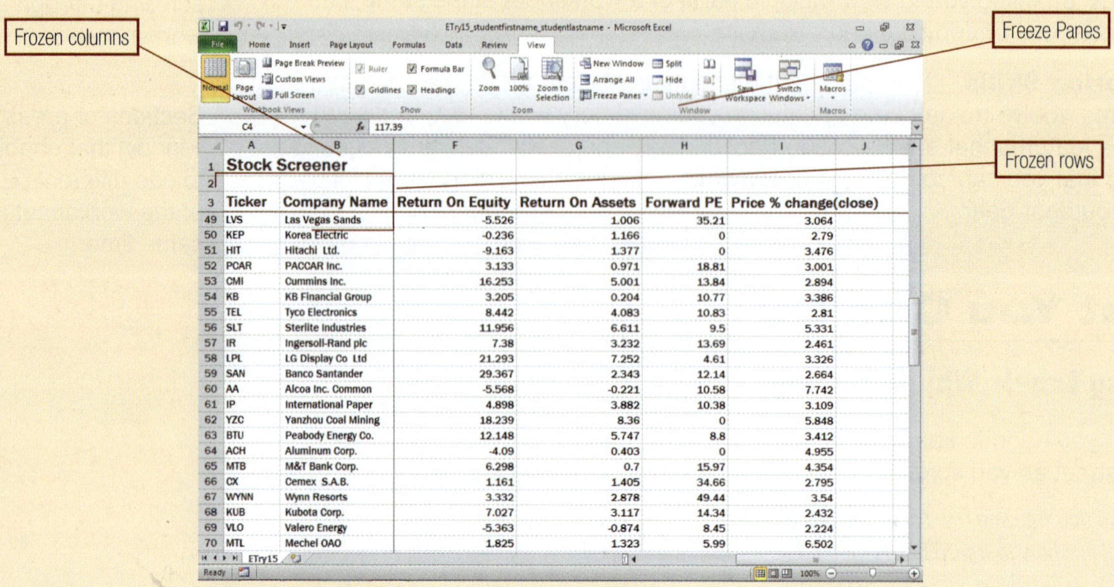

Splitting a Worksheet into Panes

- When you need to view different parts of a large worksheet at the same time, possibly at different zoom levels, split the worksheet horizontally or vertically into **panes**.

  ✓ *Panes also do not affect the appearance of a printout.*

- To split a worksheet, use the Split button in the Window group of the View tab.
- Click a cell to specify where the panes appear. The pane divider bars appear to the left of and above the selected cell.
- You also can drag the horizontal or vertical split boxes on the scroll bars to split the window into panes. Use the split box at the top of the vertical ruler to split the window horizontally. Use the split box found at the right end of the horizontal ruler to split the window vertically.
- When you position the insertion point in a cell in row 1 and use the Split command, the vertical panes scroll together when scrolling up and down, and independently when scrolling left to right.
- When you position the insertion point in a cell in column A and use the Split command, the horizontal panes scroll together when scrolling left to right, and independently when scrolling up and down.
- When you need to cancel the split, click the Split button again.

Try It! Splitting a Worksheet into Panes

1. In the **ETry15_studenfirstname_studentlastname** file, click cell C15 to select it.
2. Click View > Split.
3. In the left panes, use the scroll bar at the bottom to scroll right so that column A scrolls out of view. Drag the vertical divider bar so that column C displays completely.
4. In the right pane, scroll right so that columns A through D scroll out of view.
5. In the bottom pane, scroll down until row 60 is visible.
6. Click View > Split.
7. Drag the split box on the vertical scroll bar down to just below row 15 to insert a horizontal split at that location.
8. Scroll left so that column A is once again visible.
9. Scroll the bottom pane down until you see the Screener Criteria Conditions in the range A112:B115.
10. Save the **ETry15_studentfirstname_studentlastname** file, and close it.

Scrolling panes

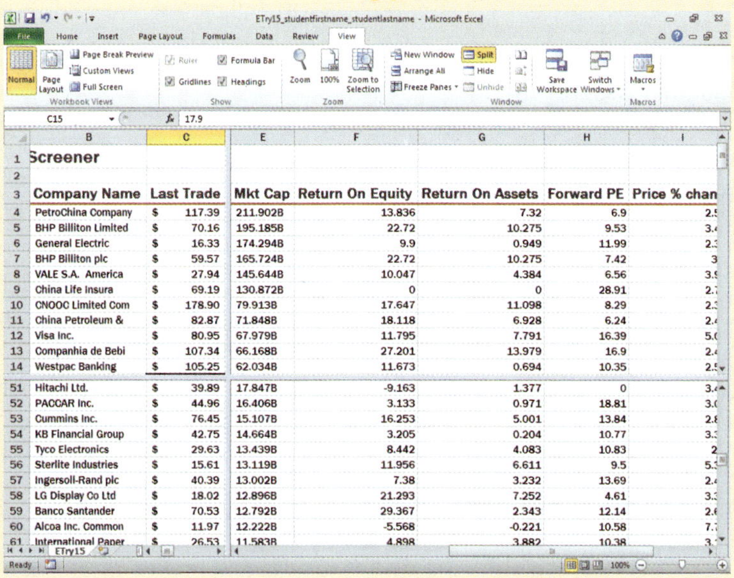

Project 31—Create It

Finishing the Data in the Inventory Worksheet

DIRECTIONS

1. Start Excel, if necessary, and open the **EProj31** file from the data files for this lesson.
2. Save the workbook as **EProj31_studentfirstname_studentlastname** in the location where your teacher instructs you to store the files for this lesson.
3. Add a header that has your name at the left, the date code in the center, and the page number code at the right, and change back to **Normal** view.
4. Scroll down to row 33, and make the following cell entries:
   a. **A33** **ZG020**
   b. **B33** **Sleeping bag, 20 degrees**
   c. **C33** **75**
   d. **D33** **3**
   e. **E33** **1**
   f. **H33** **3**
5. Press CTRL + HOME.
6. Click cell **A7** to select it.
7. Click **View > Freeze Panes** > **Freeze Panes**.
8. Scroll down again so that row 34 is visible, and make the following cell entries.
   a. **A34** **ZG030**
   b. **B34** **Sleeping bag, 30 degrees**
   c. **C34** **70**
   d. **D34** **5**
   e. **E34** **2**
   f. **H34** **8**
9. **With your teacher's permission,** print the worksheet. Submit the printout or the file for grading as required.
10. Save and close the file.

Project 32—Apply It

Using Panes to Finish the Inventory Worksheet

DIRECTIONS

1. Start Excel, if necessary, and open the **EProj32** file from the data files for this lesson.
2. Save the workbook as **EProj32_studentfirstname_studentlastname** in the location where your teacher instructs you to store the files for this lesson.
3. Add a header that has your name at the left, the date code in the center, and the page number code at the right, and change back to **Normal** view. You will need to click **OK** when a message tells you that Page Layout View is not compatible with frozen panes.
4. Click cell **D20**, and split the window into panes.
5. Scroll down the bottom pane to display the range title *Inventory Evaluation*.
6. In cell **C49**, enter a formula that sums the values in the range **F7:F34**, entering that range in the formula by dragging over it in the upper-right pane.
7. In cell **C50**, enter a formula that sums the Value column entries in the upper-right pane. Adjust the position of the vertical split divider if needed once you enter the formula, and widen the column if necessary.
8. In cell **C51**, enter a formula that calculates a carrying cost of 2.5% of the Item Value you just calculated.
9. In cell **C52**, enter a formula that calculates the average of the Current Stock Percentage entries. Your worksheet should resemble Figure 15-1.
10. **With your teacher's permission,** print the worksheet. Submit the printout or the file for grading as required.
11. Save and close the file, and exit Excel.

Figure 15-1

	A	B	C	D	E	F	G	H	I	J
15	BS113	Backpacker grill	$ 4.00	5	4	9	$ 36.00	10	90.00%	
16	CK101	Open country mess kit	$ 6.50	4	3	7	$ 45.50	10	70.00%	
17	CK102	Camp cook set	$ 50.00	2	1	3	$ 150.00	4	75.00%	
18	FL103	Emergency tinder	$ 1.50	9	7	16	$ 24.00	15	106.67%	
19	FL104	Fire paste	$ 2.00	12	6	18	$ 36.00	24	75.00%	
20	FL105	Liquid fuel, 1 gal.	$ 3.00	18	15	33	$ 99.00	36	91.67%	
21	FL108	Canister fuel, 170 g	$ 2.00	20	5	25	$ 50.00	36	69.44%	
22	FL109	Canister fuel, 300 g	$ 2.50	21	13	34	$ 85.00	36	94.44%	
23	WJ101	Water carrier, 2L	$ 9.00	10	2	12	$ 108.00	15	80.00%	
24	WJ102	Water carrier, 32 oz	$ 4.50	12	6	18	$ 81.00	24	75.00%	
25	WJ103	Water carrier, 48 oz.	$ 5.00	3	15	18	$ 90.00	24	75.00%	
26	WJ104	Dromedary, 6L	$ 15.00	6	6	12	$ 180.00	15	80.00%	
27	WJ105	Water bag, 4L	$ 10.00	10	2	12	$ 120.00	15	80.00%	
28	WT101	Water purifier, portable	$ 80.00	15	5	20	$1,600.00	20	100.00%	
29	WT103	Water purifier, camp	$ 25.00	12	0	12	$ 300.00	12	100.00%	
30	ZG005	Day pack, light	$ 35.00	3	1	4	$ 140.00	5	80.00%	
31	ZG009	Rugged pack, frameless	$ 55.00	2	2	4	$ 220.00	3	133.33%	
32	ZG010	Rugged pack, light frame	$ 65.00	2	1	3	$ 195.00	3	100.00%	
33	ZG020	Sleeping bag, 20 degrees	$ 75.00	3	1	4	$ 300.00	3	133.33%	
34	ZG030	Sleeping bag, 30 degrees	$ 70.00	5	2	7	$ 490.00	8	87.50%	
35										
47										
48		Inventory Evaluation								
49		Items in Stock	297							
50		Item Value	$5,308.00							
51		Carrying Cost	$ 132.70							
52		Average Inventory Level	86.87%							
53										

Sheet1 Sheet2 Sheet3

Lesson 16

Using Conditional Formatting and Find and Replace

➤ What You Will Learn

Applying Conditional Formatting
Using Find and Replace

Software Skills Conditional formatting is a volatile type of formatting that changes depending on what the values or calculated results in the cells are. This type of formatting enables you to identify key data, and it updates automatically if you update worksheet values and formulas. The Find and Replace function in Excel works just like it does in Word, enabling you to update text information by changing spellings and words globally. You learn to use both of these features in this lesson.

Application Skills You are the CFO for Telson Tech, a small manufacturer of custom circuit boards. You are finalizing a Profit & Loss statement that compares this year's sales, expenses, and profit information with data from last year. You will use Find and Replace to fix some text errors, and then use conditional formatting to help evaluate the financial performance of your company.

WORDS TO KNOW

Color scales
A type of conditional formatting that applies a background fill color that varies depending on the relative value stored in each of the formatted cells.

Conditional formatting
Variable formatting that changes the formatting applied based on the contents of the cells in the formatting range.

Data bars
A type of conditional formatting that creates filled background bars reflecting the relative value stored in each of the formatted cells.

Highlight cells rules
A method of applying conditional formatting based on how cell contents compare with a specified criterion, such as a Less Than comparison.

Icon sets
A type of conditional formatting that includes one of a set of icons reflecting the relative value stored in each of the formatted cells.

Top/Bottom rules
Conditional formatting rules that format the highest or lowest values in the formatted range, or those that are above or below average.

What You Can Do

Applying Conditional Formatting

- When you want cells to have different formatting depending on their contents, you can apply **conditional formatting**.
- Excel 2010 offers more forms of conditional formatting than its predecessors. You can now apply these types of conditional formatting to a cell or range:
  - Use **highlight cells rules** to apply specified formatting to cells only when the contents meet a certain rule or criterion, such as being greater than 100 or text that contains a particular phrase.
  - To format the cells holding the highest or lowest values in a range, use **top/bottom rules** conditional formatting. You can find the top or bottom 10 items or top or bottom 10%, or format values that are above or below average.
  - The **data bars** conditional formatting method creates a colored horizontal bar in every cell. The length of the colored bars varies according to the values in the cells, basically creating a chart of the data right within the range holding the values.
  - Use the **color scales** type of conditional formatting when you want to apply different cell fill colors depending on the values in the cells.
  - If you prefer graphical indicators of the relative values in cells, use **icon sets** conditional formatting. You can choose variations from four different types of icons, including ones that indicate ratings.
- To apply conditional formatting to a selected range, click the Conditional Formatting button in the Styles group of the Home tab. Click an overall conditional formatting type from the menu that appears, and then choose the specific type of conditional formatting to apply.
- You can create a custom conditional format using the New Rule command, clear conditional formatting using the Clear Rules command, or edit a conditional format with the Manage Rules choice.

Try It! Applying Conditional Formatting

1. Start Excel.
2. Open the **ETry16** file from the data files for this lesson.
3. Save the workbook as **ETry16_studentfirstname_studentlastname** in the location where your teacher instructs you to store the files for this lesson.
4. Add a header that has your name at the left, the date code in the center, and the page number code at the right, and change back to Normal view.
5. Select the range with Q1 sales data, excluding the column titles.

   ✓ *The worksheet has predefined names for each of the ranges with quarterly sales (SalesQ1 through SalesQ4) and the average data (Average).*
6. Click Home > Conditional Formatting > Highlight Cell Rules > Greater Than.
7. In the Greater Than dialog box, change the suggested value to **3000**. Open the with drop-down list and click Green Fill with Dark Green Text. Click OK.
8. Select the range with Q2 sales data.
9. Click Home > Conditional Formatting > Top/Bottom Rules > Bottom 10 Items.
10. In the Bottom 10 Items dialog box, change the suggested value to **5**. Click OK.
11. Select the range with Q3 sales data.

(continued)

Try It! Applying Conditional Formatting *(continued)*

12 Click Home > Conditional Formatting > Data Bars > Gradient Fill > Orange Data Bar.

13 Select the range with Q4 sales data.

14 Click Home > Conditional Formatting > Color Scales > Green-Yellow-Red Color Scale. (It's the first choice in the first row.)

15 Select the range with Average sales data.

16 Click Home > Conditional Formatting > Icon Sets > Ratings > 3 Stars.

17 Reselect the range with the Q2 sales data.

18 Click Home > Conditional Formatting > Manage Rules.

19 In the Conditional Formatting Rules Manager dialog box, click the Edit Rule button.

20 Under Edit the Rule Description, change the entry in the center text box to **15** and click the % of the selected range check box to check it, then click OK.

21 Click OK in the Conditional Formatting Rules Manager dialog box.

22 Save the **ETry16_studentfirstname_studentlastname** file, and leave it open to use in the next Try It.

Applying conditional formatting

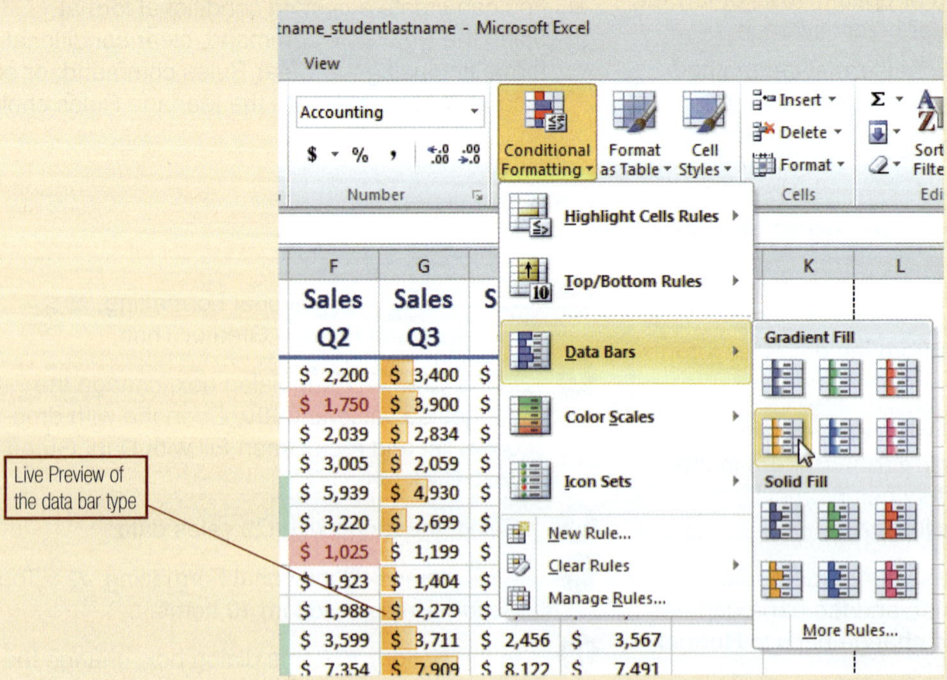

Using Find and Replace

- Word Chapter 2, Lesson 18 covers the Find and Replace feature that enables you to correct words or phrases throughout a word processing document. Excel also offers Find and Replace, and you can use it to replace all or part of a cell entry.
- To open the Find and Replace dialog box, click Home > Find & Select > Replace.
- The feature works in Excel like it does in Word. Enter Find what and Replace with entries. Then, either use the Find Next and Replace buttons to replace selected entries, or Replace All to replace all entries.
- Click the Options button in the Find and Replace dialog box to display additional choices, such as the ability to find and replace formatting or search the entire workbook rather than just the current sheet.

Try It! Using Find and Replace

1. In the **ETry16_studenfirstname_studentlastname** file, select cell A1.

   ✓ *As for a spell check, it's a good practice to start a find and replace from the top of the sheet.*

2. Click Home > Find & Select > Replace.
3. Type **Mens** in the Find what text box, press TAB, and type **M**.
4. Click the Options button to display all the options, and click the Match entire cell contents check box to check it.
5. Click the Replace All button, then click OK in the dialog box informing you that Excel made 12 replacements. Note that a number of entries in column B are replaced.
6. Change the Find what and Replace with entries to **Womens** and **W**, respectively, click the Replace All button, and click OK.
7. Change the Find what and Replace with entries to **White** and **Ivory**, respectively.
8. Click the Find Next button seven times to skip the first six instances of White in column D, rows 5 through 10.
9. Click the Replace button six times to replace the second six instances of White in rows 11 through 16.
10. Click the Match entire cell contents check box to clear it, and then click the Close button to close the Find and Replace dialog box.
11. Save the **ETry16_studentfirstname_studentlastname** file, and close it.

Project 33—Create It

Replacing Terms in the P&L Worksheet

DIRECTIONS

1. Start Excel, if necessary, and open the **EProj33** file from the data files for this lesson.
2. Save the workbook as **EProj33_studentfirstname_studentlastname** in the location where your teacher instructs you to store the files for this lesson.
3. Add a header that has your name at the left, the date code in the center, and the page number code at the right, and change back to **Normal** view.
4. Click **Home > Find & Select > Replace**.
5. Select the existing entry in the **Find what** text box, if any. Otherwise type **Operations** in the text box, and press TAB.
6. Type **Operating** in the **Replace with** box, and click the **Find Next** button.
7. Click **Replace** to replace the first match in cell A15.
8. Click in the worksheet, and press CTRL + HOME to return to cell A1.
9. Select the existing entry in the **Find what** text box in the Find and Replace dialog box, type **Expensives**, and press TAB.
10. Type **Expenses** in the **Replace with** box.
11. Click the **Replace All** button, and then click **OK** in the message box.
12. Click the **Close** button to close the Find and Replace dialog box.
13. **With your teacher's permission,** print the worksheet. Submit the printout or the file for grading as required.
14. Save and close the file.

Project 34—Apply It

Adding Conditional Formatting in the P&L Worksheet

DIRECTIONS

1. Start Excel, if necessary, and open the **EProj34** file from the data files for this lesson.
2. Save the workbook as **EProj34_studentfirstname_studentlastname** in the location where your teacher instructs you to store the files for this lesson.
3. Add a header that has your name at the left, the date code in the center, and the page number code at the right, and change back to **Normal** view.
4. Select the following noncontiguous cells and ranges (using the CTRL key):
   a. **D11**
   b. **D13:E13**
   c. **D21:E21**
   d. **D23:E23**
   e. **D27:E27**
5. Apply the **Green-White Color Scale** conditional format to the selection.

   ✓ *This formatting will apply deeper green shades to the revenue and profit items that have improved the most.*
6. Select the following noncontiguous cells and ranges:
   a. **D12 :E12**
   b. **D16:E19**
   c. **D25:E25**
7. Apply the **Red-White Color Scale** conditional format to the selection.

   ✓ *This formatting will apply deeper red shades to the expense items that have worsened (increased) the most.*
8. Select cell **B5**. Apply a highlight cell rules conditional format that changes the cell formatting to a Light Red Fill if the margin fell below 50%.
9. Select cell **B6**. Apply a highlight cell rules conditional format that changes the cell formatting to a Green Fill with Dark Green Text if the return exceeds 10%.
10. **With your teacher's permission,** print the worksheet. Submit the printout or the file for grading as required.
11. Save and close the file, and exit Excel.

Lesson 17

Rotating Entries and Resolving Errors

WORDS TO KNOW

Rotate
To change the angle of the contents of a cell.

➤ What You Will Learn

Rotating Cell Entries
Resolving a #### Error Message

Software Skills Rotating cell entries provides another choice you can use to better organize worksheet data and makc it more attractive. One formatting problem—having columns that are two narrow—produces an #### error message. In this lesson, you learn how to apply rotation and how to fix column width errors.

Application Skills You are the Payroll Manager at Whole Grains Bread. Your assistant worked on a version of the payroll worksheet, and introduced errors in the column formatting, so you need to make corrections. You also want to use rotated cell entries to improve worksheet formatting.

What You Can Do

Rotating Cell Entries

- You can **rotate** the entry in a cell to change the angle of the entry.
- The Orientation button in the Alignment group of the Home tab offers five preset rotation choices.
  - Angle Counterclockwise: 45 degrees, right end angled up.
  - Angle Clockwise: -45 degrees, left end angled up.
  - Vertical Text: Does not rotate the letters, but stacks them top to bottom.
  - Rotate Text Up: 90 degrees, right end up.
  - Rotate Text Down: -90 degrees, left end up.

- You also can specify a custom rotation in the Orientation area on the Alignment tab in the Format Cells dialog box. The Format Cell Alignment command at the bottom of the Orientation menu is another way to display that dialog box.
- You can use rotation in conjunction with other formatting methods, such as cell merging.

Try It! Rotating Cell Entries

1. Start Excel.
2. Open the **ETry17** file from the data files for this lesson.
3. Save the workbook as **ETry17_ studentfirstname_studentlastname** in the location where your teacher instructs you to store the files for this lesson.
4. Add a header that has your name at the left, the date code in the center, and the page number code at the right, and change back to Normal view.
5. Drag over the range A5:A10 to select it.
6. Click Home > Merge & Center drop-down arrow > Merge Cells.
7. Click Home > Orientation > Angle Counterclockwise.
8. Repeat the techniques in steps 6 and 7 to merge and rotate the following ranges:
   A11:A16
   A17:A22
   A23:A28
9. Double-click the right border of the column A column header to AutoFit the column width to the rotated values.
10. Click Home > Border drop-down arrow > Bottom Border to apply bottom borders to these ranges:
    A10:I10
    A16:I16
    A22:I22
    A28:I28
11. Save the **ETry17_studentfirstname_ studentlastname** file, and leave it open to use in the next Try It.

Rotating a cell entry

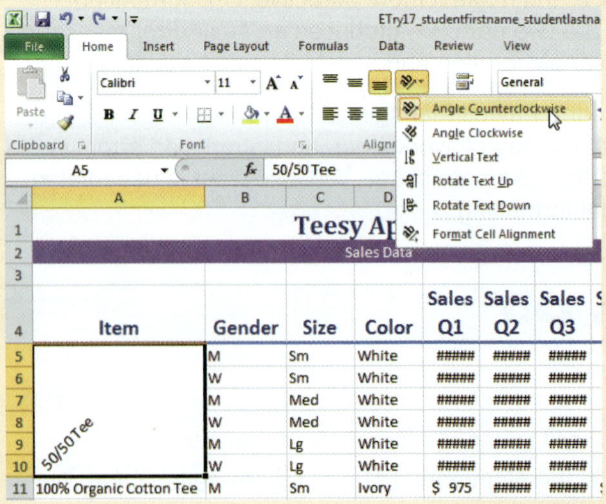

Resolving a #### Error Message

- If a column is too narrow to display a value, formula result, or date entry in a cell, the cell will fill with pound signs (#).
- You can correct this error by using any technique to increase the column width until all #### errors disappear from the column.

Try It! Resolving a #### Error Message

1. In the **ETry17_studenfirstname_studentlastname** file, double-click the right border of the column E column header to resize the column. All #### errors should disappear from the column.
2. Drag over the column headers for columns F through H to select those columns.
3. Click Home > Format > AutoFit Column Width. All #### errors should disappear from the selected columns.
4. Save the **ETry17_studentfirstname_studentlastname** file, and close it.

Project 35—Create It

Fixing Column Widths in the Payroll Worksheet

DIRECTIONS

1. Start Excel, if necessary, and open the **EProj35** file from the data files for this lesson.
2. Save the workbook as **EProj35_studentfirstname_studentlastname** in the location where your teacher instructs you to store the files for this lesson.
3. Add a header that has your name at the left, the date code in the center, and the page number code at the right, and change back to **Normal** view.
4. Click the column **E** column header.
5. Click **Home > Format > AutoFit Column Width**.
6. Drag over the column headers for columns **I** and **J** to select them.
7. Double-click the right border of the column **I** column header. Your worksheet should look like Figure 17-1.
8. **With your teacher's permission,** print the worksheet. Submit the printout or the file for grading as required.
9. Save and close the file.

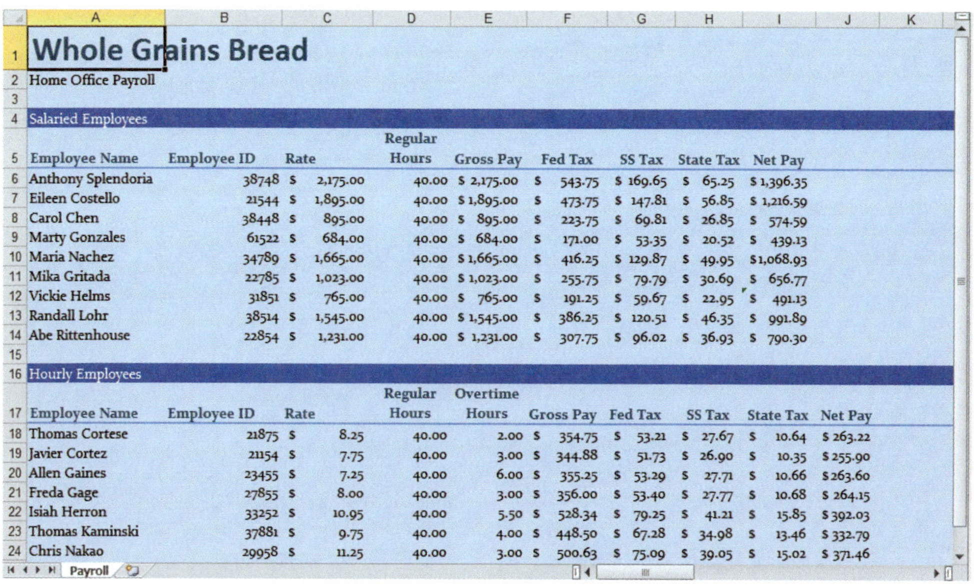

	A	B	C	D	E	F	G	H	I	J
1	Whole Grains Bread									
2	Home Office Payroll									
3										
4	Salaried Employees									
5	Employee Name	Employee ID	Rate	Regular Hours	Gross Pay	Fed Tax	SS Tax	State Tax	Net Pay	
6	Anthony Splendoria	38748	$ 2,175.00	40.00	$ 2,175.00	$ 543.75	$ 169.65	$ 65.25	$ 1,396.35	
7	Eileen Costello	21544	$ 1,895.00	40.00	$ 1,895.00	$ 473.75	$ 147.81	$ 56.85	$ 1,216.59	
8	Carol Chen	38448	$ 895.00	40.00	$ 895.00	$ 223.75	$ 69.81	$ 26.85	$ 574.59	
9	Marty Gonzales	61522	$ 684.00	40.00	$ 684.00	$ 171.00	$ 53.35	$ 20.52	$ 439.13	
10	Maria Nachez	34789	$ 1,665.00	40.00	$ 1,665.00	$ 416.25	$ 129.87	$ 49.95	$1,068.93	
11	Mika Gritada	22785	$ 1,023.00	40.00	$ 1,023.00	$ 255.75	$ 79.79	$ 30.69	$ 656.77	
12	Vickie Helms	31851	$ 765.00	40.00	$ 765.00	$ 191.25	$ 59.67	$ 22.95	$ 491.13	
13	Randall Lohr	38514	$ 1,545.00	40.00	$ 1,545.00	$ 386.25	$ 120.51	$ 46.35	$ 991.89	
14	Abe Rittenhouse	22854	$ 1,231.00	40.00	$ 1,231.00	$ 307.75	$ 96.02	$ 36.93	$ 790.30	
15										
16	Hourly Employees									
17	Employee Name	Employee ID	Rate	Regular Hours	Overtime Hours	Gross Pay	Fed Tax	SS Tax	State Tax	Net Pay
18	Thomas Cortese	21875	$ 8.25	40.00	2.00	$ 354.75	$ 53.21	$ 27.67	$ 10.64	$ 263.22
19	Javier Cortez	21154	$ 7.75	40.00	3.00	$ 344.88	$ 51.73	$ 26.90	$ 10.35	$ 255.90
20	Allen Gaines	23455	$ 7.25	40.00	6.00	$ 355.25	$ 53.29	$ 27.71	$ 10.66	$ 263.60
21	Freda Gage	27855	$ 8.00	40.00	3.00	$ 356.00	$ 53.40	$ 27.77	$ 10.68	$ 264.15
22	Isiah Herron	33252	$ 10.95	40.00	5.50	$ 528.34	$ 79.25	$ 41.21	$ 15.85	$ 392.03
23	Thomas Kaminski	37881	$ 9.75	40.00	4.00	$ 448.50	$ 67.28	$ 34.98	$ 13.46	$ 332.79
24	Chris Nakao	29958	$ 11.25	40.00	3.00	$ 500.63	$ 75.09	$ 39.05	$ 15.02	$ 371.46

Figure 17-1

Project 36—Apply It

Rotating Labels in the Payroll Worksheet

DIRECTIONS

1. Start Excel, if necessary, and open the **EProj36** file from the data files for this lesson.
2. Save the workbook as **EProj36_studentfirstname_studentlastname** in the location where your teacher instructs you to store the files for this lesson.
3. Add a header that has your name at the left, the date code in the center, and the page number code at the right, and change back to **Normal** view.
4. Select rows 4 and 16 (at the same time), and delete them from the sheet.
5. Insert a new column A, and move the entries in cells **B1:B2** left to **A1:A2**.
6. Select the range **A5:A13**, and merge it into one cell.
7. Enter **Salaried** in the merged cell A5, apply the **Accent1** cell style, and increase the text size to **24**.
8. Change the Orientation for the merged cell A5 to **Rotate Text Up**.
9. Repeat the techniques used in steps 6 through 8 to merge **A16:A22** and create a rotated label that says **Hourly**.
10. Select column **C** and double-click its right column border to AutoFit the column width. Your worksheet should look like Figure 17-2.
11. **With your teacher's permission,** print the worksheet. Submit the printout or the file for grading as required.
12. Save and close the file, and exit Excel.

Figure 17-2

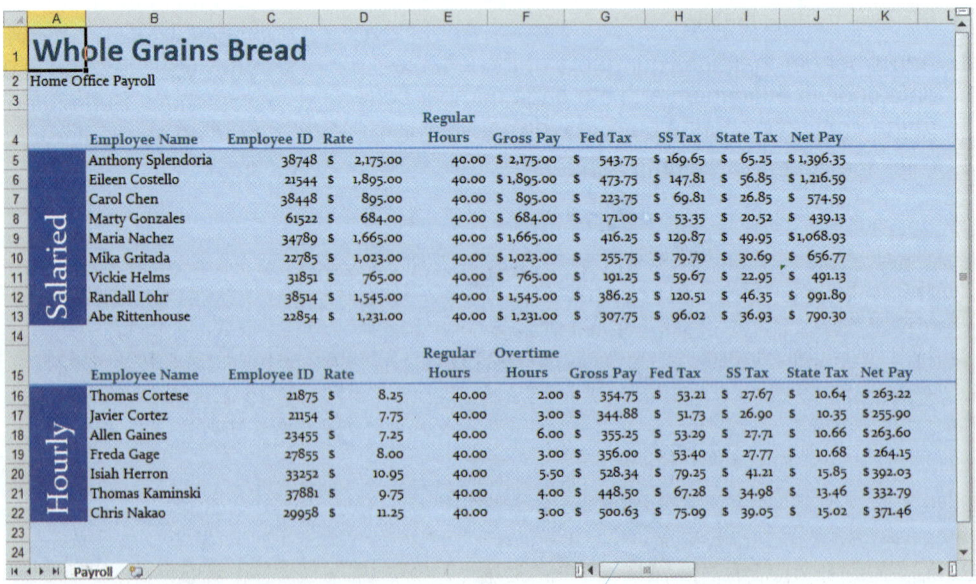

Lesson 18

Adding Print Titles and Scaling a Printout

➤ What You Will Learn

- Printing Titles
- Changing Orientation
- Scaling to Fit

Software Skills A few of the options available for adjusting a printout make a great difference in how easy it is to read the worksheet data. Repeating rows or columns with labels on multipage printouts ensures that the data will be identified on every page; choosing the right page orientation ensures enough columns will fit on screen; and scaling a printout to fit to a specified number of pages helps ensure that rows or columns aren't "orphaned" from the rest of the data. This lesson explains how to handle these three aspects of printing.

Application Skills You are the Marketing Director of Cleen-R Systems, a company that makes water filtration systems and sells them directly to the public. You are reviewing data from the U.S. Geological Survey to identify areas in Florida with poor water quality to target your marketing efforts to those areas. You need to print the source data, so you want to add print titles, work with orientation, and scale the printout.

WORDS TO KNOW

Orientation
The setting that determines whether the worksheet will be printed with the paper in a Portrait (vertical) or Landscape (horizontal) format.

Print titles
Row and column labels that reprint on each page of a printout.

Scaling
Reducing or enlarging worksheet information to fit on a specified number of pages.

What You Can Do

Printing Titles

- Using the Sheet tab of the Page Setup dialog box, you can specify rows or columns with the **print titles** that need to appear on every page of a printout.

  ✓ *Print titles do not affect or replace worksheet headers or footers.*

- You also can use the Print Titles button in the Page Setup group of the Page Layout tab on the Ribbon to add print titles.

  ✓ *Click the dialog box launcher for the Page Setup group to open the Page Setup dialog box.*

- The row and column labels make it possible for you to identify the data on every page, which is useful when the sheet has many rows or many columns of information.

Try It! Printing Titles

1. Start Excel.
2. Open the **ETry18** file from the data files for this lesson.
3. Save the workbook as **ETry18_studentfirstname_studentlastname** in the location where your teacher instructs you to store the files for this lesson.
4. Add a header that has your name at the left, the date code in the center, and the page number code at the right, and change back to Normal view.
5. Click Page Layout > Print Titles.
6. On the Sheet tab in the Page Setup dialog box, click in the Rows to repeat at top text box, click the Collapse Dialog button, and then click the row 3 row header. The row address for row 3, which holds the labels for the columns of data, appears in the box.
7. Click OK.
8. Save the **ETry18_studenfirstname_studentlastname** file, and leave it open to use in the next Try It.

Specifying print titles

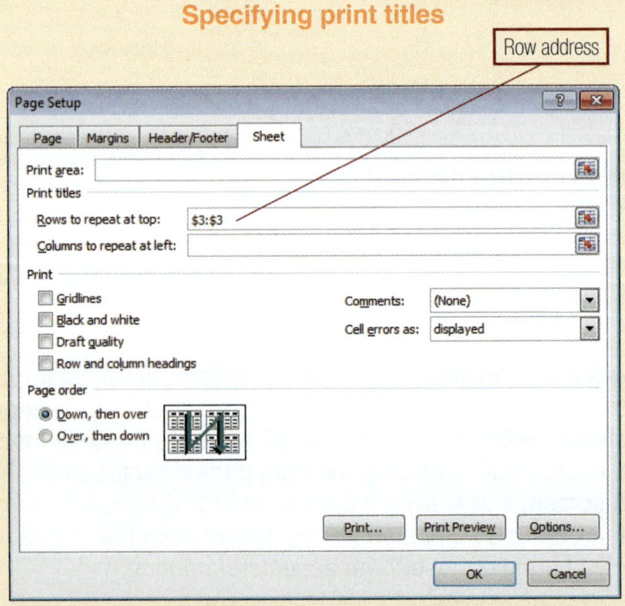

Changing Orientation

- You can change the **orientation** to help a worksheet fit better on paper.
- The default orientation is Portrait (tall or vertical).
- Changing to Landscape (wide or horizontal) orientation allows for more columns to fit on each page when a worksheet has many columns.
- Change orientation on the Page tab of the Page Setup dialog box, or use the Orientation button choices in the Page Setup group of the Page Layout tab.

Try It! Changing Orientation

1. In the **ETry18_studenfirstname_studentlastname** file, click Page Layout > Orientation > Landscape.
2. Save the **ETry18_studentfirstname_studentlastname** file, and leave it open to use in the next Try It.

Scaling to Fit

- You can **scale** the data to print to a larger or smaller size to help it fill a page or print on fewer pages.
- Specify scaling in the Scaling section of the Page tab of the Page Setup dialog box.
- You can scale the printout to a % normal size, or specify how many pages wide and tall it should be.

✓ *For many worksheets, changing to Landscape orientation and then scaling to 1 page wide prevents orphaned columns on a nearly blank page.*

- You also can use the choices in the Scale to Fit group on the Page Layout tab to specify the printout Width and Height in number of pages or a Scale percentage.

Try It! Scaling to Fit

1. In the **ETry18_studentfirstname_studentlastname** file, click the Page Layout tab, and then click the dialog box launcher for the Scale to Fit group.
2. On the Page sheet, click the Fit to button, and then adjust the accompanying text box entries to set up the printout to be 1 page(s) wide by 2 tall.
3. Click the Print Preview button.
4. At the bottom of Backstage view, click the Next Page (right arrow) button to display the second page of the printout.
5. Save the **ETry18_studentfirstname_studentlastname** file, and close it.

Project 37—Create It

Add Prints Titles on the Water Data Worksheet

DIRECTIONS

1. Start Excel, if necessary, and open the **EProj37** file from the data files for this lesson.
2. Save the workbook as **EProj37_studentfirstname_studentlastname** in the location where your teacher instructs you to store the files for this lesson.
3. Add a header that has your name at the left, the date code in the center, and the page number code at the right for each sheet, and change back to **Normal** view.
4. Click **Page Layout > Print Titles**.
5. Click in the **Rows to repeat at top** text box and click the Collapse Dialog button.
6. Click the **row 1 row header** to enter its address in the text box, and click **OK**.
7. **With your teacher's permission,** print the worksheet. Submit the printout or the file for grading as required.
8. Save and close the file.

Project 38—Apply It

Change Orientation and Scale the Water Data Worksheet

DIRECTIONS

1. Start Excel, if necessary, and open the **EProj38** file from the data files for this lesson.
2. Save the workbook as **EProj38_studentfirstname_studentlastname** in the location where your teacher instructs you to store the files for this lesson.
3. Add a header that has your name at the left, the date code in the center, and the page number code, and change back to **Normal** view.
4. Change the orientation to **Landscape**.
5. Scale the printout to 1 page wide by 4 pages tall.
6. Click **File > Print** to preview the printout, and review the various pages.
7. **With your teacher's permission,** print the worksheet. Submit the printout or the file for grading as required.
8. Save and close the file, and exit Excel.

Lesson 19

Managing Worksheets and Performing Multi-worksheet Operations

➤ What You Will Learn

Inserting, Deleting, Copying, Moving, and Renaming Worksheets
Changing the Color of a Worksheet Tab
Hiding Sheets
Grouping Worksheets for Editing and Formatting

Software Skills Use workbook sheets to divide and present data in logical chunks. For example, rather than placing an entire year's sales on one sheet, create a sales sheet for each month. You can add, delete, move, and rename sheets as needed. You also can group sheets to work on them simultaneously, such as applying the same formatting to all the selected sheets.

Application Skills As the Manager of Spa Services at Serenity Health Club, you are reviewing the popularity of four services provided by a particular group of associates. You've developed a worksheet to total the invoiced amounts for these services on a daily basis. You've created the first day's sheet, and need to copy and update it for additional days of the week.

WORDS TO KNOW

Active sheet tab
The selected worksheet; the tab name of an active sheet is bold.

Grouping
Worksheets that are selected as a unit; any action performed on this unit will affect all the worksheets in the group.

What You Can Do

Inserting, Deleting, Copying, Moving, and Renaming Worksheets

- By default, each new workbook file contains three sheets named Sheet1 through Sheet3.
- The sheet tab displays the name of the sheet. The **active sheet tab** name appears in bold.
- You can add or delete worksheets as needed, using the Insert and Delete drop-down lists in the Cells group of the Home tab. You also can use the Insert Worksheet tab that appears to the right of the right-most sheet in the workbook.
- You also can right-click a sheet tab to display a shortcut menu that allows you to insert, delete, rename, move, and copy worksheets.
- You do not need to delete unused sheets from a workbook, since they do not take up much room in the file; however, if you plan on sharing the file, you may want to remove unused sheets to create a more professional look.
- When you copy a worksheet, you copy all of its data and formatting. However, changes you later make to the copied sheet do not affect the original sheet.
- Moving sheets enables you to place them in a logical order within the workbook.
- Renaming sheets make it easier to keep track of the data on individual sheets.

Try It! Inserting, Deleting, Copying, Moving, and Renaming Worksheets

1. Start Excel.
2. Open the **ETry19** file from the data files for this lesson.
3. Save the workbook as **ETry19_studentfirstname_studentlastname** in the location where your teacher instructs you to store the files for this lesson.
4. Add a header that has your name at the left, the date code in the center, and the page number code at the right, and change back to Normal view.
5. Click the Insert Worksheet tab to insert a new, blank sheet named Sheet2.
6. Click Sheet1, and then click Sheet2.
7. Click Home > Delete drop-down arrow > Delete Sheet. Excel removes the new sheet from the workbook.
8. Right-click the Sheet1 tab and click Rename.
9. Type **2012**, and press ENTER.
10. Right-click the 2012 sheet tab, and click Move or Copy.

Shortcut menu with commands for working with sheets

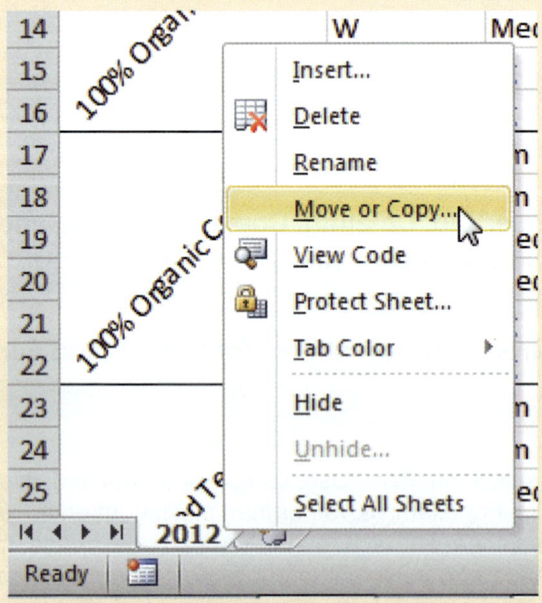

11. In the Move or Copy dialog box, click (move to end) in the Before sheet list, click the Create a copy check box to check it, and click OK. The new sheet appears, with the name 2012 (2).
12. Double-click the name on the new sheet tab, type **2013**, and press ENTER.

(continued)

Try It! Inserting, Deleting, Copying, Moving, and Renaming Worksheets *(continued)*

13. Select the 2012 sheet. Drag it to the right of the 2013 sheet tab. As you drag, the mouse pointer includes a page and a black triangle shows you the move location. When you release the mouse button, the sheet moves into that new position.

14. Create a copy of the 2012 sheet, name the copy **2014**, and move it to the far left to make it the first sheet.

15. Save the **ETry19_studentfirstname_ studentlastname** file, and leave it open to use in the next Try It.

Changing the Color of a Worksheet Tab

- Change the color of a worksheet's tab to further distinguish sheets with different types of data.
- Choosing a tab color from the current theme colors enables you to maintain a color-coordinated look. If you change themes, the colors in the worksheet and the colors of your tabs will change to those in the new theme.
- If you change the color of a sheet tab, that color appears when the tab is not selected.
- When a colored sheet tab is clicked, its color changes to white, with a small line of its original color at the bottom of the tab. For example, an orange sheet tab changes to white with a thin orange line at the bottom.

Try It! Changing the Color of a Worksheet Tab

1. In the **ETry19_studenfirstname_ studentlastname** file, right-click the 2014 sheet tab, point to Tab Color, and click the Purple, Accent 4 color in the top row.

2. Right-click the 2013 sheet tab, point to Tab Color, and click the Olive Green, Accent 3 color in the top row.

3. Right-click the 2012 sheet tab, point to Tab Color, and click the Orange, Accent 6 color in the top row.

4. Save the **ETry19_studentfirstname_ studentlastname** file, and leave it open to use in the next Try It.

Hiding Sheets

- Hide a worksheet temporarily when you need to put sensitive data out of sight.
- Hiding a sheet simply hides its sheet tab from view.
- The Home > Format > Hide & Unhide submenu includes the Hide Sheet and Unhide Sheet commands. You also can right-click the sheet tab and use the Hide and Unhide commands.
- Hiding provides a simple layer of protection, but does not provide any real security for confidential data because the Unhide commands become active whenever a sheet is hidden.
- If you rename your worksheets and hide the ones you don't want seen, it's a little harder for a user to detect that a sheet is hidden because the sheet names are no longer sequential.

Try It! Hiding Sheets

1. In the **ETry19_studentfirstname_ studentlastname** file, click the 2013 sheet tab to select it.

2. Click Home > Format > Hide & Unhide > Hide Sheet.

3. Right-click the 2012 sheet tab, and click Hide.

4. Click Home > Format > Hide & Unhide > Unhide Sheet.

5. Make sure that 2013 is selected in the Unhide sheet list of the Unhide dialog box, and click OK.

6. Save the **ETry19_studentfirstname_ studentlastname** file, and leave it open to use in the next Try It.

Grouping Worksheets for Editing and Formatting

- If you want to work on several worksheets simultaneously, select multiple worksheets and create a **grouping**.
- Grouped sheet tabs appear white when selected, the name of the active sheet tab appears in bold, and [Group] appears in the title bar.
- To group adjacent sheets, click the first sheet tab and SHIFT +click on the last one. Or, CTRL +click to select nonadjacent sheets.
- When you select a grouping, any editing, formatting, or new entries you make to the active sheet are simultaneously made to all the sheets in the group.
- For example, you can select a group of sheets and format, move, copy, or delete them in one step. You can also add, delete, change, or format the same entries into the same cells on every selected worksheet.
- Remember to deselect the grouping when you no longer want to make changes to all the sheets in the group. Right-click one of the selected sheet tabs, and click Ungroup Sheets.

Try It! Grouping Worksheets for Editing and Formatting

1. In the **ETry19_studentfirstname_studentlastname** file, click the 2014 sheet tab, and then SHIFT +click the 2013 sheet tab.
2. Select the range E5:H28.
3. Click Home > Clear > Clear Contents.
4. Select cell A2.
5. Click Home > Cell Styles > Accent2.
6. Right-click the 2014 sheet tab, and click Ungroup Sheets.
7. Click the 2013 sheet tab. The changes you made appear on this tab as well as the 2014 tab.
8. Save the **ETry19_studentfirstname_studentlastname** file, and close it.

Project 39—Create It

Setting Up Sheets in the Services Tracking Worksheet

DIRECTIONS

1. Start Excel, if necessary, and open the **EProj39** file from the data files for this lesson.
2. Save the workbook as **EProj39_studentfirstname_studentlastname** in the location where your teacher instructs you to store the files for this lesson.
3. Add a header that has your name at the left, the date code in the center, and the sheet name code at the right, and change back to **Normal** view.
4. Click the **Insert Worksheet** tab to the right of the Monday sheet tab. A new, blank Sheet1 appears.
5. Right-click the tab for the new sheet, and click **Rename**. Type **Notes**, and press ENTER .
6. Right-click the **Monday** sheet tab, and click **Move or Copy**.
7. In the Move or Copy dialog box, click **(move to end)**, click the **Create a copy** check box to check it, and click **OK**.
8. Double-click the new sheet tab, type **Tuesday**, and press ENTER .
9. Right-click the new sheet tab, point to **Tab Color**, and click **Red, Accent 2, Lighter 40%**.
10. Repeat Steps 6 to 9 to create another copy of the Monday sheet, naming the copy **Wednesday** and assigning the **Olive Green, Accent 3, Lighter 40%** color to the sheet tab.
11. Drag the **Notes** sheet tab to the far right of the other tabs, and reselect the **Monday** sheet. The tabs should now appear as shown in Figure 19-1.

12. **With your teacher's permission,** print the **Monday** worksheet. Submit the printout or the file for grading as required.
13. Save and close the file.

Figure 19-1

Project 40—Apply It

Formatting and Editing Sheets in the Services Tracking Worksheet

DIRECTIONS

1. Start Excel, if necessary, and open the **EProj40** file from the data files for this lesson.
2. Save the workbook as **EProj40_studentfirstname_studentlastname** in the location where your teacher instructs you to store the files for this lesson.
3. On each sheet, add a header that has your name at the left, the date code in the center, and the sheet name code at the right, and change back to **Normal** view.
4. Group the **Monday**, **Tuesday**, and **Wednesday** sheets.
5. Increase the font size in cell **A3** to **16**.
6. Select **row 11**, wrap the text, apply bold, and align the text to the center.
7. Adjust column widths as needed.
8. Change the entry in cell **C7** to **165**.
9. Ungroup the sheets.
10. Make sure that your changes have been applied to all three sheets. Your workbook should look like Figure 19-2.
11. **With your teacher's permission,** print one of the worksheets. Submit the printout or the file for grading as required.
12. Save and close the file, and exit Excel.

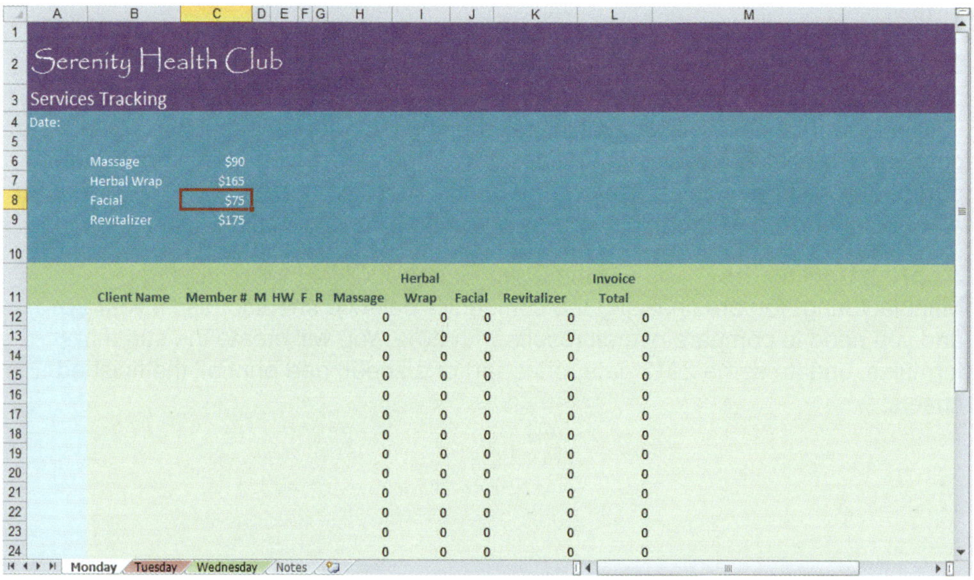

Figure 19-2

Lesson 20

Summary Worksheets and Advanced Printing

➤ What You Will Learn

- Constructing Formulas that Summarize Data from Other Sheets
- Changing Values in a Detail Worksheet to Update a Summary Worksheet
- Printing a Selection
- Printing All the Worksheets in a Workbook

Software Skills You often need to combine data from different worksheets to perform summary calculations. When you do this, you can still change data on the individual worksheets. Excel recalculates the summary formula results to reflect the changes. Excel also gives you great flexibility in printing. If you need to print only part of a worksheet, you can select and print a specific area. Or, if you need to print all worksheets in a workbook to share comprehensive information, you can do so.

Application Skills You are the Chief Financial Officer for Hyland Manufacturing. You are finalizing the company's balance sheet for fiscal year 2013, and you need to compare overall results with 2012. You will create the summary formulas, update some 2013 data, print part of a sheet, and print all the finished sheets.

What You Can Do

Constructing Formulas that Refer to Cells in Another Worksheet

- A formula on one worksheet can refer to cells in another worksheet in the same workbook file.

  ✓ *Formulas also can refer to cells in other workbook files.*

- As when using a named range for another sheet, a reference to a cell on another sheet includes the sheet name and an exclamation point, as in Income!E9.

  ✓ *Lesson 13 covered using named ranges.*

- You can type in references to cells on another sheet, or to save time, enter the reference by pointing (clicking the sheet tab and then clicking the cell to enter in the formula).

Try It! Constructing Formulas that Refer to Cells in Another Worksheet

1. Start Excel.
2. Open the **ETry20** file from the data files for this lesson.
3. Save the workbook as **ETry20_studentfirstname_studentlastname** in the location where your teacher instructs you to store the files for this lesson.
4. Click the Qtr 1 sheet tab, and then SHIFT +click the Summary sheet tab to group the sheets. (You are grouping the sheets to apply the header to all three sheets.)
5. Add a header that has your name at the left, the date code in the center, and the sheet name code at the right, and change back to Normal view.
6. Right-click the Summary sheet tab, and click Ungroup Sheets.
7. Click cell B5 on the Summary sheet.
8. Type **=sum(**, click the Qtr 1 sheet tab, click cell B5 on that sheet, and type a **,** (comma).
9. Click the Qtr 2 sheet tab, click cell B5 on that sheet, press CTRL + ENTER.
10. Fill the formula down through cell B10.
11. Click cell C5 in the Summary sheet.
12. Type **=sum(**, click the Qtr 1 sheet tab, click cell D5 on that sheet, and type a **,** (comma).

    ✓ *If a Formula AutoComplete tip appears in the way, you can drag it to another location before clicking cell D5.*

    Formula referencing other sheets

    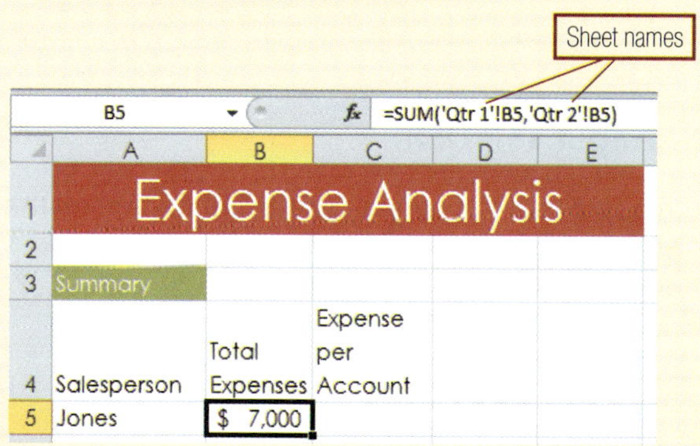

13. Click the Qtr 2 sheet tab, click cell D5 on that sheet, and press CTRL + ENTER.
14. Fill the formula down through cell D10, and apply the Currency [0] cell style to the selected range.
15. Save the **ETry20_studentfirstname_studentlastname** file, and leave it open to use in the next Try It.

Changing Values in a Detail Worksheet to Update a Summary Worksheet

- Formulas that summarize or perform calculations using data from other sheets work just like regular formulas.
- Just change entries on the referenced sheets as desired, and formulas on the summary sheet will recalculate results accordingly.

Try It! Changing Values in a Detail Worksheet to Update a Summary Worksheet

1. In the **ETry20_studenfirstname_ studentlastname** file, review the data calculated on the Summary sheet. For example, the totals for Thomas are $13,198 and $3,300 respectively.
2. Click the Qtr 2 sheet tab.
3. Change the entries in the range B5:B10 to these values:
   4250
   3300
   4599
   6654
   4952
   7300
4. Click the Summary sheet tab, and review its data again. Now the totals for Thomas are $11,198 and $2,800.
5. Save the **ETry20_studentfirstname_ studentlastname** file, and leave it open to use in the next Try It.

Printing a Selection

- In some cases, you may prefer not to print all the data on a sheet. For example, you may want to print only the data that performs a certain set of calculations.
- To print an area of the worksheet, select that range. Then, when you click File > Print, select Print Selection using the first drop-down list under Settings. (It normally says Print Active Sheets, until you change it.)

Try It! Printing a Selection

1. In the **ETry20_studentfirstname_ studentlastname** file, click the Qtr 1 sheet tab.
2. Select the range A13:B14.
3. Click File > Print.

(continued)

Try It! Printing a Selection *(continued)*

4. Click the top option under Settings, which initially reads Print Active Sheets, and click Print Selection on the menu. The Preview immediately shows you that only the selection will print. You could then click the Print button to send it to the printer.

5. Click Save to save your changes to the file, and return to the Home tab.

6. Leave the **ETry20_studentfirstname_studentlastname** file open to use in the next Try It.

Printing a worksheet selection.

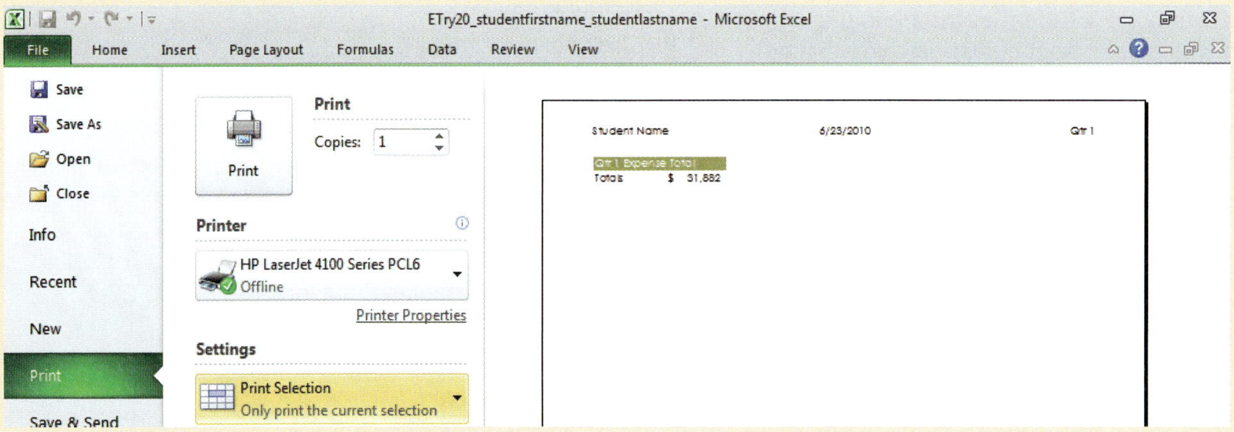

Printing All the Worksheets in a Workbook

- Workbooks with multiple sheets of data often contain information that needs to be shared with others for making business decisions.
- Excel enables you to print all the sheets in a workbook file in a single print operation, to save you the trouble of printing each sheet individually.
- Click File > Print, select Print Entire Workbook using the first drop-down list under Settings. (It normally says Print Active Sheets, until you change it.)

Try It! Printing All the Worksheets in a Workbook

1. In the **ETry20_studentfirstname_studentlastname** file, click File > Print.

2. Click the top option under Settings, which by default reads Print Active Sheets but in this instance will read Print Selection due to the last Try IT, and click Print Entire Workbook on the menu.

3. Use the Next button below the preview to view the print preview of all three sheets.

4. Save the **ETry20_studentfirstname_studentlastname** file, and close it.

Project 41—Create It

Adding Summary Formulas in the Balance Sheet Workbook

DIRECTIONS

1. Start Excel, if necessary, and open the **EProj41** file from the data files for this lesson.
2. Save the workbook as **EProj41_studentfirstname_studentlastname** in the location where your teacher instructs you to store the files for this lesson.
3. Click the **2013 Balance Sheet** sheet tab, and then SHIFT +click the **Summary** sheet tab to group the sheets. (You are grouping the sheets to apply the header to all three sheets.)
4. Add a header that has your name at the left, the date code in the center, and the sheet name code at the right, and change back to **Normal** view.
5. Right-click a grouped sheet tab and click **Ungroup Sheets** to ungroup.
6. Click the **Summary** sheet tab, and then click cell **E4**.
7. Type **=**, click the **2013 Balance Sheet** tab, click cell **B22** on that sheet, and type a **-** (minus).
8. Click the **2012 Balance Sheet** tab, click cell **B22** on that sheet, and press CTRL + ENTER. Review the formula results.
9. Click cell **E5**.
10. Type **=**, click the **2013 Balance Sheet** tab, click cell **E22** on that sheet, and type a **-** (minus).
11. Click the **2012 Balance Sheet** tab, click cell **E22** on that sheet, and press CTRL + ENTER. Review the formula results.
12. Format the range **E4:E5** with the **Currency [0]** cell style. Your workbook should look like Figure 20-1.
13. **With your teacher's permission,** print the **Summary** sheet. Submit the printout or the file for grading as required.
14. Save and close the file.

Figure 20-1

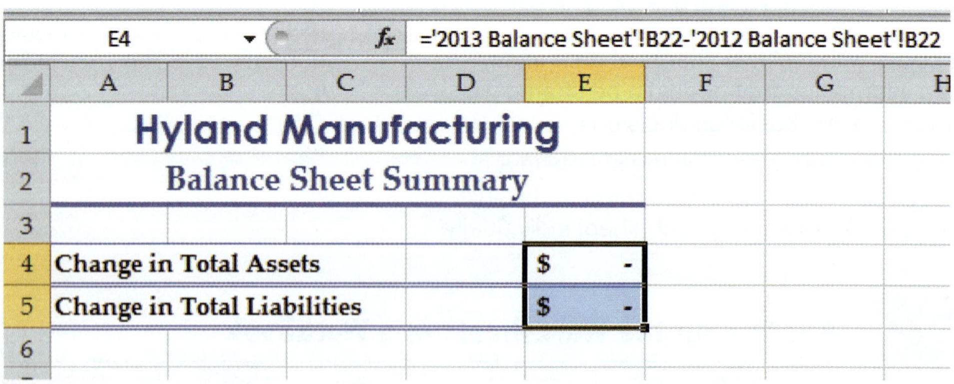

Project 42—Apply It

Printing a Selection and All Sheets in the Balance Sheet Workbook

DIRECTIONS

1. Start Excel, if necessary, and open the **EProj42** file from the data files for this lesson.
2. Save the workbook as **EProj42_studentfirstname_studentlastname** in the location where your teacher instructs you to store the files for this lesson.
3. Group the three sheets.
4. Add a header that has your name at the left, the date code in the center, and the sheet name code at the right, and change back to **Normal** view.
5. Ungroup the sheets.
6. On the **2013 Balance Sheet**, change the following entries:
   B6 302
   B9 77
   B17 506
   E7 1252
   E9 1187
   E15 2445
7. Go to the **Summary** sheet, and review the recalculated summary information.
8. Go back to the **2013 Balance Sheet**.
9. Select the range **A4:B38**, and **with your teacher's permission, print the range**. The printout preview should look like Figure 20-2.
10. **With your teacher's permission**, print all sheets in the workbook. Submit the printouts or the file for grading as required.
11. Save and close the file, and exit Excel.

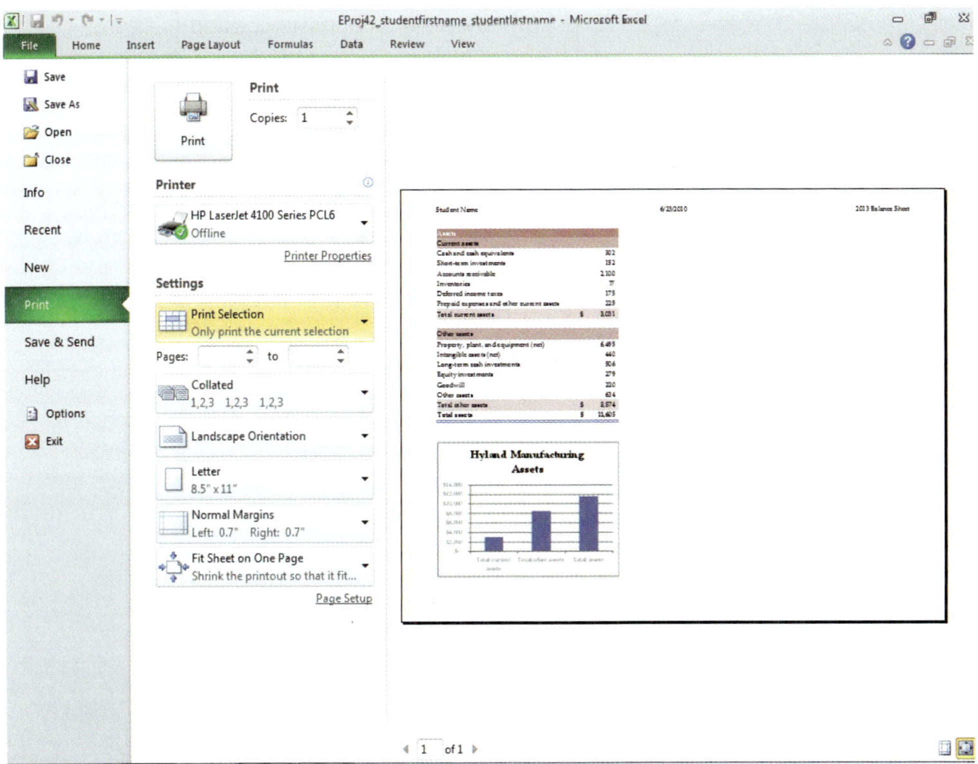

Figure 20-2

Chapter Assessment and Application

Project 43—Make It Your Own

Client Activity Worksheet

You have a business called Fry Landscape Services. You have created a worksheet to record and evaluate monthly client activity. You need to complete the sheet with some additional formulas, and try different formatting options, such as using tables and conditional formatting, to see what will suit your data analysis needs best.

DIRECTIONS

1. Start Excel, if necessary, and open the **EProj43** file from the data files for this chapter.
2. Save the workbook as **EProj43_studentfirstname_studentlastname** in the location where your teacher instructs you to store the files for this chapter.
3. Add a header that has your name at the left, the date code in the center, and the sheet name code at the right, and change back to **Normal** view.
4. Select the range **A4:D32**, and convert it to a table.
5. Apply the **Table Style Light 20** table style.
6. Add a total row, and adjust it so a *Sum total* displays for the **Fee** column only.
7. In cell **G5**, enter a formula that sums only the fees that have been paid.
8. In the range **G7:G10**, enter formulas that sum only the fees paid for each type of service.
9. Rename **Sheet1** to **Version1**.
10. Copy the **Version1** sheet, naming the copy **Version2** and placing it after the copied sheet.
11. Delete the **Sheet 3** sheet, and hide the **Sheet 2** sheet.
12. On the **Version2** sheet, convert the table back to a range.
13. Apply conditional formatting to the **Fee** column that highlights values over $100 with a **Yellow Fill with Dark Yellow Text**.
14. Apply conditional formatting to the Paid column that highlights *No entries* with **Light Red Fill with Dark Red Text**.
15. To the range with the calculated paid values **(G7:G10)**, apply one of the Blue Data Bar conditional formats (either gradient or solid).
16. In both sheets, replace the Customer name *Tayson* with **Tyler**. Your sheet should resemble Illustration A.
17. Set **row 4** as the print titles on both the visible sheets.
18. **With your teacher's permission,** print both worksheets. Submit the printouts or the file for grading as required.
19. Save and close the file, and exit Excel.

Illustration A

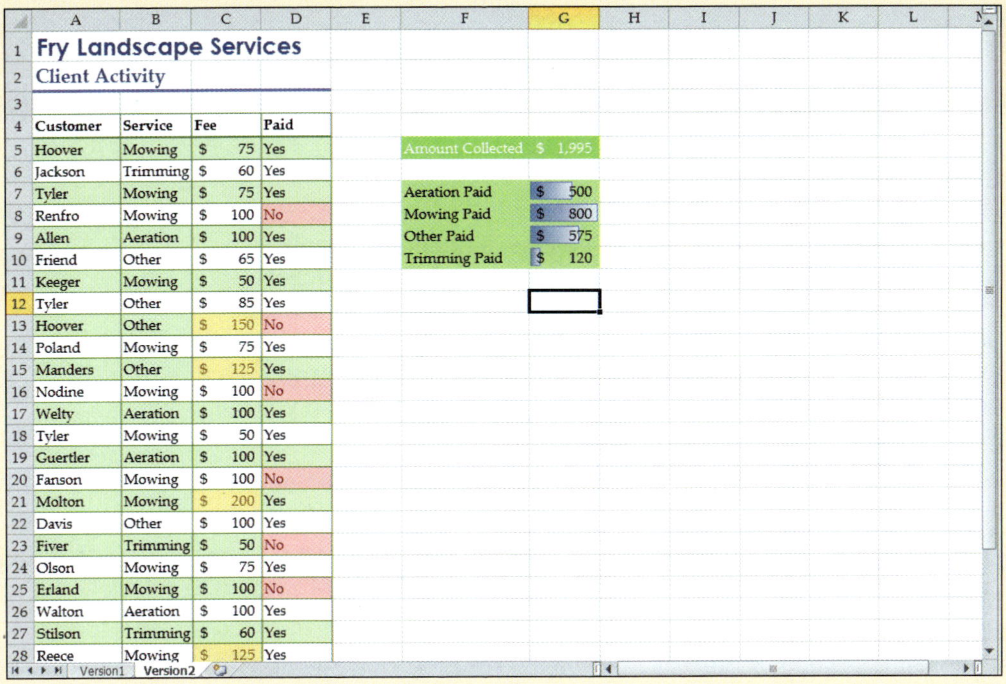

Fry Landscape Services

Client Activity

Customer	Service	Fee	Paid
Hoover	Mowing	$ 75	Yes
Jackson	Trimming	$ 60	Yes
Tyler	Mowing	$ 75	Yes
Renfro	Mowing	$ 100	No
Allen	Aeration	$ 100	Yes
Friend	Other	$ 65	Yes
Keeger	Mowing	$ 50	Yes
Tyler	Other	$ 85	Yes
Hoover	Other	$ 150	No
Poland	Mowing	$ 75	Yes
Manders	Other	$ 125	Yes
Nodine	Mowing	$ 100	No
Welty	Aeration	$ 100	Yes
Tyler	Mowing	$ 50	Yes
Guertler	Aeration	$ 100	Yes
Fanson	Mowing	$ 100	No
Molton	Mowing	$ 200	Yes
Davis	Other	$ 100	Yes
Fiver	Trimming	$ 50	No
Olson	Mowing	$ 75	Yes
Erland	Mowing	$ 100	No
Walton	Aeration	$ 100	Yes
Stilson	Trimming	$ 60	Yes
Reece	Mowing	$ 125	Yes

Amount Collected	$ 1,995
Aeration Paid	$ 500
Mowing Paid	$ 800
Other Paid	$ 575
Trimming Paid	$ 120

Version1 Version2

Project 44—Master It

Fundraising Worksheet

You are the Executive Director of Crossmont Services, a nonprofit organization that provides food assistance to needy families in Crossmont County. Your organization is holding a ball as a fundraiser. You created a budget for the ball and just entered actual information after the event. Now you need to evaluate the actual information to see if the event was a financial success. You will work with a summary worksheet and use formatting to help identify trouble spots so you can plan the event more effectively next year.

DIRECTIONS

1. Start Excel, if necessary, and open the **EProj44** file from the data files for this chapter.
2. Save the workbook as **EProj44_ studentfirstname_studentlastname** in the location where your teacher instructs you to store the files for this chapter.
3. Group **Sheet1** through **Sheet3**.
4. Add a header that has your name at the left, the sheet name code in the center, and the page number code at the right, and change back to **Normal** view.
5. Format cell **A1** with the **Title** cell style.
6. Format range **A2:E2** with the **Heading3** cell style.
7. Format the range **A4:E4** with the **Heading3** cell style, and rotate it using the **Angle Counterclockwise** setting.
8. In cell **D2**, enter the date and time using the **NOW** function.
9. Adjust column widths as needed, and then ungroup the worksheets.
10. Rename the sheets as follows:
    Sheet1 **Expenses**
    Sheet2 **Income**
    Sheet3 **Summary**
11. On the **Expenses** sheet, select the range **C5:C13**. Review the AutoCalculate results on the Status bar.
12. In cells **B14** and **C14** of the **Expenses** sheet, enter formulas using the SUM function to calculate the values above.
13. In cells **B9** and **C9** of the **Income** sheet, enter formulas using the SUM function to calculate the values above.
14. In cells **B5:C5** of the **Summary** sheet, enter formulas that summarize the applicable data from the other two sheets.
15. On the **Income** sheet, change the actual ticket sales value to **53500**.
16. Return to the **Summary** sheet to review the recalculated results. Review the revised results, which appear in Illustration B.
17. **With your teacher's permission,** print all worksheets in the workbook in one print operation. Submit the printouts or the file for grading as required.
18. Save and close the file, and exit Excel.

Illustration B

	A	B	C	D	E
1	Crossmont Services				
2	Fundraising Ball Budget			6/23/2012 19:59	
3					
4		Estimated	Actual	Difference $	Difference %
5	Event Profit	$ 52,200	$53,275	$ 1,075	2.06%
6					

Chapter 3

Charting Data

Lesson 21
Building Basic Charts
Projects 45-46

- Understanding Chart Basics
- Selecting Chart Data
- Reviewing Chart Elements
- Creating a Chart
- Changing Chart Types
- Selecting a Chart
- Resizing, Copying, Moving, or Deleting a Chart

Lesson 22
Showing Percentages with a Pie Chart
Projects 47-48

- Calculating Percentages
- Creating a Pie Chart on a Chart Sheet

Lesson 23
Enhancing a Pie Chart
Projects 49-50

- Applying 3-D to a Pie Chart
- Rotating Slices in a Pie Chart
- Exploding and Coloring a Pie Chart
- Formatting the Chart Area of a Pie Chart

Lesson 24
Adding Special Elements to a Chart or Sheet
Projects 51-52

- Inserting a Text Box in a Chart
- Updating a Chart
- Inserting WordArt in a Worksheet

Lesson 25
Completing Chart Formatting
Projects 53-54

- Changing Data Series Orientation
- Formatting a Chart
- Resizing, Moving, or Deleting a Chart Element
- Changing Chart Text
- Enhancing the Chart Plot Area
- Formatting Category and Value Axes

Lesson 26
Comparing and Analyzing Data
Projects 55-56

- Using Parentheses in a Formula
- Calculating a Value After an Increase
- Performing What-If Analysis
- Creating a Line Chart to Compare Data

Lesson 27
Chart Printing and Publishing
Projects 57-58

- Printing a Chart
- Preparing and Printing a Chart Sheet
- Publishing a Chart to the Internet/Intranet

Lesson 28
Using Charts in Other Files
Projects 59-60

- Pasting a Picture of a Chart
- Embedding a Chart in a Word Document
- Linking a Chart
- Editing a Linked or Embedded Chart

Lesson 29
Making Special Purpose Charts
Projects 61-62

- Creating Organization Charts
- Creating Other SmartArt Diagrams

End of Chapter Assessments
Projects 63-64

Lesson 21

Building Basic Charts

➤ What You Will Learn

Understanding Chart Basics
Selecting Chart Data
Reviewing Chart Elements
Creating a Chart
Changing Chart Types
Selecting a Chart
Resizing, Copying, Moving, or Deleting a Chart

Software Skills A chart presents Excel data in a graphical format—making the relationship between data items easier to understand. To present your data in the best format, you must select the proper chart type. For example, if you wanted to highlight your department's recent reduction in overtime, you might use a column or bar chart. Or, to compare your division's sales with other divisions, you might use a pie chart.

Application Skills The modifications you made to your daily bread sales worksheet is working out very well. Now, as manager of a Whole Grains Bread store, you're ready to analyze the data further with charts. Being able to visually compare the sales of the various items in your retail store will help you to produce the right products you need to maximize profits. In this lesson, you'll add two charts.

WORDS TO KNOW

Categories
In most cases, each column of charted worksheet data contains a category. Selecting multiple rows of chart data creates multiple categories. The chart displays categories along the horizontal axis.

Chart
A graphic that compares and contrasts worksheet data in a visual format.

Chart sheet
A chart that occupies its own worksheet.

Data marker
The shape—bar, column, line, pie slice, and so on—representing each data point of a chart.

Data points
The specific values plotted on a chart.

Data series
A set of related data points to be charted. In most cases, each row of charted worksheet data holds a data series. Selecting multiple columns of data for a chart creates multiple data series. The chart presents each data series in its own color bar, line, or column.

Embedded chart
A chart placed as an object within a worksheet.

What You Can Do

Understanding Chart Basics

- **Charts** provide a way of presenting and comparing data in a graphical format.
- You can create **embedded charts** or **chart sheets**.

- When you create an embedded chart, the chart exists as an object in the worksheet alongside the data.
- When you create a chart sheet, the chart exists on a separate sheet in the workbook.
- All charts are linked to the charted data, which appears in the **plot area**. (The plot area is contained within the overall chart area.) When you change worksheet data linked to the charted **data points**, the **data markers** in the chart plot area change automatically.

Selecting Chart Data

- To create a chart, you first select the data to plot.
- The selection should not contain blank columns or rows.
- If the data is not in a single range, press CTRL and select each range separately, making sure not to select blank rows or columns that may separate the ranges.
- You can select multiple ranges to plot on a single chart.
- You can hide columns or rows you do not wish to chart.
- The selection should include the labels for the data when possible.
- A blank cell in the upper-left corner of a selection tells Excel that the data below and to the right of the blank cell contains labels for the values to plot.
- Excel assumes each row includes a series. However, you may change the orientation as desired.

Reviewing Chart Elements

- As you move the mouse pointer over a chart, the name of the chart element appears in a ScreenTip.
- A chart may include some or all of the parts shown in Figure 21-1.

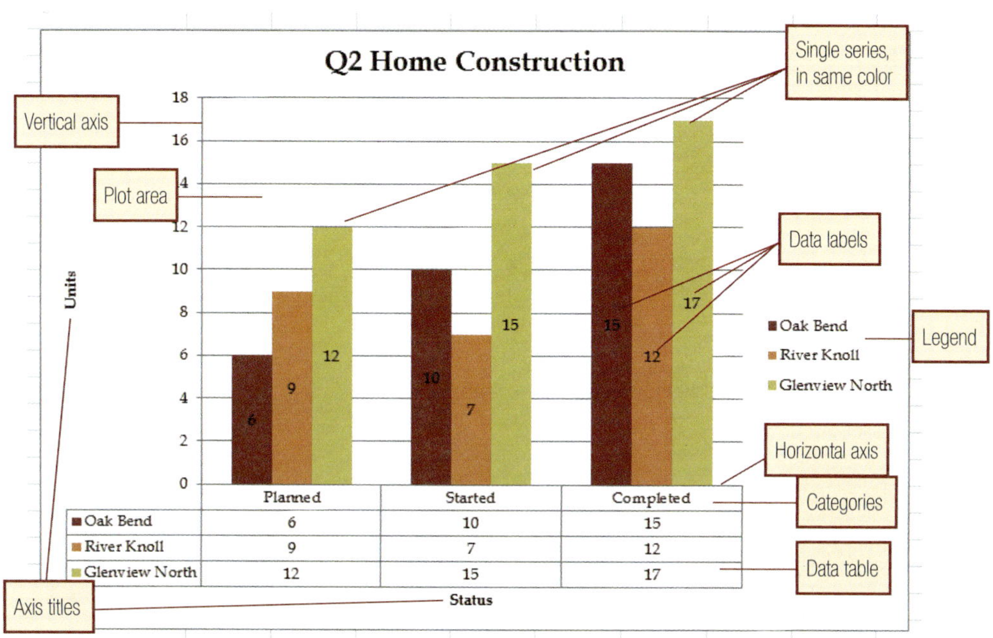

Figure 21-1

WORDS TO KNOW

Horizontal axis
The horizontal scale of a chart on which categories are plotted, sometimes called the X axis.

Legend
A key that identifies each of the data series in a chart.

Plot area
The area that holds the data points on a chart.

Vertical axis
The vertical scale of a chart on which the values from each category is plotted, sometimes called the Y axis.

- In this example, each community is a **data series** listed on its own row in the worksheet. On the chart, each data series is represented on the chart by a different data marker—columns in the example.
- The **legend** at the right is a key that identifies the series by name.
- Each kind of data for each item is a data point. For each series in the example there are three data points—Planned, Started, and Completed—as noted on the **horizontal axis** (X axis). These are the **categories** of data.
- If desired, you can identify each specific data point by displaying data labels. These labels appear on or near the data markers.
- For charts that use axes (generally all charts except pie charts and some 3-D charts), the **vertical axis** or Y axis provides the scale for the values being charted.

✔ *For bar charts the axes are reversed. The vertical axis charts categories and the horizontal axis charts values.*

✔ *3-D charts typically have a third axis representing the amount of 3-D rotation.*

- The horizontal axis title describes the categories data. (Status in the example.)
- The vertical axis title describes the types of values being plotted. (Units in the example.)
- The chart title identifies the chart overall and axis titles describe the axes. You have to add these titles when you want them to appear.
- So a user can easily view the data that's plotted on the chart, you can add a data table below the chart.
- The data table looks like a small worksheet, and it lists the data used to create the chart.

Try It! Reviewing Chart Elements

1. Start Excel.
2. Open the **ETry21** file from the data files for this lesson.
3. Save the file as **ETry21_studentfirstname_studentlastname** in the location where your teacher instructs you to store the files for this lesson.
4. On the Example sheet, scroll down until you can see the entire chart.
5. Move the mouse pointer over the title at the top of the chart. A ScreenTip that reads *Chart Title* appears.
6. Using Figure 21-1 as a guide, move the mouse pointer over these areas of the chart to view the ScreenTips, verifying that you've identified the correct parts of the chart:
   - Legend
   - Any data marker for the Oak Bend series
   - Any data marker for the River Knoll series
   - Any data marker for the Glenview North series
   - Plot area
   - Vertical axis
   - Title for each axis
   - Data table
7. Save the changes to **ETry21_studentfirstname_studentlastname**, and leave it open to use in the next Try It.

Creating a Chart

- The first step to creating a chart is selecting the data to chart on the worksheet, as discussed earlier in the lesson.
- Create charts using the buttons in the Charts group on the Insert tab.
- The buttons in the group enable you to create each type of common chart: Column, Line, Pie, Bar, Area, and Scatter. The Other Charts button also enables you to create Stock, Surface, Doughnut, Bubble, and Radar charts.
- Each chart type contains chart subtypes, which are variations on the selected chart type.

✔ *After selecting data to chart, press ALT + F1 to insert an embedded default column chart on the worksheet.*

✔ *Lesson 25 explains how to use the Chart Tools contextual tabs to work with elements, such as adding chart text.*

Try It! Creating a Chart

1. In the **ETry21_studentfirstname_ studentlastname** file, select the Practice sheet.
2. Add a header that has your name at the left, the date code in the center, and the page number code at the right, and then change back to Normal view.
3. Drag over the range A5:D8 to select it.
4. Click Insert > Bar > 3-D Bar > Clustered Bar in 3-D.
5. Drag the new chart so that its upper-left corner is over cell F2. Notice how the charted data is selected in the worksheet.
7. Leave the data selected, and press ALT + F1. A default bar chart appears.
8. Drag the new chart so that its upper-left corner is over cell F16. Compare how the different chart types present the same data.
9. Save the changes to **ETry21_studentfirstname _studenlastname**, and leave it open to use in the next Try It.

A new bar chart

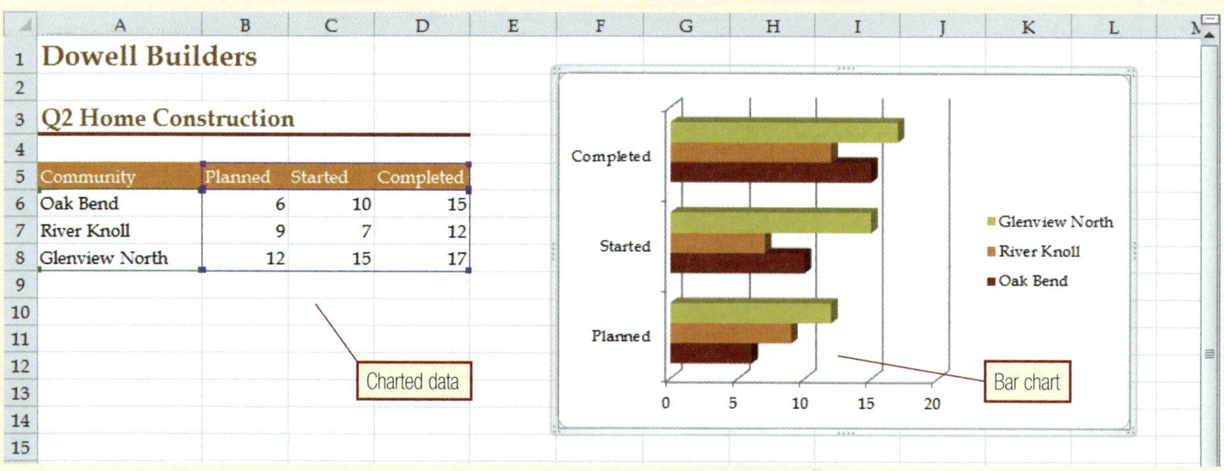

Changing Chart Types

- After creating a chart, you can easily change its chart type.
- Select the chart and click Change Chart Type in the Type group of the Chart Tools Design tab to open the Change Chart Type dialog box.
- Column charts, the default chart type, compare individual or sets of values. The height of each bar corresponds to its value in the worksheet, relative to other values in the chart.

  ✔ *Most chart types also have 3-D subtypes.*

- Line charts connect points of data, making them effective for showing changes over time, such as trends.
- Circular pie charts show the relationship of each value in a single series to the total for the series. The size of a pie wedge represents the percentage that value contributes to the total, and adding data labels clarifies the proportions even more.

  ✔ *Charting one more series of data in a pie chart results in an inaccurate chart, because Excel will combine all selected series into a single chart.*

- A bar chart is basically a column chart turned on its side. Like column charts, bar charts compare the values of various items.
- Area charts are like "filled-in" line charts; use area charts to track changes over time.
- Scatter charts, also called XY charts, represent data points as dots. The dots for each series appear in a different color. Any overall direction to the position of the dots reveals a trend.
- Excel also offers many specialty chart types such as Stock, Surface, Doughnut, Bubble, and Radar.

Figure 21-2

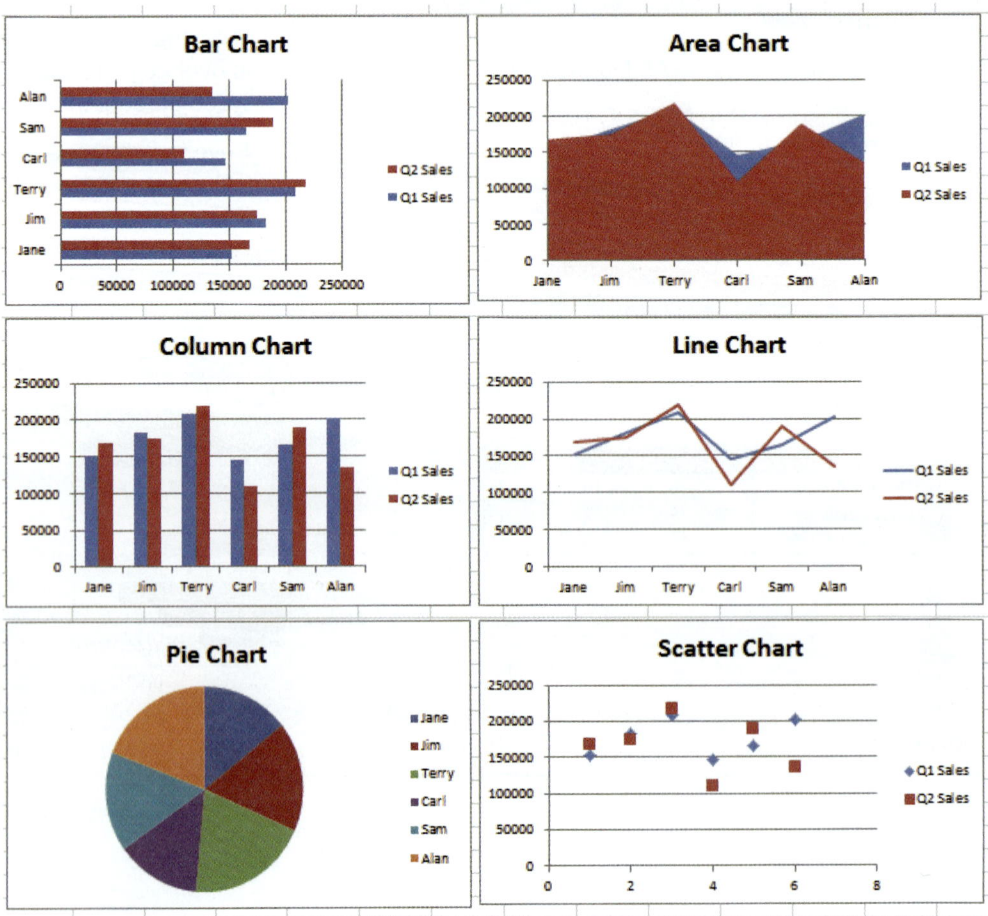

Try It! Changing Chart Types

1. In the **ETry21_studentfirstname_studentlastname** file, click the bar chart that you created first (positioned starting in cell F2) to select it.
2. Click Chart Tools Design > Change Chart Type. The Change Chart Type dialog box appears.
3. In the list at the left, click the Area chart type.
4. Scroll down if needed, and click the 3-D Area choice under Area.
5. Click OK. Observe the changes. You determine that the 3-D Area chart is too imprecise for the data, so you will change the chart again.
6. Click Chart Tools Design > Change Chart Type. The Change Chart Type dialog box appears.
7. In the list at the left, click the Line chart type.
8. Scroll the subtypes if needed, and click the Line with Markers choice under Line.
9. Click OK.
10. Save the changes to **ETry21_studentfirstname_studentlastname**, and leave it open to use in the next Try It.

Selecting a Chart

- You can copy a chart and then edit it to produce a different chart that uses the same worksheet data.
- To resize, copy, move, or format a chart, you must first select it by clicking anywhere on the chart.
- A selected chart is surrounded by a border with evenly spaced dotted handles at the corners and middle of each side.

✔ *You use these handles to resize a chart.*

- Once the chart itself is selected, click individual chart elements such as an axis or title to select it.
- To select a particular chart element, use the Chart Elements drop-down list in the Current Selection group on the Chart Tools Layout tab.

Try It! Selecting a Chart

1. In the **ETry21_studentfirstname_studentlastname** file, click the column chart with the upper-left corner in cell F16. The border with the dotted handles appears.
2. Click the line chart above it to select it, instead.
3. Click the legend on the line chart to select it.
4. Save the changes to **ETry21_studentfirstname_studentlastname**, and leave it open to use in the next Try It.

Resizing, Copying, Moving, or Deleting a Chart

- You can resize, copy, or move an embedded chart as needed using the same methods as for moving and resizing other objects.
- You can't resize a chart on a chart sheet; however, you can copy or move the chart around on the sheet.
- You can move a chart on a chart sheet to another sheet, creating an embedded object. You can reverse the process when needed to change an embedded chart into a chart sheet.
- If you copy a chart, you can change the copied chart type to present data in a different way, such as using another chart type.

Try It! Resizing, Copying, Moving, or Deleting a Chart

1. In the **ETry21_studentfirstname_ studentlastname** file, click the border of the line chart itself to reselect the whole chart.
2. Press DEL.
3. Click the column chart, and drag it up so that its upper-left corner starts at cell F2.
4. With the chart still selected, click Home > Copy.
5. Click the Sheet2 sheet tab.
6. Click Home > Paste.
7. With the chart still selected, drag it down so its upper-left corner is on cell B3.
8. Drag the lower-right handle down to cell K21 to increase the chart size.
9. Close **ETry21_studenfirstname_student lastname**, saving all changes, and exit Excel.

Project 45—Create It

Add the First Chart

DIRECTIONS

1. Start Excel, if necessary, and open the **EProj45** file from the data files for this lesson.
2. Save the file as **EProj45_studentfirstname_ studentlastname** in the location where your teacher instructs you to store the files for this lesson.
3. Group the sheets. Add a header that has your name at the left, the date code in the center, and the page number code at the right, and change back to **Normal** view. Ungroup the sheets.
4. Select the product names in the range **A6:L6**.
5. Scroll down, press and hold CTRL, and drag over the daily sales figures in the range **A31:L31**.
6. Click **Insert** > **Line** > **2-D Line** > **Line with Markers**.
7. With the new chart still selected, click **Home** > **Cut**.
8. Click the **Charts** sheet tab.
9. Click **Home** > **Paste**.
10. Drag the chart so its upper-left corner is in cell **B2**.
11. Drag the lower-right corner of the chart down and to the right, through cell **J23**. Your chart should resemble Figure 21-3.
12. **With your teacher's permission**, print the **Charts** worksheet. Submit the printout or the file for grading as required.
13. Close the workbook, saving all changes, and exit Excel.

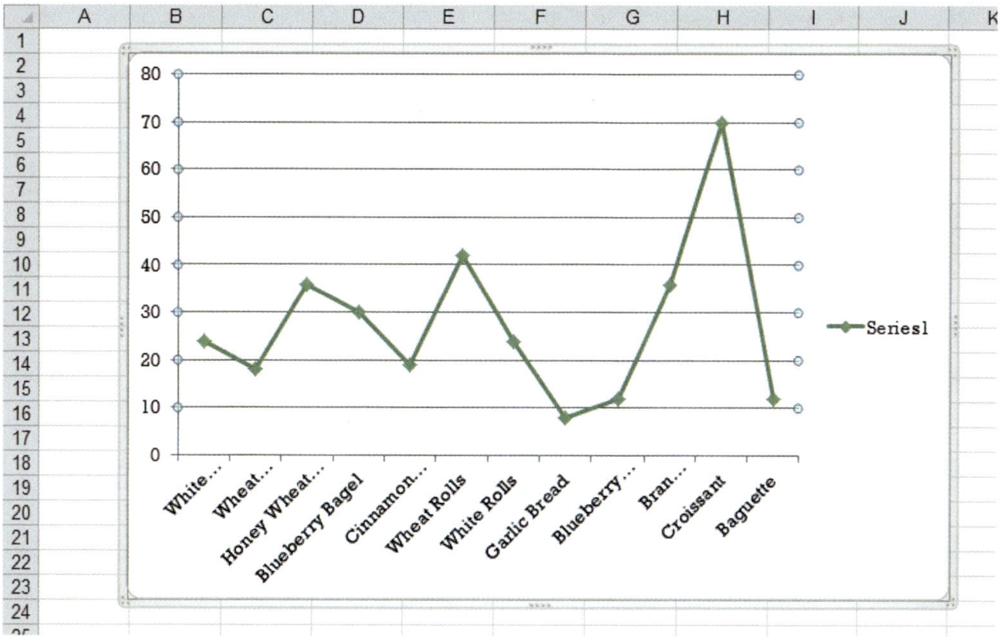

Figure 21-3

Project 46—Apply It

Add and Change Charts

DIRECTIONS

1. Start Excel, if necessary, and open the **EProj46** file from the data files for this lesson.
2. Save the file as **EProj46_studentfirstname_studentlastname** in the location where your teacher instructs you to store the files for this lesson.
3. Group the sheets. Add a header that has your name at the left, the date code in the center, and the page number code at the right, and change back to **Normal** view. Ungroup the sheets.
4. Go to the **Daily Sales** sheet and scroll down to the Daily Summary area.
5. Select the nonadjacent ranges **A38:A39** and **D38:D39**.
6. Insert a pie chart using the **Pie in 3-D** subtype.
7. Cut the new pie chart from the **Daily Sales** sheet, and paste it on the **Charts** sheet.
8. Drag the chart down so its upper-left corner is over cell **A25**.
9. Resize the chart so that its lower-right cell is over cell **J45**.
10. Scroll up and select the line chart.
11. Change the chart type to a column chart, **Clustered Cylinder** subtype.
12. Deselect the chart.
13. **With your teacher's permission**, print the **Charts** worksheet. Submit the printout or the file for grading as required.
14. Close the workbook, saving all changes, and exit Excel.

Lesson 22

Showing Percentages with a Pie Chart

➤ What You Will Learn

Calculating Percentages
Creating a Pie Chart on a Chart Sheet

Software Skills Finding relative percentages of values provides a way to measure performance or compare parts to a whole. You can build formulas from scratch to calculate percentages, or you can create a pie chart, which automatically calculates percentages. You also can place a pie chart on a separate chart sheet so you can print it separately and manage it more easily.

Application Skills You are the vice president of sales for Telson Tech. You are performing a review of quarterly sales, and you want to review how the sales made by individual sales reps contribute to overall revenue. You also want to calculate 5% bonus values. You will develop formulas to find percentages, and create reviewing percentages via a pie chart.

What You Can Do

Calculating Percentages

- A percentage is a calculation of proportion. It tells you how much one value represents when compared with a total.
- Calculate a percentage of a total by dividing the individual value by the total value.

  ✔ *For example, if you want to find the chocolate ice cream sales percentage of total ice cream sales, substitute the division operator for "percentage of" to see how to structure your formula: =chocolate sales/total sales.*

- If you know the percentage you need to calculate of a value, use multiplication and specify the percentage as a decimal.

✔ *For example, if you want to calculate 25% of total sales, change the percentage to a decimal and substitute the multiplication operator for "of" to see how to structure your formula: =.25*total sales.*

Try It! Calculating Percentages

1. Start Excel.
2. Open the **ETry22** file from the data files for this lesson.
3. Save the file as **ETry22_studentfirstname_studentlastname** in the location where your teacher instructs you to store the files for this lesson.
4. Add a header that has your name at the left, the date code in the center, and the page number code at the right, and change back to Normal view.
5. Click cell J4 to select it.
6. Use the method of your choice to enter the formula that calculates the first student's sales as a percentage of the Weekly Total sales: **=I4/E22**.
7. Press F4 to make the reference to cell E22 an absolute reference, which changes the formula to =I4/$E$22, and press CTRL + ENTER.
8. Use the fill handle to fill the formula down through cell J9.
9. Use the same process to create formulas in cells J12:J14 to calculate each type of candy's percentage of Weekly Total sales.
10. In cell G17, enter a formula that calculates 33% of the Weekly Total sales in cell E22, or **=.33*E22**.
11. Save the changes to **ETry22_studentfirstname_studentlastname**, and leave it open to use in the next Try It.

Finding a percentage

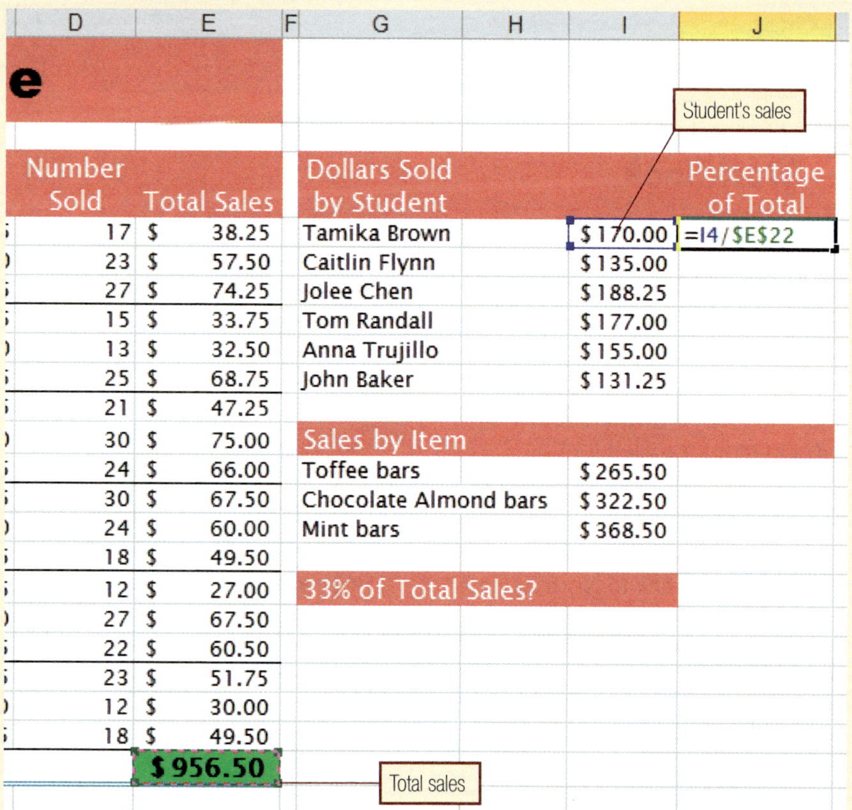

D	E	F	G	H	I	J
e						
Number Sold	Total Sales		Dollars Sold by Student			Percentage of Total
17	$ 38.25		Tamika Brown		$170.00	=I4/$E$22
23	$ 57.50		Caitlin Flynn		$135.00	
27	$ 74.25		Jolee Chen		$188.25	
15	$ 33.75		Tom Randall		$177.00	
13	$ 32.50		Anna Trujillo		$155.00	
25	$ 68.75		John Baker		$131.25	
21	$ 47.25					
30	$ 75.00		Sales by Item			
24	$ 66.00		Toffee bars		$265.50	
30	$ 67.50		Chocolate Almond bars		$322.50	
24	$ 60.00		Mint bars		$368.50	
18	$ 49.50					
12	$ 27.00		33% of Total Sales?			
27	$ 67.50					
22	$ 60.50					
23	$ 51.75					
12	$ 30.00					
18	$ 49.50					
	$956.50					

Creating a Pie Chart on a Chart Sheet

- A pie chart automatically calculates the total of the values in the selected range, and represents each individual value as a percentage of that total.

  ✔ *Lesson 25 will explain how to make changes such as adding percentage data labels to pie slices, and Lesson 23 will explain other changes specific to working with slices.*

- After you create a pie chart, you can move it to its own chart sheet using the Move Chart button in the Location group on the Chart Tools Design tab.
- This opens the Move Chart dialog box, where you can click New sheet, enter a chart sheet name, and then click the OK button.
- Or, you can select data to chart and press F11 to create a column chart on a new chart sheet, and then change the chart to a pie chart.
- When you insert a header or footer on a chart sheet, the Page Setup dialog box appears, with the Header/Footer tab selected. Click the Custom Header or Custom Footer button, and then use the dialog box that appears to specify what information appears in each section of the header or footer.

Try It! Creating a Pie Chart on a Chart Sheet

1. In the **ETry22_studentfirstname_studentlastname** file, use CTRL to select the nonadjacent ranges G4:G9 and I4:I9.
2. Click Insert > Pie > Pie.
3. Click Chart Tools Design > Move Chart.
4. Click the New sheet option button, and type **Student Pie Chart** as the name for the new sheet.
5. Click OK. Review the chart.
6. Close **ETry22_studentfirstname_studentlastname**, saving all changes, and exit Excel.

Project 47—Create It

Add Percentage Calculations in the Q3 Sales Workbook

DIRECTIONS

1. Start Excel, if necessary, and open the **EProj47** file from the data files for this lesson.
2. Save the file as **EProj47_studentfirstname_studentlastname** in the location where your teacher instructs you to store the files for this lesson.
3. Add a header that has your name at the left, the date code in the center, and the page number code at the right, and change back to Normal view.
4. In cell **F5**, enter the formula **=E5/$E$9**, and press CTRL + ENTER.
5. Drag the fill handle to fill the formula down through cell **F8**.
6. In cell **G5**, enter the formula **=.05*E5**, and press CTRL + ENTER.
7. Drag the fill handle to fill the formula down through cell **G8**, as shown in Figure 22-1.
8. **With your teacher's permission**, print the worksheet. Submit the printout or the file for grading as required.
9. Close the workbook, saving all changes, and exit Excel.

	A	B	C	D	E	F	G	H
1	Telson Tech							
2	Q3 Sales							
3								
4	Rep	July	August	September	Total	Percentage	5% Bonus	
5	Parker	$ 65,000	$ 45,982	$ 68,256	$179,238	27.96%	$ 8,962	
6	Jones	$ 35,990	$ 62,834	$ 51,045	$149,869	23.38%	$ 7,493	
7	Anderson	$ 51,030	$ 22,930	$ 73,454	$147,414	22.99%	$ 7,371	
8	Chen	$ 46,113	$ 29,288	$ 89,224	$164,625	25.68%	$ 8,231	
9	Total	$198,133	$161,034	$281,979	$641,146			
10								

Figure 22-1

Project 48—Apply It

Add a Pie Chart on a Chart Sheet in the Q3 Sales Workbook

DIRECTIONS

1. Start Excel, if necessary, and open the **EProj48** file from the data files for this lesson.
2. Save the file as **EProj48_studentfirstname_studentlastname** in the location where your teacher instructs you to store the files for this lesson.
3. Select the nonadjacent ranges **A5:A8** and **E5:E8**.
4. Insert a pie chart using the **Pie in 3-D** subtype.
5. Move the chart to its own sheet named **Sales Percentage Pie**. The finished chart should resemble Figure 22-2.
6. Add a header to the chart sheet that has your name at the left, the date code in the center, and the page number code at the right, and change back to **Normal** view.
7. **With your teacher's permission**, print the chart sheet. Submit the printout or the file for grading as required.
8. Close the workbook, saving all changes, and exit Excel.

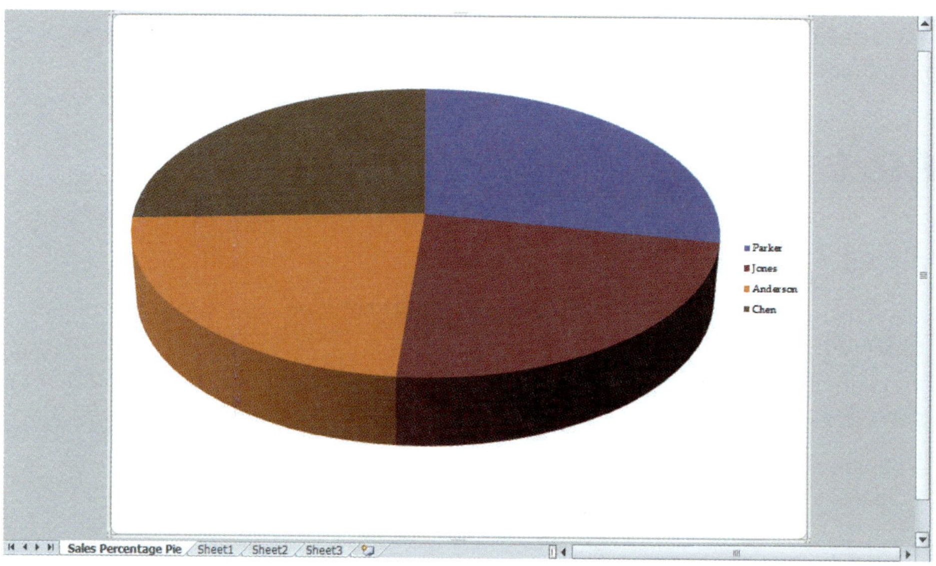

Figure 22-2

Lesson 23

Enhancing a Pie Chart

WORDS TO KNOW

Chart area
The overall background for the chart and all its elements, such as titles.

Explode
To move a pie slice away from the pie chart, for emphasis.

➤ What You Will Learn

Applying 3-D to a Pie Chart
Rotating Slices in a Pie Chart
Exploding and Coloring a Pie Chart
Formatting the Chart Area of a Pie Chart

Software Skills With the themes available in Excel, even a basic pie chart looks attractive. However, you can present the data even more effectively by working with several pie chart formatting settings. You can work with the amount of 3-D applied to the pie chart, rotate the slices to a new position, explode a slice or change slice color, and add formatting to the area behind the chart.

Application Skills As vice president of sales for Telson Tech, you are continuing the review of quarterly sales. You've received updates to the sales data, so you want to make those changes, and then enhance the pie chart by working with 3-D settings, exploding the slice for the leading salesperson, and more. You'll explore those options in this lesson.

What You Can Do

Applying 3-D to a Pie Chart

- As you saw in Lesson 22, some of the pie chart subtypes are three-dimensional (3-D) rather than two dimensional (2-D).
- You can change the amount of 3-D applied to a pie chart using one of the 3-D subtypes.

✔ *Some users believe that excessive 3-D distorts the appearance of the chart, making interpreting the data more difficult.*

- If the chart does not use a 3-D subtype, change to a 3-D subtype and then adjust the rotation.
- You can adjust rotation for either an embedded chart or chart on a chart sheet. Be sure to select the embedded chart to change it.
- Use the 3-D Rotation button in the Background group on the Chart Tools Layout tab to open the Format Chart Area dialog box.
- With 3-D Rotation selected in the list at the left of the Format Chart Area dialog box, change the X and Y percentage entries under Rotation to adjust the amount of horizontal and vertical rotation, respectively.

Try It! Applying 3-D to a Pie Chart

1. Start Excel.
2. Open the **ETry23** file from the data files for this lesson.
3. Save the file as **ETry23_studentfirstname_studentlastname** in the location where your teacher instructs you to store the files for this lesson.
4. Display the Student Pie Chart sheet, if necessary, and add a header that has your name at the left, the date code in the center, and the page number code at the right, and change back to Normal view.
5. Make sure the chart is selected. Click Chart Tools Design > Change Chart Type, click the Pie in 3-D subtype under Pie, and then click OK.
6. Click Chart Tools Layout > 3-D Rotation.
7. Under Rotation, edit the Y value to read 50°. Live Preview shows how the chart will look.
8. Click Close.
9. Save the changes to **ETry23_studentfirstname_studentlastname**, and leave it open to use in the next Try It.

Rotating the pie chart

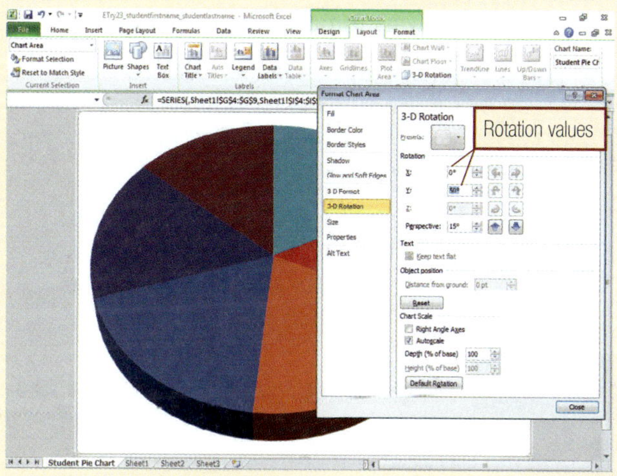

Rotating Slices in a Pie Chart

- You can rotate a pie chart's slices to help enhance a chart's appearance. For example, a pie chart might look best visually with the thinnest slices at the bottom.
- You have to select the pie chart itself (all the slices) to apply the rotation. Click the pie to do so.

✔ *To make sure you've selected the pie chart itself, click Chart Tools Layout > Chart Elements drop-down list > Series 1.*

- Click Chart Tools Layout > Format Selection to open the Format Data Series dialog box with the series option selected. Under Angle of first slide, drag the slider between No Rotation and Full Rotation to determine how far to rotate it.

Try It! Rotating Slices in a Pie Chart

1. In the ETry23_studentfirstname_studentlastname file, with the chart sheet and chart still selected, click Chart Tools Layout > Chart Elements drop-down list > Series 1.
2. Click Chart Tools Layout > Format Selection.
3. Under Angle of first slice, drag the slider right to a setting of 280.
4. Click Close.
5. Save the changes to ETry23_studentfirstname_studentlastname, and leave it open to use in the next Try It.

Exploding and Coloring a Pie Chart

- You can **explode** a pie slice to separate it from the others and emphasize it.
- To explode a single slice, first click the pie, then click the slice to select it individually. Drag the selected slice away from the rest of the slices.

  ✔ *You also can display the Format Data Series dialog box, make sure Series Options is selected at the left, and under Pie Explosion, drag the slider to explode all the slices.*

- You also can change the coloring for the entire chart or a single slice or data point. These techniques apply no matter what the chart type.
- Select the slice to change. Right-click it and then click Format Data Point. In the Format Data Point dialog box, click Fill at the left. Click Solid fill, and then use the Color button to select a color. Note that you also can fill a slice with a gradient, picture, or pattern.
- To recolor the entire chart, click Chart Tools Design, and then click the More button in the Chart Styles group to display a gallery of styles. Click the desired style to apply it.

  ✔ *Chart styles typically do not change any separate formatting you've applied previously, such as changing rotation.*

Try It! Exploding and Coloring a Pie Chart

1. In the ETry23_studentfirstname_studentlastname file, with the chart sheet and chart still selected, click Chart Tools Design > Chart Styles > More.
2. Click Style 12 from the gallery, which is fourth from the left in the second row.
3. Click the chart, and then right-click the slice for Jolee Chen, who was the top seller. It is the bright red slice beside the legend. Click Format Data Point on the shortcut menu.
4. Click Fill in the list at the left side of the Format Data Point dialog box.
5. Under Fill, click the Solid fill option button. Click the Color button, and then click Green under Standard Colors.
6. Click Close.
7. With the green slice still selected, drag it away from the pie to explode it.
8. Save the changes to ETry23_studentfirstname_studentlastname, and leave it open to use in the next Try It.

Formatting the Chart Area of a Pie Chart

- The **chart area** is the background that holds all of the elements of the chart, including the plot area.
- You can fill the chart area with a solid color, gradient, picture or texture, or pattern, just as for individual data points and series.

  ✔ *Use the techniques described here to change the formatting of the chart area for any type of chart.*

- Click Chart Tools Layout > Chart Elements drop-down arrow > Chart Area to select the chart area, and then use the Format Selection button in the same group to open the Format Chart Area dialog box, where you can apply the formatting.
- Be careful when applying a picture or texture fill. If the fill is too busy looking, it can make other elements of the chart, such as axis labels, difficult to read.

Try It! Formatting the Chart Area of a Pie Chart

1. In the **ETry23_studentfirstname_studentlastname** file, with the chart sheet and chart still selected, click Chart Tools Layout > Chart Elements drop-down arrow > Chart Area.
2. Click Chart Tools Layout > Format Selection.
3. Make sure the Fill is selected in the list at the left, and click the Gradient fill option button.
4. Click the Preset colors button, and then click the Silver choice, which is third from left on the bottom row.
5. Click Close.
6. Close **ETry23_studentfirstname_studentlastname**, saving all changes, and exit Excel.

Project 49—Create It

Q3 Sales Worksheet Data Changes

DIRECTIONS

1. Start Excel, if necessary, and open the **EProj49** file from the data files for this lesson.
2. Save the file as **EProj49_studentfirstname_studentlastname** in the location where your teacher instructs you to store the files for this lesson.
3. On the **Sales Percentage Pie** chart sheet, add a header that has your name at the left, the date code in the center, and the page number code at the right, and change back to **Normal** view.
4. Click the **Sheet1** sheet tab.
5. Right-click the row **7** row header, and click **Insert**.
6. Enter the following data across the new row to cell E7:

   Bronsky
   8504
   9250
   11904
   15172
7. Select cells **F6:G6**, and use the fill handle to fill the formulas down to row 7.
8. Change the entry in cell **B8** to **31030**.
9. Click the **Sales Percentage Pie** sheet tab to return to that sheet. As shown in Figure 23-1, the chart has automatically updated to reflect the data changes.
10. **With your teacher's permission**, print the chart sheet. Submit the printout or the file for grading as required.
11. Close the workbook, saving all changes, and exit Excel.

Figure 23-1

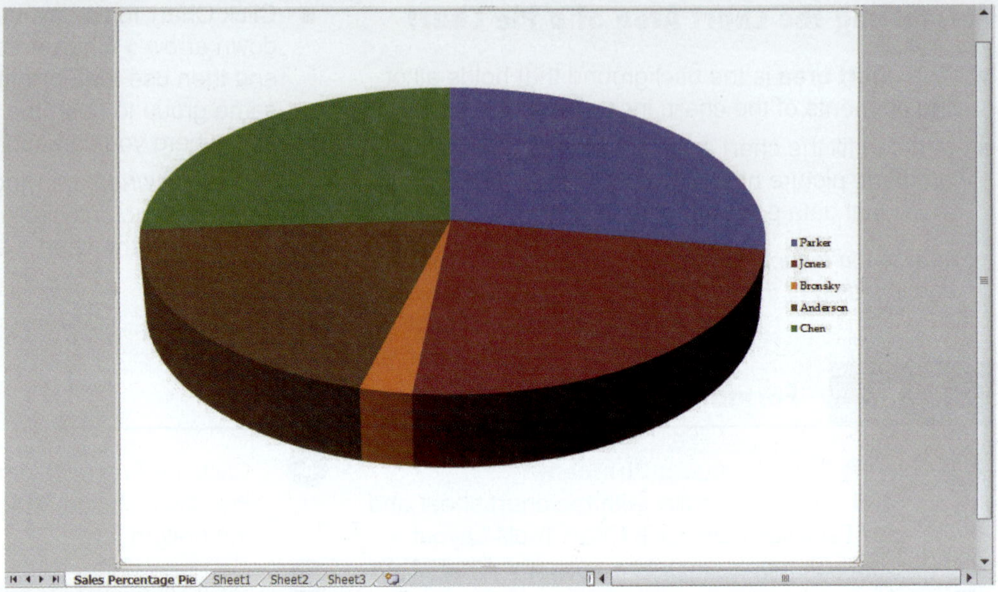

Project 50—Apply It

Working with Slices and Chart Area on the Chart Sheet in the Q3 Sales Worksheet

DIRECTIONS

1. Start Excel, if necessary, and open the **EProj50** file from the data files for this lesson.
2. Save the file as **EProj50_studentfirstname_studentlastname** in the location where your teacher instructs you to store the files for this lesson.
3. On the **Sales Percentage Pie** chart sheet, add a header that has your name at the left, the date code in the center, and the page number code at the right, and change back to **Normal** view.
4. Make sure the chart is selected by clicking in the chart area.
5. In the Format Chart Area dialog box, display the 3-D Rotation options and change the **Y** value under Rotation to **20°**.
6. Open the Format Data Series dialog box, drag the slider under **Angle of first slice** right to a setting of **150**, and then click Close.
7. Explode the blue slice for **Parker** at the bottom of the chart.
8. Format the exploded slide to fill it with the **Granite** texture.
9. Apply a **Brown, Accent 4, Lighter 60%** solid fill to the chart area.
10. **With your teacher's permission**, print the chart sheet. Submit the printout or the file for grading as required.
11. Close the workbook, saving all changes, and exit Excel.

Lesson 24

Adding Special Elements to a Chart or Sheet

➤ What You Will Learn

Inserting a Text Box in a Chart
Updating a Chart
Inserting WordArt in a Worksheet

Software Skills Even though a chart is graphical in itself, you can still enhance it with other elements. For example, you can add a text box with information to elaborate on a particular data point, or use WordArt to create a jazzy title. You also can change the actual data charted.

Application Skills As vice president of sales for Telson Tech, you continue to work with the quarterly sales worksheet and chart. You need to add a chart title, and you will create a WordArt object to serve that purpose. You also will add a text box to explain the exploded pie slice, and update chart information.

WORDS TO KNOW

Text box
A free-floating box added to a sheet or chart that contains any text you specify and that can be formatted separately.

WordArt
A free-floating text object added to a sheet or chart, to which you can apply special formatting effects.

What You Can Do

Inserting a Text Box in a Chart

- When you need to be able to position some text freely on a worksheet or chart, insert a **text box**.
- The text box can hold any text you specify, and it can be sized, positioned, and formatted as desired.
- To insert the box on an embedded chart or chart sheet, make sure the chart is selected first.
- Click Insert > Text Box, and then drag on the worksheet, chart, or chart sheet to create the initial box.

- Type the desired text.
- If adding the text box on a chart, you also can click Chart Tools Layout > Text Box to create the text box.
- Click a text box to reselect it, and use the Home tab and Drawing Tools Format tab choices to apply the desired formatting.

Try It! Inserting a Text Box in a Chart

1. Start Excel.
2. Open the **ETry24** file from the data files for this lesson.
3. Save the file as **ETry24_studentfirstname_studentlastname** in the location where your teacher instructs you to store the files for this lesson.
4. On the Student Pie Chart Sheet, add a header that has your name at the left, the date code in the center, and the page number code at the right, and change back to Normal view.
5. Click Insert > Text Box.
6. Drag on the exploded pie slice to create the text box.
7. Type **Great job!** in the text box.
8. Drag over the text in the text box.
9. Using the tools in the Font group of the Home tab, increase the font size to 20 and change the font color to White, Background 1. Also resize the text box if needed so the text is on one line.
10. Save the changes to **ETry24_studentfirstname_studentlastname**, and leave it open to use in the next Try It.

Updating a Chart

- In Lesson 23, you saw how adding data within the range of charted data was automatically added to the pie chart and changes made to the chart data also resulted in automatic chart updates. In other cases, you may need to make your own changes to the charted data to update the chart.
- For example, you may want to sort the charted range to present the data in a different order, or remove part of the charted range from the chart.
- Make any changes you want to the chart data first.

  ✔ *Sorting data does change the order of the pie slices, so be sure to fix that.*

- Then, with the chart selected, click Chart Tools > Design > Select Data. Change the entry in the Chart data range text box as needed, either by typing a new range or using the Collapse Dialog button.

  ✔ *If the chart is on the chart sheet, Excel automatically displays the sheet holding the charted data.*

Try It! Updating a Chart

1. In the **ETry24_studentfirstname_studentlastname** file, click the Sheet1 sheet to select it.
2. Select the range G3:J9.
3. Click Data > Sort to sort the data by the Percentage of Total field. Set the sort order from largest to smallest, making sure that the My data has headers check box is checked. This sort order will enable you to eliminate the bottom three contributors from the chart.
4. Click the Student Pie Chart sheet tab.
5. Select the chart and click Chart Tools Design > Select Data.
6. Click the Collapse Dialog button and edit the selected ranges to G4:G6 and I4:I6.
7. Expand the dialog box and click OK.
8. Drag the green slice back to the rest of the pie, right-click it, and click Reset to Match Style.

(continued)

Try It! **Updating a Chart** *(continued)*

9. Select the *Great job!* text box and drag it over the top slice for Jolee Chen, the top seller.
10. Click below the legend to deselect the text box.
11. Save the changes to **ETry24_studentfirstname_studentlastname**, and leave it open to use in the next Try It.

Inserting WordArt in a Worksheet

- You create a **WordArt** object to add decorative text anywhere on a worksheet, as well as in a chart sheet.

  ✔ *You also can apply WordArt styles to titles in a chart. See Lesson 25 to see more about adding and working with chart text.*

- When you create WordArt, you choose from a gallery of styles that are compatible with the theme applied to the workbook file.
- Click Insert > WordArt, and then click a style in the gallery that appears. Type the text, and click outside the WordArt object to finish creating it.
- Click the WordArt object to reselect it. You can format it using the choices on the Drawing Tools Format contextual tab.

Try It! **Inserting WordArt in a Worksheet**

1. In the **ETry24_studentfirstname_studentlastname** file, with the chart sheet and chart selected, click Insert > WordArt.
2. In the gallery, click the Fill - Red, Accent 2, Matte Bevel style, which is on the bottom row, third from left. The WordArt object appears with placeholder text.
3. Type **Top**, press ENTER, and type **Sellers**.
4. Drag the WordArt object to the upper-right corner of the chart area.

   ✔ *The S in Sellers can overlap the pie a bit. If WordArt text is too large or small, you can drag over it and use choices in the Font group on the Home tab to change its size.*

5. Click below the legend to deselect the WordArt.
6. Close **ETry24_studentfirstname_studentlastname**, saving all changes, and exit Excel.

Project 51—Create It

Add a WordArt Title to the Q3 Sales Workbook

DIRECTIONS

1. Start Excel, if necessary, and open the **EProj51** file from the data files for this lesson.
2. Save the file as **EProj51_studentfirstname_studentlastname** in the location where your teacher instructs you to store the files for this lesson.
3. On the **Sales Percentage Pie** chart sheet, add a header that has your name at the left, the date code in the center, and the page number code at the right, and change back to **Normal** view.
4. With the chart sheet displayed, click **Insert > WordArt**.
5. In the gallery, click the **Fill - Orange, Accent 3, Powder Bevel** style, which is fourth from the left in the fifth row.
6. Type **Q3 Sales by Rep**.
7. Drag the WordArt object above the chart, and click outside it to deselect it.
8. **With your teacher's permission**, print the chart sheet. Submit the printout or the file for grading as required.
9. Close the workbook, saving all changes, and exit Excel.

Project 52—Apply It

Add a Text Box and Change the Charted Data in the Q3 Sales Workbook

DIRECTIONS

1. Start Excel, if necessary, and open the **EProj52** file from the data files for this lesson.
2. Save the file as **EProj52_studentfirstname_studentlastname** in the location where your teacher instructs you to store the files for this lesson.
3. On the **Sales Percentage Pie** sheet, add a header that has your name at the left, the date code in the center, and the page number code at the right, and change back to **Normal** view.
4. On **Sheet1**, select the range **A4:G9**, and sort the data by the **Total** column, from smallest to largest, making sure that the **My data has headers** check box is checked.
5. Go back to the Sales Percentage Pie sheet, and click **Chart Tools Design > Select Data**.
6. Use the method of your choice to change the selected ranges to **A6:A9** and **E6:E9**, to eliminate the Bronsky data.
7. Drag the exploded slice back to the pie, right-click it, and click **Reset to Match Style**.
8. Rotate the pie so that the brown slice for Parker is at the lower right, and then explode that slice.
9. Add a text box at the center-bottom with the following text:
   Bronsky data eliminated because she was in training.
   Parker was top seller.
10. Format the text box text with the **Fill - Indigo Accent 1, Metal Bevel, Reflection** WordArt style. The WordArt Styles are found on the Drawing Tools Format tab.
11. Deselect the text box.
12. **With your teacher's permission**, print the chart sheet. Submit the printout or the file for grading as required.
13. Close the workbook, saving all changes, and exit Excel.

Lesson 25

Completing Chart Formatting

➤ What You Will Learn

Changing Data Series Orientation
Formatting a Chart
Resizing, Moving, or Deleting a Chart Element
Changing Chart Text
Enhancing the Chart Plot Area
Formatting Category and Value Axes

Software Skills There are many ways in which you can enhance your chart: you can add and format chart text, add color or a pattern to the chart plot area, and format the value and category axes so that the numbers are easier to read.

Application Skills The charts you created to analyze daily bread sales at your Whole Grains Bread retail store are almost completed. Before printing, you want to format them to make them more professional looking and easier to understand.

WORDS TO KNOW

Chart layout
A formatting arrangement that specifies the location and sizes of chart elements, such as the chart title and legend.

Object
Any element on a worksheet or chart that can be manipulated independently. Some chart elements are also objects.

Tick marks
Lines of measurement along the category and value axis.

What You Can Do

Changing Data Series Orientation

- When you create a chart, Excel assumes the data series are arranged in rows.
- For example, if you had a worksheet with several stores listed in different rows, and sales for each month listed in columns, then each store would be a different data series, and be represented with a unique color.
- If you switched the orientation of the data series from columns to rows, then the sales in the columns would become the series rather than the categories.
- Use the Switch Row/Column button in the Data group on the Chart Tools Design tab to change the data orientation for the selected chart.

Try It! Changing Data Series Orientation

1. Start Excel.
2. Open the **ETry25** file from the data files for this lesson.
3. Save the file as **ETry25_studentfirstname_studentlastname** in the location where your teacher instructs you to store the files for this lesson.
4. Group the sheets. Add a header that has your name at the left, the date code in the center, and the page number code at the right, and change back to Normal view. Ungroup the sheets.
5. Click the Practice sheet tab, and then click the chart.
6. Click Chart Tools Design > Switch Row/Column. The statuses become the series and the communities become the categories.
7. Save the changes to **ETry25_studentfirstname_studentlastname**, and leave it open to use in the next Try It.

Formatting a Chart

- When a chart is created, it contains a legend, and labels along each axis.
- Apply a different **chart layout** to add common features such as a chart title, axis titles, and data table.
- You can also select individual chart elements such as a legend or a chart title, and add or remove them from your chart layout to personalize it.
- In addition to its default chart layout, every new chart is formatted with a default style.
- The Chart Layouts and Chart Styles galleries are found on the Chart Tools Design tab.
- As you learned in Lesson 23, you can quickly recolor and format the selected chart by simply changing chart styles. The technique presented in that lesson works for any chart type.
- Regardless of the style you select, you can still apply manual formatting to any selected chart element using special Format dialog boxes.

Try It! Formatting a Chart

1. In the **ETry25_studentfirstname_studentlastname** file, click the Large Chart sheet tab to select it.
2. Click the chart to select it.
3. Click Chart Tools Design > Chart Layouts More button, and click Layout 9, which is third from the left in the third row of the gallery. The layout adds a placeholder chart title and axis titles.
4. Click Chart Tools Design > Chart Styles More button, and click Style 42, which is second in the last row of the gallery. This applies a dark background and lighter formatting to the chart.
5. Click the Chart Title placeholder.
6. Click Home > Font Color drop-down arrow, and apply the Dark Red, Accent 5, Lighter 40% color.
7. Save the changes to **ETry25_studentfirstname_studentlastname**, and leave it open to use in the next Try It.

Chart formatting tools

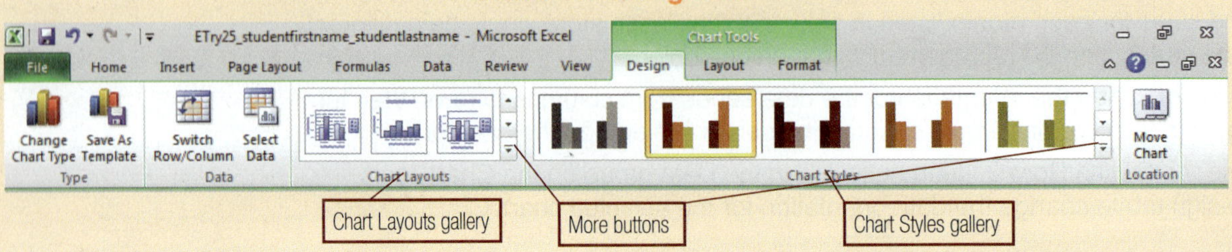

Resizing, Moving, or Deleting a Chart Element

- Before you can resize, move, or delete a chart element, also called an **object**, you must select it first.
- By resizing, moving, or deleting the parts of your chart, you may make it more attractive and easier to read.
- If you resize an object that contains text, the font size of the text changes correspondingly.
- When you delete an object from a chart, the remaining parts of the chart are enlarged to fill the gap.
- You can change the value represented by a column or bar by resizing it.

Try It! Resizing, Moving, or Deleting a Chart Element

1. In the **ETry25_studenfirstname_studentlastname** file, on the Large Chart sheet with the chart selected, click the legend to select it.
2. Drag the legend down to the lower-right corner of the chart area.
3. Drag the legend's upper-left sizing handle up and to the left, so that the legend's left boundary nearly touches the chart plot area and the top boundary aligns with the second horizontal line above the horizontal axis.
4. Click the horizontal Axis Title placeholder to select it.
5. Press DEL to delete the placeholder.
6. Save the changes to **ETry25_studentfirstname_studentlastname**, and leave it open to use in the next Try It.

Changing Chart Text

- You can edit chart text or change its formatting. For example, you can change the size, font, and attributes of a chart's title.
- Usually, you can select a new text object or placeholder, type the new text, and press ENTER to update the text. You also can click within a text box and edit the text, and then click outside the text box to finish the change.
- The Labels group on the Chart Tools Layout tab provides options for displaying individual chart labels and varying their position.
- For example, click Chart Tools > Layout > Data Labels, and then click the desired position to add data labels to the chart data points. Clicking More Data Label Options at the bottom of the menu enables you to determine the type of value displayed, such as percentages on pie chart slices, to change the number format, and more. For charts with multiple series, you have to format the data labels for each series independently.

Try It! Changing Chart Text

1. In the **ETry25_studentfirstname_studentlastname** file, on the Large Chart sheet with the chart still selected, click the Chart Title placeholder to select it if necessary.
2. Type **Buildout Status**, and press ENTER.
3. Click the vertical Axis Title placeholder to select it.
4. Type **Units**, and press ENTER.
5. Click Home > Increase Font Size four times to make the axis title larger.
6. Click Chart Tools Layout > Data Labels > Inside End to add data labels to the column chart bars.
7. Click one of the data labels for the Glenview North series, click Chart Tools Format > Text Fill drop-down arrow, and then click Automatic to change the text color to black to make it more readable.
8. Click above the legend to deselect all objects.
9. Save the changes to **ETry25_studentfirstname_studentlastname**, and leave it open to use in the next Try It.

Enhancing the Chart Plot Area

- In Lesson 23, you learned how to apply a background to the chart area. You can use that same method to apply a fill to the chart area for any chart type.
- You also can apply a separate fill to the smaller plot area.
- You can:
  - Add a border around the background area.
  - Apply a color to the background.
  - Apply a fill effect, such as gradient (a blend of two colors), texture (such as marble), pattern (such as diagonal stripes), or picture (a graphic file).
  - Add a shadow effect behind the border.
  - Shape the corners to create a 3-D look.
- To select the plot area, click it or choose Chart Tools Layout > Chart Elements > Plot Area. Then, click Chart Tools Layout > Format Selection to display the Format Plot area dialog box, where you can make your selections.
- You also can use the choices in the Chart Tools Format Shape Styles group to change the plot area formatting.
- To remove a plot area fill quickly, click Chart Tools > Layout > Plot Area > None.

Try It! Enhancing the Chart Plot Area

1. In the **ETry25_studentfirstname_studentlastname** file, in the Large Chart sheet, click Chart Tools Layout > Chart Elements drop-down list arrow > Plot Area.
2. Click Chart Tools Layout > Plot Area > None to remove the current plot area fill.
3. Click Chart Tools Format > Shape Fill > Brown, Text 2, Lighter 60% (fourth choice in the third row of theme colors).
4. Click above the legend to deselect the plot area.
5. Save the changes to **ETry25_studentfirstname_studentlastname**, and leave it open to use in the next Try It.

Formatting the plot area

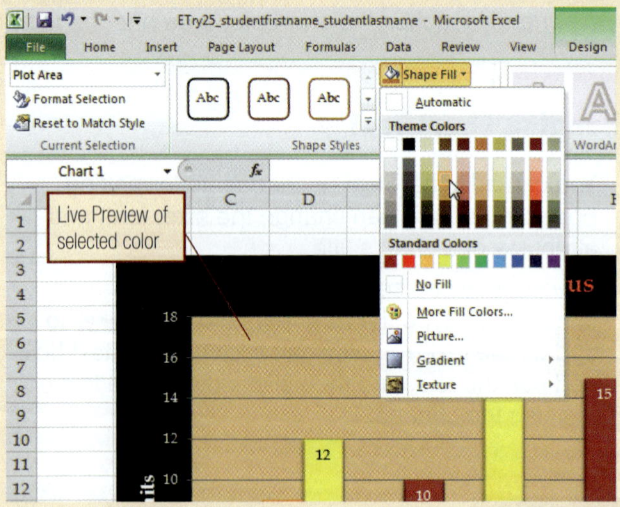

Formatting Category and Value Axes

- Categories and data series are plotted along the category or horizontal axis.
- The vertical or value axis provides a scale for the values of the data for most chart types. (For example, for bar charts, the axes are reversed.)
- You can change the font, size, color, attributes, alignment, and placement of text or numbers along both the category and value axes.
- You can add a color fill, border, line, shadow, or 3-D effect to the labels along either axis.
- You can also change the appearance of the **tick marks**, or add or remove gridlines.
- In addition, you can adjust the scale used along the value axis.
- Use the Chart Tools Layout > Axes submenus to control whether either axis displays overall.
- Use the Chart Tools Layout > Gridlines submenus to control whether the axis includes major gridlines, minor gridlines, or both.
- After selecting an axis, use Chart Tools Layout > Format Selection to see more detailed settings.

Try It! **Formatting Category and Value Axes**

1. In the **ETry25_studentfirstname_studentlastname** file, with the Large Chart sheet and chart selected, click Chart Tools Layout > Axes > Primary Vertical Axis > More Primary Vertical Axis Options. The Format Axis dialog box opens.
2. Make sure Axis Options is selected in the list at the left. Beside Minor unit, click the Fixed option button, and change the entry in the accompanying text box to 1.
3. Open the Minor tick mark type drop-down list, and click Inside.
4. Click Close.
5. Close **ETry25_studentfirstname_studentlastname**, saving all changes, and exit Excel.

Project 53—Create It

Changing the Data Orientation and Layout on a Daily Sales Chart

DIRECTIONS

1. Start Excel, if necessary, and open the **EProj53** file from the data files for this lesson.
2. Save the file as **EProj53_studentfirstname_studentlastname** in the location where your teacher instructs you to store the files for this lesson.
3. Group the sheets. Add a header that has your name at the left, the date code in the center, and the page number code at the right, and change back to **Normal** view. Ungroup the sheets.
4. Click the **Charts** sheet tab to select it.
5. Click the bottom pie chart and press the DEL key to remove it.
6. Click the top chart to select it, and click **Home** > **Copy**.
7. Click cell **B25**, and click **Home** > **Paste**.
8. Click **Chart Tools Design** > **Switch Row/Column**.
9. Scroll up and compare the appearance of the top chart with that of the bottom chart. As shown in Figure 25-1, changing the data orientation reduced the categories but increased the number of series.
10. **With your teacher's permission**, print the **Charts** sheet. Submit the printout or the file for grading as required.
11. Close the workbook, saving all changes, and exit Excel

Figure 25-1

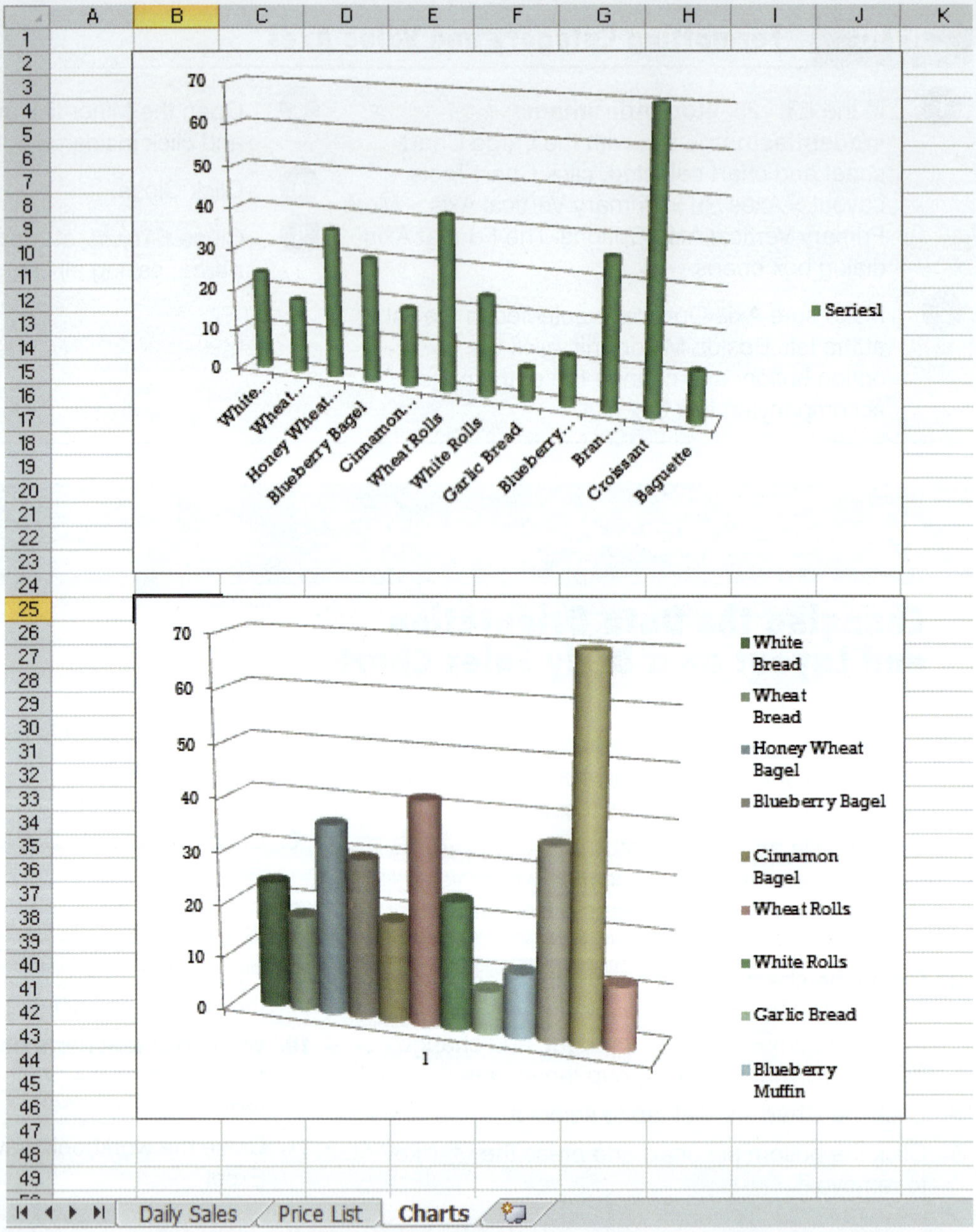

Project 54—Apply It

Finishing the Daily Sales Charts

DIRECTIONS

1. Start Excel, if necessary, and open the **EProj54** file from the data files for this lesson.
2. Save the file as **EProj54_studentfirstname_studentlastname** in the location where your teacher instructs you to store the files for this lesson.
3. Group the sheets. Add a header that has your name at the left, the date code in the center, and the page number code at the right, and change back to **Normal** view. Ungroup the sheets.

4. Click the **Charts** sheet tab.
5. Select the horizontal axis for the top chart, and format it so it displays without axis labels.
6. On the same chart display data labels that are the category names.
7. Use the Format Data Labels dialog box to show the category name only and apply the **Rotate all text 270°** alignment setting.
8. Select the **Croissant** data label, and move it just to the left of the top of its data point cylinder, within the plot area.
9. Delete the legend.
10. Add a chart title above the chart that reads **Daily Sales**.
11. Add a **Rose, Accent 6, Darker 10%** fill to the plot area.
12. Select the data marker (cylinder) for the Croissant data point, and change its fill color to **Green, Accent 1, Darker 50%**.
13. Scroll down and select the bottom chart.
14. Apply the **Style 10** chart style to highlight the cylinders.
15. Make it wider so all the entries can display.
16. Delete the horizontal axis category name.
17. Add a rotated vertical axis title that reads **Unit Sales**. Increase its font size to **16** pts.
18. Add a **Pink tissue paper** texture fill set to **25%** transparency to the chart area.
19. Scroll to compare the charts. They should resemble Figure 25-2.
20. **With your teacher's permission**, print the **Charts** sheet. Submit the printout or the file for grading as required.
21. Close the workbook, saving all changes, and exit Excel.

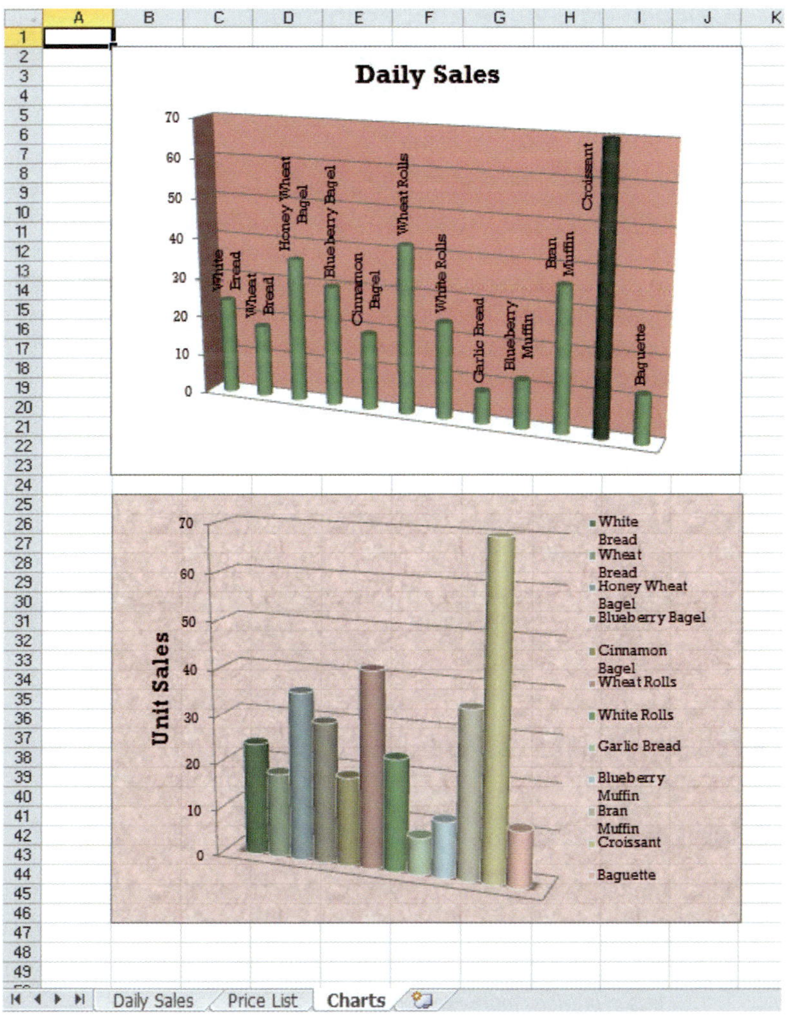

Figure 25-2

Lesson 26

Comparing and Analyzing Data

WORDS TO KNOW

What-if analysis
Using formulas and other tools in Excel to examine the results of changing particular data, for planning purposes.

➤ What You Will Learn

Using Parentheses in a Formula
Calculating a Value After an Increase
Performing What-If Analysis
Creating a Line Chart to Compare Data

Software Skills Forecasting is an important business function. You can't plan for the future unless you can anticipate how various scenarios will develop and play out numerically. Excel offers a number of techniques that you can use to evaluate data based on your answer to the question, "What if?" In this lesson, you will explore the use of parentheses in formulas, calculating a value based on a percentage increase, creating a formula that performs a basic what-if analysis, and using a line chart to visualize the what-if scenario.

Application Skills You are the CEO for Cantrell Resources, a firm that provides temporary labor, placement, and payroll services. The state legislature in your state is debating a possible increase in the state income tax for next year. You are already anticipating that gross wages will increase by 1.9% for the coming year, so you want to examine how different increased state tax levels will affect quarterly withholding taxes for your firm. In this lesson, you will add the formulas and chart needed to make these projections.

What You Can Do

Using Parentheses in a Formula

- Parentheses, along with operator precedence, control the order of calculations in formulas.

✔ *Excel Lesson 7 first introduced the concept of how to use parentheses in formulas. This lesson provides more examples.*

- When there are multiple nested pairs of parentheses, Excel calculates from the innermost pair, working outwards.
- Improperly placed parentheses can cause logic flaws in a formula that might not necessarily be flagged with an error message or indicator in Excel. So you should take care to examine the use of parentheses if formula results are not what you'd expected.

Try It! Using Parentheses in a Formula

1. Start Excel.
2. Open the **ETry26** file from the data files for this lesson.
3. Save the file as **ETry26_studentfirstname_studentlastname** in the location where your teacher instructs you to store the files for this lesson.
4. Add a header that has your name at the left, the date code in the center, and the page number code at the right, and change back to Normal view.
5. Select cell F6 and enter **=((B6/C6)+(D6/E6))/2**.

   ✔ *The parentheses cause the formula to calculate the individual quarterly averages, and then to average the two values.*
6. Copy the formula down the column using the fill handle.
7. Save the changes to **ETry26_studentfirstname_studentlastname**, and leave it open to use in the next Try It.

Calculating a Value After an Increase

- In Lesson 22, you learned how to calculate the percentage of a total value represented by a single value. In that case, you create a formula that divides the individual value by the total value to yield the percentage.
- You also learned in that lesson that to find a particular percentage of a value, you convert the percentage to a decimal, and then multiply.
- Calculating the result of an increase works the same as the latter method, in most cases. That's because increases are often stated in terms of percentage increases.
- So while you still convert to a decimal and multiply, you first add 1 (to represent 100% of the original value) to the decimal, so the result reflects the original value with the percentage increase added. Say you pay a $215 membership fee this year and that value is in cell B2. The fee will go up 15% next year, and that value (.15) is in cell B3. To find the new fee, use the formula =(1+B3)*B2, or simply =1.15*B2.

Try It! Calculating a Value After an Increase

1. In the **ETry26_studenfirstname_studentlastname** file, select cell G6.
2. Assume that Q3 travel expenses will be 2% more than the average for the first two quarters. Enter the formula **=F6*1.02** in the cell.
3. Copy the formula down the column.
4. Save the changes to **ETry26_studentfirstname_studentlastname**, and leave it open to use in the next Try It.

A formula that calculates an increase

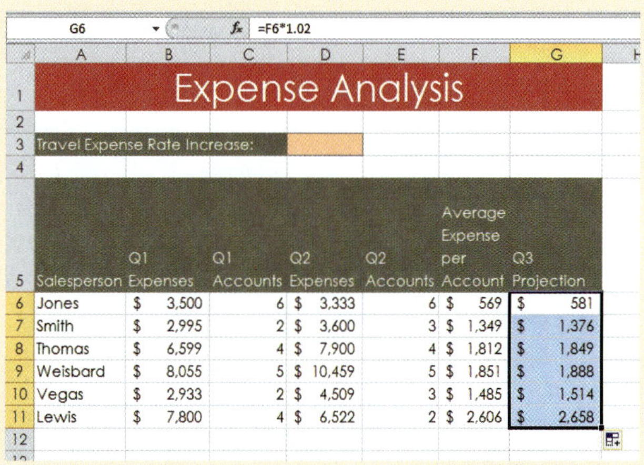

Performing What-If Analysis

- A what-if analysis entails looking at how future results might change based on varying inputs or data.
- For example, businesses often want to plan for sales increases or decreases, tax increases or decreases, or other expense increases or decreases.
- You can perform some what-if analyses in Excel simply by creating formulas that refer to an input cell whose entry you can change to see differing results.

✔ *Excel Lesson 31 covers built-in tools that help automate what-if analysis. These tools include what-if data tables, Goal Seek, and Solver.*

Try It! Performing What-If Analysis

1. In the **ETry26_studenfirstname_studentlastname** file, select cell G6.
2. Change the formula to calculate the increased projected quarterly expense amount by the input cell D3, using an absolute reference to D3. In other words, the formula should read **=F6*(1+$D$3)**.
3. Use the fill handle to copy the formula down the column.
4. Enter **2.5** in cell D3. Note how the column G values update.
5. Enter **3.5** in cell D3. Review the new values in column G again.
6. Save the changes to **ETry26_studentfirstname_studentlastname**, and leave it open to use in the next Try It.

Creating a Line Chart to Compare Data

- Line charts provide a great data analysis tool.
- Not only do line charts identify data points, but they also show how data changed between data points. You can draw the lines further to anticipate how data might change beyond the charted timeframes.
- When performing what-if analysis, charting the most recent actual data and the projected data as separate series provides an idea of how the projected data varies based on changes in projected inputs.

Try It! Creating a Line Chart to Compare Data

1. In the **ETry26_studenfirstname_studentlastname** file, select the nonadjacent ranges A5:A11 and F5:G11.
2. Click Insert > Line > Line with Markers.
3. Drag the chart down below the sheet data.
4. Change the entry in cell D3 to **7.5**. View the results in the chart.
5. Close **ETry26_studentfirstname_studentlastname**, saving all changes, and exit Excel.

(continued)

Try It! Creating a Line Chart to Compare Data *(continued)*

A line chart that shows a what-if analysis result

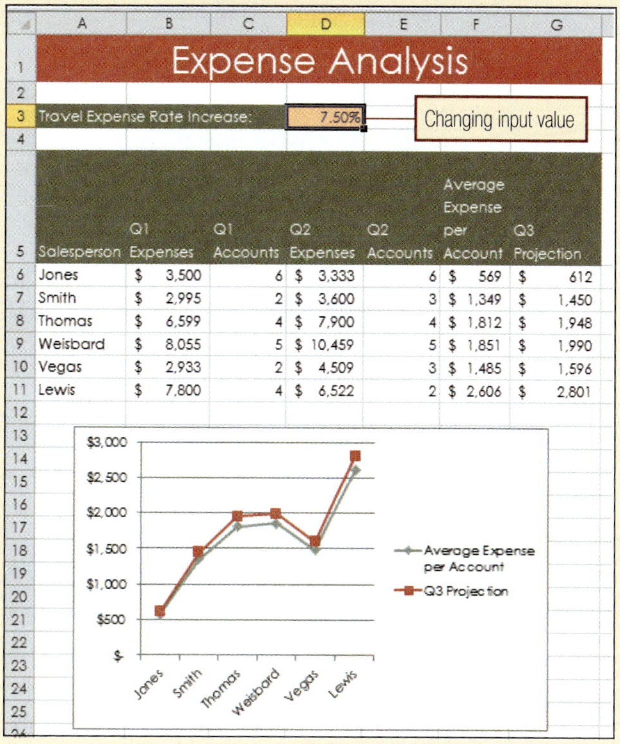

Project 55—Create It

Calculating Tax Withholding in the Projections Workbook

DIRECTIONS

1. Start Excel, if necessary, and open the **EProj55** file from the data files for this lesson.
2. Save the file as **EProj55_studentfirstname_studentlastname** in the location where your teacher instructs you to store the files for this lesson.
3. Add a header that has your name at the left, the date code in the center, and the page number code at the right, and change back to **Normal** view.
4. Click cell **B14**.
5. Enter a formula that adds the 2012 tax rates and multiplies by the Q1 2012 wages. It should be **=($B$7+$B$8+$B$9)*B13**.
6. Use the fill handle to fill the formula across the row, and increase column widths as needed.
7. Copy the formula from cell **B14** to cell **B16**.
8. Edit the absolute references in the copied formula in cell B16 to refer to column C.
9. Use the fill handle to fill the formula across the row, as shown in Figure 26-1.
10. **With your teacher's permission**, print the worksheet. Submit the printout or the file for grading as required.
11. Close the workbook, saving all changes, and exit Excel.

Figure 26-1

	A	B	C	D	E	F
1	Cantrell Resources					
2	2013 Projections					
3						
4	Proposed State Tax Increase					
5						
6		2012	2013			
7	Av. Federal Tax Rate	25.00%	25.00%			
8	State Tax Rate	6.00%	6.00%			
9	Other Payroll Taxes	15.30%	15.30%			
10						
11						
12		Q1	Q2	Q3	Q4	Total
13	2012 Wages	$ 626,254	$ 832,999	$ 709,241	$ 906,888	$ 3,075,382
14	2012 Withholding	$289,955.60	$385,678.54	$328,378.58	$419,889.14	$1,423,901.87
15	2013 Wages (+1.9%)					
16	2013 Withholding	$ -	$ -	$ -	$ -	$ -
17						

Project 56—Apply It

Calculating and Charting the What If Analysis in the Projections Workbook

DIRECTIONS

1. Start Excel, if necessary, and open the **EProj56** file from the data files for this lesson.
2. Save the file as **EProj56_studentfirstname_studentlastname** in the location where your teacher instructs you to store the files for this lesson.
3. Add a header that has your name at the left, the date code in the center, and the page number code at the right, and change back to **Normal** view.
4. Select cell **C8**, and enter a formula that multiples 1 plus the input rate in cell **C4** times the previous tax rate in cell **B8**.
5. In cell **B15**, create a formula that increases the wages in cell **B13** by **1.9%**. Fill the formula across the row and adjust column widths as needed.
6. Enter **1** as the base rate in cell **C4**.
7. Select the noncontiguous ranges **A12:E12**, **A14:E14**, and **A16:E16**.
8. Insert a line chart using the **Line with Markers** subtype.
9. Adjust the vertical axis to start from a minimum value of **250000**.
   - ✔ *Use the Fixed option button for Minimum in the Axis Options choices in the Format Axis dialog box.*
10. Remove the decimal places from the axis display.
    - ✔ *See the Number choices in the Format Axis dialog box.*
11. Increase the size of the chart as desired and position it below the data.
12. Change the entry in cell **C4** to **4**. Observe the calculations in the data and the chart.
13. **With your teacher's permission**, print the worksheet. Submit the printout or the file for grading as required.
14. Close the workbook, saving all changes, and exit Excel.

Lesson 27

Chart Printing and Publishing

➤ What You Will Learn

Printing a Chart
Preparing and Printing a Chart Sheet
Publishing a Chart to the Internet/Intranet

WORDS TO KNOW

Intranet
A private network of computers within a business or organization.

Publish
The process of saving data to an intranet or Internet.

Software Skills After creating a chart, you may want to print it out so you can share your data with others. You can print the chart with the rest of the worksheet data, or simply print just the chart, which is even easier when the chart is on a separate chart sheet. Another way to share your information is to publish your chart to the Internet, or to your company's intranet. You can even make your online chart *interactive*, so that users can change the data in the chart as well as view it. This is especially useful when the data for the chart comes from several sources, such as different departments in your company.

Application Skills You are the CFO of Restoration Architecture and you've been preparing an important report for the CEO on fourth quarter revenues. The most important part is the chart you've prepared. You're going to print it out for inclusion in the final report.

What You Can Do

Printing a Chart

- Embedded charts typically print with the worksheet on which they are located.
- If you select an embedded chart before choosing the Print command, you will only be able to print the chart.
- Typical print settings, such as changing the orientation and scaling, are available when printing a chart.

Try It! Printing a Chart

1. Start Excel.
2. Open the **ETry27** file from the data files for this lesson.
3. Save the file as **ETry27_studentfirstname_studentlastname** in the location where your teacher instructs you to store the files for this lesson.
4. On the Example sheet, add a header that has your name at the left, the date code in the center, and the page number code at the right, and change back to Normal view.
5. Make sure the Example sheet is selected.
6. Click File > Print. Examine the preview of the printout.
7. **With your teacher's permission**, click the Print button to print the sheet and chart.
8. Save the changes to **ETry27_studentfirstname_studentlastname**, and leave it open to use in the next Try It.

Preparing and Printing a Chart Sheet

- When printing a chart sheet, the Print Active Sheet option is selected by default so that only the chart sheet prints. You would have to change that setting to print the whole workbook.
- When you insert a header or footer on a chart sheet using Insert > Header & Footer, the Page Setup dialog box appears with the Header/Footer tab selected. Use the Custom Header or Custom Footer button to build the header or footer.

  ✔ *You also have to use this method to add a header or footer to an embedded chart if you want to print it by itself.*

- The File > Print command also enables you to print the chart sheet.

Try It! Preparing and Printing a Chart Sheet

1. In the **ETry27_studentfirstname_studentlastname** file, click the Large Chart sheet.
2. Click Insert > Header & Footer.
3. Click the Custom Header button. The Header dialog box appears.
4. Using the sections in the dialog box, add a header that has your name at the left, the date code in the center, and the page number code at the right, and then click OK twice.
5. Click File > Print. Examine the preview of the printout. Notice that the Large Chart sheet is using a different orientation than the Example sheet.
6. Under Settings in the center area of the dialog box, click the orientation drop-down list and click Landscape Orientation, if necessary.
7. **With your teacher's permission**, click the Print button to print the chart.
8. Save the changes to **ETry27_studentfirstname_studentlastname**, and leave it open to use in the next Try It.

Publishing a Chart to the Internet/Intranet

- The process of saving worksheet data to the Internet or your company's **intranet** is called **publishing**.
- To publish a chart on the Internet or an intranet, Excel converts the chart to HTML format.
- There are actually two different HTML formats: Web Page (HTM) and Single File Web Page (MHT).
- HTM or HTML format is the standard Web page format in which the text and page format is stored in one file, and the graphics and other elements are stored in separate files linked to the main file.
- MHT or MHTML format is a single file Web page format in which the text, page format, and supporting graphics for a Web page are stored in one file.
- Both formats work perfectly well in most Web browsers; the MHT format does make it easier to relocate a Web page file if needed.
- If the chart is an embedded chart, the chart and its supporting data is published.

✔ *You also can publish a chart sheet or the entire workbook.*

- Choose the Web format to save to from the Save as type drop-down list in the Save As dialog box. After choosing one of the Web formats, click the Publish button to open the Publish as Web Page dialog box, where you can navigate to a Web destination.

✔ *In the Publish as Web Page dialog box, you must also open the Choose drop-down list under Item to publish, and then click Entire workbook. Otherwise, only the current sheet will be published, even if you chose Entire workbook in the Save As dialog box.*

- Once your data is published, you can republish it when needed to update the data.
- You can also have Excel automatically republish the data whenever you change the workbook, using the AutoRepublish option in the Publish as Web Page dialog box.
- You also can save Web page data on your hard disk, and transfer it to a Web location using another method.

✔ *If you do so, be sure to transfer all the subfolders and contents created when the Web page was published; otherwise it will not display correctly.*

- Using an HTML editor, you can make changes to the Web page after it's saved to improve its appearance as desired.

Try It! Publishing a Chart to the Internet/Intranet

1. In the **ETry27_studentfirstname_studentlastname** file, make sure the Large Chart sheet is selected.
2. Click File > Save As.
3. Open the Save as type drop-down list, and click Single File Web Page.
4. Click the Change Title button, type **Progress in Construction** as the title, and click OK.
5. Click the Selection: Chart button.
6. Click the Publish button.
7. If necessary, use the Browse button to specify the location where your teacher instructs you to store the files for this lesson.
8. Click Publish.
9. If the sheet opens in the system's Web browser, view it, and then close the browser.
10. Close **ETry27_studentfirstname_studentlastname**, saving all changes, and exit Excel.

Publishing settings

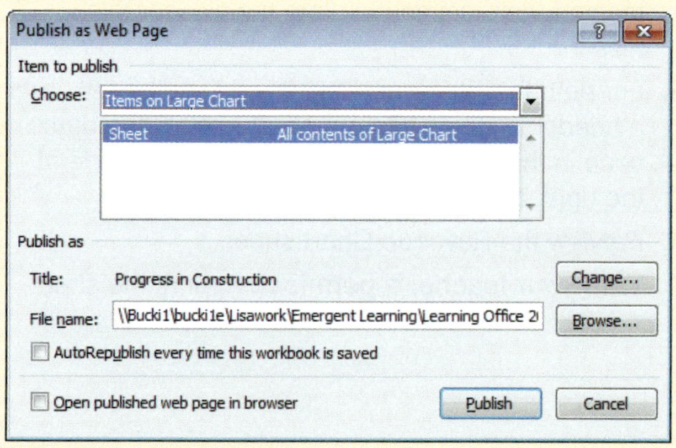

Project 57—Create It

Print Data and a Chart

DIRECTIONS

1. Start Excel, if necessary, and open the **EProj57** file from the data files for this lesson.
2. Save the file as **EProj57_studentfirstname_studentlastname** in the location where your teacher instructs you to store the files for this lesson.
3. For the **Data** sheet, add a header that has your name at the left, the date code in the center, and the page number code at the right, and change back to **Normal** view.
4. Click **File > Print**. Notice that the right side of the data and chart are cut off, and that 1 of 2 appears at the bottom of the preview to indicate the number of pages in the file.
5. Under Settings, change the orientation to **Landscape**, if necessary.
6. **With your teacher's permission**, print the worksheet. Submit the printout or the file for grading as required.
7. On the **Data** sheet, click the chart to select it.
8. Click **File > Print**. Notice that the preview shows the chart only, but no header or footer.
9. Click **Home** to return to the worksheet without printing.
10. Close the workbook, saving all changes, and exit Excel.

Project 58—Apply It

Publish a Chart Sheet for the Web

DIRECTIONS

1. Start Excel, if necessary, and open the **EProj58** file from the data files for this lesson.
2. Save the file as **EProj58_studentfirstname_studentlastname** in the location where your teacher instructs you to store the files for this lesson.
3. For both the **Revenue Chart** and **Data** sheets, add a header that has your name at the left, the date code in the center, and the page number code at the right, and change back to **Normal** view.
4. Preview the Revenue Chart sheet.
5. **With your teacher's permission**, print the sheet.
6. Save the chart sheet as a Single File Web Page, adding a title of **Q4 Revenue Chart**.
7. In the Publish as Web Page dialog box, click the **Open published web page in browser** check box to select it if it isn't already selected.
8. Finish publishing, and view the published chart in the Web browser program.
9. Close the browser.
10. **With your teacher's permission**, print the worksheet. Submit the printout or the file for grading as required.
11. Close the workbook, saving all changes, and exit Excel.

Lesson 28

Using Charts in Other Files

➤ What You Will Learn

Pasting a Picture of a Chart
Embedding a Chart in a Word Document
Linking a Chart
Editing a Linked or Embedded Chart

Software Skills You can link or embed an Excel chart into another document, such as a Word document. If the source data is likely to change, you should link the data to its source, so that your chart will automatically update. This is especially useful when the source data is updated by several different people in your organization. You can also embed the chart in your Word document to ensure that your changes will not affect the original data.

Application Skills As CFO of Hyland Manufacturing, you need to prepare an executive summary of balance sheet data for the board of directors. You've prepared the charts, and you need to incorporate the charts in the executive summary document. You will use various methods to incorporate the charts in the Word document.

WORDS TO KNOW

Embed
To insert an object in a destination document so that it can still be edited by the source application. When you double-click an embedded object, the source application (or its tools) appear, so you can edit the object. The original object remains unchanged because no link exists.

Link
A reference in a destination document to an object (such as a chart) in a source document. Changes to the linked object in the source document are automatically made to the object in the destination document.

What You Can Do

Pasting a Picture of a Chart

- The simplest way to include an Excel chart within another document, such as a Word document, is to paste its picture.
- The advantage of using a picture of a chart is that it will not significantly affect the size of your Word file.
- The disadvantage of using a chart picture is that the data is static—meaning if the data changes in the original Excel workbook, the picture of the chart is not updated.

- To update the picture, you would need to change the data in Excel and paste a new picture.
- After pasting the chart, click the Paste Options button that appears to the lower-right of the chart and then click Picture to paste the chart as a picture.

Try It! Pasting a Picture of a Chart

1. Start Excel.
2. Open the **ETry28a** file from the data files for this lesson. Click Enable Content, and then No in the Security Warning dialog box.
3. Save the file as **ETry28a_studentfirstname_studentlastname** in the location where your teacher instructs you to store the files for this lesson.
4. Start Word.
5. Open the **ETry28b** file from the data files for this lesson.
6. Save the document as **ETry28b_studentfirstname_studentlastname** in the location where your teacher instructs you to store the files for this lesson.
7. Press CTRL + END and type your name.
8. Press ↑ three times to position the insertion point where you'd like the chart to appear.
9. In the **ETry28a_studentfirstname_studentlastname** workbook, on the Expenses tab, click the chart.
10. Click Home > Copy.
11. In the **ETry28b_studentfirstname_studentlastname** Word document, click Home > Paste.
12. Click the Paste Options button, and click Picture.
13. Drag the sizing handle in the upper-left corner of the chart to make the chart smaller, so it will fit within the margins of the page.
14. Save the changes to **ETry28b_studentfirstname_studentlastname**, and leave it open to use in the next Try It.

Embedding a Chart in a Word Document

- When you **embed** a chart in a Word document, the chart data is also copied to the Word file and stored there.
- Making data or formatting changes to an embedded chart does not affect the original data or chart, since there is no link to the original chart.

✔ *Although this lesson discusses pasting charts into another document, you can use these same procedures to embed worksheet data rather than chart data. You also can use these procedures to share data in PowerPoint. See Excel Lesson 40 to learn more about using Paste Special.*

- An embedded chart in the destination file may also be displayed as an icon.
- After pasting the chart, click the Paste Options button that appears to the lower right of the chart and then click either Use Destination Theme & Embed Workbook or Keep Source Formatting & Embed Workbook to insert the chart.

✔ *Rather than pasting and then choosing a paste method, you can use the Home > Paste Options list to choose the paste method when performing the initial paste. This is true of all the procedures covered in this lesson.*

Try It! Embedding a Chart in a Word Document

1. In the **ETry28b_studenfirstname_studentlastname** Word file, double-click the pasted chart picture. Notice that Excel does not open.

   ✔ *If a Format dialog box opens, click Close to close it.*

2. With the picture selected, press DEL to remove the picture from the file.
3. Click Home > Paste.

   ✔ *Because the chart is already on the Clipboard, there is no need to copy it again. However, if you copy any other data or information in a situation like this, you would need to return to Excel and select and copy the chart again.*

4. Click the Paste Options button, and click Keep Source Formatting & Embed Workbook.
5. Click the chart. Notice that the Chart Tools contextual tabs appear on Word's Ribbon.
6. Save the changes to **ETry28b_studentfirstname_studentlastname**, and leave it open to use in the next Try It.

Linking a Chart

- If you want to be able to edit your chart after pasting it into another document, you can **link** the chart.
- When you paste a chart into a destination file (Word document) as a linked chart, it remains connected to its source data (in Excel).
- When you change the data or chart formatting in a linked chart and open the destination file again, the link causes the destination chart to update as well.
- The link also enables you to start Excel from within the destination file (from within Word, for example), display the chart, and make your changes.
- To maintain the link, the files must remain in their original locations.
- Linked data in the destination file may also be displayed as an icon.
- After pasting the chart, click the Paste Options button that appears to the lower right of the chart and then click either Use Destination Theme & Link Data or Keep Source Formatting & Link Data to establish the link.

Try It! Linking a Chart

1. In the **ETry28b_studenfirstname_studentlastname** Word file, double-click the pasted chart picture. Notice that Excel does not open.
2. With the embedded chart selected, press DEL to remove the chart from the file.
3. Click Home > Paste.
4. Click the Paste Options button, and click Use Destination Theme & Link Data.
5. Click the chart. Notice that the Chart Tools contextual tabs appear on Word's Ribbon.
6. Save the changes to **ETry28b_studentfirstname_studentlastname**, and leave it open to use in the next Try It.

Editing a Linked or Embedded Chart

- Because linked data is stored in the source document, you can open that document in Excel to edit a linked chart. Save the source document to preserve the changes.
- When you change the worksheet data in Excel, the corresponding chart is updated.
- Open the destination document and the chart is either updated automatically or when you manually update the link.
- You can open Excel from within the destination document if you like, rather than starting Excel separately.
- Click a linked or embedded chart to display Excel's Chart Tools contextual tabs in the destination application.

✔ *When you make formatting changes to a chart either in the source or destination workbook for a linked chart, those changes do not flow between the two chart locations.*

- Right-click a linked or embedded chart and click Edit Data to open the Excel window for editing data.
- If the data is linked, the source document opens in Excel. If the data is embedded, the Excel window shows the Chart name in the title bar, indicating the data is stored in the destination file, with the embedded chart.
- Make the changes you need. For a linked chart, save the source worksheet and close the Excel window. For an embedded chart, simply close the Excel window.
- If you've updated a source linked chart and the updates don't appear in the destination document, click the chart in the destination document and click Chart Tools Design > Refresh Data.

Try It! Editing a Linked or Embedded Chart

1. In Word, save the **ETry28b_studentfirstname_studentlastname** file and close it.
2. In the **ETry28a_studentfirstname_studentlastname** Excel file, select the chart title.
3. Edit the title to read **Projected 2013 Expenses**.
4. Click cell A6 and change its entry to **Computers & Software**.
5. Change the entries for book expenses in cells B4 and C4 to **375** and **450**, respectively.
6. Close **ETry28a_studentfirstname_studentlastname**, saving all changes, and exit Excel.
7. In Word, open the **ETry28b_studentfirstname_studentlastname** file.
8. Notice that the changes to the book expenses and the new series name appear in the chart. The title change does not, because that is a formatting change.
9. Close **ETry28b_studentfirstname_studentlastname**, saving all changes, and exit Word.

Project 59—Create It

Paste a Picture of a Chart in the Executive Summary Document

DIRECTIONS

1. Start Excel, if necessary, and open **EProj59a** from the data files for this lesson.
2. Save the file as **EProj59a_studentfirstname_studentlastname** in the location where your teacher instructs you to store the files for this lesson.
3. Open **EProj59b** from the data files for this lesson.
4. Save the document as **EProj59b_studentfirstname_studentlastname** in the location where your teacher instructs you to store the files for this lesson.
5. Add the date and your name where indicated at the top of the document, adding a tab or spaces as desired.
6. In the **EProj59a_studentfirstname_studentlastname** Excel file, click the **2013 Chart Sheet** tab.
7. Click the top chart to select it.
8. Click **Home > Copy**.
9. In the **EProj59b_studentfirstname_studentlastname** Word document, click below the Asset Summary heading, and click **Home > Paste**.
10. Click the **Paste Options** button, and click **Picture**. The picture appears in the document.
11. **With your teacher's permission**, print the Word document. Submit the printout or the file for grading as required.
12. Close both files, saving all changes, and exit Word and Excel.

Project 60—Apply It

Link and Embed Charts in the Executive Summary Document

DIRECTIONS

1. Start Excel, if necessary, and open **EProj60a** from the data files for this lesson.
2. Save the file as **EProj60a_studentfirstname_studentlastname** in the location where your teacher instructs you to store the files for this lesson.
3. Open **EProj60b** from the data files for this lesson.
4. Save the document as **EProj60b_studentfirstname_studentlastname** in the location where your teacher instructs you to store the files for this lesson.
5. In the **EProj60b_studentfirstname_studentlastname** document, add the date and your name where indicated at the top of the document, adding a tab or spaces as desired.
6. Add a footer that has your name at the left, the date code in the center, and the page number code at the right.
7. Delete the chart under the Asset Summary heading.
8. Switch back to the Excel file, and click the **2013 Chart Sheet** tab.
9. Select and copy the top chart.
10. Switch back to the Word document, and paste the chart as a linked object under the Asset Summary heading, using the **Destination** theme.
11. Repeat the process to paste and link the bottom chart under the Liability Summary heading. Review the appearance of both charts.
12. Switch back to the Excel file, and click the **2013 Balance Sheet** sheet tab.
13. Change the entry in cell **B15** to **4095**.
14. Change the entry in cell **E19** to **1813**.
15. Close **EProj60a_studentfirstname_studentlastname**, saving all changes, and exit Excel.
16. In the Word document, review the changes to the charts, particularly the Liabilities chart.
17. **With your teacher's permission**, print the Word document. Submit the printout or the file for grading as required.
18. Close the document, saving all changes, and exit Word.

Lesson 29

Making Special Purpose Charts

WORDS TO KNOW

Organization chart
Displays the relationships within an organization, such as the managers in an office, the people they manage, and who they report to.

SmartArt graphic
A pre-drawn graphic used to illustrate a specific data relationship, such as a list, process, cycle, hierarchy, matrix, pyramid, or other relationship.

➤ What You Will Learn

Creating Organization Charts
Creating Other SmartArt Diagrams

Software Skills With an organization chart, you can easily show the relationship between objects or people. For example, you could show how your department is organized. With other conceptual charts, you could show the progress of a project—from conception to completion, areas of overlapping responsibility within a department or on a group project, or the cycle of events with a school or calendar year.

Application Skills You are the Chief Operating Officer (COO) of Hyland Manufacturing. The company has developed a new manufacturing process, and you need to provide information about it to key customers to reassure them that their future orders will be handled seamlessly under the new process. You will create two SmartArt diagrams to send—one that illustrates the process itself, and another that is an organization chart of the team managing the process.

What You Can Do

Creating Organization Charts

- To show relationships within a group such as an office, the government, or a school, create an **organization chart**.
- An organization chart is just one of many **SmartArt graphics** you can insert on a worksheet.
- Click Insert > SmartArt to open the Choose a SmartArt Graphic dialog box. Click the Hierarchy category in the list at the left, click one of the layouts that appears in the center of the list, and then click OK.
- When you start an organization chart, Excel provides a sample chart showing several basic relationships.

- Enter data for the organization chart using the Text Pane, which displays a bulleted list that shows the relationship between people.
- You can paste this list from another source or enter it manually.
- Use the Add Shape button on the SmartArt Tools Design tab to add the desired relationships.
- You can add shapes before, after, above, or below the currently selected shape. You can also add an assistant shape.
- If you add a shape before or after, that shape is placed on the same level in the hierarchy as the current shape.
- If you add a shape above or below, the shape is placed above or below the current shape in the organizational hierarchy.
- An assistant shape is placed out to one side, indicating a different relationship than an employee-manager or employee-employee relationship.
- Shapes (relationships) you don't need for your chart may be easily removed as well. Select the shape box, and press DEL.
- For other graphics such as charts, you can select from predefined layouts and styles and apply them with a single click. The SmartArt Tools Design tab offers Layouts and SmartArt Styles galleries.
- You can also apply your own formatting (outlines, fills, shadows, glows, and other effects) to individual shapes and the background. These choices are on the SmartArt Tools Format tab.
- Format the text of individual shapes or the whole chart.
- Using the Layout button in the Create Graphic group of the SmartArt Tools Design tab, you can change the way in which relationships are displayed within the chart.

✔ *If you've already created an organization chart or other SmartArt graphic in Word or PowerPoint, you can save time by simply copying and pasting it into Excel.*

Try It! Creating Organization Charts

1. Start Excel and create a new blank workbook file.
2. Save the file as **ETry29_studentfirstname _studentlastname** in the location where your teacher instructs you to store the files for this lesson.
3. Add a header that has your name at the left, the date code in the center, and the page number code at the right, and change back to Normal view.
4. Click Page Layout > Orientation >Landscape.
5. Click Insert > SmartArt.
6. In the list at the left, click Hierarchy.
7. In the list in the middle, click the third layout in the top row, Name and Title Organization Chart, and then click OK.
8. In the Text Pane that appears to the left of the chart (click SmartArt Tools Design > Text Pane if it doesn't appear), type the names, clicking the next placeholder after finishing each one:
   Aliyah Brown
   Linda Williams
   Bill Whittaker
   Marlow Aronstein
   Katie Martin
9. Click the title box for each shape, and type the following titles:
   President
   Assistant
   HR Director
   Product Director
   Sales Director
10. Click the Katie Martin shape, and click SmartArt Tools Design > Add Shape drop-down arrow > Add Shape Below.
11. In the new shape, add **Ron Crane** and **Deputy Sales Director** as the name and title.
12. Click SmartArt Tools Design > SmartArt Styles More, and click Polished, the the first style under 3-D.
13. Click the Linda Williams shape to select it.
14. Click SmartArt Tools Format > Shape Fill > Olive Green, Accent 3, Darker 25%.
15. Click the border for the SmartArt shape itself to select it rather than the individual box.

(continued)

Try It! Creating Organization Charts (continued)

16 Click SmartArt Tools Format > Shape Fill > Dark Blue, Text 2, Lighter 80%.

17 Click SmartArt Tools Design > Text Pane to hide the Text Pane.

✔ *Use the same command to redisplay the Text Pane when needed.*

18 Drag the chart up so its upper-left corner is over cell B2.

19 Save the changes to **ETry29_studentfirstname_studentlastname**, and leave it open to use in the next Try It.

Organization chart with names and titles added

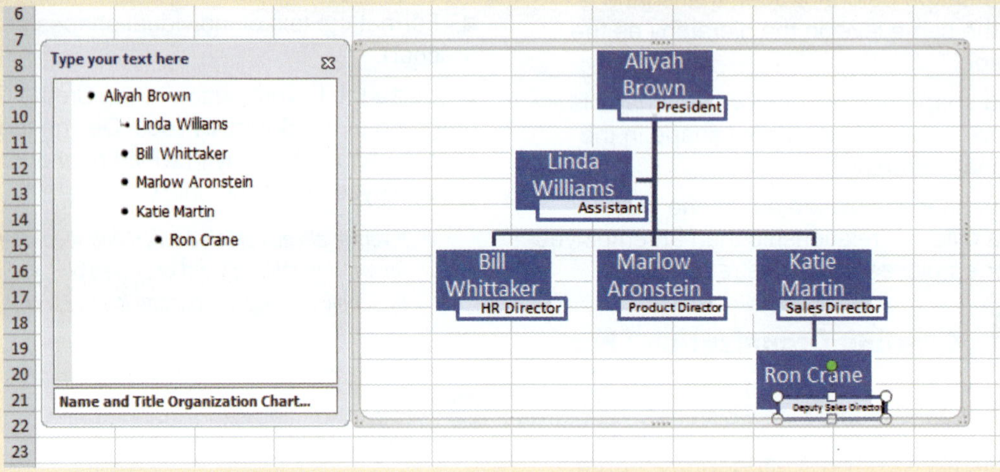

Creating Other SmartArt Diagrams

- In addition to organization charts, Excel enables you to create several other types of conceptual charts via the Choose a SmartArt Graphic dialog box.
- You can choose these overall diagram types from the list at the left side of the dialog box.

✔ *You can use the Office.com choice to see the latest added diagrams available for download.*

- There are numerous layouts available for each of the SmartArt diagram types.
- After you create the diagram, you can easily change from one layout to another until you find the one that properly conveys the relationship between your data items. Use SmartArt Tools Design > Layouts More to see the layouts. The More Layouts choice at the bottom of the menu even enables you to change to another type of diagram.

Try It! Creating Other SmartArt Diagrams

1 In the **ETry29_studentfirstname_studentlastname** file, click Insert > SmartArt.

2 In the list at the left, click Cycle.

3 In the list in the middle, click the first layout in the second row, Continuous Cycle, and then click OK.

4 Drag the new chart down below the organization chart, scrolling down if needed.

5 Click SmartArt Tools Design > Text Pane to display the Text Pane.

6 In the Text Pane, type the following text for the boxes, clicking the next placeholder after finishing each one:
Startup
Initial Diagnostics
Operational Cycle
Cleaning Cycle
Auto Power Cycle

(continued)

Try It! Creating Other SmartArt Diagrams *(continued)*

7. Click SmartArt Tools Design > Text Pane to hide the Text Pane.
8. With the mouse pointer still in the Auto Power Cycle box, click SmartArt Tools Design > Add Bullet.
9. Type **Manual power cycle every 14 days**.
10. Click SmartArt Tools Design > SmartArt Styles > Change Colors > Colorful > Colorful Range-Accent Colors 2 to 3.
11. Click the chart border to select the chart itself.
12. Click SmartArt Tools Format > Shape Fill > Gradient > Dark Variations > From Center (second on the second row).
13. Click SmartArt Tools Design > Layouts More button > More Layouts.
14. In the list at the left, click List.
15. In the list in the middle, click the second layout in the second row, Vertical Box List, and then click OK.
16. Close **ETry29_studentfirstname_studentlastname**, saving all changes, and exit Excel.

Completed cycle diagram

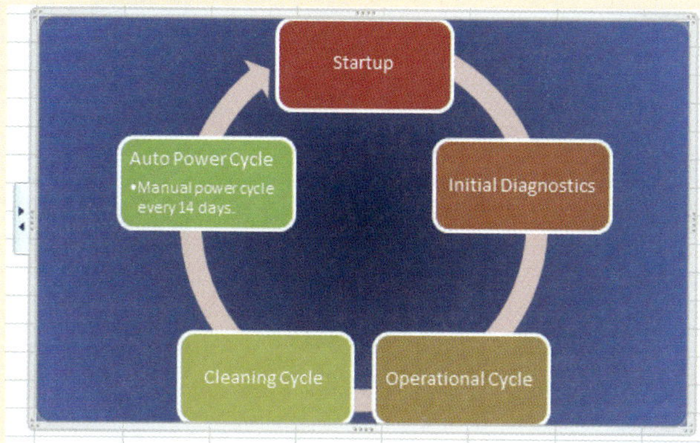

Project 61—Create It

Creating the Process Diagram

DIRECTIONS

1. Start Excel, if necessary, and open **EProj61** from the data files for this lesson.
2. Save the file as **EProj61_studentfirstname_studentlastname** in the location where your teacher instructs you to store the files for this lesson.
3. Add a header that has your name at the left, the date code in the center, and the page number code at the right, and change back to **Normal** view.
4. Click **Insert > SmartArt**.
5. In the list at the left, click **Process**.
6. In the middle list, click **Vertical Chevron List**, the third layout in the fifth row, and then click **OK**.
7. In the Text Pane, add the following text:
   Rapid Prototyping
      Reduced Time
      Reduced Waste
   Production Pilot
      Build Process
      Document Process
   Testing
      Safety Testing
      Performance Testing
8. After the last entry, press ENTER and then SHIFT + TAB. This creates another shape at the top level.
9. Type **Production Release**, press ENTER and then TAB. This indents to the bullet-level shape

10. Type **Continuous Quality Improvement**, press ENTER, and then type **RFID Tracking**.
11. Click **SmartArt Tools Design** > **Text Pane** to hide the Text Pane.
12. Drag the diagram up so its upper-left corner is on cell **B4**.
13. **With your teacher's permission**, print the worksheet. Submit the printout or the file for grading as required.
14. Close the workbook, saving all changes, and exit Excel

Figure 29-1

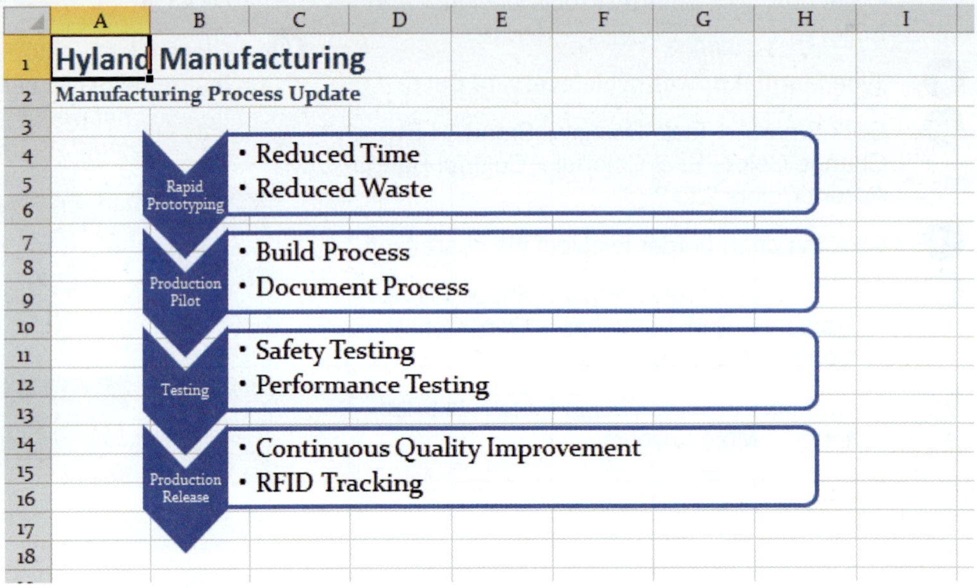

Project 62—Apply It

Creating the Organization Chart and Formatting Diagrams

DIRECTIONS

1. Start Excel, if necessary, and open **EProj62** from the data files for this lesson.
2. Save the file as **EProj62_studentfirstname_studentlastname** in the location where your teacher instructs you to store the files for this lesson.
3. Add a header that has your name at the left, the date code in the center, and the page number code at the right, and change back to **Normal** view.
4. Create an organization chart using the **Horizontal Organization Chart** layout.
5. Delete the Assistant shape.
6. Enter **Production Director** in the top level box.
7. Enter **Engineering Manager**, **Quality Manager**, and **Production Manager** in the lower-level boxes.
8. Right-click the Engineering Manager box, and then click **Change Shape** > **Pentagon**. The Pentagon shape is a Block Arrow. Apply the Pentagon shape to the other two lower-level boxes.
9. Drag the organization chart below the process chart, so its upper-left corner is over cell **B20**.
10. Apply the **Inset** SmartArt style to both charts.
11. Apply the **Dark 2 Fill** colors under Primary Theme Colors to both charts.
12. Deselect both charts.
13. **With your teacher's permission**, print the worksheet. Submit the printout or the file for grading as required.
14. Close the workbook, saving all changes, and exit Excel.

Chapter Assessment and Application

Project 63—Make It Your Own

Investment Portfolio

You are a certified financial planner with Solid Investments, LLC. You are putting some sample data together to help illustrate stock performance and investment potential and risk for new clients who are also new to investing overall. You will chart historical stock price data, create formulas that show how a sample portfolio of investments will change if the market goes up or down, and chart that sample portfolio data.

DIRECTIONS

1. Start Excel, if necessary, and open **EProj63** from the data files for this chapter.
2. Save the file as **EProj63_studentfirstname_studentlastname** in the location where your teacher instructs you to store the files for this chapter.
3. Group the named sheets. Add a header that has your name at the left, the date code in the center, and the page number code at the right, and change back to **Normal** view. Ungroup the sheets.
4. On the **Ford Historical Prices** sheet, Select the range **A5:E27**, and insert a **Stock** chart using the **Open-High-Low-Close** subtype. Stock charts are found via the **Other Charts** button in the Charts group.
5. Apply the **Layout 1** layout to the chart, and the **Style 37** chart style.
6. Change the scale of the primary vertical axis so that its minimum value is **9**. This scales the data bars so that they are easier to interpret.
7. Change the chart title to **Ford June 2010**.
8. Drag the chart so its upper-left corner is over cell **H3**.
9. Go to the **Portfolio Analysis** tab.
10. In cell **E8**, enter a formula that will recalculate the value from the Total column based on an increase percentage entered in cell **D4**. Use an absolute reference to cell D4. Copy the formula down the column.
11. In cell **F8**, enter a formula that will recalculate the value from the Total column based on a decrease percentage entered in cell **D5**. Use an absolute reference to cell D5. (Hint: You can use a similar formula to the one you created in step 11, but subtract, instead.) Copy the formula down the column.
12. To test your formulas, enter **7** in cell **D4** and **5** in cell **D5**. Verify that the values in column E increased by 7% and that the values in column F decreased by 5%. If not, correct your formulas.
13. Select the ranges **D7:F7** and **D13:F13** and insert a **Clustered Column** chart.
14. Remove the chart legend and add a title above the chart that reads **Sample Portfolio Results.**
15. Move the chart so its upper-left corner is over cell **H4**.
16. **With your teacher's permission**, print both worksheets, scaling each sheet to fit on one page. Submit the printouts or the file for grading as required.
17. Close the workbook, saving all changes, and exit Excel.

Project 64—Master It

Sales Data Chart and Web Page

You are the CFO for Teesy Apparel, a T-shirt manufacturer. You have developed a worksheet with quarterly sales data that also tracks sales by product line and size. You need to chart all this information for future production planning, and create a SmartArt diagram that ranks potential new product ideas. After you chart the data, you will publish the data as a Single File Web Page to the company intranet to give the planning team easier access.

DIRECTIONS

1. Start Excel, if necessary, and open **EProj64** from the data files for this chapter.
2. Save the file as **EProj64_studentfirstname_studentlastname** in the location where your teacher instructs you to store the files for this chapter.
3. Add a header that has your name at the left, the date code in the center, and the page number code at the right, and change back to **Normal** view.
4. Create a **Clustered Column** chart of the quarterly sales totals on its own chart sheet. Name the sheet **Q Sales**.
5. If necessary, use the Select Data Source dialog box to assign the range **='Sales Data'!$E$4:$H$4** as the axis label range. (Hint: Select one of the existing horizontal, or category, axis labels entries and click Edit.)
6. Hide the display of the legend, and add a title above the chart that reads **Strong Quarterly Product Sales**. Apply chart **Style 30** to the chart
7. On the **Sales Data** sheet, create **Pie in 3-D** charts for the Sales by Product Line and Sales by Size data, placing each chart on its own sheet and giving the sheets appropriate names.
8. Apply the **Layout 1** layout to each pie chart, and make the chart title the same as the sheet name.
9. Apply a solid fill of **Purple, Accent 4, Lighter 80%** to each of the pie chart areas.
10. Explode the smallest slice for each pie chart.
11. Rename Sheet2 as **Potential Products**.
12. Insert a **Matrix** SmartArt diagram that uses the **Grid Matrix** layout.
13. Open the Text Pane, and use it to add these entries to the diagram:
    Organic Cotton Socks
    Organic Cotton Sweatshirts
    Natural Dyes Line
    Children's Tees
14. Hide the Text Pane, apply **Colorful-Accent Colors** to the diagram, and drag it to the upper-left corner of the worksheet.
15. Delete the **Sheet3** sheet.
16. On the **Sales Data** sheet, select cell **A1**. Publish the entire workbook as a **Single File Web Page**, adding **Teesy Apparel** as a title. (Hint: In the Publish as Web Page dialog box, remember to also open the Choose drop-down list under Item to publish, and then click Entire workbook. Also make sure the File name text box uses the correct file name, rather than Page.mht.)
17. The workbook opens in your Web browser. The file has a tab for every tab in the worksheet, as shown in Illustration A. Click the various tabs to review the charts that you have created. Close the Web browser when you finish.
18. **With your teacher's permission**, print all worksheets in the workbook, scaling each to fit a single page. Submit the printouts or the file for grading as required.
19. Close the workbook, saving all changes, and exit Excel.

Illustration A

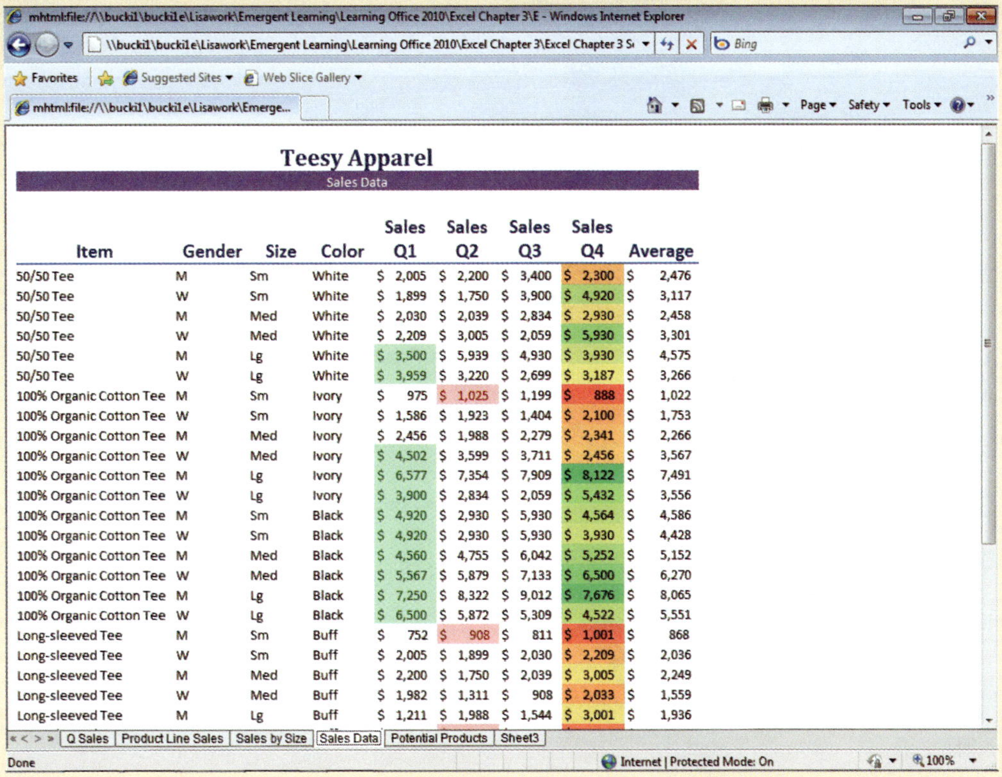

Teesy Apparel

Sales Data

Item	Gender	Size	Color	Sales Q1	Sales Q2	Sales Q3	Sales Q4	Average
50/50 Tee	M	Sm	White	$ 2,005	$ 2,200	$ 3,400	$ 2,300	$ 2,476
50/50 Tee	W	Sm	White	$ 1,899	$ 1,750	$ 3,900	$ 4,920	$ 3,117
50/50 Tee	M	Med	White	$ 2,030	$ 2,039	$ 2,834	$ 2,930	$ 2,458
50/50 Tee	W	Med	White	$ 2,209	$ 3,005	$ 2,059	$ 5,930	$ 3,301
50/50 Tee	M	Lg	White	$ 3,500	$ 5,939	$ 4,930	$ 3,930	$ 4,575
50/50 Tee	W	Lg	White	$ 3,959	$ 3,220	$ 2,699	$ 3,187	$ 3,266
100% Organic Cotton Tee	M	Sm	Ivory	$ 975	$ 1,025	$ 1,199	$ 888	$ 1,022
100% Organic Cotton Tee	W	Sm	Ivory	$ 1,586	$ 1,923	$ 1,404	$ 2,100	$ 1,753
100% Organic Cotton Tee	M	Med	Ivory	$ 2,456	$ 1,988	$ 2,279	$ 2,341	$ 2,266
100% Organic Cotton Tee	W	Med	Ivory	$ 4,502	$ 3,599	$ 3,711	$ 2,456	$ 3,567
100% Organic Cotton Tee	M	Lg	Ivory	$ 6,577	$ 7,354	$ 7,909	$ 8,122	$ 7,491
100% Organic Cotton Tee	W	Lg	Ivory	$ 3,900	$ 2,834	$ 2,059	$ 5,432	$ 3,556
100% Organic Cotton Tee	M	Sm	Black	$ 4,920	$ 2,930	$ 5,930	$ 4,564	$ 4,586
100% Organic Cotton Tee	W	Sm	Black	$ 4,920	$ 2,930	$ 5,930	$ 3,930	$ 4,428
100% Organic Cotton Tee	M	Med	Black	$ 4,560	$ 4,755	$ 6,042	$ 5,252	$ 5,152
100% Organic Cotton Tee	W	Med	Black	$ 5,567	$ 5,879	$ 7,133	$ 6,500	$ 6,270
100% Organic Cotton Tee	M	Lg	Black	$ 7,250	$ 8,322	$ 9,012	$ 7,676	$ 8,065
100% Organic Cotton Tee	W	Lg	Black	$ 6,500	$ 5,872	$ 5,309	$ 4,522	$ 5,551
Long-sleeved Tee	M	Sm	Buff	$ 752	$ 908	$ 811	$ 1,001	$ 868
Long-sleeved Tee	W	Sm	Buff	$ 2,005	$ 1,899	$ 2,030	$ 2,209	$ 2,036
Long-sleeved Tee	M	Med	Buff	$ 2,200	$ 1,750	$ 2,039	$ 3,005	$ 2,249
Long-sleeved Tee	W	Med	Buff	$ 1,982	$ 1,311	$ 908	$ 2,033	$ 1,559
Long-sleeved Tee	M	Lg	Buff	$ 1,211	$ 1,988	$ 1,544	$ 3,001	$ 1,936

Chapter 4

Advanced Functions, PivotCharts, and PivotTables

Lesson 30
Using Advanced Functions to Predict Trends
Projects 65-66

- Creating Predictions and Estimations
- Using FORECAST
- Using TREND
- Using GROWTH

Lesson 31
Using Advanced Functions for Data Analysis
Projects 67-68

- Using the PMT Function
- Creating What-If Data Tables
- Solving a Problem with Goal Seek
- Using Solver to Resolve Problems

Lesson 32
Using Lookup Functions
Projects 69-70

- Creating Lookup Functions

Lesson 33
Understanding PivotTables and PivotCharts
Projects 71-72

- Creating PivotTables
- Using the PivotTable Field List
- Enhancing PivotTables and Creating PivotCharts

End of Chapter Assessments
Projects 73-74

Lesson 30

Using Advanced Functions to Predict Trends

WORDS TO KNOW

Sparklines
A tiny chart that can be used to show trend patterns.

Step
Used to calculate a future value. The step is the difference between two existing values.

Trend
A mathematical prediction of future values based on the relationship between existing values.

➤ What You Will Learn

Creating Predictions and Estimations
Using FORECAST
Using TREND
Using GROWTH

Software Skills When it comes to business accounting, a crystal ball that predicts the future would come in handy pretty often. Imagine being able to predict sales so accurately you never order too many parts, carry too much inventory, or schedule too much staff. Excel doesn't come with a crystal ball, but it does provide some nifty equivalents, among them the FORECAST, TREND, and GROWTH functions.

Application Skills You are the owner of a Whole Grains Bread store in Salem, Washington, and you've been looking for a way to manage inventory more effectively. After learning about Excel's forecasting functions, you've decided to give them a try and see how good they are at predicting your future inventory needs.

What You Can Do

Creating Predictions and Estimations

- In Excel, you can use the AutoFill feature to create a series of data, such as April, May, June.
- You can also use AutoFill to predict many kinds of future values.

- AutoFill calculates future values by examining the **trend** of existing values.
- With AutoFill, you can choose from two different trend formulas: linear or growth.
  - Linear trend—the **step** is calculated by determining the average difference between the existing values. The step is then added to the second value.

    ✓ *For example, in the series 21, 37, the next value would be 53 (37-21=16; 16+37=53).*
  - Growth trend—the step is calculated by dividing the second selected value by the first selected value. The step is then multiplied by the second value.

    ✓ *For example, in the series 21, 37, the next value would be 65.19048 (37/21=1.761905; 37*1.761905=65.19048).*
- To determine which tool to use, follow this pattern:
  - If existing values seem to follow a straight curve, use the linear trend method.
  - If existing values seem to go up and down a lot, use the growth trend method.
- You can also create a linear trend or growth trend estimate using the Fill button in the Editing group on the Home tab.
- You can use **Sparklines**, as shown in Figure 30-1, to quickly show a trend graphically inside a single cell.

Figure 30-1

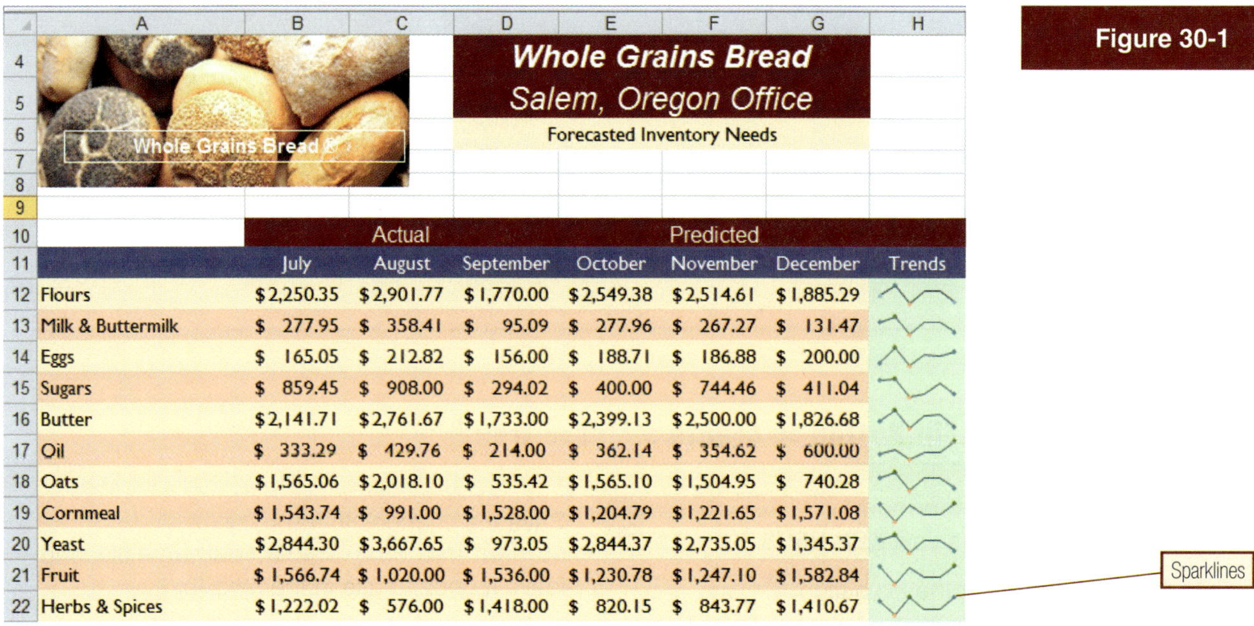

	A	B	C	D	E	F	G	H
4	Whole Grains Bread			Whole Grains Bread				
5				Salem, Oregon Office				
6				Forecasted Inventory Needs				
7								
8								
9								
10		Actual			Predicted			
11		July	August	September	October	November	December	Trends
12	Flours	$2,250.35	$2,901.77	$1,770.00	$2,549.38	$2,514.61	$1,885.29	
13	Milk & Buttermilk	$ 277.95	$ 358.41	$ 95.09	$ 277.96	$ 267.27	$ 131.47	
14	Eggs	$ 165.05	$ 212.82	$ 156.00	$ 188.71	$ 186.88	$ 200.00	
15	Sugars	$ 859.45	$ 908.00	$ 294.02	$ 400.00	$ 744.46	$ 411.04	
16	Butter	$2,141.71	$2,761.67	$1,733.00	$2,399.13	$2,500.00	$1,826.68	
17	Oil	$ 333.29	$ 429.76	$ 214.00	$ 362.14	$ 354.62	$ 600.00	
18	Oats	$1,565.06	$2,018.10	$ 535.42	$1,565.10	$1,504.95	$ 740.28	
19	Cornmeal	$1,543.74	$ 991.00	$1,528.00	$1,204.79	$1,221.65	$1,571.08	
20	Yeast	$2,844.30	$3,667.65	$ 973.05	$2,844.37	$2,735.05	$1,345.37	
21	Fruit	$1,566.74	$1,020.00	$1,536.00	$1,230.78	$1,247.10	$1,582.84	
22	Herbs & Spices	$1,222.02	$ 576.00	$1,418.00	$ 820.15	$ 843.77	$1,410.67	

Try It! Using AutoFill to Complete a Series and Create Trends

1. Start Excel, and open **ETry30** from the data files for this lesson.
2. Save the file as **ETry30_studentfirstname_studentlastname** in the location where your teacher instructs you to store the files for this lesson.
3. Select cells B2:G2.
4. Click the AutoFill handle ✛ and drag to the right to cell J2.

(continued)

Try It! Using AutoFill to Complete a Series and Create Trends *(continued)*

5. Select cells B3:G3.
6. Right-click the AutoFill handle, and drag to the right to cell J3.
7. Release the mouse button at cell J3.

AutoFill shortcut menu

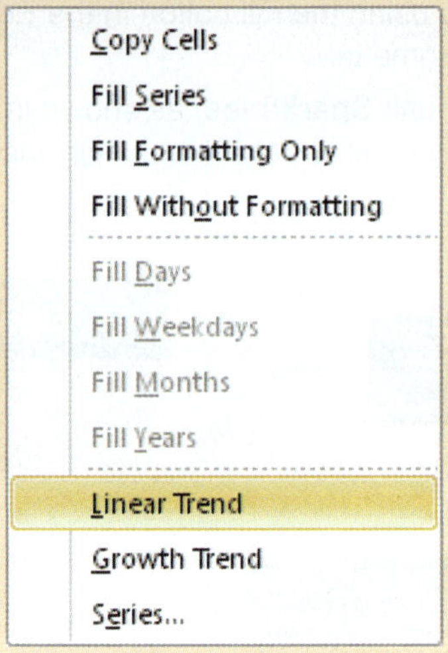

8. In the shortcut menu, select Linear Trend.
9. Select cells B4:G4.
10. Right-click the AutoFill handle, and drag to the right to cell J4.
11. Release the mouse button at cell J4.
12. In the shortcut menu, select Growth Trend.
13. Save the changes to the **ETry30_studentfirstname_studentlastname** file, and leave it open to use in the next Try It.

Try It! Using the Fill Button to Create a Linear Trend

1. In the **ETry30_studentfirstname_studentlastname** file, select cells B5:J5.
2. On the Home tab, click the Fill button and then click Series.
3. Choose Rows as the direction to fill.
4. Select Linear as the Type.

   ✓ *If you want to create an estimate based on more than one set of numbers, select Trend instead.*

   ✓ *If you want, you can enter a specific Step or Stop value.*
5. Click OK.
6. Save the changes to the **ETry30_studentfirstname_studentlastname** file, and leave it open to use in the next Try It.

The Series dialog box

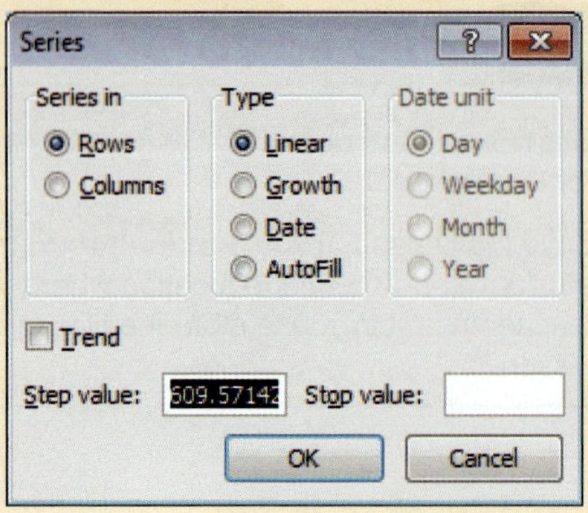

Try It! Using Sparklines to Instantly Chart Trends

1. In the ETry30_studentfirstname_studentlastname file, select cells B5:J5.
2. On the Insert tab, click one of the following options in the Sparklines group:
   - Click the Insert Line Sparkline button to show the trend in a line chart.
   - Click the Insert Column Sparkline button to show the trend in a column chart.
   - Click the Insert Win/Loss Sparkline button to show the trend in a Win/Loss chart.
3. In the Create Sparklines dialog box, enter L5 in the Location Range box.

   ✓ *If necessary, click the Collapse Dialog Box button to hide the dialog box so that you can select cell L5. When you're finished, click the Expand Dialog button.*
4. Click OK.
5. Save the changes to the ETry30_studentfirstname_studentlastname file, and leave it open to use in the next Try It.

The Create Sparklines dialog box

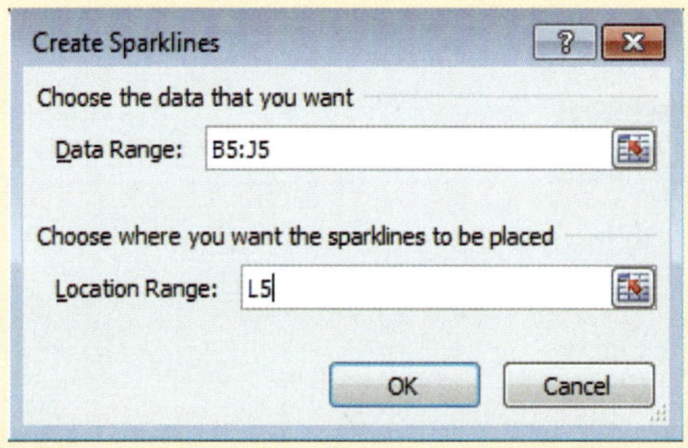

Using FORECAST

- The FORECAST function uses a "linear trend" formula to calculate future values.
- FORECAST examines the x-values and their relationship to the y-values, and then, given a new x-value, it calculates the matching y-value.
- Use FORECAST when existing values follow more or less a straight line, with little or no variance (ups or downs).
- FORECAST plots new values along a straight line formed by existing values.
- The FORECAST function requires two sets of related variables—x values and y values.

Try It! Using the FORECAST Function

1. In the ETry30_studentfirstname_studentlastname file, click D14.
2. Type =.
3. Type FORECAST.

   ✓ *Notice that when you begin typing the name of the function, Excel provides a list of functions. You can double-click the function of your choice instead of typing the entire name.*
4. Type (.
5. Select D13.
6. Type , .
7. Select B3:J3.
8. Type , .
9. Select B2:J2.
10. Type), and press ENTER.
11. Save the changes to the ETry30_studentfirstname_studentlastname file, and leave it open to use in the next Try It.

Using TREND

- TREND, like FORECAST, plots new values along the straight line formed by the plotted positions of existing values.
- Use the TREND function when existing values follow more or less a straight line when plotted on a chart.
- The TREND function uses a "linear trend" method of calculating future values.
- You only need known y-values to make a prediction using TREND.
- You can input known x-values in the TREND equation to improve the accuracy of the prediction.
- If you also input a new x-value as an argument, it will produce the same result as FORECAST.
- TREND uses the formula, y=mx+b to plot new values along a straight line.
- If you tell TREND to set the value of b to zero, the x value will be adjusted to begin plotting its trend line at zero.

Try It! Using the TREND Function

1. In the **ETry30_studentfirstname_studentlastname** file, click D15.
2. Type **=**.
3. Type **TREND**.
4. Type **(**.
5. Select cells B4:J4 and skip to Step 6.

   OR

   If desired, add known x-value(s):
   - Type **,** .
   - Select B2:J2.

   If desired, add new x-value(s):
   - Type **,** .
   - Select D13.

   If desired, set the intercept to zero:
   - Type **,** .
   - Type **FALSE**
6. Type **)** .
7. Press ENTER.
8. Save the changes to the **ETry30_studentfirstname_studentlastname** file, and leave it open to use in the next Try It.

Using GROWTH

- The GROWTH function predicts future values using an exponential growth formula, y=b*m^x.
- The trend line created by the GROWTH function is curved, not straight.
- Like TREND, the GROWTH function requires only known y-values.
- You can improve the accuracy by supplying known x-values and new x-values if they're available.

Try It! Using the GROWTH Function

1. In the ETry30_studentfirstname_studentlastname file, click D16.
2. Type =.
3. Type GROWTH.
4. Type (.
5. Select B5:J5.
6. Type ,.
7. Select B2:J2.
8. Type ,.
9. Select D13 and skip to Step 10.

   OR

   If desired, set the intercept to zero:
   - Type ,.
   - Type FALSE.
10. Type).
11. Press ENTER.
12. Save the changes to the ETry30_studentfirstname_studentlastname file, and close Excel.

Project 65—Create It

Inventory Projections

DIRECTIONS

1. Click Start > Microsoft Excel 2010, if necessary.
2. Click File > Open and browse to the location where your data files are located and
3. Double-click EProj65.
4. Save the workbook as EProj65_studentfirstname_studentlastname in the location where your teacher instructs you to store the files for this lesson.
5. Add a header that has your name at the left, the date code in the center, and the page number code at the right.
6. Switch to the FORECAST sheet, if necessary. Click cell E13.
7. Type =FORECAST(.
8. Click cell E12 and press F4 twice. This will make the row part of the address absolute.

   ✓ *You want to use the value entered in row 12 of each column as the new x-value for the y-value you wish to calculate.*
9. Type , (comma), and select the range B13:D13.
10. Press F4 three times to make the column part of the range address absolute.

    ✓ *As you copy the formula, you want it to always refer to the known y-values in columns B, C, and D.*
11. Type , (comma), and select the range B12:D12.
12. Press F4 to make the range address absolute.

    ✓ *As you copy the formula, you want it to always refer to the known x-values in cells B12:D12, which correspond to the new x value entered in row 12 of columns E through G.*
13. Type), and press ENTER to complete the formula.
14. Select cell E13. On the Home tab, click Copy to place the formula on the Office Clipboard.
15. SHIFT +click cell G22 to select the cells where you want to enter the projected fourth quarter data.
16. On the Home tab, click the Paste down arrow and select Formulas to fill the range E13:G22 while maintaining the worksheet formatting. Your worksheet should look like Figure 30-2.
17. Click the Save button on the Quick Access Toolbar.
18. **With your teacher's permission,** print the FORECAST worksheet. Submit the printout or the file for grading as required.
19. Close the file.

Figure 30-2

Whole Grains Bread
Salem, Oregon Office
Forecasted Inventory Needs

	Actual			Predicted		
	July	August	September	October	November	December
Flours	$ 2,250	$ 2,902	$ 1,770	$ 2,000	$ 3,000	$ 1,600
Milk & Buttermilk	$ 278	$ 358	$ 95	$ 174	$ 401	$ 84
Eggs	$ 165	$ 213	$ 156	$ 162	$ 214	$ 141
Sugars	$ 859	$ 908	$ 294	$ 529	$ 1,044	$ 322
Butter	$ 2,142	$ 2,762	$ 1,733	$ 1,932	$ 2,843	$ 1,567
Oil	$ 333	$ 430	$ 214	$ 268	$ 456	$ 193
Oats	$ 1,565	$ 2,018	$ 535	$ 981	$ 2,256	$ 471
Cornmeal	$ 1,544	$ 991	$ 1,528	$ 1,507	$ 1,011	$ 1,705
Yeast	$ 2,844	$ 3,668	$ 973	$ 1,783	$ 4,100	$ 856
Fruit	$ 1,567	$ 1,020	$ 1,536	$ 1,521	$ 1,043	$ 1,712
Herbs & Spices	$ 1,222	$ 576	$ 1,418	$ 1,305	$ 547	$ 1,608

Project 66—Apply It

Inventory Projections

DIRECTIONS

1. Start Excel, if necessary, and open the **EProj66** file from the data files for this lesson.
2. Save the workbook as **EProj66_studentfirstname_studentlastname** in the location where your teacher instructs you to store the files for this lesson.
3. Add a header that has your name at the left, the date code in the center, and the page number code at the right.
4. On the **TREND** worksheet, use a simple **TREND** formula to calculate the Flours projection for October.
5. Copy the formula for the rest of the year.
6. In cell **E13**, create a **TREND** formula that projects inventory expenses for Milk & Buttermilk based on its relationship to the flours usage.

   ✓ *Hint: Use the Flours expense for July-Sept as the known x-values and the Flours expense for October as the new x-value.*

7. Use this TREND formula to project the rest of the expenses for the fourth quarter. (Keep the existing formatting.)
8. On the **GROWTH** worksheet, use a simple **GROWTH** formula to calculate the Flours projection for October.
9. Copy the formula for the rest of the year.
10. In cell **E13**, create a **GROWTH** formula that projects inventory expenses for Milk & Buttermilk based on its relationship to the flours usage.

    ✓ *Hint: Use the Flours expense for July-Sept as the known x-values and the Flours expense for October as the new x-value.*

11. Use this **GROWTH** formula to project the rest of the expenses for the fourth quarter. (Keep the existing formatting.)
12. Apply the Accounting formatting to all expenses in the workbook, and widen columns as needed. Your worksheet should look like Figure 30-3.

13. Check the spelling in the workbook.
14. **With your teacher's permission,** print the **TREND** and **GROWTH** worksheets. Submit the printouts or the file for grading as required.
15. Save your changes, close the workbook, and exit Excel.

Figure 30-3

Whole Grains Bread

Salem, Oregon Office

Forecasted Inventory Needs

	Actual			Predicted		
	July	August	September	October	November	December
Flours	$ 2,250.35	$ 2,901.77	$ 1,770.00	$ 2,549.38	$ 2,514.61	$ 1,885.29
Milk & Buttermilk	$ 277.95	$ 358.41	$ 95.09	$ 277.96	$ 267.27	$ 131.47
Eggs	$ 165.05	$ 212.82	$ 156.00	$ 188.71	$ 186.88	$ 156.57
Sugars	$ 859.45	$ 908.00	$ 294.02	$ 769.29	$ 744.46	$ 411.04
Butter	$ 2,141.71	$ 2,761.67	$ 1,733.00	$ 2,399.13	$ 2,365.14	$ 1,826.68
Oil	$ 333.29	$ 429.76	$ 214.00	$ 362.14	$ 354.62	$ 242.63
Oats	$ 1,565.06	$ 2,018.10	$ 535.42	$ 1,565.10	$ 1,504.95	$ 740.28
Cornmeal	$ 1,543.74	$ 991.00	$ 1,528.00	$ 1,204.79	$ 1,221.65	$ 1,571.08
Yeast	$ 2,844.30	$ 3,667.65	$ 973.05	$ 2,844.37	$ 2,735.05	$ 1,345.37
Fruit	$ 1,566.74	$ 1,020.00	$ 1,536.00	$ 1,230.78	$ 1,247.10	$ 1,582.84
Herbs & Spices	$ 1,222.02	$ 576.00	$ 1,418.00	$ 820.15	$ 843.77	$ 1,410.67

WORDS TO KNOW

Data table
A method of performing what-if analysis, involving a column (and possibly a row) of variables and a formula that Excel solves over and over, using each of the variables. The result is a table of answers.

Goal Seek
A method of performing what-if analysis in which the result (the goal) is known, but the value of a single dependent variable is unknown.

Input cell
A cell in a data table to which your formula refers. Excel copies a variable into this cell, solves the formula, and then goes on to the next variable to create a series of answers.

Solver
A method of performing what-if analysis in which the result is known, but more than a single variable is unknown. Also, there may be additional constraints upon the final result.

Substitution values
A special name given to the variables used in a data table.

Variable
An input value that changes depending on the desired outcome.

What-if analysis
Excel's term for a series of tools that perform calculations involving one or more variables.

Lesson 31

Using Advanced Functions for Data Analysis

➤ What You Will Learn

Using the PMT Function
Creating What-If Data Tables
Solving a Problem with Goal Seek
Using Solver to Resolve Problems

Software Skills What-if analysis allows you to determine the optimal values for a given situation. For example, if you know that you can only spend a maximum of $32,000 this year on new computers, you could adjust the monthly budget amount so you could spend the total amount by the end of the year and yet still remain within your department's monthly budgetary constraints.

Application Skills As the owner of Restoration Architecture, you're always watching the bottom line. You're preparing a bid for the renovation of your town's library, and you want to run the numbers through Excel before submitting it. Specifically, you want to use Solver to help you analyze what you can afford to pay the plumbers on the job (the last remaining labor cost for which you need bids) and yet maintain a decent profit. Then, you'll create data tables to compute the cost of the small construction loan you'll need if you get the job, and the estimated amount of any increased costs you might encounter if the job runs over deadline.

What You Can Do

Using the PMT Function

- You can use the PMT (payment) function to calculate a loan payment amount given the principal, interest rate, and number of payment periods.

✓ *The PMT result is equal to your principal and interest for the loan, but does not include any other payment parts such as taxes, escrow, points, closing fees, and so on.*

- The arguments for the PMT function are: =PMT(rate,nper,pv).
  - rate: Interest rate per period (for example, annual interest rate/12).
  - nper: Number of payment periods (for example, years*12).
  - pv (present value): The total amount that a series of future payments is worth now (for example, the principal).

    ✓ *The principal is the amount of the loan, minus any down payment amount.*

- For example, if you wish to calculate a monthly payment for a $175,000 loan at a 9% rate of interest for 25 years, you must enter **.09/12** as the monthly rate and enter **25*12** to get the number of monthly payment periods (nper) per year: **=PMT(.09/12,25*12,175000)**
- Both the rate and the number of payment periods (nper) must be in the same format, such as monthly or annually.
- You must enter the present value as a negative to get a positive number for the result, as in: **=PMT(.09/12,25*12,-175000)**

Try It! Using the PMT Function

1. Start Excel, and open the **ETry31** file from the data files for this lesson.
2. Save the file as **ETry31_studentfirstname_studentlastname** in the location where your teacher instructs you to store the files for this lesson.
3. On the PMT worksheet, click D7.
4. Type **=**.
5. Type **PMT**.
6. Type **(**.
7. Click cell D6, and type **/12**.

   ✓ *This breaks the interest rate into a monthly amount. The rate is a percentage, so you would enter 9% or .09.*
8. Type **,**.
9. Click cell D5, and type ***12**.

   ✓ *For example, 3*12. The term is the number of years.*
10. Type **,**.
11. Type **–** (minus), and click cell D4.

    ✓ *When you type a minus sign before the principal, the payment amount will appear as a positive amount.*
12. Type **)**.

(continued)

Try It! Using the PMT Function *(continued)*

13 Press ENTER.

14 Save the changes to the **ETry31_studentfirstname_studentlastname** file, and leave it open to use in the next Try It.

Loan payment calculation using PMT

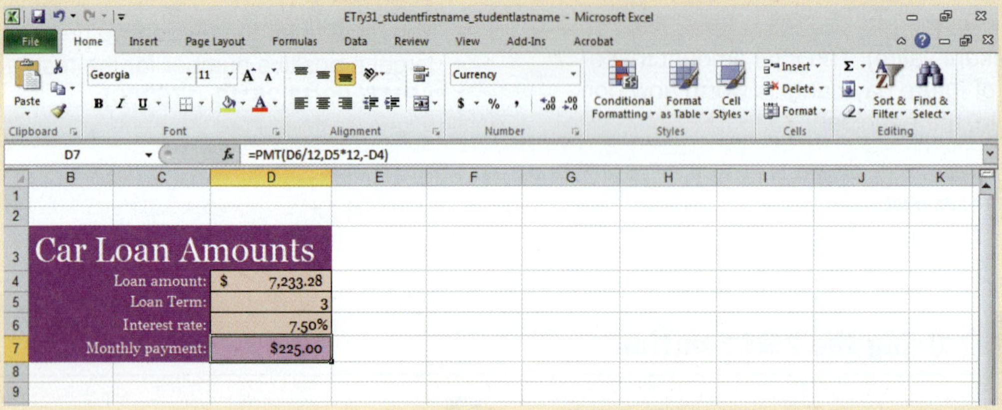

Creating What-If Data Tables

- Use **what-if analysis** to evaluate different situations and find the best solution.
- For example, a what-if table can help you figure out the maximum mortgage you can afford if you want to keep your payments at $1,000 per month given various interest rates.
- The **variables** used in a data table are called **substitution values**, because Excel substitutes each value in the given formula when evaluating the what-if situation.
- Excel uses the **input cell** as a working area during the analysis—it can be blank, or it can contain one of the variables (typically, the first one in the variables list).

  ✓ *The what-if formula must refer to this input cell.*

- Excel places each variable into the input cell as it solves each equation.
- **Data tables** can be either one-input or two-input.
- In a one-input data table, you enter one series of variables, which are then substituted in a formula to come up with a series of answers.
  - You can enter the variables, such as the varying interest rates in this example, in a single column or a single row.
  - You then enter a formula in a cell either one row up and one column to the right, or one row down and one column to the left (for variables entered in a row).
  - The formula points to the input cell, which typically contains a value equal to the first variable in your list.
- In a two-input data table, you enter two series of variables, thus increasing the number of possible solutions.

  ✓ *For example, you can enter both the loan rates and several different loan terms (15-, 20-, 25-, or 30-year) to determine what amounts you can afford under varying plans.*

- In a two-input data table, you enter one set of variables in a row, and the other set in a column to the left of the first row variable.
  - You enter the formula in the cell intersected by the variable row and variable column.
  - The formula refers to two input cells, which again can be blank, or may be filled with the first variable.
- After entering the variables, formula, and input cell precisely, you use a command on the Data tab to generate the values in the input table.

Try It! Creating a One-Input Data Table

1. In the **ETry31_studentfirstname_studentlastname** file, select the One Input Table worksheet.
2. In cell C12, type **=D8**, and press ENTER.

   ✓ *To enter additional formulas, type them in the cells to the right of the formula cell (if you entered variables in a column), or in the cells below the formula cell (if you entered variables in a row).*
3. Select the range B12:C19.

   ✓ *Select cells containing the formula and substitution values.*

   ✓ *Do not select the input cell.*
4. On Data tab, click the What-If Analysis button, and then click Data Table.
5. In the Column input cell box, cell D7 type **D8**.
6. Click OK.
7. Save the changes to the **ETry31_studentfirstname_studentlastname** file, and leave it open to use in the next Try It.

A one-variable what-if analysis

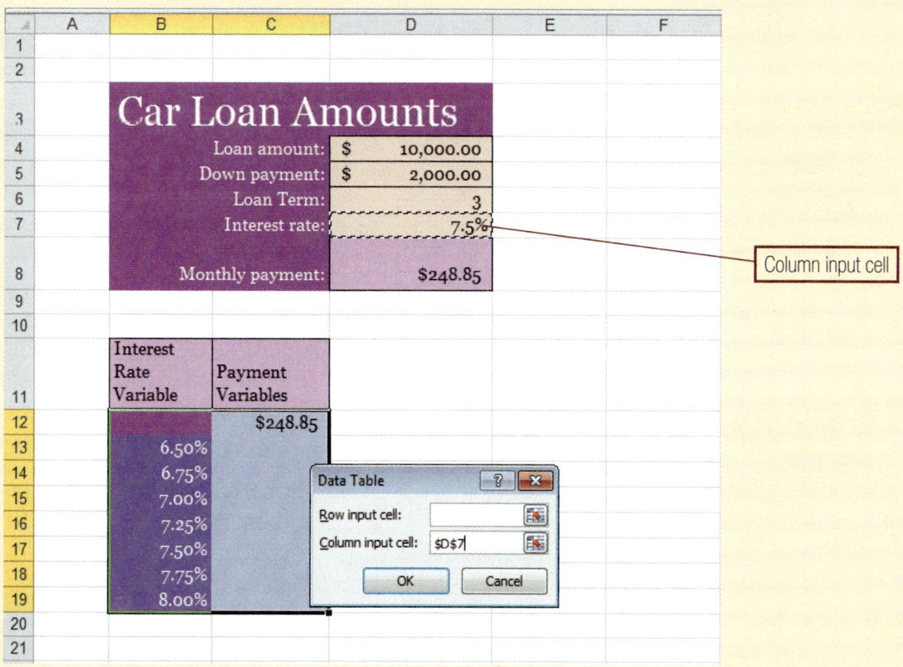

Try It! Creating a Two-Input Data Table

1. In the **ETry31_studentfirstname_studentlastname** file, select the Two Input Table worksheet.
2. In cell B6, type **=C21**, and press ENTER.
3. Select B6:I13, or all the cells in the data table range.

   ✓ *Select cells containing the formula and the substitution values.*

4. On the Data tab, click the What-If Analysis button, and then click Data Table.
5. In the Column input cell box, click cell C18.
6. In the Row input cell, type **C20**.
7. Click OK.
8. Save the changes to the **ETry31_studentfirstname_studentlastname file**, and leave it open to use in the next Try It.

A two-variable what-if analysis

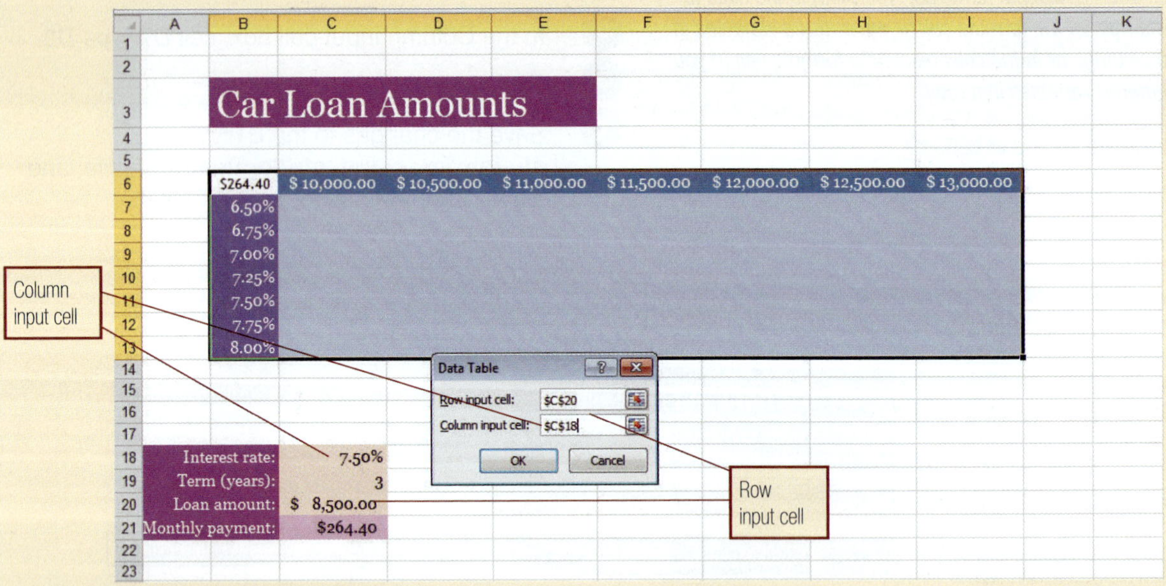

Solving a Problem with Goal Seek

- Use **Goal Seek** when you know the result (the goal), but you do not know the value of one of the input variables.
- Goal Seek tests possible variables until it finds the input value that produces the desired result.
- For example, you could use Goal Seek to determine the exact amount you could borrow at 9.25% and keep the payment at $1,000 a month.

Try It! Using Goal Seek

1. In the **ETry31_studentfirstname_studentlastname** file, select the Goal Seek worksheet.
2. On the Data tab, click the What-If Analysis button, and then click Goal Seek.
3. In the Set cell box, type **D9**.
4. In the To value box, type **350**.
5. In the By changing cell box, type **D6**.
6. Click OK.

   ✓ *Goal Seek finds a solution and displays it in the Goal Seek Status dialog box. The values on the worksheet are also changed.*

7. Click the OK button to keep the changed cell values.
8. Save the changes to the **ETry31_studentfirstname_studentlastname** file, and leave it open to use in the next Try It.

The Goal Seek Status dialog box

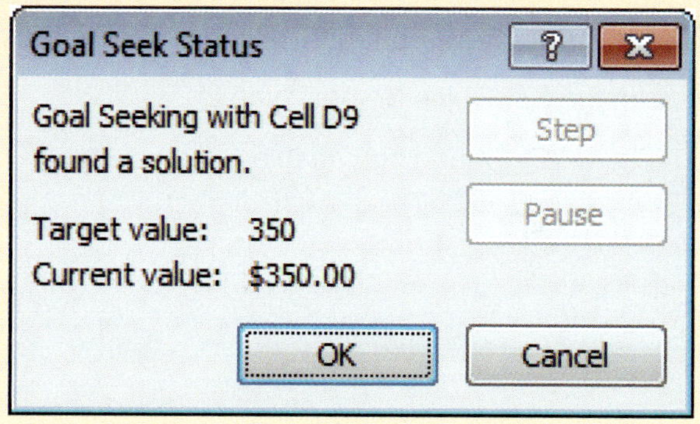

Using Solver to Resolve Problems

- With **Solver**, you can resolve problems involving more than one variable with a known result.
- For example, you could use Solver to determine the exact amount you could borrow, spending $1,000 a month, using various interest rates and various down payments.

  ✓ *Use the Value Of option if you plan to solve for a specific result.*

- You can use Solver to determine the best solution to a problem that fits within the constraints you set.

  ✓ *You can also solve problems with multiple variables using a PivotTable, which is covered in Lesson 33.*

Try It! Activating the Solver

1. In the **ETry31_studentfirstname_studentlastname** file, click File > Options.
2. In the Excel Options dialog box, click Add-Ins.
3. In the Manage drop-down arrow, select Excel Add-ins, and then click Go.
4. In the Add-Ins dialog box, check Solver Add-in and then click OK.
5. Save the changes to the **ETry31_studentfirstname_studentlastname** file, and leave it open to use in the next Try It.

Try It! Using Solver

1. In the **ETry31_studentfirstname_studentlastname** file, select the Solver worksheet.
2. On the Data tab, in the Analysis group, click Solver.
3. In the Solver Parameters dialog box, click Max.
4. In the Set Objective box, type **I4**.
5. In the By Changing Variable Cells box, type **F5**.
6. Click the Add button to add a constraint.
7. In the Cell Reference box, type **F5**.
8. Select <= from the descriptor drop-down list.
9. In the Constraint box, type **I17**.
10. Click OK.

✓ *Note that the cell reference in the Solver Parameters dialog box makes your cell references absolute.*

The Solver Parameters dialog box

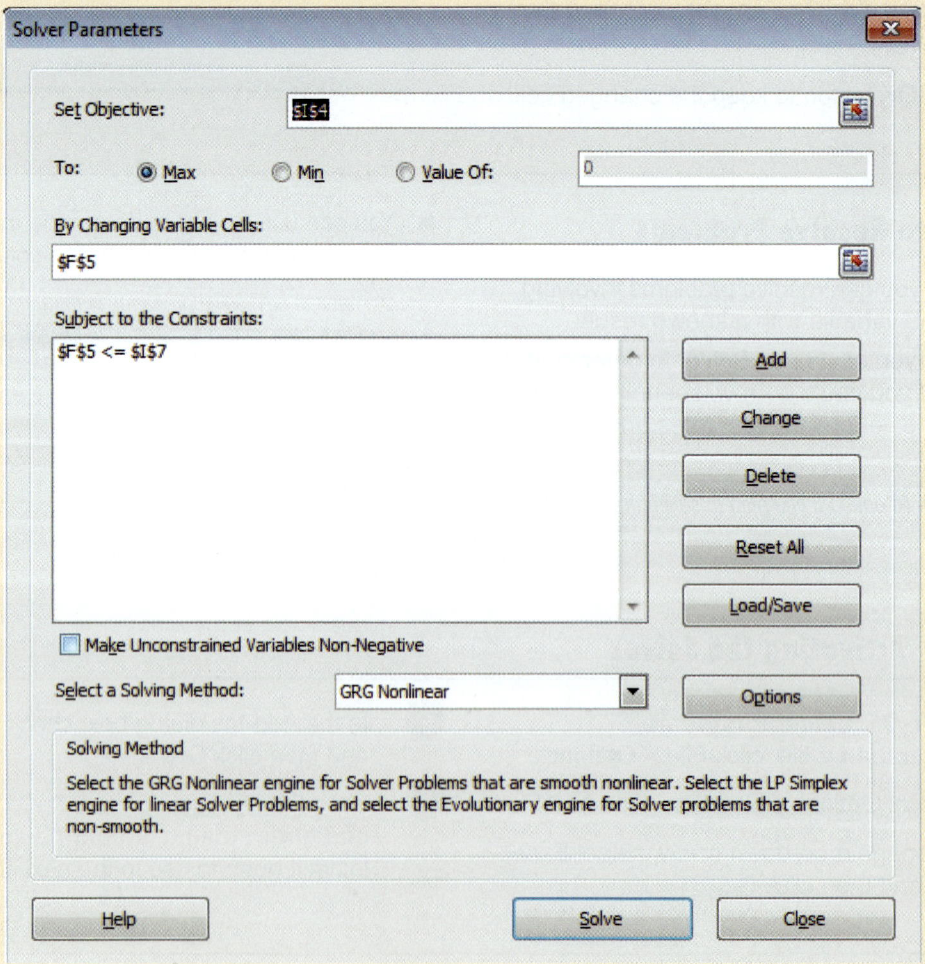

(continued)

Try It! **Using Solver** *(continued)*

11 Click Solve.

✓ *Solver finds a solution and displays it in a dialog box. The values on the worksheet are also changed.*

12 Click OK to keep the changed cell values.

✓ *You can save the scenario, restore your previous values, or print reports from the dialog box that appears.*

13 Save the changes to the **ETry31_studentfirstname_studentlastname** file, and close Excel.

Project 67—Create It

Bid Projections

DIRECTIONS

1. Start Excel, if necessary, and open the **EProj67** file from the data files for this lesson.
2. Save the workbook as **EProj67_studentfirstname_studentlastname** in the location where your teacher instructs you to store the files for this lesson.
3. Add a header that has your name at the left, the date code in the center, and the page number code at the right.
4. Select the **Bid Sheet** worksheet, if necessary.
5. On the **Data** tab, click the **Solver** button. The Solver Parameters dialog box opens.
6. In the **Set Objective** box, click the **Collapse Dialog box** button.
7. Click cell **E14**. Click the **Expand Dialog box** button.
8. Click **Value Of** and type **300000** in the text box.
9. In the **By Changing Variable Cells** box, the click the **Collapse Dialog box** button.
10. Click cells **B20** and **D7**. Expand the dialog box.
11. Click **Add** to open the Add Constraint dialog box.
12. In the **Cell Reference** box, type **B20**. Click **greater than or equal** from the descriptor list.
13. Type **22** in the **Constraint** box.
14. Click **Add** to add a second constraint.
15. In the **Cell Reference** box, type **D7**. Click **less than or equal** from the descriptor list.
16. Type **10** in the **Constraint** box. Click **OK** to return to the Solver Parameters dialog box.
17. Click **Solve**. Select **Keep Solver Solution** and click **OK**. Your document should look like the one shown in Figure 31-1.
18. **With your teacher's permission,** print the **Bid Sheet** worksheet. Submit the printout or the file for grading as required.
19. Save and close the file.

Figure 31-1

Bid Sheet - Old Highland Library Renovation

Profit 9%

	Base Bid	Alt #1	Alt #2	Base Bid + Alt
Materials	$ 173,081.00	$ 33,673.00	$ 7,619.00	$ 214,373.00
Labor	$ 45,044.00	$ 9,897.75	$ 4,914.75	$ 59,856.50
Profit	$ 20,498.12	$ 4,094.53	$ 1,177.85	$ 41,134.43
Total Bid	$ 238,623.12	$ 47,665.28	$ 13,711.60	$ 300,000.00

My estimate on the bid maximum	$ 300,000.00
Minimum profit I need	$ 0.10
Maximum I can pay plumbers	$ 22.00

Project 68—Apply It

Bid Projections

DIRECTIONS

1. Start Excel, if necessary.
2. Open the **EProj68** file from the data files for this lesson.
3. Save the workbook as **EProj68_studentfirstname_studentlastname** in the location where your teacher instructs you to store the files for this lesson.
4. Add a header that has your name at the left, the date code in the center, and the page number code at the right.
5. Create a two-input what-if analysis on the **Labor** worksheet. Set up the table as shown in Figure 31-2:
   a. Type the following formula in cell C19: **=H19*H20**.
   ✓ *This calculates the changes in cost when construction finishes early or late.*
   b. Use the data range **C19:F25**.
   c. Use **H20** for the **Row input cell**.
   d. Use **H19** for the **Column input cell**.
6. Create another two-input table on the **Loan** worksheet. Set up the table as shown in Figure 31-3:
   a. In cell **A9**, create a PMT formula using the values in cells **C6**, **C7**, and **F6**.
   ✓ *Be sure to enter the principle value as a negative.*
   b. Use the data range **A9:F15**.
   c. Use **C7** for the **Row input cell**.
   d. Use **C6** for the **Column input cell**.
7. Widen the columns as necessary.
8. Spell check the workbook.
9. **With your teacher's permission,** print the **Labor** and **Loan** worksheets. Submit the printout or the file for grading as required.
10. Save your changes, close the workbook, and exit Excel.

Figure 31-2

Estimated Labor Costs - Old Highland Library Renovation

	Hours Estimated to Complete Work					Labor Cost		
	Base Bid	Alt #1	Alt #2	Totals Hours	Hourly Rate Current Quotes	Base Bid	Alt #1	Alt #2
Masonry	215.00			215.00	$ 29.75	$ 6,396.25	$ -	$ -
Carpentry	1,245.00	325.00	114.00	1,684.00	$ 18.75	$ 23,343.75	$ 6,093.75	$ 2,137.50
Electrical	322.00	95.00	85.75	502.75	$ 27.00	$ 8,694.00	$ 2,565.00	$ 2,315.25
Roofers	96.00	21.00		117.00	$ 15.00	$ 1,440.00	$ 315.00	$ -
Plumbing	235.00	42.00	21.00	298.00	$ 22.00	$ 5,170.00	$ 924.00	$ 462.00
Total Bid	2,113.00	483.00	220.75	2,816.75		$ 45,044.00	$ 9,897.75	$ 4,914.75

			Alt #2	Alt #1	Base
		$ 4,423.28	$ 4,914.75	$ 9,897.75	$ 45,044.00
Estimated Cost Reductions/Increases for Schedule Changes	1-Week Early	90%	4,423.28	8,907.98	40,539.60
	On Time	100%	4,914.75	9,897.75	45,044.00
	1 Week Late	112%	5,504.52	11,085.48	50,449.28
	2 Weeks Late	126%	6,192.59	12,471.17	56,755.44
	3 Weeks Late	132%	6,487.47	13,065.03	59,458.08
	4 Weeks Late	141%	6,929.80	13,955.83	63,512.04

$ 4,914.75
90%

Figure 31-3

Construction Loan - Old Highland Library Renovation

Loan amount	$ 55,000.00	Term in months	6
Loan rate	5.25%		

$9,307.54	5.25%	5.50%	5.75%	6.00%	6.25%
$55,000.00	$ 9,308	$ 9,314	$ 9,321	$ 9,328	$ 9,334
$60,000.00	$ 10,154	$ 10,161	$ 10,168	$ 10,176	$ 10,183
$65,000.00	$ 11,000	$ 11,008	$ 11,016	$ 11,024	$ 11,032
$70,000.00	$ 11,846	$ 11,855	$ 11,863	$ 11,872	$ 11,880
$75,000.00	$ 12,692	$ 12,701	$ 12,710	$ 12,720	$ 12,729
$80,000.00	$ 13,538	$ 13,548	$ 13,558	$ 13,568	$ 13,577

Lesson 32

Using LOOKUP Functions

WORDS TO KNOW

Range name
The name given to a set of adjacent cells. You might name a range in order to make it more convenient to reference that range in a formula or a function, such as VLOOKUP.

Table
A series of columns and rows used to organize data. Each column typically represents a different field, and each row represents an entire record.

➤ What You Will Learn

Creating Lookup Functions

Software Skills With the lookup functions, you can look up information in a table based on a known value. For example, you can look up the salesperson assigned to a particular client. At the same time, you can look up that client's address and phone number. You can also look up the sales discount for a particular customer or calculate the bonuses for a group of salespeople based on a bonus structure. If needed, you can nest a function, such as SUM, within a lookup function in order to look up a sum total within a table. For example, you might want to look up the total cost of the items in an invoice to calculate the cost of delivering them.

Application Skills After learning about the power of Excel's lookup functions, you've decided to use them to make tax time a bit easier. In this exercise, you'll add several lookup functions to your income tax worksheets.

What You Can Do

Creating Lookup Functions

- The lookup functions, VLOOKUP and HLOOKUP, locate a value in a **table**.
- Use the VLOOKUP (vertical lookup) function to look up data in a particular column in the table.
- The VLOOKUP function uses this format: =VLOOKUP(item,table-range,column-position)
  - *Item* is the text or value for which you are looking.
    - The item to look up must be located in the first column of the VLOOKUP table.
    - Upper- and lowercase are treated the same.

- If an exact match is not found, the next smallest value is used.

  ✓ *You can use a function here to calculate the item's value. For example, you can use the SUM function to calculate the total cost of items on an invoice and look up the delivery costs in another table to determine the total cost of the invoice.*

- *Table-range* is the range reference or **range name** of the lookup table.
  - Do not include the row containing the column labels.
  - If you are going to copy the lookup function, you should express the range as an absolute reference or as a range name.
- *Column-position* is the column number in the table from which the matching value should be returned.

  ✓ *The far-left column of the table is one; the second column is two, etc.*

- Use the HLOOKUP (horizontal lookup) function to look up data in a particular row in the table.
- You may use a similar formula in a horizontal lookup table: =HLOOKUP(item,table-range,row-position).
  - *Item* is the text or value for which you are looking.
  - *Table-range* is the range reference or range name of the lookup table.

    ✓ *Do not include the column that contains the row labels in this range.*

  - *Row-position* is the row number in the table from which the matching value should be returned.

Try It! Inserting the VLOOKUP Function

1. Start Excel, and open **ETry32** file from the data files for this lesson.
2. Save the file as **ETry32_studentfirstname_studentlastname** in the location where your teacher instructs you to store the files for this lesson.
3. Click cell I18.
4. Type **=**.
5. Type **VLOOKUP(**.

   ✓ *This function's syntax appears in a ScreenTip underneath the selected cell formula. You can click the function's name in the ScreenTip in order to display the related Help screen.*

6. Type **.0725** in the lookup_value position.

   ✓ *This can be an actual value or item or a reference to the cell containing the value or item.*

   ✓ *You can click a cell in the worksheet to insert a cell reference.*

7. Type **,**.
8. Type **B6:I13** for the table_array.

   ✓ *You can also select cells in the worksheet for the cell range.*

9. Type **,**.
10. Type **4** for the col_index_num (column number).
11. Type **)**, and press ENTER.
12. Save the changes to the **ETry32_studentfirstname_studentlastname** file, and leave it open to use in the next Try It.

Try It! Inserting an HLOOKUP Function Using the Function Wizard

1. In the **ETry32_studentfirstname_ studentlastname** file, select cell I19.
2. Type **=**.
3. Type **HLOOKUP(**.
4. Click the Insert Function button on the formula bar.

   ✓ *This opens the Function Wizard that can help you format the function's arguments.*

5. In the Lookup_value box, type **10500**.
6. In the Table_array box, click the Collapse Dialog box button, select cells B6:I13, and then click the Expand Dialog button.

   ✓ *You can use the Collapse Dialog box and Expand Dialog box buttons to hide or expand the dialog box for the selection, if necessary.*

7. In the Row_index_num box, type **MATCH(0.0675,B7:B13)+1**.

   ✓ *By using the MATCH function, you can have the HLOOKUP function locate the appropriate row index item for you.*

8. Click OK.
9. Save the changes to the **ETry32_ studentfirstname_studentlastname** file, and close Excel.

The Function Arguments dialog box

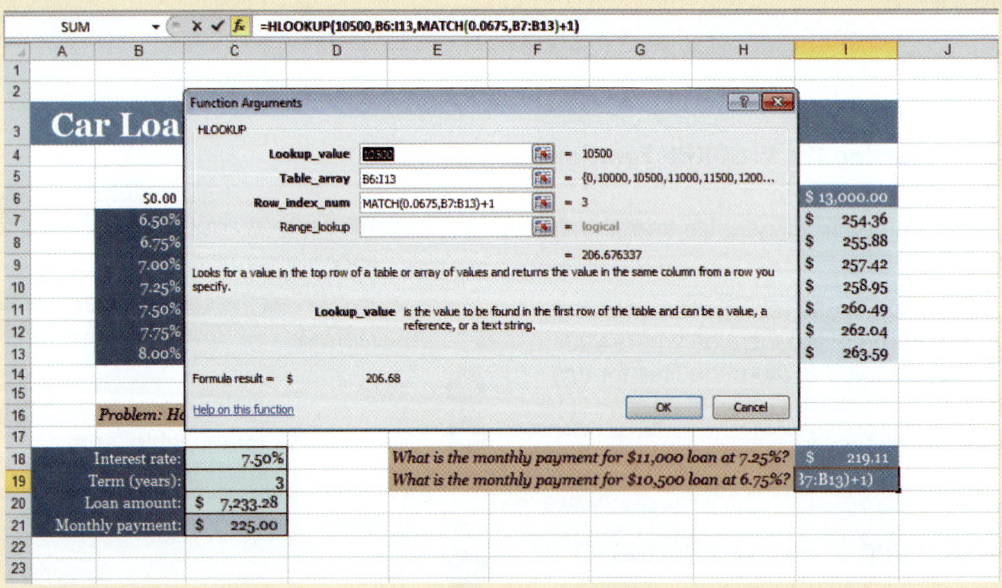

Project 69—Create It

Income Tax Calculations

DIRECTIONS

1. Start Excel, if necessary, and open the **EProj69** file from the data files for this lesson.
2. Save the workbook as **EProj69_studentfirstname_studentlastname** in the location where your teacher instructs you to store the files for this lesson.
3. Add a header that has your name at the left, the date code in the center, and the page number code at the right.
4. Select the **1040** worksheet, if necessary.
5. Click cell **F50**. You'll use this cell to enter a formula to look up your tax based on the provided taxable amount.
6. Type **=VLOOKUP(**. Click the Insert Function button *fx* on the formula bar to open the Function Arguments dialog box.
7. In the **Lookup_value** box, click the **Collapse Dialog box** button, click cell **F49**, and then click the **Expand Dialog box** button.
8. In the **Table_array** box, click the **Collapse Dialog box** button, click the **Tax Table** worksheet, select **A4:C304**, and then click the **Expand Dialog box** button.
9. In the **Column_index_num** box, type **2** (the married filing joint column).
10. Click **OK**. Your worksheet should look like Figure 32-1.
11. **With your teacher's permission,** print the **1040** worksheet. Submit the printout or the file for grading as required.
12. Save the file, and close Excel.

Figure 32-1

	B	C	D	E	F
46	Deduction (married jointly)				$ 7,850.00
47	Subtract line 38 from line 36				$ 78,530.23
48	Multiply $3,000 by tot. exemptions...				$ 12,000.00
49	Taxable income				$ 66,530.23
50	**Tax**				$ 11,758.00
51	Alternative minimum tax				
52	**Add lines 42 and 43**				$ 11,758.00
53	Foreign tax credit				
54	Credit for child and dependent care expenses			$ 682.00	
55	Credit for elderly or disabled				
56	Education credits				
57	Retirement savings credit				
58	Child tax credit			$ 1,200.00	
59	Adoption credit				
60	Credits from form 8396 or 8859				
61	Other credits from form 3800 or 8801				
62	Total credits				$ 1,882.00
63	Subtract line 54 from line 44				$ 9,876.00
64	Self-employment tax				
65	Social security tax and medicare tax on tip income				
66	Tax on IRAs				
67	Advanced EIC payments				
68	Household employment taxes				
69	**Total tax**				$ 9,876.00
70	Federal income tax withheld			$ 9,761.40	
71	2010 estimated tax payments				
72	Earned income credit				
73	Excess social security tax and tier 1 RRTA tax withheld				
74	Additional child tax credit				
75	Amount paid with extension to file				
76	Other payments				
77	**Total payments**				$ 9,761.40
78	This is the amount you OVERPAID				$ -
79	Amount to be refunded to you				$ -
80	Amount to be applied to 2011 tax				
81	The amount you OWE				$ 114.60

Amount you owe

Project 70—Apply It

Income Tax Calculations

DIRECTIONS

1. Start Excel, if necessary, and open **EProj70** from the data files for this lesson.
2. Save the workbook as **EProj70_studentfirstname_studentlastname** in the location where your teacher instructs you to store the files for this lesson.
3. Select the **Student Loan** worksheet, if necessary.
4. Add a header that has your name at the left, the date code in the center, and the page number code at the right.
5. In cell **F7**, enter a formula to look up the deduction limit, which is based on your filing status. Make sure the formula takes the following into consideration:
   a. Use the **IF** function to determine your filing status.
   b. If the text entered in cell **B7** is equal to "married, filing jointly," then use an **HLOOKUP** function that looks up the value **2** in the table, and displays the dollar amount shown below it.
   c. If the text in cell **B7** is anything else, use **HLOOKUP** to look up the value **1** and display the dollar amount below it.
   d. The **Row Index** for both **HLOOKUP** functions is 2, because the dollar amounts are located in row 2 of the table.
6. Widen columns as needed.
7. Save your changes, and close the workbook.
8. Open the **EProj70_Tax** file from the data files for this lesson.
9. Save the file as **EProj70_Tax_studentfirstname_studentlastname** in the location where your teacher instructs you to store the files for this lesson.
10. Test your new formulas by changing an amount in the **EProj70_Tax_studentfirstname_studentlastname** workbook:
    a. On the **Itemized Deductions** worksheet, in cell **D9**, enter the amount of your real estate taxes (the tax on your home): **$2,345**.
    b. Switch to the **1040** sheet, and notice that the tax amount in cell F50 has changed from what it was (as shown in Figure 32-1 on the previous page), and that you are now due a refund, as shown in Figure 32-2.
11. Widen columns as needed.
12. **With your teacher's permission,** print sheet **1040**. Submit the printout or the file for grading as required.
13. Save your changes, close the workbook, and exit Excel.

Figure 32-2

	A	B	C	D	E	F	G
46	38	Deduction (married jointly)				$ 9,475.31	
47	39	Subtract line 38 from line 36				$ 76,904.92	
48	40	Multiply $3,000 by tot. exemptions...				$ 12,000.00	
49	41	Taxable income				$ 64,904.92	
50	42	Tax				$ 11,326.00	
51	43	Alternative minimum tax					
52	44	Add lines 42 and 43				$ 11,326.00	
53	45	Foreign tax credit					
54	46	Credit for child and dependent care expenses			$ 682.00		
55	47	Credit for elderly or disabled					
56	48	Education credits					
57	49	Retirement savings credit					
58	50	Child tax credit			$ 1,200.00		
59	51	Adoption credit					
60	52	Credits from form 8396 or 8859					
61	53	Other credits from form 3800 or 8801					
62	54	Total credits				$ 1,882.00	
63	55	Subtract line 54 from line 44				$ 9,444.00	
64	56	Self-employment tax					
65	57	Social security tax and medicare tax on tip income					
66	58	Tax on IRAs					
67	59	Advanced EIC payments					
68	60	Household employment taxes					
69	61	Total tax				$ 9,444.00	
70	62	Federal income tax withheld			$ 9,761.40		
71	63	2010 estimated tax payments					
72	64	Earned income credit					
73	65	Excess social security tax and tier 1 RRTA tax withheld					
74	66	Additional child tax credit					
75	67	Amount paid with extension to file					
76	68	Other payments					
77	69	Total payments				$ 9,761.40	
78	70	This is the amount you OVERPAID				$ 317.40	
79	71a	Amount to be refunded to you				$ 317.40	
80	72	Amount to be applied to 2011 tax					
81	73	The amount you OWE				$ -	

Refund amount

Lesson 33

Understanding PivotTables and PivotCharts

➤ What You Will Learn

Creating PivotTables
Using the PivotTable Field List
Enhancing PivotTables and Creating PivotCharts

Software Skills PivotTables make it easier to analyze complex data. For example, if you had a database containing lots of information, such as sales data by product, store, region, and salesperson, you can summarize it in a PivotTable. With the table, you can display totals by region for each product, or you can rearrange the table to display sales totals by office and individual salesperson. You can also combine the tables to display totals by region, office, salesperson, and product. The flexibility of the PivotTable is its greatest asset.

Application Skills As the Inventory Manager at Voyager Travel Adventures, you are well aware of the inventory problems at the Logan store. Sometimes the store carries too much of an item, and other times, it carries so little there is nothing on the floor to sell. Carrying too many items that don't sell wastes space that costs a lot to rent and makes it difficult to restock the items you do carry. Carrying low inventory on popular items causes customers to get frustrated when they are told they have to come back. You want to use the inventory figures from the previous month to create several PivotTables and PivotCharts that will help you see quickly where the problems are.

WORDS TO KNOW

Database
An organized collection of records. For example, in an employee database, one record might include:

Employee name
Date of hire
Address
Phone number
Salary rate

Field
A single part of a record, such as "Phone number." Multiple related fields, such as one employee's name, address, phone number, etc., make up one record.

PivotChart
A chart based on PivotTable data.

PivotTable
A rearrangeable table that allows you to analyze complex data in a variety of ways.

Report filter
A field from the database that you can use to filter or limit the data displayed within the PivotTable.

What You Can Do

Creating PivotTables

- A **PivotTable** allows you to summarize complex data, such as a company's sales or accounting records.
- The advantage of the PivotTable over a regular table of information is that it lets you quickly change how data is summarized.
- For example, you can change from a report that summarizes sales data by region and office to one that summarizes the same data by salesperson and product.
- The source data for your PivotTable can be an external **database**, text file, or query file, or a named range or table within an Excel workbook.

	A	B	C	D	E
1					
2					
3	Customer	KNJ Pharmacies			
4					
5	Sum of Total Sale	Column Labels			
6	Row Labels	Bludadoze	Havcore	Pardox	Grand Total
7	10/8/2011	35097			35097
8	10/13/2011			11958	11958
9	10/17/2011			29874	29874
10	10/20/2011	21554	16654		38208
11	10/22/2011		12354	18944	31298
12	10/26/2011			17954	17954
13	10/30/2011		37894		37894
14	Grand Total	56651	66902	78730	202283

Figure 33-1

Try It! Creating PivotTables with Excel Data

1. Start Excel, and open **ETry33** from the data files for this lesson.
2. Save the file as **ETry33_studentfirstname_studentlastname** in the location where your teacher instructs you to store the files for this lesson.
3. Click cell A5.
4. On the Insert tab, click the Insert PivotTable button.

✓ *The range or table containing the cell you selected earlier should appear in the Select a table or range box. If the selection is wrong, you can select the correct range yourself.*

5. Select Existing Worksheet.
6. In the Location box, type **PivotTable!$A$5**.

(continued)

Try It! **Creating PivotTables with Excel Data** *(continued)*

7. Click OK.

8. Save the changes to the **ETry33_studentfirstname_studentlastname** file, and leave it open to use in the next Try It.

Create PivotTable dialog box

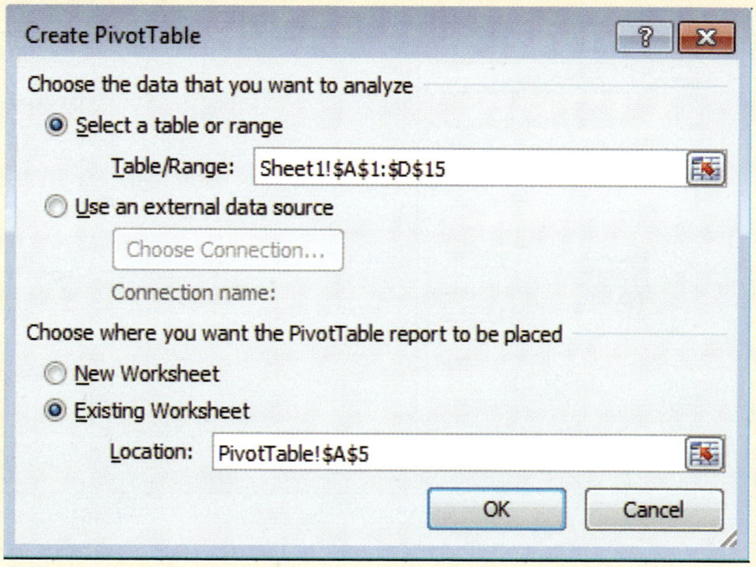

Using the PivotTable Field List

- The PivotTable Field List allows you to control each of the **fields** (columns) in your original data.
- When you insert a PivotTable in a worksheet, Excel creates the framework for your PivotTable. You then use the items on the PivotTable Field List to arrange (and rearrange) the data to create the table you want.
- To change the way your data is summarized, just drag the field name into the report area boxes at the bottom of the PivotTable Field List pane.
- The PivotTable has three basic areas into which you can drag your fields: the Row Labels area, the Column Labels area, and the body area (the Values area).
- Drag numerical items into the Values area to summarize them.

  ✓ *The default format for values on the PivotTable is a sum of the items.*

  ✓ *To modify the format of the data, click the field item in the Values area and choose Value Field Settings. Then choose the type of value you want, such as Sum, and click OK.*

  ✓ *In the sample PivotTable shown in Figure 33-1, the Total Sale item was placed in the body area of the PivotTable.*

- Drag items into the Row Labels area to have them appear as the rows of the table. Items that you drag into the Column Labels area appear in the columns of the table.

  ✓ *In the sample PivotTable shown in Figure 33-1, the Sales Date item was added to the row area, and the Drug Purchased item was added to the column area of the table (see Figure 33-2 to see where to add the items).*

- You can also filter the entire table by dragging a field to the Report Filter area.
- When you use **Report filters**, only the items relating to a particular category are displayed.

  ✓ *In the sample PivotTable shown in Figure 33-1, the Customer item was added to the Report Filter area.*

Figure 33-2

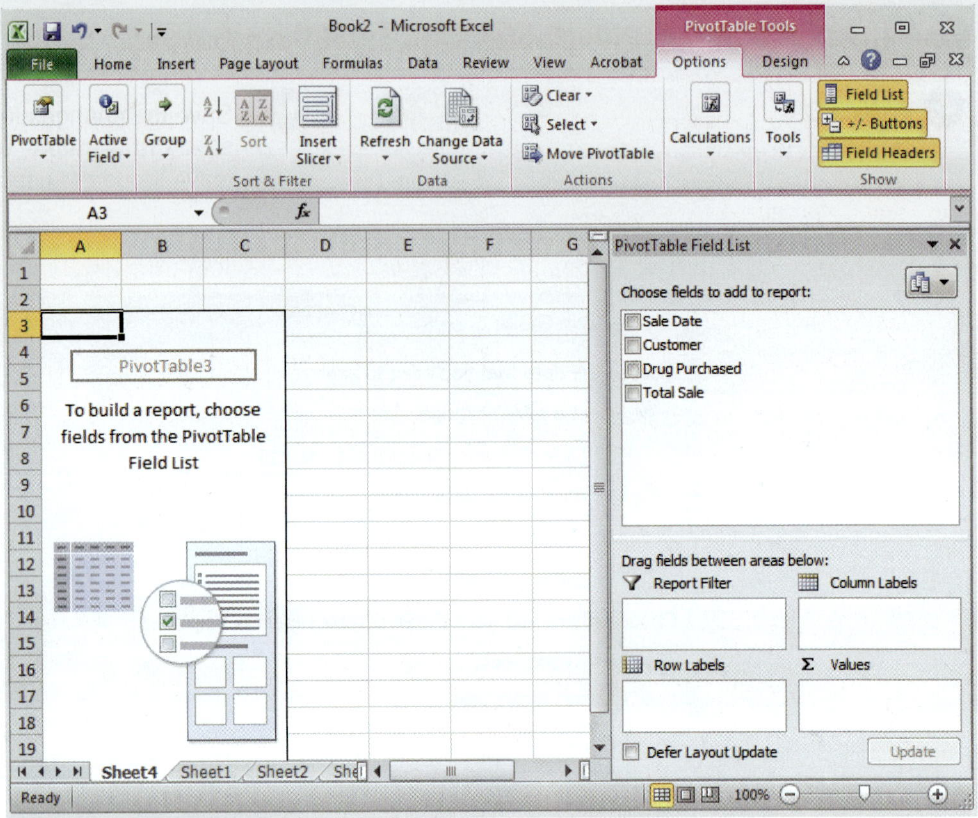

- When you add an item to a PivotTable, that item becomes a button with a down arrow.
- You can limit what's displayed in the PivotTable by clicking the down arrow on the appropriate item and selecting the item(s) you want to display.

✓ *For example, you could click the down arrow on a Sale Date field, and choose a specific date. The PivotTable data would be limited to just activity on that date.*

✓ *In the sample PivotTable shown in Figure 33-1 on page 558 the down arrow on the Customer button was clicked, and "KNJ Pharmacies" was selected. A user could further limit the report to display only the drug sales for Bludadoze and Pardox, or only the sales for 10/22.*

Try It! Using the PivotTable Field List

1. In the **ETry33_studentfirstname_studentlastname** file, click in the PivotTable Field List on the PivotTable worksheet.

   ✓ *If you don't see the PivotTable Field List, click the PivotTable box on the worksheet.*

2. In the PivotTable Field List pane, drag the Drug Purchased field into the Column Labels area.

   ✓ *If you don't want to see the changes to the PivotTable as you go, click the Defer Layout Update option. Then, when you're ready, click the Update button.*

3. Drag the Sale Date field from the PivotTable Field List into the Row Labels area.

4. Drag the Total Sale field to the Values area.

   ✓ *This item is typically a numerical item, such as total sales.*

(continued)

Try It! Using the PivotTable Field List *(continued)*

5. If you wish to display only items related to a particular category, you can add a report filter as well by dragging the Customer field to the Report Filter area.

   ✓ *To remove an item from the table, just deselect it in the PivotTable Field List.*

6. To rearrange a table, drag fields from area to area at the bottom of the PivotTable Field List.

7. Save the changes to the **ETry33_studentfirstname_studentlastname** file, and leave it open to use in the next Try It.

The PivotTable Field List and the PivotTable

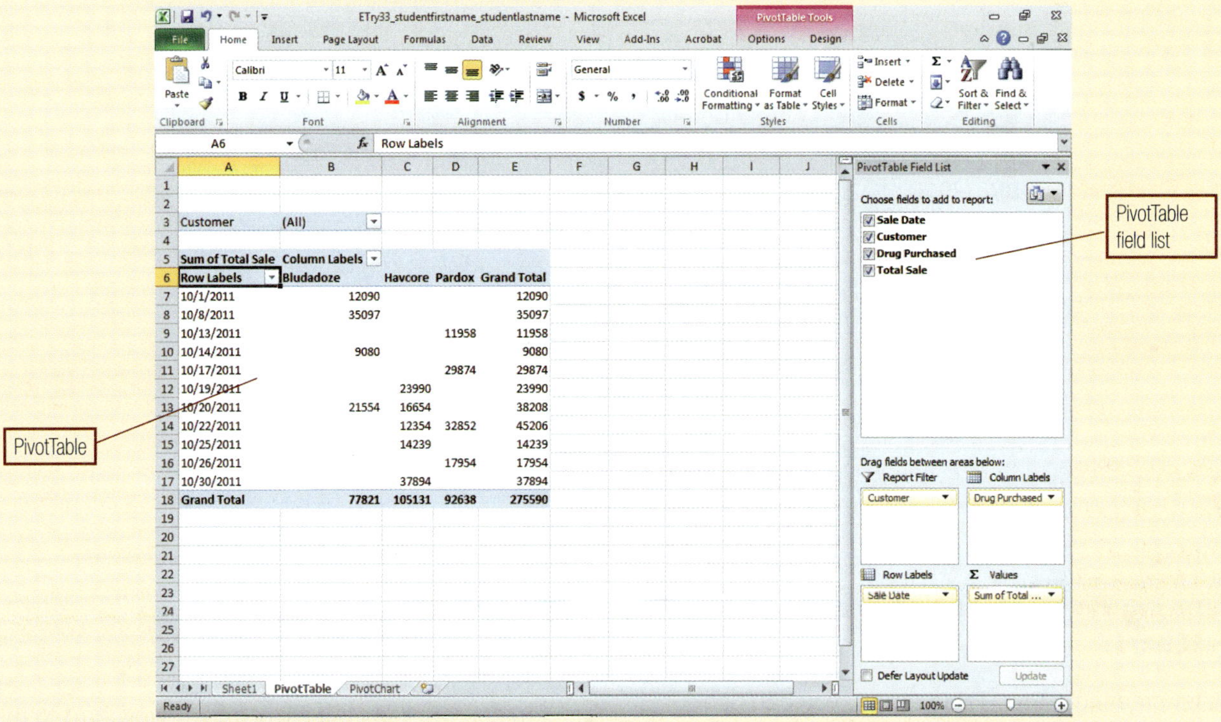

Try It! Limiting Report Data

1. In the **ETry33_studentfirstname_studentlastname** file, click anywhere within the PivotTable on the PivotTable worksheet.

2. Click the Customer down arrow, or the down arrow button for the field you want to change.

3. Select KNJ Pharmacies.

(continued)

Try It! Limiting Report Data *(continued)*

4. Click OK.

5. Save the changes to the **ETry33_studentfirstname_studentlastname** file, and leave it open to use in the next Try It.

The Filtered PivotTable

	A	B	C	D	E	F
1						
2						
3	Customer	KNJ Pharmacies				
4						
5	**Sum of Total Sale**	**Column Labels**				
6	**Row Labels**	**Bludadoze**	**Havcore**	**Pardox**	**Grand Total**	
7	10/8/2011	35097			35097	
8	10/13/2011			11958	11958	
9	10/17/2011			29874	29874	
10	10/20/2011	21554	16654		38208	
11	10/22/2011		12354	18944	31298	
12	10/26/2011			17954	17954	
13	10/30/2011		37894		37894	
14	**Grand Total**	**56651**	**66902**	**78730**	**202283**	
15						

PivotTable drop-down arrows allow you to filter data

Enhancing PivotTables and Creating PivotCharts

- After creating a PivotTable report, you can use Excel's built in PivotTable designs to make your report look professional.
- After creating a PivotTable report, you can create a **PivotChart** that illustrates the data summarized in the report.

✓ *You can create a PivotChart without creating a PivotTable first, although most users create the table prior to creating the chart.*

- You can publish your PivotTable/PivotChart to the Internet or your company's intranet.

Try It! Changing the Appearance of a PivotTable

1. In the **ETry33_studentfirstname_studentlastname** file, click inside the PivotTable.

2. On the PivotTable Tools Design tab, click the More button.

3. Select Pivot Style Dark 2, or another style of your choosing.

4. Save the changes to the **ETry33_studentfirstname_studentlastname** file, and leave it open to use in the next Try It.

Try It! Creating a PivotChart from a PivotTable

1. In the **ETry33_studentfirstname_studentlastname** file, click inside the PivotTable.
2. On the PivotTable Tools Options tab, click the PivotChart button.
3. Select the Area type, and then select 3-D Area as the chart subtype.
4. Click OK.

   ✓ *You can filter the data on the chart as you might filter the data on a PivotTable; simply select the items you want to show from the appropriate drop-down buttons on the chart.*

   ✓ *You can format a PivotChart as you would a regular chart.*
5. Save the changes to the **ETry33_studentfirstname_studentlastname** file, and leave it open to use in the next Try It.

A PivotChart

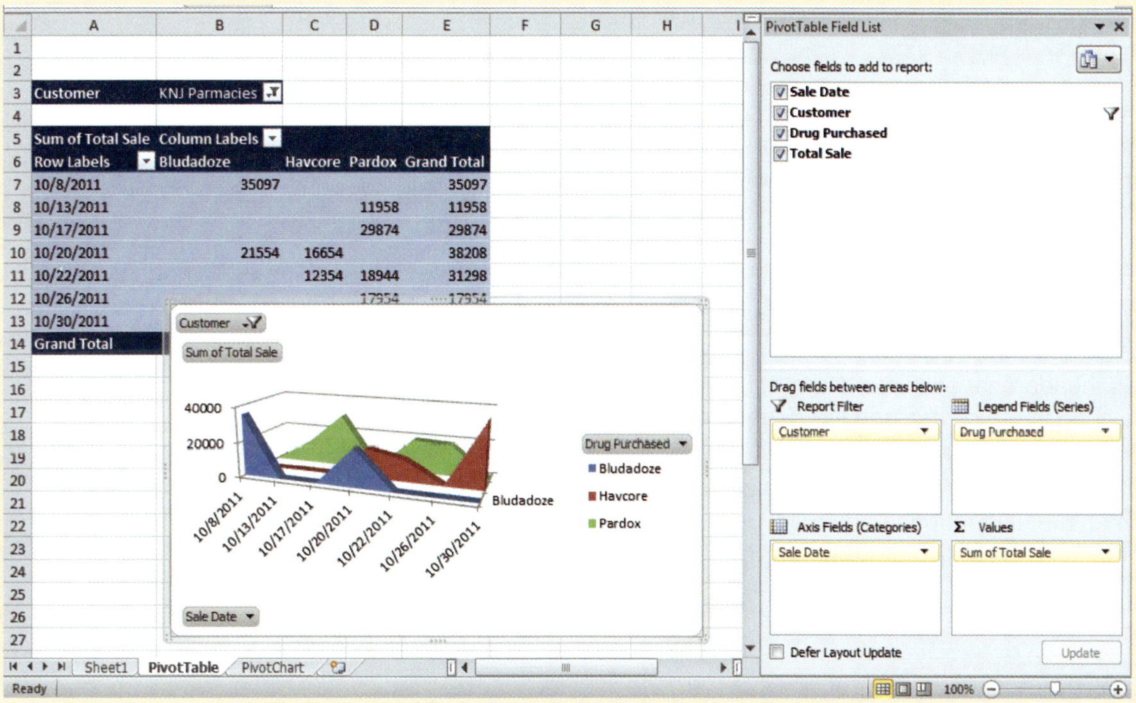

Try It! **Moving a PivotChart**

1. In the **ETry33_studentfirstname_studentlastname** file, click inside the PivotChart.
2. On the PivotChart Tools Design tab, click the Move Chart button.
3. Select Object in, and click the down arrow.
4. Select PivotChart, and click OK.
5. Click on the PivotChart worksheet to see the chart again.
6. Save the changes to the **ETry33_studentfirstname_studentlastname** file, and close the workbook.

Project 71—Create It

Inventory Analysis

DIRECTIONS

1. Start Excel, if necessary, and open **EProj71** from the data files for this lesson.
2. Save the workbook as **EProj71_studentfirstname_studentlastname** in the location where your teacher instructs you to store the files for this lesson.
3. Add a header that has your name at the left, the date code in the center, and the page number code at the right.
4. Click cell **A9** on the **Total Inventory** worksheet to indicate the data range for the PivotTable.
5. On the **Insert** tab, click the **PivotTable** button. The Create PivotTable dialog box opens.
6. In the Table/Range box, make sure the data range is **'Total Inventory'!$A$8:$L$134**, indicating that the range consists of cells A8:L134 on the Total Inventory worksheet.
7. Click **Existing Worksheet** to place the PivotTable in that location.
8. In the **Location** box, click the **Collapse Dialog box** button, click the **PivotTable** worksheet tab, and then click cell **A11**.
9. Click **OK**. A blank PivotTable appears with the PivotTable Field List on the right, as shown in Figure 33-3.
10. Submit the changes to the workbook for grading as required.
11. Save and close the file.

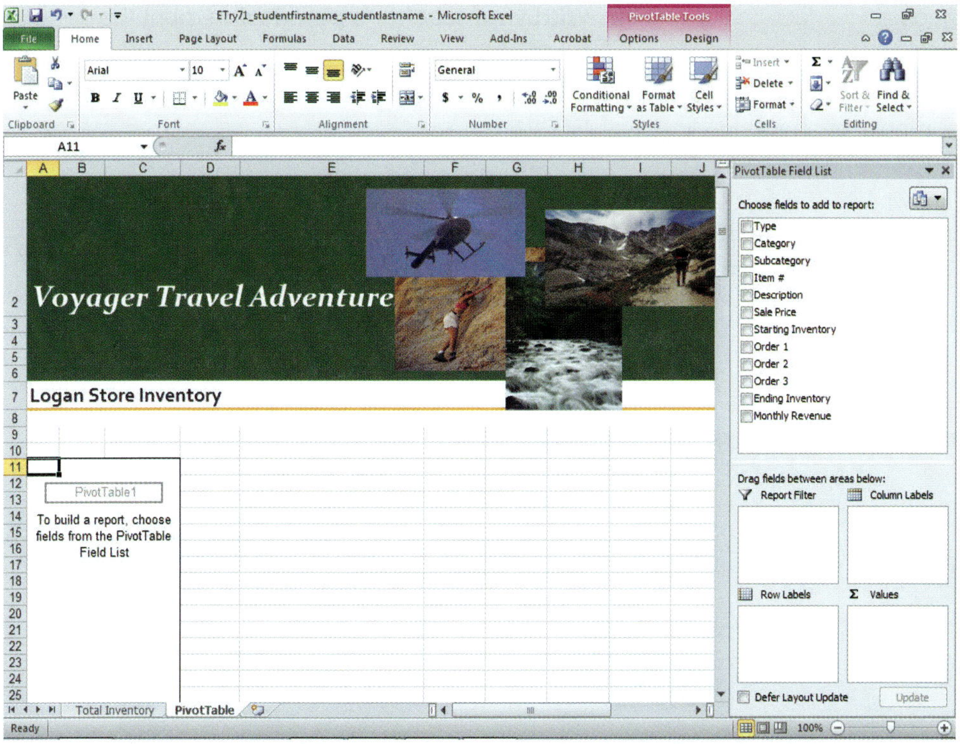

Figure 33-3

Project 72—Apply It

Inventory Analysis

DIRECTIONS

1. Start Excel, if necessary.
2. Open the **EProj72** file from the data files for this lesson.
3. Save the workbook as **EProj72_studentfirstname_studentlastname** in the location where your teacher instructs you to store the files for this lesson.
4. Add a header that has your name at the left, the date code in the center, and the page number code at the right.
5. Click cell **A11** on the **PivotTable** worksheet to open the PivotTable Field List and set up the table as follows:
   a. Drag the **Category** field to the **Row Labels** area.
   b. Drag the **Subcategory** field to the **Column Labels** area.
   c. Drag the **Monthly Revenue** field to the **Values** area.
   d. Drag the **Type** field to the **Report Filter** area.
   e. Click the **Type** drop-down arrow, select **Men**, and click **OK**.
6. Format the table as shown in Figure 33-4:
   a. Change the PivotTable Style as shown.
   b. Change the cell formats as shown.

7. Spell check the entire workbook.
8. **With your teacher's permission,** print the **PivotTable** sheet.
9. Create a PivotChart from your table as shown in Figure 33-5:
   a. Apply the Chart Type as shown.
   b. Make sure the data shown matches Figure 33-5.
   b. Place the chart on the **PivotChart** worksheet.
10. **With your teacher's permission,** print the **PivotChart** sheet.
11. Save your changes, close the workbook, and exit Excel.

Figure 33-4

Logan Store Inventory

Type	Men

Sum of Monthly Revenue	Column Labels		
Row Labels	Backpack	Footwear	Grand Total
Backcountry	$ 518,075	$ 36,000	$ 554,075
Skate		$196,650	$ 196,650
Ski		$126,300	$ 126,300
Snowboard		$ 40,500	$ 40,500
Grand Total	$ 518,075	$399,450	$ 917,525

Figure 33-5

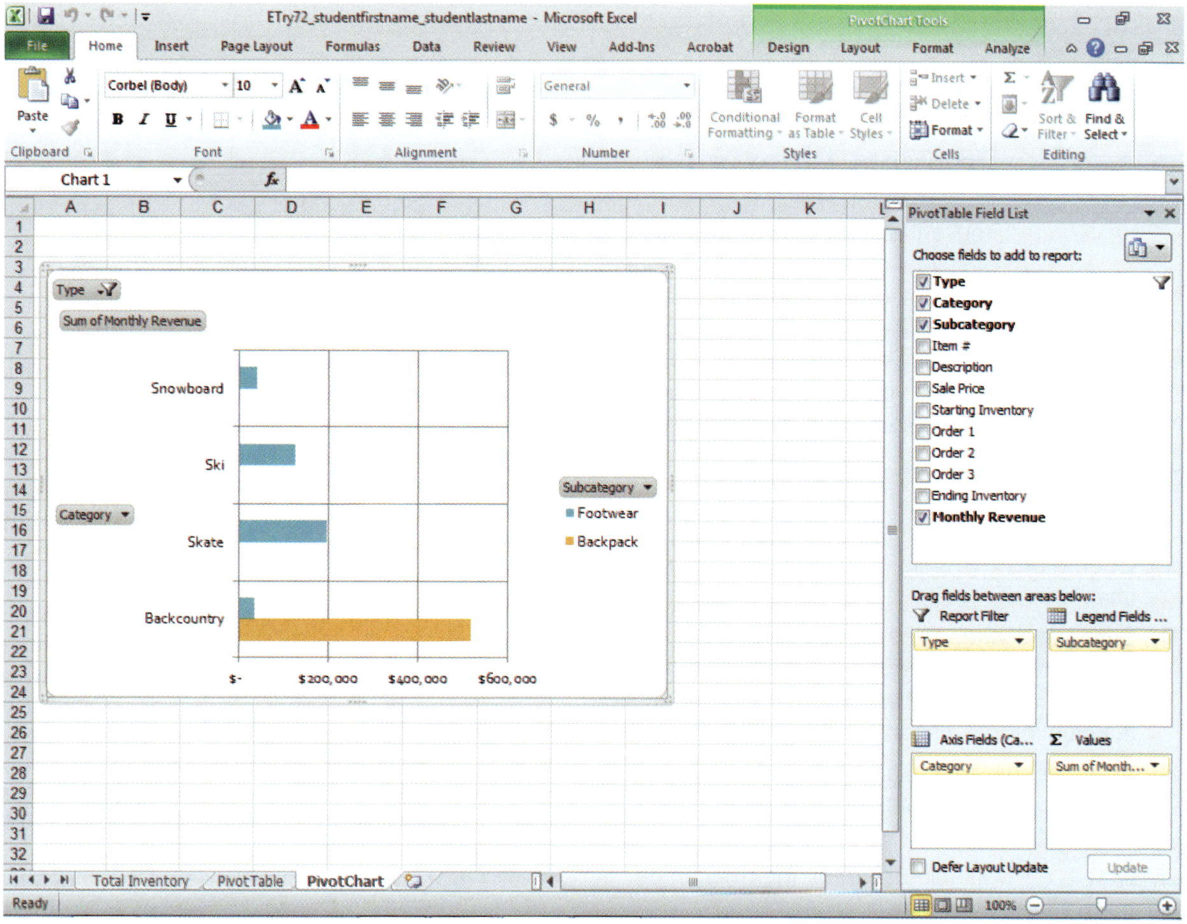
ETry72_studentfirstname_studentlastname - Microsoft Excel
PivotChart Tools
File
Home
Insert
Page Layout
Formulas
Data
Review
View
Add-Ins
Acrobat
Design
Layout
Format
Analyze
Chart 1
Type
Sum of Monthly Revenue
Snowboard
Ski
Skate
Backcountry
Category
Subcategory
Footwear
Backpack
$-
$200,000
$400,000
$600,000
PivotTable Field List
Choose fields to add to report:
Type
Category
Subcategory
Item #
Description
Sale Price
Starting Inventory
Order 1
Order 2
Order 3
Ending Inventory
Monthly Revenue
Drag fields between areas below:
Report Filter
Legend Fields ...
Axis Fields (Ca...
Values
Sum of Month...
Defer Layout Update
Update
Total Inventory
PivotTable
PivotChart
Ready
100%

Chapter Assessment and Application

Project 73—Make It Your Own

Revenue PivotTable

You're the owner of Whole Grains Bread company, and you want to analyze the past year's sales for each of your stores. You've compiled a database of revenues, and with it you'll create a PivotTable you can rearrange as you like, creating as many different revenue reports as you wish. After creating a PivotTable that lists quarterly revenues by city, you'll use its data to predict possible earnings amounts for next year. Finally, you'll use Solver to help you decide on the best price for a new product you'll introduce in your Oregon stores—tomato basil focaccia.

DIRECTIONS

1. Start Excel, if necessary.
2. Open the **EProj73** file from the data files for this chapter.
3. Save the workbook as **EProj73_studentfirstname_studentlastname** in the location where your teacher instructs you to store the files for this lesson.
4. Add a header that has your name at the left, the date code in the center, and the page number code at the right.
5. Create a PivotTable using the information on the **Revenue** worksheet:
   a. Place the table on the Analysis worksheet, beginning in cell **A10**.
   b. Show each city on its own row.
   c. Show the quarterly totals in separate columns.
   d. Display gross sales in the body of the report.
   e. Add a report filter that allows you to display each state separately if you want.
   f. Apply a currency format, no decimal places, to all numerical data.
   g. Display only the Oregon stores.
   h. Apply **Pivot Style Medium 5 style**.
   i. Spell check the worksheet.
   k. **With your teacher's permission,** print the PivotTable **Analysis** worksheet (see Illustration A).
6. Copy the table data:
   a. Make sure that all cities and states are displayed by removing the **State** field from the **Report Filter** box.
   b. Select the range **B12:F27**, and copy it.
   c. Use Paste Special to paste only the values starting in cell **B9** of the **Forecast** worksheet.
7. Use the GROWTH function to predict future sales (see Illustration B):
   a. In cell **F9** of the **Forecast** worksheet, enter a formula that calculates the predicted sales for Bend, OR.
   b. Use the actual sales in cells **B9:E9** as the basis for the prediction.
   c. Copy the formula to the range **F9:I24**.
8. Adjust column widths as needed.
9. Spell check the **Forecast** worksheet.
10. **With your teacher's permission,** print the **Forecast** worksheet.
11. Use Solver to change the proposed price of tomato basil focaccia (cell **C15** of the **New Product** sheet) so that the projected weekly profit (cell **C19**) equals **$1,200** (see Illustration C):
    a. Allow the coupon discount in cell **D18** to also be changed as needed.
    b. Set constraints that limit the price point to a value between **$3.75** and **$4.25**.
    c. Set constraints that limit the coupon discount (cell **D18**) to a value between **0.50** and **0.75**.
12. Spell check the entire workbook.
13. **With your teacher's permission,** print the **New Product** worksheet.
14. Save your changes, close the workbook, and exit Excel.

Illustration A

Whole Grains Bread
Salem, Oregon
Analysis

State	OR				
Sum of Sales	Qtr				
City	1	2	3	4	Grand Total
Bend	$261,200	$237,455	$242,394	$287,320	$1,028,369
Eugene	$259,659	$236,054	$285,625	$285,625	$1,066,963
Portland 1	$599,700	$545,181	$659,670	$659,670	$2,464,220
Portland 2	$608,767	$507,306	$595,618	$730,521	$2,442,212
Salem	$308,167	$315,100	$343,607	$301,388	$1,268,261
Three Sisters	$242,945	$220,859	$232,863	$267,240	$963,908
Grand Total	**$2,280,439**	**$2,061,955**	**$2,359,776**	**$2,531,763**	**$9,233,934**

Illustration B

Whole Grains Bread
Salem, Oregon

	Actual Sales				Predicted Sales			
City	Qtr 1	Qtr 2	Qtr 3	Qtr 4	Qtr 1	Qtr 2	Qtr 3	Qtr 4
Bend, OR	$ 261,200	$ 237,455	$ 242,394	$ 287,320	$ 244,846	$ 242,534	$ 259,685	$ 270,397
Eugene, OR	$ 259,659	$ 236,054	$ 285,625	$ 285,625	$ 247,575	$ 257,196	$ 287,537	$ 266,580
Larkspur 1, CA	$ 346,056	$ 364,269	$ 328,753	$ 328,753	$ 355,046	$ 347,835	$ 327,575	$ 341,191
Larkspur 2, CA	$ 577,597	$ 481,331	$ 693,117	$ 693,117	$ 527,272	$ 567,162	$ 702,020	$ 607,406
Olympia, WA	$ 202,075	$ 212,711	$ 222,687	$ 191,972	$ 210,425	$ 214,899	$ 210,157	$ 197,797
Portland 1, OR	$ 599,700	$ 545,181	$ 659,670	$ 659,670	$ 571,791	$ 594,011	$ 664,085	$ 615,684
Portland 2, OR	$ 608,767	$ 507,306	$ 595,618	$ 730,521	$ 544,495	$ 553,147	$ 650,073	$ 646,595
Redmond, WA	$ 624,611	$ 567,829	$ 730,795	$ 687,073	$ 599,229	$ 633,362	$ 719,262	$ 639,333
Salem, OR	$ 308,167	$ 315,100	$ 343,607	$ 301,388	$ 315,726	$ 324,630	$ 326,999	$ 304,328
San Bernardino, CA	$ 298,663	$ 311,757	$ 283,282	$ 286,119	$ 304,836	$ 298,813	$ 283,464	$ 295,290
San Diego, CA	$ 288,124	$ 261,931	$ 28,392	$ 316,936	$ 215,827	$ 114,099	$ 69,116	$ 332,763
San Francisco, CA	$ 688,752	$ 510,187	$ 836,834	$ 929,815	$ 586,571	$ 642,158	$ 888,198	$ 752,087
Seattle 1, WA	$ 781,587	$ 710,534	$ 671,774	$ 859,746	$ 727,054	$ 704,892	$ 740,179	$ 812,139
Seattle 2, WA	$ 427,087	$ 547,547	$ 533,858	$ 333,127	$ 506,932	$ 523,765	$ 441,479	$ 389,708
Spokane, WA	$ 248,896	$ 292,819	$ 211,562	$ 211,562	$ 269,966	$ 252,974	$ 209,169	$ 237,979
Three Sisters, OR	$ 242,945	$ 220,859	$ 232,863	$ 267,240	$ 228,472	$ 228,373	$ 246,539	$ 251,103
Grand Total	$ 6,763,888	$ 6,322,869	$ 6,900,830	$ 7,369,984	$ 6,456,062	$ 6,499,852	$ 7,025,535	$ 6,960,380
Average	$ 422,743	$ 395,179	$ 431,302	$ 460,624	$ 403,504	$ 406,241	$ 439,096	$ 435,024

Illustration C

Whole Grains Bread
Salem, Oregon

Analysis of Possible Profits from New Tomato Basil Focaccia				
			High	Low
ingredient cost	$ 1.76	Percent who liked item	89%	85%
No. can make in one hour	17	Weekly customers	13,050	11,500
Labor cost	$ 1.10	Customers who might buy	11,549	9,775
Total cost	$ 2.86	Estimate of likely sales	1,386	1,173
Price point	$ 4.25			
Weekly revenues	$ 4,985			
Minus cost	$ 3,358			
Minus coupons	$ 427	$ 0.50		
Weekly profit	$ 1,200			

Project 74—Master It

Lemonade Stand Projections

It's difficult to run any business, no matter how simple. Customer purchases are based on many things, some of them outside of your control, such as the weather and social trends. You might think that running a lemonade stand is easy, but it's not, as you'll find in this exercise. First, you'll gather data for 30 days of lemonade sales. You'll get the opportunity to make business decisions based on the weather and the cost of making your lemonade. In the end, you'll analyze your data using a PivotTable, and make predictions on future sales.

DIRECTIONS

1. Start Excel, if necessary.
2. Open the**EProj74** file from the data files for this chapter.
3. Save the file as **EProj74_studentfirstname_studentlastname** in the location where your teacher instructs you to store the files for this lesson.
4. Add a header that has your name at the left, the date code in the center, and the page number code at the right.
5. In the **Day** column, enter the values **1** to **30**.
6. In the **Day of Week** column, enter the days of the week, beginning with today. For example, start with Monday.
7. In the **Gross Profit** column, enter a formula that calculates revenue (the number of glasses sold multiplied by the amount you're charging per glass).
8. In the **Advertising** column, enter a formula that calculates the cost of advertising your stand (**0.25** per sign).
9. In the **Cost to Make Lemonade** column, enter a formula that calculates your cost—the cost per glass times the number of glasses you made that day.
10. Finally, enter a formula to calculate your profit in the **Net Profit** column.
11. In the first cell under **Money at Start of Day**, enter **$3**.
12. In the **Money at End of Day** column, enter a formula that adds the net profit to the Money at Start of Day. Copy the formula down to cell O5.
13. In the second cell under **Money at Start of Day**, enter a formula that displays the value in the first cell under **Money at End of Day**.
14. Copy cells **N5** and **O5**. Highlight cells **N6:O33** and click **Home > Paste** to record 30 days' worth of lemonade sales. Format the worksheet to create a professional appearance. If necessary, make up the sales data for the 30 days of sales.
15. Use the data to create a PivotTable so you can analyze your results. Place the PivotTable on the **PivotTable** worksheet.
16. Modify the PivotTable to show the effects of weather and price on the number of glasses sold. You might also want to see if the day of the week had any effect on sales—your choice
17. Format the PivotTable, similar to that shown in Illustration D.
18. Use **Paste** to copy the values and formats in the **Gross Profit, Advertising, Cost to Make Lemonade**, and **Net Profit** data to the **Forecast** worksheet. Copy the data in the **Day** and **Day of Week** columns as well.
19. Use this data and the **TREND** function to predict another 15 days' worth of gross profit.
20. Use the **FORECAST** function to predict the advertising costs, and the cost to make lemonade.
21. Use a regular formula to calculate the predicted net profits.
22. After entering data, adjust column widths, and spell check the worksheets. The sheet should look similar to that shown in Illustration E.
23. **With your teacher's permission,** print the **Forecast** and **PivotTable** worksheets.
24. Save your changes, close the workbook, and exit Excel.

Illustration D

Lemonade Sales Analysis

Day of Week	(All)

Sum of Glasses	Column Labels						
Row Labels	$ -	$ 0.10	$ 0.12	$ 0.20	$ 0.25	$ 0.30	Grand Total
Cloudy				31	32	2	65
Cool				13	12	1	26
Storms					0	1	1
Sunny				18	20		38
Hot						216	216
Hot						176	176
Sunny						40	40
Rainy	0	0	1	0			1
Cool							
Storms	0	0	1	0			1
Sunny					60	161	221
Cool						2	2
Hot						80	80
Sunny					60	79	139
Grand Total	**0**	**0**	**1**	**31**	**92**	**379**	**503**

Illustration E

Forecasted Sales

Day	Day of Week	Gross Profit	Advertising	Cost to Make Lemonade	Net Profit
1	Monday	$ 7.50	$ 0.50	$ 2.10	$ 4.90
2	Tuesday	$ 3.60	$ 0.50	$ 2.40	$ 0.70
3	Wednesday	$ 0.12	$ 0.25	$ 0.72	$ (0.85)
4	Thursday	$ -	$ -	$ 0.12	$ (0.12)
5	Friday	$ 0.60	$ 0.75	$ 4.80	$ (4.95)
6	Saturday	$ 6.00	$ 0.50	$ 1.40	$ 4.10
7	Sunday	$ 1.00	$ 0.50	$ 1.50	$ (1.00)
8	Monday	$ 9.00	$ 0.75	$ 3.00	$ 5.25
9	Tuesday	$ 7.50	$ 0.50	$ 2.00	$ 5.00
10	Wednesday	$ 5.00	$ 0.50	$ 2.00	$ 2.50
11	Thursday	$ 15.00	$ 0.75	$ 3.50	$ 10.75
12	Friday	$ -	$ 0.50	$ 3.50	$ (4.00)
13	Saturday	$ 0.30	$ 0.50	$ 1.20	$ (1.40)
14	Sunday	$ -	$ -	$ 0.50	$ (0.50)
15	Monday	$ 0.30	$ 0.75	$ 1.60	$ (2.05)
16	Tuesday	$ 13.80	$ 0.75	$ 5.40	$ 7.65
17	Wednesday	$ 7.50	$ 0.50	$ 4.25	$ 2.75
18	Thursday	$ 9.00	$ 0.75	$ 2.40	$ 5.85
19	Friday	$ 12.00	$ 0.75	$ 3.60	$ 7.65
20	Saturday	$ 2.00	$ 0.50	$ 1.80	$ (0.30)
21	Sunday	$ 12.00	$ 0.75	$ 2.40	$ 8.85
22	Monday	$ 2.60	$ 0.50	$ 1.40	$ 0.70
23	Tuesday	$ 12.00	$ 0.75	$ 4.40	$ 6.85
24	Wednesday	$ -	$ -	$ -	$ -
25	Thursday	$ -	$ 0.50	$ 1.50	$ (2.00)
26	Friday	$ -	$ -	$ 0.15	$ (0.15)
27	Saturday	$ 8.70	$ 0.75	$ 3.20	$ 4.75
28	Sunday	$ 7.50	$ 0.50	$ 4.00	$ 3.00
29	Monday	$ -	$ -	$ 0.48	$ (0.48)
30	Tuesday	$ -	$ -	$ -	$ -
31	Wednesday	$ 4.67	$ 0.47	$ 2.16	$ 2.04
32	Thursday	$ 4.68	$ 0.47	$ 2.18	$ 2.02
33	Friday	$ 4.69	$ 0.47	$ 2.17	$ 2.05
34	Saturday	$ 4.70	$ 0.47	$ 2.19	$ 2.04
35	Sunday	$ 4.70	$ 0.49	$ 2.23	$ 1.99
36	Monday	$ 4.71	$ 0.47	$ 2.10	$ 2.14
37	Tuesday	$ 4.71	$ 0.47	$ 2.14	$ 2.11
38	Wednesday	$ 4.72	$ 0.47	$ 2.13	$ 2.12
39	Thursday	$ 4.72	$ 0.46	$ 2.13	$ 2.13
40	Friday	$ 4.73	$ 0.46	$ 2.16	$ 2.10
41	Saturday	$ 4.73	$ 0.46	$ 2.17	$ 2.10
42	Sunday	$ 4.73	$ 0.47	$ 2.20	$ 2.06
43	Monday	$ 4.73	$ 0.46	$ 2.12	$ 2.15
44	Tuesday	$ 4.73	$ 0.45	$ 2.11	$ 2.17
45	Wednesday	$ 4.73	$ 0.46	$ 2.12	$ 2.15

Chapter 1

Getting Started with Access 2010

Lesson 1
Planning a Database
Projects 1-2

- Exploring Database Concepts
- Analyzing a Database Management System
- Analyzing Access Objects and Database Organization
- Understanding How Access Tables Are Related
- Planning Database Tables and Relationships
- Planning the Field Types

Lesson 2
Creating a Database with Access
Projects 3-4

- Starting Access and Creating a New Blank Database
- Exploring the Access Window
- Creating Table Fields in Datasheet View
- Saving, Closing, and Reopening a Table
- Creating Additional Tables
- Closing and Opening a Database
- Saving a Copy of a Database

Lesson 3
Modifying and Adding Data to a Table
Projects 5-6

- Adding Records
- Using Special Field Types
- Editing Records
- Selecting Records
- Deleting Records

Lesson 4
Modifying Fields in a Datasheet
Projects 7-8

- Changing Field Properties from Datasheet View
- Adding a Field
- Renaming a Field
- Moving a Column
- Hiding and Unhiding Columns
- Changing Datasheet Column Widths
- Freezing Columns

Lesson 5
Importing and Protecting Data
Projects 9-10

- Understanding Data Import Options
- Importing Data from Excel to an Existing Table
- Importing Data from Excel to a New Table
- Previewing and Printing a Table
- Opening a Database Exclusively
- Setting a Database Password
- Changing Database Properties

Lesson 6
Using Table Templates and Design View
Projects 11-12

- Creating a New Database Using a Template
- Creating a Table with a Template
- Changing the View of the Navigation Pane
- Opening a Table in Design View
- Creating a Table in Design View
- Setting a Primary Key
- Managing the Field List
- Changing a Field's Data Type
- Modifying a Field's Properties

Lesson 7
Creating Other Objects
Projects 13-14

- Using the Simple Query Wizard to Create a Query
- Creating a Quick Form
- Entering Records Using a Form
- Creating and Modifying a Quick Report
- Previewing and Printing a Report

End of Chapter Assessments
Projects 15-16

Lesson 1

Planning a Database

➤ What You Will Learn

Exploring Database Concepts
Analyzing a Database Management System
Analyzing Access Objects and Database Organization
Understanding How Access Tables Are Related
Planning Database Tables and Relationships
Planning the Field Types

Software Skills Before diving into the Access software, you should familiarize yourself with basic database concepts. This includes how Access stores data, how tables are related, and how support objects such as forms, queries, and reports interact with table data.

Application Skills You have been asked to help plan a database for a friend's new jewelry business. In this lesson, you will use paper and pencil to sketch out a database design for her, including the tables and fields she should include.

WORDS TO KNOW

Database
An organized collection of information about a subject.

Database management system
A computer program that includes both the stored database and the tools required to use the database.

Datasheet view
A spreadsheet-like view of a table in which each record is a row and each field is a column.

Field
A piece of data stored about each record in a table. For example, ZIP Code is a field in an address book.

Form
A view of a table or query's data, designed for lookup or input of records.

Primary key
The field that uniquely identifies each record in a table.

Object
An item in an Access database, such as a table, query, form, or report.

Query
A specification that describes how a set of records should be sorted, filtered, calculated, or presented.

Record
The stored information about one particular instance, such as one person's data in an address book.

What You Can Do

Exploring Database Concepts

- A **database** is an organized collection of information about a subject.
- Examples of databases include a recipe card file, the telephone book, a list of tracks on your portable music player, or a filing cabinet full of documents relating to clients.
- A name, address, and phone listing in an address book is an example of a **record** in a common paper database. To update an address of a friend in Denver, you would search for the name, erase or cross out the existing address, and write in the new address.

Figure 1-1

Some examples of database records

Name: Jim Ferrara
Address: 84 Winthrop Road
City: Denver
State: CO
ZIP: 80209
Telephone: 303-555-5576
Note: Note new address and phone number

Part Number: 001759
Part Description: Socket wrench
Cost: $3.50
List price: $14.99
Date received: 2/23/11

- While updating one or two addresses in a paper database may not take a lot of effort, searching for all friends in one city or sorting all clients who have done business with you in the last month would take considerable effort.
- Many people prefer to store their databases on computers to make them easier to find and update.

Analyzing a Database Management System

- A **database management system** includes both the database information and the tools to use the database. These tools allow you to input, edit, and verify your data.
- Microsoft Office Access is a popular personal computer database management system. Access makes it easy to organize and update information electronically.
- An Access database file can contain several types of objects, including **tables**, **forms**, **queries**, and **reports**. Each Access database file is stored with an .accdb extension for Access 2007 and 2010 format files, or an .mdb extension for Access 2003 and earlier versions.
- With Access, you can sort, find, analyze, and report on information in your database. For example, in a sales management database you can find all clients who bought a mountain bike in the last year and create mailing labels in order to send them an announcement of a new bike trails book.
- You can share data created in Access with other Microsoft Office applications, especially Word and Excel.

WORDS TO KNOW

Relational database
A database that contains (or can contain) multiple tables with relationships between them.

Report
A printable layout of the data from a table or query.

Table
A collection of records that share the same fields.

Analyzing Access Objects and Database Organization

- The four main types of objects are tables, queries, forms, and reports. Two additional types, macros and modules, are not covered in this book.
- All Access database information is stored in tables. Each table contains information about a particular topic. For example, a sales inventory database may have separate tables for clients, products, and sales.
- Each row of an Access table is a record. A record is a set of details about a specific item. For example, a record for a client may contain the client's name, address, and phone number. A record about a product could include the part number, serial number, and price.
- Each column of an Access table is a **field**. Fields provide the categories for the details describing each record. In the client example above, there would be separate fields for name, address, and phone number. Each column is headed by a field name.
- The most common way to look at a table in Access is in **Datasheet view**. In Datasheet view, the table appears in a spreadsheet-like row and column format, with each row representing a record and each column representing a field.

Figure 1-2

Tables store information in rows and columns

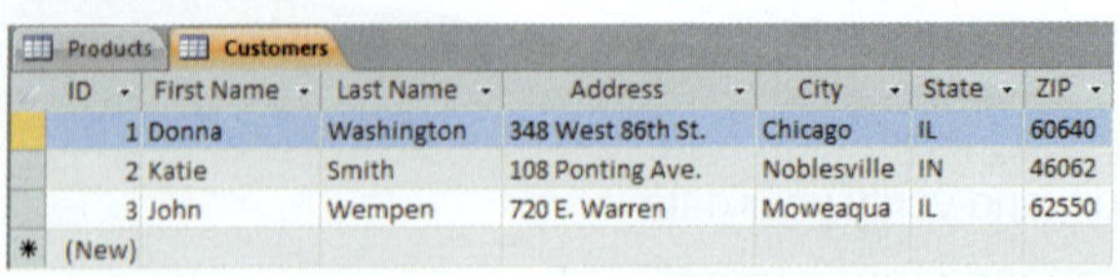

- A form is a window for viewing the data in one or more tables. Forms make it easy to view, input, and edit data because forms typically show all the information for one record on a single page.
- A query allows you to see or work with a portion of a table by limiting the number of fields and by selecting specific records. For example, you might want to see only the name, city, state, and ZIP of customers who live in Illinois.

Figure 1-3

Forms provide a friendly interface for data entry and lookup

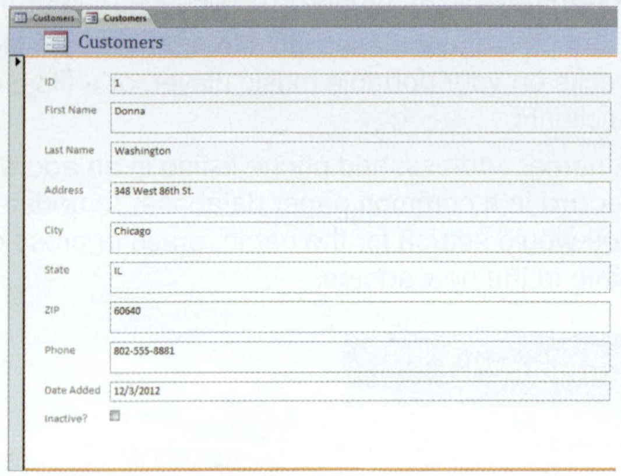

Figure 1-4

Queries sort, filter, and summarize data

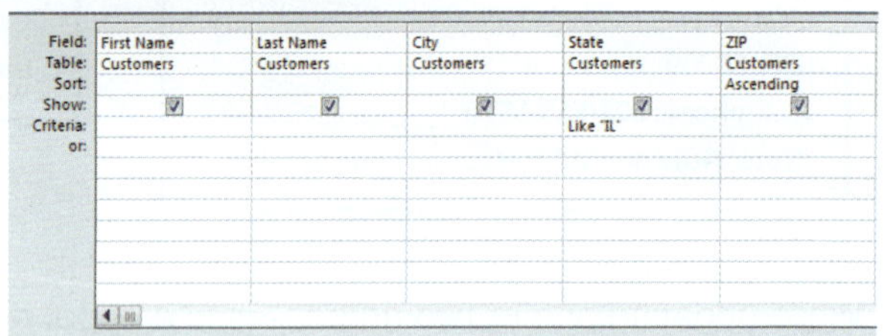

A report is formatted information from a table or query that you can send to a printer. Reports can include a detailed list of records, calculated values, and totals from the records, mailing labels, or a chart summarizing the data.

Figure 1-5

Reports provide attractive printable views of table or query data

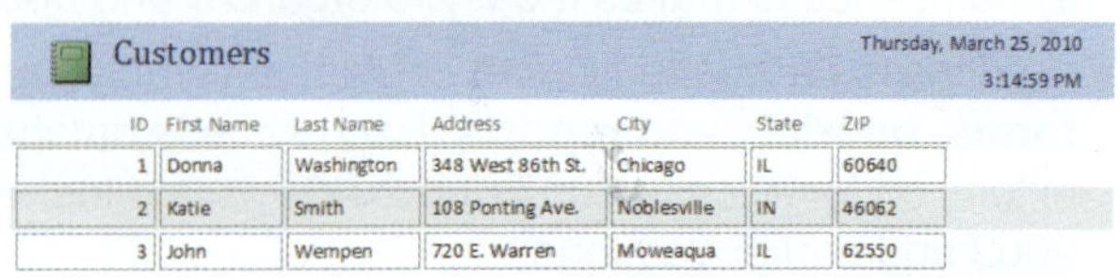

Understanding How Access Tables Are Related

- Database tables that share common fields are related. Most Access databases have multiple tables that are related to each other, which means you can use Access to create a **relational database**.

- A relational database breaks the "big picture" into smaller, more manageable pieces. For example, if you were gathering information about a new product line, each type of information—product, suppliers, customers—would be stored in its own, related table rather than in one large, all-inclusive table.
- You relate one table to another through a common field. For example, for a retail business's database, the Order Details table will have a Product field that also appears in the Products table.

Figure 1-6

Relationships between tables allow you to pull data from multiple tables for queries, reports, and forms

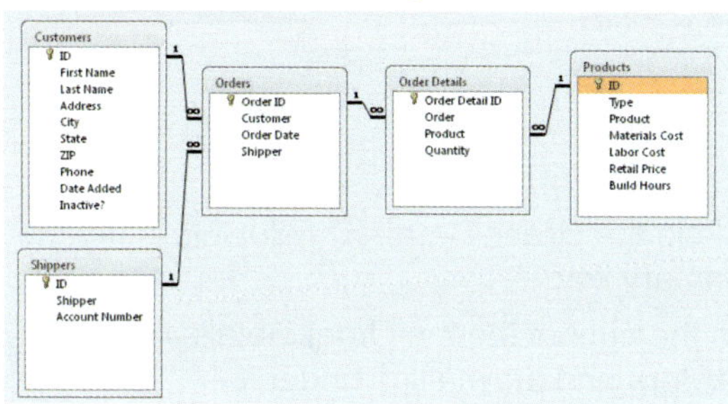

- This capability to store data in smaller, related tables gives a relational database great efficiency, speed, and flexibility in locating and reporting information.

Planning Database Tables and Relationships

- Before you create a database, you must decide which fields you want to include and if you need a single table or more than one. Consider what information the database will store and how the information will be used.
- To begin, make a list of the fields you want to store in your database, such as last name, first name, address, phone, and so on.
- Think about the ways you will want to search or sort the data, and plan the fields to support them. For example, if you want to sort by last name, make sure you have separate fields for first and last names. The same goes for city, state, and postal code.
- As you are listing the fields to include, group them according to their purpose. For example, you might have fields for information about your products, fields for information about your customers, and so on. Each of those groups will form a separate table in your database.
- Having multiple tables helps avoid needless repetition, which is not only tedious for data entry people but also potentially introduces errors. For example, you might want to store customer and order information separately so that you don't have to repeat a customer's mailing address every time he or she places an order.
- Each table should have a field in which each record will be unique, such as an ID number field. This field will be the table's **primary key**.
- Plan the relationships between your tables. Make sure that tables to be related have a common field. For example, the ID field in a Customers table might link to the Customer ID field in the Orders table.

  ✓ *Relationships between tables are covered more thoroughly in Chapter 2, Lesson 8.*

- When you've finished identifying fields and tables, you are ready to create your new database file and create the tables within it.

Try It! Planning a Pets and Owners Database

1. On a blank sheet of paper, write **Pets** and draw a line under it.
2. Under the line, write all the fields that you might need for a table that stores information about pets. The first field should be a **Pet ID** field. Make sure you include an **Owner** field somewhere in the list.
3. Write **Owners** next to **Pets** and draw a line under it.
4. Under the line, write all the fields that you might need for a table that stores information about pet owners. The first field should be an **Owner ID** field.
5. Draw a line to connect the Owner ID field from the Owners table to the Owner field in the Pets table.

Planning the Field Types

- Each field will have a field type in Access, which determines what types of values will be stored in it. Some common field types are Number, Text, and Date/Time.
- In general, any fields that will hold alphabetic text should have the Text type. This includes fields that may contain a mixture of letters, numbers, and symbols. Memo and Hyperlink fields are considered text, too.
- Phone numbers and ZIP codes are usually set up as Text fields, because the numbers they contain will never be used for calculations.
- A Yes/No field is a logical field that has only two possible values. You would use it in situations where every record is one or the other, such as Male/Female, Married/Unmarried, or Active/Not Active.

✓ *When there is a relationship between fields, the fields must have the same type. For example, in the preceding Try It example, the Owner ID field will be a Number type, so the Owner field in the Pets table must be a Number type also. The pet owner will be referred to in the Pets table by his or her ID number, rather than by a first and last name. This ensures that there is no confusion if several people have the same name.*

Project 1—Create It

Jewelry Business Database

DIRECTIONS

1. Start with a blank sheet of paper. Turn it sideways, so you are writing across the wide edge, and write your name in the upper-right corner.
2. In the upper-left corner, write **Products** and draw a line under it.
3. Under the line, write this list of fields to include in a **Products** table:

   Product ID

   Type

   Name

   Materials Cost

   Labor Cost

   Retail Price

   Build Hours
4. Circle the **Product ID** field; this is the table's primary key.
5. To the right of the Products list, write **Order Details** and draw a line under it.
6. Under the line, write this list of fields to include in an **Order Details** table:

   Order Detail ID

   Order

   Product

   Quantity
7. Circle the **Order Detail ID** field; this is the table's primary key.
8. To the right of the the Order Details list, write **Orders** and draw a line under it.
9. Under the line, write this list of fields to include in an **Orders** table:

   Order ID

   Order Date

   Customer ID

   Salesperson

   Shipper
10. Circle the **Order ID** field; this is the table's primary key.
11. Draw a straight line between the **Order ID** field in the **Orders** table and the **Order** field in the **Order Details** table. This represents a relationship.

    ✓ *Notice that this relationship involves the primary key in one table and a field that is not the primary key in another table. This is typical of most relationships in Access.*
12. Draw a straight line between the **Product ID** field in the **Products** table and the **Product** field in the **Order Details** table. This represents another relationship.
13. If your teacher requests it, turn in the database planning sheet you have created.

Project 2—Apply It

Jewelry Business Database

DIRECTIONS

1. Complete Project 1, or open and print the file **AProj02.pdf.** from the data files for this lesson, and write your name at the top of the page. (You will be working on paper for this project.) Write your name at the top of the page.
2. On the paper, fill in a list of fields you want to include in the **Shippers** table.

   Suppose you were an employee of the company, shipping an order to a customer. What information would you need about the shipping company you were going to use (such as FedEx, UPS, or the U.S. Postal Service)?

   ✓ *At a minimum you should include Shipper Name and Account Number.*

3. On the paper, fill in a list of fields you want to include in the **Employees** table:

   Think about what information about an employee would be needed in the process of fulfilling a customer's order.

   Besides the person's first and last names, you may want to include his or her position in the company.

   This is not a Human Resources database, so you do not need to include contact information for each employee (such as mailing address or phone number). However, you might want to include a field that contains some way to contact that employee, in case there are questions.

4. On the paper, fill in a list of fields you want to include in the **Customers** table.

   Think about what information you would need to gather about a customer in order to complete an order. For example, you need a name, mailing address, and at least one way to contact the customer if there is a problem with the order.

   You may also want to include an e-mail address for sending an order confirmation. If you plan to address the customer with a prefix, such as Mr. or Ms., make sure you include a field for that, too.

5. Circle the primary key fields in the **Customers**, **Employees**, and **Shippers** tables.
6. Draw lines between the primary key fields in the **Customers**, **Employees**, and **Shippers** tables and the corresponding fields in the **Orders** table.
7. Write **Auto** to the right of each primary key field.
8. Write **Number** to the right of each field that is connected via a line to one of the primary key fields.
9. Write the appropriate field type next to each of the remaining fields in each table. Choose from this list:
   - Text
   - Number
   - Date/Time
   - Currency
   - Yes/No
   - Hyperlink

   ✓ *The Account Number field for a shipper should be set to Text because some account numbers may contain letters.*

   ✓ *Use the Hyperlink type for e-mail addresses and Web sites.*

10. If your teacher requests it, turn in the database planning sheet you have created.

Lesson 2

Creating a Database with Access

WORDS TO KNOW

Extension
A suffix at the end of a file name that indicates its type, such as .accdb.

Object
An item, such as a table, query, form, or report, in an Access database file that is used to store, display, or manage data.

➤ What You Will Learn

Starting Access and Creating a New Blank Database
Exploring the Access Window
Creating Table Fields in Datasheet View
Saving, Closing, and Reopening a Table
Creating Additional Tables
Closing and Opening a Database
Saving a Copy of a Database

Software Skills You can create a new database in Access, and then add tables to it containing any fields you like. When you finish, you can close and save the design changes to the table. A database file contains multiple objects such as tables, all stored under a single file name. That file can be opened or closed as well.

Application Skills You have been asked to start a database for a friend's new jewelry business. In this lesson, you will start a new blank database file and populate it with two tables: one for customers and one for products.

What You Can Do

Starting Access and Creating a New Blank Database

- The database file contains all Access **objects**, including tables, forms, queries, and reports. Each database file is stored with an .accdb **extension** for Access 2007 and 2010 format files, or an .mdb extension for Access 2003 and earlier versions.
- You must create a database file, or open an existing one, before you can enter any data or create any objects (such as tables or queries).
- If creating a new database, you can start from scratch with a blank one, or you can start with a template that contains one or more database objects already.
  - ✓ *You will learn how to create a database from a template in Chapter 1, Lesson 6.*

Try It! Starting Access and Creating a New Database

1. Click Start > All Programs > Microsoft Office > Microsoft Access 2010.
2. In the File Name box, type **ATry02_studentfirstname_studentlastname**.
3. If necessary, click the Browse button to browse to the location where your teacher instructs you to store the files for this lesson, and click OK.
4. Click Create.
5. Leave the **ATry02_studentfirstname_studentlastname** database open to use in the next Try It.

Create a new database

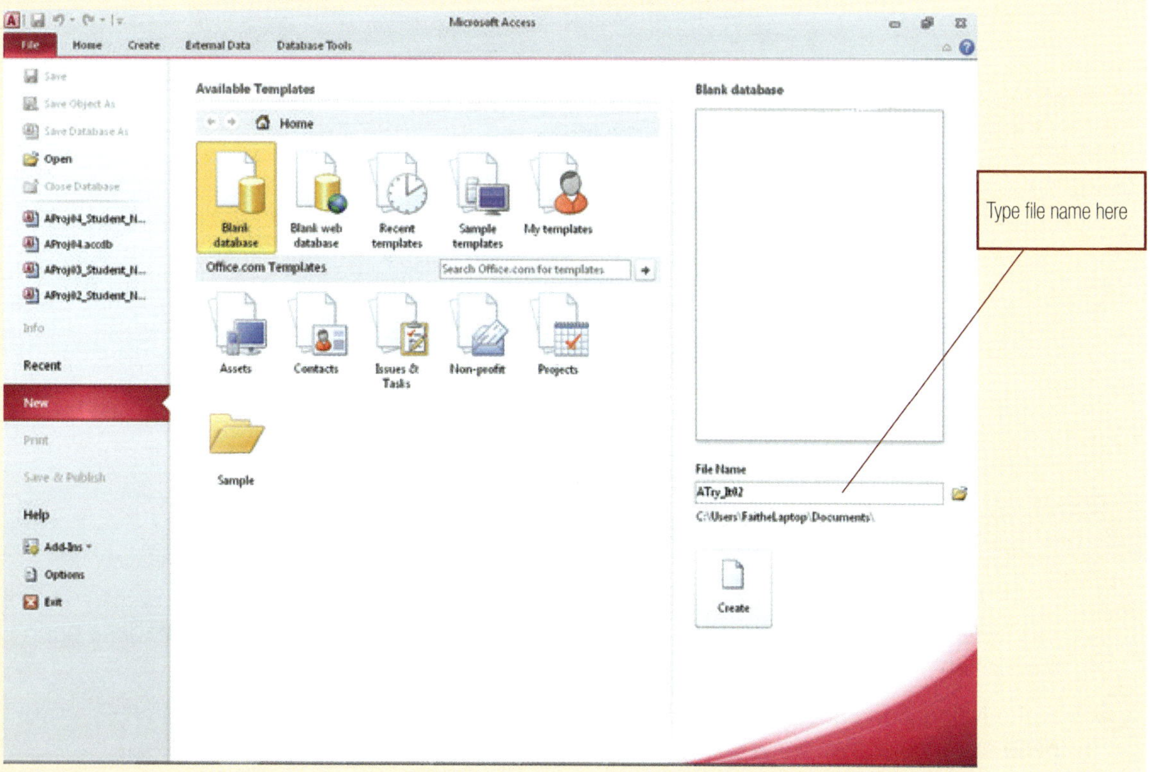

Exploring the Access Window

- After creating a new blank database, the main Access window appears and a new blank table opens.
- Across the top is the Ribbon, and the status bar is at the bottom, just like in other Office applications.
- At the left is the Navigation pane. By default, it shows all Access objects grouped by type. An object is a table, query, report, form, or other item used to store, display, or manage Access data. You can collapse the Navigation pane to save space onscreen and then expand it when you need it again.
- In the center is the open object—in this case a blank table in Datasheet view. Each open object has a tab that shows its name. The name is Table 1 for now because you have not yet saved it and given it a more descriptive name.
- At the right a field list may appear, but it is empty at this point. You can close the field list (if it appears) to make more room to work with the table.

Access opens a new table when you create a new blank database

Figure 2-1

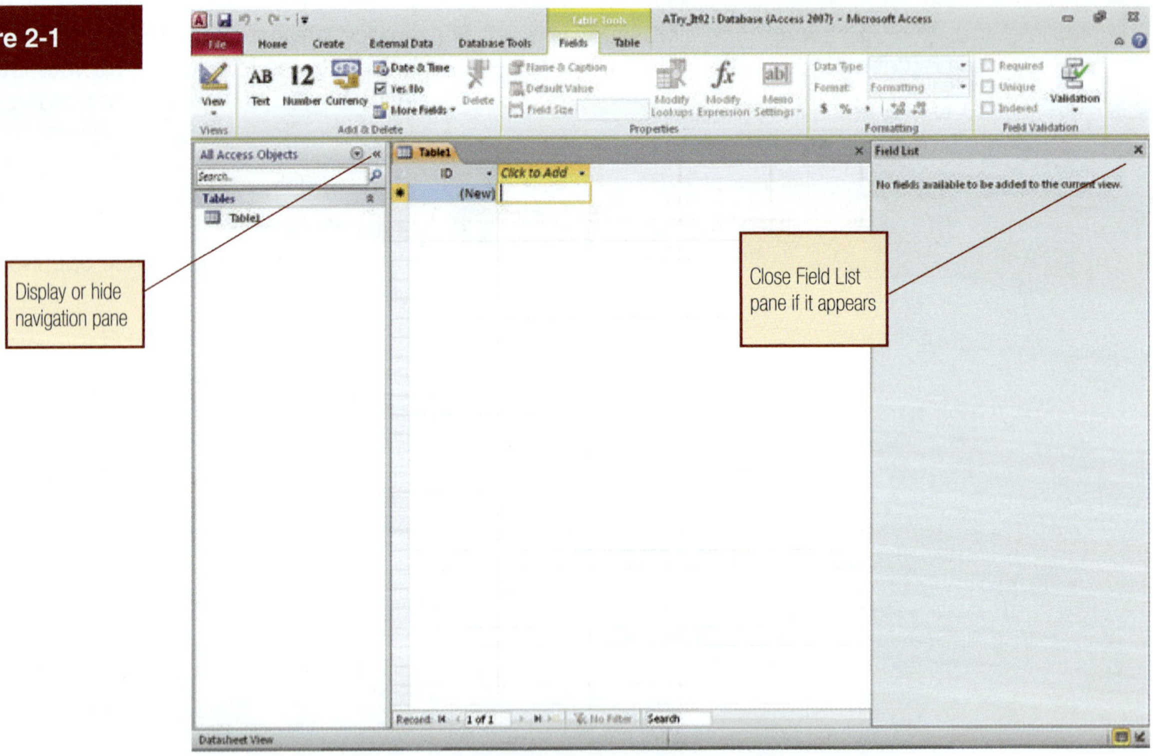

Try It! Collapsing and Expanding the Navigation Pane

1. In the ATry02_studentfirstname_studentlastname database, click « in the Navigation pane. The Navigation pane collapses.
2. In the Navigation pane, click ». The Navigation pane expands again.
3. Leave the ATry02_studentfirstname_studentlastname database open to use in the next Try It.

Try It! Closing and Reopening the Field List

1. In the **ATry02_studentfirstname_studentlastname** database, click the Close ☒ button on the Field List. The field list closes.
2. Press ALT + F8. The field list reopens.
3. Leave the **ATry02_studentfirstname_studentlastname** database open to use in the next Try It.

Creating Table Fields in Datasheet View

- Access enables you to create table fields in either Datasheet or Design view. This lesson shows you how to do it in Datasheet view (the easiest method).

  ✓ *You will learn how to create Design view in Chapter 1, Lesson 6.*

- When creating field names, try whenever possible to use concise, descriptive names.
- An ID field is created automatically by default for each table created in Datasheet view. This field is set to be unique and automatically numbered for each record.

Try It! Creating a Field in a Datasheet

1. In the **ATry02_studentfirstname_studentlastname** database, in the open datasheet, click *Click to Add*.
2. Click Text on the menu of field types.
3. Type **First Name**.
4. Press ENTER.
5. Leave the **ATry02_studentfirstname_studentlastname** database open to use in the next Try It.

Add a field

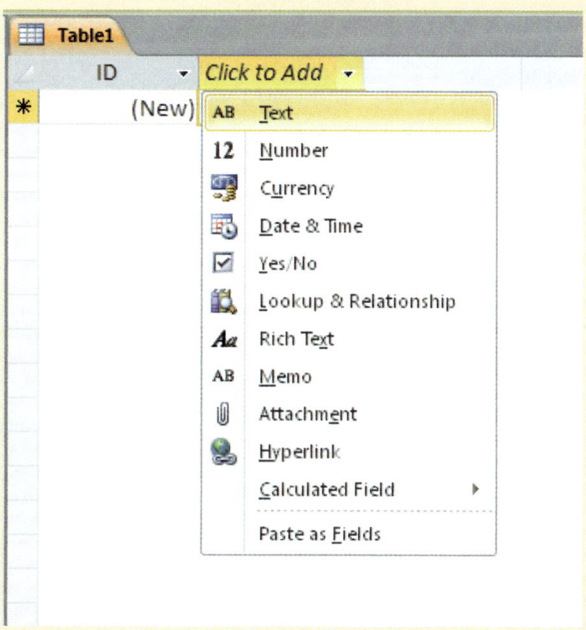

Saving, Closing, and Reopening a Table

- When you are finished creating the fields in the table, you should save your work.
- When you close a table, you are prompted to save if you have made any structural modifications to it. This includes adding and removing fields as well as changing field properties.
- Saving is necessary only when making changes to the table's structure; any records you enter in the table (covered in Lesson 3) are saved automatically.

Try It! Saving and Closing a Table

1. In the **ATry02_studentfirstname_studentlastname** database, right-click the Table1 tab and click Close, or click the Close button ☒ in the upper right corner of the Table1 datasheet.
2. Click Yes.
3. Type **Address Book**.
4. Click OK.
5. Leave the **ATry02_studentfirstname_studentlastname** database open to use in the next Try It.

Try It! Opening a Table

1. In the **ATry02_studentfirstname_studentlastname** database, click » to expand the Navigation pane if it is collapsed.
2. Double-click the **Address Book** table in the Navigation pane.
3. Leave the **ATry02_studentfirstname_studentlastname** database open to use in the next Try It.

Open a table from the Navigation pane

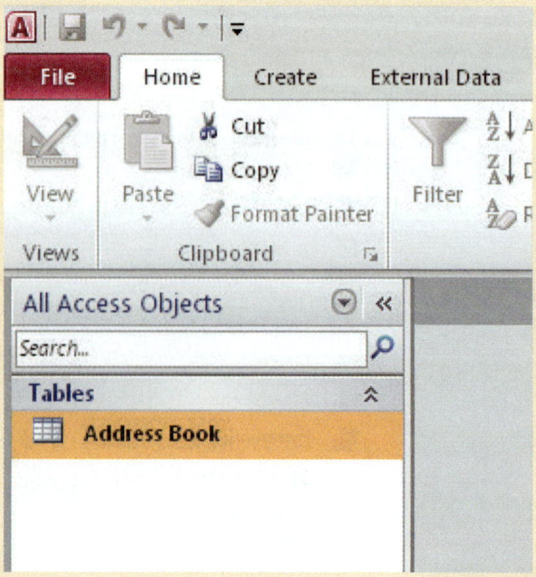

Creating Additional Tables

- Many databases have more than one table. As you learned in Lesson 1, having multiple tables and connecting them together using relationships helps reduce or eliminate redundancy in a database and reduces the likelihood of data entry errors.

Try It! Creating Additional Tables

1. In the ATry02_studentfirstname_studentlastname database, on the Create tab, click Table.
2. On the Fields tab, click Text AB. A new field appears, ready to be named.
3. Type **Event** and press ENTER. The field type list appears for the next field to be created.
4. On the field type list, click Number 12.
5. Type **Attendees** and press ENTER.
6. Click the Save button on the Quick Access Toolbar.
7. Type **Events**.
8. Click OK.
9. Leave the ATry02_studentfirstname_studentlastname database open to use in the next Try It.

Closing and Opening a Database

- When you exit Access, you automatically close the open database and save your changes to it. You can also choose to close a database without exiting Access.
- Opening a different database closes the open one; you can have only one database open at once.
- Opening a database file is much like opening any other file in an Office application. You can either choose a recently used database from the File, Recent menu, or click File > Open to select from the Open dialog box.

Try It! Closing a Database

1. In the ATry02_studentfirstname_studentlastname database, click File > Close Database. The File menu remains open.

Try It! Opening a Database from the Recent List

1. In the File menu is not already open, open it.
2. Click Recent.
3. Click ATry01.

Try It! Opening a Database with the Open Dialog Box

1. If the **ATry02_studentfirstname_studentlastname** database is open, close it.
2. Click File > Open.
3. If needed, navigate to a different location.
4. In the Open dialog box, click **ATry02_studentfirstname_studentlastname**.
5. Click Open.
6. Leave the **ATry02_studentfirstname_studentlastname** database open to use in the next Try It.

Saving a Copy of a Database

- Many of the projects in this section of the textbook begin with you opening a database file and then saving it under a different name. To do this, you must be able to save a copy of a database.
- After saving a copy of a database, the copy opens and the original closes.

  ✓ *Depending on the location you save the copy to, certain features may be disabled. If you see an information bar with an Enable Content button, click the Enable Content button.*

Figure 2-2

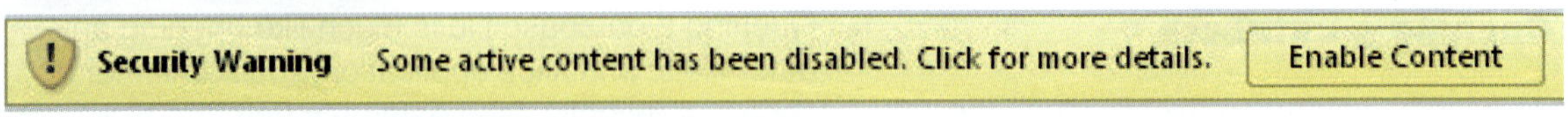

Try It! Saving a Copy of a Database

1. In the **ATry02_studentfirstname_studentlastname** database, Click File > Save Database As. The Save As dialog box opens.
2. If necessary, navigate to the location where your teacher instructs you to store the files for this lesson.
3. In the File Name box, type **ATry02_studentfirstname_studentlastname-copy**.
4. Click Save.
5. If the information bar appears, click Enable Content.
6. Click File > Exit to exit Access.

Project 3—Create It

Jewelry Business Database

DIRECTIONS

1. Click **Start > All Programs > Microsoft Office > Microsoft Access 2010**.
2. In the File Name box, type **AProj03_ studentfirstname_studentlastname** with your own first and last name substituted.
3. Click the **Browse** icon to the right of the box, browse to the location where your teacher instructs you to store the files for this lesson, and click OK.
4. Click **Create**. A new blank table opens.
5. Click **Click to Add**. A list of field types appears, as shown in Figure 2-3.
6. Click **Text**.
7. Type **First Name** and press ENTER.
8. Right-click the **Table1** tab and click **Close**.
9. When asked if you want to save, click **Yes**.
10. Type **Customers**, as shown in Figure 2-4, and press ENTER.
11. On the **Create** tab, click **Table**. A new table opens.
12. On the **Fields** tab, click **Text** AB. A new text field appears.
13. Type **Type**, and press ENTER. A list of field types appears for the next new field.
14. Click the **Close** button in the upper-right corner of the datasheet.
15. When asked if you want to save, click **Yes**.
16. Type **Products**, and press ENTER.
17. Click **File > Close Database** to close the database.

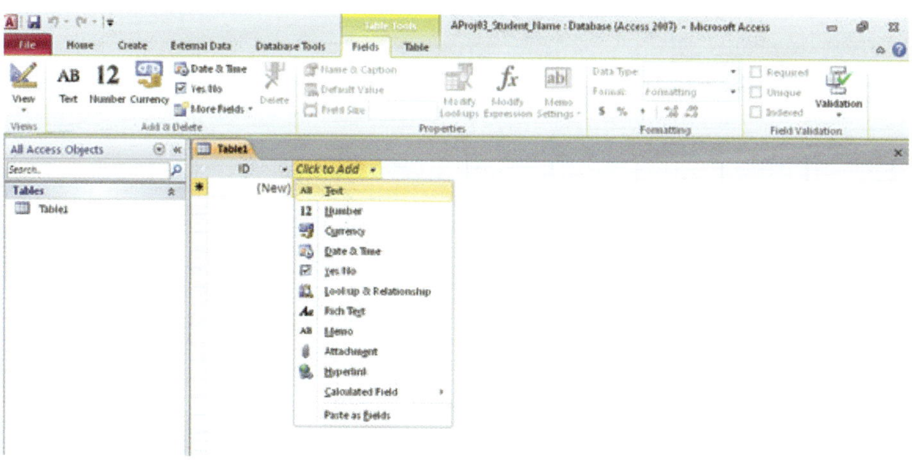

Figure 2-3

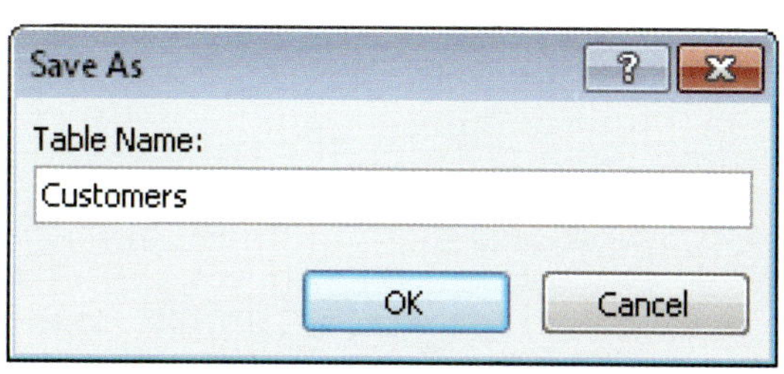

Figure 2-4

Project 4—Apply It

Jewelry Business Database

DIRECTIONS

1. Start Access, if necessary.
2. Open **AProj04** from the data files for this lesson.
3. Save the database as **AProj04_ studentfirstname_studentlastname** with your own first and last name substituted.
4. Open the Navigation pane if it is hidden, and enable active content if it is blocked.
5. Open the Customers table in Datasheet view and enter the following additional fields, in the order listed:

Field	Type
Date Added	Date & Time
Inactive?	Yes/No

6. Close the **Customer** table.
7. Open the **Products** table in Datasheet view and enter the following additional fields, in the order listed:

Field	Type
Product	Text
Materials Cost	Currency
Labor Cost	Currency
Retail Price	Currency
Build Hours	Number

8. Close the **Products** table.
9. Close the database and, if instructed, submit it to your teacher for grading.

Lesson 3

Modifying and Adding Data to a Table

➤ What You Will Learn

- Adding Records
- Using Special Field Types
- Editing Records
- Selecting Records
- Deleting Records

WORDS TO KNOW

Multi-valued field
A field that can contain more than one separate entry per record.

Software Skills After creating a table, the next step is to enter records into it. This data entry forms the basis of your database.

Application Skills You will enter records for products and customers into your friend's jewelry business database. You also will make edits to existing records.

What You Can Do

Adding Records

- When you enter records, they are stored in a table. A table is the only object type that can hold records. Most of the other types of objects are simply ways of looking at the data from one or more tables.
- To enter records in a datasheet, type the information you want in a field and press TAB or ENTER to go to the next field. To skip a field, Tab past it or click to move the insertion point to a different field.
- When you enter data in the last field for a record, pressing TAB or ENTER moves the cursor to first field of the next record. If you are at the last record of the table, this will automatically create a new record.
- Unlike other Microsoft Office applications where you have to choose the Save command, Access automatically saves a record when you go to another record.

Try It! Adding Records to a Table

1. Open the **ATry03** database from the data files for this lesson. Save it as **ATry03_studentfirstname_studentlastname**. Click Enable Content if necessary any time you see a security warning.
2. Double-click the Events table. It opens in Datasheet view.
3. Press TAB to move past the ID field. It is auto-numbered.
4. Type **Paws for a Cause** and press TAB.
5. In the Sponsor column, type **Hamilton County Humane Society** and press TAB.
6. In the Location column, type **Hamilton County Humane Society** and press TAB.
7. In the Attendees column, type **200** and press TAB.
8. Press TAB to move past the Contact field without entering data.
9. Right-click the Events tab and click Close.
10. Leave the **ATry03_studentfirstname_studentlastname** database open to use in the next Try It.

Using Special Field Types

- Depending on the way the database is set up, some fields may not be simple text boxes; instead they may be drop-down lists or check boxes.
- A check box appears in a logical (yes/no) field. Mark the check box by clicking it to choose Yes, or leave it cleared to choose No.
- A field with a drop-down list will have a down arrow to its right when selected. Click that arrow to open a menu, and then click your selection from the menu.
- Some drop-down list fields are **multi-valued fields**; you can mark or clear any or all of the check boxes on the list.
- A field that is set up for hyperlinks accepts either Web addresses (http://) or e-mail addresses. If you enter an e-mail address, you must precede the address with mailto. For example, mailto:fwempen@wholegrainsbread.com.

Try It! Using Special Field Types

1. In the **ATry03_studentfirstname_ studentlastname** database, double-click Address Book to open that table's datasheet.
2. In the first record, click in the State field, and then click the down arrow.
3. Click IN on the drop-down list.
4. Click in the E-mail field.
5. Type **tom@sycamoreknoll.com**, and press TAB to move to the next field.
6. Click the down arrow in the Special Needs field.
7. Mark the Handicap Parking and Wheelchair access check boxes and click OK.

   ✓ *It is important to click OK after making selections; otherwise the changes will not be saved.*
8. In the Inactive field, mark the check box.
9. Right-click the Address Book tab and click Close.
10. Leave the **ATry03_studentfirstname_ studentlastname** database open to use in the next Try It.

Select values for a multi-valued field

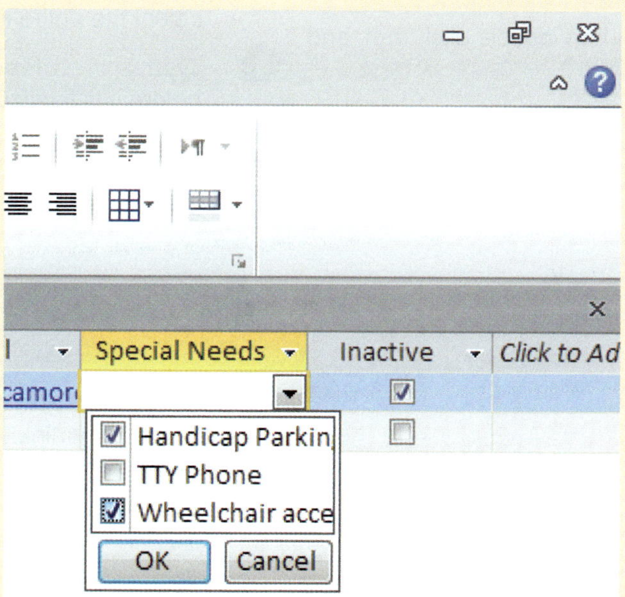

Editing Records

- You may want to correct field information after you enter it. You can delete and add text in the same way you would in Word or Excel. Click to position the insertion point.
- While you are making changes to a record, a pencil icon appears on the record selector button (to the left of the record). The pencil indicates that any changes are not currently saved.
- Press BACKSPACE to remove text before the insertion point or press DEL to remove text after the insertion point. You can also drag the mouse pointer to select text and then press DEL to remove the text.
- Select text and type new text to replace the selected text. You can double-click on a word to select a word, then type to replace it.
- If you move the mouse pointer to the beginning of a field, the pointer changes to a white plus sign. Click to select the entire content of that field.
- If you want to undo your changes, press ESC once to undo the change to the current field and press ESC again to undo all changes to the current record.
- Changes are automatically saved to the record when you go to another record or close the table or form.

Try It! Editing Field Data

1. In the **ATry03_studentfirstname_ studentlastname** database, double-click Address Book to open that table's datasheet.
2. In the First Name column, double-click Tom, and type **Thomas** to replace it.
3. In the Address column, click to move the insertion point after the "a" in Wander. Press BACKSPACE once and type **o**.
4. In the Last Name column, position the mouse pointer to the upper-left part of the field so you see a large white plus sign, and then click to select the entire field.
5. Type **Jones**. Press ESC to cancel the change before it is finalized.
6. Leave the **ATry03_studentfirstname_ studentlastname** database open to use in the next Try It.

Editing a Hyperlink

- A hyperlink field such as an e-mail address activates an e-mail or Web application when clicked on; therefore you cannot edit it normally.
- One way to edit it is to delete it and retype it. To delete it, select it and press DEL.
- To edit it, right-click it and point to Hyperlink, then click Edit Hyperlink. An Edit Hyperlink box appears in which you can edit the address.

✓ *When you edit the hyperlink in the Edit Hyperlink dialog box, you make the change in two places. The Text to Display box content determines what will appear in the datasheet, and the E-mail Address box content determines where the hyperlink will go when clicked. Changing the Text to Display is not required, but it may cause confusion if it is different than the actual hyperlink.*

Try It! Editing a Hyperlink

1. In the **ATry03_studentfirstname_studentlastname** database, with the Address Book table open in Datasheet view, right-click the e-mail address.
2. Point to Hyperlink, and click Edit Hyperlink.
3. In the Text to display box, change the e-mail address to **thomas@sycamoreknoll.com**.
4. In the E-mail address box, change the e-mail address to **thomas@sycamoreknoll.com**.

   ✓ *Do not remove the mailto: portion of the entry.*

5. Click OK.
6. Right-click the Address Book tab and click Close.
7. Leave the **ATry03_studentfirstname_studentlastname** database open to use in the next Try It.

Create an e-mail hyperlink

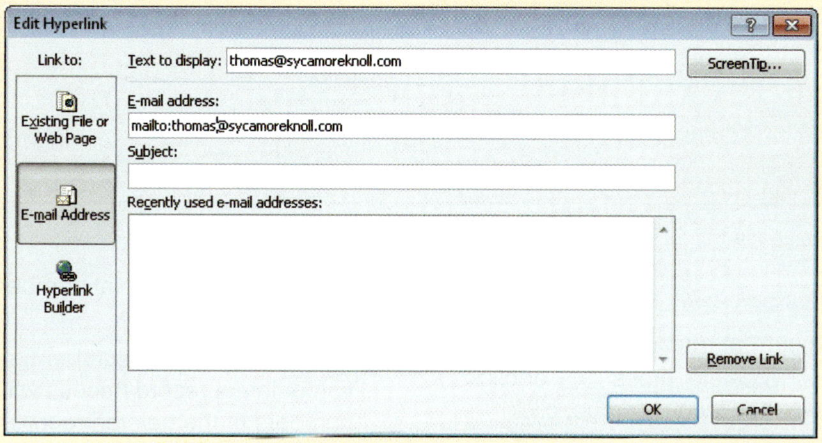

Selecting Records

- To select a single record, click the record selector button to its left.
- To select multiple contiguous (adjacent) records, select the first one and then hold down Shift as you click the record selector of the last one.
- Press CTRL + A to select all records in the entire table.

Try It! Selecting Records

1. In the **ATry03_studentfirstname_studentlastname** database, double-click the States table to open its datasheet.
2. Click the record selector for the AR record.

Select a record by clicking its record selector

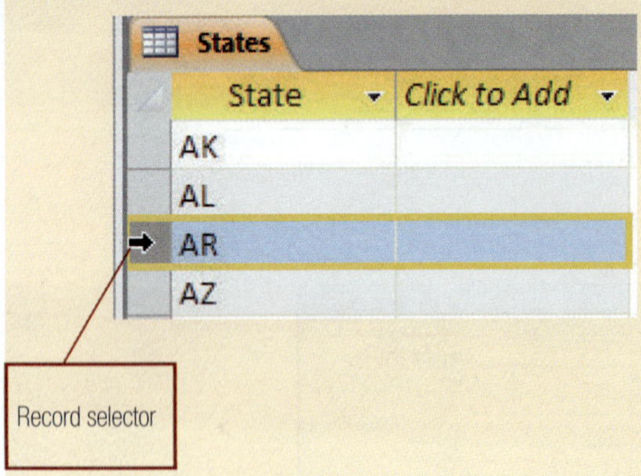

3. Hold down the SHIFT key and click the record selector for the MA record.
4. Release the SHIFT key.
5. Click any record to cancel the selection.
6. Press CTRL + A to select all records.
7. Click any record to cancel the selection.
8. Right-click the States tab and click Close to close the datasheet.
9. Leave the **ATry03_studentfirstname_studentlastname** database open to use in the next Try It.

Deleting Records

- You can delete the current record or one or more contiguous records. To delete, press DEL or click the Home tab and in the Records group, click Delete.
- When you delete one or more records, Access will ask you to confirm the deletion. After you click Yes, you cannot reverse the deletion.
- Access shows the total number of records at the bottom of the window.
- If you have an AutoNumber field in the table, when you delete a record Access will not reuse the numbers of the deleted records.

Try It! Deleting Records

1. In the **ATry03_studentfirstname_studentlastname** database, double-click the Address Book table to open its datasheet.
2. Click the record selector for the first (and only) record.
3. Press DEL.
4. Click Yes to confirm.
5. Click File > Exit to exit Access.

Project 5—Create It

Jewelry Business Database

DIRECTIONS

1. Start Access, if necessary.
2. Open **AProj05** from the data files for this lesson. If a security warning bar appears, click **Enable Content**.
3. Save the database as **AProj05_studentfirstname_studentlastname** to the location where your teacher instructs you to store the files for this lesson.
4. Double-click the **Customers** table in the navigation pane to open it in Datasheet view.
5. Press [TAB] to move past the **ID** field. (It is automatically filled in.)

   ✓ *It is okay that the number in the ID column is something other than 1. Every time this file is used for this exercise, the number increments because Access never reuses an automatically assigned number. In a table where it is important to be able to control the numbers assigned as ID numbers, you would set the field type to Number rather than AutoNumber for the ID field.*

6. In the **First Name** field, type **Ann** and press [TAB].
7. In the **Last Name** field, type **Brown** and press [TAB].
8. In the **Address** field, type **108 Ponting Street** and press [TAB].
9. In the **City** field, type **Macon** and press [TAB].
10. In the **State** field, type **IL** and press [TAB].
11. In the **ZIP** field, type **62544** and press [TAB].
12. In the **Phone** field, type **317-555-8281** and press [TAB].
13. In the **Date Added** field, type today's date in this format: **10/15/2012**. Press [TAB]. Your entry should look like Figure 3-1.
14. Press [TAB] to skip the Inactive check box without marking it.
15. Press [TAB] again to move the cursor to the next row.
16. Double-click the name in the **First Name** field (*Ann*) and type **Jennifer**.
17. Double-click the name in the **City** field (*Macon*) and type **Decatur**.
18. Click at the end of the current entry in the **ZIP** field to move the insertion point there.
19. Press [BACKSPACE] twice.
20. Type **22**, changing the entry to read **62522**.
21. Right-click the **Customers** tab and click **Close**.
22. Close the database and, if instructed, submit it to your teacher for grading.

Figure 3-1

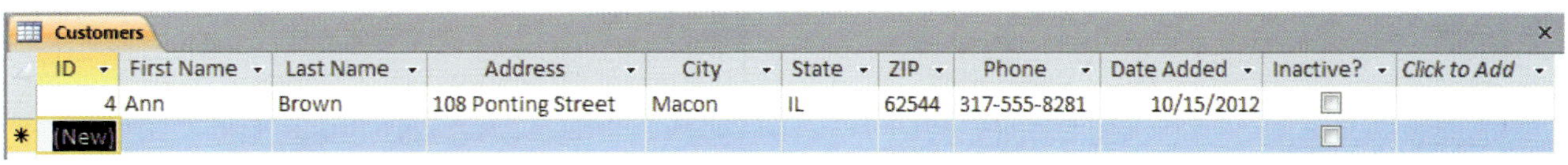

Figure 3-2

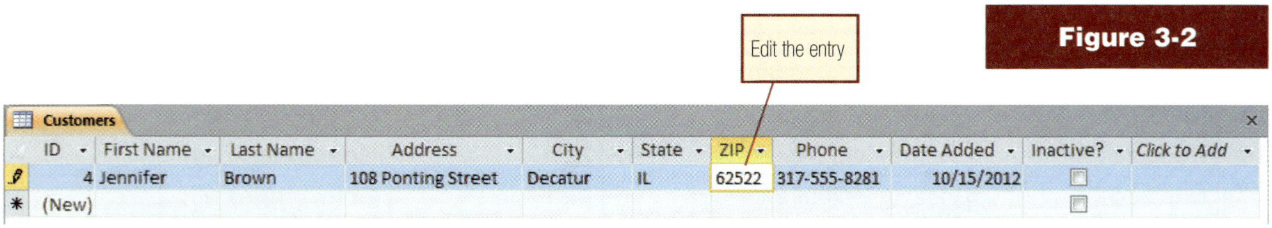

Project 6—Apply It

Jewelry Business Database

DIRECTIONS

1. Start Access, if necessary.
2. Open **AProj06** from the data files for this lesson. If a security warning bar appears, click **Enable Content**.
3. Save the database as **AProj06_studentfirstname_studentlastname** to the location where your teacher instructs you to store the files for this lesson.
4. Open the **Customers** table in Datasheet view, and enter the following records. Use today's date as the Date Added:

   Carrie Fulton
   211 West Eckhardt Street
   Pana, IL 61722
   217-555-2273

   Felicia Adamson
   775 North Main Street
   Noblesville, IN 46060
   317-555-1125

   Norman Eichmann
   55110 Old Church Lane
   Boston, MA 02134
   502-555-7755

5. Set Norman Eichmann's record to be Inactive by marking the check box in the **Inactive** column.
6. Change Carrie Fulton's last name to **Strong**.
7. Close the **Customers** table.
8. Open the **Products** table in Datasheet view.
9. Enter the records from the table at the bottom of the page in the **Products** table. Skip the fields (that is, leave them blank) that are not specified in the table.
10. Enter materials costs for each necklace:
    - Silver: **$10.00**.
    - Yellow gold: **$20.00**.
    - White gold: **$30.00**.
11. For the labor cost for each product, enter **$20.00**.
12. For the build hours for each product, enter **1**.
13. Delete all the silver necklaces.
14. Close the **Products** table.
15. If instructed, submit database file to your teacher for grading.

Type	Product	Size	Material
Necklace	Clover Necklace	22"	Sterling Silver
Necklace	Clover Necklace	22"	Gold, Yellow, 14K
Necklace	Clover Necklace	22"	Gold, White, 18K
Necklace	Starfish Necklace	22"	Sterling Silver
Necklace	Starfish Necklace	22"	Gold, Yellow, 14K
Necklace	Starfish Necklace	22"	Gold, White, 18K
Necklace	Heart Necklace	22"	Sterling Silver
Necklace	Heart Necklace	22"	Gold, Yellow, 14K
Necklace	Heart Necklace	22"	Gold, White, 18K

Lesson 4

Modifying Fields in a Datasheet

➤ What You Will Learn

- Setting Field Properties
- Adding a Field
- Renaming a Field
- Deleting a Field
- Moving a Column
- Hiding and Unhiding Columns
- Changing Datasheet Column Widths
- Freezing Columns

Software Skills It is best to edit a table's structure before putting data into it, but occasionally you may need to make changes after data has been entered. In this lesson, you will learn how to modify a table's structure and layout in Datasheet view.

Application Skills In your friend's jewelry business database, you have been asked to make the datasheet easier to read. You will do this by renaming and moving some fields, hiding some columns, and widening other columns so their entries are not truncated.

WORDS TO KNOW

Column header
The top block in a vertical column on a datasheet, containing the field name.

Freeze
To set a field so that it always remains onscreen, in the left-most position, as you scroll left-to-right.

Required field
A field for which each record must contain an entry.

Unique field
A field for which each record must contain a unique entry.

What You Can Do

Setting Field Properties

- On the Table Tools Fields tab, you can set several common properties for the active field.
- Changing the field type changes the way the data is stored in the field and may also change the type of data that is allowed in the field.

✓ *Field types are described in more detail in Chapter 1, Lesson 6.*

✓ *If the current data in that field violates the rules for the new field type, an error message appears, and any data that violates the rules is deleted. For example, if you change a field that contains text to a Number field any character-based entries are removed.*

- In a **required field**, each record must include an entry in that field. An error message appears and the record is not saved if that field is empty.
- In a **unique field**, each record must include a different entry for that field (no duplicates). For example, Social Security Number might be a unique field in a personnel database

✓ *There are many other properties you can set for a field; some of these can only be changed in Design view. Lesson 6 explains how to modify field properties in Design view.*

Try It! Changing the Field Type

1. Open the **ATry04** database from the data files for this lesson, and save it as **ATry04_studentfirstname_studentlastname**. Enable content if necessary.
2. Open the Address Book table in Datasheet view.

Choose Hyperlink as the field type

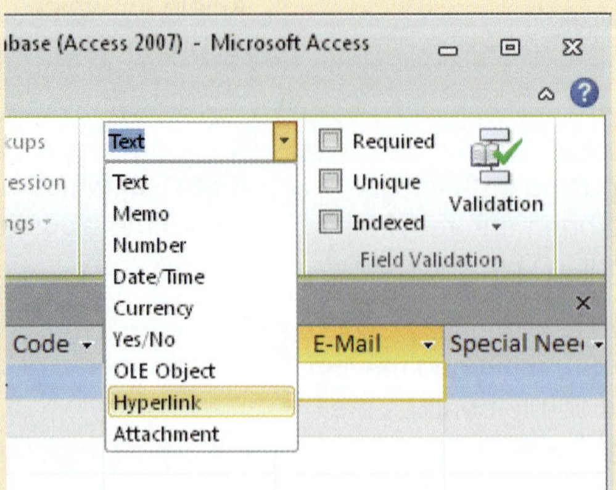

3. Click in the E-Mail field in the first (and only) record.
4. On the Table Tools Fields tab, open the Data Type drop-down list and click Hyperlink.

   ✓ *You can change an AutoNumber field to a Number field, but you can't change back again. You would need to delete that field and recreate it if you needed to make it an AutoNumber field again.*

5. Leave the **ATry04_studentfirstname_studentlastname** database open to use in the next Try It.

Try It! Making a Field Required

1. In the **ATry04_studentfirstname_studentlastname** database, click the Last Name field.

Require a field for each record

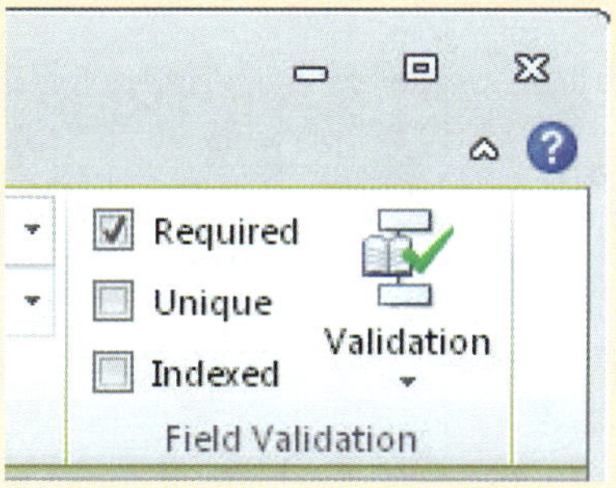

2. On the Table Tools Fields tab, click the Required check box.
3. Leave the **ATry04_studentfirstname_studentlastname** database open to use in the next Try It.

Try It! Making a Field Unique

1. In the **ATry04_studentfirstname_studentlastname** database, click the E-Mail field.
2. On the Table Tools Fields tab, click the Unique check box.
3. Leave the **ATry04_studentfirstname_studentlastname** database open to use in the next Try It.

Adding a Field

- There are three ways to create a new field on a datasheet:
  - Use the *Click to Add* empty column to the right of the existing fields on the datasheet, as you did when creating fields in Lesson 2. You can then move the new column to a different location in the sheet as you will learn later in this lesson.
  - Right-click and click Insert Field to add a new column quickly with default settings. The column's name will be a placeholder (Field1, for example). You can rename it.
  - Use one of the buttons on the Table Tools Fields tab in the Add & Delete group to insert a field of a specific type, such as Text, Number, and so on.
- When you insert a field, it appears to the left of the field that was selected when you issued the command.
- If you have already entered data in the table, you will need to go back and fill in the value for the new field for each record.

Try It! Adding a Field by Right-Clicking

1. In the **ATry04_studentfirstname_studentlastname** database, right-click the First Name field.
2. Click Insert Field. A new text field appears with a generic name.
3. Leave the **ATry04_studentfirstname_studentlastname** database open to use in the next Try It.

Insert a new field by right-clicking

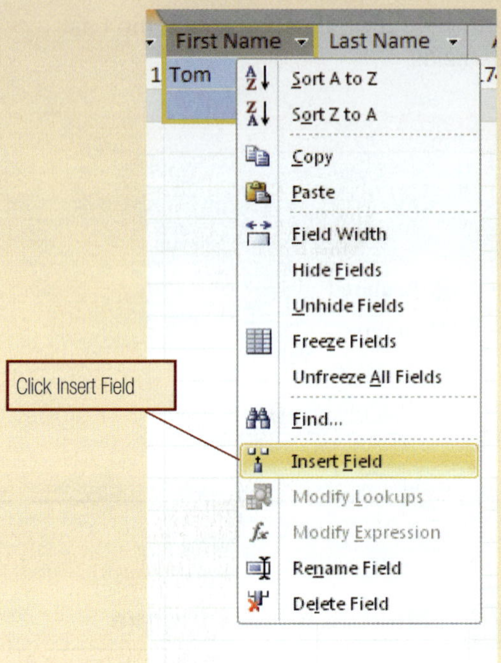

Try It! Adding a Field from the Ribbon

1. In the **ATry04_studentfirstname_studentlastname** database, click in the **Last Name** field.
2. On the Table Tools Fields tab, click the Text button AB.
3. Leave the **ATry04_studentfirstname_studentlastname** database open to use in the next Try It.

Insert a new field from the Ribbon

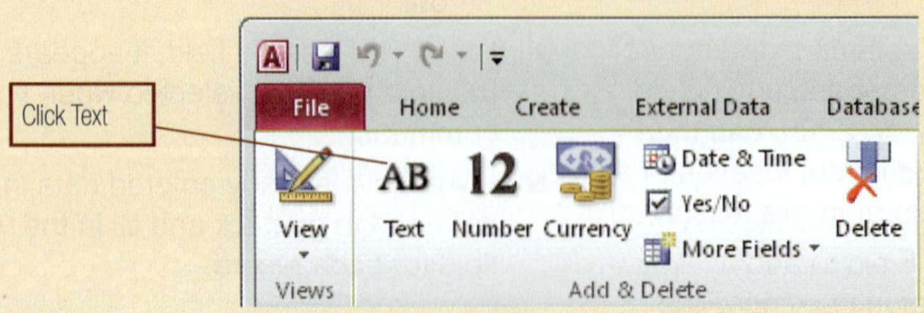

Renaming a Field

- When you insert new fields, they have generic names; you will want to change these to more descriptive names.
- You might also sometimes need to rename existing fields. For example, you might decide to omit spaces from field names for easier data sharing with other database applications.

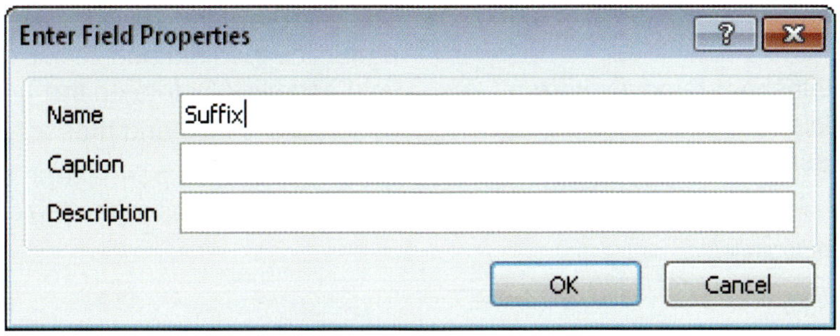

Figure 4-1

Try It! Renaming a Field

1. In the **ATry04_studentfirstname_studentlastname** database, double-click the Field1 column heading.

   OR

   Right-click anywhere in the Field1 column and click Rename Field.

2. Type **Prefix** and press ENTER .
3. Click anywhere in the Field2 column.
4. On the Table Tools Fields tab, click Name & Caption .
5. The Enter Field Properties dialog box opens. In the Name text box, change the name to **Suffix**.
6. Click OK.
7. Leave the **ATry04_studentfirstname_studentlastname** database open to use in the next Try It.

Moving a Column

- The easiest way to move a column is by dragging it. Click a **column header** to select it, hold the mouse button down, and then drag. A black vertical line shows where the column will be placed. When you release the mouse button, the column drops into the new location.

✓ *The changes you make to the field order, by moving columns, are made permanent when you save the table. If you do not want the changes to be permanent, do not save the changes to the table when prompted (when closing it).*

Try It! Moving a Column

1. In the **ATry04_studentfirstname_studentlastname** database, click the E-Mail column heading.
2. Click and hold the mouse button down over the E-Mail column heading, and drag the field to the left of the Phone field. Then release the mouse button.
3. Leave the **ATry04_studentfirstname_studentlastname** database open to use in the next Try It.

Deleting a Field

- Deleting a field from the datasheet removes it from the table's structure and deletes all data in it. Do not delete a field from the datasheet unless you want it permanently gone.

  ✓ *If you just want the field temporarily hidden, use the Hide Column(s) command, described later in this chapter.*

- There are several ways to delete a field. You can right-click the field and click Delete Field, select the field and click Delete on the Table Tools Fields tab, or select the field and press DEL.
- Deleting a field is permanent, even if you do not save your changes to the table.

Try It! Deleting a Field

1. In the **ATry04_studentfirstname_studentlastname** database, click the the E-Mail field and click Delete Field.
2. Click Yes to confirm.
3. If you see a message about deleting one or more indexes, click Yes to confirm.
4. Leave the **ATry04_studentfirstname_studentlastname** database open to use in the next Try It.

Hiding and Unhiding Columns

- If you don't want to view or print certain columns in Datasheet view, you can hide them.
- Hiding a column does not remove it from the table structure, and it does not delete any data it contains.

Try It! Hiding and Unhiding Columns

1. In the **ATry04_studentfirstname_studentlastname** database, right-click the column header of the Inactive field and click Hide Fields.
2. Right-click the column header of the Phone field (or any other visible field) and click Unhide Fields.
3. In the Unhide Columns dialog box, click to mark next to the Inactive field's check box.
4. Click Close.
5. Leave the **ATry04_studentfirstname_studentlastname** database open to use in the next Try It.

Mark the check box to unhide a column

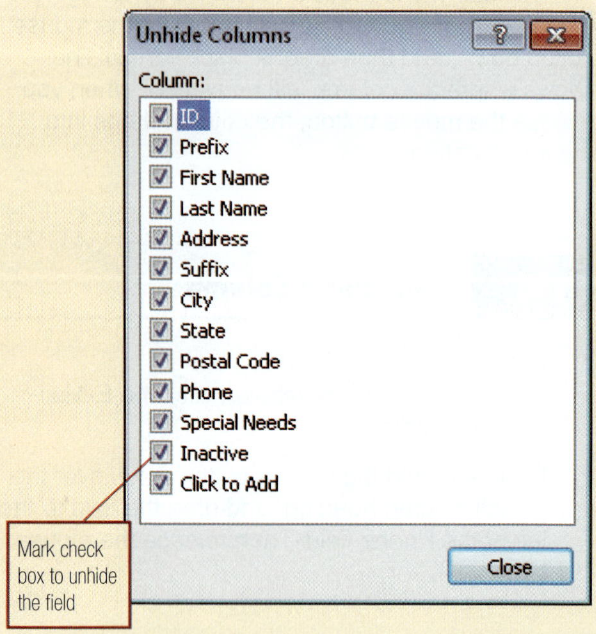

Changing Datasheet Column Widths

- If the field entry is too wide to see in Datasheet view, you can change the width to display more of the column.
- Column width does not affect the field size (that is, the maximum number of characters the field can contain); column width is only for your convenience when viewing the datasheet.
- You can change column width for automatic fit to the widest entry, drag its width manually, or specify an exact width (in number of characters).

Try It! Changing Datasheet Column Widths

1. In the **ATry04_studentfirstname_studentlastname** database, position the mouse pointer between the column headings for the Address and the City columns.
2. Double-click. The Address column widens to accommodate the widest (and only) entry.

Double-click to autosize a column

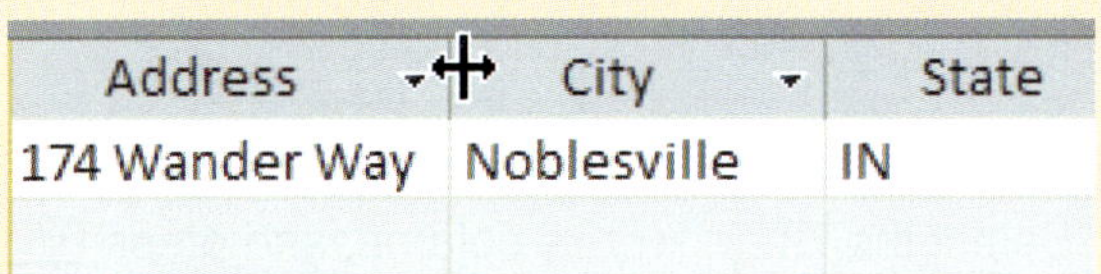

3. Position the mouse pointer between the column headings for Special Needs and Inactive.
4. Hold down the left mouse button and drag to the right approximately one inch; then release the mouse button.
5. If the Special Needs column label still appears truncated, repeat step 2 to widen the column further.
6. Select the Prefix column.
7. Right-click the Prefix column heading. Right-click and select Field Width.
8. In the Column Width dialog box, enter **7**.

   ✓ *Column width is measured in characters.*
9. Click OK.
10. Leave the **ATry04_studentfirstname_studentlastname** database open to use in the next Try It.

Freezing Fields

- If there are too many columns, you may not be able to see all fields at once in Datasheet view.
- If certain fields are important to view at all times, you can **freeze** them so that they remain on the screen as you scroll to the left or right.
- If you freeze a certain number of contiguous columns starting with the left-most column, they will simply appear fixed as you scroll from side to side.
- If you freeze individual columns that are not already at the left-most edge of the table, they will be moved to the left edge when you freeze them. After unfreezing them, you will need to move them back to their original locations manually.

Try It! **Freezing Fields**

1. In the **ATry04_studentfirstname_studentlastname** database, select the ID, Prefix, First Name, Last Name, and Suffix columns.

   ✓ *If you did not do the earlier Try It exercises, you might not have a Prefix or Suffix column; if not, omit them. To select multiple columns, click in the first column and drag to the last one.*

2. Right-click the selection, and click Freeze Fields.
3. Scroll the datasheet to the right.

   ✓ *Notice that the frozen fields remain in view.*

4. Right-click any field.
5. Click Unfreeze All Fields.
6. Right-click the Address Book tab and click Close.
7. Click Yes when prompted to save changes.
8. Click File > Exit to exit Access.

Project 7—Create It

Jewelry Business Database

DIRECTIONS

1. Start Access, if necessary.
2. Open **AProj07** from the data files for this lesson. If a security warning bar appears, click **Enable Content**.
3. Save the database as **AProj07_studentfirstname_studentlastname** to the location where your teacher instructs you to store the files for this lesson.
4. In the Navigation pane, double-click the **Products** table to open it in Datasheet view.
5. Double-click between the **Product** and **Size** column headings to widen the **Product** field to accommodate the longest entry in it.
6. Drag the divider between the **Material** and **Materials Cost** fields to the right to widen the column enough that the entries in the Material column are not truncated.
7. Right-click the **Size** field, and click **Field Width**.
8. In the Column Width box, type **6** and click **OK**.
9. Select the **Build Hours** column, and press DEL to delete it; click **Yes** to confirm.
10. Select the **Retail Price** field, and drag its column (by the heading) to the left of the **Materials Cost** field.
11. Select the **Retail Price**, **Materials Cost**, and **Labor Cost** fields.
12. Right-click the selection, and click **Hide Fields**.
13. Double-click the **Type** column heading and type **Category**, renaming it.
14. Select the **Product** column.
15. On the Table Tools Fields tab, click **Text**, adding a new text field.
16. Type **Description** and press ENTER, replacing the generic Field1 name with the new field name.
17. Close the database and, if instructed, submit it to your teacher for grading.

Project 8—Apply It

Jewelry Business Database

DIRECTIONS

1. Start Access, if necessary.
2. Open **AProj08** from the data files for this lesson. If a security warning bar appears, click **Enable Content**.
3. Save the database as **AProj08_studentfirstname_studentlastname** to the location where your teacher instructs you to store the files for this lesson.
4. Open the **Customers** table in Datasheet view.
5. Change the column widths of all columns so that they are no wider than needed, and yet no entries are truncated.
6. Hide the **Inactive?** column.
7. Change the data type on the **ID** field to **Number**.
8. Delete the **Date Added** column.
9. Redisplay the **Inactive?** column, and hide the **Click to Add** column.
10. Close the **Customers** table, saving your changes.
11. Open the **Products** table in Datasheet view.
12. Change the width on the **Description** field to **30**.
13. AutoFit the **ID**, **Category**, and **Material field** widths to their contents.
14. Move the **Description** field to the rightmost position.
15. Freeze the **Product** field.
16. Close the **Products** table, saving your changes.
17. Close the database.
18. If instructed, submit your database to your teacher for grading.

Lesson 5

Importing and Protecting Data

WORDS TO KNOW

Append
To add to the end of.

Collate
To order copies of a multipage document so that complete sets are together.

Encrypt
To add protection to a file so others cannot read it.

Exclusive mode
A mode in which only one user at a time can work with a file.

Wizard
A series of dialog boxes that guide you step-by-step through a process.

➤ What You Will Learn

Understanding Data Import Options
Importing Data from Excel to an Existing Table
Importing Data from Excel to a New Table
Previewing and Printing a Table
Opening a Database Exclusively
Setting a Database Password
Changing Database Properties

Software Skills Sometimes it is easier to import data from other sources than to type it into a table from scratch. In this lesson, you will learn how to import Excel data into an existing table and into a new table. You will also learn how to print a table and how to set a database password to protect it.

Application Skills You have received some additional data for your friend's jewelry business database and now you need to incorporate it into the database file in Access. You also need to print a copy of the Customers table and password-protect the database file.

What You Can Do

Understanding Data Import Options

- Data may be imported from a wide variety of sources, including text files, other Access databases, Excel files, SharePoint lists, XML files, and more. The procedure for doing so is roughly the same for all types: a **wizard** walks you through the process.
- You can import data from the External Data tab's Import & Link group. Buttons are available there for each of several types of data sources. The More button opens a menu of additional less-common formats from which you can import.
- Importing from Excel is simple since the data is already pre-delimited into columns. Use the Excel button in the Import group of the External Data tab to get started.
- You can import into an existing table, create a new table, or create a link to the original data source.

✓ *You cannot directly import from a Word table, but you can import the Word data into Excel, save it as an Excel file, and then open it in Access.*

The Import & Link group on the External Data tab contains options for importing many types of data

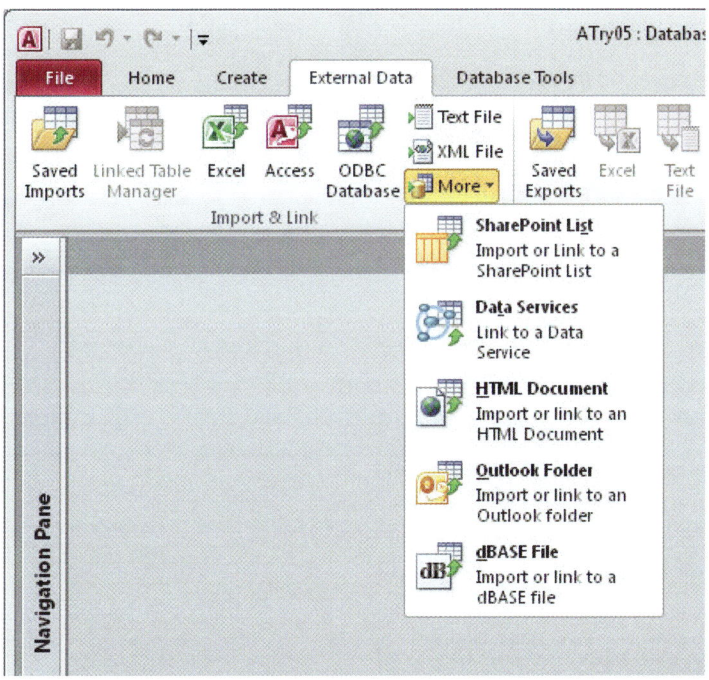

Figure 5-1

Importing Data from Excel to an Existing Table

- When you import into an existing table, the records are **appended** to the end of the table. In Datasheet view, they appear at the bottom of the datasheet.
- Importing into an existing table works only if the fields have the same names and if the data fits into the fields as they are defined in Access. For example, data in a State field where the entire state names are spelled out would not import into a State field in Access that had a length limit of two characters. You might have to edit the data in Excel before importing to correct such problems.

Try It! Importing Data to an Existing Table

1. Open the file **ATry05** from the data files for this Lesson and save it as **ATry05_studentfirstname_studentlastname**.
2. On the External Data tab, in the Import & Link group, click Excel.
3. Click Browse and navigate to the folder containing the data files for this lesson.
4. Select **ATry05data**, and click Open.

   ✓ *The file's path and name appear in the File name box.*
5. Click Append a copy of the records to the table.
6. Make sure that Address Book is selected on the drop-down list.
7. Click OK.
8. Click Next.
9. Click Next.
10. Click Finish.
11. Click Close.
12. Leave the **ATry05_studentfirstname_studentlastname** database open to use in the next Try It.

Choose which table to append the records to

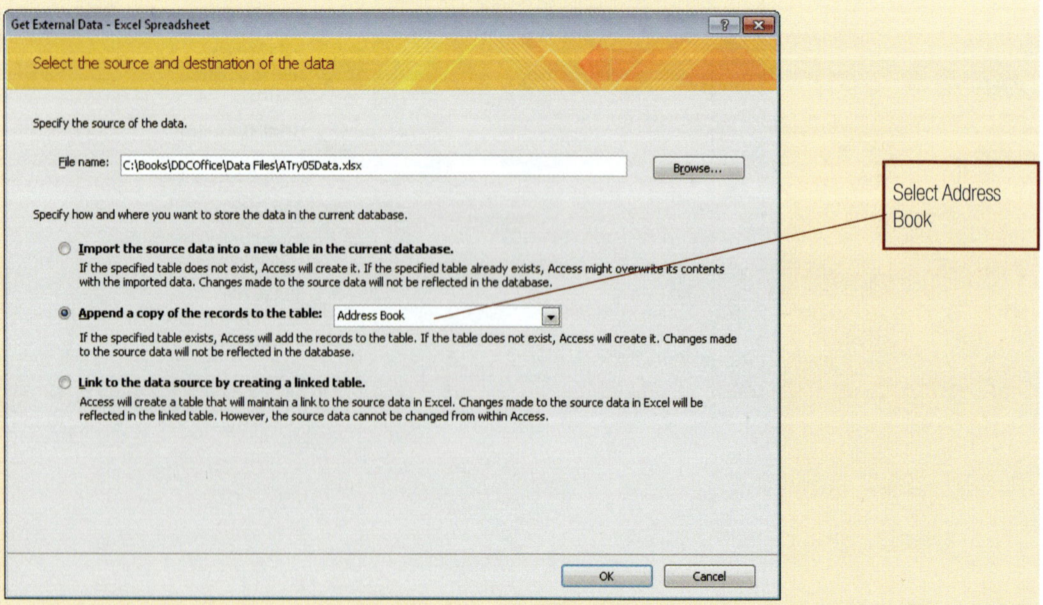

Importing Data from Excel to a New Table

- When importing data that does not fit in any of the existing tables, you can import it into a new table created on-the-spot. You do not have to create the new table beforehand.
- As part of the import process, you have the opportunity to set the fields' data types.
- You can also exclude certain fields from the import if desired.

Try It! Importing Data into a New Table

1. Open the **ATry05_studentfirstname_studentlastname** file if it is not already open. On the External Data tab, in the Import & Link group, click Excel.
2. Click Browse, and navigate to the folder containing the data files for this lesson.
3. Select the Excel file **ATry05data** and click Open.

   ✓ *The file's path and name appear in the File name box.*
4. Click OK.
5. Click Sheet2.
6. Click Next.
7. Click Next.
8. Click the Customer column to select it.
9. Open the Data Type list and click Integer.
10. Click the Salesperson column to select it.
11. Mark the Do not import field (Skip) check box.
12. Click Next.
13. Click Choose my own primary key.

    ✓ *The Order ID field is selected by default in the drop-down list box.*
14. Click Next. In the Import to Table text box, type **Orders**, replacing the default name (Sheet2).
15. Click Finish.
16. Click Close.
17. Leave the **ATry05_studentfirstname_studentlastname** database open to use in the next Try It.

Select a data type

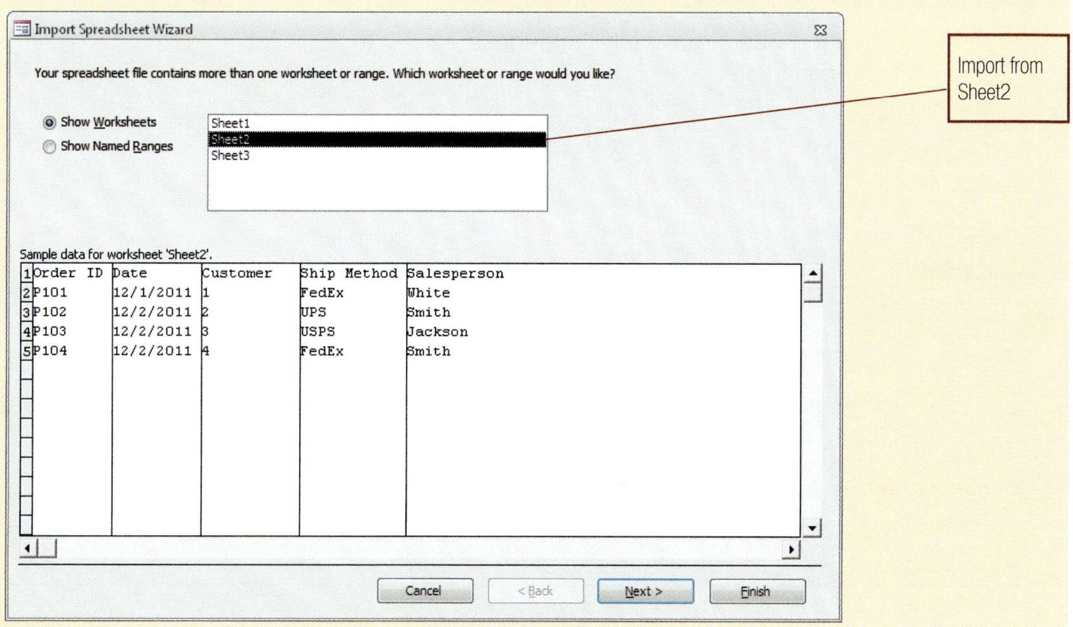

Previewing and Printing a Table

- Print all the records in the open datasheet by choosing File > Print > Print. The Print dialog box appears. From here you can set the printer, the print range, the number of copies, and more.

  ✓ *To print only certain records, select them before printing.*

- The Name drop-down arrow in the Print dialog box allows you to choose a different printer.
- To print selected records, click the record selector to the left of one or more records in Datasheet or Form view. Then click File > Print > Print and choose to print Selected Record(s) in the Print dialog box.
- If desired, type more than 1 in the Number of Copies box, and then check **Collate** if you want to print the document in a complete set; or leave Collate unchecked if you want to print multiple copies of page 1, then page 2, and so on.
- Choose File > Print > Print Preview to see a screen preview of what your printing will look like.
- While in Print Preview, click the Zoom button to toggle between zooming in and zooming out. You can also click the arrow below the Zoom button for a menu with more zoom options.
- The Navigation buttons at the bottom of the screen in Print Preview allow you to see the first, previous, specific, next, or last page.

Try It! Previewing a Datasheet

1. In the file **ATry05_studentfirstname_studentlastname**, open the Address Book table in Datasheet view.
2. Click File > Print, and then click Print Preview.
3. Click the preview of the page to zoom in.
4. Click the preview of the page again to zoom out.
5. Click the Next Page arrow ▸ at the bottom of the screen to view the second page.
6. On the Print Preview tab in the Page Layout group, click Landscape to preview the page in Landscape orientation.
7. Click Portrait to return to Portrait orientation.
8. In the Zoom group, click Two Pages to see two pages at a time.
9. Click One Page to return to single-page view.
10. Click Close Print Preview.
11. Leave the **ATry05_studentfirstname_studentlastname** database open to use in the next Try It.

Try It! Printing a Datasheet

1. In the file **ATry05_studentfirstname_studentlastname**, open the Address Book table in Datasheet view if it is not already open.
2. Click File > Print, and then click Print.
3. In the Print dialog box, click the Pages option button.
4. In the From box, type **1**.
5. In the To box, type **1**.
6. **With your teacher's permission**, click OK to print the datasheet; otherwise, click Cancel.

Opening a Database Exclusively

- To set a database password, you have to open the database in **exclusive mode** (no one else can be working in the database.) Open Exclusive is most often used to ensure that only one user at a time is trying to change the design of database objects.
- In the Open dialog box, choose the down arrow on the Open button and select Open Exclusive.

Try It! Opening a Database Exclusively

1. If any database is currently open, click File > Close Database to close it.
2. Click File > Open. The Open dialog box appears. Navigate to the data files for this lesson.
3. Click ATry05_studentfirstname_studentlastname.
4. Click the down arrow on the Open button.
5. Click Open Exclusive.
6. Leave the ATry05_studentfirstname_studentlastname database open to use in the next Try It.

Open the file exclusively

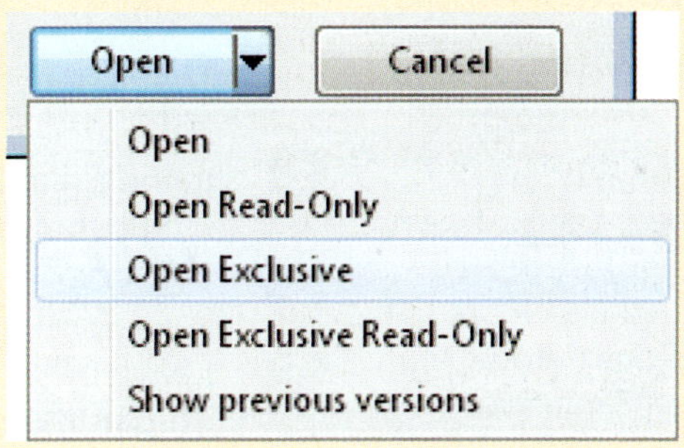

Setting a Database Password

- Password-protecting a database prevents others who do not know the password from using the database. Password protecting in Office applications is also called **encrypting**.
- When you set a password, you must type the password again to verify accuracy. The password does not show when you type; asterisks display instead. Note that passwords are case-sensitive.
- You have to type the password again when you want to remove the password. If you forget your password, you will not be able to open the database.

Try It! Setting a Database Password

1. Open **ATry05_studentfirstname_studentlastname** exclusively, if you have not already done so.
2. Click File > Info, and then click Encrypt with Password. The Set Database Password dialog box opens.
3. Type **secure** in the Password box. Then retype the password in the Verify box.
4. Click OK.
5. If a warning appears about row-level locking, click OK.
6. Click File > Close Database.

Set a database password

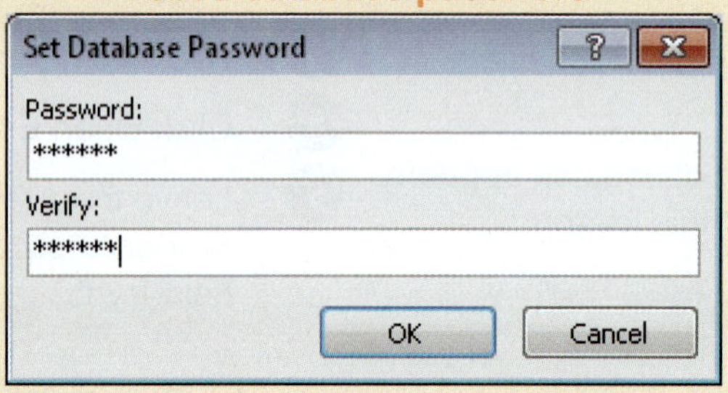

Try It! Opening a Password-Protected Database

1. Open the **ATry05_studentfirstname_studentlastname** database file.

   OR

   To open it exclusively, click the down arrow on the Open button and click Open Exclusive.
2. In the Enter Database Password dialog box, type **secure**.
3. Click OK.
4. Leave the **ATry05_studentfirstname_studentlastname** database open to use in the next Try It.

Try It! Removing the Password from a Database

1. Open **ATry05_studentfirstname_studentlastname** exclusively, if it is not already open. You may need to close it and then reopen.)
2. Click File > Info, and then click Decrypt Database. Type the database password in the Unset Database Password dialog box.
3. Click OK.
4. Leave the **ATry05_studentfirstname_studentlastname** database open to use in the next Try It.

Changing Database Properties

- Database properties can help others identify a file when it is stored on a file server, and they can help you remember why you created a database and what data it holds.
- Database properties include Title, Subject, Author, Manager, Company, Category, Keywords, Comments, and so on. You can also create custom properties to store information specific to your situation.

Try It! Modifying Database Properties

1. In **ATry05_studentfirstname_studentlastname**, choose File > Info > View and edit database properties. A Properties dialog box appears.
2. On the Summary tab in the Title box, change the text to **Try It Lesson 5**.
3. In the Author box, replace the name with your own name.
4. In the Keywords box, type **Lessons**.
5. Click the Custom tab.
6. On the Name list, click Editor.
7. In the Value box, type **Joe Smith**.
8. Click Add.
9. Click OK.
10. Click Exit to exit Access.

Project 9—Create It

Jewelry Business Database

DIRECTIONS

1. Start Access, if necessary.
2. Open **AProj09** from the data files for this lesson. If a security warning bar appears, click **Enable Content**.
3. Save the database as **AProj09_studentfirstname_studentlastname** to the location where your teacher instructs you to store the files for this lesson.
4. Click **File > Info** and then click **View and edit database properties**.
5. In the Title box, change the entry to **Jewelry Database**, as shown in Figure 5-2.
6. In the Author box, change the entry to your full name.
7. Click **OK**.

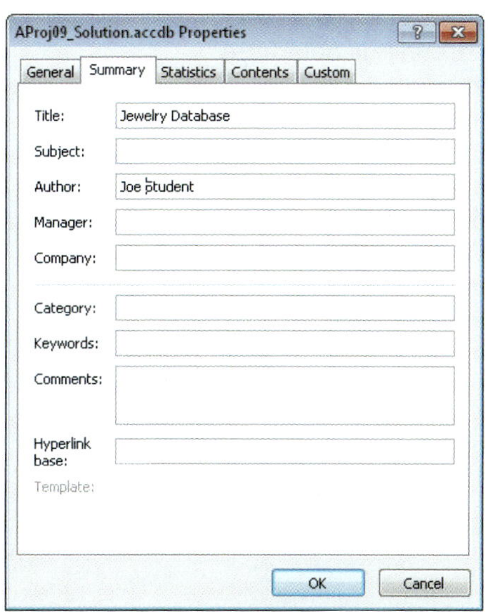

Figure 5-2

8. On the Ribbon, click **External Data** tab in the Import & Link group, click **Excel**.
9. Click Browse.
10. Navigate to the folder containing the data files for this lesson, and select **AProj09data.xls**. Then click **Open**.
11. Click **Append a copy of the records to the table**.
12. Open the drop-down list and choose **Products**.
13. Click **OK**. The Import Spreadsheet Wizard opens.
14. Click **Next** to accept the Products tab as the data source.
15. Click **Finish**.
16. Click **Close**.
17. Open the **Products** table in Datasheet view.
18. **If your teacher has instructed you to submit a printout as part of this assignment**, do the following:
    a. Click **File > Print**, and then click **Print**.
    b. Click **OK**.
19. Close the database and, if instructed, submit it to your teacher for grading.

Project 10—Apply It

Jewelry Business Database

DIRECTIONS

1. Start Access, if necessary.
2. Open **AProj10** exclusively from the data files for this lesson. If a security warning bar appears, click **Enable Content**.
3. Save the database as **AProj10_studentfirstname_studentlastname** to the location where your teacher instructs you to store the files for this lesson.
4. Import data from **AProj10data.xlsx** into two new tables: **Shippers** and **Salespeople**. Pull data from the corresponding sheets in the data file.
5. Set a password for the database: **admin**.
6. Open the **Shippers** table in Datasheet view and, **with your teacher's permission**, print one copy of it. Write your name on the printout if your teacher wants you to submit it for grading.
7. In the database's Properties box, add a Manager: **Molly Kashon**.
8. Close the database and, if instructed, submit it to your teacher for grading.

Lesson 6

Using Table Templates and Design View

➤ What You Will Learn

- Creating a New Database Using a Template
- Creating a Table with a Template
- Changing the View of the Navigation Pane
- Opening a Table in Design View
- Creating a Table in Design View
- Setting a Primary Key
- Managing the Field List
- Changing a Field's Data Type
- Modifying a Field's Properties

Software Skills Access provides a number of database templates that you can use to jumpstart project design. These templates include multiple tables with relationships already established between them in some cases. You can also create tables on your own in Design view, where you have access to a full range of property settings, not just the abbreviated set that are available in Datasheet view.

Application Skills In this lesson, you will explore one of the templates that comes with Access. Then you will return to the jewelry business database you have been working with to add more tables to it in Design view. You will set a primary key and customize field properties.

WORDS TO KNOW

Caption
Alternate text that appears instead of a field's actual name in datasheets, forms, and reports.

Composite key
Two or more fields that collectively define the primary key by unique combinations of their values.

Field description
An optional brief comment or explanation of a field. The field description appears in the status bar at the bottom of the window when the field is selected.

Field properties
Characteristics of a field.

Field selector
In Table Design view, the gray rectangle to the left of the field name. Click it to select that field; drag it up or down to move the field in the field list.

Primary key
The field that uniquely identifies each record in a table.

Table Design view
A view in which you can add, edit, and delete fields from a table, change field types and descriptions, set a primary key, and more.

Template
A database that contains formatting, styles, and sample text that you can use to create new databases.

What You Can Do

Creating a New Database Using a Template

- If the database you plan to create is for some common purpose, such as to store information about events or projects, you may find it easier to use a **template** than to build the database from scratch.
- Some templates come preinstalled with Access, and many others are available via Office Online.

Try It! Creating a New Database Using a Template

1. Start Access. It starts in Backstage view, with New selected.

   ✓ *If Access is already open, click File > New.*

2. Click Sample templates.
3. Click Events.
4. In the File Name box, type **ATry06_studentfirstname_studentlastname**.
5. Click Create and enable content if necessary.
6. Leave the **ATry06_studentfirstname_studentlastname** database open to use in the next Try It.

Create a database with a template

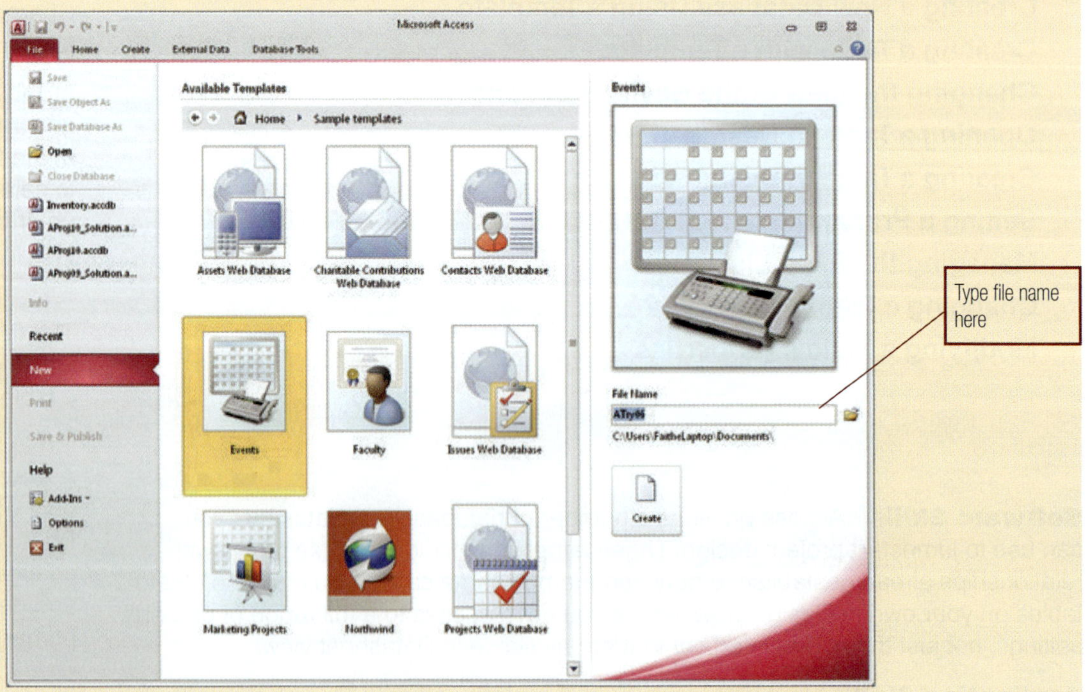

Changing the View of the Navigation Pane

- Some templates default to a different arrangement of objects in the Navigation pane than you may be used to; you can change the view from the drop-down menu on the Navigation pane header bar.

Try It! Changing the View of the Navigation pane

1. In the **ATry06_studentfirstname_studentlastname** database, if necessary, click the Navigation pane bar to display it.
2. Click the Supporting Objects heading to expand the list of objects.
3. Click the down arrow button at the top of the pane.
4. Click Object Type. The Navigation pane changes to show objects grouped by type.
5. Leave the **ATry06_studentfirstname_studentlastname** database open to use in the next Try It.

Select a view of the navigation pane

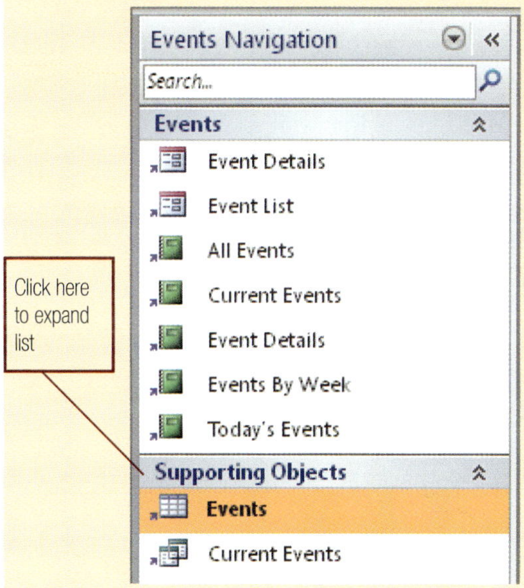

The objects are now grouped by type

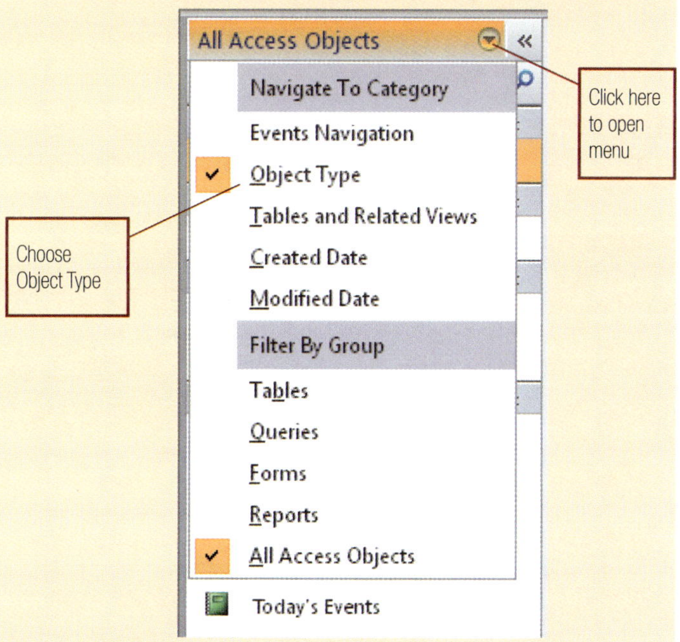

Creating a Table with a Template

- Access 2010 comes with the following table templates: Comments, Contacts, Issues, Tasks, and Users. The fields in these table templates are predefined and formatted appropriately for the data they hold.
- When you create a table based on a template, you also have the option of creating relationships between the new table and the existing ones in the database.

✓ *You will learn about relationships in Chapter 2, Lesson 8.*

Try It! Creating a Table with a Template

1. In the **ATry06_studentfirstname_studentlastname** database, on the Create tab, click Application Parts and then Tasks.
2. If prompted to close all open objects, click Yes.
3. In the Create Relationship dialog box, click There is no relationship.
4. Click Create. The new table appears on the Tables list in the Navigation pane.
5. Double-click the Tasks table to open it. Examine its fields.
6. Leave the **ATry06_studentfirstname_studentlastname** database open to use in the next Try It.

Create a table based on the Tasks table template

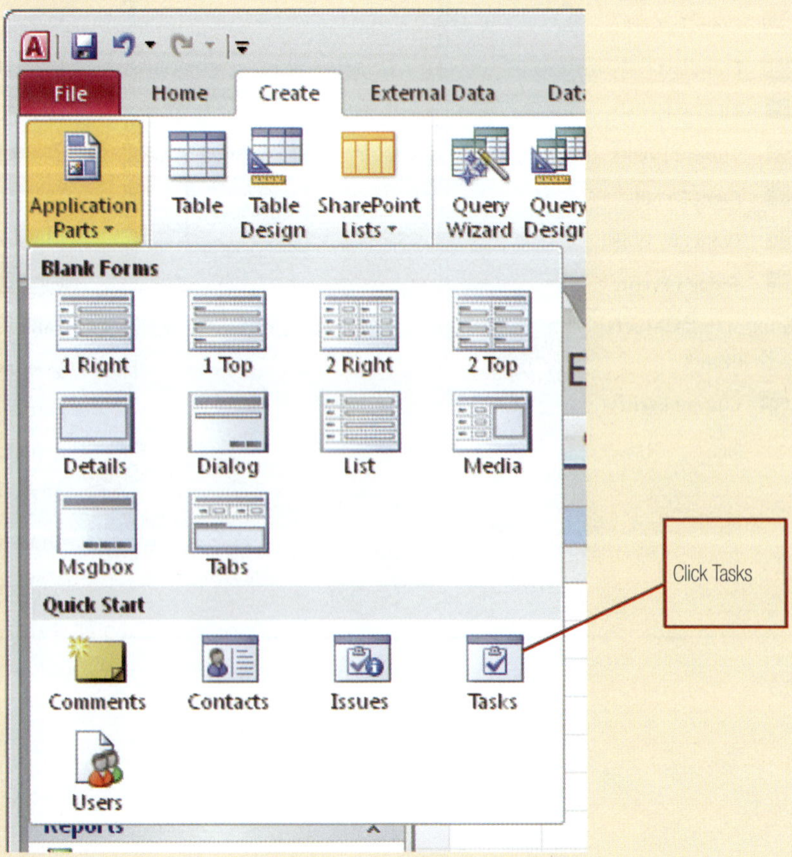

Opening a Table in Design View

- You can make changes to a table's structure in **Table Design view**.
- The table fields and their types are listed in the top part of the Design view window.
- The properties for the selected field are shown in the bottom part of the Design view window.

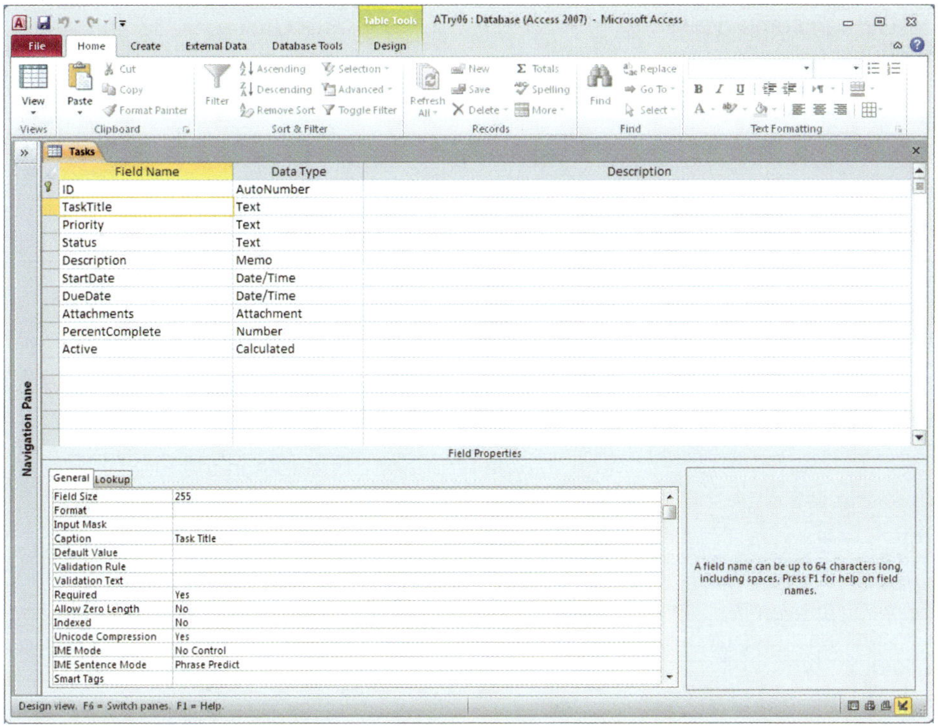

Figure 6-1

Try It! Opening a Table in Design View

1. In the **ATry06_studentfirstname_ studentlastname** database, right-click the Tasks table.

   ✓ *The Tasks table should already be open in Datasheet view from the previous steps.*

2. Click Design View.
3. Click the TaskTitle field, and examine the field properties for it.
4. Click the StartDate field, and examine the field properties for it.
5. Right-click the table's tab, and click Close to close the table.
6. Leave the **ATry06_studentfirstname_ studentlastname** database open to use in the next Try It.

Creating a Table in Design View

- To start a new table using Design view, click the Create tab. In the Tables group, click Table Design.
- Enter the field names in the Field Name column. Although you may use up to 64 characters, you should keep the name short.
- In the Data Type column, you identify what kind of information the field will store. Click the drop-down arrow to choose from the list of data types. You can also type the first letter of the data type to select it.
- The **field description** is optional. In the Field Description cell, you can enter comments or hints about the intended use and/or limitations of the field. The text you type for the field description will appear on the status bar when the user is in this field in Datasheet view or on a form.

Try It! Creating a Table in Design View

1. In the **ATry06_studentfirstname_studentlastname** database, on the Create tab in the Tables group, click Table Design.
2. In the Field Name column, type **LocID** and press TAB.
3. Open the Data Type drop-down list, choose AutoNumber and then press TAB.

   ✓ *Instead of choosing from the list, you can type the first letter of the data type option to select it.*

4. In the Field Description column, type **Automatically assigned** and press TAB.
5. In the next row, type **Location** in the Field Name column and press TAB.
6. Press TAB to accept the default field type (Text).
7. Press TAB to skip the Field Description column for this field.
8. In the next row, type **Capacity** in the Field Name column and press TAB.
9. Open the Data Type drop-down list, choose Number, and then press TAB.
10. Type **Number of people** in the Field Description cell.
11. Click the Save button on the Quick Access Toolbar.
12. In the Save As dialog box, type **Locations**.
13. Click OK.

    ✓ *A warning appears that there is no primary key.*

14. Click No.
15. Leave the **ATry06_studentfirstname_studentlastname** database open to use in the next Try It.

Enter the fields to use for the table

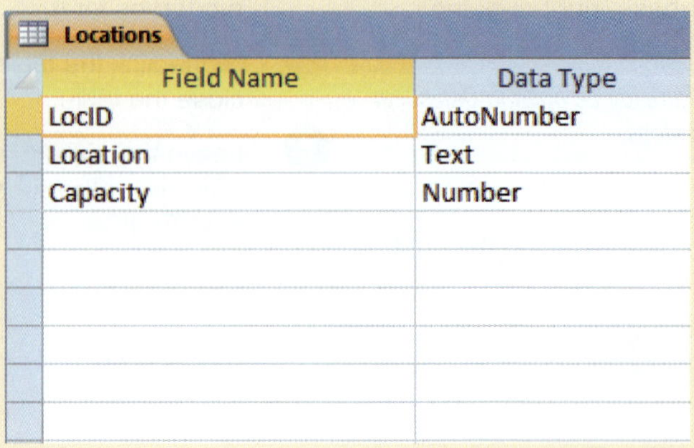

Setting a Primary Key

- As explained in Lesson 1, a table can have a **primary key** field that contains unique data for each record. The primary key field helps avoid duplicate records in a table.
- For the primary key field, choose a field that will be unique for each record. FirstName and LastName would not be good choices for the primary key because different records could have the same value. For an employee database, the primary key could be the employee's Social Security number, for example. You could also create an ID field to be the primary key field, as in the previous steps (the LocID field).
- In Design view, you can choose an existing field to be your primary key by selecting it and then clicking the Primary Key button. The field selected as the primary key appears with a key symbol to its left.

  ✓ *When you attempt to save a new table without choosing a primary key field, Access asks whether you want a primary key field to be created automatically. If you do so, the new field receives the name "ID".*

- A **composite key** exists when two or more fields together form the primary key. For example, if you designate both FirstName and LastName as keys, then no record can have the same combination of those two fields, but duplicates can occur in either of those fields individually. To create a composite key, select two or more fields and click Primary Key.

Try It! Setting a Primary Key

1. In the **ATry06_studentfirstname_studentlastname** database, with the Locations table open in Design view, click the LocID field.
2. On the Table Tools Design tab in the Tools group, click Primary Key. A key symbol appears to the left of that field.
3. Leave the **ATry06_studentfirstname_studentlastname** database open to use in the next Try It.

Select the primary key field

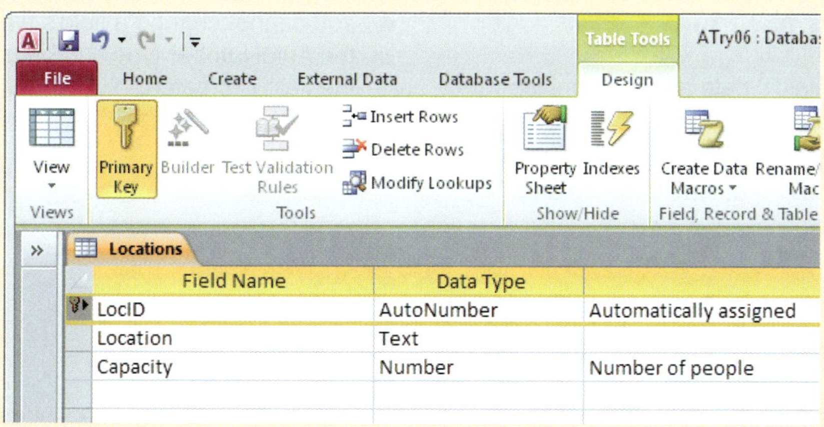

Managing the Field List

- You can add fields, delete fields, and reorder a table's fields, in Design view.
- To add a field at the bottom of the field list, simply type it into the next blank row.
- To add a field at some other position in the list, you can either insert a blank row using the Insert Rows command, or you can add the field to the bottom of the list and then reorder the list.
- Drag fields up or down on the list to reorder them. Drag a field by its **field selector** (the gray box to the left of the field name).

Try It! Managing the Field List

1. In the ATry06_studentfirstname_studentlastname database, with the Locations table open in Design view, click the Capacity field.
2. On the Table Tools Design tab in the Tools group, click Insert Rows.
3. In the new row, type City in the Field Name column and press TAB.
4. In the first blank row in the field list, type State in the Field Name column and press TAB.
5. Click the field selector to the left of the State field.
6. Holding the mouse button down, drag the field selector up until the black horizontal line appears below the City field; then release the mouse button.
7. Click the field selector for the City field.
8. On the Table Tools Design tab in the Tools group, click Delete Rows.
9. Leave the ATry06_studentfirstname_studentlastname database open to use in the next Try It.

Changing a Field's Data Type

- As you learned, a field's data type determines what can be stored in it.
- You can change any field's data type in Design view. Just select a different type from the drop-down list.
- You cannot change a field's type to AutoNumber; the AutoNumber type can be assigned only when the field is created.

The field types are described in the following table:

Data Type	Description
Text	Includes any characters up to a maximum of 255 characters (determined by field size). If the data includes a mix of numbers and any amount of letters, choose Text. Examples include name and address fields. ✓ *The default data type is Text.*
Memo	Use this data type when Text is not large enough. Like Text, this data type can also have letters and numbers but can be much larger—up to 65,536 characters. Don't use Memo unless you need that extra length, however, because you can't perform certain actions (indexing, for example) on a memo field.
Number	Includes various forms of numerical data that can be used in calculations.
Date/Time	Date and time entries in formats showing date, time, or both.
Currency	Use for currency values with up to four digits after the decimal place. This data type is more accurate for large numbers than the Number data type, but generally takes up more space.
AutoNumber	This is typically used to create an identification number for each record. The value for each record increases by one.
Yes/No	Only two possible values can be in this field. Options include Yes/No, True/False, or On/Off. The default style shows a check box with a ☑ for *Yes* or blank ☐ for *No*.
OLE Object	This data type allows you to place another file type into your record. Within the field, you can insert a picture (a company logo, for example), a Word document (employee resume), or an Excel spreadsheet (client summary chart).
Hyperlink	This allows you to insert a Web address that will launch when you click it in Datasheet view or on a form. You could also type a path and file name to a file on your hard drive or a network drive.
Attachment	Allows you to attach files from word processing programs, spreadsheets, graphics editing programs, and so on.
Calculated	A new data type available only in Access 2010. You can specify one or more other fields plus a math operation to derive the value of a calculated field.
Lookup Wizard	Creates a lookup column, which creates a list of values from which to choose when entering data.

Try It! Changing a Field's Data Type

1. In the **ATry06_studentfirstname_studentlastname** database, in the Field Name column, type **Rental** in the first empty row and press TAB.
2. In the Data Type column, open the drop-down list and choose Number.
3. Reopen the drop-down list and choose Currency.
4. Leave the **ATry06_studentfirstname_studentlastname** database open to use in the next Try It.

Modifying a Field's Properties

- When a field is selected, its **field properties** appear in the lower half of the Design view window. Field properties specify settings for the field, such as maximum entry length and default value.
- Different field types result in different properties being available. For example, numeric field types have a Decimal Places property that text fields do not.
- In some cases, multiple types of fields may have a property with the same name, but with different options available. For example, a numeric field has a Format property for which you can choose Currency, General, Fixed, and so on; a Yes/No field also has a Format property, with choices such as True/False and Yes/No.
- All field types have the **Caption** property. This field enables you to specify a caption that will appear as the field column heading in Datasheet view and also in forms and reports in which the field is inserted.

  ✓ *Captions are useful when you want to use an abbreviated or cryptic name for the field but still make it look friendly in the forms, reports, and datasheets that the end-user interacts with. For example, you might have a field named UserFirstName, but on the datasheets and forms you want it to appear as First Name (with a space between the two words).*

- The Field Size property for a text-based field defines the maximum number of characters it can contain.
- For a numeric field, choose a Field Size option on the drop-down list. The main reason to set a field size is to keep the database file as small as possible; use the field size that uses the fewest bytes per entry and still stores what you want to store.
- The table below shows the most commonly used field sizes for numeric fields.

  ✓ *Use the Long Integer data type for a numeric field that will have a relationship to an AutoNumber field in another table, because you probably don't know at the outset how big a database is going to get and how many records a table will end up containing.*

- Another commonly used field property is Default Value. This property enables you to set a default value for a field, filled in automatically in each new record. This can save you data entry time. For example, if nearly all your customers live in a certain state, you could set the Default Value of the State field to that state, eliminating the need to retype the state name for each record.

Field Size	Decimal Places	Valid Range	Bytes Used Per Record
Byte	No	0 to 255	1
Integer	No	-32,768 to 32,767	2
Long Integer	No	-2,147,483,648 to 2,147,483,647	4
Single	Yes	3.4 x 1038 to 3.4 x 1038	4
Double	Yes	-1.797 x 10308 to +1.797 x 10308	8

Try It! Modifying a Field's Properties

1. In the **ATry06_studentfirstname_ studentlastname** database, in the Locations table in Design view, select the LocID field.
2. In the Caption property, type **ID**.
3. Select the Capacity field.
4. Open the drop-down list for the Format property and choose General Number.
5. Select the Rental field.
6. In the Default Value property, type **500**.
7. Click the Save button on the Quick Access Toolbar.
8. On the Home tab in the Views group, click View . The table appears in Datasheet view.

   ✓ *Notice that the LocID field's column heading appears as ID.*

   ✓ *Notice that the Rental field contains $500.00 for the empty record.*

9. Click File > Exit to exit Access.

Project 11—Create It

Sales Pipeline Database

DIRECTIONS

1. Start Access. If Access is already running, click **File > New**.
2. Click **Sample templates**.
3. Click **Sales Pipeline**.
4. Click the **Browse** icon to the right of the File Name box.
5. Navigate to the location where your teacher instructs you to store the files for this lesson.
6. In the File Name box, type **AProj11_studentfirstname_studentlastname**.
7. Click **OK**.
8. Click **Create**.
9. Click **Enable Content**.
10. Display the Navigation pane. Click the **down arrow** button at the top of the Navigation pane.
11. Click **Object Type**.
12. On the Create tab in the **Templates** group, click **Application Parts** and then click **Comments**.
13. Click **Yes** to close all open objects.
14. Click **There is no relationship**.
15. Click **Create**.
16. In the Navigation pane, right-click the **Comments** table and click **Design View**.
17. Click the **CommentDate** field.
18. Click **Insert Rows**.
19. In the new row, type **EnteredBy** in the Field Name column, as in Figure 6-2, and press TAB.
20. Click in the **Caption** box in the Field Properties area at the bottom of the window and type **By**, as in Figure 6-3.
21. Click the **Save** button on the Quick Access Toolbar to save the changes to the table.
22. Close the database and, if instructed, submit it to your teacher for grading.

Figure 6-2

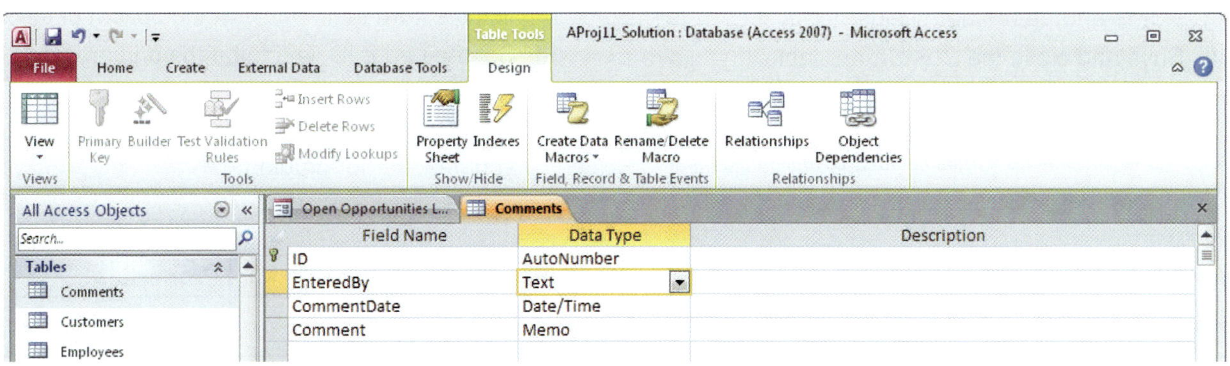

Figure 6-3

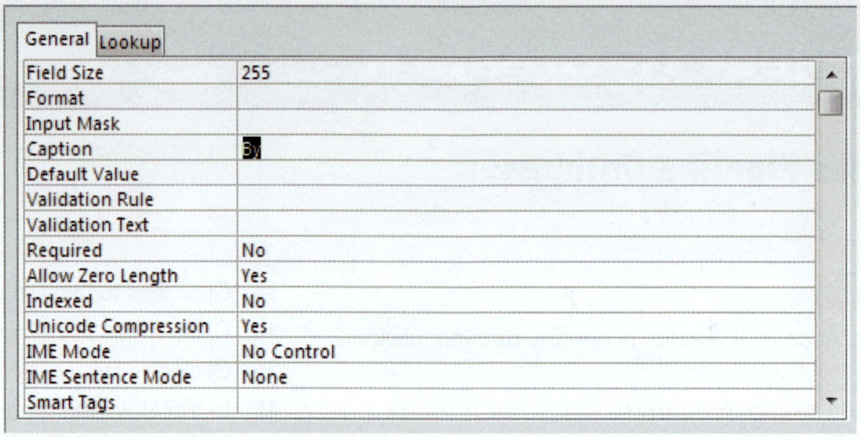

Project 12—Apply It

Jewelry Business Database

DIRECTIONS

1. Start Access, if necessary.
2. Open **AProj12** from the data files for this lesson. If a security warning bar appears, click **Enable Content**.
3. Save the database as **AProj12_ studentfirstname_studentlastname** in the location where your teacher instructs you to store the files for this lesson.
4. Open the **Customers** table in Design view.
5. Change the **Field Size** property to **50** for the **First Name** and **Last Name** fields.
6. Save and close the **Customers** table. If you see a warning about data possibly being lost, click **Yes**.

   ✓ *The warning in step 6 is not important because there are currently no entries in either of those fields that exceed 50 characters.*

7. Open the **Shippers** table in Datasheet view, and edit the values in the **ID** field to remove the letters. For example, **S1** becomes 1.
8. Switch to Design view, and change the field type for the **ID** field to **Number**.
9. Change the field size for the **ID** field to **Integer**.
10. Open the **Salespeople** table in Design view, and make **Employee ID** the primary key field.
11. Close all open tables, saving all changes to them.
12. Start a new table in Design view. Add the following fields shown in the table at the bottom of the page.
13. Set the Order ID field to be the primary key.
14. Save the table as **Orders** and close it.
15. Close the database and, if instructed, submit it to your teacher for grading.

Field Name	Data Type	Description	Properties
Order ID	AutoNumber		
Order Date	Date/Time		Format = Short Date
Customer	Number	Numeric because it is related to the Customer ID field.	

Lesson 7

Creating Other Objects

➤ What You Will Learn

- Using the Simple Query Wizard to Create a Query
- Creating a Quick Form
- Entering Records Using a Form
- Creating and Modifying a Quick Report
- Previewing and Printing a Report

Software Skills In addition to tables, you can create a variety of other objects in Access. These objects support and organize table data in a different way. This lesson shows you how to create a query, a form, and a report.

Application Skills Now that the structure of the jewelry business database is complete, you will create a query, two forms, and a report, to show your friend examples of what Access can do.

WORDS TO KNOW

Form
A view of a table or query's data designed for input or look-up of records.

Query
A specification that describes how a set of records should be sorted, filtered, calculated, or presented.

Report
A printable layout of the data from a table or query.

Print Preview
A view that shows you exactly how a report will look when printed.

What You Can Do

Using the Simple Query Wizard to Create a Query

- A **query** is a set of rules that defines how a certain table (or group of tables) should be displayed onscreen (usually in a datasheet).
- Queries are very versatile. Here are some of the things a query can do:
  - Show only certain fields
  - Show only certain records
  - Combine the data from multiple tables
  - Create new calculated fields based on the data from other fields
  - Sort the records alphabetically or numerically based on one or more fields
  - Show summary statistics
- The Simple Query Wizard creates a basic query—that shows only the fields you specify (from the table or tables choice you select).

Try It! Creating a Simple Query

1. Start Access and open the file **ATry07** from the data files for this lesson If a warning appears, click Enable Content. Save the file as **ATry07_studentfirstname_studentlastname**.
2. On the Create tab, click Query Wizard. The New Query dialog box opens.
3. Select Simple Query Wizard, and click OK.
4. Open the Tables/Queries list, and choose Table: Members.
5. Click the FirstName field and click >.
6. Click the LastName field and click >.
7. Click the Phone field and click >.
8. Click Next.
9. Enter **Phone Listing** as the title for the query.
10. Click Finish. Close the Phone Listing query.
11. Leave the **ATry07_studentfirstname_studentlastname** database open to use in the next Try It.

Select the fields to include in the query

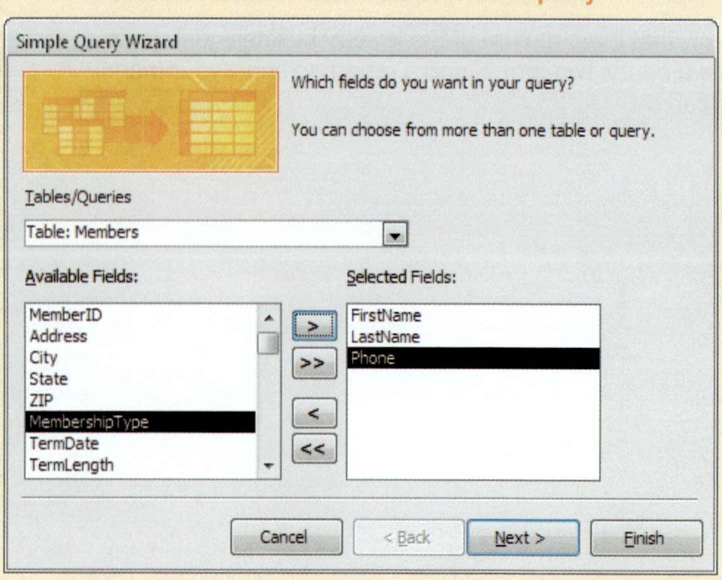

Creating a Quick Form

- A **form** provides an attractive interface to use for data entry and look-up. There are a number of ways to create forms, which you will learn more about in Chapter 3.
- The simplest type of form is a Quick Form. It is a basic form that uses all the fields in the selected table and arranges them in a single vertical column.
- A multiple-items displays multiple records in a table format, similar to a datasheet.

Try It! Creating a Quick Form

1. In the **ATry07_studentfirstname_studentlastname**, select the Classes table in the Navigation pane. (Don't open it, just click it once.)
2. On the Create tab in the Forms group, click Form. The form appears.
3. Click the Save button on the Quick Access Toolbar. The Save As dialog box opens.
4. Type **Classes Form** in the Save As dialog box, and click OK to save it.

   ✓ *Including "Form" in the name differentiates the form from the table named Classes.*
5. Right-click the form's tab and click Close.
6. Leave the **ATry07_studentfirstname_studentlastname** database open to use in the next Try It.

A new form appears based on the Classes table

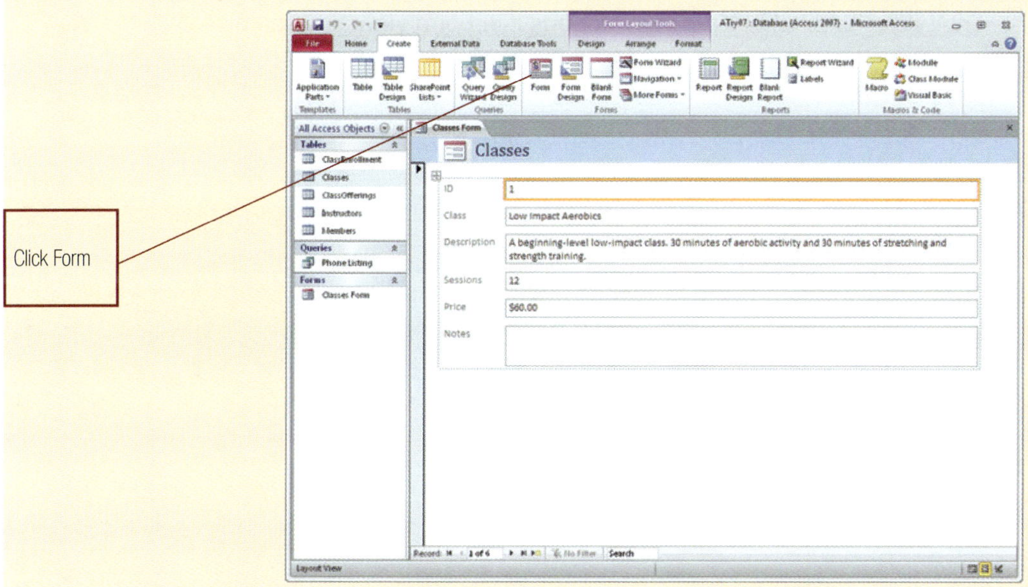

Try It! Creating a Multiple-Items Form

1. In **ATry07_studentfirstname_studentlastname**, select the Members table in the Navigation pane. (Don't open it, just click it once.)
2. On the Create tab in the Forms group, click More Forms and then click Multiple Items. The form appears.
3. Click the Save button on the Quick Access Toolbar. The Save As dialog box opens.
4. Type **Members Form** in the Save As dialog box, and click OK to save it.
5. Right-click the form's tab and click Close.
6. Leave the **ATry07_studentfirstname_studentlastname** database open to use in the next Try It.

Entering Records Using a Form

- An advantage of a form over a datasheet is that records are easier to review. For example, the Quick Form you created in the previous section shows one record at a time.
- When working with a form, navigation controls appear at the bottom. You can use them to move between records, and to clear the form so you can add a new record.
- Entering data in a multi-item form works the same way as a single-item form; move to the next field by pressing TAB.
- When you create a form, it opens in Layout view. Layout view enables you to see the form, complete with data, while making changes to its structure.
- You cannot enter records in Layout view; you must switch to Form view. Closing and reopening the form opens it in Form view. You can also click the View button to switch views.

This form shows one record at a time

Figure 7-1

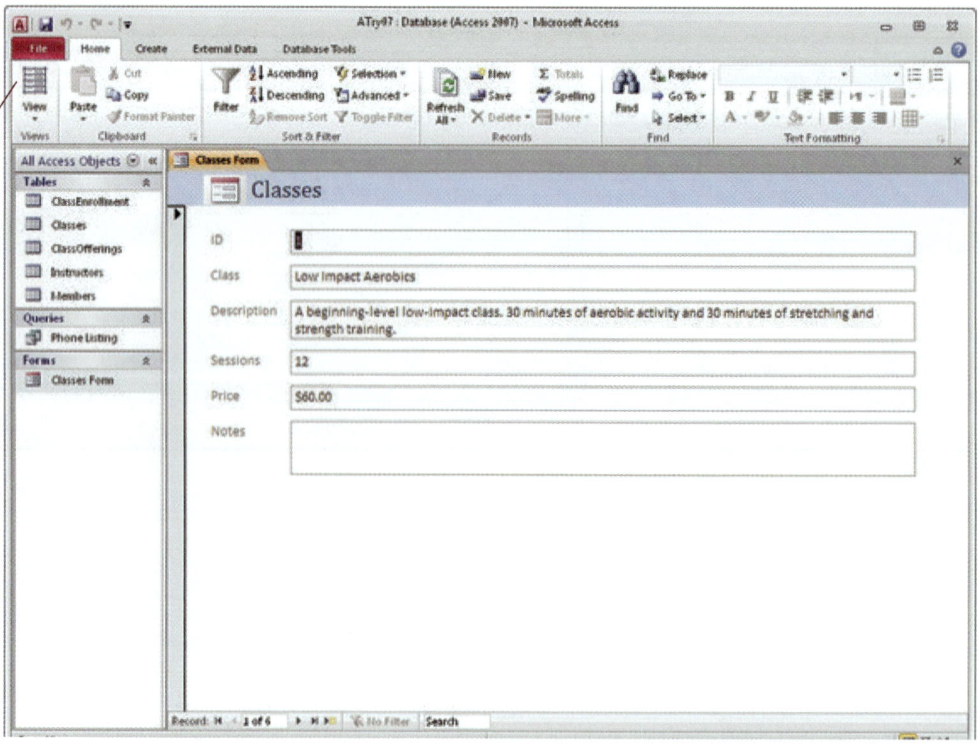

Click Views button to switch views

Try It! Entering Records in a Form

1. In the **ATry07_studentfirstname_studentlastname** database, double-click Classes Form in the Navigation pane to open the form in Form view.
2. Click the New (blank) record button in the navigation controls.
3. Press TAB to move past the ID field.
4. In the Class field, type **Intro to Pilates**, and then press TAB.
5. In the Description field, type **Beginning-level Pilates workout. No previous experience required**. Then, press TAB.
6. In the Sessions field, type **8**, and then press TAB.
7. In the Price field, type **120.00**, and then press TAB.
8. In the navigation controls, click the First record button.
9. Close all open objects.
10. Leave the **ATry07_studentfirstname_studentlastname** database open to use in the next Try It.

Creating and Modifying a Quick Report

- A **report** is a view of a table or query that's designed to be printed. A report contains the same data as the datasheet but is much more attractive and readable.
- After a report is created, it appears in Layout view by default. Just like with Form view, Layout view enables you to see the report, complete with data, while making changes to its structure.
- In Layout view, you can remove certain fields if they are not necessary. Select the field you want to remove and press DEL.
- You can also change the orientation from portrait to landscape, providing more room for field columns.
- You can change the widths of the report columns. Drag the right edge of a column to the right or left.

Try It! Creating a Report

1. In the **ATry07_studentfirstname_studentlastname** database, select the Members table in the Navigation pane. (Do not open it.)
2. On the Create tab in the Reports group, click Report. A new report appears.
3. Click the Save button on the Quick Access Toolbar.
4. Click OK to save the report with the name **Members**.
5. Leave the **ATry07_studentfirstname_studentlastname** database open to use in the next Try It.

Try It! Deleting Fields from a Report Layout

1. In the file **ATry07_studentfirstname_ studentlastname** database, with the Members report open in Layout view, scroll to the right so the Membership Type field is visible, and click it.
2. On the Report Layout Tools Arrange tab, in the Rows & Columns group, click Select Column.
3. Press DEL.
4. Click the Notes field.
5. On the Report Layout Tools Arrange tab, in the Rows & Columns group, click Select Column.
6. Press DEL.
7. On the Report Layout Tools Page Setup tab, in the Page Layout group, click Landscape.
8. Leave the **ATry07_studentfirstname_ studentlastname** database open to use in the next Try It.

Select and delete a column

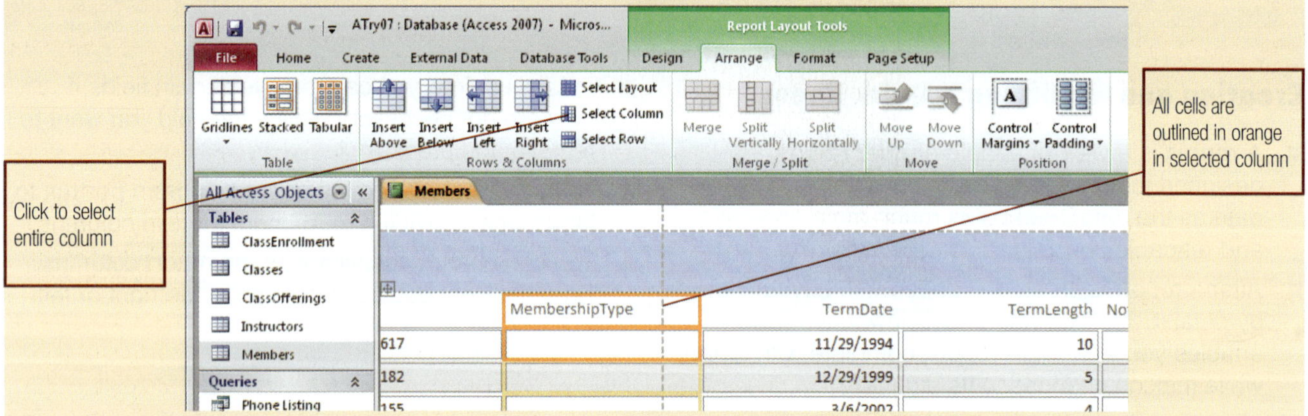

Try It! Changing Column Widths in a Report

1. In the **ATry07_studentfirstname_studentlastname** database, with the Members report open in Layout view, click in the ID field and then position the mouse pointer over the right edge of any cell in the ID column.
2. Drag to the left until the ID column is as narrow as possible while not wrapping text to additional lines.

   ✓ *If the row height becomes taller, that means the column is too narrow, and the text in at least one row is wrapping. Increase the field width until the row height returns to normal.*
3. Click in the First column, so that an orange border appears around those field entries.
4. Position the mouse pointer over the right edge of any cell in the First column.
5. Drag to the left until the First column is as narrow as possible while not truncating any entries or the field heading.
6. Repeat this process for each field in the report until all columns are as narrow as possible without truncating any entries.
7. Leave the **ATry07_studentfirstname_studentlastname** database open to use in the next Try It.

Previewing and Printing a Report

- After a report is created, it appears in Layout view. Layout view is useful for modifying the report's layout, but it does not show the report exactly as it will be printed. For example, it does not show the margins.
- **Print Preview** lets you see exactly how the report will look when printed. You also can adjust page setup options such as margins and page orientation in Print Preview.
- The navigation buttons at the bottom of the Print Preview window allow you to move from page to page within a report.
- In Print Preview, the mouse pointer displays as a magnifying glass. Click anywhere in the report display to toggle between a view of the whole and the most recent zoom value. You can set the zoom value from the Zoom button's menu on the Print Preview tab.

  ✓ *Report view is similar to Print Preview but designed for on-screen viewing. In Report view, you do not have the capability of zooming in and out on the content as in Print Preview. Report view is a more no-frills display method.*
- You can print a report from Print Preview (using the Print button).
- You can also print a report without entering Print Preview by using the File > Print > Print command. This opens the Print dialog box, which you learned about in Lesson 5.

Try It! **Previewing and Printing a Report**

1. In the ATry07_studentfirstname_studentlastname database, with the Members report still open, right-click its tab and click Print Preview.
2. On the Print Preview tab, in the Page Size group, click Margins and click Normal. This changes the document margins.
3. Click the mouse anywhere on the report. It zooms in. Click again to zoom out.
4. On the Print Preview tab, in the Print group, click Print. The Print dialog box opens.
5. **With your teacher's permission**, click OK to print your work; otherwise, click Cancel.
6. On the Print Preview tab, click Close Print Preview.
7. With the Members report open, click File > Print > Print.
8. **With your teacher's permission**, click OK to print your work; otherwise, click Cancel.
9. With the Members report open, click File > Print, and then, **with your teacher's permission**, click Quick Print.
10. Right-click the Members tab and click Close.
11. When prompted to save changes, click Yes.
12. Close the database file and exit Access.

Project 13—Create It

Jewelry Business Database

DIRECTIONS

1. Start Access, if necessary.
2. Open **AProj13** from the data files for this lesson. If a security warning bar appears, click **Enable Content**.
3. Save the database as **AProj13_studentfirstname_studentlastname** in the location where your teacher instructs you to store the files for this lesson.
4. On the Navigation pane, click the **Products** table (do not open it).
5. On the **Create** tab, in the Reports group, click **Report**.
6. Click the **Save** button on the Quick Access Toolbar.
7. Type **Product Report** and click **OK**.
8. Right-click the report's tab and click **Close**.
9. On the Navigation pane, click the **Shippers** table (do not open it).
10. On the **Create** tab, click **Form**. A new form appears.
11. Click the **Save** button on the Quick Access Toolbar.
12. Type **Shippers Form** and click **OK**.
13. Right-click the form's tab and click **Form View**.
14. Click the **New (blank) record** button in the navigation controls at the bottom of the window.
15. In the **ID** field, type **4** and press TAB.
16. In the **Shipper** field, type **DHL** and press TAB.
17. In the **Account** field, type **D3857**.
18. Right-click the form's tab and click **Close**.
19. Close the database and, if instructed, submit it to your teacher for grading.

Project 14—Apply It

Jewelry Business Database

DIRECTIONS

1. Start Access, if necessary.
2. Open **AProj14** from the data files for this lesson. If a security warning bar appears, click **Enable Content**.
3. Save the database as **AProj14_ studentfirstname_studentlastname** in the location where your teacher instructs you to store the files for this lesson.
4. Use the Simple Query Wizard to create a query that uses the following fields from the **Customers** table:

   First Name

   Last Name

   Address

   City

   State

   ZIP

   Name the query **Customer Mailing Query**.
5. Create a report based on the **Customer Mailing Query**. Save the report as **Customer Mailing Report**.

   ✓ *Notice that the title text at the top of the report says "Customer Mailing Query" because that is what the report was based on. You can change the title by double-clicking the label and retyping it.*
6. Resize the columns in the report layout so that the entire report fits on one page. (Use Print Preview to check.)
7. **With your teacher's permission**, print the report and write your name on the printout.
8. Close the report, saving your changes to it.

   ✓ *You may run into a problem with the Page 1 of 1 box at the bottom of the page being too far to the right and preventing the entire report from appearing on a single page. You can drag that box's right border to the left to shrink it in size and make it fit on the page.*
9. Create a new form for the **Salespeople** table. Name it **Salespeople Form**.
10. Use the new form to enter the following salespeople into the database:

    Employee ID: **557-22-333**

    First: **Rosa**

    Last: **Gonzalez**

    Position: **Manager**

    Commission: **7%**

    Employee ID: **441-22-571**

    First: **Pete**

    Last: **Sanchez**

    Position: **Assistant**

    Commission: **4%**
11. Close the database and, if instructed, submit it to your teacher for grading.

Chapter Assessment and Application

Project 15—Make It Your Own

Create a New Database

You are responsible for creating a new database for The BFF Travel Club, a group of friends who take vacations together. They will need to store data about members, destinations, and trips. In this exercise, you will design the structure of the database and start creating the tables for it.

DIRECTIONS

1. Write your name at the top of a blank sheet of paper.
2. Make two headings at the top of the paper: **Members** and **Trips**. Beneath each heading, list the fields to include in the table. Make sure that you:
   - Include a field in each table that will be unique for each record.
   - Include enough information about each member to be able to contact him or her in multiple ways in the **Members** table.
   - Think about what you would want to know about a trip if you were planning to go on it, and include fields that contain that information in the **Trips** table.
3. Start Access, and create a new blank database, saving it in the location where your teacher instructs you to store the files for this chapter. Name the file **AProj15_studentfirstname_studentlastname**.
4. Using any method you have learned so far, create the two tables, including the fields you have decided to include. Make sure each table has a primary key and uses the appropriate data types for each field.
5. Open the **Trips** table in Datasheet view.
6. Using the Internet, locate information about a guided tour of China that lasts at least seven days, and enter it into the **Trips** table. If you find that you need different fields, make changes in Design view.
7. Open the **Members** table in Datasheet view, and enter your own name and contact information in it. If you find that you need different fields, make changes in Design view.
8. Create a form for the **Members** table, and name it **Members Form**.
9. Using the form, enter one other person (real or fictional) into the **Members** table.
10. Close the database, and reopen it exclusively.
11. Set a password of **trip** for the database.
12. Create a report from the **Members** table and name it **Member Report**. Set it in Landscape orientation, and tighten up the field widths as much as possible. **With your teacher's permission**, print one copy of the report, and write your name on the printout. Save and close the report.
13. Close the database and, if instructed, submit it for grading along with your handwritten worksheet from steps 1-2 and the printout from step 12 if you printed one.

Project 16—Master It

Create a New Database with a Template

You are responsible for creating a new database for Succeed, a private tutoring company that offers a summer school program. In this project you will use an Access template to get a head start on the database, and then customize it as needed for the organization.

DIRECTIONS

1. Start Access, and create a new database based on the **Student Database** template (available from Office.com in the Education category). Name the file **AProj16_studentfirstname_studentlastname**.
2. This database includes two pop-up windows: Help and Getting Started. Close both of these windows. Also, close the **Student List** form (which opens by default when you open the database).
3. Import the data from **AProj16data.xlsx** from the data files for this chapter into the **Students** table.
4. Open the **Students** table in Datasheet view, and widen columns as needed so that all entries and field names are visible.
5. Freeze the **ID**, **Last Name**, and **First Name** columns.
6. Hide the **Insurance Carrier** and **Insurance Number** fields. Then, close the **Students** table.
7. Open the **Students$_ImportErrors** table. This table was generated when you imported the records in step 3. It lists the problems that occurred with the import. Examine the errors, and then close and delete this table. (To delete a table, right-click it in the Navigation pane and click **Delete**.)
8. Open the **Student Attendance** table in Datasheet view and enter the following records. **With your teacher's permission**, print the datasheet, and write your name on the printout.

Student	Attendance Date	Status
Jessica Brown	01/09/2012	Present
Ralph Garcia	01/09/2012	Present
Shannon Jackson	01/09/2012	Present
Jessica Brown	01/10/2012	Absent – Excused
Ralph Garcia	01/10/2012	Present
Shannon Jackson	01/10/2012	Present
Jessica Brown	01/11/2012	Absent – Excused
Ralph Garcia	01/11/2012	Present
Shannon Jackson	01/11/2012	Present
Jessica Brown	01/12/2012	Absent – Excused
Ralph Garcia	01/12/2012	Present
Shannon Jackson	01/12/2012	Present
Jessica Brown	01/13/2012	Present
Ralph Garcia	01/13/2012	Absent – Excused
Shannon Jackson	01/13/2012	Present

9. In the database's **Properties box**, set the title to **Success** and change the author name to your full name.
10. Create a form based on the **Guardians** table, and name the form **Guardian Form**.
11. Create a report based on the **Student Attendance** table, and name it **Attendance Report**. **With your teacher's permission**, print one copy of it and write your name on the printout. Compare this printout to the one from step 8 to see the difference between a report and a datasheet.
12. Close the database, and reopen it exclusively.
13. Assign a password of **attend** to the database.
14. Close the database, and, if instructed, submit it to your teacher for grading along with your printouts if you were instructed to print.

Chapter 2

Working with Queries

Lesson 8
Managing Relationships Between Tables
Projects 17-18

- Renaming a Table
- Relating Tables
- Enforcing Referential Integrity
- Deleting Relationships
- Showing Related Records
- Printing a Relationship Report

Lesson 9
Finding, Replacing, and Sorting Data
Projects 19-20

- Finding Data
- Replacing Data
- Searching with Wildcards
- Sorting Records in a Table
- Sorting Records Using Multiple Fields
- Removing a Sort

Lesson 10
Filtering Data
Projects 21-22

- Filtering by Selection
- Filtering for Multiple Selections
- Filtering with Comparison Operators
- Filtering by Form
- Saving Filter Results as a Query

Lesson 11
Creating a Query in Design View
Projects 23-24

- Understanding Data Analysis
- Exploring Data Mining Tools, Techniques, and Ethics
- Understanding Database Trends
- Understanding Queries
- Creating a New Select Query in Design View
- Running a Query
- Saving and Printing a Query

Lesson 12
Creating a Multi-Table Query
Projects 25-26

- Creating a Query Based on More Than One Table
- Sorting Query Results
- Reordering Fields in a Query
- Using All Fields of a Table
- Changing a Column Name
- Creating a New Query from an Existing Query
- Saving a Query with a Different Name

Lesson 13
Using Criteria in a Query
Projects 27-28

- Specify Text Criteria in a Query
- Specify Numeric Criteria in a Query
- Specify Criteria Using a Field Not Displayed in the Query Results
- Using Null Criteria to Find Blank Fields

Lesson 14
Using Comparison Operators
Projects 29-30

- Using Comparison Operators
- Using Wildcards and the Like Operator
- Using the Between…And Comparison Operator
- Using the In Operator
- Combining Criteria

Lesson 15
Using Calculated Fields
Projects 31-32

- Understanding Calculated Fields
- Creating a Calculated Field in a Table
- Using Calculated Fields in a Query

Lesson 16
Summarizing Data in Queries
Projects 33-34

- Understanding Summary Queries
- Summarizing with the Simple Query Wizard
- Summarizing Data in Query Design View

End of Chapter Assessments
Projects 35-36

Lesson 8

Managing Relationships Between Tables

➤ What You Will Learn

- Renaming a Table
- Relating Tables
- Enforcing Referential Integrity
- Deleting Relationships
- Showing Related Records
- Printing a Relationship Report

Software Skills In a multi-table database, relationships are the key to tying the tables together to form a cohesive database system. When you create relationships between tables, you associate a field in one table with an equivalent field in another. Then the two tables can be used in queries, forms, and reports together, even if there is not a one-to-one relationship between entries. In this lesson, you will learn how to create and manage the relationships between tables.

Application Skills In the jewelry business database that you created in Chapter 1, you will create relationships between the tables that will enable the business owner to enter, edit, and manage the data in multiple tables more easily.

WORDS TO KNOW

Cascade delete
When a record in a parent table is deleted, Access deletes all the related records from the child table where the value from the primary key matches the value in the foreign key.

Cascade update
When the primary key field is updated in a relationship, the corresponding foreign key value(s) in the child table's related records automatically updates.

Child field
Related field from the child table of the relationship.

Child table
The second table of a relationship. When creating a relationship, this is generally the "many" side of the relationship. One record from the parent table (such as clients) can be related to one or more records of the child table (such as sales).

Foreign key
A field in the child table that is related to the primary key in the parent table.

Master field
The related field from the main (parent) table of the relationship.

WORDS TO KNOW

One-to-many relationship
A relationship in which the value of the linked field in the parent table is different for each record, but the value of the linked field in the child table can be the same in multiple records.

Orphan
A value in the foreign key that does not have a corresponding primary key in the parent table.

Parent table
The main table of a relationship. When creating a relationship, this is the "one" side of the relationship and contains the primary key.

Referential integrity A property of a relationship between two tables. When Referential Integrity is on, the child table cannot contain a foreign key value that does not have a corresponding value in the primary key of the parent table.

Subdatasheet
A child table related to the main (parent) table.

What You Can Do

Renaming a Table

- Tables can be renamed at any time. When you rename a table, all references to it in the database are automatically changed, too. For example, if you have a form or report based on a certain table, they automatically change to refer to the table by its new name.

Try It! Renaming a Table

1. Start Access and open the database **ATry08** from the data files for this lesson and save it as **ATry08_studentfirstname_studentlastname**. Enable content if necessary any time you are prompted to do so.
2. In the Navigation pane, right-click the Members table and click Rename.
3. Type Students and press ENTER .
4. Leave the **ATry08_studentfirstname_studentlastname** database open to use in the next Try It.

Rename the table from the Navigation pane

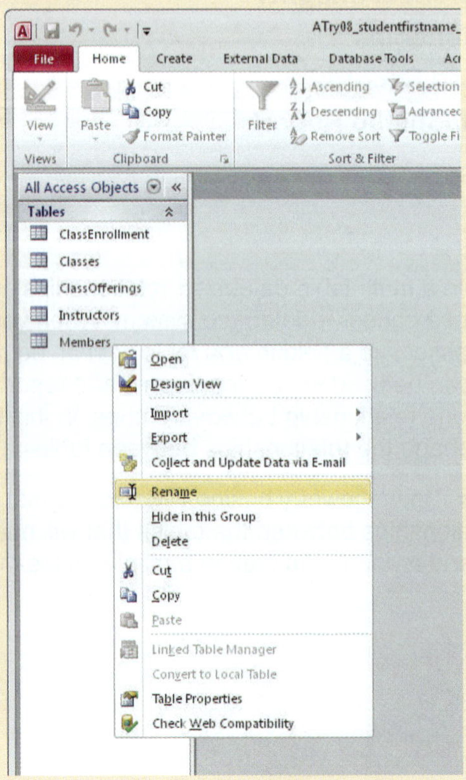

Relating Tables

- To create a relationship between two tables, the same field (or equivalents) must appear in both tables. It is not required that the field names be identical, but they should contain the same type of data.
- In most cases, the field is unique in one table (usually the primary key) but not unique in the other. This results in a **one-to-many relationship**.
- The related field in the second table is called the **foreign key**. The foreign key field must have the same data type as the related primary key, unless the primary key is an AutoNumber type. In that case, the foreign key field must be a Number type. In Figure 8-1, the foreign key is the Instructor field in the ClassOfferings table.
- The table containing the primary key field being linked is in the **parent table**, and that field is the "one" side of the relationship, indicated by a "1" in the Relationships window. In Figure 8-1, the parent table is Instructors.
- The table containing the foreign key field is the **child table**, and that field is the "many" side of the relationship, indicated by an infinity sign (∞) in the Relationships window. In Figure 8-1, the child table is ClassOfferings.

Figure 8-1

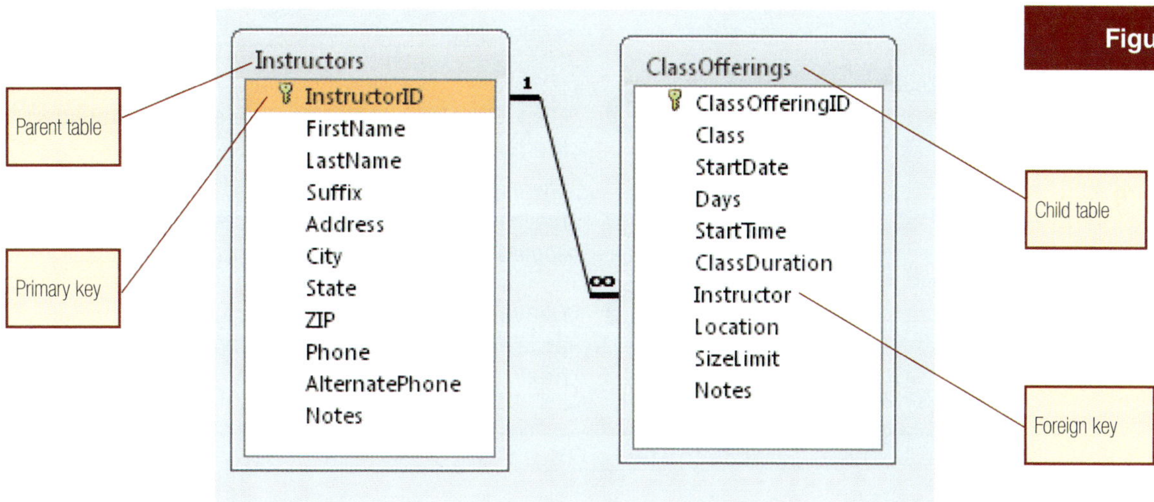

Try It! Creating Relationships

1. The database **ATry08_studentfirstname_studentlastname** should be open. On the Database Tools tab, in the Relationships group, click the Relationships button.
2. Drag the Classes table from the Navigation pane into the Relationships grid (the large blank space in the center).
3. Drag the ClassOfferings table into the Relationships pane.

Add ClassOfferings to the Relationships pane

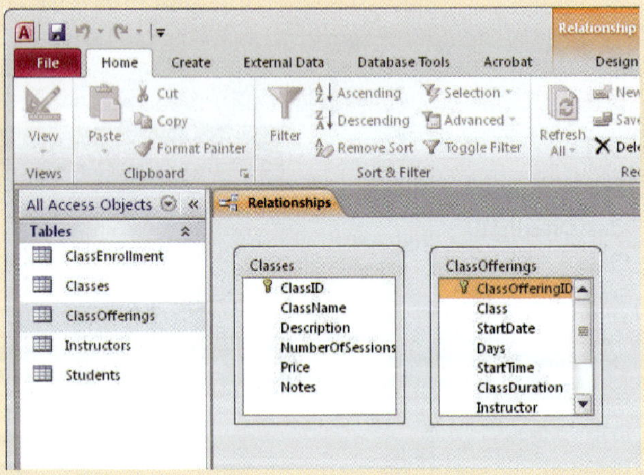

4. Drag the ClassID field from the Classes table and drop it on the Class field in the ClassOfferings table. The Edit Relationships window opens.

Create a relationship

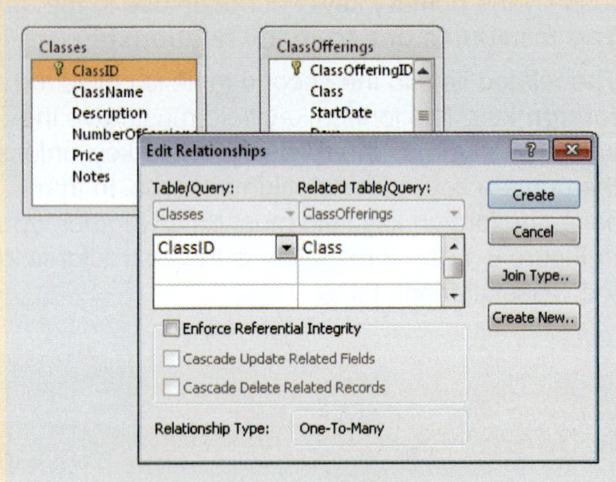

5. Click Create. A connector line appears between the two fields.

   ✓ *There is no 1 or infinity symbol (∞) on the line because referential integrity was not enforced. You will learn about that in the next section.*

6. Leave the **ATry08_studentfirstname_studentlastname** database open to use in the next Try It.

Creating Relationships

- There are two ways to add more tables to the Relationships grid. You can drag them from the Navigation pane, as you did in the preceding steps, or you can use the Show Table dialog box.

✓ *The Show Table dialog box may appear automatically the first time you open the Relationships tab. It did not in the preceding steps because the Relationships tab had already been previously displayed in that database before you opened it.*

Try It! Showing Additional Tables

1. In the ATry08_studentfirstname_studentlastname database, on the Relationship Tools Design tab, click the Show Table button. The Show Table dialog box opens.
2. Click Students.
3. Hold down the CTRL key and click ClassEnrollment.
4. Click Add. Those two tables appear on the Relationships grid.
5. Click Close.

   ✓ *In this database, relationships between the two tables you just added were already created. The relationships still existed even when the tables involved were not shown on the Relationships grid.*
6. Leave the ATry08_studentfirstname_studentlastname database open to use in the next Try It.

Enforcing Referential Integrity

- In the Edit Relationships dialog box, you can choose to Enforce **Referential Integrity** so that you won't have an **orphan** in the child table. For example, you won't be able to enter an order for a customer that does not exist.
- If you select Enforce Referential Integrity, you can choose two additional options: Cascade Update Related Fields and Cascade Delete Related Records.
- **Cascade Update** Related Fields means that when you change the value in the primary key of the parent table, the related foreign key field in all related records of the child table will automatically change as well. If you don't check this box, Access will display an error message when you try to change the primary key.
- **Cascade Delete** Related Records means that when you delete the record in the parent table, all related records in the child table will be deleted as well. If you don't check this box, Access will display an error message when you try to delete the record in the parent table.
- When referential integrity is enabled, the parent table shows a "1" next to the primary key, and the child table most often shows an infinity symbol next to the foreign key.
- If the two related fields are primary keys, you'll see a "1" on both fields.

Try It! Creating a New Relationship with Referential Integrity

1. In the database **ATry08_studentfirstname_studentlastname**, with the Relationships tab displayed, drag the Instructors table onto the grid.
2. Drag the InstructorID field from the Instructors table onto the Instructor field in the ClassOfferings table. The Edit Relationships dialog box opens.
3. Click to mark the Enforce Referential Integrity check box.
4. Click to mark the Cascade Update Related Fields check box.

   ✓ *Cascade Update is used because if an instructor's ID changes, you want the ID updated in all related tables, too.*

5. Click to mark the Cascade Delete Related Records check box.

   ✓ *Cascade Delete is used because if an instructor is deleted, you want the Instructor field in ClassOfferings to be cleared, not left with the old instructor.*

6. Leave the **ATry08_studentfirstname_studentlastname** database open to use in the next Try It.

Enforce referential integrity for a relationship

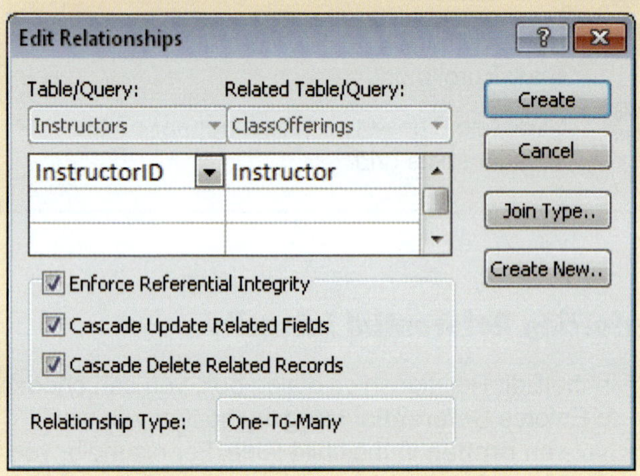

Try It! Modifying an Existing Relationship to Enforce Referential Integrity

1. In the database **ATry08_studentfirstname_studentlastname** database, with the Relationships tab displayed, double-click the connector line between the ClassID field in the Classes table and the Class field in the ClassOfferings table. The Edit Relationships dialog box opens.

   ✓ *The ClassID and Class table names should appear in the dialog box. If the dialog box appears blank, you did not double-click in the right spot; cancel and try again.*

2. Click to mark the Enforce Referential Integrity check box.
3. Click to mark the Cascade Update Related Fields check box.
4. Click to mark the Cascade Delete Related Records check box.
5. Click OK.
6. Leave the **ATry08_studentfirstname_studentlastname** database open to use in the next Try It.

Deleting Relationships

- Deleting a relationship is sometimes necessary, either because it was erroneously created or because the structure of the database has changed or needs to change. For example, in order to create a lookup (covered in Chapter 3), you may need to delete an existing relationship between tables.

Try It! Deleting and Recreating a Relationship

1. In the database **ATry08_studentfirstname_studentlastname** database, with the Relationships tab displayed, click the connector line between the Classes and ClassOfferings tables. The line appears bold.

   ✓ *If the line does not appear bold, you have not clicked in the right spot.*

2. Press DEL.
3. Click Yes.
4. Drag the ClassID field from the Classes table to the Class field in the ClassOfferings table to recreate the relationship.
5. Click Create.
6. Right-click the Relationships tab and click Close.
7. Click Yes.
8. Leave the **ATry08_studentfirstname_studentlastname** database open to use in the next Try It.

Showing Related Record

- You can view the parent table and the child table in Datasheet view. After you create a relationship between tables, return to the Datasheet view of the parent table and click the plus sign (+) on the left edge of a record to see the related rows from the child table.
- If you have more than one child table, you can change the **subdatasheet** attached to the datasheet.

Try It! Showing Related Records

1. In the database **ATry08_studentfirstname_studentlastname**, in the Navigation pane, double-click Classes. The Classes table opens in Datasheet view.
2. Click the plus sign to the left of the first class's record. The related records from the ClassOfferings table appear as a subdatasheet.
3. Click the plus sign next to the first record in the ClassOfferings subdatasheet. The related records in the Instructors table appear in a sub-subdatasheet.
4. Click the minus signs to collapse the subdatasheets.
5. Right-click the Classes tab and click Close to close the datasheet.
6. Leave the **ATry08_studentfirstname_studentlastname** database open to use in the next Try It.

View the subdatasheet

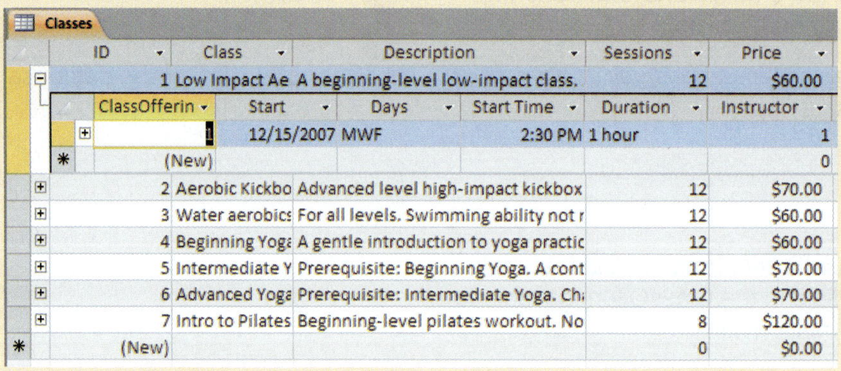

Try It! Changing the Subdatasheet

1. In the database **ATry08_studentfirstname_ studentlastname**, open the ClassOfferings table in Datasheet view.
2. Expand the subdatasheet for the first record.

   ✓ *Notice that the subdatasheet shows the Instructors table.*
3. Collapse the subdatasheet.
4. On the Home tab, in the Records group, click More, click Subdatasheet, and then click Subdatasheet again. The Insert Subdatasheet dialog box opens.
5. Click ClassEnrollment.

   ✓ *Recommended **master fields** and **child fields** in each table appear in the bottom of the dialog box. You can change those if needed, but they are usually right. If those boxes are empty, it means there is no usable relationship between the open datasheet's table and the selected table.*
6. Click OK.
7. Expand the subdatasheet.

   ✓ *Notice that the subdatasheet now shows the ClassEnrollment table. There are no records in that table right now so it shows a blank row.*

Choose a different subdatasheet

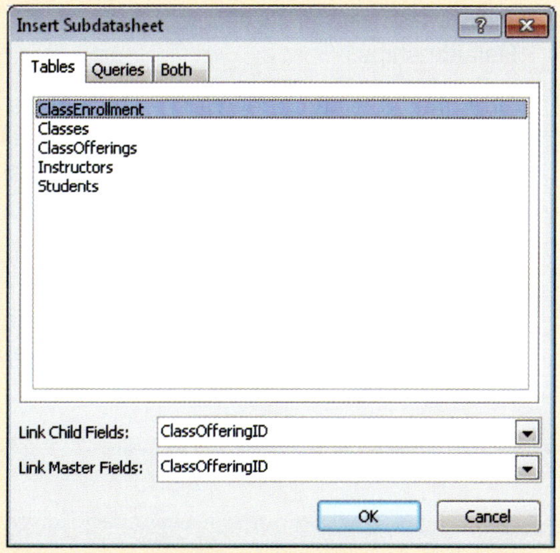

8. Right-click the ClassOfferings tab, and click Close to close the datasheet.
9. Click Yes to save the changes.
10. Leave the **ATry08_studentfirstname_ studentlastname** database open to use in the next Try It.

Printing a Relationship Report

- A relationship report is a hard-copy printout of the relationships between the tables in the database. Having one can be useful in documenting the database (for example, in a business environment where more than one person makes changes to the database's structure).

Try It! Printing a Relationship Report

1. In the database **ATry08_studentfirstname_studentlastname**, click Database Tools > Relationships.
2. Drag the tables around in the Relationships grid to make an attractive arrangement where all tables are visible and the lines between them are clear.

   ✓ *You can drag a table by its title bar at the top.*
3. On the Relationship Tools Design tab, in the Tools group, click Relationship Report. A report appears in Print Preview.
4. On the Print Preview tab, click Print. The Print dialog box opens.
5. **With your teacher's permission**, click OK to print. Otherwise, click Cancel.
6. Click Close Print Preview to exit from Print Preview. The report appears in Design view.
7. Right-click the Report1 tab and click Close.
8. Click No to discard changes. The report is not saved.
9. Click File > Close Database.

Project 17—Create It

Jewelry Business Database

DIRECTIONS

1. Start Access, if necessary, and open **AProj17** from the data files for this lesson. If a security warning bar appears, click **Enable Content**.
2. Save the database as **AProj17_studentfirstname_studentlastname** in the location where your teacher instructs you to store the files for this lesson.
3. Click **Database Tools** > **Relationships**. The Show Table dialog box opens.
4. Click **Customers**, hold down the Shift key, and click **Shippers**. All tables become selected.

Figure 8-2

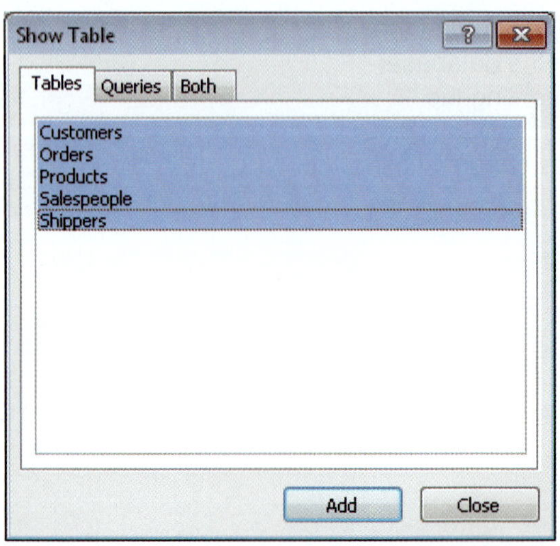

5. Click **Add**. All tables are added to the Relationships grid.
6. Click **Close** to close the Show Table dialog box.
7. Drag the **ID** field from the **Shippers** table to the Shipper field in the Orders table.
8. Mark the **Enforce Referential Integrity** check box.
9. Mark the **Cascade Update Related Fields** check box.
10. Click **Create**. An error appears, because the fields do not have the same field size.
11. Click **OK** to clear the error message.
12. Click **Cancel** to close the Edit Relationships dialog box.
13. In the Relationships grid, right-click the **Orders** table and click **Table Design**.

    ✓ *Note the Field Size setting for the Shipper field. It is Long Integer.*

14. Close the **Orders** table without saving changes.
15. In the Relationships grid, right-click the **Shippers** table and click **Table Design**.
16. Select the **ID** field.
17. In the Field Size property for the ID field, set the size to **Long Integer**.
18. Click **Save** on the Quick Access Toolbar.
19. Right-click the **Shippers** tab, and click Close to close the table.
20. On the Relationships grid, drag the **ID** field from the Shippers table to the **Shipper** field in the Orders table.
21. Click **Enforce Referential Integrity**.
22. Click **Cascade Update Related Fields**.

    ✓ *The relationship line is partly obscured by the table(s). You can drag the tables around on the grid to make the line easier to see if desired.*

23. Click **Create**. The relationship is created.
24. Right-click the **Relationships** tab and click **Close**.
25. Click **Yes** to save your work.
26. Click **File** > **Close Database**.
27. Submit your database file to your teacher for grading.

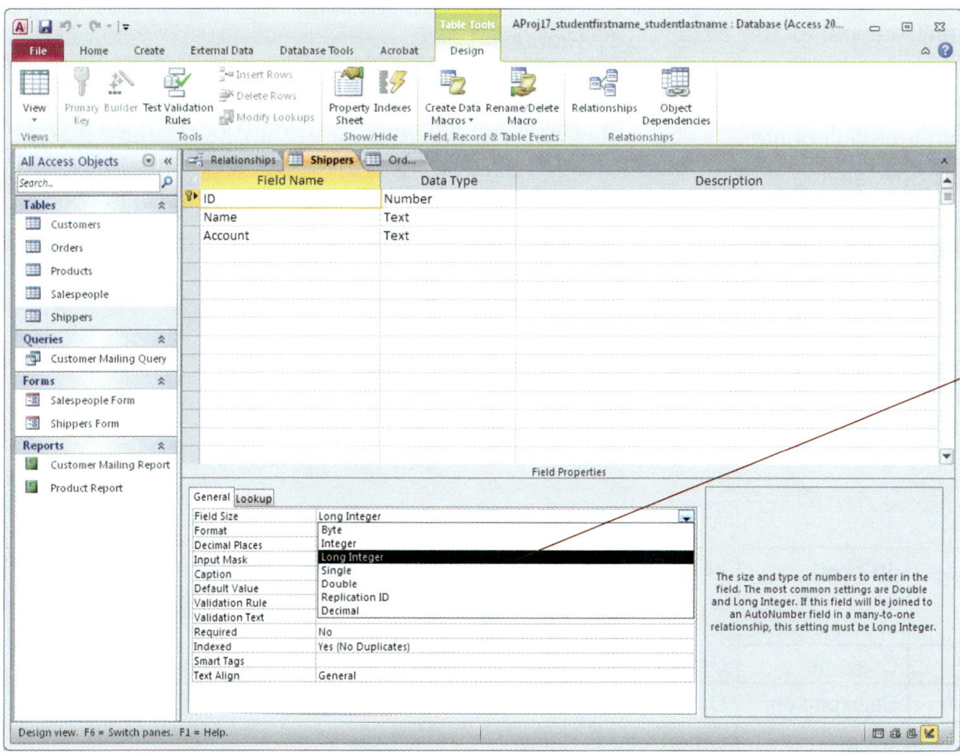

Figure 8-3

Project 18—Apply It

Jewelry Business Database

DIRECTIONS

1. Start Access, if necessary, and open **AProj18** from the data files for this lesson. If a security warning bar appears, click **Enable Content**.
2. Save the database as **AProj18_studentfirstname_studentlastname** in the location where your teacher instructs you to store the files for this lesson.
3. Open the **Relationships** grid.
4. Add the **OrderDetails** table to the grid.
5. Create the following relationships as shown in table at bottom of the page.
6. Arrange the tables on the Relationships grid so that no connector lines cross. Figure 8–4 shows one possible arrangement.
7. Edit the last relationship you created (between the Products and Order Details tables) to turn off Cascade Delete.
8. **If instructed to by your teacher**, print one copy of a **Relationships** report to your default printer.
9. Close the **Relationships** window, saving your changes.
10. Open the **Orders** table in Datasheet view, and enter the following record:

    Order ID (**AutoNumber**)

    Order Date: **12/1/2012**

    Customer: **1**

    Shipper: **1**

    Salesperson: **081-48-281**

    ✓ *You must have at least one record in a table in order for the subdatasheet to be visible. The plus sign that opens the subdatasheet does not appear until you enter a record.*
11. Open the subdatasheet for the first record. Notice that it shows data from the Customers table.
12. Collapse the subdatasheet.
13. Set the datasheet to show records from the **OrderDetails** table as the subdatasheet.
14. Using the subdatasheet, enter the following records in the **OrderDetails** table:

    OrderDetailID: (**AutoNumber**)

    Product: **2**

    Quantity: **2**

    OrderDetailID: (**AutoNumber**)

    Product: **3**

    Quantity: **1**
15. Close the datasheet, saving your changes to it when prompted.
16. Close the database, and submit the file to your teacher for grading.

From Field	In Table	To Field	In Table	Enforce Referential Integrity?	Cascade Update?	Cascade Delete?
ID	Customers	Customer	Orders	Yes	Yes	Yes
Employee ID	Salespeople	Salesperson	Orders	Yes	Yes	No
Order ID	Orders	Order	OrderDetails	Yes	Yes	Yes
ID	Products	Product	OrderDetails	Yes	Yes	Yes

Figure 8-4

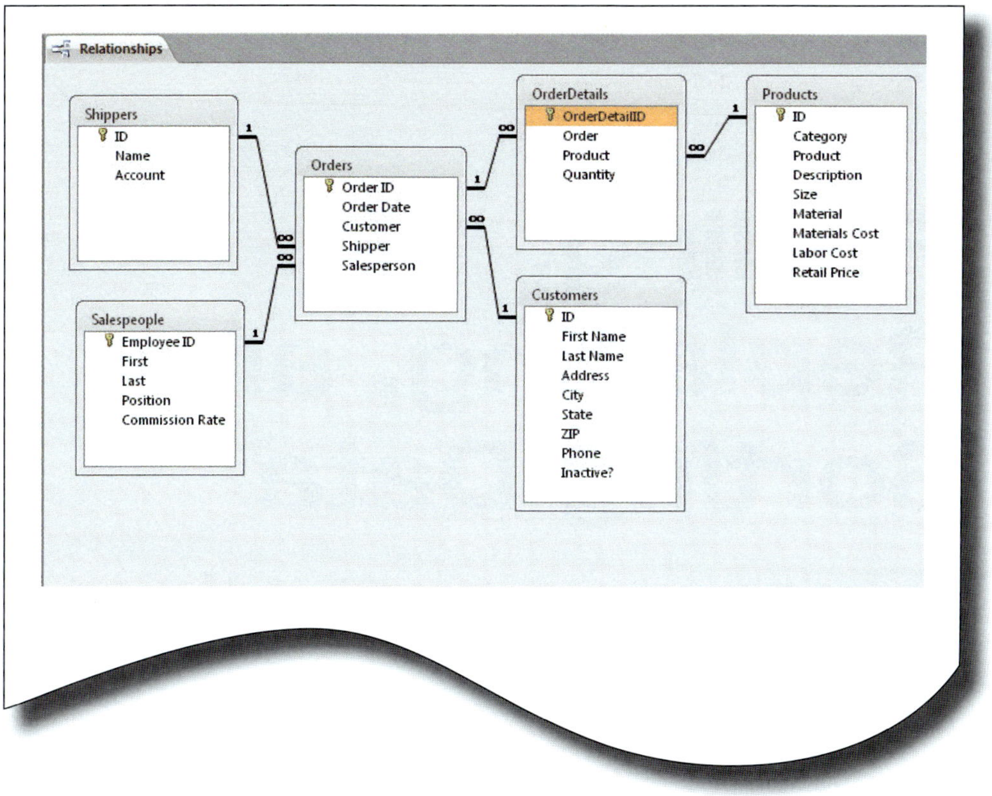
Relationships
Shippers
ID
Name
Account
Orders
Order ID
Order Date
Customer
Shipper
Salesperson
OrderDetails
OrderDetailID
Order
Product
Quantity
Products
ID
Category
Product
Description
Size
Material
Materials Cost
Labor Cost
Retail Price
Salespeople
Employee ID
First
Last
Position
Commission Rate
Customers
ID
First Name
Last Name
Address
City
State
ZIP
Phone
Inactive?

WORDS TO KNOW

Ascending
From A to Z or 1 to 9.

Descending
From Z to A or 9 to 1.

Find
To locate text within a record that matches characters you type.

Multiple sort
To use more than one field to sort. If there are duplicates for the first field, the second field is used to organize the records for each set of duplicated values in the first field.

Replace
To substitute new text after finding a string of text.

Sort
To arrange records alphabetically or numerically according to a specific field.

Wildcard
A character (? or *) that signifies one or more unspecified characters when finding text.

Lesson 9

Finding, Replacing, and Sorting Data

➤ What You Will Learn

- Finding Data
- Replacing Data
- Searching with Wildcards
- Sorting Records in a Table
- Sorting Using Multiple Fields
- Removing a Sort

Software Skills One of the primary purposes of a database is to store data so you can look it up later. You use Find procedures to locate data and Find and Replace procedures to locate data and change it to something else. You can search on an exact match or use wildcards that help you find information if you don't know the exact spelling. You can also sort records according to one or multiple fields to find things more easily.

Application Skills You have received updated information that needs to be input into the jewelry database. In this lesson, you will use the Find and Replace features to make the needed changes. You will also sort tables and create printouts of the records in the new sort order.

What You Can Do

Finding Data

- You can find and replace data in Datasheet view and in Form view.
- Move to the field where you want to search for data (unless you want to search all fields). Then open the Find and Replace dialog box to begin your search.
- The Find and Replace dialog box contains options for how to search for data. The options include:
  - *Find What*
    Type the word or phrase you want to look for. You can include **wildcards**. You can also pick from your last six searches.
  - *Look In*
    This defaults to the current field. You can choose this field for the entire table or form from the drop-down list.
  - *Match*
    Using the text in the Find What text box, find an exact match using the entire field, any part of the field, or the start of the field.
  - *Search*
    You can choose to search the entire list or in a particular direction through the records.
  - *Match Case*
    Check this box if you want the capitalization of the Find What entry to match the case of the value in the field exactly. For example, "Broadway" will not match with "broadway."
  - *Search Fields As Formatted*
    Find exact matches for date and number formats. When checked, 2/21/99 will not match February 21, 1999. When unchecked, these two dates will match.
- Click Find Next to find the next record that matches (in the direction indicated in the Search box).

Try It! Finding Data

1. Start Access and open the file **ATry09** from the data files for this lesson and save it as **ATry09_studentfirstname_studentlastname**.
2. Open the Students table in Datasheet view
3. Click anywhere in the TermDate field.
4. On the Home tab, in the Find group, click Find.
5. In the Find and Replace dialog box, type **2004** in the Find What box.
6. Open the Match drop-down list, and choose Any Part of Field.
7. Click Find Next. The selection highlight jumps to the first record with 2004 as part of the date.
8. Click Find Next again. A message appears that it was not found.

Find records that contain 2004 anywhere in the TermDate field

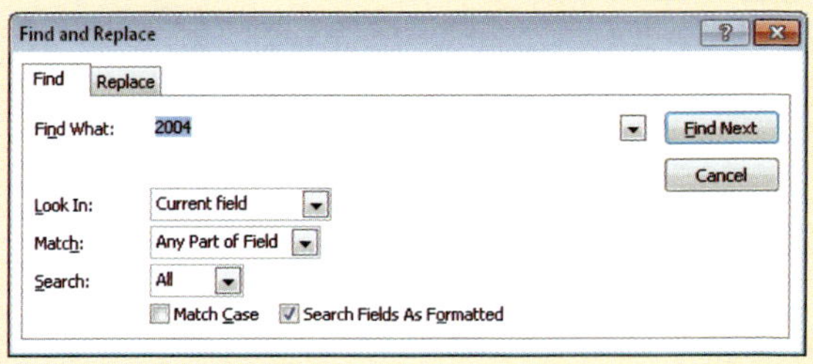

9. Click OK.
10. Leave the **ATry09_studentfirstname_studentlastname** database open to use in the next Try It.

Replacing Data

- When you have text that needs to be replaced with other text, you can manually edit it after finding it (as in the previous section).
- Alternately, you can use the Replace tab of the Find and Replace dialog box. For example, if area code 303 changes to 720, you can replace each occurrence of 303 with 720.
- If the text is found, you can click Replace to replace the text in the current record or Replace All to replace all occurrences in all records. Unless you are sure you won't create errors in your database, you should choose Replace rather than Replace All.

Try It! Replacing Data

1. In the database **ATry09_studentfirstname_studentlastname**, in the Students table in Datasheet view, click in the first record in the Notes field.
2. Click Home > Replace. The Find and Replace dialog box opens with the Replace tab displayed.
3. In the Find What box, type **Lifetime**.
4. In the Replace With box, type **Unlimited**.
5. Open the Match drop-down list and click Any Part of Field if it is not already selected there.
6. Click Find Next. The first occurrence appears.
7. Click Replace. That occurrence is replaced and the next occurrence appears.
8. Click Replace All to replace all additional occurrences at once.
9. In the confirmation box, click Yes.
10. Click Cancel to close the Find and Replace dialog box.
11. Leave the **ATry09_studentfirstname_studentlastname** database open to use in the next Try It.

Replace all instances of Lifetime with Unlimited

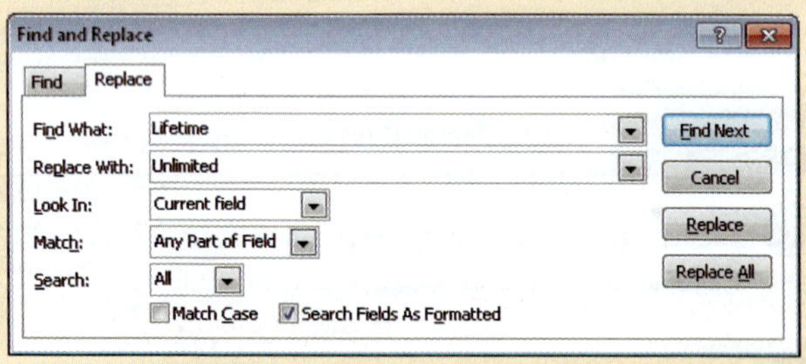

Searching with Wildcards

- You can use wildcards in the Find What text box if you don't know the exact spelling, but do know some of the characters.
- The most common wildcard is the asterisk (*). The asterisk can replace any number of characters. For example, Sm*th will find Smyth, Smith, and Smooth.
- You can use more than one asterisk. Sm*th* will find Smith, Smooth, Smothers, and Smythe.

✓ *To speed up filling in the Find or Replace dialog boxes, you don't need to change the Match choice from the default Whole Field option. Type *Broadway* to find a record when Broadway is anywhere within the field.*

- The question mark (?) wildcard is a substitute for an unknown single character. For example, ?oss will find Boss and Hoss, but not Floss.

Try It! **Searching with Wildcards**

1. In the database **ATry09_studentfirstname_ studentlastname**, in the Students table in Datasheet view, click anywhere in the Last field.
2. Click Home > Find.
3. In the Find What box, type **H???**.
4. Open the Match drop-down list and click Whole Field.
5. Click Find Next.
6. In the Find What box, delete the current entry and type ***g**.
7. Click Find Next.
8. Click Cancel to close the Find and Replace dialog box.
9. Leave the **ATry09_studentfirstname_ studentlastname** database open to use in the next Try It.

Sorting Records in a Table

- Sorting rearranges records in order by one or more fields. Most types of fields can be sorted.
- You can **sort** in **ascending** order (A to Z or 1 to 9) or **descending** order (Z to A or 9 to 1). You can sort a table by any field.
- Some reasons to sort might be to:
  - See groups of data (for example, all clients who live in New York or all of yesterday's sales).
  - See information organized from smallest or largest values.
  - Group all records that have blanks in a field.
  - Look for duplicate records.

  ✓ *You can also use filters and queries to sort records (discussed later in this chapter).*
- Before sorting, you must first move the insertion point to the field you want to sort. For example, if you want to sort a table of clients by last name in ascending order, move to the Last Name field.
- You can sort by fields with Text, Number, Currency, Date/Time, and Yes/No data types. You cannot sort fields that have Memo, Hyperlink, or OLE Object data types.
- If you save a table or form after sorting, the sort order becomes a property of the table or form. You can change this property by sorting on a different field.
- To remove a sort, you can either sort by a different field or remove all sorts with the Remove Sort command on the Home tab.
- If there is no primary key, records within a table (and its corresponding forms) are placed in input order when you remove the sort.
- If there is a primary key, records are ordered by the primary key when you remove the sort.

Try It! Sorting Records in a Table

1. In the database **ATry09_studentfirstname_studentlastname**, in the Students table in Datasheet view, click anywhere in the Last field column.
2. On the Home tab, in the Sort & Filter group, click Ascending . The records are sorted in A to Z order by last name. An up-pointing arrow appears on the field name to show it is sorted.
3. Click Home > Descending . The records are sorted in Z to A order by last name. A down-pointing arrow appears on the field name to show it is sorted.
4. Click Home > Remove Sort . The records go back to their default order.
5. Leave the **ATry09_studentfirstname_studentlastname** database open to use in the next Try It.

Sort records by last name

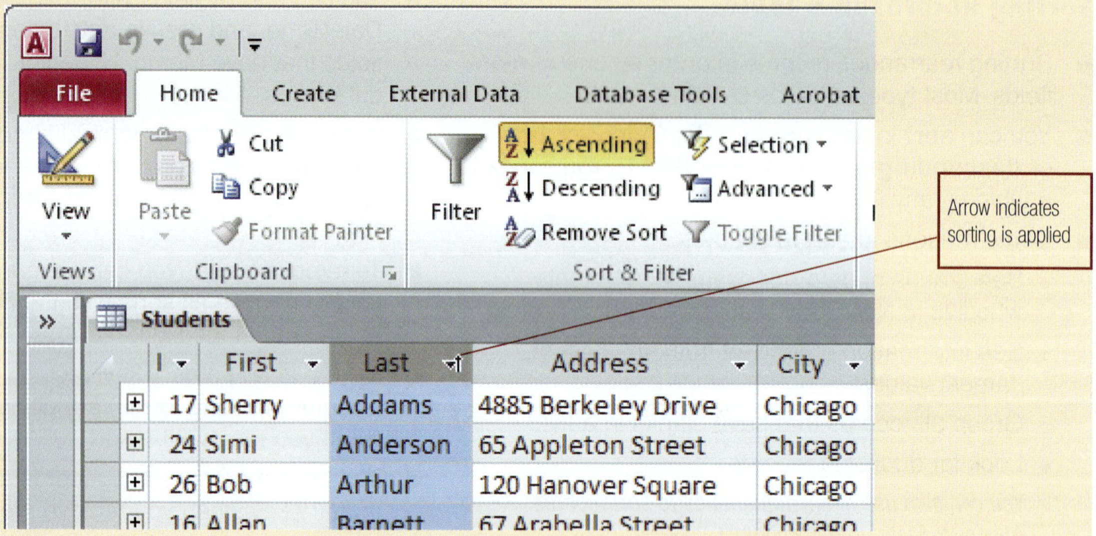

Sorting Using Multiple Fields

- With a multiple sort, you can sort by more than one column. For example, you could sort by State and then by City. All the records containing CA as the state, for example, would be grouped together, and then all the records with San Diego as the city would be grouped within the CA grouping.
- The two (or more) columns that you sort by must be adjacent on the datasheet. You might need to rearrange the fields to prepare to do the sort

✓ *To rearrange the columns in a datasheet, drag a field's heading to the right or left. If you do not want the rearrangement to be permanent, drag them back to their original positions after sorting, or do not save your changes when you close the datasheet.*

- When you sort by multiple columns, columns are sorted in left-to-right priority. In other words, Access sorts first by the leftmost selected column, then by the next-to-leftmost, and so on.

Try It! Sorting Using Multiple Fields

1. In the database **ATry09_studentfirstname_studentlastname**, in the Students table in Datasheet view, drag the TermLength field to the left of the TermDate field.
2. Select the TermLength field. Hold down SHIFT, and click the TermDate field to also select it.
3. Click Home > Descending. The records are sorted first by term length and then by term date.
4. Click Remove Sort.
5. Click File > Close Database.
6. When prompted to save changes, click No.

Project 19—Create It

Jewelry Business Database

DIRECTIONS

1. Start Access, if necessary, and open **AProj19** from the data files for this lesson. If a security warning bar appears, click **Enable Content**.
2. Save the database as **AProj19_studentfirstname_studentlastname** in the location where your teacher instructs you to store the files for this lesson.
3. Double-click the **Products** table in the Navigation pane to open it in Datasheet view.
4. Click anywhere in the **Description** column.
5. Click **Home > Replace**.
6. In the Find What box, type **filagree**.
7. In the Replace With box, type **filigree**.
8. Open the Match drop-down list and click Any Part of Field.
9. Click Replace All.
10. Click **Yes**.
11. Click **Cancel**.
12. Click anywhere in the **Material** column.
13. Click **Home > Sort Ascending**.
14. Click the **Save** button on the Quick Access Toolbar to save the changes to the datasheet.
15. **With your teacher's permission**, do the following:
    a. Click **File > Print > Print**.
    b. If necessary, choose the printer on which you have been instructed to print.
    c. Click **OK**.
    d. Write your name on the printout.
16. Click **File > Close Database**, and submit the database file to your teacher for grading.

Project 20—Apply It

Jewelry Business Database

DIRECTIONS

1. Start Access, if necessary, and open **AProj20** from the data files for this lesson. If a security warning bar appears, click **Enable Content**.
2. Save the database as **AProj20_studentfirstname_studentlastname** in the location where your teacher instructs you to store the files for this lesson.
3. Open the **Customers** table in Datasheet view. Use Find to locate the record where the phone number is 502-555-7755. Edit the number to **502-555-7756**.
4. Sort the Customers table in ascending order by State and City (First by state, then by city).

   ✓ *You will need to move the State field before the City field temporarily; then move it back to its original position after performing the sort, before the next step. You may need to change the settings of the Look In and Match drop-down lists.*
5. **With your teacher's permission**, print one copy of the datasheet. Write your name on the printout.
6. Save the changes to the table and close it.
7. Open the **Products** table in Datasheet view.
8. In the **Material** field, replace all instances of **Gold, White** with **White Gold**.
9. In the Material field, replace all instances of **Gold, White** with **White Gold**.
10. Sort the table in descending order by the **Material** field.
11. **With your teacher's permission**, print one copy of the datasheet. Write your name on the printout.
12. Save the changes to the table and close it.
13. Submit your database file to your teacher for grading.

Lesson 10

Filtering Data

➤ What You Will Learn

- Filtering by Selection
- Filtering for Multiple Selections
- Filtering with Comparison Operators
- Filtering by FormForm
- Saving Filter Results as a Query

Software Skills Sometimes you will want to look at all records that match certain criteria. Although you could sort a list, it may be easier to isolate (filter) only the records you want to see. Then when you use the navigation buttons or keys to move through records, you see only relevant records.

Application Skills Your friend for whom you have created the jewelry database would like to filter the data in various ways and be able to recall the filters quickly later. You will create several filters and save each one as a reusable query.

WORDS TO KNOW

Comparison operator
A word or symbol representing a comparison to be applied to a value, such as less than (<) or equal to (=) for a numeric value, or Begins With or Ends With for a text value.

Filter
To display only certain records.

Filter by Selection
To filter based on the data in the currently-selected record and field.

Filter by Form
To use a form that allows you to enter criteria for the filter.

What You Can Do

Filtering by Selection

- When you **filter** records, you see a subset of the records in the datasheet or form. The number of records that match the filter displays to the right of the navigation buttons at the bottom of the datasheet or form.
- **Filter By Selection** is the easiest way to filter your records. You can choose to filter for only records that equal or do not equal—or contain or do not contain—the current selection.

Try It! Filtering by Selection

1. Start Access and open the **ATry10** file from the data files for this lesson. Save it as **ATry10_studentfirstname_studentlastname**.
2. Open the Students table in Datasheet view.
3. In record 6, double-click *Unlimited* in the Notes field to select the word.
4. Click Home, click the Selection button, and then click Contains "Unlimited." Only the records that contain that value are shown.
5. On the Home tab, in the Sort & Filter group, click Toggle Filter to remove the filter.
6. In record 6, right-click Unlimited and, on the shortcut menu, click Contains "Unlimited."
7. Right-click Unlimited again and, on the shortcut menu, click Clear filter from Notes.
8. Leave the **ATry10_studentfirstname_studentlastname** database open to use in the next Try It.

Filter by a specific value using the Ribbon

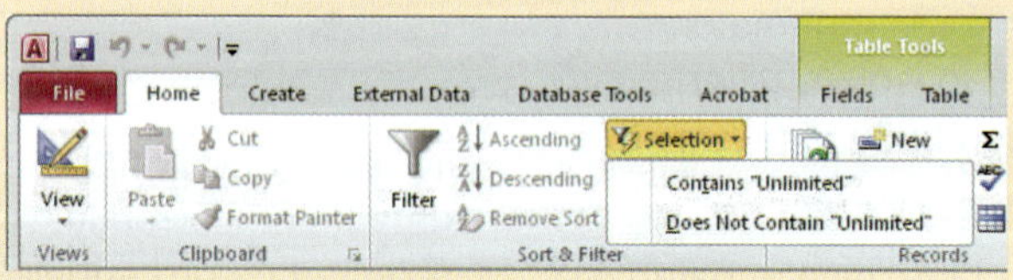

Filtering for Multiple Values

- You can also filter for multiple values at once. (That is, you can specify multiple values for that field that will all be included in the filter.) For example, you might want a filter on the ZIP field to include several different ZIP codes.

Try It! Filtering with Comparison Operators

1. In the database **ATry10_studentfirstname_ studentlastname**, in the Students table in Datasheet view, right-click any value in the TermDate column. A shortcut menu opens.
2. Point to Date Filters and then click Last Year. The records are filtered to show only the ones for the previous year.
3. Click Toggle Filter to remove the filter.
4. Right-click any value in the First column.
5. Point to Text Filters, and click Begins With.
6. In the Custom Filter dialog box, type **L** and click OK. The list is filtered to show only people with a first name beginning with L.
7. Click Toggle Filter to remove the filter.
8. Right-click the Students tab, and click Close to close the datasheet. If prompted to save changes, click Yes.
9. Leave the **ATry10_studentfirstname_ studentlastname** database open to use in the next Try It.

Filter using a data filter on the shortcut menu

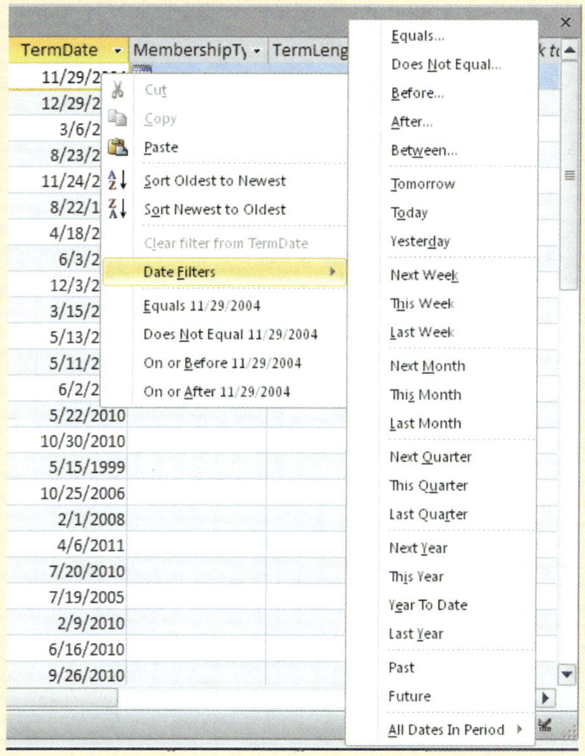

Filtering by Form

- Filter By Form gives you options to filter on multiple fields and to use wildcards in the filter criteria. (Wildcards were covered in Lesson 9.)
- The Filter by Form interface enables you to do any of the following in each field:
  - Directly type in the value you want.
  - Click the drop-down arrow to the right of the field, and choose from the existing entries in the field.
  - Use wildcards: Type the value with a wildcard asterisk (*) for any number of characters or question mark (?) for one character.
  - Use criteria: Type > (greater than), < (less than), >= (greater than or equal to), or <= (less than or equal to) and then a number or text string.

  ✓ *When using greater than or less than, put quotation marks around criteria that should be interpreted alphabetically (such as A being before B in the alphabet), or hash marks (#) around criteria that should be interpreted numerically.*

  - Type *Between firstvalue and secondvalue*. For example, *Between 1/1/99 and 3/31/99*.
  - Type *IS NULL* to find empty fields, or *IS NOT NULL* to find non-empty ones.
- If you have entries in multiple fields on the Look for tab, Access finds all records that match for all entries. For example, if *Smith* is in Last Name and *Denver* is in City, records that have both Smith and Denver show.

✓ *When you use Filter By Form on a Memo type field, the only choices are Null or Not Null. If you want to Filter By Form on such a field more precisely, you must change its field type to Text.*

- If you have an entry on the Look for tab and then an entry on the Or tab(s), Access finds all records that match any of the entries. For example, if Smith is on the Look for tab and Denver is on the Or tab, Access will find all the Smiths whether or not they live in Denver and all people who live in Denver whether or not their name is Smith.
- Click Toggle Filter to filter the data or to remove the filter.
- From Filter by Form view, you can click Home > Advanced > Close to return to the form or datasheet without filtering data, or you can click Toggle Filter twice (once to apply the filter and then again to remove it).

Filter by Form enables more complex filter criteria

Figure 10-1

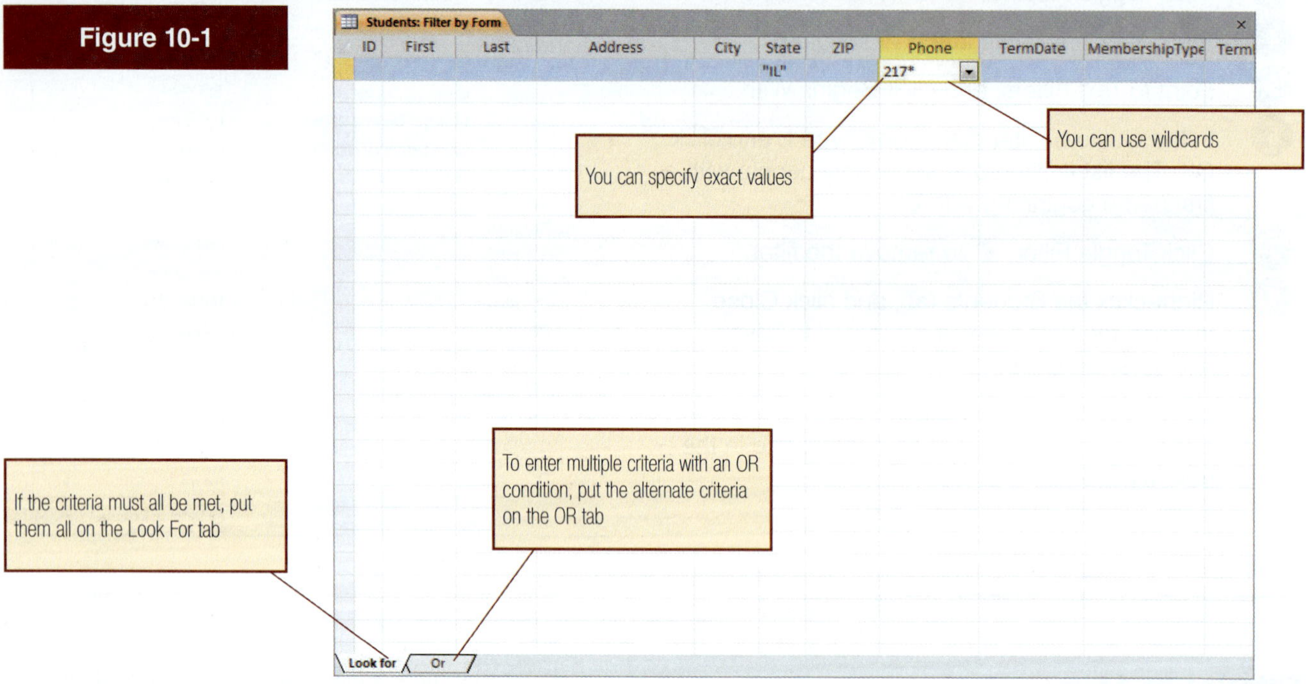

Try It! Filtering by Form

1. In **ATry10_studentfirstname_studentlastname**, in the Students table in Datasheet view, click Home, click the Advanced button, and then click Filter By Form.
2. If there are any criteria already entered in the form, remove them.
3. Click in the TermLength field, click the drop-down arrow, and choose 10.
4. In the Last field, type **Like "C*"**.
5. Click the Or tab at the bottom of the window.
6. Open the arrow TermLength field and choose 10.
7. In the Last field, type **Like "A*"**.
8. Click Toggle Filter . Two records appear in the filter.
9. Click Home > Advanced > Clear All Filters.
10. Leave the **ATry10_studentfirstname_studentlastname** database open to use in the next Try It.

Saving Filter Results as a Query

- When you save a filter to use later, you save it as a query. Queries are covered in more detail in the remaining lessons in this chapter.
- The resulting query will be available from the Navigation pane just like any other query.

Try It! Saving a Filter as a Query

1. In the database **ATry10_studentfirstname_studentlastname**, in the Students table in Datasheet view, click Home > Advanced > Filter By Form.
2. Open the TermLength drop-down arrow and choose 10.
3. Click Home > Advanced > Save As Query. The Save As Query dialog box opens.
4. Type **Term Length 10** and click OK.
5. Click Home > Advanced > Close to close the filter form without running the filter.
6. Click File > Close Database.

Save the filter as a query

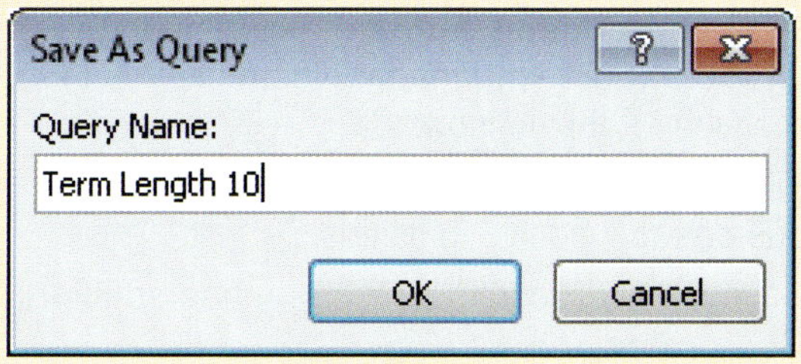

Project 21—Create It

Jewelry Business Database

DIRECTIONS

1. Start Access, if necessary, and open **AProj21** from the data files for this lesson. If a security warning bar appears, click **Enable Content**.
2. Save the database as **AProj21_studentfirstname_studentlastname** in the location where your teacher instructs you to store the files for this lesson.
3. Double-click the **Products** table to open it.
4. Click the down arrow on the **Category** heading, opening the menu.
5. Click **Select All** to clear all check boxes.
6. Click the **Bracelet** and **Necklace** check boxes.
7. Click **OK**.
8. **With your teacher's permission**, do the following to print the datasheet:
   a. Click **File** > **Print** > **Print**.
   b. Click **OK**.
9. Click **Home** > **Advanced** > **Filter By Form**.
10. Click **Home** > **Advanced** > **Save as Query**.
11. Type **Necklaces and Bracelets**.
12. Click **OK**.
13. Click **File** > **Close Database**, saving your changes when prompted.
14. Submit your database file to your teacher for grading.

Project 22—Apply It

Jewelry Business Database

DIRECTIONS

1. Start Access, if necessary, and open **AProj22** from the data files for this lesson. If a security warning bar appears, click **Enable Content**.
2. Save the database as **AProj22_studentfirstname_studentlastname** in the location where your teacher instructs you to store the files for this lesson.
3. Filter the **Customers** table to show only the customers who live in Illinois.
4. Save the filter results as a query named **Illinois Customers**.
5. Filter the **Products** table to show only necklaces that are made of any type of yellow gold. The results should contain 4 records.

   ✓ *Here's one way to do step 5: First set up a query for multiple values (all the values that contain Yellow in the Material field), and then use Filter By Form to add the additional criteria of Necklace in the Category field.*
6. Save the filter results as a query named **Yellow Gold Necklaces**.
7. Filter the **Salespeople** table to show only people whose position is **Manager**.
8. Save the filter results as a query named **Managers**.
9. Close the database, saving your changes, and submit it to your teacher for grading.

Lesson 11

Creating a Query in Design View

➤ What You Will Learn

- Understanding Data Analysis
- Exploring Data Mining Tools, Techniques, and Ethics
- Understanding Database Trends
- Understanding Queries
- Creating a New Select Query in Design View
- Running a Query
- Saving and Printing a Query

Software Skills It can be challenging to make sense of a large amount of data. Performing data analysis can extract the information you need. This can be done in Access with sorting, filtering, queries, and reports. In this lesson, you will learn about the tools and techniques of data analysis and create queries.

Application Skills In the jewelry database, you will create several queries that extract information (data analysis) from the raw data. You will also create a query that displays hidden fields in a table and enter data in those fields.

WORDS TO KNOW

Cloud computing
A model where data and programs are stored on the Internet; users do not own the infrastructure and pay only for the level of services used.

Data analysis
Using software tools to evaluate digital data so you can use the information in meaningful ways.

Data mining
Using data analysis to find patterns in data.

Query
A defined set of operations to be performed on a table (or on the results from another query).

Query Design view
A view that allows you to choose the fields in a query, to sort, and to set criteria.

Query design grid The lower half of the Query Design view that shows the field name, table name, sort order, show box, and criteria rows for selecting records.

Select query
A query that sorts and filters a table or other query to extract certain fields and records based on criteria you specify. This is by far the most common type of query.

Virtualization
A variety of technologies that allow for more efficient use of hardware and other resources.

What You Can Do

Understanding Data Analysis

- Data analysis is the process of evaluating information so you can use it in meaningful ways.
- You can use database tools in programs such as Excel or Access to perform data analysis. For example, you can use query and report calculation features in Access to analyze the data, or export the data to Excel and calculate or chart it there to find trends.
- You can also do quick data analysis by sorting or filtering records, whether or not you save as a query. You did basic data analysis in the previous two lessons.
- Data analysis can also include charting. Charting data lets you see a visual representation of the information, which can make it easier to spot trends and make comparisons.

Try It! Analyzing Data

1. Start Access and open **ATry11** from the data files for this lesson. Save it as **ATry11_studentfirstname_studentlastname**.
2. Open the ClassEnrollment table in Datasheet view.
3. Click the ClassID field, and click Home > Sort Ascending, to sort the records by the class being taken.
4. Count the number of records that have a ClassID of 1.
5. Close the ClassEnrollment table, saving changes when prompted.
6. Open the Students table in Datasheet view.
7. Click in the TermDate field, and then choose Home > Filter > Date Filters > Before.
8. In the Custom Filter dialog box, type **01/01/2010** and click OK.
9. Click Home > Advanced > Filter By Form.
10. Open the TermLength drop-down list and click 10.
11. Click the Or tab at the bottom of the screen.
12. Open the Notes field's drop-down list and click Is Not Null.
13. Click Toggle Filter. Eight records display.
14. Right-click the Students tab and click Close. When prompted to save your changes, click No.
15. Leave the **ATry11_studentfirstname_studentlastname** database open to use in the next Try It.

Exploring Data Mining Tools, Techniques, and Ethics

- **Data mining** involves using a variety of tools to identify patterns in data and to use that data to make strategic business decisions.
- For example, a supermarket may track your purchases and use data mining to identify the brands you buy most often. It can then send you coupons or special offers to encourage you to try a different brand.
- Data mining is most often performed on samples of data, rather than the full dataset. A representative sample is easier to work with, and if it is a truly random sample, it will likely produce the same results as working with the complete dataset.
- Querying, filtering, and charting tools in database and spreadsheet programs provide basic data mining capabilities, but more sophisticated data mining software is also available that performs actions.

- Organizations should establish data mining guidelines to ensure that the process is not used for unethical or illegal purposes. For example, an insurance company may not use data mining to identify and discriminate against customers who require expensive medications.
- All employees should be aware of the guidelines, and procedures should be in place for handling ethical breaches of those policies.

Understanding Database Trends

- Data collection and analysis occurs everywhere in society. Retail stores track buying patterns, hospitals track medical care, social networking sites track friend requests, and mobile phones track calling patterns.
- Businesses, organizations, and the government use the information collected in databases to help guide strategic planning, customize products for individuals, and develop new products and services.
- Trends in both hardware and software are leading to more powerful and customizable databases.
- Two trends to watch include **virtualization** and **cloud computing**:
  - Virtualization is when a variety of technologies are combined to allow for more efficient use of hardware and other resources, such as a server hosting multiple operating system environments for multiple customers with each customer accessing his or her applications and data remotely.
  - Cloud computing is when programs and data are stored on Internet servers, relieving customers of the responsibility of owning and maintaining the infrastructure, yet providing access to the information and tools they need at any time, from any location.

Understanding Queries

- **Queries** are like advanced sort/filters, except you can save a query and store it in the database window. In Lesson 10, you learned how to save a custom filter as a query.
- Like sorting/filtering, queries let you sort and define criteria to select the records you want to see.
- Unlike sorting/filtering, a query enables you to choose a subset of fields to display. You need not hide the columns you don't want; they simply don't appear in the query results.
- You can also use certain fields in the query as filters without including those fields in the query output.
- Queries also make possible some specialized operations like performing calculations on field values and placing the result in a new column in a datasheet.
- Queries, like tables, can be used as a starting point for reports or forms.
- There are several kinds of queries, but the most common type is a **select query**. The main purpose of a **select query** is to extract fields and records from a larger table and present the results in a specific sort order.

Creating a New Select Query in Design View

- **Query Design v**iew is a view in which you can define the structure of the query, including choosing the fields to include, the order in which those fields will appear, which field to sort the results by (if any), and what criteria to use for filtering records.
- Query Design view consists of two sections. At the top are field lists with which the tables/queries work. At the bottom is the **query design grid**, where you place the individual fields (one per column) and define how they should be acted upon.

Figure 11-1

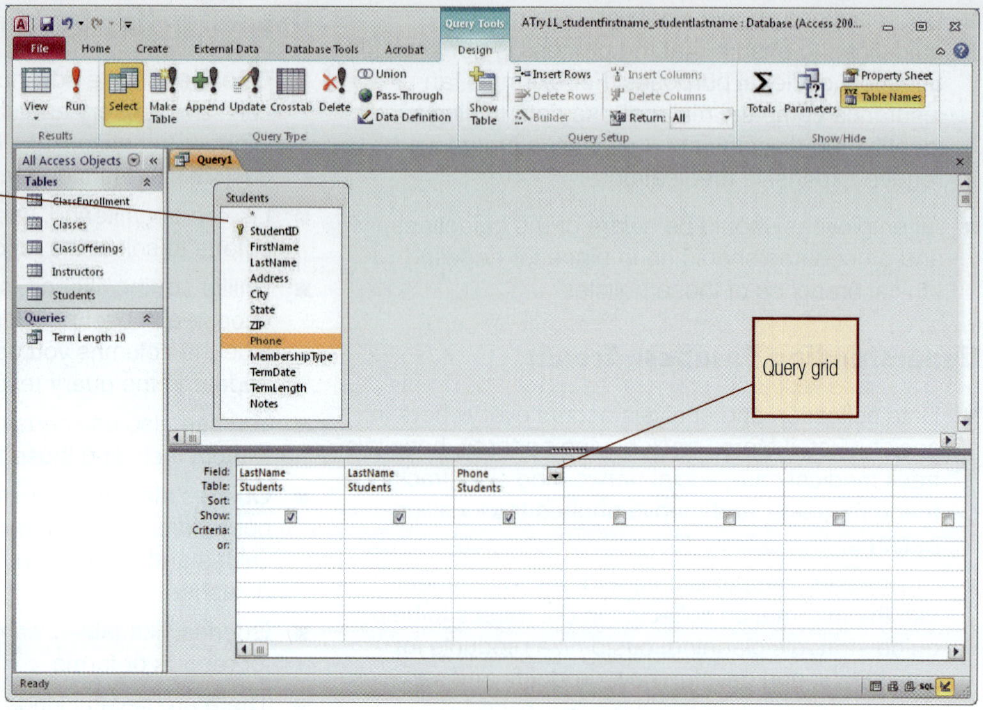

Try It! Starting a New Query in Design View

1. In the database **ATry11_studentfirstname_studentlastname**, click the Create tab. In the Queries group, click Query Design. The Show Table dialog box opens.
2. Click Students, and then click Add. Click Close to close the dialog box.
3. Drag the bottom border of the Students window down, expanding the box so that all fields are visible.
4. Leave the **ATry11_studentfirstname_studentlastname** database open to use in the next Try It.

Add the Students table to the query design

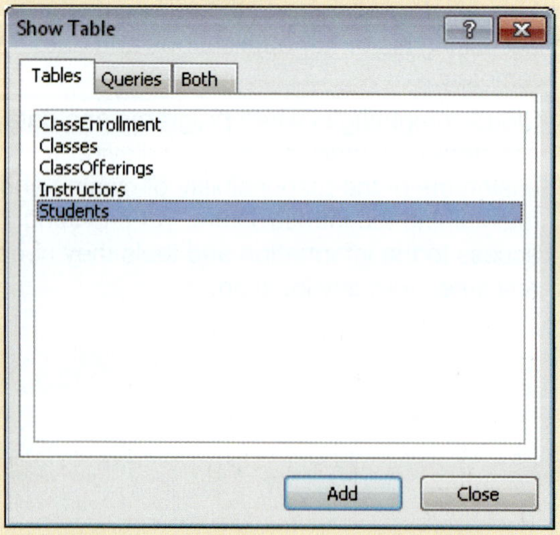

Starting a New Query in Design View

- After adding the table(s), you select individual fields and place them in the query grid at the bottom of the screen.
- The order in which you place the fields in the query design (from left to right in the query grid) determines the column order for the resulting datasheet.
- You can choose a field in any of the following ways:
  - Double-click on the field in the Field List to place the field to the right of the previous field.
  - Drag the field from the Field List to a field in the query design grid to insert this field where you want it in the grid. To place a field between two existing fields in the grid, drop the new field on top of the one that it should be to the right of.
  - Click on the drop-down arrow or type in the Field cell to choose a field from the list of fields.
- If you make a mistake in adding a certain field to the query grid, you can remove it by selecting it and pressing DEL ; or, on the Query Design Tools tab, in the Query Setup group, click Delete Columns.

Try It! Adding Fields to a Query

1. In the database **ATry11_studentfirstname_studentlastname** in Query Design view, double-click LastName on the Students table field list. LastName is added to the grid.
2. Drag FirstName from the Student table field list and drop it onto the LastName field in the grid, placing FirstName to the left of LastName.
3. Click in the Field row for the first empty column in the grid.
4. Click the drop-down list arrow in the cell, and click Phone on the menu that appears.
5. Double-click the Membership Type field to place it in the next empty column of the grid.
6. Leave the **ATry11_studentfirstname_studentlastname** database open to use in the next Try It.

Add the Membership Type field

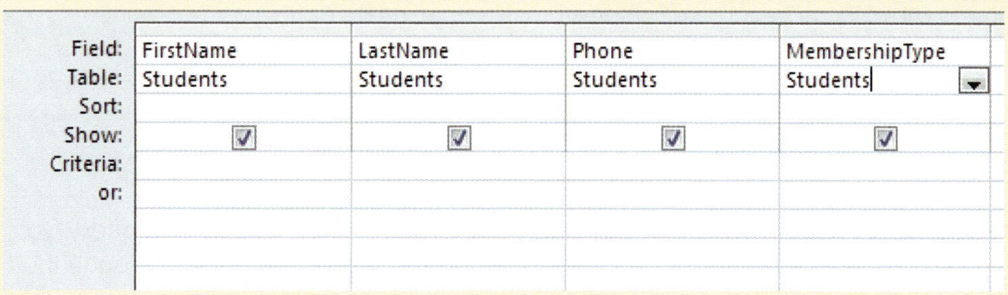

Try It! Removing Fields from the Query

1. In the database **ATry11_studentfirstname_studentlastname**, click anywhere in the Membership Type field's column.
2. Click Query Tools Design > Delete Columns.
3. Leave the **ATry11_studentfirstname_studentlastname** database open to use in the next Try It.

Running a Query

- There are two ways to see the results of a query. One is to switch to Datasheet view to preview the results. The other is to run the query with the Run button !.
- For a select query, there is no real difference between these two methods. However, when you get into action queries that actually perform operations on the data rather than just displaying it, the difference becomes important.
- Query results appear in Datasheet view, just like a table.

Try It! Running a Query

1. In the database **ATry11_studentfirstname_studentlastname**, on the Query Tools Design tab, in the Results group, click Run !. The query results appear.
2. Click Home > View > Design View. Query Design view reappears.
3. Click Query Tools Design > View > Datasheet View. Datasheet view reappears.
4. Leave the **ATry11_studentfirstname_studentlastname** database open to use in the next Try It.

Saving and Printing a Query

- When you close a query, if you have made design changes to it, you are prompted to save your work. You can also save a query from Design view before you are ready to close it.
- The first time you save a query, you will be prompted for a name. Although the name can be a maximum of 64 characters including spaces, you should keep the name short and use no spaces.
- Query results appear in Datasheet view, so you can print them just as you would print any other datasheet.

Try It! Saving and Printing a Query

1. In the database **ATry11_studentfirstname_ studentlastname**, click the Save button on the Quick Access Toolbar.
2. Type **Phone List**.
3. Click OK.
4. If the query does not already appear in Datasheet view, right-click its tab and click Datasheet View.
5. Click File > Print > Print.
6. **With your teacher's permission**, click OK; otherwise, click Cancel.
7. Close the database and exit Access.

Project 23—Create It

Jewelry Business Database

DIRECTIONS

1. Start Access, if necessary, and open **AProj23** from the data files for this lesson. If a security warning bar appears, click **Enable Content**.
2. Save the database as **AProj23_ studentfirstname_studentlastname** in the location where your teacher instructs you to store the files for this lesson.
3. Click **Create > Query Design** .
4. In the Show Table dialog box, click **Customers**, and click **Add**.
5. Click **Close**.
6. Drag the bottom of the Customers window down until all fields are visible.
7. Double-click the **First Name** field.
8. Double-click the **Last Name** field.
9. Double-click the **City** field.
10. Double-click the **State** field.
11. Double-click the **ZIP** field.
12. Drag the **Address** field into the grid and drop it on the City field, placing it between Last Name and City.
13. Click the **Save** button on the Quick Access toolbar.
14. Type **Mailing List** and click **OK**.
15. Click **Query Tools Design** > **Run** ! to run the query.
16. Right-click the query's tab and click **Close**.
17. Close the database, and submit it to your teacher for grading.

Project 24—Apply It

Jewelry Business Database

DIRECTIONS

1. Start Access, if necessary, and open **AProj24** from the data files for this lesson. If a security warning bar appears, click **Enable Content**.
2. Save the database as **AProj24_studentfirstname_studentlastname** to the location where your teacher instructs you to store the files for this lesson.
3. Open the **Mailing List** query in Design view.

   ✓ *One way to open the Mailing List in Design view is to right-click the query in the Navigation pane and click Design View.*

4. Add the **ID** field to the query grid in the leftmost position.
5. Close the query, saving your changes.
6. Create a new query using Query Design view, based on the **Products** table.

   ✓ *Note that some extra fields that appear on the field list do not show up in Datasheet view for this table. That's because these fields have been hidden. When you create a query, you have access to all the fields in the table, even the hidden ones.*

7. Add the **Product**, **Material**, **Materials Cost**, and **Labor Cost** fields to the query grid, in that order.
8. Run the query to display its datasheet.
9. In the **Materials Cost** and **Labor Cost** fields in the datasheet, enter the following values, as shown in table at bottom of the page.
10. Save the query as **Production Costs** and close it.
11. Create a new query based on the **Salespeople** table. Include these fields: **Employee ID**, **First**, **Last**, and **Position**.
12. Save the query as **Sales List** and close it.
13. Rename the query **Salesperson List**.
14. Close the database, and submit to your teacher for grading.

Product	Material	Materials Cost	Labor Cost
Curb Chain	Yellow Gold, 10K	$100.00	$10.00
Curb Chain	White Gold, 14K	$120.00	$10.00
Curb Chain	Sterling Silver	$60.00	$10.00
Frog Bracelet	Sterling Silver	$50.00	$25.00
Snake Bracelet	Sterling Silver	$50.00	$30.00
Hoop Earrings	Yellow Gold, 10K	$40.00	$20.00
Hoop Earrings	White Gold, 14K	$50.00	$20.00
Hoop Earrings	Yellow Gold, 10K	$40.00	$20.00
Hoop Earrings	White Gold, 14K	$50.00	$20.00
Knot Earrings	White Gold, 14K	$40.00	$30.00
Knot Earrings	Yellow Gold, 10K	$30.00	$30.00
Knot Earrings	Sterling Silver	$10.00	$30.00
Three-Diamond Pendant	Yellow Gold, 10K	$350.00	$50.00

Lesson 12

Creating a Multi-Table Query

➤ What You Will Learn

- Creating a Query Based on More Than One Table
- Sorting Query Results
- Reordering Fields in a Query
- Using All Fields of a Table
- Changing a Column Name
- Creating a New Query from an Existing Query
- Saving a Query with a Different Name

WORDS TO KNOW

Alias
An alternative name for a field.

Software Skills One of the main uses for queries is to join the data from two or more tables into a single datasheet of results. This involves adding multiple tables that have relationships among them to the query design. In this lesson, you will learn how to open a query in Design view and make changes to it, including adding more tables and fields and sorting the results.

Application Skills In the jewelry business database, you will continue building more complex and useful queries for your friend to use to analyze her business data. In this lesson, you will build several multi-table queries that will help her see the relationships between the tables more clearly.

What You Can Do

Creating a Query Based on More than One Table

- You can use fields from as many tables as you like in a query. The only requirement is that the tables all be related to one another in some way.
- There are many benefits to creating queries based on multiple tables. For example, if you have a table that represents related records from another table as numeric entries, it is not always obvious what the numeric entries represent. In Figure 12-1, for example, the ClassEnrollment table shows the classes and students as ID numbers, rather than names.
- In contrast, a datasheet based on a table that combines values from the ClassEnrollment, ClassOfferings, Classes, and Students tables can show all that data in text form, making it easier to understand and interpret. See Figure 12-2.

Figure 12-1

ClassEnrollment

Enrollment I	Class ID	Student ID	Click to Add
1	1	1	
2	1	11	
3	1	24	
4	1	4	
5	1	7	
6	2	15	
7	2	36	
8	2	2	
9	2	9	
10	2	31	
11	2	14	
* (New)	0	0	

Figure 12-2

Query1

Class	Start	Days	First	Last
Low Impact Aerobics	12/15/2007	MWF	Leroy	Critchfield
Low Impact Aerobics	12/15/2007	MWF	Robert	Kroeker
Low Impact Aerobics	12/15/2007	MWF	Simi	Anderson
Low Impact Aerobics	12/15/2007	MWF	Abdul	Norcutt
Low Impact Aerobics	12/15/2007	MWF	Margaret	Faderman
Aerobic Kickboxing	12/15/2007	TTh	Jacob	Hill
Aerobic Kickboxing	12/15/2007	TTh	Marjorie	Pratt
Aerobic Kickboxing	12/15/2007	TTh	Juliana	Smith
Aerobic Kickboxing	12/15/2007	TTh	Anna	Roecher
Aerobic Kickboxing	12/15/2007	TTh	Abby	McNally
Aerobic Kickboxing	12/15/2007	TTh	Melissa	Wilson
*				

Try It! Creating a Multi-Table Query

1. Start Access and open **ATry12** from the data files for this lesson and save it as **ATry12_studentfirstname_studentlastname**.
2. Click Create > Query Design.
3. In the Show Table dialog box, click Classes and hold down SHIFT, and click Instructors.
4. Click Add and then click Close. Three tables are added.
5. Drag the bottom of the Instructors table down so that all fields are visible.
6. Double-click the FirstName field in the Instructors table.
7. Double-click the LastName field in the Instructors table.
8. Double-click the ClassName field in the Classes table.
9. Double-click the Days, StartTime, and Location fields in the ClassOfferings table, in that order.
10. Click Query Tools Design > Run ! to see the query results. Two records are displayed.
11. Click Home > View > Design View to return to Design view.
12. Press CTRL + S to open the Save As dialog box.
13. In the Save As dialog box, type **Class Offerings Query** and click OK.
14. Leave the **ATry12_studentfirstname_studentlastname** database open to use in the next Try It.

Sorting Query Results

- In the query's design, you can specify that the resulting datasheet be sorted in a certain way. You can sort by one field, or by more than one.
- As with other sorts, the second-level sort applies only in the event of a duplicate value in the first-level sort field.
- If you choose multiple fields to be sorted, the sort order is left to right in the query grid.

✓ *If you want to sort in a different order than left to right, there's a workaround. Add a second copy of a field to the query grid and set it to be sorted. Then clear the check box in the Show row for that field so that copy of the field doesn't appear in the results.*

Try It! Sorting Query Results

1. In the database **ATry12_studentfirstname_studentlastname** in Query Tools Design view, click in the Sort row for LastName field.
2. Click the drop-down arrow and choose Ascending.
3. Click in the Sort row for the ClassName field.
4. Click the drop-down arrow and choose Ascending.
5. Leave the **ATry12_studentfirstname_studentlastname** database open to use in the next Try It.

Sort by LastName

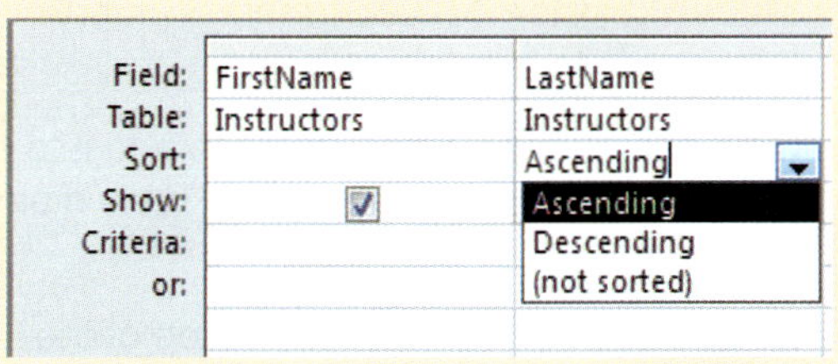

Reordering Fields in a Query

- To reorder the fields in the query grid, select a field, and then drag it to the right or left.
- To select a field, click the thin gray bar immediately above the field name.

Try It! Reordering Fields in a Query

1. In the database **ATry12_studentfirstname_studentlastname** in Query Design view, click the thin gray bar above the FirstName field. The column becomes selected.
2. Drag the bar to the right to place the field to the right of the Location field.
3. Click the thin gray bar above the LastName field.
4. Drag the bar to the right to place the field to the right of the FirstName field.
5. Click Run ! to preview the query results and then close the query. Click Yes to save the query.
6. Leave the **ATry12_studentfirstname_studentlastname** database open to use in the next Try It.

Select the field by clicking the gray bar above it

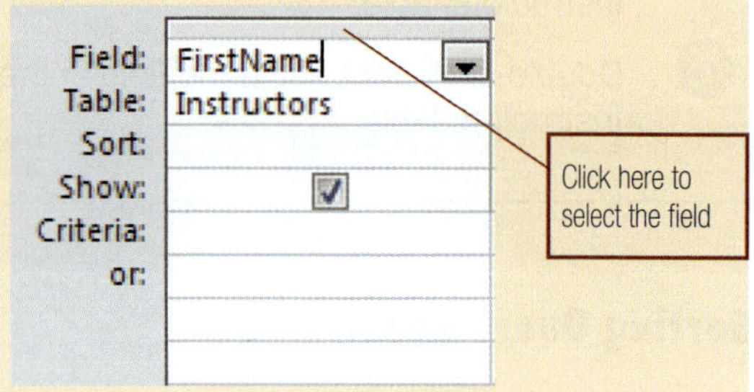

Using All Fields of a Table

- If you want to include all the fields from a table in the query, drag or double-click the asterisk (*) at the top of the table's field list into the query grid.

Try It! Using All Fields of a Table

1. In the database **ATry12_studentfirstname_studentlastname**, click Create > Query Design to start a new query.
2. Double-click the Classes table to add it to the query, and then close the Show Table dialog box.
3. Double-click the asterisk at the top of the Classes table field list.
4. Click Run ! to preview the query results. All fields appear.
5. Click Home > View to return to Design view.
6. Right-click the query tab and click Close. Click No when prompted to save your changes.
7. Leave the **ATry12_studentfirstname_studentlastname** database open to use in the next Try It.

Changing a Column Name

- Sometimes when you include a field from a different table, that field's name doesn't make sense in the new context. You can rename the column headings in the query results to show different names. This new name is called an **alias**.
- To assign an alias, in the Field row of the query grid, add the new name in front of the official name, separated by a colon. For example, if the field's actual name is Last and you want the column name to be Salesperson, you would type Salesperson: in front of Last.

Try It! Changing a Column Name

1. In the database **ATry12_studentfirstname_studentlastname**, right-click the Phone List query in the Navigation pane and click Design View.
2. In the query grid, click to place the insertion point to the left of Phone in the Field row.
3. Type **Telephone:**. The entry in the Field row should now appear as *Telephone:Phone*.
4. Click Run ! to run the query.
5. Right-click the query's tab and choose Close. Do not save changes.
6. Leave the **ATry12_studentfirstname_studentlastname** database open to use in the next Try It.

Saving a Query with a Different Name

- You might sometimes want to have several similar queries in the same database. You don't have to recreate the query for each version; you can open the query in Design view, make changes, and then save it with a different name.

Try It! Saving a Query with a Different Name

1. In the database **ATry12_studentfirstname_studentlastname**, in the Navigation pane, right-click the Phone List query and select Design View.
2. Double-click the Notes field to add it to the query grid.
3. Click File > Save Object As. The Save As dialog box opens.
4. In the Save Phone List To box, type **Phone List with Notes**.
5. Click OK.
6. Click the Home tab to exit from Backstage view.
7. Click the Phone List with Notes query in the Navigation pane to display its results in Datasheet view.
8. Close all open objects and close the database.

Project 25—Create It

Jewelry Business Database

DIRECTIONS

1. Start Access, if necessary, and open **AProj25** from the data files for this lesson. If a security warning bar appears, click **Enable Content**.
2. Save the database as **AProj25_studentfirstname_studentlastname** to the location where your teacher instructs you to store the files for this lesson.
3. Click **Create > Query Design**.
4. In the Show Table dialog box, click **Customers**. Then hold down the CTRL key and click **Orders**.
5. Click **Add** to add both tables to the query, and then click **Close**.
6. On the Customers field list, click **First Name**. Then hold down the CTRL key and click **Last Name**.
7. Drag the selected fields to the lower grid.
8. Double-click the **Order Date** field in the Orders table to place it into the grid.
9. Click **Query Tools Design** > **Run** ! to run the query.
10. Click the **Save** button on the Quick Access Toolbar.
11. In the Save As box, type **Customers and Orders** and click **OK**.
12. Close the database, and submit to your teacher for grading.

Project 26—Apply It

Jewelry Business Database

DIRECTIONS

1. Start Access, if necessary, and open **AProj26** from the data files for this lesson. If a security warning bar appears, click **Enable Content**.
2. Save the database as **AProj26_studentfirstname_studentlastname** to the location where your teacher instructs you to store the files for this lesson.
3. Save a copy of the **Illinois Customers** query. Name the copy **Indiana Customers**.
4. Modify the Indiana Customers query design so that it shows Indiana customers, rather than Illinois customers.

   ✓ *To do so, change the state in the Criteria row of the grid from IL to IN.*

5. Run the **Indiana Customers** query to make sure it shows Indiana customers and then close it.
6. Open the **Customers and Orders** query in Design view, and add the **Shippers** and **Salespeople** tables.
7. Place the **Name** field from the Shippers table in the grid to the left of all other fields.
8. Select the **Name** column and drag it to the right of all other fields.
9. Place the **Last** field from the Salespeople table in the grid to the right of all other fields
10. Assign an alias of **Shipper** to the **Name** field.
11. Assign an alias of **Salesperson** to the **Last** field.
12. Run the query to confirm that it works, and that the aliases appear correctly. Then save and close the query.
13. Create a new query in Design view that uses the **Orders**, **Products**, and **OrderDetails** tables.
14. Place the following fields in the grid: **Order Date** from the Orders table, **Product** from the Products table, and **Quantity** from the OrderDetails table.
15. Set the query to be sorted in **Ascending** order, first by **Order Date** and then by **Product**.
16. Save the query as **Product Ordering**, run it to check the results, and close it.
17. Close the database, and submit your database to your teacher for grading.

Lesson 13

Using Criteria in a Query

WORDS TO KNOW

Criteria
Filtering specifications that determine what records will be included in a query.

Null
A lack of an entry in a field.

➤ What You Will Learn

Specifying Text Criteria in a Query
Specifying Numeric Criteria in a Query
Specifying Criteria Using a Field Not Displayed in the Query Results
Using Null Criteria to Find Blank Fields

Software Skills Criteria (which is the plural of criterion) enable you to apply filters to query results so that only certain records are displayed. In this lesson, you learn how to apply basic text and numeric criteria and how to use criteria based on a field that does not appear in the query results.

Application Skills In the jewelry database, you will create queries that filter the data based on multiple criteria, both numeric and text-based. These queries will provide the business owner with useful information about her business.

What You Can Do

Specifying Text Criteria in a Query

- **Criteria** are filtering specifications that you apply to individual fields. Criteria are very similar to the filters you learned how to create in Lesson 10.
- Criteria can be text-based, numeric, or logical. You can specify an exact value, use one or more wildcards, or enter a formula with a comparison operator such as < (less than) or = (equal to).
- When using text-based criteria, the text must be enclosed in quotation marks. If you forget the quotation marks, Access adds them for you automatically.

✓ *Lesson 14 covers using wildcards in text criteria.*

- If you want to specify more than one possible value, you can enter the second one in the Or row in the query grid. This works for both text and numeric criteria.
- There is no limit to the number of Or lines you can use. However, for practical purposes, you may want to use a wildcard or a comparison operator, as described in Lesson 14, if you have more than two or three possible values to accept.

Try It! Specifying Text Criteria

1. Start Access and open the files **ATry13** from the data files for this lesson. Save it as **ATry13_studentfirstname_studentlastname**.
2. Right-click the Classes Being Offered query, and click Design View.
3. In the Criteria row for the Days field, type **MWF** and press TAB. Access automatically encloses the text with quotation marks.
4. Click Query Tools Design > Run !. The query results show only classes that have MWF in the Days field.
5. Click Home > View to return to Design view.
6. In the Or row below where you typed MWF, type **TTh**.
7. Click Run ! to run the query again. This time, records that match either entry appear.
8. Right-click the Classes Being Offered tab and click Close. Click No when prompted to save changes.
9. Leave the **ATry13_studentfirstname_studentlastname** database open to use in the next Try It.

Enter MWF for the Days criteria

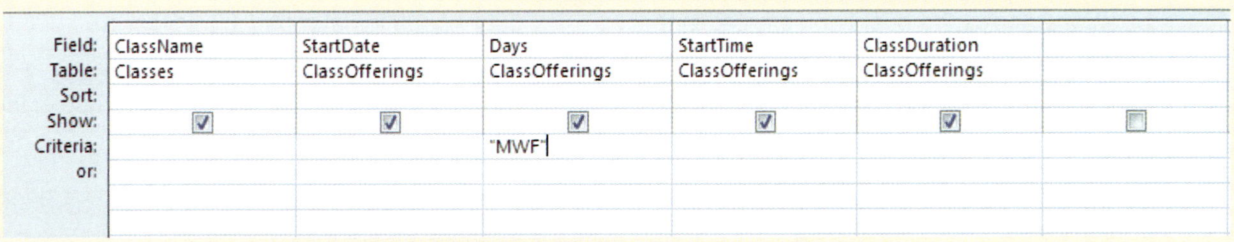

Specifying Numeric Criteria in a Query

- Numeric criteria are not enclosed in quotation marks; they are entered as regular numbers in the Criteria row.

Try It! Specifying Numeric Criteria in a Query

1. In **ATry13_studentfirstname_ studentlastname**, click Create > Query Design. In the Show Table dialog box, double-click the Students table and then click Close.
2. In the field list, double-click the FirstName, LastName, and TermLength fields to add them to the grid.
3. In the Criteria row for the TermLength field, type **5**.
4. Click Run. The query results show only people with a term length of 5.
5. Click View to return to Design view. Leave the query open for later use in this lesson.
6. Leave the **ATry13_studentfirstname_ studentlastname** database open to use in the next Try It.

Specifying Criteria Using a Field Not Displayed in the Query Results

- You can filter query results based on a criterion that does not appear in the query results themselves. To do this, you add the criteria to the query grid, but then clear the Show check box for the unwanted field(s).

Try It! Filtering by an Undisplayed Field

1. In **ATry13_studentfirstname_ studentlastname**, the query you created in the previous steps should be open in Design view. In the query grid, click to clear the Show check box for the TermLength field.
2. Click Run. The query results show only the people with a term length of 5, but the TermLength field does not appear.
3. Click View to return to Design view.
4. Mark the Show check box again for the TermLength field.
5. Clear the 5 from the Criteria row. Leave the query open for later use in this lesson.
6. Leave the **ATry13_studentfirstname_ studentlastname** database open to use in the next Try It.

Clear the Show check box

Field:	FirstName	LastName	TermLength
Table:	Students	Students	Students
Sort:			
Show:	☑	☑	☐
Criteria:			5
or:			

Using Null Criteria to Find Blank Fields

- **Null** is the word that Access uses to describe a field that is empty. This is different from a zero value, or a text field in which you have clicked and pressed the spacebar. (A space, technically, is a character. A null field contains no characters.)
- You can create a filter criterion based on whether or not a field is null. The words you use for this are Is *Null* and *Is Not Null*, respectively. Enter those words directly in the Criteria row, without quotation marks.

Try It! **Filtering for Null Values**

1. In **ATry13_studentfirstname_studentlastname**, in the Criteria row for the TermLength field, type **Is Null**.
2. Click Run. The query results show only where that field is empty.
3. Click View to return to Design view.
4. In the Criteria row for the TermLength field, replace Is Null with **Is Not Null**.
5. Click Run. The query results show only records where that field is not empty.
6. Close the database file without saving your changes.

Project 27—Create It

Jewelry Business Database

DIRECTIONS

1. Start Access, if necessary, and open **AProj27** from the data files for this lesson. If a security warning bar appears, click **Enable Content**.
2. Save the database as **AProj27_studentfirstname_studentlastname** to the location where your teacher instructs you to store the files for this lesson.
3. Right-click the **Product Ordering** query, and click **Design View**.
4. In the Criteria row for the Quantity field, type **1**. Refer to Figure 13-1.
5. Click **Run** to run the query and confirm that only records where the Quantity is 1 appear. Then click **View** to return to Query Design view.
6. In the Or row under the Quantity field, type **2**.
7. Click **Run** to run the query. This time records appear where the Quantity is either 1 or 2.
8. Click **View** to return to Query Design view.
9. Click **File** > **Save Object As**. Type **Orders with 1 or 2 Quantity** and click OK.
10. Close the database, and submit it to your teacher for grading.

Figure 13-1

Field:	Order Date	Product	Quantity
Table:	Orders	Products	OrderDetails
Sort:	Ascending	Ascending	
Show:	☑	☑	☑
Criteria:			1
or:			

Project 28—Apply It

Jewelry Business Database

DIRECTIONS

1. Start Access, if necessary, and open **AProj28** from the data files for this lesson. If a security warning bar appears, click **Enable Content**.
2. Save the database as **AProj28_ studentfirstname_studentlastname** in the location where your teacher instructs you to store the files for this lesson.
3. Create a new query in Design view, and add the **Product Ordering** query to it as a data source.
4. Add all fields to the query grid by adding the asterisk (*) from the field list to the grid.
5. Add the **Product** field to the query grid, and set up a criterion so that the query includes only records where the Product field equals **Curb Chain**.
6. Clear the **Show** check box for the Product field.
7. Run the query and make sure that only one copy of the Product field appears and only curb chain records are displayed.
8. Save the query as **Curb Chain Sales**.
9. Create a new query in Design view, and add the **Products** table to it as a data source.
10. Add all fields to the query grid by adding the asterisk (*) from the field list to the grid.
11. Add the Size field to the query grid, and set up a criterion so that the query includes only records where the Size field is null (empty).
12. Clear the **Show** check box for the Size field. Refer to Figure 13-2.
13. Run the query and make sure only records where the Size field is empty are displayed. You may want to turn on the display of the Size field in the query results temporarily to check.
14. Save the query as **One Size Items**.
15. Close the database, and submit to your teacher for grading.

Figure 13-2

Field:	Products.*	Size
Table:	Products	Products
Sort:		
Show:	☑	☐
Criteria:		Is Null
or:		

Lesson 14

Using Comparison Operators

➤ What You Will Learn

- Using Comparison Operators
- Using Wildcards and the Like Operator
- Using the Between...And Comparison Operator
- Using the In Operator
- Combining Criteria

WORDS TO KNOW

Comparison operator
A symbol or word that represents a comparison to be performed between values.

Software Skills Although you can use multiple Or lines in the query grid to allow for multiple criteria, it is often easier to write an expression that defines the characteristics of the values you want to include. You can do this with wildcards and comparison operators.

Application Skills In this lesson, you will continue writing queries for the jewelry business database using wildcards and comparison operators to construct more complex filters.

What You Can Do

Using Comparison Operators

- Comparison operators represent comparisons between two values. For example, in the formula x=y, the equals sign (=) is a comparison operator.
- When using comparison operators with text, enclose the text in quotation marks. When using them with dates, enclose the dates in # (hash signs). If you forget to add those signs, Access will in most cases add them for you.
- Here are the symbols you can use for comparison operators:

Symbol	Meaning	Example
<	Less Than	<30
<=	Less Than or Equal To	<=#1/1/2011
>	Greater Than	>100
>=	Greater Than or Equal To	>=500
<>	Not Equal To	<>"Denver"

Try It! Using a Comparison Operator in a Query

1. Start Access and open the file **ATry14** from the data files for this lesson. Save the file as **ATry14_studentfirstname_studentlastname**.
2. Right-click the Classes Under $70 query and select Design View.
3. Double-click the Price field to place it in the grid.
4. In the Criteria row for the Price field, type **<70**.
5. Click to clear the Show checkbox for the Price field.
6. Click Query Design Tools > Run ! to run the query.
7. Click the Save button on the Quick Access Toolbar to save the query.

Enter <70 for the Price criteria

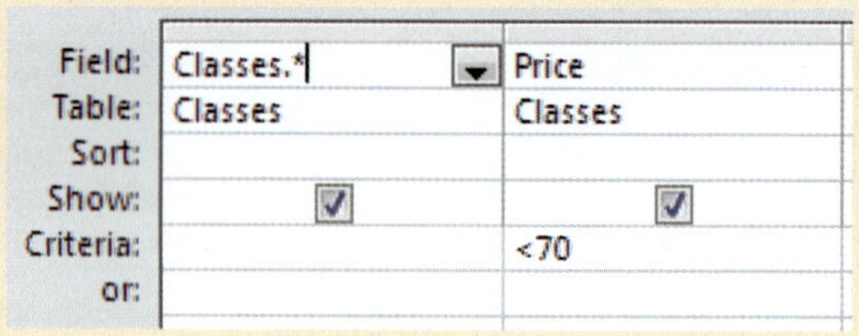

8. Right-click the query's tab and click Close.
9. Leave the **ATry14_studentfirstname_studentlastname** database open to use in the next Try It.

Using Wildcards and the Like Operator

- Wildcards work in queries the same as in filters (see Lesson 10).
- The asterisk (*) substitutes for any number of characters; the question mark (?) substitutes for any single character.
- If you want to find records where the field includes the text you specify, but not necessarily as the entire entry, precede the criterion with the word *Like*. Then include text and a wildcard character.
- When greater-than or less-than comparison operators are used with text, alphabetical order is used. For example, <="F*" includes entries that begin with letters that come before F alphabetically.

Symbol	EXample	Example
Like	Like "den*"	Find entries that begin with *den* and include any other text following it.
	Like "den??"	Find entries that begin with *den* and exactly two other characters following it.
	Like "*den"	Find entries that end with *den*, with any text before it.
	Like "??den"	Find entries that contain exactly two characters followed by *den*.
	Like "*den*"	Find entries that contain *den* and optionally other characters before and/or after them.

Try It! Using Wildcards and the Like Operator in a Query

1. In the file **ATry14_studentfirstname_studentlastname**, right-click the Beginning Classes query and click Design View.
2. Double-click the Description field to add it to the grid.
3. In the Criteria row for the Description field, type **Like "*Beginning*"**.

   ✓ *Make sure you type the asterisks on both sides of the word, inside of the quotation marks.*
4. Click Run ! to run the query. Three records should appear.
5. Click the Save button on the Quick Access Toolbar.

Place an asterisk * at the start and end of the word

Field:	Classes.*	Description
Table:	Classes	Classes
Sort:		
Show:	☑	☑
Criteria:		Like "*Beginning*"
or:		

6. Right-click the query's tab and click Close.
7. Leave the **ATry14_studentfirstname_studentlastname** database open to use in the next Try It.

Using the Between...And Operator

- The word *Between* is used as a comparison operator to specify a range of values.
- For example, *Between #1/1/2011# and #1/15/2011#* finds values that fall between those two dates, inclusive.

Try It! Using the Between...And Operator in a Query

1. In the file **ATry14_studentfirstname_studentlastname** database, right-click the Classes Between $60 and $80 query and select Design View.
2. Double-click the Price field to add it to the grid.
3. In the Criteria row for the Price field, type **Between 60 and 80**.
4. Click to clear the Show check box for the Price field.
5. Click Run ! to run the query. Six records should appear.
6. Click the Save button on the Quick Access toolbar to save the query.

Set up Between criteria for the Price field

Field:	Classes.*	Price
Table:	Classes	Classes
Sort:		
Show:	☑	☐
Criteria:		Between 60 And 80
or:		

7. Right-click the query's tab and click Close.
8. Leave the **ATry14_studentfirstname_studentlastname** database open to use in the next Try It.

Using the In Operator

- The word *In* is used as a function to specify a list of values. For example, *In ("NM","NY","CA")* would include any fields that contained any of those values.

Try It! Using the In Operator in a Query

1. In the file **ATry14_studentfirstname_studentlastname** database, right-click the Term Length 1, 5, or 10 query and click Design View.
2. Double-click the TermLength field to add it to the grid.
3. In the Criteria row for the TermLength field, type **In (1, 5, 10)**.
4. Click Run to run the query. Fifteen records should appear.
5. Click the Save button on the Quick Access toolbar to save the query.

Set up In criteria for the TermLength field

Field:	Students.*	TermLength
Table:	Students	Students
Sort:		
Show:	☑	☐
Criteria:		In (1,5,10)
or:		

7. Right-click the query's tab and click Close.
8. Leave the **ATry14_studentfirstname_studentlastname** database open to use in the next Try It.

Combining Criteria with AND or OR Operators

- As you saw in the previous lesson, you can use the additional rows under the Criteria row to enter OR conditions.
- As an alternative, you can use an OR operator to combine criteria. For example, "GA" OR "CA" would find either value, just the same as if you had entered "GA" in the Criteria row and "CA" in the Or row.
- To use multiple criteria and restrict the results to records where both are matched, use the AND operator. For example, >5 AND <10 finds values between 5 and 10 (but not including 5 or 10 themselves).

Try It! Using the Or Operator in a Query

1. In the file **ATry14_studentfirstname_studentlastname** database, right-click the Date Not 2006 query and click Design View.
2. Double-click the TermDate field to add it to the grid.
3. In the Criteria row for the TermDate field, type **<#1/1/2006# OR >#12/31/2006#**.

   ✓ *You can widen the TermDate column by dragging so the criteria are not truncated. It makes no difference in how the query functions, however.*
4. Click Run to run the query. Thirty-four records should appear.
5. Click the Save button on the Quick Access toolbar to save the query.

Use an Or operator for the TermDate field

Field:	Students.*	TermDate
Table:	Students	Students
Sort:		
Show:	☑	☐
Criteria:		<#1/1/2006# Or >#12/31/2006#
or:		

6. Right-click the query's tab and click Close.
7. Click File > Close Database.

Project 29—Create It

Jewelry Business Database

DIRECTIONS

1. Start Access, if necessary, and open **AProj29** from the data files for this lesson. If a security warning bar appears, click **Enable Content**.
2. Save the database as **AProj29_studentfirstname_studentlastname** to the location where your teacher instructs you to store the files for this lesson.
3. In the Navigation pane, right-click the **Product Ordering** query and click **Design View**.
4. In the Criteria line for the Quantity field, type **Between 2 And 10**. Refer to Figure 14-1.
5. Click **Run**. Notice that the records all have quantities from 2 to 10, inclusive.
6. Click **View** to return to Design view.
7. Click **File** > **Save Object As**. Type **Order Quantities 2 to 10** and click **OK**.
8. Click the **Order Quantities 2 to 10** tab and click **Close** to close the query.
9. Close the database, and submit it to your teacher for grading.

Field:	Order Date	Product	Quantity
Table:	Orders	Products	OrderDetails
Sort:	Ascending	Ascending	
Show:	☑	☑	☑
Criteria:			Between 2 And 10
or:			

Figure 14-1

Project 30—Apply It

Jewelry Business Database

DIRECTIONS

1. Start Access, if necessary, and open **AProj30** from the data files for this lesson. If a security warning bar appears, click **Enable Content**.
2. Save the database as **AProj30_studentfirstname_studentlastname** in the location where your teacher instructs you to store the files for this lesson.
3. Open the **Products Basic** query in Design view.
4. Use the **Like** operator to create a criterion that includes records with the word "**starfish**" anywhere in the Product field. Run the query to check it (it should return 2 records) and then return to Design view.
5. Save the query as **Starfish Products**.
6. Save the query again as **Animal Products**, and then modify the criteria to show any animal names (Starfish, Frog, or Snake). Run the query (it should return 4 records), and then save and close it.

   ✓ *Use multiple Or criteria.*
7. In Query Design view, create a new query that uses all the fields from the Product Ordering query, but shows only odd-numbered quantities less than 10. (In other words, 1, 3, 5, 7, or 9.) Name the query **Odd-Numbered Quantities**.

   ✓ *Use the In operator.*
8. In Query Design view, create a new query that uses all the fields from the Product Ordering query, but shows only orders placed on 12/14/2012. Name the query **Orders 12/14/2012**.
9. Close the database, and submit to your teacher for grading.

Lesson 15

Using Calculated Fields

➤ What You Will Learn

Understanding Calculated Fields
Creating a Calculated Field in a Table
Using Calculated Fields in a Query

WORDS TO KNOW

Calculated field
A field that contains the result of a computation performed on one or more other fields.

Software Skills You can insert calculations in database objects. You can create calculated fields directly within the table's design, or you can create calculated fields in a query's design grid.

Application Skills In the jewelry business database you have been working on, you will add several calculated fields that will make the business's data easier to understand. You will add a Cost to Make field to the Products table, and you will construct a new query that calculates prices at various discount levels.

What You Can Do

Understanding Calculated Fields

- A **calculated field** contains the result of a computation performed on one or more other fields.
- A calculated field can perform a math operation on a single field. For example, you might have a Markup field that multiplies the Wholesale cost of an item by 1.5.
- A calculated field can perform a math operation on multiple fields. For example, you might have a Cost field that consists of adding the LaborCost field to the MaterialCost field.

Creating a Calculated Field in a Table

- A new feature in Access 2010 is the ability to create calculated fields in tables; in previous versions, you could only create them on forms, reports, or queries.
- Calculated fields are added to a table in table Design view; create a new field and set its data type to Calculated.
- When constructing a calculated field, you use the Expression Builder. This is a dialog box that provides help for building math and logical functions.
- First you choose from the Expression Elements list. This list contains the following elements:
  - Table: The name of the table you are working with. Selecting it allows you to select individual fields from the table to use in the calculation.
  - Functions: Type of operation to be performed in the calculation; same types of functions as provided in Excel.
  - Constants: These are values such as True, False, and Null.
  - Operators: Symbols that represent math operations such as + (addition) or * (multiplication).
- Depending on your choice of expression element, the other two columns change in content to help you narrow down further what you want. For example, Operators is the category chosen, <All> is the Expression Category, and * is the Expression Value.
- Once you locate the expression value you want, double-click it to add it to the expression at the top of the dialog box.
- Using the Expression Builder's lists is optional; if you remember the syntax of the formula you want, you can type it at the top of the Expression Builder window rather than building it by selecting from the lists.

Try It! Creating a Calculated Field in a Table

1. Start Access and open the file **ATry15** from the data files for this lesson. Save the file as **ATry15_studentfirstname_studentlastname**.
2. Right-click the Classes table and click Design View .
3. Click in the Notes row, and click Table Tools Design > Insert Rows . A new row appears.
4. In the Field Name column, type **Discount Price**.
5. In the Data Type column, open the drop-down list and click Calculated. The Expression Builder opens.
6. Click Classes in the Expression Elements list.
7. In the Expression Categories list, double-click the Price field.
8. Click Operators in the Expression Elements list.
9. In the Expression Values list, double-click the asterisk (*).
10. Click at the end of the formula in the top of the dialog box and type **.85**.
11. Click OK.

    ✓ *Notice that in the field's properties, the Expression row contains the formula you just created.*
12. Click Table Tools Design > View . A message appears that you must save.
13. Click Yes to save and to display the datasheet with the new field.

    ✓ *Notice that the calculated field does not show the discount price in Currency format. You can optionally go back to table Design view and set the field's Format property to Currency.*
14. Leave the **ATry15_studentfirstname_studentlastname** database open to use in the next Try It.

Using Calculated Fields in a Query

- If you don't want a calculated field to appear as a regular part of the table, you can instead create a query based on that table and put the calculated field in the query.
- Creating a calculated field in a query involves constructing a field in the query grid. In the Field Name row, you type a new field name (that doesn't currently exist). Then you type a colon and then the expression that performs the desired calculation. For example, see Figure 15-1, where a new field named Sale Price is created.
- To set the new field's format, right-click it in the query grid and choose Properties. Then select a format from the Format property on the Property Sheet.

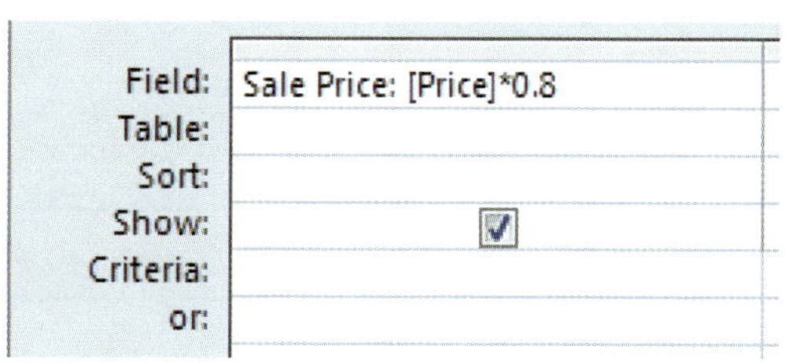

Figure 15-1

Try It! Using Calculated Fields in a Query

1. In **ATry15_studentfirstname_studentlastname**, right-click the Expiration Check query and click Design View.
2. In the first blank column in the query grid, in the Field Name row, type **ExpirationDate:**.
   ✓ *Make sure you type the colon after the text.*
3. Click Query Tools Design > Builder. The Expression Builder opens.
4. In the Expression Elements list, click Expiration Check. Then double-click TermLength.
5. In the Expression Elements list, click Operators. Then in the Expression Values list, double-click *.
6. Type **365+**.
7. Click Expiration Check again, and then double-click TermDate.
8. Click OK. The formula appears in the Field Name row.
   ✓ *You can drag to widen the column to see the entire formula if desired.*
9. Click Run to see the results of the query, including the new calculated field.
   ✓ *If your get a message indicating a syntax error, delete <<Expr>> in the formula and then run the query.*
10. Click the Save button on the Quick Access Toolbar.
11. Right-click the query tab, and click Close All.
12. Close the database file and exit Access.

Set up criteria with the Expression Builder

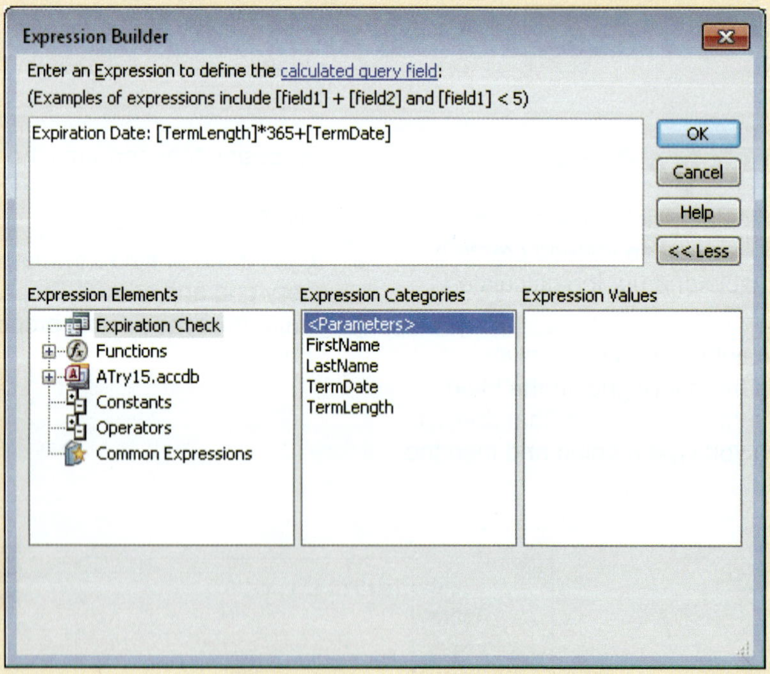

Project 31—Create It

Jewelry Business Database

DIRECTIONS

1. Start Access, if necessary, and open **AProj31** from the data files for this lesson. If a security warning bar appears, click **Enable Content**.
2. Save the database as **AProj31_studentfirstname_studentlastname** to the location where your teacher instructs you to store the files for this lesson.
3. Right-click the **Products** table and click **Design View**.
4. Click **Retail Price** and click **Table Tools Design** > **Insert Rows**.
5. In the Field Name column for the new field, type **Cost To Make**.
6. In Data Type column, open the drop-down list and click **Calculated**.
7. In the Expression Builder window, click **Products** on the Expression Elements list.
8. Double-click **Materials Cost**.
9. Type **+**.
10. Double-click **Labor Cost**. Refer to Figure 15-2.
11. Click **OK**.
12. Click **View**.
13. When prompted to save, click **Yes**.
14. Scroll the datasheet to the right to see the new field.
15. Right-click the table's tab and click **Close**.
16. Right-click the **Gross Sales by Product** query and click **Design View**.
17. In the first empty column, in the Field Name row, type **Gross Sale: [Quantity]*[Retail Price]**.
18. Click **Save** on the Quick Access Toolbar.
19. Click **Query Tools Design** > **Run** to view the query results.
20. Close the database, and submit it to your teacher for grading.

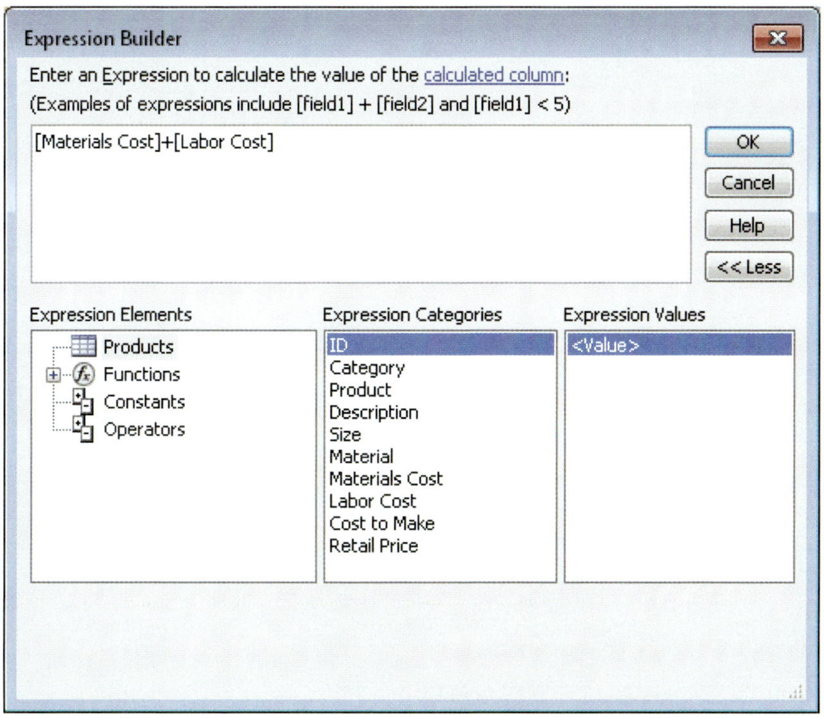

Figure 15-2

Project 32—Apply It

Jewelry Business Database

DIRECTIONS

1. Start Access, if necessary, and open **AProj32** from the data files for this lesson. If a security warning bar appears, click **Enable Content**.
2. Save the database as **AProj32_studentfirstname_studentlastname** in the location where your teacher instructs you to store the files for this lesson.
3. Open the **Products** table in Design view.
4. Delete the **Retail Price** field from the table, and replace it with a calculated field named **Retail Price** that multiplies the Cost to Make field's value by 2.2.
5. Set the new Retail Price field's format to **Currency**.
6. Save your work and view the table in Datasheet view to check it.
7. Create a new query in Design view using the **Products** table.
8. Add the **ID** and **Retail Price** fields to the query grid.
9. Create a new calculated field named **10% Off** that shows the Retail Price multiplied by 0.9.

   ✓ *You multiply by 0.9 because you want to calculate 90% of the original price.*

10. Create a new calculated field named **20% Off** that shows the Retail Price multiplied by 0.8.
11. Create additional calculated fields named **30% Off**, **40% Off**, and **50% Off** that multiply the Retail Price by 0.7, 0.6, and 0.5 respectively.
12. Set each of the new fields' formats to **Currency**.

    ✓ *To set a query field format, click in the field name, click Property Sheet on the Query Tools Design tab, click the Format drop-down arrow, and click Currency.*

13. Save the new query as **Discount Prices**, and run the query to check your results.
14. Submit your database file to your teacher for grading.

Lesson 16

Summarizing Data in Queries

➤ What You Will Learn

Understanding Summary Queries
Summarizing with the Simple Query Wizard
Summarizing Data in Query Design View

WORDS TO KNOW

Aggregate function
Functions that summarize grouped data. These functions include sum, count, average, minimum, and maximum.

Software Skills Sometimes it can be difficult to see the meaning in data if there's too much of it shown in too much detail. It is often helpful to create summary queries that help you pull statistics out of a large pool of data.

Application Skills The jewelry business owner would like to know which of her products are selling the best and how much profit she is making. You will help her by creating queries that summarize the raw sales data.

What You Can Do

Summarizing with the Simple Query Wizard

- When you create a query that includes numeric data fields, the Simple Query Wizard gives you the option of either a detail or a summary query.
- When you choose Summary, the Summary Options button becomes available. Click it and then choose one or more **aggregate functions** for the query, such as AVG, MIN, or MAX. The functions available depend on the data type. For text fields, the only option available is to count the records.

- Using the Simple Query Wizard to create a summary query has many advantages, including the ability to group data (such as for a whole month of dates together rather than each individual date separately) without having manually to write the complex code required to show the data in groups.
- Therefore, the best way to create a summary query is to use the wizard and then edit the query as needed in Query Design view.

Try It! Summarizing with the Simple Query Wizard

1. Start Access and open the file **ATry16** from the data files for this lesson. Save the file as **ATry16_studentfirstname_studentlastname** in the location where your teacher instructs you to store the files for this lesson.
2. Click Create > Query Wizard.
3. In the New Query dialog box, click Simple Query Wizard and click OK.

   ✓ *In the Tables/Queries list, Students is already selected.*
4. Open the Tables/Queries list and click Table:Students.
5. In the Available Fields list, click TermLength and click the > button.
6. Click Next.
7. Click Summary, and then click Summary Options.
8. In the Summary Options dialog box, click the Avg check box.
9. Click OK.
10. Click Next.
11. In the What title do you want for your query box, type **Average Term Length**.
12. Click Finish. The query results appear in a datasheet.

    ✓ *The results consist of a single field, containing a single value: the average of all records.*
13. Leave the **ATry16_studentfirstname_studentlastname** database open to use in the next Try It.

Summarizing Data in Query Design View

- You can also create a summary query manually in query Design view.
- To create a summary query in Design view, click the Totals button in the Show/Hide group on the Query Tools Design tab. This adds a new row, Total, to the query design grid.
- The default value for each field in the Total row is Group By. The summary will be grouped by each of the fields with this setting.

✓ *Include only the essential fields in a summary query. A field should not be present in the query unless it is being used as a criterion, calculated, or grouped by.*

- You can open the drop-down list for the Total row and choose an aggregate function for the field on which you want to calculate.

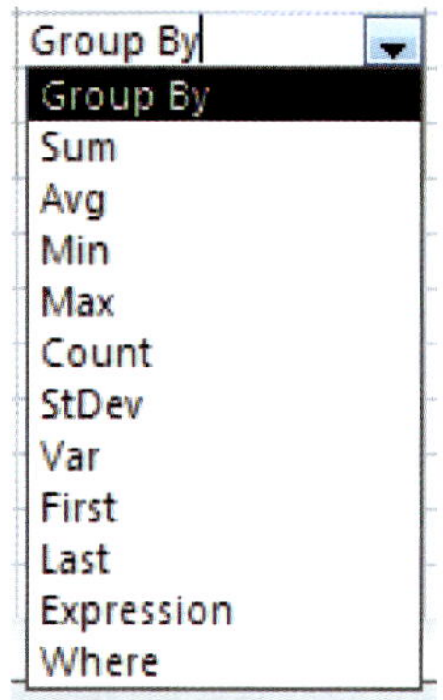

Figure 16-2

✓ *Some of the aggregate functions require the data to be numeric, such as Sum; others, such as Count, will work on any data type.*

- If you want to show just the calculation(s) for the entire table, do not use any Group By fields.

Here are the aggregate functions you can choose from:

Use	To
Sum	Total numeric values by each Group By field
Avg	Total numeric values and divide by the number of records in each Group By field.
Min	Find the lowest value in each Group By field. If the Min field is text, the function finds the first alphabetical value. If the field is a number, the function finds the lowest number. If the field is a date, the function finds the earliest date.
Max	Find the highest value in each Group By field. If the Max field is text, the function finds the last alphabetical value. If the field is a number, the function finds the largest number. If the field is a date, the function finds the latest date.
Count	Find the number of records in each Group By field.
StDey	Calculate the standard deviation of the number by each Group By field. This is used to see how close all the values are to the average.
Var	Calculate the variance of the number by each Group By field. This is another measure of how close the values are to the average.
First	Find the field's first record input for each Group By field.
Last	Find the field's last record input for each Group By field.
Expression	If you have a calculated field (for example, Quantity*Price), you can choose Expression in the Total row and enter a formula such as Sum([Quantity]*[Price]) in the Field row.
Where	Refer the query to the Criteria row. This enables you to include fields in the query purely for criteria purposes without grouping or calculating by that field.

Try It! Summarizing Data in Query Design View

1. In the **ATry16_studentfirstname_studentlastname**, double-click the Class Enrollments query to view its datasheet.
2. Right-click the query's tab and click Design View.
3. Click Query Tools Design > Totals Σ. The Total row appears in the query grid.
4. Open the drop-down list for the Totals row in the EnrollmentID column and click Count.
5. Click Run ! to display the query results.

   ✓ *Note how the results differ from the results you saw in step 1.*
6. Close the database without saving any changes.

Project 33—Create It

Jewelry Business Database

DIRECTIONS

1. Start Access, if necessary, and Open **AProj33** from the data files for this lesson. If a security warning bar appears, click **Enable Content**.
2. Save the database as **AProj33_studentfirstname_studentlastname** in the location where your teacher instructs you to store the files for this lesson.
3. Click **Create** > **Query Wizard** .
4. Click **Simple Query Wizard** and click **OK**.
5. Open the drop-down list and click **Query: Product Ordering**.
6. Double-click the **Product** and **Quantity** fields to add them to the Selected Fields list, as shown in Figure 16-3. Then click **Next**.
7. Click **Summary**, and then click **Summary Options**.
8. In the Summary Options dialog box, mark the **Sum**, **Min**, and **Max** check boxes.
9. Mark the **Count Records in OrderDetails** check box.
10. Click **OK**.
11. Click **Next**.
12. In the What title do you want for your query box, type **Product Order Statistics**.
13. Click **Finish**. The query results appear in a datasheet.
14. Right-click the query's tab and click **Close**. Click **Yes** if prompted to save your changes.
15. Close the database, and submit it to your teacher for grading.

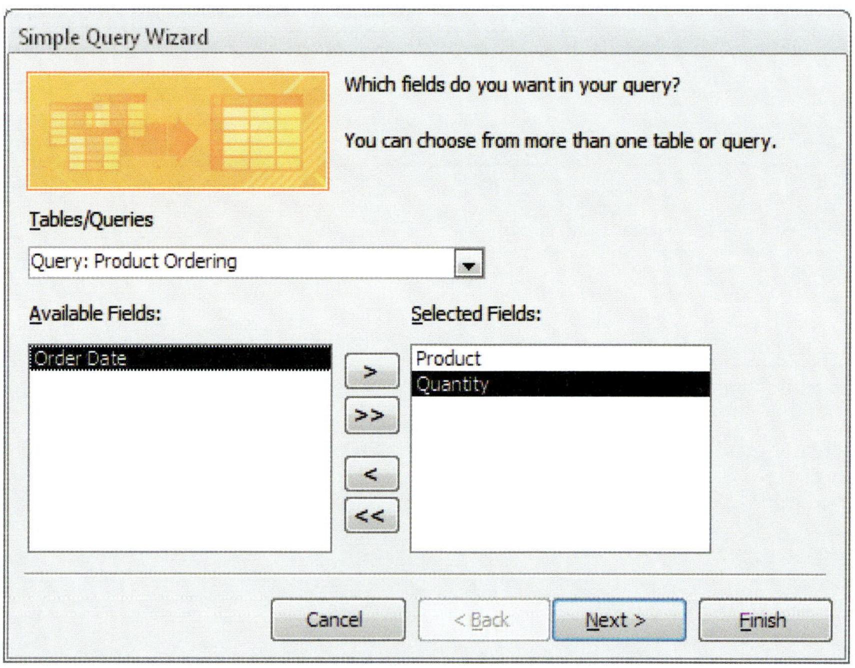

Figure 16-3

Project 34—Apply It

Jewelry Business Database

DIRECTIONS

1. Start Access, if necessary, and open **AProj34** from the data files for this lesson. If a security warning bar appears, click **Enable Content**.
2. Save the database as **AProj34_studentfirstname_studentlastname** in the location where your teacher instructs you to store the files for this lesson.
3. In Design view, create a new query based on the Customers table that counts the number of customers from each state. Name it **Customers By State**.

   ✓ *This query should consist of two copies of the State field: one set to Group By and one set to Count.*
4. In Design view, create a new query that averages the sales commission for the Salespeople table. Name it **Average Sales Commission**.

   ✓ *This query should consist of one copy of the Commission Rate field, with its Total row set to Avg.*
5. Apply the Percent format to the average. To do this, select the field and open its Property Sheet. Set the Format value to Percent.
6. Use the Simple Query Wizard to create a query based on the **Products** table that includes the **Category** and **Retail Price** fields. The query should show the Average of the retail prices by Category. Name it **Average Retail Price**.
7. Submit your database file to your teacher for grading.

Chapter Assessment and Application

Project 35—Make It Your Own

Little League Database

You are the assistant coach of a little league team and have been given the responsibility of maintaining the database for the team. You have inherited a database that contains several tables, but no queries. You will create relationships between the tables and create several queries that can help extract data from them.

DIRECTIONS

1. Open the file **AProj35** from this Chapter and save it as **AProj35_studentfirstname_studentlastname** in the location where your teacher instructs you to store the files for this Chapter.
2. Open the **Relationships** window, and add all the tables except Venues to the layout.
3. Create the following relationships (with no referential integrity enforced) as shown in table at bottom of the page.
4. Edit the last two relationships created to enforce referential integrity. Choose both **Cascade Update** and **Cascade Delete** for each.
   - ✓ *You cannot enforce referential integrity on the first relationship created because neither field involved in the relationship is the primary key field in its table.*
5. Arrange the tables in the Relationships window so that none of the relationship lines cross. Then close the Relationships window, saving your changes.
6. Create a new query using the Simple Query Wizard that shows people's names from the **Roster** table (First and Last names) and also shows the name and description of the equipment each person owns (from the **Equipment** table). Name the query **Equipment Ownership**.
   - ✓ *To include fields from multiple tables in the query, make your selections from the first one, and then choose a different table/query from the Table/Query drop-down list in the Wizard.*
   - ✓ *When the query results appear in the datasheet, you may want to widen the columns so all the text fits without being truncated. This is optional.*
7. Using Query Design view, create a query that uses the **Categories** and **Roster** tables. Show all fields from the Roster table except Category. Include the **MembershipCategory** field from the **Categories** table, and set its criteria to **Active**, but hide it from the query results. Name the query **Active Players**.
8. Display the **Equipment** table in datasheet view. Filter it to show only items where the Item Type is **Bat**. Save the results of the filter as a new query named **Equipment:Bats**.
9. Copy the **Equipment:Bats** table, and name the copy **Equipment:Balls**. Edit the Equipment:Balls query so that it shows balls, rather than bats.
10. Close the database, and submit it to your teacher for grading.

From	To
ItemType in the **ItemType** table	**ItemType** in the **Equipment** table
CategoryID in the **Categories** table	**Category** in the **Roster** table
ID in the **Roster** table	**Owner** in the **Equipment** table

Project 36—Master It

Book Collection Database

A friend who collects antique books has asked for your help in developing a database for his collection. He has three tables created already, and now would like some queries. You will create several queries for him, to give him some examples of how Access can help him understand his data.

DIRECTIONS

1. Open the file **AProj36** from the data files for this Chapter and save it as **AProj36_studentfirstname_studentlastname** in the location where your teacher instructs you to store the files for this Chapter.
2. Open the Relationships window and enforce referential integrity between the **Books** and **Authors** tables. Use **Cascade Update** and **Cascade Delete**. Then close the Relationships window.
3. Create a query that shows all the fields for only the books (in the **Books** table) where the **Notes** field is not null. Name the query **Book Notes**.
4. Open the Books table in Datasheet view and sort the list in Ascending order by Author and then by **Date Published**.

   ✓ *You will need to temporarily rearrange the columns to perform the sort; then put them back the way they were after sorting.*
5. Save the filter/sort as a query named **Books Sorted by Author and Date**. Do not save the changes to the table itself.
6. Create a query that shows all the fields for only authors who were born after 1850. Name the query **Authors Born After 1850**.
7. Create a calculated field in the Authors table named **Age At Death** that calculates how old the author was when he or she died. Place the new field immediately before Nationality.
8. Create a query that provides the author's first and last name and the earliest publication date for each author. (Use the MIN function.) Name it **First Published**.
9. Close the database, and submit it to your teacher for grading.

Chapter 3

Working with Forms and Reports

Lesson 17
Creating a Lookup List
Projects 37-38

- Creating a Lookup
- Creating a Value List
- Looking Up Field Values from Another Table
- Creating a Multivalued Field

Lesson 18
Creating an Input Mask
Projects 39-40

- Understanding Input Masks
- Creating an Input Mask Using the Input Mask Wizard
- Creating an Input Mask Using the Input Mask Properties Box

Lesson 19
Creating and Using a Form
Projects 41-42

- Understanding Forms
- Creating a Form with a Wizard
- Applying a Theme to a Form
- Adding Records to a Table by Using a Form
- Navigating Records in a Form
- Deleting Records from a Table by Using a Form
- Printing a Form

Lesson 20
Working with a Form in Layout View
Projects 43-44

- Understanding Layout View
- Creating a Form in Layout View
- Sizing a Control
- Moving Controls in the Layout
- Deleting a Control
- Adjusting the Control Margins and Control Padding
- Changing Control Formatting

Lesson 21
Working with a Form in Design View
Projects 45-46

- Exploring Design View and Resizing Fields
- Selecting and Moving Controls
- Resetting Tab Order
- Changing the Form Size
- Inserting an Unbound Label
- Creating a New Form in Design View

Lesson 22
Working with Form Sections
Projects 47-48

- Understanding Sections
- Displaying and Resizing Sections
- Inserting a Form Title
- Adding Date/Time Codes
- Moving Controls Between Sections

Lesson 23
Creating a Report
Projects 49-50

- Understanding Access Reports
- Creating and Formatting a Report in Layout View
- Creating a Report Using the Report Wizard
- Modifying a Report in Design View
- Working with Print Preview and Report Views
- Printing a Report

Lesson 24
Modifying a Report in Design View
Projects 51-52

- Working with Report Sections
- Moving a Control Between Sections
- Adding Page Number Codes
- Sorting and Grouping Records in a Report
- Adding a Calculated Field to a Report

Lesson 25
Creating Labels
Projects 53-54

- Understanding Labels
- Using the Label Wizard

End of Chapter Assessments
Projects 55-56

Lesson 17

Creating a Lookup List

➤ What You Will Learn

Creating a Lookup
Creating a Value List
Looking Up Field Values from Another Table
Creating a Multivalued Field

WORDS TO KNOW

Lookup field
A list of values from which to choose when entering information in a field.

Multivalued field
A field that can store more than one entry simultaneously.

Software Skills Some fields store data that can contain only a limited range of valid values, such as Marital Status (single, married, etc.) or Gender (male, female). To simplify data entry and prevent entry errors, you can create a lookup for a field that presents the user who is entering records with a drop-down list of options from which to choose. You can also set up fields that hold more than one value and that allow users to select from multiple check boxes during data entry.

Application Skills Your friend has been using the jewelry database you created, but finds data entry awkward. You will help her by creating lookups for some of the fields.

What You Can Do

Creating a Lookup

- If the appropriate values for a certain field are limited, such as gender or marital status, consider using a **lookup field**.
- A lookup field appears as a drop-down list during data entry, and you can choose from the list rather than typing an entry. This minimizes data entry errors and ensures consistent formatting (such as capitalization).

- When you enter data for a record, an arrow appears within the lookup field indicating that you can choose from a list of options.
- You can use the Lookup Wizard to create a lookup field with values you enter. This is most appropriate for short lists that do not change frequently.
- You can also use the Lookup Wizard to create a lookup field that looks up values from another table. This is most appropriate for long lists or lists that frequently need updating.
- To create a lookup for a field, go to table Design view and change the field's type to Lookup Wizard. The Lookup Wizard will run automatically.

Creating a Value List

- The Lookup Wizard provides a list in which you can type the values you want to appear on the list.
- This method works well when the values on the list will seldom or never change. If the values change frequently, use the table lookup method instead.

✓ *When creating your list, try to enter the values in a useful order. An alphabetical list of states, for example, is easier to use than one that doesn't have a recognizable order. A list of prospect levels might be ordered by the frequency with which they are used.*

Try It! Creating a Lookup with a Typed Value List

1. Open the database **ATry17** from the data files for this lesson.
2. Save the database as **ATry17_studentfirstname_studentlastname** in the location where your teacher instructs you to store the files for this lesson.
3. In the Navigation pane, right-click the Students table and click Design View.
4. Open the Data Type list for the Gender field and click Lookup Wizard.
5. Click I will type in the values that I want.
6. Click Next.
7. In the Col1 column, in the first blank row, type **Male**.
8. Click in the next blank row and type **Female**.
9. Click Next.
10. Click the Limit to List check box.
11. Click Finish.
12. Click the Save button on the Quick Access Toolbar.
13. Leave the **ATry17_studentfirstname_studentlastname** database open to use in the next Try It.

Type the list items

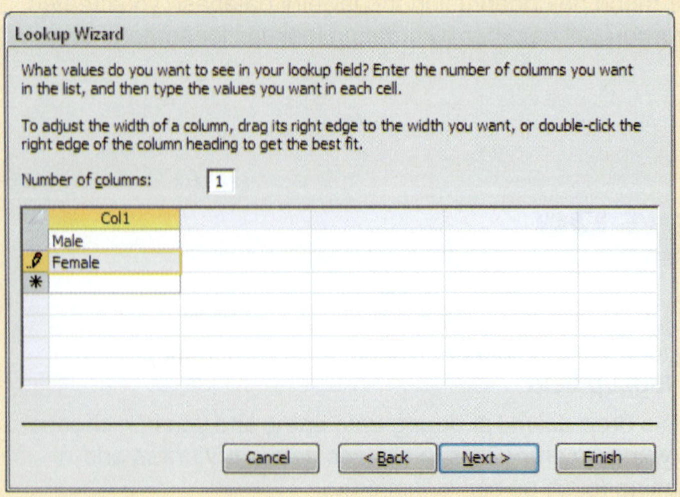

Try It! Using a Lookup List

1. In the **ATry17_studentfirstname_ studentlastname** file, click Home > View to view the datasheet.
2. For the first record (Leroy Critchfield), click the Gender field.
3. Click the down arrow to open the drop-down list.
4. Click Male.
5. Right-click the table's tab and click Close to close it.
6. Leave the **ATry17_studentfirstname_ studentlastname** database open to use in the next Try It.

A lookup list provides the values you enter to the user

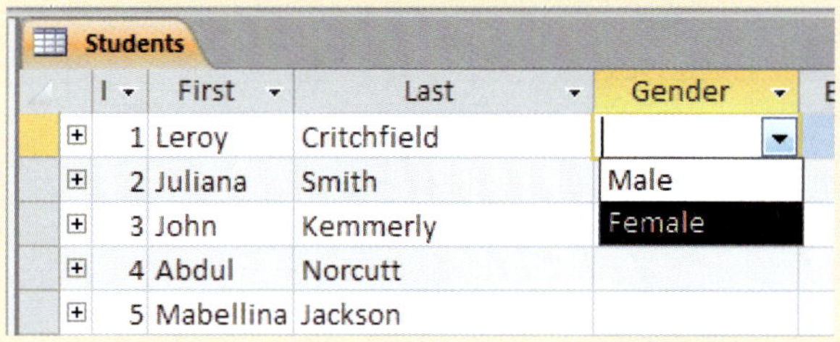

Looking Up Field Values from Another Table

- If your list often varies, or is long, you might find it easier to create a separate table for the list instead, and then create a lookup field that looks into that table.
- Before creating the lookup, you must first create the additional table. Then, run the Lookup Wizard and select the table to be used.
- Creating a lookup also produces a relationship between the tables, which will be reflected in the Relationships window. The relationship it creates does not enforce referential integrity, but you can edit it to do so later.
- The Lookup Wizard first helps you choose the lookup table or query.

  ✓ *If there is already a relationship between the two tables, you can't create the lookup until you delete the relationship from the Relationships window. The Lookup Wizard will recreate the relationship.*

- When setting up a lookup based on another table, you are prompted to sort by a particular field if desired, in Ascending or Descending order. This enables the lookup list to display values in a different order than they appear in the table being referenced. If you do not choose a sort order, the values will appear in the same order as in the table.

Try It! Deleting an Existing Relationship

1. In the **ATry17_studentfirstname_ studentlastname** file, click Database Tools > Relationships .
2. Click the relationship line between the Classes and ClassOfferings tables and press DEL . Click Yes to confirm the deletion.
3. Right-click the Relationships tab and click Close. Click Yes to save the changes if prompted.
4. Leave the **ATry17_studentfirstname_ studentlastname** database open to use in the next Try It.

Try It! Creating a Lookup with Values from Another Table

1. In the **ATry17_studentfirstname_studentlastname** file, in the Navigation pane, right-click the ClassOfferings table and click Design View.
2. Open the Data Type list for the Class field and click Lookup Wizard.
3. Click Next.
4. Click Table: Classes and click Next.

Select the table for use for the lookup

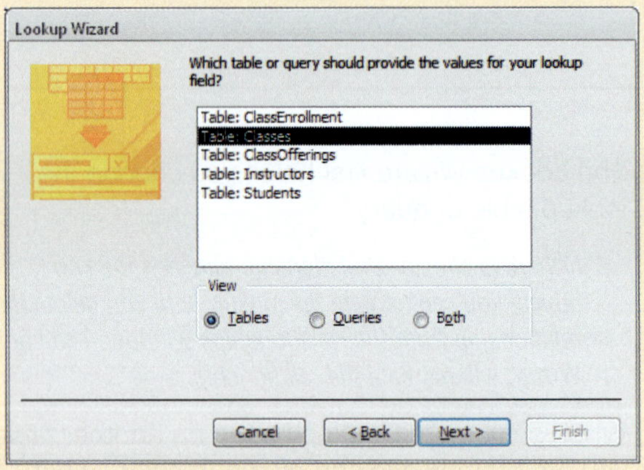

5. Click the ClassName field and click > to move it to the Selected Fields list.

   ✓ *If the table you choose for the lookup has a primary key field, Access will automatically include it even if you don't select it. The wizard calls it a Key Column. You can choose whether or not to display it in step 8.*

6. Click Next.
7. Open the 1 drop-down list and click ClassName, then click Next.
8. Slightly widen the column by dragging its column heading to the right.

   ✓ *You can clear the Key Column check box to display the primary key field on which the relationship is based. In this exercise, you will leave the Key Column checkbox checked.*

Select the field by which to sort

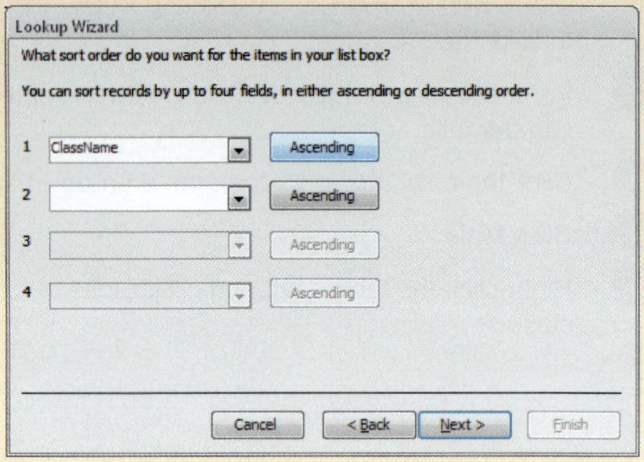

9. Click Next to accept the list, and then click Finish.
10. When prompted to save the table, click Yes.
11. Click Home > View to switch to Datasheet view.
12. In the first row, open the drop-down list for the Class field to view the new list.
13. Right-click the table's tab and click Close.
14. Leave the **ATry17_studentfirstname_studentlastname** database open to use in the next Try It.

Widen the column if necessary to see the entries

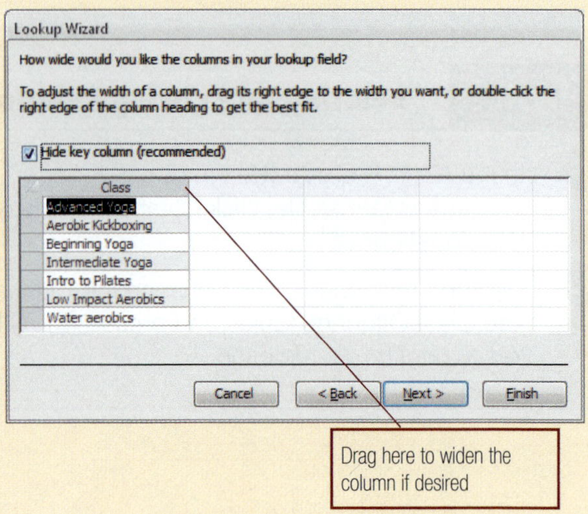

Creating a Multivalued Field

- On the last step of the Lookup Wizard, you also have the opportunity to allow multiple values. If you mark the Allow Multiple Values check box, you will then be able to store multiple values in a single field.
- Rather than selecting from a simple drop-down list, with a multivalued field you select individual check boxes from the list, and you can mark as many as you like. You learned about using this type of field in Lesson 3.

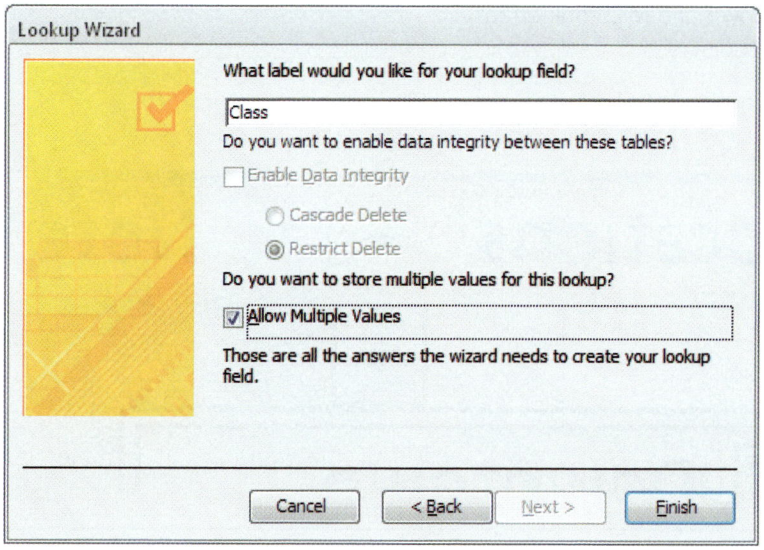

Figure 17-1

Try It! Creating a Multivalued Field

1. In the **ATry17_studentfirstname_studentlastname** file, right-click the Instructors table in the Navigation pane and click Design View.
2. Open the Data Type list for the Locations field and click Lookup Wizard.
3. Click I will type in the values that I want, and click Next.
4. In the Col1 column, in the first row, type **Downtown**. In the second row, type **Millbrook**. In the third row, type **Glendale**. In the fourth row, type **Castleton**. Then, click Next.
5. Click the Allow Multiple Values check box.
6. Click Finish.
7. Click Yes to confirm.
8. Click the Save button on the Quick Access Toolbar.
9. Leave the **ATry17_studentfirstname_studentlastname** database open to use in the next Try It.

Try It! Using a Multivalued Field

1. In the **ATry17_studentfirstname_studentlastname** file, click Home > View to view the datasheet.
2. In the first record, open the drop-down list in the Locations field.
3. Click to mark the Downtown and Millbrook check boxes.
4. Click OK.
5. Close the **ATry17_studentfirstname_studentlastname** file and exit Access.

Select multiple values using checkboxes

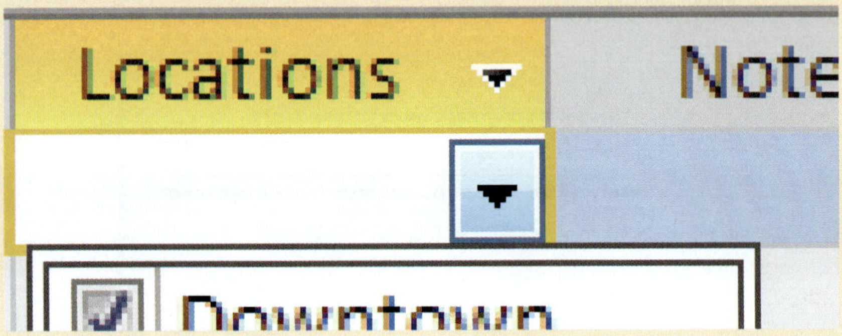

Project 37—Create It

Jewelry Business Database

DIRECTIONS

1. Start Access, if necessary, and open **AProj37** from the data files for this lesson. If a security warning bar appears, click **Enable Content**.
2. Save the database as **AProj37_studentfirstname_studentlastname** in the location where your teacher instructs you to store the files for this lesson.
3. Click **Database Tools** > **Relationships** to open the Relationships window.
4. Click the relationship between Shippers and Orders, and press DEL. Click **Yes** to confirm the deletion.
5. Click **Relationship Tools Design** > **Close**.
6. In the Navigation pane, right-click the **Orders** table and click **Design View**.
7. Open the **Data Type** drop-down list for the Shipper field and click **Lookup Wizard**.
8. Click **Next**.
9. Click **Table:Shippers** and click **Next**.
10. Click the **Name** field and click > to select it. See Figure 17-2. Then, click **Next**.
11. Click **Next** to bypass setting a sort order.
12. Click **Next** to accept the default column.
13. Click **Finish** to accept the default name.
14. Click **Yes** to save the table.

15. Right-click the **Orders** tab and click **Close**.
16. Click **Database Tools** > **Relationships**.
17. Select the relationship line between Shippers and Orders. It turns bold.
18. Click **Relationship Tools Design** > **Edit Relationships**.
19. Click to mark the **Enforce Referential Integrity** check box.
20. Click to mark the **Cascade Update Related Fields** check box. See Figure 17-3.
21. Click **OK**.
22. Click **File** > **Close Database**, and submit your database file to your teacher for grading.

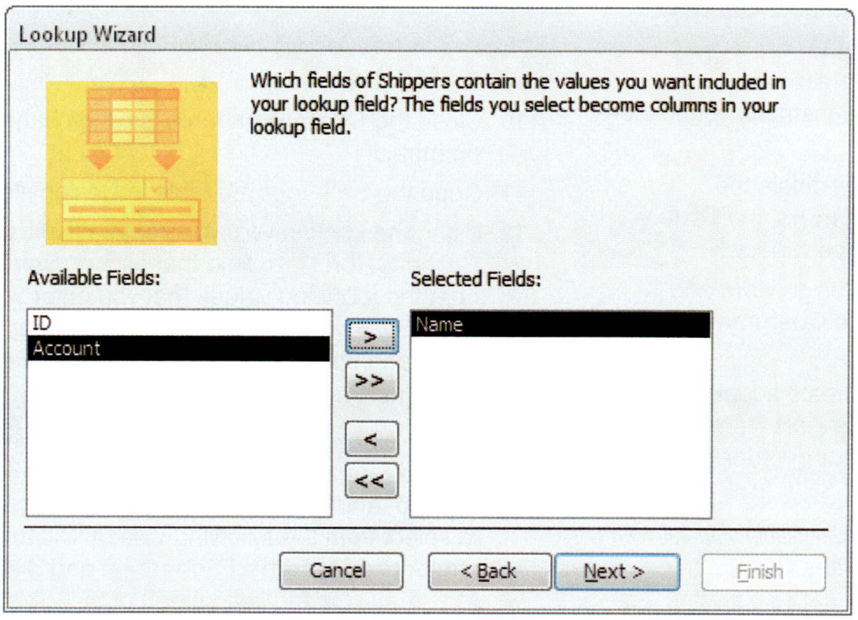

Figure 17-2

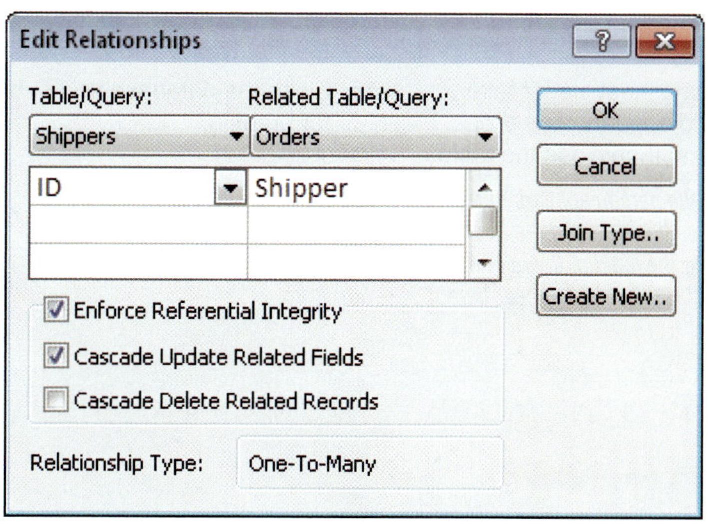

Figure 17-3

Project 38—Apply It

Jewelry Business Database

DIRECTIONS

1. Start Access, if necessary, and open **AProj38** from the data files for this lesson. If a security warning bar appears, click **Enable Content**.
2. Save the database as **AProj38_studentfirstname_studentlastname** in the location where your teacher instructs you to store the files for this lesson.
3. In the Relationships window, delete the relationship between **Customers** and **Orders**. Then, close the Relationships window.
4. Open the **Orders** table in Design view, and change the data type for the **Customer** field to **Lookup Wizard**.
5. Using the Lookup Wizard, create a lookup to **Table:Customers** using the **First Name** and **Last Name** fields. Sort in **Ascending** order by **Last Name**.

   ✓ *The lookup wizard recreates the relationship between the Customers and Orders tables.*

6. Reopen the Relationships window, and edit the relationship between the **Orders** and **Customers** tables to turn on **Enforce Referential Integrity** and **Cascade Update Related Fields**. Then, close the Relationships window.
7. Open the **Orders** table in Datasheet view. Make sure that the **Customer** field appears as a drop-down list for each record, and then close the table.

   ✓ *Notice that the first name of the person appears in the Customer field. That's because you selected the First Name field first when creating the lookup; if you had selected the Last Name field first, it would appear here instead.*

8. Open the **Customers** table in Design view.
9. Change the **State** field's data type to **Lookup Wizard**, and create a lookup to the States table, sorted in Ascending order.

   ✓ *This table has only one field, and it's already set up as the primary key.*

10. Close the **Customers** table, saving changes if prompted.
11. Open the **Salespeople** table in Design view.
12. Using the Lookup Wizard, create a lookup for the **Commission Rate** field that allows users to select from the following values that you enter yourself: **4%**, **5%**, **6%**, and **7%**. Save the changes to the table, and check your work in Datasheet view.
13. Open the **Products** table in Design view.
14. Create a new field, at the bottom of the field list, named **Special**. Set its Data Type to **Lookup Wizard**, and create a lookup that allows users to select from the following values: **Craftsman Collection**, **Modified Schedule**, and **Special Materials**. On the last screen of the Wizard, mark the **Allow Multiple Values** check box.
15. View the **Products** table in Datasheet view and set the **Special** field to **Craftsman Collection** for the first two records.
16. Close the database and submit it to your teacher for grading.

Lesson 18

Creating an Input Mask

➤ What You Will Learn

Understanding Input Masks
Creating an Input Mask Using the Input Mask Wizard
Creating an Input Mask Using the Input Mask Properties Box

WORDS TO KNOW

Input mask
A pattern to follow for entering data in a field.

Software Skills Especially when multiple people use a database, inconsistencies can develop that can cause data analysis problems. For example, some people might enter phone numbers with parentheses around the area code and others may not, or someone may enter the wrong number of digits for a ZIP code. An input mask can help users enter data correctly.

Application Skills Your friend with the jewelry business is getting ready to hire an assistant and would like the database to be as foolproof as possible. You will assist her by creating input masks for common field types like phone numbers and ZIP codes.

What You Can Do

Understanding Input Masks

- An **input mask** is like a frame that the data is poured into. You use it to ensure that data is entered correctly in specified fields.
- The Input Mask Wizard works only with fields of the Text or Date/Time data types. You can manually create an input mask for a Number or Currency data field.

- An input mask streamlines data entry by displaying "helper" characters, such as parentheses around the area code in a phone number or a dash between the fifth and sixth digits of a 9-digit ZIP code.

  ✓ *When you add an input mask to a table field, any future forms you create based on that table will also use that input mask. However, any existing forms are not affected (unless you delete the affected field from the form and then reinsert it). Forms are covered in Lessons 19, 20, and 21.*

- If you click in a field with an input mask, you will be entering data at a specific position in the input mask, which is not necessarily at the beginning. This can cause errors if there are required characters. Pressing HOME moves the insertion point to the beginning of the field. You can avoid the problem altogether by and pressing TAB from the previous field, rather than clicking.
- An input mask does not affect data already entered in the table.

Try It! Using an Input Mask

1. Start Access, and open the database **ATry18** from the data files for this lesson.
2. Save the database as **ATry18_studentfirstname_studentlastname** in the location where your teacher instructs you to store the files for this lesson.
3. Open the Students table in Datasheet view.
4. Click in the Birthdate field for Leroy Critchfield.
5. Press HOME to move the insertion point to the beginning of the field.
6. Type **04/12/1959**.

   ✓ *You do not have to type the slashes; they are already in the field because of the existing input mask.*

7. Click Home > Design View to switch to Design view.
8. Click the Birthdate field.
9. In the Properties section, examine the text in the Input Mask box.

   ✓ *Notice the codes there: 99/99/0000;0;_. This code creates the mask. Later in this lesson, you will learn what this code means.*

10. Leave the **ATry18_studentfirstname_studentlastname** database open to use in the next Try It.

Creating an Input Mask Using the Input Mask Wizard

- The easiest way to create an input mask is to use the Input Mask Wizard. The wizard walks you through the steps for creating any of several common mask types, such as date, ZIP code, Social Security number, or phone number.
- You can fine-tune the input mask by manually editing its codes within the wizard if you like. You will learn about manually editing mask codes in the next section.

  ✓ *Be careful that your input mask doesn't conflict with the Format property for the field. For example, if your date format is set to Short Date, don't specify an input mask of Medium Date. The input mask and the format will both work, but users may be confused as to which format is correct.*

- The wizard lets you specify which placeholder character to use. This is the character that appears in the field before you enter the number. By default, it is an underscore for most mask types, but you can change it to some other character, such as * or #.
- For some mask types, the wizard lets you specify whether or not helper characters should be stored in the field. For example, for a ZIP code, you might have a number like 09123-2842. The dash displays onscreen as part of the mask, to help users input the data. You can choose to not have the dash be stored though, in which case Access stores the data as 091232842.

  ✓ *Storing helper characters (or not) is an issue for two reasons. One is that each extra character takes up space, making the database file larger. Another is that if you export data to some other program, it may be beneficial or detrimental to have the helper characters included, depending on the program and the usage.*

Try It! Creating an Input Mask using the Input Mask Wizard

1. In the **ATry18_studentfirstname_studentlastname** file, with the Students table open in Design view, click the ZIP field.
2. Click in the Input Mask property. A Build button appears.
3. Click the Build button. The Input Mask Wizard runs.
4. Click Zip Code.
5. Click Next. The code displays for the mask.
6. Open the Placeholder character drop-down list and click #.
7. Click Next.
8. Click Next to accept the default data storage (without the symbols in the mask).
9. Click Finish. The mask is created, and the code for it appears in the Input Mask property.
10. Leave the **ATry18_studentfirstname_studentlastname** database open to use in the next Try It.

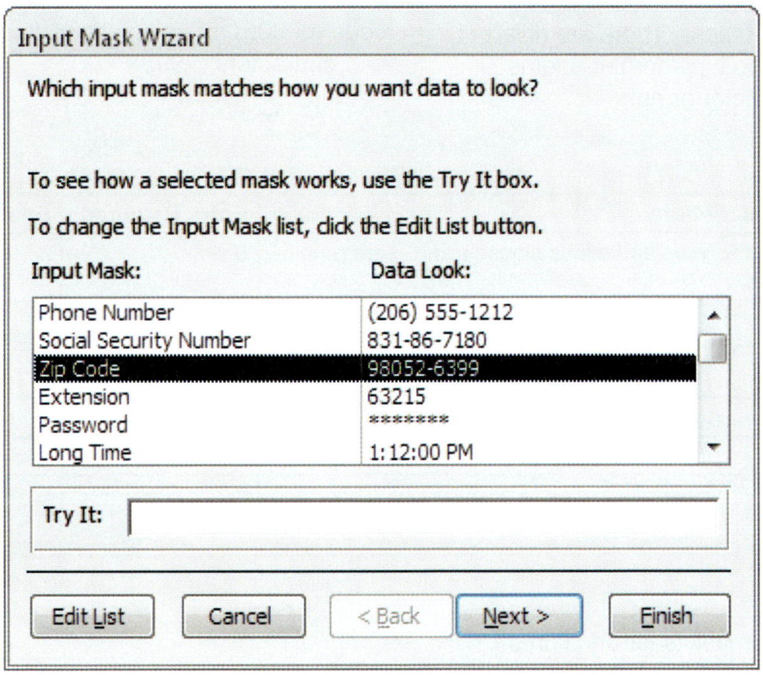

Figure 18-1

Creating an Input Mask the Input Mask Properties Box

- You can also enter your own input mask by typing characters in a specified format directly in the Input Mask dialog box.
- Alternately, you can use the Wizard to create the mask and then edit it manually to fine-tune it.
- There are up to three sections for the input mask. Each section is separated with a semi-colon:

Section	Description	What to type
First	Input mask characters	Type codes shown in the following table.
Second	Store extra characters such as parentheses with the number	Type 0 for yes, or 1 (or leave blank) for no.
Third	Placeholder character to be used	Type any character, such as an underscore. If you want a blank space, type a space in quotation marks.

- The following table shows the characters to use in the first section of the input mask. There are different symbols used depending on whether the user is required to enter that character or not.
- For example, 00000-9999 requires a five-digit ZIP code (00000), but also allows for an optional extra four characters (9999).

Data	Description	Entry Required	Entry Optional
Number	0 or 9. Plus and minus signs (+ and -) are prohibited.	0	9
Number or space	Leading and trailing spaces are blanks but removed when the field is saved. Plus and minus signs (+ and -) are permitted.	1	#
Letter	Any alphabet character	L	?
Letter or number	Any numeral or any alphabet characters	A	a
Any character or space	Any	&	C

- The second section of the mask is for additional characters or special instructions, as shown in the following table:

. , : ; - /	Decimal, thousand, date, and time separators. Depends on Windows settings.
\	Any character following this symbol is displayed literally.
" "	Any characters within quotes are displayed literally.
>	Converts the following characters to uppercase.
<	Converts the following characters to lowercase.

- For example, an input mask for a 9-digit ZIP code might look like this: 00000-9999;;_. The 00000 specifies five required digits. The 9999 specifies four optional digits. The first semicolon marks the end of the first section. The second section is empty, so another semicolon immediately follows. The _ character is the placeholder.
- The input mask "("999") "999"-"9999;;_ uses quotation marks to include literal characters for the parentheses and the dash. It could also be written as \(999\)999\-9999;;_ instead, but you lose the additional space following the closing parenthesis.
- Adding an exclamation point at the beginning of the code string like this !\(999") "000\-0000;;_ enables you to put numbers anywhere in the field. If you only enter 7 numbers even at the beginning of the field, the number will display to the right of the parentheses. For example, as you type the number, 5554567, it will show (555) 456-7, but after the number is entered, it will display as ( ) 555-4567.

Try It! Modifying an Input Mask

1. In the **ATry18_studentfirstname_studentlastname** file, in the Students table in Design view, select the ZIP field.
2. In the Input Mask property, delete the # at the end of the code and type an underscore _ to replace it.
3. Leave the **ATry18_studentfirstname_studentlastname** database open to use in the next Try It.

Try It! Manually Creating an Input Mask

1. In the **ATry18_studentfirstname_studentlastname** file, in the Students table in Design view, select the Phone field.
2. In the Input Mask property, type the following: **!\(999") "000\-0000;;_**.
3. Close the **ATry18_studentfirstname_studentlastname** file and exit Access.

Project 39—Create It

Jewelry Business Database

DIRECTIONS

1. Start Access, if necessary, and open **AProj39** from the data files for this Lesson. If a security warning bar appears, click **Enable Content**.
2. Save the database as **AProj39_studentfirstname_studentlastname** in the location where your teacher instructs you to store the files for this lesson.
3. Right-click the **Orders** table, and click **Design View**.
4. Click the **Order Date** field, and then click in the **Input Mask** property for that field.
5. Click the **Build** button.
6. Click **Short Date**, and click **Finish**.

   ✓ *You do not have to go all the way through the wizard if you want to accept the default settings.*

7. Click the **Save** button on the Quick Access Toolbar.
8. Click **Home** > **View** to switch to Datasheet view.
9. Enter a new record in the table:

   Order Date: **12/16/2012**

   Customer: **Jennifer Brown**

   Shipper: **UPS**

   Salesperson: **TR**

10. Right-click the table's tab and click **Close**.
11. Right-click the **Customers** table, and click **Design View**.
12. Click the **ZIP** field, and click in the **Input Mask** property.
13. Type **00000;;_** in the Input Mask property.
14. Click the **Save** button on the Quick Access Toolbar.
15. Click **File** > **Close Database** and submit your database file to your teacher for grading.

Project 40—Apply It

Jewelry Business Database

DIRECTIONS

1. Start Access, if necessary, and open **AProj40** from the data files for this lesson. If a security warning bar appears, click **Enable Content**.
2. Save the database as **AProj40_studentfirstname_studentlastname** in the location where your teacher instructs you to store the files for this lesson.
3. Open the **Customers** table in Design View.
4. Set up an input mask for the **Phone** field that requires all 10 digits and stores the parentheses as part of the field entry.
5. Save and close the table.
6. Open the **Orders** table in Design View.
7. Manually create an input mask for the **Salesperson** field that requires exactly two alphabetic characters.
8. Switch to Datasheet view, and enter the following new record. As you do so, try to enter an extra character in the Salesperson field. Access will not let you because of the input mask.

   Order Date: **12/16/2012**

   Customer: **Norman Eichmann**

   Shipper: **UPS**

   Salesperson: **AA**

9. Close the database and submit it to your teacher for grading.

Lesson 19

Creating and Using a Form

➤ What You Will Learn

- Understanding Forms
- Creating a Form with a Wizard
- Applying a Theme to a Form
- Adding Records to a Table by Using a Form
- Navigating Records in a Form
- Deleting Records from a Table by Using a Form
- Printing a Form

Software Skills If your table contains many fields, entering records in Datasheet view can become cumbersome. Many people find it easier to create a data entry form that displays all the fields on-screen at once, one record at a time.

Application Skills As you add more information to the jewelry database, you're finding that you're spending too much time scrolling through the records in Datasheet view. You've decided to create forms to help navigate through the information.

WORDS TO KNOW

Form
An alternative view of a table or query displaying the fields in an easy-to-enter arrangement, usually one record at a time.

Split form
A form that shows a related table in a separate pane below the form.

Form Design view
A view in which you can edit the controls on a form.

Control
An item such as a text box, label, or line on a form or report.

AutoFormat
A feature that applies a formatting template to a form, including background and fonts.

What You Can Do

Understanding Forms

- A **form** is an alternative view of a table or query, displaying the fields in an easy-to-enter arrangement, usually one record at a time.
- A form is connected to one or more tables or queries. When you add data to a form, it automatically fills in the underlying table(s).
- To create a quick form, display a table datasheet and then click the Form button in the Forms group on the Create tab. This type of form is very basic and might not be formatted exactly the way you want. You can edit it later if needed.
- A form appears in Layout view after you create it. This view shows the form approximately as it will appear in use, but its layout can also be edited.
- A **split form** is one that shows a related table in a separate pane below the main form. To create a split form, display a table datasheet. On the Create tab, in the Forms group, click the More Forms button, and click Split Form.
- If you use the Form button to create a quick form from a datasheet that has a related datasheet, Access creates a subform on the form. This is different from a split form in that the subform is embedded in the main form; there are not two separate panes.

Figure 19-1

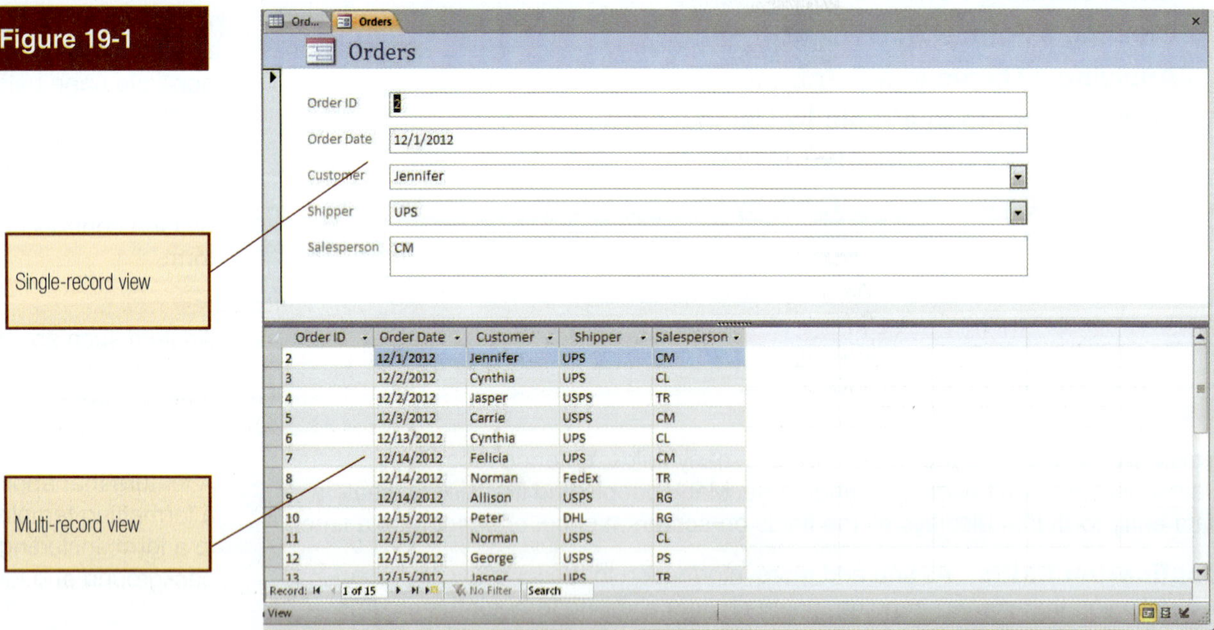

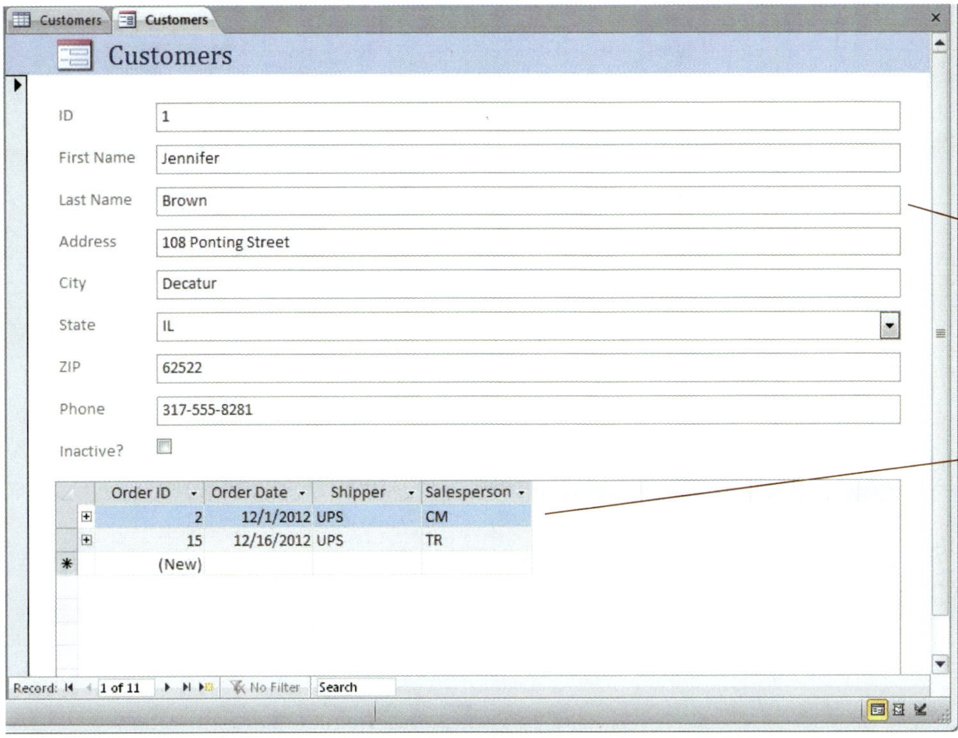

Figure 19-2

Try It! Creating a Quick Form

1. Start Access, and open the database **ATry19** from the data files for this lesson. Click Enable Content if a security message appears.
2. Save the database as **ATry19_studentfirstname_studentlastname** in the location where your teacher instructs you to store the files for this lesson.
3. In the Navigation pane, double-click the Students table.
4. Click Create > Form . A new form appears, with the Class Enrollment table in the subform.
5. Right-click the form's tab and click Close. Do not save changes.
6. In the Students table datasheet, click Create > More Forms > Split Form. A new split form appears.
7. Right-click the form's tab and click Close. Do not save changes.
8. Right-click the Students table tab and click Close.
9. Leave the **ATry19_studentfirstname_studentlastname** database open to use in the next Try It.

Creating a Form with a Wizard

- The Form Wizard asks questions in a series of dialog boxes, walking you step-by-step through the process of selecting tables/queries, fields, and formatting.

Try It! Creating a Form with a Wizard

1. In the **ATry19_studentfirstname_studentlastname** file, click Create > Form Wizard.
2. In the Form Wizard dialog box, open the Tables/Queries list and click Table:Classes.
3. Click >> to move all the fields to the Selected Fields list.
4. Click Next.
5. Click Next to accept Columnar as the layout.
6. Click Finish. The new form appears. It is already saved; you do not need to re-save it.
7. Leave the **ATry19_studentfirstname_studentlastname** database open to use in the next Try It.

Applying a Theme to a Form

- You can apply a theme to a form, as you do in other Office applications. The theme controls the form's colors and fonts.
- Unlike in other Microsoft Office applications, however, there is no visual effect formatting applied by a theme—only colors and fonts.
- You can also apply a color or font theme separately.

Try It! Applying a Theme to a Form

1. In the **ATry19_studentfirstname_studentlastname** file, with the Classes form open from the previous steps, on the Home tab, in the Views group, click the down arrow on the View button, and click Layout View.

   ✓ *You must switch to Layout or Design view before applying a theme.*

2. Click Form Layout Tools Design > Themes.
3. Click the Black Tie theme.

   ✓ *Black Tie is the rightmost theme in the second row in the Built-In section of the list.*

4. With the Classes form open in Layout view, click Form Layout Tools Design > Colors.
5. Click the Angles color theme.
6. With the Classes form open in Layout view, click Form Layout Tools Design > Fonts.
7. Click the Apex font theme.
8. Leave the **ATry19_studentfirstname_studentlastname** database open to use in the next Try It.

Applying Records to a Table by Using a Form

- To use a form, you must display it in Form view. Layout view closely resembles Form view in appearance, but records cannot be added or edited in Layout view.
- To start a new record, click the New (blank) record button at the bottom of the form. This clears the form, so a new record can be inserted. Then, enter data in the fields, pressing Tab to move to the next field or Shift+Tab to the previous field.

  ✓ *You can also individually click in each field to move the insertion point into it.*

- When you press Tab in the last field of the record, Access saves that record and clears the form for you to start another new record.

Try It! Adding a Record to a Table by Using a Form

1. In the **ATry19_studentfirstname_studentlastname** file, with the Classes form open from the previous steps, on the Home tab, click the down arrow on the View button, and click Form View .
2. Click the New (blank) record button at the bottom of the form.
3. Press TAB to move past the ID field.

   ✓ *The ID field is an AutoNumber field.*

4. Type **Beginning Gymnastics** and press TAB.
5. Type **An introduction to gymnastics for adults with no previous gymnastics experience** and press TAB.
6. Type **8** and press TAB.
7. Type **120** and press TAB.
8. Press TAB to move past the Discount Price field.

   ✓ *The Discount Price field is a calculated field.*

9. Type **Ages 18 and older only** in the Notes field.
10. Press TAB. The record is saved and a new blank record opens.
11. Leave the **ATry19_studentfirstname_studentlastname** database open to use in the next Try It.

Navigating Records in a Form

- It is important to know how to move between records, especially in a form where only one record appears at a time.
- The navigation buttons at the bottom of the form control which record is displayed. You can use the buttons to move to the first, previous, next, or last record, or you can enter a specific record number in the Current Record text box.

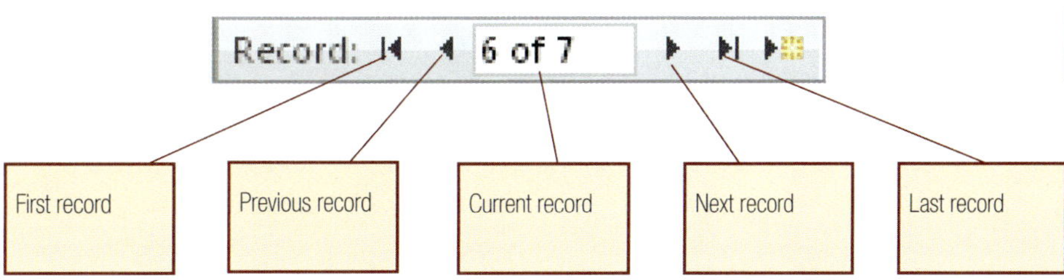

Figure 19-3

Try It! Navigating Records in a Form

1. In the **ATry19_studentfirstname_ studentlastname** file, with the Classes form open from the previous steps, click the First record button. The Low Impact Aerobics record appears.
2. Click Next record button. The Aerobic Kickboxing record appears.
3. Click the Last record button. The Beginning Gymnastics record appears.
4. Leave the **ATry19_studentfirstname_ studentlastname** database open to use in the next Try It.

Deleting Records from a Table by Using a Form

- You can also delete records from the form. To do so, display the record you want to delete (or select it, if it is a form that displays more than one record at a time), and then delete the record using any method.
- You can use either of these methods to delete a record from Form view:
  - On the Home tab, in the Records group, click the Delete drop-down arrow, and then click Delete Record.
  - Click the selection bar to the left of the form to select the record and then press DEL.

Figure 19-4

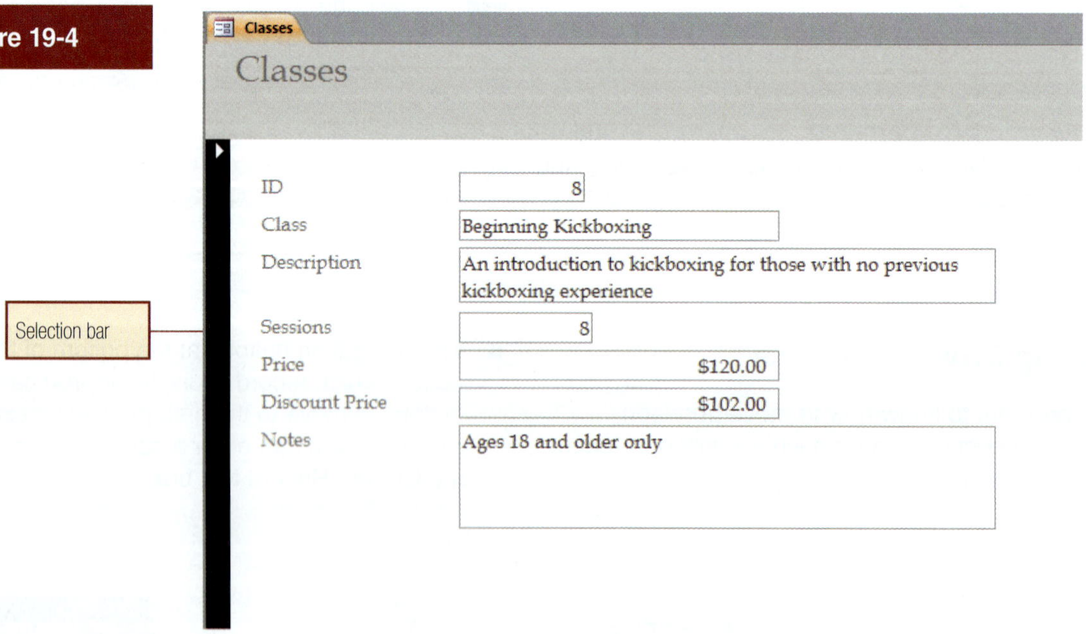

Try It! Deleting a Record from a Form

1. In the **ATry19_studentfirstname_studentlastname** file, with the Classes form open, click the Last record button to make sure the Beginning Gymnastics record is displayed.
2. Click Home > Delete drop-down arrow > Delete Record.
3. Click Yes to confirm.
4. Click Yes to confirm.
5. Leave the **ATry19_studentfirstname_studentlastname** database open to use in the next Try It.

Printing a Form

- Printing a form may be useful if you want people to fill out paper copies of it for later entry in a database.

Try It! Printing a Form

1. In the **ATry19_studentfirstname_studentlastname** file, with the Classes form open, click File > Print > Print. The Print dialog box opens.
2. **With your teacher's permission**, click OK to print. Otherwise, click Cancel.
3. Leave the **ATry19_studentfirstname_studentlastname** database open to use in the next Try It.

Project 41—Create It

Jewelry Business Database

DIRECTIONS

1. Start Access, if necessary, and open **AProj41** from the data files for this lesson. If a security warning bar appears, click **Enable Content**.
2. Save the database as **AProj41_studentfirstname_studentlastname** in the location where your teacher instructs you to store the files for this lesson.
3. Double-click the **Orders** table to open it in Datasheet view.
4. Click **Create** > **Form** .
5. Click the **Save** button on the Quick Access Toolbar.
6. In the Save As dialog box, type **Orders and Details Form** and click OK.

7. Right-click the form's tab and click **Close All**.
8. Double-click the **Products** table to open it in Datasheet view.
9. Click **Create** > **More Forms** > **Split Form**.
10. Click the **Save** button on the Quick Access Toolbar.
11. In the Save As dialog box, type **Products Split Form** and click **OK**.
12. Click **File** > **Close Database** and submit your database file to your teacher for grading.

Project 42—Apply It

Jewelry Business Database

DIRECTIONS

1. Start Access, if necessary, and open **AProj42** from the data files for this lesson. If a security warning bar appears, click **Enable Content**.
2. Save the database as **AProj42_studentfirstname_studentlastname** in the location where your teacher instructs you to store the files for this lesson.
3. Use the Form Wizard to create a form for the Salespeople table. Use all the fields, and use the Justified layout. Name the form **Salespeople Form**.
4. Apply the **Clarity** theme to the form.

   ✓ *The ID field is an AutoNumber field.*
5. Apply the **Verve** color theme to the form.
6. Enter a new salesperson using the form:

   Employee ID: **GC**

   First Name: **Garry**

   Last Name: **Cutler**

   Position: **Manager**

   Commission Rate: **7%**
7. **With your teacher's permission**, print one copy of the form and write your name on the printout.
8. Use the Form Wizard to create a form for the Shippers table. Use all the fields, and the **Tabular** layout. Name the form **Shippers Form**.
9. Close the database and submit it to your teacher for grading as well as the printout if you printed one.

Lesson 20

Working with a Form in Layout View

➤ What You Will Learn

- Understanding Layout View
- Creating a Form in Layout View
- Sizing a Control
- Moving Controls in the Layout
- Deleting a Control
- Adjusting the Control Margins and Control Padding
- Changing Control Formatting

Software Skills Layout view provides an easy interface for arranging, moving, sizing, and formatting the controls on a form. It is easier to manage these operations in Layout view than in Design view, covered in the next lesson.

Application Skills In the jewelry database you have created, you have decided that some of the forms need visual enhancement. You will improve the forms' appearances using Layout view.

WORDS TO KNOW

Control
A generic term for any object on a form or report.

Control margin
The spacing on the inside of the control.

Control padding
The spacing on the outside of the control.

Label
A control that contains descriptive text, such as the name of a field or the form's title.

Text box
A control that pulls information from a table or query and displays it on a form or report.

What You Can Do

Understanding Layout View

- Layout view enables you to create forms by dragging fields onto a grid in which the fields and labels automatically align neatly.
- Each object on the form is generically referred to as a control. A **control** can be a **label**, a **text box** (the field itself), or some other type of object, such as a drop-down list or a picture.
- When you place a field on a form, the field itself appears as a text box, and its name appears in a label adjacent to the text box. Depending on the form's layout, that label may be either to the left of the field or above it.
- The default layout is a stacked layout, which shows each field and its label on a separate row. See Figure 20-1.
- The alternative is a tabular layout, in which the labels appear across the top and the fields themselves appear beneath the names.
- To select a field or label in Layout view, click it. An orange border appears around it.
- To select more than one (for example, to apply formatting to more than one control at a time), hold down Ctrl as you click each one.

Figure 20-1

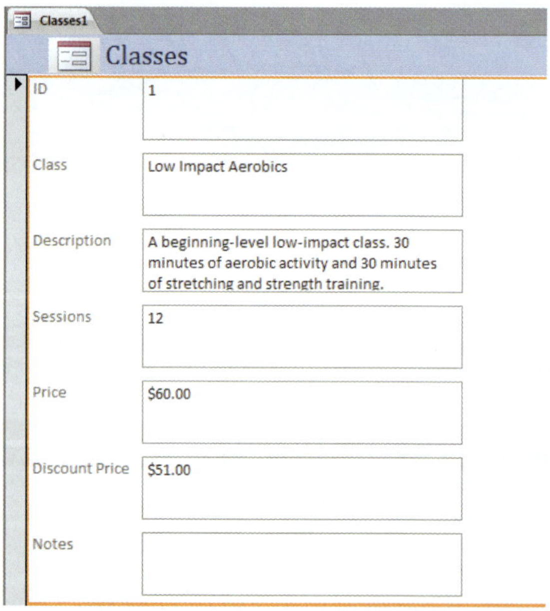

Figure 20-2

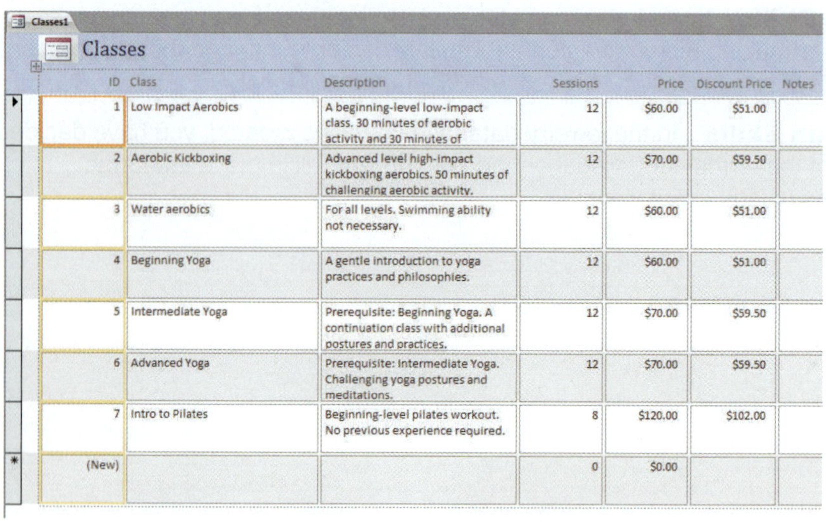

Try It! Selecting Fields in Layout View

1. Start Access and open the file **ATry20** from the data files for this lesson.
2. Save the database as **ATry20_studentfirstname_studentlastname** in the location where your teacher instructs you to store the files for this lesson.
3. Right-click the Classes form, and click Layout View.

   ✓ *Make sure you right-click the Classes form, not the Classes table. The Classes form is in the Forms section of the Navigation pane.*
4. Click the ID field's label. The label appears with an orange box around it.
5. Click the ID field's text box (where the ID number appears). The text box appears with an orange box around it.
6. Hold down CTRL and click the ID field's label. Both the label and the text box appear with orange boxes around them.
7. Continue holding down CTRL and click on each of the other labels and text boxes on the form, until they all have orange boxes around them.
8. Click Format Layout Tools Arrange > Tabular. The layout changes to a tabular one.
9. Press CTRL + Z to undo the last action. The form returns to the default stacked layout.
10. Click outside the fields to deselect them.
11. Right-click the form's tab and click Close. When prompted to save changes, click No.
12. Leave the **ATry20_studentfirstname_studentlastname** database open to use in the next Try It.

Select the label and the text box

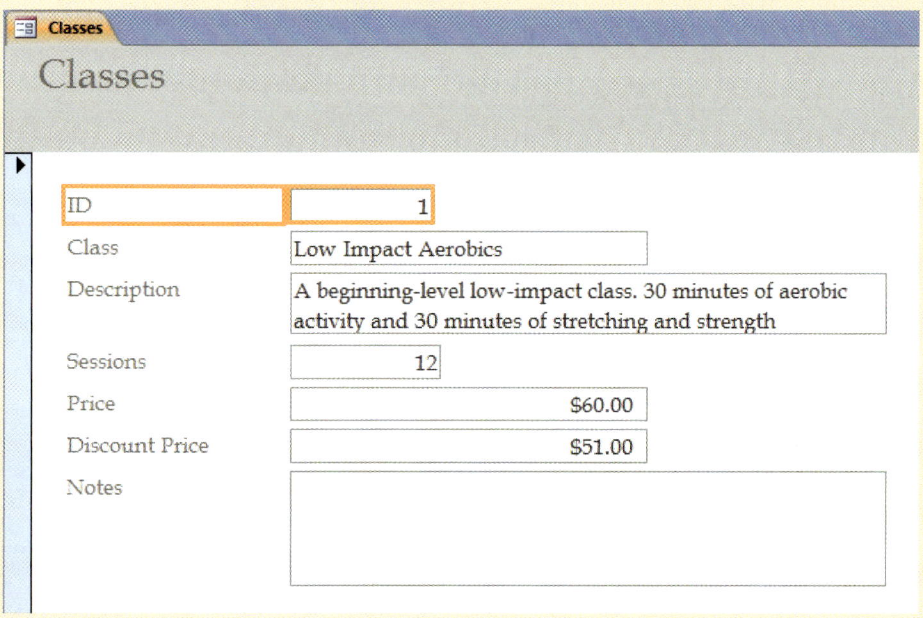

Creating a Form in Layout View

- Layout view enables you to drag-and-drop fields onto the form without worrying about precise placement. As you add and remove fields from the layout in Layout view, the others move automatically to accommodate them.
- You can later switch to Design view to fine-tune their placement if desired, as described in Lesson 21.

Try It! Creating a Form in Layout View

1. In the **ATry20_studentfirstname_ studentlastname** file, click the Classes table in the Navigation pane.
2. Click Create > Blank Form . A blank form opens, with the Field List pane on the right.

   ✓ *If you did not click the Classes table in step 1, the list of fields from the Classes table does not appear automatically. In that case you must click Show All Tables and then click the plus sign next to the Classes table to open its field list.*
3. Drag the ClassID field from the field list to the top of the blank form.
4. Drag the ClassName field onto the form.
5. Drag each of the remaining fields from the Classes table onto the form, in the order they appear in the field list.

   ✓ *The label column appears truncated; this is normal at this point.*
6. Click the Save button on the Quick Access Toolbar. In the Save As dialog box, type **Alternate Class Form** and click OK.
7. Leave the **ATry20_studentfirstname_ studentlastname** database open to use in the next Try It.

Place the remaining fields on the form

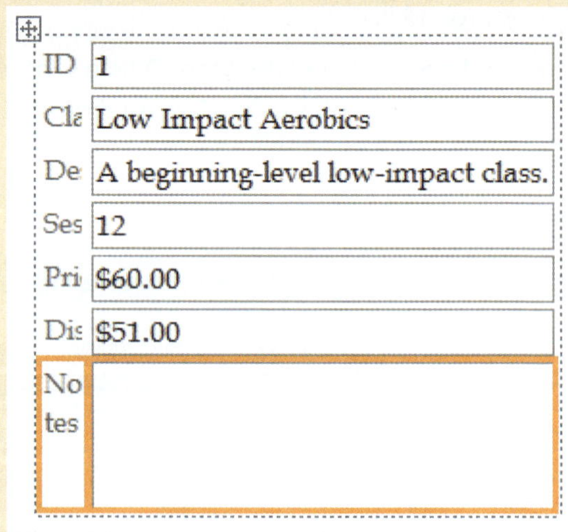

Place the ClassID field on the form

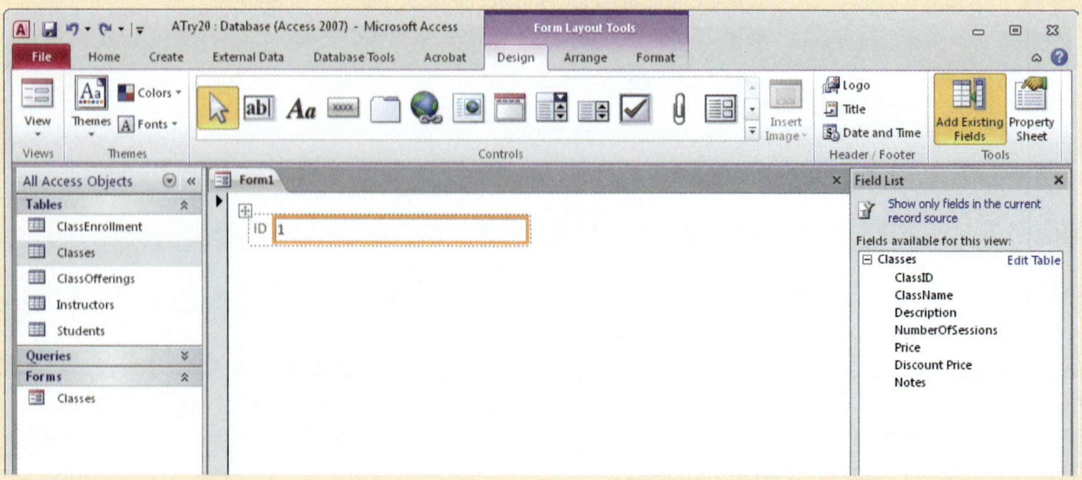

Sizing a Control

- You can resize a control by dragging its border. Select the desired control, and then position the mouse pointer over the border and drag.
- Resizing one control in a column also automatically resizes all other controls in that column so the columns stay even.

✓ *You can double-click the right edge of a selected control to auto-size it to fit. However, all other controls in that column are resized to that new size as well, even if they need to be wider to avoid being truncated. Therefore, double-clicking to resize works best when performed on the control in that column that requires the greatest width.*

Try It! Sizing a Control

1. In the **ATry20_studentfirstname_studentlastname** file, with the Alternate Class form open in Layout view, click the ID label.
2. Position the mouse pointer at the right edge of the orange selection box, so the pointer becomes a double-headed arrow.
3. Drag to the right until the column is wide enough to accommodate all entries.
4. Click the Discount Price label to select it.
5. Position the mouse pointer over the right edge of the Discount Price label, so the pointer turns to a double-headed arrow.
6. Double-click to auto-size the label to fit, and all the other labels change size to match.
7. Leave the **ATry20_studentfirstname_studentlastname** database open to use in the next Try It.

Auto-size the Discount Price label

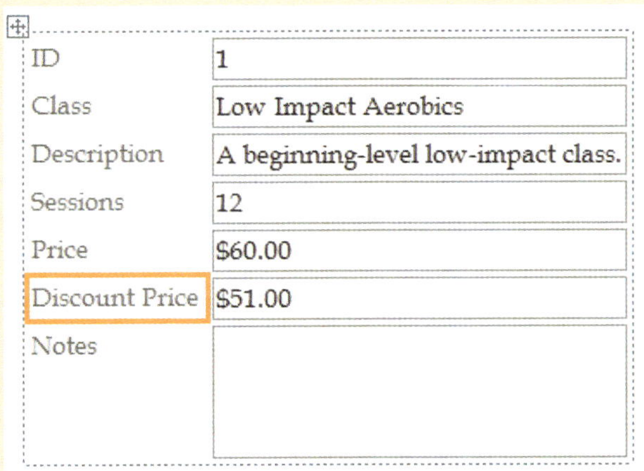

Moving Controls in a Layout

- If you want to move both the field and its associated label, you must select them both. Otherwise they move separately.
- To move a control, select it (and any associated controls) position the mouse pointer over it so a four-headed arrow appears and drag to the new location.
- To rearrange controls in a stacked layout, drag them up or down. To rearrange controls in a tabular layout, drag them to the left or right.

✓ *Fields within a layout can only be rearranged, not moved around freely on the form. If you need to place a control outside of the layout grid, use Design view, covered in the next lesson.*

✓ *After reordering the fields, you might need to reset the tab order for the form so that pressing* TAB *moves the insertion point from one field to another in the right order. In Access 2010, tab order must be changed in Design view, covered in the next lesson.*

Try It! Moving Controls in a Layout

1. In the **ATry20_studentfirstname_studentlastname** file, with the Alternate Class form open in Layout view, click the Description label.
2. Hold down CTRL and click the Description field (text box.)
3. Position the mouse pointer over the Description label and text box so the pointer becomes a four-headed arrow.
4. Drag the field down to the bottom position in the form. A yellow horizontal line shows where it is moving.
5. Position the mouse pointer over the bottom border of the Description field. The mouse pointer becomes a vertical double-headed arrow.
6. Drag down to enlarge the Description field to two lines of text. Position the mouse pointer over the right edge of the field and drag to the right to display all text.
7. Leave the **ATry20_studentfirstname_studentlastname** database open to use in the next Try It.

Resize the Description field after moving it

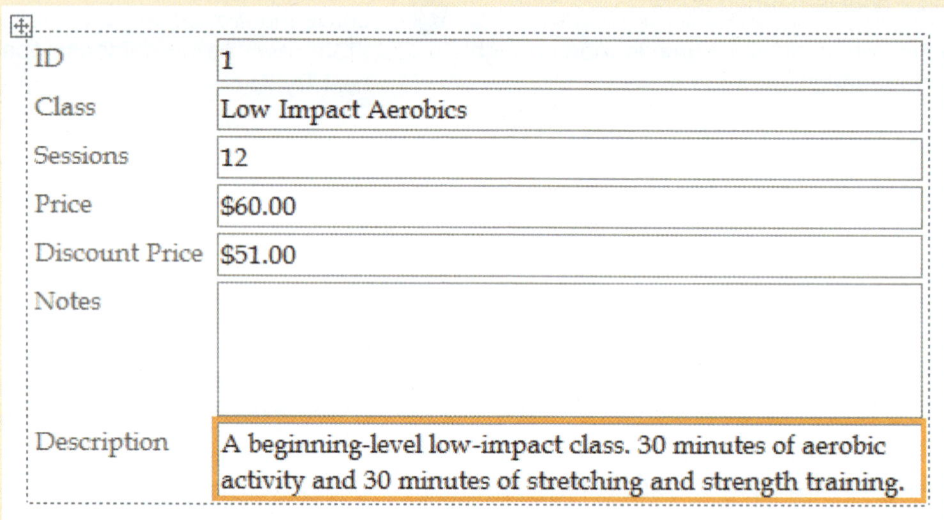

Deleting a Control

- To delete a field or other control, select the field's text box (not its label) and press DEL. The field and its associated label are both deleted.
- If you select the label (rather than the field itself) before pressing DEL, only the label is deleted; the field remains.

Try It! Deleting a Control

1. In the ATry20_studentfirstname_ studentlastname file, with the Alternate Class form open in Layout view, click the ID field.
2. Press DEL . Both the field and the label are removed.
3. Press CTRL + Z to undo the last action.
4. Click the ID label and press DEL . Only the label is deleted.
5. Click the ID field and press DEL . The field is deleted.
6. Leave the ATry20_studentfirstname_ studentlastname database open to use in the next Try It.

Adjusting the Control Margins and Control Padding

- Each control has its own individual margins and padding. **Control padding** is the space on the outside of the control (that is, between it and another control). **Control margin** is the space on the inside of the control (that is, between the text inside the control and the control's border).
- Both are controlled using buttons in the Position group on the Form Layout Tools Arrange tab. Each has four possible settings: None, Narrow, Medium, and Wide. The settings apply only to the selected fields/labels.

Try It! Adjusting the Control Margins and Control Padding

1. In the ATry20_studentfirstname_ studentlastname file, with the Alternate Class Form open in Layout view, press CTRL + A to select all controls on the form.
2. Click Form Layout Tools Arrange > Control Margins .
3. Click Narrow.
4. Click Form Layout Tools Arrange > Control Padding .
5. Click Medium.
6. Click outside the fields to deselect them.
7. Leave the ATry20_studentfirstname_ studentlastname database open to use in the next Try It.

Select narrow control margins

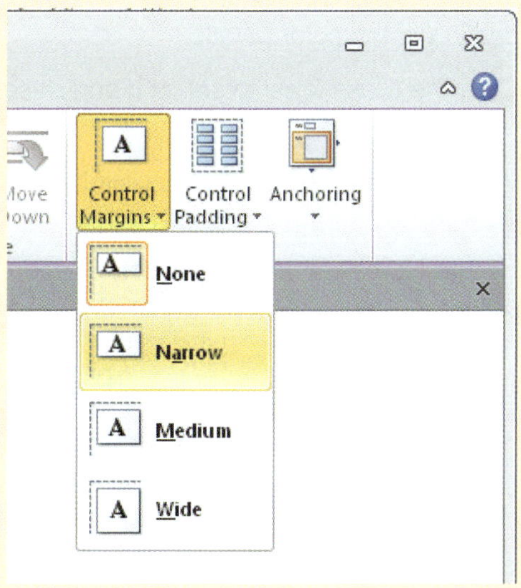

Changing Control Formatting

- While a control on a form is selected, you can use the controls in the Font group on either the Form Layout Tools Format tab or the Home tab to do any of the following:
  - Change the item's font or font size.
  - Apply bold, italic, or underlined font styles.
  - Choose left-aligned, centered, or right-aligned.
  - Choose the color of the background, text, and border.
  - Choose the style and width of the line or of the border surrounding the box.
- If you make an error while formatting, choose the Undo command immediately after a change.
- To copy formatting from one control to another, select a control with the formatting you want to copy, click the Format Painter button, and then click the object to change.
- If you want to change multiple objects with Format Painter, double-click the Format Painter button and click on each control you want to change. Click the Format Painter button again to turn it off.

Try It! Changing Control Formatting

1. In the **ATry20_studentfirstname_studentlastname** file, with the Alternate Class form open in Layout view, click the Class label.
2. Hold down CTRL and click each of the other labels, so all labels are selected.

   ✓ *Do not select the fields themselves.*
3. Click Home > Bold **B**, or press CTRL + B.
4. Click Home > Font Color arrow and click the bright-red square from the Standard Colors section of the color palette.
5. Click the Class label to select it and deselect all other labels.
6. In the Text Formatting group, click the Font drop-down arrow and click 14.
7. On the Home tab, in the Clipboard group, double-click the Format Painter button.
8. Click each of the other labels to copy the new font size to them.
9. Close the **ATry20_studentfirstname_studentlastname** file and exit Access.

Choose Red as the color for the labels

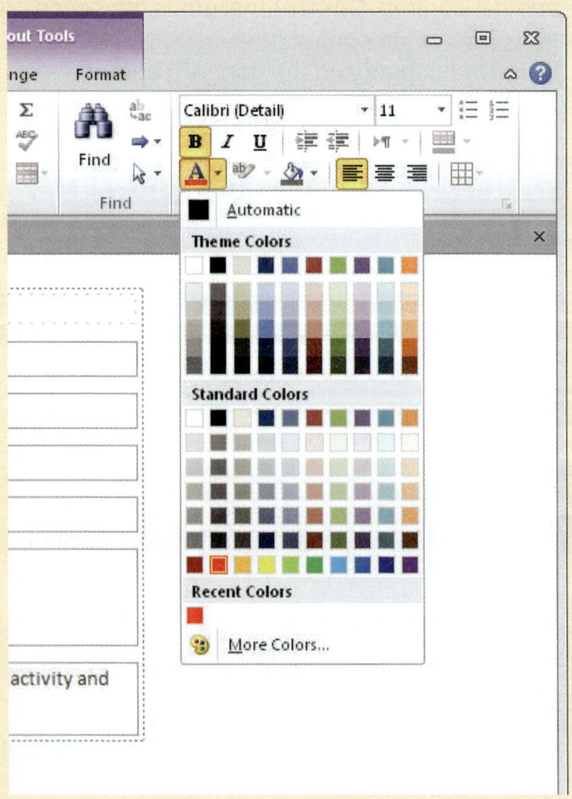

Project 43—Create It

Jewelry Business Database

DIRECTIONS

1. Start Access, if necessary, and open **AProj43** from the data files for this lesson. If a security warning bar appears, click **Enable Content**.
2. Save the database as **AProj43_studentfirstname_studentlastname** in the location where your teacher instructs you to store the files for this lesson.
3. Click **Create** > **Blank Form**.
4. In the Field List pane, click **Show All Tables** if the list of tables does not already appear.
5. In the Field List pane, click the plus sign next to **Customers** to display the fields for that table. Refer to Figure 20-1.
6. Drag the **First Name** field from the field list to the form.
7. Drag the **Last Name** field from the field list to the form.
8. Click **Form Layout Tools Arrange** > **Tabular** to change the form to a tabular layout.
9. Drag the **ID** field onto the form, to the left of the First Name field.

   ✓ *When dragging, position the mouse pointer so a vertical yellow line appears to the left of the First Name field, and then release the mouse button.*
10. Position the mouse pointer at the right edge of the **ID** field (selected) and drag to the left, resizing the column to fit the current content.
11. Click the ID field's label to select it.
12. Hold down CTRL and click the **First Name** label, and then the **Last Name** label.
13. Click **Home** > **Italic** *I*, or press CTRL + I.
14. Click the **Save** button on the Quick Access Toolbar.
15. In the Save As dialog box, type **Customer Basics** and click **OK**.
16. Close the database and submit it to your teacher for grading.

Figure 20-1

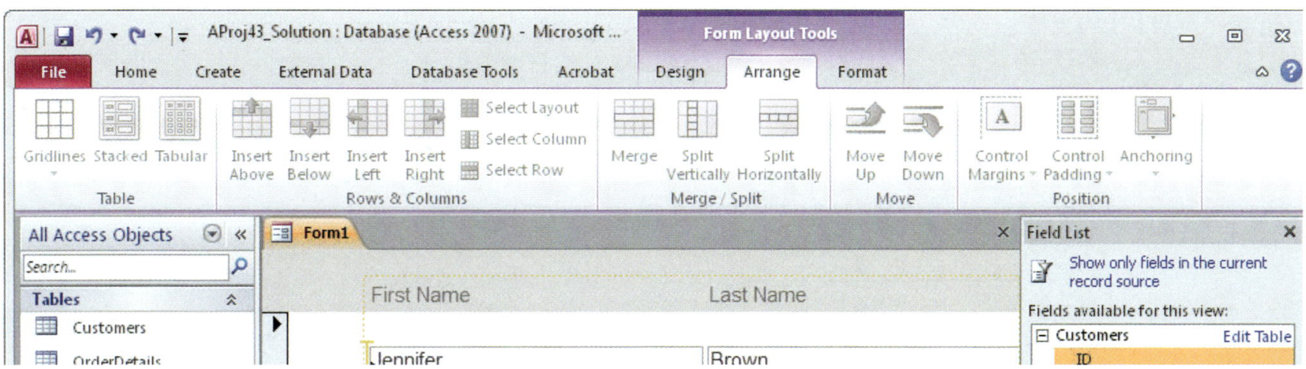

Project 44—Apply It

Jewelry Business Database

DIRECTIONS

1. Start Access, if necessary, and open **AProj44** from the data files for this lesson. If a security warning bar appears, click **Enable Content**.
2. Save the database as **AProj44_studentfirstname_studentlastname** in the location where your teacher instructs you to store the files for this lesson.
3. Create a new form in Layout view, with Stacked layout, that uses the **Category**, **Product**, **Size**, and **Material** fields from the **Products** table, in that order.
4. Move the **Material** field to immediately follow the Category field.
5. Right-align all the labels.
6. Apply a green text color to the labels.
7. Change the label text size to 12 point.
8. Widen the column containing the fields to approximately twice its original width.
9. Widen the column containing the labels to approximately twice its original width.
10. Save the form as **Product Basics**, and close it.
11. Open the **Shippers** form in Layout view.
12. In the **Name** column, drag the bottom border of one of the fields upward to shrink the height to match the height of the ID field. Do the same thing for the **Account** field.
13. Set the **Control Margins** for all fields on the form to **Narrow**. (Do not include the labels.)
14. Save and close the form.
15. Open the **Orders and Details Form** in Layout view.
16. In the subform, widen the **Product** column so none of the names are truncated.
17. On the main part of the form, widen the column containing the labels so that the **Salesperson** field does not overflow onto an additional line.
18. Save and close the form.
19. Close the database and submit it to your teacher for grading.

Lesson 21

Working with a Form in Design View

WORDS TO KNOW

Layout selector
The four-headed arrow button in the upper left corner of a layout, visible in Design view when a field or label in the layout is selected.

Selection handles
Squares around the border of a control that can be dragged to resize the control.

Tab order
The sequence in which the insertion point moves from field to field when you press TAB .

Unbound
Not connected to a particular field.

➤ What You Will Learn

Exploring Design View and Resizing Fields
Selecting and Moving Controls
Resetting Tab Order
Changing the Form Size
Inserting an Unbound Label
Creating a New Form in Design View

Software Skills In a form's Design view, you can fine-tune the form's layout, including moving controls around individually. You can also apply formatting and adjust form controls as you do in Layout view.

Application Skills In your friend's jewelry business database, you will make changes to forms that cannot be made in Layout view, such as changing the form's size and adding explanatory labels. You will use Design view to make these changes.

What You Can Do

Exploring Design View and Resizing Fields

- Form Design view consists of a layout grid on which you place fields, labels, and other controls. You can drag them around freely on that grid.
- You can do almost everything in Design view that you can do in Layout view, plus you can add other controls such as drop-down lists, check boxes, and even charts and graphics.

- In Design view, you can place codes on the form that display the date and time, record or page numbers, and other information by using functions similar to those in Excel. These are typically placed in the header or footer, which are covered in Lesson 22.
- You can also fine-tune placement of items more precisely in Design view and move fields separately from their labels and vice-versa.

  ✓ *Click the Grid button on the Arrange tab to toggle the dotted grid display on or off in Design view.*

- Fields behave differently depending on whether they are in a layout. A layout is a tabular structure that automatically arranges and organizes the fields, as you saw in Lesson 20. To determine whether a layout is in use, click any label or field. If a **layout selector** appears above and to the left of the fields, a layout is present.
- If you created the form in Layout view or with the Form Wizard, the fields are already in a stacked or tabular layout.
- If you manually create a form in Design view, the fields are free-floating and there is no layout grid. Fields are also free-floating on forms that were upgraded from Access 2003 and earlier versions.

  ✓ *The layout grid in Access is very much like a table in Word. That same symbol is present when working in a table in Word, but it is called the table selector.*

- You can drag a control's right border to resize it. This does not change the number of characters that can be stored in the field; that's controlled in the table properties. It only changes the width of the on-screen control that displays the field value.
- When you resize a control that is part of a layout, all the controls in that column are resized. When you resize a free-floating control, only that control is resized.

Try It! Exploring Design View and Resizing Fields

1. Start Access and open the file **ATry21** file from the data files for this lesson.
2. Save it as **ATry21_studentfirstname_studentlastname** in the location where your teacher instructs you to store the files for this lesson.
3. In the navigation pane, right-click Classes With Layout and click Design View.
4. Click the ID label.

   ✓ *Notice the four-headed arrow in the upper left corner of the layout and the dashed border that surrounds the fields.*

   ✓ *All the fields and their labels are exactly the same width.*

5. Position the mouse pointer at the right edge of the selected ID label and drag to the left.

   ✓ *All the fields are resized the same amount.*

6. In the Navigation pane, right-click Classes Without Layout and click Design View .
7. Click the text box (the field itself) for the ClassID field.

   ✓ *There is no layout selector.*

   ✓ *Some fields have different widths than others. This is permitted only when a layout is not being used.*

8. Position the mouse pointer at the right edge of the selected ClassID field and drag to the left.

   ✓ *Only the ClassID field is resized.*

9. Leave the **ATry21_studentfirstname_studentlastname** database open to use in the next Try It.

(continued)

Try It! **Exploring Design View and Resizing Fields** *(continued)*

Resize the ClassID field

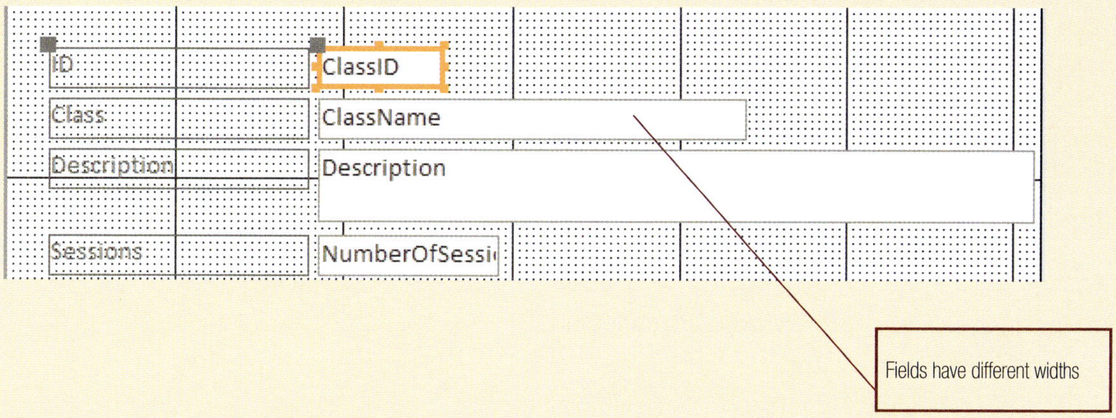

Selecting and Moving Controls

- When you click a control that is part of a layout, an orange border appears around it, just like in Layout view.
- Also, like in Layout view, you can drag the right edge of a label or field to change its width as you saw in the preceding steps. Whether the change is made only to that control or to all controls in that column depends on whether or not a layout is in use.
- You can drag a control to move it.
- When you drag a control that is part of a layout, you can only drag it to different positions within the layout; you cannot drag it outside of the layout. The label and field move together, regardless of which one you drag.
- When you drag a free-floating control (that is, a control that is not part of a layout), you can place it anywhere you like.

  ✓ *You cannot drag a control from one section to another. However, you can cut a control (CTRL + Z) and then select a different section and paste it (CTRL + Z). Sections are covered in Lesson 22.*

- When working with free-floating controls, each control has a large square selection handle in its upper left corner. You can drag the control by that square to move it independently of any associated controls.
- To select multiple controls, click on the first control, hold down the CTRL or SHIFT key, and click on additional controls. You can also "lasso" controls by dragging a box around them.

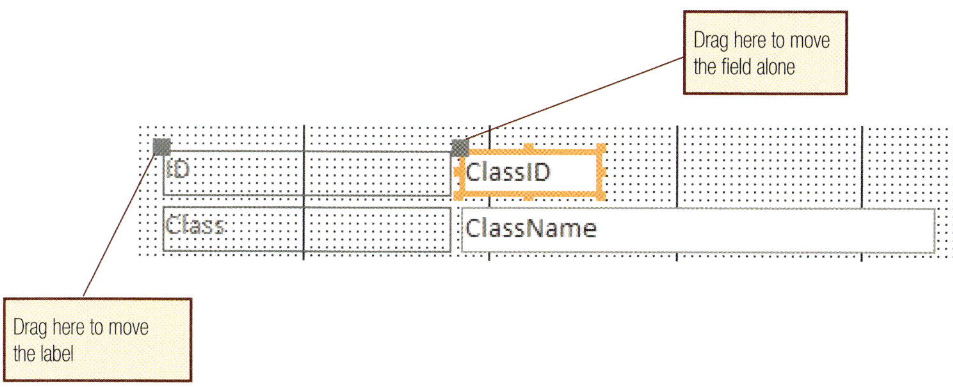

Figure 21-1

Try It! Moving Fields on a Form

1. In the **ATry21_studentfirstname_ studentlastname** file, open Classes With Layout in Design view, if it is not already open.
2. On the Classes With Layout form, click the Description field.
3. Drag the Description field between the Discount Price and Notes fields.
4. Open Classes Without Layout in Design view, if it is not already open.
5. On the Classes Without Layout form, click the Description field.
6. Point to the border of the Description field, but not over the large square in the upper left corner.
7. Drag the field to a new position on the form. Both the field and the label move.
8. Press CTRL + Z to undo the move.
9. Point to the large square in the upper-left corner of the Description field.
10. Drag the field to a new position on the form. Only the field moves, not its label.
11. Press CTRL + Z to undo the move.
12. Leave the **ATry21_studentfirstname_ studentlastname** database open to use in the next Try It.

Resetting Tab Order

- **Tab order** is the sequence in which pressing the Tab key moves from one field to another. The default tab order is from top to bottom on a stacked form, or from left to right on a tabular form.
- If you add or move controls on a form based on a layout, Access automatically adjusts the tab order. For example, earlier in this lesson when you moved the Description field on the Classes With Layout form, Access reset the tab order to reflect the Description field's new position.
- However, if you add or move controls on a form without a layout, you have to change the tab order manually.
- You might also want to set an alternate tab order so that users don't have to tab past a seldom-used field, such as Suffix or Middle Initial during data entry, or past an automatically entered field, such as a calculated or AutoNumber field.

Try It! Resetting Tab Order

1. In the **ATry21_studentfirstname_studentlastname** file, with the Classes With Layout form open in Design view, click Form Design Tools Design > Tab Order .
2. In the Tab Order dialog box, drag the ClassID field to the bottom of the list. (Drag the gray box to the left of the field name.)
3. Click OK.
4. Click Form Design Tools Design > Tab Order to reopen the dialog box.
5. Click Auto Order.
6. Click OK.
7. Leave the **ATry21_studentfirstname_studentlastname** database open to use in the next Try It.

Drag a field up or down in the Tab Order dialog box

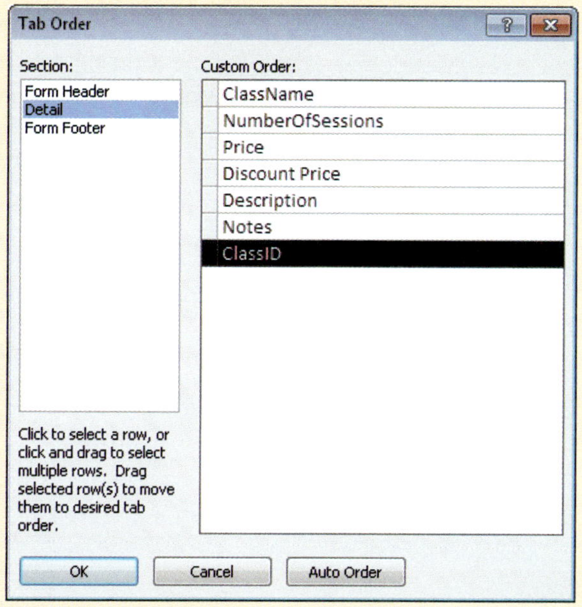

Changing the Form Size

- By default, forms appear on tabs in Access 2010, so form size is not an issue; the form is as large as the tabbed page on which it displays, which is in turn determined by the size of the Access window.
- However, it is also possible to set a form to display in its own window, in which case the form size is important because it specifies the size of the window.

✓ *Setting a form to appear in a window is beyond the scope of this book.*

- Form size is also (and more commonly) an issue if you want to add additional controls to a form in Design view. The form may need to be enlarged to accommodate the additional controls.

Try It! Changing the Form Size

1. In the **ATry21_studentfirstname_studentlastname** file, with the Classes With Layout form open in Design view, position the mouse pointer at the right edge of the form.
2. Drag to the right to expand the form horizontally approximately 2 inches.

   ✓ *Use the ruler above the work area to gauge the distance.*

3. Leave the **ATry21_studentfirstname_studentlastname** database open to use in the next Try It.

(continued)

Try It! Changing the Form Size *(continued)*

Drag to enlarge the form horizontally

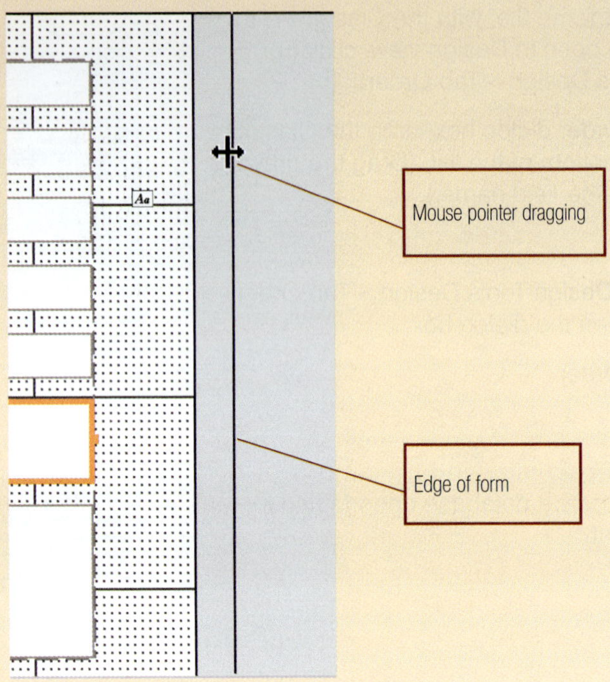

Inserting an Unbound Label

- An **unbound control** is one that is not associated with any particular field.
- The simplest type of unbound control is a label. Most of the labels on a form are connected to fields, but a form can also contain other labels too.

Try It! Inserting an Unbound Label

1. In the **ATry21_studentfirstname_studentlastname** file, if you have not already done so, follow the preceding steps, so there is 2" of extra space at the right edge of the Classes With Layout form in Design view.
2. Click Form Design Tools Design > Label .
3. On the form, in the blank space to the right of the fields, drag to draw a rectangular box, approximately 2" by 2" square.
4. In the new box, type **Note: Not all classes are offered every quarter**.
5. Click the outside of the box to select its border. The border appears orange.
6. Position the mouse pointer on the selection handle at the bottom of the box, and drag upward to size the box to fit the text.
7. Right-click the form's tab and click Close. Click Yes when prompted to save changes. If the Classes Without Layout form is still open, close it and save its changes.
8. Leave the **ATry21_studentfirstname_studentlastname** database open to use in the next Try It.

(continued)

Try It! **Inserting an Unbound Label** *(continued)*

Draw a text box in the newly created space

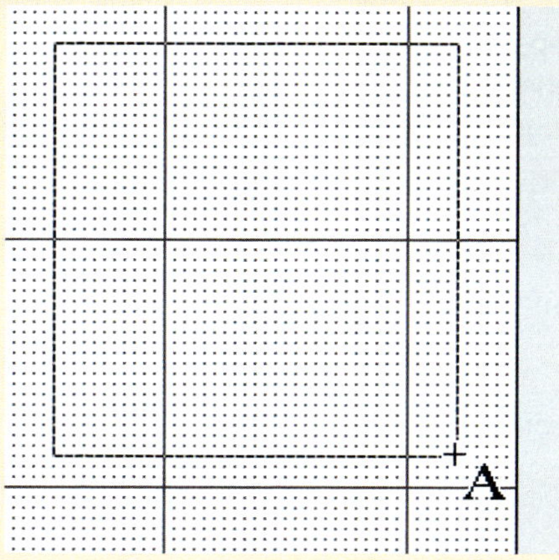

Resize the text box to fit the text

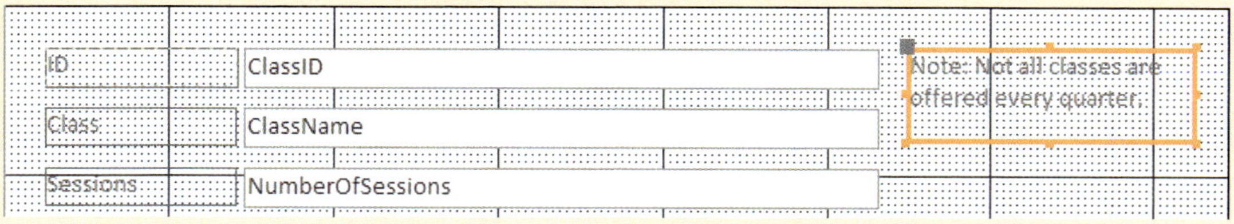

Creating a New Form in Design View

- It is not ideal to create a form in Design view from scratch because positioning the fields can be time-consuming and tricky. However, some forms with special requirements may be more conveniently created in Design view.

Try It! Creating a New Form in Design View

1. In the **ATry21_studentfirstname_studentlastname** file, if you have not already done so, follow the preceding steps, so there is 2" of extra space at the right edge of the Classes With Layout form in Design view.
2. Click Create > Form Design.
3. Click Form Design Tools Design > Add Existing Fields. The Field List pane opens.
4. Click Show all tables.
5. Click the plus sign ⊞ to the left of Class Enrollment.
6. Double-click the EnrollmentID field. It appears on the form.
7. Double-click the ClassOfferingID field.
8. Double-click the StudentID field.
9. Press CTRL + A to select all the fields on the form.
10. Click Form Design Tools Arrange > Stacked. The fields are placed in a stacked layout.
11. Close the **ATry21_studentfirstname_studentlastname** database without saving the changes to the new form, and exit Access.

Place the fields on the form

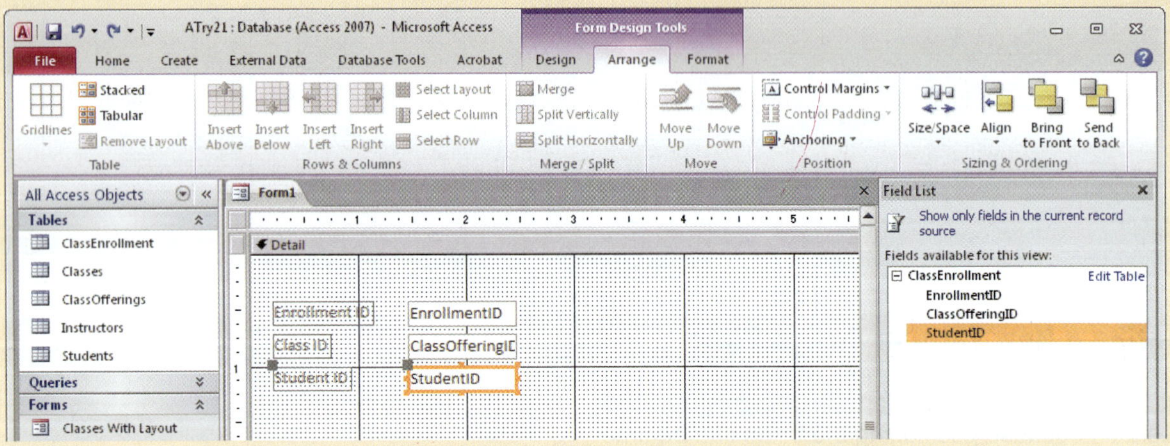

Project 45—Create It

Jewelry Business Database

DIRECTIONS

1. Start Access, if necessary, and open **AProj45** from the data files for this lesson. If a security warning bar appears, click **Enable Content**.
2. Save the database as **AProj45_studentfirstname_studentlastname** in the location where your teacher instructs you to store the files for this lesson.
3. Click **Create** > **Form Design** .
4. If the Field List pane does not appear already, click Form Design Tools Design > Add Existing Fields to display it.
5. Click **Show all tables**.
6. Click the **plus sign** next to Order Details.
7. Double-click the **OrderDetailID** field to add it to the form.
8. Double-click the **Order** field.
9. Double-click the **Quantity** field.
10. Double-click the **Product** field.
11. Click the **Close** button on the Field List pane to close it.
12. Press CTRL + A to select all the fields on the form.
13. Drag the selected fields down 1" on the form.
14. Click **Form Design Tools Design** > **Label** .
15. Drag to create a label box above the fields.
16. In the label box, type **Order Details**.
17. Click outside the label box to move the insertion point out of it.
18. Click the border of the label box to select it.
19. Click **Home** > **Font Size** arrow > **20**.
20. Click the **Save** button on the Quick Access Toolbar.
21. In the Save As dialog box, type **Order Detail Form** and click **OK**.
22. Close the database, and submit it to your teacher for grading.

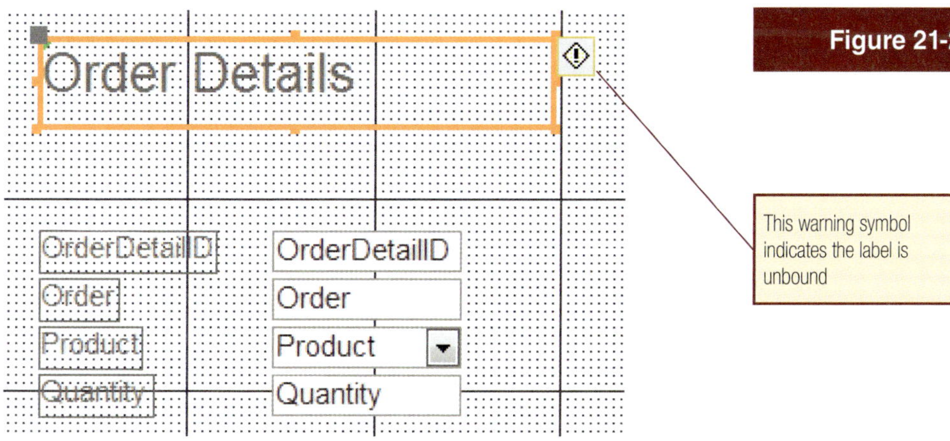

Figure 21-2

Project 46—Apply It

Jewelry Business Database

DIRECTIONS

1. Start Access, if necessary, and open **AProj46** from the data files for this lesson. If a security warning bar appears, click **Enable Content**.
2. Save the database as **AProj46_studentfirstname_studentlastname** in the location where your teacher instructs you to store the files for this lesson.
3. Open the **Order Detail Form** in Design view.
4. Change the order of the last three fields to Order, Product, and Quantity.
5. Change the tab order to reflect the new field order.
6. Select all the fields, and place them in a stacked layout.
7. Widen the field column by approximately 1".
8. Close the form, saving your changes.
9. Open the **Customer Basics** form in Design view.
10. Select all fields, and remove them from the layout using the Remove Layout command.
11. Resize the field lengths so they are about the same size as shown in Figure 21-3.
12. Close the database and submit it to your teacher for grading.

Figure 21-3

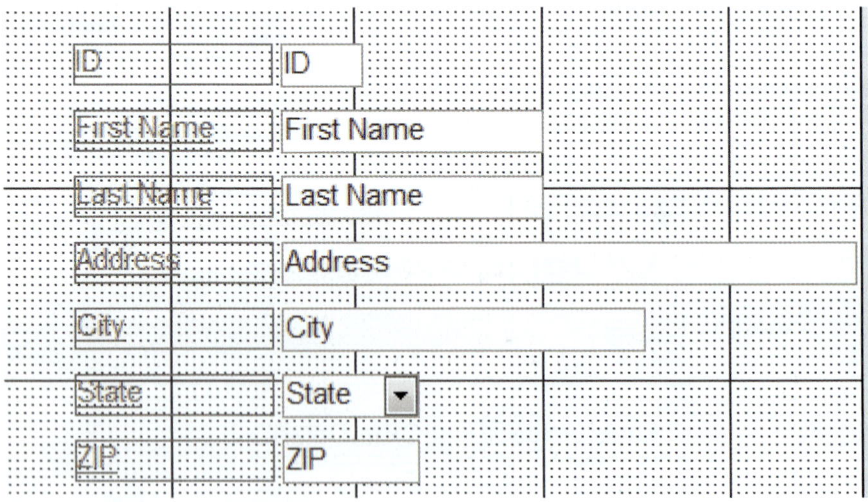

Lesson 22

Working with Form Sections

➤ What You Will Learn

- Understanding Sections
- Displaying and Resizing Sections
- Inserting a Form Title
- Adding Date/Time Codes
- Moving Controls Between Sections

Software Skills One major benefit of working with a form in Design view is the ability to add and customize additional sections, such as the form header and footer. The header is typically used for a form title; the footer may contain codes such as page numbering or date/time codes.

Application Skills In the jewelry business database, you will enhance the forms by adding and formatting their header and footer sections.

WORDS TO KNOW

Form footer
An area at the bottom of the form, below the Detail area, in which you can enter explanatory text, graphics, or other information that applies to the form as a whole.

Form header
An area at the top of the form, above the Detail area, in which you can enter titles, explanatory text, graphics, or anything else that applies to the form as a whole.

Page footer
Same as form footer except it applies to individual printed pages.

Page header
Same as form header except it applies to individual printed pages instead of to the form as a whole.

Section
An area of a form or report layout designed for a specific purpose. For example, the Detail section contains the fields and the Form Header section contains the form title.

What You Can Do

Understanding Sections

- A form can have multiple sections. The Detail section is the main one, where the fields are placed.
- Headers and footers on a form provide a place to enter information and objects that relate to the entire form or entire page, rather than to an individual record. They are managed from Design view.

- Forms that you create via the Form Wizard or via the Form button (or Split Form button) automatically have a form header set up. Forms that you create via Design view or via the Blank Form button (Layout view) do not.
- On-screen, headers and footers appear at the top and bottom of a form (or page, on a multipage form). See Figure 22-1.
- In Design view, there are separate areas for each section, each with its own divider bar at the top. See Figure 22-2.
- There are two kinds of headers possible in a form: page header and form header.
- Whatever you enter in the page header appears on each page of a multipage form or printout. You might place a page numbering code here, for example, to print a page number at the top of each page.
- The **page header** and footer print at the top and bottom of the page but do not display in Form view.
- Page headers are not typically used, because a typical form is only one page long when printed, so it would be redundant to have both a form header and a page header.
- Whatever you enter on the **form header** appears only once, at the top of the on-screen form or at the beginning of the printout, regardless of the number of pages in the printout.
- The **form footer** displays in Form view and on the last page of a printout. The form's footer is a good place for controls that you always want to see if the detail section requires scrolling.
- Footers work the same way; you can have a **page footer** and a form footer that appear on the bottom of each page and at the bottom of the last page respectively.
- To select a section, click its bar. To select the entire form (all sections), click the Select All button in the upper left corner of the form.

Figure 22-1

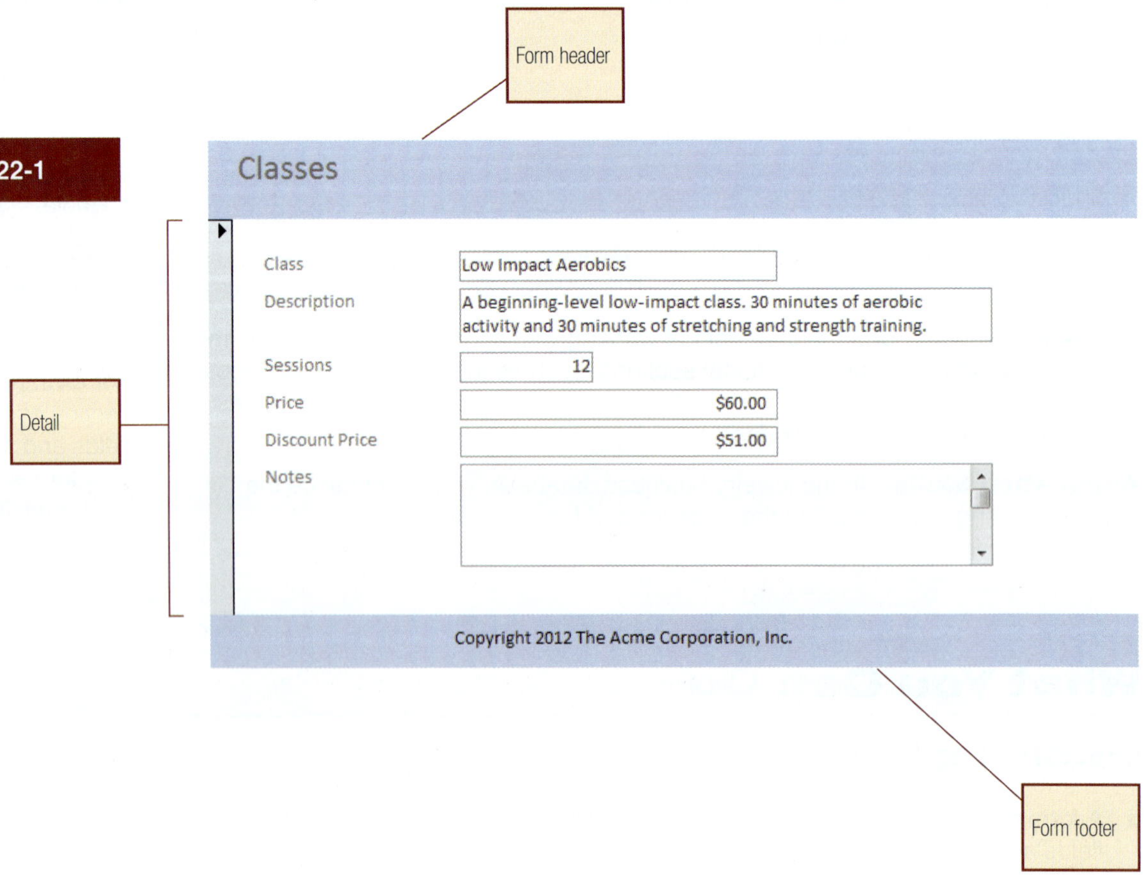

Figure 22-2

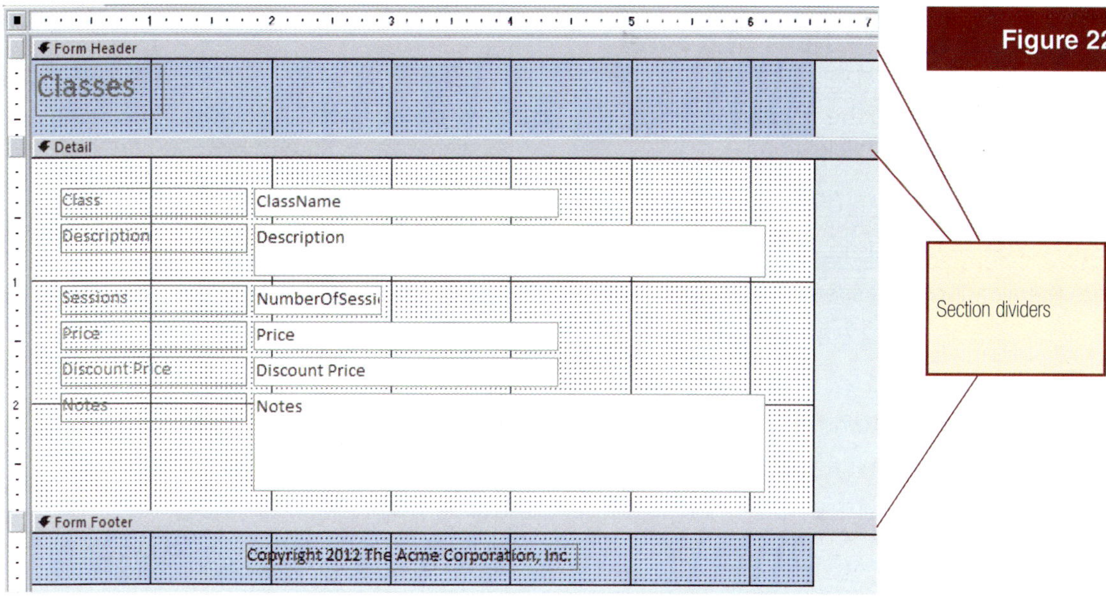

Figure 22-3

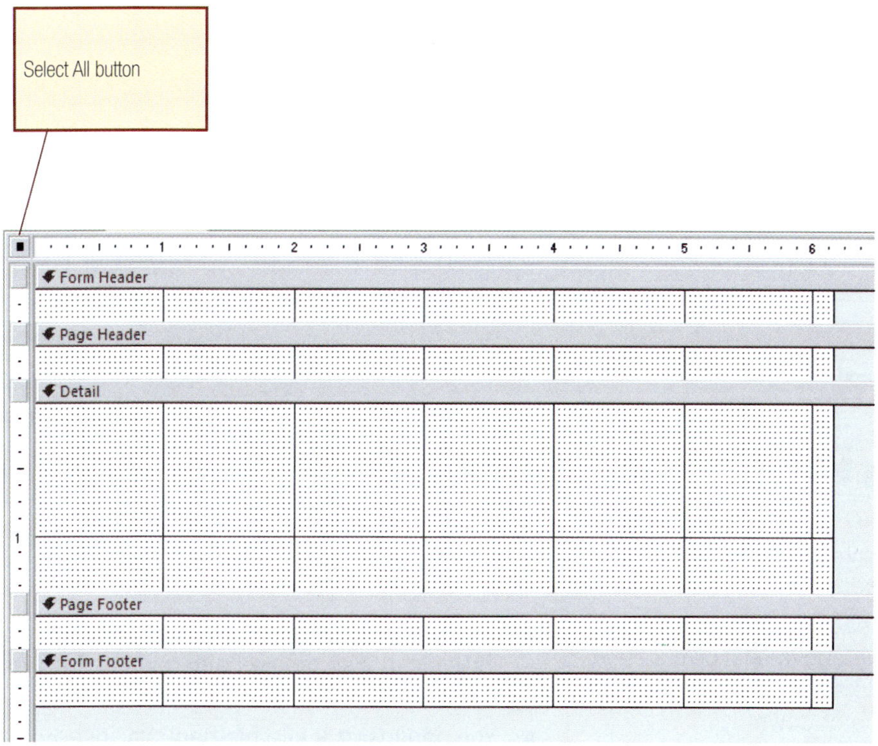

Try It! Selecting Sections of a Form

1. Start Access and open the database **ATry22** from the data files for this lesson.
2. Save the database as **ATry22_studentfirstname_studentlastname** in the location where your teacher instructs you to store the files for this lesson.
3. Right-click the Sections form and click Design View.
4. Click the Detail bar. It turns black, indicating it is selected.
5. Click the Select All button. The button appears with a black square in it, and the previously selected bar becomes unselected.
6. Right-click the form's tab and click Close.
7. Leave the **ATry22_studentfirstname_studentlastname** database open to use in the next Try It.

The selected section's header bar is black

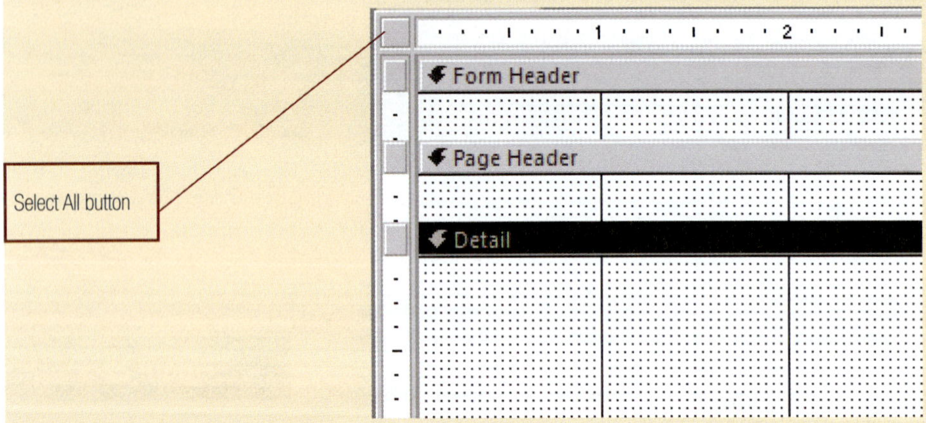

Displaying and Resizing Sections

- Depending on how the form was created, certain sections besides Detail may already be displayed and may already contain controls.
- You can drag the bars for each section up or down to increase or decrease the above section's size. For example, to change the size of the Form Header area, drag the Detail bar up or down.
- The headers and footers are paired, so you cannot display one and hide the other. However, you can resize a section to its smallest size (0" in height), effectively hiding it. In this way, you can have a form with a header but no footer or vice-versa.
- Refer to the vertical and horizontal rulers on-screen to help gauge the size of the header or footer when printed. However, the actual size that appears on-screen will depend on the monitor size and resolution.
- Hiding a header/footer pair does not just make them invisible; it also deletes any content that was in those sections.
- You can insert a title by manually inserting an unbound label box, as you learned in Lesson 21, in the Form Header section.
- You can also use the Title command to insert a title. The Title command not only inserts an unbound label, but also formats it and, if the Form Header section is not already displayed, it displays it all in one step.

Try It! Displaying and Resizing Sections

1. In the **ATry22_studentfirstname_studentlastname** file, click Create > Form Design. A new form appears (Detail section only).
2. Right-click the new form and click Page Header/Footer. The page header and page footer appear.
3. Right-click the new form and click Page Header/Footer again. The page header and page footer are removed.
4. Right-click the new form and click Form Header/Footer. The form header and footer appear.
5. Click the Detail bar to select that section.
6. Drag the Detail bar downward ½", increasing the height of the Form Header section.
7. Drag the Form Footer bar upward 1", decreasing the height of the Detail section.
8. Drag the bottom edge of the form footer upward until it touches the Form Footer bar, collapsing the form footer so it no longer appears.
9. Click Form Design Tools > Title. A Form1 title placeholder appears in the Form Header.
10. Type **Commerce**. The new text replaces the placeholder.
11. Click outside the label to accept the new text entry.
12. Leave the **ATry22_studentfirstname_studentlastname** database open to use in the next Try It.

Increase the height of the form header section

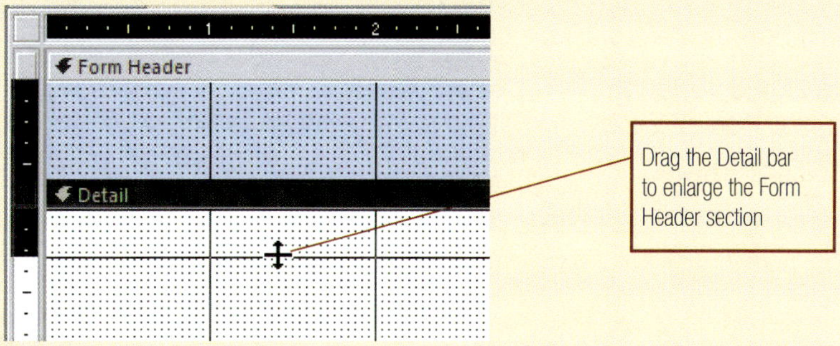

Collapse the form footer section

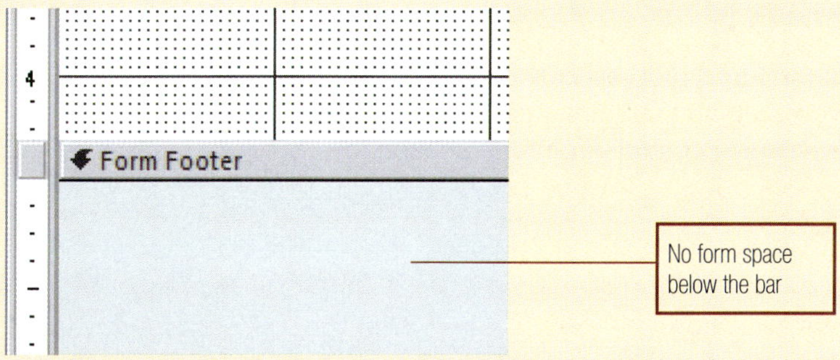

Adding Date/Time Codes

- You can add a date and/or time code to the form. It will appear in Form view and also when you print the form. The date/time is automatically updated from the computer's internal clock.
- When you choose to insert a date/time code, the Date and Time dialog box appears. You can choose to include the date, time, or both. You can also choose among three formats for each.
- A date/time code is always placed in the form header; you cannot choose where to insert it. You can, however, move it to another section after its insertion. (See the next section.)

Try It! Adding a Date Code

1. In the **ATry22_studentfirstname_studentlastname** file, click Form Design Tools Design > Date and Time. The Date and Time dialog box opens.
2. Clear the Include Time check box.
3. Click OK. An =Date( ) code appears in the top right corner of the Form Header.
4. Click Home > View arrow > Form View to see how the date will look on the form.
5. Click Home > View arrow > Design View to return to Design view.
6. Leave the **ATry22_studentfirstname_studentlastname** database open to use in the next Try It.

Select a format for the date code

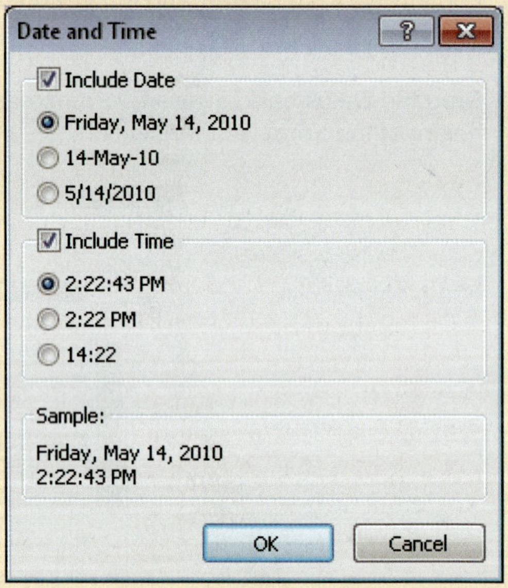

Moving Controls Between Sections

- You cannot drag-and-drop controls between sections. However, you can use the Cut and Paste commands to move controls from one section to another.

Try It! **Moving Control Between Sections**

1. In the **ATry22_studentfirstname_studentlastname** file, in Design view, click the Date code that you just inserted. The frame's border appears orange.
2. Press CTRL + X to cut the code to the Clipboard.
3. Click the Form Footer bar to select that section.
4. Press CTRL + V to paste the code from the Clipboard.
5. Close the form without saving changes to it.
6. Close the **ATry22_studentfirstname_studentlastname** file, and exit Access.

Project 47—Create It

Jewelry Business Database

DIRECTIONS

1. Start Access, if necessary, and open **AProj47** from the data files for this lesson. If a security warning bar appears, click **Enable Content**.
2. Save the database as **AProj47_studentfirstname_studentlastname** in the location where your teacher instructs you to store the files for this lesson.
3. In the Navigation pane, right-click the **Customer Basics** form and click **Design View**.
4. Position the mouse pointer between the Form Header and Detail bars and drag downward 1" to enlarge the Form Header area.
5. Click **Form Design Tools Design** > **Title** to place a title placeholder in the header.
6. Type **Basic Customer Information**, replacing the placeholder.
7. Drag the Detail bar upward until it almost touches the bottom of the title box, tightening up the unused space in the Form Header area.
8. Close the database, and submit it to your teacher for grading.

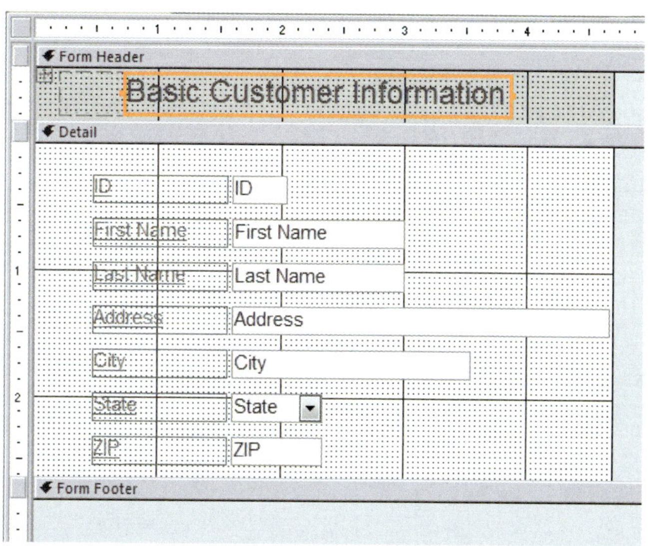

Figure 22-4

Project 48—Apply It

Jewelry Business Database

DIRECTIONS

1. Start Access, if necessary, and open **AProj48** from the data files for this lesson. If a security warning bar appears, click **Enable Content**.
2. Save the database as **AProj48_ studentfirstname_studentlastname** to the location where your teacher instructs you to store the files for this lesson.
3. Open the **Customer Basics** form in Design view.
4. Enlarge the Form Footer section by 1" vertically.
5. Insert a code for the current time. It appears in the Form Header.
6. Move the time code into the Form Footer and place it at the right edge of the form.
7. Drag the bottom of the form upward until it almost touches the bottom of the time placeholder, tightening up the unused space in the Form Footer area.
8. Save and close the form.
9. Open the **Product Basics** form in Design view.
10. Display the page header and footer.
11. In the Page Header, place the label **Product Information**. Change the font size of the label to 22.

    ✓ *You can place title manually as a label, or you can use the Title command to place it in the Form Header and then move it into the Page Header.*
12. Close the database, and submit to your teacher for grading.

Figure 22-5

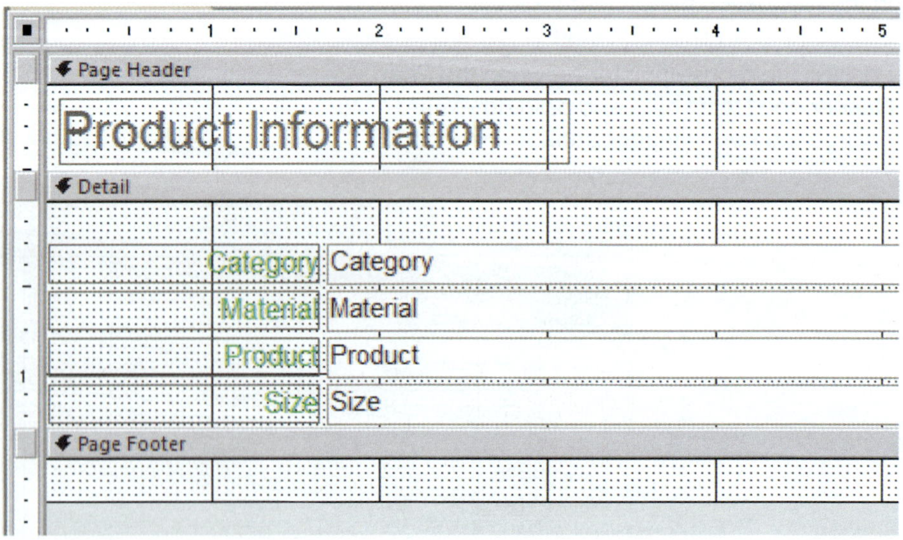

Lesson 23

Creating a Report

➤ What You Will Learn

Understanding Access Reports
Creating and Formatting a Report in Layout View
Creating a Report Using the Report Wizard
Modifying a Report in Design View
Working with Print Preview and Report View
Printing a Report

WORDS TO KNOW

Print Preview
A view of the report as it will appear when printed.

Report
A way to present your data for printing with formatting enhancements.

Report Design view
A view of the report that lets you change its appearance and content.

Software Skills Reports give you much more flexibility in producing output than simply printing tables and queries. You can print records in a tabular format that looks like a datasheet but with more attractive fonts, and you can print records one below the other in a columnar format.

Application Skills After seeing your printouts of queries and tables, your friend has been asking if you could make the printouts more readable. You realize it is time to learn about reports.

What You Can Do

Understanding Access Reports

- You can print tables, queries, and forms, but the printouts may not be attractive. Reports, on the other hand, are designed specifically for printed output. Reports give you more options for formatting, calculating, and totaling your data.
- There are four main types of report layouts:
  - In a tabular report, each row is a record and each column is a field. It's similar to the printout you get when printing a datasheet.

- In a columnar report, all the fields for each record appear together, followed by those for the next record, and so on.
- In a justified report, the field names appear above the fields for each individual record, arranged in blocks.
- In a mailing label report, records are arranged in blocks across and down the page, ready to print on a sheet of self-stick labels. Label reports are covered in Lesson 25.

■ There are four views for working with reports:

- Design: Uses a grid to arrange fields and other controls precisely; enables you to add non-field controls like formulas and labels. The layout does not look exactly as it will when printed, so you must switch between this view and others to check your work.

✓ *Report Design view works very much like Form Design view, which you learned about earlier in this chapter.*

- Layout: Shows the report approximately as it will look when printed and is editable. You can add and remove fields, resize controls, and so on.

✓ *Report Layout view is very much like Form Layout view.*

- Report: Shows the report optimized for on-screen viewing. The report is not editable in this view.
- Print Preview: Shows the report exactly as it will look when printed. The report is not editable in this view. Print Preview and Report views are very similar.

Figure 23-1

Columnar Report

Classes

Class	Low Impact Aerobics
Description	A beginning-level low-impact class. 30 minutes of aerobic activity and 30 minu
Sessions	12
Price	$60.00
Class	Aerobic Kickboxing
Description	Advanced level high-impact kickboxing aerobics. 50 minutes of challenging aeı
Sessions	12
Price	$70.00
Class	Water aerobics
Description	For all levels. Swimming ability not necessary.
Sessions	12
Price	$60.00

Figure 23-2

Tabular Report

Classes

Class	Description	Sessions	Price
Low Impact Aerobics	A beginning-level low-impact class. 30 minutes of aerob	12	$60.00
Aerobic Kickboxing	Advanced level high-impact kickboxing aerobics. 50 min	12	$70.00
Water aerobics	For all levels. Swimming ability not necessary.	12	$60.00
Beginning Yoga	A gentle introduction to yoga practices and philosophie	12	$60.00
Intermediate Yoga	Prerequisite: Beginning Yoga. A continuation class with	12	$70.00
Advanced Yoga	Prerequisite: Intermediate Yoga. Challenging yoga post	12	$70.00
Intro to Pilates	Beginning-level pilates workout. No previous experienc	8	$120.00

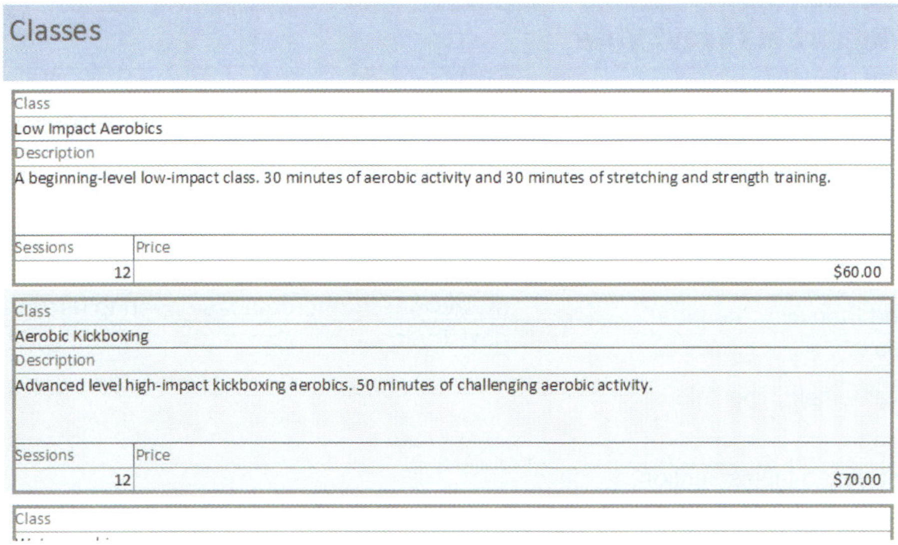

Figure 23-3

Justified Report

Try It! Creating and Viewing a Tabular Report

1. Start Access and open the database **ATry23** from the data files for this lesson.
2. Save the database as **ATry23_studentfirstname_studentlastname** in the location where your teacher instructs you to store the files for this lesson.
3. In the Navigation pane, click the Classes table.
4. Click Create > Report. A tabular report is created.
5. In the Views group, click the View arrow and click Report View.
6. Right-click the report's tab, and click Design View to switch to Design view.
7. Right-click the report's tab and click Close. When prompted to save changes, click No.
8. Leave the **ATry23_studentfirstname_studentlastname** database open to use in the next Try It.

Creating and Formatting a Report in Layout View

- Report Layout view is very similar to form Layout view. You can drag fields onto the report, and then drag them around to rearrange them. You can also resize fields and labels the same as on a form by dragging the right border of the desired control.
- You can format the controls on a report the same as on a form. Use the formatting buttons on the Home tab to control fonts, font sizes and colors, and text alignment.

Try It! Creating a Report in Layout View

1. In the **ATry23_studentfirstname_ studentlastname** file, click Create > Blank Report . A blank report opens in Layout view.

   ✓ *If the Field List pane does not appear, click Report Layout Tools Design > Add Existing Fields.*

2. Click Show all tables, and then click the plus sign to the left of Classes.
3. Double-click the ClassName field. The field is added to the form.
4. In the Fields available in related tables section, click the plus sign to the left of ClassOfferings, and then double-click the StartDate field.
5. Click the plus sign to the left of Instructors, and then double-click the LastName field.
6. Click outside the fields to deselect them; then click once on any row in the Class column.
7. Position the mouse pointer at the right edge of the Class field and drag to the right, widening the column so that the longest entry fits on a single row.
8. Click any field in the Start column, and click Home > Align Text Left .
9. Right-click the report's tab and click Close. Click No when asked if you want to save your work.
10. Leave the **ATry23_studentfirstname_ studentlastname** database open to use in the next Try It.

Format and align the fields

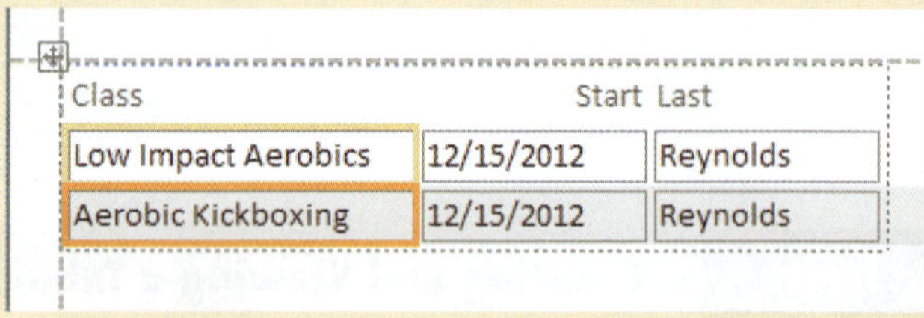

Creating a Report Using the Report Wizard

- The Report Wizard works like other wizards you have already used in Access.
- You choose the table/query and fields, the layout, and other options for the report, and then Access creates it according to your specifications.
- You can group the records in a report by one or more fields, and then sum, count, or perform some other calculation for each group. For example, you could count the number of clients from each ZIP code.
- You can also specify a sort order. Grouping takes precedence over sorting, so for example, if you group by ZIP and then sort by LastName, the records within each ZIP code will be sorted by LastName.

Try It! Creating a Report Using the Report Wizard

1. In the **ATry23_studentfirstname_studentlastname** file, click Create > Report Wizard.
2. Open the Tables/Queries list and click Table:ClassOfferings.
3. Click >> to select all the fields, then click Next.
4. The Instructor field is already selected for grouping. Click Next to accept it.
5. Open the 1 drop-down list and click Class. Then, click Next.
6. Under Layout, click Block.
7. Under Orientation, click Portrait. Then, click Next.
8. For the title of the report, type **Class Offerings Report**.
9. Click Finish. The report opens in Print Preview.
10. Leave the **ATry23_studentfirstname_studentlastname** database open to use in the next Try It.

Modifying a Report in Design View

- Report Design view is similar to Form Design view. You can move individual controls around by dragging them, cut and paste controls between sections, add titles and dates, and so on.

✓ *Tabular reports contain the field labels in the Page Header section and the fields themselves in the Detail section. It can be tricky to move fields and their labels when they exist in different sections; it is often better to rearrange fields in Layout view for this reason.*

Try It! Modifying a Report in Design View

1. In the **ATry23_studentfirstname_studentlastname** file, right-click the open report's tab, and click Design View.
2. Click the Instructor label in the Page Header section.
3. Hold down CTRL, and click the Instructor field in the Detail section.
4. Position the mouse pointer over the border of either selected control and drag to the left, moving the label and field to the left edge of the report.
5. Click the Class label in the Page Header section.
6. Hold down CTRL, and click the Class field in the Detail section.
7. Position the mouse over the left selection handle on either selected control and drag to the left until almost touching the right edge of the Instructor field/label, enlarging both the field and the label controls.
8. Click the ClassOfferingID label in the Page Header section and press DEL.
9. Click the ClassOfferingID field in the Detail section and press DEL.
10. Click the Start label in the Page Header section, and click Home > Align Text Left.
11. Click the StartDate field in the Detail section and click Home > Align Text Left.
12. Leave the **ATry23_studentfirstname_studentlastname** database open to use in the next Try It.

Working with Print Preview and Report View

- **Print Preview** lets you see exactly how the report will look when printed. It also contains page setup options like margins and page orientation.
- In Print Preview, the mouse pointer displays as a magnifying glass. Click anywhere in the report display to toggle between a view of the whole and the most recent zoom value. You can set the zoom value from the Zoom button's menu on the Print Preview tab.
- The navigation buttons at the bottom of the Print Preview window are similar to those for tables, queries, and forms, except they are for moving from page to page within a report.
- **Report view** is similar to Print Preview but designed for onscreen viewing.
- In Report view, you do not have the capability of zooming in and out on the content like in Print Preview. Report view is more of a "no-frills" display method.

Try It! Working with Print Preview and Report View

1. In the ATry23_studentfirstname_ studentlastname file, click Home > View arrow > Report View to switch to Report view.
2. Click the View arrow again and click Print Preview to switch to Print Preview.
3. Click anywhere on the report. The view zooms out.
4. Click again on the report. The view zooms in.
5. Drag the View slider to the right. The report zooms in even more.
6. Click anywhere on the report. The view zooms out again.

Drag the slider to zoom in

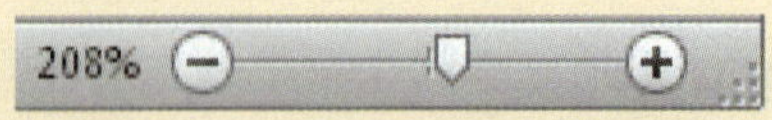

7. Click Print Preview > Landscape button .
8. In the Page Size group, click the Margins button, and then click Wide.
9. Click Close Print Preview.
10. Leave the ATry23_studentfirstname_ studentlastname database open to use in the next Try It.

Printing a Report

- Reports are designed to be printed, so you will probably want to print a report after finalizing its appearance.

Try It! Printing a Report

1. In the ATry23_studentfirstname_ studentlastname file, with the report displayed in Report View, click File > Print > Print.

   ✓ *If you are in Print Preview, you can click the Print button on the Print Preview.*
2. **With your teacher's permission**, click OK in the Print dialog box. Otherwise, click Cancel.
3. Close the ATry23_studentfirstname_ studentlastname file and exit Access.

Project 49—Create It

Jewelry Business Database

DIRECTIONS

1. Start Access, if necessary, and open **AProj49** from the data files for this lesson. If a security warning bar appears, click **Enable Content**.
2. Save the database as **AProj49_studentfirstname_studentlastname** to the location where your teacher instructs you to store the files for this lesson.
3. Click **Create** > **Report Wizard** .
4. Open the **Tables/Queries** list and click **Query:Customers and Orders**.
5. Click >> to include all fields, then click **Next**.
6. Click **By Salespeople** and click **Next**.
7. For Grouping Levels, click **Order Date** and click **>** to set it as a grouping field. See Figure 23-4. Then, click **Next**.
8. Click **Next** to skip the sorting criteria selection.
9. Under Layout, click **Block**. Then, click **Next**.
10. For the report's title, type **Orders by Salesperson**. Then, click **Finish**.
11. Close the database, and submit your database to your teacher for grading.

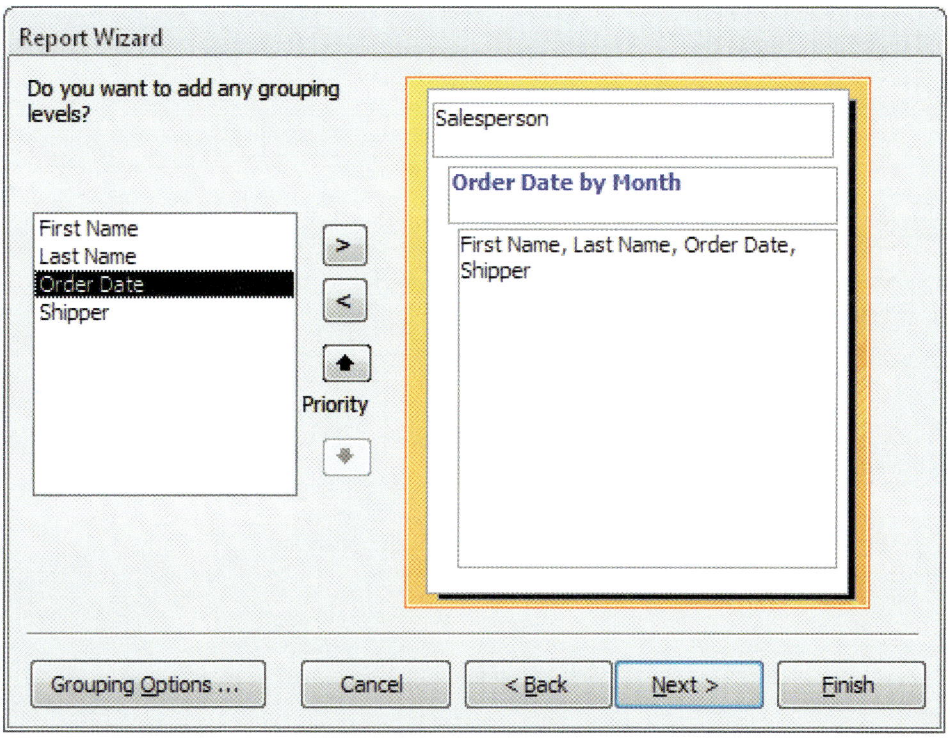

Figure 23-4

Project 50—Apply It

Jewelry Business Database

DIRECTIONS

1. Start Access, if necessary, and open **AProj50** from the data files for this lesson. If a security warning bar appears, click **Enable Content**.
2. Save the database as **AProj50_studentfirstname_studentlastname** to the location where your teacher instructs you to store the files for this lesson.
3. Open the **Orders by Salesperson** report.
4. Adjust the column widths so no fields or labels are truncated or overlapping, as in Figure 23-5.
5. Set the horizontal alignment for the **Order Date** field to **Left**.
6. Save and close the report.
7. Open the **Products** table in Datasheet view, and create a tabular report from it using the **Report** command.
8. Change the report's orientation to **Landscape**.
9. From either Layout or Design view, adjust the column widths as needed to tighten up the design as much as possible without truncating any fields or labels.
10. Save the report as **Products Report** and close it.
11. Create a new report in Layout view that uses the **Name** and **Account** fields from the Shippers table. Save the report as **Shipper List**.
12. View the Shipper List report in Print Preview.
13. **With your teacher's permission**, print one copy of the report and write your name on the printout.
14. Close the database, and submit to your teacher for grading. If you printed in step 13, also submit your printout.

Figure 23-5

Orders by Salesperson

Salesperson	Order Date by Month	First Name	Last Name	Order Date	Shipper
Gonzalez	December 2012	Allison	Norville	12/14/2012	USPS
		Peter	Washington	12/15/2012	DHL
Leffler	December 2012	Cynthia	Green	12/2/2012	UPS
		Cynthia	Green	12/13/2012	UPS
		Felicia	Adamson	12/15/2012	USPS
		Norman	Greenburg	12/15/2012	USPS
Mueller	December 2012	Jennifer	Brown	12/1/2012	UPS
		Carrie	Strong	12/3/2012	USPS
		Felicia	Adamson	12/14/2012	UPS
Rodriguez	December 2012	Jasper	Garrett	12/2/2012	USPS
		Norman	Eichmann	12/14/2012	FedEx
		Jasper	Garrett	12/15/2012	UPS
		Jennifer	Brown	12/16/2012	UPS
Sanchez	December 2012	George	Colvin	12/15/2012	USPS

Monday, May 17, 2010 Page 1 of 1

Lesson 24

Modifying a Report in Design View

➤ What You Will Learn

- Working with Report Sections
- Moving a Control Between Sections
- Adding Page Number Codes
- Sorting and Grouping Records in a Report
- Adding a Calculated Field to a Report

WORDS TO KNOW

Calculated field
A formula on the report that performs a math operation on the records and presents a result, such as counting the number of records, summing the values in a particular field, or multiplying the amount in one field by the amount in another field.

Software Skills Report Design view enables you to make more extensive changes to a report than are possible in Layout view. You can add calculated fields to a report, for example, and move controls between sections. Access also enables you to sort and group data in a report, from either Design or Layout view.

Application Skills You are not quite satisfied with the reports you have created so far for the jewelry database, and would like to improve them further. You will add sorting and grouping to reports, and add a calculated field.

What You Can Do

Working with Report Sections

- Header and footer sections in the report Design view work just as they do in a form's Design view. You can right-click the report and click the applicable header/footer name to turn it on or off.
- In reports, there can also be additional headers and footers for the grouping you set up. For example, if you group by salesperson, there will be a Salesperson header and Salesperson footer. You will learn about grouping later in this lesson.

Try It! Working with Report Sections

1. Start Access and open the database **ATry24** from the data files for this lesson.
2. Save the database as **ATry24_studentfirstname_studentlastname** in the location where your teacher instructs you to store the files for this lesson.
3. In the Navigation pane, right-click the Class Offerings Report and click Design View.
4. Position the mouse pointer between the Instructor Header and Detail sections and drag downward, creating a ½" height for the Instructor Header section.
5. Leave the **ATry24_studentfirstname_studentlastname** database open to use in the next Try It.

Moving a Control Between Sections

- Most fields should stay in the Detail section; however, all other controls can be moved to any section you wish.
- For example, suppose you have a code that prints today's date in the Page Footer. If you want that date to appear only once in the report, at the very end, you could move that control to the Report Footer section.
- In a report that contains grouping, you might also want to move certain fields or labels into the header section for that field.
- You must use cut-and-paste to move a control between sections; drag-and-drop will not work.

Try It! Moving a Control Between Sections

1. In the **ATry24_studentfirstname_studentlastname** file, with the Class Offerings Report open in Design view, click the Instructor field in the Detail section.
2. Press CTRL + X to cut the control to the Clipboard.
3. Click the bar for the Instructor Header section.
4. Press CTRL + V to paste the control.
5. Drag the Detail bar up slightly, closing up the extra space between the Detail bar and the Instructor field.
6. Click Report Design Tools Design > View > Report View to preview the report in Report view.
7. Click Home > View arrow > Design View to return to Design view.
8. Leave the **ATry24_studentfirstname_studentlastname** database open to use in the next Try It.

(continued)

Try It! Moving a Control Between Sections *(continued)*

Decrease the height of the Instructor Header section

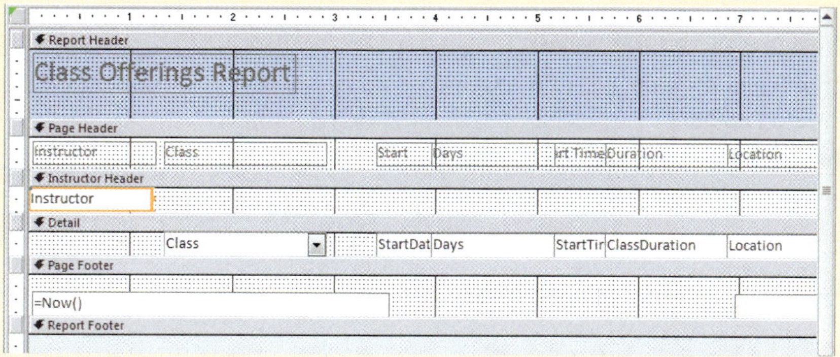

Adding Page Number Codes

- Page numbering codes are added to a report automatically when you create it with the Report Wizard. You can also manually insert page numbering codes.
  - A page numbering code is a function that consists of a combination of placeholders and literal text. The literal text portions are enclosed in quotation marks. For example: ="Page " & [Page].
  - = signals that it is a function.
  - "Page " is literal text.
  - & is a concatenation operator that joins the literal text to what follows it.
  - [Page] is a code that inserts the correct page number.
- You can manually type a page numbering code into an unbound text box, but there is seldom any need to do so because you can use the Page Numbers command in the Header/Footer group on the Report Design Tools Design tab instead.

Try It! Adding Page Number Codes

1. In the **ATry24_studentfirstname_studentlastname** file, with the Class Offerings Report open in Design view, click Report Design Tools Design > Page Numbers. The Page Numbers dialog box opens.
2. Click the Page N of M option.
3. Click the Bottom of Page [Footer] option.
4. Open the Alignment drop-down list and click Right.
5. Click OK. The code is placed in the report.
6. Click Home > Report View to see the page number.
7. Right-click the report tab and click Close. Click Yes to save changes.
8. Leave the **ATry24_studentfirstname_studentlastname** database open to use in the next Try It.

Open the Page Numbers dialog box

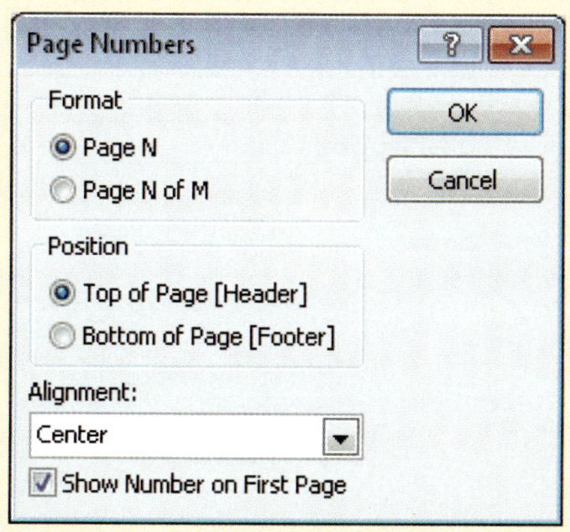

Adding Sorting and Grouping

- If you created the report with the Report Wizard, you were prompted to set a grouping level and sort order. You can also create and manage grouping and sorting from Design view or Layout view.
- To change the properties of a group, click one of the down-pointing arrows on its bar.
- For example, to change the field on which the report is grouped, click the down arrow following the Group on statement.
- For more options, click the More arrow. More settings appear, each with its own down-pointing arrow you can click to select from a list.
- A grouping also includes sorting. For example, you can also change the sort order for groups.
- You can also set up sorting without the grouping by clicking the Add a sort button in the Group, Sort, and Total pane.

Try It! Adding Sorting and Grouping

1. In the **ATry24_studentfirstname_studentlastname** file, click the Classes table in the Navigation pane.
2. Click Create > Report . A report opens in Layout view.
3. Right-click the report tab and click Design View.
4. Click Report Design Tools Design > Group & Sort .

   ✓ *The Group, Sort, and Total pane appears at the bottom of the Access window.*

5. Click Add a group and then click Price. The report changes so that the classes with the same price are grouped together.
6. Leave the **ATry24_studentfirstname_studentlastname** database open to use in the next Try It.

Group the report by Price

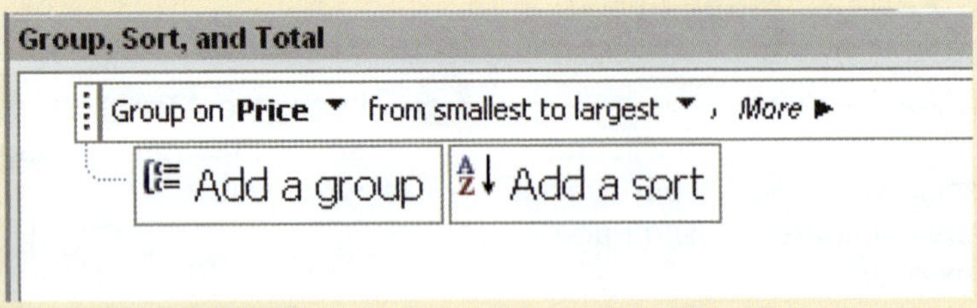

Try It! Changing Group Options

1. In the **ATry24_studentfirstname_studentlastname** file, in the Price group, click the down arrow to the right of from smallest to largest, and click from largest to smallest.

   ✓ *The order in which the groups are presented in the report is reversed.*

2. Click More. Additional grouping options appear.
3. Click the down arrow to the right of without a footer section, and click with a footer section.
4. Beneath the Price group, click Add a sort and, on the menu that appears, click NumberOfSessions.
5. Click Report Design Tools Design > Report View to see the grouped and sorted report. Right-click the report's tab and click Close. Click No when prompted to save changes.
6. Leave the **ATry24_studentfirstname_studentlastname** database open to use in the next Try It.

Adding a Calculated Field to a Report

- A **calculated field** is a formula on the report that performs a math operation on the records and presents a result, such as counting the number of records, summing the values in a particular field, or multiplying the amount in one field by the amount in another field.
- For simple calculated fields, you can use the Totals command in the Grouping & Totals group on the Report Layout Tools Design tab (in Layout view) or on the Report Design Tools Design tab (in Design view), and select a function from the menu that appears.
- You can also insert an unbound text box and type a function directly in it. Insert a Text Box control to draw a text box, and then in that box type the function.
- Here are some tips for creating your own calculations:
  - Each formula begins with an equals sign.
  - To reference a field name, use square brackets. For example, =[Price]*[Quantity]
  - A function requires parentheses after it. If there are any arguments, they are placed in the parentheses; otherwise the parentheses are empty. For example, =Now() or =Sum([quantity]).
  - To refer to all records, use an asterisk *. For example, =Count(*) counts all records.

Try It! Adding a Calculated Field to a Report

1. In the **ATry24_studentfirstname_ studentlastname** file, in the Navigation pane, right-click the Enrollment by Class report and click Design View .
2. Position the mouse between the ClassName Footer and the Page Footer bar and drag downward ½", creating some space in the ClassName Footer area.
3. Click the ClassName Footer bar to select that section.
4. Click Report Design Tools Design > Text Box .
5. Click in the ClassName Footer section. An unbound text box appears.
6. Click outside the control to deselect it. Then, click the label box that overlaps the text box to the left.
7. Press DEL. The label is deleted but the text box remains.
8. Click in the text box. The Unbound placeholder text disappears.
9. Type **=Count([ClassName])** in the text box.
10. Click Home > View arrow > Report View to view the report in Report view and check your work. Close the report, saving changes.
11. Close the **ATry24_studentfirstname_ studentlastname** file and exit Access.

An unbound text box appears

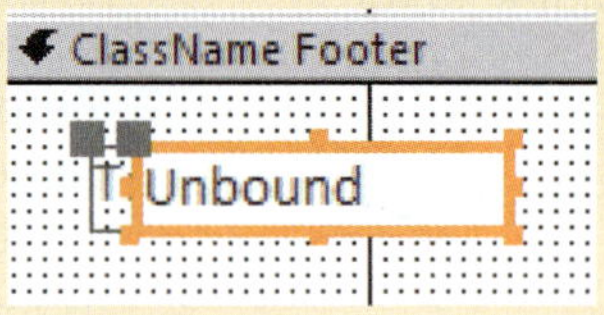

Select the label box that overlaps the text box to the left

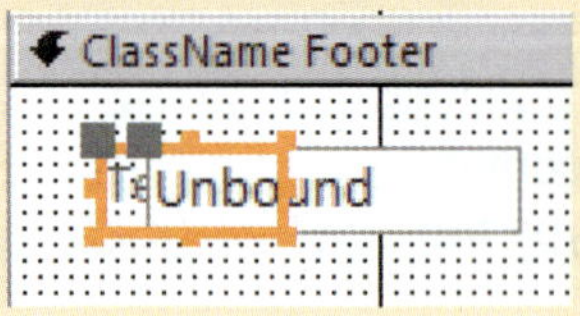

Project 51—Create It

Jewelry Business Database

DIRECTIONS

1. Start Access, if necessary, and open **AProj51** from the data files for this lesson. If a security warning bar appears, click **Enable Content**.
2. Save the database as **AProj51_studentfirstname_studentlastname** to the location where your teacher instructs you to store the files for this lesson.
3. In the Navigation pane, right-click the **Orders by Salesperson** report and click **Layout View**.
4. Click **Report Layout Tools Design > Page Numbers**.
5. Click **Bottom of Page (Footer)** if it is not already selected.
6. Open the **Alignment** drop-down list and click **Outside**.
7. Click **OK**.
8. Click **Report Layout Tools Design > Group & Sort**.
9. Next to Group on Salesperson, click **More**.
10. Click the down arrow to the right of with **no totals**.
11. Click the **Show Subtotal in Group Footer** check box. The count of records appears beneath each salesperson.
12. View the report in Report View. Click the **Save** button on the Quick Access Toolbar.
13. Close the database, and submit it to your teacher for grading.

Project 52—Apply It

Jewelry Business Database

DIRECTIONS

1. Start Access, if necessary, and open **AProj52** from the data files for this lesson. If a security warning bar appears, click **Enable Content**.
2. Save the database as **AProj52_studentfirstname_studentlastname** to the location where your teacher instructs you to store the files for this lesson.
3. Open the **Orders by Date** report in Design View.
4. Group the report by **Order Date**.
5. Cut and paste the **Order Date** field from the Detail section into the **Order Date Header** section and position it below the **Order Date** label.
6. In the Report Footer section, insert an unbound text box.
7. Move the text box's label so that it is fully visible, and change its text to **Total Quantity Ordered**.
8. In the unbound text box, type **=SUM([Quantity])**.
9. Position both the label and the text box at the right margin, so that when you preview it in Report view, it appears as shown in Figure 24-1.
10. Save your work, and close the report.
11. Open the **Products Report** in Layout view, and sort it by **Product**.
12. Save and close the report.
13. Close the database and submit it to your teacher for grading.

Figure 24-1

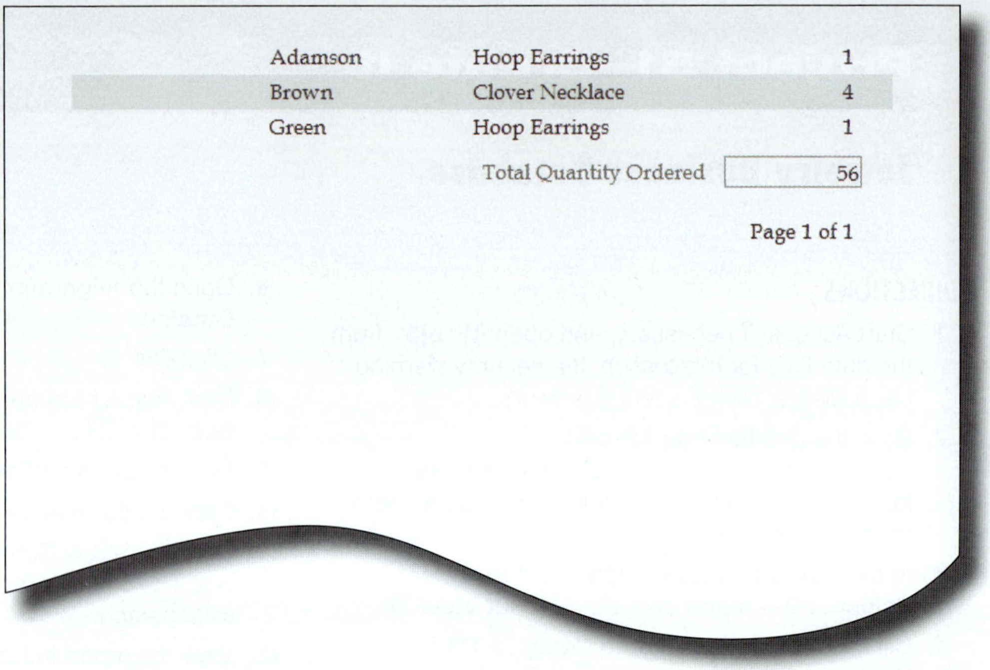

Adamson	Hoop Earrings	1
Brown	Clover Necklace	4
Green	Hoop Earrings	1
	Total Quantity Ordered	56

Page 1 of 1

Lesson 25

Creating Labels

➤ What You Will Learn

Understanding Labels
Using the Label Wizard

WORDS TO KNOW

Label Wizard
A series of dialog boxes that guides you through the creation of labels.

Software Skills You can create mailing labels using Microsoft Office applications. You can create them in Word by merging them with a data source. In Access, you can create labels using a table or query as the data source.

Application Skills Your friend has prepared a catalog of her jewelry items and wants to mail them to customers. You will create mailing labels to affix to the catalogs. You will also create product labels to identify boxes in her storage warehouse.

What You Can Do

Understanding Labels

- In label format, records are arranged in blocks across and down the page. This format is used to make mailing labels and includes field values, not field names.
- Labels usually are printed on special self-adhesive labels. A variety of manufacturers make such labels, and Access provides automatic formatting for many of the self-adhesive label styles available.
- Although mailing labels are the most common type of label, you can also find labels for diskettes, manila folders, and DVD cases. If you create a database that contains information on your video collection, you can create labels from the database to identify the videos.
- In Access, labels are a type of report.

Using the Label Wizard

- The Label Wizard helps you set up a labels report quickly and easily.
- Before running the Label Wizard, determine the brand and model number of the labels. If you do not have this information, measure one of the labels with a ruler so you can choose an equivalent that is the same size.

Try It! Using the Label Wizard

1. Start Access and open the file **ATry25** from the data files for this lesson.
2. Save the database as **ATry25_studentfirstname_studentlastname** in the location where your teacher instructs you to store the files for this lesson.
3. In the Navigation pane, click the Students table.
4. Click Create > Labels.
5. Open the Filter by manufacturer drop-down list and click Avery if it is not already selected.
6. From the Product number list, click 5160. Then, click Next.
7. Open the Font size drop-down list and click 9. Then, click Next.
8. Click the FirstName field and then click the > button.
9. Press the spacebar once, click the LastName field, and then click the > button.
10. Press ENTER to move to the next line. Click the Address field and click the > button.
11. Press ENTER, click the City field, and then click the > button.
12. Type a comma and then press the spacebar once.
13. Click the State field and click the > button.
14. Press the spacebar twice, click the ZIP field, and then click the > button.
15. Click Next.
16. Click LastName and click > to specify that the labels will be sorted by last name. Then, click Next.
17. Click Finish. A warning appears about some data not being displayed.
18. Click OK. The labels appear in a report in Print Preview.
19. Close the **ATry25_studentfirstname_studentlastname** file and exit Access.

Project 53—Create It

Jewelry Business Database

DIRECTIONS

1. Start Access, if necessary, and open **AProj53** from the data files for this lesson. If a security warning bar appears, click **Enable Content**.
2. Save the database as **AProj53_ studentfirstname_studentlastname** to the location where your teacher instructs you to store the files for this lesson.
3. In the Navigation pane, click the **Products** table.
4. Click **Create** > **Labels** .
5. Click **5963** as the label model, and click **Next**.

✓ *Avery should already be selected as the label manufacturer; if not, select it before step 5.*

6. Open the **Font size** drop-down list, click **16**, and then click **Next**.
7. Click **Product**, click **>**, and then press ENTER.
8. Click **Size**, click **>**, and then press ENTER.
9. Click **Material**, click **>**, and then press ENTER.
10. Click **Finish** to accept all remaining default settings.
11. Click **OK** to accept the warning that some data may not be displayed.
12. Close the database and submit it to your teacher for grading.

Project 54—Apply It

Jewelry Business Database

DIRECTIONS

1. Start Access, if necessary, and open **AProj54** from the data files for this lesson. If a security warning bar appears, click **Enable Content**.
2. Save the database as **AProj54_ studentfirstname_studentlastname** to the location where your teacher instructs you to store the files for this lesson.
3. Start the Label Wizard based on the **Customers** table.
4. You do not have the label manufacturer and model number, so browse through the available products and find a label that has the following qualities:
   - 2 labels per row
   - 2" tall
   - 4" wide
   - Sheet fed
5. Format the label text with dark blue color, 9-point font size, Normal font weight, and Times New Roman font.
6. Include all the fields needed for a postal mailing, in the correct order and format.
7. Sort the labels by ZIP.
8. Accept the default name for the report.
9. Open the completed report in Design view, and make the text bold for the FirstName and LastName fields. Save your changes and preview the labels in Print Preview.
10. **With your teacher's permission**, print one copy of the first page of the label report, and write your name on the printout.
11. Close the database and submit it to your teacher for grading.

Chapter Assessment and Application

Project 55—Make It Your Own

Medical Office Time Cards

You are a consultant for a medical office where employee data and time cards are stored in an Access database. So far there are only tables and queries in the database. You will create forms and reports that make the data easier to store and retrieve.

DIRECTIONS

1. Start Access, if necessary, and open **AProj55** from the data files for this chapter. If a security warning bar appears, click **Enable Content**.
2. Save the database as **AProj55_studentfirstname_studentlastname** in the location where your teacher instructs you to store the files for this chapter.
3. Open the **Employees** table in Design view.
4. Set up the **Positions** table as a lookup for the Position field in the **Employees** table, with the positions sorted in Ascending order.
   ✓ *You may see a warning that some data may be lost; this is okay.*
5. Create an input mask for the **ZIP** field using any standard format you like.
   ✓ *The format you use must be valid for mailings in the United States.*
6. Create an input mask for the **HomePhone** field in which all 10 digits are required. Use any other settings you like.
7. Copy the input mask code you just created into the **CellPhone** and **Pager** fields' Input Mask property.
8. Close the **Employees** table, saving your changes.
9. Using the **Create** > **Form** command, create a form for entering data in the **Timecards** table. Save it as **Time Card Entry**.
10. Using the Form Wizard, create a columnar form for entering new employees in the **Employees** table. Use all the fields. Save it as **Employees Form**.
11. Using the Report Wizard, create a report that shows a list of all employees (first and last names), grouped by position. Use the **Positions** field from the Positions table, and the **FirstName** and **LastName** fields from the Employees table. Sort by **LastName**. Use the Block layout. Name the report **Employees by Position**.
12. In Design view, remove the extraneous shading from certain rows by doing the following:
    a. Click the appropriate header to select the section. Click **Report Design Tools Design** > **Property Sheet** .
    b. Click the **Format** tab in the Property Sheet task pane.
    c. Open the drop-down list for the **Alternate Back Color** property and click **No Color**.
13. In Layout view, widen the **Positions** field column's width so the longest entry is not truncated.
14. Create a quick report (**Create** > **Report**) based on the **Hours Worked** query. Save it as **Hours Worked Report**.
15. Close the database, and submit it to your teacher for grading,

Project 56—Master It

Book Collection Database

A friend who collects antique books has asked for your help in continuing to develop a database for his collection. His database currently consists of several tables and queries you created for him earlier. Now you will build forms and reports for him as well.

DIRECTIONS

1. Start Access, if necessary, and open **AProj56** from the data files for this chapter. If a security warning bar appears, click **Enable Content**.
2. Save the database as **AProj56_studentfirstname_studentlastname** in the location where your teacher instructs you to store the files for this chapter.
3. Open the **Authors** table in Design view.
4. For the **Born** field, manually construct an input mask that requires exactly 4 digits.
5. Copy the input mask to the **Died** field.
6. Use the Lookup Wizard to create a lookup for the **Nationality** field that looks up values from the **Countries** table.
7. Create a new form in Layout view that includes all the fields from the **Books** table, in the order they appear in the table.
8. Widen the columns for both the labels and the fields so that nothing is truncated.
9. Switch to Design View, and display the **Form Header** and **Form Footer** sections.
10. In the Form Header, insert a title of **Books**.
11. In the Form Footer, insert a code that shows the current date (but not the time).

    ✓ *The Date & Time command inserts the code in the Form Header; cut-and-paste it to the Form Footer.*
12. Save the form as **Book Information** and close it.
13. In Layout view, create a new tabular report that lists the books from the **Books** table. Include the **Title**, **Author**, and **Date Published** fields in that order.
14. Adjust the column widths as needed so that no entries wrap to more than one row and nothing is truncated.
15. Group the report by **Author**.
16. Include a count of the number of books for the author in each Author group footer.
17. Save the report as **Books by Author**. **With your teacher's permission**, print one copy of the first page of the report, and write your name on the printout.
18. Close the database, and submit it to your teacher for grading.

Chapter 1

Getting Started with PowerPoint

Lesson 1
Getting Started with PowerPoint
Projects 1-2

- About PowerPoint
- Starting PowerPoint
- Saving a Presentation
- Closing a Presentation
- Opening an Existing Presentation
- Exploring the PowerPoint Window
- Entering Text Using Placeholders
- Applying a Theme
- Checking Spelling in a Presentation

Lesson 2
Working with Slides
Projects 3-4

- Inserting New Slides
- Selecting Slide Layout
- Moving from Slide to Slide
- Changing List Levels
- Printing a Presentation

Lesson 3
Working with Headers, Footers, and Speaker Notes
Projects 5-6

- Reusing Slides from Other Presentations
- Adding Speaker Notes
- Changing Slide Size and Orientation
- Inserting Headers and Footers

Lesson 4
Inserting and Formatting Pictures
Projects 7-8

- Inserting a Picture from a File
- Formatting Pictures Using Styles and Artistic Effects

Lesson 5
Formatting Text
Projects 9-10

- Finding and Replacing Text in a Presentation
- Selecting Text and Placeholders
- Changing the Appearance of Text Using Font Sizes, Styles, and Colors
- Copying Text Formatting
- Using Undo and Redo
- Clearing Formatting

Lesson 6
Aligning Text
Projects 11-12

- Aligning Text
- Adjusting Line Spacing
- Adjusting Paragraph Spacing
- Moving and Copying Text
- Using AutoFit Options
- Adjusting and Formatting Placeholders

Lesson 7
Displaying the Presentation Outline
Projects 13-14

- Displaying the Presentation Outline
- Viewing a Presentation in Reading View

Lesson 8
Arranging Slides
Projects 15-16

- Copying, Duplicating, and Deleting Slides
- Rearranging Slides in Slide Sorter View

Lesson 9
Adding Slide Transitions
Projects 17-18

- Identifying Guidelines for Using Graphics, Fonts, and Special Effects in Presentations
- Evaluating and Selecting Appropriate Sources of Information
- Adding Slide Transitions
- Controlling Slide Advance

End-of-Chapter Assessments
Projects 19-20

Lesson 1

Getting Started with PowerPoint

WORDS TO KNOW

Presentation
A set of slides or handouts that contains information you want to convey to an audience.

Normal View
PowerPoint's default view that displays the Slide pane, the Notes pane, and the Slides/Outline pane.

Placeholders
Designated areas in PowerPoint layouts that can be used to easily insert text, graphics, or multimedia objects.

Slide Layout
Prearranged sets of placeholders for various types of slide content.

Theme
Formatting feature that applies a background, colors, fonts, and effects to all slides in a presentation.

➤ What You Will Learn

About PowerPoint
Starting PowerPoint
Saving a Presentation
Closing a Presentation
Opening an Existing Presentation
Exploring the PowerPoint Window
Entering Text Using Placeholders
Applying a Theme
Checking Spelling in a Presentation

Software Skills PowerPoint's many features make it easy to create both simple and sophisticated presentations. One way to create a new slide show is to start with the default blank presentation that displays when PowerPoint opens. Once a presentation is open, you can enter text and apply a theme to give it a consistent design.

Application Skills Wynnedale Medical Center has contacted you about preparing a presentation announcing their new laser eye surgery unit. In this lesson, you start a new presentation and explore basic features such as placeholders and themes.

What You Can Do

About PowerPoint

- PowerPoint is a presentation graphics program that lets you create slide shows you can present using a computer projection system or publish as interactive Web pages.

- A **presentation** can include handouts, outlines, and speaker notes as well as slides.
- PowerPoint slides may contain text and various other types of content, such as clip art, pictures, movies, tables, or charts.
- You can create all the slide content in PowerPoint or import data from other Microsoft Office programs such as Word and Excel to create slide content.
- You use Microsoft Windows to start PowerPoint.
- When PowerPoint starts, it displays a single blank slide you can use to start a new presentation. The default slide is intended to be the first slide of the presentation, so it is set up for you to add the presentation's title and subtitle.
- The title slide is only one of several different slide types you can use to create a new presentation. You will learn more about **slide layouts** in Lesson 2.

Starting PowerPoint

- To use PowerPoint 2010 you must first start it so it is running on your computer.

Try It! Starting PowerPoint

1. Click Start > All Programs. If necessary, scroll down until you see the Microsoft Office folder icon.
2. Click the Microsoft Office folder icon.
3. Click Microsoft PowerPoint.

OR

1. Click Start.
2. Click PowerPoint in the list of recently used programs.

OR

1. Double-click the PowerPoint shortcut icon on the desktop.

OR

1. Click the PowerPoint icon on the Taskbar.

Saving a Presentation

- PowerPoint supplies the default title *Presentation* and a number (for example, *Presentation1*) in the title bar of each new presentation. You should change this default title to a more descriptive title when you save a new presentation so that you can work on it again later.
- By default, a new presentation is saved in XML format, the standard for Office 2007 and Office 2010 applications, giving the file an extension of .pptx.
- If you wish to use a presentation with earlier versions of PowerPoint, you can save the file in PowerPoint 97-2003 Presentation format. You can also save the presentation in several other formats, such as PDF or XPS, or as a template or show.

✓ *You will save presentations as templates and shows in later lessons.*

Try It! Saving a Presentation

1. If necessary, start PowerPoint.
2. Click Save on the Quick Access Toolbar.

   OR

   a. Click File.
   b. Click Save.
3. Select the File name text box if it is not selected already.
4. Type **PTry01_studentfirstname_studentlastname**.

(continued)

Try It! Saving a Presentation *(continued)*

✓ *Replace the text studentfirstname with your own first name, and studentlastname with your own last name. For example, if your name is Mary Jones, type PTry_Mary_Jones.*

5 Use the Navigation pane to navigate to the location where your teacher tells you to store the files for this lesson.

✓ *Refer to Lesson 1 of the Basics section of this book for information on navigating in Windows Explorer.*

6 Click Save or press ENTER.

Closing a Presentation

- Closing a PowerPoint presentation can be done in the same manner as closing other Microsoft Office documents and spreadsheets.
- Make sure to save your work before closing.

Try It! Closing a Presentation

1 In the **PTry01_studentfirstname_studentlastname** file, click File > Exit.

OR

1 Press CTRL + W to close the file.

OR

1 Click Close to close the file and PowerPoint.

Opening an Existing Presentation

- Open an existing presentation to modify, add, or delete material.
- PowerPoint makes it easy to open presentations on which you have recently worked by listing them in the Recent Documents list that you access in the Backstage view showing Recent Presentations.
- If you do not see the presentation on this list, you can use the Open command and the Open dialog box to navigate to the presentation you want to open.

Try It! Opening an Existing Presentation

1 Click File > Open.

2 In the Open dialog box, use the Navigation pane to navigate to the location where your teacher tells you to store the files for this lesson.

3 Select **PTry01_studentfirstname_studentlastname** (the file you saved with your first and last name in an earlier Try It), then click Open.

4 Leave **PTry01_studentfirstname_studentlastname** open for use in the next Try It.

Exploring the PowerPoint Window

- PowerPoint, like other Microsoft Office 2010 applications, displays the Ribbon interface that groups commands on tabs across the top of the window below the title bar.
- The status bar displays information about the presentation, such as the slide number and theme name.
- A presentation opens by default in **Normal view**, which displays the Slide pane, the Notes pane, and the Slides/Outline pane. You will learn more about these views in a later Lesson.
- Normal view, the default view, allows you to work with slides in several ways:
  - Use the Slide pane to insert and modify slide content.
  - Use the Notes pane to add text for personal reference, such as material you want to remember to cover during the presentation. Notes recorded in the Notes pane can also be printed along with the slide to use as audience handouts.
  - The Slides tab in the Slides/Outline pane shows a small version of all slides in the presentation and can be used to quickly select slides or reorganize them.
  - The Outline tab, behind the Slides tab in the Slides/Outline pane, lets you view all slide content in outline format.

Try It! Exploring the PowerPoint Window

1. In the **PTry01_studentfirstname_studentlastname** file, move your mouse pointer over each window element shown in the figure.
2. Save the **PTry01_studentfirstname_studentlastname** file and leave it open to use in the next Try It.

The PowerPoint Window

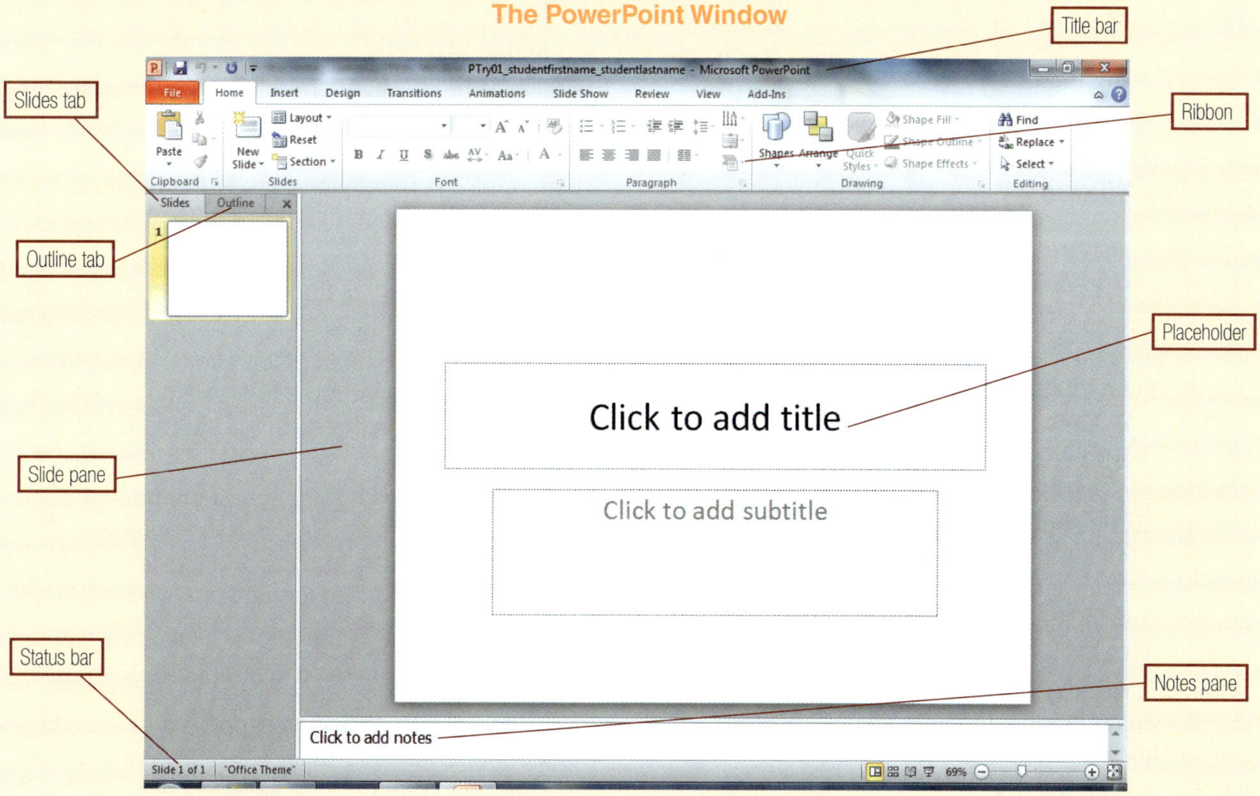

Entering Text Using Placeholders

- PowerPoint displays **placeholders** to define the arrangement and location of text and other objects you can add to slides.
- The title slide you see when creating a new presentation has two placeholders: one for the title and one for the subtitle.
- To insert text in a placeholder, click inside the placeholder and begin typing. When you click the placeholder, PowerPoint selects the box with a dashed outline, displays sizing handles you can use to resize the placeholder, and displays a blinking insertion point that shows where text will appear when typed.
- Different types of slides in a presentation have different types of placeholders. In the previous illustration, the slide offers a title placeholder and a subtitle placeholder. Other types of slides offer content placeholders in which you can insert a bulleted list or other types of content such as a table, a chart, or a picture.

Try It! Entering Text Using Placeholders

1. In the **PTry01_studentfirstname_studentlastname** file, click once in the Title placeholder to select it and position the insertion point.
2. Type **Premier Soccer Club** in the Title placeholder.
3. Click the Click to add subtitle placeholder. Type **Top Travel Soccer Competition for Boys and Girls**.

   ✓ *Note: The Subtitle text will appear in a lighter, gray font, compared to the Title.*
4. Save the **PTry01_studentfirstname_studentlastname** file and leave it open to use in the next Try It.

Applying a Theme

- In PowerPoint 2010, **themes** are used as a means of supplying graphical interest for a presentation.
- A theme provides a background, a color palette, a selection of fonts for titles and text, distinctive bullets, and a range of special effects that can be applied to shapes. The theme also controls the layout of placeholders on slides.
- Themes are located in the Themes group on the Design tab, as shown in Figure 1-1. The size of the PowerPoint window determines how many theme thumbnails display in the group. If you have created custom themes, they display along with PowerPoint's built-in themes.
- When you rest the pointer on a theme thumbnail, the slide in the Slide pane immediately displays the theme elements. This Live Preview feature makes it easy to choose a graphic look for slides—if you don't like the look of the theme, simply move the pointer off the theme to return to the previous appearance or point at a different theme to try another appearance.
- Themes have names that you can see if you rest the pointer on a theme thumbnail.
- By default, the Themes group shows only a few of the available themes. To see all themes, click the More button in the theme scroll bar to display a gallery of themes.
- The gallery shows the theme (or themes) currently used in a presentation in the This Presentation area. Options at the bottom of the gallery allow you to search for other themes or save the current theme for future use.

  ✓ *You will learn how to change and save a theme in Chapter 3.*
- Clicking a theme thumbnail applies it to all slides in the presentation. You can also choose to apply the theme to one or more selected slides in the presentation.

Figure 1-1

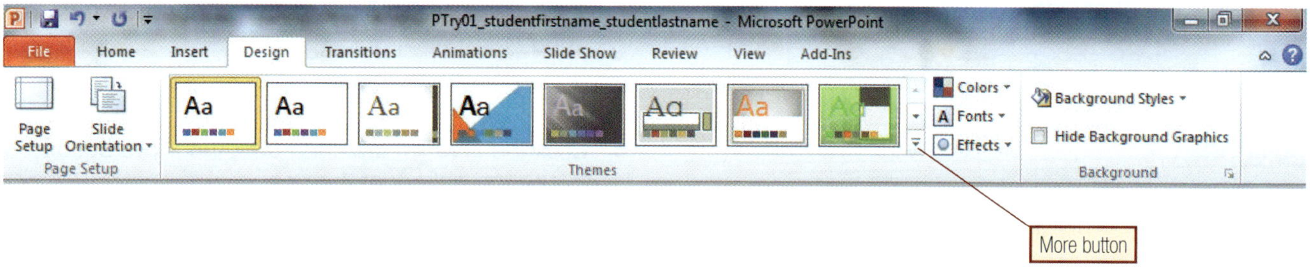

Try It! Applying a Theme

1. In the **PTry01_studentfirstname_ studentlastname** file, click the Design tab.
2. Click the More button to display all themes.
3. Point to several themes in the gallery to see them previewed in the presentation.
4. Click the Perspective theme to apply it to the presentation.
5. Save the **PTry01_studentfirstname_ studentlastname** file and leave it open to use in the next Try It.

Checking Spelling in a Presentation

- PowerPoint provides two methods of spell checking in your presentation: automatic and manual.
- Automatic spell checking works while you're typing, displaying a wavy red line under words PowerPoint doesn't recognize. Right-click a wavy underline to see a list of possible correctly spelled replacements.
- To check spelling manually, use the Spelling button on the Review tab. The process of checking spelling in a presentation using the Spelling dialog box is similar to that in other Microsoft Office applications.

Try It! Checking Spelling in a Presentation

1. In the **PTry01_studentfirstname_ studentlastname** file, click the subtitle text and select the entire subtitle.
2. Type **The Top Travil Soccer Clubb for Boys and Girls**.

   ✓ *Note: "Travil" and "Clubb" should be typed incorrectly for purposes of the Try It.*
3. Right-click on **Travil** to see a list of suggested spellings. Click **Travel** to replace with the correct spelling.
4. Click the Review tab, and then click Spelling.
5. Click Change in the Spelling dialog box to replace the misspelled word Clubb with Club.
6. Click OK.
7. Close the **PTry01_studentfirstname_ studentlastname** file, saving all changes, and exit PowerPoint.

Project 1—Create It

Laser Surgery Presentation

DIRECTIONS

1. Click **Start** > **Microsoft Office** > **Microsoft PowerPoint 2010**, if necessary.
2. Click **File** > **Save As**. The Save As dialog box opens. Navigate to the folder your teacher tells you to use when saving your work. Type **PProj01_studentfirstname_studentlastname** in the File name text box, then click **Save**.
3. Click on the title placeholder and enter the text **Wynnedale Medical Center**.
4. Click on the subtitle placeholder and enter the text **Laser Eye Surgery Unit**.
5. Click the **Design** tab, then click the **More** button to see the gallery of themes.
6. Click the **Austin** theme to apply it, as shown in Figure 1-2.
7. Click **Review** > **Spelling** to check spelling in the presentation.
8. Click **Ignore All** to skip changing the spelling of Wynnedale, then click **OK**.
9. Click **Save** to save your work, then click **File** > **Exit** to close the file and close PowerPoint.

Figure 1-2

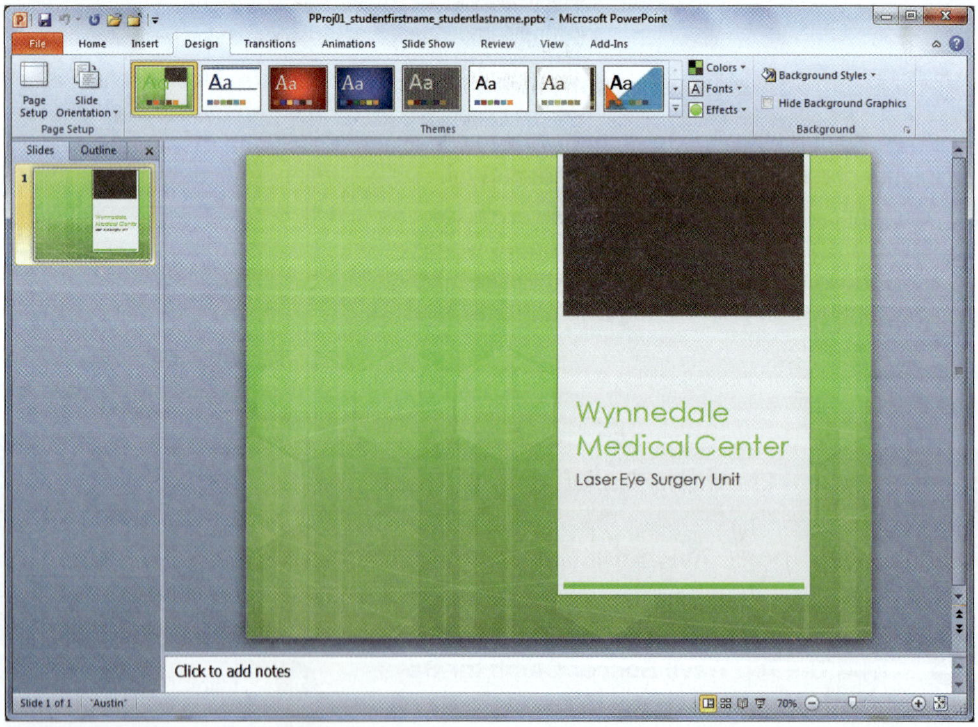

Project 2—Apply It

Laser Surgery Presentation

DIRECTIONS

1. Start PowerPoint, if necessary.
2. Open **PProj02** from the data files for this lesson.
3. Save the presentation as **PProj02_studentfirstname_studentlastname** in the location where your teacher instructs you to store the files for this lesson.
4. Click in the subtitle placeholder, click following the word Unit, press ENTER, and type the following text: ***Find out if Laser Surgery is right for you.***
5. Apply the **Metro** theme to the presentation.
6. Check the spelling.
7. Close the presentation, saving all changes, and exit PowerPoint.

Lesson 2

Working with Slides

WORDS TO KNOW

Active Slide
The slide currently selected or displayed.

➤ What You Will Learn

Inserting New Slides
Selecting Slide Layout
Moving from Slide to Slide
Changing List Levels
Printing a Presentation

Software Skills In PowerPoint, you can quickly and easily add new slides to a presentation. After adding new slides, you can change the slide layout and change the level of an item in a bulleted list. It's easy to move from one slide to the other, and you can also preview your slide show before printing it or presenting it.

Application Skills In this lesson, you continue to work with the Wynnedale Medical Center presentation. You will add more content to the presentation using slides with different layouts.

What You Can Do

Inserting New Slides

- Most presentations consist of a number of slides. Use the New Slide button on the Home tab to add a slide to a presentation.
- If you simply click the New Slide button, PowerPoint adds the kind of slide you are most likely to need. With the default title slide displayed, for example, PowerPoint will assume the next slide should be a Title and Content slide.
- If the **active slide**—the currently displayed slide—uses a layout other than Title Slide, PowerPoint inserts a new slide with the same layout as the one currently displayed.
- A new slide is inserted immediately after the active slide.

Try It! Inserting New Slides

1. Start PowerPoint and open **PTry02** from the data files for this lesson.
2. Save the file as **PTry02_studentfirstname_studentlastname** in the location where your teacher instructs you to store the files for this lesson.
3. Click Home > New Slide.
4. Press CTRL + M to add another slide.
5. Save the **PTry02_studentfirstname_studentlastname** file and leave it open to use in the next Try It.

Selecting Slide Layout

- To specify a particular layout for a slide, click the down arrow on the New Slide button to display a gallery of slide layout choices.
- A slide layout arranges the standard objects of a presentation—titles, charts, text, clip art—on the slide to make it attractive. Each layout provides placeholders for specific types of content.
- PowerPoint 2010 has many fewer layout choices than some previous versions of PowerPoint offered, but layouts are multifunctional. Rather than having a layout that offers side-by-side text and a layout that offers side-by-side content, for example, PowerPoint 2010 has one layout that allows you to insert side-by-side content of any type, including text, graphics, charts, or movies.
- The New Slide drop down gallery also provides options to Duplicate Selected Slides, add new Slides from Outline, and Reuse Slides.

Try It! Selecting Slide Layout

1. In the **PTry02_studentfirstname_studentlastname** file, click the New Slide button down arrow. A gallery of available slide types appears as shown in the figure.
2. Click the Two Content slide.
3. Click New Slide > Duplicate Selected Slides.
4. Save the **PTry02_studentfirstname_studentlastname** file and leave it open to use in the next Try It.

The New Slide gallery

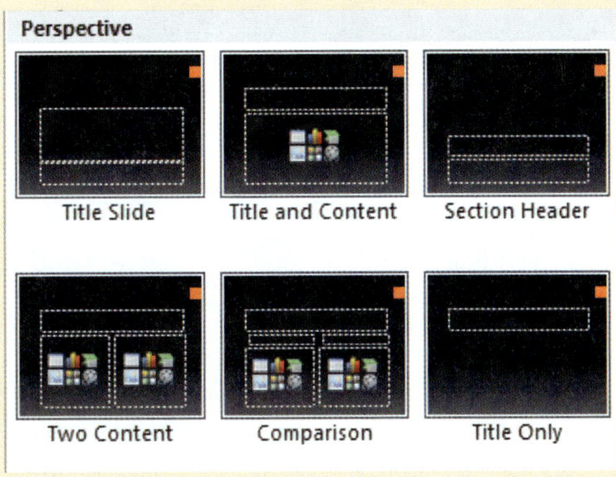

Moving from Slide to Slide

- Most presentations include multiple slides. You will need to move from slide to slide in Normal view to enter text and modify the presentation.
- PowerPoint offers a variety of ways to select and display slides. Click in the scroll bar or drag the scroll box to display slides, or use the Previous Slide and Next Slide buttons at the bottom of the scroll bar to move through the slides.
- You can also select slides by clicking them in the Slides tab.

Try It! Moving from Slide to Slide

1. In the **PTry02_studentfirstname_studentlastname** file, click slide 3 in the Slides tab.
2. Click the Next Slide button.
3. Press PG UP twice.
4. Click in the scroll bar three times. You should now be on slide 5, as shown by the highlighted slide in the Slides tab.
5. Save the **PTry02_studentfirstname_studentlastname** file and leave it open to use in the next Try It.

Changing List Levels

- You can enter or modify text in the Outline tab if desired. As you type the text in the Outline tab, it appears on the current slide in the Slide pane.
- Slide text content consists mostly of bulleted items. First-level bullets are supplied on content placeholders. PowerPoint supplies formatting for five levels of bullets. Each subordinate level uses a smaller font size than the previous level and a different bullet character.
- Create subordinate levels of bullets as you type by pressing Tab at the beginning of a line. You can also use the Increase List Level and Decrease List Level buttons in the Paragraph group on the Home tab to apply subordinate level formatting.
- Themes supply bullet characters for all levels of bullets in specific sizes and colors. If you change a theme, you will notice that the bullet characters change along with colors, fonts, backgrounds, and placeholder layout.
- You can change the bullets for a text placeholder using the Bullets and Numbering dialog box.

Try It! Changing List Levels

1. In the **PTry02_studentfirstname_studentlastname** file, click slide 2 in the Slides tab.
2. Click the Outline tab. Notice that slide 2 is highlighted as your current location within the presentation.
3. Type **Tryouts Begin Next Week**. The text you entered should appear as the title of slide 2.
4. Press the down arrow and type **All Age Groups Invited**. The text you entered should appear as the title of slide 3.
5. Press ENTER and type **Directions to Fields**. The text you entered should appear as the title of slide 4.

   ✓ *Note that pressing Enter added a new slide to the presentation.*

(continued)

Try It! Changing List Levels *(continued)*

6. Click at the end of the text in slide 2 in the Outline tab and press ENTER . A new slide is added after slide 2.

   ✓ *Make sure you don't click on the slide 2 icon at the left of the Outline tab. Pressing Enter if the entire slide is selected will delete the slide.*

7. Click Home > Increase List Level . This deletes the new slide and positions the cursor for new text to be entered into the body of slide 2.

8. Type **Club tryouts start Wednesday, June 8** and press ENTER .

9. Press TAB. Type **4 p.m. for under-11** and press ENTER .

10. Type **5 p.m. for all others**. Your presentation should look like the one shown in the figure below. Note the different levels of outline in the slide 2 bullet points.

11. Save the **PTry02_studentfirstname_ studentlastname** file and leave it open to use in the next Try It.

Insert bullet text in the Outline tab

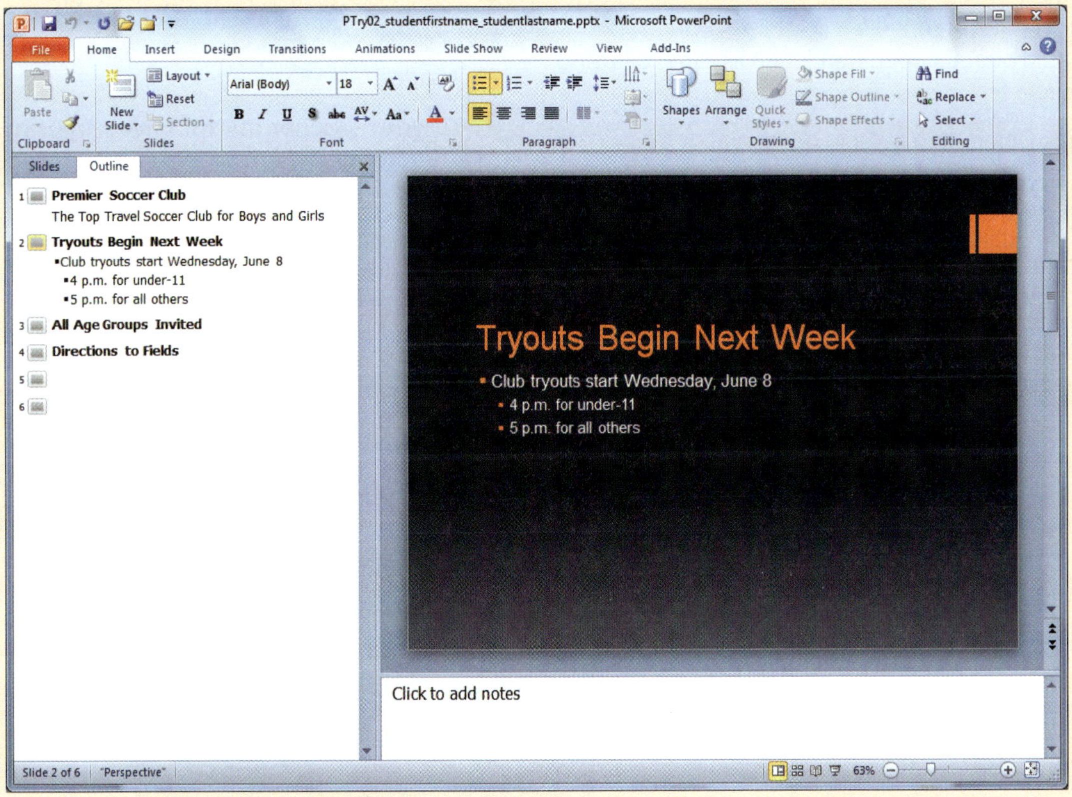

Printing a Presentation

- Printing PowerPoint materials is similar to printing pages in other Microsoft Office programs, with a few exceptions.
- A presentation can be printed in various formats: as slides, notes pages, handouts, or as an outline. You choose the settings for these formats by clicking the File tab and then clicking the Print tab, shown in the illustration in the following Try It.
- Among the options you can choose are:
  - Which slides to print and number of copies to print.
  - What material (slides, notes pages, handouts, or outline) to print.
  - Whether to print in grayscale, color, or black and white.
  - If handouts are to be printed, how many slides per page and the order in which the slides display on the page.
  - Whether the material should be scaled (sized) to fit the page or framed by a box.
  - Whether comments and markup annotations should be printed.
  - Whether hidden slides should be printed.

Try It! Printing a Presentation

1. In the **PTry02_studentfirstname_studentlastname** file, click File > Print. You should see a screen that looks like the following figure.
2. Click Color, then select Grayscale.
3. Click Full Page Slides, then select Outline.
4. Click Outline, then select 3 Slides.
5. Click Grayscale, then select Color.
6. Click Print All Slides, then select Print Current Slide.
7. **If your teacher instructs you to print the Try It activity,** click Print.
8. Close **PTry02_studentfirstname_studentlastname**, saving all changes, and exit PowerPoint.

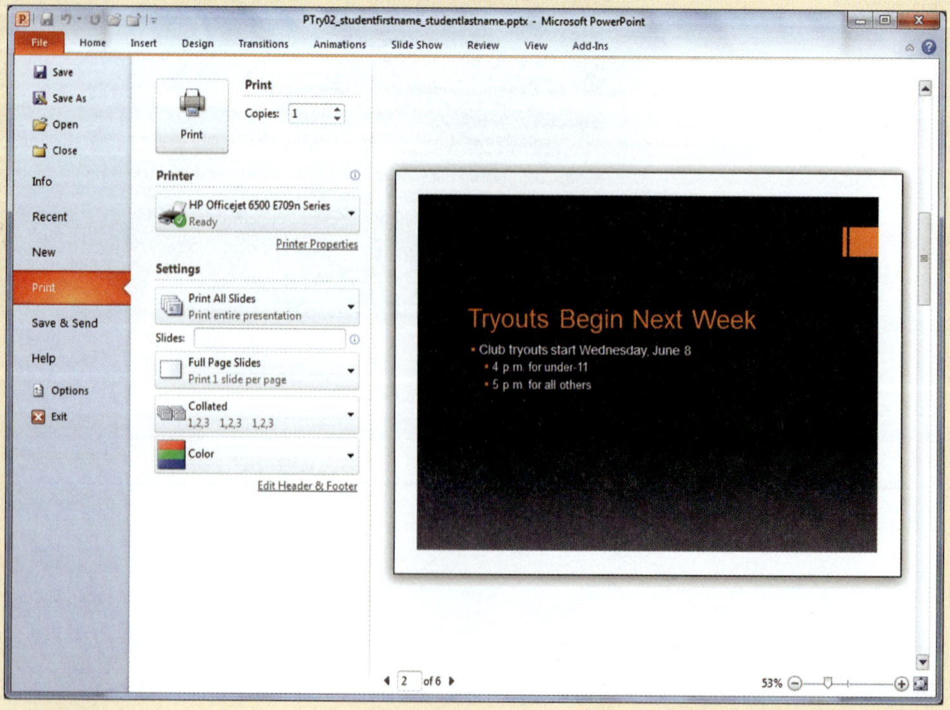

The Print Tab

Project 3—Create It

Laser Surgery Presentation

DIRECTIONS

1. Start PowerPoint if necessary and open **PProj03** from the data files for this lesson. Save the file as **PProj03_studentfirstname_studentlastname** in the location where your teacher instructs you to store files for this lesson.
2. Click on slide 3 to display it in the slide pane.
3. On the Home tab, click the New Slide drop-down arrow, then click Two Content.
4. Click in the Title placeholder and type **Laser Eye Surgery Facts**.
5. Click in the left content placeholder and type the first bullet item, **LASIK is the most common refractive surgery**.
6. Click on the Outline tab, then click just to the right of the word surgery on the outline of the current slide.
7. Press ENTER and type the next bullet item, **Relative lack of pain**.
8. Click **Review** > **Spelling** to check spelling in the presentation, then click OK.
9. **With your teacher's permission,** click **File** > **Print**. Select **Print All Slides**, then click **Print** to print the presentation.
10. Click **Save** to save your work, then click **File** > **Exit** to close the file and close PowerPoint.

Project 4—Apply It

Laser Surgery Presentation

DIRECTIONS

1. Start PowerPoint, if necessary.
2. Open **PProj04** from the data files for this lesson.
3. Save the presentation as **PProj04_ studentfirstname_studentlastname** in the location where your teacher instructs you to store the files for this lesson.
4. Move to slide 4 and enter the two additional bullets in the left content placeholder:

   Almost immediate results (within 24 hours)

   Both nearsighted and farsighted can benefit
5. Apply the **Clarity** theme to the presentation, and then move through the slides to see how the new theme has changed the appearance of slides.
6. Change the layout of slide 4 to Title and Content. Your presentation should look like the one shown in Figure 2-1.
7. Check the spelling.
8. **With your teacher's permission,** print the presentation.
9. Close the presentation, saving all changes, and exit PowerPoint.

Figure 2-1

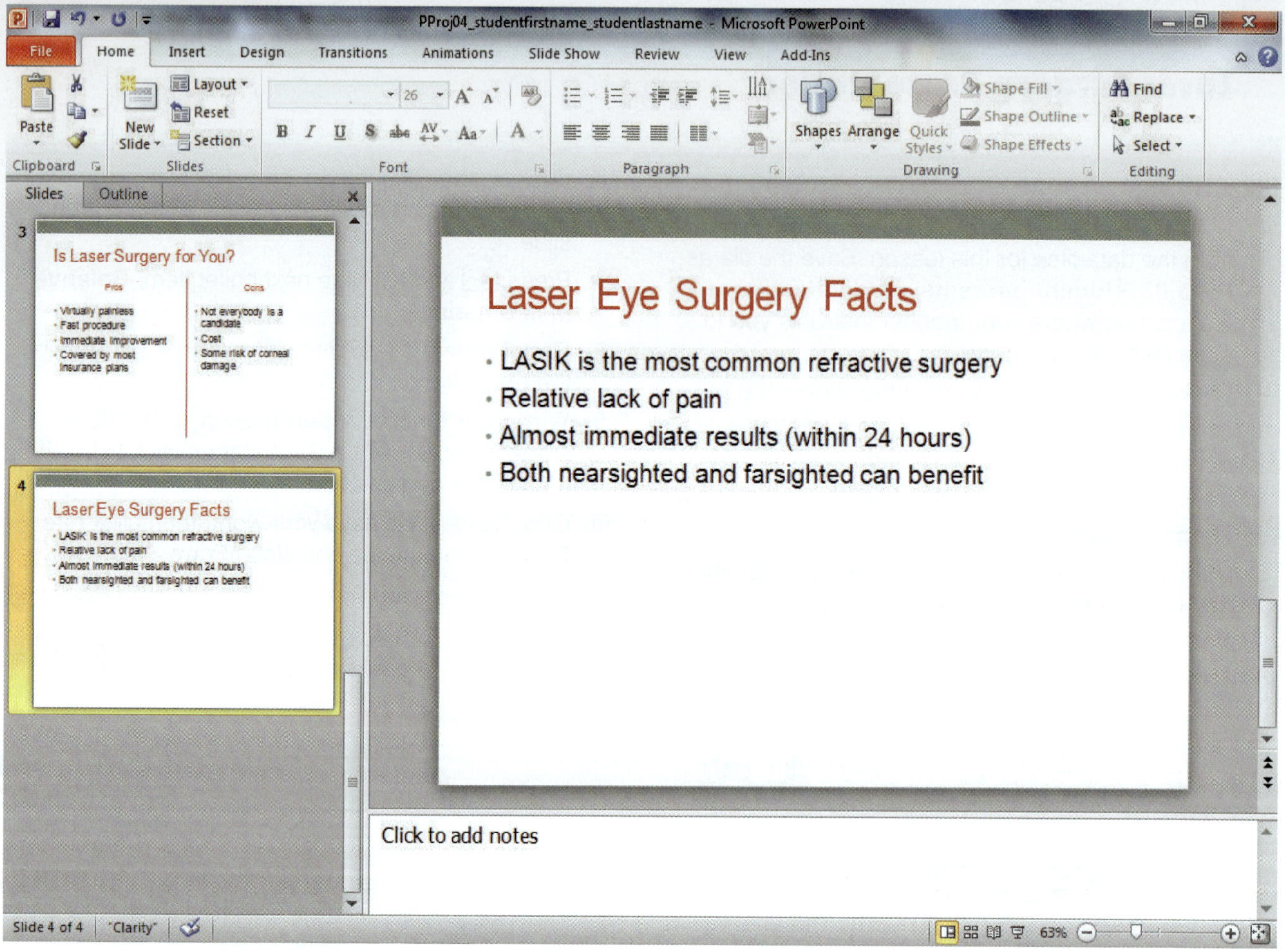
PProj04_studentfirstname_studentlastname - Microsoft PowerPoint
File
Home
Insert
Design
Transitions
Animations
Slide Show
Review
View
Add-Ins
Paste
Layout
Reset
New Slide
Section
Clipboard
Slides
Font
Paragraph
Shapes
Arrange
Quick Styles
Shape Fill
Shape Outline
Shape Effects
Drawing
Find
Replace
Select
Editing
Slides
Outline
Is Laser Surgery for You?
Laser Eye Surgery Facts
LASIK is the most common refractive surgery
Relative lack of pain
Almost immediate results (within 24 hours)
Both nearsighted and farsighted can benefit
Click to add notes
Slide 4 of 4
"Clarity"
63%

Lesson 3

Working with Headers, Footers, and Speaker Notes

➤ What You Will Learn

- Reusing Slides from Other Presentations
- Adding Speaker Notes
- Changing Slide Size and Orientation
- Inserting Headers and Footers

Software Skills PowerPoint makes it easy to reuse slides from other presentations by inserting them into your presentation. Footers, dates, and numbers provide additional information on slides to help users navigate and work with presentations. Notes pages allow you to easily refer to slide notes during a presentation, while handouts can give the audience a helpful reference of what has been covered in the presentation.

Application Skills In this lesson, you will add existing slides to a new travel adventures presentation. You will also work with the Wynnedale presentation. You will add notes and footer information to both presentations and change slide size and orientation.

WORDS TO KNOW

Handouts
Printed copies of the presentation for the audience to refer to during and after the slide show.

Landscape orientation
A slide or printout is wider than it is tall.

Portrait orientation
A slide or printout is taller than it is wide.

Footer
An area at the bottom of a slide in which you can enter a date, slide number, or other information.

Header
An area at the top of a slide in which you can enter a date or other information that repeats for each page.

What You Can Do

Reusing Slides from Other Presentations

- You will find that preparing presentations can be a time-consuming process, especially as you venture into more complex formatting and content. It makes sense to reuse slides whenever you can to save time.
- Borrowing slides from other presentations can also help to ensure consistency among presentations, an important consideration when you are working with a number of presentations for a company or organization.
- You can find the Reuse Slides command on the New Slide drop-down list. This command opens the Reuse Slides task pane where you can specify the presentation file to open. The slides are then displayed in the task pane. To see the content more clearly, rest the pointer on a slide in the current presentation. To insert a slide, simply click it.
- By default, slides you insert this way take on the formatting of the presentation they're inserted into (the destination presentation).
- If you want to retain the original formatting of the inserted slides, click the Keep source formatting check box at the bottom of the Reuse Slides task pane.

✓ *This is also covered in Lesson 19.*

Try It! Reusing Slides from Other Presentations

1. Start PowerPoint and open **PTry03a** from the data files for this lesson.
2. Save the file as **PTry03a_studentfirstname_studentlastname** in the location where your teacher instructs you to store the files for this lesson.
3. Click slide 4 in the Slides tab to select it.
4. Click Home > New Slide drop-down arrow, then click Reuse Slides.
5. In the Reuse Slides pane, click Browse and then click Browse File. Navigate to the location where the files for this lesson are stored and open **PTry03b**. The slides from this presentation appear in the Reuse Slides pane, as shown in the figure at the right.
6. Point to the first slide to view the slide content in a larger format. Point to each of the slides to see their content as well.
7. Click *June Calendar* to insert it into the destination presentation.

✓ *Note that the inserted slide takes on the theme and formatting of the destination presentation.*

8. Click on the remaining four slides in the Reuse Slides pane to insert them in the presentation.
9. Click the Close button on the Reuse Slides pane to close the pane.
10. Save the **PTry03a_studentfirstname_studentlastname** file and leave it open to use in the next Try It.

The Reuse Slides pane

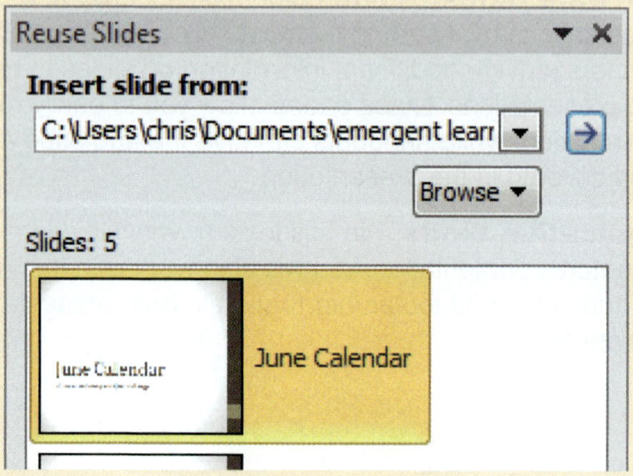

Adding Speaker Notes

- Strictly speaking, you do not need to "create" either notes pages or **handouts** in PowerPoint. Notes pages and handouts are simply another way to view and print existing slides.
- To view notes pages before printing, you can use Notes Page view. To view handouts, you can go to Backstage view and click Full Page Slides to see the various Handout formats available. The 3 Slides handout configuration provides lines next to each slide for audience members to take notes.
- By default, notes pages display a page number and handouts display a date and a page number. You can add information such as date and time, header, page number, and footer to both notes pages and handouts by adding **headers** and **footers**, covered later in this Lesson.
- You can use the Handout Master view and Notes Master view to see what handouts and Notes pages will look like and adjust settings before printing.

Try It! Adding Speaker Notes

1. In the **PTry03a_studentfirstname_studentlastname** file, click slide 5 in the Slides tab.
2. Click View > Notes Page.
3. Click in the Notes placeholder and type **Tell them about what's coming up in June.**
4. Press PG UP. Click in the Notes placeholder of slide 4 and type **Remind them that membership is free.**
5. Click File > Print. Click Full Page Slides, then click 3 Slides.
6. Click View > Handout Master. Click Close Master View.
7. Save the **PTry03a_studentfirstname_studentlastname** file and leave it open to use in the next Try It.

Changing Slide Size and Orientation

- By default, slides are displayed in **landscape orientation**—they are wider than they are tall—and notes pages and handouts are displayed in **portrait orientation**—they are taller than they are wide.
- In some instances, you may want to reverse the usual orientation of slides to display them in portrait orientation. You can use the Slide Orientation button on the Design tab to quickly switch from one orientation to another.

  ✓ *If your presentation includes graphics, they may become distorted when orientation is changed.*

- For more control over orientation and slide size, use the Page Setup dialog box.
- Slides are initially sized for an on-screen show on a screen that uses a standard 4:3 aspect ratio. You can change slide sizes to better fit the type of output device, such as a wide-screen display with a 16:9 aspect ratio.
- You can also select a size that will work best for a particular paper size, for 35mm slides, for overheads, or even for a custom size that you specify in the Width and Height boxes.

Try It! Changing Slide Size and Orientation

1. In the **PTry03a_studentfirstname_ studentlastname** file, click View > Normal.
2. Click Design > Slide Orientation > Portrait.
3. Click Design > Page Setup.
4. Click Landscape, then click On-screen Show (16:10) from the Slides sized for drop-down list, then click OK.
5. Save the **PTry03a_studentfirstname_ studentlastname** file and leave it open to use in the next Try It.

Inserting Headers and Footers

- You can add several types of information that repeat for each slide to help organize or identify slides.
  - Use a slide **footer** to identify a presentation's topic, author, client, or other information.
  - Add the date and time to a slide footer so you can tell when the presentation was created or updated.
  - Include a slide number in the footer to identify the slide's position in the presentation.
- Use the Header and Footer dialog box to specify these options. Note that you can choose a fixed date or a date that updates each time the presentation is opened. You can also choose to not display the information on the title slide, apply the information only to the current slide, or apply it to all slides.
- If you are working with notes pages or handouts, you can use the options on the Notes and Handouts tab to add a **header** in addition to date and time, slide number, and footer.

Try It! Inserting Headers and Footers

1. In the **PTry03a_studentfirstname_ studentlastname** file, click Insert > Header & Footer.

The Header and Footer dialog box

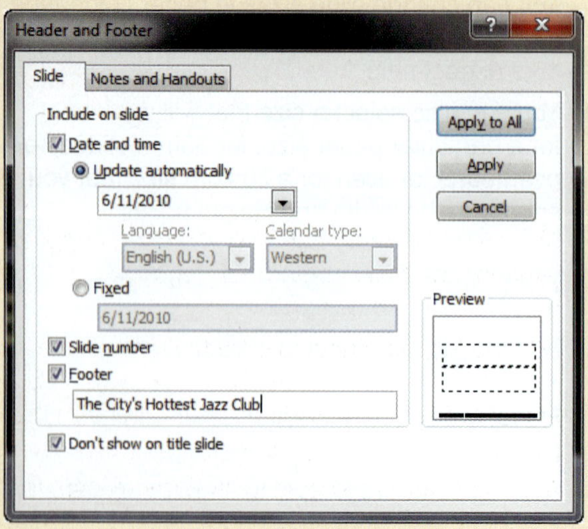

2. Click the Slide tab in the Header and Footer dialog box, then click Date and time.
3. Click Slide number and Don't show on title slide.
4. Click Footer, and type **The City's Hottest Jazz Club**. The dialog box should look like the one shown in the illustration at the left.
5. Click the Notes and Handouts tab, then click Header and type **The City's Hottest Jazz Club**.
6. Click Apply to All. Click through the slides to view the footers.
7. On slide 5, click View > Notes Page to view the notes page headers and footers.
8. Close **PTry03a_studentfirstname_ studentlastname**, saving all changes, and exit PowerPoint.

Project 5—Create It

Travel Adventures Presentation

DIRECTIONS

1. Start PowerPoint if necessary and open **PProj05a** from the data files for this lesson. Save the file as **PProj05a_studentfirstname_studentlastname** in the location where your teacher instructs you to store files for this lesson.
2. Click on slide 3 to display it in the Slide pane.
3. Click **Home** > **New Slide** drop-down arrow. Then click **Reuse Slides**.
4. In the Reuse Slides pane, click **Browse** and then click **Browse File**. Navigate to the location where the files for this lesson are stored and open **PProj05b**.
5. Point to the second slide to view the slide content in a larger format. Click **Adventure Travel Packages** to insert it into the destination presentation.

   ✓ *Note that the inserted slide takes on the theme and formatting of the destination presentation.*
6. Click the **Close** button on the Reuse Slides pane to close the pane.
7. Click slide 2, then click **View** > **Notes Page**.
8. Click in the Notes placeholder and type **Be sure to mention special group rates.**
9. Press PG DN. Click in the Notes placeholder of slide 3 and type **Also tell them about special rates on the Web site.**
10. Click **Insert** > **Header & Footer**.
11. Click the **Slide** tab in the Header and Footer dialog box, then click **Date and time**.
12. Click **Slide number** and **Don't show on title slide**.
13. Click **Footer** and type **Everywhere You Want to Go**. Click **Apply to All**.
14. Click **Design** > **Slide Orientation** > **Portrait.**
15. Click **View** > **Normal** and scroll through the slides to see the new layout.

   ✓ *Note that the two headings on Slide 1 are overlapping.*
16. Click **Design** > **Slide Orientation** > **Landscape**.
17. Click **Review** > **Spelling** to check spelling in the presentation, then click **OK**.
18. **With your teacher's permission,** click **File** > **Print**. Select **Print All Slides**, then click **Print** to print the presentation.
19. Click **Save** to save your work, then click **File** > **Exit** to close the file and close PowerPoint.

Project 6—Apply It

Laser Surgery Presentation

DIRECTIONS

1. Start PowerPoint, if necessary.
2. Open **PProj06a** from the data files for this lesson.
3. Save the presentation as **PProj06a_studentfirstname_studentlastname** in the location where your teacher instructs you to store the files for this lesson.
4. Move to slide 4, and then choose to reuse slides from another presentation. Browse to **PProj06b**, and insert both slides from the presentation. Close the Reuse Slides pane.
5. Move to slide 5 and note that the main heading overlaps the body content. Change the presentation theme to **Elemental**.
6. Add the following note to slide 5: **Compare surgery cost to the cost of glasses or contacts**. Add the following note to slide 6: **Make sure potential patients know that the surgery is painless**.
7. Add the following footers to all slides except for the title slide: **Date and time**, **Slide number**, and the following footer: **Clear Vision in a Day**.

8. Change the slide aspect ratio to **16:10**. Your presentation should look like the one in Figure 3-1.
9. Check the spelling.
10. **With your teacher's permission,** print the presentation.
11. Close the presentation, saving all changes, and exit PowerPoint.

Figure 3-1

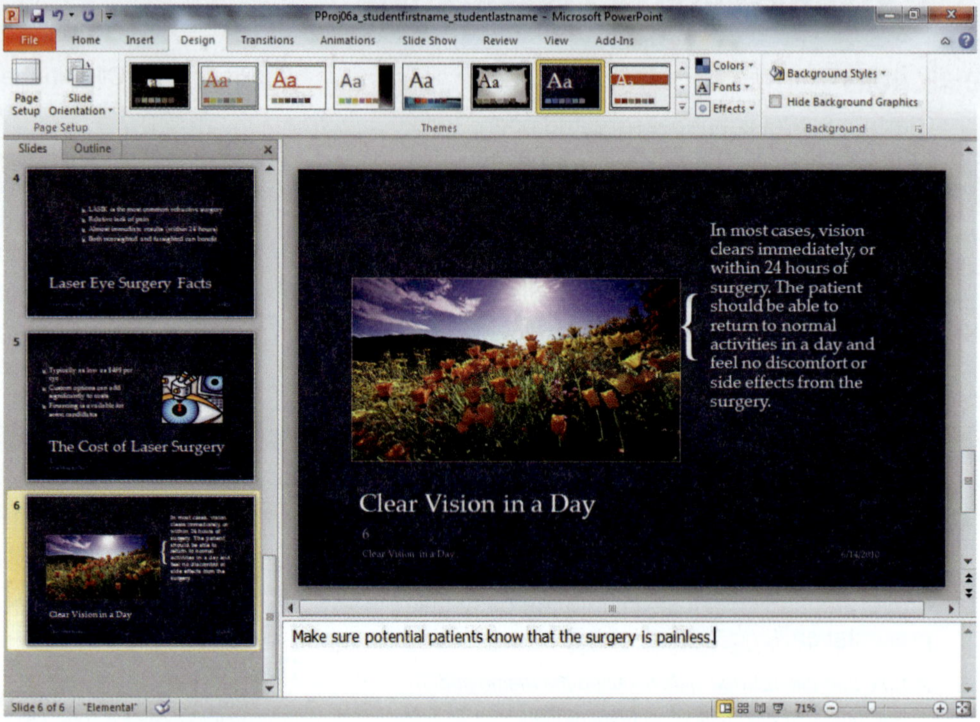

Lesson 4

Inserting and Formatting Pictures

➤ What You Will Learn

Inserting a Picture from a File
Formatting Pictures Using Styles and Artistic Effects

WORDS TO KNOW

Crop
Remove a portion of a picture that you don't want.

Scaling
Specifying a percentage of original size to enlarge or reduce the size of an object.

Software Skills You can insert your own pictures in a presentation and then use the enhanced picture tools to adjust the picture's appearance and apply special effects.

Application Skills A local environmental group, Planet Earth, has asked you to prepare a presentation they can show on Earth Day. In this exercise, you begin the presentation by inserting and formatting several pictures.

What You Can Do

Inserting a Picture from a File

- You can use Microsoft Office clip art graphics or photos to illustrate your slides, as you will learn in Chapter 2. But in some instances, you may want to include your own pictures of specific locations, events, or people.
- You can scan your own pictures into the computer using a scanner. Using the scanner and computer, you can save the scanned image to the folder where you store your photos.
- Use the Insert Picture from File icon in any content placeholder or the Picture button on the Insert tab to place your own picture file on a slide. This command opens the Insert Picture dialog box so you can navigate to and select the picture you want to insert.

Try It! Inserting a Picture from a File

1. Start PowerPoint and open PTry04 from the data files for this lesson.
2. Save the file as PTry04_studentfirstname_studentlastname in the location where your teacher instructs you to store the files for this lesson.
3. Go to slide 2 and click the Insert Picture from File icon in the content placeholder.
4. Navigate to the location where files for this lesson are stored, and select the Skyline image, then click Insert.
5. Press CTRL + M to add a new slide, and type The Haystack at Cannon Beach in the title placeholder.
6. Click in the content placeholder, then click Insert > Picture. Navigate to the location where files for this lesson are stored, and select the PTry04_Haystack image, then click Insert.
7. Save the PTry04_studentfirstname_studentlastname file, and leave it open to use in the next Try It.

Formatting Pictures Using Styles and Artistic Effects

- Once you have inserted a picture, you can resize a picture by dragging a corner handle, or reposition it by dragging it to a new location.
- For more control over the formatting process, use the tools on the Picture Tools Format tab to modify and enhance a picture. Options on this tab allow you to create interesting and unusual picture effects as well as specify a precise size.
- Use the tools in the Adjust group to change brightness or contrast. You can also recolor a picture using the current theme colors.
- The Picture Styles group lets you apply a number of interesting styles to your pictures. You can also choose a shape in which to enclose the picture, select border options, or apply standard effects such as shadows or reflections.
- The Size group allows you to **crop** a picture to remove portions of the picture you don't need. You can restore the hidden portion of the picture by using the Crop tool again.
- Once you are certain the picture has the right appearance, you can compress the picture to remove the hidden portions. This action reduces the presentation's file size and makes it more efficient.
- The Size group also supplies width and height settings that allow you to precisely size a picture. Click the Size dialog box launcher to open the Format Picture dialog box, where you can adjust the size or **scale** the picture to a percentage of its original size. You can scale any drawing object, including clip art graphics and shapes you draw yourself.

Try It! Formatting Pictures Using Styles and Artistic Effects

1. In the PTry04_studentfirstname_studentlastname file, click slide 2 and click the picture.
2. Click the upper-left corner handle and drag it up and to the left to enlarge the picture. Then click and drag the photograph to the right side of the slide, in line with the blue graphic above, as shown in the illustration on the next page.
3. Click Picture Tools Format > Corrections and then click the far-right image in the Sharpen and Soften row.
4. Click Picture Tools Format > Color and select Saturation: 200% in the Color Saturation row.

(continued)

Try It! Formatting Pictures Using Styles and Artistic Effects *(continued)*

5. Click Picture Tools Format and select Soft Edge Rectangle from the Picture Styles gallery.

6. Click Picture Tools Format > Crop > Crop to activate the crop tool. Click the bottom middle handle and drag it up to remove most of the trees from the picture.

7. Click Crop again to complete the crop.

8. Click slide 3 and click the picture. Click Picture Tools > Picture Effects > Soft Edges > 25 Point.

9. Click Picture Tools Format > Artistic Effects, then select Glow Diffused.

10. Close **PTry04_studentfirstname_studentlastname**, saving all changes, and exit PowerPoint.

Click and Drag to Change Picture Size and Position

Project 7—Create It

Planet Earth Presentation

DIRECTIONS

1. Start PowerPoint if necessary and open **PProj07** from the data files for this lesson. Save the file as **PProj07_studentfirstname_studentlastname** in the location where your teacher instructs you to store files for this lesson.
2. Click on the **Insert Picture from File** icon in the content placeholder to the right of the Planet Earth text.
3. Navigate to the location where files for this lesson are stored and select the **PProj07_earthpic** image, then click **Insert**.
4. Click **Picture Tools Format** > **Corrections** and then click the image to the right of the current image in Brightness and Contrast to increase the image brightness by 20%.
5. Right-click the image and click **Format Picture** to open the Format Picture dialog box. Click and drag to select the **0** in the Contrast box and type **25%**. Click **Close**.
6. Click **Picture Tools Format** > **Crop** > **Crop**, then click and drag the bottom middle handle up a half inch. Click **Crop** again to crop the picture.
7. Click **Picture Tools Format** and type **3.9"** in the Height box, as shown in Figure 4-1.
8. Click the **Compress Pictures** button, then click **OK**.
9. Click **Review** > **Spelling** to check spelling in the presentation, then click **OK**.
10. **With your teacher's permission,** click **File** > **Print**. Select **Print All Slides**, then click **Print** to print the presentation.
11. Click **Save** to save your work, then click **File** > **Exit** to close the file and close PowerPoint.

Figure 4-1

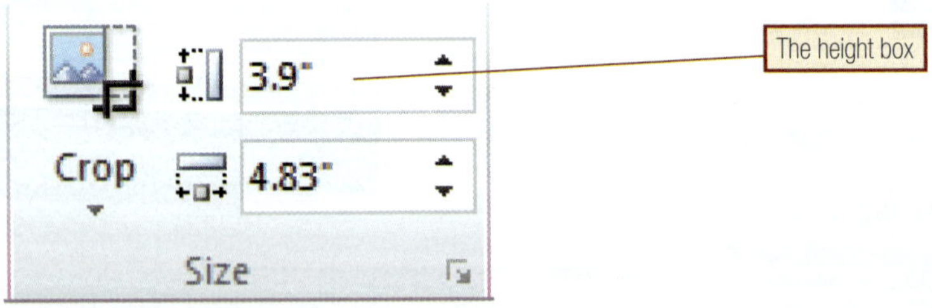

Project 8—Apply It

Planet Earth Presentation

DIRECTIONS

1. Start PowerPoint, if necessary.
2. Open **PProj08** from the data files for this lesson.
3. Save the presentation as **PProj08_studentfirstname_studentlastname** in the location where your teacher instructs you to store the files for this lesson.
4. Insert the **PProj08_Dolphin** image in slide 2.
5. Increase the image brightness by 20%.
6. Recolor the image to **Sky Blue, Accent color 3 Dark**.
7. Apply the **Pencil Sketch** Artistic Effect to the image. Your presentation should look like the one in Figure 4-2.
8. Compress the picture using document resolution.
9. Check the spelling.

10. **With your teacher's permission,** print the presentation.

11. Close the presentation, saving all changes, and exit PowerPoint.

Figure 4-2

Lesson 5

Formatting Text

WORDS TO KNOW

Format Painter
A tool that lets you copy text formatting from one text selection and apply it to any other text in the presentation.

➤ What You Will Learn

Finding and Replacing Text in a Presentation
Selecting Text and Placeholders
Changing the Appearance of Text Using Font Sizes, Styles, and Colors
Copying Text Formatting
Using Undo and Redo
Clearing Formatting

Software Skills Although themes and theme fonts are designed to produce a pleasing appearance, you may sometimes wish to modify the appearance of text by changing font, font style, size, or color. Use the Format Painter to copy formatting from one slide to another.

Application Skills Great Grains Bakery, a company that sells fresh-baked breads and other bakery items at various locations around your area, wants you to help them create a presentation to display at a trade show. In this lesson, you explore ways to improve the appearance of text in the presentation. You will also modify a presentation about an Internet acceptable use policy.

What You Can Do

Finding and Replacing Text in a Presentation

- As with other Microsoft Office 2010 applications, you can search for specific text in a PowerPoint presentation and replace it with new text. You can use the Find and Replace buttons in the Editing group of the Home tab to do this.
- You can also use the Replace Fonts command to find and replace text fonts throughout a presentation. Just indicate the font you want to replace, and the new font you want to use.

Try It! Finding and Replacing Text in a Presentation

1. Start PowerPoint and open **PTry05** from the data files for this lesson.
2. Save the file as **PTry05_studentfirstname_studentlastname** in the location where your teacher instructs you to store the files for this lesson.
3. Click Home > Find and type **walkathon** in the Find dialog box. Click Find Next.
4. Click Replace and type **Walkathon** in the Replace dialog box. Click Replace to change the selected text. Click Find Next.
5. Click OK and then click Close.
6. Click Home > Replace > Replace Fonts. The font Book Antiqua, which is used throughout the presentation, should be highlighted in the Replace list box.
7. Click to select Agency FB in the With list box, click Replace, then click Close.
8. Save the **PTry05_studentfirstname_studentlastname** file and leave it open to use in the next Try It.

Selecting Text and Placeholders

- Manipulating text in a presentation requires you to know some basics about selecting text and placeholders to ensure you are working efficiently.
- As in a word processing document, you can select text by dragging the insertion point over it, highlighting the selected text. You can also double-click a single word to select it.
- As you are working with text in a placeholder, the placeholder displays a dashed line, sizing handles, and a rotation handle.
- You can also select the placeholder by clicking its outline with the four-headed pointer. The selected placeholder has a solid outline.
- While a placeholder is selected, any change you make using text tools will apply to all text in the placeholder.
- When you want to make a change to all text in a placeholder, it is speedier to select the placeholder rather than drag over the text to select it.

Try It! Selecting Text and Placeholders

1. In the **PTry05_studentfirstname_studentlastname** file, go to slide 2, then click and drag to select **Homeless** in the slide title. Note the dashed line, sizing handles and rotation handle shown in the following figure.

Placeholder Tools with Selected Text

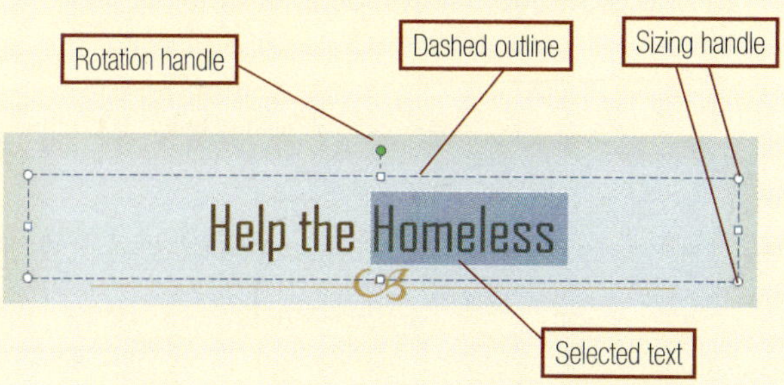

2. Move the mouse arrow down below the rule until it changes to a four-headed pointer, then click to select the slide content placeholder.
3. Double-click the word **homeless** in the second bullet to select it.
4. Move the mouse arrow slightly over the selected word to make the Mini toolbar appear. This toolbar can be used to change formatting of the selected text.
5. Save the **PTry05_studentfirstname_studentlastname** file and leave it open to use in the next Try It.

Changing the Appearance of Text Using Font Sizes, Styles, and Colors

- PowerPoint's themes guarantee a presentation with a sophisticated design, and that includes the appearance of text. You can, however, easily customize text appearance to emphasize it or to make your presentation more readable, interesting, or unique.
- Text appearance attributes include font family, size, color, style, and special effects. You can also change the case of text to control use of uppercase and lowercase letters.
- You can change text attributes using techniques similar to those that you used in Word and Excel:
  - Select text or a placeholder and then use the options in the Font group on the Home tab of the Ribbon. Commands in this group allow you to change font, font size, font style, and font color. You can also increase or decrease font size by set increments and clear formatting to restore default appearance.
  - You can use the Mini toolbar that appears near selected text to modify text appearance as well as adjust paragraph features such as alignment, indents, and bullet formatting.
- You can open the Font dialog box by clicking the Font group's dialog box launcher to change multiple attributes at one time and then apply them all at once.
- Note that effects such as superscript and subscript that are not available on Ribbon buttons are available in this dialog box.
- The Character Spacing option on the Home tab and in the Font dialog box allows you to control the amount of space between characters from very tight to very loose, or you can set a specific spacing amount.

Try It! Changing the Appearance of Text Using Font Sizes, Styles, and Colors

1. In the **PTry05_studentfirstname_studentlastname** file, click slide 4 and click the content placeholder.
2. Click Home > Font drop-down list, then click Book Antiqua in the Theme Fonts section of the Font drop-down list.
3. Click and drag to select the title **How to Get Involved.** Click Home > Font Color and then select Dark Red, Accent 5, Lighter 60% from the Theme Colors.
4. Click Home > Text Shadow.
5. With the title still selected, Click Home > Character Spacing > Loose.
6. With the title still selected, click Home > Font Size drop-down list > 66.
7. Double-click **Walkathon** in the second bullet, then click the Font dialog box launcher. Click Equalize Character Height, then click OK.
8. Save the **PTry05_studentfirstname_studentlastname** file and leave it open to use in the next Try It.

Copying Text Formatting

- Just as in Word, you can quickly copy and apply text formatting in PowerPoint by using the **Format Painter**.
- You can copy text and object formatting and apply it to one or multiple text blocks or objects.

Try It! Copying Text Formatting

1. In the **PTry05_studentfirstname_studentlastname** file, click slide 5 and click the title placeholder.
2. Click Home > Format Painter.
3. Click the title placeholder in slide 4 to apply the formatting.
4. Save the **PTry05_studentfirstname_studentlastname** file and leave it open to use in the next Try It.

Using Undo and Redo

- PowerPoint contains an Undo feature, as in other Microsoft Office applications, which reverses the most recent action or a whole series of previous actions.
- The Redo button allows you to redo actions after you undo them, if you change your mind.
- You can find the Undo and Redo buttons on the Quick Access Toolbar.

Try It! Using Undo and Redo

1. In the **PTry05_studentfirstname_studentlastname** file, click slide 4 and click Undo in the Quick Access Toolbar.
2. Now click Redo in the Quick Access Toolbar.
3. Click the Undo drop-down list arrow to see a list of the most recent actions you can undo. Click Text Shadow. Notice that all the subsequent actions are also undone.
4. Save the **PTry05_studentfirstname_studentlastname** file and leave it open to use in the next Try It.

Clearing Formatting

- You can use the Reset button to clear formatting you have added to text and return the position, size, and formatting of the slide placeholders to the default settings.

Try It! Clearing Formatting

1. In the **PTry05_studentfirstname_studentlastname** file, go to slide 5.
2. Click Reset. The placeholder formatting returns to the default settings.
3. Close **PTry05_studentfirstname_studentlastname**, saving all changes, and exit PowerPoint.

Project 9—Create It

Great Grains Bakery Presentation

DIRECTIONS

1. Start PowerPoint if necessary and open **PProj09** from the data files for this lesson. Save the file as **PProj09_studentfirstname_studentlastname** in the location where your teacher instructs you to store files for this lesson.
2. Click **Home** > **Find** and type **Breads, baguettes, and bagels** in the Find dialog box. Click **Find Next**.
3. Click **Replace** and type **Breads and baguettes** in the Replace with text box. Click **Replace All**.
4. Click **OK**. Click **Close**.
5. Click **Home** > **Replace** > **Replace Fonts**. The font Arial, which is used throughout the presentation, should be highlighted in the Replace list box.
6. Click to select **Agency FB** in the With list box, click **Replace**, then click **Close**.
7. Click to select slide 3, then select the title placeholder.
8. Click **Home** > **Font** drop-down list, then click **Arial (Headings)** in the Theme Fonts section of the Font drop-down list.
9. Click **Home** > **Font Color** drop-down list and then select **Indigo, Accent 5** from the Theme Colors.
10. Click **Home** > **Character Spacing** > **Loose** and then click **Home** > **Font Size drop-down list** > **54**. Click **Home** > **Text Shadow**.
11. Click **Home** > **Format Painter**. Click the title placeholder in slide 4. Use the Format Painter to apply the title placeholder formatting to all the remaining slides.
12. Click slide 5 and click **Undo** in the Quick Access Toolbar. Then click **Redo**.
13. Click **Reset**, then click **Undo**. Your presentation should look like the one shown in Figure 5-1.
14. Click **Review** > **Spelling** to check spelling in the presentation, then click **OK**.
15. **With your teacher's permission,** click **File** > **Print**. Select **Print All Slides**, then click **Print** to print the presentation.
16. Click **Save** to save your work, then click **File** > **Exit** to close the file and close PowerPoint.

Figure 5-1

Project 10—Apply It

Acceptable Use Policy Presentation

DIRECTIONS

1. Start PowerPoint, if necessary.
2. Open **PProj10** from the data files for this lesson.
3. Save the presentation as **PProj10_studentfirstname_studentlastname** in the location where your teacher instructs you to store the files for this lesson.
4. Replace the word **teacher** with **instructor** throughout the presentation.

   ✓ *Be sure to check capitalization and punctuation throughout after replacing.*

5. On slide 2, change the title font to **Calibri, 40 point**. Change the font color to Theme Color **Blue, Accent 2**, and apply the **Shadow** effect.
6. Copy this text formatting to the titles of all the slides in the presentation, including the title slide.
7. On slide 2, change the bullet list font to **Calibri, 28 point**. Change the font color to Theme Color **Gray-50%, Accent 6**.
8. Copy this text formatting to the bullet lists of all the slides in the presentation.
9. On slide 6, use Undo or the Reset button to remove copied formatting from the sub-bullets.
10. On slide 6, format the sub-bullet font as **Calibri, 22 point, Gray-50%, Accent 6**. Your presentation should look like the one shown in Figure 5-2.
11. Check the spelling.
12. **With your teacher's permission,** print the presentation.
13. Close the presentation, saving all changes, and exit PowerPoint.

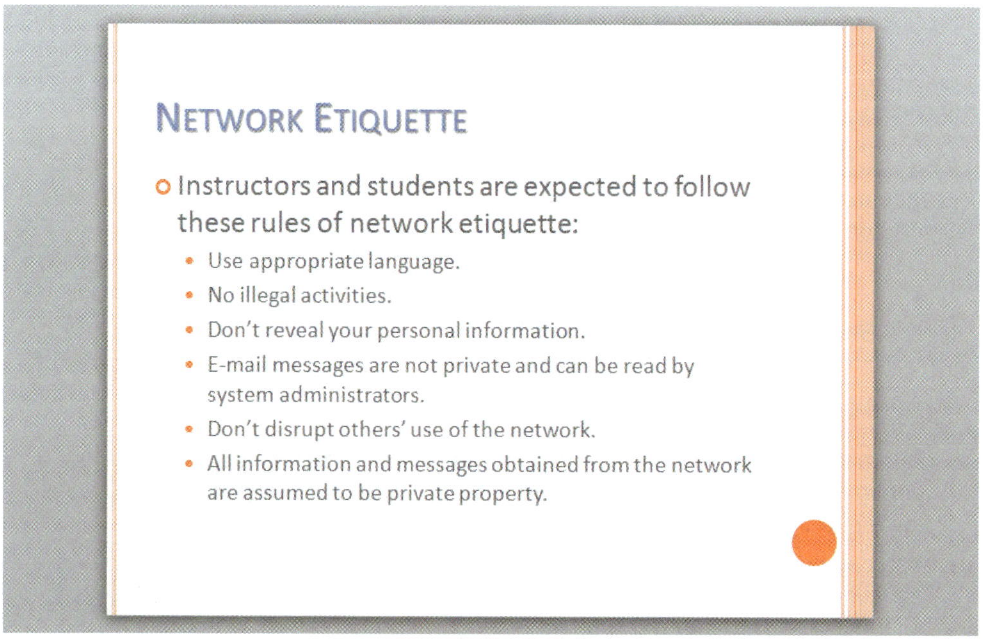

Figure 5-2

Lesson 6

Aligning Text

WORDS TO KNOW

AutoFit
PowerPoint feature designed to reduce font size to fit text in the current placeholder.

➤ What You Will Learn

Aligning Text
Adjusting Line Spacing
Adjusting Paragraph Spacing
Moving and Copying Text
Using AutoFit Options
Adjusting and Formatting Placeholders

Software Skills Other ways to modify the appearance of text on a slide include changing text alignment and tweaking paragraph spacing. Move or copy text from slide to slide just as you would in a document. You can also move, resize, copy, or delete any placeholder on a slide or any object on a slide.

Application Skills In this lesson, you will work on the presentations for Great Grains Bakery and the Holmes Medical Center by modifying list items, text alignment, text, and the position and size of placeholders.

What You Can Do

Aligning Text

- Themes also control the alignment of text in placeholders. You can left-align, center, right-align, or justify text in any placeholder to add interest or enhance text appearance.
- You can change alignment of any paragraph of text in a text placeholder without affecting other paragraphs of text. In a title placeholder, however, changing alignment of one paragraph realigns all paragraphs in that placeholder.
- Use buttons in the Paragraph group on the Home tab to align text. You can also use the Mini toolbar to apply left, center, or right alignment or use the Paragraph dialog box, discussed in the next section, to specify alignment.
- You can also click the Align Text button in the in the Paragraph group on the Home tab to adjust the vertical alignment of text within a placeholder. Settings include Top, Middle, and Bottom.

Try It! Aligning Text

1. Start PowerPoint and open **PTry06** from the data files for this lesson.
2. Save the file as **PTry06_studentfirstname_studentlastname** in the location where your teacher instructs you to store the files for this lesson.
3. Go to slide 6 and click on the text placeholder underneath the slide title.
4. Click Home > Align Text Left.
5. Click Home > Justify.
6. Double-click on any word in the text placeholder, then move the arrow over the Mini toolbar and click Align Text Right.
7. Click Home > Paragraph dialog box launcher. Click Centered in the Alignment drop-down list, then click OK.
8. Go to slide 3 and click on the text placeholder. Click Home > Align Text > Middle.
9. Save the **PTry06_studentfirstname_studentlastname** file and leave it open to use in the next Try It.

Adjusting Line Spacing

- You can also change the spacing between lines of text in a placeholder.
- Use the Line Spacing button to apply line spacing options similar to those you would use in Word: 1.5, 2.0, and so on. Line spacing affects all lines of a paragraph.
- With the insertion point in a single paragraph in a placeholder, the new line spacing option applies only to that paragraph. To adjust line spacing for all items in a placeholder, select them or select the placeholder.
- From the Line Spacing drop-down list, you can click Line Spacing Options to open the Paragraph dialog box for more customized line spacing options.
- In the Paragraph dialog box, you can specify Single, Double, Exact, Multiple, or 1.5 Lines of spacing.
- If you choose Exact or Multiple spacing, you can specify the exact amount of space you want between lines or the number of lines of space you want between lines by using the At text box in the Paragraph dialog box.

Try It! Adjusting Line Spacing

1. In the **PTry06_studentfirstname_studentlastname** file, click slide 2 and click in the second bullet of text in the text placeholder.
2. Click Home > Line Spacing > 2.0.
3. This spacing is too large. Click Home > Line Spacing > 1.5.
4. This spacing is still a bit too large. Click Home > Line Spacing > Line Spacing Options.
5. In the Paragraph dialog box, click Exactly in the Line Spacing drop-down list, then enter **32** in the At text box and click OK.
6. Click in the third bullet of text in the text placeholder. Click Home > Line Spacing, then roll the arrow over all the line spacing options to see the effect on the paragraph.
7. Move the arrow away from the drop-down list without changing the spacing.
8. Click to select the entire text placeholder. Click Home > Paragraph dialog box launcher.
9. In the Paragraph dialog box, click Exactly in the Line Spacing drop-down list, then enter **32** in the At text box and click OK.
10. Click Home > Align Text > Middle.
11. Save the **PTry06_studentfirstname_studentlastname** file and leave it open to use in the next Try It.

Adjusting Paragraph Spacing

- Adjust paragraph spacing between bullets or other paragraphs to make text easier to read or to control space on a slide.
- For greater control over paragraph spacing, use the Paragraph dialog box. You can choose alignment and indention settings as well as specify a space before and/or after each paragraph and choose a line spacing option.

Try It! Adjusting Paragraph Spacing

1. In the **PTry06_studentfirstname_studentlastname** file, click slide 2 and click the text placeholder to select it.
2. Click Home > Paragraph dialog box launcher.
3. In the Paragraph dialog box, click in the Before text text box and enter **0.5"** to change the indentation.
4. Click in the By text box and enter **0.5"** and click First line in the Indentation drop-down list.
5. Click in the Before text box and enter **10 pt**. Click OK.
6. Save the **PTry06_studentfirstname_studentlastname** file and leave it open to use in the next Try It.

Moving and Copying Text

- As you review a slide or presentation, you may rearrange the text to make it easier to follow.
- Just as in Word, you can move text in PowerPoint using drag-and-drop or cut-and-paste methods.
- Use the drag-and-drop method to move text to a nearby location, such as within the same placeholder or on the same slide, or from the Outline pane to a slide.
- When you move text, a vertical line moves with the mouse to help you position the text.
- Use the cut-and-paste method to move text between two locations that are some distance apart, such as from one slide to another or from one presentation to another.

Try It! Moving and Copying Text

1. In the **PTry06_studentfirstname_studentlastname** file, click slide 5 and select the text in the second bullet.
2. Click and drag the text in the second bullet down beneath the next bullet text, *Volunteer your services*.
3. Open the file **PTry06_support** from the location where the files for this lesson are stored.
4. In the **PTry06_studentfirstname_studentlastname** file, click slide 6, then click Home > New Slide > Title and Content.
5. In the **PTry06_support** file, click slide 1 and select the text in the title placeholder. Press CTRL + C.
6. Go to slide 7 of the **PTry06_studentfirstname_studentlastname** file, click in the title placeholder, then press CTRL + V.
7. Save the **PTry06_studentfirstname_studentlastname** file and leave it open to use in the next Try It. Leave the **PTry06_support** file open to use in the next Try It as well.

Using AutoFit Options

- If you enter more text than a placeholder can handle—such as a long slide title or a number of bullet entries—PowerPoint will by default use **AutoFit** to fit the text in the placeholder. AutoFit reduces font size or line spacing (or both) to fit the text into the placeholder.
- You can control AutoFit options using the AutoFit Options button that displays near the bottom left corner of a placeholder.

Try It! Using AutoFit Options

1. In the **PTry06_support** file, click slide 1 and select all three bullets of text in the text placeholder. Press CTRL + C.
2. In the **PTry06_studentfirstname_studentlastname** file, go to slide 7 and click in the text placeholder, then press CTRL + V.
3. In the **PTry06_support** file, click slide 2 and select all three bullets of text in the text placeholder. Press CTRL + C.
4. In the **PTry06_studentfirstname_studentlastname** file, go to slide 7 and click in the text placeholder after the three bullets of text you previously inserted, then press CTRL + V. Note that PowerPoint has used AutoFit to fit the text in the placeholder.
5. Click AutoFit Options > Change to Two Columns.

AutoFit to Two Columns

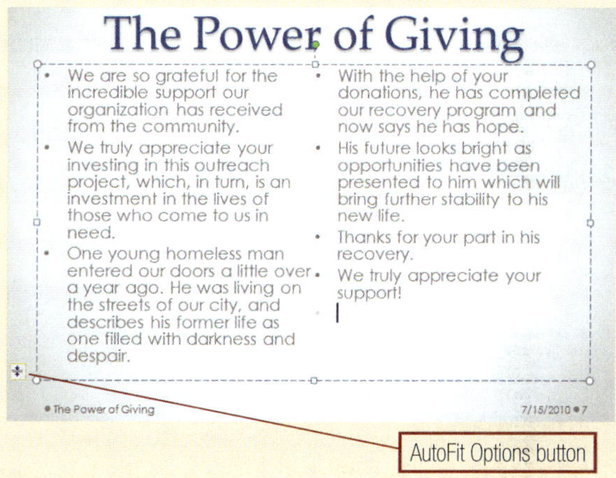

6. Click AutoFit Options > Split Text Between Two Slides.
7. Save the **PTry06_studentfirstname_studentlastname** file and leave it open to use in the next Try It. Also leave the **PTry06_support** file open to use in the next Try It.

Adjusting and Formatting Placeholders

- You can move or size any text or object placeholder to make room on the slide for other objects such as text boxes or images.
- You can also delete any placeholder to remove it from a slide, or copy a placeholder to use on another slide or in another presentation.
- To move, copy, size, or delete a placeholder and everything in it, select the placeholder so that its border becomes a solid line.
  - To move the placeholder, drag it by its border or use cut-and-paste to remove it from one slide and paste it on another.
  - To copy the placeholder, use copy-and-paste. A pasted placeholder appears in the same location on the new slide as on the original slide.
  - Delete a placeholder by simply pressing Delete while it is selected.
  - To resize a placeholder, drag one of the sizing handles at the corners and centers of the sides of the placeholder box.
- PowerPoint 2010 makes it easy to format a placeholder in interesting ways. Use a Quick Style, for example, to apply color and other effects to an entire placeholder.
- You can also apply a fill, outline, or other shape effect to a placeholder, just as you would to a drawing shape.

Try It! Adjusting and Formatting Placeholders

1. In the **PTry06_studentfirstname_studentlastname** file, go to slide 8, then click Home > New Slide > Title and Content.
2. In the **PTry06_support** file, go to slide 3 and click to select the title placeholder. Press CTRL + C.
3. In the **PTry06_studentfirstname_studentlastname** file, go to slide 9, then click to select the title placeholder. Press CTRL + V.
4. Click the bottom center sizing handle and drag it up to resize the title placeholder.
5. In the **PTry06_support** file, go to slide 3 and click to select the text placeholder. Press CTRL + C.
6. In the **PTry06_studentfirstname_studentlastname** file, go to slide 9, then click to select the text placeholder. Press CTRL + V.
7. Click the right center sizing handle of the text placeholder and drag it left to the center of the slide to resize the text placeholder.
8. Go to slide 4 and click to select the text placeholder. Click the center top sizing handle of the text placeholder and drag it down slightly to move the text away from the title.
9. Click Home > Quick Styles, then move the arrow over the various Quick Styles in the palette to see how they look in the text placeholder. Click on the Quick Style of your choice to apply it.
10. Save the **PTry06_studentfirstname_studentlastname** presentation and close the file. Close the **PTry06_support** file without saving and exit PowerPoint.

Project 11—Create It

Holmes Medical Center Presentation

DIRECTIONS

1. Start PowerPoint if necessary and open **PProj11** from the data files for this lesson. Save the file as **PProj11_studentfirstname_studentlastname** in the location where your teacher instructs you to store files for this lesson.
2. Go to slide 5 and click the text placeholder. Click **Home** > **Align Text Left**.
3. Go to slide 4 and click the text placeholder. Click **Home** > **Align Text** > **Middle**.
4. Now click **Home** > **Line Spacing** > **1.5**.
5. Go to slide 2 and click the text placeholder. Click **Home** > **Line Spacing** > **1.5**.
6. Go to slide 5 and click the text placeholder. Click **Home** > **Line Spacing** > **1.5**.
7. Go to slide 3 and click the left text placeholder. Click **Home** > **Paragraph** dialog box launcher.
8. In the Paragraph dialog box, click in the **Before text** text box and enter **0.5"** to change the indentation.
9. Click in the **By** text box and enter **0.5"** and click First line in the Indentation drop-down list. Click **OK**.
10. Click the right text placeholder. Click **Home** > **Paragraph** dialog box launcher.
11. In the Paragraph dialog box, click in the **Before text** text box and enter **0.5"** to change the indentation.
12. Click in the **By** text box and enter **0.5"** and click **First line** in the Indentation drop-down list. Click **OK**.
13. Go to slide 6 and click the picture. Drag the picture to align with the title placeholder at the left.
14. Click the center right sizing handle and drag it to the left to display the entire right text placeholder. Your slide should look similar to the one in Figure 6-1.

Figure 6-1

15. Click **File** > **Open** and navigate to the location where the files for this lesson are stored. Open **PProj11_integrated**.
16. Select the text in the text placeholder. Press CTRL + C.
17. Go to slide 5 in the **PProj11_studentfirstname_studentlastname** file, click after the last text bullet, press ENTER, then press CTRL + V.
18. Click to select the text placeholder, then click the bottom center sizing handle and drag it down to expand the text placeholder. PowerPoint AutoFits the text to the new placeholder size.
19. Select the text in the placeholder, then click **Home** > **Line Spacing** > **1.0**.
20. Click **Review** > **Spelling** to check spelling in the presentation. Click **Ignore All** for *Wynnedale* and *waveforming*, then click **OK**.
21. **With your teacher's permission,** click **File** > **Print**. Select **Print All Slides**, then click **Print** to print the presentation.
22. Click **Save** to save your work, then click **File** > **Exit** to close the files and close PowerPoint.

Project 12—Apply It

Great Grains Bread Presentation

DIRECTIONS

1. Start PowerPoint, if necessary.
2. Open **PProj12** from the data files for this lesson.
3. Save the presentation as **PProj12_studentfirstname_studentlastname** in the location where your teacher instructs you to store the files for this lesson.
4. On slide 1, center the title and subtitle.
5. On slide 2, change the paragraph indent of the four bullet items under *Breads* and the three bullet items under *Sweet specialties* to: **0.55"** indentation before text.
6. On slide 3, position the insertion point after the first bullet item, press ENTER, and type **Franchises available**. Move the last bullet item on the slide to be the first bullet item.

7. On slide 4, copy the first item and paste it at the end of the list. Add an exclamation point at the end of the word *Quality* in item 5. Then change the word *FOUR* in the slide title to **FIVE**.
8. Change the line spacing for all items in the text placeholder to **1.5**.
9. On slide 5, delete the *Turbinado sugar* and *Gourmet sea salt* items and then drag the bottom of the placeholder upwards to redistribute the items so the *Fair trade* item is positioned in the right column. Your slide should look like the one shown in Figure 6-2.
10. On slide 6, select the text placeholder on top of the photo and delete it.
11. Select the photo and drag it to the left, to the middle of the background area.
12. Right-align the text in the placeholder to the right of the photo.
13. Copy the subtitle placeholder from slide 1 and paste it on slide 6. Move it below the photo and resize the placeholder to be the same width as the photo. Click the **Bullets** button on the Home tab to remove bullet formatting if necessary.
14. Apply a Quick Style to the placeholder. You may need to change the text color to make it stand out against the Quick Style formatting.
15. Check the spelling.
16. **With your teacher's permission,** print the presentation.
17. Close the presentation, saving all changes, and exit PowerPoint.

Figure 6-2

Lesson 7

Displaying the Presentation Outline

➤ What You Will Learn

Displaying the Presentation Outline
Viewing a Presentation in Reading View

Software Skills Use PowerPoint views to work with the outline when doing detailed editing work and to view a finished presentation.

Application Skills In this lesson, you begin work on a presentation for a charity foundation, as well as the presentation for Voyager Travel Adventures by editing text in Outline view and viewing the finished presentations in Reading view.

What You Can Do

Displaying the Presentation Outline

- It is sometimes easier to edit a presentation that has lots of text using the presentation outline.
- To display the outline, click the Outline tab in the Slides/Outline pane at the left of the Normal view window.
- The outline of the presentation displays in the pane. You can cut, copy, and edit text here as you would within slide placeholders and within Word.

✓ *Note: You will learn how to insert new slides from an outline in Microsoft Word in Lesson 19.*

Try It! Displaying the Presentation Outline

1. Start PowerPoint and open **PTry07** from the data files for this lesson.
2. Save the file as **PTry07_studentfirstname_studentlastname** in the location where your teacher instructs you to store the files for this lesson.
3. Click the Outline tab of the Slides/Outline pane in Normal view.

   ✓ *Note that the outline of the current slide is highlighted in the Outline tab.*
4. Read the presentation by scrolling through the outline using the scroll bar at the right of the Outline tab.
5. Click at the end of each every bullet in the outline (not including the titles of the slides) and insert a period.

   ✓ *Note that the slide displayed in the Slide pane changes as you click on bullets of subsequent slides. The Outline tab is good for this kind of detailed editing work.*
6. Save the **PTry07_studentfirstname_studentlastname** file and leave it open to use in the next Try It.

Viewing a Presentation in Reading View

- Reading view can be used instead of full-screen Slide Show view to see how a presentation will appear when you deliver it to an audience.
- Reading view includes a simple control menu you can use to copy slides and move around the presentation.
- Reading view is also useful for someone who wants to display your presentation on their computer, rather than on a large screen with Slide Show view.

Try It! Viewing a Presentation in Reading View

1. In the **PTry07_studentfirstname_studentlastname** file, click Reading View on the Status bar.
2. Click Next and Previous to scroll through the presentation.
3. Click Menu > Go to Slide > 4 Fair Use of Material.
4. Click Menu > Full Screen.
5. Click the left mouse button to advance to the next slide.
6. Right-click to display the shortcut menu, then click End Show.
7. Click Normal on the Status bar to return to Normal view.
8. Close **PTry07_studentfirstname_studentlastname**, saving all changes, and exit PowerPoint.

Project 13—Create It

The Power of Giving Presentation

DIRECTIONS

1. Start PowerPoint if necessary and open **PProj13** from the data files for this lesson. Save the file as **PProj13_studentfirstname_studentlastname** in the location where your teacher instructs you to store files for this lesson.
2. Go to slide 1 and click the Outline tab of the Slides/Outline pane in **Normal** view.
3. Click after *services* in the third bullet of slide 4, then press ENTER.
4. In the new fourth bullet, delete **or** and capitalize the word **every** to start the new bullet.

   ✓ *Note the changes as they appear in the slide displayed in the Slide pane.*
5. Delete the period at the end of the final bullet.
6. Click **Reading View** on the Status bar.
7. Click **Next** and **Previous** to scroll through the presentation.
8. Click **Menu** > **Go to Slide** > **3 Giving Can Mean...**.
9. Click **Menu** > **Full Screen**.
10. Click the left mouse button to advance to the next slide.
11. Right-click to display the shortcut menu, then click **End Show**.
12. If necessary, click **Normal** on the Status bar to return to Normal view.
13. Click **Review** > **Spelling** to check spelling in the presentation. Click **OK**.
14. **With your teacher's permission,** click **File** > **Print**. Select **Print All Slides**, then click **Print** to print the presentation.
15. Click **Save** to save your work, then click **File** > **Exit** to close the file and close PowerPoint.

Project 14—Apply It

Travel Adventures Presentation

DIRECTIONS

1. Start PowerPoint, if necessary.
2. Open **PProj14** from the data files for this lesson.
3. Save the presentation as **PProj14_studentfirstname_studentlastname** in the location where your teacher instructs you to store the files for this lesson.
4. Display the presentation in the **Outline** tab.
5. On slide 2, add the text shown in Figure 7-1.

   ✓ *Remember, you can press ENTER in the Outline tab to enter a new bullet in the list, and press TAB to decrease the level of an item within the outline.*

6. View the presentation in **Reading** view, then return to **Normal** view.
7. Check the spelling.
8. **With your teacher's permission,** print the presentation.
9. Close the presentation, saving all changes, and exit PowerPoint.

Figure 7-1

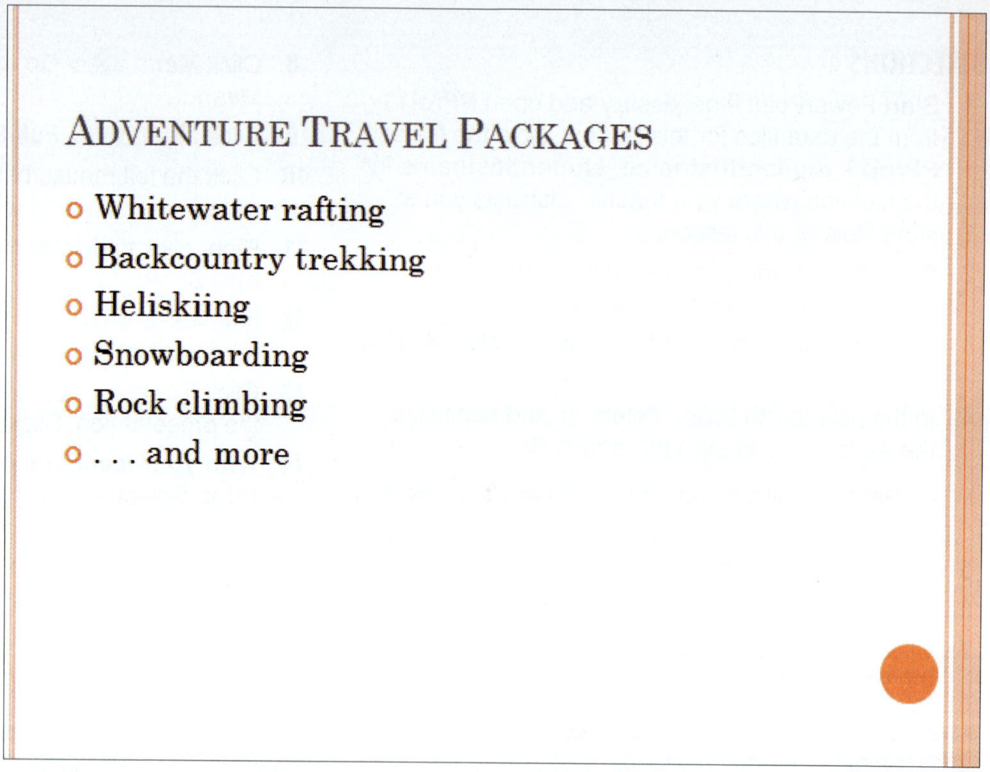

Lesson 8

Arranging Slides

➤ What You Will Learn

Copying, Duplicating, and Deleting Slides
Rearranging Slides In Slide Sorter View

Software Skills As you work on a presentation, you often need to copy, delete, or rearrange slides. Slide Sorter view is the best view to use when arranging slides in a presentation.

Application Skills In this lesson, you begin work on presentations for Restoration Architecture, a local architecture firm, as well as starting a presentation on strategic planning. You will modify these presentations by copying, moving, and deleting slides in Slide Sorter view.

What You Can Do

Copying, Duplicating, and Deleting Slides

- In the course of working with a presentation, you may often need to create slides similar to one another. You can simplify this process by copying or duplicating slides.
  - Copy a slide if you want to paste the copy some distance from the original or in another presentation.
  - Duplicate a slide to create an identical version immediately after the original slide.
- To remove a slide from the presentation, delete it using the Cut button on the Home tab, or press DEL. Note that PowerPoint does not ask you if you're sure you want to delete a slide—the slide is immediately deleted. If you change your mind about the deletion, use Undo to restore the slide.

Try It! Copying, Duplicating, and Deleting Slides

1. Start PowerPoint and open **PTry08** from the data files for this lesson.
2. Save the file as **PTry08_studentfirstname_studentlastname** in the location where your teacher instructs you to store the files for this lesson.
3. Click Slide Sorter, then click slide 3.
4. Click Home > Copy.
5. Click in the space between slides 4 and 5, then click Paste.

   ✓ *Note that a large vertical blinking cursor appears in the space between two slides when you have clicked there or dragged a slide there.*
6. Click slide 8, then click Home > Copy > Duplicate.
7. With slide 8 selected, click Home > Cut.
8. Save the **PTry08_studentfirstname_studentlastname** file and leave it open to use in the next Try It.

Rearranging Slides in Slide Sorter View

- Another task you must frequently undertake when working with slides is to rearrange them. Slide Sorter view is your best option for moving slides from one place in a presentation to another.
- Rearrange slides in Slide Sorter view by simply dragging a slide to a new location.
- You can also rearrange slides in the Slides tab in Normal view, using the same dragging technique. This is an easy process in a presentation that has only a few slides, but for a large presentation, Slide Sorter view is the better choice because you can see more slides at a time without scrolling.

Try It! Rearranging Slides in Slide Sorter View

1. In the **PTry08_studentfirstname_studentlastname** file, click slide 5 and drag it to the end of the presentation, after slide 8.
2. Select slide 8 and press DEL.
3. Click slide 7 and drag it to the position between slides 5 and 6.
4. Click slide 2 and drag it after slide 7.
5. Again, click slide 2 and drag it after slide 7.
6. Close **PTry08_studentfirstname_studentlastname**, saving all changes, and exit PowerPoint.

Project 15—Create It

Restoration Architecture Presentation

DIRECTIONS

1. Start PowerPoint if necessary and open **PProj15** from the data files for this lesson. Save the file as **PProj15_studentfirstname_studentlastname** in the location where your teacher instructs you to store files for this lesson.
2. Click **Slide Sorter**, then click slide 11.
3. Click **Home** > **Copy** > **Duplicate**.
4. Click and drag slide 12 to the space between slides 4 and 5.
5. Click and drag slide 11 to the space between slides 4 and 5.

6. Click **File** > **Open** and navigate to the location where the files for this lesson are stored. Open **PProj15_gallery**.
7. Click **Slide Sorter**, then hold the CTRL key down while you click to select slides 1, 2, and 3.
8. Click **Home** > **Copy**.
9. In the **PProj15_studentfirstname_studentlastname** presentation, click between slides 6 and 7, then click **Home** > **Paste**.
10. Click slide 15, then press DEL. Your presentation should look like the one shown in Figure 8-1.
11. **With your teacher's permission,** click **File** > **Print**. Select **Full Page Slides** > **6 Slides Horizontal**, then click **Print** to print the presentation.
12. Click **Save** to save your work, then click **File** > **Exit** to close both the **PProj15_studentfirstname_studentlastname** and **PProj15_gallery** files and close PowerPoint.

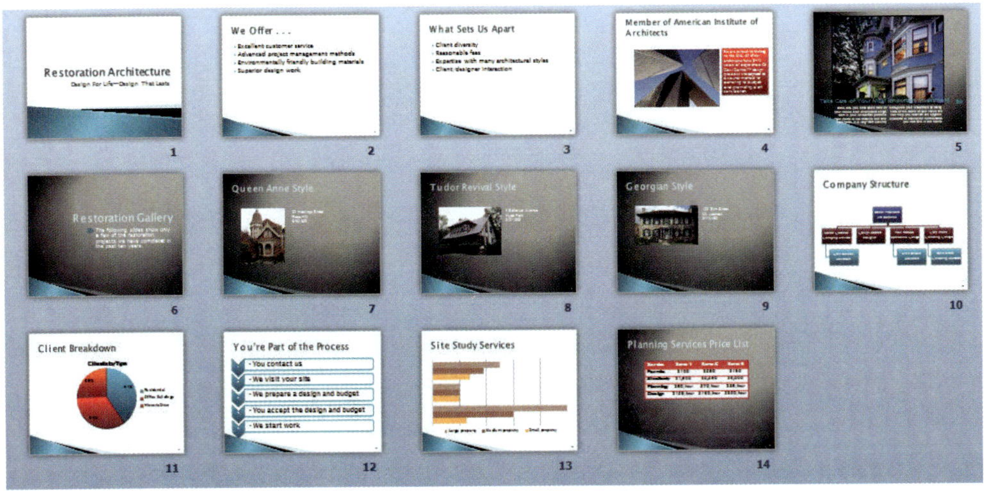

Figure 8-1

Project 16—Apply It

Recommending a Strategy Presentation

DIRECTIONS

1. Start PowerPoint, if necessary.
2. Open **PProj16** from the data files for this lesson.
3. Save the presentation as **PProj16_studentfirstname_studentlastname** in the location where your teacher instructs you to store the files for this lesson.
4. Change to Slide Sorter view.
5. Move slide 2 to follow slide 3.
6. Duplicate slide 4.
7. Double-click slide 5 to return to Normal view and change the title of slide 5 to **Additional Options**.
8. Open **PProj16_slide.**
9. Copy the slide and then paste it after slide 5 in **PProj16_studentfirstname_studentlastname**.
10. Change to Slide Sorter view again to view the sequence of the slides, which should look like that shown in Figure 8-2.
11. Check the spelling.
12. **With your teacher's permission,** print the presentation.
13. Close both presentations, saving all changes, and exit PowerPoint.

Figure 8-2

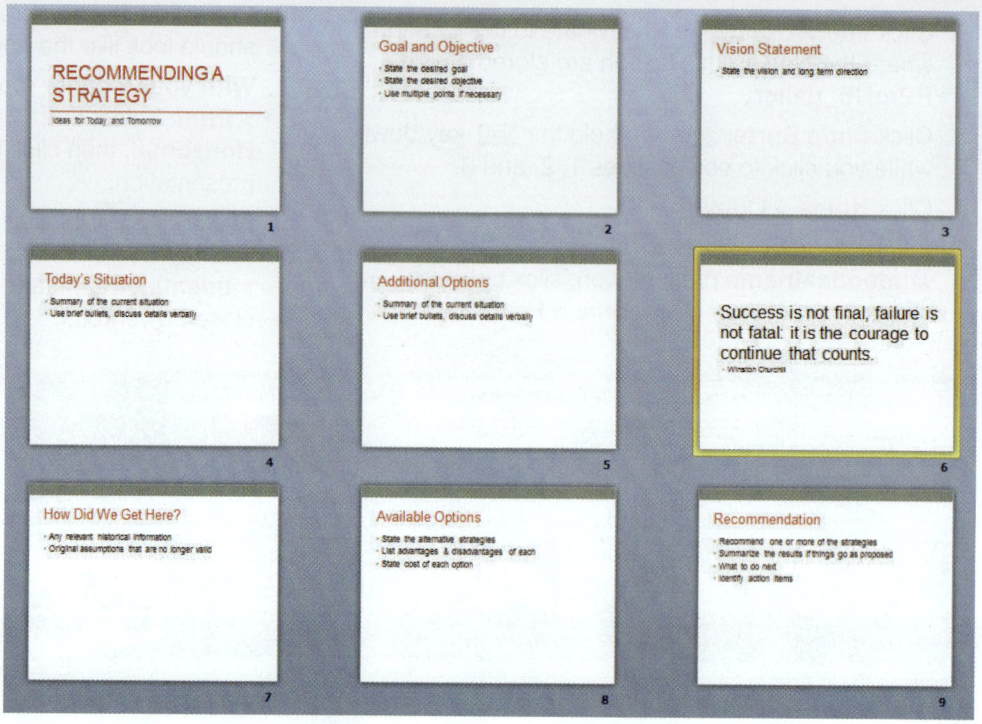
RECOMMENDING A STRATEGY
Ideas for Today and Tomorrow
1
Goal and Objective
State the desired goal
State the desired objective
Use multiple points if necessary
2
Vision Statement
State the vision and long term direction
3
Today's Situation
Summary of the current situation
Use brief bullets, discuss details verbally
4
Additional Options
Summary of the current situation
Use brief bullets, discuss details verbally
5
Success is not final, failure is not fatal: it is the courage to continue that counts.
Winston Churchill
6
How Did We Get Here?
Any relevant historical information
Original assumptions that are no longer valid
7
Available Options
State the alternative strategies
List advantages & disadvantages of each
State cost of each option
8
Recommendation
Recommend one or more of the strategies
Summarize the results if things go as proposed
What to do next
Identify action items
9

Lesson 9

Adding Slide Transitions

➤ What You Will Learn

Identifying Guidelines for Using Graphics, Fonts, and Special Effects in Presentations

Evaluating and Selecting Appropriate Sources of Information

Adding Slide Transitions

Controlling Slide Advance

WORDS TO KNOW

Transitions
The visual effects used when one slide moves off of the screen and another moves onto the screen.

Advance slide timing
A setting that controls the amount of time a slide displays on the screen.

Software Skills PowerPoint allows you to add transitions to make your slides more visually interesting during a presentation. After you set up the transitions, you can rehearse the show to make sure you have allowed enough time for the audience to view slide content.

Application Skills In this lesson, you continue to work on the presentation for the charity organization as well as the Holmes Medical Center laser surgery unit by adding appropriate slide transitions.

What You Can Do

Identifying Guidelines for Using Graphics, Fonts, and Special Effects in Presentations

- When working with graphic information such as a PowerPoint presentation, keep in mind that you should avoid overloading a presentation with too many graphics, fonts, and special effects.
- Make sure all graphics you use, including photos, clip art, and custom shapes, fit with the color scheme of the slide or presentation, and serve a purpose for conveying your message.
- PowerPoint Themes make it easy to provide visual interest with color and fonts that are combined in a pleasing way. You can modify fonts to make key information stand out or provide additional visual appeal to a presentation.

- Make sure that all text stands out against placeholder backgrounds and is large enough to be readable. Also, make sure you're using text effects such as bold, italic, and underline in an appropriate way. And don't get too carried away with special effects like drop shadows.
- PowerPoint also provides a wide variety of slide transitions and special effects to provide interest and movement as you present a slide show. Again, make sure that the effects you use are appropriate to the visual theme and the message of the presentation.
- In most cases, simpler, more subtle transition effects will prove to be most effective, and won't detract from the message you're delivering.

Evaluating and Selecting Appropriate Sources of Information

- When doing research for a project or presentation, it's important to evaluate and select appropriate sources of information, whether the source is print, electronic, video, or a person you interview.
- Use Internet search engines and bookmarks to locate and access information. Basic and advanced search techniques will help you pinpoint exactly what you need to find using search engines, directories, biographical dictionaries, and other research tools.
- Be sure to evaluate the accuracy and validity of the information you find by understanding the author's point of view, credentials, and any potential bias that might come as a result of his or her position.
- Finding information on the Internet often gives a source more credibility than it may deserve. It's important to be able to decide what is someone's opinion, and what is a fact backed up by research and data.
- As always, cite the sources of the information, and request permission to use if necessary.

Adding Slide Transitions

- PowerPoint provides **transitions** that you can use to make the slide show more interesting. You can apply transitions in either Normal view or Slide Sorter view using tools on the Transitions tab.
- The Transition gallery offers almost 60 different transitions. If you are in Normal view, clicking on a transition previews the transition on the current slide. In Slide Sorter view, select a transition from the gallery to apply it and see a preview of the effect.
- The Transition gallery organizes transition effects by Subtle, Exciting, and Dynamic Content.
- The Transitions tab offers several other important options. You can:
  - Select a sound effect or sound clip to accompany the transition.
  - Choose a duration for the transition effect.
  - Choose how to advance slides: by clicking the mouse or automatically based on a specific time lapse. This option is discussed further in the next section.
  - Apply settings to all slides at the same time.
  - After you have applied a transition, you can use the Preview button to review all effects you have applied to the slides.

Try It! Adding Slide Transitions

1. Start PowerPoint and open PTry09 from the data files for this lesson.
2. Save the file as PTry09_studentfirstname_studentlastname in the location where your teacher instructs you to store the files for this lesson.
3. With slide 1 selected, click Transitions, then double-click Reveal.

   ✓ *Note that a star with lines appears next to the slide thumbnail in the Slides pane at left to indicate a transition has been applied.*
4. Go to slide 2 and then double-click Fade from the Transitions gallery.
5. Go to slide 3, then double-click Flash from the Transitions gallery.

(continued)

Try It! Adding Slide Transitions *(continued)*

6. Go to slide 4, then double-click Random Bars from the Transitions gallery.
7. Go to slide 5, then double-click Ripple from the Transitions gallery.
8. Go to slide 6, then double-click Fly Through from the Transitions gallery.
9. Go to slide 1, then click Transitions > Preview. Click Slide Sorter, then click each slide and Preview the transition.
10. Click Normal, go to slide 1, then click Sound > Drum Roll. Click Apply to All.
11. Click Slide Show > From Beginning to view the transitions with the sound. Click to exit the slide show.
12. Try experimenting with the different Effect Options by clicking Transition > Effect Options.
13. You can also try changing the duration of transitions by entering times in the duration text box, or clicking the up or down arrows to increase or decrease the time.
14. Save the **PTry09_studentfirstname_studentlastname** file and leave it open to use in the next Try It.

Controlling Slide Advance

- By default, you advance slides in a presentation manually by clicking the mouse button or a keyboard key. If you do not want to advance slides manually, you can have PowerPoint advance each slide automatically.
- **Advance slide timing** defines the amount of time a slide is on the screen before PowerPoint automatically advances to the next slide.
- You can set advance slide timing on the Transitions tab for individual slides or for all slides in a presentation. Set advance slide timing in seconds or minutes and seconds.
- Even if you set advance timings for your slides, you can also choose to advance a slide manually.
- The advance slide timing for each slide is indicated in Slide Sorter view by a number below the slide.

Try It! Controlling Slide Advance

1. In the **PTry09_studentfirstname_studentlastname** file, click Slide Sorter.
2. Click slide 1, then click Advance Slide After and type **5**.
3. Click Apply To All.
4. Click Sound > No Sound, then click Apply To All.
5. Click Slide Show > From Beginning to view the transitions without the sound. Click to exit the slide show.
6. Close **PTry09_studentfirstname_studentlastname**, saving all changes, and exit PowerPoint.

Project 17—Create It

The Power of Giving Presentation

DIRECTIONS

1. Start PowerPoint if necessary and open **PProj17** from the data files for this lesson. Save the file as **PProj17_studentfirstname_studentlastname** in the location where your teacher instructs you to store files for this lesson.
2. Go to slide 1 and click **Transitions**, then double-click **Wipe** from the Transitions gallery.
3. Go to slide 2 and double-click **Wipe** from the Transitions gallery.
4. Go to slide 3 and double-click **Cover** from the Transitions gallery.
5. Go to slide 4 and double-click **Flip** from the Transitions gallery.
6. Go to slide 5 and double-click **Doors** from the Transitions gallery.
7. Go to slide 6 and double-click **Conveyor** from the Transitions gallery.
8. Go to slide 7 and double-click **Shape** from the Transitions gallery.
9. Go to slide 1, click **Slide Sorter**, then click each slide to preview the transition.
10. Click **Normal**, go to slide 1, then click **Sound** > **Chime**.
11. Click **Transitions** > **Effect Options** > **From Left**.
12. Click **Advance Slide After**, then enter **5** in the text box. Click **Apply To All**.
13. Click **Slide Show** > **From Beginning** to view the transitions. Click to exit the slide show.
14. **With your teacher's permission,** click **File** > **Print**. Select **Full Page Slides** > **6 Slides Horizontal**, then click **Print** to print the presentation.
15. Click **Save** to save your work, then click **File** > **Exit** to close the **PProj17_studentfirstname_studentlastname** file and close PowerPoint.

Project 18—Apply It

Laser Surgery Presentation

DIRECTIONS

1. Start PowerPoint, if necessary.
2. Open **PProj18** from the data files for this lesson.
3. Save the presentation as **PProj18_studentfirstname_studentlastname** in the location where your teacher instructs you to store the files for this lesson.
4. Apply several different slide transitions to the slides. View the slides in Slide Show view to see the transitions.
5. Apply the **Laser** sound to the first slide and the last slide.
6. Choose to advance all slides after 5 seconds.
7. View the presentation as a slide show, without clicking the mouse to advance each slide.
8. Check the spelling.
9. **With your teacher's permission,** print the presentation.
10. Close the presentation, saving all changes, and exit PowerPoint.

Chapter Assessment and Application

Project 19—Make It Your Own

Aquatic Center Presentation

The student athletics council has asked you to update a presentation about the benefits of the campus aquatics center. Follow the guidelines below to make a stronger case for all members of the local community to use the aquatics center.

DIRECTIONS

1. Start PowerPoint. Save a new blank file as **PProj19_studentfirstname_studentlastname** in the location where your teacher tells you to save the files for this project.
2. Apply a theme from the themes available on the Design tab. Pick one that you think is appropriate for the audience. Apply a different color theme if the colors in the design you chose are not bright and cheerful.
3. On slide 1, type **Campus Recreation Center** in the Title placeholder. In the subtitle placeholder, type your full name.
4. Add two new **Title and Content** slides. On slide 2, type **CRC Introduces . . .** in the Title placeholder. In the content placeholder, type the following bullets:
   - **The Bedard Aquatics Center**
     - **Lap pool—50 meters by 25 yards, with 1 meter and 3 meter diving boards**
     - **Leisure pool—features a current channel, vortex, and water wall**
     - **Whirlpool—temperature ranges from 101 degrees to 104 degrees**
5. On slide 3, type **Why We're Talking** in the Title placeholder. In the content placeholder, type the following bullets:
   - **The Aquatics Center is currently underused**
   - **Maintaining fitness is a lifelong goal for students, faculty, staff, and community members**
   - **Surveys suggest the university community is interested in regular visits to the CRC**
   - **Talking about the Center will increase that interest**
6. Open the file **PProj19_swim** from the data files for this chapter and copy the slides from this presentation. Paste the slides after slide 3 of **PProj19_studentfirstname_studentlastname**. Close the **PProj19_swim** file. Reset slide 6 if the chart overlaps the title.
7. Move slide 3 to the end of the presentation.
8. Go to the new slide 3, titled **Specific Programs**, and select the content placeholder. Change the text formatting to **Calibri, 36 pt**. Change the font color to one of the Theme colors. Be sure to choose one that stands out enough to be readable.
9. Use the Format Painter to apply this text formatting to the level 1 bullets in slides 4 and 7.
10. If necessary, use text AutoFit options to resize the text on slide 7.
11. Display the presentation outline and promote the three bullets under *The Bedard Aquatics Center* to the same level as the first bullet. (Right-click each item and click Promote.)
12. Change the slide layout of slide 5 to **Two Content**. In the right placeholder, insert the picture **PProj19_youthswim** from the location where the data files for this chapter are stored.
13. Move the picture up to align with the top of the chart at left. Apply a picture style and artistic effect of your choice.
14. In Slide Sorter view, move slides 3 and 4 after slide 6.
15. Insert a footer that includes the **Date and time**, the **Slide number**, and your full name. Don't show these on the title slide. Include the page number on notes and handouts pages.
16. Add speaker's notes to slide 5 that say **Don't forget to mention unlimited lap swimming hours!**

17. Find **university** and replace with **University**. Be sure to match case when you replace. Replace the **Calibri** font with **Agency FB** throughout the presentation.
18. On slide 5, adjust line spacing to **1.5**.
19. Add slide transitions, sounds, and timings of your choosing.
20. View the presentation in Reading view.
21. Check spelling, and, **with your instructor's permission,** print one copy of your presentation.
22. Close the presentation, saving changes, and exit PowerPoint.

Project 20—Master It

Franchise Sales Presentation

As a new sales manager for Great Grains Bakery, you have been asked by one of representatives if you can help him spruce up his presentation for customers and potential franchisees. Follow the guidelines below to add stronger introductory slides to the presentation, additional photos and text formatting, as well as a new theme and transitions.

DIRECTIONS

1. Start PowerPoint, if necessary, and open **PProj20** from the data files for this chapter. Save the file as **PProj20_studentfirstname_studentlastname** in the location where your teacher tells you to save the files for this project.
2. Apply a theme from the themes available on the Design tab. Pick one that you think is appropriate for the audience. Adjust placement of the objects on slide 4 if necessary.
3. Insert three new slides before slide 1. Make the first new slide a **Title** slide, the second new slide a **Two Content** slide, and the third new slide should be a **Title and Content** slide.
4. On slide 1, type **Great Grains Bakery** in the Title placeholder. In the subtitle placeholder, enter **Fresh to You Each Day**.
5. On slide 2, type **A Variety of Baked Goods** in the Title placeholder. In the left content placeholder, type the following bullets:
   - **Breads**
   - **Croissants**
   - **Bagels**
   - **Muffins**
   - **Rolls**
6. On slide 2, in the right content placeholder, type the following bullets:
   - **Sweet specialties**
   - **Pastries**
   - **Cookies**
   - **Cakes**
7. On slide 3, type **Fresh Is Best!** in the Title placeholder. In the content placeholder, type the following bullets:
   - **Locally grown herbs**
   - **Whole grain flours**
   - **Fresh creamery butter**
   - **Free range eggs**
   - **Locally produced honey**
   - **Fair trade coffee and chocolate**
   - **Certified organic fruits and vegetables**
   - **Local and imported cheeses**
8. Change the title and text fonts throughout the presentation to a font, font size, and font color of your choice. Check all slides for text alignment and fit within placeholders after making the change.
9. Insert the **PProj20_bagel** picture on a slide of your choice; resize and position appropriately. Add picture styles and formatting to the photo you inserted and the photo on slide 7.
10. Change the footer to show only your full name.
11. Add speaker's notes to slide 6 that say **Remind seminar audiences that franchises are going fast!**
12. In Slide Sorter view, move slides 6 and 7 after slide 9. Copy slide 5 and add it to the end of the presentation.
13. Add slide transitions, sounds, and timings of your choosing.
14. View the presentation in Reading view.
15. Check spelling, and, **with your instructor's permission,** print one copy of your presentation.
16. Close the presentation, saving changes, and exit PowerPoint.

Chapter 2

Working with Lists and Graphics

Lesson 10
Working with Bulleted and Numbered Lists
Projects 21-22

- Removing a Bullet Symbol from a Bullet Point
- Changing a Bulleted List to a Numbered List
- Modifying the Bulleted List Style
- Changing Bullets on the Slide Master

Lesson 11
Using Clip Art and Pictures
Projects 23-24

- Inserting Clip Art
- Resizing and Positioning Clip Art
- Inserting a Photo from the Clip Art Task Pane
- Removing the Background from a Picture

Lesson 12
Inserting Symbols and Text Boxes
Projects 25-26

- Inserting Symbols
- Inserting and Formatting a Text Box
- Using Multiple Columns in a Text Box

Lesson 13
Drawing and Formatting Shapes
Projects 27-28

- Using Rulers, Guides, and Gridlines
- Drawing Shapes
- Moving and Sizing Shapes
- Applying Fills and Outlines
- Applying Shape Effects
- Applying Shape Styles
- Adding Text to Shapes

Lesson 14
Positioning and Grouping Shapes
Projects 29-30

- Stacking Objects
- Grouping Objects
- Duplicating Objects
- Aligning and Distributing Objects

Lesson 15
Creating WordArt
Projects 31-32

- Understanding WordArt
- Applying WordArt Styles to Existing Text
- Inserting and Formatting WordArt

Lesson 16
Creating SmartArt Diagrams
Projects 33-34

- Creating a SmartArt Diagram
- Adding, Removing, and Resizing Shapes in a Diagram
- Reordering Diagram Content
- Changing the Diagram Type
- Changing the Color and Style of a Diagram
- Creating Picture-Based SmartArt

Lesson 17
Creating a Photo Album
Projects 35-36

- Creating a Photo Album

End of Chapter Assessments
Projects 37-38

Lesson 10

Working with Bulleted and Numbered Lists

WORDS TO KNOW

Layout Master
A template on which individual slides that use a certain layout are based.

Picture bullet
A graphic specifically designed to be used as a bullet character.

Slide Master
A template on which the individual slides in the presentation are based.

➤ What You Will Learn

Removing a Bullet Symbol from a Bullet Point
Changing a Bulleted List to a Numbered List
Modifying the Bulleted List Style
Changing Bullets on the Slide Master

Software Skills Bullet points are the most common format for presenting data in a PowerPoint presentation. Sometimes, though, the default bulleted list needs a little uplift to keep it from being repetitive. This lesson shows you how to make some changes to a bulleted list, including how to convert it into a list that doesn't use bullets at all.

Application Skills At Wynnedale Medical, the manager you have created a presentation for has commented that she does not like the bullet character in the draft presentation. You will change to a different bullet character, and demonstrate on a few slides how the presentation might look with numbered lists or with no bullets at all.

What You Can Do

Removing a Bullet Symbol from a Bullet Point

- In some cases, you may not want bullets at all. Sometimes a regular paragraph is more appropriate for a slide than a series of bulleted items.

- You can easily remove the bullets from paragraphs with the Bullets button on the Home tab. This button is an on/off toggle for the Bullets feature.

✓ *The Bullets button also has a drop-down list for selecting a different bullet character. You will learn how to switch characters later in this chapter.*

Try It! Removing a Bullet Symbol from a Bullet Point

1. Start PowerPoint and open **PTry10** from the data files for this lesson.
2. Save the presentation as **PTry10_studentfirstname_studentlastname** in the location where your teacher instructs you to store the files for this lesson.
3. Click to move the insertion point into the first bulleted paragraph on slide 2.
4. Click Home > Bullets. The bullet character is toggled off.
5. Click Home > Bullets. The bullet character is toggled back on again.
6. Save the changes to the **PTry10_studentfirstname_studentlastname** file and leave it open to use in the next Try It.

Changing a Bulleted List to a Numbered List

- Numbered lists are almost identical to bulleted ones except they use consecutive numbers rather than using the same character for each paragraph.
- Use a numbered list whenever the order of the items is significant, such as in step-by-step instructions.

✓ *Avoid using numbered lists when the order is not significant, because the audience may erroneously read significance into it.*

Try It! Changing a Bulleted List to a Numbered List

1. In the **PTry10_studentfirstname_studentlastname** file, click slide 6 to display it.
2. Drag across the entire bulleted list to select it.

   OR

   Click to move the insertion point into the bulleted list and press CTRL + A to select all.
3. Click Home > Numbering. The list becomes numbered.
4. Save the changes to the **PTry10_studentfirstname_studentlastname** file and leave it open to use in the next Try It.

Modifying the Bulleted List Style

- There are two ways of modifying a bulleted list's style. You can manually edit the individual paragraphs or lists that you want to specifically affect, or you can change the overall style for bulleted lists on the Slide Master.
- A wide variety of bullet characters are available, including symbols and pictures. You can select a bullet character from any font installed on your PC, or from a large collection of **picture bullets**.
- Changes to the default bullet are made in the Bullets and Numbering dialog box.

Try It! Modifying the Bulleted List Style

1. In the **PTry10_studentfirstname_studentlastname** file, click slide 2 to display it.
2. Click anywhere in the bulleted list and press CTRL + A to select all.
3. On the Home tab, in the Paragraph group, click the down arrow on the Bullets button, opening its menu.
4. Click the small round bullets on the menu. The bullets change.
5. With the bulleted list still selected from the previous steps, click the down arrow on the Bullets button again.
6. Click Bullets and Numbering to open the Bullets and Numbering dialog box.
7. Click the Customize button. The Symbol dialog box opens.
8. If the Wingdings font is not already selected in the Font list, open the Font list and click Wingdings.

Select a symbol

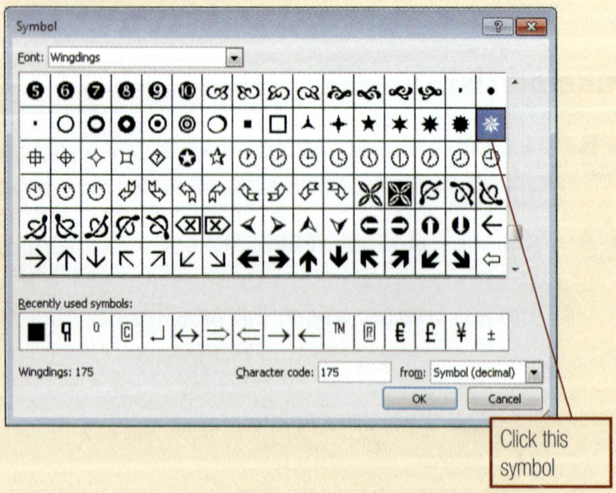

✓ *You can choose any character from any font as a bullet symbol. Wingdings is a font designed specifically for this purpose, but you may have others available that have interesting bullet characters, too.*

9. Click a fancy star symbol in Symbol dialog box. and click OK.
10. Click the up increment arrow next to the Size text box 10 times, increasing the size of the bullet to 110%.
11. Open the Color button's palette and click Dark Red, Accent 5 color from the theme colors.
12. Click OK. The bullets on the slide change.
13. Save the changes to the **PTry10_studentfirstname_studentlastname** file and leave it open to use in the next Try It.

Select a color

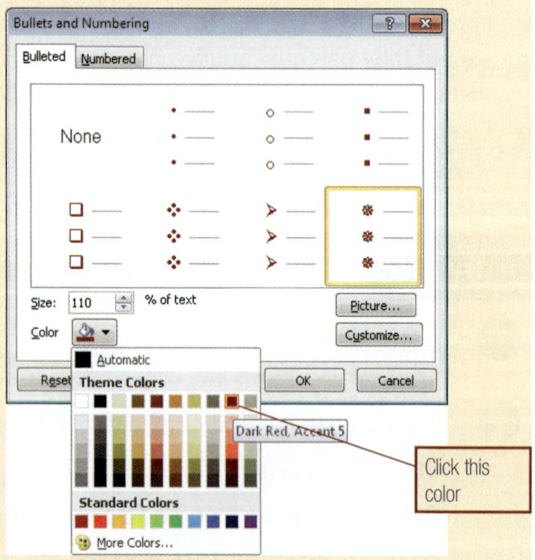

Try It! Using a Picture as a Bullet Character

1. In the **PTry10_studentfirstname_studentlastname** file, click slide 3 to select it.
2. Click anywhere in the bulleted list and press CTRL + A to select all.
3. On the Home tab, in the Paragraph group, click the down arrow on the Bullets button, opening its menu.
4. Click Bullets and Numbering.
5. Click Picture. The Picture Bullet dialog box opens.
6. Scroll through the list and click on a green sphere graphic. Click OK. The bullet character changes.
7. Save the changes to the **PTry10_studentfirstname_studentlastname** file, and leave it open to use in the next Try It.

Changing Bullets on the Slide Master

- The **Slide Master** is the template on which each slide is based. When you modify the Slide Master, all slides that use that template are affected. If you want to affect all the bullets in the presentation, regardless of the slide layout, make the changes here.
- A slide master has one or more Layout Masters. Each **Layout Master** determines the placement of the text boxes and other placeholders for a certain slide layout. If you want to affect the bullets only on slides that use a certain layout, make the changes on that particular layout's Layout Master.

Try It! Changing Bullets on the Slide Master

1. In the **PTry10_studentfirstname_studentlastname** file, click View > Slide Master.
2. In the Slides pane at the left, click the top thumbnail image on the list (the Slide Master itself).
3. On the Slide Master slide, click in the paragraph that reads *Click to edit Master text styles*.
4. On the Home tab, click the down arrow on the Bullets button and click the white circles preset.

   ✓ *Only the bullet character for the first level of bullets changes. You can specify a different character for each of the preset levels here if desired.*
5. On the Slide Master tab, click Close Master View to return to the presentation.

   ✓ *Notice that the slides you manually changed earlier in this lesson are not affected by the new bullet character selection. That's because manual settings override the automatic ones.*

Change the bullet on the Slide Master

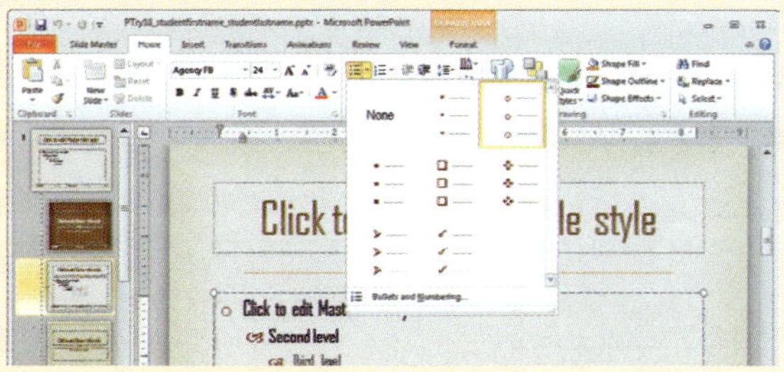

6. Click slide 2 in the Slides pane, click in the bulleted list, and press CTRL + A to select all.
7. Click Home > Bullets, removing the old bullet character.
8. Click Bullets again, applying the new default bullet character (the circle).
9. Repeat steps 6–8 for slide 3.
10. Save the changes to the **PTry10_studentfirstname_studentlastname** file and leave it open to use in the next Try It.

Try It! Changing the Bullets on a Layout Master

1. In the **PTry10_studentfirstname_studentlastname** file, click View > Slide Master .

2. In the Slides pane at the left, click the fifth thumbnail image from the top (the Two Content Layout).

3. Click in the left placeholder box of the layout and press CTRL + A to select all levels of bullets in that box.

4. On the Home tab, open the Bullets buttons list and click the filled square bullet character.

5. Click Slide Master > Close Master View .

6. Save the **PTry10_studentfirstname_studentlastname** file and close it.

Choose a filled square bullet for only one placeholder box, in only this one layout

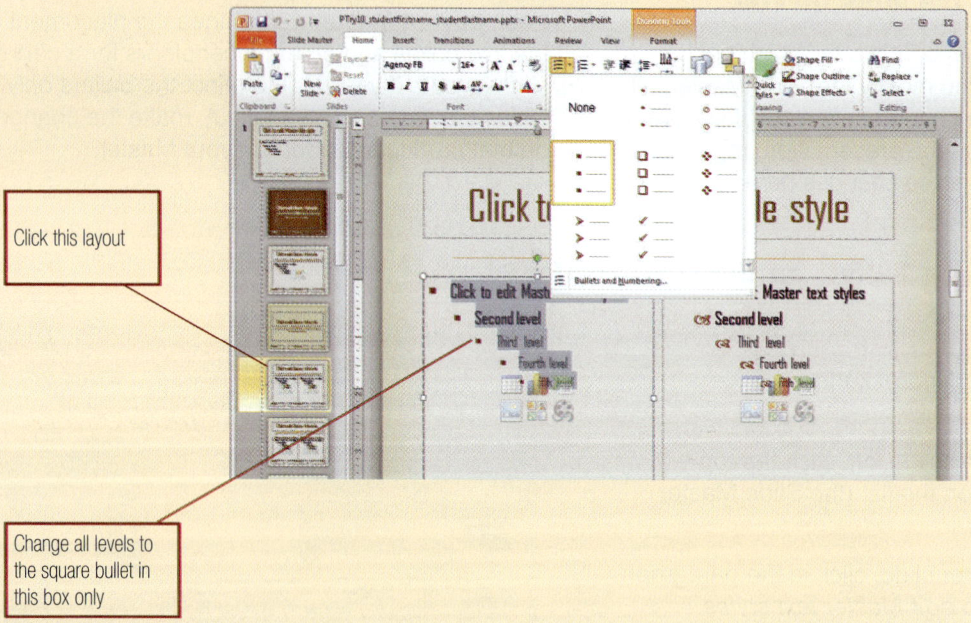

Project 21—Create It

Laser Surgery Presentation

DIRECTIONS

1. Start PowerPoint if necessary, and open **PProj21** from the data files for this lesson.
2. Save the presentation as **PProj21_studentfirstname_studentlastname** in the location where your teacher instructs you to store the files for this lesson.
3. Display slide 1, and click **Insert** > **Text Box**. Click at the bottom of the slide and type your full name.

   ✓ *Remember to replace the sample text studentfirstname with your own first name and studentlastname with your own last name.*
4. Click **View** > **Slide Master**.
5. Click the top slide in the Slides pane (the Slide Master).
6. Click in the bulleted list area, and press CTRL + A to select all.
7. On the **Home** tab, click the down arrow on the Bullets button, opening a menu.
8. Click **Bullets and Numbering**. The Bullets and Numbering dialog box opens.
9. Click **Customize**. The Symbol dialog box opens.
10. Open the Font drop-down list and click **ZapfDingbats**.

    ✓ *If you do not have this font, choose Wingdings.*
11. Click a check mark symbol.
12. Click **OK** to close the Symbol dialog box.
13. Click **OK** to close the Bullets and Numbering dialog box.
14. Click **Slide Master** > **Close Master View**.
15. Browse through the slides. Each slide should use the check mark bullet.
16. **With your teacher's permission**, print slide 2 of the presentation.

    ✓ *Refer to Lesson 2 of the Basics section of this book for information on printing a file.*
17. Close the presentation, saving changes, and exit PowerPoint.

Project 22—Apply It

Laser Surgery Presentation

DIRECTIONS

1. Start PowerPoint if necessary, and open **PProj22** from the data files for this lesson.
2. Save the presentation as **PProj22_studentfirstname_studentlastname** in the location where your teacher instructs you to store the files for this lesson.
3. Display slide 1, and place a text box at the bottom of the slide containing your full name.
4. Open Slide Master view, and change the bullet character for all slides (all layouts) to a picture bullet. Choose any yellow sphere from the Picture Bullet dialog box.
5. On the Title and Content Layout Master, change only the first-level bullet character to any red sphere picture bullet. Set the bullet size to 100% of Text.
6. Close Master view.
7. Remove the bullet from the paragraph on slide 7.
8. Convert the bullet points on slide 6 to a numbered list.
9. Browse the presentation in Slide Sorter view, looking at the bullets on the slides. See Figure 10-1.

   ✓ *Notice that slides 3 and 5 use the yellow bullet because they do not use the Title and Content layout. The slides that use Title and Content as their layout appear with red bullets.*

10. **With your teacher's permission**, print the presentation as handouts (6 slides per page).
11. Close the presentation, saving changes, and exit PowerPoint.

Figure 10-1

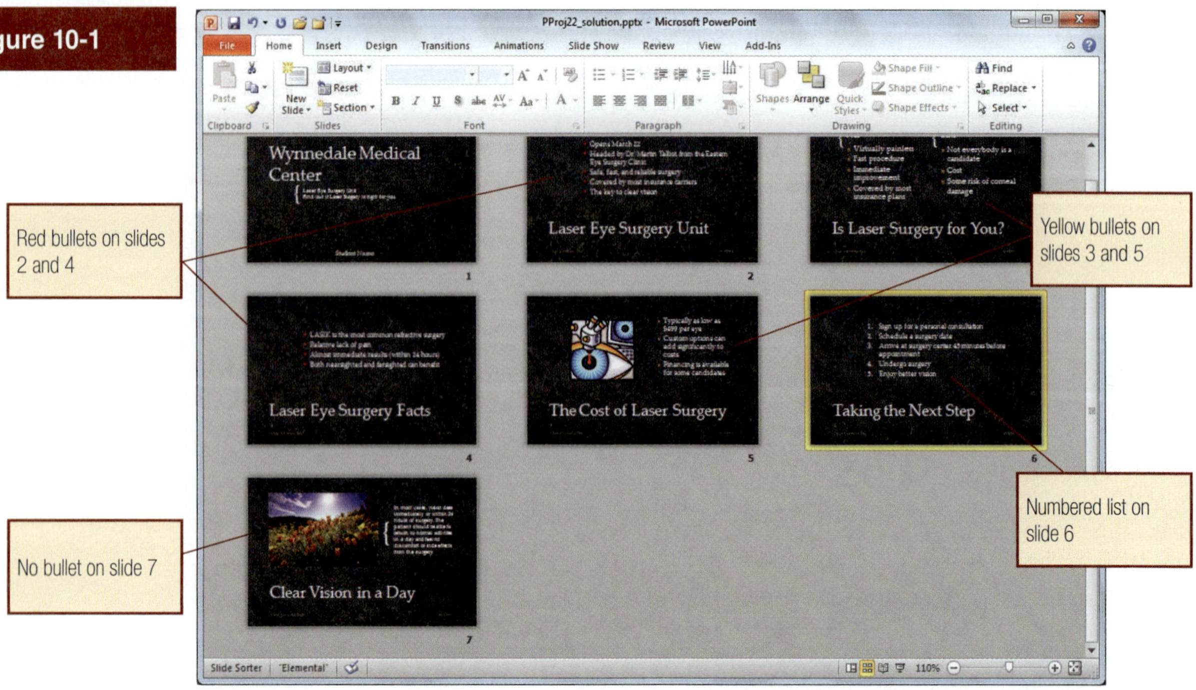

Lesson 11

Using Clip Art and Pictures

➤ What You Will Learn

Inserting Clip Art
Resizing and Positioning Clip Art
Inserting a Photo from the Clip Art Task Pane
Removing the Background from a Picture

Software Skills Clip art can be a tremendous asset to you as you create presentations. Your copy of PowerPoint includes free access to a huge library of ready-made drawings on Microsoft's Web site. You can access them through the Clip Art feature in PowerPoint.

Application Skills In this lesson, you continue to work with the Wynnedale Medical Center presentation. You will select appropriate clip art images and insert them in the presentation to enhance its appearance.

WORDS TO KNOW

Clip art
Generic, reusable drawings of common people, places, things, and concepts.

Keyword
A descriptive word attached to an image, used for searching and indexing the image library.

What You Can Do

Inserting Clip Art

- **Clip art** can be used in any Office application, but is especially suitable for PowerPoint because of the graphical focus of most slides.
- If you are connected to the Internet when you search for clips, PowerPoint automatically searches the large Office.com collection of clips. Otherwise, fewer clips are returned when you search, from the much smaller collection stored on your hard disk.

- You can find clip art by searching for specific **keywords**. Each clip art image has one or more keywords assigned to it that describe it. For example, a picture of a dog might include the keywords *dog, pup, canine, animal,* and *pet*.
- If the slide contains an open Content placeholder, you can place the clip art using that. You can also insert clip art on any slide without using a placeholder.

Try It! Inserting Clip Art

1. Start PowerPoint and open **PTry11** from the data files for this lesson.
2. Save the presentation as **PTry11_studentfirstname_studentlastname** in the location where your teacher instructs you to store the files for this lesson.
3. Click slide 8 in the Slides pane.
4. In the empty placeholder on slide 8, click the Clip Art icon. The Clip Art task pane opens.
5. In the Search for box in the Clip Art task pane, type **Donation** and press ENTER.
6. Click a clip that shows people making a donation (any kind). The clip appears in the placeholder.
7. Click slide 4 in the Slides pane.
8. In the search results in the Clip Art task pane, locate another suitable donation clip and click it. It appears in the center of slide 4.
9. Save the changes to the **PTry11_studentfirstname_studentlastname** file, and leave it open to use in the next Try It

Resizing and Positioning Clip Art

- When you insert a clip art image in a placeholder, the placeholder determines the starting size and position.
- When you insert a clip art image without a placeholder, the clip appears in the center of the slide, at a default size.
- You can resize a clip by dragging one of the selection handles (circles) on its border.
- You can move a clip by dragging the clip itself. Position the mouse pointer inside the clip's frame, away from any selection handles, and drag.
- Another way to size and position a clip is with the Size tab in the Format Picture dialog box. Right-click the clip, click Size and Position on the shortcut menu, and then enter exact settings in the dialog box.

Try It! Resizing and Positioning Clip Art

1. In the **PTry11_studentfirstname_studentlastname** file, on slide 4, click the clip to select it (if not already selected). Selection handles appear around it.
2. Drag the clip so its upper left corner is at the 4" mark on the horizontal ruler (right of center) and at the 1" mark on the vertical ruler (above center).

   ✓ *If the ruler is not displayed, click View > Ruler to turn it on.*
3. Drag the bottom left selection handle on the clip so the bottom left corner is at the 1" mark on the horizontal ruler (right of center).
4. Click slide 8 in the Slides pane.

(continued)

Try It! Resizing and Positioning Clip Art *(continued)*

5. Right-click the clip art and click Size and Position. The Format Picture dialog box opens with the Size tab displayed.
6. Enter 4" in the Height box.

   ✓ *The value in the Width box will change automatically in proportion.*

7. Click the Position tab.
8. Enter 1.5" for both the Vertical and Horizontal positions. (Measurements are from the top left corner.)
9. Click Close.
10. Save the changes to the **PTry11_studentfirstname_studentlastname** file, and leave it open to use in the next Try It.

Reposition the clip art on the slide

Inserting a Photo from the Clip Art Task Pane

- Through the Clip Art task pane, you can insert more types of content than just clip art. Microsoft's online library of images also includes photographs, sounds, and video clips.
- To search the online library of photos, perform a search in which the file type is set to Photographs.

  ✓ *You can also insert your own pictures with the Insert > Picture command. This command is the same as in Word. It is covered in Chapter 1 (Lesson 8) of the Word section.*

Try It! Inserting a Photo from the Clip Art Task Pane

1. In the PTry11_studentfirstname_studentlastname file, display slide 5.
2. Click Insert > Clip Art to open the Clip Art task pane.
3. In the Search for box, type Careers and press ENTER.
4. Open the Results Should Be drop-down list and mark the check box for Photographs. Clear all other check boxes.
5. Press ENTER. Photos appear from Microsoft's library of stock photography.
6. Click a career-related photo, such as a classified ad job search. The photo is placed on the slide.
7. Click the Close button on the Clip Art task pane to close it.
8. Size and position the photo, just as with a clip art image, so that it looks attractive on the slide and does not overlap any text.
9. Save the changes to the PTry11_studentfirstname_studentlastname file, and leave it open to use in the next Try It.

Removing the Background from a Picture

- In some photos, the background detracts from the main image. Using a graphics program, you can cut out the part of the image you want to use.
- PowerPoint 2010 also provides this capability, so you can remove a photo's background without leaving PowerPoint.
- Using the default settings may produce strange effects on some pictures; you can fine-tune where the dividing lines are between the foreground and background of the image if PowerPoint does not guess them correctly.

Try It! Removing the Background from a Picture

1. In the PTry11_studentfirstname_studentlastname file, display slide 3.
2. Click Insert > Picture. The Insert Picture dialog box opens.
3. Navigate to the folder containing the data files for this lesson, and click PTry11a.jpg.
4. Click Insert. The picture appears on the slide.
5. Resize and reposition the picture so that it is attractive and does not overlap any text.
6. Select the photo and click Picture Tools Format > Remove Background. Purple shading appears on the areas of the image that will be cropped, and a Background Removal tab appears.
7. Click Keep Changes.
8. Save the PTry11_studentfirstname_studentlastname file and close it.

Project 23—Create It

Laser Surgery Presentation

DIRECTIONS

1. Start PowerPoint, if necessary, and open **PProj23** from the data files for this lesson.
2. Save the presentation as **PProj23_studentfirstname_studentlastname** in the location where your teacher instructs you to store the files for this lesson.
3. Display slide 1, and click **Insert** > **Text Box**. Click at the bottom of the slide and type your full name.
4. Click slide 2, and click **Insert** > **Picture**.
5. Navigate to the folder containing the data files for this lesson, click **PProj23a.jpg**, and click **Insert**.
6. Drag the picture to place it to the left of the bulleted list.
7. Click slide 5 to display it.
8. Click the **Clip Art** placeholder icon.
9. In the Clip Art task pane, open the **Results Should Be** drop-down list.
10. Mark the **Illustrations** check box, and clear all other check boxes. Click away from the list to close it.
11. Click in the Search For box and type **dollar bill**. Click **Go** or press ENTER.
12. Click any of the found clips to insert it on the slide.

    ✓ *Try to find a clip that fits the content of the list as well as possible.*
13. **With your teacher's permission**, click **File** > **Print**. Select **Print All Slides**, and then click **Print** to print the presentation.
14. Close the presentation, saving changes, and exit PowerPoint.

Project 24—Apply It

Laser Surgery Presentation

DIRECTIONS

1. Start PowerPoint, if necessary, and open **PProj24** from the data files for this lesson.
2. Save the presentation as **PProj24_studentfirstname_studentlastname** in the location where your teacher instructs you to store the files for this lesson.
3. Display slide 1, and insert a text box at the bottom of the slide and type your full name.
4. On slide 2, position the clip art to the left of the bulleted list.
5. Size the clip art so it is the same height as the list.
6. On slide 4, insert **PProj24a.jpg** from the data files for this lesson.
7. Size the picture to be exactly **2"** high.
8. Position the picture to be **0.5"** horizontally and **1"** vertically from the upper left corner of the slide.

9. On slide 7, in the placeholder, insert **PProj24b.jpg** from the data files for this lesson.
10. Remove the background from the picture.

    ✓ *Notice that PowerPoint does not include all of the person's body by default. You can fix this by dragging the bottom left corner of the dotted outline inside the picture frame out to the edge of the picture. See Figure 11-1.*

11. Enlarge the picture to about **4"** in height. Use the vertical ruler to gauge size.
12. **With your teacher's permission**, print the presentation as handouts, 6 slides per page.
13. Close the presentation, saving changes, and exit PowerPoint.

Figure 11-1

Lesson 12

Inserting Symbols and Text Boxes

➤ What You Will Learn

Inserting Symbols
Inserting and Formatting a Text Box
Using Multiple Columns in a Text Box

Software Skills Not all characters are available for insertion by typing on the keyboard. Some characters such as ® and © are available only as symbols. In this lesson you will learn how to insert symbols in a presentation. You will also learn how to manually create text boxes that are not a part of a slide layout, and to format the text in multiple columns in a single text box.

Application Skills In the Wynnedale Medical Center presentation, you will add a copyright notice to the first page. You will adjust a text placeholder to present text in two columns. You will also add customer testimonials to a page, using manually placed text boxes that you format in colorful ways.

WORDS TO KNOW

Symbol
A typographical character that is neither a letter nor a number. Some symbols can be typed on a keyboard, and others must be inserted.

Text box
A non-placeholder container for text that you can position anywhere on a slide.

What You Can Do

Inserting Symbols

- As you learned in Word, **symbols** are characters that are neither alphabetic nor numeric. Most of them cannot be typed from the keyboard. Symbols can include decorative characters, foreign language characters, and mathematical or punctuation characters.

- You can insert symbols from the Symbols dialog box. You have a choice of fonts there. You can choose Normal Text, which uses the same font as the default used for bullet paragraphs in the presentation, or some other font.

  ✓ *If you want decorative characters instead, you can choose a font such as Zapf Dingbats or Wingdings, both of which are specifically designed for symbol use.*

Try It! Inserting Symbols

1. Start PowerPoint and open **PTry12** from the data files for this lesson.
2. Save the presentation as **PTry12_studentfirstname_studentlastname** in the location where your teacher instructs you to store the files for this lesson.
3. Display slide 1, and click to place the insertion point immediately after the word *Giving* in the title.
4. Click Insert > Symbol . The Symbol dialog box opens.
5. If (normal text) does not appear in the Font box, open its drop-down list and select (normal text).
6. Scroll through the symbols, and click the TM (trademark) symbol. It is in the next-to-the-bottom row.
7. Click Insert.
8. Click Close. The symbol appears in the title.
9. Save the changes to the **PTry12_studentfirstname_studentlastname** file, and leave it open to use in the next Try It.

The Insert Symbol dialog box

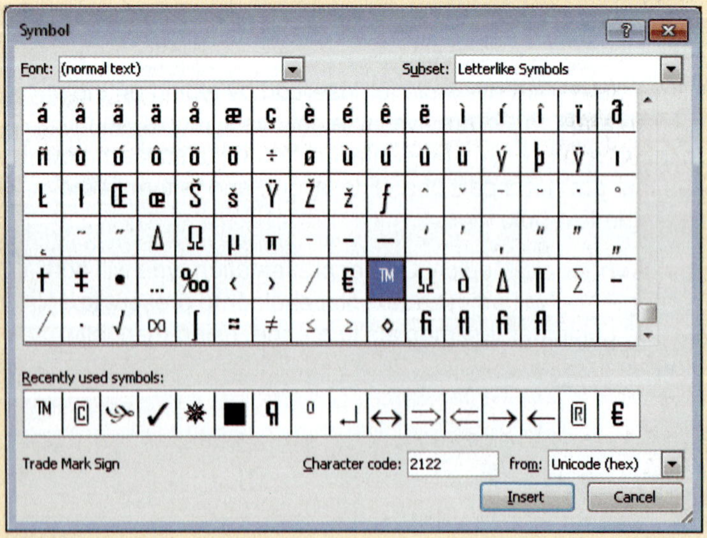

Inserting and Formatting a Text Box

- A **text box** is a container for text that you can position anywhere on a slide. It is not a placeholder, and not part of a slide layout. Like other slide objects, text boxes are inserted from the Insert tab.
- There are two ways to use the Text Box tool. After selecting Insert > Text Box, you can:
  - Click on the slide and start typing. This creates a text box in which the text does not wrap; the text box just keeps getting wider to accommodate your text.
  - Drag on the slide to define the size and shape of the text box, and then click inside it and start typing. This creates a text box in which text wraps to multiple lines automatically.
- You can resize a text box as you would any other object, by dragging the selection handles.
- You can format a text box as you would any other object. This includes adding a border, shading, and special effects. Use the tools in the Drawing group on the Home tab, or use the Drawing Tools Format contextual tab. You can also right-click the border of the text box and click Format Shape.

  ✓ *Lesson 13 covers object formatting in detail. The same basic formatting commands work for all types of objects, including drawn shapes and text boxes.*

- In the Format Shape dialog box, you can use the Text Box tab to control how the text appears in the text box (alignment, margins, and so on.)

Try It! Inserting a Text Box

1. In the **PTry12_studentfirstname_studentlastname** file, in the Slides pane, click between slides 6 and 7, and press ENTER, creating a new slide there.
2. With the new slide displayed, click Home > Layout > Title Only.
3. In the title placeholder, type **What People Are Saying**.
4. Click Insert > Text Box.
5. On the slide, drag the mouse pointer to create a box that is at least 4" wide and 3" high. Use the rulers to gauge size.

   ✓ *Notice that PowerPoint accepts the width you dragged, but the height snaps back to a much smaller size—the size of a single line of text at the default size. This is normal. The text box will expand vertically as you type.*

6. Type the text shown at the right. To manually insert a line break between the end of the quotation and the person's name, press SHIFT + ENTER.
7. Save the changes to the **PTry12_studentfirstname_studentlastname** file, and leave it open to use in the next Try It.

Type this text in the text box

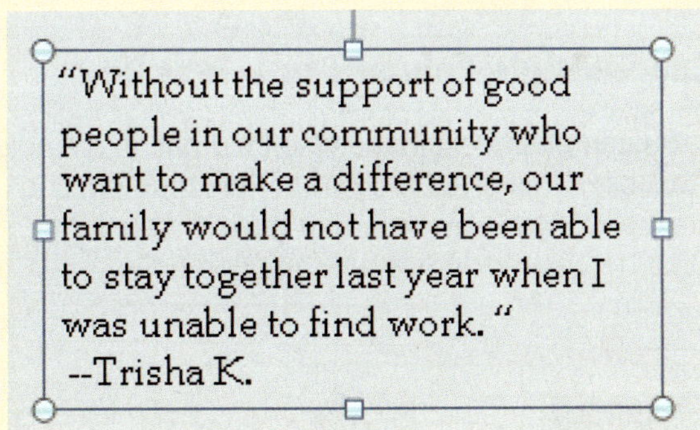

Try It! Formatting a Text Box

1. In the **PTry12_studentfirstname_studentlastname** file, click the outer border of the text box. This selects the box itself, and not the text inside.
2. On the Drawing Tools Format tab, click the More button in the Shape Styles group to open the Shape Styles gallery.
3. Click the second style in the bottom row.
4. Click Drawing Tools Format > Edit Shape > Change Shape and click a rounded rectangle.
5. Click Drawing Tools Format > Shape Effects > Reflection and click the first reflection type in the Reflection Variations section.
6. Click Drawing Tools Format > Shape Effects > 3-D Rotation and click the second sample in the first row of the Perspective section. When you are finished, the text box should look like that shown in the figure on the right.
7. Save the changes to the **PTry12_studentfirstname_studentlastname** file, and leave it open to use in the next Try It.

The formatted text box

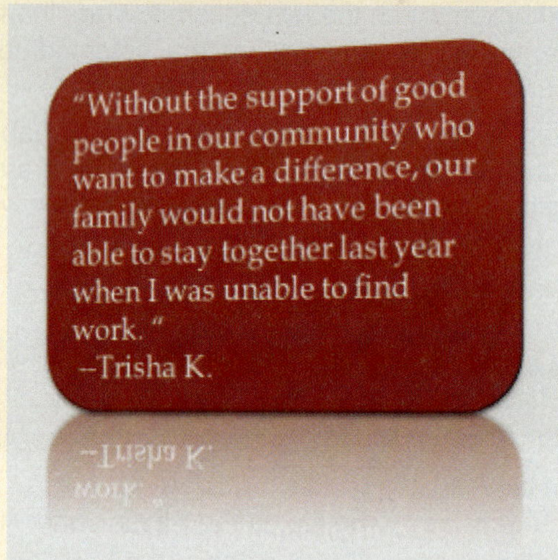

Using Multiple Columns in a Text Box

- You can place text in multiple columns in a single text box. This gives a different look than placing two text boxes side-by-side, and makes it easier to move text between columns after making edits.
- Use the Columns dialog box, accessed from the Columns drop-down list, to select the number of columns and space between them.

Try It! Using Multiple Columns in a Text Box

1. In the **PTry12_studentfirstname_studentlastname** file, in the Slides pane, click between slides 7 and 8, and press ENTER, creating a new slide there.
2. With the new slide displayed, click Home > Layout > Title Only.
3. In the title placeholder, type **In the News**.
4. Click Insert > Text Box.
5. On the slide, drag the mouse pointer to create a box that runs from the 4" mark on the ruler at the left to the 4" mark on the right.

✓ *The height you drag does not matter because PowerPoint will make the box as tall as needed for the content.*

continued

Try It! Using Multiple Columns in a Text Box *(continued)*

6. Type the following paragraphs into the new text box:

   In a recent study at Purdue University, it was shown that the return on investment (ROI) for investing in job skills training programs for people living below the poverty line is approximately 5:1.

   How is this money generated? When you train people who are currently receiving government assistance, they can get jobs and stop needing those payments. In addition, they begin paying income taxes, sales taxes, and property taxes as income rises and property is purchased.

7. Click Home > Columns > Two Columns.
8. Click Home > Columns > More Columns. The Columns dialog box opens.
9. In the Spacing text box, type **0.2"**.
10. Click OK.
11. Position the insertion point at the end of the first paragraph and press ENTER once, forcing the second paragraph to begin at the top of the second column.

    ✓ *Unfortunately PowerPoint lacks a Column Break command like the one Word has.*

12. Save the **PTry12_studentfirstname_studentlastname** file and close it.

The Columns dialog box

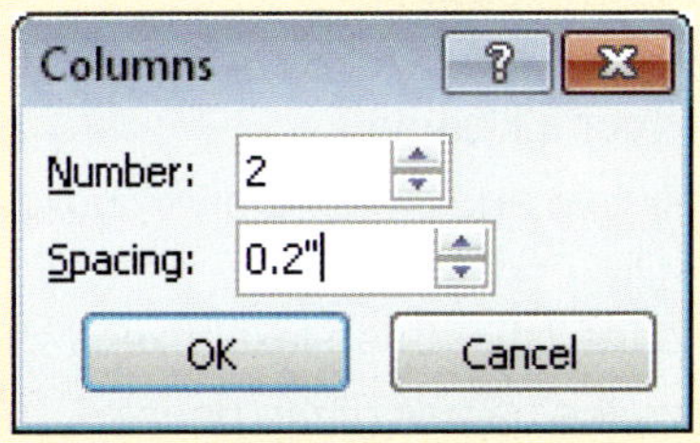

Project 25—Create It

Laser Surgery Presentation

DIRECTIONS

1. Start PowerPoint, if necessary, and open **PProj25** from the data files for this lesson.
2. Save the presentation as **PProj25_studentfirstname_studentlastname** in the location where your teacher instructs you to store the files for this lesson.
3. Click slide 1 to display it.
4. Click **Insert** > **Text Box**. Click at the top of the slide and type your full name.
5. Click **Insert** > **Text Box**.
6. Drag to create a 7" wide text box at the bottom of the slide. Center it horizontally.
7. In the text box, type **Copyright** and press SPACEBAR once.
8. Click **Insert** > **Symbol**.
9. Click the Copyright symbol © and click **Insert**. Then click **Close**.
10. Press SPACEBAR again.
11. Type **2011 Wynnedale Medical Group, LLC**.
12. Press CTRL + A to select all the text in the text box.
13. Press CTRL + E to center the text.
14. On the **Home** tab, in the Font group, open the **Size** drop-down list and click **10**.
15. Close the presentation, saving changes, and exit PowerPoint.

Project 26—Apply It

Laser Surgery Presentation

DIRECTIONS

1. Start PowerPoint, if necessary, and open **PProj26** from the data files for this lesson.
2. Save the presentation as **PProj26_studentfirstname_studentlastname** in the location where your teacher instructs you to store the files for this lesson.
3. On slide 1, insert a text box at the top of the slide, and type your full name.
4. Move to slide 6 and create the text boxes shown in Figure 12-1.
   a. Create the other three text boxes.
   b. Italicize the names of the people.
   c. On the **Drawing Tools Format** tab, use four different colors of presets from the bottom row of the palette of Shape Styles.
5. Move to slide 7 and set the text box that contains the numbered list to **Two Columns**.
6. Decrease the height of the text box so that items 1 and 2 appear in the first column and the other items appear in the second column. See Figure 12-2.
7. Check the spelling.
8. **With your teacher's permission**, print the presentation as handouts, six slides per page.
9. Close the presentation, saving changes, and exit PowerPoint.

Figure 12-1

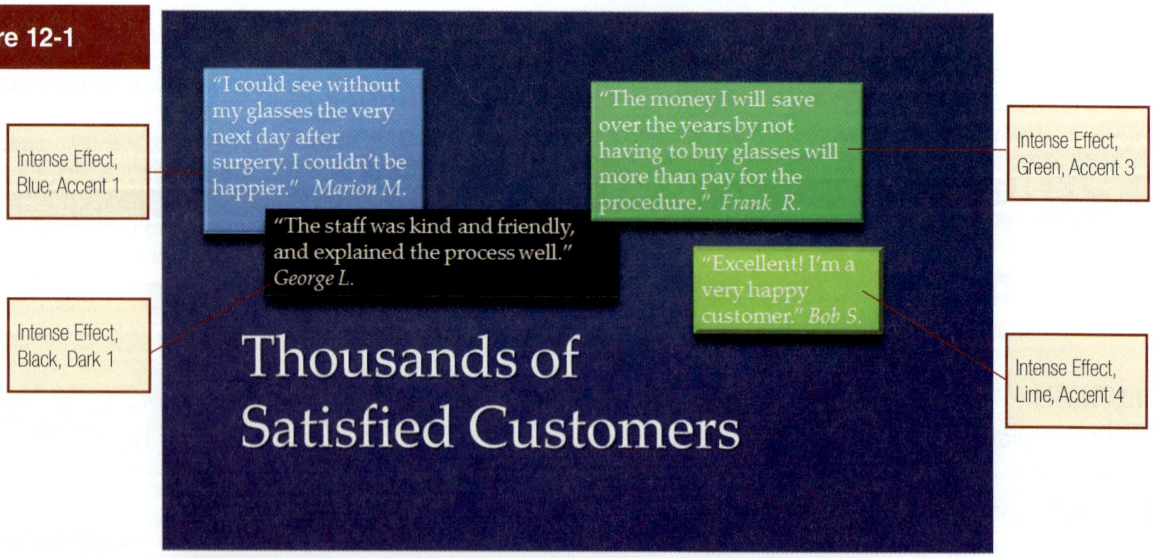

Figure 12-2

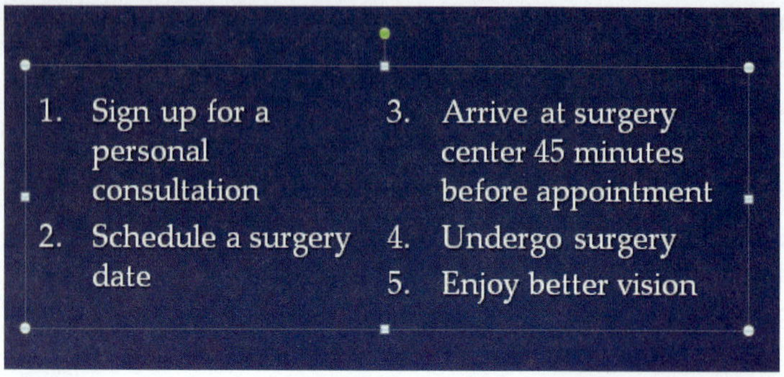

Lesson 13

Drawing and Formatting Shapes

➤ What You Will Learn

- Using Rulers, Guides, and Gridlines
- Drawing Shapes
- Moving and Sizing Shapes
- Applying Fills and Outlines
- Applying Shape Styles
- Applying Shape Effects
- Adding Text to Shapes

Software Skills Use PowerPoint's many drawing tools to help enhance a presentation. You might use rulers and guides or the grid to line up text or drawing objects, for example. Use shape tools to draw logos, illustrations, or other objects to add to slides.

Application Skills A friend who works for Kelly Greenery, a landscaping company, has asked you to create a simple logo that he can use in his marketing presentations. You will use PowerPoint's Shapes tools to construct a logo.

WORDS TO KNOW

Aspect ratio
The proportion of width to height for an object.

Gridlines
A regular grid of dotted lines displayed on a slide to help arrange objects.

Guides
Nonprinting vertical and horizontal lines you can use to align objects on a slide.

Shape effects
Special effects such as glow, shadow, 3D rotation, and soft edges applied to drawn shapes.

Shape Styles
Preset combinations of shape effects that can be applied as a single formatting action.

Snap
To change position to align precisely with a gridline.

What You Can Do

Using Rulers, Guides, and Gridlines

- PowerPoint provides a vertical and horizontal ruler that you can show or hide at any time. You can use these rulers to adjust indents or add tabs to text. You can also use rulers to align objects on the slide.
- The ruler's origins (0 measurement on the ruler) change depending on whether you're using text or an object. The origin appears on the edge of the ruler when you're working with text and in the center point of the ruler when you're working with an object.
- As you move the mouse pointer, an indicator moves on each ruler showing your horizontal and vertical locations.
- **Guides** are alignment tools that help you line up objects and text. PowerPoint supplies one vertical and one horizontal guide that you can move and copy, as shown in Figure 13-1.
- PowerPoint's **gridlines** display as a grid of dotted lines over the entire slide. Like guides, they can help you line up objects or position them attractively on the slide.
- By default, objects **snap** to the grid as they are drawn or positioned on the slide, even if the gridlines are not currently displayed. Generally this is an advantage, but if you find you want to position an object more exactly, you can turn off the snapping feature or hold down Alt while dragging to temporarily disable the snapping feature.

Figure 13-1

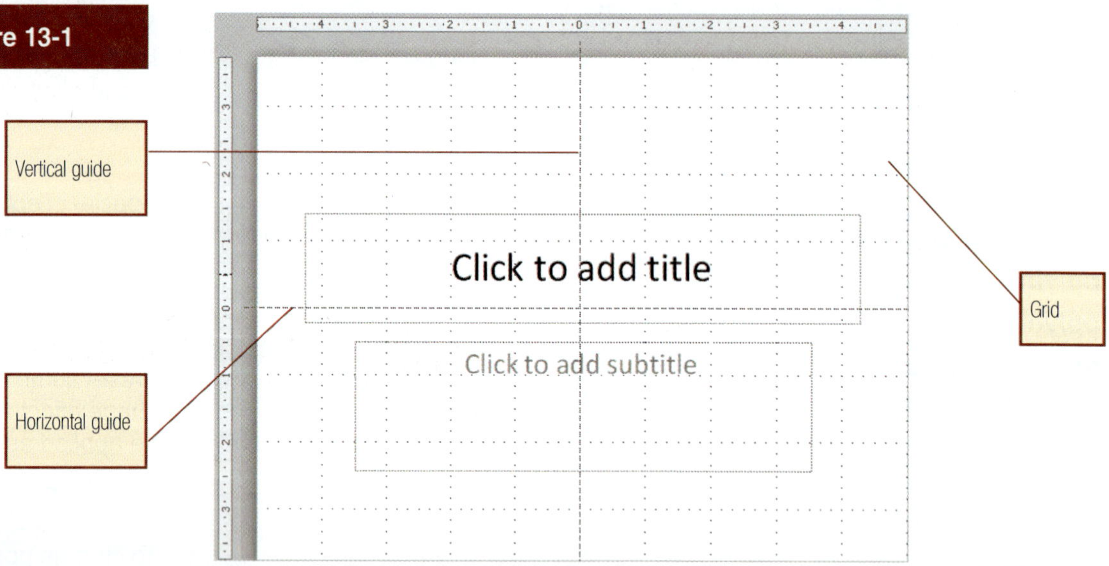

Try It! Turning On Rulers, Gridlines, and Guides

1. Start PowerPoint and start a new blank presentation.
2. Save the presentation as **PTry13_studentfirstname_studentlastname** in the location where your teacher instructs you to store the files for this lesson.
3. Click the View tab.
4. If the Ruler check box is not already marked, click to mark it.
5. If the Gridlines check box is not already marked, click to mark it.
6. If the Guides check box is not already marked, click to mark it.
7. Save the changes to the **PTry13_studentfirstname_studentlastname** file, and leave it open to use in the next Try It.

Try It! Adjusting Grid and Guide Settings

1. In the **PTry13_studentfirstname_ studentlastname** file, position the mouse pointer over the dashed vertical guide and click and hold the left mouse button.

   ✓ *The mouse pointer changes to show 0.00.*

2. Drag to the right until the mouse pointer shows 1.50, and then release the mouse button.

3. On the View tab, click the dialog box launcher for the Show group. The Grid and Guides dialog box opens.

4. Click the Snap objects to grid check box if it is not already marked.

5. Open the Spacing drop-down list and click 1/16".

   ✓ *PowerPoint converts the measurement to decimal automatically in the Spacing text box: 0.063".*

6. Click OK.

7. Save the changes to the **PTry13_ studentfirstname_studentlastname** file, and leave it open to use in the next Try It.

The Grid and Guides dialog box

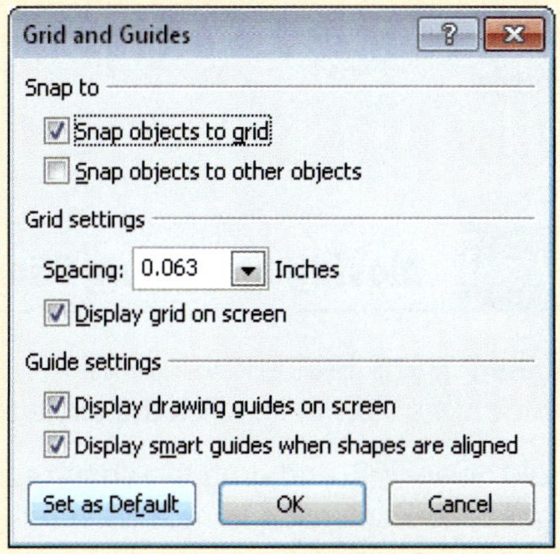

Drawing Shapes

- Use the shapes on the Home tab or Drawing Tools tab to draw basic objects such as lines, rectangles, and circles as well as more complex shapes such as stars, banners, and block arrows.
- The Shapes gallery is divided into several sections that organize shapes of various kinds. Click a shape and then drag on the slide to draw it. You control the size as you draw.
- If you click on the slide instead of dragging, you get a default-sized shape.
- You can hold down SHIFT as you drag to constrain the shape to its original **aspect ratio**. For example, if you draw an oval while holding down SHIFT, it's a perfect circle; if you draw a rectangle, it's a perfect square.

Try It! Drawing Shapes

1. In the **PTry13_studentfirstname_ studentlastname** file, click Home > Layout > Blank to switch to a blank layout with no placeholders.

2. Click Insert > Shapes. In the Stars and Banners section, click the five-pointed star.

3. Hold down SHIFT and draw a star in the center of the slide, approximately 4" x 4".

   ✓ *Each square in the grid is 1".*

4. Click Insert > Shapes. In the Basic Shapes section, click the oval.

5. Hold down SHIFT and draw a circle to the left of the star, approximately 3" in diameter.

6. Save the changes to the **PTry13_ studentfirstname_studentlastname** file, and leave it open to use in the next Try It.

Moving and Sizing Shapes

- You can move, size, copy, and delete drawing objects just like any other PowerPoint object.
  - To move a shape, drag it.

    ✓ *You can also display the Format Shape dialog box and enter precise position measurements on the Position tab there.*

  - To size a shape, drag one of its selection handles.

    ✓ *You can also display the Format Shape dialog box and enter precise size measurements on the Size tab there. You can also enter a precise height and width on the Drawing Tools Format tab, in the Size group.*

  - To delete a shape, select it and press DEL .
  - To nudge an object (move it in small increments), hold down CTRL while pressing an arrow key in the direction you want it to move.
- Some shapes also have one or more yellow diamond resize handles that you can use to adjust the appearance of the shape.

Try It! Moving and Sizing Shapes

1. In the **PTry13_studentfirstname_studentlastname** file, click the circle to select it.
2. Hold down SHIFT and drag the shape's bottom right corner selection handle, to shrink the circle to approximately 2" in diameter.
3. On the Drawing Tools Format tab, click in the Shape Height box and type 2.5".
4. Click in the Shape Width box and type 2.5".
5. Drag the circle to the upper right corner of the slide.
6. Right-click the circle and click Format Shape. The Format Shape dialog box opens.
7. Click the Position tab.
8. In the Horizontal box, type **0.5"**.
9. In the Verical box, type **0.5"**.
10. Click Close.
11. Click Insert > Shapes and in the Block Arrows section, click the up arrow.
12. Drag on the slide to place a block arrow to the right of the star, approximately 4" high and 2" wide.

    ✓ *Two yellow diamonds appear on it: one on the arrowhead and one on the arrow shaft.*

13. Drag the diamond on the arrowhead to change the shape of the arrowhead.
14. Drag the diamond on the arrow shaft to change the width of the shaft.
15. Save the changes to the **PTry13_studentfirstname_studentlastname** file, and leave it open to use in the next Try It.

Modify the arrow by dragging the yellow diamonds

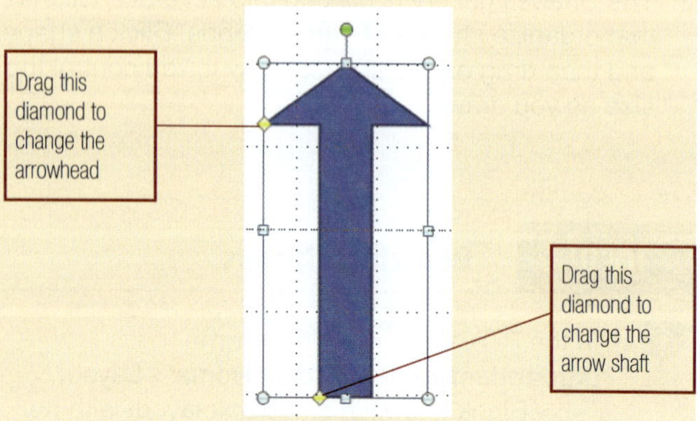

Applying Fills and Outlines

- By default, shapes are formatted with the current theme colors. The fill is the Accent 1 color in the theme (the fifth color) and the outline is the Text 2 color (the fourth color).
- On the Drawing Tools Format tab, you can use the Shape Fill and Shape Outline drop-down lists to format a shape differently from the default.
- You can also right-click the shape and choose Format Shape for access to the Format Shape dialog box, where a wider variety of formatting options are available.

Try It! Applying Fills and Outlines

1. In the **PTry13_studentfirstname_studentlastname** file, click the star to select it.
2. Click the Drawing Tools Format tab.
3. Click the Shape Fill drop-down arrow, opening its menu.
4. Click the yellow square under Standard Colors.
5. Click the Shape Outline drop-down arrow, opening its menu.
6. Click More Outline Colors.
7. In the Colors dialog box, click the Standard tab.
8. Click an orange hexagon.
9. Click OK.
10. Right-click the star and click Format Shape.
11. In the Format Shape dialog box, click the Line Style tab.
12. In the Width box, type **1 pt**.
13. Click the Dash Type button, opening its menu, and choose the Square Dot dash style (the third style on the list).
14. Click Close to close the dialog box.
15. Save the changes to the **PTry13_studentfirstname_studentlastname** file, and leave it open to use in the next Try It.

Select a fill color

Select an outline color

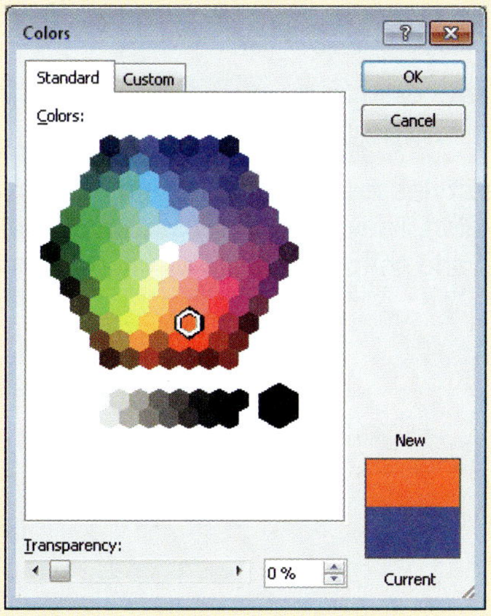

Applying Shape Effects

- **Shape effects** are special formatting options you can apply to objects in PowerPoint 2007/2010 presentations. They are not available in backward-compatible presentations (97-2003).
- The available effects include shadows, reflections, soft edges, bevels, and 3D rotation. After opening the Shape Effects menu, you point to a submenu name and then click one of the presets from the submenu that appears.

✓ *The shape effect you choose does not affect the color or border of the object. However, some effects hide the shape's outline.*

- Each of the effect submenus has an Options command at the bottom that opens the Format Shape dialog box with the corresponding tab selected. For example, the Shadow Options command opens it to the Shadow tab.

Try It! Applying Shape Effects

1. In the **PTry13_studentfirstname_studentlastname** file, click the circle to select it.
2. Click Drawing Tools Format > Shape Effects > Preset and click the second preset in the first row of the Presets section.
3. Click Shape Fill, and click the light green square in the Standard section.

   ✓ *Notice that the effect remains, even though you have changed the color.*
4. Click Shape Effects > Bevel > Riblet (the second effect in the third row of the Bevel section).
5. Save the changes to the **PTry13_studentfirstname_studentlastname** file, and leave it open to use in the next Try It.

Applying Shape Styles

- **Shape styles** are the next step up in formatting automation. They apply combinations of color, outline, and shape effects in a single action.
- Each shape style is available in any of the current theme's colors. You can also apply a shape style and then manually change the color if you like.

Try It! Applying Shape Styles

1. In the **PTry13_studentfirstname_studentlastname** file, click the star to select it.
2. On the Drawing Tools Format tab, in the Shape Styles group, click the More button to open the Shape Styles gallery.
3. Click the style in the lower right corner of the gallery.
4. Click the block arrow shape.
5. Click the More button to open the Shape Styles gallery again.
6. Click the first style in the fourth row of the gallery.
7. Save the changes to the **PTry13_studentfirstname_studentlastname** file, and leave it open to use in the next Try It.

Click the shape style to apply

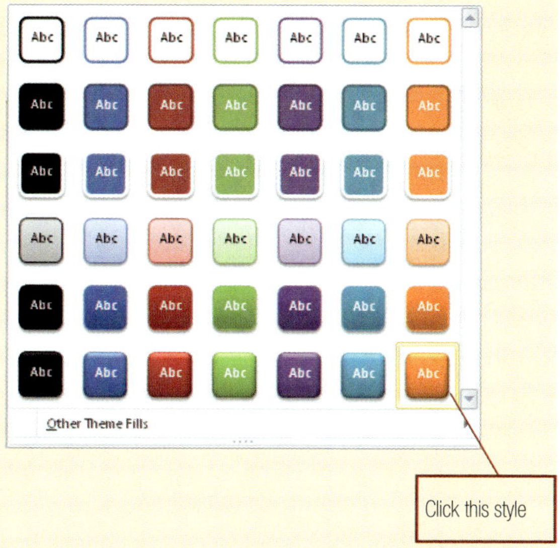

Adding Text to Shapes

- You can add text to any filled shape. Simply click on the shape and start typing. PowerPoint handles line length and text wrap. This allows you, in effect, to have any shape of text box you want, not just rectangular.
- You can edit and format text in a shape just as you would edit text in a text box. For a special effect, you can change text direction so that text reads from top to bottom or bottom to top.

Try It! Adding Text to a Shape and Rotating the Text

1. In the **PTry13_studentfirstname_studentlastname** file, click the block arrow to select it.
2. Type **Check out our specials**. The text appears in the shaft of the arrow, with only a few characters per line.
3. Right-click the block arrow and click Format Shape.
4. In the Format Shape dialog box, click the Text Box tab.
5. Open the Text Direction drop-down list and click Rotate All Text 270°.
6. Click Close to close the dialog box. The text now runs vertically in the shape.
7. Save the **PTry13_studentfirstname_studentlastname** file and close it.

Project 27—Create It

Kelly Greenery Logo

DIRECTIONS

1. Start PowerPoint, if necessary, and start a new blank presentation.
2. Save the presentation as **PProj27_studentfirstname_studentlastname** in the location where your teacher instructs you to store the files for this lesson.
3. Click **Home** > **Layout** > **Blank** to switch to a blank layout.
4. Click **Insert** > **Text Box**. Click at the bottom of the slide and type your full name.
5. On the View tab, clear the **Guides** check box if it is marked. Leave the Gridlines check box marked.
6. Click **Insert** > **Shapes**. Click the oval in the Basic Shapes section.
7. Drag on the slide to create an oval in the center of the slide that is approximately 8" wide and 4" tall.
8. On the **Drawing Tools Format** tab, in the Shape Styles group, click the **More** button to open the Shape Styles gallery.
9. Click the light green style in the next-to-last row.
10. With the oval selected, type **Kelly Greenery**.
11. Press CTRL + A to select all the text you just typed.
12. On the Home tab, open the **Font** drop-down list and click **Algerian**.
13. Open the Size drop-down list and click **44**.
14. Click the arrow on the **Font Color** button and click the black square in the theme colors (second square in the top row).
15. On the **Drawing Tools Format** tab, click **Shape Effects** > **Preset** and click the rightmost preset in the first row of the Presets section.

    ✓ *The finished logo is shown in Figure 13-3.*
16. Close the presentation, saving changes, and exit PowerPoint.

Figure 13-3

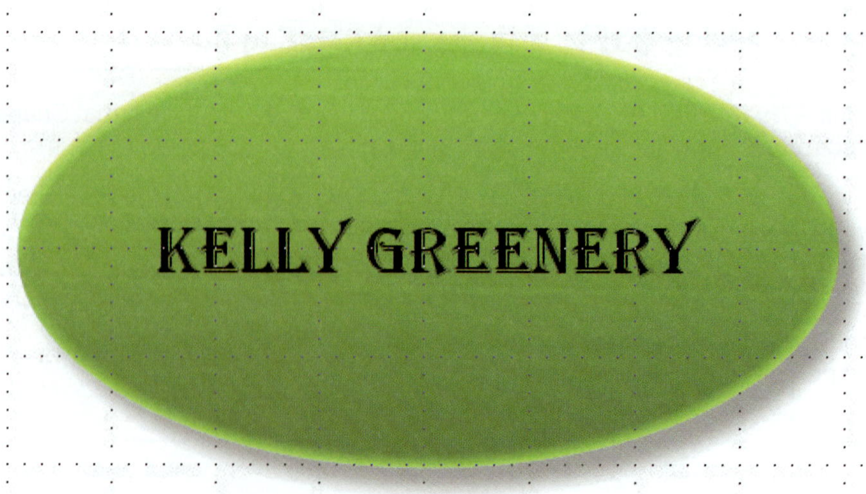

Project 28—Apply It

Kelly Greenery Logo

DIRECTIONS

1. Start PowerPoint and open **PProj28** from the data files for this lesson.
2. Save the presentation as **PProj28_studentfirstname_studentlastname** in the location where your teacher instructs you to store the files for this lesson.
3. Create a text box at the bottom of the slide and type your name in it.
4. Set the height and width of the oval to exactly **4"** high and **8"** wide.
5. Remove the Bevel effect from the oval.
6. Apply an **Offset Diagonal Bottom Right** shadow using Shape Effects.
7. Change the shape fill to the Orange standard color.
8. Apply a 3-point dark green outline to the oval.
9. Apply that same shade of green to the text in the oval.
10. If gridlines are displayed, turn them off. The finished logo is shown in Figure 13-4.
11. **With your teacher's permission**, print the presentation.
12. Close the presentation, saving changes, and exit PowerPoint.

Figure 13-4

Lesson 14

Positioning and Grouping Shapes

WORDS TO KNOW

Group
To combine multiple shapes or other objects into a collective unit that can be controlled as a single object.

Stack
To overlap objects, and control the order in which overlapping objects appear.

➤ What You Will Learn

Stacking Objects
Grouping Objects
Duplicating Objects
Aligning and Distributing Objects

Software Skills Many of the drawings you create with the Shapes tools in PowerPoint will consist of multiple shapes that overlap each other. When a graphic consists of several pieces, you need to know how to combine and position them to make a cohesive whole.

Application Skills The Kelly Greenery logo you have been working on currently consists of several separate drawn shapes. You will stack the pieces in the correct order, and then group them into a single object that the customer can use as his business's logo. You will also fix the problem of the yellow background showing through part of the clip art image.

What You Can Do

Stacking Objects

- As you create objects on a slide, they **stack** from the "back" (the first object created) to the "front" (the last object created). You can think of this process as a series of layers stacked on top of each other with an object on each layer.

- Use the Drawing Tools Format tab's arrangement tools to change an object's stack order:
  - Bring to Front and Send to Back move the object all the way to the top or bottom of the stack, respectively.
  - Bring Forward and Send Backward move an object back or forward one layer at a time.
- To make it easy to select objects for arranging or other manipulation, use the Selection and Visibility pane. Access it from the Drawing Tools Format tab.
- The Selection and Visibility pane shows all objects currently displayed on the slide. To select any object, click it in the Selection and Visibility pane. You can also click on the visibility symbol (the open eye) to hide an object.

✓ *You can click on an object name to open the default name for editing and supply your own names for objects. Meaningful names for objects can also help you when you are creating animations for slide objects.*

Try It! Stacking Objects

1. Start PowerPoint and open **PTry14** from the data files for this lesson.
2. Save the presentation as **PTry14_studentfirstname_studentlastname** in the location where your teacher instructs you to store the files for this lesson.
3. Click any of the shapes, and then click Drawing Tools Format > Selection Pane. The Selection and Visibility pane opens.
4. In the Selection and Visibility pane, click the eye symbol next to Oval 4. The circle disappears and the button changes to a blank. Click the blank button to make the circle reappear.
5. Click the circle to select it. Then hold down SHIFT and drag a corner selection handle on the circle to expand it so it is large enough to completely cover the star. Drag it to reposition it so it is directly over the star.

Select any object easily in this pane

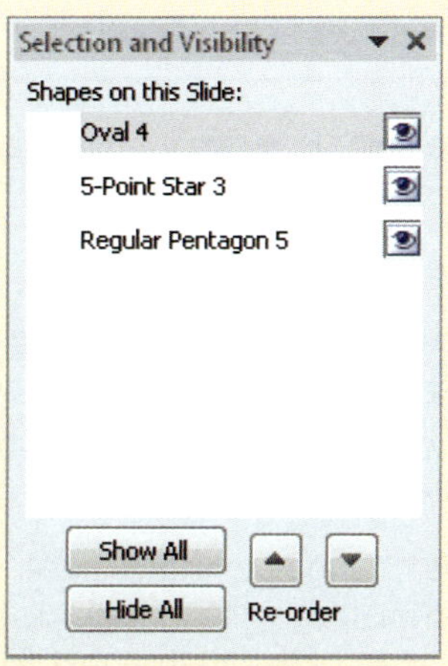

6. With the circle still selected, on the Drawing Tools Format tab, click the arrow to the right of the Send Backward button and click Send to Back.
7. Adjust the size and position of the circle so that the tips of the star barely touch the edges of the circle.
8. Click the pentagon, either on the slide or in the Selection and Visibility pane.
9. Click the arrow to the right of the Bring Forward button and click Bring to Front.
10. Position the pentagon on top of the star, at its center.
11. Click Drawing Tools Format > Selection Pane to turn off the Selection and Visibility pane.
12. Click View > Gridlines to turn off the gridlines. The design should look like that shown in the following figure.
13. Save the changes to the **PTry14_studentfirstname_studentlastname** file, and leave it open to use in the next Try It.

Arrange and stack the pieces of the design

Grouping Objects

- You can **group** the objects within a drawing so that they can be treated as a single object. Grouping objects makes them easier to copy, move, or resize.
- You can ungroup objects when you want to work with the objects individually again.
- Some changes can be made to the individual elements of a grouped object without ungrouping it, such as changing the colors.
- To select the objects to be grouped, you can hold down CTRL as you click on each one, or you can drag a lasso around all the objects to be included. To lasso a group, drag to draw an imaginary box around them.

Try It! Grouping Objects

1. In the **PTry14_studentfirstname_studentlastname** file, drag to lasso all the drawn shapes. Each one appears with its own selection handles.
2. Click Drawing Tools Format > Group > Group. The group now has a single set of selection handles.
3. Hold down SHIFT and drag the bottom right corner of the shape inward to shrink it in size by 1".

   ✓ *All shapes are resized together because they are all part of the group.*
4. Click to select the object if it is not already selected.
5. Click Drawing Tools Format > Group > Ungroup. The shapes become ungrouped.
6. Click Drawing Tools Format > Group > Group again, because you will need the objects grouped for the next steps.
7. Save the changes to the **PTry14_studentfirstname_studentlastname** file, and leave it open to use in the next Try It.

Duplicating Objects

- After drawing an object, you may want to duplicate it rather than drawing additional objects from scratch. For example, if you need three circles that are all exactly the same size, duplicating the first one twice ensures that they are identical.
- You can duplicate either with drag-and-drop, or with copy-and-paste.

Try It! Duplicating an Object

1. In the **PTry14_studentfirstname_studentlastname** file, select the object, and on the Drawing Tools Format tab, enter a Height and Width of 2" each.

   ✓ *This makes the shape small enough that multiple copies of it will fit on the slide.*
2. Select the object and press CTRL + C. It is copied to the Clipboard.
3. Press CTRL + V. A copy is pasted on the slide.
4. Drag the copy to move it so it does not overlap the original.
5. Click the original object.
6. Hold down the CTRL key and drag the original to a different spot on the slide. It is copied there.

   ✓ *Now you have three copies of the shape, which you will use in the next Try It.*
7. Save the changes to the **PTry14_studentfirstname_studentlastname** file, and leave it open to use in the next Try It.

Aligning and Distributing Objects

- Sometimes it is important that the objects on a slide be precisely aligned, either with one another or with the slide itself. PowerPoint has several commands to help you accomplish this.
- The Align command aligns objects by their top, bottom, right side, left side, or center. It can also be used to place one or more objects in relation to the slide itself. In Figure 14-1, the shapes are top-aligned.
- The Distribute command equalizes the spacing among objects.
- On the Align button's menu is an Align to Slide command that is a toggle. When it is turned on, a check mark appears by it.
- When this command is on, the Align and Distribute commands apply to the object in relation to the slide, as well as in relation to the other selected objects.
- When this command is on, you can use Align or Distribute on a single object. When this command is off, the minimum number of selected objects to use Align is 2, and the minimum to use Distribute is 3.

Figure 14-1

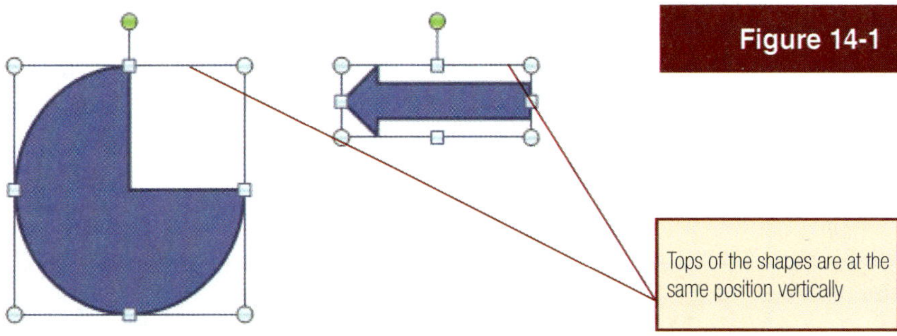

Figure 14-2

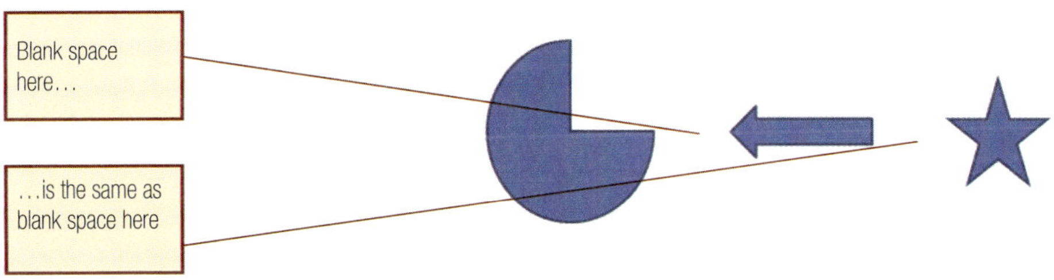

Try It! Aligning and Distributing Objects

1. In the **PTry14_studentfirstname_studentlastname** file, manually drag the three copies of the object so that they are in a single horizontal row in the center of the slide.

   ✓ *The placement does not have to be precise. In fact, the results will be more obvious if one of them is slightly higher than the others.*

2. Click one copy, hold down CTRL, and click the other two copies to also select them.
3. Click Drawing Tools Format > Align > Align Top.
4. Click Drawing Tools Format > Align > Distribute Horizontally.
5. To confirm that they are aligned, click View > Gridlines to turn on the gridlines. Click the Gridlines check box to turn off gridlines again when finished.
6. Save the **PTry14_studentfirstname_studentlastname** file and close it.

Project 29—Create It

Kelly Greenery Logo

DIRECTIONS

1. Start PowerPoint, if necessary, and open **PProj29** from the data files for this lesson.
2. Save the presentation as **PProj29_studentfirstname_studentlastname** in the location where your teacher instructs you to store the files for this lesson.
3. Click **Insert** > **Text Box**. Click at the bottom of the slide and type your full name.
4. Select the star.
5. Hold down CTRL and drag the star to the right, making a copy of it.
6. Repeat step 4 three more times, so you have a total of five stars.
7. Drag a lasso around all five stars to select them.
8. Click **Drawing Tools Format** > **Align** > **Align Selected Objects**.
9. Click **Drawing Tools Format** > **Align** > **Distribute Horizontally**.
10. Click **Drawing Tools Format** > **Align** > **Align Middle**.
11. Click **Drawing Tools Format** > **Group** > **Group**. The stars are now a single object.
12. Select the clip art image.
13. Click **Picture Tools Format** > **Bring Forward**.
14. Select the oval, the stars, and the banner.
15. Click **Drawing Tools Format** > **Align** > **Align Center**.
16. Click **Drawing Tools Format** > **Group** > **Group**. The finished logo is shown in Figure 14-3.
17. **With your teacher's permission**, click **File** > **Print**. Select **Print All Slides**, and then click **Print** to print the presentation.
18. Close the presentation, saving changes, and exit PowerPoint.

Figure 14-3

Project 30—Apply It

Kelly Greenery Logo

DIRECTIONS

1. Start PowerPoint, if necessary, and open **PProj30** from the data files for this lesson.
2. Save the presentation as **PProj30_studentfirstname_studentlastname** in the location where your teacher instructs you to store the files for this lesson.
3. Insert a text box at the bottom of the slide, and type your full name in it.
4. Draw an oval that covers up as much of the clip art graphic as possible, while not overrunning its border. See Figure 14-4.
5. Remove the outline (border) from the oval and change its fill color to white.
6. Use the **Send Backward** command to send the oval behind the clip art.

   ✓ *Now the part of the clip art that overlaps the yellow oval does not show yellow.*
7. Group the clip art, the white oval, and the yellow oval into a single object.
8. Apply an orange outline to the stars.
9. Select everything on the slide, and group all the pieces into a single object.
10. Center the logo on the slide vertically and horizontally.

    ✓ *Here's one way: On the Align button's menu, make sure Align to Slide is marked. Then use the Distribute Vertically and Distribute Horizontally commands.*
11. **With your teacher's permission**, print one copy of the slide. The finished logo is shown in Figure 14-5.
12. Close the presentation, saving changes, and exit PowerPoint.

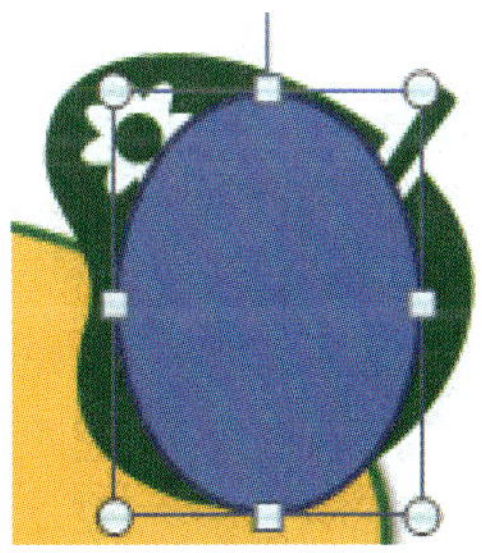

Figure 14-4

Figure 14-5

Lesson 15

Creating WordArt

WORDS TO KNOW

WordArt
Text that is formatted with graphical effects.

➤ What You Will Learn

Understanding WordArt
Applying WordArt Styles to Existing Text
Inserting and Formatting WordArt

Software Skills WordArt enables you to apply special effects to text to make it appear more graphical. Using WordArt you can create logos and decorative text without a stand-alone graphics program.

Application Skills Your friend at Kelly Greenery likes the logo you created for him, but would like some alternatives to choose from. You will create two alternate company logos using a combination of clip art and WordArt.

What You Can Do

Understanding WordArt

- Use **WordArt** to create a graphic from text. WordArt is useful whenever you want text to be both readable and decorative.
- WordArt is similar to drawn shapes in the ways you can format it. For example, you can apply a fill, an outline, and various formatting effects and styles to it. This formatting is the same as it is with shapes, which you learned about in the previous two lessons.
- The Transform command is unique to WordArt. It modifies the shape of the text to make it conform to a path. Choose a transformation from the Text Effects button's Transform submenu, as shown in Figure 15-1.

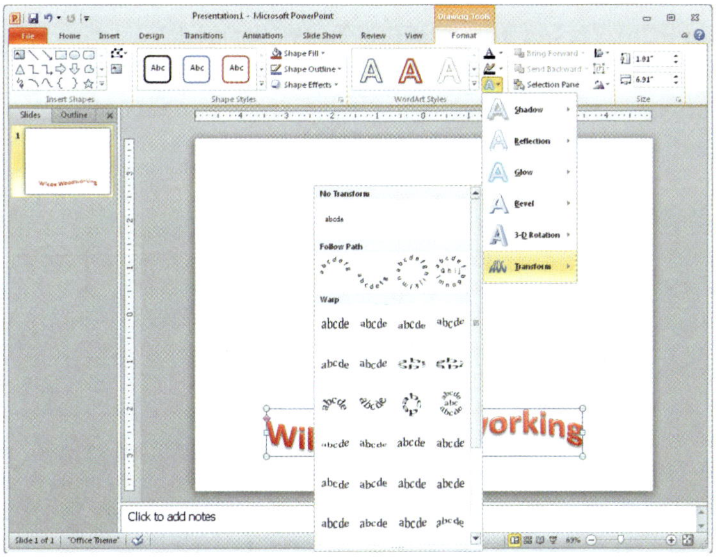

Figure 15-1

Applying WordArt Styles to Existing Text

- Any text can be easily turned into WordArt. Select any existing text, and then on the Drawing Tools Format tab, use the WordArt Styles group's commands and lists to select the effects that you want.
- When applying WordArt presets from the WordArt Styles gallery, there are two sections in the gallery:
  - Applies to Selected Text: These effects can be applied to individual characters and words in a text box without affecting the entire text box.
  - Applies to All Text in the Shape: These effects apply to the entire text box.

Try It! Applying WordArt Styles to Existing Text

1. Start a new blank presentation and save it as **PTry15_studentfirstname_studentlastname** in the location where your teacher instructs you to store the files for this lesson.
2. Click Home > Layout > Blank to change to a blank layout.
3. Click Insert > Text Box .
4. Click on the slide, and type **Lowe Insurance**.
5. Press CTRL + A to select all the text.
6. Click the Drawing Tools Format tab.
7. Click the More button in the WordArt Styles group to open the WordArt Styles gallery.
8. Click the bottom right style in the Applies to Selected Text section of the gallery.
9. Click the text box containing the WordArt.
10. Click the More button in the WordArt Styles group to open the WordArt Styles gallery.
11. Click Clear WordArt.
12. Save the changes to the **PTry15_studentfirstname_studentlastname** file, and leave it open to use in the next Try It.

(continued)

Try It! Applying WordArt Styles to Existing Text *(continued)*

Select a WordArt style

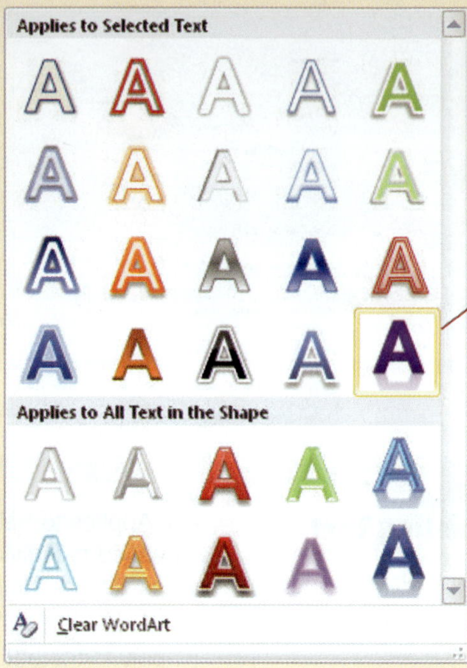

Click this style

Inserting and Formatting WordArt

- You can also insert WordArt from scratch. This creates a text box and applies a WordArt style to it in a single step.

Try It! Inserting WordArt

1. In the **PTry15_studentfirstname_studentlastname** file, click Insert > WordArt. A palette of WordArt samples appears.

   ✓ *These samples are the same as the ones that appeared in the WordArt Styles list you saw in the preceding steps.*

2. Click the second sample in the fourth row.

   ✓ *A WordArt object appears, with generic text. The text is highlighted, so if you type something, it will be replaced.*

3. Type **Apex Industries**. Your text replaces the generic text.

4. Save the changes to the **PTry15_studentfirstname_studentlastname** file, and leave it open to use in the next Try It.

Try It! Formatting WordArt

1. In the **PTry15_studentfirstname_studentlastname** file, with the WordArt object selected, click Drawing Tools Format > Text Effects > Transform. A gallery of transformation options appears, as you saw in Figure 15-1.
2. In the Warp section, click the first sample in the second row (Chevron Up).
3. Drag the pink diamond at the left edge of the WordArt down as far as it will go.

   ✓ *The WordArt shape is further transformed.*
4. With the insertion point in the WordArt, press CTRL + A to select all the text.

   ✓ *If you do not select all the text, the formatting applies only to the word where the insertion point was.*
5. Click Drawing Tools Format > Text Fill. A palette of colors appears.
6. Click the light blue square in the Standard Colors section.
7. Click Drawing Tools Format > Text Outline. A palette of colors appears.
8. Click the medium blue square in the Standard Colors section.
9. Click Drawing Tools Format > Text Outline.

The transformed WordArt object

10. Point to the Weight command. A submenu appears.
11. Click the solid 1½ point line.
12. With the insertion point in the WordArt, press CTRL + A to select all the text.
13. Click Drawing Tools Format > Text Effects > Shadow.
14. Click the first shadow in the Perspective section.
15. Click Drawing Tools Format > Text Effects > Bevel.
16. Click the fourth sample in the third row of the Bevel section (Art Deco).
17. Click Drawing Tools Format > Text Effects > 3-D Rotation.
18. Click the fourth sample in the second row of the Parallel section (Off Axis 2 Left).
19. Click away from the WordArt object to deselect it. It should look like the following figure.
20. Save the **PTry15_studentfirstname_studentlastname** file and close it.

The finished WordArt object

Project 31—Create It

Kelly Greenery Logo

DIRECTIONS

1. Start PowerPoint, if necessary, and open **PProj31** from the data files for this lesson.
2. Save the presentation as **PProj31_studentfirstname_studentlastname** in the location where your teacher instructs you to store the files for this lesson.
3. Click **Insert** > **Text Box**. Click at the bottom of the slide and type your full name.
4. Click **Insert** > **WordArt** and click the fourth sample in the third row.
5. Type **Kelly Greenery**.
6. Drag the WordArt so that the last letter overlaps the trunk of the tree graphic.
7. Press CTRL + A to select all the text.
8. Click **Drawing Tools Format** > **Text Fill** and click the light green square in the Standard section.
9. Click **Drawing Tools Format** > **Text Outline** and click **No Outline**.
10. Click **Drawing Tools Format** > **Text Effects** > **Transform** and click the first sample in the fifth row of the Warp section (Wave 1).
11. Click the WordArt, hold down CTRL, and click the clip art.
12. Click **Drawing Tools Format** > **Group** > **Group**.

    Your slide should look like Figure 15-2.
13. **With your teacher's permission**, click **File** > **Print**. Select **Print All Slides**, and then click **Print** to print the presentation.
14. Close the presentation, saving changes, and exit PowerPoint.

Figure 15-2

Project 32—Apply It

Kelly Greenery Logo

DIRECTIONS

1. Start PowerPoint, if necessary, and open **PProj32** from the data files for this lesson.
2. Save the presentation as **PProj32_studentfirstname_studentlastname** in the location where your teacher instructs you to store the files for this lesson.
3. Insert a text box at the bottom of the slide, and type your full name in it.
4. Insert WordArt that uses the second sample in the sixth row of the WordArt gallery. (It is the shiny orange sample.)
5. Replace the placeholder text with **Kelly Greenery**.
6. Apply the **Arch Up** transformation from the Follow Path section of the **Text Effects** > **Transform** menu.
7. Apply a bright green fill to the text, matching the bright green in the clip art image as closely as possible.
8. Apply a dark green outline to the WordArt text.
9. Apply a green **Glow** effect to the WordArt. (Use the green sample from the top row.)
10. Increase the height of the WordArt frame to **3"** and position the WordArt so it is arched over the clip art.
11. **With your teacher's permission**, print one copy of the slide. The finished logo is shown in Figure 15-3.
12. Close the presentation, saving changes, and exit PowerPoint.

Figure 15-3

Lesson 16

Creating SmartArt Diagrams

WORDS TO KNOW

SmartArt
Professionally designed graphics that organize and display information in various graphic types such as lists, processes, or hierarchical displays.

SmartArt style
The shading and texture effects on the shapes used in the diagram. Some of the styles make the shapes look raised or shiny, for example.

➤ What You Will Learn

Creating a SmartArt Diagram
Adding, Removing, and Resizing Shapes in a Diagram
Reordering Diagram Content
Changing the Diagram Type
Changing the Color and Style of a Diagram
Creating Picture-Based SmartArt

Software Skills SmartArt enables you to combine graphics with text to present information in a much more interesting and attractive layout than a plain bulleted list provides.

Application Skills In the Wynnedale Medical Center presentation, most of the information is presented in bulleted lists. In this lesson, you will switch over some of those lists to SmartArt, for a more interesting and graphical presentation.

What You Can Do

Creating a SmartArt Diagram

- **SmartArt** is a tool that enables you to place text in graphical containers that make it more interesting to read. These container graphics are specially designed to arrange items in conceptually relevant ways, such as in an organization chart, cycle diagram, or pyramid.

- You can insert a SmartArt graphic in a content slide layout, or you can add it without a placeholder using the SmartArt button on the Insert tab. You can also, if desired, convert a bulleted list to a SmartArt graphic.
- Each SmartArt diagram has a fly-out text pane where you can edit its content. Click the arrow button to the left of the diagram to open the text pane. You can also make text edits directly in the shapes.

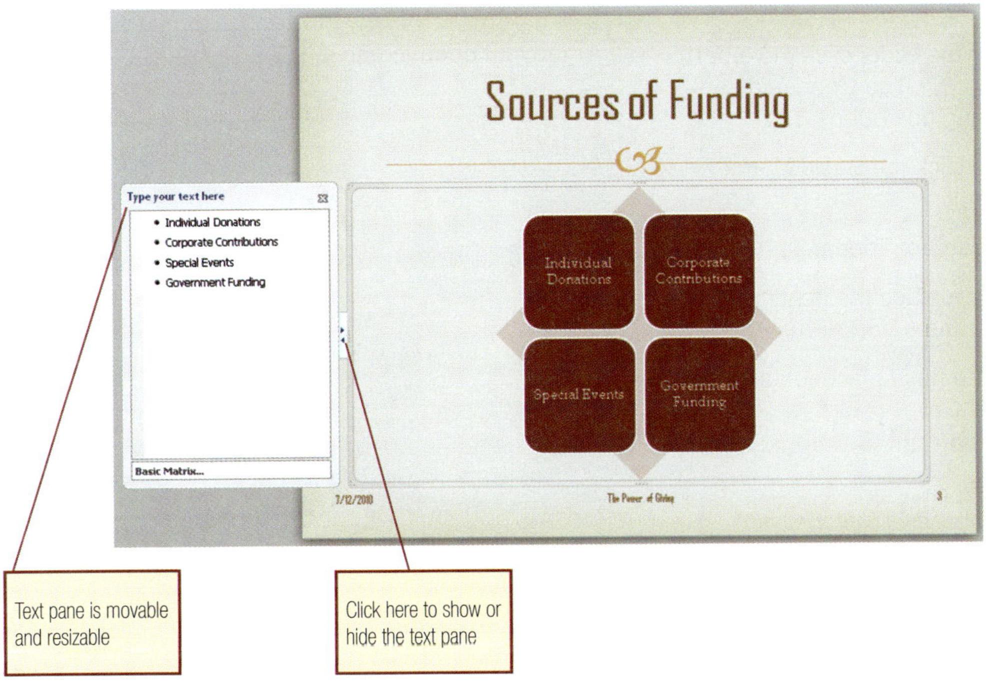

Figure 16-1

Try It! Converting a Bulleted List to SmartArt

1. Start PowerPoint and open **PTry16** from the data files for this lesson.
2. Save the presentation as **PTry16_studentfirstname_studentlastname** in the location where your teacher instructs you to store the files for this lesson.
3. Display slide 6. Click in the numbered list and press CTRL + A to select all the text.
4. Right-click the selected list and click Convert to SmartArt. A palette of samples appears.
5. Point to the Basic Timeline design (second design in the fourth row). The design is previewed behind the list.
6. Click the Continuous Block Process design (first design in the fourth row). The design is applied to the list.
7. Display slide 9. Click in the content area and press CTRL + A to select all the text.
8. Right-click the selected text and click Convert to SmartArt.
9. Click the Horizontal Bulleted List (the first sample in the second row). The design is applied to the list.

   ✓ *Because this slide contained a multilevel bulleted list, the subordinate levels appear as mini lists within the main shapes.*
10. Save the changes to the **PTry16_studentfirstname_studentlastname** file, and leave it open to use in the next Try It.

Try It! Inserting a New SmartArt Object

1. In the **PTry16_studentfirstname_studentlastname** file, in the Slides pane, click between slides 2 and 3 and press ENTER, inserting a new blank slide.
2. In the content area on the slide, click the Insert SmartArt Graphic icon. The Choose a SmartArt Graphic dialog box opens.
3. Click Matrix, and then click the Basic Matrix design (the first design).
4. Click OK. An empty diagram appears.
5. In the upper right box, replace the [text] placeholder with **Individual Donations**.
6. Replace the other three [text] placeholders (going clockwise) with **Corporate Contributions**, **Government Funding**, and **Special Events**.

   ✓ *Notice that the text resizes automatically to fit.*
7. In the title placeholder at the top of the slide, type **Sources of Funding**.
8. Save the changes to the **PTry16_studentfirstname_studentlastname** file, and leave it open to use in the next Try It.

Fill in the placeholders on the new diagram

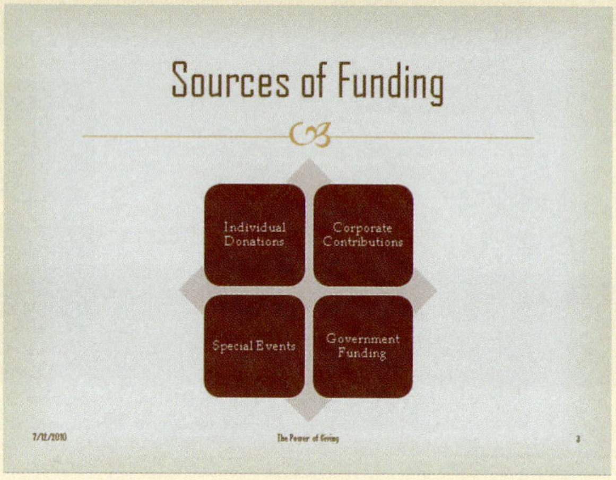

Adding, Removing, and Resizing Shapes in a Diagram

- Each diagram begins with a default number of shapes, but you can add or remove them as needed. Use the commands on the SmartArt Tools Design tab.

  ✓ *There are some exceptions; some diagram types require a certain number of shapes in them. For such diagrams the Add Shape command is unavailable.*
- You can also resize each shape individually. Drag its selection handles to do so, just as you would any drawn shape. Instead of dragging, you can also use the Smaller or Larger buttons on the SmartArt Tools Format tab.

Try It! Adding, Removing, and Resizing a Shape

1. In the **PTry16_studentfirstname_studentlastname** file, on slide 7, select the last shape ("Follow up to assess progress").
2. Press DEL. The shape is removed and the other shapes resize to fill the space.
3. With the rightmost shape selected on the diagram on slide 7, click SmartArt Tools Design > Add Shape. A new shape appears.

   ✓ *The Add Shape button has a down arrow you can click to choose where the new shape will be added, but you don't need it in these steps because you want the new shape in the default position, to the right of the selected shape.*

4. Click in the new shape and type the text that appeared in the deleted shape before ("Follow up to assess progress").
5. On slide 7, click the first rounded rectangle in the diagram to select it.
6. Hold down CTRL and click on each of the other rounded rectangles.
7. Position the mouse pointer on a top selection handle on any of the selected shapes and drag upward 1/2". The height of each of the rectangles changes equally.
8. Click SmartArt Tools Format > Smaller. Then, click it again to make the shapes one more step smaller.
9. Save the changes to the **PTry16_studentfirstname_studentlastname** file, and leave it open to use in the next Try It.

Reordering Diagram Content

- Even though each shape in a SmartArt diagram is individually movable, you should not drag shapes to reorder them in a SmartArt diagram, because it interrupts the automatic flow of the layout. Instead you should use the reordering commands on the SmartArt Tools Design tab.
- The Promote and Demote commands change the level of the text within the diagram hierarchy. This is like promoting and demoting bulleted list levels on a text-based layout.

Try It! Reordering Diagram Content

1. In the **PTry16_studentfirstname_studentlastname** file, file, on slide 3, click the top left rounded rectangle to select it.
2. Click SmartArt Tools Design > Move Down. The content of that shape is moved one position in the layout.

   ✓ *Notice that it moved to the right, and not literally down. In this case, down means to move it down in the flow one position, regardless of the direction of the flow. If the diagram's flow was top-to-bottom, moving "down" might even be up in the diagram.*

3. On slide 10, click in the *Get friends involved* bullet point in the second column.
4. Click SmartArt Tools Design > Promote. That bullet point becomes its own separate column.
5. Click SmartArt Tools Design > Demote. The text goes back to being a bullet point in the center column.
6. Click SmartArt Tools Design > Right to Left. The diagram changes its flow direction, so that the right and left columns switch places.
7. Save the changes to the **PTry16_studentfirstname_studentlastname** file, and leave it open to use in the next Try It.

Changing the Diagram Type

- There are many diagram types to choose from. If you don't like the original diagram type you started with, you can easily switch to another.
- The diagram types are arranged in categories, but there is some overlap; some designs appear in more than one category.
- On the SmartArt Tools Design tab, you can open a gallery of layouts and choose the one you want to apply to the diagram.

Try It! Changing the Diagram Type

1. In the **PTry16_studentfirstname_studentlastname**, click slide 10 to display it.
2. Click the SmartArt to make the SmartArt tabs available.
3. On the SmartArt Tools Design tab, in the Layouts group, click the More button to open the gallery of design samples.
4. Point at several different samples, and see previews of them on the slide, behind the open menu.
5. Click the Vertical Bracket List (first sample in the second row). The diagram changes to that layout.
6. Save the changes to the **PTry16_studentfirstname_studentlastname** file, and leave it open to use in the next Try It.

Changing the Color and Style of a Diagram

- A SmartArt diagram's colors are determined by the color theme in use in the presentation. You can choose different combinations of those theme colors.
- **SmartArt style** refers to the shading and texture effects on the shapes used in the diagram. Some of the styles make the shapes look raised or shiny, for example.

Try It! Changing the Style and Color of a Diagram

1. In the **PTry16_studentfirstname_studentlastname**, click slide 10 to display it if it is not already displayed.
2. Select the SmartArt object's frame if it is not already selected.
3. On the SmartArt Tools Design tab, click the More button in the SmartArt Styles group to open a gallery of style choices.
4. Click Polished (the first sample in the first row of the 3D section). It is applied to the diagram.
5. On slide 10, with the diagram still selected, click SmartArt Tools Design > Change Colors. A palette of color presets appears.
6. Point to several of the presets, and see them previewed on the slide behind the open menu.
7. Click the fourth sample in the Colorful section. It is applied to the diagram.

   ✓ *The Colorful section's presets use a different color from the theme for each of the major shapes. Most of the other preset types stick to a single color.*
8. Save the changes to the **PTry16_studentfirstname_studentlastname** file, and leave it open to use in the next Try It.

Creating Picture-Based SmartArt

- Some of the SmartArt layouts include picture placeholders. These are useful for providing small pieces of artwork, either to illustrate points being made in the text or as decoration.
- The main difference with this type of layout is that you have an extra step after inserting the SmartArt and typing the text—you must click each picture placeholder and select a picture to insert into it.

Try It! Creating Picture-Based SmartArt

1. In the **PTry16_studentfirstname_studentlastname** file, on slide 5, select the clip art and press DEL to remove.
2. Select the bulleted list.
3. Right-click the bulleted list and click Convert to SmartArt > More SmartArt Graphics. The Choose a SmartArt Graphic dialog box opens.
4. Click the Picture category.
5. Click Captioned Pictures (the second sample in the second row.)
6. Click OK.
7. On the SmartArt diagram, double-click the Insert Picture from File icon in the leftmost picture placeholder. The Insert Picture dialog box opens.
8. Navigate to the folder containing the files for this lesson.
9. Click **PTry16a.jpg** and click Insert. The picture appears in the placeholder.
10. Using this same process, insert **PTry16b.jpg** and **PTry16c.jpg** in the other two placeholders on the slide.
11. Save the **PTry16_studentfirstname_studentlastname** file and close it.

Project 33—Create It

Laser Surgery Presentation

DIRECTIONS

1. Start PowerPoint, if necessary, and open **PProj33** from the data files for this lesson.
2. Save the presentation as **PProj33_studentfirstname_studentlastname** in the location where your teacher instructs you to store the files for this lesson.
3. Display slide 1, and click **Insert** > **Text Box**. Click at the top of the slide and type your full name.
4. On slide 3, click in the content area and press CTRL + A to select all.
5. Right-click the selection and point to **Convert to SmartArt**.
6. Click the Radial List (first sample in the third row). The list changes to a diagram.
7. Click the picture placeholder in the large circle on the SmartArt diagram.
8. In the Insert Picture dialog box, navigate to the data files for this lesson and click **PProj33a.jpg**.
9. Click **Insert**.
10. On the **SmartArt Tools Design** tab, click the **More** button in the SmartArt Styles group to open the SmartArt Styles gallery.
11. Click **Polished** (the first sample in the 3D section).
12. **With your teacher's permission**, print one copy of the presentation as handouts, 6 slides per page.
13. Close the presentation, saving changes, and exit PowerPoint.

Project 34—Apply It

Laser Surgery Presentation

DIRECTIONS

1. Start PowerPoint, if necessary, and open **PProj34** from the data files for this lesson.
2. Save the presentation as **PProj34_studentfirstname_studentlastname** in the location where your teacher instructs you to store the files for this lesson.
3. Place a text box containing your full name at the top of slide 1.
4. On slide 4, convert the bulleted list to the Vertical Block List SmartArt design.
   ✓ *You can determine a sample's name by hovering the mouse over it.*
5. Change the SmartArt Style to **Moderate Effect**.
6. Change the colors to the first sample in the Colorful section of the color list. Figure 16-2 shows the finished slide.
7. On slide 5, change the colors for the SmartArt to the **Colored Fill** colors in the Accent 3 section of the color list.
8. On slide 8, convert the numbered list to the **Staggered Process** SmartArt.
   ✓ *You will need to open the Choose a SmartArt Graphic dialog box to find this design. After right-clicking the list, choose More SmartArt Graphics, and then look in the Process category.*
9. Drag the bottom of the SmartArt frame down **1"** on the slide, enlarging the diagram.
10. Change the colors for the diagram to the third sample in the Colorful section of the color list.
11. Change the SmartArt Style to **Polished** (the first sample in the 3D section of the SmartArt Styles gallery). Figure 16-3 shows the finished slide.
12. Close the presentation, saving changes, and exit PowerPoint.

Figure 16-2

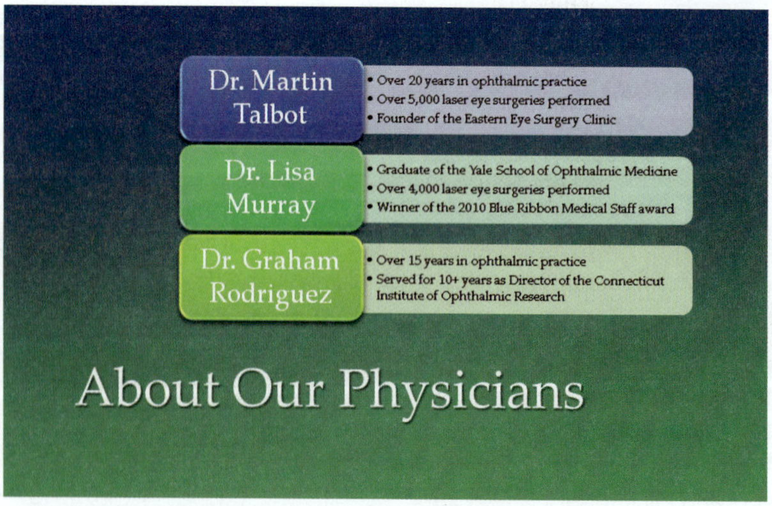

Sign up for a personal consultation
Schedule a surgery date
Arrive at surgery center 45 minutes before appointment
Undergo surgery
Enjoy better vision
Taking the Next Step
8
Clear Vision in a Day
7/13/2010

Figure 16-3

Lesson 17

Creating a Photo Album

WORDS TO KNOW

Photo album
A special type of presentation in which the main point is to display photos.

➤ What You Will Learn

Creating a Photo Album

Software Skills A photo album presentation enables you to display multiple photographs with very little text, to let the pictures tell their own stories. PowerPoint has a special Photo Album feature that makes it easy to create and modify photo albums in PowerPoint.

Application Skills Orchard School, a small private school in your area, has asked you to help create a photo album of pictures to market the school to local families. You will create a photo album with the pictures they have given you so far, as an example of what can be done in PowerPoint.

What You Can Do

Creating a Photo Album

- A **photo album** presentation doesn't have placeholders for bulleted lists or other text; it is designed to efficiently display and organize photos.
- In a photo album presentation you can easily import and arrange many photo files. You can change the order of the photos at any time.
- You can also choose from a variety of picture frame styles.
- You should edit a photo album presentation via the Photo Album dialog box as much as possible, rather than manually editing it. This allows PowerPoint's photo album management features to remain in operation, such as automatically reordering the pictures across multiple slides when you rearrange picture order in the dialog box.

Try It! Creating a Photo Album

1. Start PowerPoint.

   ✓ *You do not need to save the presentation file yet because the Photo Album feature creates a brand-new presentation file.*

2. Click Insert > Photo Album. The Photo Album dialog box opens.
3. Click the File/Disk button. The Insert New Pictures dialog box opens.
4. Navigate to the location where data files for this lesson are stored and click **PTry17a.jpg**.
5. Hold down the CTRL key and click **PTry17b**, **PTry17c**, **PTry17d**, and **PTry17e**.
6. Click Insert. The file names appear on the Pictures in album list.
7. Click **PTry17b** on the list, and then click the Decrease Brightness button.
8. Open the Picture layout drop-down list and click 2 Pictures.
9. Open the Frame shape drop-down list and click Rounded Rectangle.
10. Click Create. The photo album is created in a new presentation file.
11. Save the presentation as **PTry17_studentfirstname_studentlastname** in the location where your teacher instructs you to store the files for this lesson, and leave it open to use in the next Try It.

Try It! Editing a Photo Album

1. In the **PTry17_studentfirstname_studentlastname** file, on the Insert tab, click the arrow below the Photo Album button to open its menu. Then, click Edit Photo Album.
2. Open the Picture layout drop-down list and click Fit to slide.
3. Click **PTry17e** on the list, and click the Move Up button four times, to move it to the top of the list.
4. Click **PTry17a** on the list, and click Remove.
5. Click Update.
6. Save the changes to the **PTry17_studentfirstname_studentlastname** file, and leave it open to use in the next Try It.

Try It! Applying a Theme to a Photo Album

1. In the **PTry17_studentfirstname_studentlastname** file, on the Insert tab, click the arrow below the Photo Album button to open its menu. Then, click Edit Photo Album.
2. Click the Browse button next to the Theme text box.
3. Click the Civic theme.
4. Click Select.
5. Click Update.
6. Save the **PTry17_studentfirstname_studentlastname** file and then close it.

Project 35—Create It

Orchard School Photo Album

DIRECTIONS

1. Start PowerPoint if necessary.
2. Click **Insert** > **Photo Album**. The Photo Album dialog box opens.
3. Click the **File/Disk** button. The Insert New Pictures dialog box opens.
4. Navigate to the location where data files for this lesson are stored and click **PProj35a.jpg**.
5. Hold down the CTRL key and click **PProj35b.jpg**.
6. Click **Insert**.
7. Open the **Picture layout** drop-down list and click **1 Picture**.
8. Click the **Browse** button next to the Theme text box.
9. Click the **Pushpin** theme, and click **Select**.
10. Click **Create**. A new presentation is created.
11. Display slide 1, and click **Insert** > **Text Box**. Click at the bottom of the slide and type your full name.
12. Save the presentation as **PProj35_studentfirstname_studentlastname** in the location where your teacher instructs you to store the files for this lesson.
13. **With your teacher's permission**, print one copy of the presentation as handouts, 6 slides per page.
14. Close the presentation and exit PowerPoint.

Project 36—Apply It

Orchard School Photo Album

DIRECTIONS

1. Start PowerPoint if necessary, and open **PProj36** from the data files for this lesson.
2. Save the presentation as **PProj36_studentfirstname_studentlastname** in the location where your teacher instructs you to store the files for this lesson.
3. At the bottom of slide 1, insert a text box and type your full name.
4. Open the Edit Photo Album dialog box, navigate to the location where data files for this lesson are stored, and add **PProj36a.jpg** through **PProj36f.jpg** to the photo album.
5. Move the **PProj35a** photo to the bottom of the list.
6. Choose **Soft Edge Rectangle** as the frame shape.
7. Remove **PProj36e**.
8. Update the photo album.
9. **With your teacher's permission**, print one copy of the presentation as handouts, 6 slides per page.
10. Close the presentation, saving changes, and exit PowerPoint.

Chapter Assessment and Application

Project 37—Make It Your Own

MyPyramid Presentation

Childhood obesity has become a serious problem in the United States, and one way to combat it is to educate children about nutrition at an early age. The United States Department of Agriculture has created MyPyramid, a way of thinking about nutrition using a pyramid graphic. The MyPyramid system is a very popular tool for educating young people about nutrition today. Information about it is available at www.MyPyramid.gov.

Using the information you find at that site, create an educational presentation for children ages 9 to 12 that explains the importance of eating a healthy balance of foods every day. On the first slide of your presentation, include an original logo that you design yourself using the shapes in PowerPoint.

DIRECTIONS

Create the Logo

1. Start PowerPoint. Save a new blank file as **PProj37_studentfirstname_studentlastname** in the location where your teacher tells you to save the files for this project.
2. Apply a theme from the themes available on the Design tab. Pick one that you think is appropriate for the audience. Apply a different color theme if the colors in the design you chose are not bright and cheerful.
3. On slide 1, type **Nutrition and You** in the Title placeholder. In the subtitle placeholder, type your full name.
4. On slide 1, use the Shapes tools to create a logo that consists of at least two shapes, stacked and grouped together, with two different fill colors chosen from the current color theme.

Assemble the Information

1. On the www.MyPyramid.gov Web site, read about the food pyramid and the recommendations for daily nutrition for children ages 9 to 12.
2. Visit the News & Media section of the site and download the jpeg version of the full-color MyPyramid graphic. Save it to your hard disk as **MyPyramid.jpg** in the location where your teacher tells you to save files for this project.

✓ *If you cannot download the logo from the Web site, use* **PProj37a.jpg** *from the data files for this chapter.*

Create the Information

1. Create a presentation of at least 9 slides (including the title slide) that explains how children ages 9 to 12 can use MyPyramid guidelines to choose what to eat each day. Include one slide explaining each of the colored stripes in the pyramid, plus whatever additional slides you think are necessary.

   The presentation should include:
   - At least one usage of the MyPyramid graphic you downloaded from the Web site.
   - At least one piece of clip art.
   - At least one symbol.
   - At least one SmartArt graphic.
   - At least one text box that is not a placeholder.
2. **With your instructor's permission**, print one copy of your presentation.
3. Close the presentation, saving changes, and exit PowerPoint.

Project 38—Master It

White River Restoration Project

The White River Restoration Society is recruiting new members to help with the cleanup and reforestation of some land they recently received as a donation. They have a basic presentation with all the text in it, but they need some graphics to make it more interesting. You will help them out by adding clip art, photos, SmartArt, and WordArt.

DIRECTIONS

1. Start PowerPoint, if necessary, and open **PProj38** from the data files for this chapter.
2. Save the presentation as **PProj38_studentfirstname_studentlastname** in the location where your teacher instructs you to store the files for this chapter.
3. At the bottom of slide 1, create a new text box and type the following:

   Copyright 2012 Friends of the White River – Student Name.
4. Insert a copyright symbol © after the word *Copyright*.
5. Format the text box as follows:
   - Format the text in the text box as 14-point and italic.
   - Apply a background fill to the text box that uses the palest shade of the light green theme color (the third color in the theme).
6. On slide 1, create a piece of WordArt with the text **White River Restoration Project**:
   - Start with the orange gradient fill sample (second sample in the fourth row).
   - Press ENTER after the word River, so the text appears on two lines.
   - Apply the **Arch Up** transformation (the first sample in the Follow Path section).
   - Size the WordArt to exactly **3"** high and **9"** wide.
   - Change the text fill color to the darkest shade of light green (the third color) in the theme color set.

Illustration A

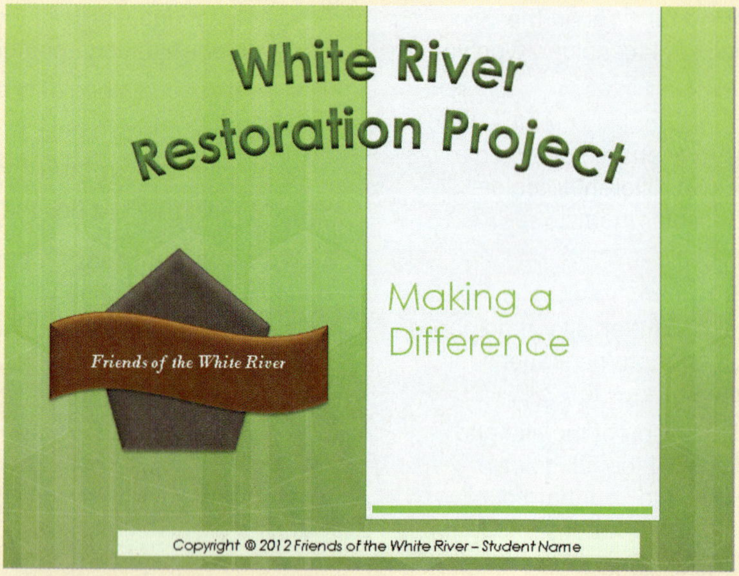

7. On slide 1, create the logo shown in Illustration A:
   - Both shapes were drawn with the Shapes feature.
   - The pentagon is gray, and the banner is brown.
   - Both have the **Preset 2** shape effect applied.
   - Type the text directly into the banner shape.
8. On the Slide Master, change the bullet character for all layouts to a picture bullet that looks like a light green square. Then, close Slide Master view.

   ✓ *Any light green square is acceptable; try to choose one that looks similar to the green background image on the slides.*
9. On slide 2, convert the bulleted list to the **Vertical Bullet List** SmartArt layout.
10. Apply the **Moderate Effect** SmartArt style to the SmartArt.
11. Change the color of the SmartArt to Colored Outline – Accent 1. Illustration B shows the finished slide.
12. On slide 4, in the empty content placeholder, insert a clip art image of people canoeing on a river.
13. From the **Picture Tools Format** tab's **Picture Effects** menu, apply the Preset 5 settings to the clip art image.
14. On slide 5, in the empty content placeholder, insert **PProj38a.jpg** from the data files for this chapter.
15. On slide 6, convert the bulleted list to a **Target** type of SmartArt layout.
16. On slide 7, remove the bullet characters from both paragraphs.
17. **With your instructor's permission**, print the presentation (6 slides per page).
18. Close the presentation, saving changes, and exit PowerPoint.

Illustration B

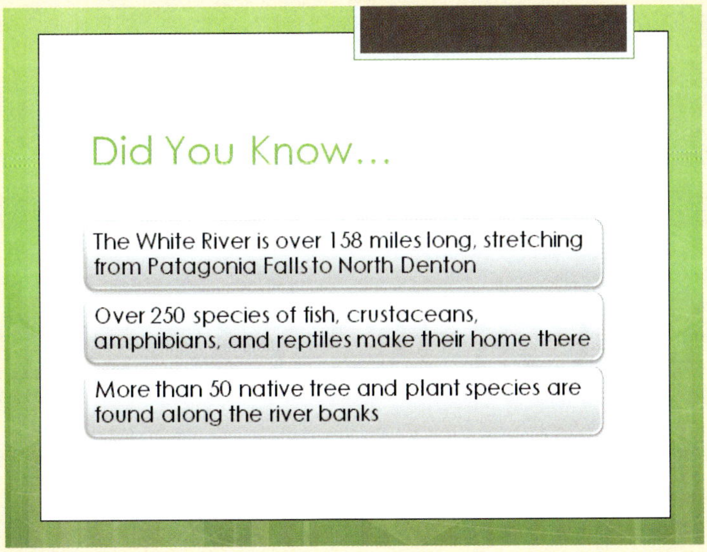

Chapter 3

Enhancing a Presentation

Lesson 18
Modifying a Theme
Projects 39-40

- Changing Background Style
- Changing Theme Colors
- Changing Theme Fonts
- Creating New Theme Fonts

Lesson 19
Modifying a Background
Projects 41-42

- Creating Slides from an Outline
- Hiding Background Graphics
- Formatting a Slide Background with a Picture
- Applying a Background Fill Color
- Resetting the Slide Background
- Reusing Slides from Other Presentations

Lesson 20
Using Effects and Animations
Projects 43-44

- Applying Entrance Effects
- Setting Effect Options
- Applying Animation Effects with Animation Painter
- Apply Animations to Objects and SmartArt Graphics

Lesson 21
Creating Multimedia Presentations
Projects 45-46

- Analyzing the Effectiveness of Multimedia Presentations
- Inserting a Video
- Editing a Video
- Applying Video Styles
- Adjusting Video Color
- Controlling a Video in a Presentation
- Inserting Sounds and Music

Lesson 22
Working with Tables
Projects 47-48

- Inserting a Table
- Formatting and Modifying a Table

Lesson 23
Working with Charts
Projects 49-50

- Inserting a Column Chart
- Formatting and Modifying a Chart
- Animating a Chart

End of Chapter Assessments
Projects 51-52

Lesson 18

Modifying a Theme

WORDS TO KNOW

Font
A set of characters with a specific size and style.

➤ What You Will Learn

Changing Background Style
Changing Theme Colors
Changing Theme Fonts
Creating New Theme Fonts

Software Skills You can change theme colors, fonts, and backgrounds to customize a presentation. You can also create new theme font combinations to easily apply in later presentations.

Application Skills In this lesson, you continue work on presentations for Integrated Health Systems' new laser eye surgery centers. You want to explore how changing theme elements might improve the appearance of a presentation you have prepared for the company's Holmes Medical Center facility.

What You Can Do

Changing Background Style

- Each theme has a specific background color, and some have background graphics or other effects such as gradients—gradations from one color to another.
- To customize a theme, you can change the background style to one of the choices offered by the current theme, such as those shown in the Background Styles gallery on the Design tab.
- Background styles use the current theme colors. You can apply a new style to all slides or to selected slides.

- As you rest your pointer on different background styles, the current slide shows what that background style will look like.
- If you want to make a more radical change to the background, click the Background dialog box launcher on the Design tab to open the Format Background dialog box where you can create a new background using a solid color, a gradient, a texture, or a picture file.

Try It! **Changing Background Style**

1. Start PowerPoint and open **PTry18** from the data files for this lesson.
2. Save the presentation as **PTry18_studentfirstname_studentlastname** in the location where your teacher instructs you to store the files for this lesson.
3. Select the words Student Name in the subtitle placeholder on slide 1 and type your first name and last name.
4. On the Design tab, click the Background Styles button.
5. Click the Style 6 to apply it to all the slides in the presentation.
6. Display slide 1.
7. On the Design tab, click the Background Styles button.
8. Right-click Style 10 in the gallery.
9. Click Apply to Selected Slides.
10. Save the changes to the **PTry18_studentfirstname_studentlastname** file, and leave it open to use in the next Try It.

Changing Theme Colors

- Each PowerPoint theme uses a palette of colors selected to work well together. These colors are automatically applied to various elements in the presentation, such as the slide background, text, shape fills, and hyperlink text.
- You can see the color palettes for each theme by clicking the Colors button on the Design tab.
- PowerPoint offers several ways to adjust theme colors:

  ✔ *If you like the layout and fonts of a particular theme but not its colors, you can choose to use the color palette of a different theme.*

  ✔ *You can change one or more colors in the current theme to customize the theme.*

- You modify theme colors in the Create New Theme Colors dialog box.
- Change a color by clicking the down arrow for a particular color to display a palette. Select a different tint or hue of a theme color, choose one of ten standard colors, or click More Colors to open the Colors dialog box and pick from all available colors.
- As soon as you change a theme color, the preview in the Create New Theme Colors dialog box also changes to show how your new color coordinates with the others in the theme.
- You can name a new color scheme and save it. It then displays in the Custom area at the top of the Theme Colors gallery. Custom colors are available to use with any theme.

  ✔ *You can delete custom theme colors by right-clicking the color palette set and selecting Delete.*

Try It! **Changing Theme Colors**

1. In the **PTry18_studentfirstname_studentlastname** file, select slide 2.
2. Hover over several color themes. Live Preview shows you how the color theme will look on your slide.
3. Click Design > Colors.
4. Select the Oriel theme.
5. Click Design > Colors.
6. Click Create New Theme Colors.

(continued)

Try It! Changing Theme Colors *(continued)*

7. In the Name box, type your first name and last name.
8. Click the down arrow for Accent 1.
9. Select Ice Blue, Accent 5, Darker 50% from the palette.
10. Click Save.
11. Save the changes to the **PTry18_studentfirstname_studentlastname** file, and leave it open to use in the next Try It.

Changing Theme Fonts

- Themes also offer a set of two specific **fonts**, one font for all titles and the other for body text such as the text in bullet lists.
- You can apply the fonts of another theme by choosing a set from the Theme Fonts gallery.
- You can create your own theme fonts if desired, or you can change the font of text in any placeholder using the tools in the Font group on the Home tab.

Try It! Changing Theme Fonts

1. In the **PTry18_studentfirstname_studentlastname** file, select slide 2.
2. Click Design > Fonts [A].
3. Scroll through the available themes.
4. Select Apex.
5. Save the changes to the **PTry18_studentfirstname_studentlastname** file, and leave it open to use in the next Try It.

Creating New Theme Fonts

- PowerPoint makes it easy to change text appearance on one or more slides.
- If you know you want to change the font for each slide, you can create your own set of theme fonts and then apply them to change text on all slides at once.
- Create a new set of theme fonts in the Create New Theme Fonts dialog box. The Sample Preview window shows you the heading and body font as you select them.
- After you name your set of theme fonts, the set appears at the top of the Theme Fonts gallery in the Custom section.

✔ *You can delete custom theme fonts by right-clicking the font set and selecting Delete.*

- If you want to change only one font throughout a presentation, you can click Home > Replace > Replace Fonts, as you learned in Chapter 1.
- If you want to make a number of changes to a presentation's fonts, you should change text on the slide master, which controls text appearance throughout the presentation.

✔ *You learn more about slide masters in Lesson 24.*

Try It! Creating New Theme Fonts

1. In the **PTry18_studentfirstname_studentlastname** file, click Design > Fonts [A].
2. Click Create New Theme Fonts.
3. Click the Heading font down arrow and select Tahoma.
4. Click the Body font down arrow and select Bookman Old Style.
5. Click Save.
6. Save the changes to the **PTry18_studentfirstname_studentlastname** file and close it.

Project 39—Create It

Customizing a Presentation

DIRECTIONS

1. Start PowerPoint, if necessary, and open **PProj39** from the data files for this lesson.
2. Save the presentation as **PProj39_studentfirstname_studentlastname** in the location where your teacher instructs you to store the files for this lesson.
3. Click at the end of the subtitle text. The placeholder becomes active.
4. Press ENTER and type **Presented by** and then add your first name and last name.
5. Move to slide 4 and click **Home** > **New Slide** > **Content with Captions**.
6. In the caption placeholder, type the text shown in Figure 18-1.
7. Click **Design** > **Fonts** > **Create New Theme Fonts**. The Create New Theme Fonts dialog box opens.
8. In the Heading font box, select **Arial** and in the Body font box, select **Corbel**. The Preview window shows you how the fonts look together.
9. Type your first name and last name in the Name box and click **Save**. The newly created Theme Font will appear at the top of the Theme Fonts gallery.
10. Click **Design** > **Colors** and select **Origin**. The new theme color is applied to all slides.
11. Click **Design** > **Background Styles**. The Background Styles gallery opens.
12. Select **Style 2** to apply the light blue color to all slides.
13. **With your teacher's permission**, print slide 4.
14. Close the workbook, saving changes, and exit PowerPoint.

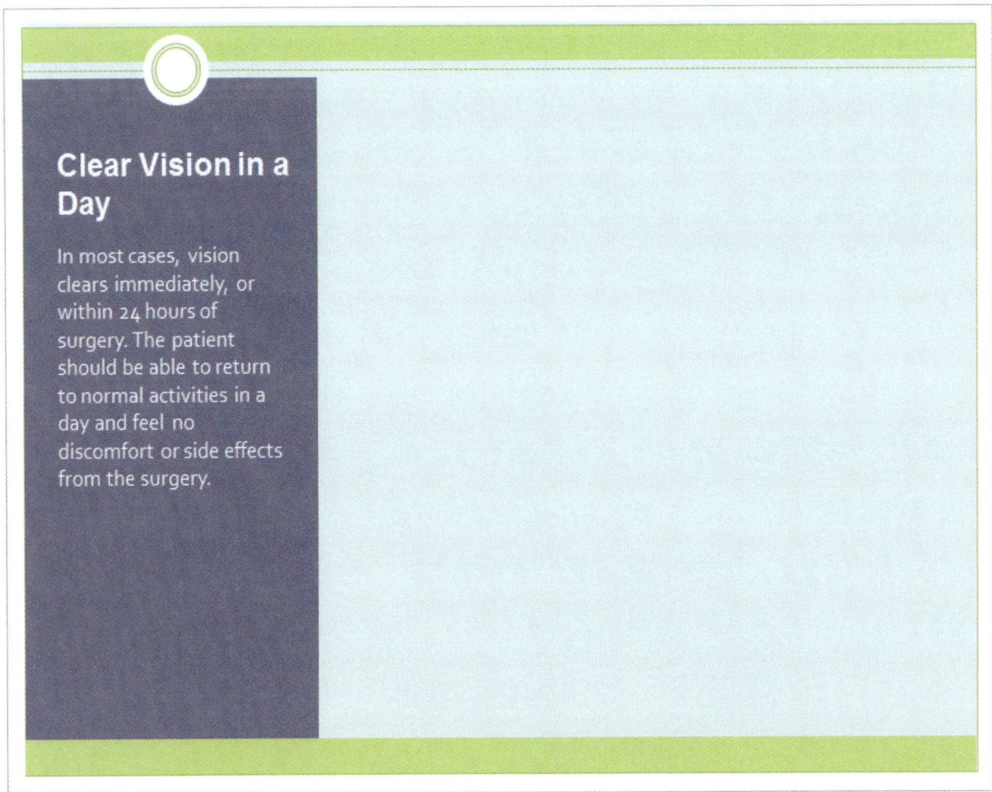

Figure 18-1

Project 40—Apply It

Customizing a Presentation

DIRECTIONS

1. Start PowerPoint, if necessary, and open **PProj40** from the data files for this lesson.
2. Save the presentation as **PProj40_studentfirstname_studentlastname** in the location where your teacher instructs you to store the files for this lesson.
3. Add an image to slide 5 to add interest.
   a. Search for an appropriate clip art photograph.
   b. Resize the image as necessary to fit in the placeholder.
4. Change the theme font to **Trek** (Franklin Gothic Medium and Franklin Gothic Book).
5. Change the background style to **Style 6**.
6. Using the Notes and Handouts tab in the Header and Footer dialog box, add your first name and last name to the footer.
7. **With your teacher's permission**, print a handout of slide 5.
8. Close the presentation, saving changes, and exit PowerPoint.

Lesson 19

Modifying a Background

➤ What You Will Learn

- Creating Slides from an Outline
- Reusing Slides from Other Presentations
- Hiding Background Graphics
- Applying a Background Fill Color
- Formatting a Slide Background with a Picture
- Resetting the Slide Background

Software Skills Word outlines can be readily imported to create slides. In some instances, you may want to hide the background graphics created as part of a theme.

Application Skills Your client, Voyager Travel Adventures, has supplied you with files they want you to use in the presentation you're creating for them. You'll also add information on each slide to help identify and organize the presentation.

What You Can Do

Creating Slides from an Outline

- You can save time by reusing text created in other programs, such as Word, in your PowerPoint presentation.
- You can use Word to help you organize the contents of a presentation and then transfer that outline to PowerPoint.
- If you want to use a Word outline to create slides, you must format the text using Word styles that clearly indicate text levels.

  ✔ *For instance, text formatted with the Word Heading 1 style become slide titles. Text styled as Heading 2 or Heading 3 becomes bulleted items.*

- You have two options for using a Word outline to create slides:
  - You can simply open the Word document in PowerPoint to create the slides. Use this option to create a new presentation directly from outline content.
  - You can use the Slides from Outline command on the New Slide drop-down list to add slides to an existing presentation.

    ✔ *You cannot use this command unless a presentation is already open.*
- When a Word document is used to create a new presentation, the slides will display the same fonts and styles used in the document. These will not change even if a new theme or theme fonts are applied.
- If you want to change the fonts in a presentation created from an outline, you need to click the Reset button on the Home tab.

  ✔ *You can also use this command to reverse changes made to slide layouts or themes.*
- The Reset function will delete the Word styles and apply the theme defaults for colors, fonts, and effects.

Figure 19-1

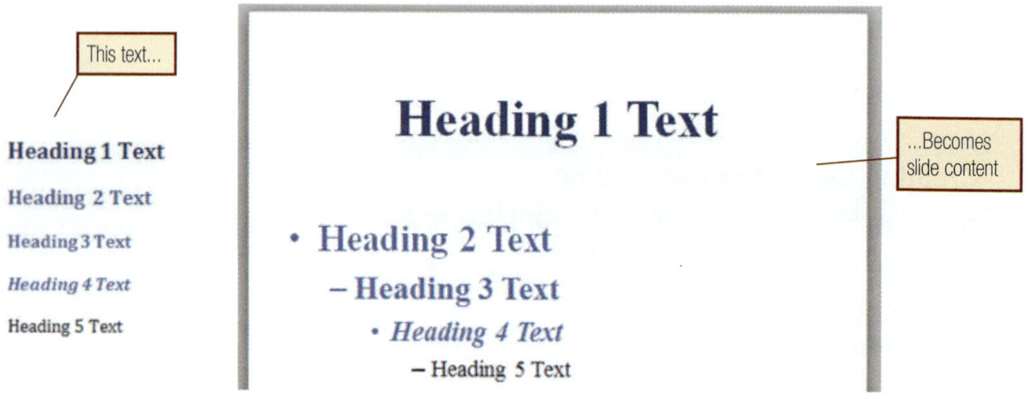

Try It! Creating Slides from an Outline

1. Start PowerPoint, click File > Open, and navigate to the location where the data files for this lesson are stored.
2. In the Open dialog box, click All PowerPoint Presentations and select All Files.
3. Select the Word document **PTry19_Giving** and click Open.
4. Scroll through the presentation to see how the Word styles are applied to the slides.
5. Save the presentation as **PTry19_Giving_studentfirstname_studentlastname** in the location where your teacher instructs you to store the files for this lesson.
6. Close the file.

Try It! Adding Slides from an Outline to an Existing Presentation

1. In PowerPoint, open **PTry19** from the data files for this lesson.
2. Save the presentation as **PTry19_studentfirstname_studentlastname** in the location where your teacher instructs you to store the files for this lesson.
3. Select slide 1 (the new slides will appear after this slide).
4. Click Home > New Slide drop-down arrow.
5. Click Slides from Outline.

(continued)

Try It! Adding Slides from an Outline to an Existing Presentation *(continued)*

6. In the Insert Outline dialog box, navigate to the location where the data files for this lesson are stored and select **PTry19_outline**.
7. Click Insert.
8. Save the changes to the **PTry19_studentfirstname_studentlastname** file, and leave it open to use in the next Try It.

Try It! Resetting a Slide

1. In the **PTry19_studentfirstname_studentlastname** file, select slides 2–4 in the Slides pane.
2. Click Home > Reset .
3. Save the changes to the **PTry19_studentfirstname_studentlastname** file, and leave it open to use in the next Try It.

Reusing Slides from Other Presentations

- Borrowing slides from other presentations is a good way to ensure consistency among presentations, which is important when you are working for a larger company.
- As you learned in Lesson 3 in Chapter 1, you can use the Reuse Slides command on the New Slide drop-down list to insert slides from another presentation into your current presentation.
- To display the slides available to reuse, specify a presentation in the Reuse Slides task pane.

  ✔ *To see the content more clearly, rest the pointer on a slide in the current presentation.*

  ✔ *To insert a slide, simply click it.*
- If you have access to a SharePoint server, you can store slides in a Slide Library so that others can access the slides. Use the Slide Library option on the Browse list to access a SharePoint Slide Library.
- By default, slides you reuse take on the formatting of the presentation they're inserted into (the destination presentation).

  ✔ *If you want to retain the original formatting of the inserted slides, click the Keep source formatting check box at the bottom of the Reuse Slides task pane.*

Try It! Reusing Slides from Other Presentations

1. In the **PTry19_studentfirstname_studentlastname** file, click Home> New Slide > Reuse Slides.
2. In the Reuse Slides task pane, click Browse and then click Browse File.
3. Navigate to the location where you are storing the files for this lesson and select **PTry19_Giving_ studentfirstname_studentlastname**.
4. Click slide 4 in the Slides pane.
5. Point to each of the slides in the Reuse Slides task pane to view their contents.
6. Click slide 2 in the Reuse Slides task pane.
7. Close the task pane.
8. Click Home > Reset .

   ✔ *You have to reset this slide because it was originally created from a Word outline and was not reset after you created the presentation from the outline.*
9. Save the changes to the **PTry19_studentfirstname_studentlastname** file, and leave it open to use in the next Try It.

(continued)

Try It! Reusing Slides from Other Presentations *(continued)*

Reusing content from another presentation

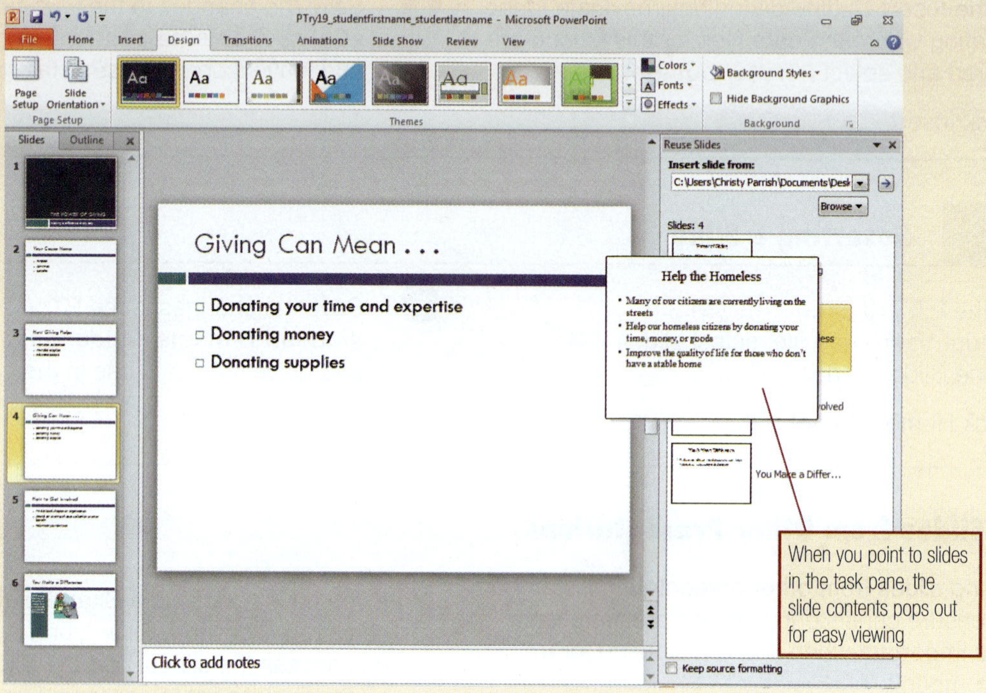

Hiding Background Graphics

- Many themes include some type of graphics such as lines or shapes that form a part of the slide background.
- You can only select and modify theme background graphics in Slide Master view.

✔ *You will learn how to create and manipulate background graphics on slide masters in Lesson 24.*

- If you don't like these background graphics, you can simply remove them from a slide by clicking Design > Hide Background Graphics.
- Remember that text colors are often chosen to contrast with the graphic background. If you hide the background graphic, the text colors might need to be changed so that they don't blend into the background.

Try It! Hiding Background Graphics

1. In the **PTry19_studentfirstname_studentlastname** file, select slide 1.
2. Click Design > Hide Background Graphics.
3. Save the changes to the **PTry19_studentfirstname_studentlastname** file, and leave it open to use in the next Try It.

Applying a Background Fill Color

- Instead of changing the entire color theme in a presentation, you can change just the background color.
- You can apply a background fill color to one slide or to the entire presentation using the Format Background dialog box.
- To open the Format Background dialog box, click the Background Styles button on the Design tab and then click Format Background.

Try It! Applying a Background Fill Color

1. In the **PTry19_studentfirstname_studentlastname** file, click the Design tab.
2. Click the Background group dialog box launcher .
3. On the Fill page, click the Color button.
4. Select Blue-Gray, Accent 6.
5. Click Apply to All. Click close.
6. Save the changes to the **PTry19_studentfirstname_studentlastname** file, and leave it open to use in the next Try It.

The Format Background dialog box

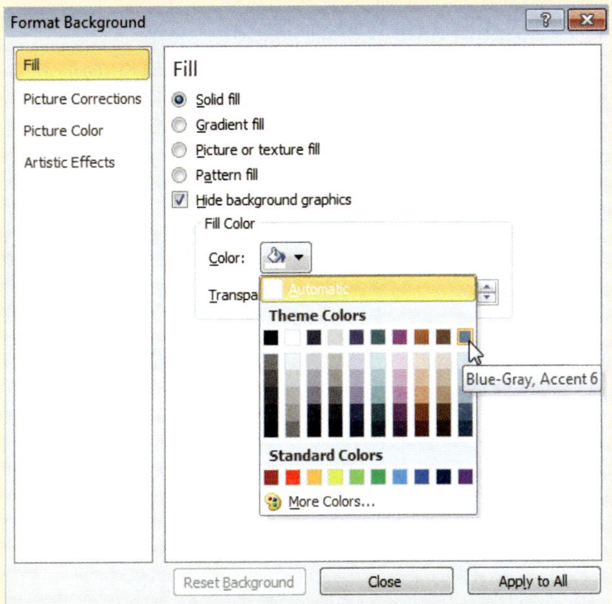

Formatting a Slide Background with a Picture

- Adding a picture to your slide background adds interest and helps convey your message.
- You can format the background with a picture using the Format Background dialog box.
- You can use clip art or image files to add graphics to the slide background.

Try It! Formatting a Slide Background with a Picture

1. In the **PTry19_studentfirstname_studentlastname** file, click the Design tab and then click the Background group dialog box launcher .
2. In the Format Background dialog box, click Picture or texture fill.

   ✔ *Note that the background of the slide automatically changes to the first texture option.*
3. Click the File button and navigate to the location where the data files for this lesson are stored.
4. Select **PTry19_soup.jpg** and click Insert.
5. Click Close to apply the graphic to the title slide.
6. Save the changes to the **PTry19_studentfirstname_studentlastname** file, and leave it open to use in the next Try It.

Resetting the Slide Background

- Remember that only changes made to individual slide backgrounds can be reset. If you apply a change to all the slides in a presentation, you cannot reverse the change using the Reset Background option.

✔ *You can, however, use the Undo button to reverse global changes.*

Try It! **Resetting the Slide Background**

1. In the PTry19_studentfirstname_studentlastname file, click Design > Background Styles > Format Background.
2. Click Reset Background. Notice that the slide background changes immediately.
3. Click Close.
4. Save the changes to the PTry19_studentfirstname_studentlastname file and close it.

Project 41—Create It

Creating a Presentation from an Outline

DIRECTIONS

1. Start PowerPoint, click **File** > **Open**, and navigate to the location where the data files for this lesson are stored.
2. In the Open dialog box, click **All PowerPoint Presentations** and select **All Files**.
3. Select the Word document **PProj41** and click **Open.**
4. Save the presentation as **PProj41_studentfirstname_studentlastname** in the location where your teacher instructs you to store the files for this lesson.
5. Click **View** > **Slide Sorter** to display all the slides in the main window.
6. Click CTRL + A to select all the slides.
7. Click **Home** > **Reset**. Each slide will revert to the default formatting and placeholders.
8. Double-click slide 1. The presentation will change to Normal view.
9. Click **Home** > **Layout** > **Title Slide**. Slide 1 changes to a Title Slide layout.
10. On the **Design** tab, click the **More** button to display the Themes gallery, and then click **Thatch**. The entire presentation changes to reflect the new Thatch theme.
11. Click **Design** > **Hide Background Graphics**. The stripes on the Title slide disappear.
12. Click **Insert** > **Header & Footer**. The Header and Footer dialog box opens.
13. Select **Footer** and type your first name and last name. Click **Apply** to apply the footer to the title slide only.
14. **With your teacher's permission**, print slide 1.
15. Close the presentation, saving changes, and exit PowerPoint.

Project 42—Apply It

Reusing Slides in a Presentation

DIRECTIONS

1. Start PowerPoint, if necessary, and open **PProj42** from the data files for this lesson.
2. Save the presentation as **PProj42_studentfirstname_studentlastname** in the location where your teacher instructs you to store the files for this lesson.
3. Use the Format Background dialog box to change the background styles as follows:
   a. Change the gradient fill color to **Aqua, Accent 5**. Apply the change to all the slides.
   b. Use the file **PProj42_Travel.jpg** located in the data files for this lesson as a picture fill on the title slide.

4. Choose to reuse slides from the presentation **PProj42_slides**, located in the data files for this lesson.
   a. Point to each slide in the task pane to see its content.
   b. Click slide 2 in the task pane to insert the slide as slide 3 in the presentation. Note that the inserted slide takes on the theme of the current presentation.
   c. Display slide 5 in the current presentation and then insert the third slide in the task pane to become slide 6. Close the task pane.
5. Insert a date that updates automatically, slide numbers, and a footer that includes your first name and last name. Do not show this information on the title slide, but apply it to all other slides. Your presentation should look like Figure 19-2.
6. Spell check the presentation.
7. **With your teacher's permission,** print the presentation as a 6 slides per page handout.
8. Close the presentation, saving changes, and exit PowerPoint.

Figure 19-2

Lesson 20

Using Effects and Animations

WORDS TO KNOW

Animate
To apply movement to text or an object to control its display during the presentation.

➤ What You Will Learn

Applying Entrance Effects
Setting Effect Options
Applying Animation Effects with Animation Painter
Applying Animations to Objects and SmartArt Graphics

Software Skills PowerPoint allows you to add transitions and animations to make your slides more visually interesting during a presentation.

Application Skills The public relations director at Holmes Medical Center has informed you that she will present the laser surgery unit slide show to a large audience. In this lesson, you will animate both text and objects.

What You Can Do

Applying Entrance Effects

- You can **animate** text and objects in a presentation to add interest or emphasize special points.
- Use the Animation gallery on the Animations tab to apply one of PowerPoint's preset animation effects. This gallery provides several animation effects from which to choose.
- Because you must select a placeholder or object before the Animation gallery becomes active, you must be in Normal view to apply these animations.

Try It! Applying Entrance Effects

1. Start PowerPoint and open PTry20 from the data files for this lesson.
2. Save the presentation as PTry20_studentfirstname_studentlastname in the location where your teacher instructs you to store the files for this lesson.
3. On slide 2, click the content placeholder.
4. On the Animations tab, click the More button, and click the Fly In animation from the gallery.
5. Save the changes to the PTry20_studentfirstname_studentlastname file, and leave it open to use in the next Try It.

Setting Effect Options

- If you want more control over animation effects, use the Animation Pane. Using the Animation Pane, you can control how the effect is applied.
- For each animation effect you use, you can modify the direction the animation takes, along with its timing.
- When you add an effect, the object name and an effect symbol display in the Animation Pane. This list represents the order in which the effects take place when the slide is viewed.
  - You can adjust the order in which effects take place using the Re-Order arrows at the bottom of the task pane.
  - The Play button allows you to preview the animations to make sure they display as you want them to.
  - To see more options for controlling an effect, click the drop-down arrow to the right of the effect item.
- The Effect Options button on the Animations tab offers options for controlling the direction and sequence of the selected animation.

Try It! Setting Effect Options

1. In the PTry20_studentfirstname_studentlastname file, click the content placeholder on slide 2.
2. Click Animations > Effect Options.
3. Click From Left.
4. Click Animations > Effect Options.
5. Click By Paragraph if that option is not already selected.
6. Save the changes to the PTry20_studentfirstname_studentlastname file, and leave it open to use in the next Try It.

The Effect Options drop-down list

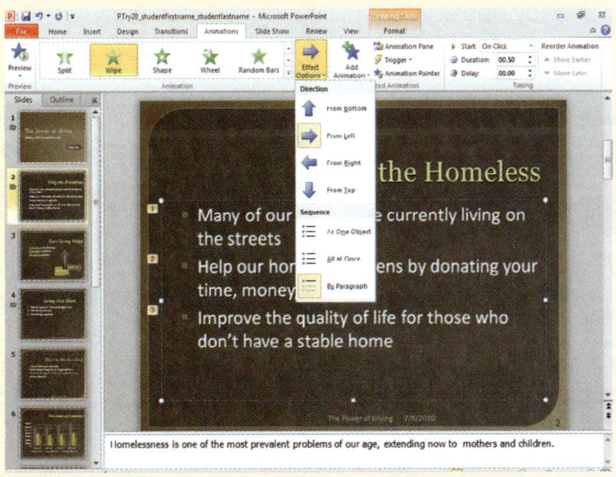

Applying Animation Effects with Animation Painter

- Creating just the right animation effect can be time-consuming. When you want to use the same animation effect on more than one slide, the best choice is to use the Animation Painter.
- Like the Format Painter, the Animation Painter duplicates the animation formatting from one placeholder to another.
- To copy the animation to another placeholder, select a placeholder that has the animation you want to use and click the Animation Painter button. Then, click the placeholder to which you want to apply it.
- To apply the animation to multiple placeholders, double-click the Animation Painter button after selecting your animation placeholder.

Try It! Applying Animation Effects with Animation Painter

1. In the **PTry20_studentfirstname_studentlastname** file, select the text placeholder on slide 2.
2. Double-click Animations > Animation Painter.
3. Click slide 4 in the Slides pane. Click the text placeholder.
4. Click slide 5 in the Slides pane. Click the text placeholder.
5. Press ESC.
6. Save the changes to the **PTry20_studentfirstname_studentlastname** file, and leave it open to use in the next Try It.

Applying Animations to Objects and SmartArt Graphics

- Effects can be used to create an interesting entrance for an object, to emphasize an object that already appears on a slide, or to accompany an object's exit from a slide.
- Objects and SmartArt graphics can be animated using the same tools that you use to animate text.

Try It! Applying Animations to Objects and SmartArt Graphics

1. In the **PTry20_studentfirstname_studentlastname** file, click the grouped graphic on slide 3.
2. In the Animations gallery, click the More button and click Teeter.
3. Save the changes to the **PTry20_studentfirstname_studentlastname** file and close it.

Project 43—Create It

Adding Animations

DIRECTIONS

1. Start PowerPoint, if necessary, and open **PProj43** from the data files for this lesson.
2. Save the presentation as **PProj43_studentfirstname_studentlastname** in the location where your teacher instructs you to store the files for this lesson.
3. Click the title placeholder on slide 1 and on the **Animations** tab, in the Animation gallery, click **Fade**. A preview of the fade animation displays.
4. Click following the word *Unit* in the subtitle. Press ENTER and type **Presented by** and then add your first name and last name.
5. Click the border of the subtitle placeholder, click the **More** button on the Animation gallery, and click **Wipe**. A preview of the Wipe animation displays.
6. Select the content placeholder on slide 2 and on the **Animations** tab, in the Animation gallery, click **Fly In**. A preview of the Fly In animation displays. Slide 1 of your presentation should look like Figure 20-1.
7. Close the presentation, saving changes, and exit PowerPoint.

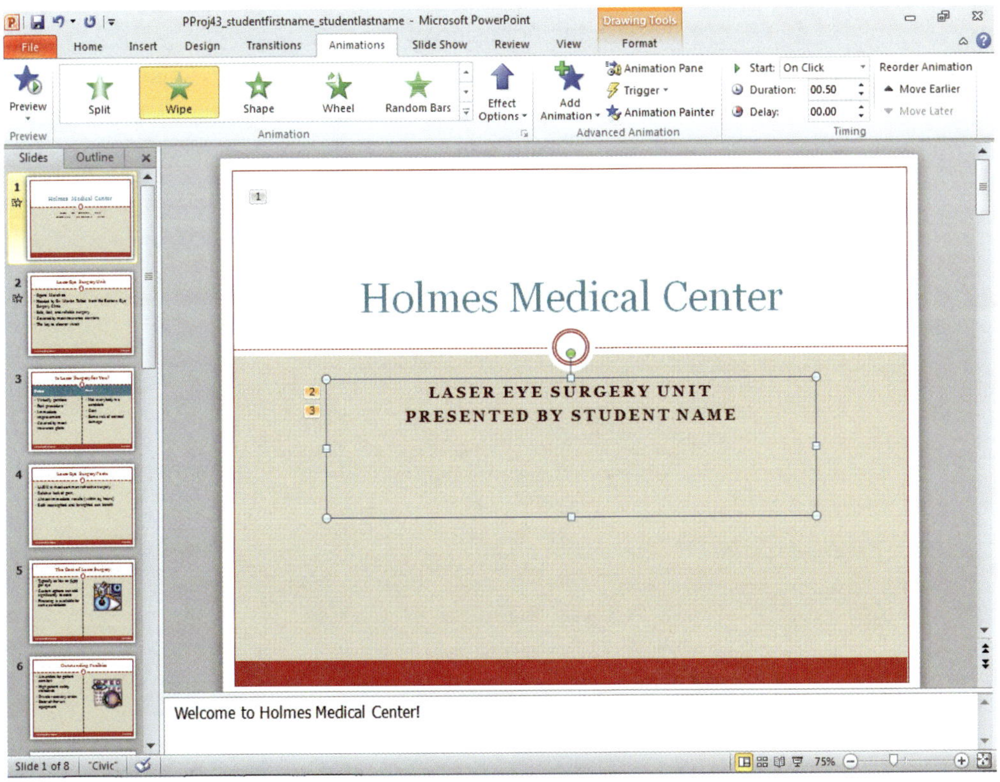

Figure 20-1

Project 44—Apply It

Adding Animations

DIRECTIONS

1. Start PowerPoint, if necessary, and open **PProj44** from the data files for this lesson.
2. Save the presentation as **PProj44_studentfirst name_studentlastname** in the location where your teacher instructs you to store the files for this lesson.
3. Use the Animation Painter to copy the animation from the presentation title to the title placeholders on slides 2 through 6.
4. Apply custom animations to each slide as follows:
   a. On slide 1, apply a **Zoom** animation effect to the subtitle.
   b. On slide 2, apply a **Fly In** entrance effect for the text placeholder. Change the direction of the effect to **From Left**.
   c. On slide 3, apply the **Grow & Turn** effect to the Cons text box.
   d. On slide 3, use the **Animation Painter** to apply the same effect to the Pros text box.
   e. On slide 4, apply the **Split** effect to the text placeholder. Use the Effect Options list to change the effect to **Vertical Out**.
   f. On slide 5, apply **Random Bars** Entrance effect to the text placeholder and the **Swivel** effect to the graphic. Modify the effects so that the text in the left-hand placeholder displays **All at Once** and then the clip art graphic displays.
   g. On slide 6, apply the same effects as slide 5.
   h. On slide 7, animate the title, text, and photo so that they all fly in from separate directions.
   i. On slide 8, apply the **Float In** effect to the WordArt graphic.
5. Change the text *Student Name* on slide 8 to your first name and last name.
6. Add an automatically updating date to the slide footer. Notice that for this theme the footer is along the right side of the slide.
7. Watch the slideshow from start to finish.
8. Close the presentation, saving changes, and exit PowerPoint.

Lesson 21

Creating Multimedia Presentations

➤ What You Will Learn

- Analyzing the Effectiveness of Multimedia Presentations
- Inserting a Video
- Editing a Video
- Applying Video Styles
- Adjusting Video Color
- Controlling a Video in a Presentation
- Inserting Sounds and Music

Software Skills PowerPoint has many tools and features, but selecting the options that make your presentation effective depends on many factors, including the topic, the audience, and the purpose. For example, a marketing presentation may be more effective if it uses lots of multimedia and animation effects, while a tutorial or training presentation may be more effective if it uses straightforward bullet text without distracting sounds and actions.

You can insert your own pictures in a presentation and then use the enhanced picture tools to adjust the picture's appearance and apply special effects. For a really dynamic presentation, add media clips such as movies and sounds.

Application Skills A local environmental group, Planet Earth, has asked you to prepare a presentation they can show on Earth Day. In this lesson, you begin the presentation by inserting and formatting a picture and several multimedia files.

What You Can Do

Analyzing the Effectiveness of Multimedia Presentations

- Always consider your audience when creating a presentation. Research the audience's needs and knowledge level, and tailor the presentation to it.
- Also consider how the presentation will be delivered. Not all presentations are delivered by a live narrator to a live audience.
  - Will it be printed? Select a light background and dark text for readability.
  - Will it be standalone? Include navigation tools for the viewer.
  - Will it run automatically in a loop? Keep it short so a viewer does not have to wait a long time for the presentation to begin anew.
  - Will it be delivered over the Internet? Make sure the audio is high quality.
- Follow general design guidelines when preparing a presentation. For example:
  - Apply a consistent theme to all slides. That means using the same font and color scheme throughout, and repeating elements such as bullets and backgrounds.
  - Limit bullet points to no more than five per slide.
  - Limit the number of fonts to two per slide.
  - Use contrasting colors when necessary to make text stand out. For example, use a dark background color such as dark green or blue and a light contrasting text color, such as yellow.
  - Avoid the use of pastels, which can be hard to read.
  - Make sure text is large enough so that even someone at the back of the room can read it. No smaller than 18 points and no larger than 48 points is usually effective.
  - Use graphics such as tables, charts, and pictures to convey key points.
  - Make sure graphics are sized to fill the slide.
  - Use consistent transitions, sounds, and animations that enhance the presentation and do not distract from the content.
- Be clear about the message you are trying to convey. For example, if you are creating a marketing presentation, be clear about what you are trying to sell. If you are creating a training presentation, be clear about what you are teaching.
- Know your time limit based on your audience. Most people will lose interest if the presentation goes on too long.
- An effective presentation has a logical progression:
  - Introduction in which you tell your audience what you are going to present.
  - Body in which you present the information.
  - Summary in which you tell your audience what you presented.
- Do not use slang, incorrect grammar, jargon, or abbreviations that your audience might not understand.
- Your role in the delivery of a live presentation is key. Dress appropriately, speak loudly and clearly, and make eye contact with your audience.
- You can assess a presentation's effectiveness by testing it on a practice audience. Ask for constructive criticism to help you improve.

Inserting a Video

- Insert a movie file using the Insert Media Clip button in a content placeholder or the Video button on the Insert tab.
- You have three options for adding a video to your presentation:
  - Insert clip art video.
  - Insert a video file saved in a format such as AVI or MPEG.
  - Insert a video from the Web.
- Clip art video files are animated graphics that play automatically on the slide. You insert these graphics as you would any other clip art graphic. You can use tools on the Picture Tools Format tab to change the appearance of the graphic, but you cannot control playback.
- When you insert a video file or a video from the Web, the Video Tools Format and Video Tools Playback tabs open. Use the tools on these tabs to modify the appearance of the video on the slide and to control playback options.

Try It! Inserting a Video from a File

1. Start PowerPoint and open **PTry21** from the data files for this lesson.
2. Save the presentation as **PTry21 _ studentfirstname_studentlastname** in the location where your teacher instructs you to store the files for this lesson.
3. Select slide 4 and click the Insert Media Clip icon in the content placeholder.

   OR

   Click Insert > Video and then click Video from File.
4. Navigate to the location where the data files for this lesson are stored and select **PTry21_video**.
5. Click Insert.
6. Save the changes to the **PTry21_ studentfirstname_studentlastname** file, and leave it open to use in the next Try It.

Insert a video from a file

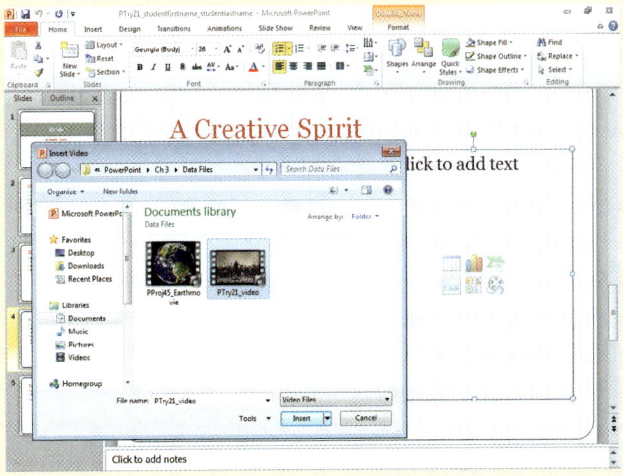

Editing a Video

- The Video Tools Format tab is very similar to the Picture Tools tab. It contains tools for changing the way the video clip looks within the slide.
- When video files are inserted into presentations, you'll see a black box effect. Rather than leaving the black margins on a video object, crop the object the way you would with a picture.

Try It! Editing a Video

1. In the **PTry21_studentfirstname_ studentlastname** file, select the video on slide 4.
2. On the Video Tools Format tab, click the Crop button.
3. Drag the left cropping handle to the right to remove the black.
4. Drag the right cropping handle to the left to remove the black.
5. On the Video Tools Format tab, click the Crop button again to save the changes to video object.
6. Save the changes to the **PTry21_ studentfirstname_studentlastname** file, and leave it open to use in the next Try It.

Cropping a video

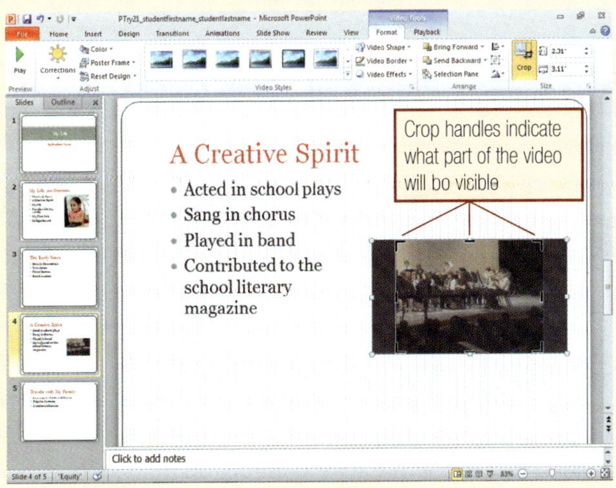

Applying Video Styles

- When you insert a video into a slide, you can format it using the same tools that you would any graphic.
- Applying a video style to a video gives it a more finished look.
- Before you settle on a video style, try several. Not all video styles are suited to every video.
- Depending on the video style you choose, you can add or change the video effects, change the color of the border, or change the shape of the video screen.

Try It! Applying Video Styles

1. In the **PTry21_studentfirstname_ studentlastname** file, select the video on slide 4.
2. On the Video Tools Format tab, click the More button to open the Video Styles gallery.
3. Move your mouse over several styles to see the live preview and then choose Drop Shadow Rectangle.
4. Save the changes to the **PTry21_ studentfirstname_studentlastname** file, and leave it open to use in the next Try It.

Apply a video style

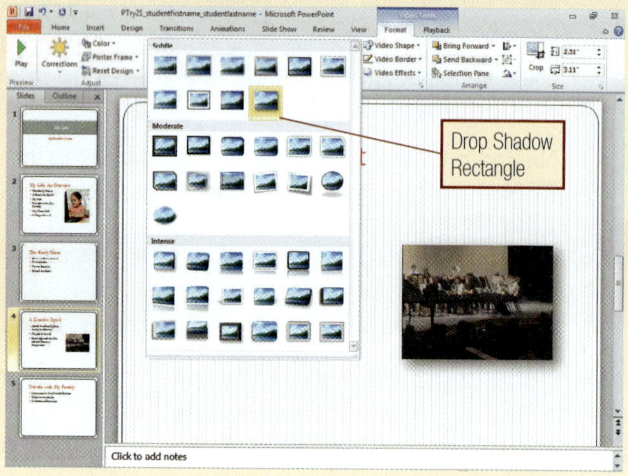

Adjusting Video Color

- You can use the same tools that you would use to change the color of a photo image in PowerPoint to change the color of a video.
- In addition to the most popular video color options—Black and White, Grayscale, Sepia, and Washout—you can also choose to tint the video in 14 different variations.
- If you don't see a color you like, you can choose More Variations to open the color palette and choose from all Windows colors.

Try It! Adjusting Video Color

1. In the **PTry21_ studentfirstname_ studentlastname** file, select the video on slide 4.
2. Click Video Tools Format > Color .
3. Choose Grayscale.
4. Save the changes to the **PTry21_ studentfirstname_studentlastname** file, and leave it open to use in the next Try It.

Controlling a Video in a Presentation

- Inserted video clips can be controlled using the standard play and pause controls on the video object.
- In addition to these controls, PowerPoint allows you to hide the movie during the presentation, play it full screen, loop it continuously, rewind it, change its arrangement relative to other objects, or scale it.

Try It! Previewing a Movie in Normal View

1. In the **PTry21 _studentfirstname_ studentlastname** file, select the video on slide 4.
2. Click Video Tools Playback > Play ▶.

   OR

   Click the Play button ▶ on the video itself.
3. Watch for a few seconds and click Video Tools Playback > Pause ⏸.

   OR

   Click the Pause button ⏸ on the video itself.
4. Save the changes to the **PTry21_ studentfirstname_studentlastname** file, and leave it open to use in the next Try It.

Try It! Viewing Videos in a Slide Show

1. In the **PTry21_studentfirstname_ studentlastname** file, select slide 4, if necessary.
2. Click Slide Show > From Current Slide.
3. Hover your mouse over the video to display the Play button.
4. Click the Play button ▶.
5. Watch the video for a few seconds and then click the slide to progress to the next slide.
6. Press ESC.
7. Select the video on slide 4, if necessary, and click Video Tools Playback > Start, and click Automatically.
8. Click Slide Show > From Current Slide. Notice that the video starts immediately.
9. Press ESC.
10. Save the changes to the **PTry21_ studentfirstname_studentlastname** file, and leave it open to use in the next Try It.

Inserting Sounds and Music

- You can add sound and music clips to your presentation to make it more interesting or to emphasize a slide. Your computer must have speakers and a sound card to play music or sounds during a presentation.
- Use the Audio button on the Insert tab to choose what kind of sound to insert: a sound file, a sound from the clip art files, or record your own sounds.
- When you insert an audio clip, a sound icon displays on the slide. You can move this icon to a new location (or even off the slide) or resize it to make it less obtrusive.

  ✔ *The sound icon must appear on the slide if you intend to control a sound by clicking it during the presentation.*
- You can choose whether to play the sound automatically or when clicked.
- Use the Audio Tools Playback tab to control sound options.

Try It! Inserting Sounds or Music from a File

1. In the **PTry21_studentfirstname_ studentlastname** file, select slide 5.
2. Click Insert > Audio.
3. Click Audio from File.
4. In the Insert Audio dialog box, navigate to the location where the data files for this lesson are stored and select **PTry21_audio.mid**.
5. Click Insert and drag the audio icon to the lower right of the slide.

(continued)

Try It! Inserting Sounds or Music from a File *(continued)*

6. On the Audio Tools Playback tab, click the Start down arrow Start:, and click Automatically.

7. Save the changes to the **PTry21_studentfirstname_studentlastname** file, and leave it open to use in the next Try It.

PowerPoint gives you complete control over audio clips

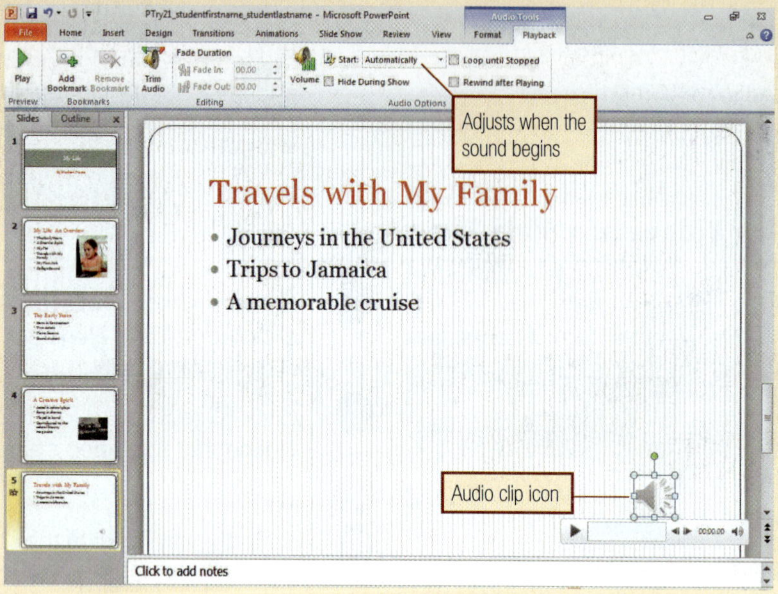

Try It! Inserting a Sound from the Clip Organizer

1. In the **PTry21_Grades_studentfirstname_studentlastname** file, select slide 1.

2. Click Insert > Audio .

3. Select Clip Art Audio.

4. In the Clip Art task pane, scroll through the audio clips to see what's available.

   ✔ *To listen to a clip, hover over the clip. When the down arrow appears, click it and select Preview/Properties. Use the play button to hear the clip. Click Close when you're done.*

5. Double-click Starter music to insert the clip.

6. Close the task pane.

7. On the Audio Tools Playback tab, click the Start down arrow Start: and click Automatically.

8. Click Slide Show > From Beginning and watch the presentation.

9. Close the **PTry21_studentfirstname_studentlastname** file, saving changes, and exit PowerPoint.

Project 45—Create It

Creating a Multimedia Presentation

DIRECTIONS

1. Start PowerPoint, if necessary, and open **PProj45** from the data files for this lesson.
2. Save the presentation as **PProj45_studentfirst name_studentlastname** in the location where your teacher instructs you to store the files for this lesson.
3. Select slide 1, click inside the subtitle placeholder, and type your first name and last name.
4. Select slide 2 and then click the **Insert Media Clip** icon in the right placeholder. The Insert Video dialog box opens.
5. Navigate to the location where the data files for this lesson are stored and select **PProj45_ earthmovie.mpeg**.
6. Click **Insert**. The video appears in the placeholder, as shown in Figure 21-1.
7. Select slide 3 and in the placeholder, click the **Insert Picture from File** icon. The Insert Picture dialog box opens.
8. Navigate to the location where the data files for this lesson are stored and select **PProj45_ earthpic.jpg**.
9. Click **Insert**. The picture appears in the placeholder.
10. Close the presentation, saving changes, and exit PowerPoint.

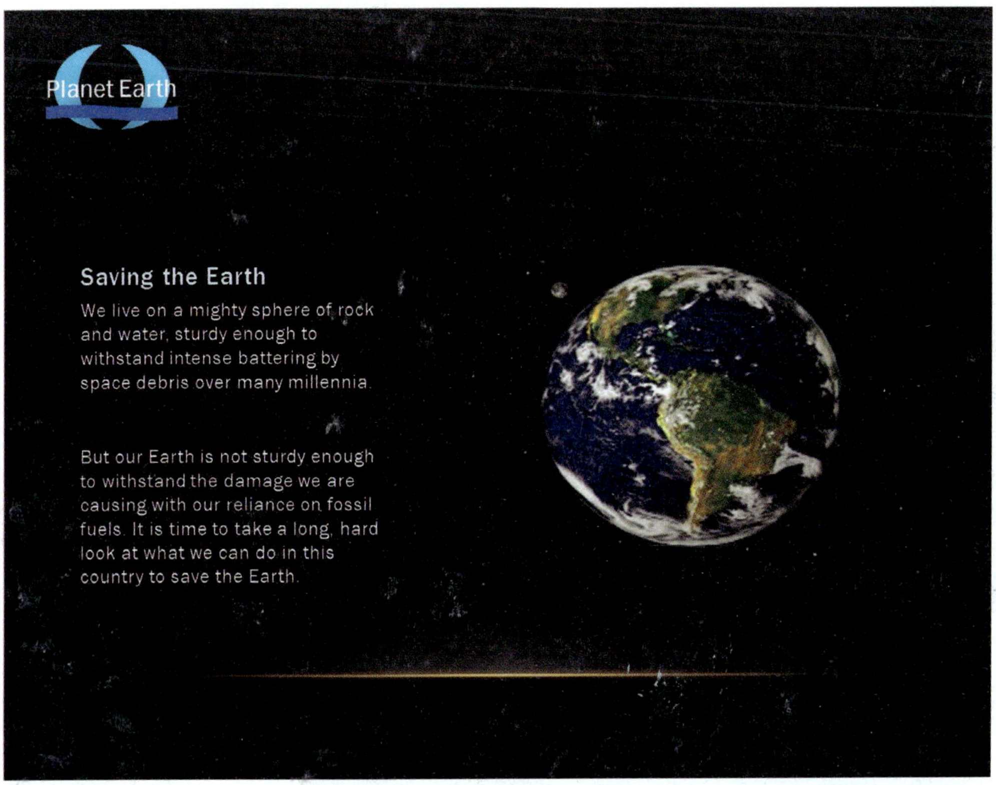

Figure 21-1

Project 46—Apply It

Creating a Multimedia Presentation

DIRECTIONS

1. Start PowerPoint, if necessary, and open **PProj46** from the data files for this lesson.
2. Save the presentation as **PProj46_studentfirstname_studentlastname** in the location where your teacher instructs you to store the files for this lesson.
3. Replace the text Student Name on the title slide with your first name and last name.
4. Modify the video clip on slide 2 as follows:
   a. Drag the movie down so that the top of it is more or less aligned with the top of the text in the placeholder to the left of the movie.
   b. Apply the **Simple Frame, White** video style to the movie.
   c. Set the movie to start automatically.
   d. Preview the movie in Normal view.
5. Format the picture on slide 3 as shown in Figure 21-2. Be sure to include the following:
   a. Adjust the brightness to make the picture 20% brighter.
   b. Adjust the contrast to 20%.
   c. Crop about a half an inch from the bottom of the picture.
   d. Apply the **Reflected Rounded Rectangle** picture style.
6. Locate a thunder sound using the Clip Art task pane. Insert the sound and choose to have it play automatically. Move the sound icon off the slide so it will not display when you show the slides.
7. View the slides in Slide Show view to see the movie and hear the sound.
8. **With your teacher's permission**, print slide 3.
9. Close the presentation, saving changes, and exit PowerPoint.

Figure 21-2

Lesson 22

Working with Tables

➤ What You Will Learn

Inserting a Table
Formatting and Modifying a Table

Software Skills Use tables to organize data in a format that is easy to read and understand. Table formats enhance visual interest and also contribute to readability.

Application Skills In this lesson, you work on a presentation for Restoration Architecture. You'll insert and format a table that lists planning services.

What You Can Do

Inserting a Table

- Use a table on a slide to organize information into rows and columns so it is easy for your audience to read and understand.
- You have two options for inserting a table on a slide:
  - Click the Insert Table icon in any content placeholder to display the Insert Table dialog box. After you select the number of columns and rows, the table structure appears on the slide in the content placeholder.
  - Click the Table button on the Insert tab to display a grid that you can use to select rows and columns. As you drag the pointer, the table columns and rows appear on the slide.

  ✔ *If you use this option on a slide that does not have a content layout, you may have to move the table to position it properly on the slide.*
- Note that the Table menu also allows you to access the Insert Table dialog box, draw a table using the Draw Table tool, or insert an Excel worksheet to organize data.

Try It! Inserting a Table

1. Start PowerPoint and open **PTry22** from the data files for this lesson.
2. Save the presentation as **PTry22_studentfirstname_studentlastname** in the location where your teacher instructs you to store the files for this lesson.
3. Select slide 2 and click the Insert Table icon in the content placeholder.
4. Type 2 in the Number of Columns scroll box.
5. Type 5 in the Number of Rows scroll box.
6. Click OK.
7. Select slide 4.
8. Click Insert > Table.
9. Drag the pointer over the grid or use arrow keys to select 5 columns and 3 rows.
10. Click or press ENTER to insert the table on the slide.
11. Save the changes to the **PTry22_studentfirstname_studentlastname** file, and leave it open to use in the next Try It.

Using the Insert Table icon to insert a table

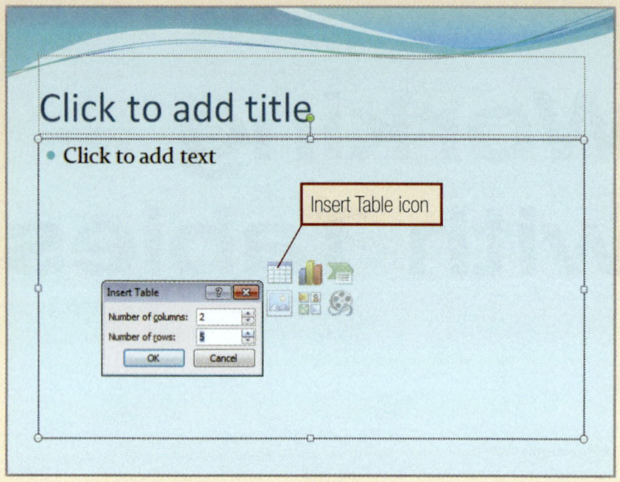

Using the Table Grid to insert a table

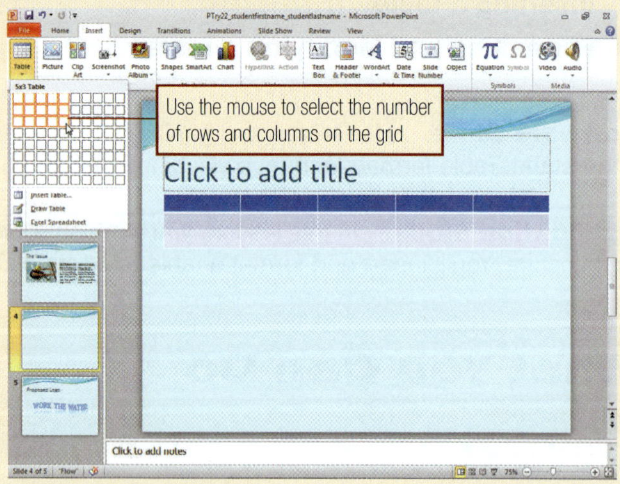

Formatting and Modifying a Table

- When a table appears on a slide, the Table Tools contextual tabs become active on the Ribbon.
- Use the Table Tools Design tab to control formatting options, such as styles, shading, borders, and effects. You can also choose to emphasize specific parts of a table.
- Use the Table Tools Layout tab to control the table structure, such as inserting or deleting rows and columns, merging or splitting cells, distributing rows or columns evenly, adjusting both horizontal and vertical alignment, changing text direction, and adjusting cell margins and table size.
- If you do not want to enter specific measurements for cells and table size, you can adjust rows, columns, or the table itself by dragging borders. You can also drag the entire table to reposition it on the slide if necessary.

Try It! Applying Table Formats

1. In the **PTry22_studentfirstname_studentlastname** file, click slide 2.
2. Click the table to select it.
3. Click the Table Styles More button to open the Table Styles gallery.
4. Click Medium Style 2 – Accent 3.
5. Select the entire table and click Table Tools Design > Borders .
6. Select All Borders.

   OR

   Click the Shading button and select a color, picture, gradient, or texture to fill table cells.
7. Click the Effects button and select from bevel, shadow, or reflection effects for the table.
8. Save the changes to the **PTry22_studentfirstname_studentlastname** file, and leave it open to use in the next Try It.

Try It! Inserting a Row or Column

1. In the **PTry22_studentfirstname_studentlastname** file, select slide 2.
2. Click one of the rows in the table to select it.
3. Click Table Tools Layout > Insert Above .

   OR

   Click the Insert Below button to insert a row below the selected cell.

   OR

   Click the Insert Left button to insert a column to the left of the selected cell.

   OR

   Click the Insert Right button to insert a column to the right of the selected cell.
4. Save the changes to the **PTry22_studentfirstname_studentlastname** file, and leave it open to use in the next Try It.

Try It! Deleting Part of the Table

1. In the **PTry22_studentfirstname_studentlastname** file, select slide 2.
2. Click one of the rows in the table to select it.
3. Click Table Tools Layout > Delete .
4. Click Delete Rows.

   OR

   Click Delete Columns to delete the selected column instead.
5. Save the changes to the **PTry22_studentfirstname_studentlastname** file, and leave it open to use in the next Try It.

Try It! Merging Table Cells

1. In the **PTry22_studentfirstname_studentlastname** file, type **Table Heading** in the first row of the table on slide 2.
2. Select the heading row and click Table Tools Layout > Merge Cells.
3. Click Table Tools Layout > Center.
4. Save the changes to the **PTry22_studentfirstname_studentlastname** file, and leave it open to use in the next Try It.

Merging table cells

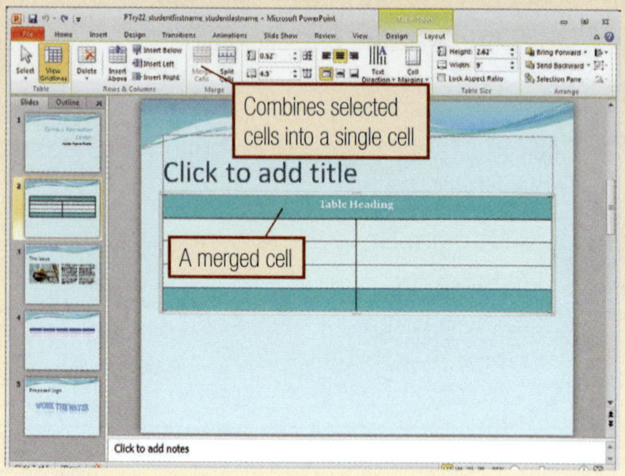

Try It! Distributing Rows Evenly

1. In the **PTry22_studentfirstname_studentlastname** file, select the third row in the table on slide 4.
2. In the Cell Size group, type 1 in the Height box.
3. Select the entire table, and click Table Tools Layout > Distribute Rows.
4. Save the changes to the **PTry22_studentfirstname_studentlastname** file and close it.

Project 47—Create It

Creating a Table

DIRECTIONS

1. Start PowerPoint, if necessary, and open **PProj47** from the data files for this lesson.
2. Save the presentation as **PProj47_studentfirstname_studentlastname** in the location where your teacher instructs you to store the files for this lesson.
3. Click the subtitle placeholder and move to the end of the text. Press ENTER three times and then type your first name and last name.
4. Click on slide 3 and then click **Home** > **New Slide** > **Title Only**. A new slide appears at the end of the presentation.
5. Click the title placeholder and type **Planning Services** as the slide title.
6. Click outside the placeholder and click **Insert** > **Table**.
7. Drag to create a table that is five rows down and five columns wide.
8. Fill in the table with the text shown in Figure 22-1.
9. On the **Table Tools Layout** tab, in the Table Size group, type **3** in the **Height** box. The table height is adjusted.
10. Click in the **Width** box and type **7.5**. The table width is adjusted and the text now all fits on a single row. Drag the table to position it as shown in Figure 22-1.
11. Select the entire table, then click **Table Tools Layout** > **Distribute Rows**. All rows are now the same height.
12. **With your teacher's permission**, print the presentation.
13. Close the presentation, saving changes, and exit PowerPoint.

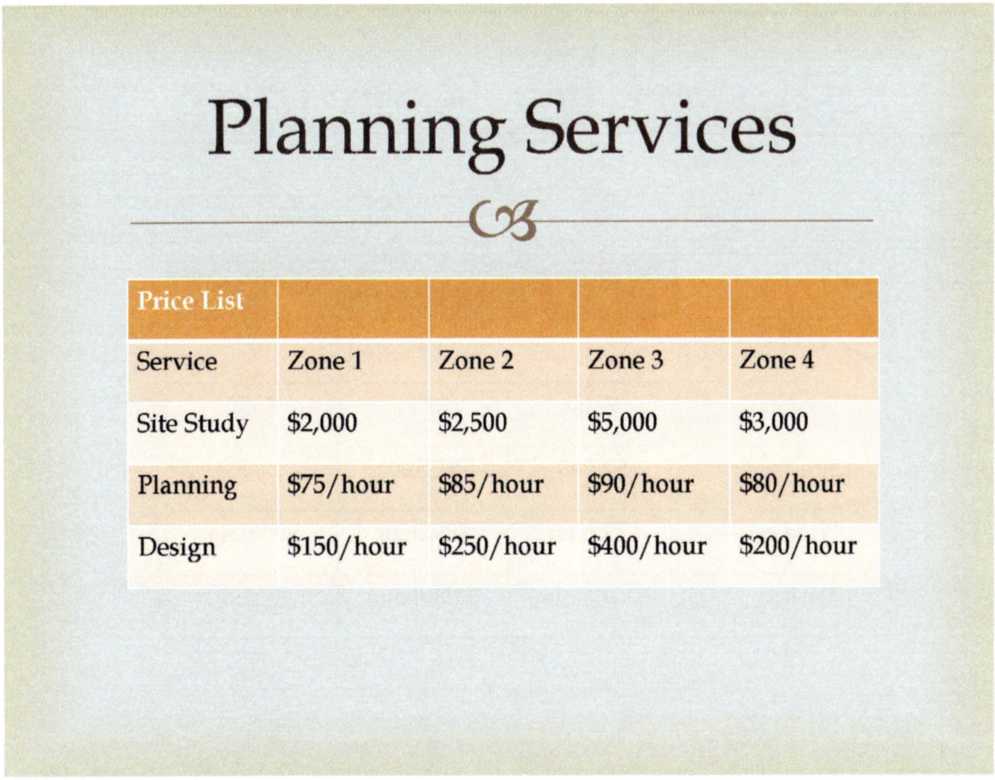

Planning Services

Price List				
Service	Zone 1	Zone 2	Zone 3	Zone 4
Site Study	$2,000	$2,500	$5,000	$3,000
Planning	$75/hour	$85/hour	$90/hour	$80/hour
Design	$150/hour	$250/hour	$400/hour	$200/hour

Figure 22-1

Project 48—Apply It

Editing a Table

DIRECTIONS

1. Start PowerPoint, if necessary, and open **PProj48** from the data files for this lesson.
2. Save the presentation as **PProj48_studentfirstname_studentlastname** in the location where your teacher instructs you to store the files for this lesson.
3. You have decided to stop offering services for Zone 4. On slide 4, delete the *Zone 4* column in the table.
4. Use the Table Tools Design tab to change the table style to **Medium Style 1 – Accent 2**. Apply All Borders to the table.
5. Center the entries in the last three columns, adjust column widths as desired, and position the table attractively on the slide.
6. Insert a row below the second row. Type the following:

   Permits $200 $350 $500
7. Merge the second, third, and fourth cell in the first row. Center the text in the cell.
8. Remove the shading in the first cell of the first row. Your slide should look like Figure 22-2.
9. Replace the text Student Name on the title slide with your first name and last name.
10. **With your teacher's permission**, print slide 4.
11. Close the presentation, saving changes, and exit PowerPoint.

Figure 22-2

Planning Services

	Zones		
Service	1	2	3
Permits	$200	$350	$500
Site Study	$2,000	$2,500	$5,000
Planning	$75/hour	$85/hour	$90/hour
Design	$150/hour	$250/hour	$400/hour

Lesson 23

Working with Charts

➤ What You Will Learn

Inserting a Chart
Formatting and Modifying a Chart
Animating a Chart

Software Skills Add charts to a presentation to illustrate data and other concepts in a graphical way that is easy to understand. Charts can be formatted or modified as needed to improve the display.

Application Skills In this lesson, you continue working on the presentation for the Campus Recreation Center. You insert a chart to show results of a usage survey.

What You Can Do

Inserting a Chart

- You can add a chart to your presentation to illustrate data in an easy-to-understand format or to compare and contrast sets of data.
- In PowerPoint 2010, you create a chart using Excel 2010 if Excel is installed on your system.

  ✔ *If you do not have Excel, charts are created using Microsoft Graph as in past versions of PowerPoint. However, you won't be able to use the advanced charting tools.*

- Excel charts are embedded in PowerPoint—an embedded object becomes part of the destination file and can be edited using the source application's tools. So, when you insert a chart in PowerPoint, you work with Excel's charting tools.
- You can insert a chart into a content slide layout or add it without a placeholder using the Chart button on the Insert tab.

- When you insert a new chart, Excel opens in a split window with sample data. The chart associated with that sample data displays on the PowerPoint slide.
- You can type replacement data in the worksheet. As you change the data, the chart adjusts on the slide. You can save the Excel worksheet data for the chart and then close the worksheet to work further with the chart on the slide.

Try It! Inserting a Chart

1. Start PowerPoint and open **PTry23** from the data files for this lesson.
2. Save the presentation as **PTry23_studentfirstname_studentlastname** in the location where your teacher instructs you to store the files for this lesson.
3. Select slide 3 and click the Insert Chart icon in the content placeholder.

   OR

   Click Insert > Insert Chart.
4. Select the Clustered Column chart type and click OK.
5. The chart is inserted on the slide and Excel opens with sample data displayed in the worksheet.
6. Close the Excel data file.
7. Save the changes to the **PTry23_studentfirstname_studentlastname** file, and leave it open to use in the next Try It.

Creating an Embedded Excel Chart in PowerPoint

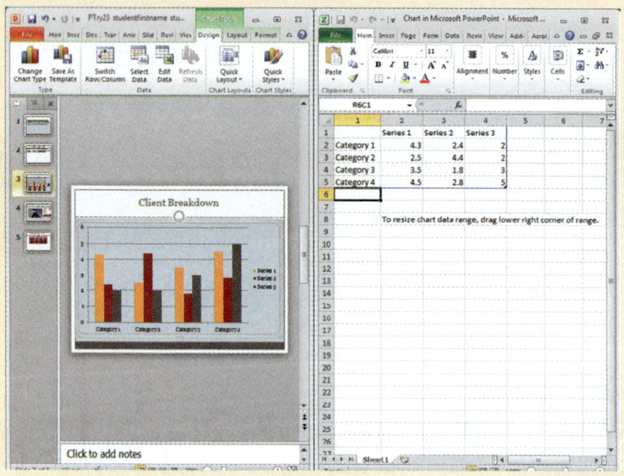

Formatting and Modifying a Chart

- When you click on a chart in PowerPoint, three content-specific tabs open on the Ribbon: Chart Tools Format, Chart Tools Design, and Chart Tools Layout.
- Use the tools on the Chart Tools Design tab to modify the chart type and edit data.
- With PowerPoint, you can choose from several chart types, including line, pie, bar, area, scatter, stock, surface, doughnut, bubble, and radar.
- Tools on the Chart Tools Layout tab help you to customize a chart by choosing what chart elements to display.
- Use the tools on the Chart Tools Format tab to select a layout or chart style, or apply special effects to the chart elements.
- You can move, copy, size, and delete a chart just like any other slide object.

Try It! Formatting and Modifying a Chart

1. In the **PTry23_studentfirstname_studentlastname** file, click the chart to select it, if necessary.
2. Click Chart Tools Design > Change Chart Type.
3. Click Clustered Bar in 3D and click OK.
4. Click the chart to select it, if necessary.

(continued)

Try It! Formatting and Modifying a Chart *(continued)*

5. On the Chart Tools Design tab, click the Chart Styles More button.

6. Select Style 34.

7. Save the changes to the **PTry23_studentfirstname_studentlastname** file, and leave it open to use in the next Try It.

The Change Chart Type dialog box

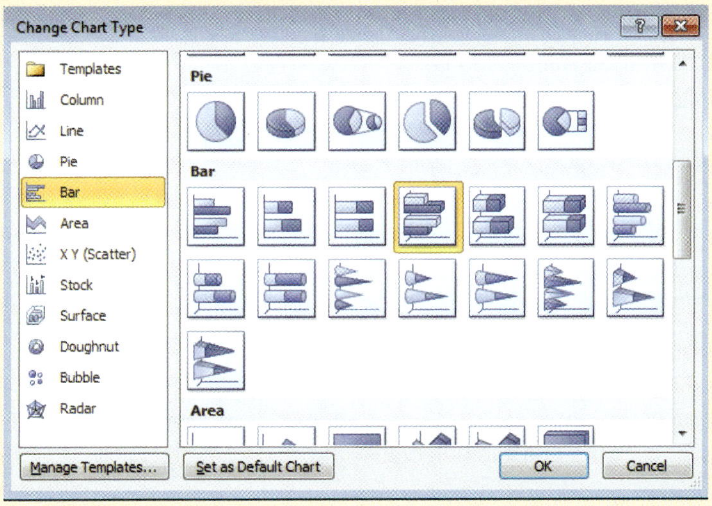

Try It! Editing the Excel Data

1. In the **PTry23_studentfirstname_studentlastname** file, click the chart to select it, if necessary.

2. Click Chart Tools Design > Edit Data.

3. In the Excel data file, click cell A2.

4. Type **Project 1**, and press ENTER.

5. Save the changes to the **PTry23_studentfirstname_studentlastname** file, and leave it open to use in the next Try It.

Try It! Switching Rows and Columns

1. Both the Excel data file and the **PTry23_studentfirstname_studentlastname** file should be open.

2. On the chart slide in PowerPoint, click Chart Tools Design >Switch Row/Column.

3. Close the Excel data file.

4. Save the changes to the **PTry23_studentfirstname_studentlastname** file, and leave it open to use in the next Try It.

Try It! Selecting Data to Chart

1. In the **PTry23_studentfirstname_studentlastname** file, click the chart to select it, if necessary.
2. Click Chart Tools Design > Select Data.
3. In the Select Data Source dialog box, select Project 1 in the Legend Entries (Series) box.
4. Click Remove to remove the Project 1 entry.
5. Click OK and close the Excel window.
6. Save the changes to the **PTry23_studentfirstname_studentlastname** file, and leave it open to use in the next Try It.

The Select Data Source dialog box

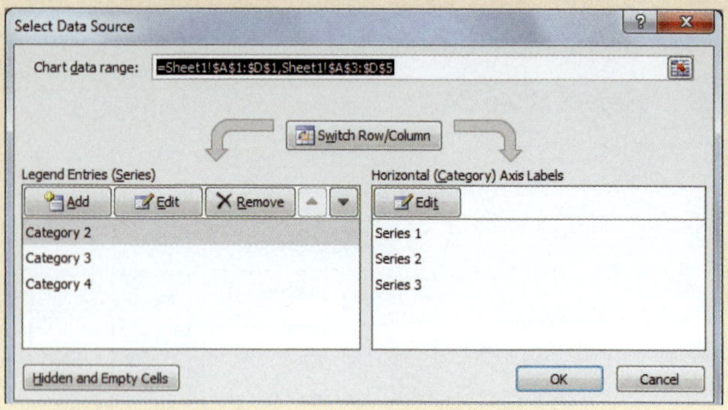

Try It! Changing Chart Layout

1. In the **PTry23_studentfirstname_studentlastname** file, click the chart to select it, if necessary.
2. Click Chart Tools Layout > Legend.
3. Select Show Legend at Bottom.
4. Click Chart Tools Layout > Chart Wall.
5. Select None.
6. Save the changes to the **PTry23_studentfirstname_studentlastname** file, and leave it open to use in the next Try It.

Animating a Chart

- You can animate charts on slides using the Animations tab.
- When you animate a chart, the entire chart is affected.

Try It! Animating a Chart

1. In the **PTry23_studentfirstname_studentlastname** file, click the chart to select it, if necessary.
2. On the Animations tab, click Fade in the Animation gallery.
3. In the Timing group, type **01:00** in the Duration scroll box.
4. In the Timing group, type **0:75** in the Delay scroll box.
5. Save the changes to the **PTry23_studentfirstname_studentlastname** file and close it.

Project 49—Create It

Adding a Chart to a Presentation

DIRECTIONS

1. Start PowerPoint, if necessary, and open **PProj49** from the data files for this lesson.
2. Save the presentation as **PProj49_studentfirstname_studentlastname** in the location where your teacher instructs you to store the files for this lesson.
3. Click the subtitle placeholder and move to the end of the text. Press ENTER and then type your first name and last name.
4. Click on slide 5 and then click **Home** > **New Slide** > **Title and Content**. A new slide appears.
5. Click the title placeholder and type **Survey Results** as the slide title.
6. Click outside the placeholder and click **Insert** > **Chart**. The Insert Chart dialog box opens.
7. Select **3-D Clustered Column** and click **OK**. An Excel data file appears.
8. Replace the sample data with the data shown in Figure 23-1. You may need to drag the lower-right corner of the range indicator to include all the data.
9. In PowerPoint, on the **Chart Tools Design** tab, click the **Chart Layouts More** button and click **Layout 3**. The layout of the chart changes and a chart title appears.
10. On the **Chart Tools Design** tab, click the **Chart Styles More** button and click **Style 26**. The chart style changes using thinner and darker columns.
11. Select the chart title and type **Visits per Week**.
12. **With your teacher's permission**, print slide 6. It should look like that shown in Figure 23-2.
13. Close the Excel data file.
14. Close the presentation, saving changes, and exit PowerPoint.

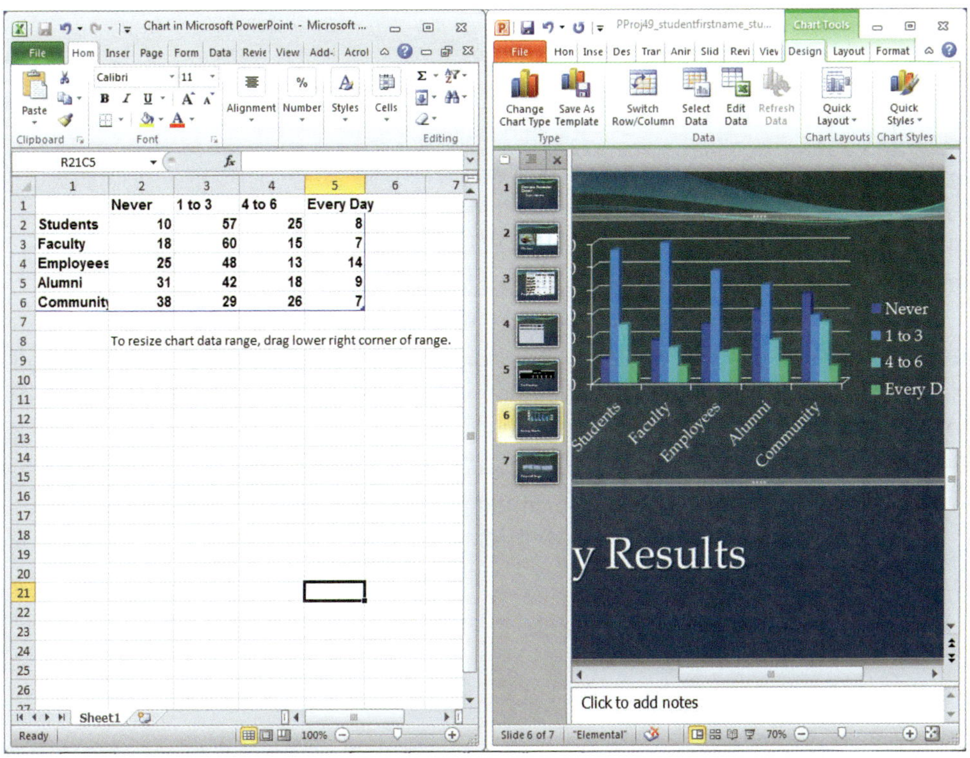

Figure 23-1

Figure 23-2

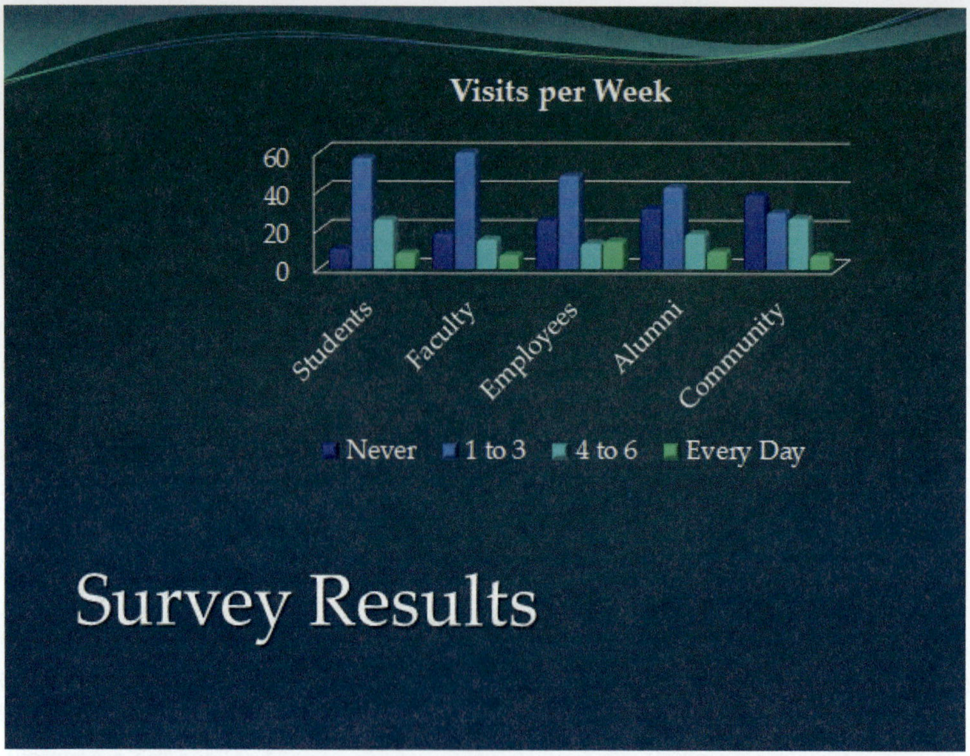

Project 50—Apply It

Modifying a Chart

DIRECTIONS

1. Start PowerPoint, if necessary, and open **PProj50** from the data files for this lesson.
2. Save the presentation as **PProj50_studentfirstname_studentlastname** in the location where your teacher instructs you to store the files for this lesson.
3. On slide 6, change the appearance of the chart as follows:
   a. Change the chart type to **Clustered Cylinder**.
   b. On the Layout tab, select the primary vertical gridlines option and then choose to display major gridlines.
4. Edit the Excel data as follows:
   a. Change the Student value for 1 to 3 to **47**.
   b. Change the Every Day value to **18**.
5. Switch the rows and columns, and then close the Excel data file.

   ✔ *If you find the Every Day data is missing from the chart, use the Select Data button to specify the correct rows and columns.*
6. Apply a **Zoom** animation to the chart.
7. Set the timing duration to **1:50**.
8. Add a slide footer to the presentation that includes your first name and last name and an automatically updating date.
9. **With your teacher's permission**, print slide 6.
10. Close the presentation, saving changes, and exit PowerPoint.

Chapter Assessment and Application

Project 51—Master It

Enhancing a Presentation

The Marketing Manager of Restoration Architecture has asked you to take a recent presentation and improve its appearance to help get it ready for an upcoming event. You'll take advantage of your new skills to change the background, theme, colors, and fonts. You'll also add animations to the slides and change the chart and table.

DIRECTIONS

1. Start PowerPoint and open **PProj51** from the data files for this chapter.
2. Save the presentation as **PProj51_studentfirstname_studentlastname** in the location where your teacher instructs you to store the files for this chapter.
3. Change the theme of the presentation to **Paper**. Note that the title doesn't change because it is a WordArt graphic.
4. Change the color theme to **Concourse**.
5. Change the background style to **Style 8**.
6. Change the font theme to **Verve**.
7. Select the chart on slide 3 and change the chart type to **Pie**.
8. Change the chart layout to **Layout 4**.
9. Change the chart style to **Style 30**.
10. Select the table object on slide 5 and change its height to **3.5"** and the width to **7"**.
11. Center-align the table on the slide.
12. Change the table style to **Themed Style 1-Accent 4**.
13. Select the WordArt graphic on slide 1 and change the WordArt style to **Fill – Gray 80%, Text 2, Outline – Background 2**.
14. Add a handout footer that includes a date that updates automatically and your first name and last name. Apply the footer to all.
15. **With your teacher's permission**, print a horizontal handouts page containing all the slides.
16. Close the presentation, saving changes, and exit PowerPoint.

Project 52—Make It Your Own

Creating an Effective Presentation

As the office manager at the Michigan Avenue Athletic Club, you have found that many staff members deliver ineffective presentations. You decide to research techniques to make presentations more effective, and create a presentation about it to deliver at the next staff meeting.

DIRECTIONS

1. Use the Internet to research the topic "Creating an effective presentation in PowerPoint."
2. Start PowerPoint and create a new presentation.
3. Save the presentation as **PProj52_studentfirstname_studentlastname** in the location where your teacher instructs you to store the files for this chapter.
4. Apply the **Flow** theme to the presentation.
5. On slide 1, the title slide, enter the title **Effective Presentations** and the subtitle **Common Sense Rules for Delivering Your Message**.
6. Insert a footer that displays today's date and your first name and last name on all slides.
7. Add at least five slides to the presentation.
   a. Slide 2 should be an introduction.
   b. Slide 3 should be bullet points.
   c. Slide 4 should include a graphic.
   d. Slide 5 should be a conclusion or summary.
   e. Slide 6 should list your sources.
   f. You may choose to include additional slides between slide 4 and slide 5 to expand the topic, if necessary.
8. Apply transitions and animations to enhance the presentation's effectiveness.
9. If you have access to multimedia objects, insert them if they can enhance the presentation's effectiveness.
10. Save the presentation.
11. Review the presentation to identify errors and problems, and assess how you might improve its effectiveness. For example, you might add slides so you can have fewer bullets per slide. You might adjust the font size or color to make it more readable. Save all changes.
12. Add notes to help you deliver the presentation.
13. Practice delivering the presentation, and then make changes to the presentation if necessary to improve its effectiveness. For example, you might want to make it longer or shorter, or change the timing for advancing between slides. Save all changes.
14. Practice delivering the presentation again, until you are comfortable with it.
15. Deliver the presentation to your class.
16. **With your teacher's permission**, print the presentation.
17. Close the presentation, saving changes, and exit PowerPoint.

Index

X

Y

Z